Engage, Assess, Apply

- **Personalize Learning with MyMarketingLab**—MyMarketingLab is an online homework, tutorial, and assessment program designed to work with this text to engage students and improve results. Within its structured environment, students practice what they learn, test their understanding, and pursue a personalized study plan that helps them better absorb course material and understand difficult concepts.

- **MediaShare for Business**—Consisting of a curated collection of business videos tagged to learning outcomes and customizable, auto-scored assignments, MediaShare for Business helps students understand why they are learning key concepts and how they will apply those in their careers. Instructors can also assign favorite YouTube clips or original content and employ MediaShare's powerful repository of tools to maximize student accountability and interactive learning, and provide contextualized feedback for students and teams who upload presentations, media, or business plans.

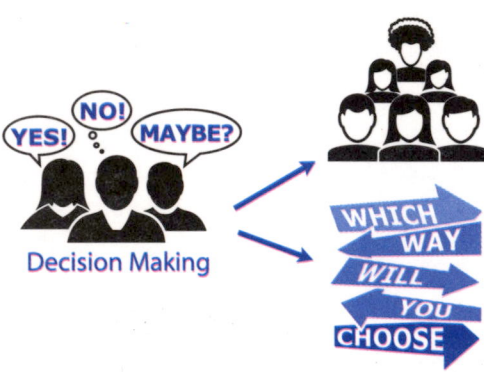

- **Branching, Decision-Making Simulations**—Put your students in the role of manager as they make a series of decisions based on a realistic business challenge. The simulations change and branch based on their decisions, creating various scenario paths. At the end of each simulation, students receive a grade and a detailed report of the choices they made with the associated consequences included.

- **Dynamic Study Modules**—Helps students study effectively on their own by continuously assessing their activity and performance in real time. Here's how it works: students complete a set of questions with a unique answer format that also asks them to indicate their confidence level. Questions repeat until the student can answer them all correctly and confidently. Once completed, Dynamic Study Modules explain the concept using materials from the text. These are available as graded assignments prior to class, and accessible on smartphones, tablets, and computers.

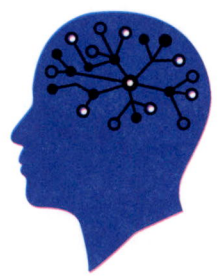

- **Enhanced eText**—Keeps students engaged in learning on their own time, while helping them achieve greater conceptual understanding of course material. The worked examples bring learning to life, and algorithmic practice allows students to apply the very concepts they are reading about. Combining resources that illuminate content with accessible self-assessment, MyLab with Enhanced eText provides students with a complete digital learning experience—all in one place.

with MyMarketingLab®

- **Reporting Dashboard**—View, analyze, and report learning outcomes clearly and easily, and get the information you need to keep your students on track throughout the course with the new Reporting Dashboard. Available via the MyLab Gradebook and fully mobile-ready, the Reporting Dashboard presents student performance data at the class, section, and program levels in an accessible, visual manner.

- **Quizzes and Tests**—Pre-built quizzes and tests allow you to quiz students without having to grade the assignments yourself.

- **Writing Space**—Better writers make great learners who perform better in their courses. Designed to help you develop and assess concept mastery and critical thinking, the Writing Space offers a single place to create, track, and grade writing assignments, provide resources, and exchange meaningful, personalized feedback with students, quickly and easily. Thanks to auto-graded, assisted-graded, and create-your-own assignments, you decide your level of involvement in evaluating students' work. The auto-graded option allows you to assign writing in large classes without having to grade essays by hand. And because of integration with Turnitin®, Writing Space can check students' work for improper citation or plagiarism.

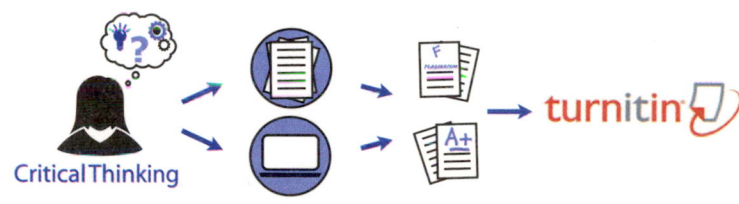

- **Learning Catalytics™**—Is an interactive, student response tool that uses students' smartphones, tablets, or laptops to engage them in more sophisticated tasks and thinking. Now included with MyLab with eText, Learning Catalytics enables you to generate classroom discussion, guide your lecture, and promote peer-to-peer learning with real-time analytics. Instructors, you can:
  - Pose a variety of open-ended questions that help your students develop critical thinking skills
  - Monitor responses to find out where students are struggling
  - Use real-time data to adjust your instructional strategy and try other ways of engaging your students during class
  - Manage student interactions by automatically grouping students for discussion, teamwork, and peer-to-peer learning

STUDENT VALUE EDITION

Principles of MARKETING

Kotler | Armstrong

17e

ISBN-13: 978-0-13-446152-6
ISBN-10: 0-13-446152-5

EAN

P Pearson

Before purchasing this text, please be sure this is the correct book for your course. Once this package has been opened, you may not be able to return it to your bookstore.

Principles of
MARKETING

Principles of
MARKETING

17e

Philip Kotler
Northwestern University

Gary Armstrong
University of North Carolina

New York, NY

Vice President, Business Publishing: Donna Battista
Director of Portfolio Management: Stephanie Wall
Portfolio Manager: Daniel Tylman
Editorial Coordinator: Linda Albelli
Vice President, Product Marketing: Roxanne McCarley
Director of Strategic Marketing: Brad Parkins
Strategic Marketing Manager: Deborah Strickland
Product Marketer: Becky Brown
Field Marketing Manager: Lenny Ann Kucenski
Product Marketing Assistant: Jessica Quazza
Vice President, Production and Digital Studio, Arts and Business: Etain O'Dea
Director of Production, Business: Jeff Holcomb

Managing Producer, Business: Ashley Santora
Operations Specialist: Carol Melville
Creative Director: Blair Brown
Manager, Learning Tools: Brian Surette
Content Developer, Learning Tools: Sarah Peterson
Managing Producer, Digital Studio, Arts and Business: Diane Lombardo
Digital Studio Producer: Darren Cormier
Digital Studio Producer: Alana Coles
Full-Service Project Management, Design, and Composition: Integra Software Services
Cover Art: MSSA/Shutterstock.com
Printer/Binder: LSC Communications
Cover Printer: Phoenix Color/Hagerstown

Library of Congress Cataloging-in-Publication Data
Names: Kotler, Philip, author. | Armstrong, Gary (Gary M.), author.
Title: Principles of marketing / Philip Kotler, Gary Armstrong.
Description: Seventeenth edition. | Hoboken: Pearson Higher Education, [2018]
Identifiers: LCCN 2016022842 | ISBN 9780134492513 | ISBN 013449251X
Subjects: LCSH: Marketing.
Classification: LCC HF5415 .K636 2018 | DDC 658.8—dc23
LC record available at https://lccn.loc.gov/2016022842

5   18

ISBN 10:   0-13-449251-X
ISBN 13: 978-0-13-449251-3

Dedication

To Kathy, Betty, Mandy, Matt, KC, Keri, Delaney, Molly, Macy, and Ben; and Nancy, Amy, Melissa, and Jessica

About the Authors

As a team, Philip Kotler and Gary Armstrong provide a blend of skills uniquely suited to writing an introductory marketing text. Professor Kotler is one of the world's leading authorities on marketing. Professor Armstrong is an award-winning teacher of undergraduate business students. Together, they make the complex world of marketing practical, approachable, and enjoyable.

Philip Kotler is S.C. Johnson & Son Distinguished Professor of International Marketing at the Kellogg School of Management, Northwestern University. He received his master's degree at the University of Chicago and his Ph.D. at M.I.T., both in economics. Dr. Kotler is the author of *Marketing Management* (Pearson), now in its fifteenth edition and the most widely used marketing textbook in graduate schools of business worldwide. He has authored more than 50 other successful books and has published more than 150 articles in leading journals. He is the only three-time winner of the coveted Alpha Kappa Psi award for the best annual article in the *Journal of Marketing*.

Professor Kotler was named the first recipient of four major awards: the *Distinguished Marketing Educator of the Year Award* and the *William L. Wilkie "Marketing for a Better World" Award*, both given by the American Marketing Association; the *Philip Kotler Award for Excellence in Health Care Marketing* presented by the Academy for Health Care Services Marketing; and the *Sheth Foundation Medal for Exceptional Contribution to Marketing Scholarship and Practice*. He is a charter member of the Marketing Hall of Fame, was voted the first Leader in Marketing Thought by the American Marketing Association, and was named the Founder of Modern Marketing Management in the *Handbook of Management Thinking*. His numerous other major honors include the Sales and Marketing Executives International *Marketing Educator of the Year Award*; the European Association of Marketing Consultants and Trainers *Marketing Excellence Award*; the *Charles Coolidge Parlin Marketing Research Award*; and the *Paul D. Converse Award*, given by the American Marketing Association to honor "outstanding contributions to science in marketing." A recent *Forbes* survey ranks Professor Kotler in the top 10 of the world's most influential business thinkers. And in a recent *Financial Times* poll of 1,000 senior executives across the world, Professor Kotler was ranked as the fourth "most influential business writer/guru" of the twenty-first century.

Dr. Kotler has served as chairman of the College on Marketing of the Institute of Management Sciences, a director of the American Marketing Association, and a trustee of the Marketing Science Institute. He has consulted with many major U.S. and international companies in the areas of marketing strategy and planning, marketing organization, and international marketing.

He has traveled and lectured extensively throughout Europe, Asia, and South America, advising companies and governments about global marketing practices and opportunities.

Gary Armstrong is Crist W. Blackwell Distinguished Professor Emeritus of Undergraduate Education in the Kenan-Flagler Business School at the University of North Carolina at Chapel Hill. He holds undergraduate and master's degrees in business from Wayne State University in Detroit, and he received his Ph.D. in marketing from Northwestern University. Dr. Armstrong has contributed numerous articles to leading business journals. As a consultant and researcher, he has worked with many companies on marketing research, sales management, and marketing strategy.

But Professor Armstrong's first love has always been teaching. His long-held Blackwell Distinguished Professorship is the only permanent endowed professorship for distinguished undergraduate teaching at the University of North Carolina at Chapel Hill. He has been very active in the teaching and administration of Kenan-Flagler's undergraduate program. His administrative posts have included Chair of Marketing, Associate Director of the Undergraduate Business Program, Director of the Business Honors Program, and many others. Through the years, he has worked closely with business student groups and has received several UNC campuswide and Business School teaching awards. He is the only repeat recipient of the school's highly regarded Award for Excellence in Undergraduate Teaching, which he received three times. Most recently, Professor Armstrong received the UNC Board of Governors Award for Excellence in Teaching, the highest teaching honor bestowed by the sixteen-campus University of North Carolina system.

Brief Contents

Contents

CHAPTER **4 Managing Marketing Information to Gain Customer Insights 98**

CHAPTER **5 Consumer Markets and Buyer Behavior 132**

CHAPTER **6 Business Markets and Business Buyer Behavior 162**

Preface

The Seventeenth Edition of Kotler/Armstrong's *Principles of Marketing*! Setting the World Standard in Marketing Education

These are exciting times in marketing. Recent surges in digital technologies have created a new, more engaging, more connected marketing world. Beyond traditional tried-and-true marketing concepts and practices, today's marketers have added a host of new-age tools for engaging consumers, building brands, and creating customer value and relationships. In these digital times, sweeping advances in "the Internet of Things"—from social and mobile media, connected digital devices, and the new consumer empowerment to "big data" and new marketing analytics—have profoundly affected both marketers and the consumers they serve.

All around the world—across five continents, more than 40 countries, and 24 languages—students, professors, and business professionals have long relied on Kotler/Armstrong's *Principles of Marketing* as the most-trusted source for teaching and learning about the latest developments in basic marketing concepts and practices. More than ever, the seventeenth edition introduces new marketing students to the fascinating world of modern marketing in a complete and authoritative yet fresh, practical, and engaging way.

Once again, we've added substantial new content and poured over every page, table, figure, fact, and example in order to make this the best text from which to learn about and teach marketing. Enhanced by MyMarketingLab, our online homework and personalized study tool, the seventeenth edition of *Principles of Marketing* remains the world standard in introductory marketing education.

Marketing: Creating Customer Value and Engagement in the Digital and Social Age

Top marketers share a common goal: putting the consumer at the heart of marketing. Today's marketing is all about creating customer value and engagement in a fast-changing, increasingly digital and social marketplace.

Marketing starts with understanding consumer needs and wants, determining which target markets the organization can serve best, and developing a compelling value proposition by which the organization can attract and grow valued consumers. Then, more than just making a sale, today's marketers want to *engage* customers and build deep customer relationships that make their brands a meaningful part of consumers' conversations and lives.

In this digital age, to go along with their tried-and-true traditional marketing methods, marketers have a dazzling set of new online, mobile, and social media tools for engaging customers anytime, anyplace to jointly shape brand conversations, experiences, and community. If marketers do these things well, they will reap the rewards in terms of market share, profits, and customer equity. In the seventeenth edition of *Principles of Marketing,* you'll learn how *customer value* and *customer engagement* drive every good marketing strategy.

What's New in the Seventeenth Edition?

We've thoroughly revised the seventeenth edition of *Principles of Marketing* to reflect the major trends and forces that affect marketing in this digital age of customer value, engagement, and relationships. Here are just some of the major and continuing changes you'll find in this edition.

- The seventeenth edition adds fresh coverage in both traditional marketing areas and on fast-changing and trending topics such as customer engagement marketing, mobile and social media, big data and the new marketing analytics, the Internet of Things, omni-channel marketing and retailing, customer co-creation and empowerment, real-time customer listening and marketing, building brand community, marketing content creation and native advertising, B-to-B social media and social selling, monetizing social media, tiered and dynamic pricing, consumer privacy, sustainability, global marketing, and much more.

- This new edition continues to build on its *customer engagement* framework—creating direct and continuous customer involvement in shaping brands, brand conversations, brand experiences, and brand community. New coverage and fresh examples throughout the text address the latest customer engagement tools, practices, and developments. See especially Chapter 1 (refreshed sections on *Customer Engagement and Today's Digital and Social Media* and *Consumer-Generated Marketing*); Chapter 4 (big data and real-time research to gain deeper customer insights); Chapter 5 (creating social influence and customer community through digital and social media marketing); Chapter 9 (customer co-creation and customer-driven new-product development); Chapter 13 (omni-channel retailing); Chapters 14 and 15 (marketing content curation and native advertising); Chapter 16 (sales force social selling); and Chapter 17 (direct digital, online, social media, and mobile marketing).

- No area of marketing is changing faster than online, mobile, social media, and other digital marketing technologies. Keeping up with digital concepts, technologies, and practices has become a top priority and major challenge for today's marketers. The seventeenth edition of *Principles of Marketing* provides thoroughly refreshed, up-to-date coverage of these explosive developments in every chapter—from online, mobile, and social media engagement technologies discussed in Chapters 1, 5, 14, 15, and 17 to "real-time listening" and "big data" research tools in Chapter 4, real-time dynamic pricing in Chapter 11, omni-channel retailing in Chapter 13, and social selling in Chapter 16. A Chapter 1 section on *The Digital Age: Online, Mobile, and Social Media Marketing* introduces the exciting new developments in digital and social media marketing. Then a Chapter 17 section on *Direct, Online, Social Media, and Mobile Marketing* digs more deeply into digital marketing tools such as online sites, social media, mobile ads and apps, online video, email, blogs, and other digital platforms that engage consumers anywhere, anytime via their computers, smartphones, tablets, internet-ready TVs, and other digital devices.

- The seventeenth edition continues to track fast-changing developments in marketing communications and the creation of marketing content. Marketers are no longer simply creating integrated marketing communications programs; they are joining with customers and media to curate customer-driven marketing content in paid, owned, earned, and shared media. You won't find fresher coverage of these important topics in any other marketing text.

- The seventeenth edition of *Principles of Marketing* continues to improve on its innovative learning design. The text's active and integrative presentation includes learning enhancements such as annotated chapter-opening stories, a chapter-opening objective outline, explanatory author comments on major chapter sections and figures, and Real Marketing highlights that provide in-depth examples of marketing concepts and practices at work. The chapter-opening layout helps to preview and position the chapter and its key concepts. Figures annotated with author comments help students to simplify and organize chapter material. New and substantially revised end-of-chapter features help to summarize important chapter concepts and highlight important themes, such as marketing ethics, financial marketing analysis, and online, mobile, and social media marketing. This innovative learning design facilitates student understanding and eases learning.

- The seventeenth edition provides 18 new end-of-chapter company cases by which students can apply what they learn to actual company situations. It also features 16 new video cases, with brief end-of-chapter summaries and discussion questions. Finally, all of the chapter-opening stories, Real Marketing highlights, and end-of-chapter features in the seventeenth edition are either new or revised.

- New material throughout the seventeenth edition highlights the increasing importance of *sustainable marketing*. The discussion begins in Chapter 1 and ends in Chapter 20, which pulls marketing together under a sustainable marketing framework. In between, frequent discussions and examples show how sustainable marketing calls for socially and environmentally responsible actions that meet both the immediate and the future needs of customers, companies, and society as a whole.

- The seventeenth edition provides new discussions and examples of the growth in *global marketing*. As the world becomes a smaller, more competitive place, marketers face new global marketing challenges and opportunities, especially in fast-growing emerging markets such as China, India, Brazil, Africa, and others. You'll find much new coverage of global marketing throughout the text, starting in Chapter 1 and discussed fully in Chapter 19.

Five Major Customer Value and Engagement Themes

The seventeenth edition of *Principles of Marketing* builds on five major customer value and engagement themes:

1. **Creating value for customers in order to capture value from customers in return.** Today's marketers must be good at *creating customer value, engaging customers,* and *managing customer relationships.* Outstanding marketing companies understand the marketplace and customer needs, design value-creating marketing strategies, develop integrated marketing programs that engage customers and deliver value and satisfaction, and build strong customer relationships and brand community. In return, they capture value from customers in the form of sales, profits, and customer equity.

   This innovative *customer-value and engagement framework* is introduced at the start of Chapter 1 in a five-step marketing process model, which details how marketing *creates* customer value and *captures* value in return. The framework is carefully developed in the first two chapters and then fully integrated throughout the remainder of the text.

2. **Customer Engagement and Today's Digital and Social Media.** New digital and social media have taken today's marketing by storm, dramatically changing how companies and brands engage consumers and how consumers connect and influence each other's brand behaviors. The seventeenth edition introduces and thoroughly explores the contemporary concept of *customer engagement marketing* and the exciting new digital and social media technologies that help brands to engage customers more deeply and interactively. It starts with two major Chapter 1 sections: *Customer Engagement and Today's Digital and Social* Media and *The Digital Age: Online, Mobile, and Social Media.* A refreshed Chapter 17 on *Direct, Online, Social Media, and Mobile Marketing* summarizes the latest developments in digital engagement and relationship-building tools. Everywhere in between, you'll find revised and expanded coverage of the exploding use of digital and social tools to create customer engagement and build brand community.

3. **Building and managing strong, value-creating brands.** Well-positioned brands with strong brand equity provide the basis upon which to build customer value and profitable customer relationships. Today's marketers must position their brands powerfully and manage them well to create valued brand experiences. The seventeenth edition provides a deep focus on brands, anchored by a Chapter 8 section on *Branding Strategy: Building Strong Brands.*

4. **Measuring and managing return on marketing.** Especially in uneven economic times, marketing managers must ensure that their marketing dollars are being well spent. In the past, many marketers spent freely on big, expensive marketing programs, often without thinking carefully about the financial returns on their spending. But all that has changed rapidly. "Marketing accountability"—measuring and managing marketing return on investment—has now become an important part of strategic marketing decision making. This emphasis on marketing accountability is addressed in Chapter 2, in Appendix 2 (*Marketing by the Numbers*), and throughout the seventeenth edition.

5. **Sustainable marketing around the globe.** As technological developments make the world an increasingly smaller and more fragile place, marketers must be good at marketing their brands globally and in sustainable ways. New material throughout the

seventeenth edition emphasizes the concepts of global marketing and sustainable marketing—meeting the present needs of consumers and businesses while also preserving or enhancing the ability of future generations to meet their needs. The seventeenth edition integrates global marketing and sustainability topics throughout the text. It then provides focused coverage on each topic in Chapters 19 and 20, respectively.

An Emphasis on Real Marketing and Bringing Marketing to Life

Principles of Marketing, seventeenth edition, takes a practical marketing-management approach, providing countless in-depth, real-life examples and stories that engage students with marketing concepts and bring modern marketing to life. In the seventeenth edition, every chapter has an engaging opening story plus *Real Marketing* highlights that provide fresh insights into real marketing practices. Learn how:

- Amazon has become the poster child for direct and digital marketing. Its passion for creating superb online customer experiences has made it one of the most powerful names on the internet.
- Wildly innovative Google (…er, Alphabet) has become an incredibly successful new product "moonshot factory," unleashing a seemingly unending flurry of diverse products, most of which are market leaders in their categories.
- Apple's outstanding success has never been about prices; it's always been about creating "life-feels-good" user experiences that make its products fly off the shelves despite their premium prices.
- Ultra-low-price Spirit Airlines is thriving despite industry-*low* customer experience ratings. You don't get much when you fly Spirit. Then again, you don't pay for what you don't get.
- Nike—by far the world's largest sports apparel company—does much more than just make and sell sports gear. The iconic brand creates customer value by building deep engagement and a sense of community with and between the Nike brand and its customers.
- Harley-Davidson's market dominance comes from a deep understanding of the emotions and motivations that underlie consumer behavior. Harley doesn't just sell motorcycles; it sells freedom, independence, power, and authenticity.
- Mighty Kellogg, the world's largest cereal maker, may be losing its Snap, Crackle, and Pop as shifts in the marketing environment change how people today eat breakfast.
- Toy market leader LEGO uses innovative marketing research—lots and lots of it—to dig out fresh customer insights, then uses the insights to create irresistible play experiences for children around the world.
- Netflix uses "big data" and sophisticated marketing analytics to personalize each customer's viewing experience. While Netflix subscribers are busy watching videos, Netflix is busy watching them—very, very closely.
- App-based car sharing service Uber is radically reshaping urban transportation channels in cities around the globe, making traditional taxi cab services innovate or risk extinction.
- Industrial giant GE has unleashed a remarkable array of digital and social media content that connects the brand with its business customers and positions the 130-year-old company as a youthful, contemporary technology leader in the new digital industrial era.
- High-flying Mountain Dew is "Doin' the Dew" with brand superfans to build a passionately loyal and engaged brand community. It doesn't just market to customers; it makes them partners in building the brand.

Beyond such features, each chapter is packed with countless real, engaging, and timely examples that reinforce key concepts. No other text brings marketing to life like the seventeenth edition of *Principles of Marketing.*

Learning Aids That Create Value and Engagement

A wealth of chapter-opening, within-chapter, and end-of-chapter learning devices help students to learn, link, and apply major concepts:

- *Integrated chapter-opening preview sections.* The active and integrative chapter-opening spread in each chapter starts with a *Chapter Preview,* which briefly previews chapter concepts, links them with previous chapter concepts, and introduces the chapter-opening story. This leads to a chapter-opening vignette—an engaging, deeply developed, illustrated, and annotated marketing story that introduces the chapter material and sparks student interest. Finally, an *Objective Outline* provides a helpful preview of chapter contents and learning objectives, complete with page numbers.
- *Real Marketing highlights.* Each chapter contains two carefully developed highlight features that provide an in-depth look at real marketing practices of large and small companies.
- *Author comments and figure annotations.* Each figure contains author comments that ease student understanding and help organize major text sections.
- *Reviewing and Extending the Concepts.* Sections at the end of each chapter summarize key chapter concepts and provide questions and exercises by which students can review and apply what they've learned. The *Objectives Review and Key Terms* section reviews major chapter concepts and links them to chapter objectives. It also provides a helpful listing of chapter key terms by order of appearance with page numbers that facilitate easy reference. A *Discussion and Critical Thinking* section provides discussion questions and critical thinking exercises that help students to keep track of and apply what they've learned in the chapter.
- *Applications and Cases.* Brief *Online, Mobile, and Social Media Marketing; Marketing Ethics;* and *Marketing by the Numbers* sections at the end of each chapter provide short applications cases that facilitate discussion of current issues and company situations in areas such as mobile and social marketing, ethics, and financial marketing analysis. A *Video Case* section contains short vignettes with discussion questions to be used with a set four- to seven-minute videos that accompanied the seventeenth edition. End-of-chapter *Company Case* sections provide all-new or revised company cases that help students to apply major marketing concepts to real company and brand situations.
- *Marketing Plan appendix.* Appendix 1 contains a sample marketing plan that helps students to apply important marketing planning concepts.
- *Marketing by the Numbers appendix.* An innovative Appendix 2 provides students with a comprehensive introduction to the marketing financial analysis that helps to guide, assess, and support marketing decisions. An exercise at the end of each chapter lets students apply analytical and financial thinking to relevant chapter concepts and links the chapter to the Marketing by the Numbers appendix.

More than ever before, the seventeenth edition of *Principles of Marketing* creates value and engagement for you—it gives you all you need to know about marketing in an effective and enjoyable total learning package!

A Total Teaching and Learning Package

A successful marketing course requires more than a well-written book. Today's classroom requires a dedicated teacher, well-prepared students, and a fully integrated teaching system. A total package of teaching and learning supplements extends this edition's emphasis on creating value and engagement for both the student and instructor. The following aids support *Principles of Marketing,* seventeenth edition.

Instructor Resources

At the Instructor Resource Center, www.pearsonhighered.com/irc, instructors can easily register to gain access to a variety of instructor resources available with this text in downloadable format. If assistance is needed, a dedicated technical support team is ready to help with the media supplements that accompany the text. Visit support.pearson.com/getsupport for answers to frequently asked questions and toll-free user support phone numbers.

The following supplements are available with this text:

- **Instructor's Resource Manual**
- **Test Bank**
- **TestGen® Computerized Test Bank**
- **PowerPoint Presentation**

Acknowledgments

No book is the work only of its authors. We greatly appreciate the valuable contributions of several people who helped make this new edition possible. As always, we owe extra-special thanks to Keri Jean Miksza for her dedicated and valuable contributions to *all* phases of the project and to her husband Pete and daughters Lucy and Mary for all the support they provide Keri during this very absorbing project.

We owe substantial thanks to Andy Norman of Drake University for his skillful help in developing chapter vignettes and highlights, company and video cases, PowerPoint presentations, and the marketing plan appendix. This and many previous editions have benefited greatly from Andy's assistance. We also thank Colette Wolfson of the Ivy Tech Community College School of Business for her dedicated efforts in preparing end-of-chapter materials. Additional thanks go to Carol Davis at California State University Monterey Bay for her work in updating the Instructor's Manual and Test Item File. Finally, we'd like to thank the professors who assisted with our work on MyMarketingLab: Arlene Green, Indian River State College; Mahmood Khan, Virginia Tech; Todd Korol, Monroe Community College; Susan Schanne, Eastern Michigan University; and Sarah Shepler, Ivy Tech Community College. All of these contributors are greatly appreciated in making the seventeenth edition of *Principles of Marketing* a robust teaching and learning system.

Many reviewers at other colleges and universities provided valuable comments and suggestions for this and previous editions. We are indebted to the following colleagues for their thoughtful input:

Reviewers

Sucheta Ahlawat, Kean University
Darrell E. Bartholomew, Rider University
Leta Beard, University of Washington
Greg Black, Metropolitan State University of Denver
Christopher P. Blocker, Colorado State University
Kathryn Boys, Virginia Tech
Rod Carveth, Naugatuck Valley Community College
Anindja Chatterjee, Slippery Rock University of Pennsylvania
Christina Chung, Ramapo College of New Jersey
Ed Chung, Elizabethtown College
Marianne Collins, Winona State University
Mary Conran, Temple University
Eloise Coupey, Virginia Tech
Deborah L. Cowles, Virginia Commonwealth University
Alan Dick, University of Buffalo
Patti Diggin, West Chester University of Pennsylvania
Frank Franzak, Virginia Commonwealth University
George J. Gannage Jr., Embry Riddle Aeronautical University
David A. Gilliam, University of Arkansas at Little Rock
Karen Gore, Ivy Tech Community College, Evansville Campus
Deborah M. Gray, Central Michigan University
Amy Handlin, Monmouth University
James Heyman, University of St. Thomas
Ken Knox, Eastern Gateway Community College
Ann T. Kuzma, Minnesota State University, Mankato
Geoffrey P. Lantos, Stonehill College

Charles Lee, Chestnut Hill College
Yun Jung Lee, Adelphi University
Carolyn A. Massiah, University of Central Florida
Samuel McNeely, Murray State University
Chip Miller, Drake University
Linda Morable, Richland College
Randy Moser, Elon University
David Murphy, Madisonville Community College
Esther Page-Wood, Western Michigan University
Ed Petkus Jr., Ramapo College of New Jersey
Tim Reisenwitz, Valdosta State University
Mary Ellen Rosetti, Hudson Valley Community College
William Ryan, University of Connecticut
James Sawhill, Washington University–Missouri
Mid Semple, SUNY Broome
Roberta Schultz, Western Michigan University
Shweta Singh, Kean University
Michaeline Skiba, Monmouth University
Joseph G. Slifko Jr., Pennsylvania Highlands Community College
J. Alexander Smith, Oklahoma City University
Deb Utter, Boston University
Donna Waldron, Manchester Community College
Wendel Weaver, Oklahoma Wesleyan University
Susan D. Williams, New Jersey City University
Douglas Witt, Brigham Young University
Poh-Lin Yeoh, Bentley University

We also owe a great deal to the people at Pearson Education who helped develop this book. Portfolio Manager Dan Tylman provided resources and support during the revision. Editorial Coordinator Linda Albelli and Project Manager Karin Williams provided valuable assistance and advice in guiding this complex revision project through development, design, and production. We'd also like to thank Director of Portfolio Management Stephanie Wall for her strong guidance and support along the way as well as the expertise of Managing Producer Ashley Santora, Director of Production Jeff Holcomb, and Product Marketer Becky Brown. We are proud to be associated with the fine professionals at Pearson. We also owe a mighty debt of gratitude to Senior Project Manager Charles Fisher, Associate Managing Editor Allison Campbell, Design Manager Emily Friel, and the rest of the team at Integra for their fine work on this edition.

Finally, we owe many thanks to our families for all of their support and encouragement—Kathy, Betty, Mandy, Matt, KC, Keri, Delaney, Molly, Macy, and Ben from the Armstrong clan and Nancy, Amy, Melissa, and Jessica from the Kotler family. To them, we dedicate this book.

Gary Armstrong
Philip Kotler

Principles of
MARKETING

1

Marketing
Creating Customer Value and Engagement

CHAPTER PREVIEW
This first chapter introduces you to the basic concepts of marketing. We start with the question: What is marketing? Simply put, marketing is engaging customers and managing profitable customer relationships. The aim of marketing is to create value for customers in order to capture value from customers in return. Next we discuss the five steps in the marketing process—from understanding customer needs, to designing customer value–driven marketing strategies and integrated marketing programs, to building customer relationships and capturing value for the firm. Finally, we discuss the major trends and forces affecting marketing in this new age of digital, mobile, and social media. Understanding these basic concepts and forming your own ideas about what they really mean to you will provide a solid foundation for all that follows.

Let's start with a good story about marketing in action at Nike, the world's leading sports apparel company and one of the best-known brands on the planet. Nike's outstanding success results from much more than just making and selling good sports gear. It's based on a customer-focused marketing strategy by which Nike creates customer value through deep brand–customer engagement and close brand community with and among its customers.

NIKE'S CUSTOMER VALUE–DRIVEN MARKETING: Engaging Customers and Building Brand Community

The Nike "swoosh"—it's everywhere! Just for fun, try counting the swooshes whenever you pick up the sports pages or watch a basketball game or tune into a televised soccer match. Over the past 50 years, through innovative marketing, Nike has built the ever-present swoosh into one of the world's best-known brand symbols.

Product innovation has always been a cornerstone of Nike's success. Nike makes outstanding shoes, clothing, and gear, whether for basketball, football, and baseball or golf, skateboarding, wall climbing, bicycling, and hiking. But from the start, a brash, young Nike revolutionized sports marketing. To build image and market share, the brand lavishly outspent competitors on big-name endorsements, splashy promotional events, and big-budget, in-your-face "Just do it" ads. Whereas competitors stressed technical performance, Nike built customer engagement and relationships.

Beyond shoes, Nike marketed a way of life, a genuine passion for sports, a "just-do-it" attitude. Customers didn't just wear their Nikes, they *experienced* them. As the company once

> Nike's outstanding success results from much more than just making good sports gear. The iconic brand delivers customer value by building deep engagement and a sense of community with and between the Nike brand and its customers.

stated on its web page, "Nike has always known the truth—it's not so much the shoes but where they take you." Nike's mission isn't to make better gear, it's to help and inspire everyday athletes to do their very best. Few brands have become more ever-present and valued than Nike in their customers' lives and conversations.

Whether customers connect with Nike through ads, in-person events at Niketown stores, a local Nike running club, a Nike+ app, or one of the company's profusion of community web and social media sites, more and more people are bonding closely with the Nike brand. Connecting once required simply outspending competitors on big media ads and celebrity endorsers that talk *at* customers. But in these digital times, Nike is forging a new kind of brand–customer connection—a deeper, more personal, more engaging one. Nike still invests heavily in traditional advertising. But the brand now spends a lion's share of its hefty marketing budget on digital and social media marketing that interacts *with* customers to build brand engagement, advocacy, and community.

Nike's innovative use of online, mobile, and social media recently earned the brand the title of "top genius" in "digital IQ" among 42 sportswear companies in one digital consultancy's rankings. Nike also placed first in creating brand "tribes"—large groups of highly engaged users—with the help of social media platforms such as Facebook, Twitter, Snapchat, Instagram, YouTube, and Pinterest. For example, the main Nike Facebook page has more than 23 million Likes. The Nike Soccer page adds another 42 million, the Nike Basketball page 7 million more, and Nike Running another 6 million. More than just numbers, Nike's social media presence engages customers at a high level, gets them talking with each other about the brand, and weaves the brand into their daily lives.

Nike excels at cross-media campaigns that integrate digital media with traditional tools to connect with customers. An example is Nike's recent "Risk Everything" campaign, specially designed around the FIFA World Cup in Brazil. The Risk Everything campaign began with captivating four- to five-minute videos embedded in Nike social media sites and its own Risk Everything website. The campaign—featuring Nike-sponsored soccer superstars such as Portugal's Cristiano Ronaldo, England's Wayne Rooney, Brazil's Neymar, and a dozen others—was built around an intense, provocative World Cup story line of taking risks to gain the glory of succeeding against rival teams and nations.

In one Risk Everything video—"Winner Stays"—two teams of young men faced off on a local soccer field for a pickup game, pretending to be (then turning into) the superstars. The scene transformed into a legendary bout on a global stage. As the video ended, a young boy stepped in for Ronaldo and under immense pressure scored the winning goal. According to one analyst, the Risk Everything videos were "the perfect blend of product placement, provocative storytelling, and real-time marketing." Although the videos were filled with Nike swooshes, products, and stars, highly engaged viewers hardly realized that they were consuming ad content.

By the end of the final World Cup match, the Risk Everything videos had produced 372 million views, 22 million engagements (Likes, comments, shares), and 650,000 uses of #riskeverything. Nike reigned as the "most-viewed brand" of the World Cup in terms of online video, trouncing rival adidas. In fact, Nike's online views accounted for an incredible one-half of all the views attributed to the event's 97 World Cup marketing campaigns—and Nike wasn't even an official sponsor. Along with the Risk Everything videos, Nike ran a full array of traditional television, print, radio, cinema, and gaming advertising. Taken as a whole, across all media, the Risk Everything campaign generated more than 6 *billion* impressions in 35 countries. Now that's customer engagement.

Nike has also created customer value and brand community through groundbreaking mobile apps and technologies.

The Nike swoosh—it's everywhere. Nike has mastered social networking, both online and off, creating deep engagement and community with and among customers.
© Steve Hellerstein/Alamy

For example, its Nike+ apps have helped Nike become a part of the daily fitness routines of millions of customers around the world. Whether your activity is running, jumping, baseball, skating, dancing, stacking sports cups, or chasing chickens, you can use the Nike+ family of apps to "unlock your potential." Nike+ apps let everyday athletes design their workouts, access coaching and training tools, track their personal progress, get extra motivation on the go, and share and compare their experiences across sports and locations with friends and others in the Nike community. Nike+ has engaged a huge global brand community, with more than 28 million registered users and a goal of 100 million users.

Thus, Nike delivers customer value well beyond the products it makes. It has built a deep kinship and sense of community with and between the Nike brand and its customers. Whether it's through local running clubs, a performance-tracking app, primetime TV ads, videos, or other content at any of its dozens of brand websites and social media pages, the Nike brand has become a valued part of customers' lives and times.

As a result, Nike remains the world's largest sports apparel company, an impressive 44 percent larger than rival adidas. It captures an even more impressive 62 percent of the U.S. sports footwear market versus number-two Skechers at only 5 percent and adidas at 4.6 percent. During the past decade, even as a sometimes-shaky economy left many sports footwear and apparel rivals gasping for breath, Nike's global sales and income have sprinted ahead by more than double.

"Connecting used to be, 'Here's some product, and here's some advertising. We hope you like it,'" notes Nike's CEO. "Connecting today is a dialogue." Says Nike's chief marketing officer, "The engagement levels we have received...drive huge momentum for our brand. This is just the beginning of how we will connect with and inspire athletes around the world." Concludes the CEO, "at Nike, there is no finish line."[1]

OBJECTIVES OUTLINE

OBJECTIVE 1-1	Define marketing and outline the steps in the marketing process. **What Is Marketing?** *(pp 4–6)*
OBJECTIVE 1-2	Explain the importance of understanding the marketplace and customers and identify the five core marketplace concepts. **Understanding the Marketplace and Customer Needs** *(pp 6–10)*
OBJECTIVE 1-3	Identify the key elements of a customer value–driven marketing strategy and discuss the marketing management orientations that guide marketing strategy. **Designing a Customer Value–Driven Marketing Strategy and Plan** *(pp 10–14)*
OBJECTIVE 1-4	Discuss customer relationship management and identify strategies for creating value *for* customers and capturing value *from* customers in return. **Managing Customer Relationships and Capturing Customer Value** *(pp 14–22)*
OBJECTIVE 1-5	Describe the major trends and forces that are changing the marketing landscape in this age of relationships. **The Changing Marketing Landscape** *(pp 22–31)*

Today's successful companies have one thing in common: Like Nike, they are strongly customer focused and heavily committed to marketing. These companies share a passion for satisfying customer needs in well-defined target markets. They motivate everyone in the organization to help build lasting customer relationships based on creating value.

Customer relationships and value are especially important today. Facing dramatic technological advances and deep economic, social, and environmental challenges, today's customers are reassessing how they engage with brands. New digital, mobile, and social media developments have revolutionized how consumers shop and interact, in turn calling for new marketing strategies and tactics. It's now more important than ever to build strong customer engagement, relationships, and advocacy based on real and enduring customer value.

We'll discuss the exciting new challenges facing both customers and marketers later in the chapter. But first, let's introduce the basics of marketing.

> **Author Comment** | Pause here and think about how you'd answer this question before studying marketing. Then see how your answer changes as you read the chapter.

What Is Marketing?

Marketing, more than any other business function, deals with customers. Although we will soon explore more-detailed definitions of marketing, perhaps the simplest definition is this one: *Marketing is engaging customers and managing profitable customer relationships.* The two-fold goal of marketing is to attract new customers by promising superior value and to keep and grow current customers by delivering value and satisfaction.

For example, Nike leaves its competitors in the dust by delivering on its promise to inspire and help everyday athletes to "Just do it." Amazon dominants the online marketplace by creating a world-class online buying experience that helps customers to "find and discover anything they might want to buy online." Facebook has attracted more than 1.5 billion active web and mobile users worldwide by helping them to "connect and share with the people in their lives." And Coca-Cola has earned an impressive 49 percent global share of the carbonated beverage market—more than twice Pepsi's share—by fulfilling its

"Taste the Feeling" motto with products that provide "a simple pleasure that makes everyday moments more special."[2]

Sound marketing is critical to the success of every organization. Large for-profit firms such as Google, Target, Procter & Gamble, Coca-Cola, and Microsoft use marketing. But so do not-for-profit organizations, such as colleges, hospitals, museums, symphony orchestras, and even churches.

● **Marketing is all around you, in good old traditional forms and in a host of new forms, from websites and mobile phone apps to videos and online social media.**

Westend61/Getty Images

You already know a lot about marketing—it's all around you. Marketing comes to you in the good old traditional forms: You see it in the abundance of products at your nearby shopping mall and the ads that fill your TV screen, spice up your magazines, or stuff your mailbox. ● But in recent years, marketers have assembled a host of new marketing approaches, everything from imaginative websites and smartphone apps to blogs, online videos, and social media. These new approaches do more than just blast out messages to the masses. They reach you directly, personally, and interactively. Today's marketers want to become a part of your life and enrich your experiences with their brands. They want to help you *live* their brands.

At home, at school, where you work, and where you play, you see marketing in almost everything you do. Yet there is much more to marketing than meets the consumer's casual eye. Behind it all is a massive network of people, technologies, and activities competing for your attention and purchases. This book will give you a complete introduction to the basic concepts and practices of today's marketing. In this chapter, we begin by defining marketing and the marketing process.

Marketing Defined

What *is* marketing? Many people think of marketing as only selling and advertising. We are bombarded every day with TV commercials, catalogs, spiels from salespeople, and online pitches. However, selling and advertising are only the tip of the marketing iceberg.

Today, marketing must be understood not in the old sense of making a sale—"telling and selling"—but in the new sense of *satisfying customer needs.* If the marketer engages consumers effectively, understands their needs, develops products that provide superior customer value, and prices, distributes, and promotes them well, these products will sell easily. In fact, according to management guru Peter Drucker, "The aim of marketing is to make selling unnecessary."[3] Selling and advertising are only part of a larger *marketing mix*—a set of marketing tools that work together to engage customers, satisfy customer needs, and build customer relationships.

Marketing

The process by which companies engage customers, build strong customer relationships, and create customer value in order to capture value from customers in return.

Broadly defined, marketing is a social and managerial process by which individuals and organizations obtain what they need and want through creating and exchanging value with others. In a narrower business context, marketing involves building profitable, value-laden exchange relationships with customers. Hence, we define **marketing** as the process by which companies engage customers, build strong customer relationships, and create customer value in order to capture value from customers in return.[4]

The Marketing Process

● **Figure 1.1** presents a simple, five-step model of the marketing process for creating and capturing customer value. In the first four steps, companies work to understand consumers, create customer value, and build strong customer relationships. In the final step, companies reap the rewards of creating superior customer value. By creating value *for* consumers, they in turn capture value *from* consumers in the form of sales, profits, and long-term customer equity.

In this chapter and the next, we will examine the steps of this simple model of marketing. In this chapter, we review each step but focus more on the customer relationship

The Marketing Process: Creating and Capturing Customer Value

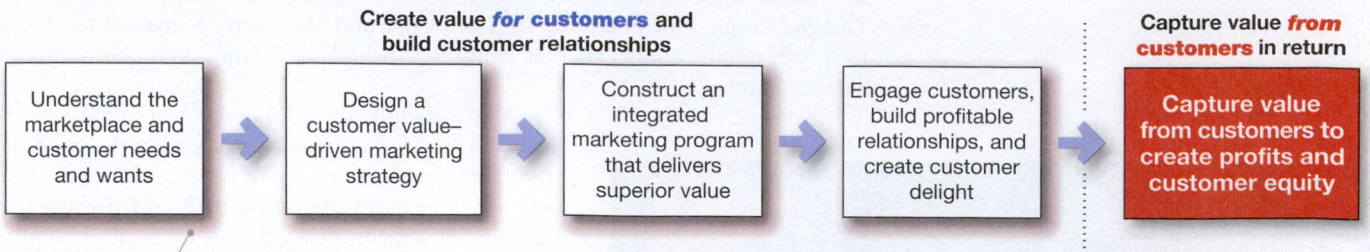

Create value **for customers** and build customer relationships

Capture value **from customers** in return

| Understand the marketplace and customer needs and wants | → | Design a customer value–driven marketing strategy | → | Construct an integrated marketing program that delivers superior value | → | Engage customers, build profitable relationships, and create customer delight | → | Capture value from customers to create profits and customer equity |

> This important figure shows marketing in a nutshell. By creating value *for* customers, marketers capture value *from* customers in return. This five-step process forms the marketing framework for the rest of the chapter and the remainder of the text.

steps—understanding customers, engaging and building relationships with customers, and capturing value from customers. In Chapter 2, we look more deeply into the second and third steps—designing value-creating marketing strategies and constructing marketing programs.

> **Author Comment** | Marketing is all about creating value for customers. So, as the first step in the marketing process, the company must fully understand customers and the marketplace.

Understanding the Marketplace and Customer Needs

As a first step, marketers need to understand customer needs and wants and the marketplace in which they operate. We examine five core customer and marketplace concepts: (1) *needs, wants, and demands*; (2) *market offerings (products, services, and experiences)*; (3) *value and satisfaction*; (4) *exchanges and relationships*; and (5) *markets*.

Customer Needs, Wants, and Demands

Needs
States of felt deprivation.

Wants
The form human needs take as they are shaped by culture and individual personality.

Demands
Human wants that are backed by buying power.

The most basic concept underlying marketing is that of human needs. Human **needs** are states of felt deprivation. They include basic *physical* needs for food, clothing, warmth, and safety; *social* needs for belonging and affection; and *individual* needs for knowledge and self-expression. Marketers did not create these needs; they are a basic part of the human makeup.

Wants are the form human needs take as they are shaped by culture and individual personality. An American *needs* food but *wants* a Big Mac, fries, and a soft drink. A person in Papua, New Guinea, *needs* food but *wants* taro, rice, yams, and pork. Wants are shaped by one's society and are described in terms of objects that will satisfy those needs. When backed by buying power, wants become **demands**. Given their wants and resources, people demand products and services with benefits that add up to the most value and satisfaction.

Companies go to great lengths to learn about and understand customer needs, wants, and demands. They conduct consumer research, analyze mountains of customer data, and observe customers as they shop and interact, offline and online. People at all levels of the company— including top management—stay close to customers:[5]

Target's energetic CEO, Brian Cornell, makes regular unannounced visits to Target stores, accompanied by local moms and loyal Target shoppers. ● Cornell likes nosing around stores and getting a real feel for what's going on. It gives him "great, genuine feedback." He and other Target executives even visit customers in their homes, opening closet doors and poking around in cupboards to understand their product choices and buying habits. Similarly, Boston Market CEO George Michel makes frequent visits to company restaurants, working in the dining room and engaging customers to learn about "the good, the bad, and the ugly." He also stays connected by reading customer messages on the Boston Market website and has even cold-called customers for insights. "Being close to the customer is critically important," says Michel. "I get to learn what they value, what they appreciate."

● **Staying close to customers: Energetic Target CEO Brian Cornell makes regular unannounced visits to Target stores, accompanied by local moms and loyal Target shoppers.**
Ackerman + Gruber

Market Offerings—Products, Services, and Experiences

Market offerings

Some combination of products, services, information, or experiences offered to a market to satisfy a need or want.

Consumers' needs and wants are fulfilled through **market offerings**—some combination of products, services, information, or experiences offered to a market to satisfy a need or a want. Market offerings are not limited to physical *products*. They also include *services*—activities or benefits offered for sale that are essentially intangible and do not result in the ownership of anything. Examples include banking, airline, hotel, retailing, and home repair services.

More broadly, market offerings also include other entities, such as *persons, places, organizations, information*, and *ideas*. For example, San Diego runs a "Happiness Is Calling" advertising campaign that invites visitors to come and enjoy the city's great weather and good times—everything from its bays and beaches to its downtown nightlife and urban scenes. And the Ad Council and the National Highway Traffic Safety Administration created a "Stop the Texts. Stop the Wrecks." campaign that markets the idea of eliminating texting while driving. The campaign points out that a texting driver is 23 times more likely to get into a crash than a non-texting driver.[6]

Marketing myopia

The mistake of paying more attention to the specific products a company offers than to the benefits and experiences produced by these products.

Many sellers make the mistake of paying more attention to the specific products they offer than to the benefits and experiences produced by these products. These sellers suffer from **marketing myopia**. They are so taken with their products that they focus only on existing wants and lose sight of underlying customer needs.[7] They forget that a product is only a tool to solve a consumer problem. A manufacturer of quarter-inch drill bits may think that the customer needs a drill bit. But what the customer *really* needs is a quarter-inch hole. These sellers will have trouble if a new product comes along that serves the customer's need better or less expensively. The customer will have the same *need* but will *want* the new product.

Smart marketers look beyond the attributes of the products and services they sell. By orchestrating several services and products, they create *brand experiences* for consumers. For example, you don't just visit Walt Disney World Resort; you immerse yourself and your family in a world of wonder, a world where dreams come true and things still work the way they should. And your local Buffalo Wild Wings restaurant doesn't just serve up wings and beer; it gives customers the ultimate "Wings. Beer. Sports." fan experience (see Real Marketing 1.1).

● Similarly, Mattel's American Girl does much more than just make and sell high-end dolls. It creates special experiences between the dolls and the girls who adore them.[8]

> To put more smiles on the faces of the girls who love their American Girl dolls, the company operates huge American Girl experiential stores in 20 major cities around the country. Each store carries an amazing selection of dolls plus every imaginable outfit and accessory. But more than just places to shop, American Girl stores are exciting destinations unto themselves, offering wonderfully engaging experiences for girls, mothers, grandmothers, and even dads or grandpas. There's an in-store restaurant where girls, their dolls, and grown-ups can sit down together for brunch, lunch, afternoon tea, or dinner. There's even a doll hair salon where a stylist can give a doll a new hairdo. American Girl also offers "perfect parties" to celebrate a birthday or any day as well as a full slate of special events, from crafts and activities to excursions. Much more than a store that sells dolls, says the company, "it's the place where imaginations can soar." A visit to American Girl creates "Fun today. Memories forever."

● Marketing experiences: American Girl does more than just make and sell high-end dolls. It creates special experiences between the dolls and the girls who adore them.

Customer Value and Satisfaction

Consumers usually face a broad array of products and services that might satisfy a given need. How do they choose among these many market offerings? Customers form expectations about the value and satisfaction that various market offerings will deliver and buy accordingly. Satisfied customers buy again and tell others about their good experiences. Dissatisfied customers often switch to competitors and disparage the product to others.

Marketers must be careful to set the right level of expectations. If they set expectations too low, they may satisfy those who buy but fail to attract enough buyers. If they set expectations too high, buyers will be disappointed. Customer value and customer satisfaction are key building blocks for developing and managing customer relationships. We will revisit these core concepts later in the chapter.

1.1   Buffalo Wild Wings: Fueling the Sports Fan Experience

"Wings. Beer. Sports." That's the long-standing motto for the fast-growing Buffalo Wild Wings restaurant chain. "B-Dubs"—as it's known to avid regulars—focuses on food and sports and "everything in between."

There's no doubt about it. Buffalo Wild Wings more than lives up to the "wings" and "beer" parts of the equation. It serves up wings in an abundant variety: boned or boneless, with five dry seasonings and 17 signature sauces ranging on the heat scale from Sweet BBQ (traditional BBQ sauce: satisfyingly sweet with no heat) to Desert Heat (smoky, sweet, and chili pepper seasoning) to Reformulated Blazin' (so good, it's scary—made with the unrelenting heat of the ghost pepper). To wash it all down, each B-Dubs restaurant pours as many as 30 different draft beers, with a full selection of domestic, import, and craft beer brands. You won't go hungry or thirsty at B-Dubs.

However, the Buffalo Wild Wings recipe for success goes much deeper than just selling wings and beer for profit. What really packs 'em in and keeps 'em coming back is the B-Dubs customer *experience*. Customers do gobble up the wings—more than 11 million wings chain-wide on last Super Bowl Sunday alone. But even more important, they come to B-Dubs to watch sports, trash talk, cheer on their sports teams, and meet old friends and make new ones—that is, a total eating and social experience. "We realize that we're not just in the business of selling wings," says the company. "We're something much bigger. We're in the business of fueling the sports fan experience. Our mission is to WOW people every day!"

Everything about B-Dubs is designed to deliver the ultimate sports experience, for any fan of any sport. The WOW begins the minute you step into any of Buffalo Wild Wings's 1,100 restaurants. This is not your average dark-and-dank sports bar. Instead, a B-Dubs is like a miniature stadium, with high ceilings, ample natural light, and brightly colored furnishings and wall coverings. The newest Buffalo Wild Wings "Stadia" restaurants are divided into barrier-free zones—including a bar area and a separate dining area. And every B-Dubs has 60 to 70 really big flat-screen TVs lining the walls, over the bar, and about everywhere else, ensuring that every table has the best seat in the house

no matter what your team or sport, including live streaming of local college and even high school events. B-Dubs creates an exciting environment that makes it the next best thing to being at the game—or something even better. "We consider ourselves to have 1,100 stadiums," says the chain's vice president for guest experience and innovation.

There's an experience for everyone at Buffalo Wild Wings. The chain appeals to a wide range of customers, from pub-loving sports nuts to families looking for an affordable evening out. Singles and couples gravitate to the bar area; families stick to the carpeted areas with booths. In addition to streaming sports events of all kinds on the big screens, B-Dubs supplies tableside tablets upon which customers can play poker or trivia games. A social jukebox feature lets guests control the music that plays on the restaurant's sound system.

It seems like there's always something happening in a B-Dubs to engage customers and enhance the experience. Take the chain's infamous Blazin' Wing Challenge—which promises a trophy-style T-shirt and a place on the Wall of Fame to any customer who can down a dozen wings with the chain's hottest signature sauce in no more than six minutes. That's no easy feat considering that the Blazin' sauce

is 60 times hotter than typical jalapeño sauce. During the six-minute binge, challengers are not allowed to use napkins or utensils, touch their faces, or eat or drink anything other than the wings (no dipping sauces, please). The menu boasts plenty of warnings, and servers advise most people not to even attempt the challenge. And before taking the plunge, each challenger signs a waiver agreeing that he or she "voluntarily assumes all risk of loss, damage, injury, illness, or death that may be sustained by him or her as a result." As you can imagine, when a challenge is announced over the PA, it usually draws a crowd.

Buffalo Wild Wings never rushes its guests. Whereas many other casual-dining restaurants have a "turn-and-burn" philosophy—cycling as many paying guests as possible through each table—at B-Dubs it's just the opposite. Buffalo Wild Wings encourages people to linger longer, enjoy the food, and soak up the ambiance.

To help make that happen, the chain has created a new staff position at each restaurant. In addition to the usual waitstaff, each table has a "Guest Experience Captain." According to B-Dubs's chief marketer, the captain is "like a host at any party," moving from table to table, chatting with guests, personalizing their experiences, and making sure their needs are met. Want a special

Customer-focused mission: The Buffalo Wild Wings mission is to provide a total eating and social environment that "fuels the sports fan experience" through in-store and online engagement.

Reprinted with permission of Buffalo Wild Wings, Inc.

game on one screen with another game on the screen next to it? Your Guest Experience Captain sees to it. Need help with a tablet? Your captain lends a hand. Want to try some new sauces? Your captain will make suggestions and even bring out samples of different sauces with complimentary fries for dipping.

Adding Guest Experience Captains is a major expense, especially when multiplied across shifts in all 1,100 stores. But Buffalo Wild Wings reasons that the captains will more than pay for themselves by enhancing the all-important guest experience, keeping customers around longer, and bringing them back more often. Buffalo Wild Wings restaurants with captains are achieving record levels of customer satisfaction and loyalty compared with those that have not yet brought captains on board. "It's just an opportunity for us to go a little deeper with the community than our competitors," says the B-Dubs marketing chief.

True to its "ultimate sports experience" mission, Buffalo Wild Wings actively engages its customers digitally and socially outside its restaurants as well as inside. In fact, the company brags that it's the number-one brand in its industry for digital fan engagement. B-Dubs's very active website draws 3 million visitors per month. The brand has more than 12 million Facebook fans, 660,000 Twitter followers, and very active YouTube and Instagram pages. It recently launched GameBreak, an app for fantasy football and other games that can be played inside or outside its restaurants. According to the company's customer experience executive, GameBreak players visit more often, stay longer, and tend to "buy that second or third beer or maybe one more basket of wings." In all, Buffalo Wild Wings creates a host of both in-store and online promotions that inspire camaraderie. "It's about giving [customers] tools to not just be spectators but advocates of the brand," says the chain.

Catering to the customer experience has paid big dividends for Buffalo Wild Wings. B-Dubs is now the nation's number-one seller of chicken wings and largest pourer of draft beer. Over the past five years, as other casual-dining restaurants have struggled with fierce competition and slow growth, B-Dubs's sales have more than tripled and profits are up 250 percent. The chain's "hottest wing coating available comes with a warning to B-Dubs' customers: 'keep away from eyes, pets, and children.' The sauce is called 'Blazin',' says one analyst. 'That term also happens to be a good description of the stock's performance lately.'"

Sources: Demitrios Kalogeropoulos, "Why Buffalo Wild Wings Is Spending More on Its Employees," *The Motley Fool*, June 24, 2015, www.fool.com/investing/general/2015/06/24/why-buffalo-wild-wings-is-spending-more-on-its-emp.aspx; Demitrios Kalogeropoulos, "3 Reasons Buffalo Wild Wings Can Keep Soaring in 2015," *The Motley Fool*, January 9, 2015, www.fool.com/investing/general/2015/01/09/3-reasons-why-buffalo-wild-wings-can-keep-soaring.aspx; Bryan Gruley, "The Sloppy Empire: How Buffalo Wild Wings Turned the Sports Bar into a $1.5 Billion Juggernaut," *Bloomberg Businessweek*, April 13–19, 2015, pp. 62–65; Tanya Dua, "The Buffalo Wild Wings Recipe for the 'Ultimate Sports Experience,'" August 4, 2015, http://digiday.com/brands/buffalo-wild-wings-recipe-ultimate-sports-experience/; and http://ir.buffalowildwings.com/financials.cfm and www.buffalowildwings.com/en/, accessed September 2016.

Exchanges and Relationships

Exchange
The act of obtaining a desired object from someone by offering something in return.

Marketing occurs when people decide to satisfy their needs and wants through exchange relationships. **Exchange** is the act of obtaining a desired object from someone by offering something in return. In the broadest sense, the marketer tries to bring about a response to some market offering. The response may be more than simply buying or trading products and services. A political candidate, for instance, wants votes; a church wants membership and participation; an orchestra wants an audience; and a social action group wants idea acceptance.

Marketing consists of actions taken to create, maintain, and grow desirable exchange *relationships* with target audiences involving a product, service, idea, or other object. Companies want to build strong relationships by consistently delivering superior customer value. We will expand on the important concept of managing customer relationships later in the chapter.

Markets

Market
The set of all actual and potential buyers of a product or service.

The concepts of exchange and relationships lead to the concept of a market. A **market** is the set of actual and potential buyers of a product or service. These buyers share a particular need or want that can be satisfied through exchange relationships.

Marketing means managing markets to bring about profitable customer relationships. However, creating these relationships takes work. Sellers must search for and engage buyers, identify their needs, design good market offerings, set prices for them, promote them, and store and deliver them. Activities such as consumer research, product development, communication, distribution, pricing, and service are core marketing activities.

Although we normally think of marketing as being carried out by sellers, buyers also carry out marketing. Consumers market when they search for products, interact with companies to obtain information, and make their purchases. In fact, today's digital technologies, from online sites and smartphone apps to the explosion of social media, have empowered consumers and made marketing a truly two-way affair. Thus, in addition to customer relationship management, today's marketers must also deal effectively with *customer-managed relationships*. Marketers are no longer asking only "How can we influence our customers?" but also "How can our customers influence us?" and even "How can our customers influence each other?"

● FIGURE | 1.2
A Modern Marketing System

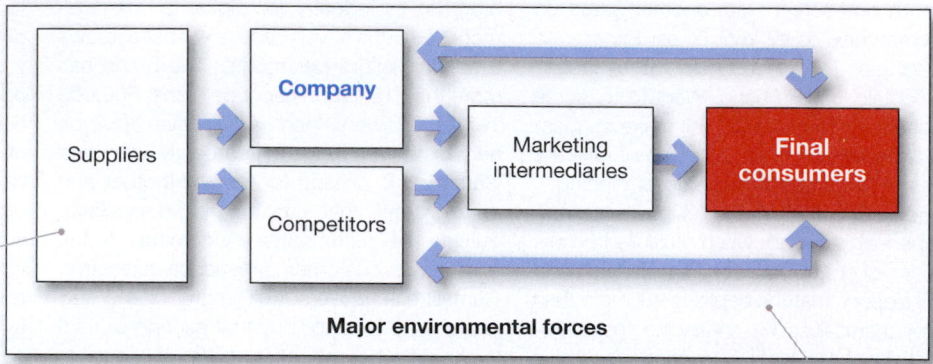

Each party in the system adds value. Walmart cannot fulfill its promise of low prices unless its suppliers provide low costs. Ford cannot deliver a high-quality car-ownership experience unless its dealers provide outstanding service.

Major environmental forces

Arrows represent relationships that must be developed and managed to create customer value and profitable customer relationships.

● **Figure 1.2** shows the main elements in a marketing system. Marketing involves serving a market of final consumers in the face of competitors. The company and competitors research the market and interact with consumers to understand their needs. Then they create and exchange market offerings, messages, and other marketing content with consumers, either directly or through marketing intermediaries. Each party in the system is affected by major environmental forces (demographic, economic, natural, technological, political, and social/cultural).

Each party in the system adds value for the next level. The arrows represent relationships that must be developed and managed. Thus, a company's success at engaging customers and building profitable relationships depends not only on its own actions but also on how well the entire system serves the needs of final consumers. Walmart cannot fulfill its promise of low prices unless its suppliers provide merchandise at low costs. And Ford cannot deliver a high-quality car-ownership experience unless its dealers provide outstanding sales and service.

Author Comment | Once a company fully understands its consumers and the marketplace, it must decide which customers it will serve and how it will bring them value.

Designing a Customer Value–Driven Marketing Strategy and Plan

Customer Value–Driven Marketing Strategy

Once it fully understands consumers and the marketplace, marketing management can design a customer value–driven marketing strategy. We define **marketing management** as the art and science of choosing target markets and building profitable relationships with them. The marketing manager's aim is to engage, keep, and grow target customers by creating, delivering, and communicating superior customer value.

Marketing management
The art and science of choosing target markets and building profitable relationships with them.

To design a winning marketing strategy, the marketing manager must answer two important questions: *What customers will we serve (what's our target market)?* and *How can we serve these customers best (what's our value proposition)?* We will discuss these marketing strategy concepts briefly here and then look at them in more detail in Chapters 2 and 7.

Selecting Customers to Serve

The company must first decide *whom* it will serve. It does this by dividing the market into segments of customers (*market segmentation*) and selecting which segments it will go after (*target marketing*). Some people think of marketing management as finding as many customers as possible and increasing demand. But marketing managers know that they cannot serve all customers in every way. By trying to serve all customers, they may not serve any customers well. Instead, the company wants to select only customers that it can serve well and profitably. For example, Nordstrom profitably targets affluent professionals; Dollar General profitably targets families with more modest means.

Ultimately, marketing managers must decide which customers they want to target and on the level, timing, and nature of their demand. Simply put, marketing management is *customer management* and *demand management*.

Choosing a Value Proposition

The company must also decide how it will serve targeted customers—how it will *differentiate and position* itself in the marketplace. A brand's *value proposition* is the set of benefits or values it promises to deliver to consumers to satisfy their needs. JetBlue promises to put "You Above All" by bringing "humanity back to travel." By contrast, Spirit Airlines gives you "Bare Fare" pricing: "Less Money. More Go." Homewood Suites by Hilton wants you to "Make yourself at home." 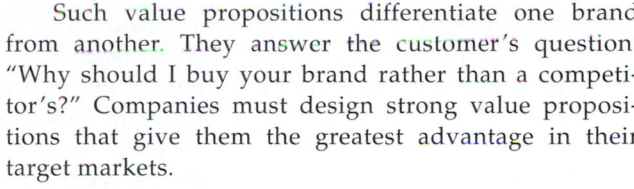 Meanwhile, the Hyatt Regency brand declares that sometimes "It's good not to be home." Its ads highlight the joys of traveling and the fun things that people do when they are traveling on business.

Such value propositions differentiate one brand from another. They answer the customer's question: "Why should I buy your brand rather than a competitor's?" Companies must design strong value propositions that give them the greatest advantage in their target markets.

● **Value propositions: The Hyatt Regency brand declares that sometimes "It's good not to be home." Its ads highlight the joys of business travel and staying at a Hyatt Regency hotel.**

Courtesy Hyatt Corporation. Photograph ©Richard Schultz-2015. Talent: Dean West.

Marketing Management Orientations

Marketing management wants to design strategies that will engage target customers and build profitable relationships with them. But what *philosophy* should guide these marketing strategies? What weight should be given to the interests of customers, the organization, and society? Very often, these interests conflict.

There are five alternative concepts under which organizations design and carry out their marketing strategies: the *production, product, selling, marketing,* and *societal marketing concepts.*

Production concept

The idea that consumers will favor products that are available and highly affordable; therefore, the organization should focus on improving production and distribution efficiency.

The Production Concept. The **production concept** holds that consumers will favor products that are available and highly affordable. Therefore, management should focus on improving production and distribution efficiency. This concept is one of the oldest orientations that guides sellers.

The production concept is still a useful philosophy in some situations. For example, both personal computer maker Lenovo and home appliance maker Haier dominate the highly competitive, price-sensitive Chinese market through low labor costs, high production efficiency, and mass distribution. However, although useful in some situations, the production concept can lead to marketing myopia. Companies adopting this orientation run a major risk of focusing too narrowly on their own operations and losing sight of the real objective—satisfying customer needs and building customer relationships.

Product concept

The idea that consumers will favor products that offer the most quality, performance, and features; therefore, the organization should devote its energy to making continuous product improvements.

The Product Concept. The **product concept** holds that consumers will favor products that offer the most in quality, performance, and innovative features. Under this concept, marketing strategy focuses on making continuous product improvements.

Product quality and improvement are important parts of most marketing strategies. However, focusing *only* on the company's products can also lead to marketing myopia. For example, some manufacturers believe that if they can "build a better mousetrap, the world will beat a path to their doors." But they are often rudely shocked. Buyers may be looking for a better solution to a mouse problem but not necessarily for a better mousetrap. The better solution might be a chemical spray, an exterminating service, a house cat, or something else that suits their needs even better than a mousetrap. Furthermore, a better mousetrap will not sell unless the manufacturer designs, packages, and prices it attractively; places it in convenient distribution channels; brings it to the attention of people who need it; and convinces buyers that it is a better product.

Selling concept
The idea that consumers will not buy enough of the firm's products unless the firm undertakes a large-scale selling and promotion effort.

The Selling Concept. Many companies follow the **selling concept**, which holds that consumers will not buy enough of the firm's products unless it undertakes a large-scale selling and promotion effort. The selling concept is typically practiced with unsought goods—those that buyers do not normally think of buying, such as life insurance or blood donations. These industries must be good at tracking down prospects and selling them on a product's benefits.

Such aggressive selling, however, carries high risks. It focuses on creating sales transactions rather than on building long-term, profitable customer relationships. The aim often is to sell what the company makes rather than to make what the market wants. It assumes that customers who are coaxed into buying the product will like it. Or, if they don't like it, they will possibly forget their disappointment and buy it again later. These are usually poor assumptions.

Marketing concept
A philosophy in which achieving organizational goals depends on knowing the needs and wants of target markets and delivering the desired satisfactions better than competitors do.

The Marketing Concept. The **marketing concept** holds that achieving organizational goals depends on knowing the needs and wants of target markets and delivering the desired satisfactions better than competitors do. Under the marketing concept, customer focus and value are the *paths* to sales and profits. Instead of a product-centered *make-and-sell* philosophy, the marketing concept is a customer-centered *sense-and-respond* philosophy. The job is not to find the right customers for your product but to find the right products for your customers.

● **Figure 1.3** contrasts the selling concept and the marketing concept. The selling concept takes an *inside-out* perspective. It starts with the factory, focuses on the company's existing products, and calls for heavy selling and promotion to obtain profitable sales. It focuses primarily on customer conquest—getting short-term sales with little concern about who buys or why.

In contrast, the marketing concept takes an *outside-in* perspective. As Herb Kelleher, the colorful founder of Southwest Airlines, once put it, "We don't have a marketing department; we have a customer department." The marketing concept starts with a well-defined market, focuses on customer needs, and integrates all the marketing activities that affect customers. In turn, it yields profits by creating relationships with the right customers based on customer value and satisfaction.

Implementing the marketing concept often means more than simply responding to customers' stated desires and obvious needs. *Customer-driven* companies research customers deeply to learn about their desires, gather new product ideas, and test product improvements. Such customer-driven marketing usually works well when a clear need exists and when customers know what they want.

In many cases, however, customers *don't* know what they want or even what is possible. As Henry Ford once remarked, "If I'd asked people what they wanted, they would have said faster horses."[9] For example, even 20 years ago, how many consumers would have thought to ask for now-commonplace products such as tablet computers, smartphones, digital cameras, 24-hour online buying, digital video and music streaming, and GPS systems in their cars and phones? Such situations call for *customer-driving* marketing—understanding customer needs even better than customers themselves do and creating products and services that meet both existing and latent needs, now and in the future. As an executive at 3M put it, "Our goal is to lead customers where they want to go before *they* know where they want to go."

● FIGURE | 1.3
Selling and Marketing
Concepts Contrasted

The selling concept takes an inside-out view that focuses on existing products and heavy selling. The aim is to sell what the company makes rather than making what the customer wants.

	Starting point	Focus	Means	Ends
The selling concept	**Factory**	Existing products	Selling and promoting	**Profits through sales volume**
The marketing concept	**Market**	Customer needs	Integrated marketing	**Profits through customer satisfaction**

The marketing concept takes an outside-in view that focuses on satisfying customer needs as a path to profits. As Southwest Airlines's colorful founder puts it, "We don't have a marketing department; we have a customer department."

● FIGURE | 1.4

Three Considerations Underlying
the Societal Marketing Concept

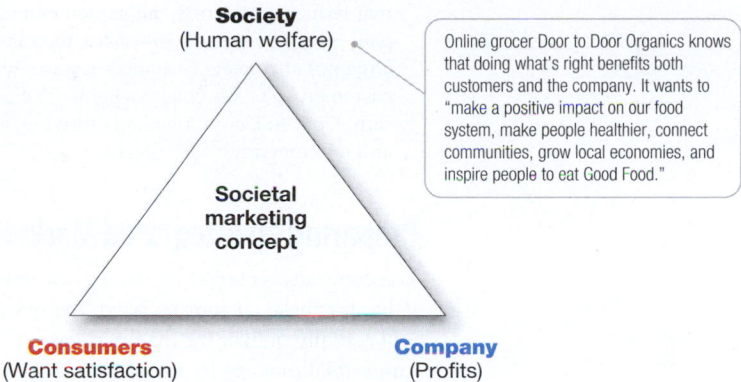

Society
(Human welfare)

Societal
marketing
concept

Online grocer Door to Door Organics knows
that doing what's right benefits both
customers and the company. It wants to
"make a positive impact on our food
system, make people healthier, connect
communities, grow local economies, and
inspire people to eat Good Food."

Consumers
(Want satisfaction)

Company
(Profits)

Societal marketing concept

The idea that a company's marketing
decisions should consider consumers'
wants, the company's requirements,
consumers' long-run interests, and
society's long-run interests.

The Societal Marketing Concept. The **societal marketing concept** questions
whether the pure marketing concept overlooks possible conflicts between consumer *short-
run wants* and consumer *long-run welfare*. Is a firm that satisfies the immediate needs and
wants of target markets always doing what's best for its consumers in the long run? The
societal marketing concept holds that marketing strategy should deliver value to customers in a way that maintains or improves both the consumer's *and society's* well-being. It
calls for *sustainable marketing,* socially and environmentally responsible marketing that
meets the present needs of consumers and businesses while also preserving or enhancing
the ability of future generations to meet their needs.

Even more broadly, many leading business and marketing thinkers are now preaching
the concept of *shared value,* which recognizes that societal needs, not just economic needs,
define markets.[10] The concept of shared value focuses on creating economic value in a way
that also creates value for society. A growing number of companies known for their hard-
nosed approaches to business—such as GE, Dow, Google, IBM, Intel, Johnson & Johnson,
Nestlé, Unilever, and Walmart—are rethinking the interactions between society and corporate performance. They are concerned not just with short-term economic gains but with the
well-being of their customers, the depletion of natural resources
vital to their businesses, the viability of key suppliers, and the economic well-being of the communities in which they operate.

One prominent marketer calls this *Marketing 3.0.* "Marketing
3.0 organizations are values-driven," he says. "I'm not talking about
being value-driven. I'm talking about 'values' plural, where values
amount to caring about the state of the world." Another marketer
calls it *purpose-driven marketing.* "The future of profit is purpose,"
he says.[11]

As ● **Figure 1.4** shows, companies should balance three
considerations in setting their marketing strategies: company profits, consumer wants, *and* society's interests. Online grocer Door to
Door Organics operates this way:[12]

● Door to Door Organics delivers fresh, high-quality, organic, natural, and local meat, dairy, produce, and groceries directly to homes,
offices, and schools in 16 states across the country. Customers order
online and receive weekly deliveries to their doorsteps year-round.
But Door to Door Organics does much more than just sell groceries
online for profit. It also dedicates itself to a deeply felt mission "to
bring more Good Food—food that positively impacts health, communities, and the environment—to more people in a sustainable
way." It wants to "make a positive impact on our food system, make
people healthier, connect communities, grow local economies, and
inspire people to eat Good Food."

● The societal marketing concept: Door to Door Organics does
more than just sell natural and organic groceries online for profit.
Its deep-felt mission is "to bring more Good Food—food that
positively impacts health, communities, and the environment—to
more people in a sustainable way."

Door to Door Organics

To meet its ambitious Good Food mission, Door to Door sources
most of what it sells from local family farms and businesses who
are "dedicated stewards of the land and use USDA-certified organic
practices that are healthier for both animals and people, better for the
soil, and reduce carbon emissions." Door to Door delivers to specified
areas on specific days of the week, maintaining a tight delivery radius

that reduces both costs and carbon emissions. And through careful food management, the company puts 44 percent less wasted food in landfills than the average grocery store. Door to Door Organics also treats customers responsibly. All deliveries carry a #JoyDelivered guarantee—if a customer isn't "absolutely delighted," the company will make it right. Thanks to its societal mission, Door to Door Organics is thriving, suggesting that doing good can benefit both the planet and the company.

Preparing an Integrated Marketing Plan and Program

The company's marketing strategy outlines which customers it will serve and how it will create value for these customers. Next, the marketer develops an integrated marketing program that will actually deliver the intended value to target customers. The marketing program builds customer relationships by transforming the marketing strategy into action. It consists of the firm's *marketing mix*, the set of marketing tools the firm uses to implement its marketing strategy.

The major marketing mix tools are classified into four broad groups, called the *four Ps* of marketing: product, price, place, and promotion. To deliver on its value proposition, the firm must first create a need-satisfying market offering (product). It must then decide how much it will charge for the offering (price) and how it will make the offering available to target consumers (place). Finally, it must engage target consumers, communicate about the offering, and persuade consumers of the offer's merits (promotion). The firm must blend each marketing mix tool into a comprehensive integrated marketing program that communicates and delivers the intended value to chosen customers. We will explore marketing programs and the marketing mix in much more detail in later chapters.

> **Author Comment** | Doing a good job with the first three steps in the marketing process sets the stage for step four, building and managing customer relationships.

Managing Customer Relationships and Capturing Customer Value

Engaging Customers and Managing Customer Relationships

The first three steps in the marketing process—understanding the marketplace and customer needs, designing a customer value–driven marketing strategy, and constructing a marketing program—all lead up to the fourth and most important step: engaging customers and managing profitable customer relationships. We first discuss the basics of customer relationship management. Then we examine how companies go about engaging customers on a deeper level in this age of digital and social marketing.

Customer Relationship Management

Customer relationship management is perhaps the most important concept of modern marketing. In the broadest sense, **customer relationship management** is the overall process of building and maintaining profitable customer relationships by delivering superior customer value and satisfaction. It deals with all aspects of acquiring, engaging, and growing customers.

Customer relationship management
The overall process of building and maintaining profitable customer relationships by delivering superior customer value and satisfaction.

Relationship Building Blocks: Customer Value and Satisfaction. The key to building lasting customer relationships is to create superior customer value and satisfaction. Satisfied customers are more likely to be loyal customers and give the company a larger share of their business.

Attracting and retaining customers can be a difficult task. Customers often face a bewildering array of products and services from which to choose. A customer buys from the firm that offers the highest **customer-perceived value**—the customer's evaluation of the difference between all the benefits and all the costs of a market offering relative to those of competing offers. Importantly, customers often do not judge values and costs "accurately" or "objectively." They act on *perceived* value.

Customer-perceived value
The customer's evaluation of the difference between all the benefits and all the costs of a marketing offer relative to those of competing offers.

To some consumers, value might mean sensible products at affordable prices. To other consumers, however, value might mean paying more to get more. For example, a Steinway piano—any Steinway piano—costs a lot. But to those who own one, a Steinway is a great value:[13]

A Steinway grand piano typically runs anywhere from $61,000 to as high as several hundred thousand dollars. The most popular model sells for about $87,000. But ask anyone who owns a Steinway grand piano, and they'll tell you that, when it comes to Steinway, price is nothing; the Steinway experience is everything. Steinway makes very high-quality pianos—handcrafting

● Perceived value: A Steinway piano—any Steinway piano—costs a lot. But a to Steinway customer, it's a small price to pay for the value of owning one.

© Westend61 GmbH/Alamy Stock Photo

Customer satisfaction

The extent to which a product's perceived performance matches a buyer's expectations.

each Steinway from more than 12,000 individual parts requires up to one full year. But, more importantly, owners get the Steinway mystique. The Steinway name evokes images of classical concert stages and the celebrities and performers who've owned and played Steinway pianos across more than 160 years. But Steinways aren't just for world-class pianists and the wealthy. Ninety-nine percent of all Steinway buyers are amateurs who perform only in their dens.

So is a Steinway piano worth its premium price compared with less expensive pianos? To many consumers, the answer is no. ● But to Steinway customers, whatever a Steinway costs, it's a small price to pay for the value of owning one. As one Steinway user puts it, "A pianist without a Steinway, for me, is the same as a singer without a voice." Says another, "My friendship with the Steinway piano is one of the most important and beautiful things in my life." Who can put a price on such feelings?

Customer satisfaction depends on the product's perceived performance relative to a buyer's expectations. If the product's performance falls short of expectations, the customer is dissatisfied. If performance matches expectations, the customer is satisfied. If performance exceeds expectations, the customer is highly satisfied or delighted.

Outstanding marketing companies go out of their way to keep important customers satisfied. Most studies show that higher levels of customer satisfaction lead to greater customer loyalty, which in turn results in better company performance. Companies aim to delight customers by promising only what they can deliver and then delivering more than they promise. Delighted customers not only make repeat purchases but also become willing marketing partners and "customer evangelists" who spread the word about their good experiences to others.

For companies interested in delighting customers, exceptional value and service become part of the overall company culture. For example, L.L.Bean—the iconic American outdoor apparel and equipment retailer—was founded on the principle that keeping customers satisfied is the key to building lasting relationships.[14]

> Year after year, L.L.Bean lands in the top 10 of virtually every list of top service companies, including J.D. Power's most recent list of "customer service champions." The customer-service culture runs deep at L.L.Bean. ● More than 100 years ago, Leon Leonwood Bean founded the company on a philosophy of complete customer satisfaction, expressed in the following guarantee: "I do not consider a sale complete until [the] goods are worn out and the customer [is] still satisfied." To this day, customers can return any item, no questions asked, even decades after purchase.
>
> The company's customer-service philosophy is perhaps best summed up in founder L.L.'s answer to the question "What is a customer?" His answer still forms the backbone of the company's values: "A customer is the most important person ever in this company—in person or by mail. A customer is not dependent on us, we are dependent on him. A customer is not an interruption of our work, he is the purpose of it. We are not doing a favor by serving him, he is doing us a favor by giving us the opportunity to do so. A customer is not someone to argue or match wits with. Nobody ever won an argument with a customer. A customer is a person who brings us his wants. It is our job to handle them profitably to him and to ourselves." Adds former L.L.Bean CEO Leon Gorman: "A lot of people have fancy things to say about customer service, but it's just a day-in, day-out, ongoing, never-ending, persevering, compassionate kind of activity."

NOTICE

I do not consider a sale complete until goods are worn out and customer still satisfied.

We will thank anyone to return goods that are not perfectly satisfactory.

Should the person reading this notice know of anyone who is not satisfied with our goods, I will consider it a favor to be notified.

Above all things we wish to avoid having a dissatisfied customer.

L.L.Bean

● Customer satisfaction: Customer service champion L.L.Bean was founded on a philosophy of complete customer satisfaction. As founder Leon Leonwood Bean put it, "I do not consider a sale complete until [the] goods are worn out and the customer [is] still satisfied."

L.L.Bean

Other companies that have become legendary for customer delight and their service heroics include Zappos.com, Amazon.com, Chick-fil-A, Nordstrom department stores, and JetBlue Airways. However, a company doesn't need to have over-the-top service to create customer delight. For example, no-frills grocery chain ALDI has highly satisfied customers, even though they have to bag their own groceries and can't use credit cards. ALDI's everyday very low pricing on good-quality products delights customers and keeps them coming back. Thus, customer satisfaction comes not just from service heroics but from how well a company delivers on its basic value proposition and helps customers solve their buying problems. "Most customers don't want to be 'wowed,'" says one marketing consultant. "They [just] want an effortless experience."[15]

Although a customer-centered firm seeks to deliver high customer satisfaction relative to competitors, it does not attempt to *maximize* customer satisfaction. A company can always increase customer satisfaction by lowering its prices or increasing its services. But this may result in lower profits. Thus, the purpose of marketing is to generate customer value *profitably*. This requires a very delicate balance: The marketer must continue to generate more customer value and satisfaction but not "give away the house."

Customer Relationship Levels and Tools. Companies can build customer relationships at many levels, depending on the nature of the target market. At one extreme, a company with many low-margin customers may seek to develop *basic relationships* with them. For example, P&G's Tide detergent does not phone or call on all of its consumers to get to know them personally. Instead, Tide creates engagement and relationships through product experiences, brand-building advertising, websites, and social media. At the other extreme, in markets with few customers and high margins, sellers want to create *full partnerships* with key customers. For example, P&G sales representatives work closely with Walmart, Kroger, and other large retailers that sell Tide. In between these two extremes, other levels of customer relationships are appropriate.

Beyond offering consistently high value and satisfaction, marketers can use specific marketing tools to develop stronger bonds with customers. For example, many companies offer *frequency marketing programs* that reward customers who buy frequently or in large amounts. Airlines offer frequent-flier programs, hotels give room upgrades to frequent guests, and supermarkets give patronage discounts to "very important customers."

These days almost every brand has a loyalty rewards program. Such programs can enhance and strengthen a customer's brand experience. For example, JetBlue's TrueBlue loyalty program offers the usual frequent-flier points and rewards but adds some nice enhancements such as no blackout dates and family sharing. More important, the TrueBlue program personalizes the customer experience. ● Each TrueBlue member has customized web and mobile pages, complete with a dashboard that shows available points, JetBlue activity history, connections with JetBlue rewards partners, and trip- and flight-planning links. The personalized pages not only make it easy for TrueBlue members to manage their points and rewards, they are also a handy one-stop trip-planning tool, all geared to an individual member's profile. As one member describes it: "Once

● Relationship marketing tools: JetBlue's TrueBlue loyalty program personalizes and strengthens the customer's brand experience, including a customized dashboard for managing points, rewards, and trips. JetBlue's pledge to members, "TrueBlue. For your loyalty, we give you ours."

JetBlue

you're an official TrueBlue member, go hog wild filling out your profile. Upload that stunning selfie with the blue filter as your member picture, pick your favorite JetBlue destinations, even create an ultimate dream itinerary to the Blue Ridge Mountains and add it to your TrueBlue Wishlist." JetBlue's pledge to members: "TrueBlue. For your loyalty, we give you ours."[16]

Significant changes are occurring in the nature of customer–brand relationships. Today's digital technologies—the internet and the surge in online, mobile, and social media—have profoundly changed the ways that people on the planet relate to one another. In turn, these events have had a huge impact on how companies and brands connect with customers and how customers connect with and influence each other's brand behaviors.

Customer Engagement and Today's Digital and Social Media

The digital age has spawned a dazzling set of new customer relationship-building tools, from websites, online ads and videos, mobile ads and apps, and blogs to online communities and the major social media, such as Twitter, Facebook, YouTube, Snapchat, and Instagram.

Customer-engagement marketing

Making the brand a meaningful part of consumers' conversations and lives by fostering direct and continuous customer involvement in shaping brand conversations, experiences, and community.

Yesterday's companies focused mostly on mass marketing to broad segments of customers at arm's length. By contrast, today's companies are using online, mobile, and social media to refine their targeting and to engage customers more deeply and interactively. The *old marketing* involved marketing brands *to* consumers. The *new marketing* is **customer-engagement marketing**—fostering direct and continuous customer involvement in shaping brand conversations, brand experiences, and brand community. Customer-engagement marketing goes beyond just selling a brand to consumers. Its goal is to make the brand a meaningful part of consumers' conversations and lives.

The burgeoning internet and social media have given a huge boost to customer-engagement marketing. Today's consumers are better informed, more connected, and more empowered than ever before. Newly empowered consumers have more information about brands, and they have a wealth of digital platforms for airing and sharing their brand views with others. Thus, marketers are now embracing not only customer relationship management but also *customer-managed relationships*, in which customers connect with companies and with each other to help forge and share their own brand experiences.

Greater consumer empowerment means that companies can no longer rely on marketing by *intrusion*. Instead, they must practice marketing by *attraction*—creating market offerings and messages that engage consumers rather than interrupt them. Hence, most marketers now combine their mass-media marketing efforts with a rich mix of online, mobile, and social media marketing that promotes brand–consumer engagement, brand conversations, and brand advocacy among customers.

For example, companies post their latest ads and videos on social media sites, hoping they'll go viral. They maintain an extensive presence on Twitter, YouTube, Facebook, Google+, Pinterest, Instagram, Snapchat, Vine, and other social media to create brand buzz. They launch their own blogs, mobile apps, online microsites, and consumer-generated review systems, all with the aim of engaging customers on a more personal, interactive level.

Take Twitter, for example. Organizations ranging from Dell, JetBlue, and Dunkin' Donuts to the Chicago Bulls, NASCAR, and the Los Angeles Fire Department have created Twitter pages and promotions. They use tweets to start conversations with and between Twitter's more than 307 million active users, address customer service issues, research customer reactions, and drive traffic to relevant articles, web and mobile marketing sites, contests, videos, and other brand activities.

Engaging customers: Life is good starts with a deeply felt, engagement-worthy sense of purpose: spreading the power of optimism. Then it creates online and social media tools that let people engage and help co-author the brand's story.

© WWPhotography/Alamy Stock Photo

Similarly, almost every company has something going on Facebook these days. Starbucks has more than 36 million Facebook "fans"; Coca-Cola has more than 96 million. And every major marketer has a YouTube channel where the brand and its fans post current ads and other entertaining or informative videos. Instagram, LinkedIn, Pinterest, Snapchat, Vine—all have exploded onto the marketing scene, giving brands more ways to engage and interact with customers. Skilled use of social media can get consumers involved with a brand, talking about it, and advocating it to others.

The key to engagement marketing is to find ways to enter targeted consumers' conversations with engaging and relevant brand messages. Simply posting a humorous video, creating a social media page, or hosting a blog isn't enough. And not all customers want to engage deeply or regularly with every brand. Successful engagement marketing means making relevant and genuine contributions to targeted consumers' lives and interactions. Consider T-shirt and apparel maker Life is good:[17]

> For starters, Life is good has an authentic, engagement-worthy sense of purpose: spreading the power of optimism. The brand is about helping people to open up, create relationships, and connect with other people. The company's infectious philosophy is best represented by the "Life is good" slogan itself and by Jake—the familiar beret-wearing, happy-go-lucky stick figure who quickly became a pop-culture icon. Life is good backs its optimism philosophy with good deeds, donating 10 percent of its net profits each year to help kids in need.
>
> Online and social media have become a perfect fit for sharing the Life is good message. Today, the brand fosters a thriving community of Optimists, with more than 2.6 million Facebook fans, 304,000 Twitter followers, 33,000 followers on Instagram, and an active YouTube channel. But the strongest engagement platform is the brand's own website, Lifeisgood.com, one of the most active customer-engagement sites found anywhere online. The site's "Live It" section gives brand fans a breath of "fresh share." It's a place where they share photos, videos, and stories showing the brand's role in their trials, triumphs, and optimism. To Life is good, true engagement is about deep meaningful relationships that go beyond the products it is selling. Says Life is good CEO Bert Jacobs: "You can't build a brand on your own; we have entered a world where customers co-author your story."

Consumer-Generated Marketing

Consumer-generated marketing
Brand exchanges created by consumers themselves—both invited and uninvited—by which consumers are playing an increasing role in shaping their own brand experiences and those of other consumers.

One form of customer-engagement marketing is **consumer-generated marketing**, by which consumers themselves play role in shaping their own brand experiences and those of others. This might happen through uninvited consumer-to-consumer exchanges in blogs, video-sharing sites, social media, and other digital forums. But increasingly, companies themselves are inviting consumers to play a more active role in shaping products and brand content.

Some companies ask consumers for new product and service ideas. For example, the LEGO Ideas website invites customers to submit and vote on ideas for new LEGO building sets. And at the My Starbucks Idea site, Starbucks collects ideas from customers on new products, store changes, and just about anything else that might make their Starbucks experience better. "You know better than anyone else what you want from Starbucks," says the company at the website. "So tell us. What's your Starbucks idea? Revolutionary or simple—we want to hear it." The site invites customers to share their ideas, vote on and discuss the ideas of others, and see which ideas Starbucks has implemented.[18]

Other companies invite customers to play an active role in shaping ads and brand content. For example, for 10 full years, PepsiCo's Doritos brand held a "Crash the Super Bowl" contest that invited 30-second ads from consumers and ran the best ones during the game. The contest attracted thousands of entries from around the world, and the hugely popular consumer-generated ads routinely finished in the top five of the *USA Today's* AdMeter rankings. Based on the success of the "Crash the Super Bowl" contest, Doritos now runs new campaigns that create fun fan-made ads and other content throughout the year.[19]

Many brands incorporate user-generated social media content into their own traditional marketing and social media campaigns. For example, Mountain Dew stirred up and employed user-generated content to create buzz around a limited-time reintroduction of its iconic Baja Blast flavor. ● It began with a discreet Rogue Wave social media campaign in which it posted tantalizing hints on Facebook, Snapchat, Instagram, and Twitter about bringing Baja Blast back. For example, on Snapchat, the brand showed quick clips of

Consumer-generated marketing: Mountain Dew stirred up user-generated content to create buzz around a limited-time reintroduction of its iconic Baja Blast drink, boosting online chatter by 170 percent.

PepsiCo

bottles. Mountain Dew fans responded with a flood of tweets and other social media chatter. "We started with discreet posts, but it didn't take long for Dew Nation to call us out and beg for the rumors to be true," says Mountain Dew's digital brand manager. "Some of our fans even created collages of all the images featuring Baja over the last few days to confirm to other members of Dew Nation that Baja was coming back." Mountain Dew then created ads on social media and men's lifestyle websites incorporating consumers' tweets. The result: Online chatter about Baja Blast shot up 170 percent.[20]

Despite the successes, however, harnessing consumer-generated content can be a time-consuming and costly process, and companies may find it difficult to mine even a little gold from all the content submitted. Moreover, because consumers have so much control over social media content, inviting their input can sometimes backfire. For example, McDonald's famously launched a Twitter campaign using the hashtag #McDStories, hoping that it would inspire heartwarming stories about Happy Meals. Instead, the effort was hijacked by Twitter users, who turned the hashtag into a "bashtag" by posting less-than-appetizing messages about their bad experiences with the fast-food chain. McDonald's pulled the campaign within only two hours, but the hashtag was still churning weeks, even months later.[21]

As consumers become more connected and empowered, and as the boom in digital and social media technologies continues, consumer brand engagement—whether invited by marketers or not—will be an increasingly important marketing force. Through a profusion of consumer-generated videos, shared reviews, blogs, mobile apps, and websites, consumers are playing a growing role in shaping their own and other consumers' brand experiences. Engaged consumers are now having a say in everything from product design, usage, and packaging to brand messaging, pricing, and distribution. Brands must embrace this new consumer empowerment and master the new digital and social media relationship tools or risk being left behind.

Partner Relationship Management

Partner relationship management
Working closely with partners in other company departments and outside the company to jointly bring greater value to customers.

When it comes to creating customer value and building strong customer relationships, today's marketers know that they can't go it alone. They must work closely with a variety of marketing partners. In addition to being good at *customer relationship management*, marketers must also be good at **partner relationship management**—working closely with others inside and outside the company to jointly engage and bring more value to customers.

Traditionally, marketers have been charged with understanding customers and representing customer needs to different company departments. However, in today's more connected world, every functional area in the organization can interact with customers. The new thinking is that—no matter what your job is in a company—you must understand marketing and be customer focused. Rather than letting each department go its own way, firms must link all departments in the cause of creating customer value.

Marketers must also partner with suppliers, channel partners, and others outside the company. Marketing channels consist of distributors, retailers, and others who connect the company to its buyers. The *supply chain* describes a longer channel, stretching from raw materials to components to final products that are carried to final buyers. Through *supply chain management*, companies today are strengthening their connections with partners all along the supply chain. They know that their fortunes rest on more than just how well they perform. Success at delivering customer value rests on how well their entire supply chain performs against competitors' supply chains.

Author | Look back at Figure 1.1.
Comment | In the first four steps of
the marketing process, the company
creates value *for* target customers and
builds strong relationships with them.
If it does that well, it can capture value
from customers in return, in the form of
loyal customers who buy and continue
to buy the company's brands.

Capturing Value from Customers

The first four steps in the marketing process outlined in Figure 1.1 involve engaging customers and building customer relationships by creating and delivering superior customer value. The final step involves capturing value in return in the form of sales, market share, and profits. By creating superior customer value, the firm creates satisfied customers who stay loyal and buy more. This, in turn, means greater long-run returns for the firm. Here, we discuss the outcomes of creating customer value: customer loyalty and retention, share of market and share of customer, and customer equity.

Creating Customer Loyalty and Retention

Good customer relationship management creates customer satisfaction. In turn, satisfied customers remain loyal and talk favorably to others about the company and its products. Studies show big differences in the loyalty between satisfied and dissatisfied customers. Even slight dissatisfaction can create an enormous drop in loyalty. Thus, the aim of customer relationship management is to create not only customer satisfaction but also customer delight.

Customer lifetime value

The value of the entire stream of
purchases a customer makes over a
lifetime of patronage.

Keeping customers loyal makes good economic sense. Loyal customers spend more and stay around longer. Research also shows that it's five times cheaper to keep an old customer than acquire a new one. Conversely, customer defections can be costly. Losing a customer means losing more than a single sale. It means losing the entire stream of purchases that the customer would make over a lifetime of patronage. For example, here is a classic illustration of **customer lifetime value**:[22]

● **Customer lifetime value: To keep customers coming back, Stew Leonard's has created the "Disneyland of dairy stores." Rule #1—The customer is always right. Rule #2—If the customer is ever wrong, reread Rule #1.**

Courtesy of Stew Leonard's

Stew Leonard, who operates a highly profitable four-store supermarket in Connecticut and New York, once said that he saw $50,000 flying out of his store every time he saw a sulking customer. Why? Because his average customer spent about $100 a week, shopped 50 weeks a year, and remained in the area for about 10 years. If this customer had an unhappy experience and switched to another supermarket, Stew Leonard's lost $50,000 in lifetime revenue. The loss could be much greater if the disappointed customer shared the bad experience with other customers and caused them to defect.

To keep customers coming back, Stew Leonard's has created what has been called the "Disneyland of Dairy Stores," complete with costumed characters, scheduled entertainment, a petting zoo, and animatronics throughout the store. From its humble beginnings as a small dairy store in 1969, Stew Leonard's has grown at an amazing pace. It's built 30 additions onto the original store, which now serves more than 300,000 customers each week. ● This legion of loyal shoppers is largely a result of the store's passionate approach to customer service. "Rule #1: The customer is always right. Rule #2: If the customer is ever wrong, reread rule #1."

Stew Leonard is not alone in assessing customer lifetime value. Lexus, for example, estimates that a single satisfied and loyal customer is worth more than $600,000 in lifetime sales, and the estimated lifetime value of a Starbucks customer is more than $14,000.[23] In fact, a company can lose money on a specific transaction but still benefit greatly from a long-term relationship. This means that companies must aim high in building customer relationships. Customer delight creates an emotional relationship with a brand, not just a rational preference. And that relationship keeps customers coming back.

Growing Share of Customer

Share of customer

The portion of the customer's purchasing
that a company gets in its product
categories.

Beyond simply retaining good customers to capture customer lifetime value, good customer relationship management can help marketers increase their **share of customer**— the share they get of the customer's purchasing in their product categories. Thus, banks want to increase "share of wallet." Supermarkets and restaurants want to get more "share of stomach." Car companies want to increase "share of garage," and airlines want greater "share of travel."

To increase share of customer, firms can offer greater variety to current customers. Or they can create programs to cross-sell and up-sell to market more products and services to existing customers. For example, Amazon is highly skilled at leveraging relationships with its 304 million customers worldwide to increase its share of each customer's spending budget:[24]

Once they log onto Amazon.com, customers often buy more than they intend, and Amazon does all it can to help make that happen. The online giant continues to broaden its merchandise assortment, creating an ideal spot for one-stop shopping. And based on each customer's purchase and search history, the company recommends related products that might be of interest. This recommendation system influences perhaps a third of all sales. Amazon's ingenious Amazon Prime two-day shipping program has also helped boost its share of customers' wallets. For an annual fee of $99, Prime members receive delivery of all their purchases within two days, whether it's a single paperback book or a 60-inch HDTV. According to one analyst, the ingenious Amazon Prime program "converts casual shoppers, who gorge on the gratification of having purchases reliably appear two days after the order, into Amazon addicts." As a result, Amazon's 54 million U.S. Prime customers now account for more than half of its U.S. sales. On average, a Prime customer spends 1.8 times more than a non-Prime customer.

Building Customer Equity

We can now see the importance of not only acquiring customers but also keeping and growing them. The value of a company comes from the value of its current and future customers. Customer relationship management takes a long-term view. Companies want to not only create profitable customers but also "own" them for life, earn a greater share of their purchases, and capture their customer lifetime value.

Customer equity

The total combined customer lifetime values of all of the company's customers.

What Is Customer Equity? The ultimate aim of customer relationship management is to produce high *customer equity*.[25] **Customer equity** is the total combined customer lifetime values of all of the company's current and potential customers. As such, it's a measure of the future value of the company's customer base. Clearly, the more loyal the firm's profitable customers, the higher its customer equity. Customer equity may be a better measure of a firm's performance than current sales or market share. Whereas sales and market share reflect the past, customer equity suggests the future. ● Consider Cadillac:[26]

In the 1970s and 1980s, Cadillac had some of the most loyal customers in the industry. To an entire generation of car buyers, the name *Cadillac* defined "The Standard of the World." Cadillac's share of the luxury car market reached a whopping 51 percent in 1976, and based on market share and sales, the brand's future looked rosy. However, measures of customer equity would have painted a bleaker picture. Cadillac customers were getting older (average age 60), and average customer lifetime value was falling. Many Cadillac buyers were on their last cars. Thus, although Cadillac's market share was good, its customer equity was not.

Compare this with BMW. Its more youthful and vigorous image didn't win BMW the early market share war. However, it did win BMW younger customers (average age about 40) with higher customer lifetime values. The result: In the years that followed, BMW's market share and profits soared while Cadillac's fortunes eroded badly. BMW overtook Cadillac in the 1980s. In recent years, Cadillac has struggled to make the Caddy cool again with edgier, high-performance designs that target a younger generation of consumers. More recently, the brand has billed itself as "The New Standard of the World" with marketing pitches based on "power, performance, and design," attributes that position it more effectively against the likes of BMW and Audi. Recent ads feature young achievers and invite consumers to "Dare Greatly" and "Drive the world forward." However, for the past decade, Cadillac's share of the luxury car market has stagnated.

● **Managing customer equity: To increase customer equity, Cadillac is making the classic car cool again among younger buyers, encouraging consumers to "Dare Greatly."**

General Motors

The moral: Marketers should care not just about current sales and market share. Customer lifetime value and customer equity are the name of the game.

Building the Right Relationships with the Right Customers. Companies should manage customer equity carefully. They should view customers as assets that need to be managed and maximized. But not all customers, not even all loyal customers, are good investments. Surprisingly, some loyal customers can be unprofitable, and some disloyal customers can be profitable. Which customers should the company acquire and retain?

The company can classify customers according to their potential profitability and manage its relationships with them accordingly. ● **Figure 1.5** classifies customers into one of four relationship groups, according to their profitability and projected loyalty.[27] Each group requires a different relationship management strategy. *Strangers* show low potential profitability and little projected loyalty. There is little fit between the company's offerings and their needs. The relationship management strategy for these customers is simple: Don't invest anything in them; make money on every transaction.

Butterflies are potentially profitable but not loyal. There is a good fit between the company's offerings and their needs. However, like real butterflies, we can enjoy them for only a short while and then they're gone. An example is stock market investors who trade shares often and in large amounts but who enjoy hunting out the best deals without building a regular relationship with any single brokerage company. Efforts to convert butterflies into loyal customers are rarely successful. Instead, the company should enjoy the butterflies for the moment. It should create satisfying and profitable transactions with them, capturing as much of their business as possible in the short time during which they buy from the company. Then it should move on and cease investing in them until the next time around.

True friends are both profitable and loyal. There is a strong fit between their needs and the company's offerings. The firm wants to make continuous relationship investments to delight these customers and engage, nurture, retain, and grow them. It wants to turn true friends into *true believers*, who come back regularly and tell others about their good experiences with the company.

Barnacles are highly loyal but not very profitable. There is a limited fit between their needs and the company's offerings. An example is smaller bank customers who bank regularly but do not generate enough returns to cover the costs of maintaining their accounts. Like barnacles on the hull of a ship, they create drag. Barnacles are perhaps the most problematic customers. The company might be able to improve their profitability by selling them more, raising their fees, or reducing service to them. However, if they cannot be made profitable, they should be "fired."

The point here is an important one: Different types of customers require different engagement and relationship management strategies. The goal is to build the *right relationships* with the *right customers*.

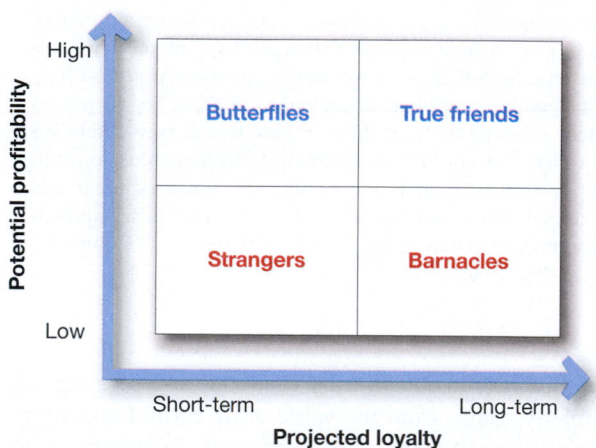

● **FIGURE | 1.5**
Customer Relationship Groups

Author | Marketing doesn't take
Comment | place in a vacuum. Now
that we've discussed the five steps in
the marketing process, let's look at how
the ever-changing marketplace affects
both consumers and the marketers
who serve them. We'll look more
deeply into these and other marketing
environment factors in Chapter 3.

The Changing Marketing Landscape

Every day, dramatic changes are occurring in the marketplace. Richard Love of HP observed, "The pace of change is so rapid that the ability to change has now become a competitive advantage." Yogi Berra, the legendary New York Yankees catcher and manager, summed it up more simply when he said, "The future ain't what it used to be." As the marketplace changes, so must those who serve it.

In this section, we examine the major trends and forces that are changing the marketing landscape and challenging marketing strategy. We look at five major developments: the digital age, the changing economic environment, the growth of not-for-profit marketing, rapid globalization, and the call for sustainable marketing practices.

The Digital Age: Online, Mobile, and Social Media Marketing

The explosive growth in digital technology has fundamentally changed the way we live—how we communicate, share information, access entertainment, and shop. Welcome to the age of the *Internet of Things* (IoT), a global environment where everything and everyone is digitally connected to everything and everyone else. More than 3.3 billion people—46 percent of the world's population—are now online; 64 percent of all American adults own smartphones. These numbers will only grow as digital technology rockets into the future.[28]

Most consumers are totally smitten with all things digital. For example, according to one study, 71 percent of Americans keep their mobile phone next to them when they sleep; 3 percent sleep with phone in hand. In just the past few years, people in the United States averaged more time per day with digital media (5.25 hours) than viewing traditional TV (4.5 hours).[29]

The consumer love affair with digital and mobile technology makes it fertile ground for marketers trying to engage customers. So it's no surprise that the internet and rapid advances in digital and social media have taken the marketing world by storm. **Digital and social media marketing** involves using digital marketing tools such as websites, social media, mobile ads and apps, online video, email, blogs, and other digital platforms to engage consumers anywhere, anytime via their computers, smartphones, tablets, internet-ready TVs, and other digital devices. These days, it seems that every company is reaching out to customers with multiple websites, newsy tweets and Facebook pages, viral ads and videos posted on YouTube, rich-media emails, and mobile apps that solve consumer problems and help them shop.

Digital and social media marketing
Using digital marketing tools such as websites, social media, mobile apps and ads, online video, email, and blogs to engage consumers anywhere, at any time, via their digital devices.

● At the most basic level, marketers set up company and brand websites that provide information and promote the company's products. Many companies also set up branded community sites, where customers can congregate and exchange brand-related interests and information. For example, Petco's Community site is a place "where pet lovers can connect, share, and learn" via a blog and discussion boards dedicated to dogs ("the bark"), cats ("the purr"), fish ("the splash"), birds ("the chirp"), reptiles ("the hiss"), and other types of pets. And Sony's PlayStation Forums site serves as a social hub for PlayStation PS4 game enthusiasts. It's a place where fans can follow social media posts about PS4, watch the latest PS4 videos, discover which PS4 games are trending on social networks, share content, and interact with other fans—all in real time.[30]

Beyond brand websites, most companies are also integrating social and mobile media into their marketing mixes.

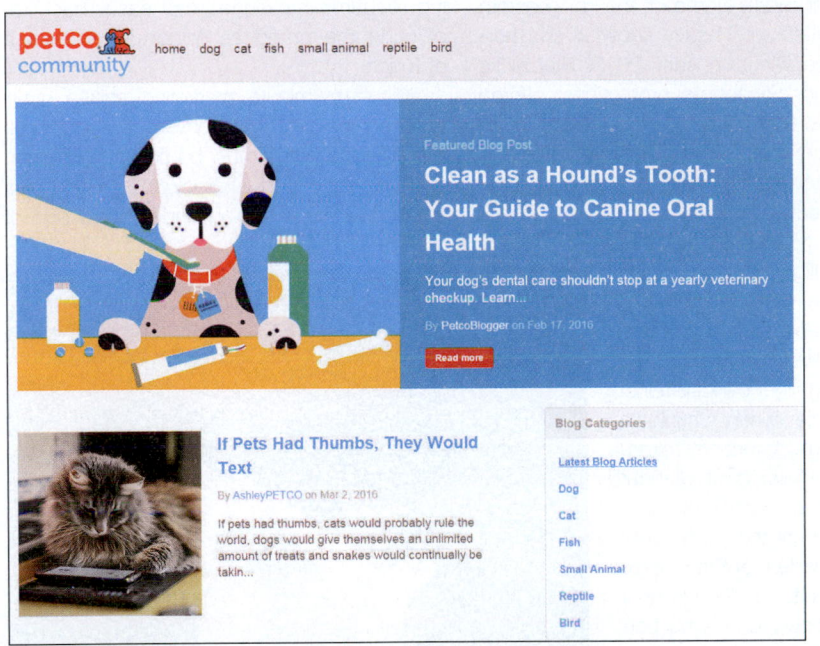

● **Branded online communities: Petco's Community site is a place where pet lovers can connect, share, and learn via a blog and discussion boards dedicated to pets of all types, from dogs and cats to birds, fish, and reptiles.**
Petco

Social Media Marketing

It's hard to find a brand website, or even a traditional media ad, that doesn't feature links to the brand's Facebook, Instagram, Twitter, Google+, YouTube, Snapchat, Pinterest, LinkedIn, or other social media sites. Social media provide exciting opportunities to extend customer engagement and get people talking about a brand.

Some social media are huge—Facebook has more than 1.59 billion active monthly members. Instagram has more than 400 million active monthly users, Twitter has more than 315 million monthly users, Google+ racks up 300 million active monthly visitors, and Pinterest draws in more than 100 million users. Reddit, the online social news community, has 234 million unique visitors each month from 185 countries. But smaller, more focused social media sites are also thriving, such as CafeMom, an online community of 20 million moms who exchange advice, entertainment, and commiseration at the community's online, Facebook, Twitter, Pinterest, YouTube, Google+, and mobile sites. Even tiny sites can attract active audiences, such as Birdpost.com for avid birdwatchers or Ravelry.com for knitters and crocheters.

Online social media provide a digital home where people can connect and share important information and moments in their lives. As a result, they offer an ideal platform for *real-time marketing,* by which marketers can engage consumers in the moment by linking brands to important trending topics, real-world events, causes, personal occasions, or other important happenings in consumers' lives (see Real Marketing 1.2).

1.2 Real-Time Marketing: Engaging Consumers in the Moment

A funny thing happened during Super Bowl XLVII in New Orleans. Early in the third quarter, the lights in the Mercedes-Benz Superdome suddenly went out. As 71,000 attendees and 106 million viewers restlessly bided their time and scratched their heads, engineers worked feverishly for a full 34 minutes to repair the power outage and bring the lights back on. But whereas the blackout was a disaster for Superdome management and CBS Sports and an annoyance for players and fans, at least one marketer saw it as an opportunity. Shortly after the blackout began, Nabisco's Oreo brand tweeted out a simple message: "Power out? No problem. You can still dunk in the dark."

That now-famous single tweet, conceived and approved within just minutes, grabbed more attention for Oreo than the brand's extravagant first-quarter advertisement. Within an hour, the "dunk in the dark" message was retweeted nearly 16,000 times and racked up more than 20,000 Facebook likes, resulting in tens of millions of favorable exposures. In the following days, Oreo received tons of media coverage and was hailed as "The Brand That Won the Blackout Bowl." Those were pretty impressive results for a one-off joke by a cookie maker.

Oreo's successful Super Bowl one-liner triggered a surge in real-time marketing. Brands of all kinds have since tried to create their own "Oreo moments" by aligning marketing content with real-world events and trending topics through timely tweets, videos, blog entries, and social media posts.

Today, many real-time marketing efforts center on major media events, such as the Super Bowl, the Grammys, and the Academy Awards. These events let marketers engage huge, ready-made audiences. For example, when its blockbuster feature *The LEGO Movie* failed to win a nomination in the Best Animated Movie category at a recent Oscars, LEGO turned the snub into an opportunity to engage viewers in real time during the Academy Awards TV spectacular. During a performance of the movie's Oscar-nominated song— "Everything Is Awesome"—performers handed out Oscars made of golden LEGO bricks to celebrities in the audience. Simultaneously, the brand tweeted coordinated real-time images and the message "#EverythingIsAwesome at

the #Oscars!" With pictures of stars such as Meryl Streep, Clint Eastwood, Oprah Winfrey, and Bradley Cooper posing with their LEGO Oscars, #LegoOscar became the number-one trending topic on Twitter.

Other companies use real-time efforts to connect their brands to current events important to customers. Starbucks has long used real-time marketing in this way. For example, after Winter Storm Nemo hit the northeastern United States with heavy snowfall and hurricane-force winds in early 2013, Starbucks Twitter and Facebook promotions offered free "Snow Day" coffee to customers in affected areas. "We wanted to make a grand [and timely] gesture," said a Starbucks digital marketer. As another example, Red Roof Inn regularly links airline flight data from flight tracking service FlightAware with Google's online search-ad system to beam real-time ads to stranded travelers facing flight cancellations. For example, when Chicago's O'Hare Airport recently experienced a major bout of flight cancellations, Red Roof managed to secure the top ad spot in three-quarters of the Google search results for "hotels near O'Hare," resulting in a 60 percent jump in bookings from those searches.

Companies sometimes set up temporary real-time command centers, or "war rooms," to created rapid responses during major events or even to counter competitor's moves. For example, with each new Apple iPhone model, at the very same time that Apple executives are on stage unveiling the features of the new phone, Samsung marketers are flooding social media with clever real-time "The next best thing is already here" responses. The strategy lets Samsung capitalize on the buzz surrounding the Apple introductions to promote its own wares.

Done right, real-time marketing can engage consumers

in the moment and make a brand more relevant. Done poorly, however, real-time engagements can come off as little more than awkward or inappropriate intrusions. Too often, brands simply toss standalone, last-minute ads or messages into social channels, hoping to "catch lightning in a bottle." But hastily prepared real-time content can fall flat or miss the mark. Worse, self-serving real-time messages can easily backfire, painting the brand as opportunistic or out of touch.

Minute-by-minute marketing strikes rarely succeed. Instead, to be consistently successful, real-time marketing must be part of a broader, carefully conceived strategy that makes the brand itself an engaging and relevant part of

Real-time marketing: Oreo's spectacularly successful "You can still dunk in the dark" tweet triggered a surge in real-time marketing, as brands of all kinds are now trying to create their own "Oreo moments" by aligning marketing content with real-world events and trending topics.

© Isabella Cassini/Alamy

consumers' lives. More than just trying to catch lightning in a bottle with one-off "Oreo moments" during showcase events, says one strategist, "keeping pace with the speed of digital culture actually requires marketers to plan ahead." Says another, "The war room has given way to a campsite—real-time marketing needs to be a built-in strategy all year round." Smart brands build agile, ongoing real-time marketing programs that listen in on the social space and respond with relevant marketing content that blends smoothly with the dynamics of customers' real-time social sharing.

For example, although the Oreo "dunk in the dark" tweet might have seemed off the cuff, it was only the latest in a long series of real-time marketing efforts designed to make Oreo a part of consumers' daily discourse. In the months preceding the Super Bowl, Oreo had successfully carried out its "Daily Twist" campaign. Each day for 100 days, the brand posted consumer-inspired Oreo cookie art tied to a relevant event. There was a Mars Rover Landing Oreo (an open-face cookie with tire tracks through its red crème filling), an Elvis Week Oreo (with an Oreo profile of the King of Rock 'n' Roll), and a Shark Week Oreo (with a jagged bite taken out of it, of course). The groundbreaking Daily Twist campaign gave Oreo a fourfold increase in Facebook shares and boosted its Instagram following from 2,200 to more than 85,000.

Oreo wages an ongoing social media and mobile campaign to engage consumers in the moment, skillfully injecting the brand into consumers' lives and conversations. For example, there was the wildly popular "Twist, Lick, Dunk" mobile game app that had 4 million users dunking 4 billion virtual Oreo cookies. Then there was the catchy 90-second "Oreo Cookie Balls" rap video, tweeted and posted on YouTube and other social media, showing clever ideas for eating and serving cookie balls during the end-of-year holiday season—it quickly went viral with more than 1.6 million views on YouTube alone. And leading up to a one Halloween season, Oreo Laboratorium, a series of brief stop-motion videos, showed different Oreo creatures and asked fans to "Name the Nomster." Such gems illustrate how Oreo keeps itself smack dab in the middle of the consumer consciousness by making real-time marketing an everyday event.

Whether connected to a social cause, a trending topic or event, a consumer's personal situation, or something else, the essential concept behind successful real-time marketing is pretty simple: Find or create ongoing connections between the brand and what's happening and important in consumers' lives, then engage consumers genuinely in the moment. One marketing executive suggests that real-time marketers should equate the practice to "meeting somebody in a social gathering—you don't accost them, instead you try to find a commonality of interest."

Sources: "Marketing in the Moments, to Reach Customers Online," *New York Times,* January 18, 2016, p. B5; Danielle Sacks, "The Story of Oreo: How an Old Cookie Became a Modern Marketing Personality," *Fast Company,* October 23, 2014, www.fastcocreate.com/3037068; Christopher Heine, "Ads in Real Time, All the Time," *Adweek,* February 18, 2013, p. 9; Christopher Palmeri, "'Lego Movie' Picks Up Tweets Not Trophies at Academy Awards," *Businessweek,* February 23, 2015, www.bloomberg.com/news/articles/2015-02-23/lego-movie-picks-up-tweets-not-trophies-at-academy-awards-show; Tanya Dua, "You Can Still Dunk in the Dark, but You Don't Need a War Room," *Digiday,* February 4, 2016, http://digiday.com/agencies/super-bowl-war-room-rip/; and www.360i.com/work/oreo-daily-twist/ and https://twitter.com/oreo/status/298246571718483968, accessed September 2016.

● NASA uses an extensive array of social media to engage and educate the next generation of space explorers. The agency invites you to "follow, share, and be a part of the conversation on popular social media sites with NASA."

NASA

Using social media might involve something as simple as a contest or promotion to garner Facebook Likes, tweets, or YouTube postings. But more often these days, large organizations of all kinds use a wide range of carefully integrated social media. For example, space agency NASA uses a broad mix of social media to educate the next generation of space explorers on its mission to "boldly go where no man has gone before." ● In all, NASA has more than 480 social media accounts spanning various topics and digital platforms. The agency has more than 14 million Facebook fans, 14.5 million Twitter followers, 8.8 million Instagram followers, and 76,000 YouTube subscribers. One of NASA's largest-ever social media campaigns supported the recent test launch of the Orion spacecraft, which will eventually carry humans to deep space destinations, such as Mars or an asteroid:[31]

The extensive campaign included a dozen or more YouTube "I'm On Board" videos starring actors from classic science-fiction TV shows, such as *Star Trek* and *The Incredible Hulk*. Even *Sesame Street*'s Elmo added his support, proudly displaying his "I'm On Board" boarding pass, chatting up astronauts, and relaying facts and launch information on the *Sesame Street* Twitter feed and other digital platforms. The campaign offered social media users a chance to put their names on a microchip aboard the space vehicle—more than a million people signed on. During the flight, NASA's social media team briefed the public through Twitter, Facebook, and Instagram posts. In all, it's a new NASA. People once followed NASA events from afar by gathering around their TV sets. Not anymore. Now, the space agency engages fans directly through interactive social media. "You can ask an astronaut a question," says NASA's social media manager. "You can...really be part of the experience in a much different way than ever before. It's not your father and grandfather's space agency anymore."

Mobile Marketing

Mobile marketing is perhaps the fastest-growing digital marketing platform. Smartphones are ever present, always on, finely targeted, and highly personal. This makes them ideal for engaging customers anytime, anywhere as they move through the buying process. For example, Starbucks customers can use their mobile devices for everything from finding the nearest Starbucks and learning about new products to placing and paying for orders.

Four out of five smartphone users use their phones to shop—browsing product information through apps or the mobile web, making in-store price comparisons, reading online product reviews, finding and redeeming coupons, and more. Almost 30 percent of all online purchases are now made from mobile devices, and mobile online sales are growing 2.6 times faster than total online sales. During this past holiday season, mobile shoppers made up more than 70 percent of traffic to Walmart.com, accounting for almost half the site's orders over the Black Friday weekend.[32]

Marketers use mobile channels to stimulate immediate buying, make shopping easier, enrich the brand experience, or all of these. ● Consider Redbox:[33]

Redbox DVD rental kiosks are unmanned, so the company has to find innovative ways to engage customers and personalize its service—most of which it does through its website and

mobile app, text messaging, and email. Customers can use the Redbox mobile app to locate Redbox kiosks, check availability of movies and games, and reserve rentals for quick pickup. Mobile customers can also join the Redbox Text Club to receive texts about the latest Redbox news, releases, and members-only deals.

Text Club members are Redbox's most valuable customers, so the company launched a 10-day-long mobile marketing campaign to increase membership. Using large call-to-action stickers on kiosks, a blast of email, and posts on its Facebook and other social media pages, Redbox offered discounts of between 10 cents and $1.50 on the next DVD rental to customers who texted the word "DEALS" to 727272. The campaign—called "The 10 Days of Deals"—generated nearly 1.5 million text messages from some 400,000 customers, resulting in more than 200,000 new Text Club members. "Mobile is like having a kiosk in your hand," explains Redbox's chief marketer. "It's an incredibly important part of our [marketing] strategy."

Although online, social media, and mobile marketing offer huge potential, most marketers are still learning how to use them effectively. The key is to blend the new digital approaches with traditional marketing to create a smoothly integrated marketing strategy and mix. We will examine digital, mobile, and social media marketing throughout the text—they touch almost every area of marketing strategy and tactics. Then, after we've covered the marketing basics, we'll look more deeply into digital and direct marketing in Chapter 17.

The Changing Economic Environment

The Great Recession of 2008 to 2009 and its aftermath hit American consumers hard. After two decades of overspending, new economic realities forced consumers to bring their consumption back in line with their incomes and rethink their buying priorities.

In today's post-recession era, consumer incomes and spending are again on the rise. However, even as the economy has strengthened, rather than reverting to their old free-spending ways, Americans are now showing a new enthusiasm for frugality. Sensible consumption has made a comeback, and it appears to be here to stay. The new consumer spending values emphasize simpler living and more value for the

● Mobile marketing: Redbox uses mobile marketing to engage its customers, personalize its service, and promote DVD rentals. Its "The 10 Days of Deals" mobile campaign generated nearly 1.5 million text messages, resulting in more than 200,000 new Redbox Text Club members.

dollar. Despite their rebounding means, consumers continue to buy less, clip more coupons, swipe their credit cards less, and put more in the bank.

Many consumers are reconsidering their very definition of the good life. "People are finding happiness in old-fashioned virtues—thrift, savings, do-it-yourself projects, self-improvement, hard work, faith, and community," says one consumer behavior expert. "We are moving from mindless to mindful consumption."[34] The new, more frugal spending values don't mean that people have resigned themselves to lives of deprivation. As the economy has improved, consumers are again indulging in luxuries and bigger-ticket purchases, just more sensibly.

In response, companies in all industries—from discounters such as Target to luxury brands such as Lexus—have realigned their marketing strategies with the new economic realities. More than ever, marketers are emphasizing the *value* in their value propositions. They are focusing on value for the money, practicality, and durability in their product offerings and marketing pitches.

For example, for years discount retailer Target focused increasingly on the "Expect More" side of its "Expect More. Pay Less." value proposition. Its carefully cultivated "upscale-discounter" image successfully differentiated it from Walmart's more hard-nosed "lowest-price" position. But when the economy soured, many consumers worried that Target's trendier assortments and hip marketing also meant higher prices. So Target has shifted its balance more toward the "Pay Less" half of the slogan, making certain that its prices are in line with Walmart's and that customers know it. Although still trendy, Target's marketing now emphasizes more practical price and savings appeals. Offering "more for your money" holds a prominent place in the Target mission. "We think a lot about your budget and how to give you the best value every time you shop with us," says the company.[35]

In adjusting to the new economy, companies may be tempted to cut their marketing budgets and slash prices in an effort to coax customers into opening their wallets. However, although cutting costs and offering selected discounts can be important marketing tactics, smart marketers understand that making cuts in the wrong places can damage long-term brand images and customer relationships. The challenge is to balance the brand's value proposition with the current times while also enhancing its long-term equity. Thus, rather than slashing prices in uncertain economic times, many marketers hold the line on prices and instead explain why their brands are worth it.

The Growth of Not-for-Profit Marketing

In recent years, marketing has also become a major part of the strategies of many not-for-profit organizations, such as colleges, hospitals, museums, zoos, symphony orchestras, foundations, and even churches. The nation's not-for-profits face stiff competition for support and membership. Sound marketing can help them attract membership, funds, and support.

● For example, not-for-profit St. Jude Children's Research Hospital has a special mission: "Finding cures. Saving children." It directly serves some 7,800 patients each year plus countless thousands more through its affiliations and clinical trials in places across the country and around the world. Families never receive a bill from St. Jude, for treatment, travel, housing, or food. To accomplish this mission, St. Jude raises the funds for its $2.4 million daily operating budget through powerhouse marketing.[36] Fundraising efforts include everything from public service announcements, celebrity endorsements, corporate partnerships, and an extensive online presence to events such as Trike-a-thons, Math-a-thons, an Up 'Til Dawn student challenge, and the St. Jude Dream Home Giveaway. St. Jude's works with more than 70 corporate partners such as Target, Domino's, Williams-Sonoma,

● **Not-for-profit marketing:** St. Jude Children's Research Hospital aggressively markets its powerful mission: "Finding cures. Saving children."
ALSAC I St. Jude

Regal Cinemas, and Expedia that participate in its annual Thanks and Giving campaign, which asks consumers to "give thanks for the healthy kids in your life, and give to those who are not." The result is a pervasive brand that brings in more than $1 billion each year from private donors—from preschoolers and professionals to eighth-graders and 80-year-olds.

Another example is the World Wildlife Fund (WWF), a global not-for-profit conservation organization whose mission is to conserve nature and protect the world's wildlife. WWF operates in 100 countries under funding from government grants, foundations, corporations, and individuals—1.2 million members in the United States and nearly 5 million members worldwide. WWF uses sophisticated marketing to raise the considerable resources it needs to accomplish its sweeping mission. Just one example is the WWF's recent cost-efficient but effective #LastSelfie Snapchat campaign:

> The idea behind the WWF #Last Selfie campaign is that the world's endangered wildlife species are disappearing from the earth as quickly as a Snapchat. To make the point, WWF sent nine-second Snapchat pictures of endangered animals to WWF followers worldwide with the message "Don't let this be my #LastSelfie," urging recipients to take a screenshot. Within only eight hours, the campaign generated 5,000 tweets viewed on 6 million timelines. Within only a week, there were 40,000 tweets reaching 120 million users. In all, the #LastSelfie campaign reached more than half of all Twitter users. It also helped WWF to meet its monthly donation target in just three days and led to a record number of animal adoptions through WWF's website. More broadly, thanks to such marketing efforts and despite its limited marketing budget, WWF raised nearly $290 million in funds last year, more than a third of it from individual donors.

Government agencies have also shown an increased interest in marketing. For example, the U.S. military has a marketing plan to attract recruits to its different services, and various government agencies are now designing social marketing campaigns to encourage energy conservation and concern for the environment or discourage smoking, illegal drug use, and obesity. Even the once-stodgy U.S. Postal Service has developed innovative marketing to sell commemorative stamps, promote its Priority Mail services, and lift its image as a contemporary and competitive organization. In all, the U.S. government is the nation's 39th largest advertiser, with an annual advertising budget of more than $980 million.[37]

Rapid Globalization

As they are redefining their customer relationships, marketers are also taking a fresh look at the ways in which they relate with the broader world around them. Today, almost every company, large or small, is touched in some way by global competition. A neighborhood florist buys its flowers from Mexican nurseries, and a large U.S. electronics manufacturer competes in its home markets with giant Korean rivals. A fledgling internet retailer finds itself receiving orders from all over the world at the same time that an American consumer goods producer introduces new products into emerging markets abroad.

American firms have been challenged at home by the skillful marketing of European and Asian multinationals. Companies such as Toyota, Nestlé, and Samsung have often outperformed their U.S. competitors in American markets. Similarly, U.S. companies in a wide range of industries have developed truly global operations, making and selling their products worldwide. Quintessentially American McDonald's now serves 70 million customers daily in more than 36,000 local restaurants in more than 100 countries worldwide—68 percent of its corporate revenues come from outside the United States. Similarly, Nike markets in 190 countries, with non-U.S. sales accounting for 52 percent of its worldwide sales.[38] Today, companies are not just selling more of their locally produced goods in international markets; they are also sourcing more supplies and components abroad and developing new products for specific markets around the world.

Thus, managers in countries around the world are increasingly taking a global, not just local, view of the company's industry, competitors, and opportunities. They are asking: What is global marketing? How does it differ from domestic marketing? How do global competitors and forces affect our business? To what extent should we "go global"? We will discuss the global marketplace in more detail in Chapter 19.

Sustainable Marketing—The Call for More Environmental and Social Responsibility

Marketers are reexamining their relationships with social values and responsibilities and with the very earth that sustains us. As the worldwide consumerism and environmentalism movements mature, today's marketers are being called on to develop *sustainable marketing* practices. Corporate ethics and social responsibility have become hot topics for almost every business. And few companies can ignore the renewed and very demanding environmental movement. Every company action can affect customer relationships. Today's customers expect companies to deliver value in a socially and environmentally responsible way.

The social responsibility and environmental movements will place even stricter demands on companies in the future. Some companies resist these movements, budging only when forced by legislation or organized consumer outcries. Forward-looking companies, however, readily accept their responsibilities to the world around them. They view sustainable marketing as an opportunity to do well by doing good. They seek ways to profit by serving immediate needs and the best long-run interests of their customers and communities.

● Sustainable marketing: Ben & Jerry's three-part "linked prosperity" mission drives it to make fantastic ice cream (product mission), manage the company for sustainable financial growth (economic mission), and use the company "in innovative ways to make the world a better place" (social mission). Both Ben & Jerry's and its products are "Made of Something Better."

Clark Brennan / Alamy Stock Photo

Some companies, such as Patagonia, Timberland, Method, Ben & Jerry's, and others, practice *caring capitalism*, setting themselves apart by being civic minded and responsible. They build social and environmental responsibility into their company value and mission statements. ● For example, Ben & Jerry's, a division of Unilever, has long prided itself on being a "values-led business," one that creates "linked prosperity" for everyone connected to the brand—from suppliers to employees to customers and communities:[39]

Under its three-part mission, Ben & Jerry's wants to make fantastic ice cream (product mission), manage the company for sustainable financial growth (economic mission), and use the company "in innovative ways to make the world a better place" (social mission). Ben & Jerry's backs its mission with actions. For example, the company is committed to using wholesome, natural, non-GMO, fair-trade-certified ingredients and buys from local farms. It employs business practices "that respect the earth and the environment," investing in wind energy, solar usage, travel offsets, and carbon neutrality. Its Caring Dairy program helps farmers develop more sustainable practices on the farm ("Caring Dairy means happy cows, happy farmers, and a happy planet"). The Ben & Jerry's Foundation awards nearly $2 million annually in grassroots grants to community service organizations and projects in communities across the nation. Ben & Jerry's also operates 14 PartnerShops, scoop shops that are independently owned and operated by community-based not-for-profit organizations. The company waives standard franchise fees for these shops.

Sustainable marketing presents both opportunities and challenges for marketers. We will revisit the topic of sustainable marketing in greater detail in Chapter 20.

Author Comment | Remember Figure 1.1 outlining the marketing process? Now, based on everything we've discussed in this chapter, we'll expand that figure to provide a road map for learning marketing throughout the remainder of the text.

So, What Is Marketing? Pulling It All Together

At the start of this chapter, Figure 1.1 presented a simple model of the marketing process. Now that we've discussed all the steps in the process, ● **Figure 1.6** presents an expanded model that will help you pull it all together. What is marketing? Simply put, marketing is the process of engaging customers and building profitable customer relationships by creating value for customers and capturing value in return.

● FIGURE | 1.6

An Expanded Model of the Marketing Process

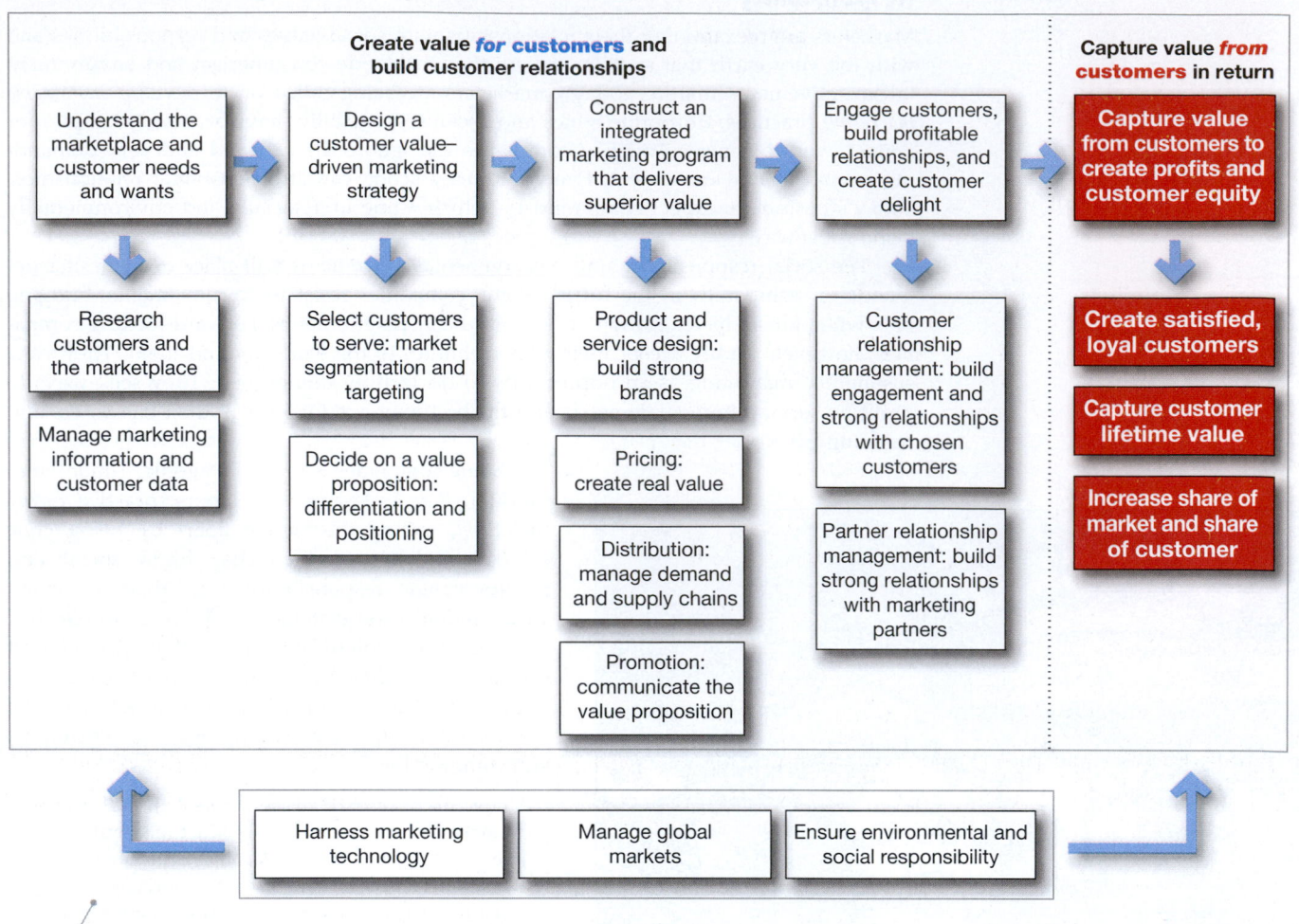

This expanded version of Figure 1.1 at the beginning of the chapter provides a good road map for the rest of the text. The underlying concept of the entire text is that marketing creates value for customers in order to capture value from customers in return.

The first four steps of the marketing process focus on creating value for customers. The company first gains a full understanding of the marketplace by researching customer needs and managing marketing information. It then designs a customer-driven marketing strategy based on the answers to two simple questions. The first question is "What consumers will we serve?" (market segmentation and targeting). Good marketing companies know that they cannot serve all customers in every way. Instead, they need to focus their resources on the customers they can serve best and most profitably. The second marketing strategy question is "How can we best serve targeted customers?" (differentiation and positioning). Here, the marketer outlines a value proposition that spells out what values the company will deliver to win target customers.

With its marketing strategy chosen, the company now constructs an integrated marketing program—consisting of a blend of the four marketing mix elements, the four Ps—that transforms the marketing strategy into real value for customers. The company develops product offers and creates strong brand identities for them. It prices these offers to create real customer value and distributes the offers to make them available to target consumers. Finally, the company designs promotion programs that engage target customers, communicate the value proposition, and persuade customers to act on the market offering.

Perhaps the most important step in the marketing process involves building value-laden, profitable relationships with target customers. Throughout the process, marketers practice customer relationship management to create customer satisfaction and delight. They engage customers in the process of creating brand conversations, experiences, and community. In creating customer value and relationships, however, the company cannot go it alone. It must work closely with marketing partners both inside the company and throughout its marketing system. Thus, beyond practicing good customer relationship management and customer-engagement marketing, firms must also practice good partner relationship management.

The first four steps in the marketing process create value *for* customers. In the final step, the company reaps the rewards of its strong customer relationships by capturing value *from* customers. Delivering superior customer value creates highly satisfied customers who will buy more and buy again. This helps the company capture customer lifetime value and greater share of customer. The result is increased long-term customer equity for the firm.

Finally, in the face of today's changing marketing landscape, companies must take into account three additional factors. In building customer and partner relationships, they must harness marketing technologies in the new digital age, take advantage of global opportunities, and ensure that they act sustainably in an environmentally and socially responsible way.

Figure 1.6 provides a good road map to future chapters of this text. Chapters 1 and 2 introduce the marketing process, with a focus on building customer relationships and capturing value from customers. Chapters 3 through 6 address the first step of the marketing process—understanding the marketing environment, managing marketing information, and understanding consumer and business buyer behavior. In Chapter 7, we look more deeply into the two major marketing strategy decisions: selecting which customers to serve (segmentation and targeting) and determining a value proposition (differentiation and positioning). Chapters 8 through 17 discuss the marketing mix variables one by one. Chapter 18 sums up customer-driven marketing strategy and creating competitive advantage in the marketplace. The final two chapters examine special marketing considerations: global marketing and sustainable marketing.

1 | Reviewing and Extending the Concepts

OBJECTIVES REVIEW AND KEY TERMS

Objectives Review

Today's successful companies—whether large or small, for-profit or not-for-profit, domestic or global—share a strong customer focus and a heavy commitment to marketing. The goal of marketing is to engage customers and manage profitable customer relationships.

OBJECTIVE 1-1   Define marketing and outline the steps in the marketing process. *(pp 4–6)*

Marketing is the process by which companies create value for customers and build strong customer relationships in order to capture value from customers in return. The marketing process involves five steps. The first four steps create value *for* customers. First, marketers need to understand the marketplace and customer needs and wants. Next, marketers design a customer-driven marketing strategy with the goal of getting, engaging, and growing target customers. In the third step, marketers construct a marketing program that actually delivers superior value. All of these steps form the basis for the fourth step: engaging customers, building profitable customer relationships, and creating customer delight. In the final step, the company reaps the rewards of strong customer relationships by capturing value *from* customers.

OBJECTIVE 1-2   Explain the importance of understanding the marketplace and customers and identify the five core marketplace concepts. *(pp 6–10)*

Outstanding marketing companies go to great lengths to learn about and understand their customers' *needs, wants,* and *demands*. This understanding helps them to design want-satisfying market offerings and build value-laden customer relationships by which they can capture *customer lifetime value* and greater *share of customer*. The result is increased long-term *customer equity* for the firm.

The core marketplace concepts are needs, wants, and demands; market offerings (products, services, and experiences); value and satisfaction; exchange and relationships; and markets. Companies address needs, wants, and demands by putting forth a value proposition, a set of benefits that they promise to consumers to satisfy their needs. The value proposition is fulfilled through a market offering, which delivers customer value and satisfaction, resulting in long-term exchange relationships with customers.

OBJECTIVE 1-3   Identify the key elements of a customer value–driven marketing strategy and discuss the marketing management orientations that guide marketing strategy. *(pp 10–14)*

To design a winning marketing strategy, the company must first decide whom it will serve. It does this by dividing the market into segments of customers (*market segmentation*) and selecting which segments it will cultivate (*target marketing*). Next, the company must decide *how* it will serve targeted customers (how it will *differentiate and position* itself in the marketplace).

Marketing management can adopt one of five competing market orientations. The *production concept* holds that management's task is to improve production efficiency and bring down prices. The *product concept* holds that consumers favor products that offer the most in quality, performance, and innovative features; thus, little promotional effort is required. The *selling concept* holds that consumers will not buy enough of an organization's products unless it undertakes a large-scale selling and promotion effort. The *marketing concept* holds that achieving organizational goals depends on determining the needs and wants of target markets and delivering the desired satisfactions more effectively and efficiently than competitors do. The *societal marketing concept* holds that generating customer satisfaction *and* long-run societal well-being through sustainable marketing strategies is key to both achieving the company's goals and fulfilling its responsibilities.

OBJECTIVE 1-4 Discuss customer relationship management and identify strategies for creating value *for* customers and capturing value *from* customers in return. (pp 14–22)

Broadly defined, *customer relationship management* is the process of engaging customers and building and maintaining profitable customer relationships by delivering superior customer value and satisfaction. *Customer-engagement marketing* aims to make a brand a meaningful part of consumers' conversations and lives through direct and continuous customer involvement in shaping brand conversations, experiences, and community. The aim of customer relationship management and customer engagement is to produce high *customer equity,* the total combined customer lifetime values of all of the company's customers. The key to building lasting relationships is the creation of superior *customer value* and *satisfaction.* In return for creating value *for* targeted customers, the company captures value *from* customers in the form of profits and customer equity.

OBJECTIVE 1-5 Describe the major trends and forces that are changing the marketing landscape in this age of relationships. (pp 22–31)

Dramatic changes are occurring in the marketing arena. The digital age has created exciting new ways to learn about and relate to individual customers. As a result, advances in digital and social media have taken the marketing world by storm. Online, mobile, and social media marketing offer exciting new opportunities to target customers more selectively and engage them more deeply. The key is to blend the new digital approaches with traditional marketing to create a smoothly integrated marketing strategy and mix.

The Great Recession caused consumers to rethink their buying priorities and bring their consumption back in line with their incomes. Even as the post-recession economy has strengthened, Americans are now showing an enthusiasm for frugality not seen in decades. The challenge is to balance a brand's value proposition with current times while also enhancing its long-term equity.

In recent years, marketing has become a major part of the strategies for many not-for-profit organizations, such as colleges, hospitals, museums, zoos, symphony orchestras, foundations, and even churches. Also, in an increasingly smaller world, many marketers are now connected *globally* with their customers, marketing partners, and competitors. Finally, today's marketers are also reexamining their ethical and societal responsibilities. Marketers are being called on to take greater responsibility for the social and environmental impacts of their actions.

Pulling it all together, as discussed throughout the chapter, the major new developments in marketing can be summed up in a single concept: *engaging customers and creating and capturing customer value.* Today, marketers of all kinds are taking advantage of new opportunities for building value-laden relationships with their customers, their marketing partners, and the world around them.

Key Terms

OBJECTIVE 1-1

Marketing (p 5)

OBJECTIVE 1-2

Needs (p 6)
Wants (p 6)
Demands (p 6)
Market offerings (p 7)
Marketing myopia (p 7)
Exchange (p 9)
Market (p 9)

OBJECTIVE 1-3

Marketing management (p 10)
Production concept (p 11)
Product concept (p 11)
Selling concept (p 12)
Marketing concept (p 12)
Societal marketing concept (p 13)

OBJECTIVE 1-4

Customer relationship management (p 14)
Customer-perceived value (p 14)

Customer satisfaction (p 15)
Customer-engagement marketing (p 17)
Consumer-generated marketing (p 18)
Partner relationship management (p 19)
Customer lifetime value (p 20)
Share of customer (p 20)
Customer equity (p 21)

OBJECTIVE 1-5

Digital and social media marketing (p 23)

DISCUSSION AND CRITICAL THINKING

MyMarketingLab

Go to **mymktlab.com** to complete the problems marked with this icon ⭐.

Discussion Questions

⭐ **1-1** Define *marketing* and outline the steps in the marketing process. (AACSB: Communication)

1-2 What is a market offering? Give a recent example of a market offering that has satisfied your need or want. (AASCB: Communication; Reflective Thinking)

⭐ **1-3** Describe the key elements of a customer-driven marketing strategy and discuss the marketing management orientations that guide marketing strategy. (AACSB: Communication; Reflective Thinking)

1-4 Discuss the concept of customer satisfaction. How do customer relationship management and customer-perceived value affect customer satisfaction? (AACSB: Communication; Reflective Thinking)

⭐ **1-5** Explain the growing importance of digital and social media marketing. (AACSB: Communication; Reflective Thinking)

Critical Thinking Exercises

1-6 Select a publicly traded company and research how much was spent on marketing activities in the most recent year of available data. What percentage of sales do marketing expenditures represent for the company? Have these expenditures increased or decreased over the past five years? Write a brief report of your findings. (AACSB Communication; Analytic Reasoning)

⭐ **1-7** Visit the Tide website at tide.com/en-us. Scroll to the bottom of the page and notice how Tide is currently connecting with customers on social media platforms including Facebook, Twitter, Pinterest, Google+, and YouTube. Click on one or more of the platforms to view ways in which Tide

is building and maintaining customer linkages while illustrating value and providing information behind the brand. Evaluate Tide's effectiveness in creating customer engagement through its web and social media sites. (AACSB: Communication, Use of IT, Reflective Thinking)

1-8 Search the internet for salary information regarding jobs in the marketing industry using www.glassdoor.com, www.payscale.com, or a similar website. Choose five different jobs in marketing. For each position, review the national average salaries and compare them to the salaries in your local area. Discuss your findings. (AACSB: Communication; Use of IT; Reflective Thinking)

APPLICATIONS AND CASES

Online, Mobile, and Social Media Marketing   The ALS Ice Bucket Challenge

In the summer of 2014, people with connections to ALS (Lou Gehrig's disease) raised awareness of the condition by urging people to post videos of themselves dumping buckets of ice water over their heads and challenge others to do the same. The efforts raised millions of dollars in online donations to the ALS Association for enhanced research and patient services. This real-time marketing campaign generated 17 million videos uploaded to social media platforms from 159 countries. Celebrities posting videos included Will Smith, Bill Gates, Oprah Winfrey, and Mark Zuckerberg. The Ice Bucket Challenge generated 70 billion video views while raising $220 million. The best part? Zero dollars were spent to promote the Ice Bucket Challenge, yet 440 million people saw it. The ALS Association has now turned the wildly successful challenge into an annual social media campaign, bringing back the original Ice Bucket Challenge #EveryAugustUntilACure.

For more information, visit www.alsa.org/fight-als/ice-bucket-challenge.

1-9 Real-time marketing is a shift for traditional marketers who can now digitally link brands to important moments in customers' lives. Explain how real-time marketing was used in the Ice Bucket Challenge. Why was this campaign successful? (AACSB: Communication; Reflective Thinking)

1-10 Create a real-time marketing campaign for a product or service of your choice to create customer engagement using online, mobile, and social media. How would you measure the success of your campaign? (AACSB: Communication; Reflective Thinking)

Marketing Ethics Is Big Brother Watching?

Retailers commonly track customers' shopping patterns and target them with special offers. For example, CVS has an Extracare card that, when swiped at checkout, applies discounts to purchases and provides rebates called Extra Bucks to be used as cash on future purchases. Behind the scenes, CVS is gathering data on customers' purchases and using aggregated data to target individuals with special offers. Customers who haven't recently shopped may receive a discount in the mail or an online offer to incentivize them to return. Frequent shoppers can scan their Extracare cards to get discounts and offers in the store.

1-11 Is it right for marketers to track consumer purchases? Should consumers be concerned with what information is being used? (AACSB: Communication; Ethical Reasoning; Reflective Thinking)

1-12 Discuss other examples of marketers using data collection to sell products. Is this ethical? (AACSB: Communication; Ethical Reasoning)

Marketing by the Numbers What's a Customer Worth?

How much are you worth to a given company if you continue to purchase its brand for the rest of your life? Many marketers are grappling with that question, but it's not easy to determine how much a customer is worth to a company over his or her lifetime. Calculating customer lifetime value can be very complicated. Intuitively, however, it can be a fairly simple net present value calculation, which incorporates the concept of the time value of money. To determine a basic customer lifetime value, each stream of profit (C, the net cash flow after costs are subtracted) is discounted back to its present value (PV) and then summed. The basic equation for calculating net present value (NPV) is:

$$NPV = \sum_{t=0}^{N} \frac{C_t}{(1 + r)^t}$$

Where,
t: time of the cash flow
N: total customer lifetime
r: discount rate
C_t: net cash flow (the profit) at time t (The initial cost of acquiring a customer would be a negative net cash flow at time 0.)

NPV can be calculated easily on most financial calculators or by using one of the calculators available on the internet, such as the one found at www.investopedia.com/calculator/NetPresentValue.aspx.

1-13 Assume that a customer shops at a local grocery store, spending an average of $200 a week and resulting in a retailer profit of $10 each week from this customer. Assuming the shopper visits the store all 52 weeks of the year, calculate the customer lifetime value if this shopper remains loyal over a 10-year life span. Also assume a 5 percent annual interest rate and no initial cost to acquire the customer. (AACSB Communication; Analytic Reasoning)

1-14 Describe ways marketers can increase the lifetime value of a customer. (AACSB Communication; Reflective Thinking)

Video Case Eskimo Joe's

Since 1975, Eskimo Joe's has been a popular watering hole in Stillwater, Oklahoma. Through word of mouth and a popular logo spread via T-shirts, it rapidly became a favorite place to grab a beer for students at Oklahoma State. But what started as a basic beer joint has grown into something much more.

When the drinking age changed from 18 to 21 in the 1980s, Eskimo Joe's had to decide how it would move forward. That challenge helped the company to recognize that its product is much more than just a cold mug of beer. Instead, people flocked to Eskimo Joe's for the fun atmosphere and customer-friendly service. This realization led to an expansion into different

businesses that have now spread the Eskimo Joe's logo all over the planet.

After viewing the video featuring Eskimo Joe's, answer the following questions:

1-15 Describe Eskimo Joe's market offering.

1-16 What is Eskimo Joe's value proposition? How does its value proposition relate to its market offering?

1-17 How does Eskimo Joe's build long-term customer relationships?

Company Case   Chick-Fil-A: Getting Better before Getting Bigger

Chick-fil-A is dominating the U.S. fast-food market. Whereas McDonald's, Subway, Burger King, and Taco Bell trudge along at the top of the heap, Chick-fil-A has quietly risen from a Southeast regional favorite to become the largest chicken chain and the eighth-largest quick-service food purveyor in the country. The chain sells significantly more food per restaurant than any of its competitors—twice that of Taco Bell or Wendy's and more than three times what the KFC Colonel fries up. And it does this without even opening its doors on Sundays. With annual revenues of more than $6 billion and annual average growth of 12.7 percent, the chicken champ from Atlanta shows no signs of slowing down.

How does Chick-fil-A do it? By focusing on customers. Since the first Chick-fil-A restaurant opened for business in the late 1960s, the chain's founders have held tenaciously to the philosophy that the most sustainable way to do business is to provide the best possible experience for customers.

Applying Some Pressure

Chick-fil-A founder S. Truett Cathy was no stranger to the restaurant business. Owning and operating restaurants in Georgia in the 1940s, '50s, and '60s, his experience led him to investigate a better (and faster) way to cook chicken. He discovered a pressure fryer that could cook a chicken breast in the same amount of time it took to cook a fast-food burger. Developing the chicken sandwich as a burger alternative, he registered the name "Chick-fil-A, Inc." and opened the first Chick-fil-A restaurant in 1967.

The company began expanding immediately, although at a substantially slower pace than the market leaders. Even today, Chick-fil-A adds only about 100 new stores each year. Although it now has more than 2,000 stores throughout the United States, that number is relatively small compared to KFC's 4,100, McDonald's 13,000, and Subway's 27,000. Chick-fil-A's controlled level of growth ties directly to its "customer first" mantra. As a family-owned operation, the company has never deviated from its core value to "focus on getting better before getting bigger." The slow-growth strategy has facilitated that ability to "get better."

As another way to perfect its business, the company has also stuck to a limited menu. The original breaded chicken sandwich remains at the core of Chick-fil-A's menu today—"a boneless breast of chicken seasoned to perfection, hand-breaded, pressure cooked in 100% refined peanut oil and served on a toasted, buttered bun with dill pickle chips." In fact, the company's trademarked slogan—"We didn't invent the chicken, just the chicken sandwich"—has kept the company on track for decades. Although it has carefully and strategically added other items to the menu, it's the iconic chicken sandwich in all its varieties that primarily drives the brand's image and the company's revenues. This focus has helped the company give customers what they want year after year without being tempted to develop a new flavor of the month.

Getting It Right

Also central to Chick-fil-A's mission is to "have a positive influence on all who come in contact with Chick-fil-A." Although seemingly a tall order to fill, this sentiment permeates every aspect of its business. Not long ago, current Chick-fil-A CEO Dan Cathy was deeply affected by a note that his wife taped to their refrigerator. In a recent visit to a local Chick-fil-A store, she had not only received the wrong order, she had been overcharged. She circled the amount on her receipt, wrote "I'll be back when you get it right" next to it, and posted it on the fridge for her husband to see.

That note prompted Dan Cathy to double-down on customer service. He initiated a program by which all Chick-fil-A employees were retrained to go the "second mile" in providing service to everyone. That "second mile" meant not only meeting basic standards of cleanliness and politeness but going above and beyond by delivering each order to the customer's table with unexpected touches such as a fresh-cut flower or ground pepper for salads.

The experience of a recent patron illustrates the level of service Chick-fil-A's customers have come to expect as well as the innovative spirit that makes such service possible:

My daughter and I stopped at Chick-fil-A on our way home. The parking lot was full, the drive-thru was packed…but the love we have for the chicken sandwiches and waffle potato fries! So we decided it was worth the wait. As we walked up the sidewalk, there were two staff members greeting every car in the drive-thru and taking orders on little tablets. A manager was making his rounds around the building outside smiling and waving at cars as they were leaving.

When we came inside, the place was packed! We were greeted immediately by the cashiers. Seth happened to take our order. He had a big smile, wonderful manners, spoke clearly and had great energy as a teenager! He gave us a number and said he'd be right out with our drinks. We were able to sit at a table as the other guests were leaving and before we could even get settled our drinks were on the table! While Seth started to walk away, our food was delivered by another very friendly person. Both myself and my 15-year-old daughter commented on how fast it all happened. We were so shocked that we started commenting on the large groups arriving behind us, and began watching in amazement, not only inside but outside!

Everyone behind the counter worked together, used manners, and smiled. The teamwork was amazing! Then Ron, a gray headed friendly man, made his way from table to table, checking on guests, giving refills, and trading coloring books for small ice cream cones with sprinkles for little kids. He checked on us twice and filled our drinks once.

Recently, the company instituted the "parent's valet service," inviting parents juggling small children to go through the drive-through, place their order, park, and make their way inside the store. By the time the family gets inside, its meal is waiting on placemats at a table with high chairs in place. But beyond the tactics that are taught as a matter of standard policy, Chick-fil-A also trains employees to look for special ways to serve—such as retrieving dental appliances from dumpsters or delivering smartphones and wallets that customers have left behind.

Give Them Something to Do

Beyond high levels of in-store service, Chick-fil-A has focused on other brand-building elements that enhance the customer experience. The brand got a big boost when the Chick-fil-A cows made their promotional debut as three-dimensional characters on billboards with the now famous slogan, "EAT MORE CHIKIN." The beloved bovines and their self-preservation message have been a constant across all Chick-fil-A promotional materials for the past 20 years. They've also been the linchpin for another Chick-fil-A customer experience–enhancing strategy—engage customers by giving them something to do.

Displaying any of the cow-themed mugs, T-shirts, stuffed animals, refrigerator magnets, laptop cases, and dozens of other items the company sells on its website certainly qualifies as "something to do." But Chick-fil-A marketers go far beyond promotional items to engage customers. For starters, there's "Cow Appreciation Day"—a day set aside every July when customers who go to any Chick-fil-A store dressed as a cow get a free meal. Last year, the 10th anniversary of this annual event, about a million cow-clad customers cashed in on the offer.

Another tradition for brand loyalists is to camp out prior to the opening of a new restaurant. Chick-fil-A encourages this ardent activity with its "First 100" promotion—an officially sanctioned event in which the company present the first 100 people in line for each new restaurant opening vouchers for a full year's worth of Chick-fil-A meals. Dan Cathy himself has been known to camp out with customers, signing T-shirts, posing for pictures, and personally handing coupons to the winners. And whereas some customer-centric giveaways are regular events, others pop up randomly. Take the most recent "family challenge," which awards a free ice cream cone to any dine-in customers who relinquish their smartphones to a "cell phone coop" for the duration of their meals.

To keep customers engaged when they aren't in the stores, Chick-fil-A has become an expert in social and digital media. Its newest app, Chick-fil-A One, jumped to the number-one spot on iTunes only hours after being announced. Nine days later, more than a million customers had downloaded the app, giving them the ability to place and customize their orders, pay in advance, and skip the lines at the register. And in a recent survey by social media tracker Engagement Labs, Chick-fil-A was ranked number one and crowned the favorite American brand on all major social media platforms, including Facebook, Twitter, and Instagram.

Every year, as the accolades roll in, it is apparent that Chick-fil-A's customer-centric culture is more than just talk. Among the many competitors, Chick-fil-A was rated number one in customer service in the most recent Consumer Reports survey of fast-food chains. In the latest annual Customer Service Hall of Fame survey, Chick-fil-A ranked second out of 151 of the best-known companies across 15 industries, trailing only Amazon. A whopping 47 percent of customers rated the company's service as "excellent," and Chick-fil-A was the only fast-food chain to make the list for the second year in a row.

After decades of phenomenal growth and success, Chick-fil-A is celebrating by firing the Richards Group, its long-standing agency of record. Additionally, the beloved cows that are so widely recognized as symbols of the brand will ease into the background of promotional materials. "The cows are an integral part of the brand. They're our mascot, if you will," says Jon Bridges, chief marketing officer for Chick-fil-A. "But they aren't the brand. The brand is bigger than that." For now, Bridges only says that the cows won't disappear. But a new "Cow-plus" is in the works, and the brand's promotional messages will expand beyond the bovines to tell engaging stories about the food, people, and service that make the brand so special. It's a risky move. With Chick-fil-A growing faster than any other major fast-food chain, it begs the question as to whether such a drastic change in the brand's symbolism will sustain its current growth for years to come, or send some customers out to pasture.

Prior to this recent announcement, one estimate has Chick-fil-A on track to add between $6 billion and $9 billion in revenues within the next decade. In that same period, giant McDonald's may add as much as $10 billion in U.S. sales but as little as only $1 billion. Clearly, all this growth is not an accident. As one food industry analyst states, "It's about trying to maintain high levels of service, high quality, not deviating dramatically, and giving customers an idea of what to expect." As long as Chick-fil-A continues to make customers the number-one priority, we can expect to find more and more access to those scrumptious chicken sandwiches.

Questions for Discussion

1-18 Give examples of needs, wants, and demands of Chick-fil-A customers, differentiating these three concepts.

1-19 Describe Chick-fil-A in terms of the value it provides customers. How does Chick-fil-A engage customers?

1-20 Evaluate Chick-fil-A's performance relative to customer expectations.

1-21 Which of the five marketing management orientations best applies to Chick-fil-A?

1-22 Can Chick-fil-A continue to provide exceptional customer service *and* sustain the level of growth it now enjoys? Why or why not?

Sources: Jessica Wohl, "Chick-fil-A Drops The Richards Group After 22 Years," *Advertising Age*, July 21, 2016, www.adage.com/print/305057; Micah Solomon, "Chick-fil-A Becomes a Customer Experience Thought Leader by Asking Families to Ditch Cell Phones," *Forbes*, March 3, 2016, www.forbes.com/sites/micahsolomon/2016/03/03/chik-fil-a-rewards-families-for-ditching-cellphones-the-genius-customer-experience-move-of-2016/#4e1830e65858; Micah Solomon, "The Chick-fil-A Way of Customer Service and Employee Engagement," *Forbes*, June 14, 2016, www.forbes.com/sites/micahsolomon/2016/06/14/the-chick-fil-a-way-of-customer-service-and-employee-engagement/#8587848660eb; Hayley Peterson, "How Chick-fil-A's Restaurants Sell Three Times as Much as KFC," *Time*, August 5, 2015, www.businessinsider.com/how-chick-fil-a-is-dominating-fast-food-2015-8; Michael B. Sauter, "2015's Customer Service Hall of Fame," *USA Today*, August 2, 2015, www.usatoday.com/story/money/business/2015/07/24/24-7-wall-st-customer-service-hall-fame/30599943/; "Chick-fil-A One Surges to No. 1 Slot in iTunes App Store," *QSR*, June 10, 2016, www.qsrmagazine.com/news/chick-fil-one-surges-no-1-slot-itunes-app-store; "Chick-fil-A Beats Amazon, Netflix in Social Media," *QSR*, January 12, 2016, www.qsrmagazine.com/news/chick-fil-beats-amazon-netflix-social-media; and www.chick-fil-a.com/Company/Highlights-Fact-Sheets and www.chick-fil-a.com/Story, accessed June 2016.

MyMarketingLab

Go to **mymktlab.com** for Auto-graded writing questions as well as the following Assisted-graded writing questions:

1-23 When implementing customer relationship management, why might a business desire fewer customers over more customers? Shouldn't the focus of marketing be to acquire as many customers as possible?

1-24 Compare and contrast needs, wants, and demands. Which one(s) can marketers influence?

2 Company and Marketing Strategy
Partnering to Build Customer Engagement, Value, and Relationships

CHAPTER PREVIEW

In the first chapter, we explored the marketing process by which companies create value for customers to capture value from them in return. In this chapter, we dig deeper into steps two and three of that process: designing customer value–driven marketing strategies and constructing marketing programs. First, we look at the organization's overall strategic planning, which guides marketing strategy and planning. Next, we discuss how, guided by the strategic plan, marketers partner closely with others inside and outside the firm to engage customers and create value for them. We then examine marketing strategy and planning—how marketers choose target markets, position their market offerings, develop a marketing mix, and manage their marketing programs. Finally, we look at the important step of measuring and managing marketing return on investment (marketing ROI).

First, let's look at Starbucks, a good company and a good marketing strategy story. Starbucks met with enormous early success by focusing not just on coffee but on the coffee-drinking experience. The company has since taken a bumpy ride from boom to bust and back to boom again. Along the way, it learned that good marketing strategy means more than just growth, sales, and profits. It means skillfully engaging customers and creating value for them. At its core, Starbucks doesn't sell just coffee, it sells "The Starbucks Experience."

STARBUCKS'S MARKETING STRATEGY: Delivering "The Starbucks Experience"

More than 30 years ago, Howard Schultz transformed the coffee industry by bringing a European-style coffeehouse to America. He believed that people needed to slow down—to "smell the coffee" and to enjoy life a little more. The result was Starbucks, founded with a whole new strategy for engaging customers and creating customer value.

Starbucks didn't sell just coffee, it sold "The Starbucks Experience"—"an uplifting experience that enriches people's lives one moment, one human being, one extraordinary cup of coffee at a time." Starbucks gave customers what it calls a "third place"—a place away from home and away from work. At Starbucks, the smells, the sound of beans grinding, watching baristas blend and brew the brand's specialty coffees—all became as much or more a part of the customer experience as the coffee itself.

Over the next two decades, customers flocked to Starbucks cafés. By 2007, some 15,000 Starbucks stores dotted the nation and globe, and the company's sales and profits rose like steam off a mug of hot java. However, Starbucks's enormous success drew a host of competitors. It seemed that every rival—from independent coffeehouses to fast-food restaurants—was peddling its own brand of premium coffee.

To maintain its phenomenal growth in the increasingly overcaffeinated marketplace, Starbucks brewed up an ambitious growth strategy. It opened new stores at a breakneck pace, seemingly *everywhere*. For example, one three-block stretch in Chicago contained six of the trendy coffee bars. In New York City, there were two Starbucks in one Macy's store. In fact, cramming so many stores so close together caused one satirical publication to run this headline: "A New Starbucks Opens in the Restroom of Existing Starbucks." The company also blanketed the country with Starbucks kiosks and coffee stands in everything from Target stores and supermarkets to hotel lobbies, and service businesses from airlines to car dealerships proclaimed, "We proudly serve Starbucks coffee."

The more Starbucks grew, however, the more it drifted away from the core mission and values that had made it so successful. The company's almost obsessive focus on growth for

> Starbucks has become America's—the world's—largest coffeehouse by skillfully engaging customers and delivering superior customer value. At its core, Starbucks doesn't sell just coffee. It sells "The Starbucks Experience."

growth's sake began to take a toll on the prized Starbucks Experience. Far from its roots as a warm and intimate coffeehouse, Starbucks began to evolve into more of a caffeine filling station. More and more, the premium brand found itself competing with the likes of—gasp!—McDonald's for many of the same customers.

Founder Howard Schultz, who had stepped down as CEO in 2000, expressed concern. In a 2007 memo to Starbucks management, Schultz lamented that the company's push for growth had "led to the watering down of the Starbucks Experience" and that Starbucks was "losing its soul." Schultz was right that something was wrong. By early 2008, when Schultz reassumed his role as Starbucks president and CEO, the company found itself in hot water. For the first time ever, the average number of transactions per U.S. store fell off and same-store sales growth slowed. Within just the previous two years, Starbucks's stock had tumbled nearly 80 percent. According to one analyst, "The financial vultures circled. Obituaries were drafted."

Instead of presiding over the brand's demise, however, Schultz reacted quickly to restore its luster. He cooled the pace of Starbucks's growth, closed underperforming locations, and replaced most of the company's top executives. Most important, Schultz laid plans to reestablish the brand's core mission and values and to refocus the company on giving customers the authentic Starbucks Experience. "As we grew rapidly and had phenomenal success," Shultz announced, "we started to lose sight of our focus on the customer and our commitment to continually and creatively enhance the Starbucks Experience." Starbucks needed to shift its focus back to customers—to "reignite the emotional attachment with customers."

To emphasize the point, at a cost of $30 million, Schultz transported 10,000 Starbucks store managers to New Orleans for a morale-building reorientation. A short time later, Starbucks dramatically closed all of its U.S. locations for three hours to conduct nationwide employee training on the basics of producing satisfying customer experiences.

Those early actions began a process of continual renewal by which Starbucks has reignited the Starbucks customer experience through new products, innovative store formats, and new platforms for engaging customers. Beyond improvements in its signature coffee products, Starbucks has developed new products that take the Starbucks Experience into new areas. For example, a few years ago, Starbucks successfully launched Via, an instant coffee that's as good at home as fresh brewed is in stores. More recently, Starbucks added Fizzio to its menu— freshly carbonated and handcrafted sodas in classic flavors.

The company is also experimenting with new store formats, such as the new high-end Starbucks Reserve Roastery and Tasting Room in Seattle that's part café, part shrine, and part working roastery. Schultz describes the new interactive store as "Niketown meets Apple meets Starbucks"—think of it as the Starbucks Experience on steroids. In another big move,

More than just coffee, Starbucks sells "The Starbucks Experience," one that "enriches people's lives one moment, one human being, one extraordinary cup of coffee at a time."
Associated Press

Starbucks purchased Teavana—a specialty tea retailer with more than 400 locations in North America. Schultz sees the Teavana acquisition as pivotal to Starbucks's renewal and reinvention. Tea is "a $90 billion global category, ripe for innovation," he says. "We're going to do for tea what we've done for coffee."

Starbucks's renewal extends the Starbucks Experience well beyond employee relearning, new products, and innovative stores formats. Over the past decade, as much as any brand, Starbucks has built customer engagement and brand community through digital and mobile platforms. Its highly successful mobile payments app, My Starbucks Rewards loyalty program, and prepaid Starbucks Cards now give Starbucks "a direct, real-time, personalized, two-way digital relationship with its customers," says the company's chief digital officer. The Starbucks Rewards mobile payment app has more than 11 million active users, and mobile payments account for 20 percent of all U.S. in-store transactions.

Today, a rejuvenated Starbucks is once again fully engaged with customers and delivering the one-of-a-kind Starbucks Experience. And once again, sales and profits are really perking. Every week, Starbucks serves more than 70 million customers face-to-face in 23,500 stores in 70 countries. Over the past six years, revenues have almost doubled and profits have shot up fivefold.

The moral of the Starbucks story: Good marketing strategy means keeping your eye squarely on delivering customer value. The objective isn't just growth or sales or profits; it's engaging customers in a meaningful way and creating value for them. If a company takes care of customer engagement and value, good performance will result. "It's not just about ringing a register and performing a task," says Schultz. "It's also about creating an emotional, enduring relationship and connection with our…customers. At our core, we celebrate the interaction between us and our customers through the coffee experience. Life happens over coffee."[1]

OBJECTIVES OUTLINE

OBJECTIVE 2-1	Explain company-wide strategic planning and its four steps. **Company-Wide Strategic Planning: Defining Marketing's Role** (pp 40–42)
OBJECTIVE 2-2	Discuss how to design business portfolios and develop growth strategies. **Designing the Business Portfolio** (pp 42–48)
OBJECTIVE 2-3	Explain marketing's role in strategic planning and how marketing works with its partners to create and deliver customer value. **Planning Marketing: Partnering to Build Customer Relationships** (pp 48–49)
OBJECTIVE 2-4	Describe the elements of a customer value–driven marketing strategy and mix and the forces that influence them. **Marketing Strategy and the Marketing Mix** (pp 50–55)
OBJECTIVE 2-5	List the marketing management functions, including the elements of a marketing plan, and discuss the importance of measuring and managing marketing return on investment. **Managing the Marketing Effort and Marketing Return on Investment** (pp 55–60)

Author | Company-wide strategic
Comment | planning guides marketing
strategy and planning. Like marketing
strategy, the company's broader strategy
must also be customer focused.

Strategic planning
The process of developing and
maintaining a strategic fit between the
organization's goals and capabilities and
its changing marketing opportunities.

Company-Wide Strategic Planning: Defining Marketing's Role

Each company must find the game plan for long-run survival and growth that makes the most sense given its specific situation, opportunities, objectives, and resources. This is the focus of **strategic planning**—the process of developing and maintaining a strategic fit between the organization's goals and capabilities and its changing marketing opportunities.

Strategic planning sets the stage for the rest of planning in the firm. Companies usually prepare annual plans, long-range plans, and strategic plans. The annual and long-range plans deal with the company's current businesses and how to keep them going. In contrast, the strategic plan involves adapting the firm to take advantage of opportunities in its constantly changing environment.

At the corporate level, the company starts the strategic planning process by defining its overall purpose and mission (see ● **Figure 2.1**). This mission is then turned into detailed supporting objectives that guide the entire company. Next, headquarters decides what portfolio of businesses and products is best for the company and how much support to give each one. In turn, each business and product develops detailed marketing and other departmental plans that support the company-wide plan. Thus, marketing planning occurs at the business-unit, product, and market levels. It supports company strategic planning with more detailed plans for specific marketing opportunities.

Defining a Market-Oriented Mission

An organization exists to accomplish something, and this purpose should be clearly stated. Forging a sound mission begins with the following questions: What *is* our business? Who is the customer? What do consumers value? What *should* our business be? These simple-sounding questions are among the most difficult the company will ever have to answer. Successful companies continuously raise these questions and answer them carefully and completely.

● **FIGURE | 2.1**
Steps in Strategic
Planning

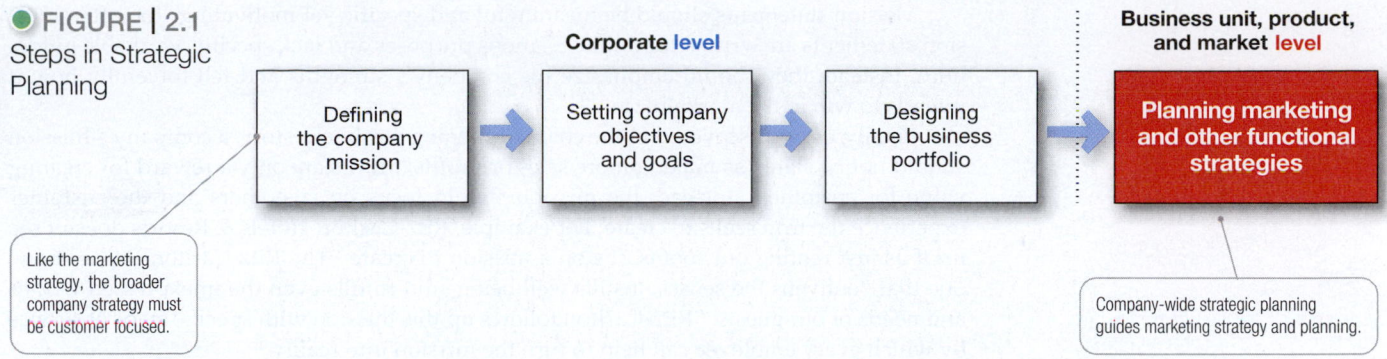

Like the marketing
strategy, the broader
company strategy must
be customer focused.

Company-wide strategic planning
guides marketing strategy and planning.

Mission statement

A statement of the organization's
purpose—what it wants to accomplish in
the larger environment.

Many organizations develop formal mission statements that answer these questions. A **mission statement** is a statement of the organization's purpose—what it wants to accomplish in the larger environment. A clear mission statement acts as an "invisible hand" that guides people in the organization.

Some companies define their missions myopically in product or technology terms ("We make and sell furniture" or "We are a chemical-processing firm"). But mission statements should be *market oriented* and defined in terms of satisfying basic customer needs. Products and technologies eventually become outdated, but basic market needs may last forever. For example, social scrapbooking site Pinterest doesn't define itself as just an online place to post pictures. Its mission is to give people a social media platform for collecting, organizing, and sharing things they love. And Microsoft's mission isn't to create the world's best software, technologies, and devices. It's to "empower every person and every organization on the planet to achieve more." ● **Table 2.1** provides several examples of product-oriented versus market-oriented business definitions.[2]

● **Table 2.1 | Product- versus Market-Oriented Business Definitions**

Company	Product-Oriented Definition	Market-Oriented Definition
Chipotle	We sell burritos and other Mexican food.	We give customers "Food With Integrity," served with a commitment toward the long-term welfare of customers and the environment.
Facebook	We are an online social network.	We connect people around the world and help them share important moments in their lives.
Home Depot	We sell tools and home repair and improvement items.	We empower consumers to achieve the homes of their dreams.
NASA	We explore outer space.	We reach for new heights and reveal the unknown so that what we do and learn will benefit all humankind.
Revlon	We make cosmetics.	We sell lifestyle and self-expression; success and status; memories, hopes, and dreams.
Ritz-Carlton Hotels & Resorts	We rent rooms.	We create "The Ritz-Carlton experience"—a memorable stay that far exceeds guests' already-high expectations.
Starbucks	We sell coffee and snacks.	We sell "The Starbucks Experience," one that enriches people's lives one moment, one human being, one extraordinary cup of coffee at a time.
Walmart	We run discount stores.	We deliver low prices every day and give ordinary folks the chance to buy the same things as rich people. "Save Money. Live Better."

Mission statements should be meaningful and specific yet motivating. Too often, mission statements are written for public relations purposes and lack specific, workable guidelines. Instead, they should emphasize the company's strengths and tell forcefully how it intends to win in the marketplace.

Finally, as we discovered in the chapter-opening Starbucks story, a company's mission should not be stated as making more sales or profits; profits are only a reward for creating value for customers. Instead, the mission should focus on customers and the customer experience the firm seeks to create. For example, Ritz-Carlton Hotels & Resorts doesn't see itself as just renting out rooms. It's on a mission to create "The Ritz-Carlton Experience," one that "enlivens the senses, instills well-being, and fulfills even the unexpressed wishes and needs of our guests." Ritz-Carlton follows up this mission with specific steps of service by which every employee can help to turn the mission into reality.[3]

Setting Company Objectives and Goals

The company needs to turn its broad mission into detailed supporting objectives for each level of management. Each manager should have objectives and be responsible for reaching them. For example, most Americans know CVS as a chain of retail pharmacies selling prescription and over-the-counter medicines, personal care products, and a host of convenience and other items. But CVS—recently renamed CVS Health—has a much broader mission. ● It views itself as a "pharmacy innovation company," one that is "helping people on their path to better health." The company's motto: "Health is everything."[4]

CVS Health's broad mission leads to a hierarchy of objectives, including business objectives and marketing objectives. CVS Health's overall business objective is to increase access, lower costs, and improve the quality of care. It does this through the products it sells at its retail pharmacies and by taking a more active role in overall health-care management through research, consumer outreach and education, and support of health-related programs and organizations.

However, such activities are expensive and must be funded through improved profits, so improving profits becomes another major objective for CVS Health. Profits can be improved by increasing sales or by reducing costs. Sales can be increased by improving customer engagement and raising the company's share of the health-care market. These goals then become the company's current marketing objectives.

● CVS Health's overall mission is to be a "pharmacy innovation company," one that is "helping people on their way to better health." Its marketing strategies and programs must support this mission.

CVS Caremark Corporation

Marketing strategies and programs must be developed to support these marketing objectives. To increase customer engagement, sales, and market share, CVS Health has reshaped and broadened its lines of products and services. For example, it recently stopped selling tobacco products, items not compatible with its "better health" mission. And it has placed CVS MinuteClinic locations in more than 1,000 of its 9,500 stores, providing walk-in medical care for more than 18 million patient visits since 2000. CVS Health has also broadened its range of customer contact activities to include tailored advising to customers managing chronic and specialty health conditions.

These are CVS Health's broad marketing strategies. Each marketing strategy must then be defined in greater detail. For example, the company's rapidly expanding MinuteClinic services will require more advertising and promotional efforts, and such efforts will need to be spelled out carefully. In this way, CVS Health's broad mission is translated into a set of specific short-term objectives and marketing plans.

Designing the Business Portfolio

Guided by the company's mission statement and objectives, management now must plan its business portfolio—the collection of businesses and products that make up the

Business portfolio

The collection of businesses and products that make up the company.

company. The best **business portfolio** is the one that best fits the company's strengths and weaknesses to opportunities in the environment.

Most large companies have complex portfolios of businesses and brands. Strategic and marketing planning for such business portfolios can be a daunting but critical task. For example, ESPN's brand portfolio consists of more than 50 business entities, ranging from multiple ESPN cable channels to ESPN Radio, ESPN.com, *ESPN The Magazine*, and even ESPN Zone sports-themed restaurants. In turn, ESPN is just one unit in the even more complex portfolio of its parent company, The Walt Disney Company. Through skillful portfolio management, however, ESPN has built a cohesive brand, unified powerfully under its mission to serve sports enthusiasts "wherever sports are watched, listened to, discussed, debated, read about, or played" (see Real Marketing 2.1).

Business portfolio planning involves two steps. First, the company must analyze its *current* business portfolio and determine which businesses should receive more, less, or no investment. Second, it must shape the *future* portfolio by developing strategies for growth and downsizing.

Analyzing the Current Business Portfolio

Portfolio analysis

The process by which management evaluates the products and businesses that make up the company.

The major activity in strategic planning is business **portfolio analysis**, whereby management evaluates the products and businesses that make up the company. The company will want to put strong resources into its more profitable businesses and phase down or drop its weaker ones.

Management's first step is to identify the key businesses that make up the company, called *strategic business units* (SBUs). An SBU can be a company division, a product line within a division, or sometimes a single product or brand. The company next assesses the attractiveness of its various SBUs and decides how much support each deserves. When designing a business portfolio, it's a good idea to add and support products and businesses that fit closely with the firm's core philosophy and competencies.

The purpose of strategic planning is to find ways in which the company can best use its strengths to take advantage of attractive opportunities in the environment. For this reason, most standard portfolio analysis methods evaluate SBUs on two important dimensions: the attractiveness of the SBU's market or industry and the strength of the SBU's position in that market or industry. The best-known portfolio-planning method was developed by the Boston Consulting Group, a leading management consulting firm.[5]

The Boston Consulting Group Approach

Growth-share matrix

A portfolio-planning method that evaluates a company's SBUs in terms of market growth rate and relative market share.

Using the now-classic Boston Consulting Group (BCG) approach, a company classifies all its SBUs according to the **growth-share matrix**, as shown in ● **Figure 2.2.** On the vertical axis, *market growth rate* provides a measure of market attractiveness. On the

● FIGURE | 2.2
The BCG Growth-Share Matrix

Under the classic BCG portfolio planning approach, the company invests funds from mature, successful products and businesses (cash cows) to support promising products and businesses in faster-growing markets (stars and question marks), hoping to turn them into future cash cows.

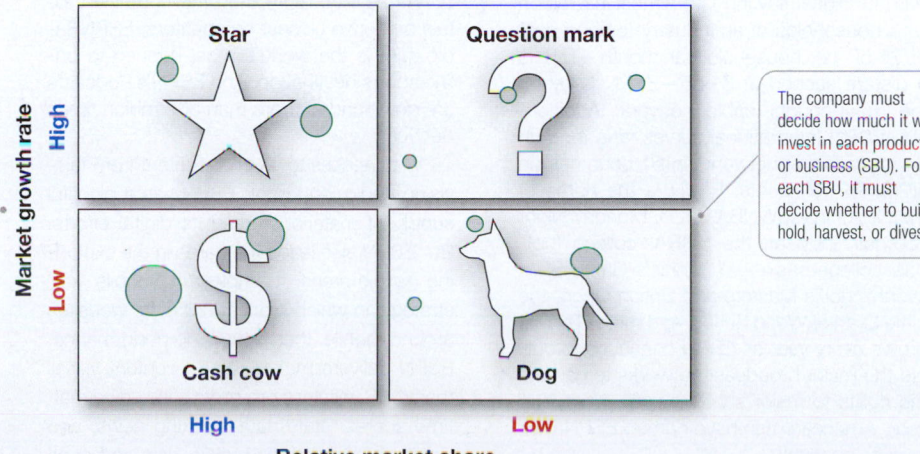

The company must decide how much it will invest in each product or business (SBU). For each SBU, it must decide whether to build, hold, harvest, or divest.

2.1 ESPN: Skillfully Managing a Complex Brand Portfolio

When you think about ESPN, you probably think of it as a cable TV network, or a magazine, or maybe a website. ESPN is all of those things. But over the years, ESPN has grown to become a huge and complex brand portfolio consisting of more than 50 different entities. Thanks to skillful portfolio management, however, ESPN is much more than just a haphazard collection of media entities. Instead, it's an immersive brand experience—a meaningful part of customers' lives. ESPN is synonymous with sports entertainment, inexorably linked with customers' sports memories, realities, and anticipations.

In 1979, entrepreneur Bill Rasmussen took a daring leap and founded the round-the-clock sports network ESPN (Entertainment and Sports Programming Network). Despite many early skeptics—seriously, a 24-hour sports network?—ESPN is now a multibillion-dollar sports empire and a "can't-live-without-it" part of the daily routines of hundreds of millions of people worldwide. Today, ESPN is as much recognized and revered as iconic megabrands such as Coca-Cola, Nike, Apple, and Google. No matter who you are, chances are good that ESPN has touched you in some meaningful way. And no matter what the sport or where, ESPN seems to be everywhere at once.

Here's a brief summary of the incredible variety of entities tied together as part of the ESPN portfolio:

Television: From its original groundbreaking cable network, the ESPN brand has sprouted eight additional U.S. networks—ESPN3D, ESPN2, ESPN Classic, ESPNEWS, ESPNU, ESPN Deportes (Spanish language), the Longhorn Network, and the SEC Network. With its signal flowing into almost 92 million U.S. households at an industry-topping cost of $6.60 per household per month—TNT is a distant second at $1.65—ESPN is by far the most-sought cable network. Additionally, ESPN International serves fans through 24 international networks in 61 countries on all seven continents. ESPN is the home of the NBA Finals, WNBA, MLB, Monday Night Football, IndyCar, the NHRA, college football, college basketball, tennis's Grand Slam events, golf's Masters and British Open, the Little League World Series, and more. This list grows every year as ESPN continues to outbid the major broadcast networks to capture the rights to major sports events. Year after year, American men have named ESPN their favorite channel.

ESPN is much more than just a haphazard collection of media entities. It's a skillfully managed brand portfolio that delivers an immersive sports entertainment experience, inexorably linked with customers' sports memories, realities, and anticipations.

Mike Windle/Stringer/Getty Images

Radio: Sports radio is thriving, and ESPN Radio is the largest sports radio network, broadcasting more than 9,000 hours of content annually to 20 million listeners through nearly 500 U.S. affiliates. Overseas, ESPN has radio and syndicated radio programs in 11 countries. ESPN Radio extends its reach even further through Sirius XM, digital distributors Slacker Radio and Tune In, and its own ESPNRadio.com.

Online: ESPN Digital Media is composed of 19 U.S. websites, including the flagship ESPN.com. These digital destinations capture nearly 82 million unique visitors and more than 7 billion minutes of usage every month. ESPN accounts for 30 percent of all online sports activity, more than the combined totals of its two closest competitors. ESPNRadio.com is the world's most-listened-to online sports destination. And ESPN's Podcasts are downloaded more than 302 million times per year.

With access to its own content from television, radio, and print, ESPN has a plentiful supply of material to feed its digital efforts. But ESPN also leads the game in the exploding mobile arena. It employs a "mobile first" strategy, in which it orients all of its websites around mobile, thus optimizing performance. ESPN delivers mobile sports content via all major U.S. wireless providers—including real-time scores, stats, late-breaking news, and video-on-demand. Its mobile sites and apps

lead the sports category in unique visitors and average audience per minute. The digital strategy has led to WatchESPN, an online and mobile destination for major ESPN channels, and ESPN3, a multi-screen live 24/7 online sports network available at no cost to tens of millions of homes that receive their high-speed internet connection from an affiliated service provider.

Publishing: When ESPN first published *ESPN The Magazine* in 1998, critics gave it little chance against mighty *Sports Illustrated*. Yet with its bold look, bright colors, and unconventional format, the ESPN publication now serves more than 16.5 million readers per issue. Digital-only consumption of *ESPN The Magazine* is soaring, whereas a relatively stagnate *Sports Illustrated* is struggling to make the shift to a digital world.

Even More: As if all this weren't enough, ESPN also manages events, including the X Games, the ESPYs, college bowls, and NCAA basketball games. It also develops ESPN-branded consumer products and services, including DVDs, video games, apparel, and even golf schools. If reading all this makes you hungry, you may be near an ESPN Zone, which includes a sports-themed restaurant, interactive games, and sports-related merchandise sales. You'll now find ESPN content in airports and on planes, in health clubs, and even on gas station video panels.

All this translates into annual revenues of $10.8 billion, making ESPN more important to its parent The Walt Disney Company than the Disneyland and Disney World theme parks combined. And ESPN accounts for more than half of Disney's total operating income.

What ties this huge collection of ESPN entities together? The brand's customer-focused mission: It wants to serve sports enthusiasts "wherever sports are watched, listened to, discussed, debated, read about, or played." ESPN has a philosophy known as "best available screen." It knows that when fans are at home, they'll watch the big 60-inch flat-screen. But during the morning hours, smartphones light up more. During the day, desktops dominate, and in the evening, tablet activity increases. And as more young "cord-cutting" cable subscribers begin to forego traditional cable options in favor of other means of streaming sports content, look for ESPN to reach them through non-cable "over-the-top" technologies. ESPN is on a crusade to know when, where, and under what conditions fans will reach for which device, and to provide the most seamless, high-quality experience for them.

It's no surprise, then, that sports fans around the world love their ESPN. To consumers everywhere, ESPN means sports. Tech savvy, creative, and often irreverent, the well-managed, ever-extending yet carefully integrated brand portfolio continues to build meaningful customer engagement and experiences. If it has to do with your life and sports—large or small—ESPN covers it for you, anywhere you are, 24/7. Perhaps the company should rename ESPN to stand for Every Sport Possible—Now.

Sources: Matthew Ingram, "When Will ESPN's Subscriber Numbers Finally Hit Bottom?" *Fortune*, November 24, 2015, http://fortune.com/2015/11/24/espn-subscriber-numbers/; Anthony Kosner, "Mobile First: How ESPN Delivers to the Best Available Screen," *Forbes*, January 30, 2012, *www.forbes.com/sites/anthonykosner/2012/01/30/mobile-first-how-espn-delivers-to-the-best-available-screen/2/*; Derek Thompson, "The Global Dominance of ESPN," *The Atlantic*, August 14, 2013, *www.theatlantic.com/magazine/archive/2013/09/the-most-valuable-network/309433/*; Lisa Richwine and Lehar Maan, "ESPN Casts Shadow Over 'Star Wars' Success at Disney," *Reuters*, February 9, 2016, www.reuters.com/article/us-walt-disney-results-idUSKCN0VI24S; and information from *http://espnmediazone.com/us/espn-inc-fact-sheet/* and *www.espn.com*, accessed September 2016.

horizontal axis, *relative market share* serves as a measure of company strength in the market. The growth-share matrix defines four types of SBUs:

1. *Stars.* Stars are high-growth, high-share businesses or products. They often need heavy investments to finance their rapid growth. Eventually their growth will slow down, and they will turn into cash cows.
2. *Cash cows.* Cash cows are low-growth, high-share businesses or products. These established and successful SBUs need less investment to hold their market share. Thus, they produce a lot of the cash that the company uses to pay its bills and support other SBUs that need investment.
3. *Question marks.* Question marks are low-share business units in high-growth markets. They require a lot of cash to hold their share, let alone increase it. Management has to think hard about which question marks it should try to build into stars and which should be phased out.
4. *Dogs.* Dogs are low-growth, low-share businesses and products. They may generate enough cash to maintain themselves but do not promise to be large sources of cash.

The 10 circles in the growth-share matrix represent the company's 10 current SBUs. The company has two stars, two cash cows, three question marks, and three dogs. The area of each circle is proportional to the SBU's dollar sales. This company is in fair shape, although not in good shape. It wants to invest in the more promising question marks to make them stars and maintain the stars so that they will become cash cows as their markets mature. Fortunately, it has two good-sized cash cows. Income from these cash cows will help finance the company's question marks, stars, and dogs. The company should take some decisive action concerning its dogs and its question marks.

Once it has classified its SBUs, the company must determine what role each will play in the future. It can pursue one of four strategies for each SBU. It can invest more in the business unit to *build* its share. Or it can invest just enough to *hold* the SBU's share at the current level. It can *harvest* the SBU, milking its short-term cash flow regardless of the long-term effect. Finally, it can *divest* the SBU by selling it or phasing it out and using the resources elsewhere.

As time passes, SBUs change their positions in the growth-share matrix. Many SBUs start out as question marks and move into the star category if they succeed. They later become cash cows as market growth falls and then finally die off or turn into dogs toward the end of the life cycle. The company needs to add new products and units continuously so that some of them will become stars and, eventually, cash cows that will help finance other SBUs.

Problems with Matrix Approaches. The BCG and other formal methods revolutionized strategic planning. However, such centralized approaches have limitations: They can be difficult, time consuming, and costly to implement. Management may find it difficult to define SBUs and measure market share and growth. In addition, these approaches focus on classifying current businesses but provide little advice for future planning.

Because of such problems, many companies have dropped formal matrix methods in favor of more customized approaches that better suit their specific situations. Moreover, unlike former strategic planning efforts that rested mostly in the hands of senior managers at company headquarters, today's strategic planning has been decentralized. Increasingly, companies are placing responsibility for strategic planning in the hands of cross-functional teams of divisional managers who are close to their markets. In this digital age, such managers have rich and current data at their fingertips and can adapt their plans quickly to meet changing conditions and events in their markets.

Portfolio planning can be challenging. For example, consider GE, the giant $117 billion industrial conglomerate operating with a broad portfolio of products in dozens of consumer and business markets:[6]

Most consumers know GE for its home appliance and lighting products, part of the company's GE Lighting unit and former GE Appliances unit. But that's just the beginning for GE. Other company units—such as GE Transportation, GE Aviation, GE Energy Connections, GE Power, GE Oil & Gas, GE Healthcare, and others—offer products and services ranging from jet engines, diesel-electric locomotives, wind turbines, and off-shore drilling solutions to aerospace systems and medical imaging equipment. GE Capital offers a breadth of financial products and services. However, in recent years, GE has been dramatically shifting its vast portfolio away from consumer products and financial services toward the goal of becoming a more focused "industrial infrastructure company," one that's on a mission to "invent the next digital industrial era, to build, move, power, and cure the world."

Currently, less than 8 percent of GE's annual revenues come from consumer products, and that percentage continues to dwindle. The company is now in the midst of selling off its huge GE Capital financial services arm, and it recently sold its entire GE Appliances division to Haier. Such portfolio decisions have huge implications for the company's future. For example, prior to the sale of its appliances unit, GE's appliance and lighting businesses alone generated more than $8.8 billion in annual revenues, more than the total revenues of companies such as JetBlue, Netflix, Harley-Davidson, or Hershey. Thus, successfully managing GE's broad portfolio takes plenty of management skill and—as GE's long-running corporate slogan suggests—lots of "Imagination at work."

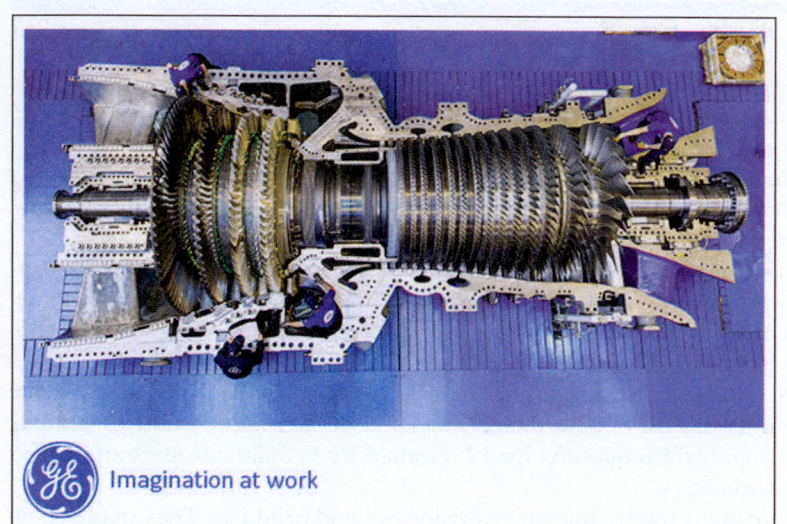

Imagination at work

● **Managing the business portfolio:** Managing GE's broad portfolio of businesses and its mission to "invent the next digital industrial era, to build, move, power, and cure the world" requires plenty of skill and lots of GE's famous "Imagination at work." This huge GE turbine weighs as much as a fully loaded Boeing 747 and can generate the power needed to supply more than 680,000 homes.
GE

Developing Strategies for Growth and Downsizing

Beyond evaluating current businesses, designing the business portfolio involves finding businesses and products the company should consider in the future. Companies need growth if they are to compete more effectively, satisfy their stakeholders, and attract top talent. At the same time, a firm must be careful not to make growth itself an objective. The company's objective must be to manage "profitable growth."

Marketing has the main responsibility for achieving profitable growth for the company. Marketing needs to identify, evaluate, and select market opportunities and lay down strategies for capturing them. One useful device for identifying growth opportunities is the **product/market expansion grid**, shown in ● **Figure 2.3**.[7] We apply it here to performance sports apparel maker Under Armour.[8]

Less than 20 years ago, Under Armour introduced its innovative line of comfy, moisture-wicking performance shirts and shorts with the mission "to make all athletes better through passion, design, and the relentless pursuit of innovation." Since then, it has grown at a torrid pace. In just the past five years, Under Armour's sales have more than

Product/market expansion grid
A portfolio-planning tool for identifying company growth opportunities through market penetration, market development, product development, or diversification.

● **FIGURE | 2.3**
The Product/Market Expansion Grid

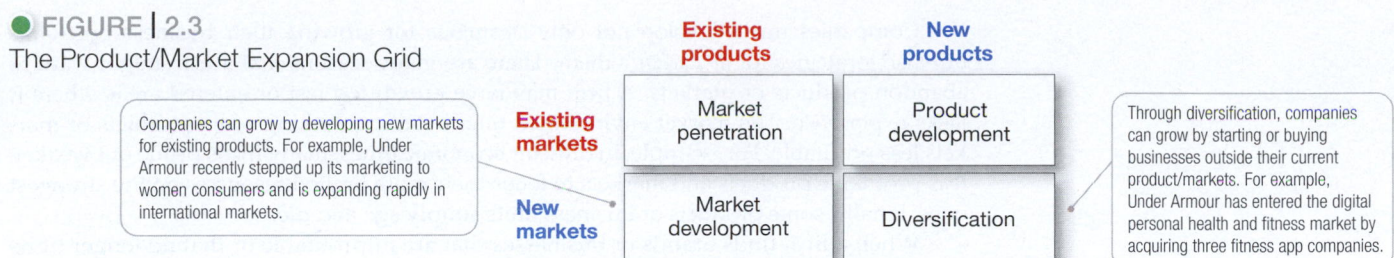

Companies can grow by developing new markets for existing products. For example, Under Armour recently stepped up its marketing to women consumers and is expanding rapidly in international markets.

	Existing products	New products
Existing markets	Market penetration	Product development
New markets	Market development	Diversification

Through diversification, companies can grow by starting or buying businesses outside their current product/markets. For example, Under Armour has entered the digital personal health and fitness market by acquiring three fitness app companies.

Market penetration
Company growth by increasing sales of current products to current market segments without changing the product.

Market development
Company growth by identifying and developing new market segments for current company products.

Product development
Company growth by offering modified or new products to current market segments.

Diversification
Company growth through starting up or acquiring businesses outside the company's current products and markets.

doubled, making it the nation's second-best-selling apparel brand behind Nike. Looking forward, the company must look for new ways to keep growing.

First, Under Armour might consider whether the company can achieve deeper **market penetration**—making more sales in its current product lines and markets. It can spur growth through marketing mix improvements—adjustments to its product design, advertising, pricing, and distribution efforts. For example, Under Armour offers an ever-increasing range of styles and colors in its original apparel lines. And it recently boosted its spending on advertising and professional athlete and team endorsements by 35 percent over previous years. The company has also added direct-to-consumer distribution channels, including its own retail stores and sales websites. Direct-to-consumer sales have tripled over the past eight years and now account for some 30 percent of total revenues.

Second, Under Armour might consider possibilities for **market development**—identifying and developing new markets for its current products. Under Armour can review new *demographic markets*. ● For instance, the company recently stepped up its marketing to women consumers, with new products and a highly acclaimed $15 million women-focused promotion campaign called "I Will What I Want." Under Armour can also pursue new *geographical markets*. For example, the brand is rapidly making a name for itself in international markets, including Japan, Europe, Canada, and Latin America. It recently opened its first-ever brand store in China. Although Under Armour's international sales grew 70 percent last year, they still account for only 12 percent of total sales, leaving plenty of room for international growth.

Third, Under Armour can consider **product development**—offering modified or new products to current markets. For example, the company added athletic shoes to its apparel lines in 2006, and it continues to introduce innovative new athletic-footwear products, such as the recently added Under Armour SpeedForm line. Sneaker sales rose 44 percent last year yet still account for only about 13 percent of total sales, again leaving plenty of growth potential.

Finally, Under Armour can consider **diversification**—starting up or buying businesses outside of its current products and markets. For example, the company recently expanded into the digital personal health and fitness tracking market by acquiring three fitness app companies—MapMyFitness, MyFitnessPal, and Endomondo. It has also partnered with IBM to add artificial fitness tracking technologies that connect fitness, sleep, and nutrition to its products and bind consumers to the brand via technology and services rather than just apparel. Under Armour might also consider moving into nonperformance leisurewear or begin making and marketing Under Armour fitness equipment. When diversifying, companies must be careful not to overextend their brands' positioning.

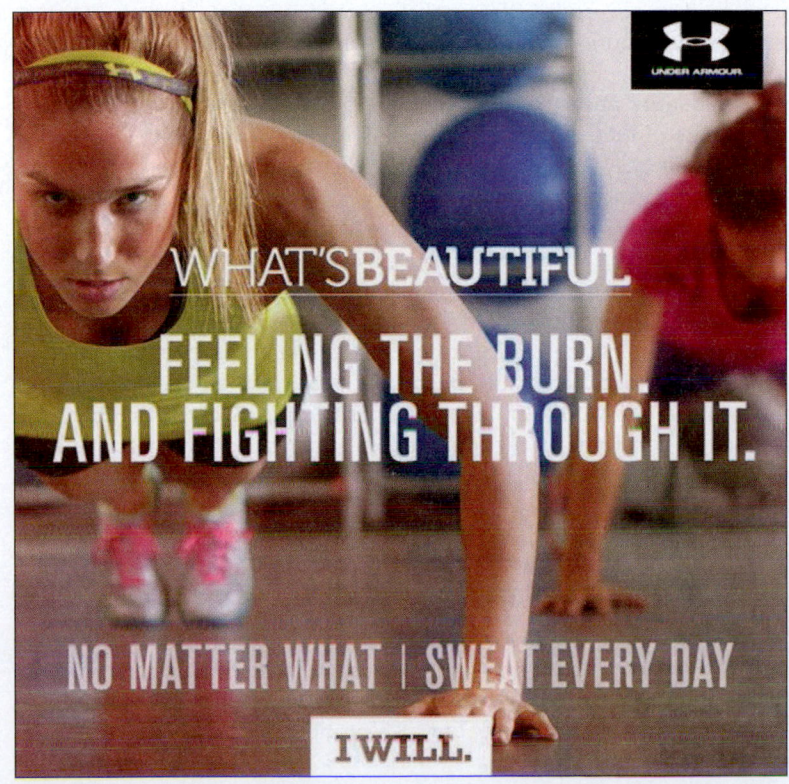

● **Strategies for growth:** Under Armour has grown at a blistering rate under its multipronged growth strategy. In recent years, the brand has stepped up its marketing to women, as in its highly acclaimed "I Will" advertising campaign.

UNDER ARMOUR, INC.

Companies must develop not only strategies for growing their business portfolios but also strategies for *downsizing* them. There are many reasons that a firm might want to abandon products or markets. A firm may have grown too fast or entered areas where it lacks experience. The market environment might change, making some products or markets less profitable. For example, in difficult economic times, many firms prune out weaker, less-profitable products and markets to focus their more limited resources on the strongest ones. Finally, some products or business units simply age and die.

When a firm finds brands or businesses that are unprofitable or that no longer fit its overall strategy, it must carefully prune, harvest, or divest them. For example, over the past several years, P&G has sold off dozens of major brands—from Crisco, Folgers, Jif, and Pringles to Duracell batteries, Right Guard deodorant, Aleve pain reliever, CoverGirl and Max Factor cosmetics, Wella and Clairol hair care products, and its Iams and other pet food brands—allowing the company to focus on household care and beauty and grooming products. And in recent years, GM has pruned several underperforming brands from its portfolio, including Oldsmobile, Pontiac, Saturn, Hummer, and Saab. Weak businesses usually require a disproportionate amount of management attention. Managers should focus on promising growth opportunities, not fritter away energy trying to salvage fading ones.

Author Comment | Marketing can't go it alone in creating customer value. Under the company-wide strategic plan, marketing must work closely with other departments to form an effective internal company value chain and with other companies in the marketing system to create an external value delivery network that jointly serves customers.

Planning Marketing: Partnering to Build Customer Relationships

The company's strategic plan establishes what kinds of businesses the company will operate and its objectives for each. Then, within each business unit, more detailed planning takes place. The major functional departments in each unit—marketing, finance, accounting, purchasing, operations, information systems, human resources, and others—must work together to accomplish strategic objectives.

Marketing plays a key role in the company's strategic planning in several ways. First, marketing provides a guiding *philosophy*—the marketing concept—that suggests the company strategy should revolve around creating customer value and building profitable relationships with important consumer groups. Second, marketing provides *inputs* to strategic planners by helping to identify attractive market opportunities and assessing the firm's potential to take advantage of them. Finally, within individual business units, marketing designs *strategies* for reaching the unit's objectives. Once the unit's objectives are set, marketing's task is to help carry them out profitably.

Customer engagement and value are the key ingredients in the marketer's formula for success. However, as noted in Chapter 1, although marketing plays a leading role, it alone cannot produce engagement and superior value for customers. It can be only a partner in attracting, engaging, and growing customers. In addition to *customer relationship management*, marketers must also practice *partner relationship management*. They must work closely with partners in other company departments to form an effective internal *value chain* that serves customers. Moreover, they must partner effectively with other companies in the marketing system to form a competitively superior external *value delivery network*. We now take a closer look at the concepts of a company value chain and a value delivery network.

Partnering with Other Company Departments

Value chain

The series of internal departments that carry out value-creating activities to design, produce, market, deliver, and support a firm's products.

Each company department can be thought of as a link in the company's internal **value chain**.[9] That is, each department carries out value-creating activities to design, produce, market, deliver, and support the firm's products. The firm's success depends not only on how well each department performs its work but also on how well the various departments coordinate their activities.

For example, True Value Hardware's goal is to create customer value and satisfaction by providing shoppers with the hardware and home improvement products they need at affordable prices along with top-notch customer service. Marketers at the retail-owned cooperative play an important role. They learn what customers need and help the 3,500 independent True Value retailers stock their store shelves with the desired products at competitive prices. They prepare advertising and merchandising programs and assist shoppers

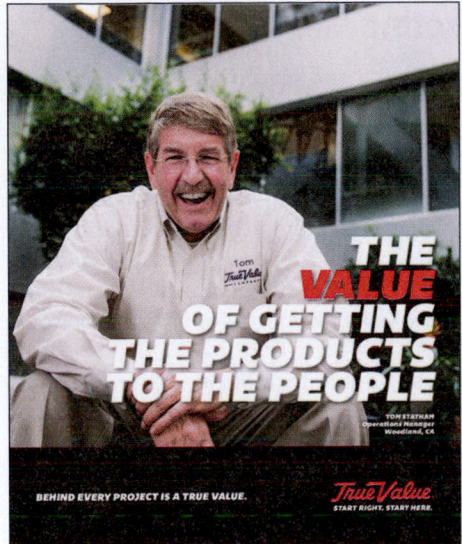 

○ The value chain: These True Value ads recognize that everyone in the organization—from marketing research analyst Jeff Alvarez to operations manager Tom Statham—must contribute to helping the chain's customers handle their home improvement projects. They form the foundation for the brand's "Behind Every Project Is a True Value" positioning.

True Value and Start Right. Start Here. are registered trademarks of True Value Company. The print ads and images are copyrighted works of authorship of True Value Company.

with customer service. Through these and other activities, True Value marketers help deliver value to customers.

However, True Value's marketers, both at the home office and in stores, need help from the company's other functions. True Value's ability to help you "Start Right. Start Here." depends on purchasing's skill in developing the needed suppliers and buying from them at low cost. True Value's information technology people must provide fast and accurate information about which products are selling in each store. And its operations people must provide effective, low-cost merchandise handling and delivery.

A company's value chain is only as strong as its weakest link. Success depends on how well each group performs its work of adding customer value and on how the company coordinates the activities of various functions. ○ True Value's marketing campaign—"Behind Every Project Is a True Value"—recognizes the importance of having everyone in the organization—from in-store managers and employees to home-office operations managers and marketing research analysts—understand the needs and aspirations of the chain's do-it-yourself customers and help them handle home improvement projects.

Ideally, then, a company's different functions should work in harmony to produce value for consumers. But, in practice, interdepartmental relations are full of conflicts and misunderstandings. The marketing department takes the consumer's point of view. But when marketing tries to improve customer satisfaction, it can cause other departments to do a poorer job *in their terms*. Marketing department actions can increase purchasing costs, disrupt production schedules, increase inventories, and create budget headaches. Thus, other departments may resist the marketing department's efforts.

Yet marketers must find ways to get all departments to "think consumer" and develop a smoothly functioning value chain. One marketing expert puts it this way: "Engaging customers today requires commitment from the entire company. We're all marketers now."[10] Thus, whether you're an accountant, an operations manager, a financial analyst, an IT specialist, or a human resources manager, you need to understand marketing and your role in creating customer value.

Partnering with Others in the Marketing System

In its quest to engage customers and create customer value, the firm needs to look beyond its own internal value chain and into the value chains of its suppliers, its distributors, and, ultimately, its customers. Consider McDonald's. People do not swarm to McDonald's only because they love the chain's hamburgers. Consumers flock to the McDonald's *system*, not only to its food products. Throughout the world, McDonald's finely tuned value delivery system delivers a high standard of QSCV—quality, service, cleanliness, and value. McDonald's is effective only to the extent that it successfully partners with its franchisees, suppliers, and others to jointly create "our customers' favorite place and way to eat."

More companies today are partnering with other members of the supply chain—suppliers, distributors, and, ultimately, customers—to improve the performance of the customer **value delivery network**. Competition no longer takes place only between individual competitors. Rather, it takes place between the entire value delivery network created by these competitors. Thus, Ford's performance against Toyota depends on the quality of Ford's overall value delivery network versus Toyota's. Even if Ford makes the best cars, it might lose in the marketplace if Toyota's dealer network provides a more customer-satisfying sales and service experience.

Value delivery network
A network composed of the company, suppliers, distributors, and, ultimately, customers who partner with each other to improve the performance of the entire system in delivering customer value.

Author | Now that we've set
Comment | the context in terms of
company-wide strategy, it's time
to discuss customer value–driven
marketing strategies and programs.

Marketing strategy
The marketing logic by which the
company hopes to create customer
value and achieve profitable customer
relationships.

Marketing Strategy and the Marketing Mix

The strategic plan defines the company's overall mission and objectives. Marketing's role is shown in ● **Figure 2.4**, which summarizes the major activities involved in managing a customer-driven marketing strategy and the marketing mix.

Consumers are in the center. The goal is to create value for customers and build profitable customer relationships. Next comes **marketing strategy**—the marketing logic by which the company hopes to create this customer value and achieve these profitable relationships. The company decides which customers it will serve (segmentation and targeting) and how (differentiation and positioning). It identifies the total market and then divides it into smaller segments, selects the most promising segments, and focuses on serving and satisfying the customers in these segments.

Guided by marketing strategy, the company designs an integrated *marketing mix* made up of factors under its control—product, price, place, and promotion (the four Ps). To find the best marketing strategy and mix, the company engages in marketing analysis, planning, implementation, and control. Through these activities, the company watches and adapts to the actors and forces in the marketing environment. We will now look briefly at each activity. In later chapters, we will discuss each one in more depth.

Customer Value–Driven Marketing Strategy

To succeed in today's competitive marketplace, companies must be customer centered. They must win customers from competitors and then engage and grow them by delivering greater value. But before it can satisfy customers, a company must first understand customer needs and wants. Thus, sound marketing requires careful customer analysis.

Companies know that they cannot profitably serve all consumers in a given market— at least not all consumers in the same way. There are too many different kinds of consumers with too many different kinds of needs. Most companies are in a position to serve some segments better than others. Thus, each company must divide up the total market, choose the best segments, and design strategies for profitably serving chosen segments. This process involves *market segmentation, market targeting, differentiation*, and *positioning*.

Market Segmentation

The market consists of many types of consumers, products, and needs. The marketer must determine which segments offer the best opportunities. Consumers can be grouped and served in various ways based on geographic, demographic, psychographic, and behavioral

● **FIGURE** | 2.4
Managing Marketing Strategies
and the Marketing Mix

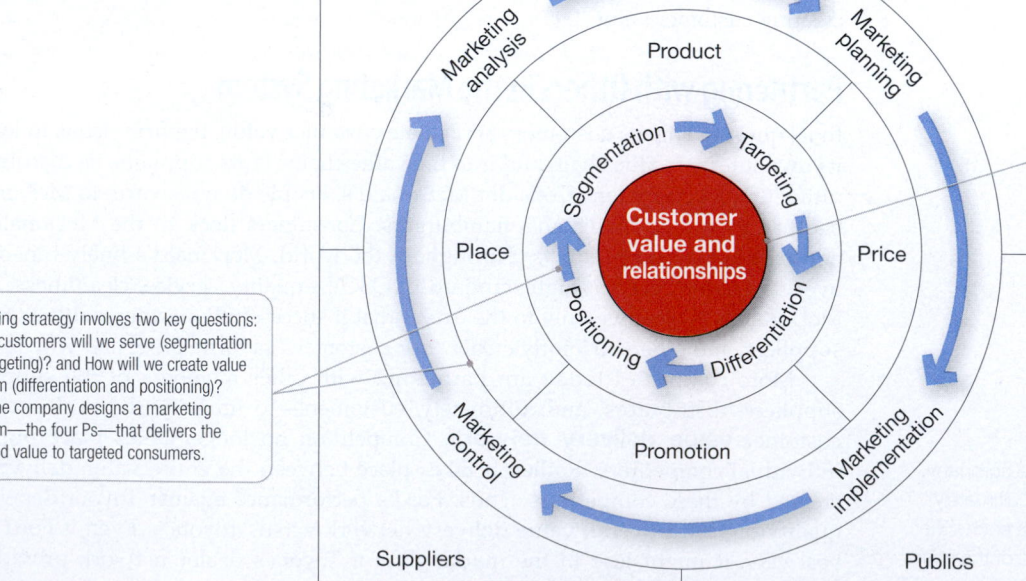

Marketing strategy involves two key questions: Which customers will we serve (segmentation and targeting)? and How will we create value for them (differentiation and positioning)? Then the company designs a marketing program—the four Ps—that delivers the intended value to targeted consumers.

At its core, marketing is all about creating customer value and profitable customer relationships.

Market segmentation
Dividing a market into distinct groups of buyers who have different needs, characteristics, or behaviors and who might require separate marketing strategies or mixes.

Market segment
A group of consumers who respond in a similar way to a given set of marketing efforts.

Market targeting
Evaluating each market segment's attractiveness and selecting one or more segments to serve.

Positioning
Arranging for a product to occupy a clear, distinctive, and desirable place relative to competing products in the minds of target consumers.

factors. The process of dividing a market into distinct groups of buyers who have different needs, characteristics, or behaviors and who might require separate marketing strategies or mixes is called **market segmentation**.

Every market has segments, but not all ways of segmenting a market are equally useful. For example, Tylenol would gain little by distinguishing between low-income and high-income pain-relief users if both respond the same way to marketing efforts. A **market segment** consists of consumers who respond in a similar way to a given set of marketing efforts. In the car market, for example, consumers who want the biggest, most comfortable car regardless of price make up one market segment. Consumers who care mainly about price and operating economy make up another segment. It would be difficult to make one car model that was the first choice of consumers in both segments. Companies are wise to focus their efforts on meeting the distinct needs of individual market segments.

Market Targeting

After a company has defined its market segments, it can enter one or many of these segments. **Market targeting** involves evaluating each market segment's attractiveness and selecting one or more segments to enter. A company should target segments in which it can profitably generate the greatest customer value and sustain it over time.

A company with limited resources might decide to serve only one or a few special segments or market niches. Such nichers specialize in serving customer segments that major competitors overlook or ignore. For example, McLaren sold only 1,653 of its very-high-performance cars last year but at very high prices—such as its 570S model at $180,000 or a made-to-order FI model starting at an eye-popping $980,000. Most nichers aren't quite so exotic. Profitable low-cost airline Allegiant Air avoids direct competition with larger major airline rivals by targeting smaller, neglected markets and new fliers. Nicher Allegiant "goes where they ain't." And small online-search start-up DuckDuckGo thrives among privacy-minded users in the shadows of search giants Google and Microsoft's Bing (see Real Marketing 2.2).

Alternatively, a company might choose to serve several related segments—perhaps those with different kinds of customers but with the same basic wants. Gap Inc., for example, targets different age, income, and lifestyle clothing and accessory segments with five different store and online brands: Gap, Banana Republic, Old Navy, Athleta, and INTERMIX. The Gap store brand breaks its segment down into even smaller niches, including Gap, GapKids, babyGap, GapMaternity, and GapBody.[11] Or a large company (for example, car companies such as Honda and Ford) might decide to offer a complete range of products to serve all market segments.

Most companies enter a new market by serving a single segment; if this proves successful, they add more segments. For example, Nike started with innovative running shoes for serious runners. Large companies eventually seek full market coverage. Nike now makes and sells a broad range of sports apparel and equipment for just about anyone and everyone in about every sport. It designs different products to meet the special needs of each segment it serves.

Market Differentiation and Positioning

After a company has decided which market segments to enter, it must determine how to differentiate its market offering for each targeted segment and what positions it wants to occupy in those segments. A product's *position* is the place it occupies relative to competitors' products in consumers' minds. Marketers want to develop unique market positions for their products. If a product is perceived to be exactly like others on the market, consumers would have no reason to buy it.

Positioning is arranging for a product to occupy a clear, distinctive, and desirable place relative to competing products in the minds of target consumers. Marketers plan positions that distinguish their products from competing brands and give them the greatest advantage in their target markets.

BMW promises "Sheer driving pleasure"; Subaru is "Confidence in motion." Coca-Cola wants you to "Taste the feeling"; Pepsi says "Live for now." Del Monte is "Bursting with Life"; Cascadian Farm products are "Certified Organic. Guaranteed Delicious." At Panera, you'll find "Food as it should be"; at Wendy's, "Quality Is Our Recipe."

Without a heart, it's just a machine.

Southwest.

● **Positioning:** Southwest's positioning as "The LUV Airline" is reinforced by the colorful heart in its new logo and plane redesign. Southwest has "always put Heart in everything it does."
Southwest Airlines Co.

Real Marketing

2.2 DuckDuckGo: Google's Tiniest, Fiercest Competitor

Google dominates U.S. online search with its massive 64 percent market share. Two other giants—Microsoft's Bing and Yahoo!—combine for another 34 percent of the market. That leaves a precious 2 percent sliver of the market for dozens of other search engines trying to get a foothold. What's more, Google and the other search giants have deep pockets from their non-search businesses, letting them spend abundantly to hold and grow market share. So how does a small search engine wannabe compete against global powerhouses? The best answer: It doesn't—at least not directly. Instead, it finds a unique market niche and runs where the big dogs don't.

Enter DuckDuckGo, a plucky search engine start-up that's carving out its own special market niche. Instead of battling Google and other giants head-on, DuckDuckGo provides a customer benefit that the market leaders can't—privacy. Then it energizes its unique niche with brand personality and user community. One look at DuckDuckGo's icon—a quirky bow-tied duck—gives you the sense that, like the small locomotive in the classic children's story, this might be "the little engine that could."

DuckDuckGo isn't just surviving in its niche, it's exploding. The company is still comparatively tiny—it averages about 3 billion searches a year compared with Google's more than 1.2 trillion. But DuckDuckGo's daily search volume has surged nearly tenfold in just the past three years, whereas Google's volume growth has lagged a bit.

When Gabriel Weinberg first launched DuckDuckGo eight years ago, most people questioned his sanity. How could a small upstart challenge the likes of mighty Google? But rather than simply mimicking Google, Weinberg went a different direction, developing a quality search engine with a key differentiating feature. DuckDuckGo now positions itself strongly on "Smarter Search. Less Clutter. Real Privacy."

DuckDuckGo focuses only on search. It offers a streamlined, clutter-free, customizable user interface with far fewer sponsored ads. As with other search engines, a DuckDuckGo query returns link-by-link search results based on third-party sources, but the results are filtered and reorganized to reduce spam. And beyond the usual search-result links, for many searches, DuckDuckGo provides direct "Instant Answers" in the form of zero-click information boxes above the search results. "When you do a search, you generally want an answer," says Weinberg. "It's our job to try to get an answer." With Instant Answers, DuckDuckGo can "help you get where you want to go in fewer clicks."

The Instant Answer feature is a good one, so good in fact that it has now been copied by Google and Bing. For example, run a Google search for "davinci" or "how long is the great wall" and along with the familiar list of blue links you'll get a white box containing a mini-biography of Leonardo Da Vinci or displaying the length of the Great Wall of China (5,500.3 miles) and other interesting facts about it.

DuckDuckGo would tell you that its Instant Answers are often better. Its answers rely not just on third-party data sources but also on the deep and diverse knowledge of its active, growing, and loyal community of users and developers. DuckDuckGo's community provides additional power behind its searches. In a Wikipedia-like fashion, DuckDuckGo users come up with ideas about what the answers should be, suggest sources, and even develop answers themselves. "DuckDuckGo is a search engine driven by community—you're on the team!" says the company. "We're not just servers and an algorithm. We're so much more."

Still, even though DuckDuckGo had Instant Answers long before Google, Google's response illustrates a typical nicher dilemma. Market leaders usually have huge resources and can quickly copy the start-up's most popular features. "At any point," notes one analyst, "the Googles or Facebooks or Apples of the world can just mimic what made you different, slam-dunking your shattered dreams into the waste bin of tech history."

Fortunately for DuckDuckGo, it has one crucial differentiator that the Googles of the world simply can't mimic. Real privacy. Google's entire model is built around personalization for customers and behaviorally targeted marketing for advertisers. That requires collecting and sharing data about users and their searches. When you search on Google, the company knows and retains in detail who you are, what you've searched for, and when you've searched. It then integrates your online identity and data with its services.

DuckDuckGo
Our vision is simple.
To give you great search results without tracking you.

Niche marketing: DuckDuckGo thrives in the shadows of giant search engine competitors by giving its user community something the Googles of the world can't mimic—real privacy.
Duck Duck Go, Inc.

By contrast, DuckDuckGo is specifically designed to be less invasive and less creepy than its competitors. DuckDuckGo doesn't know who you are. It doesn't log user IP addresses or use cookies to track users over time or other online locations. Users don't have accounts. In fact, DuckDuckGo doesn't even save user search histories. Perhaps most important, when users click on DuckDuckGo's search results links, the linked websites don't receive any information generated by the search engine. As one privacy advocate puts it, "DuckDuckGo is a solid search engine that lets you surf the web without leaving behind a bunch of bread crumbs for Uncle Sam or anyone else to follow. … The sites you visit are being kept at arm's length."

So DuckDuckGo has become the preferred search engine for people concerned about online privacy, and that's a fast-growing group. "If you look at the logs of people's search sessions, they're the most personal thing on the internet," Weinberg says. "Unlike Facebook, where you choose what to post, with search you're typing in medical and financial problems and all sorts of other things." Today, more and more people are thinking about the privacy implications of their search histories. "It was extreme at the time," says Weinberg of DuckDuckGo's early privacy positioning. But today, he adds, "It's

become obvious why people don't want to be tracked."

How does DuckDuckGo make money? Last year, Google made 90 percent of its $74.5 billion of revenue from search-related advertising, and most of that business involved large-scale, behaviorally targeted advertising that relies on the very tracking tools that DuckDuckGo shuns. However, even without tracking users, smaller DuckDuckGo can be profitable. It simply focuses on the other part of Google's business—delivering contextual search ads based on the topic of the search itself. So when users search for "curved OLED TVs," DuckDuckGo shows ads and links for TV manufacturers and retailers who've paid for the associated key words.

Thus, in many ways, DuckDuckGo is David to Google's Goliath. But unlike David, DuckDuckGo isn't out to slay the giant. It knows that it can't compete head-on with

the Googles and Bings of the world—it doesn't even try. Then again, given the depth of consumer engagement and loyalty that DuckDuckGo engenders in its own small corner of the online search market, Google and the other giants may find it difficult to compete with DuckDuckGo for privacy-minded users. DuckDuckGo is currently the nation's 11th-most-popular search engine based on unique monthly visitors. And as privacy grows in importance, so will DuckDuckGo.

That's what niche marketing is all about—a well-defined brand engaging a focused customer community with meaningful brand relationships that even large and resourceful competitors can't crack. Smart niching has made DuckDuckGo "Google's tiniest, fiercest competitor," says the analyst. "Our vision is simple," says DuckDuckGo. "To give you great search results without tracking you."

Sources: "comScore Releases February 2016 U.S. Desktop Search Engine Rankings," March 16, 2016, www.comscore.com/Insights/Rankings/comScore-Releases-January-2016-US-Desktop-Search-Engine-Rankings; "DuckDuckGo Direct Queries per Day," *https://duckduckgo.com/traffic.html*, accessed July 2016; John Paul Titlow, "Inside DuckDuckGo, Google's Tiniest, Fiercest Competitor," *Fast Company*, February 20, 2014, *www.fastcompany.com/3026698/inside-duckduckgo-googles-tiniest-fiercest-competitor*; Susan Adams, "The Founder of DuckDuckGo Explains Why Challenging Google Isn't Insane," *Forbes*, February 19, 2016, www.forbes.com/sites/forbestreptalks/2016/02/19/the-founder-of-duckduckgo-explains-how-to-get-customers-before-you-have-a-product-and-why-challenging-google-isnt-insane/#5899487d593c; "Top 15 Most Popular Search Engines—March 2016," *www.ebizmba.com/articles/search-engines*, accessed July 2016; and *https://duckduckgo.com/about*, accessed September 2016.

Such deceptively simple statements form the backbone of a product's marketing strategy. For example, from its founding, Southwest Airlines has positioned itself as "The LUV Airline," a positioning recently reinforced by the colorful heart in its new logo and plane graphics design. As recent Southwest advertising affirms, "Without a heart, it's just a machine." The airline has "always put Heart in everything it does."

In positioning its brand, a company first identifies possible customer value differences that provide competitive advantages on which to build the position. A company can offer greater customer value by either charging lower prices than competitors or offering more benefits to justify higher prices. But if the company *promises* greater value, it must then *deliver* that greater value. Thus, effective positioning begins with **differentiation**—actually *differentiating* the company's market offering to create superior customer value. Once the company has chosen a desired position, it must take strong steps to deliver and communicate that position to target consumers. The company's entire marketing program should support the chosen positioning strategy.

Differentiation
Actually differentiating the market offering to create superior customer value.

Developing an Integrated Marketing Mix

After determining its overall marketing strategy, the company is ready to begin planning the details of the **marketing mix**, one of the major concepts in modern marketing. The marketing mix is the set of tactical marketing tools that the firm blends to produce the response it wants in the target market. The marketing mix consists of everything the firm can do to engage consumers and deliver customer value. The many possibilities can be collected into four groups of variables—the four Ps. **Figure 2.5** shows the marketing tools under each P.

Marketing mix
The set of tactical marketing tools—product, price, place, and promotion—that the firm blends to produce the response it wants in the target market.

- *Product* means the goods-and-services combination the company offers to the target market. Thus, a Ford Escape consists of nuts and bolts, spark plugs, pistons, headlights, and thousands of other parts. Ford offers several Escape models and dozens of optional features. The car comes fully serviced and with a comprehensive warranty that is as much a part of the product as the tailpipe.

- *Price* is the amount of money customers must pay to obtain the product. For example, Ford calculates suggested retail prices that its dealers might charge for each Escape. But Ford dealers rarely charge the full sticker price. Instead, they negotiate the price with each customer, offering discounts, trade-in allowances, and credit terms. These actions adjust prices for the current competitive and economic situations and bring them into line with the buyer's perception of the car's value.
- *Place* includes company activities that make the product available to target consumers. Ford partners with a large body of independently owned dealerships that sell the company's many different models. Ford selects its dealers carefully and strongly supports them. The dealers keep an inventory of Ford automobiles, demonstrate them to potential buyers, negotiate prices, close sales, and service the cars after the sale.
- *Promotion* refers to activities that communicate the merits of the product and persuade target customers to buy it. Ford spends nearly $2.5 billion each year on U.S. advertising to tell consumers about the company and its many products.[12] Dealership salespeople assist potential buyers and persuade them that Ford is the best car for them. Ford and its dealers offer special promotions—sales, cash rebates, and low financing rates—as added purchase incentives. And Ford's Facebook, Twitter, YouTube, Instagram, and other social media platforms engage consumers with the brand and with other brand fans.

An effective marketing program blends the marketing mix elements into an integrated marketing program designed to achieve the company's marketing objectives by engaging consumers and delivering value to them. The marketing mix constitutes the company's tactical tool kit for establishing strong positioning in target markets.

Some critics think that the four Ps may omit or underemphasize certain important activities. For example, they ask, "Where are services? Just because they don't start with a *P* doesn't justify omitting them." The answer is that services, such as banking, airline, and retailing services, are products too. We might call them *service products*. "Where is packaging?" the critics might ask. Marketers would answer that they include packaging as one of many product decisions. All said, as Figure 2.5 suggests, many marketing activities that might appear to be left out of the marketing mix are included under one of the four Ps. The issue is not whether there should be four, six, or ten Ps so much as what framework is most helpful in designing integrated marketing programs.

● FIGURE | 2.5
The Four Ps of the Marketing Mix

Product
Variety
Quality
Design
Features
Brand name
Packaging
Services

Price
List price
Discounts
Allowances
Payment period
Credit terms

Target customers

Intended positioning

The marketing mix—or the four Ps—consists of tactical marketing tools blended into an integrated program that actually engages target customers and delivers the intended customer value.

Promotion
Advertising
Personal selling
Sales promotion
Public relations
Direct and digital

Place
Channels
Coverage
Locations
Inventory
Transportation
Logistics

There is another concern, however, that is valid. It holds that the four Ps concept takes the seller's view of the market, not the buyer's view. From the buyer's viewpoint, in this age of customer value and relationships, the four Ps might be better described as the four As:[13]

Four Ps	Four As
Product	Acceptability
Price	Affordability
Place	Accessibility
Promotion	Awareness

Under this more customer-centered framework, *acceptability* is the extent to which the product exceeds customer expectations; *affordability* the extent to which customers are willing and able to pay the product's price; *accessibility* the extent to which customers can readily acquire the product; and *awareness* the extent to which customers are informed about the product's features, persuaded to try it, and reminded to repurchase. The four As relate closely to the traditional four Ps. Product design influences acceptability, price affects affordability, place affects accessibility, and promotion influences awareness. Marketers would do well to think through the four As first and then build the four Ps on that platform.

> **Author Comment** | So far we've focused on the *marketing* in marketing management. Now, let's turn to the *management*.

Managing the Marketing Effort and Marketing Return on Investment

Managing the Marketing Effort

In addition to being good at the *marketing* in marketing management, companies also need to pay attention to the *management*. Managing the marketing process requires the five marketing management functions shown in ● **Figure 2.6**—*analysis, planning, implementation, organization,* and *control*. The company first develops company-wide strategic plans and then translates them into marketing and other plans for each division, product, and brand. Through implementation and organization, the company turns the plans into actions. Control consists of measuring and evaluating the results of marketing activities and taking corrective action where needed. Finally, marketing analysis provides the information and evaluations needed for all the other marketing activities.

SWOT analysis
An overall evaluation of the company's strengths (S), weaknesses (W), opportunities (O), and threats (T).

Marketing Analysis

Managing the marketing function begins with a complete analysis of the company's situation. The marketer should conduct a **SWOT analysis** (pronounced "swat" analysis), by

● **FIGURE** | 2.6
Managing Marketing: Analysis, Planning, Implementation, and Control

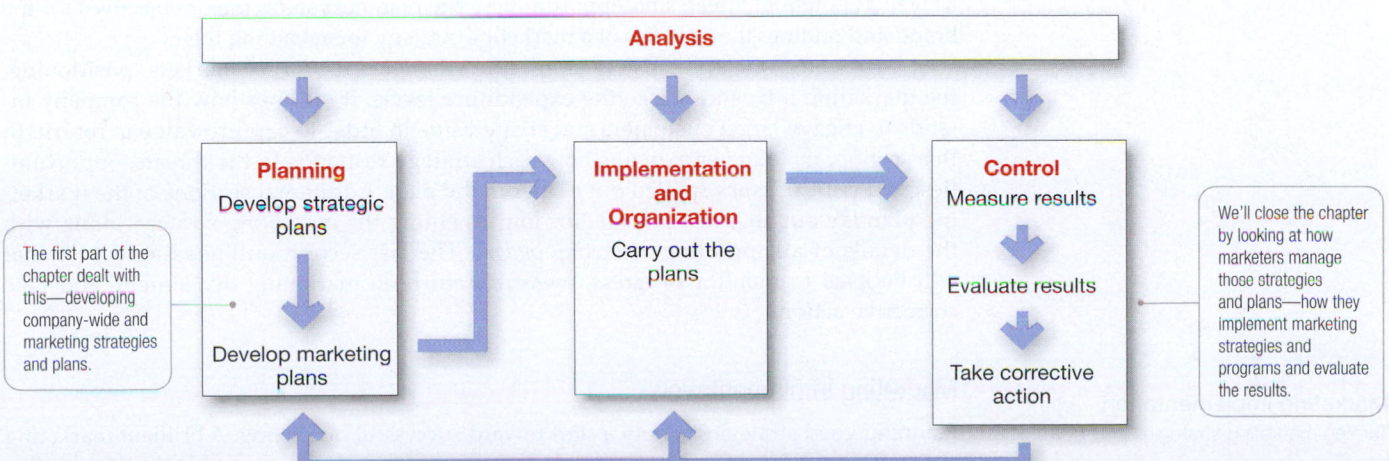

● FIGURE | 2.7

SWOT Analysis: Strengths (S),
Weaknesses (W), Opportunities (O),
and Threats (T)

Internal

The goal of SWOT analysis is to match the company's strengths to attractive opportunities in the environment while eliminating or overcoming the weaknesses and minimizing the threats.

External

Strengths Internal capabilities that may help a company reach its objectives	**Weaknesses** Internal limitations that may interfere with a company's ability to achieve its objectives
Opportunities External factors that the company may be able to exploit to its advantage	**Threats** Current and emerging external factors that may challenge the company's performance

Hang on to this figure! SWOT analysis (pronounced "swat" analysis) is a widely used tool for conducting a situation analysis. You'll find yourself using it a lot in the future, especially when analyzing business cases.

Positive   **Negative**

which it evaluates the company's overall strengths (S), weaknesses (W), opportunities (O), and threats (T) (see ● **Figure 2.7**). Strengths include internal capabilities, resources, and positive situational factors that may help the company serve its customers and achieve its objectives. Weaknesses include internal limitations and negative situational factors that may interfere with the company's performance. Opportunities are favorable factors or trends in the external environment that the company may be able to exploit to its advantage. And threats are unfavorable external factors or trends that may present challenges to performance.

The company should analyze its markets and marketing environment to find attractive opportunities and identify threats. It should analyze company strengths and weaknesses as well as current and possible marketing actions to determine which opportunities it can best pursue. The goal is to match the company's strengths to attractive opportunities in the environment while simultaneously eliminating or overcoming the weaknesses and minimizing the threats. Marketing analysis provides inputs to each of the other marketing management functions. We discuss marketing analysis more fully in Chapter 3.

Marketing Planning

Through strategic planning, the company decides what it wants to do with each business unit. Marketing planning involves choosing marketing strategies that will help the company attain its overall strategic objectives. A detailed marketing plan is needed for each business, product, or brand. What does a marketing plan look like? Our discussion focuses on product or brand marketing plans.

● **Table 2.2** outlines the major sections of a typical product or brand marketing plan. (See Appendix 1 for a sample marketing plan.) The plan begins with an executive summary that quickly reviews major assessments, goals, and recommendations. The main section of the plan presents a detailed SWOT analysis of the current marketing situation as well as potential threats and opportunities. The plan next states major objectives for the brand and outlines the specifics of a marketing strategy for achieving them.

A *marketing strategy* consists of specific strategies for target markets, positioning, the marketing mix, and marketing expenditure levels. It outlines how the company intends to engage target customers and create value in order to capture value in return. In this section, the planner explains how each strategy responds to the threats, opportunities, and critical issues spelled out earlier in the plan. Additional sections of the marketing plan lay out an *action program* for implementing the marketing strategy along with the details of a supporting *marketing budget*. The last section outlines the *controls* that will be used to monitor progress, measure return on marketing investment, and take corrective action.

Marketing Implementation

Marketing implementation
Turning marketing strategies and plans into marketing actions to accomplish strategic marketing objectives.

Planning good strategies is only a start toward successful marketing. A brilliant marketing strategy counts for little if the company fails to implement it properly. **Marketing implementation** is the process that turns marketing *plans* into marketing *actions* to accomplish

● **Table 2.2** | **Contents of a Marketing Plan**

Section	Purpose
Executive summary	Presents a brief summary of the main goals and recommendations of the plan for management review, helping top management find the plan's major points quickly.
Current marketing situation	Describes the target market and the company's position in it, including information about the market, product performance, competition, and distribution. This section includes the following: • A *market description* that defines the market and major segments and then reviews customer needs and factors in the marketing environment that may affect customer purchasing. • A *product review* that shows sales, prices, and gross margins of the major products in the product line. • A review of *competition* that identifies major competitors and assesses their market positions and strategies for product quality, pricing, distribution, and promotion. • A review of *distribution* that evaluates recent sales trends and other developments in major distribution channels.
Threats and opportunities analysis	Assesses major threats and opportunities that the product might face, helping management to anticipate important positive or negative developments that might have an impact on the firm and its strategies.
Objectives and issues	States the marketing objectives that the company would like to attain during the plan's term and discusses key issues that will affect their attainment.
Marketing strategy	Outlines the broad marketing logic by which the business unit hopes to engage customers, create customer value, and build customer relationships, plus the specifics of target markets, positioning, and marketing expenditure levels. How will the company create value for customers in order to capture value from customers in return? This section also outlines specific strategies for each marketing mix element and explains how each responds to the threats, opportunities, and critical issues spelled out earlier in the plan.
Action programs	Spells out how marketing strategies will be turned into specific action programs that answer the following questions: *What* will be done? *When* will it be done? *Who* will do it? *How* much will it cost?
Budgets	Details a supporting marketing budget that is essentially a projected profit-and-loss statement. It shows expected revenues and expected costs of production, distribution, and marketing. The difference is the projected profit. The budget becomes the basis for materials buying, production scheduling, personnel planning, and marketing operations.
Controls	Outlines the controls that will be used to monitor progress, allow management to review implementation results, and spot products that are not meeting their goals. It includes measures of return on marketing investment.

strategic marketing objectives. Whereas marketing planning addresses the *what* and *why* of marketing activities, implementation addresses the *who, where, when*, and *how*.

Many managers think that "doing things right" (implementation) is as important as, or even more important than, "doing the right things" (strategy). The fact is that both are critical to success, and companies can gain competitive advantages through effective implementation. One firm can have essentially the same strategy as another yet win in the marketplace through faster or better execution. Still, implementation is difficult—it is often easier to think up good marketing strategies than it is to carry them out.

In an increasingly connected world, people at all levels of the marketing system must work together to implement marketing strategies and plans. At John Deere, for example, marketing implementation for the company's residential, commercial, agricultural, and industrial equipment requires day-to-day decisions and actions by thousands of people both inside and outside the organization. Marketing managers make decisions about target segments, branding, product development, pricing, promotion, and distribution. They talk with engineering about product design, with manufacturing about production and inventory levels, and with finance about funding and cash flows. They also connect with outside people, such as advertising agencies to plan ad campaigns and the news media to obtain publicity support. The sales force urges and supports independent John Deere dealers and large retailers like Lowe's in their efforts to convince residential, agricultural, and industrial customers that "Nothing Runs Like a Deere."

Marketing Department Organization

The company must design a marketing organization that can carry out marketing strategies and plans. If the company is very small, one person might do all the research, selling, advertising, customer service, and other marketing work. As the company expands, however, a marketing department emerges to plan and carry out marketing activities. In large companies, this department contains many specialists—product and market managers, sales managers and salespeople, market researchers, and advertising and social media experts, among others.

To head up such large marketing organizations, many companies have now created a *chief marketing officer* (or CMO) position. This person heads up the company's entire marketing operation and represents marketing on the company's top management team. The CMO position puts marketing on equal footing with other "C-level" executives, such as the chief operating officer (COO) and the chief financial officer (CFO). As a member of top management, the CMO's role is to champion the customer's cause—to be the "chief customer officer." To that end, British Airways even went so far as to rename its top marketing position as Director of Customer Experience.[14]

● **Marketers must continually plan their analysis, implementation, and control activities.**

Pressmaster/Adobe Photo

Modern marketing departments can be arranged in several ways. The most common form of marketing organization is the *functional organization*, under which different marketing activities are headed by a functional specialist—a sales manager, an advertising manager, a marketing research manager, a customer service manager, or a new product manager. A company that sells across the country or internationally often uses a *geographic organization*, assigning sales and marketing people to specific countries, regions, and districts. Companies with many very different products or brands often create a *product management organization*. For companies that sell one product line to many different types of markets and customers who have different needs and preferences, a *market* or *customer management organization* might be best. Large companies that produce many different products flowing into many different geographic and customer markets usually employ some *combination* of the functional, geographic, product, and market organization forms.

Marketing organization has become an increasingly important issue in recent years. More and more, companies are shifting their brand management focus toward *customer management*—moving away from managing only product or brand profitability and toward managing customer profitability and customer equity. They think of themselves not as managing portfolios of brands but as managing portfolios of customers. And rather than managing the fortunes of a brand, they see themselves as managing customer-brand engagement, experiences, and relationships.

Marketing control
Measuring and evaluating the results of marketing strategies and plans and taking corrective action to ensure that the objectives are achieved.

Marketing Control

Because many surprises occur during the implementation of marketing strategies and plans, marketers must practice constant **marketing control**—evaluating results and taking corrective action to ensure that the objectives are attained. Marketing control involves four steps. Management first sets specific marketing goals. It then measures its performance in the marketplace and evaluates the causes of any differences between expected and actual performance. Finally, management takes corrective action to close the gaps between goals and performance. This may require changing the action programs or even changing the goals.

Operating control involves checking ongoing performance against the annual plan and taking corrective action when necessary. Its purpose is to ensure that the company achieves the sales, profits, and other goals set out in its annual plan. It also involves determining the profitability of different products, territories, markets, and channels. *Strategic control* involves looking at whether the company's basic strategies are well matched to its opportunities. Marketing strategies and programs can quickly become outdated, and each company should periodically reassess its overall approach to the marketplace.

Author | Measuring marketing
Comment | return on investment has
become a major emphasis. But it can
be difficult. For example, a Super Bowl
ad reaches more than 100 million
consumers but may cost more than $4
million for 30 seconds of airtime. How
do you measure the return on such an
investment in terms of sales, profits,
and building customer engagement
and relationships?

Marketing return on investment (marketing ROI)
The net return from a marketing investment divided by the costs of the marketing investment.

Measuring and Managing Marketing Return on Investment

Marketing managers must ensure that their marketing dollars are being well spent. In the past, many marketers spent freely on big, expensive marketing programs and flashy advertising campaigns, often without thinking carefully about the financial returns on their spending. Their goal was often a general one—to "build brands and consumer preference." They believed that marketing produces intangible creative outcomes, which do not lend themselves readily to measures of productivity or return.

However, those free-spending days have now been replaced by a new era of marketing measurement and accountability. More than ever, today's marketers are being held accountable for linking their strategies and tactics to measurable marketing performance outcomes. One important marketing performance measure is **marketing return on investment** (or **marketing ROI**). *Marketing ROI* is the net return from a marketing investment divided by the costs of the marketing investment. It measures the profits generated by investments in marketing activities.

Marketing ROI can be difficult to measure. In measuring financial ROI, both the *R* and the *I* are uniformly measured in dollars. For example, when buying a piece of equipment, the productivity gains resulting from the purchase are fairly straightforward. As of yet, however, there is no consistent definition of marketing ROI. For instance, returns such as engagement, advertising, and brand-building impact aren't easily put into dollar returns.

A company can assess marketing ROI in terms of standard marketing performance measures, such as brand awareness, sales, or market share. Many companies are assembling such measures into *marketing dashboards*—meaningful sets of marketing performance measures in a single display used to monitor strategic marketing performance. Just as automobile dashboards present drivers with details on how their cars are performing, the marketing dashboard gives marketers the detailed measures they need to assess and adjust their marketing strategies. For example, VF Corporation uses a marketing dashboard to track the performance of its more than 30 lifestyle apparel brands—including Wrangler, Lee, The North Face, Vans, Nautica, 7 For All Mankind, Timberland, and others. VF's marketing dashboard tracks brand equity and trends, share of voice, market share, online sentiment, and marketing ROI in key markets worldwide, not only for VF brands but also for competing brands.[15]

Increasingly, however, beyond standard performance measures, marketers are using customer-centered measures of marketing impact, such as customer acquisition, customer engagement, customer experience, customer retention, customer lifetime value, and customer equity. These measures capture not only current marketing performance but also future performance resulting from stronger customer relationships. ● **Figure** 2.8 views marketing expenditures as investments that produce returns in the form of more profitable customer relationships.[16] Marketing investments result in improved customer value, engagement, and satisfaction, which in turn increase customer attraction and retention. This increases individual customer lifetime values and the firm's overall customer equity. Increased customer equity, in relation to the cost of the marketing investments, determines return on marketing investment.

● FIGURE | 2.8

Marketing Return on Investment

Source: Adapted from Roland T. Rust, Katherine N. Lemon, and Valerie A. Zeithaml, "Return on Marketing: Using Consumer Equity to Focus Marketing Strategy," *Journal of Marketing,* January 2004, p. 112. Used with permission.

Beyond measuring marketing return on investment in terms of standard performance measures such as sales or market share, many companies are using customer relationship measures, such as customer satisfaction, engagement, retention, and equity. These are more difficult to measure but capture both current and future performance.

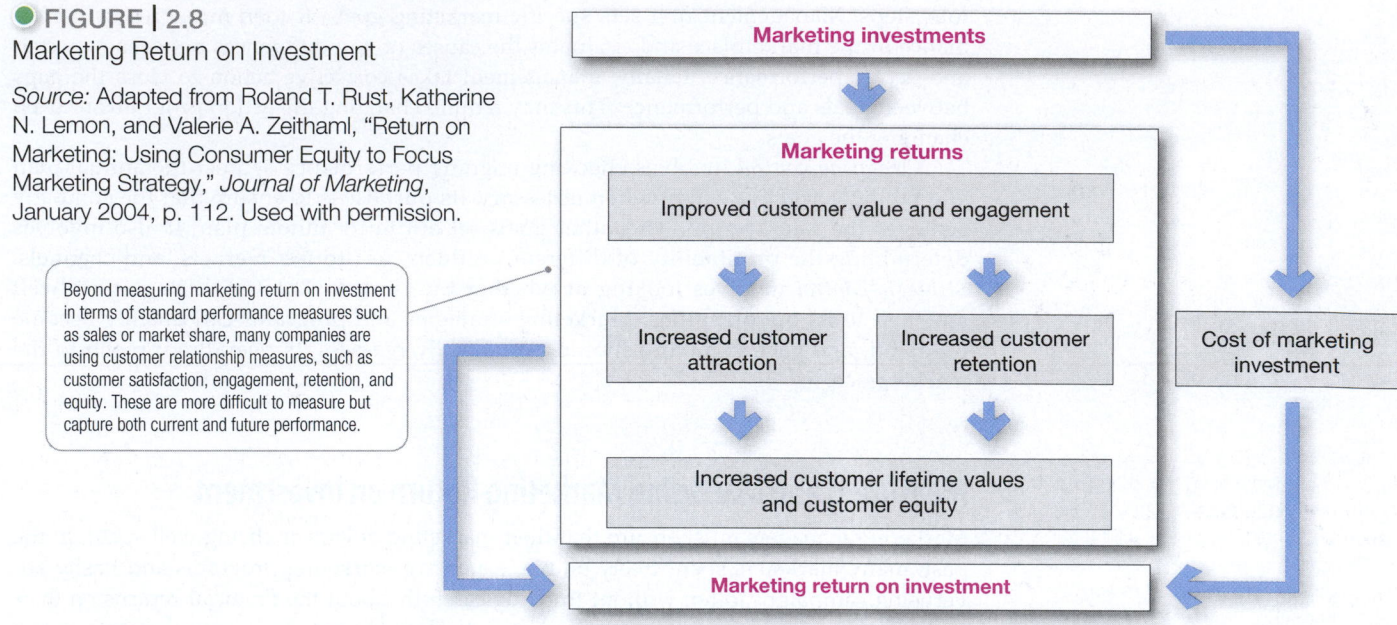

As one chief marketing officer says, "You have to be able to move on to those deeper engagement metrics, which show that for the money that I'm spending, here are the various programs that are working in terms of driving engagement with customers and ultimately driving purchase behavior and revenue."[17]

2 | Reviewing and Extending the Concepts

OBJECTIVES REVIEW AND KEY TERMS

Objectives Review

In Chapter 1, we defined marketing and outlined the steps in the marketing process. In this chapter, we examined company-wide strategic planning and marketing's role in the organization. Then we looked more deeply into marketing strategy and the marketing mix and reviewed the major marketing management functions. So you've now had a pretty good overview of the fundamentals of modern marketing.

OBJECTIVE 2-1 Explain company-wide strategic planning and its four steps. *(pp 40–42)*

Strategic planning sets the stage for the rest of the company's planning. Marketing contributes to strategic planning, and the overall plan defines marketing's role in the company.

Strategic planning involves developing a strategy for long-run survival and growth. It consists of four steps: (1) defining the company's mission, (2) setting objectives and goals, (3) designing a business portfolio, and (4) developing functional plans. The company's mission should be market oriented,

realistic, specific, motivating, and consistent with the market environment. The mission is then transformed into detailed supporting goals and objectives, which in turn guide decisions about the business portfolio. Then each business and product unit must develop detailed marketing plans in line with the company-wide plan.

OBJECTIVE 2-2 Discuss how to design business portfolios and develop growth strategies. *(pp 42–48)*

Guided by the company's mission statement and objectives, management plans its business portfolio, or the collection of businesses and products that make up the company. The firm wants to produce a business portfolio that best fits its strengths and weaknesses to opportunities in the environment. To do this, it must analyze and adjust its current business portfolio and develop growth and downsizing strategies for adjusting the future portfolio. The company might use a formal portfolio-planning method. But many companies are now designing more-customized portfolio-planning approaches that better suit their unique situations.

OBJECTIVE 2-3 Explain marketing's role in strategic planning and how marketing works with its partners to create and deliver customer value. *(pp 48–49)*

Under the strategic plan, the major functional departments—marketing, finance, accounting, purchasing, operations, information systems, human resources, and others—must work together to accomplish strategic objectives. Marketing plays a key role in the company's strategic planning by providing a marketing concept philosophy and inputs regarding attractive market opportunities. Within individual business units, marketing designs strategies for reaching the unit's objectives and helps to carry them out profitably.

Marketers alone cannot produce superior value for customers. Marketers must practice partner relationship management, working closely with partners in other departments to form an effective *value chain* that serves the customer. And they must also partner effectively with other companies in the marketing system to form a competitively superior value delivery network.

OBJECTIVE 2-4 Describe the elements of a customer value–driven marketing strategy and mix and the forces that influence them. *(pp 50–55)*

Customer engagement, value, and relationships are at the center of marketing strategy and programs. Through market segmentation, targeting, differentiation, and positioning, the company divides the total market into smaller segments, selects segments it can best serve, and decides how it wants to bring value to target consumers in the selected segments. It then designs an integrated marketing mix to produce the response it wants in the target market. The marketing mix consists of product, price, place, and promotion decisions (the four Ps).

OBJECTIVE 2-5 List the marketing management functions, including the elements of a marketing plan, and discuss the importance of measuring and managing marketing return on investment. *(pp 55–60)*

To find the best strategy and mix and to put them into action, the company engages in marketing analysis, planning, implementation, and control. The main components of a marketing plan are the executive summary, the current marketing situation, threats and opportunities, objectives and issues, marketing strategies, action programs, budgets, and controls. Planning good strategies is often easier than carrying them out. To be successful, companies must also be effective at implementation—turning marketing strategies into marketing actions.

Marketing departments can be organized in one way or a combination of ways: functional marketing organization, geographic organization, product management organization, or market management organization. In this age of customer relationships, more and more companies are now changing their organizational focus from product or territory management to customer relationship management. Marketing organizations carry out marketing control, both operating control and strategic control.

More than ever, marketing accountability is the top marketing concern. Marketing managers must ensure that their marketing dollars are being well spent. In a tighter economy, today's marketers face growing pressures to show that they are adding value in line with their costs. In response, marketers are developing better measures of marketing return on investment. Increasingly, they are using customer-centered measures of marketing impact as a key input into their strategic decision making.

Key Terms

OBJECTIVE 2-1

Strategic planning (p 40)
Mission statement (p 41)

OBJECTIVE 2-2

Business portfolio (p 43)
Portfolio analysis (p 43)
Growth-share matrix (p 43)
Product/market expansion grid (p 46)
Market penetration (p 47)
Market development (p 47)

Product development (p 47)
Diversification (p 47)

OBJECTIVE 2-3

Value chain (p 48)
Value delivery network (p 49)

OBJECTIVE 2-4

Marketing strategy (p 50)
Market segmentation (p 51)
Market segment (p 51)

Market targeting (p 51)
Positioning (p 51)
Differentiation (p 53)
Marketing mix (p 53)

OBJECTIVE 2-5

SWOT analysis (p 55)
Marketing implementation (p 56)
Marketing control (p 58)
Marketing return on investment (marketing ROI) (p 59)

DISCUSSION AND CRITICAL THINKING

Discussion Questions

2-1 Define *strategic planning* and briefly describe the four steps that lead managers and the firm through the strategic planning process. Discuss the role marketing plays in this process. (AASCB: Communication)

⭐ **2-2** Name and define the four product/market growth strategies in the product/market expansion grid. Provide an example of a company implementing each strategy. (AACSB: Communication; Reflective Thinking)

2-3 Describe the differences between a value chain and a value delivery network. (AACSB: Communication, Reflective Thinking)

⭐ **2-4** Discuss the elements of the integrated marketing mix. Explain how marketers use these tools to position products and services. (AACSB: Communication; Reflective Thinking)

2-5 Why must marketers practice marketing control, and how is it done? (AACSB: Communication)

Critical Thinking Exercises

2-6 As a student you have individual experiences with your college or university. These may include managing the application process, enrolling, orientation, choosing a major, setting schedules, and many more. Conduct a SWOT analysis for your school from your perspective. Discuss how your SWOT analysis would provide strategic insight for future decisions at your college or university. (AACSB: Communication; Reflective Thinking)

⭐ **2-7** Examine Starbucks and determine how its marketers have positioned the company relative to the competition. How has Starbucks used differentiation to create customer value? (AACSB: Communication)

2-8 Create a mission statement for a nonprofit organization you would be interested in starting. Have another student evaluate your mission statement while you evaluate the other student's statement, suggesting areas of improvement. (AACSB: Communication; Reflective Thinking)

APPLICATIONS AND CASES

Online, Mobile, and Social Media Marketing Google's (Alphabet's) Mission

Founded in 1998 as an internet search engine, Google's mission statement remains the same to this day: to "organize the world's information and make it universally accessible and useful." Google is certainly successful, with revenues growing from $3.2 billion in 2002 to $74.5 billion in 2015, 90 percent of which comes from advertisers. Google is expanding rapidly into other areas well beyond its search engine, such as self-driving cars, smart contact lenses that measure a person's blood sugar levels, internet-bearing balloons to create internet hotspots anywhere on earth, and even magnetic nanoparticles to search for disease within the human bloodstream. In fact, Google has innovated into so many diverse new ventures that it recently created a broader organization—a parent holding company called Alphabet—to contain them all. Google/Alphabet has been on a buying frenzy recently, purchasing security, biotech, and robotic companies in a quest to capitalize on the Internet of Things (IoT) phenomenon. Experts predict there will be 25 million connected devices in our homes and workplaces by 2020. Google recently announced its new IoT operating system, dubbed Brillo (after the Brillo scrubbing pad because it is a scrubbed-down version of its Android operating system), targeted to developers of smart products connected to the internet, such as ovens, thermostats, and even toothbrushes. It's also developed Weave, the corresponding IoT language that will allow smart products to speak to each other. Perhaps one day you will be sitting in your Google/Alphabet self-driving car, streaming the news, checking your blood sugar, and cooling your home by turning down your thermostat on the way home from work.

2-9 Conduct research on Google/Alphabet to learn more about its products and services. Some say the time has come for Google to create a new mission statement. Do you agree? Explain. (AACSB: Communication; Reflective Thinking)

2-10 Create a new mission statement for Google/Alphabet that will take it through the rest of this century. (AACSB: Communication; Reflective Thinking)

Marketing Ethics Creating Value or Distracting Consumers?

In early 2014, Chipotle Mexican Grill announced that it would stop using genetically modified ingredients (GMOs) in its restaurants. Many observers applauded this move. However, critics of the fast-food chain cited a lack of evidence to support its anti-GMO stance. They suspected that Chipotle's anti-GMO claim was simply a ploy to distract consumers from a larger issue: the company's risky sanitation practices. Chipotle's anti-GMO policies may have won the burrito chain some health-conscious customers, but at the same time customers were becoming sick after eating at some Chipotle locations, calling into question the firm's food handling and safety practices.

Steve Ells, founder and co-CEO of Chipotle, said the GMO decision was "another step toward the visions we have of changing the way people think about and eat fast food. Just because food is served fast doesn't mean it has to be made with cheap raw ingredients, highly processed with preservatives and fillers and stabilizers and artificial colors and flavors." However, ridding Chipotle's supply chain of genetically altered components proved difficult. The chain discovered GMOs in basic ingredients such as baking powder, cornstarch, canola and soy oils, corn

meal, and sugar. And many non-GMO ingredients were in short supply. For example, at one point, Chipotle found that it could not supply all its locations with enough non-GMO pork to make carnitas. Given the supply chain challenges, Chipotle decided to use non-GMO products in its food preparation but to continue to serve some soft drinks with sweeteners derived from genetically engineered corn.

2-11 Has Chipotle's focus on eliminating GMOs created value for its customers? Defend this market strategy. (AACSB: Communication; Ethical Reasoning)

2-12 From an ethics standpoint, discuss Chipotle's focus on sourcing non-GMO food products versus attention to food safety. The company's oversights in food safety resulted in numerous customers becoming ill (E. coli, norovirus, and salmonella). Discuss the challenges Chipotle faces in overcoming the negative image that resulted. (AACSB: Communication; Reflective Thinking; Ethical Reasoning)

Marketing by the Numbers Apple vs. Microsoft

In 2014, Apple reported profits of more than $50 billion on sales of $182 billion. For that same period, Microsoft posted a profit of almost $30 billion on sales of $88 billion. So Apple is a better marketer, right? Sales and profits provide information to compare the profitability of these two competitors, but between these numbers is information regarding the efficiency of marketing efforts in creating those sales and profits. Appendix 2, Marketing by the Numbers, discusses other marketing profitability measures beyond the return on marketing investment (marketing ROI) measure described in this chapter. Review the Appendix to answer the questions using the following information from the two companies' incomes statements (all numbers are in thousands):

	Apple	**Microsoft**
Sales	$182,795,000	$86,833,000
Gross Profit	$ 70,537,000	$59,899,000
Marketing Expenses	$ 8,994,750	$15,474,000
Net Income (Profit)	$ 52,503,000	$27,759,000

2-13 Calculate profit margin, net marketing contribution, marketing return on sales (or marketing ROS), and marketing return on investment (or marketing ROI) for each company. Which company is performing better? (AACSB: Communication; Use of IT; Analytic Thinking)

2-14 Go to Yahoo! Finance (*http://finance.yahoo.com/*) and find the income statements for two other competing companies. Perform the same analyses for these companies that you performed for the previous question. Which company is doing better overall and with respect to marketing? For marketing expenses, use 75 percent of the company's reported "Selling General and Administrative" expenses, as not all of the expenses in that category are marketing expenses. (AACSB: Communication; Analytic Reasoning; Reflective Thinking)

Video Case Konica

Konica Minolta has been in business since 1873. For decades, it was a successful photo company selling cameras, equipment, and supplies primarily to final consumers. But dramatic changes in the marketing environment forced the company to reevaluate its marketing strategy and ultimately to abandon what had been its primary industry.

Today, Konica Minolta has a successful business-to-business strategy centered on office equipment and print products for commercial printers. The company has also developed a healthcare and medical group, an optics group, and a division that produces components for mobile phones and televisions. With the

advent and growth of social media, Konica Minolta's marketing strategy continues to evolve.

After viewing the video featuring Konica Minolta, answer the following questions:

2-15 What is Konica Minolta's mission?

2-16 What market conditions led Konica Minolta to reevaluate its marketing strategy?

2-17 How has Konica Minolta modified its marketing mix? Are these changes in line with its mission?

Company Case Facebook: Making the World More Open and Connected

The world has rapidly gone online, social, and mobile. And no company is more online, social, and mobile than Facebook. In spite of the growing number of social media options, Facebook continues to dominate. In little more than a decade, it has accumulated more than 1.6 billion active monthly users—more than 20 percent of the world's total population—and some 1.5 billion people now access the network on a mobile device. More than a billion Facebook members already log on daily, and five new Facebook profiles are created every second. In the United States, more collective time is spent on Facebook than on any other website. Together, the Facebook community uploads 350 million photos, "Likes" 4.5 billion items, and shares 4.75 billion pieces of content daily.

Having achieved such phenomenal impact in such a short period of time, Facebook's success can be attributed to tenacious focus on its mission—"to give people the power to share and make the world more open and connected." It's a place where friends and family meet, share their stories, display their photos, pass along information, and chronicle their lives. Hordes of people have made Facebook their digital home 24/7.

From Simple Things

Initially, carrying out this mission was relatively simple. When CEO Mark Zuckerberg and friends launched "thefacebook.com" in 2004, it was for Harvard students only. Still, with its clean design ("No Disneyland, no 'Live nude girls.'"), the fledgling site attracted a lot of attention when it racked up more than 1,200 registered users by the end of the first day. Within the first month, more than half of Harvard's undergraduate student body had joined. The massive response demonstrated tremendous untapped demand. At first, the social network grew one university campus at a time. But it wasn't long before Facebook was open to the public and people everywhere were registering by the millions.

As it grew, Facebook's interface was a work in progress. Features were added and modified in order to appeal to everyone. The network's growth and development also gave it the ability to target specific kinds of content to well-defined user segments. However, Facebook's "all things to all people" approach left many users, especially younger ones, visiting Facebook less and shifting time to more specialized competing social networks. To meet that growing threat, Facebook shifted gears from a "one site for all" approach to a multi-app strategy of providing "something for any and every individual." According to Zuckerberg, "Our vision for Facebook is to create a set of products that help you share any kind of content you want with any audience you want."

As the first move under its multi-app strategy, Facebook paid a then-stunning $1 billion to acquire Instagram, the surging photo-sharing app. Although Facebook already had its own photo-sharing features, the Instagram acquisition brought a younger, 27-million-strong user base into the Facebook fold. And rather than incorporating Instagram as just another Facebook feature, Facebook maintained Instagram as an independent brand with its own personality and user base. Instagram and Facebook customers can choose their desired level of integration, including Instagram membership without a Facebook account. "The fact that Instagram is connected to other services beyond Facebook is an important part of the experience," says Zuckerberg.

Not long after the Instagram acquisition, in its quest to add unique new products and user segments, Facebook announced the creation of Creative Labs, a Facebook division charged with developing single-purpose mobile apps. It also unveiled the new division's first product—Paper, a mobile app that provides easy and personalized access to Facebook's News Feed. Although the core Facebook mobile app already provided access to this content, Paper let users organize the feed by themes, interests, and sources, serving it all up in a full-screen, distraction-free layout.

On the heels of Paper came another stunning Facebook mega-acquisition. Dwarfing its Instagram deal, Facebook paid a shocking $19 billion for standalone messaging app WhatsApp. Facebook's own Messenger had already grown quickly to 200 million users. But similar to Instagram, WhatsApp immediately gave Facebook something it could not easily build on its own— an independent brand with more than 450 million registered international users, many of whom were not on Facebook.

By developing and acquiring such new products and apps, Facebook is doing what it does best—growing its membership and giving its diverse users more ways and reasons to connect and engage. Facebook's fuller portfolio lets users meet their individual needs within the broadening Facebook family.

To the Stratosphere

As Facebook develops more reasons for more users to connect and engage, it also pursues technologies that might leave some observers scratching their heads. For example, a few years ago, the social media giant paid $2 billion to acquire Oculus VR, the virtual reality start-up. In the past year, Facebook has also developed its own 360-degree stereoscopic 3D video camera with 17 lenses—a device it calls Facebook Surround360. Why these acquisitions and developments? According to Zuckerberg, it has to do with "first steps."

When Zuckerberg took his first steps, his parents noted the event in his baby book. When one of his cousins first walked some time later, Mom and Dad captured the moment with a photo. When his niece learned to walk, the video camera was rolling. But for his own daughter, Zuckerberg wanted to take it to the next level. "When Max takes her first step, we'll be able to capture the whole scene, not just write down the date or take a photo or take a little 2D video," Zuckerber says. "The people we want to share this with...can go there. They can experience *that moment*."

Zuckerberg's wanting to broadcast his daughter's first steps as though others were there is just one more example of how Facebook constantly focuses on its central mission—to connect the world. "Over time, people get richer and richer tools to communicate and express what they care about," says Zuckerberg. Facebook anticipates that this kind of video could lead to an entirely new mode of communication, one that could extend to Facebook's own Oculus virtual reality headset.

As much as 3D virtual reality video sounds like a long shot, it's easy pickings compared to Facebook's biggest current initiative. Zuckerberg has been spanning the globe, addressing everyone from global leaders to fellow entrepreneurs and making a case for what he sees as the most critical social endeavor of our time—making the internet a basic human right, like health care or clean water. As he tells it, lack of free and open access to information is the greatest barrier to prosperity for the world's impoverished. Yet almost 5 billion people are not yet connected to the internet. Zuckerberg and the Facebook team aim to eliminate that barrier by making the internet accessible to all.

To this end, Facebook has created its own innovation think tank called the Connectivity Lab. This group will have a satellite orbiting above sub-Saharan Africa within a year. But satellites are expensive, so the group is also working on other options. The most promising option is known internally as Aquila—a sleek, boomerang-shaped drone that has the wingspan of a Boeing 737, weighs less than 1,000 pounds, and can to stay aloft at 65,000 feet for months at a time. Soon to be tested, Aquila will receive radio signals from a ground station, relay those signals via lasers to transponders on the ground, and convert the signals to Wi-Fi or 4G networks. Facebook's vision is to eventually have 10,000 Aquilas flying the friendly skies around planet earth.

Giving It All Away

Although Facebook spent more than five years building its user base and paying almost no attention to generating income, it is now making up for lost time. In the past five years, Facebook's revenues have gone viral—from $2 billion to $18 billion, a ninefold increase to its top line. With a 20 percent margin, its bottom line isn't doing too badly either. And although Facebook has experimented with various ways to generate income, the vast majority of its income comes via tried-and-true online advertising.

With all the development of fancy technologies such as drones, lasers, virtual reality, and 3D video, you might think that Facebook intends to diversify into new businesses that could generate cash and profits. But nothing could be further from the truth. In fact, as Facebook launches these and other technologies, it is giving away the designs for free. Years ago when Facebook built its own servers and data centers, it promptly open-sourced the designs and let the world have them for nothing. It did the same with big data analytics tools such as Cassandra and Hadoop. Although that might seem like throwing away money, it's right in line with Facebook's mission. Whereas most companies define themselves by a craft, such as making the best consumer electronic gadgets or solving companies' efficiency problems, Facebook has been built around a single-minded goal of connecting everyone in the world and giving them the tools they need "to share anything and everything in a natural way."

For that reason, Facebook focuses on what it does best—being the best social network. Rather than becoming distracted by developing multiple business units and trying to make money through diversified means, it remains focused on building its user base and treating its core social media products as works in process. To those who view the projects coming out of the Connectivity Lab as unrelated, Zuckerberg points out, "They're actually incredibly focused in terms of the mission. The real goal is to build the community. A lot of times, the best way to advance the technology is to work on it as a community."

With many companies already working on the very technologies that Facebook is trying to advance, it might seem that Facebook isn't adding much. But Zuckerberg is impatient, and he feels that the tech world is providing too little, too late. For example, Facebook's laser drones will be able to shower entire rural areas, villages, and cities with extremely high bandwidth at higher speeds with more economical costs than the systems currently being employed and developed by telecom companies. "We need certain technologies to exist in the world, so we will build those," says Zuckerberg. "We're not selling [servers] or cameras or connectivity services. But if no one else is building them, we're going to."

Whatever its future, Facebook seems to have barely scratched the surface when it comes to fulfilling its mission. Its new multi-app, multi-segment strategy, combined with its massive, closely knit social structure, gives Facebook staggering potential. And moving the world toward internet access for all will help make Facebook's portfolio of apps and products available to everyone. For years, a popular saying around Facebook has been "We are one percent done with our mission." These days, those who manage Facebook might concede that they've made progress—say, to maybe 2 percent. For skeptics, consider how Facebook got started:

> It was a few nights after [Zuckerberg] launched the website. He and his computer science buddy were getting pizza and talking. Zuckerberg told his friend that someone was going to build a social network, because it was too important not to exist. But he didn't guess, back then, that he'd be the guy to do it. There were older people and bigger companies. So why, then, was Zuckerberg the one to build Facebook? "I think it's because we cared. A lot of times, caring about something and believing in it trumps," he says. "I couldn't connect the dots going forward on Facebook from the beginning. To me, that's a lot of the story of [Facebook's future] too."

Questions for Discussion

2-18 Is Facebook's mission statement market oriented? Explain.

2-19 How is Facebook's strategy driven by its mission?

2-20 Is it wise for Facebook to give away it technologies for free? Why or why not?

2-21 As it moves forward in fulfilling its mission, what challenges does Facebook face in the future?

Sources: Based on information from Cade Metz, "How Will Zuckerberg Rule the World? By Giving Facebook's Tech Away," *Wired*, April 12, 2016, www.wired.com/2016/04/mark-zuckerberg-giving-away-facebooks-tech-free/; Jessi Hempel, "Inside Facebook's Ambitious Plan to Connect the Whole World," *Wired*, January 19, 2016, www.wired.com/2016/01/facebook-zuckerberg-internet-org/; Sarah Kessler, "With Paper, Facebook Stops Trying to Be Everything for Everyone," *Fast Company*, January 30, 2014, www.fastcompany.com/3025762/with-paper-facebook-stops-trying-to-be-everything-for-everyone; Josh Constine, "Zuck Says Ads Aren't the Way to Monetize Messaging," *Techcrunch*, February 19, 2014, www.techcrunch.com/2014/02/19/whatsapp-will-monetize-later/; and information from www.facebook.com/facebook/info/?tab=page_info and www.zephoria.com/top-15-valuable-facebook-statistics/, accessed June 2016.

MyMarketingLab

Go to **mymktlab.com** for Auto-graded writing questions as well as the following Assisted-graded writing questions:

2-22 How are marketing departments organized? Which organization is best?

2-23 Explain the roles of market segmentation, market targeting, differentiation, and positioning in implementing an effective marketing strategy.

3 Analyzing the Marketing Environment

CHAPTER PREVIEW

So far, you've learned about the basic concepts of marketing and the steps in the marketing process for engaging and building profitable relationships with targeted consumers. Next, we'll begin digging deeper into the first step of the marketing process—understanding the marketplace and customer needs and wants. In this chapter, you'll see that marketing operates in a complex and changing environment. Other actors in this environment—suppliers, intermediaries, customers, competitors, publics, and others—may work with or against the company. Major environmental forces—demographic, economic, natural, technological, political, and cultural—shape marketing opportunities, pose threats, and affect the company's ability to engage customers and build customer relationships. To develop effective marketing strategies, a company must first understand the environment in which marketing operates.

To start, let's look at Kellogg, the world's largest cereal maker and one of its most recognized and respected brands. Kellogg's cereals have been staples in American homes for generations. However, as demographic, cultural, lifestyle, and other environmental shifts have changed how people eat breakfast, mighty Kellogg has had difficulty adapting. The storied company now finds itself battling to bring modern breakfast eaters back to its table.

KELLOGG: Losing Its Snap, Crackle, and Pop?

For more than 109 years, ever since the Kellogg brothers of Battle Creek, Michigan, first perfected the process of making toasted corn flakes, the morning bowl of cereal has been a daily ritual in U.S. homes. Generations of sleepy-eyed Americans have bellied up to the breakfast table, filled a bowl with crunchy goodness, and munched their way through enough fuel to fortify them until lunch.

That morning ritual has made Kellogg the world's largest cereal maker. For more than a century, the company's storied brands—such as Kellogg's Corn Flakes, Frosted Flakes, Froot Loops, Rice Krispies, Frosted Mini-Wheats, Raisin Bran, and Special K—have helped define the American breakfast experience.

From its origins, Kellogg has capitalized on environmental trends and shifts, even led them. Before Kellogg, most people ate leftovers for breakfast, a sure-fire path to late-morning indigestion. Then John and Will Kellogg patented the process for making a healthy alternative, "flaked cereal," leading to their first successful product, Kellogg's Corn Flakes. When television appeared in 1950s, Kellogg pioneered the pairing of its cereal brands with familiar animated mascots, such as Tony the Tiger for Frosted Flakes, Toucan Sam for

Froot Loops, and Snap, Crackle, and Pop for Rice Krispies. And when cereal sales waned in the 1980s, Kellogg almost single-handedly grew the entire cereal category by 50 percent in just five years by targeting baby boomers with products positioned on nutrition and convenience.

But in recent years, amid a flurry of demographic, cultural, and lifestyle changes, Kellogg's bowl-of-cereal breakfast has lost a lot of its allure. Today, as people increasingly reach for granola bars or Greek yogurt, cold cereal consumption has dipped. As breakfast-eating behavior has changed, however, Kellogg has not. As a result, in recent years, Kellogg's overall revenues and profits have lost their snap, crackle, and pop. Its morning-foods sales—which account for the lion's share of its overall revenues—have been hardest hit. Last year, for example, sales of 19 of Kellogg's 25 top cereals dropped by as much as 14 percent.

Americans simply aren't eating as much cereal these days. Gone are the times when families gathered around the breakfast table before Dad headed off to work while Mom stayed home, made lunches, and got the kids off to school. Cold cereal fit well with that routine. But now, with both parents often working, it's a grab-and-go breakfast

> Kellogg is the world's largest cereal maker. But as demographic, cultural, lifestyle, and other shifts in the marketing environment change how people eat breakfast, mighty Kellogg finds itself battling to bring modern breakfast eaters back to its table.

world, with little time to linger over a bowl of Raisin Bran and the morning newspaper. "For a while, breakfast cereal was convenience food," says one food historian. "But convenience is relative. It's more convenient [now] to grab a breakfast bar, yogurt, a piece of fruit, or a breakfast sandwich at some fast-food place than to eat a bowl of breakfast cereal." Kellogg does market some grab-and-go breakfast lines—such as Eggo frozen waffles, Pop-Tarts toaster pastries, and Nutri-Grain cereal bars. But the modest gains in those products have done little to offset the bigger losses from Kellogg's powerhouse cereals.

There's another major lifestyle trend affecting Kellogg's cereal business—Americans have become more health-conscious. Increasingly, consumers are looking for food with attributes such as "low-carb," "gluten-free," "organic," and "non-GMO" (genetically modified organisms). That presents a big problem for Kellogg, which churns out box after box of carb-heavy, processed foods made from corn, oats, wheat, and rice.

Increased health concerns also add new weight to long-standing claims by food activists that the cereal industry is peddling junk food to children. "Many of the kid-oriented cereals have a fair amount of sugar in them," says one Kellogg critic. "Their Eggo waffles are mostly white flour. Pop-Tarts are white flour and sugar. For a company that started out as a health-food company, they've turned into something very different." For some discerning breakfast eaters, says one analyst, "Tony the Tiger and Toucan Sam may seem less like friendly childhood avatars and more like malevolent sugar traffickers."

Kellogg has responded to some of these concerns. Over the years it has lowered the amount of sugar in its top-selling children's cereals, added gluten-free and GMO-free cereal varieties, and added healthier extensions such as Raisin Bran with Cranberries and Special K Red Berries, a current best seller. In 2000, Kellogg also purchased Kashi, a California-based health-food cereal brand known for natural and organic ingredients. Leveraging Kellogg's resources and know-how, Kashi's annual revenues grew from $25 million to more than $600 million in less than a decade.

But moves toward a healthier Kellogg have been compromised by decisions that seemed at odds with shifting customer lifestyles and preferences. For example, at the same time that Kellogg was adding healthier options to its mainstream brands, it was weighing down its more wholesome brands like Special K and Kashi with less-than-healthy extensions—such as Special K Chocolatey Pretzel Bars, Special K Fudge Brownie Bites, Kashi GoLean Vanilla Graham Clusters cereal, and Kashi Blueberry Frozen Waffles—all processed foods loaded with carbs and calories. Kashi also now sells cookies, crackers, pizzas, and frozen entrees in addition to breakfast foods. As a result, these "healthier" Kellogg brands have suffered setbacks. Last year, some Special K versions posted double-digit declines. And the Kashi brand is now struggling with both its identity and its sales. "Kashi is a brand that has lost its way," says an analyst. "Many of its varieties are not organic. Many have GMOs."

For generations, Kellogg's storied cereal brands have helped to define the American breakfast experience. But as modern American lifestyles and breakfast-eating behaviors have changed, Kellogg has lost some of its snap, crackle, and pop.

Associated Press

Kellogg has plans to reenergize its breakfast sales, such as restoring Kashi's credibility among health-food shoppers and repositioning Special K from a diet brand to one with broader appeal to health-conscious consumers. And the company is busy developing new on-trend breakfast products. Kellogg has also reduced its reliance on cereals with the acquisitions of big snack brands such as Pringles and Keebler—cereal now accounts for 45 percent of its business, down from 70 percent 15 years ago.

Still, some analysts wonder if Kellogg's heart is really into keeping up with new health and lifestyle trends. For example, its recent unveiling of a new gluten-free Special K was largely overshadowed by the enthusiastic introduction of peanut butter and jelly Pop-Tarts, a product largely out of sync with where the U.S. food culture is heading. And although Kellogg has already put 15 new GMO-free cereals on supermarket shelves, behind the scenes the company is spending millions to defeat ballot initiatives in three Western states that would require companies to identify GMO ingredients on their labels. Finally, the Pringles and Keebler acquisitions were more off-trend than on, and they moved the company farther away from its breakfast-foods core.

Despite its recent woes, Kellogg remains a strong, iconic brand. Kellogg's CEO doesn't seem all that worried: "The company has been around for 109 years," he says. "We have the time. We have a plan to turn it around." Some analysts, however, paint a more ominous picture. "Carbs, sugar, and stubbornness are killing Kellogg," says one. Whatever their views, all observers agree that Kellogg is at a critical juncture. As consumers change, Kellogg must change with them. The company's difficulties provide a cautionary tale of what can happen when a company—even a dominant market leader—fails to adapt to its changing marketing environment. Companies that understand and adapt well to their environments can thrive. Those that don't risk their very survival.[1]

OBJECTIVES OUTLINE

OBJECTIVE 3-1	Describe the environmental forces that affect the company's ability to serve its customers. **The Microenvironment and Macroenvironment** *(pp 68–72)*
OBJECTIVE 3-2	Explain how changes in the demographic and economic environments affect marketing decisions. **The Demographic and Economic Environments** *(pp 72–80)*
OBJECTIVE 3-3	Identify the major trends in the firm's natural and technological environments. **The Natural and Technological Environments** *(pp 80–84)*
OBJECTIVE 3-4	Explain the key changes in the political and cultural environments. **The Political–Social and Cultural Environments** *(pp 84–90)*
OBJECTIVE 3-5	Discuss how companies can react to the marketing environment. **Responding to the Marketing Environment** *(pp 90–92)*

Marketing environment
The actors and forces outside marketing that affect marketing management's ability to build and maintain successful relationships with target customers.

A company's **marketing environment** consists of the actors and forces outside marketing that affect marketing management's ability to build and maintain successful relationships with target customers. Like Kellogg, companies must constantly watch and adapt to the changing environment—or, in many cases, lead those changes.

More than any other group in the company, marketers must be environmental trend trackers and opportunity seekers. Although every manager in an organization should watch the outside environment, marketers have two special aptitudes. They have disciplined methods—marketing research and marketing intelligence—for collecting information and developing insights about the marketing environment. They also spend more time in customer and competitor environments. By carefully studying the environment, marketers can adapt their strategies to meet new marketplace challenges and opportunities.

Microenvironment
The actors close to the company that affect its ability to serve its customers—the company, suppliers, marketing intermediaries, customer markets, competitors, and publics.

The Microenvironment and Macroenvironment

The marketing environment consists of a *microenvironment* and a *macroenvironment*. The **microenvironment** consists of the actors close to the company that affect its ability to engage and serve its customers—the company, suppliers, marketing intermediaries, customer markets, competitors, and publics. The **macroenvironment** consists of the larger societal forces that affect the microenvironment—demographic, economic, natural, technological, political, and cultural forces. We look first at the company's microenvironment.

Macroenvironment
The larger societal forces that affect the microenvironment—demographic, economic, natural, technological, political, and cultural forces.

Author | The microenvironment
Comment | includes all the actors close to the company that affect, positively or negatively, its ability to create value for and relationships with customers.

The Microenvironment

Marketing management's job is to build relationships with customers by creating customer value and satisfaction. However, marketing managers cannot do this alone. ● **Figure 3.1** shows the major actors in the marketer's microenvironment. Marketing success requires building relationships with other company departments, suppliers, marketing intermediaries, competitors, various publics, and customers, which combine to make up the company's value delivery network.

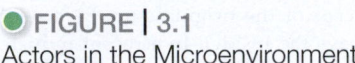

● FIGURE | 3.1
Actors in the Microenvironment

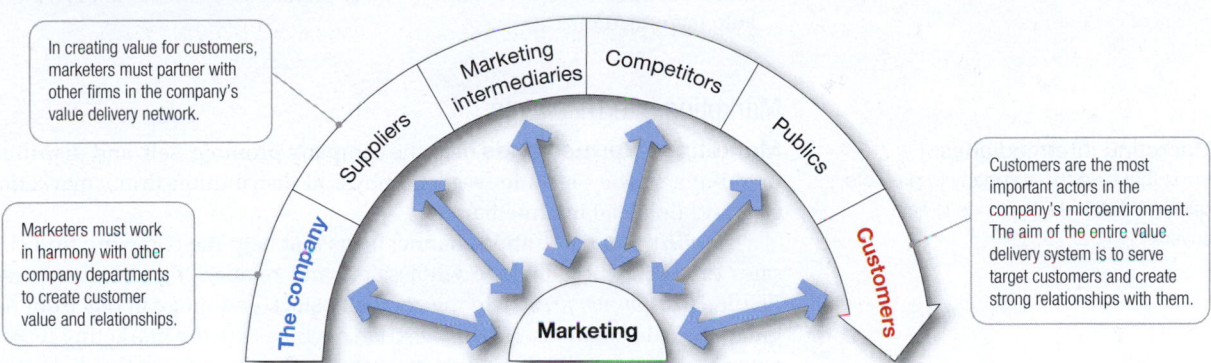

In creating value for customers, marketers must partner with other firms in the company's value delivery network.

Marketers must work in harmony with other company departments to create customer value and relationships.

Customers are the most important actors in the company's microenvironment. The aim of the entire value delivery system is to serve target customers and create strong relationships with them.

The Company

In designing marketing plans, marketing management takes other company groups into account—groups such as top management, finance, research and development (R&D), purchasing, operations, human resources, and accounting. All of these interrelated groups form the internal environment. Top management sets the company's mission, objectives, broad strategies, and policies. Marketing managers make decisions within these broader strategies and plans. Then, as we discussed in Chapter 2, marketing managers must work closely with other company departments. With marketing taking the lead, all departments—from manufacturing and finance to legal and human resources—share the responsibility for understanding customer needs and creating customer value.

Suppliers

Suppliers form an important link in the company's overall customer value delivery network. They provide the resources needed by the company to produce its goods and services. Supplier problems can seriously affect marketing. Marketing managers must watch supply availability and costs. Supply shortages or delays, natural disasters, and other events can cost sales in the short run and damage customer satisfaction in the long run. Rising supply costs may force price increases that can harm the company's sales volume.

Most marketers today treat their suppliers as partners in creating and delivering customer value. ● For example, Honda knows the importance of building close relationships with its extensive network of suppliers, who furnish everything from fuel tanks, brake controls, and seating systems to production equipment and office supplies.[2]

In the United States alone, American Honda purchases more than $23 billion worth of auto parts and materials annually from 557 strategic suppliers in 34 states. It spends billions of dollars more on maintenance, repair, and operations (MRO) supplies and services from another 16,800 suppliers. Outside purchases represent about 75 percent of the cost of making a Honda vehicle. So Honda views strategic suppliers as key players in its success and develops deep relationships and teamwork with them. "These suppliers are literally considered extensions of Honda," says one insider.

For example, Honda requires that strategic suppliers open up their books and give Honda full access to their financial information. This helps Honda purchasing associates, Honda engineers, and supplier engineers to work as a team to achieve target costs and quality standards, often improving suppliers' performance and profit margins in the process. Supplier personnel also participate in Honda training programs on leadership, finance, quality, and other topics. And Honda meets formally each year with strategic suppliers to review the previous year's results and set goals for the coming year. As a result of such teamwork, Honda has developed healthy, long-term

● **Suppliers: Through close teamwork, Honda has developed healthy, long-term supplier relationships. Strategic suppliers are considered extensions of Honda to the benefit of both partners.**

(right) © Ian Dagnall/Alamy Stock; (left) Bloomberg via Getty Images

supplier relationships. "Almost 100 percent of the original suppliers selected in the late 1980s are still Honda suppliers today," says the insider. In a recent industry survey, automotive suppliers rated Honda the "most preferred" customer among the world's top six auto manufacturers.

Marketing Intermediaries

Marketing intermediaries
Firms that help the company to promote, sell, and distribute its goods to final buyers.

Marketing intermediaries help the company promote, sell, and distribute its products to final buyers. They include resellers, physical distribution firms, marketing services agencies, and financial intermediaries.

Resellers are distribution channel firms that help the company find customers or make sales to them. These include wholesalers and retailers that buy and resell merchandise. *Physical distribution firms* help the company stock and move goods from their points of origin to their destinations. *Marketing services agencies* are the marketing research firms, advertising agencies, media firms, and marketing consulting firms that help the company target and promote its products to the right markets. *Financial intermediaries* include banks, credit companies, insurance companies, and other businesses that help finance transactions or insure against the risks associated with the buying and selling of goods.

Like suppliers, marketing intermediaries form an important component of the company's overall value delivery network. Thus, today's marketers recognize the importance of working with their intermediaries as partners rather than simply as channels through which they sell their products. For example, when Coca-Cola signs on as the exclusive beverage provider for a fast-food chain, such as McDonald's, Wendy's, or Subway, it provides much more than just soft drinks. ● It also pledges powerful marketing support:[3]

● **Partnering with intermediaries: Coca-Cola provides its retail partners with much more than just soft drinks. It also pledges powerful marketing support.**

Bloomberg via Getty Images

Coca-Cola assigns cross-functional teams dedicated to understanding the finer points of each retail partner's business. It conducts a staggering amount of research on beverage consumers and shares these insights with its partners. It analyzes the demographics of U.S. zip code areas and helps partners determine which Coke brands are preferred in their areas. Coca-Cola has even studied the design of drive-through menu boards to better understand which layouts, fonts, letter sizes, colors, and visuals induce consumers to order more food and drink. Based on such insights, the Coca-Cola food service solutions group develops marketing programs and merchandising tools that help its retail partners improve their beverage sales and profits. Its website, www.CokeSolutions.com, provides retailers with a wealth of information, business solutions, merchandising tips, advice on digital and social media marketing, and techniques on how to go green. "At Coca-Cola we always strive to be our customers' most valued partner," says Coca-Cola's vice president of Foodservice Customer Marketing. Such intense partnering has made Coca-Cola a runaway leader in the U.S. fountain-soft-drink market.

Competitors

The marketing concept states that, to be successful, a company must provide greater customer value and satisfaction than its competitors do. Thus, marketers must do more than simply adapt to the needs of target consumers. They also must gain strategic advantage by positioning their offerings strongly against competitors' offerings in the minds of consumers.

No single competitive marketing strategy is best for all companies. Each firm should consider its own size and industry position compared with those of its competitors. Large firms with dominant positions in an industry can use certain strategies that smaller firms cannot afford. But being large is not enough. There are winning strategies for large firms, but there are also losing ones. And small firms can develop strategies that give them better rates of return than large firms enjoy.

Publics

Public
Any group that has an actual or potential interest in or impact on an organization's ability to achieve its objectives.

The company's marketing environment also includes various publics. A **public** is any group that has an actual or potential interest in or impact on an organization's ability to achieve its objectives. We can identify seven types of publics:

- *Financial publics.* This group influences the company's ability to obtain funds. Banks, investment analysts, and stockholders are the major financial publics.
- *Media publics.* This group carries news, features, editorial opinions, and other content. It includes television stations, newspapers, magazines, and blogs and other social media.
- *Government publics.* Management must take government developments into account. Marketers must often consult the company's lawyers on issues of product safety, truth in advertising, and other matters.
- *Citizen-action publics.* A company's marketing decisions may be questioned by consumer organizations, environmental groups, minority groups, and others. Its public relations department can help it stay in touch with consumer and citizen groups.
- *Internal publics.* This group includes workers, managers, volunteers, and the board of directors. Large companies use newsletters and other means to inform and motivate their internal publics. When employees feel good about the companies they work for, this positive attitude spills over to the external publics.
- *General public.* A company needs to be concerned about the general public's attitude toward its products and activities. The public's image of the company affects its buying behavior.
- *Local publics.* This group includes local community residents and organizations. Large companies usually work to become responsible members of the local communities in which they operate.

● For example, home-improvement retailer The Home Depot gives back to its local publics through its charitable giving arm, The Home Depot Foundation:[4]

● **Publics:** The Home Depot Foundation gives back to local communities through support for local nonprofits, grants, and countless Team Depot volunteer hours. Its mission is simple: Improve the homes and lives of people.

THE HOME DEPOT name and logo are trademarks of Home Depot Product Authority, LLC, used under license.

The Home Depot Foundation has a simple mission: Improve the homes and lives of people. Through its support for local nonprofits, grants, and countless employee volunteer hours, the foundation focuses on repairing and refurbishing homes and facilities for veterans in addition to natural disaster relief. For example, when natural disasters strike, The Home Depot Foundation provides disaster relief supplies, resources, and volunteers to help rebuild homes and communities. It also awards Community Impact Grants to fund local community projects.

The Home Depot Foundation is now placing a special emphasis on helping military veterans who face growing financial and physical hardships at home as they return to civilian life. The goal is "to ensure every veteran has a safe place to call home." To that end, the foundation provides Veteran Housing Grants to nonprofits that help develop and repair housing for veterans. And through Team Depot—the company's employee-led volunteer program—dedicated Home Depot employees volunteer their time in local communities to create a meaningful impact on veterans' lives. "From retrofitting a wounded warrior's home to helping make a housing facility move-in ready," says the company, "our Team Depot associates work with local nonprofit organizations to improve the homes and lives of thousands of deserving veteran families." Since its establishment in 2002, The Home Depot Foundation has invested more than $380 billion in its local communities.

A company can prepare marketing plans for these major publics as well as for its customer markets.

Suppose the company wants a specific response from a particular public, such as goodwill, favorable word of mouth and social sharing, or donations of time or money. The company would have to design an offer to this public that is attractive enough to produce the desired response.

Customers

Customers are the most important actors in the company's microenvironment. The aim of the entire value delivery network is to engage target customers and create strong relationships with them. The company might target any or all of five types of customer markets. *Consumer markets* consist of individuals and households that buy goods and services for personal consumption. *Business markets* buy goods and services for further processing or use in their production processes, whereas *reseller markets* buy goods and services to resell at a profit. *Government markets* consist of government agencies that buy goods and services to produce public services or transfer the goods and services to others who need them. Finally, *international markets* consist of these buyers in other countries, including consumers, producers, resellers, and governments. Each market type has special characteristics that call for careful study by the seller.

> **Author Comment** | The macroenvironment consists of broader forces that affect the actors in the microenvironment.

The Macroenvironment

The company and all of the other actors operate in a larger macroenvironment of forces that shape opportunities and pose threats to the company. ● **Figure 3.2** shows the six major forces in the company's macroenvironment. Even the most dominant companies can be vulnerable to the often turbulent and changing forces in the marketing environment. Some of these forces are unforeseeable and uncontrollable. Others can be predicted and handled through skillful management. Companies that understand and adapt well to their environments can thrive. Those that don't can face difficult times. One-time dominant market leaders such as Xerox, Sears, and Sony have learned this lesson the hard way. In the remaining sections of this chapter, we examine these forces and show how they affect marketing plans.

The Demographic and Economic Environments

The Demographic Environment

> **Author Comment** | Changes in demographics mean changes in markets, so they are very important to marketers. We first look at the biggest demographic trend—the changing age structure of the population.

Demography is the study of human populations in terms of size, density, location, age, gender, race, occupation, and other statistics. The demographic environment is of major interest to marketers because it involves people, and people make up markets. The world population is growing at an explosive rate. It now exceeds 7.3 billion people and is expected to grow to more than 8 billion by the year 2030.[5] The world's large and highly diverse population poses both opportunities and challenges.

Changes in the world demographic environment have major implications for business. Thus, marketers keep a close eye on demographic trends and developments in their

● FIGURE | 3.2
Major Forces in the Company's Macroenvironment

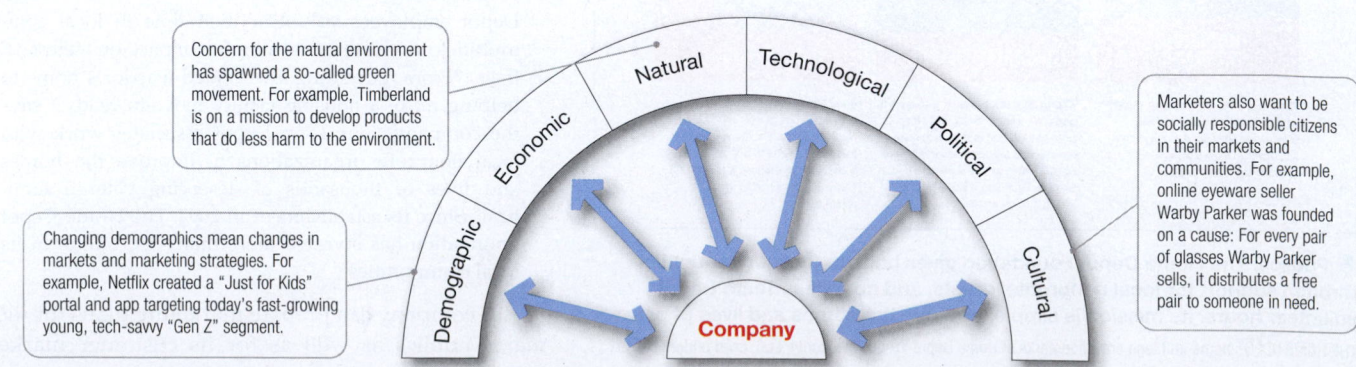

Concern for the natural environment has spawned a so-called green movement. For example, Timberland is on a mission to develop products that do less harm to the environment.

Changing demographics mean changes in markets and marketing strategies. For example, Netflix created a "Just for Kids" portal and app targeting today's fast-growing young, tech-savvy "Gen Z" segment.

Marketers also want to be socially responsible citizens in their markets and communities. For example, online eyeware seller Warby Parker was founded on a cause: For every pair of glasses Warby Parker sells, it distributes a free pair to someone in need.

Demography
The study of human populations in terms of size, density, location, age, gender, race, occupation, and other statistics.

Baby boomers
The 78 million people born during the years following World War II and lasting until 1964.

Generation X
The 49 million people born between 1965 and 1976 in the "birth dearth" following the baby boom.

markets. They analyze changing age and family structures, geographic population shifts, educational characteristics, and population diversity. Here, we discuss the most important demographic trends in the United States.

The Changing Age Structure of the Population

The U.S. population currently stands at nearly 323 million and may reach almost 364 million by 2030.[6] The single most important demographic trend in the United States is the changing age structure of the population. Primarily because of falling birthrates and longer life expectancies, the U.S. population is rapidly getting older. In 1970, the median age was 28; by 2016, it was 38.[7] This aging of the population will have a significant impact on markets and those who service them.

The U.S. population contains several generational groups. Here, we discuss the four largest groups—the baby boomers, Generation X, the millennials, and Generation Z—and their impact on today's marketing strategies.

The Baby Boomers. The post–World War II baby boom produced 78 million **baby boomers**, who were born between 1946 and 1964. Over the years, the baby boomers have been one of the most powerful forces shaping the marketing environment. The youngest boomers are now in their 50s; the oldest are in their early 70s and well into retirement.

The baby boomers are the wealthiest generation in U.S. history, what one analyst calls "a marketer's dream." Today's baby boomers account for about 26 percent of the U.S. population but control an estimated 70 percent of the nation's disposable income and half of all consumer spending.[8] The boomers constitute a lucrative market for financial services, new housing and home remodeling, new cars, travel and entertainment, eating out, health and fitness products, and just about everything else. And contrary to the popular belief that they are staid in their ways, one recent survey found that 82 percent of boomers are open to new brands. Says a researcher, "Changing and trying new brands helps boomers feel like they are staying current."[9]

It would be a mistake to think of older boomers as phasing out or slowing down. Rather than viewing themselves that way, many of today's boomers see themselves as entering new life phases. More active boomers have no intention of abandoning their youthful lifestyles as they age. For example, adults over 50 now account for 80 percent of luxury travel spending in America. Boomers are also digitally active and increasingly social media savvy. They are the fastest-growing shopper demographic online, outspending younger generations two to one. They are also the fastest-growing social media users, with an 80 percent surge in Facebook usage over the past four years.[10]

Thus, although boomers buy lots of products that help them deal with issues of aging—from vitamins to blood pressure monitors to Good Grips kitchen tools—they tend to appreciate marketers who appeal to their youthful thinking rather than their advancing age. ● For example, Walgreens recently launched a campaign called "Carpe Med Diem," telling older boomers how to "seize the day" to get more out of life and their Medicare Part D prescription coverage at Walgreens, not just with savings on prescriptions but also with products that make them look and feel good.[11] One "Carpe Med Diem" ad features an active and stylish boomer-age woman with purple highlights in her hair and the headline "Who says blonds have more fun." In another ad, two boomer women pick up their prescriptions at Walgreens but also load up on sunscreen before heading out to a nude beach, where they drop their clothes and enjoy some fun in the sun. "Walgreen's has you covered," says the ad. "Who says that being on Medicare has to stop you from being edgy?"

Generation X. The baby boom was followed by a "birth dearth," creating another generation of 49 million people born between 1965 and 1976. Author Douglas Coupland calls them **Generation X** because they lie in the shadow of the boomers.

Carpe **MED** Diem

Save on Medicare Part D with helpful info and more

Walgreens

● **Targeting baby boomers: Walgreen's Carpe Med Diem campaign appeals to older boomers' youthful thinking rather than advancing age. "Who says that being on Medicare has to stop you from being edgy?"**
Walgreen Co.

Considerably smaller than the boomer generation that precedes them and the millennials who follow, the Generation Xers are a sometimes-overlooked consumer group. Although they seek success, they are less materialistic than the other groups; they prize experience, not acquisition. For many of the Gen Xers who are parents, family comes first—both children and their aging parents—and career second.

From a marketing standpoint, the Gen Xers are a more skeptical bunch. They are sensible shoppers who research products heavily before they consider a purchase, prefer quality to quantity, and tend to be less receptive to overt marketing pitches. They are more receptive to irreverent ad pitches that make fun of convention and tradition. The first to grow up in the internet era, Generation X is a connected generation that embraces the benefits of new technology.

The Gen Xers, now in their 40s, have grown up and are taking over. They have increasingly displaced the lifestyles, culture, and values of the baby boomers. They are firmly into their careers, and many are proud homeowners with growing families. They are the most educated generation to date, and they possess hefty annual purchasing power. Although Gen Xers make up less than a quarter of all U.S. adults, they pull in 29 percent of the nation's total income.

With so much potential, many brands and organizations focus on Gen Xers as a prime target segment. For example, a full 82 percent of Gen Xers own their own homes, making them an important segment for home-and-hearth marketers. ● Home-improvement retailer Lowe's markets heavily to Gen X homeowners, urging them to "Never Stop Improving." Through ads, online videos, and a substantial social media presence, Lowe's provides ideas and advice on a wide range of indoor and outdoor home-improvement projects and problems, providing solutions that make life simpler for busy Gen X homeowners and their families. Its myLowe's app is like a 24/7 home-improvement concierge that lets customers build room-by-room profiles of their homes, archive their Lowe's purchases, build product lists with photos, receive reminders for things like changing furnace filters, and even consult with store employees online as they plan out home-improvement projects.[12]

● Targeting Gen Xers: Lowe's markets heavily to Gen X homeowners with ideas and advice on home-improvement projects and problems, urging them to "Never Stop Improving."

Bryan Bedder/Stringer/Getty Images

Millennials (or Generation Y)
The 83 million children of the baby boomers born between 1977 and 2000.

Millennials. Both the baby boomers and Gen Xers will one day be passing the reins to the **millennials** (also called **Generation Y** or the echo boomers). Born between 1977 and 2000, these children of the baby boomers number 83 million or more, dwarfing the Gen Xers and becoming larger even than the baby boomer segment. In the post-recession era, the millennials are the most financially strapped generation. Facing higher unemployment and saddled with more debt, many of these young consumers have near-empty piggy banks. Still, because of their numbers, the millennials make up a huge and attractive market, both now and in the future.

One thing that all millennials have in common is their comfort with digital technology. They don't just embrace technology; it's a way of life. The millennials were the first generation to grow up in a world filled with computers, mobile phones, satellite TV, iPods and iPads, and online social media. As a result, they engage with brands in an entirely new way, such as with mobile or social media.

Compared with other generational groups, millennials tend to be frugal, practical, connected, mobile, and impatient. More than sales pitches from marketers, millennials seek authenticity and opportunities to shape their own brand experiences and share them with others. One AT&T marketer identifies what she calls "universal Millennial truths: being transparent, authentic, immediate, and versatile."[13]

Many brands are now fielding specific products and marketing campaigns aimed at millennial needs and lifestyles. ● For example, many financial services firms are shedding their once-stodgy images to make their brands more appealing to millennial consumers. Consider Fifth Third Bank:[14]

Fifth Third Bank knows that waiting is hard for time-crunched millennials. So it launched a new campaign called "No Waiting" that shows how its mobile app takes the wait out of banking. The

Targeting millennials: Fifth Third Bank's "No Waiting" campaign engages impatient, social-media-savvy millennials with anything-but-stodgy videos demonstrating how its mobile app takes the wait out of banking.

Fifth Third Bank

Generation Z

People born after 2000 (although many analysts include people born after 1995) who make up the kids, tweens, and teens markets.

campaign targets younger consumers who are increasingly put off by the traditional banking world. The "No Waiting" campaign includes TV spots but also a full slate of digital video and social media content, even a novel mobile game, aimed at engaging impatient, social-media-savvy millennials. ● The anything-but-stodgy digital videos provide humorous side-by-side comparisons showing that a check can be deposited using the Fifth Third Bank app faster than a hamster can eat five cheese balls or faster than an accordion player can play "Mary Had a Little Lamb." The campaign also features an animated mobile game, "TXTvsTXT," that tests a user's texting speed. Something you wouldn't expect from a bank, the mobile game offers a quirky way for text-savvy millennials to test their finger-clicking skills, challenge friends on Facebook, and earn badges ranging from "molasses hands" to "turbo twiddler." Millennials "want it fast, whether in a text conversation or checking your balance on the Fifth Third Bank mobile app," says Fifth Third's chief marketer. "Our mobile banking takes the wait out of banking and we believe [this campaign] tells that story in a fun engaging way."

Generation Z. Hard on the heels of the millennials is **Generation Z**, young people born after 2000 (although many analysts include people born after 1995 in this group). The approximately 82 million Gen Zers make up the important kids, tweens, and teens markets. They spend an estimated $44 billion annually of their own money and influence up to $600 billion of family spending.[15] These young consumers also represent tomorrow's markets—they are now forming brand relationships that will affect their buying well into the future.

Even more than the millennials, the defining characteristic of Gen Zers is their utter fluency and comfort with digital technologies. Generation Z takes smartphones, tablets, internet-connected game consoles, wireless internet, and digital and social media for granted—they've always had them—making this group highly mobile, connected, and social. On average, connected Gen Zers receive more than 3,000 texts per month. "If they're awake, they're online," quips one analyst. They have "digital in their DNA," says another.[16]

Gen Zers blend the online and offline worlds seamlessly as they socialize and shop. According to recent studies, despite their youth, more than half of all Generation Z tweens and teens do product research before buying a product or having their parents buy it for them. Of those who shop online, more than half *prefer* shopping online in categories ranging from electronics, books, music, sports equipment, and beauty products to clothes, shoes, and fashion accessories.

Companies in almost all industries market products and services aimed at Generation Z. For example, many retailers have created special lines or even entire stores appealing to Gen Z buyers and their parents—consider Abercrombie Kids, Gap Kids, Old Navy Kids, and Pottery Barn Kids. The Justice chain targets only tween girls, with apparel and accessories laser-focused on their special preferences and lifestyles. Although these young buyers often have their mothers in tow, "the *last* thing a 10- or 12-year-old girl wants is to look like her mom," says Justice's CEO. Justice's stores, website, and social media pages are designed with tweens in mind. "You have to appeal to their senses," says the CEO. "They love sensory overload—bright colors, music videos, a variety of merchandise, the tumult of all of that."[17]

Marketing to Gen Zers and their parents presents special challenges. Traditional media are still important to this group. Magazines such as *J-14* and *Twist* are popular with some Gen Z segments, as are TV channels such as Nickelodeon and the Disney Channel. But marketers know they must meet Gen Zers where they hang out and shop. Increasingly, that's in the online and mobile worlds. Although the under-13 set remains barred from social media such as Periscope, Snapchat, and Instagram, at least officially, social media will play a crucial marketing role as the kids and tweens grow into their teens and early twenties.

Today's kids are notoriously fickle and hard to pin down. The key is to engage these young consumers and let them help to define their brand experiences. ● For example, to engage young consumers more deeply, The North Face even invites them to help design its outdoor apparel and gear:[18]

The North Face Youth Design Team holds focus groups at summer camps with tweens 9 to 12 year olds and their parents to get their input on the brand's outdoor clothing for kids. "We find that

● Targeting Generation Z: The North Face engages young consumers directly and lets them help to define their brand experiences. Such efforts have helped to make The North Face one of today's hottest brands among teens and tweens.

VF Corporation

these kids are just beginning to have their own personal style and are also beginning to influence their parents in their purchases," says a North Face marketer. To engage kids even further, The North Face recently launched a design contest in which it invited young would-be artists ages 6 to 12 to submit new apparel and gear designs that represent what the brand's "Never Stop Exploring" mantra means to them. The 10 winners will see their artwork featured in the brand's youth collection. "Kids are our main source of inspiration," says a Youth Design Team marketer. "It's important that we make things that are 'fun,' and how fun would it be to have kids help design our product?" Such engagement efforts have helped to make The North Face one of today's hottest brands among teens and tweens.

An important Generation Z marketing concern involves children's privacy and their vulnerability to marketing pitches. Companies marketing to this group must do so responsibly or risk the wrath of parents and public policy makers.

Generational Marketing. Do brands need to create separate products and marketing programs for each generation? Some experts warn that marketers need to be careful about turning off one generation each time they craft a product or message that appeals effectively to another. Others caution that each generation spans decades of time and many socioeconomic levels. For example, marketers often split the baby boomers into three smaller groups—leading-edge boomers, core boomers, and trailing-edge boomers—each with its own beliefs and behaviors. Similarly, they split Generation Z into kids, tweens, and teens.

Thus, marketers need to form more precise age-specific segments within each group. More important, defining people by their birth date may be less effective than segmenting them by lifestyle, life stage, or the common values they seek in the products they buy. We will discuss many other ways to segment markets in Chapters 5 and 7.

The Changing American Family

The traditional household consists of a husband, wife, and children (and sometimes grandparents). Yet the historic American ideal of the two-child, two-car suburban family has lately been losing some of its luster.

In the United States, fewer than half of today's households contain married couples, down from 76 percent in 1940. Married couples with children under 18 represent only 19 percent of the nation's 125 million households. Married couples without children represent 23 percent, and single parents are another 14 percent. A full 34 percent are nonfamily households—singles living alone or unrelated adults of one or both sexes living together.[19]

More people are divorcing or separating, choosing not to marry, marrying later, remarrying, or marrying without intending to have children. Currently, 15 percent of all new marriages are interracial or interethnic, and 7.3 percent of same-sex couple households are raising children.[20] ● The changing composition of today's modern American families is increasingly reflected in popular movies and television shows, such as *Modern Family*, the award-winning TV sitcom about an extended nontraditional family. Marketers must consider the special needs of nontraditional households because they are now growing more rapidly than traditional households. Each group has distinctive needs and buying habits.

● The American family: The changing composition of American families is increasingly reflected in popular movies and television shows, such as *Modern Family*, the award-winning TV sitcom about an extended nontraditional family.

Mitch Haddad/Getty Images

The number of working women has also increased greatly, growing from 38 percent of the U.S. workforce in 1970 to 47 percent of the workforce today. American women now make up 40 percent of primary family breadwinners in households with children under 18. Among households made up of married couples with children, 60 percent are dual-income households; only the husband works in 27 percent. Meanwhile, more men also stay home with their children and manage the household while their wives go to work.[21]

Companies are now adapting their marketing to reflect the changing dynamics of American families. For example, whereas fathers were once ignored or portrayed as dolts in family-oriented ads, today's advertisers are showing more caring and capable dads. One recent Samsung Galaxy phone ad, for instance, features a dad swaddling and calming his newborn son while Mom runs errands. When the anxious mom calls home to check in, the newly minted swaddle master replies, "We're having a dudes' day here. We're fiiiiine. You take the *weekend* if you want to."

Other ads reflect the evolving diversity in modern American households. For example, Campbell Soup's recent "Your Father" commercial—part of the brand's "Made for Real. Real Life" campaign—features a real-life same-sex couple feeding their son Campbell's Star Wars soup as they mimic Darth Vader's famous Star Wars line "I am your father." The commercial, like others in the campaign, aligns the brand with the company's purpose: "Real food that matters for real life moments." Similarly, General Mills ran a series of commercials for Cheerios featuring an interracial couple and their daughter portraying typical young family scenarios—from the daughter pouring Cheerios on her sleeping dad's chest after learning that Cheerios are good for your heart to her negotiating for a new puppy after learning that she is going to have a baby brother. Said a General Mills marketer, "At Cheerios, we know there are many kinds of families and we celebrate them all."[22]

Geographic Shifts in Population

This is a period of great migratory movements between and within countries. Americans, for example, are a mobile people, with about 12 percent of all U.S. residents moving each year. Over the past two decades, the U.S. population has shifted toward the Sunbelt states. The West and South have grown, whereas the Midwest and Northeast states have lost population.[23] Such population shifts interest marketers because people in different regions buy differently. For example, people in the Midwest buy more winter clothing than people in the Southeast.

Also, for more than a century, Americans have been moving from rural to metropolitan areas. In the 1950s, they made a massive exit from the cities to the suburbs. Today, the migration to the suburbs continues. And more and more Americans are moving to "micropolitan areas," small cities located beyond congested metropolitan areas, such as Minot, North Dakota; Boone, North Carolina; Traverse City, Michigan; and Concord, New Hampshire. These smaller micros offer many of the advantages of metro areas—jobs, restaurants, diversions, community organizations—but without the population crush, traffic jams, high crime rates, and high property taxes often associated with heavily urbanized areas. Ten percent of the U.S. population now resides in micropolitan areas.[24]

The shift in where people live has also caused a shift in where they work. For example, the migration toward micropolitan and suburban areas has resulted in a rapid increase in the number of people who "telecommute"—work at home or in a remote office and conduct business by phone or the internet. This trend, in turn, has created a booming SOHO (small office/home office) market. Increasing numbers of people are working from home with the help of electronic conveniences such as PCs, tablets, smartphones, and broadband internet access. One recent study estimates that 37 percent of employed individuals do some or all of their work at home.[25]

Many marketers are actively courting the lucrative telecommuting market. ● For example, online applications such as Citrix's GoToMeeting, Sqwiggle, and Cisco's WebEx help connect people who telecommute or work remotely. With such applications, people

● Telecommuting: Applications like Citrix's GoToMeeting help people meet and collaborate online via computer, tablet, or smartphone, no matter what their work location.
Citrix Systems, Inc.

can meet and collaborate online via computer, tablet, or smartphone, no matter what their work location. And companies ranging from Salesforce.com to Google and IBM offer cloud computing applications that let people collaborate anywhere and everywhere through the internet and mobile devices.

Additionally, for telecommuters who can't work fully at home, companies such as ShareDesk, DaVinci, and Regus rent out fully equipped shared office space. For a daily, monthly, or yearly fee, telecommuters who work away from a main office can rent shared space that includes the same amenities of a regular office, from networked computers, printers, and copiers to conference rooms and lounge spaces.

A Better-Educated, More White-Collar, More Professional Population

The U.S. population is becoming better educated. For example, in 2012, 88 percent of the U.S. population over age 25 had completed high school and 32 percent had a bachelor's degree or better, compared with 66 percent and 16 percent, respectively, in 1980.[26] The workforce also is becoming more white collar. Job growth is now strongest for professional workers and weakest for manufacturing workers. Between 2014 and 2024, of 30 detailed occupations projected to have the fastest employment growth, most require some type of postsecondary education.[27] The rising number of educated professionals will affect not just what people buy but also how they buy.

Increasing Diversity

Countries vary in their ethnic and racial makeup. At one extreme is Japan, where almost everyone is Japanese. At the other extreme is the United States, with people from virtually all national origins. The United States has often been called a melting pot, where diverse groups from many nations and cultures have melted into a single, more homogenous whole. Instead, the United States seems to have become more of a "salad bowl" in which various groups have mixed together but have maintained their diversity by retaining and valuing important ethnic and cultural differences.

Marketers now face increasingly diverse markets, both at home and abroad, as their operations become more international in scope. The U.S. population is about 62.2 percent non-Hispanic white, with Hispanics at 17.4 percent and African Americans at 13.2 percent. The U.S. Asian American population now totals more than 5.4 percent of the total U.S. population, with the remaining groups being Native Hawaiian, Pacific Islander, American Indian, Eskimo, or Aleut. Moreover, one in eight people living in the United States—more than 13 percent of the population—was born in another country. The nation's ethnic populations are expected to explode in coming decades. By 2060, Hispanics will be about 28 percent of the population, African Americans will be about 14 percent, and Asian Americans will increase to 9 percent.[28]

Most large companies, from P&G, Walmart, Allstate, and Wells Fargo to McDonald's and Southwest Airlines, now target specially designed products, ads, and promotions to one or more of these groups. For example, Southwest Airlines's outreach to Asian Americans includes being the title sponsor for the Chinese New Year Festival and Parade in San Francisco, the biggest nighttime parade in the United States and the second-biggest in North America after the Macy's Thanksgiving Day parade:[29]

祝福，是一張雙程機票

Blessings. They're a two-way ticket.

Southwest Airlines Chinese
New Year Festival & Parade
San Francisco
March 7–8, 2015

Southwest. | Chinese New Year Festival & Parade

● Serving diverse customer communities: Southwest Airlines reaches out to Asian American consumers through its title sponsorship of San Francisco's Chinese New Year Festival and Parade and through ads like this one, which pass along "cleverly constructed well wishes and cheerful nods to the community."
Southwest Airlines Co.

San Francisco's Chinese New Year Festival and Parade typically draws hundreds of thousands of spectators and is broadcast on English- and Asian-language TV stations to viewers around the world. Consumers in the affluent, fast-growing Asian American segment travel often. And they are concentrated in a few key areas such as California and New York, making them easy to pinpoint. That makes them an ideal target for Southwest. The Chinese New Year Festival and Parade event also aligns well with Southwest's preference for grassroots marketing programs that position it as a hometown carrier targeting local "passion points," in this case a cultural and family-related celebration. ● To support its title sponsorship, Southwest ties its brand to the Lunar New Year through promotional efforts ranging from floats and ticket-giveaway contests to "cleverly constructed well wishes and cheerful nods to the community" on street pole banners, bus shelters, billboards, and traditional broadcast and print ads. Something must be working right—Southwest has been the event's title sponsor for more than 15 years.

Diversity goes beyond ethnic heritage. For example, many major companies explicitly target gay and lesbian consumers. According to one estimate, the 6 to 7 percent of U.S. adults who identify themselves as lesbian, gay, bisexual, or transgender (LGBT) have buying power of more than $884 billion.[30] As a result of TV shows such as *Modern Family, Transparent,* and *Gotham*; movies like *Brokeback Mountain* and *Carol*; and openly gay celebrities and public figures such as Neil Patrick Harris, Ellen DeGeneres, David Sedaris, and Apple CEO Tim Cook, the LGBT community has increasingly emerged in the public eye.

Brands in a wide range of industries are now targeting the LGBT community with gay-specific ads and marketing efforts—from Amazon, adidas, Allstate, and Apple to Kaiser Permanente, Wells Fargo, Macy's, and Best Buy. For example, Allstate recently ran an "Everyone deserves to be in good hands" campaign with ads featuring same-sex couples and the hashtag #OutHoldingHands. Last Valentine's Day, adidas posted an image on Instagram featuring a same-sex couple and quoting the Beatles' "The Love You Take Is Equal to the Love You Make." Macy's and Best Buy run regular ads for their wedding registries featuring same-sex couples. And Frito-Lay launched a limited-edition Doritos Rainbows, multi-colored chips demonstrating the brand's "expression of inclusion and support for individuality."

Wells Fargo recently became one of the first banks to feature an LGBT couple in a national TV ad campaign. The heartwarming commercial, featuring a lesbian couple adopting a deaf child, is part of a nine-commercial series that also spotlights other diverse customer groups ranging from Asian Americans to small business owners. Says a Wells Fargo representative, "We…embrace diversity in every aspect, internally and externally. Diversity and inclusion is something we live internally very strongly. This [campaign] is a very important and natural progression of [that value] in how we serve our customers."[31]

Another attractive diversity segment is the 53 million U.S. adults with disabilities—a market larger than African Americans or Hispanics—representing anywhere from $200 to $500 billion in annual spending power. Most individuals with disabilities are active consumers. For example, one study found that the segment spends $17.3 billion on 73 million business or leisure trips every year. And because people with disabilities typically travel with one or more other adults, the economic impact is estimated to be at least double that amount.[32]

How are companies trying to reach consumers with disabilities? Many marketers now recognize that the worlds of people with disabilities and those without disabilities are one in the same. Marketers such as McDonald's, Verizon Wireless, Nike, Samsung, Nordstrom, Toyota, and Apple have featured people with disabilities in their mainstream marketing. For instance, a recent Apple iPad Air commercial features real-life travel writer Chérie King traveling the world with her iPad Air in hand, helping her along as she travels through diverse global settings. She communicates back home, posts photos, writes articles, and lets her iPad translate what she wants to say to shop keepers and others who don't speak English. Only at the very end of the commercial is her disability revealed—she is deaf.[33]

As the population in the United States grows more diverse, successful marketers will continue to diversify their marketing programs to take advantage of opportunities in fast-growing segments.

The Economic Environment

Markets require buying power as well as people. The **economic environment** consists of economic factors that affect consumer purchasing power and spending patterns. Economic factors can have a dramatic effect on consumer spending and buying behavior. For example, until fairly recently, American consumers spent freely, fueled by income growth, a boom in the stock market, rapid increases in housing values, and other economic good fortunes. They bought and bought, seemingly without caution, amassing record levels of debt. However, the free spending and high expectations of those days were dashed by the Great Recession of 2008–2009.

Economic environment
Economic factors that affect consumer purchasing power and spending patterns.

As a result, as discussed in Chapter 1, consumers have now adopted a back-to-basics sensibility in their lifestyles and spending patterns that will likely persist for years to come. They are buying less and looking for greater value in the things they do buy. In turn, *value marketing* has become the watchword for many marketers. Marketers in all industries are looking for ways to offer today's more financially frugal buyers greater value—just the right combination of product quality and good service at a fair price.

 **Economic environment: Consumers adopted a new back-to-basics sensibility in their lifestyles and spending patterns. To serve the tastes of these more financially frugal buyers, companies like Target are emphasizing the "pay less" side of their value propositions.**
Associated Press

You'd expect value pitches from the sellers of everyday products.  For example, as Target has shifted emphasis toward the "Pay Less" side of its "Expect More. Pay Less." slogan, the once-chic headlines at the Target.com website have been replaced by more practical appeals such as "Our lowest prices of the season," "Slam dunk deals," and "Free shipping, every day." However, these days, even luxury-brand marketers are emphasizing good value. For example, Tiffany has long been known for selling high-end "fine jewelry" and "statement jewelry" at prices of $5,000 to $50,000 or more. However, when the Great Recession eroded Tiffany's high-end sales, the company began offering affordable luxury items—what it calls "fashion jewelry"—priced at as little as $100 to $500. Such relatively affordable items now account for about one-quarter of Tiffany's sales.[34]

Marketers should pay attention to *income distribution* as well as income levels. Over the past several decades, the rich have grown richer, the middle class has shrunk, and the poor have remained poor. The top 5 percent of American earners capture 22 percent of the country's adjusted gross income, and the top 20 percent of earners capture 51 percent of all income. In contrast, the bottom 40 percent of American earners get just 11 percent of the total income.[35]

This distribution of income has created a tiered market. Many companies—such as Nordstrom and Neiman Marcus—aggressively target the affluent. Others—such as Dollar General, Five Below, and Family Dollar—target those with more modest means. Still other companies tailor their marketing offers across a range of markets, from the less affluent to the very affluent. For example, Ford offers cars ranging from the low-priced Ford Fiesta, starting at $14,090, to the luxury Lincoln Navigator SUV, starting at $63,195.

Changes in major economic variables, such as income, cost of living, interest rates, and savings and borrowing patterns, have a large impact on the marketplace. Companies watch these variables by using economic forecasting. Businesses do not have to be wiped out by an economic downturn or caught short in a boom. With adequate warning, they can take advantage of changes in the economic environment.

The Natural and Technological Environments

The Natural Environment

Author Comment | Today's enlightened companies are developing *environmentally sustainable* strategies in an effort to create a world economy that the planet can support indefinitely.

Natural environment
The physical environment and the natural resources that are needed as inputs by marketers or that are affected by marketing activities.

The **natural environment** involves the physical environment and the natural resources that are needed as inputs by marketers or that are affected by marketing activities. At the most basic level, unexpected happenings in the physical environment—anything from weather to natural disasters—can affect companies and their marketing strategies. For example, during a recent cold winter—in which the term *polar vortex* gusted into the American vocabulary—sales suffered across a wide range of businesses, from florists and auto dealers to restaurants, airlines, and tourist destinations. In contrast, the severe weather boosted demand for products such as salt, snowblowers, winter clothing, and auto repair centers.

Although companies can't prevent such natural occurrences, they should prepare for dealing with them. For example, shipping companies such as FedEx and UPS maintain corps of meteorologists on their staffs to anticipate weather conditions that might inhibit on-time deliveries around the world. "Someone awaiting a package in Bangkok doesn't care if it snowed in Louisville, Kentucky," says a UPS meteorologist. "They want their stuff."[36]

At a broader level, environmental sustainability concerns have grown steadily over the past several decades. In many cities around the world, air and water pollution have reached dangerous levels. World concern continues to mount about the possibilities of global warming, and many environmentalists fear that we soon will be buried in our own trash.

Marketers should be aware of several trends in the natural environment. The first involves growing *shortages of raw materials*. Air and water may seem to be infinite resources, but some groups see long-run dangers. Air pollution chokes many of the world's large cities, and water shortages are already a big problem in some parts of the United States and the world. By 2030, more than one in three people in the world will not have enough water to drink.[37] Renewable resources, such as forests and food, also have to be used wisely. Nonrenewable resources, such as oil, coal, and various minerals, pose a serious problem. Firms making products that require these scarce resources face large cost increases even if the materials remain available.

A second environmental trend is *increased pollution*. Industry will almost always damage the quality of the natural environment. Consider the disposal of chemical and nuclear wastes; the dangerous mercury levels in the ocean; the quantity of chemical pollutants in the soil and food supply; and the littering of the environment with nonbiodegradable bottles, plastics, and other packaging materials.

A third trend is *increased government intervention* in natural resource management. The governments of different countries vary in their concern and efforts to promote a clean environment. Some, such as the German government, vigorously pursue environmental quality. Others, especially many poorer nations, do little about pollution, largely because they lack the needed funds or political will.

In the United States, the Environmental Protection Agency (EPA) was created in 1970 to create and enforce pollution standards and conduct pollution research. In the future, companies doing business in the United States can expect continued strong controls from government and pressure groups. Instead of opposing regulation, marketers should help develop solutions to the materials and energy problems facing the world.

Environmental sustainability
Developing strategies and practices that create a world economy that the planet can support indefinitely.

Concern for the natural environment has spawned an **environmental sustainability** movement. Today, enlightened companies go beyond what government regulations dictate. They are developing strategies and practices that create a world economy that the planet can support indefinitely. Environmental sustainability means meeting present needs without compromising the ability of future generations to meet their needs.

Many companies are responding to consumer demands with more environmentally responsible products. Others are developing recyclable or biodegradable packaging, recycled materials and components, better pollution controls, and more energy-efficient operations. ● Consider Walmart, for example. Through its own environmental sustainability actions and its impact on the actions of suppliers, Walmart has emerged in recent years as the world's super "eco-nanny":[38]

When it comes to sustainability, perhaps no company in the world is doing more good these days than Walmart. That's right—big, bad Walmart. The giant retailer is now one of the world's biggest crusaders for the cause of saving the world for future generations. For starters, Walmart is rolling out new high-efficiency stores, each one saving more energy than the last. These stores use wind turbines to generate energy, high-output linear fluorescent lighting to reduce what energy stores do use, and native landscaping to cut down on watering and fertilizer. Store heating systems burn recovered cooking oil from the deli fryers and motor oil from the Tire and Lube Express centers. All organic waste, including produce, meats, and paper, is hauled off to a company that turns it into mulch for the garden. Walmart is committed to eventually using 100 percent renewable energy in all of its stores and distribution centers (it's currently at 26 percent) and sending zero waste to landfills (currently down to just 19 percent).

● The natural environment: Walmart has emerged in recent years as the world's super "eco-nanny" through its own sustainability practices and its impact on the actions of its huge network of suppliers.
AP Images/PRNewsFoto/Walmart; Bebay/iStockphoto

Walmart not only is greening up its own operations but has also laid down the eco-law to its vast network of suppliers to get them to do the same, asking them to examine the carbon life cycles of their products and rethink how they source, manufacture, package, and transport these goods. It has developed the Walmart Sustainability Index program, which helps suppliers understand, monitor, and enhance the sustainability of their products and the supply chain. As a result, Walmart suppliers have cut energy, water, materials, toxic ingredients, and other inputs while creating less waste and fewer emissions—for themselves as well as for Walmart stores and consumers. With its immense buying power, Walmart can humble even the mightiest supplier. When imposing its environmental demands on suppliers, Walmart has even more clout than government regulators. Whereas the EPA can only level nominal fines, Walmart can threaten a substantial chunk of a supplier's business.

Companies are learning that what's good for customer well-being and the planet can also be good business. For example, Walmart's eco-charge is about more than just doing the right thing. It also makes good business sense. More efficient operations and less wasteful products are not only good for the environment but also save Walmart money. Lower costs, in turn, let Walmart do more of what it has always done best—save customers money.

Many companies today are looking to do more than just good deeds. More and more, companies are making environmental sustainability a part of their core missions. For example, outdoor apparel and equipment maker Patagonia donates 1 percent of its revenue annually to environmental causes and adheres fiercely to a "Five Rs" mantra: "reduce, repair, reuse, recycle, and reimagine." But more than just implementing sustainability practices, Patagonia wants to "reimagine a world where we take only what nature can replace." It recently took sustainability to a whole new level when it told its customers, "Don't buy our products" (see Real Marketing 3.1).

The Technological Environment

The **technological environment** is perhaps the most dramatic force now shaping our destiny. Technology has released such wonders as antibiotics, robotic surgery, smartphones, and the internet. It also has released such horrors as nuclear missiles and assault rifles. It has released such mixed blessings as the automobile, television, and credit cards. Our attitude toward technology depends on whether we are more impressed with its wonders or its blunders.

New technologies can offer exciting opportunities for marketers. For example, what would you think about having tiny little transmitters implanted in all the products you buy that would allow tracking of the products from their point of production through use and disposal? How about a bracelet with a chip inserted that would let you make and pay for purchases, receive personalized specials at retail locations, or even track your whereabouts or those of friends? Or how about "beacon" technology that would do all those things using your smartphone? On the one hand, such technologies would provide many advantages to both buyers and sellers. On the other hand, they could be a bit scary. Either way, with the advent of such technologies as radio-frequency identification (RFID), GPS, and Bluetooth, it's already happening.

Technological environment
Forces that create new technologies, creating new product and market opportunities.

Many firms are already using RFID technology to track products and customers at various points in the distribution channel. For example, Walmart has strongly encouraged suppliers shipping products to its distribution centers to apply RFID tags to their pallets. And retailers such as American Apparel, Macy's, and Bloomingdales are now installing item-level RFID systems in their stores. Fashion and accessories maker Burberry even uses chips imbedded in items and linked to smartphones to provide personalized, interactive experiences for customers in its stores and at runway shows.[39]

● Disney is taking RFID technology to new levels with its cool MagicBand RFID wristband:[40]

Wearing a MagicBand at The Walt Disney World Resort opens up a whole new level of Disney's famed magic. After registering for cloud-based MyMagic+ services, with the flick of your wrist you can enter a park or attraction, buy dinner or souvenirs, or even unlock your hotel room. But Disney has only begun to tap the MagicBand's potential for personalizing guest experiences. Future applications could be truly magical. Imagine, for example, the wonder of a child who receives a warm hug from Mickey Mouse or a bow from Prince Charming, who then greets the child by name and wishes her a happy birthday. Imagine animatronics that interact with nearby guests based on personal information supplied in advance. You get separated from family or friends? No problem. A quick scan of your MagicBand at a nearby directory could pinpoint the locations of your entire party. Linked to your Disney phone app, the MagicBand could trigger in-depth information about park features, ride wait times, FastPass check-in alerts, and your reservations schedule. Of course, the MagicBand also offers Disney a potential mother lode of digital data on guest activities and movements in minute detail, helping to improve guest logistics, services, and sales. If all this seems too Big Brother-ish, there will be privacy options—for example, letting parents opt out of things like characters knowing children's names. In all, such digital technologies promise to enrich the Disney experience for both guests and the company.

● **Marketing technology: Disney is taking RFID technology to new levels with its cool new MagicBand RFID wristband.**
Bob Croslin

3.1 Patagonia's "Conscious Consumption"— Telling Consumers to Buy *Less*

Patagonia—the high-end outdoor clothing and gear company—was founded on a mission of using business to help save the planet. More than 40 years ago, mountain-climber entrepreneur Yvon Chouinard started the company with this enduring mission: "Build the best product, cause no unnecessary harm, use business to inspire and implement solutions to the environmental crisis." Now, Chouinard and Patagonia are taking that mission to new extremes. They're actually telling consumers "don't buy our products."

It started a few years ago with a full-page *New York Times* ad on Black Friday, the day after Thanksgiving and busiest shopping day of the year, showing Patagonia's best-selling R2 jacket and pronouncing "Don't Buy This Jacket." Patagonia backed the ad with messaging in its retail stores and at its website and social media pages. To top things off, Patagonia customers received a follow-up email prior to Cyber Monday—the season's major online shopping day—reasserting the brand's buy less message. Here's part of what it said:

Because Patagonia wants to be in business for a good long time—and leave a world inhabitable for our kids—we want to do the opposite of every other business today. We ask you to buy less and to reflect before you spend a dime on this jacket or anything else.

The environmental cost of everything we make is astonishing. Consider the R2 Jacket shown, one of our best sellers. To make it required 135 liters of water, enough to meet the daily needs (three glasses a day) of 45 people. Its journey from its origin as 60% recycled polyester to our Reno warehouse generated nearly 20 pounds of carbon dioxide, 24 times the weight of the finished product. This jacket left behind, on its way to Reno, two-thirds its weight in waste. And this is a 60% recycled polyester jacket, knit and sewn to a high standard. But, as is true of all the things we can make and you can buy, this jacket comes with an environmental cost higher than its price.

There is much to be done and plenty for us all to do. Don't buy what you don't need. Think twice before you buy anything. [Work with us] to reimagine a world where we take only what nature can replace.

A for-profit firm telling its customers to buy *less*? It sounds crazy. But that message is right on target with Patagonia's reason for being. Founder Chouinard contends that capitalism is on an unsustainable path. Today's companies and customers are wasting the world's resources by making and buying low-quality goods that they buy mindlessly and throw away too quickly. Instead, Chouinard and his company are calling for *conscious consumption,* asking customers to think before they buy and to stop consuming for consumption's sake.

Coming from Patagonia, a company that spends almost nothing on traditional advertising, the paradoxical "Don't Buy This Jacket" ad had tremendous impact. The internet was soon ablaze with comments from online journalists, bloggers, and customers regarding the meaning and motivation behind Patagonia's message. Analysts speculated about whether the ad would help or harm sales—whether it would engage customers and build loyalty or be perceived as little more than a cheap marketing gimmick.

But to Patagonia, far from a marketing gimmick, the campaign expressed the brand's deeply held philosophy of sustainability. The purpose was to increase awareness of and participation in the Patagonia Common Threads Initiative, which urges customers to take a pledge to work together with the company to consume more responsibly. Common Threads rests on five Rs of joint action toward sustainability:

Reduce: **WE** make useful gear that lasts a long time. **YOU** don't buy what you don't need.
Repair: **WE** help you repair your Patagonia gear. **YOU** pledge to fix what's broken.
Reuse: **WE** help find a home for Patagonia gear you no longer need. **YOU** sell or pass it on.
Recycle: **WE** take back your Patagonia gear that is worn out. **YOU** pledge to keep your stuff out of the landfill and incinerator.
Reimagine: **TOGETHER** we reimagine a world where we take only what nature can replace.

● **Environmental sustainability: A for-profit firm telling its customers to buy *less* sounds crazy. But it's right on target with Patagonia's reason for being. The company wants to "reimagine a world where we take only what nature can replace."**

Property of Patagonia, Inc. Used with permission.

So Patagonia's conscious consumption solution seems pretty simple. Making, buying, repairing, and reusing higher-quality goods results in less consumption, which in turn uses fewer resources and lowers costs for everyone. Patagonia has always been committed to the idea of quality as a cure for overconsumption. It makes durable products with timeless designs, products that customers can keep and use for a long time. Then, through programs like its Worn Wear Initiative, Patagonia uses social media to let customers share stories about their long-lasting gear and to inspire people to keep their clothing in circulation for as long as possible. In Patagonia's words:

> At the end of the day, we can tinker with our supply chain, improve sourcing, use all-recycled fabrics, and give away millions of dollars to environmental organizations until the cows come in, but nothing is more important and impactful than keeping our clothing in use for as long as possible.

So on that Black Friday weekend, while other companies were inundating customers with promotions that encouraged them to "buy, buy, buy," Patagonia stood on its founding principles. It said, "Hey, look: Only purchase what you need," explains Rob BonDurant, vice president of marketing and communications at Patagonia. "The message, 'Don't buy this jacket,' is obviously super counterintuitive to what a for-profit company would say, especially on a day like Black Friday, but honestly [it] is what we really were after, [communicating] this idea of evolving capitalism and conscious consumption that we wanted to effect."

Not just any company can pull off something like this—such a message can only work if it is real. Patagonia didn't just suddenly stick an ad in the *New York Times* on Black Friday. It had been sending—and living—this message for decades. Can other companies follow Patagonia's lead? "If it is [just] a marketing campaign, no," says BonDurant. "If it is a way they live their lives and do their business, absolutely. You can't just apply it to your messaging or to a particular window of time. It has to be done 24 hours a day, 365 days a year."

Pushing conscious consumption doesn't mean that Patagonia wants customers to stop buying its products. To the contrary, like other for-profit brands, Patagonia really does care about doing well on Black Friday and the rest of the holiday season. As a company that sells products mostly for cold-weather activities, Patagonia reaps a whopping 40 percent of its revenues during the final two months of the year. But to Patagonia, business is about more than making money. And according to BonDurant, the "Don't Buy This Jacket" campaign has more than paid for itself with the interest and involvement it created for the Common Threads Initiative. As an added bonus, however, the campaign also boosted sales. During the first year of the campaign, Patagonia's sales surged by almost a third.

"It is not enough just to make good products anymore," says BonDurant. "There also has to be a message that people can buy into, that people feel they are a part of, that they can be solutions-based. That is what [Patagonia's "buy only what you need"] communication efforts are really all about." But what's good for customers and the planet is also good for Patagonia. Says founder Chouinard, "I know it sounds crazy, but every time I have made a decision that is best for the planet, I have made money. Our customers know that—and they want to be part of that environmental commitment."

Sources: Based on information from Danielle Sacks, "Any Fight Worth Fighting—That's the Attitude We Take," *Fast Company*, February 2015, pp. 34–36; Ryan Bradley, "The Tao Rose," *Fortune*, September 15, 2015, pp. 155–160; Katherine Ling, "Walking the Talk," *Marketing News*, March 15, 2012, p. 24; Kyle Stock, "Patagonia's 'Buy Less' Plea Spurs More Buying," *Bloomberg Businessweek*, August 28, 2013, www.businessweek.com/printer/articles/147326-patagonias-buy-less-plea-spurs-more-buying; "How a Clothing Company's Anti-Consumerist Message Boosted Business," *PBS*, August 20, 2015, www.pbs.org/newshour/bb/clothing-companys-anti-consumerist-message-boosted-business/; "How Patagonia Is Recycling Bottles into Jackets," *Earth911*, March 4, 2016, www.earth911.com/business-policy/how-patagonia-is-recycling-bottles-into-jackets/; and www.patagonia.com/us/common-threads?src=112811_mt1, http://wornwear.patagonia.com/, and www.patagonia.com/us/environmentalism, accessed September 2016.

The technological environment changes rapidly, creating new markets and opportunities. However, every new technology replaces an older technology. Transistors hurt the vacuum-tube industry, digital photography hurt the film business, and digital downloads and streaming are hurting the DVD and book businesses. When old industries fight or ignore new technologies, their businesses decline. Thus, marketers should watch the technological environment closely. Companies that do not keep up will soon find their products outdated. If that happens, they will miss new product and market opportunities.

As products and technologies become more complex, the public needs to know that these items are safe. Thus, government agencies investigate and ban potentially unsafe products. In the United States, the Food and Drug Administration (FDA) has created complex regulations for testing new drugs. The Consumer Product Safety Commission (CPSC) establishes safety standards for consumer products and penalizes companies that fail to meet them. Such regulations have resulted in much higher research costs and longer times between new product ideas and their introduction. Marketers should be aware of these regulations when applying new technologies and developing new products.

Political environment

Laws, government agencies, and pressure groups that influence and limit various organizations and individuals in a given society.

The Political–Social and Cultural Environments

The Political and Social Environment

Marketing decisions are strongly affected by developments in the political environment. The **political environment** consists of laws, government agencies, and pressure groups that influence or limit various organizations and individuals in a given society.

Legislation Regulating Business

> **Author Comment** | Even the strongest free-market advocates agree that the system works best with at least some regulation. But beyond regulation, most companies *want* to be socially responsible. We'll dig deeper into marketing and social responsibility in Chapter 20.

Even the strongest advocates of free-market economies agree that the system works best with at least some regulation. Well-conceived regulation can encourage competition and ensure fair markets for goods and services. Thus, governments develop *public policy* to guide commerce—sets of laws and regulations that limit business for the good of society as a whole. Almost every marketing activity is subject to a wide range of laws and regulations.

Legislation affecting business around the world has increased steadily over the years. The United States and many other countries have many laws covering issues such as competition, fair-trade practices, environmental protection, product safety, truth in advertising, consumer privacy, packaging and labeling, pricing, and other important areas (see **Table 3.1**).

Understanding the public policy implications of a particular marketing activity is not a simple matter. In the United States, there are many laws created at the national, state, and local levels, and these regulations often overlap. For example, aspirin products sold in Dallas are governed by both federal labeling laws and Texas state advertising laws. Moreover, regulations are constantly changing; what was allowed last year may now be prohibited, and what was prohibited may now be allowed. Marketers must work hard to keep up with changes in regulations and their interpretations.

Business legislation has been enacted for a number of reasons. The first is to *protect companies* from each other. Although business executives may praise competition, they sometimes try to neutralize it when it threatens them. Therefore, laws are passed to define and prevent unfair competition. In the United States, such laws are enforced by the Federal Trade Commission (FTC) and the Antitrust Division of the Attorney General's office.

The second purpose of government regulation is to *protect consumers* from unfair business practices. Some firms, if left alone, would make shoddy products, invade consumer privacy, mislead consumers in their advertising, and deceive consumers through their packaging and pricing. Rules defining and regulating unfair business practices are enforced by various agencies.

The third purpose of government regulation is to *protect the interests of society* against unrestrained business behavior. Profitable business activity does not always create a better quality of life. Regulation arises to ensure that firms take responsibility for the social costs of their production or products.

International marketers will encounter dozens, or even hundreds, of agencies set up to enforce trade policies and regulations. In the United States, Congress has established federal regulatory agencies, such as the FTC, the FDA, the Federal Communications Commission, the Federal Energy Regulatory Commission, the Federal Aviation Administration, the Consumer Product Safety Commission, the Environmental Protection Agency, and hundreds of others. Because such government agencies have some discretion in enforcing the laws, they can have a major impact on a company's marketing performance.

New laws and their enforcement will continue to increase. Business executives must watch these developments when planning their products and marketing programs. Marketers need to know about the major laws protecting competition, consumers, and society. They need to understand these laws at the local, state, national, and international levels.

Increased Emphasis on Ethics and Socially Responsible Actions

Written regulations cannot possibly cover all potential marketing abuses, and existing laws are often difficult to enforce. However, beyond written laws and regulations, business is also governed by social codes and rules of professional ethics.

Socially Responsible Behavior. Enlightened companies encourage their managers to look beyond what the regulatory system allows and simply "do the right thing." These socially responsible firms actively seek out ways to protect the long-run interests of their consumers and the environment.

Almost every aspect of marketing involves ethics and social responsibility issues. Unfortunately, because these issues usually involve conflicting interests, well-meaning people can honestly disagree about the right course of action in a given situation. Thus, many industrial and professional trade associations have suggested codes of ethics. And more companies are now developing policies, guidelines, and other responses to complex social responsibility issues.

The boom in online, mobile, and social media marketing has created a new set of social and ethical issues. Critics worry most about online privacy issues. There has been an explosion in the amount of personal digital data available. Users themselves supply some of it. They voluntarily place highly private information on social media sites, such as Facebook or LinkedIn, or on genealogy sites that are easily searched by anyone with a computer or a smartphone.

However, much of the information is systematically developed by businesses seeking to learn more about their customers, often without consumers realizing that they are under the microscope. Legitimate businesses track consumers' online browsing and buying behavior and collect, analyze, and share digital data from every move consumers make at

● Table 3.1 | Major U.S. Legislation Affecting Marketing

Legislation	Purpose
Sherman Antitrust Act (1890)	Prohibits monopolies and activities (price-fixing, predatory pricing) that restrain trade or competition in interstate commerce.
Federal Food and Drug Act (1906)	Created the Food and Drug Administration (FDA). It forbids the manufacture or sale of adulterated or fraudulently labeled foods and drugs.
Clayton Act (1914)	Supplements the Sherman Act by prohibiting certain types of price discrimination, exclusive dealing, and tying clauses (which require a dealer to take additional products in a seller's line).
Federal Trade Commission Act (1914)	Established the Federal Trade Commission (FTC), which monitors and remedies unfair trade methods.
Robinson-Patman Act (1936)	Amends the Clayton Act to define price discrimination as unlawful. Empowers the FTC to establish limits on quantity discounts, forbid some brokerage allowances, and prohibit promotional allowances except when made available on proportionately equal terms.
Wheeler-Lea Act (1938)	Makes deceptive, misleading, and unfair practices illegal regardless of injury to competition. Places advertising of food and drugs under FTC jurisdiction.
Lanham Trademark Act (1946)	Protects and regulates distinctive brand names and trademarks.
National Traffic and Safety Act (1958)	Provides for the creation of compulsory safety standards for automobiles and tires.
Fair Packaging and Labeling Act (1966)	Provides for the regulation of the packaging and labeling of consumer goods. Requires that manufacturers state what the package contains, who made it, and how much it contains.
Child Protection Act (1966)	Bans the sale of hazardous toys and articles. Sets standards for child-resistant packaging.
Federal Cigarette Labeling and Advertising Act (1967)	Requires that cigarette packages contain the following statement: "Warning: The Surgeon General Has Determined That Cigarette Smoking Is Dangerous to Your Health."
National Environmental Policy Act (1969)	Establishes a national policy on the environment. The 1970 Reorganization Plan established the Environmental Protection Agency (EPA).
Consumer Product Safety Act (1972)	Establishes the Consumer Product Safety Commission (CPSC) and authorizes it to set safety standards for consumer products as well as exact penalties for failing to uphold those standards.
Magnuson-Moss Warranty Act (1975)	Authorizes the FTC to determine rules and regulations for consumer warranties and provides consumer access to redress, such as the class action suit.
Children's Television Act (1990)	Limits the number of commercials aired during children's programs.
Nutrition Labeling and Education Act (1990)	Requires that food product labels provide detailed nutritional information.
Telephone Consumer Protection Act (1991)	Establishes procedures to avoid unwanted telephone solicitations. Limits marketers' use of automatic telephone dialing systems and artificial or prerecorded voices.
Americans with Disabilities Act (1991)	Makes discrimination against people with disabilities illegal in public accommodations, transportation, and telecommunications.
Children's Online Privacy Protection Act (2000)	Prohibits websites or online services operators from collecting personal information from children without obtaining consent from a parent and allowing parents to review information collected from their children.
Do-Not-Call Implementation Act (2003)	Authorizes the FTC to collect fees from sellers and telemarketers for the implementation and enforcement of a national Do-Not-Call Registry.
CAN-SPAM Act (2003)	Regulates the distribution and content of unsolicited commercial email.
Financial Reform Law (2010)	Created the Bureau of Consumer Financial Protection, which writes and enforces rules for the marketing of financial products to consumers. It is also responsible for enforcement of the Truth-in-Lending Act, the Home Mortgage Disclosure Act, and other laws designed to protect consumers.

their online sites. Critics worry that these companies may now know *too* much and might use digital data to take unfair advantage of consumers. Although most companies fully disclose their internet privacy policies and most try to use data to benefit their customers, abuses do occur. As a result, consumer advocates and policy makers are taking action to protect consumer privacy. In Chapters 4 and 20, we discuss these and other societal marketing issues in greater depth.

Cause-Related Marketing. To exercise their social responsibility and build more positive images, many companies are now linking themselves to worthwhile causes. These days, every product seems to be tied to some cause. For example, the P&G "Tide Loads of Hope" program provides mobile laundromats and loads of clean laundry to families in disaster-stricken areas—P&G washes, dries, and folds clothes for these families for free. Shake Shack runs an annual Great American Shake Sale: If you donate at least $2 at the register to Share Our Strength's No Kid Hungry program dedicated to ending child hunger in America, you get a $5 shake free on your next visit. ● And AT&T joined forces with competitors Verizon, Sprint, and T-Mobile to spearhead the "It Can Wait" campaign, which addresses the texting-while-driving epidemic by urging people of all ages to take the pledge to never text and drive. The campaign's cause-related message: "No text is worth the risk. It can wait."[41]

● Cause-related marketing: AT&T joined forces with competitors Verizon, Sprint, and T-Mobile to spearhead the "It Can Wait" campaign, which urges people of all ages to take the pledge to never text and drive.
Courtesy of AT&T Intellectual Property. Used with permission.

Some companies are founded on cause-related missions. Under the concept of "values-led business" or "caring capitalism," their mission is to use business to make the world a better place. For example, Warby Parker—the online marketer of low-priced prescription eyewear—was founded with the hope of bringing affordable eyewear to the masses. The company sells "eyewear with a purpose." For every pair of glasses Warby Parker sells, it distributes a free pair to someone in need. The company also works with not-for-profit organizations that train low-income entrepreneurs to sell affordable glasses. "We believe that everyone has the right to see," says the company.[42]

Cause-related marketing has become a primary form of corporate giving. It lets companies "do well by doing good" by linking purchases of the company's products or services with benefiting worthwhile causes or charitable organizations. Beyond being socially admirable, Warby Parker's Buy a Pair, Give a Pair program also makes good economic sense, for both the company and its customers. "Companies can do good in the world while still being profitable," says Warby Parker co-founder Neil Blumenthal. "A single pair of reading glasses causes, on average, a 20 percent increase in income. Glasses are one of the most effective poverty alleviation tools in the world."[43]

Cause-related marketing has also stirred some controversy. Critics worry that cause-related marketing is more a strategy for selling than a strategy for giving—that "cause-related" marketing is really "cause-exploitative" marketing. Thus, companies using cause-related marketing might find themselves walking a fine line between increased sales and an improved image and facing charges of exploitation. However, if handled well, cause-related marketing can greatly benefit both the company and the cause. The company gains an effective marketing tool while building a more positive public image. The charitable organization or cause gains greater visibility and important new sources of funding and support. Spending on cause-related marketing in the United States skyrocketed from only $120 million in 1990 to $2 billion in 2016.[44]

Cultural environment
Institutions and other forces that affect society's basic values, perceptions, preferences, and behaviors.

Author Comment | Cultural factors strongly affect how people think and how they consume, so marketers are keenly interested in the cultural environment.

The Cultural Environment

The **cultural environment** consists of institutions and other forces that affect a society's basic values, perceptions, preferences, and behaviors. People grow up in a particular society that shapes their basic beliefs and values. They absorb a worldview that defines their relationships with others. The following cultural characteristics can affect marketing decision making.

The Persistence of Cultural Values

People in a given society hold many beliefs and values. Their core beliefs and values have a high degree of persistence. For example, most Americans believe in individual freedom, hard work, getting married, and achievement and success. These beliefs shape more specific attitudes and behaviors found in everyday life. *Core* beliefs and values are passed on from parents to children and are reinforced by schools, businesses, religious institutions, and government.

Secondary beliefs and values are more open to change. Believing in marriage is a core belief; believing that people should get married early in life is a secondary belief. Marketers have some chance of changing secondary values but little chance of changing core values. For example, family-planning marketers could argue more effectively that people should get married later than not get married at all.

Shifts in Secondary Cultural Values

Although core values are fairly persistent, cultural swings do take place. Consider the impact of popular music groups, movie personalities, and other celebrities on young people's hairstyle and clothing norms. Marketers want to predict cultural shifts to spot new opportunities or threats. The major cultural values of a society are expressed in people's views of themselves and others as well as in their views of organizations, society, nature, and the universe.

People's Views of Themselves. People vary in their emphasis on serving themselves versus serving others. Some people seek personal pleasure, wanting fun, change, and escape. Others seek self-realization through religion, recreation, or the avid pursuit of careers or other life goals. Some people see themselves as sharers and joiners; others see themselves as individualists. People use products, brands, and services as a means of self-expression, and they buy products and services that match their views of themselves.

Marketers can position their brands to appeal to specific self-view segments. For example, consider Sperry, maker of storied Sperry Top-Sider boat shoes:[45]

> Sperry first introduced its iconic Top-Sider shoes in 1935 as the perfect non-slip boat shoe for rough seas and slippery decks. That nautical legacy remains an important part of Sperry's positioning. The brand's recent "Odysseys Await" marketing campaign confirms that the sure-footed shoes are built for adventurous soles who can't stay put. The campaign targets "intrepid consumers"—active millennials who view themselves as adventurous, authentic, bold, and creative. "There's a certain section of Millennials that really look at life as an opportunity," says a Sperry marketer. They "want to have meaningful experiences and align with brands that provide opportunities for such." The "Odysseys Await" campaign reconnects the brand with the sea, featuring intrepid consumers having nautical adventures, jumping off boats, sailing, and diving off cliffs. Headlines such as "The best stories are written with your feet," "Keep your laces tight and your plans loose," "Try living for a living," and "If Earth has an edge, find it" suggest that Sperry Top-Siders are more than just shoes. They are the embodiment of customers' self-views and lifestyles.

People's Views of Others. People's attitudes toward and interactions with others shift over time. In recent years, some analysts have voiced concerns that the digital age would result in diminished human interaction, as people buried themselves in social media pages or emailed and texted rather than interacting personally. Instead, today's digital technologies seem to have launched an era of what one trend watcher calls "mass mingling." Rather than interacting less, people are using social media and mobile communications to connect more than ever. Basically, the more people meet, network, text, and socialize online, the more likely they are to eventually meet up with friends and followers in the real world.

However, these days, even when people are together, they are often "alone together." Groups of people may sit or walk in their own little bubbles, intensely connected to tiny screens and keyboards. One expert describes the latest communication skill as "maintaining eye contact with someone while you text someone else; it's hard but it can be done," she says. "Technology-enabled, we are able to be with one another, and also 'elsewhere,' connected to wherever we want to be."[46] Thus, whether the new technology-driven

● People's views of others: Today's digital technologies have launched a new era of mass mingling. However, even when people are together, they are often "alone together"—immersed in their own little bubbles, intensely connected to tiny screens and keyboards.

Dmitriy Shironosov/123RF

communication is a blessing or a curse is a matter of much debate.

This new way of interacting strongly affects how companies market their brands and communicate with customers. Consumers increasingly tap digitally into networks of friends and online brand communities to learn about and buy products and to shape and share brand experiences. As a result, it is important for brands to participate in these networks too.

People's Views of Organizations. People vary in their attitudes toward corporations, government agencies, trade unions, universities, and other organizations. By and large, people are willing to work for major organizations and expect them, in turn, to carry out society's work.

The past two decades have seen a sharp decrease in confidence in and loyalty toward America's business and political organizations and institutions. In the workplace, there has been an overall decline in organizational loyalty. Waves of company downsizings bred cynicism and distrust. In just the past decade, major corporate scandals, rounds of layoffs resulting from the Great Recession, the financial meltdown triggered by Wall Street bankers' greed and incompetence, and other unsettling activities have resulted in a further loss of confidence in big business. Many people today see work not as a source of satisfaction but as a required chore to earn money to enjoy their nonwork hours. This trend suggests that organizations need to find new ways to win consumer and employee confidence.

People's Views of Society. People vary in their attitudes toward their society—patriots defend it, reformers want to change it, and malcontents want to leave it. People's orientation to their society influences their consumption patterns and attitudes toward the marketplace.

American patriotism has been increasing gradually for the past two decades. One annual consumer survey shows that some brands are highly associated with patriotism, such as Jeep, Coca-Cola, Disney, Levi Strauss, Harley-Davidson, Gillette, and Apple. Marketers respond with renewed "Made in America" pitches and ads with patriotic themes. For example, last summer Coca-Cola launched a limited-edition red, white, and blue flag can surrounding the July 4 holiday with the patriotic song lyric "I'm proud to be an American" on the label. Apple recently kicked off a $100 million "Made in America" push with the introduction of a new high-end Mac Pro personal computer. The Mac Pro, "the most powerful Mac ever," is built in Austin, Texas, with components made domestically. And Jeep's recent patriotic "Portraits" Super Bowl ad—which featured famous and ordinary faces of Americans who've driven Jeeps through 75 years of wars, peace, boom times, and bust—resonated strongly with Americans. "We don't make Jeep," concludes the ad, "you do."[47]

Although most such marketing efforts are tasteful and well received, waving the red, white, and blue can sometimes prove tricky. Flag-waving promotions can be viewed as corny or as token attempts to cash in on the nation's emotions. For example, some critics note that, so far, Apple's "Made in America" push hasn't had much real impact. The Mac Pro contributes less than 1 percent of Apple's total revenues. More than 70 percent of the company's revenues come from its iPhone and iPad products, both built in China. Marketers must take care when appealing to patriotism and other strong national emotions.

People's Views of Nature. People vary in their attitudes toward the natural world—some feel ruled by it, others feel in harmony with it, and still others seek to master it. A long-term trend has been people's growing mastery over nature through technology and the belief that nature is bountiful. More recently, however, people have recognized that nature is finite and fragile; it can be destroyed or spoiled by human activities.

This renewed love of things natural has created a sizable market of consumers who seek out everything from natural, organic, and nutritional products to fuel-efficient cars

 Riding the trend toward all things natural: Annie's is out to create a happier and healthier world with nourishing foods and responsible conduct that is "forever kind to the planet."

General Mills Marketing, Inc.

and alternative medicines. These consumers make up a sizable and growing market. For example, food producers have also found fast-growing markets for natural and organic products. In total, the U.S. organic/natural food market now generates $45 billion in annual retail sales and will grow to an estimated $200 billion by 2019.[48]

Annie's Homegrown, a General Mills company, caters to this market with sustainable, all-natural food products—from mac and cheese to pizzas, pastas, snacks, and salad dressings—made and sold in a sustainable way:[49]

 Annie's is out to create a happier and healthier world with nourishing foods and responsible conduct that is "forever kind to the planet." Annie's products are made from simple, natural ingredients grown by its farm partners. The products contain "no artificial anything," says the company. "If it's not real, it's not Annie's." The company works closely with its food supply-system partners to jointly raise the bar for sustainability and organics. Annie's also makes sustainable practices a top priority with its packaging—more than 90 percent of Annie's packaging by weight is recyclable. Finally, Annie's gives back to the community through programs such as sustainable agriculture scholarships, school garden programs, and support for like-minded organizations dedicated to making the planet a better place to live and eat.

People's Views of the Universe. Finally, people vary in their beliefs about the origins of the universe and their place in it. Although most Americans practice religion, religious conviction and practice have been dropping off gradually through the years. According to a recent poll, 22 percent of Americans now say they are not affiliated with any particular faith, up from about 17 percent just seven years prior. Among Americans ages 18 to 29, more than one-third say they are not currently affiliated with any particular religion.[50]

However, the fact that people are dropping out of organized religion doesn't mean that they are abandoning their faith. Some futurists have noted a renewed interest in spirituality, perhaps as a part of a broader search for a new inner purpose. People have been moving away from materialism and dog-eat-dog ambition to seek more permanent values—family, community, earth, faith—and a more certain grasp of right and wrong. Rather than calling it "religion," they call it "spirituality." One recent survey found that whereas Americans have become less religious in recent years, the share of people who feel a deep sense of "spiritual peace and well-being" as well as a deep sense of "wonder about the universe" has risen.[51] This changing spiritualism affects consumers in everything from the television shows they watch and the books they read to the products and services they buy.

Author Comment | Rather than simply watching and reacting to the marketing environment, companies should take proactive steps.

Responding to the Marketing Environment

Someone once observed, "There are three kinds of companies: those who make things happen, those who watch things happen, and those who wonder what's happened." Many companies view the marketing environment as an uncontrollable element to which they must react and adapt. They passively accept the marketing environment and do not try to change it. They analyze environmental forces and design strategies that will help the company avoid the threats and take advantage of the opportunities the environment provides.

Other companies take a *proactive* stance toward the marketing environment. Rather than assuming that strategic options are bounded by the current environment, these firms develop strategies to change the environment. Companies and their products often create and shape new industries and their structures, products such as Ford's Model T car, Apple's iPod and iPhone, Google's search engine, and Amazon's online marketplace.

Even more, rather than simply watching and reacting to environmental events, proactive firms take aggressive actions to affect the publics and forces in their marketing environment. Such companies hire lobbyists to influence legislation affecting their industries and stage media events to gain favorable press coverage. They take to the social media and run blogs to shape public opinion. They press lawsuits and file complaints with regulators to keep competitors in line, and they form contractual agreements to better control their distribution channels.

By taking action, companies can often overcome seemingly uncontrollable environmental events. For example, whereas some companies try to hush up negative talk about their products, others proactively counter false information. McDonald's did this when a photo went viral showing unappetizing "mechanically separated chicken" (also known as "pink goop") and associating it with the company's Chicken McNuggets:[52]

> McDonald's quickly issued statements disclaiming the pink goop photo as a hoax and noting that McNuggets are made using only boneless white breast meat chicken in a process that never produces anything remotely resembling the weird pink substance. But McDonald's took its response an important step further. It created its own nearly three-minute social media video giving a tour of a company processing plant in Canada, showing the step-by-step process by which McNuggets are made. In the process, fresh chicken breasts are ground and seasoned, stamped into four nugget shapes (balls, bells, boots, and bow ties), battered, flash-fried, frozen, packaged, and shipped out to local McDonald's restaurants where they are fully cooked. There's not a trace of the gross pink goop anywhere in the process. The proactive video itself went viral, garnering more than 3.5 million YouTube views in less than six weeks. As a follow-up, McDonald's launched an "Our Food. Your Questions." campaign inviting consumers to submit questions about its food-making processes via Facebook, Twitter, YouTube, and other social media. It then addressed the top concerns in a series of "behind-the-scenes" webisodes.

Marketing management cannot always control environmental forces. In many cases, it must settle for simply watching and reacting to the environment. For example, a company would have little success trying to influence geographic population shifts, the economic environment, or major cultural values. But whenever possible, smart marketing managers take a *proactive* rather than *reactive* approach to the marketing environment (see Real Marketing 3.2).

Real Marketing

3.2 In the Social Media Age: When the Dialogue Gets Nasty

Marketers have hailed the internet and social media as the great new way to engage customers and nurture customer relationships. In turn, today's more-empowered consumers use the new digital media to share their brand experiences with companies and with each other. All of this back and forth helps both the company and its customers. But sometimes, the dialogue can get nasty. Consider the following examples:

- Upon receiving a severely damaged computer monitor via FedEx, YouTube user goobie55 posts footage from his security camera. The video clearly shows a FedEx delivery man hoisting the monitor package over his head and tossing it over goobie55's front gate without ever attempting to ring the bell, open the gate, or walk the package to the door. The video—with FedEx's familiar purple and orange logo prominently displayed on everything from the driver's shirt to the

package and the truck—goes viral, with 5 million hits in just five days. TV news and talk shows go crazy discussing the clip.
- A young creative team at Ford's ad agency in India produces a Ford Figo print ad and releases it to the internet without approval. The ad features three women—bound, gagged, and scantily clad—in the hatch of a Figo, with a caricature of a grinning Silvio Berlusconi (Italy's sex-scandal-plagued ex-prime minister) at the wheel. The ad's tagline: "Leave your worries behind with Figo's extra-large boot (trunk)." Ford quickly pulls the ad, but not before it goes viral. Within days, millions of people around the world have viewed the ad, causing an online uproar and giving Ford a global black eye.
- When eight-year-old Harry Winsor sends a crayon drawing of an airplane he's designed to Boeing with a suggestion that the company might want to manufacture it, the company responds with a stern, legal-form letter. "We do not accept unso-

licited ideas," the letter states. "We regret to inform you that we have disposed of your message and retain no copies." The embarrassing blunder would probably go unnoticed were it not for the fact that Harry's father—John Winsor, a prominent ad exec—blogs and tweets about the incident, making it instant national news.

Extreme events? Not anymore. The internet and social media have turned the traditional power relationship between businesses and consumers upside down. In the good old days, disgruntled consumers could do little more than bellow at a company service rep or shout out their complaints from a street corner. Now, armed with only a laptop or smartphone, they can take it public, airing their gripes to millions on blogs, social media sites, or even hate sites devoted exclusively to their least favorite corporations. "A consumer's megaphone is now [sometimes] more powerful than a brand's," says one ad agency executive. "Individuals can bring a huge company to its knees ... simply by sharing their experiences and opinions on Facebook, Yelp, Twitter, Instagram, or other social forums."

"I hate" and "sucks" sites are almost commonplace. These sites target some highly respected companies with some highly disrespectful labels: Walmartblows. com, PayPalSucks.com (aka NoPayPal), IHateStarbucks.com, DeltaREALLYsucks.com, and UnitedPackageSmashers.com (UPS), to name only a few. "Sucks" videos on YouTube and other video sites also abound. For example, a search of "Apple sucks" on YouTube turns up more than 600,000 videos; a search for Microsoft finds 143,000 videos. An "Apple sucks" search on Facebook links to hundreds of groups. If you don't find one you like, try "Apple suks" or "Apple sux" for hundreds more.

Some of these sites, videos, and other online attacks air legitimate complaints that should be addressed. Others, however, are little more than anonymous, vindictive slurs that unfairly ransack brands and corporate reputations. Some of the attacks are only a passing nuisance; others can draw serious attention and create real headaches.

How should companies react to online attacks? The real quandary for targeted companies is figuring out how far they can go to protect their images without fueling the already-raging fire. One point on which all experts seem to agree: Don't try to retaliate in kind. "It's rarely a good idea to lob bombs at the fire starters," says one analyst. "Preemption, engagement, and diplomacy are saner tools." Such criticisms are often based on real consumer concerns and unresolved anger. Hence, the best strategy might be to proactively monitor these sites and respond honestly to the concerns they express.

For example, Boeing quickly took responsibility for mishandling aspiring Harry Winsor's designs, turning a potential PR disaster into a positive. It called and invited young Harry to visit Boeing's facilities. On its corporate Twitter site, it confessed, "We're experts at airplanes but novices in social media. We're learning as we go." In response to its Figo ad fiasco, Ford's chief marketing officer issued a deep public apology, citing that Ford had not approved the ads and that it had since modified its ad review process. Ford's ad agency promptly fired the guilty creatives.

Similarly, FedEx drew praise by immediately posting its own YouTube video addressing the monitor-smashing incident. In the video, FedEx Senior Vice President of Operations Matthew Thornton stated that he had personally met with the aggrieved customer, who had

Today's empowered consumers: Boeing's embarrassing blunder over young Harry Winsor's airplane design made instant national news. However, Boeing quickly took responsibility and turned the potential PR disaster into a positive.
John Winsor

accepted the company's apology. "This goes directly against all FedEx values," declared Thornton. The FedEx video struck a responsive chord. Numerous journalists and bloggers responded with stories about FedEx's outstanding package handling and delivering record.

Many companies have now created teams of specialists that monitor online conversations and engage unhappy consumers. For example, the social care team at Southwest Airlines includes a chief Twitter officer who tracks Twitter comments and monitors Facebook groups, an online representative who checks facts and interacts with bloggers, and another person who takes charge of the company's presence on sites such as YouTube, Instagram, Flickr, and LinkedIn. So if someone posts an online comment, the company can respond promptly in a personal way.

Not long ago, Southwest's team averted what could have been a major PR catastrophe when a hole popped open in a plane's fuselage

on a flight from Phoenix to Sacramento. The flight had Wi-Fi, and the first passenger tweet about the incident, complete with a photo, was online in only nine minutes—11 minutes before Southwest's official dispatch channel report. But Southwest's monitoring team picked up the social media chatter and was able to craft a blog post and other social media responses shortly after the plane made an emergency landing in Yuma, Arizona. By the time the story hit the major media, the passenger who had tweeted initially was back on Twitter praising the Southwest crew for its professional handling of the situation.

Thus, by monitoring and proactively responding to seemingly uncontrollable events in the environment, companies can prevent the negatives from spiraling out of control or even turn them into positives. Who knows? With the right responses, Walmartblows.com might even become Walmartrules.com. Then again, probably not.

Sources: See Matt Wilson, "How Southwest Airlines Wrangled Four Social Media Crises," *Ragan.com*, February 20, 2013, www.ragan.com/Main/Articles/How_Southwest_Airlines_wrangled_four_social_media_46254.aspx#; Vanessa Ko, "FedEx Apologizes after Video of Driver Throwing Fragile Package Goes Viral," *Time*, December 23, 2011, http://newsfeed.time.com/2011/12/23/fedex-apologizes-after-video-of-driver-throwing-fragile-package-goes-viral/; Michelle Conlin, "Web Attack," *BusinessWeek*, April 16, 2007, pp. 54–56; "Boeing's Social Media Lesson," May 3, 2010, http://mediadecoder.blogs.nytimes.com/2010/05/03/boeings-social-media-lesson/; Brent Snavely, "Ford Marketing Chief Apologizes for Ads," *USA Today*, March 27, 2013; Benet J. Wilson, "Southwest Airlines Steps Up Its Social Media Game during Jonas Snowstorm," *Airways News*, February 3, 2016, http://airwaysnews.com/blog/2016/02/03/swa-sm-jonas/; and www.youtube.com/watch?v=C5ulH0VTg_o, accessed September 2016.

3 | Reviewing and Extending the Concepts

OBJECTIVES REVIEW AND KEY TERMS

Objectives Review

In this and the next two chapters, you'll examine the environments of marketing and how companies analyze these environments to better understand the marketplace and consumers. Companies must constantly watch and manage the *marketing environment* to seek opportunities and ward off threats. The marketing environment consists of all the actors and forces influencing the company's ability to transact business effectively with its target market.

OBJECTIVE 3-1 Describe the environmental forces that affect the company's ability to serve its customers. (pp 68–72)

The company's *microenvironment* consists of actors close to the company that combine to form its value delivery network or that affect its ability to serve customers. It includes the company's *internal environment*—its several departments and management levels—as it influences marketing decision making. *Marketing channel firms*—suppliers, marketing intermediaries, physical distribution firms, marketing services agencies, and financial intermediaries—cooperate to create customer value. *Competitors* vie with the company in an effort to serve customers better. Various *publics* have an actual or potential interest in or impact on the company's ability to meet its objectives. Finally, five types of customer *markets* exist: consumer, business, reseller, government, and international markets.

The *macroenvironment* consists of larger societal forces that affect the entire microenvironment. The six forces making up the company's macroenvironment are demographic, economic, natural, technological, political/social, and cultural forces. These forces shape opportunities and pose threats to the company.

OBJECTIVE 3-2 Explain how changes in the demographic and economic environments affect marketing decisions. (pp 72–80)

Demography is the study of the characteristics of human populations. Today's *demographic environment* shows a changing age structure, shifting family profiles, geographic population shifts, a better-educated and more white-collar population, and increasing diversity. The *economic environment* consists of factors that affect buying power and patterns. The economic environment is characterized by more frugal consumers who are seeking greater value—the right combination of good quality and service at a fair price. The distribution of income also is shifting. The rich have grown richer, the middle class has shrunk, and the poor have remained poor, leading to a two-tiered market.

OBJECTIVE 3-3 Identify the major trends in the firm's natural and technological environments. (pp 80–84)

The *natural environment* shows three major trends: shortages of certain raw materials, higher pollution levels, and more government intervention in natural resource management. Environmental concerns create marketing opportunities for alert companies. The *technological environment* creates both opportunities and challenges. Companies that fail to keep up with technological change will miss out on new product and marketing opportunities.

OBJECTIVE 3-4 Explain the key changes in the political and cultural environments. (pp 84–90)

The *political environment* consists of laws, agencies, and groups that influence or limit marketing actions. The political environment has undergone changes that affect marketing worldwide: increasing legislation regulating business, strong government agency enforcement, and greater emphasis on ethics and socially responsible actions. The *cultural environment* consists of institutions and forces that affect a society's values, perceptions, preferences, and behaviors. The environment shows trends toward new technology-enabled communication, a lessening trust of institutions, increasing patriotism, greater appreciation for nature, a changing spiritualism, and the search for more meaningful and enduring values.

OBJECTIVE 3-5 Discuss how companies can react to the marketing environment. (pp 90–92)

Companies can passively accept the marketing environment as an uncontrollable element to which they must adapt, avoiding threats and taking advantage of opportunities as they arise. Or they can take a *proactive* stance, working to change the environment rather than simply reacting to it. Whenever possible, companies should try to be proactive rather than reactive.

Key Terms

OBJECTIVE 3-1

Marketing environment (p 68)
Microenvironment (p 68)
Macroenvironment (p 68)
Marketing intermediaries (p 70)
Public (p 71)

OBJECTIVE 3-2

Demography (p 72)
Baby boomers (p 73)
Generation X (p 73)
Millennials (Generation Y) (p 74)
Generation Z (p 75)
Economic environment (p 79)

OBJECTIVE 3-3

Natural environment (p 80)
Environmental sustainability (p 81)
Technological environment (p 82)

OBJECTIVE 3-4

Political environment (p 84)
Cultural environment (p 87)

DISCUSSION AND CRITICAL THINKING

MyMarketingLab

Go to **mymktlab.com** to complete the problems marked with this icon ✪.

Discussion Questions

3-1   Name and describe the types of publics in a company's marketing environment. (AASCB: Communication)

3-2   What are marketing intermediaries, and are they important for marketers? (AACSB: Communication; Reflective Thinking)

✪ **3-3**   Describe Generation Z. What differentiates GenZers from other demographic groups, such as baby boomers, Generation X, and millennials? (AACSB: Communication; Reflective Thinking)

3-4   Discuss the impact of the changing age structure of the population on consumer spending and buying behavior. Why is this trend important to marketers? (AACSB: Communication; Reflective Thinking)

✪ **3-5**   Why should marketers pay close attention to the cultural environment? (AACSB: Communication)

Critical Thinking Exercises

✪ **3-6**   In 1965, more than 40 percent of American adults were smokers. That percentage has now fallen to less than 18 percent. Tobacco companies have dealt with this threat by developing new markets overseas and also developing alternative nicotine products such as electronic cigarettes (e-cigarettes). Research this product and the regulatory environment regarding this product, then write a report advising tobacco companies on the opportunities and threats posed by this technology. (AACSB: Communication; Reflective Thinking)

3-7   Form a small group and discuss cultural trends in the United States. Research one of them in depth and create a presentation on the trend's impact on marketing. (AACSB: Communication; Reflective Thinking)

3-8   Visit www.causemarketingforum.com to learn about companies that have won Halo Awards for outstanding cause-related marketing programs. Present an award-winning case study to your class. (AACSB: Communication; Use of IT)

APPLICATIONS AND CASES

Online, Mobile, and Social Media Marketing Sharing Economy

Changes in the technological environment have created amazing opportunities for new business models while at the same time threatening traditional ones. For example, Airbnb has shaken up the hospitality industry by allowing people to rent out spare rooms or their entire homes to strangers. The Uber and Lyft ridesharing businesses allow consumers to find a ride from people looking to earn extra money with their vehicles. And with Uber you don't have to worry about having enough cash or giving your credit card to the driver—payments and tips are all done through the Uber app. Traditional hotel and cab companies are crying foul, claiming that these businesses are not playing by the same regulatory rules to which they are subject. Others are concerned about safety amid reports of riders allegedly being attacked, kidnappings, and driver accidents, questioning the thoroughness

of background checks of the 160,000-plus Uber drivers around the world. Some countries, states, and cities in the United States have banned Uber because of these issues.

3-9   Describe how Uber's business model works and the role technology has played in its success. What are the arguments for banning these types of businesses? What are the arguments for defending them? (AACSB: Communication; Use of IT; Reflective Thinking)

3-10   Describe examples of two other businesses based on the sharing economy model and create a new business idea based on this concept. (AACSB: Communication; Reflective Thinking)

Marketing Ethics How Young Is Too Young?

Walmart rolled out a cosmetics line aimed at girls as young as nine years old. According to the *Wall Street Journal*, Walmart introduced this line called geoGirl to meet the demands of "tween" girls. The geoGirl line was developed free

of chemicals (phthalates and parabens), synthetic colors, and fragrances, allowing marketers to promote the "environmentally friendly" product offering to parents. Capitalizing on this demand trend, Target launched the Hello Kitty line. Tween boys are not to be left out: Axe markets a line of chocolate-scented body spray, and Old Spice developed Swagger body wash. Recently, focus has been placed on girls' self-images as they near the teen years. Some child development experts say makeup for young girls places too much emphasis on appearance while others say a little lipstick shouldn't cause much concern.

3-11 Is it an appropriate business strategy to use a popular movement such as environmentalism to market an unrelated product?

3-12 Apart from the question of placing undue emphasis on a child's appearance, what factors should marketers consider in developing campaigns for these types of products?

Marketing by the Numbers Demographic Trends

Marketers are interested in demographic trends related to variables such as age, ethnicity, and population. The U.S. Census Bureau provides considerable demographic information that is useful for marketers. For example, the following table provides a sample of such population data (see www.censusscope. org/2010Census/PDFs/RaceEth-States.pdf):

	2000		2010	
State	**Total**	**Hispanic**	**Total**	**Hispanic**
Georgia	8,186,453	435,227	9,687,653	853,689
Michigan	9,938,444	323,877	9,883,640	436,358
California	33,871,648	10,966,556	37,253,956	14,013,719

3-13 What percentage change in the total and Hispanic populations occurred in each state between 2000 and 2010? What conclusions can be drawn from this analysis? (AACSB: Communication; Analytical Reasoning; Reflective Thinking)

3-14 Research another demographic trend and create a presentation to marketers regarding the significance of the trend you analyzed. (AACSB: Communication; Reflective Thinking)

Video Case Burger King

In the fast-food burgers business, french fries are perhaps more important than the burgers themselves. System-wide, Burger King sells 56 million orders of french fries every month—one order of fries for every two customers. But nothing is exempt from the impact of marketing environment forces. As health trends drove some companies to cut back on fatty foods, Burger King saw its french fry sales dip.

So Burger King decided to let people have their fries and eat them to. To bring health-conscious customers back to the counter, Burger King introduced Satisfries—french fries with 30 percent less fat and 20 percent fewer calories than its regular fries. In a product category that has seen little if any innovation,

Satisfries could be a big game changer. Still, reduced fat and calories may not be enough to make a difference to health-food lovers. And at 30 to 40 cents more per item, Satisfries may end up as little more than a fry fiasco.

After viewing the video featuring Burger King, answer the following questions:

3-15 Considering marketing environment forces, describe how Burger King went about developing its new Satisfries.

3-16 With Satisfries, has Burger King truly created customer value, or is it just chasing trends? Explain.

Company Case Fitbit: Riding the Fitness Wave to Glory

It was 2009. James Park and Eric Friedman were at a breaking point. They'd been flitting around Asia for months, setting up the supply chain for their company's first product, the Fitbit Tracker. Having raised capital to launch the product with nothing more than a circuit board in a balsa wood box, they were now on the verge of pushing the button to start the assembly line. But with thousands of orders to fill, they discovered that the antenna on the device wasn't working properly. They stuck a piece of foam on the circuit board and called it "good enough." Five thousand customers received shiny new Fitbit Trackers just in time for the holidays.

Getting a start-up company off the ground is challenging. Getting a hardware start-up to succeed is near impossible, especially when you're the pioneer. But with so many changes in the marketing environment, Park and Friedman knew they had something special. Pedometers had been selling for years,

following personal fitness and wellness trends. But those devices were low-tech and limited in the information they provided consumers. And with the seemingly endless demand for high-tech gadgetry, Park and Friedman saw big potential for using sensors in small, wearable devices.

The two entrepreneurs were correct. In just seven years, Fitbit has marketed more than a dozen different products and sold millions of units. Last year alone, the company shipped 21 million devices—almost double the previous year's number—ringing up $1.86 billion in revenues and $116 million in profits. Fitbit created what is now a fast-growing segment—wearable tech. Amid its best year to date, Fitbit went public with an initial public offering of $4.1 billion. How did the company go from a balsa wood box to sitting atop an exploding industry? To hear Park tell it, "It was the right product at the right time at the right price point."

A Magical Device

Although Park's response may seem simplistic, it's right on. Coming up with a product that delivers the right benefits to consumers at precisely the time they need them is the key to any new product launch. In Fitbit's case, consumers were hungry for this small device that could not only track steps taken but calculate distance walked, calories burned, floors climbed, and activity duration and intensity, all from an unobtrusive spot—clipped on a pants pocket. What's more, the Fitbit Tracker could track sleep quality based on periods of restlessness, the amount of time before falling asleep, and the amount of time actually sleeping.

Even more enticing to consumers, the device could upload data to a computer and make them available on the Fitbit website. At the site, users could overview their physical activity, set and track goals, and keep logs on food eaten and additional activities not tracked by the device. To top things off, the explosion of social media and sharing personal information went hand in hand with what users were uploading. By design, Park and Friedman put more into Fitbit's software than its own hardware, recognizing that other hardware device companies like Garmin had shortchanged the software aspect.

But Fitbit's success can also be attributed to new models. Recognizing that gadgets have a limited life span and that competition would attempt to improve on its offerings, Fitbit has made development a constant process. From the original Tracker to its current Blaze smartwatch with GPS, heart-rate monitor, and the ability to display smartphone notifications for calls, texts, calendar alerts, Fitbit has stayed ahead in giving consumers what they want.

An Unexpected Opportunity

Still, Fitbit's path to success has been challenging. One big challenge the company has faced from the start is customer retention. Like many diets and pieces of exercise equipment, users are drawn to the "wow" factor of something that can improve their health and wellness but quickly fizzle out. And if users stop using a device, they are far less likely to purchase the "new-and-improved" version, much less recommend it to anyone else. But an interesting thing happened as Fitbit got things rolling. The company received a flood of calls and messages from corporate human resource departments. Perplexed as to why businesses would want to buy Fitbit devices in bulk, the company assigned a point person to find out.

It turned out that corporate America was going through a push to enroll employees in wellness programs. The reasons for this push extended far beyond concerns about employee health and well-being. Healthy employees provide major benefits for a company. They call in sick less often and are generally more productive. They also cost less in terms of health-care benefits. And although diet and exercise can't erase every poor health condition, they can have a big effect on health factors such as blood pressure, cholesterol levels, and blood sugar levels—conditions related to common diseases such as heart disease, stroke, and diabetes. So it's no wonder that companies have an incentive to do whatever they can to motivate employees to take better care of themselves.

As Fitbit talked to companies, it discovered that most were struggling to enroll even a small proportion of employees in their workforce wellness programs—many had less than 20 percent compliance. One problem was that—even as the latest fitness wearables from Fitbit and its competitors were showing up around offices everywhere—participation in corporate wellness programs often required the use of a bulky corporate-issued tracker, better known as an analog pedometer. "Can you imagine asking engineers to wear a janky old pedometer and write down their steps?" mused Amy McDonough, Fitbit's corporate point person. Fitbit, of course, offered a much more high-tech option, letting individuals easily track more complex data and letting HR departments easily compile and analyze the data as well. Fitbit's bulk sales to corporations started rolling in.

Much to Fitbit's pleasant surprise, Fitbit products sold through corporations versus those sold to individuals had noticeably higher retention rates. Fitness trackers in corporate wellness programs were often used in wellness challenges—maintain a minimum of 10,000 steps a day and get free vacation days or a discount on health insurance premiums. It might seem logical that people would stop using their devices once a challenge ended. But when IBM gave out 40,000 Fitbits to employees over a two-year period, it found not only that 96 percent of employees routinely logged their health data and eating habits but that 63 percent of employees continued to wear their Fitbits months after the challenge concluded.

Other companies noted even greater tangible benefits. Cloud-services start-up Appirio bought Fitbit devices for 400 employees. Armed with data from the wearables, Appirio was able to convince its health insurance provider, Anthem, that the increased health benefits were translating into lower health-care costs. This gave Appirio the leverage to negotiate lower premiums, shaving $280,000 off its annual bill.

Today, Fitbit's well division offers tools specifically designed for employers, such as dashboards, dedicated service support, and webinars. Corporate clients include BP America, Kimberly-Clark, Time Warner, and Barclays. Target offered Fitbit Zip trackers to 335,000 of its employees. Corporate sales currently account for 10 percent of Fitbit revenues. But the corporate share of the sales will increase, as adoption in that sector is growing at a faster rate than in consumer markets. Founder Park claims that the use of Fitbits in employee wellness programs is having an impact not only on health and well-being but on job safety as well. Companies have also experienced improvements in office cultures as a result of the unified effort among coworkers to achieve fitness goals together—a factor that is also likely boosting retention numbers in the corporate setting.

Encountering Hurdles

With high growth rates and plenty of market potential, it would seem that the sky is the limit for Fitbit. But Fitbit still faces numerous obstacles. For starters, privacy issues have increased as technology creates new ways to gather and share information. In Fitbit's early days, information logged by users was public by default. That meant that as users integrated their information into social networks, their fitness, eating, sleeping, and in some cases sexual activities were being posted for all to see. That was easily remedied by making "private" the default setting. But general concerns about what happens with uploaded personal data remain, even amid assurances from Fitbit that it does not analyze individual data or sell or share consumer data.

But other privacy matters haven't been so easily managed. Fitness trackers and the data they generate are not regulated. That means that any organization bound by compliance with the U.S. Health Insurance Portability and Accountability Act (HIPAA) has had to tread lightly when adopting a digital tracking device. Fitbit has always been proactive on privacy and information security issues, leading the industry by working with Congress on legislation in this area. Fitbit recently achieved HIPAA compliance, which goes a long way toward putting employers' fears about privacy and security to rest.

But other concerns remain on the part of both employers and employees. Even as Fitbit and its corporate customers do all they can to allay privacy concerns, many employees have expressed concerns that companies will misuse the data. Concern about what data are being collected and how they are being used has led some employees to wonder whether their Fitbits could be telling employers if they are recovering from a wild night of partying, calling in sick when they really aren't, or feeling nervous in a meeting or even if they become pregnant.

Although the overall benefits of integrating a Fitbit device into wellness programs and the associated challenges seem clear, there are negative outcomes as well. Health experts point to the potential for a cultural divide between the "dos" and the "do nots." Employees with disabilities, chronic ailments, or even unhealthy habits may opt out of such programs. Particularly in programs that use leaderboards and group incentives, the result can be to celebrate the fit but demoralize those who are not. And rewards given to those who participate as well as those who succeed are viewed as penalties for those who opt out.

Cheaters are also a concern. Yes, some participants in wellness programs have found ways to fool their Fitbits. For example, a dog can trigger 13,000 to 30,000 steps per day with a Fitbit attached to its collar, easily exceeding the standard 10,000-step goal. Social media sites have erupted with shared practices. "Want to cheat your Fitbit? Try a puppy or a power drill," suggests one Tweet with a link to instructions. Other methods for logging steps include putting it in the dryer, shaking the fist, attaching it to small children, playing the piano, leading music, and whisking a bowl of chocolate-chip cookie batter. Even the vibrations from riding a Harley or a lawnmower can do the trick.

Beyond these concerns that stand in the way of more widespread acceptance and use, perhaps Fitbit's greatest challenge is competition. With a dominant market share in the rapidly growing product category that it created, you might think the Fitbit has it made. However, as digital technologies advance on all fronts, it has become apparent that a fitness tracker is not a product. It's a feature. That became painfully apparent when the Apple Watch hit the market. The Apple Watch wowed the public as a wrist-worn extension of the iPhone with practically unlimited app potential. Its fitness tracking features seemed to minimize those of Fitbit's products. And if Apple can jump Fitbit's train as one simple addition to a far more robust product, what other companies and devices might make their way into Fitbit's territory? And on the software and analytics side, Apple Health and Google Fit seem poised to corner the market with compatibility across mobile platforms.

But Fitbit is hard at work differentiating its wares and positioning itself as more than just a maker of fitness trackers. It has already introduced its own smartwatch. And its "next big leap" is to move beyond fitness tracking into medical diagnosis. By partnering with organizations that can link Fitbit's products with more detailed clinical research, Fitbit devices could soon replace blood glucose meters and even alert users to dangerous health conditions and disease. If Fitbit can successfully position itself on strengths that competitors have a hard time replicating, the sky may be the limit.

Questions for Discussion

3-17 What microenvironmental factors have affected Fitbit since it opened for business?

3-18 What macroenvironmental factors have affected Fitbit?

3-19 How should Fitbit overcome the threats and obstacles it faces?

3-20 What factors in the marketing environment not mentioned in this case could affect Fitbit?

Sources: Based on information from Christina Farr, "Fitbit at Work," *Fast Company*, May 2016, pp. 27–30; Robert Hof, "How Fitbit Survived as a Hardware Startup," *Forbes*, February 4, 2014, www.forbes.com/sites/roberthof/2014/02/04/how-fitbit-survived-as-a-hardware-startup/#5e2a544e4f42; Lance Whitney, "Fitbit Still Tops in Wearables, but Market Share Slips," *Cnet*, February 23, 2016, www.cnet.com/news/fitbit-still-tops-in-wearables-market/; Jen Wieczner, "Fitbit Users Are Finding Creative Ways to Cheat," *Fortune*, June 10, 2016, http://fortune.com/2016/06/10/fitbit-hack-cheat/.

MyMarketingLab

Go to **mymktlab.com** for Auto-graded writing questions as well as the following Assisted-graded writing questions:

3-21 What is environmental sustainability and why has it grown in importance for marketers?

3-22 Discuss a recent change in the technological environment that impacts marketing. How has it affected buyer behavior and how has it changed marketing?

PART 1: Defining Marketing and the Marketing Process (Chapters 1–2)
PART 2: Understanding the Marketplace and Consumer Value (Chapters 3–6)
PART 3: Designing a Customer Value–Driven Strategy and Mix (Chapters 7–17)
PART 4: Extending Marketing (Chapters 18–20)

4 Managing Marketing Information
to Gain Customer Insights

CHAPTER PREVIEW

In this chapter, we continue our exploration of how marketers gain insights into consumers and the marketplace. We look at how companies develop and manage information about important marketplace elements: customers, competitors, products, and marketing programs. To succeed in today's marketplace, companies must know how to turn mountains of marketing information into fresh customer insights that will help them engage customers and deliver greater value to them.

Let's start with a story about marketing research and customer insights in action. Over the past decade, The LEGO Group has used innovative marketing research to gain deep insights into how children really play and then used those insights to create compelling play experiences for children all over the world. In the process, it has rescued itself from near bankruptcy to become the world's biggest toy maker. As one analyst puts it, The LEGO Group has now become "the Apple of Toys."

THE LEGO GROUP: Digging Out Fresh Customer Insights

Classic LEGO plastic bricks have been fixtures in homes around the world for more than 65 years. Last year, The LEGO Group (TLG) produced a record 55 *billion* LEGO bricks, enough to construct a continuous line stretching around the world more than 20 times. It put its popular constructions sets and toys into the eager hands of an estimated 100 million customers annually in 130 countries. TLG is now the world's largest toy company, ahead of competitors Mattel and Hasbro. And whereas Mattel and Hasbro are facing flat or declining sales, TLG's sales are exploding. In the past 10 years, its revenues have quadrupled to more than $5.7 billion, growing nearly 25 percent last year alone.

But just over a decade ago, TLG was near bankruptcy, spiraling downward and losing money at a rate of $1 million a day. The problem: The classic toy company had fallen out of touch with its customers. In the age of the internet, video games, mobile devices, and high-tech playthings, traditional toys such as LEGO bricks had been pushed to the back of the closet. So, in 2004, the company set out to rebuild its aging products and approaches, brick by brick.

The LEGO makeover, however, didn't start with engineers working in design labs. First, TLG had to reconnect with

> The LEGO Group uses innovative marketing research—lots and lots of it—to dig out fresh customer insights, then uses the insights to create irresistible play experiences for children around the world. LEGO is now the world's number-one toy maker.

customers. So it started with marketing research—lots and lots of it—listening to customers and learning in depth how children around the world really play. It created a Global Insights Team, a group of marketing researchers charged with finding innovative new ways to dig out fresh customer insights.

Beyond traditional research methods and data analytics, TLG used innovative immersive research approaches to understand the deeper motivations underlying LEGO purchases and play. For example, TLG research teams conducted up-close-and-personal ethnographic studies. They embedded researchers with families, observed children at play, interviewed their parents, shopped with families, and studied the inside workings of toy stores. This immersive research produced a lot of "Aha! Moments," customer insights that shattered many of the brand's decades-old traditions.

For example, TLG had long held fast to a "keep it simple" mantra. From the beginning, it had offered only basic play sets—bricks, building bases, beams, doors, windows, wheels, and slanting roof tiles—with few or no instructions. The philosophy was that giving children unstructured building sets would stimulate their imaginations and foster creativity. But the research showed that this concept just wasn't cutting it in today's modern, tech-rich world. Today's children get bored easily, and in the current fast-moving environment, they are exposed to many more characters, themes, and technologies. However, counter to previous assumptions that kids seek only instant gratification, TLG found that today's children welcome challenging tasks, such as putting together complex LEGO sets.

Responding to such insights, TLG shifted toward more-specialized, more-structured play experiences. It now churns out a seemingly endless assortment of themed product lines and specific building

The LEGO Group's innovative marketing research produced lots of "Aha! Moments," helping the brand to recast its classic, colorful bricks into modern, tech-rich play experiences for children around the world.
(left) Bloomberg via GettyImages; (right) © incamerastock / Alamy Stock Photo

projects, complete with detailed instructions. So instead of just buying a set of basic square LEGO bricks and building their own houses or cars, children can now buy specialized kits to construct anything from fire trucks and helicopters to crave-worthy ninja castles. To add variety and familiarity, TLG also offers an ever-changing assortment of licensed lines based on everything from *Star Wars* and *DC Comics* to *Marvel Super Heroes* and *Disney Princesses*. And to satisfy children's needs for skill-mastery challenges, TLG has developed involving play experiences such as LEGO MINDSTORMS, a series of building sets complete with hardware and software for making customizable robots that are programmable from a smartphone app. The latest incarnation of LEGO MINDSTORMS, EV3, is a 601-piece kit that includes software, motors, and sensors that control robot movements and speech.

Another customer insight that emerged from the ethnographic research is that kids no longer draw meaningful distinctions between digital and physical play. To children today, the two worlds blend together into one. This insight led to TLG's "One Reality" products, which combine digital and real-world play experiences that involve building with LEGO bricks alongside software running on a phone or tablet app. For example, the LEGO Fusion line lets children build physical models with actual LEGO bricks, scan their creations using a phone or tablet app, and bring them to life in a virtual world. In LEGO Fusion Town Master, for instance, kids create a miniature virtual LEGO city, then run the city as its mayor in an app. Town Master was one of last year's hottest-selling Christmas toys.

TLG's marketing researchers have also discovered important differences between how boys and girls play, leading to the launch of girl-focused lines such as LEGO Friends. Both boys and girls like the construction aspects of LEGO bricks. However, boys tend to be more drawn to narrative—as reflected in popular boy-focused, story-based product lines such as Ninjago and Legends of Chima. In contrast, girls tend to use their sets for role-play, as reflected in the pink- and purple-accented LEGO Friends, which focuses on community and friendship themes. The development of LEGO Friends took four years, based on research involving 3,500 girls and their mothers around the world seeking to understand what girls who had not previously played with LEGO products might want in a construction toy. LEGO Friends has been a major hit with girls in markets ranging from the United States and Germany to China.

Of course, kids aren't the only ones playing with LEGO bricks. The classic brick sets have a huge fan base of adults who never got over the toys of their youth. Hundreds of thousands of AFOLs (Adult Fans of LEGO) around the globe spend large sums on LEGO products. These adults maintain thousands of LEGO fan sites and blogs and organize get-togethers such as the annual BrickFest fan festival. TLG actively taps into the AFOL community for new customer insights and ideas. It has created a roster of customer ambassadors who provide regular input, and it even invites customers to participate directly in the product development process. For example, it once invited 250 LEGO train-set enthusiasts to visit its New York office to assess new designs. The result was the LEGO Santa Fe Super Chief set, which sold out the first 10,000 units in less than two weeks with virtually no marketing. Similarly, TLG used customer co-creation to develop its most popular product ever, LEGO MINDSTORMS.

Thus, over the past decade, thanks to customer insight–driven marketing research, The LEGO Group has reconnected with both its customers and the times. TLG probably knows as much about how children play as any organization on earth, and it has parlayed that knowledge into compelling, profitable play experiences for the world's children. As one analyst concludes, "In the last 10 years, LEGO has grown into nothing less than the Apple of Toys: a profit-generating, design-driven miracle built around premium, intuitive, highly covetable [play experiences that its young] fans can't get enough of."[1]

OBJECTIVES OUTLINE

OBJECTIVE 4-1	Explain the importance of information in gaining insights about the marketplace and customers. **Marketing Information and Customer Insights** *(pp 100–102)*
OBJECTIVE 4-2	Define the marketing information system and discuss its parts. **Assessing Information Needs and Developing Data** *(pp 102–106)*
OBJECTIVE 4-3	Outline the steps in the marketing research process. **Marketing Research** *(pp 106–116)*
OBJECTIVE 4-4	Explain how companies analyze and use marketing information. **Analyzing and Using Marketing Information** *(pp 116–120)*
OBJECTIVE 4-5	Discuss the special issues some marketing researchers face, including public policy and ethics issues. **Other Marketing Information Considerations** *(pp 120–125)*

AS THE LEGO STORY highlights, good products and marketing programs begin with good customer information. Companies also need an abundance of information on competitors, resellers, and other actors and marketplace forces. But more than just gathering information, marketers must *use* the information to gain powerful *customer and market insights*.

> **Author Comment** | Marketing information by itself has little value. The value is in the *customer insights* gained from the information and how marketers use these insights to make better decisions.

Marketing Information and Customer Insights

To create value for customers and build meaningful relationships with them, marketers must first gain fresh, deep insights into what customers need and want. Such customer insights come from good marketing information. Companies use these customer insights to develop a competitive advantage.

For example, when it began six years ago, social media site Pinterest needed to differentiate itself from the dozens, even hundreds, of existing social networking options.[2]

Pinterest's research uncovered a key customer insight: Many people want more than just Twitter- or Facebook-like places to swap messages and pictures. They want a way to collect, organize, and share things on the internet related to their interests and passions. So Pinterest created a social scrapbooking site where people can create and share digital pinboards—theme-based image collections of things that inspire them. "Pinterest is your own little internet of only the things you love," says the company.

Thanks to this unique customer insight, Pinterest has been wildly popular. Today, more than 100 million active monthly Pinterest users collectively pin more than 5 million articles a day and view more than 2.5 billion Pinterest pages a month. In turn, more than a half-million businesses use Pinterest to engage and inspire their customer communities. For example, L.L.Bean has 5.1 million Pinterest followers, Nordstrom has 4.3 million followers, and Lowe's has 3.4 million followers. Some 47 percent of U.S. online shoppers have purchased something as a result of a Pinterest recommendation.

Although customer and market insights are important for building customer value and engagement, these insights can be very difficult to obtain. Customer needs and buying motives are often anything but obvious—consumers themselves usually can't tell you exactly what they need and why they buy. To gain good customer insights, marketers must effectively manage marketing information from a wide range of sources.

Marketing Information and Today's "Big Data"

With the recent explosion of information technologies, companies can now generate and find marketing information in great quantities. The marketing world is filled to the brim with information from innumerable sources. Consumers themselves are now generating tons of marketing information. Through their smartphones, PCs, and tablets—via online browsing and blogging, apps and social media interactions, texting and video, and geolocation data—consumers now volunteer a tidal wave of bottom-up information to companies and to each other.

Far from lacking information, most marketing managers are overloaded with data and often overwhelmed by it. This problem is summed up in the concept of **big data**. The term *big data* refers to the huge and complex data sets generated by today's sophisticated information generation, collection, storage, and analysis technologies. Every year, the people and systems of the world generate about a trillion gigabytes of information. That's enough data to fill 2.47 trillion good old CD-ROMs, a stack tall enough to go to the moon and back four times. A full 90 percent of all the data in the world has been created in just the past two years.[3]

Big data presents marketers with both big opportunities and big challenges. Companies that effectively tap this glut of data can gain rich, timely customer insights. However, accessing and sifting through so much data is a daunting task. For example, when a large consumer brand such as Coca-Cola or Apple monitors online discussions about its brand in tweets, blogs, social media posts, and other sources, it might take in a stunning 6 million public conversations a day, more than 2 billion a year. That's far more information than any manager can digest. Thus, marketers don't need *more* information; they need *better* information. And they need to make better *use* of the information they already have.

Managing Marketing Information

The real value of marketing information lies in how it is used—in the **customer insights** that it provides. Based on such thinking, companies ranging from PepsiCo, Starbucks, and McDonald's to Google and GEICO have restructured their marketing information and research functions. They have created *customer insights teams*, whose job it is to develop actionable insights from marketing information and work strategically with marketing decision makers to apply those insights. Consider PepsiCo:[4]

> Years ago, PepsiCo's various marketing research departments were mainly data providers. But not anymore. Today they are integrated "customer insights teams" charged with delivering insights at the center of the brand, the business, and consumers. The teams gather insights from a rich and constantly evolving variety of sources—ranging from grocery store cash registers, focus groups and surveys, and subconscious measures to mingling with and observing customers in person and monitoring their digital and social media behaviors. The teams continually evaluate new methods for uncovering consumer truths that might predict market behavior. Then the insights teams use the data and observations, tempered by intuitive judgment, to form actionable consumer insights with real business implications. Finally, they share these insights with brand teams from Pepsi, Mountain Dew, Aquafina, and other PepsiCo brands to help them make better decisions.
>
> Beyond just transmitting data and findings through traditional fact-based presentations, reports, and spreadsheets, the Consumer Insights teams share their insights in more engaging, accessible, and digestible ways. ● For example, the PepsiCo North America Beverages (NAB) Consumer Insights team has even developed a consumer insights app that disseminates custom-designed data and content to marketing and brand decision makers. More than just collecting and distributing data, the PepsiCo consumer insights teams are strategic marketing partners. "We drive decisions that ultimately lead to sustainable growth," says a senior PepsiCo consumer strategy and insights executive. "And everything we do impacts the bottom line."

Thus, companies must design effective marketing information systems that give managers the right information, in the right form, at the right time and help them to use this information to create customer value, engagement, and stronger customer relationships. A **marketing information system (MIS)** consists of people and procedures dedicated to assessing information needs, developing the needed information, and helping decision makers use the information to generate and validate actionable customer and market insights.

Big data
The huge and complex data sets generated by today's sophisticated information generation, collection, storage, and analysis technologies.

Customer insights
Fresh marketing information-based understandings of customers and the marketplace that become the basis for creating customer value, engagement, and relationships.

Marketing information system (MIS)
People and procedures dedicated to assessing information needs, developing the needed information, and helping decision makers to use the information to generate and validate actionable customer and market insights.

● **Consumer insights: PepsiCo's "consumer insights teams" wring actionable insights out of the glut of marketing data. They have even developed a consumer insights app to share custom-designed content with brand decision makers.**

PepsiCo

● **Figure 4.1** shows that the MIS begins and ends with information users—marketing managers, internal and external partners, and others who need marketing information and insights. First, it interacts with these information users to assess information needs. Next, it interacts with the marketing environment to develop needed information through internal company databases, marketing intelligence activities, and marketing research. Finally, the MIS helps users to analyze and use the information to develop customer insights, make marketing decisions, and manage customer engagement and relationships.

Assessing Information Needs and Developing Data

Assessing Marketing Information Needs

> Author Comment | The marketing information system begins and ends with users—assessing their information needs and then delivering information and insights that meet those needs.

The marketing information system primarily serves the company's marketing and other managers. However, it may also provide information to external partners, such as suppliers, resellers, or marketing services agencies. For example, Walmart's Retail Link system gives key suppliers access to information on everything from customers' buying patterns and store inventory levels to how many items they've sold in which stores in the past 24 hours.[5]

A good marketing information system balances the information users would *like* to have against what they really *need* and what is *feasible* to offer. Some managers will ask for whatever information they can get without thinking carefully about what they really need. And in this age of big data, some managers will want to collect and store vast amounts of digital data simply because technology lets them. But too much information can be as harmful as too little. In contrast, other managers may omit things they ought to know, or they may not know to ask for some types of information they should have. The MIS must monitor the marketing environment to provide decision makers with information and insights they should have to make key marketing decisions.

Finally, the costs of obtaining, analyzing, storing, and delivering information can mount quickly. The company must decide whether the value of insights gained from additional information is worth the costs of providing it, and both value and cost are often hard to assess.

> Author Comment | The problem isn't *finding* information; in this "big data" age, the world is bursting with information from a glut of sources. The real challenge is to find the *right* information—from inside and outside sources—and turn it into customer insights.

Developing Marketing Information

Marketers can obtain the needed information from *internal data, marketing intelligence,* and *marketing research.*

● **FIGURE | 4.1**
The Marketing
Information System

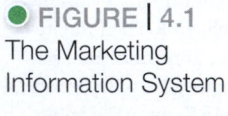

This chapter is all about managing marketing information to gain customer insights. And this important figure organizes the entire chapter. Marketers start by assessing user information needs. Then they develop the needed information using internal data, marketing intelligence, and marketing research processes. Finally, they make the information available to users in the right form at the right time.

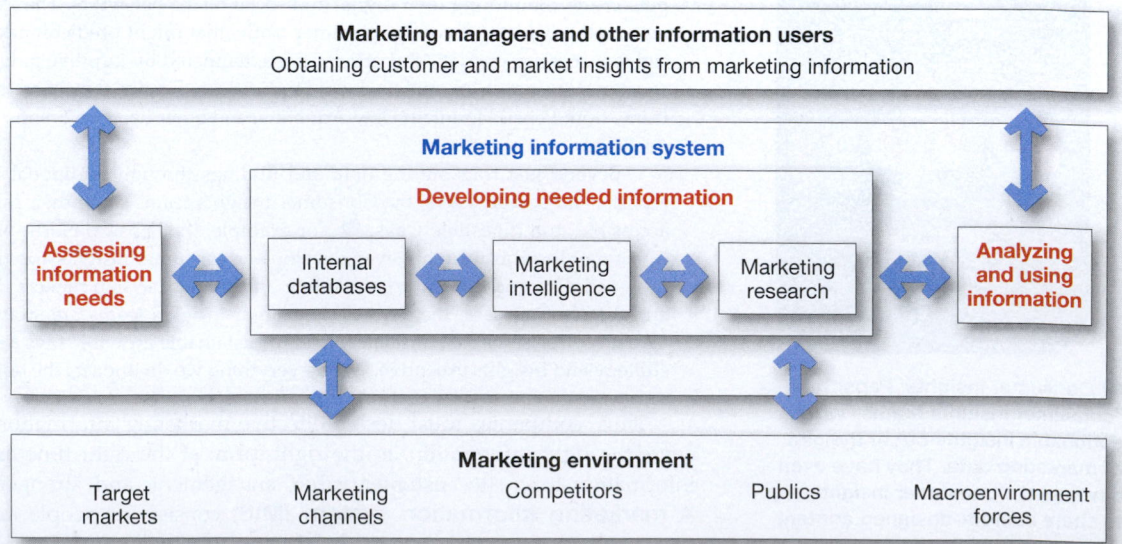

Internal Data

Internal databases
Collections of consumer and market information obtained from data sources within the company network.

Many companies build extensive **internal databases**, collections of consumer and market information obtained from data sources within the company's network. Information in an internal database can come from many sources. The marketing department furnishes information on customer characteristics, in-store and online sales transactions, and web and social media site visits. The customer service department keeps records of customer satisfaction or service problems. The accounting department provides detailed records of sales, costs, and cash flows. Operations reports on production, shipments, and inventories. The sales force reports on reseller reactions and competitor activities, and marketing channel partners provide data on sales transactions. Harnessing such information can provide powerful customer insights and competitive advantage.

For example, insurance and financial services provider USAA uses its internal database to create an incredibly loyal customer base:[6]

● **Internal data: Financial services provider USAA uses its extensive database to tailor its services to the specific needs of individual customers, creating incredible loyalty.**

Courtney Young

● USAA provides financial services to U.S. military personnel and their families, largely through direct marketing via the phone, the internet, and mobile channels. It maintains a huge customer database built from customer purchasing histories and information collected directly through customer surveys, transaction data, and browsing behavior at its online sites. USAA uses the database to tailor direct marketing offers to the needs of individual customers. For example, for customers looking toward retirement, it sends information on estate planning. If the family has college-age children, USAA sends those children information on how to manage their credit cards.

One delighted reporter, a USAA customer, recounts how USAA even helped him teach his 16-year-old daughter to drive. Just before her birthday, but before she received her driver's license, USAA sent a "package of materials, backed by research, to help me teach my daughter how to drive, help her practice, and help us find ways to agree on what constitutes safe driving later on, when she gets her license." Through such skillful use of its database, USAA serves each customer uniquely, resulting in legendary levels of customer satisfaction and loyalty. More important, the $24 billion company retains 98 percent of its customers.

Internal databases usually can be accessed more quickly and cheaply than other information sources, but they also present some problems. Because internal information is often collected for other purposes, it may be incomplete or in the wrong form for making marketing decisions. Data also age quickly; keeping the database current requires a major effort. Finally, managing and mining the mountains of information that a large company produces require highly sophisticated equipment and techniques.

Competitive Marketing Intelligence

Competitive marketing intelligence
The systematic monitoring, collection, and analysis of publicly available information about consumers, competitors, and developments in the marketing environment.

Competitive marketing intelligence is the systematic monitoring, collection, and analysis of publicly available information about consumers, competitors, and developments in the marketplace. The goal of competitive marketing intelligence is to improve strategic decision making by understanding the consumer environment, assessing and tracking competitors' actions, and providing early warnings of opportunities and threats. Marketing intelligence techniques range from observing consumers firsthand to quizzing the company's own employees, benchmarking competitors' products, online research, and monitoring social media buzz.

Good marketing intelligence can help marketers gain insights into how consumers talk about and engage with their brands. Many companies send out teams of trained observers to mix and mingle personally with customers as they use and talk about the company's products. Other companies—such as PepsiCo, Mastercard, Kraft, and Dell—have set up sophisticated digital command centers that routinely monitor brand-related online consumer and marketplace activity (see Real Marketing 4.1).

4.1 Social Media Command Centers: Listening to and Engaging Customers in Social Space

Today's social space is alive with buzz about brands and related happenings and trends. As a result, many companies are now setting up state-of-the-art social media command centers with which they track or even help shape the constant barrage of social media activity surrounding their brands.

Some social media command centers are event-specific. For example, Jaguar set up "The Villain's Lair," a social media command center for the express purpose of managing engagement with its Super Bowl ads featuring famous movie villains. But many other organizations, ranging from financial institutions and consumer products companies to not-for-profit organizations, have opened permanent digital command centers to harness the power of today's burgeoning social media chatter.

For example, Mastercard's digital intelligence command center—called the Conversation Suite—monitors, analyzes, and responds in real time to millions of online conversations around the world. It monitors online brand-related conversations across 43 markets and 26 languages. It tracks social networks, blogs, online and mobile video, and traditional media—any and every digital place that might contain relevant content or commentary on Mastercard.

At Mastercard's Purchase, New York, headquarters, Conversation Suite staff huddle with managers from various Mastercard departments and business units in front of a giant 40-foot LED screen that displays summaries of ongoing global brand conversations, refreshed every four minutes. A rotating group of marketing and customer service people spends two or three hours a day in the command center. "It's a real-time focus group," says a Mastercard marketing executive. "We track all mentions of Mastercard and any of our products, plus the competition."

Mastercard uses what it sees, hears, and learns in the Conversation Suite to improve its products and marketing, track brand performance, and spark meaningful customer conversations and engagement. Mastercard is even training "social ambassadors," who can join online conversations and engage customers and brand influencers directly. "Today, almost everything we do [across the company] is rooted in insights we're gathering

from the Conversation Suite," says another manager. "[It's] transforming the way we do business."

PepsiCo's Gatorade was one of the first brands to set up a social media command center, called Gatorade Mission Control. The center conducts extensive real-time monitoring of brand-related social media activity. Whenever someone mentions anything related to Gatorade (including competitors, Gatorade athletes, and sports nutrition-related topics) on major social media or blogs, it pops up in various visualizations and dashboards on one of six big screens. Gatorade Mission Control staffers also monitor digital ad, web, and mobile site traffic, producing a consolidated picture of the brand's internet image. Gatorade uses what it sees and learns at the center to improve its products, marketing, and interactions with customers.

Gatorade Mission Control also lets the brand engage consumers in real time, sometimes adding to or even shaping the online discourse. For example, during Game One of the 2014 NBA Finals, when then-Miami Heat forward LeBron James was carried off the court with leg cramps, Twitter exploded with comments that Gatorade had failed

to prevent James's cramps. Although the former Gatorade spokesman had recently switched to rival Powerade, a Coca-Cola brand, most fans still associated King James with Gatorade. However, at the same time that fans were tweeting concerns about the brand, the Gatorade Mission Control team was countering with its own humorous responses, such as "The person cramping isn't our client. Our athletes can take the Heat." When one fan tweet asked where Gatorade was when LeBron James needed it, the team replied, "Waiting on the sidelines, but he prefers to drink something else." Thus, real-time social media monitoring helped Gatorade turn potentially negative online chatter into a game-winning shot at the buzzer.

All kinds of organizations are now setting up social media command centers, even not-for-profits. For example, the American Red Cross partnered with Dell to create its Digital Operations Center in Washington, DC, which helps the humanitarian relief organization improve its responses to emergencies and natural disasters. The Red Cross got serious about monitoring social media after an opinion poll revealed that 80 percent of Americans expect emergency responders

Competitive marketing intelligence: Mastercard's digital intelligence command center—called the Conversation Suite—monitors, analyzes, and responds in real time to millions of brand-related conversations across 43 markets and 26 languages around the world.

Mastercard

to monitor social networks, and one-third presumed that they could get help during a disaster within an hour if they posted or tweeted a request. Modeled after Dell's own iconic social media center, the Red Cross Digital Operations Center broke new ground with an innovative digital volunteer program, adding thousands of trained volunteers around the country to help handle the massive volume of social media traffic that occurs during a disaster.

The Digital Operations Center helps improve the Red Cross's everyday relief efforts, such as responses to an apartment fire in a large metropolitan area. "Not only are we scanning the social media landscape looking for actionable intelligence," says a Red Cross manager, "we are also scanning the social space to see if there are people out there who need information and emotional support."

But it's the major disasters that highlight the center's biggest potential. For example, during the week of Hurricane Sandy, one of the biggest natural disasters in U.S. history, the Digital Operations Center played a crucial role in directing Red Cross relief efforts. In addition to the usual data from government partners, on-the-ground assessments, and damage reports from traditional media, the center pored through and acted on millions tweets, Facebook posts, blog entries, and

photos posted online. In all, it tracked more than 2 million posts and responded directly to thousands of people. In at least 88 cases, social media posts had a direct effect on Red Cross actions. "We put trucks in areas where we saw a greater need, we moved cots to a shelter where we needed more supplies," says the Red Cross manager. Even a lack of social media activity was an important indicator. A social media "black hole" in a specific area probably meant that factors were preventing people in that area from tweeting and that they needed help.

So whether it's Mastercard, Gatorade, or the American Red Cross, a social media

command center can help marketers scour the digital environment, analyze brand-related conversations in real time to gain marketing insights, and respond quickly and appropriately. Ultimately, social media listening gives consumers another voice, to the benefit of both customers and the brand. "It enables us to give the public a seat at our response table," says the Red Cross manager. Wells Fargo's Director of Social Media agrees: "Consumers want to be a part of how companies serve them," she says. "Our nirvana is that if someone offers us an idea, tip, or feedback that really helps us, we respond directly."

Sources: "Mastercard Conversation Suite Video," http://newsroom.mastercard.com/videos/mastercard-conversation-suite-video/, accessed September 2016; Sheila Shayon, "Mastercard Harnesses the Power of Social with Innovative Conversation Suite," *brandchannel,* May 7, 2013, www.brandchannel.com/home/post/2013/05/07/Mastercard-Conversation-Suite-050713.aspx; Giselle Abramovich, "Inside Mastercard's Social Command Center," *Digiday,* May 9, 2013, http://digiday.com/brands/inside-mastercards-social-command-center/; Anthony Shop, "Social Media Lessons from Gatorade Mission Control," *Socialmediadriver.com,* August 28, 2013, http://socialdriver.com/2013/08/28/social-media-lessons-from-gatorade-mission-control/; Evan Hanson, "PepsiCo Drinks In Gatorade's Social Media Performance at Game One of NBA Finals," *24/7 Wallstreet,* June 7, 2014, http://247wallst.com/general/2014/06/07/pepsico-drinks-in-gatorades-social-media-performance-at-game-one-of-nba-finals/#ixzz3O6SWtQJt; Ariel Schwartz, "How the Red Cross Used Tweets to Save Lives during Hurricane Sandy," *Fast Company,* October 31, 2013, www.fastcoexist.com/3020923/how-the-red-cross-used-tweets-to-save-lives-during-hurricane-sandy; "Gatorade Mission Control," *YouTube,* www.youtube.com/watch?v=YPBUZOX36DQ, accessed September 2016; and "Examples of Ten Social Media Command Centers," *Salesforce,* www.exacttarget.com/sites/exacttarget/files/10-Examples-of-Social-Media-Command-Centers.pdf, accessed June 2016.

Companies also need to actively monitor competitors' activities. They can monitor competitors' web and social media sites. For example, Amazon's Competitive Intelligence arm routinely purchases merchandise from competing sites to analyze and compare their assortment, speed, and service quality. Companies can use the internet to search specific competitor names, events, or trends and see what turns up. And tracking consumer conversations about competing brands is often as revealing as tracking conversations about the company's own brands.

Firms use competitive marketing intelligence to gain early insights into competitor moves and strategies and to prepare quick responses. For example, Samsung routinely monitors real-time social media activity surrounding the introductions of Apple's latest iPhones, iPads, and other devices to quickly shape marketing responses for its own Galaxy S smartphones and tablets. At the same time that Apple CEO Tim Cook is onstage unveiling the latest much-anticipated new models, Samsung marketing strategists are huddled around screens in a war room hundreds of miles away watching the introductions unfold. They carefully monitor not only each new device feature as it is presented but also the gush of online consumer commentary flooding blogs and social media channels. Even as the real-time consumer and competitive data surge in, the Samsung team is drafting responses. Within only a few days, just as Apple's new models are hitting store shelves, Samsung is already airing TV, print, and social media responses that rechannel the excitement toward its own Galaxy line.

Much competitor intelligence can be collected from people inside the company—executives, engineers and scientists, purchasing agents, and the sales force. The company can also obtain important intelligence information from suppliers, resellers, and key customers. Intelligence seekers can also pour through any of thousands of online databases. Some are free. For example, the U.S. Security and Exchange Commission's database provides a huge stockpile of financial information on public competitors, and the U.S.

Patent Office and Trademark database reveals patents that competitors have filed. For a fee, companies can also subscribe to any of the more than 3,000 online databases and information search services, such as Hoover's, LexisNexis, and Dun & Bradstreet. Today's marketers have an almost overwhelming amount of competitor information only a few keystrokes away.

The intelligence game goes both ways. Facing determined competitive marketing intelligence efforts by competitors, most companies take steps to protect their own information. One self-admitted corporate spy advises that companies should try conducting marketing intelligence investigations of themselves, looking for potentially damaging information leaks. They should start by "vacuuming up" everything they can find in the public record, including job postings, court records, company advertisements and blogs, web pages, press releases, online business reports, social media postings by customers and employees, and other information available to inquisitive competitors.[7]

The growing use of marketing intelligence also raises ethical issues. Some intelligence-gathering techniques may involve questionable ethics. Clearly, companies should take advantage of publicly available information. However, they should not stoop to snoop. With all the legitimate intelligence sources now available, a company does not need to break the law or accepted codes of ethics to get good intelligence.

> Author Comment | Whereas marketing intelligence involves actively scanning the general marketing environment, marketing research involves more focused studies to gain customer insights related to specific marketing decisions.

Marketing Research

In addition to marketing intelligence information about general consumer, competitor, and marketplace happenings, marketers often need formal studies that provide customer and market insights for specific marketing situations and decisions. For example, Starbucks wants to know how customers would react to a new breakfast menu item. Yahoo! wants to know how web searchers will react to a proposed redesign of its site. Or Samsung wants to know how many and what kinds of people will buy its next-generation, ultrathin televisions. In such situations, managers will need marketing research.

Marketing research
The systematic design, collection, analysis, and reporting of data relevant to a specific marketing situation facing an organization.

Marketing research is the systematic design, collection, analysis, and reporting of data relevant to a specific marketing situation facing an organization. Companies use marketing research in a wide variety of situations. For example, marketing research gives marketers insights into customer motivations, purchase behavior, and satisfaction. It can help them to assess market potential and market share or measure the effectiveness of pricing, product, distribution, and promotion activities.

Some large companies have their own research departments that work with marketing managers on marketing research projects. In addition, these companies—like their smaller counterparts—frequently hire outside research specialists to consult with management on specific marketing problems and to conduct marketing research studies. Sometimes firms simply purchase data collected by outside firms to aid in their decision making.

The marketing research process has four steps (see ● **Figure 4.2**): defining the problem and research objectives, developing the research plan, implementing the research plan, and interpreting and reporting the findings.

Defining the Problem and Research Objectives

Marketing managers and researchers must work together closely to define the problem and agree on research objectives. The manager best understands the decision for which information is needed, whereas the researcher best understands marketing research and how to obtain the information. Defining the problem and research objectives is often the hardest step in the research process. The manager may know that something is wrong without knowing the specific causes.

> This first step is probably the most difficult but also the most important one. It guides the entire research process. It's frustrating and costly to reach the end of an expensive research project only to learn that you've addressed the wrong problem!

● FIGURE | 4.2
The Marketing
Research Process

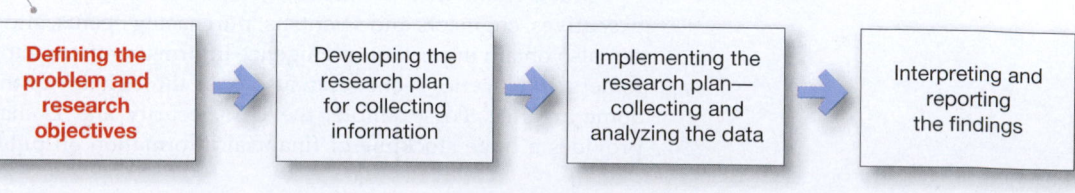

| Defining the problem and research objectives | → | Developing the research plan for collecting information | → | Implementing the research plan—collecting and analyzing the data | → | Interpreting and reporting the findings |

Exploratory research

Marketing research to gather preliminary information that will help define problems and suggest hypotheses.

Descriptive research

Marketing research to better describe marketing problems, situations, or markets, such as the market potential for a product or the demographics and attitudes of consumers.

Causal research

Marketing research to test hypotheses about cause-and-effect relationships.

After the problem has been defined carefully, the manager and the researcher must set the research objectives. A marketing research project might have one of three types of objectives. The objective of **exploratory research** is to gather preliminary information that will help define the problem and suggest hypotheses. The objective of **descriptive research** is to describe things, such as the market potential for a product or the demographics and attitudes of consumers who buy the product. The objective of **causal research** is to test hypotheses about cause-and-effect relationships. For example, would a 10 percent decrease in tuition at a private college result in an enrollment increase sufficient to offset the reduced tuition? Managers often start with exploratory research and later follow with descriptive or causal research.

The statement of the problem and research objectives guides the entire research process. The manager and the researcher should put the statement in writing to be certain that they agree on the purpose and expected results of the research.

Developing the Research Plan

Once researchers have defined the research problem and objectives, they must determine the exact information needed, develop a plan for gathering it efficiently, and present the plan to management. The research plan outlines sources of existing data and spells out the specific research approaches, contact methods, sampling plans, and instruments that researchers will use to gather new data.

Research objectives must be translated into specific information needs. For example, suppose that Chipotle Mexican Grill wants to know how consumers would react to the addition of drive-thru service to its restaurants. U.S. fast-food chains generate an estimated 24 percent of sales through drive-thrus. However, Chipotle—the sustainability-minded fast-casual restaurant that positions itself on "Food With Integrity"—doesn't offer drive-thru service. Adding drive-thrus might help Chipotle leverage its strong brand position and attract new sales. The proposed research might call for the following specific information:

● A decision by Chipotle Mexican Grill to add drive-thru service would call for marketing research that provides lots of specific information.

Chipotle Mexican Grill, Inc.

- ● The demographic, economic, and lifestyle characteristics of current Chipotle customers: Do current counter-service customers also use drive-thrus? Are drive-thrus consistent with their needs and lifestyles? Or would Chipotle need to target a new segment of consumers?
- The characteristics and usage patterns of the broader population of fast-food and fast-casual diners: What do they need and expect from such restaurants? Where, when, and how do they use them, and what existing quality, price, and service levels do they value? The new Chipotle service would require strong, relevant, and distinctive positioning in the crowded fast-food market.
- Impact on the Chipotle customer experience: Would drive-thrus be consistent with a higher-quality fast-casual experience like the one Chipotle offers?
- Chipotle employee reactions to drive-thru service: Would restaurant employees support drive-thrus? Would adding drive-thrus disrupt operations and their ability to deliver high-quality food and service to inside customers?
- Forecasts of both inside and drive-thru sales and profits: Would the new drive-thru service create new sales and customers or simply take sales away from current inside operations?

Chipotle's marketers would need these and many other types of information to decide whether to introduce drive-thru service and, if so, the best way to do it.

The research plan should be presented in a *written proposal*. A written proposal is especially important when the research project is large and complex or when an outside firm carries it out. The proposal should cover the management problems addressed, the research objectives, the information to be obtained, and how the results will help management's decision making. The proposal also should include estimated research costs.

To meet the manager's information needs, the research plan can call for gathering secondary data, primary data, or both. **Secondary data** consist of information that already exists somewhere, having been collected for another purpose. **Primary data** consist of information collected for the specific purpose at hand.

Gathering Secondary Data

Researchers usually start by gathering secondary data. The company's internal database provides a good starting point. However, the company can also tap into a wide assortment of external information sources.

Companies can buy secondary data from outside suppliers. For example, Nielsen sells shopper insight data from a consumer panel of more than 250,000 households in 25 countries worldwide, with measures of trial and repeat purchasing, brand loyalty, and buyer demographics. Experian Simmons carries out a full spectrum of consumer studies that provide a comprehensive view of the American consumer. The U.S. Yankelovich MONITOR service by The Futures Company sells information on important social and lifestyle trends. These and other firms supply high-quality data to suit a wide variety of marketing information needs.[8]

Using *commercial online databases*, marketing researchers can conduct their own searches of secondary data sources. ● General database services such as ProQuest and LexisNexis put an incredible wealth of information at the fingertips of marketing decision makers. Beyond commercial services offering information for a fee, almost every industry association, government agency, business publication, and news medium offers free information to those tenacious enough to find their websites or apps.

Internet search engines can also be a big help in locating relevant secondary information sources. However, they can also be very frustrating and inefficient. For example, a Chipotle marketer Googling "fast-food drive-thru" would come up with more than 6.8 million hits. Still, well-structured, well-designed online searches can be a good starting point to any marketing research project.

Secondary data can usually be obtained more quickly and at a lower cost than primary data. Also, secondary sources can sometimes provide data an individual company cannot collect on its own—information that either is not directly available or would be too expensive to collect. For example, it would be too expensive for a consumer products brand such as Coca-Cola or Tide to conduct a continuing retail store audit to find out about the market shares, prices, and displays of its own and competitors' brands. But those marketers can buy store sales and audit data from IRI, which provides data from 34,000 retail stores in markets around the nation.[9]

Secondary data can also present problems. Researchers can rarely obtain all the data they need from secondary sources. For example, Chipotle will not find existing information regarding consumer reactions about new drive-thru service that it has not yet installed. Even when data can be found, the information might not be very usable. The researcher must evaluate secondary information carefully to make certain it is *relevant* (fits the research project's needs), *accurate* (reliably collected and reported), *current* (up-to-date enough for current decisions), and *impartial* (objectively collected and reported).

Secondary data

Information that already exists somewhere, having been collected for another purpose.

Primary data

Information collected for the specific purpose at hand.

● General database services such as Dialog, ProQuest, and LexisNexis put an incredible wealth of information at the fingertips of marketing decision makers.

Primary Data Collection

Secondary data provide a good starting point for research and often help to define research problems and objectives. In most cases, however, the company must also collect primary data. ● Table 4.1 shows that designing a plan for primary data collection calls for a number of decisions on *research approaches, contact methods*, the *sampling plan*, and *research instruments*.

Research Approaches

Research approaches for gathering primary data include observation, surveys, and experiments. We discuss each one in turn.

Observational research
Gathering primary data by observing relevant people, actions, and situations.

Observational Research. **Observational research** involves gathering primary data by observing relevant people, actions, and situations. For example, food retailer Trader Joe's might evaluate possible new store locations by checking traffic patterns, neighborhood conditions, and the locations of competing Whole Foods, Fresh Market, and other retail chains.

Researchers often observe consumer behavior to glean customer insights they can't obtain by simply asking customers questions. For instance, Fisher-Price has established an observation lab in which it can observe the reactions little tots have to new toys. The Fisher-Price Play Lab is a sunny, toy-strewn space where lucky kids get to test Fisher-Price prototypes under the watchful eyes of designers who hope to learn what will get them worked up into a new-toy frenzy. In the lab, some 3,500 kids participate each year testing 1,200 products annually. "Our designers watch and learn from how [children] play," says a Fisher-Price child research manager. "It really helps us make better products."[10]

Marketers not only observe what consumers do but also observe what consumers are saying. As discussed earlier, marketers now routinely listen in on consumer conversations on blogs, social media, and websites. Observing such naturally occurring feedback can provide inputs that simply can't be gained through more structured and formal research approaches.

Ethnographic research
A form of observational research that involves sending trained observers to watch and interact with consumers in their "natural environments."

A wide range of companies now use **ethnographic research**. Ethnographic research involves sending observers to watch and interact with consumers in their "natural environments." The observers might be trained anthropologists and psychologists or company researchers and managers. For example, Coors insights teams frequent bars and other locations in a top-secret small-town location—they call it the "Outpost"—within a day's drive of Chicago. The researchers use the town as a real-life lab, hob-knobbing anonymously with bar patrons, supermarket shoppers, restaurant diners, convenience store clerks, and other townspeople to gain authentic insights into how middle American consumers buy, drink, dine, and socialize around Coors and competing beer brands.[11]

Global branding firm Landor launched Landor Families, an ongoing ethnographic study that has followed 11 French families intensely for the past seven years. Landor researchers visit the families twice a year in their homes, diving deeply into both their refrigerators and their food shopping behaviors and opinions. The researchers also shop with the families at their local supermarkets and look over their shoulders while they shop online. The families furnish monthly online reports detailing their shopping behaviors and opinions. The Landor Families study provides rich behavioral insights for Landor clients such as Danone, Kraft Foods, and Procter & Gamble. Today's big data analytics can provide important insights into the whats, whens, and wheres of consumer buying. The Landor Families

● **Table 4.1 | Planning Primary Data Collection**

Research Approaches	Contact Methods	Sampling Plan	Research Instruments
Observation	Mail	Sampling unit	Questionnaire
Survey	Telephone	Sample size	Mechanical instruments
Experiment	Personal	Sampling procedure	
	Online		

FAMILIES

"THERE IS NO **BETTER** WAY TO **UNDERSTAND** PEOPLE THAN TO ~~FAX~~ OBSERVE THEM IN REAL LIFE."

● The Landor Families ongoing ethnographic study has followed 11 French families intensely for the past seven years, diving deeply into both their refrigerators and their food shopping behaviors. Says Landor, "There is no better way to understand people than to observe them in real life."

Landor

Survey research
Gathering primary data by asking people questions about their knowledge, attitudes, preferences, and buying behavior.

Experimental research
Gathering primary data by selecting matched groups of subjects, giving them different treatments, controlling related factors, and checking for differences in group responses.

program is designed to explore the whys. ● According to Landor, "There is no better way to understand people than to observe them in real life."[12]

Observational and ethnographic research often yields the kinds of details that just don't emerge from traditional research questionnaires or focus groups. Whereas traditional quantitative research approaches seek to test known hypotheses and obtain answers to well-defined product or strategy questions, observational research can generate fresh customer and market insights that people are unwilling or unable to provide. It provides a window into customers' unconscious actions and unexpressed needs and feelings.

However, some things simply cannot be observed, such as attitudes, motives, or private behavior. Long-term or infrequent behavior is also difficult to observe. Finally, observations can be very difficult to interpret. Because of these limitations, researchers often use observation along with other data collection methods.

Survey Research. **Survey research**, the most widely used method for primary data collection, is the approach best suited for gathering descriptive information. A company that wants to know about people's knowledge, attitudes, preferences, or buying behavior can often find out by asking them directly.

The major advantage of survey research is its flexibility; it can be used to obtain many different kinds of information in many different situations. Surveys addressing almost any marketing question or decision can be conducted by phone or mail, online, or in person.

However, survey research also presents some problems. Sometimes people are unable to answer survey questions because they cannot remember or have never thought about what they do and why they do it. People may be unwilling to respond to unknown interviewers or about things they consider private. Respondents may answer survey questions even when they do not know the answer just to appear smarter or more informed. Or they may try to help the interviewer by giving pleasing answers. Finally, busy people may not take the time, or they might resent the intrusion into their privacy.

Experimental Research. Whereas observation is best suited for exploratory research and surveys for descriptive research, **experimental research** is best suited for gathering causal information. Experiments involve selecting matched groups of subjects, giving them different treatments, controlling unrelated factors, and checking for differences in group responses. Thus, experimental research tries to explain cause-and-effect relationships.

For example, before adding a new sandwich to its menu, McDonald's might use experiments to test the effects on sales of two different prices it might charge. It could introduce the new sandwich at one price in one city and at another price in another city. If the cities are similar and if all other marketing efforts for the sandwich are the same, then differences in sales in the two cities could be related to the price charged.

Contact Methods

Information can be collected by mail, by telephone, by personal interview, or online. Each contact method has its own particular strengths and weaknesses.

Mail, Telephone, and Personal Interviewing. *Mail questionnaires* can be used to collect large amounts of information at a low cost per respondent. Respondents may give more honest answers on a mail questionnaire than to an unknown interviewer in person or over the phone. Also, no interviewer is involved to bias respondents' answers. However, mail questionnaires are not very flexible; all respondents answer the same questions in a fixed order. And mail surveys usually take longer to complete and response rates are often low.

As a result, more and more marketers are now shifting to faster, more flexible, and lower-cost email, online, and mobile phone surveys.

Telephone interviewing is one of the best methods for gathering information quickly, and it provides greater flexibility than mail questionnaires. Interviewers can explain difficult questions and, depending on the answers they receive, skip some questions or probe on others. Response rates tend to be higher than with mail questionnaires, and interviewers can ask to speak to respondents with the desired characteristics or even by name.

However, with telephone interviewing, the cost per respondent is higher than with mail, online, or mobile questionnaires. Also, people may not want to discuss personal questions with an interviewer. The method introduces interviewer bias—the way interviewers talk, how they ask questions, and other differences that may affect respondents' answers. Finally, in this age of do-not-call lists and promotion-harassed consumers, potential survey respondents are increasingly hanging up on telephone interviewers rather than talking with them.

Personal interviewing takes two forms: individual interviewing and group interviewing. *Individual interviewing* involves talking with people in their homes or offices, on the street, or in shopping malls. Such interviewing is flexible. Trained interviewers can guide interviews, explain difficult questions, and explore issues as the situation requires. They can show subjects actual products, packages, advertisements, or videos and observe reactions and behavior. However, individual personal interviews may cost three to four times as much as telephone interviews.

Focus Group Interviewing. *Group interviewing* consists of inviting small groups of people to meet with a trained moderator to talk about a product, service, or organization. Participants normally are paid a small sum for attending. A moderator encourages free and easy discussion, hoping that group interactions will bring out deeper feelings and thoughts. At the same time, the moderator "focuses" the discussion—hence the name **focus group interviewing**.

Focus group interviewing
Personal interviewing that involves inviting small groups of people to gather for a few hours with a trained interviewer to talk about a product, service, or organization. The interviewer "focuses" the group discussion on important issues.

In traditional focus groups, researchers and marketers watch the focus group discussions from behind a one-way mirror and video-record sessions for later study. Through videoconferencing and internet technology, marketers in far-off locations can look in and listen, even participate, as a focus group progresses.

Focus group interviewing has become one of the major qualitative marketing research tools for gaining fresh insights into consumer thoughts and feelings. In focus group settings, researchers not only hear consumer ideas and opinions, they also can observe facial expressions, body movements, group interplay, and conversational flows. However, focus group studies present some challenges. They usually employ small samples to keep time and costs down, and it may be hard to generalize from the results. Moreover, consumers in focus groups are not always open and honest about their real feelings, behaviors, and intentions in front of other people.

To overcome these problems, many researchers are tinkering with the focus group design. Some companies are changing the environments in which they conduct focus groups to help consumers relax and elicit more authentic responses. For example, Lexus hosts "An Evening with Lexus" dinners in customers' homes with groups of luxury car buyers to learn up close and personal why they did or did not buy a Lexus. Other companies use *immersion groups*—small groups of consumers who interact directly and informally with product designers without a focus group moderator present.

Research and innovation consultancy The Mom Complex uses such immersion groups to help brand marketers from companies such as Unilever, Johnson & Johnson, Kimberly-Clark, Kellogg, Playskool, and Walmart understand and connect with their "mom customers":[13]

According to The Mom Complex, America's 80 million moms control 85 percent of household purchases, yet three out of four moms say marketers have no idea what it's like to be a mother. To change that, The Mom Complex arranges "Mom Immersion Sessions," in which brand marketers interact directly with groups of mothers, who receive $100 in compensation for a two-hour session. Rather than the usual focus group

New focus group designs: The Mom Complex uses "Mom Immersion Sessions" to help brand marketers understand and connect directly with their "mom customers" on important brand issues.
© caia image/Alamy

practice of putting the marketers behind a one-way mirror to observe groups of moms discussing their brands, the participants and marketers sit in the same room. Guided by a discussion facilitator, the moms begin by educating the marketers about the realities of motherhood—"the raw, real ugly truth about being a mom." Then the moms and marketers work together to address specific brand issues—whether it's new product ideas, current product problems, or positioning and communications strategy. The goal is to "turn the challenges of motherhood into growth opportunities for brands."

Individual and focus group interviews can add a personal touch as opposed to more numbers-oriented, big data research. They can provide rich insights into the motivations and feelings behind the numbers and analytics. "Focus groups are the most widely used qualitative research tool," says one analyst, "and with good reason. They foster fruitful discussion and can provide unique insight into customers' and potential customers' needs, wants, thoughts, and feelings." Things really come to life when you hear people say them.[14]

Online Marketing Research. The internet has had a dramatic impact on how marketing research is conducted. Increasingly, researchers are collecting primary data through **online marketing research**: internet and mobile surveys, online focus groups, consumer tracking, experiments, and online panels and brand communities.

Online research can take many forms. A company can use the internet or mobile technology as a survey medium: It can include a questionnaire on its web or social media sites or use email or mobile devices to invite people to answer questions. It can create online panels that provide regular feedback or conduct live discussions or online focus groups. Researchers can also conduct online experiments. They can experiment with different prices, headlines, or product features on different web or mobile sites or at different times to learn the relative effectiveness of their offers. They can set up virtual shopping environments and use them to test new products and marketing programs. Or a company can learn about the behavior of online customers by following their click streams as they visit the online site and move to other sites.

The internet is especially well suited to *quantitative* research—for example, conducting marketing surveys and collecting data. More than 90 percent of all Americans now use the internet, making it a fertile channel for reaching a broad cross-section of consumers.[15] As response rates for traditional survey approaches decline and costs increase, the internet is quickly replacing mail and the telephone as the dominant data collection methodology.

Internet-based survey research offers many advantages over traditional phone, mail, and personal interviewing approaches. The most obvious advantages are speed and low costs. By going online, researchers can quickly and easily distribute surveys to thousands of respondents simultaneously via email or by posting them on selected online and mobile sites. Responses can be almost instantaneous, and because respondents themselves enter the information, researchers can tabulate, review, and share research data as the information arrives.

Online research also usually costs much less than research conducted through mail, phone, or personal interviews. Using the internet eliminates most of the postage, phone, interviewer, and data-handling costs associated with the other approaches. Moreover, sample size and location have little impact on costs. Once the questionnaire is set up, there's little difference in cost between 10 respondents and 10,000 respondents on the internet or between local or globally distant respondents.

Its low cost puts online research well within the reach of almost any business, large or small. In fact, with the internet, what was once the domain of research experts is now available to almost any would-be researcher. ● Even smaller, less sophisticated researchers can use online survey services such as Snap Surveys (www.snapsurveys.com) and SurveyMonkey (www.surveymonkey.com) to create, publish, and distribute their own custom online or mobile surveys in minutes.

Online marketing research
Collecting primary data through internet and mobile surveys, online focus groups, consumer tracking, experiments, and online panels and brand communities.

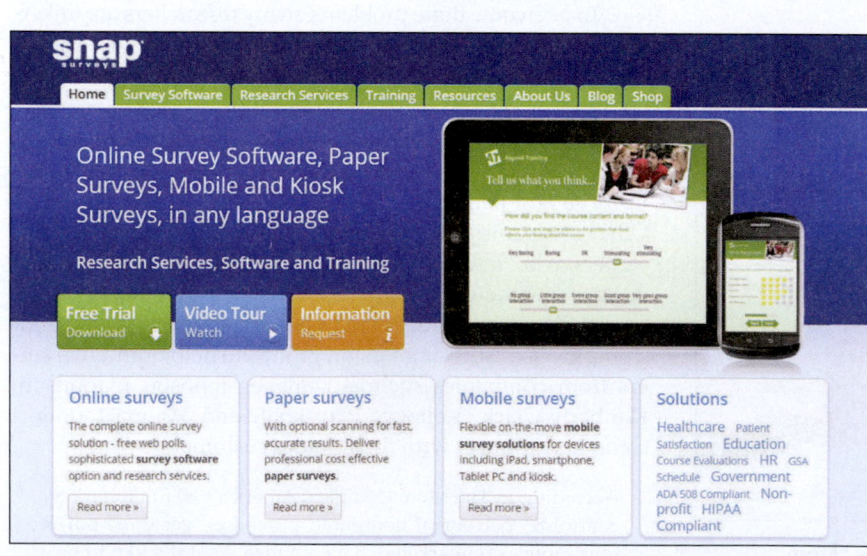

● **Online research: Thanks to survey services such as Snap Surveys, almost any business, large or small, can create, publish, and distribute its own custom online or mobile surveys in minutes.**

Reproduced with permission from Snap Surveys. www.snapsurveys.com

Online focus groups
Gathering a small group of people online with a trained moderator to chat about a product, service, or organization and gain qualitative insights about consumer attitudes and behavior.

Internet-based surveys also tend to be more interactive and engaging, easier to complete, and less intrusive than traditional phone or mail surveys. As a result, they usually garner higher response rates. The internet is an excellent medium for reaching the hard-to-reach consumer—for example, the often-elusive teen, single, affluent, and well-educated audiences. It's also good for reaching people who lead busy lives, from working mothers to on-the-go executives. Such people are well represented online, and they can respond in their own space and at their own convenience.

Just as marketing researchers have rushed to use the internet for quantitative surveys and data collection, they are now also adopting *qualitative* internet-based research approaches, such as online focus groups, blogs, and social networks. The internet can provide a fast, low-cost way to gain qualitative customer insights.

A primary qualitative internet-based research approach is **online focus groups**. ● For example, online research firm FocusVision offers its InterVu service, which harnesses the power of the internet to conduct focus groups with participants at remote locations, anywhere in the world, at any time. Using their own webcams, InterVu participants can log on to focus sessions from their homes or offices and see, hear, and react to each other in real-time, face-to-face discussions.[16] Such focus groups can be conducted in any language and viewed with simultaneous translation. They work well for bringing together people from different parts of the country or world at low cost. Researchers can view the sessions in real time from just about anywhere, eliminating travel, lodging, and facility costs. Finally, although online focus groups require some advance scheduling, results are almost immediate.

● Online focus groups: FocusVision's InterVu service lets focus group participants at remote locations see, hear, and react to each other in real-time, face-to-face discussions.

FocusVision

Although growing rapidly, both quantitative and qualitative internet-based research have some drawbacks. One major problem is controlling who's in the online sample. Without seeing respondents, it's difficult to know who they really are. To overcome such sample and context problems, many online research firms use opt-in communities and respondent panels.

Alternatively, many companies have now developed their own "insight communities" from which they obtain customer feedback and insights. For example, NASCAR has built an online community of 12,000 core fans called the NASCAR Fan Council from which it obtains quick and relevant feedback from fans. Similarly, women's magazine *Allure* formed its own insight community—called Beauty Enthusiasts, now 35,000 members strong—from which it solicits feedback both on its own content and on advertisers' brands. When Beauty Enthusiast members first join the community, they provide detailed information about their demographics, product needs, and preferences. Brands can then interact online with specific segments of the Beauty Enthusiasts community about brand perceptions, product ideas, beauty trends, and marketing moves. Says one analyst, "The feedback combines the precision of quantitative research with the qualitative results of focus groups, as people write their reactions to products in their own words."[17]

Online Behavioral and Social Tracking and Targeting. Thus, in recent years, the internet has become an important tool for conducting research and developing customer insights. But today's marketing researchers are going even further—well beyond online surveys, focus groups, and online communities. Increasingly, they are listening to and watching consumers by actively mining the rich veins of unsolicited, unstructured, "bottom-up" customer information already coursing around the internet. Whereas traditional marketing research provides more logical consumer responses to structured and intrusive research questions, online listening provides the passion and spontaneity of unsolicited consumer opinions.

Tracking consumers online might be as simple as scanning customer reviews and comments on the company's brand site or on shopping sites such as Amazon.com or BestBuy.com. Or it might mean using sophisticated online-analysis tools to deeply analyze the mountains of consumer brand-related comments and messages found in blogs or on social media sites. Listening to and engaging customers online can provide valuable insights into what consumers are saying or feeling about a brand. It can also provide opportunities for building positive brand experiences and relationships. Many companies now excel at listening online and responding quickly and appropriately. As noted previously, more and more companies are setting up social media command centers with which they scour the digital environment and analyze brand-related comments and conversations to gain marketing insights.

Information about what consumers do while trolling the vast digital expanse—what searches they make, the online and mobile sites they visit, how they shop, and what they buy—is pure gold to marketers. And today's marketers are busy mining that gold. Then, in a practice called **behavioral targeting**, marketers use the online data to target ads and offers to specific consumers. For example, if you place an Apple iPad in your Amazon.com shopping cart but don't buy it, you might expect to see some ads for that very type of tablet the next time you visit your favorite ESPN site to catch up on the latest sports scores.

The newest wave of web analytics and targeting takes online eavesdropping even further—from *behavioral* targeting to *social* targeting. Whereas behavioral targeting tracks consumer movements across online sites, social targeting also mines individual online social connections and conversations from social networking sites. Research shows that consumers shop a lot like their friends and are much more likely to respond to ads from brands friends use. So, instead of just having a Zappos.com ad for running shoes pop up because you've recently searched online for running shoes (behavioral targeting), an ad for a specific pair of running shoes pops up because a friend that you're connected to via Twitter just bought those shoes from Zappos.com last week (social targeting).

Behavioral targeting
Using online consumer tracking data to target advertisements and marketing offers to specific consumers.

Online listening, behavioral targeting, and social targeting can help marketers to harness the massive amounts of consumer information swirling around the internet. However, as marketers get more adept at trolling blogs, social networks, and other internet and mobile domains, many critics worry about consumer privacy. ● At what point does sophisticated online research cross the line into consumer stalking? Proponents claim that behavioral and social targeting benefit more than abuse consumers by feeding back ads and products that are more relevant to their interests. But to many consumers and public advocates, following consumers online and stalking them with ads feels more than just a little creepy.

Regulators and others are stepping in. The Federal Trade Commission (FTC) has recommended the creation of a "Do Not Track" system (the online equivalent to the "Do Not Call" registry)—which would let people opt out of having their actions monitored online. However, progress has been mixed. Meanwhile, many major internet browsers and social media have heeded the concerns by adding extended privacy features to their services.[18]

● **Marketers watch what consumers say and do online, then use the resulting insights to personalize online shopping experiences. Is it sophisticated online research or "just a little creepy"?**

Andresr/Shutterstock.com

Sampling Plan

Marketing researchers usually draw conclusions about large groups of consumers by studying a small sample of the total consumer population. A **sample** is a segment of the population selected for marketing research to represent the population as a whole. Ideally, the sample should be representative so that the researcher can make accurate estimates of the thoughts and behaviors of the larger population.

Sample
A segment of the population selected for marketing research to represent the population as a whole.

Designing the sample requires three decisions. First, *who* is to be studied (what *sampling unit*)? The answer to this question is not always obvious. For example, to learn about the decision-making process for a family automobile purchase, should the subject be the husband, the wife, other family members, dealership salespeople, or all of these? Second, *how many* people should be included (what *sample size*)? Large samples give more reliable results than small samples. However, larger samples usually cost more, and it is not necessary to sample the entire target market or even a large portion to get reliable results.

Finally, *how* should the people in the sample be *chosen* (what *sampling procedure*)? ● **Table 4.2** describes different kinds of samples. Using *probability samples*, each population member has a known chance of being included in the sample, and researchers can calculate confidence limits for sampling error. But when probability sampling costs too much or takes too much time, marketing researchers often take *nonprobability samples* even though their sampling error cannot be measured. These varied ways of drawing samples have different costs and time limitations as well as different accuracy and statistical properties. Which method is best depends on the needs of the research project.

● Table 4.2 | Types of Samples

Probability Sample

Simple random sample	Every member of the population has a known and equal chance of selection.
Stratified random sample	The population is divided into mutually exclusive groups (such as age groups), and random samples are drawn from each group.
Cluster (area) sample	The population is divided into mutually exclusive groups (such as blocks), and the researcher draws a sample of the groups to interview.

Nonprobability Sample

Convenience sample	The researcher selects the easiest population members from which to obtain information.
Judgment sample	The researcher uses his or her judgment to select population members who are good prospects for accurate information.
Quota sample	The researcher finds and interviews a prescribed number of people in each of several categories.

Research Instruments

In collecting primary data, marketing researchers have a choice of two main research instruments: *questionnaires* and *mechanical devices*.

Questionnaires. The questionnaire is by far the most common instrument, whether administered in person, by phone, by email, or online. Questionnaires are very flexible—there are many ways to ask questions. Closed-ended questions include all the possible answers, and subjects make choices among them. Examples include multiple-choice questions and scale questions. Open-ended questions allow respondents to answer in their own words. In a survey of airline users, Southwest Airlines might simply ask, "What is your opinion of Southwest Airlines?" Or it might ask people to complete a sentence: "When I choose an airline, the most important consideration is…" These and other kinds of open-ended questions often reveal more than closed-ended questions because they do not limit respondents' answers.

Open-ended questions are especially useful in exploratory research, when the researcher is trying to find out *what* people think but is not measuring *how many* people think in a certain way. Closed-ended questions, on the other hand, provide answers that are easier to interpret and tabulate.

Researchers should also use care in the *wording* and *ordering* of questions. They should use simple, direct, and unbiased wording. Questions should be arranged in a logical order. The first question should create interest if possible, and difficult or personal questions should be asked last so that respondents do not become defensive.

Mechanical Instruments. Although questionnaires are the most common research instrument, researchers also use mechanical instruments to monitor consumer behavior. For example, Nielsen Media Research attaches people meters to television sets in selected homes to record who watches which programs. Retailers use checkout scanners to record shoppers' purchases. Other marketers use mobile phone GPS technologies to track consumer movements in and near their stores.

Still other researchers apply *neuromarketing*, using EEG and MRI technologies to track brain electrical activity to learn how consumers feel and respond. Neuromarketing measures, often combined with *biometric* measures (such as heart rates, respiration rates, sweat levels, and facial and eye movements), can provide companies with insights into what turns consumers on and off regarding their brands and marketing. For example, research firm Nielsen and the Ad Council used neuromarketing to improve the effectiveness of an ad for the Shelter Pet Project, a public service campaign focused on increasing adoption rates for pets in shelters:[19]

● Using neuroscience methods, Nielsen charted how people's brains responded to an existing Shelter Pet Project public service ad and the ad's canine star, Jules the dog. Researchers used a combination of EEG and eye-tracking measurements to determine the second-by-second,

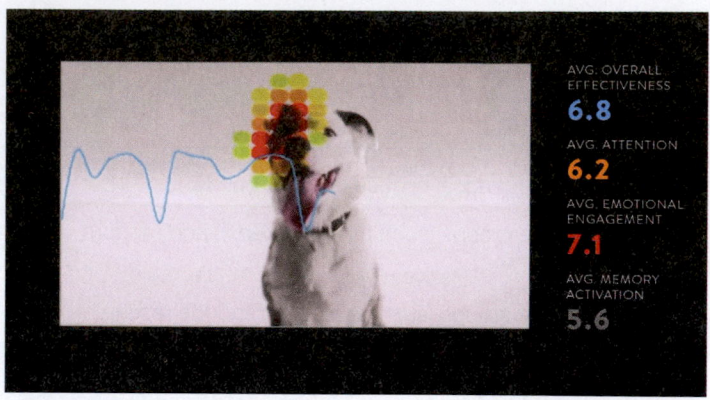

AVG. OVERALL
EFFECTIVENESS
6.8

AVG. ATTENTION
6.2

AVG. EMOTIONAL
ENGAGEMENT
7.1

AVG. MEMORY
ACTIVATION
5.6

● **Neuromarketing helped improve the effectiveness of ads for the Shelter Pet Project, increasing viewer attention, emotional engagement, and memory recall and more than doubling traffic to the organization's website.**

scene-by-scene impact of the ad on viewer attention, emotional engagement, and memory activation. They discovered that viewer attention and emotional engagement jumped when Jules was on the screen. They also learned that the end of the ad caused confusion, with Jules, the logo, and the website URL all competing for viewer attention. The creative team re-edited the ad, increasing Jules's onscreen moments and sharpening the ad's ending and call to action. A second round of neuroscience tests showed that the recrafted ad held viewers' attention better, kept them more consistently engaged, and improved ad recall. As a result, in the first three months after the launch of the refreshed ad, traffic to the Shelter Pet Project website more than doubled, a change that may have real life-or-death implications for shelter pets.

Although neuromarketing techniques can measure consumer involvement and emotional responses second by second, such brain responses can be difficult to interpret. Thus, neuromarketing is usually used in combination with other research approaches to gain a more complete picture of what goes on inside consumers' heads.

Implementing the Research Plan

The researcher next puts the marketing research plan into action. This involves collecting, processing, and analyzing the information. Data collection can be carried out by the company's marketing research staff or outside firms. Researchers should watch closely to make sure that the plan is implemented correctly. They must guard against problems with data collection techniques and technologies, data quality, and timeliness.

Researchers must also process and analyze the collected data to isolate important information and insights. They need to check data for accuracy and completeness and code them for analysis. The researchers then tabulate the results and compute statistical measures.

Interpreting and Reporting the Findings

The market researcher must now interpret the findings, draw conclusions, and report them to management. The researcher should not try to overwhelm managers with numbers and fancy statistical techniques. Rather, the researcher should present important findings and insights that are useful in the major decisions faced by management.

However, interpretation should not be left only to researchers. Although they are often experts in research design and statistics, the marketing manager knows more about the problem and the decisions that must be made. The best research means little if the manager blindly accepts faulty interpretations from the researcher. Similarly, managers may be biased. They might tend to accept research results that show what they expected and reject those that they did not expect or hope for. In many cases, findings can be interpreted in different ways, and discussions between researchers and managers will help point to the best interpretations. Thus, managers and researchers must work together closely when interpreting research results, and both must share responsibility for the research process and resulting decisions.

Author Comment | We've talked generally about managing customer relationships throughout the book. But here, *customer relationship management* (CRM) has a much narrower data-management meaning. It refers to capturing and using customer data from all sources to manage customer interactions, engage customers, and build customer relationships.

Analyzing and Using Marketing Information

Information gathered from internal databases, competitive marketing intelligence, and marketing research usually requires additional analysis. Managers may need help applying the information to gain customer and market insights that will improve their marketing decisions. This help may include advanced analytics to learn more about the relationships within sets of data. Information analysis might also involve the application of analytical models that will help marketers make better decisions.

Once the information has been processed and analyzed, it must be made available to the right decision makers at the right time. In the following sections, we look deeper into analyzing and using marketing information.

Customer Relationship Management (CRM)

The question of how best to analyze and use individual customer data presents special problems. In the current *big data* era, most companies are awash in information about their customers and the marketplace. Still, smart companies capture information at every possible customer *touch point*. These touch points include customer purchases, sales force contacts, service and support calls, web and social media site visits, satisfaction surveys, credit and payment interactions, market research studies—every contact between a customer and a company.

Unfortunately, this information is usually scattered widely across the organization or buried deep in separate company databases. To overcome such problems, many companies are now turning to **customer relationship management (CRM)** to manage detailed information about individual customers and carefully manage customer touch points to maximize customer loyalty.

CRM consists of sophisticated software and analysis tools from companies such as Salesforce.com, Oracle, Microsoft, and SAS that integrate customer and marketplace information from all sources, analyze it, and apply the results to build stronger customer relationships. CRM integrates everything that a company's sales, service, and marketing teams know about individual customers, providing a 360-degree view of the customer relationship. For example, MetLife recently developed a CRM system that it calls "The MetLife Wall":[20]

> One of the biggest customer service challenges for MetLife's sales and service reps used to be quickly finding and getting to customer information—different records, transactions, and interactions stored in dozens of different company data locations and formats. The MetLife Wall solves that problem. The Wall uses a Facebook-like interface to serve up a consolidated view of each MetLife customer's service experience. The innovative CRM system draws customer data from 70 different MetLife systems containing 45 million customer agreements and 140 million transactions. It puts all of a given customer's information and related links into a single record on a single screen, updated in near real time. Now, thanks to The MetLife Wall—with only a single click instead of the 40 clicks it used to take—sales and service reps can see a complete view of a given customer's various policies, transactions, and claims filed and paid along with a history of all the interactions the customer has had with MetLife across the company's many touch points, all on a simple timeline. The Wall has given a big boost to MetLife's customer service and cross-selling efforts. According to a MetLife marketing executive, it's also had "a huge impact on customer satisfaction."

By using CRM to understand customers better, companies can provide higher levels of customer service and develop deeper customer relationships. They can use CRM to pinpoint high-value customers, target them more effectively, cross-sell the company's products, and create offers tailored to specific customer requirements.

Big Data and Marketing Analytics

As noted at the start of the chapter, today's big data can yield big results. But simply collecting and storing huge amounts of data has little value. Marketers must sift through the mountains of data to mine the gems—the bits that yield customer insights. As one marketing executive puts it, "It's actually [about getting] *big insights* from big data. It's throwing away 99.999 percent of that data to find things that are actionable." Says another data expert, "*right* data trumps *big* data."[21] That's the job of *marketing analytics*.

Marketing analytics consists of the analysis tools, technologies, and processes by which marketers dig out meaningful patterns in big data to gain customer insights and gauge marketing performance.[22] Marketers apply marketing analytics to the large and complex sets of data they collect from web, mobile, and social media tracking; customer transactions and engagements; and other big data sources. For example, Netflix maintains a bulging customer database and uses sophisticated marketing analytics to gain insights, which it then uses to fuel recommendations to subscribers, decide what programming to offer, and even develop its own exclusive content in the quest to serve its customers better (see Real Marketing 4.2).

Another good example of marketing analytics in action comes from food products giant Kraft, whose classic brands—from JELL-O, Miracle Whip, and Kraft Macaroni and

---

Customer relationship management (CRM)
Managing detailed information about individual customers and carefully managing customer touch points to maximize customer loyalty.

Marketing analytics
The analysis tools, technologies, and processes by which marketers dig out meaningful patterns in big data to gain customer insights and gauge marketing performance.

Real Marketing

4.2 Netflix Streams Success with Big Data and Marketing Analytics

Americans now watch more movies and TV programs streamed online than they watch on DVDs and Blu-ray discs. And with its rotating library of more than 60,000 titles, Netflix streams more movie and program content by far than any other video service. Netflix's 81.5 million paid subscribers watch some 3.8 billion hours of movies and TV programs every month. A remarkable 51 percent of all Americans have streamed Netflix content during the past year.

All of this comes as little surprise to avid Netflixers. But members might be startled to learn that while they are busy watching Netflix videos, Netflix is busy watching *them*—watching them very, very closely. Netflix tracks and analyzes heaps of customer data in excruciating detail. Then it uses the big data insights to give customers exactly what they want. Netflix knows in depth what its audience wants to watch, and it uses this knowledge to fuel recommendations to subscribers, decide what programming to offer, and even develop its own exclusive content.

No company knows its customers better than Netflix. The company has mind-boggling access to real-time data on member viewing behavior and sentiments. Every day, Netflix tracks and parses member data on tens of millions of searches, ratings, and "plays." Netflix's bulging database contains every viewing detail for each individual subscriber—what shows they watch, at what time of day, on what devices, at what locations, even when they hit the pause, rewind, or fast-forward buttons during programs. Netflix supplements this already-massive database with consumer information purchased from Nielsen, Facebook, Twitter, and other sources. Finally, the company employs experts to classify each video on hundreds of characteristics, such as talent, action, tone, genre, color, volume, scenery, and many, many others. Using this rich base of big data, Netflix builds detailed subscriber profiles based on individual viewing habits and preferences. It then uses these profiles to personalize each customer's viewing experience. According to Netflix, there are 69 million different versions of Netflix, one for each individual subscriber worldwide.

For example, Netflix uses data on viewing history to make personalized recommendations.

Wading through 60,000 titles to decide what to watch can be overwhelming. So when new customers sign up, Netflix asks them to rate their interest in movie and TV genres and to rate specific titles they have already seen. It then cross-references what people like with other similar titles to predict additional movies or programs customers will enjoy.

But that's just the beginning. As customers watch and rate more and more video content, and as Netflix studies the details of their viewing behavior, the predictions become more and more accurate. Netflix often comes to know individual customer viewing preferences better than customers themselves do. How accurate are Netflix's recommendations? Seventy-five percent of viewing activity results from these suggestions. That's important. The more subscribers watch, the more likely they are to stay with Netflix—viewers who watch at least 15 hours of content each month are 75 percent less likely to cancel. Accurate recommendations increase average viewing time, keeping subscribers in the fold.

Increased viewing also depends on offering the right content in the first place. But adding new programming is expensive—content licensing fees constitute the lion's share of Netflix's cost of goods sold. With so many new and existing movies and TV programs on the market, Netflix must be very selective in what it adds to its content inventory. Once again, it's big data and marketing analytics to the rescue. Just as Netflix analyzes its database to come up with subscriber recommendations, it uses the data to assess what additional titles customers might enjoy and how much each is worth. The goal is to maximize subscriber "happiness-per-dollar-spent" on new titles. "We always use our in-depth knowledge about what our members love to watch to decide what's available on Netflix," says a Netflix marketer. "If you keep watching, we'll keep adding more of what you love."

To get even more viewers watching even more hours, Netflix uses its extensive big data insights to add its own exclusive video content—things you can see only on Netflix. In its own words, Netflix wants "to become HBO faster than HBO can become Netflix." For example, Netflix stunned the media industry when it outbid both HBO and AMC by paying a stunning $100 million for exclusive rights to air the first two seasons of *House of Cards*, a U.S. version of a hit British political drama produced by Hollywood bigwigs David Fincher and Kevin Spacey.

Netflix, big data, and CRM: While members are busy watching Netflix videos, Netflix is busy watching *them*—watching them very, very closely. Then it uses the big data insights to give customers exactly what they want.

© OJO Images Ltd/Alamy (photo); PR NEWSWIRE (logo)

To outsiders, the huge investment in *House of Cards* seemed highly risky. However, using its powerful database, Netflix was able to predict accurately which and how many existing members would watch the new *House of Cards* regularly and how many new members would sign up because of the show. Netflix also used its viewer knowledge to pinpoint and personalize promotion of the exclusive series to just the right members. Before *House of Cards* premiered, based on their profiles, selected subscribers saw one of 10 different trailers of the show aimed at their specific likes and interests.

Thanks to Netflix's big data and marketing analytics prowess, *House of Cards* was a smash hit. It brought in 3 million new subscribers in only the first three months. These new subscribers alone covered almost all of the $100 million investment. More important, a Netflix survey revealed that for the average *House of Cards* viewer, 86 percent were less likely to cancel because of the new program. Such success came as no surprise to Netflix. Its data had predicted that the

program would be a hit before the director ever shouted "action."

Based on the success of *House of Cards*, Netflix has developed a number of other original series, including *Hemlock Grove, Lillyhammer, Orange Is the New Black, Bad Samaritans, Marco Polo*, and the animated series *BoJack Horseman*. For traditional broadcast networks, the average success rate for new television shows is 35 percent. In contrast, Netflix is batting almost 70 percent. To continue the momentum, Netflix committed to spending a dazzling $6 billion in new original content in 2016. Such investments promise an ever-growing slate of new and continuing

Netflix original series, specials, documentaries, and films.

As more and more high-quality video streams out of Netflix, more success streams in. Netflix's sales have surged 36 percent during the past two years. Last year alone, membership grew by more than 20 percent. Netflix thrives on using big data and marketing analytics to know and serve its customers. The company excels at helping customers figure out just what they want to watch and offering just the right content profitably. Says Netflix's chief communications officer, "Because we have a direct relationship with consumers, we *know* what people like to watch, and that helps us [immeasurably]."

Sources: Shalini Ramachandram, "Netflix Drops on Weak-Growth Forecast," *Wall Street Journal*, April 19, 2016, www.wsj.com/articles/netflix-adds-more-users-than-expected-1461010680; David Carr, "Giving Viewers What They Want," *New York Times*, February 25, 2013, p. B1; Trey Williams, "Netflix Has Star-Studded Original Content Up Its Sleeve," October 14, 2015, www.marketwatch.com/story/netflix-has-star-studded-original-content-up-its-sleeve-2015-08-26; Zach Bulygo, "How Netflix Uses Analytics to Select Movies, Create Content, and Make Multimillion Dollar Decisions," *Kissmetrics*, September 6, 2013, http://blog.kissmetrics.com/how-netflix-uses-analytics/; Craig Smith, "By the Numbers: 50+ Amazing Netflix Statistics and Facts," *Expanded Ramblings*, April 18, 2016, http://expandedramblings.com/index.php/netflix_statistics-facts/; and www.netflix.com, accessed September 2016.

Cheese to Oscar Mayer, Philadelphia Cream Cheese, Lunchables, and Planters nuts—are found in 98 percent of all North American households:[23]

● Kraft has a treasure trove of marketing data, gathered from years of interactions with customers and from its social media monitoring hub called Looking Glass. Looking Glass tracks consumer trends, competitor activities, and more than 100,000 brand-related conversations daily in social media and on blogs. Kraft also reaps data from customer interactions with its *Kraft Food & Family* magazine, email communications, and the more than 100 web and social media sites that serve its large brand portfolio. In all, Kraft has 18 years' worth of customer data across 22,000 different attributes.

Kraft applies high-level marketing analytics to this wealth of data to mine nuggets of customer insight. Then it uses these insights to shape big data–driven marketing strategies and tactics, from developing new products to creating more focused and personalized web, mobile, and social media content. For example, Kraft's analytics have identified more than 500 custom target segments.

● Marketing analytics: Food products giant Kraft reaps a treasure trove of data from customers of its classic brands, then applies high-level marketing analytics to mine nuggets of customer insights.
Bloomberg/Getty Images

Within these segments, Kraft knows in detail what consumers need and like. Says one analyst, it knows "their dietary [characteristics and] restrictions—gluten free, a diabetic, low calorie, big snacks, feeding a big family, whether they are new cooks." Kraft uses this knowledge to personalize digital interactions with individual customers, down to the fine details. "If Kraft knows you're not a bacon user," says the analyst, "you will never be served a bacon ad." Thus, sophisticated analytics let Kraft target the right customer with the right message in the right medium at the right moment.

The benefits of customer relationship management and big data analytics don't come without costs or risks. The most common mistake is to view CRM and marketing analytics as technology processes only. Or they get buried in the big data details and miss the big picture.[24] Yet technology alone cannot build profitable customer relationships. Companies can't improve customer relationships by simply installing some new software. Instead, marketers should start with the fundamentals of managing customer relationships and *then* employ high-tech data and analytics solutions. They should focus first on the R— it's the *relationship* that CRM is all about.

Distributing and Using Marketing Information

Marketing information has no value until it is used to make better marketing decisions. Thus, the marketing information system must make information readily available to managers and others who need it, when they need it. In some cases, this means providing managers with regular performance reports, intelligence updates, and reports on the results of research studies.

But marketing managers may also need access to nonroutine information for special situations and on-the-spot decisions. For example, a sales manager having trouble with a large customer may want a summary of the account's sales and profitability over the past year. Or a brand manager may want to get a sense of the amount of the social media buzz surrounding the recent launch of a new product. These days, therefore, information distribution involves making information available in a timely, user-friendly way.

Many firms use company *intranet* and internal CRM systems to facilitate this process. These systems provide ready access to research and intelligence information, customer transaction and experience information, shared reports and documents, and more. For example, the CRM system at phone and online gift retailer 1-800-Flowers.com gives customer-facing employees real-time access to customer information. When a repeat customer calls, the system immediately pulls up data on previous transactions and other contacts, helping reps make the customer's experience easier and more relevant. For instance, if a customer usually buys tulips for his wife, the rep can talk about the best tulip selections and related gifts. Such connections result in greater customer satisfaction and loyalty and greater sales for the company. "We can do it in real time," says a 1-800-Flowers.com executive, "and it enhances the customer experience."[25]

In addition, companies are increasingly allowing key customers and value-network members to access account, product, and other data on demand through *extranets*. Suppliers, customers, resellers, and select other network members may access a company's extranet to update their accounts, arrange purchases, and check orders against inventories to improve customer service. ● For example, online shoes and accessories retailer Zappos considers suppliers to be "part of the Zappos family" and a key component in its quest to deliver "WOW" through great customer service. So it treats suppliers as valued partners, including sharing information with them. Through its ZUUL extranet (Zappos Unified User Login), thousands of suppliers are given full access to brand-related Zappos's inventory levels, sales figures, and even profitability. Suppliers can also use ZUUL to interact with the Zappos creative team and to enter suggested orders for Zappos buyers to approve.[26]

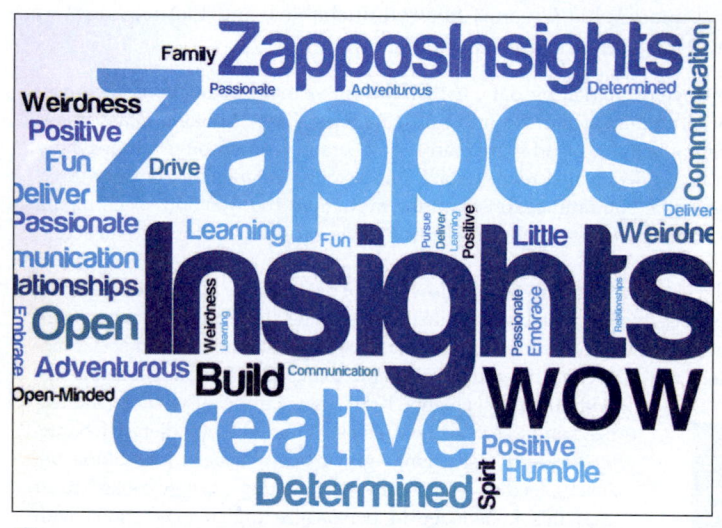

● Extranets: Zappos shares marketing information and insights with suppliers through its ZUUL extranet. It considers suppliers to be "part of the Zappos family."

Zappos

Thanks to modern technology, today's marketing managers can gain direct access to a company's information system at any time and from virtually anywhere. They can tap into the system from a home office, customer location, airport, or the local Starbucks—anyplace they can connect on a laptop, tablet, or smartphone. Such systems allow managers to get the information they need directly and quickly and tailor it to their own needs.

> **Author Comment** | We finish this chapter by examining three special marketing information topics.

Other Marketing Information Considerations

This section discusses marketing information in two special contexts: marketing research in small businesses and nonprofit organizations and international marketing research. Then we look at public policy and ethics issues in marketing research.

Marketing Research in Small Businesses and Nonprofit Organizations

Just like larger firms, small businesses and not-for-profit organizations need market information and the customer insights that it can provide. However, large-scale research studies are beyond the budgets of most small organizations. Still, many of the marketing research techniques discussed in this chapter can be used by smaller organizations in a less formal manner and at little or no expense. ● Consider how one small business owner conducted market research on a shoestring before even opening his doors:[27]

After a string of bad experiences with his local dry cleaner, Robert Byerley decided to open his own dry-cleaning business. But before jumping in, he conducted plenty of market research. He needed a key customer insight: How would he make his business stand out from the others? To start, Byerley spent an entire week online, researching the dry-cleaning industry. To get input from potential customers, using a local marketing firm, Byerley held focus groups on the store's name, look, and brochure. He also took clothes to the 15 best competing cleaners in town and had focus group members critique their work. Based on his research, he made a list of features for his new business. First on his list: quality. His business would stand behind everything it did. Not on the list: cheap prices. Creating the perfect dry-cleaning establishment simply didn't fit with a discount operation.

With his research complete, Byerley opened Bibbentuckers, a high-end dry cleaner positioned on high-quality service and convenience. It featured a bank-like drive-thru area with curbside delivery. A computerized barcode system read customer cleaning preferences and tracked clothes all the way through the cleaning process. Byerley added other differentiators, such as decorative awnings, TV screens, and refreshments (even "candy for the kids and a doggy treat for your best friend"). "I wanted a place … that paired five-star service and quality with an establishment that didn't look like a dry cleaner," he says. The market research yielded results. Today, Bibbentuckers is a thriving eight-store operation.

● Before opening Bibbentuckers dry cleaner, owner Robert Byerley conducted research to gain insights into what customers wanted. First on the list: quality.
Bibbentuckers

Thus, small businesses and not-for-profit organizations can obtain good marketing insights through observation or informal surveys using small convenience samples. Also, many associations, local media, and government agencies provide special help to small organizations. For example, the U.S. Small Business Administration offers dozens of free publications and a website (www.sba.gov) that give advice on topics ranging from starting, financing, and expanding a small business to ordering business cards. Other excellent research resources for small businesses include the U.S. Census Bureau (www.census.gov) and the Bureau of Economic Analysis (www.bea.gov). Finally, small businesses can collect a considerable amount of information at very little cost online. They can check out online product and service review sites, use internet search engines to research specific companies and issues, and scour competitor and customer web, mobile, and social media sites.

In summary, secondary data collection, observation, surveys, and experiments can all be used effectively by small organizations with small budgets. However, although these informal research methods are less complex and less costly, they still must be conducted with care. Managers must think carefully about the objectives of the research, formulate questions in advance, recognize the biases introduced by smaller samples and less skilled researchers, and conduct the research systematically.[28]

International Marketing Research

International researchers follow the same steps as domestic researchers, from defining the research problem and developing a research plan to interpreting and reporting the results. However, these researchers often face more and different problems. Whereas domestic researchers deal with fairly homogeneous markets within a single country, international researchers deal with diverse markets in many different countries. These markets often vary greatly in their levels of economic development, cultures and customs, and buying patterns.

Nielsen Pop Quiz #19

HOW MANY COUNTRIES
DOES IT TAKE TO BE THE
WORLD'S LEADING GLOBAL
INFOR MATION COMPANY?

WANT THE ANS WER?
JUST ASK NIELSEN.

● **Some of the largest research services firms have large international organizations. Nielsen has offices in more than 100 countries.**

In many foreign markets, the international researcher may have a difficult time finding good secondary data. Whereas U.S. marketing researchers can obtain reliable secondary data from dozens of domestic research services, many countries have almost no research services at all. Some of the largest international research services operate in many countries. ● For example, The Nielsen Company (the world's largest marketing research company) has offices in more than 100 countries, from Schaumburg, Illinois, to Hong Kong to Nicosia, Cyprus.[29] However, most research firms operate in only a relative handful of countries. Thus, even when secondary information is available, it usually must be obtained from many different sources on a country-by-country basis, making the information difficult to combine or compare.

Because of the scarcity of good secondary data, international researchers often must collect their own primary data. However, obtaining primary data may be no easy task. For example, it can be difficult simply to develop good samples. U.S. researchers can use current telephone directories, email lists, census tract data, and any of several sources of socioeconomic data to construct samples. However, such information is largely lacking in many countries.

Once the sample is drawn, the U.S. researcher usually can reach most respondents easily by phone, by mail, online, or in person. However, reaching respondents is often not so easy in other parts of the world. Researchers in Mexico cannot rely on phone, internet, and mail data collection—most data collection is conducted door to door and concentrated in three or four of the largest cities. In some countries, few people have computers, let alone internet access. For example, whereas there are 84 internet users per 100 people in the United States, there are only 43 internet users per 100 people in Mexico. In Madagascar, the number drops to 2 internet users per 100 people. In some countries, the postal system is notoriously unreliable. In Brazil, for instance, an estimated 30 percent of the mail is never delivered; in Russia, mail delivery can take several weeks. In many developing countries, poor roads and transportation systems make certain areas hard to reach, making personal interviews difficult and expensive.[30]

Cultural differences from country to country cause additional problems for international researchers. Language is the most obvious obstacle. For example, questionnaires must be prepared in one language and then translated into the languages of each country researched. Responses then must be translated back into the original language for analysis and interpretation. This adds to research costs and increases the risks of error. Even within a given country, language can be a problem. For example, in India, English is the language of business, but consumers may use any of 14 "first languages," with many additional dialects.

Translating a questionnaire from one language to another is anything but easy. Many idioms, phrases, and statements mean different things in different cultures. For example, a Danish executive noted, "Check this out by having a different translator put back into English what you've translated from English. You'll get the shock of your life. I remember [an example in which] 'out of sight, out of mind' had become 'invisible things are insane.'"[31]

Consumers in different countries also vary in their attitudes toward marketing research. People in one country may be very willing to respond; in other countries, nonresponse can be a major problem. Customs in some countries may prohibit people from talking with strangers. In certain cultures, research questions often are considered too personal. For example, in many Muslim countries, mixed-gender focus groups are taboo, as is videotaping female-only focus groups. In some countries, even when respondents are *willing* to respond, they may not be *able* to because of high functional illiteracy rates.

Despite these problems, as global marketing grows, global companies have little choice but to conduct these types of international marketing research. Although the costs and problems associated with international research may be high, the costs of not doing it—in terms of missed opportunities and mistakes—might be even higher. Once recognized, many of the problems associated with international marketing research can be overcome or avoided.

Public Policy and Ethics in Marketing Research

Most marketing research benefits both the sponsoring company and its consumers. Through marketing research, companies gain insights into consumers' needs, resulting in more satisfying products and services and stronger customer relationships. However, the misuse of marketing research can also harm or annoy consumers. Two major public policy and ethics issues in marketing research are intrusions on consumer privacy and the misuse of research findings.

Intrusions on Consumer Privacy

Many consumers feel positive about marketing research and believe that it serves a useful purpose. Some actually enjoy being interviewed and giving their opinions. However, others strongly resent or even mistrust marketing research. They don't like being interrupted by researchers. They worry that marketers are building huge databases full of personal information about customers. Or they fear that researchers might use sophisticated techniques to probe our deepest feelings, track our internet and mobile device usage, or peek over our shoulders as we shop and then use this knowledge to manipulate our buying. A recent survey showed that more than 90 percent of Americans feel that they have lost control over the collection and use by companies of their personal data and information they share on social media sites.[32]

For example, Target made some of its customers very uneasy recently when it used their buying histories to figure out that they had a baby on the way, including eerily accurate estimates of child gender and due date:[33]

Target gives every customer a Guest ID number, tied to his or her name, credit card, or email address. It then tracks the customer's purchases in detail, along with demographic information from other sources. By studying the buying histories of women who'd previously signed up for its baby registries, Target found that it could develop a "pregnancy prediction" score for each customer based on her purchasing patterns across 25 product categories. It used this score to start sending personalized books of coupons for baby-related items to expectant parents, keyed to their pregnancy stages.

The strategy seemed to make good marketing sense—by hooking parents-to-be, Target could turn them into loyal buyers as their families developed. However, the strategy hit a snag when an angry man showed up at his local Target store, complaining that his high school-aged daughter was receiving Target coupons for cribs, strollers, and maternity clothes. "Are you trying to encourage her to get pregnant?" he demanded. The Target store manager apologized. But when he called to apologize again a few days later, he learned that Target's marketers had, in fact, known about the young woman's pregnancy before her father did. It turns out that many other customers were creeped out that Target knew about their pregnancies before they'd told even family and close friends. And they wondered what else Target might be tracking and profiling. As one reporter concluded: "The store's bull's-eye logo may now send a shiver...down the closely-watched spines of some [Target shoppers]."

● **Consumer privacy: Target made some customers uneasy when it used their buying histories to figure out things about them that even their family and friends didn't know. The chain's bull's-eye logo may now "send a shiver...down the closely-watched spines of some Target shoppers."**

©Ken Wolter/Shutterstock

When mining customer information, marketers must be careful not to cross over the privacy line. But there are no easy answers when it comes to marketing research and privacy. For example, is it a good or bad thing that some retailers use mannequins with cameras hidden in one eye to record customer demographics and shopping behavior in order to serve them better? Should we applaud or resent companies that monitor consumer posts on Facebook, Twitter, Instagram, YouTube, or other social media in an effort to be more responsive? Should we worry when marketers track consumers' mobile phone usage to issue location-based information, ads, and offers? Consider this example:[34]

> SAP's Consumer Insight 365 service helps mobile service providers to "extract data about subscribers [and their] mobile-centric lifestyles." It ingests as many as 300 mobile web surfing, text messaging, phone call, and other mobile events per day for each of 20 to 25 million mobile subscribers across multiple carriers. The data tell marketers in detail where customers are coming from and where they go. According to one analyst, by combining the mobile data with other information, the service can tell businesses "whether shoppers are checking out competitor prices on their phones or just emailing friends. It can tell them the age ranges and genders of people who visited a store location between 10 a.m. and noon, and link location and demographic data with shoppers' web browsing histories. Retailers might use the information to arrange store displays to appeal to certain customer segments at different times of the day, or to help determine where to open new locations." Although such information can help marketers target customers with more useful offers, it might be "a little too close for comfort" from a consumer privacy viewpoint.

Increasing consumer privacy concerns have become a major problem for the marketing research industry. Companies face the challenge of unearthing valuable but potentially sensitive consumer data while also maintaining consumer trust. At the same time, consumers wrestle with the trade-offs between personalization and privacy. They want to receive relevant, personalized offers that meet their needs, but they worry or resent that companies may track them too closely. The key question: When does a company cross the line in gathering and using customer data?

Failure to address privacy issues could result in angry, less cooperative consumers and increased government intervention. As a result, the marketing research industry is considering several options for responding to intrusion and privacy issues. One example is the Marketing Research Association's "Your Opinion Counts" and "Respondent Bill of Rights" initiatives to educate consumers about the benefits of marketing research and distinguish it from telephone selling and database building.[35]

Most major companies—including Facebook, Apple, Microsoft, IBM, American Express, and even the U.S. government—have now appointed a chief privacy officer (CPO), whose job is to safeguard the privacy of customers. In the end, however, if researchers provide value in exchange for information, customers will gladly provide it. For example, Amazon's customers don't mind if the firm builds a database of previous purchases as a way to provide future product recommendations. This saves time and provides value. The best approach is for researchers to ask only for the information they need, use it responsibly to provide customer value, and avoid sharing information without the customer's permission.

Misuse of Research Findings

Research studies can be powerful persuasion tools; companies often use study results as claims in their advertising and promotion. Today, however, many research studies appear to be little more than vehicles for pitching the sponsor's products. In fact, in some cases, research surveys appear to have been designed just to produce the intended effect. For example, a Black Flag survey once asked: "A roach disk…poisons a roach slowly. The dying roach returns to the nest and after it dies is eaten by other roaches. In turn these roaches become poisoned and die. How effective do you think this type of product would be in killing roaches?" Not surprisingly, 79 percent said effective.

Few advertisers openly rig their research designs or blatantly misrepresent the findings—most abuses tend to be more subtle "stretches." Or disputes arise over the validity, interpretation, and use of research findings. Almost any research results can be variously interpreted depending on the researchers' bias and viewpoints.

Recognizing that marketing research can be abused, several associations—including the American Marketing Association, the Marketing Research Association, and the Council of American Survey Research Organizations (CASRO)—have developed codes of research ethics and standards of conduct. For example, the CASRO Code of Standards and Ethics for Survey Research outlines researcher responsibilities to respondents, including confidentiality, privacy, and avoidance of harassment. It also outlines major responsibilities in reporting results to clients and the public.[36]

In the end, however, unethical or inappropriate actions cannot simply be regulated away. Each company must accept responsibility for policing the conduct and reporting of its own marketing research to protect consumers' best interests as well as its own.

4 | Reviewing and Extending the Concepts

OBJECTIVES REVIEW AND KEY TERMS

Objectives Review

To create value for customers and build meaningful relationships with them, marketers must first gain fresh, deep insights into what customers need and want. Such insights come from good marketing information. As a result of the recent explosion of "big data" and digital technologies, companies can now obtain great quantities of information, often even too much. Consumers themselves are now generating a tidal wave of bottom-up information through their smartphones, PCs, and tablets via online browsing and blogging, apps and social media interactions, and texting and video. The challenge is to transform today's vast volume of consumer information into actionable customer and market insights.

OBJECTIVE 4-1 Explain the importance of information in gaining insights about the marketplace and customers. *(pp 100–102)*

The marketing process starts with a complete understanding of the marketplace and consumer needs and wants. Thus, the company needs to turn sound consumer information into meaningful *customer insights* by which it can produce superior value for its customers. The company also requires information on competitors, resellers, and other actors and forces in the marketplace. Increasingly, marketers are viewing information not only as an input for making better decisions but also as an important strategic asset and marketing tool.

OBJECTIVE 4-2 Define the marketing information system and discuss its parts. *(pp 102–106)*

The *marketing information system* (*MIS*) consists of people and procedures for assessing information needs, developing the needed information, and helping decision makers use the information to generate and validate actionable customer and market insights. A well-designed information system begins and ends with users.

The MIS first *assesses information needs*. The MIS primarily serves the company's marketing and other managers, but it may also provide information to external partners. Then the MIS *develops information* from internal databases, marketing intelligence activities, and marketing research. *Internal databases* provide information on the company's own operations and departments. Such data can be obtained quickly and

cheaply but often need to be adapted for marketing decisions. *Marketing intelligence* activities supply everyday information about developments in the external marketing environment, including listening and responding to the vast and complex digital environment. *Market research* consists of collecting information relevant to a specific marketing problem faced by the company. Last, the marketing information system helps users analyze and use the information to develop customer insights, make marketing decisions, and manage customer relationships.

OBJECTIVE 4-3 Outline the steps in the marketing research process. *(pp 106–116)*

The first step in the marketing research process involves *defining the problem and setting the research objectives*, which may be exploratory, descriptive, or causal research. The second step consists of *developing a research plan* for collecting data from primary and secondary sources. The third step calls for *implementing the marketing research plan* by gathering, processing, and analyzing the information. The fourth step consists of *interpreting and reporting the findings*. Additional information analysis helps marketing managers apply the information and provides them with sophisticated statistical procedures and models from which to develop more rigorous findings.

Both *internal* and *external* secondary data sources often provide information more quickly and at a lower cost than primary data sources, and they can sometimes yield information that a company cannot collect by itself. However, needed information might not exist in secondary sources. Researchers must also evaluate secondary information to ensure that it is *relevant, accurate, current*, and *impartial*.

Primary research must also be evaluated for these features. Each primary data collection method—*observational, survey*, and *experimental*—has its own advantages and disadvantages. Similarly, each of the various research contact methods—mail, telephone, personal interview, and online—has its own advantages and drawbacks.

OBJECTIVE 4-4 Explain how companies analyze and use marketing information. *(pp 116–120)*

Information gathered in internal databases and through marketing intelligence and marketing research usually requires more analysis. To analyze individual customer data, many companies have now acquired or developed special software and analysis techniques—called *customer relationship management (CRM)*—that integrate, analyze, and apply the mountains of individual customer data to gain a 360-degree view of customers and build stronger the customer relationships. They apply *marketing analytics* to dig out meaningful patterns in big data and gain customer insights and gauge marketing performance.

Marketing information has no value until it is used to make better marketing decisions. Thus, the MIS must make the information available to managers and others who make marketing decisions or deal with customers. In some cases, this means providing regular reports and updates; in other cases, it means making nonroutine information available for special situations and on-the-spot decisions. Many firms use company intranets and extranets to facilitate this process. Thanks to modern technology, today's marketing managers can gain direct access to marketing information at any time and from virtually any location.

OBJECTIVE 4-5 **Discuss the special issues some marketing researchers face, including public policy and ethics issues.** *(pp 120–125)*

Some marketers face special marketing research situations, such as those conducting research in small business, not-for-profit, or international situations. Marketing research can be conducted effectively by small businesses and nonprofit organizations with limited budgets. International marketing researchers follow the same steps as domestic researchers but often face more and different problems. All organizations need to act responsibly concerning major public policy and ethical issues surrounding marketing research, including issues of intrusions on consumer privacy and misuse of research findings.

Key Terms

OBJECTIVE 4-1

Big data (p 101)
Customer insights (p 101)
Marketing information system
    (MIS) (p 101)

OBJECTIVE 4-2

Internal databases (p 103)
Competitive marketing
    intelligence (p 103)

OBJECTIVE 4-3

Marketing research (p 106)
Exploratory research (p 107)
Descriptive research (p 107)
Causal research (p 107)
Secondary data (p 108)
Primary data (p 108)
Observational research (p 109)
Ethnographic
    research (p 109)
Survey research (p 110)

Experimental research (p 110)
Focus group interviewing (p 111)
Online marketing research (p 112)
Online focus groups (p 113)
Behavioral targeting (p 114)
Sample (p 114)

OBJECTIVE 4-4

Customer relationship management
    (CRM) (p 117)
Marketing analytics (p 117)

DISCUSSION AND CRITICAL THINKING

MyMarketingLab

Go to **mymktlab.com** to complete the problems marked with this icon ⭐.

Discussion Questions

⭐ **4-1** What is *big data,* and what opportunities and challenges does it provide for marketers? (AACSB: Communication; Reflective Thinking)

⭐ **4-2** Explain how marketing intelligence differs from marketing research. Which is more valuable to a company? Why? (AACSB: Communication; Reflective Thinking)

⭐ **4-3** What is customer relationship management (CRM)? How are firms integrating this information into their marketing and general business practices? Provide an example of CRM in a firm. (AACSB: Communication, Reflective Thinking)

4-4 Marketers make heavy use of both primary and secondary data. What is primary data? What is secondary data? What are possible benefits or drawbacks of using each of these data types? (AACSB: Communication, Reflective Thinking)

4-5 What are the similarities and differences when conducting research in another country versus the domestic market? What research strategies might a company use to address the differences in various markets? (AACSB: Communication, Reflective Thinking)

Critical Thinking Exercises

4-6 In a small group, identify a problem faced by a local business or charitable organization and propose a research project addressing that problem. Develop a research proposal that implements each step of the marketing research process. Discuss how the research results will help the business or organization. (AACSB: Communication; Reflective Thinking)

4-7 Suppose you are conducting market research for your favorite soda brand. Sales have been lagging for two quarters, and you are determined to find out why. You decide to host an in-person focus group to gain customer insights into your brand's current product offerings. You are also interested in obtaining feedback on a new product that your brand plans to launch in the next six months. Determine the makeup of your focus group. Who should be invited to the focus group, and why? What types of information would you want to obtain? Identify possible questions to present to the focus group. (AACSB: Communication; Reflective Thinking)

4-8 Conduct an online search to learn more about the marketing research industry. Develop a presentation describing the variety of jobs in the marketing research field along with the compensation for those jobs. Create a graphical representation to communicate your findings. (AACSB: Communication; Use of IT; Reflective Thinking)

APPLICATIONS AND CASES

Online, Mobile, and Social Media Marketing The Trail You Leave Behind

Marketers are always interested in collecting as much valuable data as possible regarding customer likes, preferences, and trends. Web activity and social media platforms such as Twitter, Facebook, Instagram, and various blog sites are gold mines for marketers. All of these access points create information that can be aggregated and used to a company's competitive advantage, which allows firms to stay in tune with what is currently trending in the marketplace. Businesses can also use these same access points to track competitor activity, which can then be used in competitive marketing intelligence.

4-9 Have you ever thought about the data you leave behind for marketers to collect? Marketers are always looking for digital footprints, which are traceable sources of online activities. Visit www.internetsociety.org/your-digital-footprint-matters and review the various resources available. Select one of the tutorials and present what you learned from the video. (AACSB: Communication, Use of IT, Reflective Thinking)

4-10 After reviewing the tutorials on http://www.internet-society.org/your-digital-footprint-matters, do you plan to alter your online habits? Are you concerned about your digital footprint and the data trail you leave behind, and do you plan to actively manage them? Why or why not? (AACSB: Communication, Use of IT, Reflective Thinking)

Marketing Ethics Metadata

Everyone generates metadata when using technologies such as computers and mobile devices to search, post, tweet, play, text, and talk. What many people don't realize, however, is that this treasure trove of date, time, and location information can be used to identify them without their knowledge. For example, in analyzing more than a million anonymous credit card transactions, researchers at the Massachusetts Institute of Technology were able to link 90 percent of the transactions to specific users with just four additional bits of metadata, such as user locations based on apps such as Foursquare, the timing of an activity such as a tweet on Twitter, or playing a mobile game. Since there are more mobile devices than there are people in the United States and 60 percent of purchases are made with a credit card, marketing research firms are gobbling up all sorts of metadata that will let them tie a majority of purchase transactions to specific individuals.

4-11 Describe at least four applications you use that provide location, time, and date information that can be tied to your identity. (AACSB Communication; Reflective Thinking)

4-12 Debate whether it is ethical for marketers to use metadata to link individual consumers with specific credit card transactions. (AACSB: Communication; Ethical Reasoning)

Marketing by the Numbers The Value of Information

Conducting research is costly, and the costs must be weighed against the value of the information gathered. Consider a company faced with a competitor's price reduction. Should the company also reduce price in order to maintain market share, or should the company maintain its current price? The company has conducted some preliminary research showing the financial outcomes of each decision under two competitor responses: the competition maintains its price or the competition lowers its price further. The company feels pretty confident that the competitor cannot lower its price further and assigns that outcome a probability (p) of 0.7, which means the other outcome would have only a 30 percent chance of occurring ($1 - p = 0.3$). These outcomes are shown in the table below:

Company action	Competitive Response	
	Maintain Price $p = 0.7$	**Reduce Price** $(1 - p) = 0.3$
Reduce Price	$160,000	$120,000
Maintain Price	$180,000	$100,000

For example, if the company reduces its price and the competitor maintains its price, the company would realize $160,000, and so on. From this information, the expected monetary value (EMV) of each company action (reduce price or maintain price) can be determined using the following equation:

$$EMV = (p)(\text{financial outcome}_p) + (1 - p)(\text{financial outcome}_{(1 - p)})$$

The company would select the action expected to deliver the greatest EMV. More information might be desirable, but is it worth the cost of acquiring it? One way to assess the value of additional information is to determine the expected value of perfect information (EMV$_{PI}$), calculated using the following equation:

$$EMV_{PI} = EMV_{certainty} - EMV_{best alternative}$$

where,

$$EMV_{certainty} = (p)(\text{highest financial outcome}_p) + (1 - p)(\text{highest financial outcome}_{(1 - p)})$$

If the value of perfect information is more than the cost of conducting the research, then the research should be undertaken (that is, EMV$_{PI}$ > cost of research). However, if the value of the additional information is less than the cost of obtaining more information, the research should not be conducted.

4-13 Calculate the expected monetary value (EMV) of both company actions. Which action should the company take? (AACSB: Communication; Analytical Reasoning)

4-14 What is the expected value of perfect information (EMV$_{PI}$)? Should the research be conducted? (AACSB: Communication; Analytical Reasoning)

Video Case Nielsen

Most people know Nielsen as the TV ratings company. In reality, however, Nielsen is a multiplatform market research company that has constantly been evolving since 1923. Its goal is to measure and track a wide range of consumer activity in order to establish a 360-degree view of individuals and market segments. To accomplish this, Nielsen has to follow consumers wherever they may be—watching TV, online, in their homes, or in stores.

How does Nielsen track all this activity? The veteran research firm has established effective methods of recording consumer activity, from retail scanner data to household panels to monitoring social networks. As data are captured, they are transferred to a Nielsen data warehouse, where they are matched to the right individual and added to the terabytes of information Nielsen already possesses. Through data sorting and analytics, Nielsen cuts through billions of daily transactions to deliver clear consumer insights to clients.

After viewing the video featuring Nielsen, answer the following questions:

4-15 What is Nielsen's expertise?

4-16 Providing a real-world example, describe how Nielsen might discover a consumer insight.

4-17 What kinds of partnerships might Nielsen need to form with other companies in order to accomplish its goals?

Company Case Campbell Soup Company: Watching What You Eat

You might think that a well-known, veteran consumer products company like the Campbell Soup Company has it made. After all, when people think of soup, they think of Campbell's. In the $5 billion U.S. soup market, Campbell dominates with a 44 percent share. Selling products under such an iconic brand name should be a snap. But if you ask Denise Morrison, CEO of Campbell, she'll tell you a different story. Just a few years ago, when Morrison took over as head of the world's oldest and best-known soup company, she faced a big challenge—reverse the declining market share of a 145-year-old brand in a mature, low-growth, and fickle market characterized by shifting consumer preferences, ever-expanding tastes, and little tolerance for price increases. Turning things around would require revitalizing the company's brands in a way that would attract new customers without alienating the faithful who had been buying Campbell products for decades.

Morrison had a plan. A core element of that plan was to maintain a laser-like focus on consumers. "The consumer is our boss," Morrison said. "[Maintaining a customer focus] requires a clear, up-to-the-minute understanding of consumers in order to create more relevant products." Morrison's plan involved transforming the traditional stagnant culture of a corporate dinosaur into one that embraces creativity and flexibility. But it also involved employing innovative methods that would allow brand managers and product developers to establish the customer understanding that was so desperately needed. In other words, marketing research at the Campbell Soup Company was about to change.

Reading Consumers' Minds

Soup is a well-accepted product found in just about everyone's pantry in the United States. However, not long ago, Campbell researchers discovered that marketing soups presents unique problems. People don't covet soup. Sure, a steaming bowl of savory soup really hits the spot after coming in out of a bitingly cold rain. But soup is not a top-of-mind meal or snack choice, and it's typically a prelude to a more interesting main course. The bottom line—consumers don't really think much about soup, making meaningful marketing research difficult.

For years, Campbell researchers relied on good old paper-and-pencil surveys and traditional interviews to gain consumer insights for making ads, labels and packaging, and the products themselves more effective. But Campbell's experience with such marketing research showed that traditional methods failed to capture important subconscious thoughts, emotions, and behaviors that consumers experience when shopping for soup.

So instead, to get closer to what was really going on inside consumers' hearts and minds, Campbell researchers began employing state-of-the-art neuroscience methods. They outfitted shoppers with special vests that measured skin-moisture levels, heart rates, depth and pace of breathing, and postures. Sensors tracked eye movements and pupil width. Then, to aid interpretation, such biometric data was combined with interviews and videos that captured each shopper's experiences.

The high-tech research produced some startling insights. Campbell knew that people hold strong emotions associated with eating soup. After all, who doesn't remember getting a hot bowl of soup from Mom when they were sick or cold? But the new biometric testing revealed that all that warmth and those positive emotions evaporated when consumers confronted the sea of nearly identical red and white Campbell's cans found on a typical grocery store soup aisle.

In the past, the top of a typical store shelf display featured a large Campbell's logo with a bright red background. But the new research showed that such signs made all varieties of Campbell's Soup blend together, creating an overwhelming browsing situation and causing shoppers to spend less time at the aisle. The biometric research methods also revealed that the soup can labels themselves were lacking—the big bowl of soup on Campbell's labels was not perceived warmly, and the large spoon filled with soup provoked no emotional response.

Based on these research insights, in an attempt to prompt and preserve important consumer emotions surrounding soup consumption, Campbell began evaluating specific aspects of its displays, labels, and packaging. This led to seemingly small but important changes. For starters, the Campbell's logo

is now smaller and lower on the shelf, minimizing the overwhelming "sea of cans" effect. To further encourage browsing, can labels now fall into different categories, each with distinguishing visual cues. Varieties like Beef Broth and Broccoli Cheese, which are typically used as ingredients in recipes, feature a narrow blue swath across the middle of the can with a "Great for Cooking" label. A green swath and the label "98% Fat Free" characterize reduced-fat varieties. Tomato Chipotle & Olive Oil, part of Campbell's "Latin Inspired" line, features a black background rather than the traditional white. And top-sellers such as Chicken Noodle, Tomato, and Cream of Mushroom feature the plain traditional label with the center medallion, immortalized by Andy Warhol's larger-than-life recreations of Campbell's soup cans. As for bringing out those warm emotions, Campbell's labels are now adorned with steam rising off a larger, more vibrant picture of the featured soup in a more modern white bowl. The non-emotional spoons are gone as well.

Can such minor label changes make a real difference? Yes, they can. Campbell claims that its sales of condensed soups are up by 2 percent since making the changes. That may not sound like much, but even a small sales bump applied to a $2 billion consumer brand means real money. The sales jump also indicates that consumers are receiving greater value through a more fulfilling shopping experience.

Diving Deeper for Insights

Although the insights from Campbell's biometric marketing research have proven valuable, it will take more to capture the attention of a new generation of customers and stay attuned to the changing nature of consumer food tastes and preferences. Additionally, the Campbell Soup Company makes and markets much more than just soup these days. Over the years, the company has added or created such brands as Pepperidge Farms, Swanson, Pace, Prego, V8, Bolthouse Farms, and Plum Organics. Today, Campbell's house of packaged food brands includes something for just about everyone. With that kind of product portfolio, maintaining and creating relevant products based on a clear, up-to-the-minute understanding of consumers is an especially daunting proposition.

To capture clear and contemporary customer insights, Campbell researchers turn to deep dive marketing research—qualitative methods employed in the fields of anthropology and other social sciences for up-close-and-personal study. Campbell researchers and marketers dive in and spend time with consumers on their own turf. "We're in their homes," says Charles Vila, Campbell's vice president of consumer and customer insights. "We are cooking with them; we're eating with them; we're shopping with them." By spending hours at a time with consumers and observing them in their natural environments, researchers can unlock deep consumer insights of which customers themselves are often not aware.

By employing deep dive marketing research methods, Campbell researchers have identified six different consumer groups, each with an extensive profile. For each of these groups, Campbell has created six fully equipped kitchens at its Camden, New Jersey, headquarters, each designed to mirror the homes of consumers in the six groups. Each kitchen has a unique design, with different appliances, different features, and, most importantly, different food in the cabinets and refrigerators.

At one end of the spectrum is the group called "Uninvolved Quick Fixers." These are individuals and families who are not acquainted with or into cooking. Their kitchens are strewn with pizza boxes, and collections of takeout menus adorn their fridges. Their stoves and ovens often look like they've never been touched. "They're doing a lot of microwaving and frozen foods," explains the manager of Campbell's test facilities.

At the other end of the spectrum is group six, the "Passionate Kitchen Masters." Their kitchens tend to be filled with well-used, high-end appliances. Their refrigerators are stuffed with fresh produce, dairy, and meats. Gourmet sauces and artisanal breads and pastas are complemented by a wide variety of spices.

Such levels of detail help Campbell marketers discover and understand existing and developing trends in each consumer group as well as in the general market. For example, ginger is in. Only a few years ago, this herb was something found only in ethnic restaurants or in obscure recipes. But now its popularity is soaring. Campbell expects that it will soon be an important ingredient for each of the six consumer segments, a valuable insight for developing new products.

Another conclusion from Campbell's deep dive is that although Passionate Kitchen Masters consume far fewer prepared and packaged foods than other consumers, they still buy a lot of ingredients—such as broth. Broth flies under the radar of most consumers. But for people who like to cook, it's a sturdy component of soups, sauces, and braised meats.

Under both the Campbell's and Swanson brands, broth is also a $400 million business for the Campbell Soup Company. Applying the 2 percent sales boost resulting from the label changes discussed earlier translates to $8 million in sales gains for broth alone. That's why Campbell researchers are so interested in consumer trends, big and small.

The main goal is to enhance the customer's food experience. For example, Thai dishes are becoming more popular for foodies. But coming up with key ingredients like lemongrass is both time consuming and expensive. "Even for confident cooks, to bring those together, to go and purchase them, and actually blend them in such a way that it actually works, that's not easy," says Campbell's vice president Dale Clemiss, who oversees the Swanson and other Campbell brands. Add that to other insights that Campbell's research has uncovered, and a new broth is born—Swanson Thai Ginger, a broth "infused with flavors of lime, soy sauce, coconut, lemongrass, cilantro, and ginger—a simple way to make delicious restaurant inspired global dishes at home."

Every marketing research method has pitfalls. So Campbell combines multiple research methods to minimize the possibility of making incorrect judgments. In addition to neuroscience and deep dive research, the company still employs traditional methods of surveys and interviews. The triangulation of data across methods allows for greater accuracy as well as the ability to cover larger consumer samples.

In the packaged foods business, every little bit helps. It's all about staying in tune with consumers and keeping up with the changes—large and small—in consumer preferences. That philosophy has worked well for the Campbell Soup Company in the past. And as Campbell has dug deeper through multiple marketing research methods, the proof is in the pudding. Over the most recent three years, Campbell's corporate revenues rose 12.6 percent while net profits returned 6 to 10 percent each year. Campbell's stock price also increased by more than 60 percent during that time. As the company website states, "For generations, people have trusted Campbell to provide authentic, flavorful, and readily available foods and beverages that connect them to each other, to warm memories, and to what's important today." With the help of Campbell's marketing research program, it looks like consumers will continue to trust Campbell for generations to come.

Questions for Discussion

4-18 What are the strengths and weaknesses of the Campbell Soup Company's marketing information system?

4-19 What objectives does Campbell have for the marketing research efforts described in this case?

4-20 Compare the effectiveness of Campbell's biometric research with its deep dive research.

4-21 Describe how traditional marketing research could be integrated with Campbell's research efforts from this case.

Sources: "Soup in the U.S.," *Euromonitor International*, December 2015, www.euromonitor.com/soup-in-the-us/report; Mark Garrison, "How Food Companies Watch What You Eat," *Marketplace*, December 2, 2013, www.marketplace.org/topics/business/how-food-companies-watch-what-you-eat; Ilan Brat, "The Emotional Quotient of Soup Shopping," *Wall Street Journal*, February 17, 2010, p. B1; Bonnie Marcus, "Campbell Soup CEO Denise Morrison Stirs the Pot to Create Cultural Change," *Forbes*, April 25, 2015, www.forbes.com/sites/bonniemarcus/2014/04/25/campbell-soup-ceo-denise-morrison-stirs-the-pot-to-create-cultural-change/; and information from www.campbellsoupcompany.com/about-campbell/ and www.google.com/finance, accessed September 2016.

MyMarketingLab

Go to **mymktlab.com** for Auto-graded writing questions as well as the following Assisted-graded writing questions:

4-22 What is neuromarketing and how is it useful in marketing research? Why is this research approach usually used with other approaches?

4-23 Describe an example in which marketing research could cause harm to participants. Many companies have a review process similar to that required for following the government's "Common Rule." Write a brief report explaining this rule and how you would apply it to your example.

5 Consumer Markets and Buyer Behavior

CHAPTER PREVIEW

You've studied how marketers obtain, analyze, and use information to develop customer insights and assess marketing programs. In this chapter, we take a closer look at the most important element of the marketplace—customers. The aim of marketing is to engage customers and affect how they think and act. To affect the *whats*, *whens*, and *hows* of buyer behavior, marketers must first understand the *whys*. In this chapter, we look at *final consumer* buying influences and processes. In the next chapter, we'll study the buyer behavior of *business customers*. You'll see that understanding buyer behavior is an essential but very difficult task.

To get a better sense of the importance of understanding consumer behavior, we begin by looking at Harley-Davidson, maker of the nation's top-selling heavyweight motorcycles. Who rides these big Harley "Hogs"? What moves them to tattoo their bodies with the Harley-Davidson bar and shield logo, abandon home and hearth for the open road, and flock to Harley rallies by the hundreds of thousands? You might be surprised by the answers to these questions, but Harley-Davidson knows them *very* well.

HARLEY-DAVIDSON: Selling Freedom, Independence, Power, and Authenticity

Few brands engender such intense loyalty as that found in the hearts of Harley-Davidson owners. Harley buyers are granitelike in their devotion to the brand. You don't see people tattooing Yamaha on their bodies, or Kawasaki or Honda. Harley-Davidson riders don't want just any motorcycle—it's *got* to be a Harley. The iconic Harley-Davidson brand is that strong.

An estimated 100,000 to 200,000 people flocked to Harley-Davidson's recent 110th anniversary celebration in Milwaukee, the city where it all began. One reporter described the epic event's opening parade as "one of the greatest spectacles in America...a thunder of Harley-Davidson pride you could literally feel as nearly 7,000 [riders] rolled through downtown Milwaukee." During the three days of rumbling fun, bikers from across the nation lounged on their low-slung Harleys, swapped biker tales, and sported T-shirts proclaiming things like "Screw it, let's ride!" and "I'd rather push a Harley than ride a Yamaha."

Riding such intense emotions, Harley-Davidson has long dominated the U.S. motorcycle market. The brand captures more than 50 percent of all U.S. heavyweight motorcycle sales.

> Harley-Davidson's market dominance comes from a deep understanding of the emotions and motivations that underlie consumer behavior. Harley doesn't just sell motorcycles; its sells freedom, independence, power, and authenticity.

And despite some lingering post-recession doldrums, its revenues and profits have been growing at a smooth-riding pace. Over the past four years, sales have grown more than 30 percent and profits have jumped almost sevenfold.

Harley-Davidson's marketers have spent a great deal of time thinking about customers and their buying behavior. They want to know who their customers are, what they think and how they feel, and why they buy a Harley-Davidson Softail rather than a Yamaha or a Kawasaki or a big Honda Gold Wing. What is it that makes Harley buyers so fiercely loyal? These are difficult questions; even Harley owners themselves don't know exactly what motivates their buying. But Harley-Davidson management puts top priority on understanding customers and what makes them tick.

Who rides a Harley-Davidson? You might be surprised. It's not the outlaw bad-boy biker that some people still associate with Harleys. The brand's motorcycles attract a different breed of bikers—older, more affluent, and better educated. Remove the helmets and the leathers of a hard-core Harley enthusiast, and there's no telling whom you'll find. It might be a guy with tattoos and unruly hair, but it's just as likely to be a CEO, investment banker, or gourmet chef.

The average Harley customer is a 50-something male with a median household income of $87,000. More than 12 percent of Harley purchases today are made by women. "Harley brings together all walks of life," says Harley's chief marketing officer. "You'll find a neurosurgeon talking and riding with a janitor. It's a family." And a big family it is. The Harley Owners Group (H.O.G.)—the official riding club of "Harley owners around the world, bound by a passion to ride"—has more than a million members. The brand's Facebook site counts more than 7 million Likes.

In recent years, the company has been extending the Harley-Davidson family beyond the core segment of older Caucasian males who now account for about two-thirds of buyers. It has crafted products

For Harley-Davidson enthusiasts, it's all about the experience. More than just bikes, the iconic company is selling self-expression, lifestyles, aspirations, and dreams.
Scott Olson/Getty Images

and programs specifically designed to attract what it calls "outreach customers," segments such as young adults ages 18 to 34, women, African Americans, and Hispanics. Last year, sales to those outreach groups grew at more than twice the rate of sales to its traditional core customers. For example, to broaden its reach, Harley-Davidson recently introduced its first all-new motorcycle platform in 13 years—its Street models—smaller, lighter, more agile, and more efficient motorcycles designed for the riding needs of young urban riders. Though smaller, these new motorcycles still carry the Harley mystique. "These new bikes are leaner, yet still have a mean streak," says Harley's CMO. "They're the real deal, made of real steel."

Harley-Davidson makes good bikes, and to keep up with its shifting market, the company has upgraded its showrooms and sales approaches. But Harley customers are buying a lot more than just a quality bike and a smooth sales pitch. To gain a better understanding of customers' deeper motivations, over the years Harley-Davidson has conducted seemingly endless surveys, focus groups, and interpretive studies that plumb the depths of customers' feelings about their Harleys. Beyond research, everyone connected with the Harley-Davidson brand—from the CEO and CMO to ad agency copywriters—attend biker events and immerse themselves deeply in the biker culture. They spend countless hours in the saddle to gain a firsthand understanding of what moves and motivates core customers.

All of the research yields strong and consistent results. No matter who they are, what they do, or where they come from, Harley-Davidson disciples share a common, deeply held attraction to the brand. The universal Harley appeals are these: freedom, independence, power, and authenticity. Harley-Davidson

doesn't just sell motorcycles. It sells self-expression, lifestyles, aspirations, and dreams. "It's all about the *experience*," says an analyst, "one forged in heavy metal thunder, living free and peeling wheel down Route 66. It's an experience that allows middle-aged accountants to don black, studded leather and forget about debits and credits for a little while."

To hard-core enthusiasts, a Harley is much more than a machine. It's a part of who they are and where they want to go in life. A Harley renews your spirits and announces your freedom and independence. A popular line at Harley-Davidson is that "Thumbing the starter of a Harley does a lot more than fire the engine. It fires the imagination." The classic look, the throaty sound, the very idea of a Harley—all contribute to its mystique. Owning this "American legend" makes you a part of something bigger, a member of the Harley-Davidson family.

The strong emotions and motivations underlying Harley consumer behavior are captured in a classic old Harley-Davidson print advertisement. The ad shows a close-up of an arm, the bicep adorned with a Harley-Davidson tattoo. The headline asks, "When was the last time you felt this strongly about anything?" The ad copy outlines the problem and suggests a solution: "Wake up in the morning and life picks up where it left off....What once seemed exciting has now become part of the numbing routine. It all begins to feel the same. Except when you've got a Harley-Davidson. Something strikes a nerve. The heartfelt thunder rises up, refusing to become part of the background. Suddenly things are different. Clearer. More real. As they should have been all along. Riding a Harley changes you from within. The effect is permanent. Maybe it's time you started feeling this strongly. Things are different on a Harley."[1]

OBJECTIVES OUTLINE

OBJECTIVE 5-1	Define the consumer market and construct a simple model of consumer buyer behavior.
	Model of Consumer Behavior *(pp 134–135)*
OBJECTIVE 5-2	Name the four major factors that influence consumer buyer behavior.
	Characteristics Affecting Consumer Behavior *(pp 135–149)*
OBJECTIVE 5-3	List and define the major types of buying decision behavior and the stages in the buyer decision process.
	Buying Decision Behavior and the Buyer Decision Process *(pp 150–154)*
OBJECTIVE 5-4	Describe the adoption and diffusion process for new products.
	The Buyer Decision Process for New Products *(pp 154–156)*

Consumer buyer behavior
The buying behavior of final consumers—individuals and households that buy goods and services for personal consumption.

Consumer market
All the individuals and households that buy or acquire goods and services for personal consumption.

THE HARLEY-DAVIDSON EXAMPLE shows that factors at many levels affect consumer buying behavior. Buying behavior is never simple, yet understanding it is an essential task of marketing management. **Consumer buyer behavior** refers to the buying behavior of final consumers—individuals and households that buy goods and services for personal consumption. All of these final consumers combine to make up the **consumer market**. The American consumer market consists of more than 323 million people who consume more than $11.9 trillion worth of goods and services each year, making it one of the most attractive consumer markets in the world.[2]

Consumers around the world vary tremendously in age, income, education level, and tastes. They also buy an incredible variety of goods and services. How these diverse consumers relate with each other and with other elements of the world around them affects their choices among various products, services, and companies. Here we examine the fascinating array of factors that affect consumer behavior.

> **Author Comment** | Despite the simple-looking model in Figure 5.1, understanding the *whys* of buying behavior is very difficult. Says one expert, "The mind is a whirling, swirling, jumbled mass of neurons bouncing around…."

Model of Consumer Behavior

Consumers make many buying decisions every day, and the buying decision is the focal point of the marketer's effort. Most large companies research consumer buying decisions in great detail to answer questions about what consumers buy, where they buy, how and how much they buy, when they buy, and why they buy. Marketers can study actual consumer purchases to find out what they buy, where, and how much. But learning about the *whys* behind consumer buying behavior is not so easy—the answers are often locked deep within the consumer's mind. Often, consumers themselves don't know exactly what influences their purchases.

The central question for marketers is this: How do consumers respond to various marketing efforts the company might use? The starting point is the stimulus-response model of buyer behavior shown in ● **Figure 5.1**. This figure shows that marketing and other stimuli enter the consumer's "black box" and produce certain responses.

Marketers want to understand how the stimuli are changed into responses inside the consumer's black box, which has two parts. First, the buyer's characteristics influence how he or she perceives and reacts to the stimuli. These characteristics include a variety of cultural, social, personal, and psychological factors. Second, the buyer's decision process itself affects his or her behavior. This decision process—from need recognition, information search, and alternative evaluation to the purchase decision and postpurchase behavior—begins long before the actual purchase decision and continues long after.

● FIGURE | 5.1
The Model of Buyer Behavior

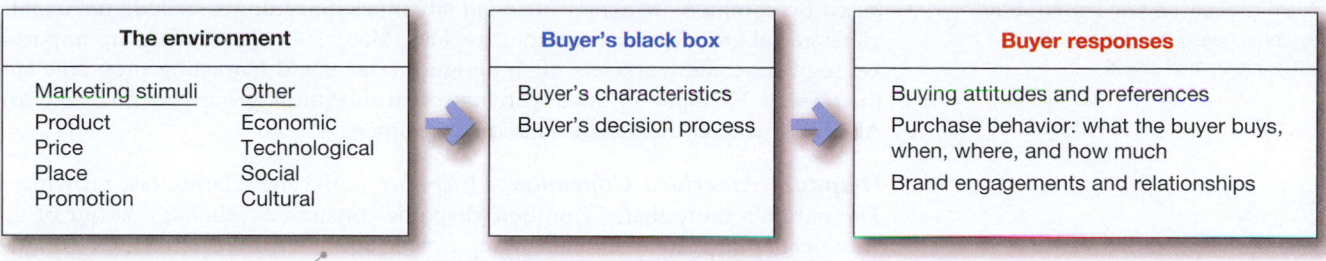

We can measure the whats, wheres, and whens of buyer behavior. But it's difficult to "see" inside the consumer's head and figure out the whys (that's why it's called the black box).

We look first at buyer characteristics as they affect buyer behavior and then discuss the buyer decision process.

Characteristics Affecting Consumer Behavior

Author Comment | Many levels of factors affect our buying behavior—from broad cultural and social influences to motivations, beliefs, and attitudes lying deep within us.

Consumer purchases are influenced strongly by cultural, social, personal, and psychological characteristics, as shown in ● **Figure 5.2**. For the most part, marketers cannot control such factors, but they must take them into account.

Cultural Factors

Cultural factors exert a broad and deep influence on consumer behavior. Marketers need to understand the role played by the buyer's *culture, subculture,* and *social class.*

Culture

Culture
The set of basic values, perceptions, wants, and behaviors learned by a member of society from family and other important institutions.

Culture is the most basic cause of a person's wants and behavior. Human behavior is largely learned. Growing up in a society, a child learns basic values, perceptions, wants, and behaviors from his or her family and other important institutions. A child in the United States normally is exposed to the following values: achievement and success, freedom, individualism, hard work, activity and involvement, efficiency and practicality, material comfort, youthfulness, and fitness and health. Every group or society has a culture, and cultural influences on buying behavior may vary greatly from both county to county and country to country.

Marketers are always trying to spot *cultural shifts* so as to discover new products that might be wanted. For example, the cultural shift toward greater concern about health and fitness has created a huge industry for health-and-fitness services, exercise equipment and clothing, organic foods, and a variety of diets.

● FIGURE | 5.2
Factors Influencing Consumer Behavior

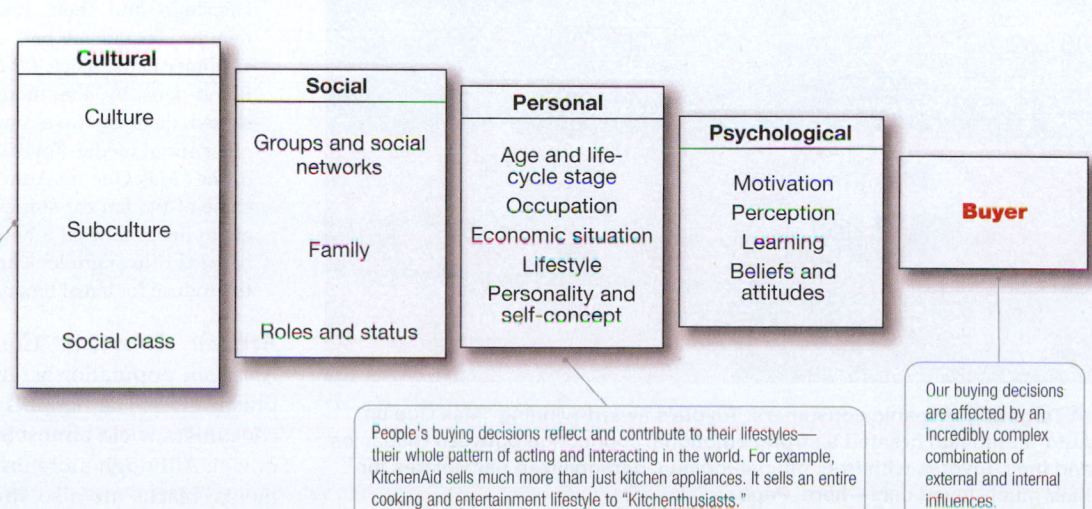

Many brands now target specific subcultures—such as Hispanic American, African American, and Asian American consumers—with marketing programs tailored to their specific needs and preferences.

People's buying decisions reflect and contribute to their lifestyles—their whole pattern of acting and interacting in the world. For example, KitchenAid sells much more than just kitchen appliances. It sells an entire cooking and entertainment lifestyle to "Kitchenthusiasts."

Our buying decisions are affected by an incredibly complex combination of external and internal influences.

Subculture

Each culture contains smaller **subcultures**, or groups of people with shared value systems based on common life experiences and situations. Subcultures include nationalities, religions, racial groups, and geographic regions. Many subcultures make up important market segments, and marketers often design products and marketing programs tailored to their needs. Examples of three such important subculture groups are Hispanic American, African American, and Asian American consumers.

Hispanic American Consumers. *Hispanics* represent a large, fast-growing market. The nation's more than 55 million Hispanic consumers (almost one out of every six Americans) have total annual buying power of $1.7 trillion. The U.S. Hispanic population will surge to more than 130 million by 2030, close to one-third of the total U.S. population. Hispanics are a youthful segment—more than 52 percent of U.S. Hispanics are below age 30.[3] Within the Hispanic market, there exist many distinct subsegments based on nationality, age, income, and other factors. A company's product or message may be more relevant to one nationality over another, such as Mexicans, Costa Ricans, Argentineans, or Cubans.

Although Hispanic consumers share many characteristics and behaviors with the mainstream buying public, there are also distinct differences. They tend to be deeply family oriented and make shopping a family affair—children have a big say in what brands they buy. Older, first-generation Hispanic consumers tend to be very brand loyal and to favor brands and sellers who show special interest in them. Younger Hispanics, however, have shown increasing price sensitivity in recent years and a willingness to switch to store brands. Befitting their youthfulness, Hispanics are more active on mobile and social networks than other segments, making digital media ideal for reaching this segment.[4]

Companies ranging from P&G, McDonald's, AT&T, Walmart, and State Farm to Google, L'Oréal, and many others have developed special targeting efforts for this fast-growing consumer segment. For example, working with its longtime Hispanic advertising agency Conill, Toyota has developed numerous Hispanic marketing campaigns that have helped make it the favorite automobile brand among Hispanic buyers. Consider its recent award-winning "Más Que un Auto" campaign:

Last fall, to celebrate its 10th year as America's most-loved auto brand among Hispanics, Toyota ran a Hispanic campaign themed "Más Que un Auto" (translation: "More than a Car"). The campaign appealed to Hispanics' special love for their cars and their penchant for giving everything and anything a superpersonal nickname, including their cars. ● The campaign offered Hispanic customers free nameplates featuring their unique car names, made with the same typeface and materials as the official Toyota nameplates. Now, along with the Toyota and model names, they could adorn their cars with personalized, official-looking brand badges of their own—whether Pepe, El Niño, Trueno ("Thunder"), Monster, or just plain Oliver, Ellie, or Rolly the Corolla.

The award-winning "Más Que un Auto" campaign created a strong emotional connection between Hispanics and their Toyotas. Within the first few months, customers had ordered more than 100,000 customer nameplates, far exceeding the goal of 25,000. Brand fans by the thousands posted pictures and shared their car love stories on campaign sites and other social media. Toyota is now shaping new phases of the "Más Que un Auto" campaign, such as turning some of the fan car stories into ads or asking customers to imagine what a how commercial featuring their beloved ride might look and then picking the best idea to produce for a real broadcast ad.[5]

African American Consumers. The U.S. *African American* population is growing in affluence and sophistication. The nation's more than 44 million black consumers wield almost $1.3 trillion in annual buying power. Although more price conscious than other segments, blacks are also strongly motivated by quality and selection. Brands are important. African American

● Targeting Hispanic consumers: Toyota's award-winning "Más Que un Auto" campaign created a strong emotional connection between Hispanics and their Toyotas with free, official-looking, personalized nameplates for their much-loved cars—here, Pepe.

Toyota Motor Sales, U.S.A. Inc.

Unplug.

Discover The Forest.org

● **Targeting African American consumers: The U.S. Forest Service and the Ad Council joined forces to create the "Discover the Forest" public service campaign to raise awareness among African American families of the benefits for children of getting outside and enjoying nature.**

The Forest Service, an agency of the U.S. Department of Agriculture, and the Ad Council

Total market strategy
Integrating ethnic themes and cross-cultural perspectives within a brand's mainstream marketing, appealing to consumer similarities across subcultural segments rather than differences.

consumers are heavy users of digital and social media, providing access through a rich variety of marketing channels.[6]

Many companies develop special products, appeals, and marketing programs for African American consumers—from carmakers like Ford and Hyundai to consumer products companies like P&G to even not-for-profits and government agencies such as the U.S. Forest Service. ● For example, the U.S. Forest Service and the Ad Council recently joined forces to create the "Discover the Forest" public service campaign to raise awareness among families of the benefits for children of getting outside and enjoying nature. One round of the campaign specifically targeted the parents of African American tweens:[7]

Although more than 245 million Americans live within 100 miles of a national forest or grassland, research shows that a majority of children in some population segments are not spending active time outdoors. For example, only 37 percent of African American children ages 6 to 12 participate frequently in outdoor activities compared with 67 percent of the broader U.S. population in that age group. To help close that gap, the U.S. Forest Service and the Ad Council created the "Discover the Forest" campaign, a series of public service messages ranging from billboards and radio commercials to interactive social media and website content. With headlines such as "Unplug," "Where Curiosity Blooms," and "Where Imagination Sprouts," the ads targeting African American families promote the discovery and imagination wonders of connecting with the great outdoors and the resulting physical, mental, health, and emotional well-being benefits. "The forest is one of those amazing places where kids can flex their imagination muscles through exploration and discovery," says a marketer associated with the campaign.

Asian American Consumers. *Asian Americans* are the most affluent U.S. demographic segment. A relatively well-educated segment, they now number more than 18.5 million (5 percent of the population), with annual buying power expected to approach $1 trillion by 2018. Asian Americans are the second-fastest-growing subsegment after Hispanic Americans. And like Hispanic Americans, they are a diverse group. Chinese Americans constitute the largest group, followed by Filipinos, Asian Indians, Vietnamese, Korean Americans, and Japanese Americans. Yet, unlike Hispanics who all speak various dialects of Spanish, Asians speak many different languages. For example, ads for the 2010 U.S. Census ran in languages ranging from Japanese, Cantonese, Khmer, Korean, and Vietnamese to Thai, Cambodian, Hmong, Hinglish, and Taglish.[8]

As a group, Asian American consumers shop frequently and are the most brand conscious of all the ethnic groups. They can be fiercely brand loyal, especially to brands that work to build relationships with them. As a result, many firms now target the Asian American market. For example, many retailers, especially luxury retailers such as Bloomingdale's, now feature themed events and promotions during the Chinese New Year, a spending season equivalent to the Christmas holidays for Chinese American consumers. They hire Mandarin-speaking staff, offer Chinese-themed fashions and other merchandise, and feature Asian cultural presentations. Bloomingdale's has even introduced seasonal, limited edition pop-up shops in many stores around the country:

● Richly designed in red, gold, and black motifs, Chinese colors of good fortune, the Bloomingdale's pop-up boutiques feature high-end Chinese-themed fashions and other merchandise created especially for the Chinese New Year celebration. Some locations sponsor entertainment such as lion dancers, Chinese tarot card readings, calligraphy, lantern making, tea tastings, and free Zodiac nail art. Shoppers in some stores are invited to select Chinese red envelopes with prizes such as gift cards in denominations of $8, $88, or $888 (eight is a lucky number in Chinese culture). In addition to the pop-up boutiques, Bloomingdale's celebrates the days and weeks leading up to the Chinese New Year with Chinese-language ads and promotions in carefully targeted traditional and online media. The retailer also has 175 Chinese-speaking associates across the country. "Chinese customers, including both tourists as well as Chinese Americans, are an important part of the overall Bloomingdale's business," says the retailer's CEO.[9]

A Total Marketing Strategy. Beyond targeting segments such as Hispanics, African Americans, and Asian Americans with specially tailored efforts, many marketers now embrace a **total market strategy**—the practice of integrating ethnic themes and

● **Targeting Asian American consumers:** Bloomingdale's celebrates the important Chinese New Year with carefully targeted ads and promotions and even special seasonal pop-up boutiques in its stores featuring Chinese-themed merchandise, events, and entertainment.

Petr Svab/Epoch Times Inc.

cross-cultural perspectives within their mainstream marketing. An example is general-market commercials for Cheerios and Honey Maid that feature interracial and blended families and couples. A total market strategy appeals to consumer similarities across subcultural segments rather than differences.[10]

Many marketers are finding that insights gleaned from ethnic consumer segments can influence their broader markets. For example, today's youth-oriented lifestyle is influenced heavily by Hispanic and African American entertainers. So it follows that consumers expect to see many different cultures and ethnicities represented in the advertising and products they consume. For instance, McDonald's takes cues from African Americans, Hispanics, and Asians to develop menus and advertising in hopes of encouraging mainstream consumers to buy smoothies, mocha drinks, and snack wraps as avidly as they consume hip-hop and rock 'n' roll. Or McDonald's might take an ad primarily geared toward African Americans and run it in general-market media.

Social Class

Social class

Relatively permanent and ordered divisions in a society whose members share similar values, interests, and behaviors.

Almost every society has some form of social class structure. **Social classes** are society's relatively permanent and ordered divisions whose members share similar values, interests, and behaviors. Social scientists have identified seven American social classes: upper upper class, lower upper class, upper middle class, middle class, working class, upper lower class, and lower lower class.

Social class is not determined by a single factor, such as income, but is measured as a combination of occupation, income, education, wealth, and other variables. In some social systems, members of different classes are reared for certain roles and cannot change their social positions. In the United States, however, the lines between social classes are not fixed and rigid; people can move to a higher social class or drop into a lower one.

Marketers are interested in social class because people within a given social class tend to exhibit similar buying behavior. Social classes show distinct product and brand preferences in areas such as clothing, home furnishings, travel and leisure activity, financial services, and automobiles.

Social Factors

A consumer's behavior also is influenced by social factors, such as the consumer's *small groups, social networks, family,* and *social roles and status.*

Groups and Social Networks

Group

Two or more people who interact to accomplish individual or mutual goals.

Many small **groups** influence a person's behavior. Groups that have a direct influence and to which a person belongs are called *membership groups*. In contrast, *reference groups* serve as direct (face-to-face interactions) or indirect points of comparison or reference in forming a person's attitudes or behavior. People often are influenced by reference groups to which they do not belong. For example, an *aspirational group* is one to which the individual wishes to belong, as when a young basketball player hopes to someday emulate basketball star LeBron James and play in the NBA.

Marketers try to identify the reference groups of their target markets. Reference groups expose a person to new behaviors and lifestyles, influence the person's attitudes and self-concept, and create pressures to conform that may affect the person's product and brand choices. The importance of group influence varies across products and brands. It tends to be strongest when the product is visible to others whom the buyer respects.

Word-of-mouth influence
The impact of the personal words and recommendations of trusted friends, family, associates, and other consumers on buying behavior.

Word-of-mouth influence can have a powerful impact on consumer buying behavior. The personal words and recommendations of trusted friends, family, associates, and other consumers tend to be more credible than those coming from commercial sources, such as advertisements or salespeople. One recent study found that only 49 percent of consumers reported that they trust or believe advertising, whereas 72 percent said they trusted family and friends and 72 percent said they trust online reviews.[11] Most word-of-mouth influence happens naturally: Consumers start chatting about a brand they use or feel strongly about one way or the other. Often, however, rather than leaving it to chance, marketers can help to create positive conversations about their brands.

Marketers of brands subjected to strong group influence must figure out how to reach **opinion leaders**—people within a reference group who, because of special skills, knowledge, personality, or other characteristics, exert social influence on others. Some experts call this group the *influentials* or *leading adopters*. When these influentials talk, consumers listen. Marketers try to identify opinion leaders for their products and direct marketing efforts toward them.

Opinion leader
A person within a reference group who, because of special skills, knowledge, personality, or other characteristics, exerts social influence on others.

Buzz marketing involves enlisting or even creating opinion leaders to serve as "brand ambassadors" who spread the word about a company's products. Consider Mercedes-Benz's award-winning "Take the Wheel" influencer campaign:[12]

> Mercedes-Benz wanted get more people talking about its all-new, soon-to-be-launched 2014 CLA model, priced at $29,900 and aimed at getting a new generation of younger consumers into the Mercedes brand. So it challenged five of Instagram's most influential photographers—everyday Gen Y consumers whose stunning imagery had earned them hundreds of thousands of fans—to each spend five days behind the wheel of a CLA, documenting their journeys in photos shared via Instagram. The photographer who got the most Likes got to keep the CLA. The short campaign really got people buzzing about the car, earning 87 million social media impressions and more than 2 million Likes. Ninety percent of the social conversation was positive. And when Mercedes launched the CLA the following month, it broke sales records.

Sometimes, everyday customers become a brand's best evangelists. For instance, Alan Klein loves the McDonald's McRib—a sandwich made of a boneless pork patty molded into a rib-like shape, slathered in BBQ sauce and topped with pickles and onion. The McRib is sold for only short time periods each year at McDonald's restaurants around the nation. Klein loves it so much that he created the McRib Locator app and website (mcrib-locator.com), where McRib fans buzz about locations where they've recently sighted the coveted sandwich.[13]

Online social networks
Online social communities—blogs, online social media, brand communities, and other online forums—where people socialize or exchange information and opinions.

Over the past several years, a new type of social interaction has exploded onto the scene—online social networking. **Online social networks** are online communities where people socialize or exchange information and opinions. Social networking communities range from blogs (Consumerist, Engadget, Gizmodo) and message boards (Craigslist) to social media sites (Facebook, Twitter, YouTube, Instagram, Snapchat, LinkedIn) and even communal shopping sites (Amazon.com and Etsy). These online forms of consumer-to-consumer and business-to-consumer dialogue have big implications for marketers.

Marketers are working to harness the power of these new social networks and other "word-of-web" opportunities to promote their products and build closer customer relationships. Instead of throwing more one-way commercial messages at consumers, they hope to use digital, mobile, and social media to become an interactive part of consumers' conversations and lives.

For example, Red Bull has an astounding 44 million friends on Facebook; Twitter and Facebook are the primary ways it communicates with college students. ● Dunkin' Donuts uses Vine personality Logan Paul to promote its Dunkin' Donuts app and DD Perks loyalty program with posts on Vine and other social media. As it turns out, Paul is a genuine Dunkin' Donuts fan, so the brand lets him figure out what to say to his more than 8.7 million Vine followers, 5.4 million Facebook fans, 2.4 million followers on Instagram, and 615 followers on Twitter.[14]

Other marketers are working to tap the army of self-made influencers already plying the internet—independent bloggers. Believe it or not, there are now almost as many people making a living as bloggers as there are lawyers. The key is to find bloggers who have strong networks of relevant readers, a credible voice, and a good fit with the brand. For example, you'll no doubt cross paths with the likes of climbers and skiers blogging for Patagonia, bikers blogging for Harley-Davidson, and foodies blogging for Whole Foods Market or Trader Joe's. And companies such as P&G, McDonald's, Walmart, and Disney

Instagram post:

loganpaul   FOLLOW

123k likes   18w

loganpaul Bruh. Does it get much better than this? Enjoying the goods on the @DunkinDonuts app :) Go download it, sign up for DD perks, and enter promo code LOGAN to get a free beverage #ad Link in bio 😊

view all 404 comments

ayita_kasa Mhhhh dunkin donuts 😍😍😍 how old are you btw?

luke.haas10 @ayita_kasa he's out of college do probably like early to mid 20's

502joseph STARBUCKS IS BETTERRRRRRRRR

kaylacaste @sev620 i hope this is me and 7 years

sev620 Me too #dreamsinlife @kaylacaste

__beanieboy__ 😊 is life isn't it

day_vaa @emielis @ericaajackk

Add a comment...

🔵 **Harnessing the power of online social networking: Dunkin' Donuts uses Vine personality Logan Paul to promote its Dunkin' Donuts app and DD Perks loyalty program with posts on Vine and other social media.**

Courtesy Logan Paul

work closely with influential "mom bloggers" or "social media moms," turning them into brand advocates (see Real Marketing 5.1).

Even Bermuda uses social media extensively. The Bermuda Tourism Authority maintains Facebook, Instagram, Pinterest, Twitter, YouTube, and other social media pages; two mobile apps, including the Bermuda's Very Own Mobile Events App; and a Discovering Bermuda blog featuring "Posts from Paradise." It also hires popular users of social media such as Instagram and trendy Tastemade—which features quirky videos about restaurants—to the island and urges them to post about their visits.[15]

We will dig deeper into online and social media as marketing tools in Chapter 17. However, although much current talk focuses on the digital, mobile, and social media, most brand conversations still take place the old-fashioned way—face to face. So effective word-of-mouth marketing programs usually begin with generating person-to-person brand conversations and integrating both offline and online social influence strategies. The goal is to get customers involved with brands and then help them share their brand passions and experiences with others in both their real and digital worlds. Consider Chubbies:[16]

> Chubbies is a small but trendy and fast-growing startup that targets young men with a line of "anti-cargo shorts" (and a retro 5 1/2-inch inseam). Until recently, the brand marketed itself only through its social media presence. Avid Chubsters actively swap influence via pictures, videos, and stories on YouTube, Facebook, Twitter, Instagram, Pinterest, and the Chubbies website and ChubsterNation blog. But now, Chubbies is building an army of face-to-face influencers in the form of 140 student ambassadors at college campuses across the country. The ambassadors— what Chubbies calls its "badass crew of thigh-liberating patriots"—spread the Chubster manifesto that "We don't do pants. We don't do cargos. We don't do capris. We do shorts and only shorts." "Pants are for work," they preach. Chubbies "are for having fun, or jumping off rocks, or playing beer pong, or climbing Everest." The ambassadors personally rally the faithful at tailgate parties and other campus events, expanding the ChubsterNation and sparking even more word of mouth for the irreverent brand.

Family

Family members can strongly influence buyer behavior. The family is the most important consumer buying organization in society, and it has been researched extensively. Marketers are interested in the roles and influence of the husband, wife, and children on the purchase of different products and services.

Husband–wife involvement varies widely by product category and by stage in the buying process. Buying roles change with evolving consumer lifestyles. For example, in the United States, the wife traditionally has been considered the main purchasing agent for the family in the areas of food, household products, and clothing. But with 71 percent of all mothers now working outside the home and the willingness of husbands to do more of the family's purchasing, all this has changed in recent years. Recent surveys show that 41 percent of men are now the primary grocery shoppers in their households, 39 percent handle most of their household's laundry, and about one-quarter say they are responsible for all of their household's cooking. At the same time, today women outspend men three to two on new technology purchases and influence more than 80 percent of all new car purchases.[17]

Such shifting roles signal a new marketing reality. Marketers in industries that have traditionally sold their products to only women or only men—from groceries and personal care products to cars and consumer electronics—are now carefully targeting the opposite sex. Other companies are showing their products in "modern family" contexts. For example, one General Mills ad shows a father packing Go-Gurt yogurt in his son's lunch as the child heads off to school in the morning, with the slogan "Dads who

5.1 Tapping Social Media Moms as Brand Ambassadors

America's moms constitute a huge market. Women account for 85 percent of all consumer purchases, and the nation's 85 million moms account $3.2 trillion worth of annual consumer spending. Moms are also heavy social media sharers and shoppers. They are 20 percent more likely than the general population to use social media, and 44 percent of moms have made a purchase on their smartphones within the past week.

Moreover, many moms rely heavily on social media to share experiences with other moms, including brand and buying experiences. For example, there are as many as 14.2 million U.S. mothers who blog, and some mom bloggers influence millions of followers. Some 55 percent of moms on social media regularly base their buying decisions on personal stories, recommendations, and product reviews that they find in blogs and other social media.

Given these pretty amazing figures, it's not surprising that many marketers now harness the power of mom-to-mom influence by creating or tapping into networks of influential social media moms and turning them into brand ambassadors. Here are just three examples: McDonald's, Walmart, and Disney.

McDonald's Mom Bloggers. McDonald's systematically reaches out to key "mom bloggers," those who influence the nation's homemakers, who in turn influence their families' eating-out choices. For example, McDonald's recently hosted 15 influential mom bloggers on an all-expenses-paid tour of its Chicago-area headquarters. The bloggers toured the facilities (including the company's test kitchens), met McDonald's USA president, and had their pictures taken with Ronald at a nearby Ronald McDonald House.

McDonald's knows that these mom bloggers have loyal followings and talk a lot about McDonald's in their blogs. So it's turning the bloggers into believers by giving them a behind-the-scenes view. McDonald's doesn't try to tell the bloggers what to say in their posts about the visit. It simply asks them to write one honest recap of their trip. However, the resulting posts (each acknowledging the blogger's connection with McDonald's) were mostly very positive. Thanks to this and other such efforts, mom bloggers around the country are now more informed about and connected with McDonald's. "I know they have

smoothies and they have yogurt and they have other things that my kids would want," says one prominent blogger. "I really couldn't tell you what Burger King's doing right now," she adds. "I have no idea."

Walmart Moms. Eight years ago, Walmart enlisted a group of 11 influential mom bloggers—originally called the ElevenMoms—to "represent the voice of all moms." Now numbering 22 and called simply the "Walmart Moms," these influential social media moms provide input to Walmart on behalf of all moms and in turn represent Walmart to their large blog followings.

Described by Walmart as "moms like you," the Walmart Moms represent a cross-section of American moms in terms of geography, ethnicity, and age. "Walmart Moms are pretty much like most moms out there," says Walmart. They "know what it's like to balance family, work, errands, searching for missing softball mitts, and everything else in between. And [they're] always looking for ways to save money and live better."

The Walmart Moms have become important and influential Walmart brand ambassadors. Though surveys, focus groups, and in-store events, the mom bloggers and their readers provide Walmart and its suppliers with key customer insights regarding its stores and products. Going the other way, the Walmart Moms create relevant written and video content—everything from money-saving tips to product reviews to craft suggestions and recipes—shared on their blogs and through links on Walmart's online and social media sites.

Walmart Moms receive product samples and compensation. Their posts often refer to products sold by Walmart and include links to the products on Walmart sites. But both Walmart and

the Walmart Moms know that their strength lies in their authenticity and in the trust they build with their readers. So with Walmart's urging and full support, the moms write whatever they please and share their sincere opinions. "Walmart does not require anything of us but to be ourselves and remain authentic to our own voice," says one mom blogger. Without that, what the Walmart Moms write and say would be viewed as little more than paid promotions.

Disney Social Media Moms. The Walt Disney Company has long recognized the power of moms in social media and the importance moms play in planning family vacations. Five years ago, the company assembled a group called Disney Social Media Moms, roughly 1,300 carefully selected mom

Harnessing the power of mom-to-mom influence: Each year, Disney invites 175 to 200 moms and their families to its Disney Social Media Moms Celebration in Florida, an affair that's a mix of public relations event, educational conference, and family vacation with plenty of Disney magic for these important mom influencers.
Mindy Marzec

bloggers (and some dads), travel bloggers, and active Disney-focused social media posters.

Disney looks for influential moms who fit the brand's family-friendly focus, use social media heavily, and are active in their communities offline as well as online. One example is Rachel Pitzel, a mother of two and CEO of ClubMomMe, a social and educational group that sponsors events for moms, expectant parents, and families and maintains an active blog. Another is Wendy Wright, a homeschooling mother of two and a prolific blogger. Wendy describes herself as a "Disney nut" (she named her cats Mickey and Minnie), and she fills her blog with advice for planning Disney park visits, tips for holding Disney-themed parties, and reviews of Disney movies.

Disney Social Media Moms aren't paid; they participate because of their passion and enthusiasm for all things Disney. However, they do receive special educational attention from Disney, inside information, and occasional perks. For example, every year, Disney invites 175 to 200 of the moms and their families for a deeply discounted, four-day trip to attend its annual Disney Social Media Moms Celebration in Florida. The celebration is a mix of public relations event, educational conference, and family vacation with plenty of Disney magic for these important mom influencers.

The Disney Social Media Moms are under no obligation to post anything about Disney, and the company doesn't tell them what to say when they do post. However, the most recent celebration generated 28,500 tweets, 4,900 Instagram photos, and 88 blog posts full of ride reviews, videos of families meeting Disney characters, and a host of overwhelmingly positive comments. "For a big chunk of our guests, it's the moms who are making [travel] decisions," says a top Disney executive. The Disney Social Media Moms effort costs the company very little but effectively harnesses the power of mom-to-mom influence to help sprinkle Disney's magical pixie dust on an important group of buyers.

Sources: See Mindy Rasledvich, "Harnessing the Power of Mom-to-Mom Influence," *Dedicated Media,* May 19, 2015, www.dedicatedmedia.com/articles/harnessing-the-power-of-mom-to-mom-influence-2; Elizabeth Segran, "On Winning the Hearts—and Dollars—of Mommy Bloggers," *Fast Company,* August 14, 2015, www.fastcompany.com/3049137; Keith O'Brien, "How McDonald's Came Back Bigger than Ever," *New York Times,* May 6, 2012, p. MM44; "Who Are Walmart Moms?" http://learn.walmart.com/Tips-Ideas/Articles/Walmart_Moms/19242/, accessed June 2016; "How Walmart Made 11 Moms Become Its Brand Ambassadors," http://crezeo.com/how-11-moms-became-walmart-brand-ambassadors/, accessed June 2016; Lisa Richwine, "Disney's Powerful Marketing Force: Social Media Moms," *Reuters,* June 15, 2015, www.reuters.com/article/us-disney-moms-insight-idUSKBN0OV0DX20150615; and "Disney Parks Social Media Moms Celebration," http://disneysmmoms.com/, accessed September 2016.

get it, get Go-Gurt." And a recent General Mills "How to Dad" campaign for Cheerios presents a dad as a multitasking superhero around the house, a departure from the bumbling dad stereotypes often shown in food ads. This dad does all the right things, including feeding this children healthy Cheerios breakfasts. "Being a dad is awesome," he proclaims in one ad. "Just like Cheerios are awesome. That's why it's the Official Cereal of Dadhood."[18]

Children also have a strong influence on family buying decisions. The nation's kids and tweens influence up to 80 percent of all household purchases, to the tune of $1.2 trillion of spending annually. ● In one recent survey, parents with teens reported that their children weigh in heavily on everything from where they eat out (95 percent) and take vacations (82 percent) to what mobile devices they use (63 percent) and cars they buy (45 percent).[19]

Roles and Status

A person belongs to many groups—family, clubs, organizations, online communities. The person's position in each group can be defined in terms of both role and status. A role consists of the activities people are expected to perform according to the people around them. Each role carries a status reflecting the general esteem given to it by society.

People usually choose products appropriate to their roles and status. Consider the various roles a working mother plays. In her company, she may play the role of a brand manager; in her family, she plays the role of wife and mother; at her favorite sporting events, she plays the role of avid fan. As a brand manager, she will buy the kind of clothing that reflects her role and status in her company. At the game, she may wear clothing supporting her favorite team.

● **Family buying influences: Children may weigh in heavily on family purchases for everything from restaurants and vacation destinations to mobile devices and even car purchases.**

Andres Rodriguez/123RF

Personal Factors

A buyer's decisions also are influenced by personal characteristics such as the buyer's *occupation, age and stage, economic situation, lifestyle,* and *personality and self-concept.*

Occupation

A person's occupation affects the goods and services bought. Blue-collar workers tend to buy more rugged work clothes, whereas executives buy more business suits. Marketers try to identify the occupational groups that have an above-average interest in their prod-

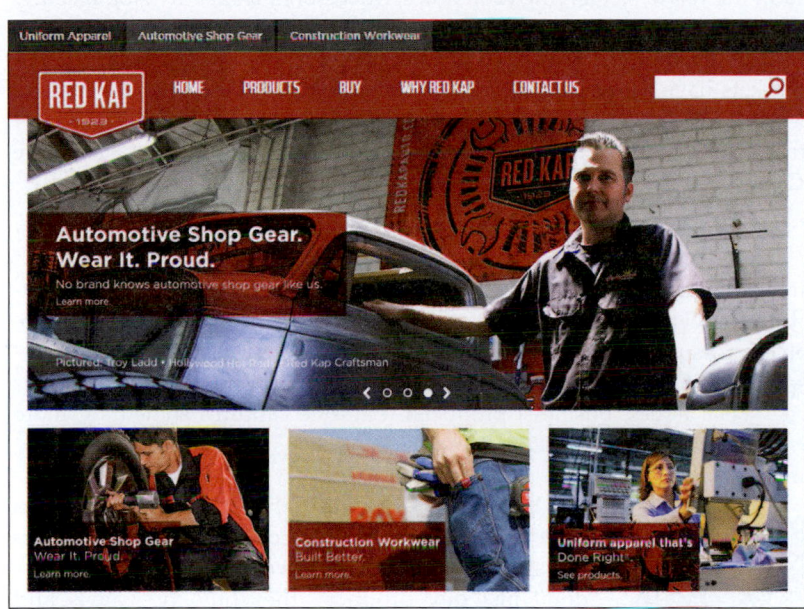

● Appealing to occupation segments: Red Kap makes rugged, durable work clothes and uniform apparel for the automotive and construction industries.

VF Corporation

ucts and services. A company can even specialize in making products needed by a given occupational group. ● For example, Red Kap makes rugged, durable work clothes and uniform apparel for the automotive and construction industries. Since 1923, the brand has lived up to its "Done Right" slogan—it makes "Workwear. Built Better." According to the company, "If there's a secret to our success, it's the quality time our design team spends in the garage. That's where our best ideas are born. Where working prototypes are tested, fine-tuned, and tested again. The result? Top-grade [workwear] that any serious gearhead can actually feel good about wearing. Comfortable, long-lasting favorites that stand up to hard days, greasy nights, and everything in between."[20]

Age and Life Stage

People change the goods and services they buy over their lifetimes. Tastes in food, clothes, furniture, and recreation are often age related. Buying is also shaped by the stage of the family life cycle—the stages through which families might pass as they mature over time. Life-stage changes usually result from demographics and life-changing events—marriage, having children, purchasing a home, divorce, children going to college, changes in personal income, moving out of the house, and retirement. Marketers often define their target markets in terms of life-cycle stage and develop appropriate products and marketing plans for each stage.

One of the leading life-stage segmentation systems is the Nielsen PRIZM Lifestage Groups system. PRIZM classifies every American household into one of 66 distinct life-stage segments, which are organized into 11 major life-stage groups based on affluence, age, and family characteristics. The classifications consider a host of demographic factors such as age, education, income, occupation, family composition, ethnicity, and housing; and behavioral and lifestyle factors such as purchases, free-time activities, and media preferences.

The major PRIZM Lifestage groups carry names such as "Striving Singles," "Midlife Success," "Young Achievers," "Sustaining Families," "Affluent Empty Nests," and "Conservative Classics," which in turn contain subgroups such as "Brite Lites, Li'l City," "Kids & Cul-de-Sacs," "Gray Power," and "Big City Blues." The "Young Achievers" group consists of hip, single 20-somethings who rent apartments in or close to metropolitan neighborhoods. Their incomes range from working class to well-to-do, but the entire group tends to be politically liberal, listen to alternative music, and enjoy lively nightlife.[21]

Life-stage segmentation provides a powerful marketing tool for marketers in all industries to better find, understand, and engage consumers. Armed with data about the makeup of consumer life stages, marketers can create targeted, actionable, personalized campaigns based on how people consume and interact with brands and the world around them.

Economic Situation

A person's economic situation will affect his or her store and product choices. Marketers watch trends in spending, personal income, savings, and interest rates. In today's more value-conscious times, most companies have taken steps to create more customer value by redesigning, repositioning, and repricing their products and services. For example, in recent years, upscale discounter Target has put more emphasis on the "Pay Less" side of its "Expect More. Pay Less." positioning promise.

Similarly, in line with worldwide economic trends, smartphone makers who once offered only premium-priced phones are now offering lower-priced models for consumers both at home and in the world's emerging economies. Microsoft's Nokia division recently targeted emerging markets with lower-end Lumia models priced well under $100. And Apple is rumored to be introducing a lower-priced version of its iPhone. As their more affluent Western markets have become saturated and more competitive, the phone makers hope that their lower-priced phones will help them to compete effectively in less-affluent emerging Eastern markets such as China and Southeast Asia against low-cost smartphone makers such as Chinese giant Xiaomi.[22]

Lifestyle

Lifestyle
A person's pattern of living as expressed in his or her activities, interests, and opinions.

People coming from the same subculture, social class, and occupation may have quite different lifestyles. **Lifestyle** is a person's pattern of living as expressed in his or her psychographics. It involves measuring consumers' major AIO dimensions—*activities* (work, hobbies, shopping, sports, social events), *interests* (food, fashion, family, recreation), and *opinions* (about themselves, social issues, business, products). Lifestyle captures something more than the person's social class or personality. It profiles a person's whole pattern of acting and interacting in the world.

When used carefully, the lifestyle concept can help marketers understand changing consumer values and how they affect buyer behavior. Consumers don't just buy products; they buy the values and lifestyles those products represent. ● For example, Title Nine markets much more than just women's apparel:

Named after the federal act that helped end gender discrimination in high school and collegiate sports, Title Nine markets "adventure-ready athletic and sportswear" that fits a sports participation and activities lifestyle. "We are evangelical about women's participation in sports and fitness," says T9. Title Nine fills its web and social media sites, catalogs, and blog with images of strong, confident, and active women running on trails wearing reflective gear, snowshoeing with their dogs, stand-up paddle boarding in tropical lagoons, and running errands in ski resort towns wearing more casual, playful clothing. Title Nine's models are all real people, and T9 highlights their lifestyles and stories through an active social media presence plus local activities sponsored by its retail shops. "They are ordinary women capable of extraordinary things," says the company. "And, like many of you, they somehow manage to weave sports and fitness into their hectic lives." That's the T9 lifestyle.

● **Lifestyles: Title Nine markets much more than just women's apparel. It sells the T9 sports participation and activities lifestyle of "ordinary women capable of extraordinary things."**
Photograph by Virginia Nowell

Marketers look for lifestyle segments with needs that can be served through special products or marketing approaches. Such segments might be defined by anything from family characteristics or outdoor interests to the foods people eat.

Personality and Self-Concept

Personality
The unique psychological characteristics that distinguish a person or group.

Each person's distinct personality influences his or her buying behavior. **Personality** refers to the unique psychological characteristics that distinguish a person or group. Personality is usually described in terms of traits such as self-confidence, dominance, sociability, autonomy, defensiveness, adaptability, and aggressiveness. Personality can be useful in analyzing consumer behavior for certain product or brand choices.

The idea is that brands also have personalities, and consumers are likely to choose brands with personalities that match their own. A *brand personality* is the specific mix of human traits that may be attributed to a particular brand. One researcher identified five brand personality traits: *sincerity* (down-to-earth, honest, wholesome, and cheerful), *excitement* (daring, spirited, imaginative, and up-to-date), *competence* (reliable, intelligent, and successful), *sophistication* (glamorous, upper class, charming), and *ruggedness* (outdoorsy and tough). "Your personality determines what you consume, what TV shows you watch, what products you buy, and [most] other decisions you make," says one consumer behavior expert.[23]

Most well-known brands are strongly associated with a particular trait: the Ford F150 with "ruggedness," Apple with "excitement," the *Washington Post* with "competence," Method with "sincerity," and Gucci with "class and sophistication." Many brands build their positioning and brand stories around such traits. For example, fast-growing lifestyle brand Shinola has crafted an "authentic, built in Detroit" persona that has made it one of America's hottest brands (see Real Marketing 5.2).

Many marketers use a concept related to personality—a person's *self-concept* (also called *self-image*). The idea is that people's possessions contribute to and reflect their identities—that is, "we are what we consume." Thus, to understand consumer behavior, marketers must first understand the relationship between consumer self-concept and possessions.

Hence, brands will attract people who are high on the same personality traits. ● For example, the MINI automobile has an instantly recognizable personality as a clever and sassy but powerful little car. MINI owners—who sometimes call themselves "MINIacs"—have a strong and emotional connection with their cars. More than targeting specific demographic segments, MINI appeals to personality segments—to people who are "adventurous, individualistic, open-minded, creative, tech-savvy, and young at heart," just like the car.[24]

● Brand personality: MINI markets to personality segments of people who are "adventurous, individualistic, open-minded, creative, tech-savvy, and young at heart"—anything but "normal"—just like the car.
Used with permission of MINI Division of BMW of North America, LLC

Psychological Factors

A person's buying choices are further influenced by four major psychological factors: *motivation, perception, learning*, and *beliefs and attitudes*.

Motivation

Motive (drive)
A need that is sufficiently pressing to direct the person to seek satisfaction of the need.

A person has many needs at any given time. Some are biological, arising from states of tension such as hunger, thirst, or discomfort. Others are psychological, arising from the need for recognition, esteem, or belonging. A need becomes a motive when it is aroused to a sufficient level of intensity. A **motive (or drive)** is a need that is sufficiently pressing to direct the person to seek satisfaction. Psychologists have developed theories of human motivation. Two of the most popular—the theories of Sigmund Freud and Abraham Maslow—carry quite different meanings for consumer analysis and marketing.

Sigmund Freud assumed that people are largely unconscious about the real psychological forces shaping their behavior. His theory suggests that a person's buying decisions are affected by subconscious motives that even the buyer may not fully understand. Thus, an aging baby boomer who buys a sporty BMW convertible might explain that he simply likes the feel of the wind in his thinning hair. At a deeper level, he may be trying to impress others with his success. At a still deeper level, he may be buying the car to feel young and independent again.

Consumers often don't know or can't describe why they act as they do. Thus, many companies employ teams of psychologists, anthropologists, and other social scientists to carry out *motivation research* that probes the subconscious motivations underlying

Real Marketing

5.2 Shinola: A Real, Authentic, "Detroit" Persona

Earlier this year, a comedy sketch on *Jimmy Kimmel Live* featured a mock TV game show that presented each of two contestants with a pair of luxury products and asked, "Which of these products is sh*t, and which is Shinola?" It wasn't much of a challenge. One product in each pair really did look like it was made from poop, whereas the other items were genuine products from the hot new American luxury brand Shinola. The contestants ended up taking home "all this beautiful sh*t from Shinola." The idea for the gag came from the very company that was the butt of the joke, Detroit-based luxury goods maker Shinola.

Shinola opened for business less than five years ago with a line of premium watches priced between $550 and $850. Its unlikely name derives from the old Shinola shoe polish brand that became a household name following a widely circulated story during World War II that a soldier had polished his commander's boots with poop because "he doesn't know sh*t from Shinola."

The original Shinola company closed its doors in 1960, but the founders of the current company purchased the rights to the unique Shinola name, replete with its mildly crude but colorful associations. In another seemingly surprising move, Shinola chose to headquarter itself in Detroit, the once-iconic symbol of gritty American manufacturing and ingenuity that had since fallen into bankruptcy and desperately hard times. Shinola prints the city's name in its logo and on every product it makes.

Since its founding, Shinola has expanded rapidly into other product categories including high-end bicycles, apparel, leather accessories, and even basketballs. Its sales are booming. Shinola is now sold in high-end department stores such as Nordstrom, Neiman-Marcus, Saks Fifth Avenue, and Bloomingdale's. The company has opened 16 retail stores of its own and faces exploding online demand for its products. And it seems Shinola is just getting started.

Such success might seem surprising. At first blush, Shinola's name and its Detroit roots seem incongruous with the luxury lines of trendy products it makes and sells. But dig deeper and you find that everything about Shinola binds together strongly under a carefully crafted, all-American brand persona. In an age of products "made in China," Shinola is on a mission to revive old-time American manufacturing. "We are a Detroit-based company dedicated to quality, craft, and creating world-class manufacturing jobs in the United States," says the company.

Why the Shinola name and why the Detroit location? "We're starting with the reinvigoration of a storied American brand, and a storied American city," says the company. Shinola "is a brand committed to turning out high-quality products in America with…American suppliers and American labor," says an analyst. "To drive home that commitment, the company selected Detroit—the buckle of the American rust belt—as its base." The brand story just wouldn't be as compelling if it was based in Chicago or San Francisco.

The brand reflects a gritty Detroit, authentically American persona. So do its products and manufacturing. Shinola began with about 100 local manufacturing employees and brought in the world's best Swiss watchmakers to train them how to build watches the old-fashioned way—by hand. As the company expanded into other lines, it remained committed to working with mostly U.S.-based suppliers. Leather goods come from the Horween tannery in Chicago, whereas bike frames and forks are hand-built by Waterford, a Wisconsin company. We are "creating a community that will thrive through excellence of craft and pride of work," says the company "where we will reclaim the making of things that are made well and define American luxury through American quality."

The roots of American ingenuity and manufacturing are evident in every facet of Shinola's products and branding, from its Wright Brothers Limited Edition Runwell bike ($2,950 and sold out), to its Bluetooth player with Gramophone speaker ($400 with a waiting list of buyers), to its limited-edition Great American Series Muhammad Ali watch, a tribute to the six principles that shaped the life of the famed fighter: conviction, respect, dedication, confidence, giving, and spirituality.

Shinola products are at once both classic and modern, with clean, functional, and authentically American designs, craftsmanship, and quality. Backed by a lifetime guarantee, they are meant to be handed down from generation to generation rather than to end up in a landfill after a few years of use.

Shinola's retail stores are the ultimate embodiment of its brand persona. Store interiors have an industrial feel—weathered brick, varnished wood, glass, stainless

Brand personality: Shinola's carefully crafted, real, authentic, "Detroit" persona has made it one of America's hottest brands.
Shinola

steel, and exposed iron trusswork. But they are also warm and inviting. According to Shinola's marketer director, "Shinola's stores are more than a place to buy stuff—they're centers of activity complete with permanent coffee bars and period events like whisky tastings or pop-up florists and barbershops." The company plans to open a dozen or more new stores each year going forward.

In another throwback to a bygone era, Shinola is committed to its employees. If you take care of your people, the company believes, they will take care of your customers and your business. Shinola pays its people above-market wages and provides amazing benefits. All employees spend time in the company's retail stores to gain a clear understanding of the customers for whom they are making products. Shinola has a promote-from-within policy. Today, many of Shinola's critical operations managers are people who started with the company as security guards, janitors, and delivery people. "We build our goods to last," says Shinola, "but of all the things we make, American jobs might just be the thing we're most proud of."

Thus, Shinola's well-crafted, deeply felt brand persona has made it special to consumers who identify with its personality. "Shinola is about pride and craft, making things that matter and last, and honoring the past as well as the future," observes a business writer. "It's a no-nonsense notion combined with a lot of nostalgia, and it's the real deal." "Consumers want something real, something authentic. You want to feel proud about something," says Shinola's marketing director. "We have good timing, a good product, and a good story." In short, nobody's confusing sh*t with Shinola anymore.

Sources: Robert Klara, "How Shinola Went from Shoe Polish to the Coolest Brand in America," *Adweek*, June 22, 2015, pp. 23–25; Helen Heller, "The Luxury-Goods Company Shinola Is Capitalizing on Detroit," *Washington Post*, November 17, 2014, www.washingtonpost.com/lifestyle/style/the-luxury-goods-company-shinola-is-capitalizing-on-detroit/2014/11/17/638f88a4-6a8f-11e4-b053-65cea7903f2e_story.html; Howard Tullman, "4 Lessons from Shinola," *Inc.*, February 17, 2015, www.inc.com/howard-tullman/4-lessons-from-shinola.html; Jack Preston, "What Does the Success of Shinola Tell Us about the City's Future?" July 29, 2015, www.virgin.com/entrepreneur/inside-detroit-what-does-the-success-of-shinola-tell-us-about-the-citys-future; and www.shinola.com/our-story and www.shinola.com/about-shinola, accessed September 2016.

consumers' emotions and behaviors toward brands. One ad agency routinely conducts one-on-one, therapy-like interviews to delve the inner workings of consumers. Another company asks consumers to describe their favorite brands as animals or cars (say, a Mercedes versus a Chevy) to assess the prestige associated with various brands. Still others rely on hypnosis, dream therapy, or soft lights and mood music to plumb the murky depths of consumer psyches.

Such projective techniques might seem pretty goofy, and some marketers dismiss such motivation research as mumbo jumbo. But many marketers use such touchy-feely approaches, now sometimes called *interpretive consumer research*, to dig deeper into consumer psyches and develop better marketing strategies.

Abraham Maslow sought to explain why people are driven by particular needs at particular times. Why does one person spend a lot of time and energy on personal safety and another on gaining the esteem of others? Maslow's answer is that human needs are arranged in a hierarchy, as shown in ● **Figure 5.3**, from the most pressing at the bottom to the least pressing at the top.[25] They include *physiological* needs, *safety* needs, *social* needs, *esteem* needs, and *self-actualization* needs.

● **FIGURE | 5.3**
Maslow's Hierarchy of Needs

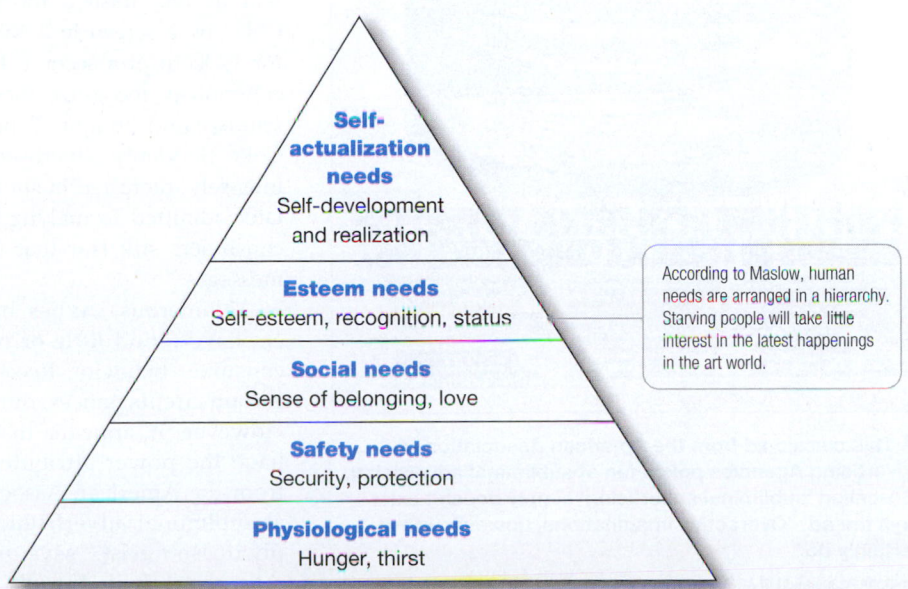

Self-actualization needs
Self-development and realization

Esteem needs
Self-esteem, recognition, status

Social needs
Sense of belonging, love

Safety needs
Security, protection

Physiological needs
Hunger, thirst

According to Maslow, human needs are arranged in a hierarchy. Starving people will take little interest in the latest happenings in the art world.

A person tries to satisfy the most important need first. When that need is satisfied, it will stop being a motivator, and the person will then try to satisfy the next most important need. For example, starving people (physiological need) will not take an interest in the latest happenings in the art world (self-actualization needs) nor in how they are seen or esteemed by others (social or esteem needs) nor even in whether they are breathing clean air (safety needs). But as each important need is satisfied, the next most important need will come into play.

Perception

Perception

The process by which people select, organize, and interpret information to form a meaningful picture of the world.

A motivated person is ready to act. How the person acts is influenced by his or her own perception of the situation. All of us learn by the flow of information through our five senses: sight, hearing, smell, touch, and taste. However, each of us receives, organizes, and interprets this sensory information in an individual way. **Perception** is the process by which people select, organize, and interpret information to form a meaningful picture of the world.

People can form different perceptions of the same stimulus because of three perceptual processes: selective attention, selective distortion, and selective retention. People are exposed to a great amount of stimuli every day. For example, individuals are exposed to an estimated 3,000 to 5,000 ad messages daily—from TV and magazine ads to billboards to social media ads and posts on their smartphones.[26] People can't possibly pay attention to all the competing stimuli surrounding them. *Selective attention*—the tendency for people to screen out most of the information to which they are exposed—means that marketers must work especially hard to attract the consumer's attention.

Even noticed stimuli do not always come across in the intended way. Each person fits incoming information into an existing mindset. *Selective distortion* describes the tendency of people to interpret information in a way that will support what they already believe. People also will forget much of what they learn. They tend to retain information that supports their attitudes and beliefs. *Selective retention* means that consumers are likely to remember good points made about a brand they favor and forget good points made about competing brands. Because of selective attention, distortion, and retention, marketers must work hard just to get their messages through.

Interestingly, although most marketers worry about whether their offers will be perceived at all, some consumers worry that they will be affected by marketing messages without even knowing it—through *subliminal advertising*. More than 50 years ago, a researcher announced that he had flashed the phrases "Eat popcorn" and "Drink Coca-Cola" on a screen in a New Jersey movie theater every five seconds for 1/300th of a second. He reported that although viewers did not consciously recognize these messages, they absorbed them subconsciously and bought 58 percent more popcorn and 18 percent more Coke. Suddenly advertisers and consumer-protection groups became intensely interested in subliminal perception. Although the researcher later admitted to making up the data, the issue has not died. Some consumers still fear that they are being manipulated by subliminal messages.

Numerous studies by psychologists and consumer researchers have found little or no link between subliminal messages and consumer behavior. Recent brain-wave studies have found that in certain circumstances, our brains may register subliminal messages. However, it appears that subliminal advertising simply doesn't have the power attributed to it by its critics.[27] ● One classic ad from the American Association of Advertising Agencies pokes fun at subliminal advertising. "So-called 'subliminal advertising' simply doesn't exist," says the ad. "Overactive imaginations, however, most certainly do."

● **This classic ad from the American Association of Advertising Agencies pokes fun at subliminal advertising. "So-called 'subliminal advertising' simply doesn't exist," says the ad. "Overactive imaginations, however, most certainly do."**

American Association of Advertising Agencies

Learning

Learning
Changes in an individual's behavior arising from experience.

When people act, they learn. **Learning** describes changes in an individual's behavior arising from experience. Learning theorists say that most human behavior is learned. Learning occurs through the interplay of drives, stimuli, cues, responses, and reinforcement.

A *drive* is a strong internal stimulus that calls for action. A drive becomes a motive when it is directed toward a particular *stimulus object*. For example, a person's drive for self-actualization might motivate him or her to look into buying a camera. The consumer's response to the idea of buying a camera is conditioned by the surrounding cues. *Cues* are minor stimuli that determine when, where, and how the person responds. The camera buyer might spot several camera brands in a shop window, hear of a special sale price, or discuss cameras with a friend. These are all cues that might influence a consumer's *response* to his or her interest in buying the product.

Suppose the consumer buys a Nikon camera. If the experience is rewarding, the consumer will probably use the camera more and more, and his or her response will be *reinforced*. Then the next time he or she shops for a camera, or for binoculars or some similar product, the probability is greater that he or she will buy a Nikon product. The practical significance of learning theory for marketers is that they can build up demand for a product by associating it with strong drives, using motivating cues, and providing positive reinforcement.

Beliefs and Attitudes

Belief
A descriptive thought that a person holds about something.

Through doing and learning, people acquire beliefs and attitudes. These, in turn, influence their buying behavior. A **belief** is a descriptive thought that a person holds about something. Beliefs may be based on real knowledge, opinion, or faith and may or may not carry an emotional charge. Marketers are interested in the beliefs that people formulate about specific products and services because these beliefs make up product and brand images that affect buying behavior. If some of the beliefs are wrong and prevent purchase, the marketer will want to launch a campaign to correct them.

Attitude
A person's consistently favorable or unfavorable evaluations, feelings, and tendencies toward an object or idea.

People have attitudes regarding religion, politics, clothes, music, food, and almost everything else. **Attitude** describes a person's relatively consistent evaluations, feelings, and tendencies toward an object or idea. Attitudes put people into a frame of mind of liking or disliking things, of moving toward or away from them. Our camera buyer may hold attitudes such as "Buy the best," "The Japanese make the best camera products in the world," and "Creativity and self-expression are among the most important things in life." If so, the Nikon camera would fit well into the consumer's existing attitudes.

Attitudes are difficult to change. A person's attitudes fit into a pattern; changing one attitude may require difficult adjustments in many others. Thus, a company should usually try to fit its products into existing attitude patterns rather than attempt to change attitudes. Of course, there are exceptions. Repositioning or extending a brand calls for changing attitudes. For example, consider the Jimmy Dean brand:[28]

> When you think of Jimmy Dean, a Tyson Foods brand, you probably think of sausage and other breakfast items, and for good reason. Jimmy Dean captures a 53 percent share of the frozen hand-held breakfast foods segment and a 36 percent share of the frozen breakfast entree segment. So when the brand recently introduced lines of lunch and dinner items, it knew it would have to change existing attitudes. The new items include pulled pork, smoked turkey, beef, and smoked sausage sandwiches and bowls with a variety of meats, potatoes, pastas, and cheeses. Half are marketed under a Jimmy Dean Delights subbrand of offerings with 300 or fewer calories.
>
> To change consumer attitudes, Jimmy Dean launched an estimated $20 million "It's not just for breakfast anymore" marketing campaign featuring its familiar sun-costumed character, who convinces disappointed food court and deli lunchers that Jimmy Dean Delight's new lunch sandwiches are a better option. "It just felt like such a natural evolution for the sun to keep shining all day long, and to go from owning morning to owning noon and owning night as well," says a Jimmy Dean advertising executive. The sunshine mascot doesn't appear in Jimmy Dean's most recent marketing campaign, "Shine On." However, the campaign builds on the character's sunny attitude and optimism to assure consumers that Jimmy Dean products are a sunny day thing.

We can now appreciate the many forces acting on consumer behavior. The consumer's choice results from the complex interplay of cultural, social, personal, and psychological factors.

Author | Some purchases are simple
Comment | and routine, even habitual.
Others are far more complex—involving
extensive information gathering
and evaluation—and are subject to
sometimes subtle influences. For
example, think of all that goes into a
new car buying decision.

Buying Decision Behavior and the Buyer Decision Process

Types of Buying Decision Behavior

Buying behavior differs greatly for a tube of toothpaste, a smartphone, financial services, and a new car. More complex decisions usually involve more buying participants and more buyer deliberation. ● **Figure 5.4** shows the types of consumer buying behavior based on the degree of buyer involvement and the degree of differences among brands.

Complex Buying Behavior

Complex buying behavior
Consumer buying behavior in situations characterized by high consumer involvement in a purchase and significant perceived differences among brands.

Consumers undertake **complex buying behavior** when they are highly involved in a purchase and perceive significant differences among brands. Consumers may be highly involved when the product is expensive, risky, purchased infrequently, and highly self-expressive. Typically, the consumer has much to learn about the product category. For example, someone buying a new car might not know what models, attributes, and accessories to consider or what prices to expect.

This buyer will pass through a learning process, first developing beliefs about the product, then attitudes, and then make a thoughtful purchase choice. Marketers of high-involvement products must understand the information-gathering and evaluation behavior of high-involvement consumers. They need to help buyers learn about product-class attributes and their relative importance. They need to differentiate their brand's features, perhaps by describing and illustrating the brand's benefits through printed promotional materials or in-depth online information and videos. They must motivate store salespeople and the buyer's acquaintances to influence the final brand choice.

Dissonance-Reducing Buying Behavior

Dissonance-reducing buying behavior
Consumer buying behavior in situations characterized by high involvement but few perceived differences among brands.

Dissonance-reducing buying behavior occurs when consumers are highly involved with an expensive, infrequent, or risky purchase but see little difference among brands. For example, consumers buying carpeting may face a high-involvement decision because carpeting is expensive and self-expressive. Yet buyers may consider most carpet brands in a given price range to be the same. In this case, because perceived brand differences are not large, buyers may shop around to learn what is available but buy relatively quickly. They may respond primarily to a good price or purchase convenience.

After the purchase, consumers might experience *postpurchase dissonance* (after-sale discomfort) when they notice certain disadvantages of the purchased carpet brand or hear favorable things about brands not purchased. To counter such dissonance, the marketer's after-sale communications should provide evidence and support to help consumers feel good about their brand choices.

Habitual Buying Behavior

Habitual buying behavior
Consumer buying behavior in situations characterized by low consumer involvement and few significant perceived brand differences.

Habitual buying behavior occurs under conditions of low-consumer involvement and little significant brand difference. For example, take table salt. Consumers have little involvement in this product category—they simply go to the store and reach for a brand. If they keep reaching for the same brand, it is out of habit rather than strong brand loyalty. Consumers appear to have low involvement with most low-cost, frequently purchased products.

● **FIGURE | 5.4**
Four Types of Buying Behavior

Source: Adapted from Henry Assael, *Consumer Behavior and Marketing Action* (Boston: Kent Publishing Company, 1987), p. 87. Used with permission of the author.

	High involvement	**Low** involvement
Significant differences between brands	Complex buying behavior	Variety-seeking buying behavior
Few differences between brands	Dissonance-reducing buying behavior	Habitual buying behavior

Buying behavior varies greatly for different types of products. For example, someone buying a new car might undertake a full information-gathering and brand evaluation process.

At the other extreme, for low-involvement products, consumers may simply select a familiar brand out of habit. For example, what brand of salt do you buy and why?

Variety-seeking buying behavior
Consumer buying behavior in situations characterized by low consumer involvement but significant perceived brand differences.

Author Comment | The actual purchase decision is part of a much larger buying process—from recognizing a need through postpurchase behavior. Marketers want to be involved throughout the entire buyer decision process.

The buying process starts long before the actual purchase and continues long after. Therefore, marketers must focus on the entire buying process, not just the purchase decision.

In such cases, consumer behavior does not pass through the usual belief-attitude-behavior sequence. Consumers do not search extensively for information about the brands, evaluate brand characteristics, and make weighty decisions about which brands to buy. Because they are not highly involved with the product, consumers may not evaluate the choice, even after purchase. Thus, the buying process involves brand beliefs formed by passive learning, followed by purchase behavior, which may or may not be followed by evaluation.

Because buyers are not highly committed to any brands, marketers of low-involvement products with few brand differences often use price and sales promotions to promote buying. Alternatively, they can add product features or enhancements to differentiate their brands from the rest of the pack and raise involvement.

For example, take something as seemingly uncomplicated as wheat flour or oatmeal. To set its brand apart, Bob's Red Mill adds an "honest-to-goodness" touch to all of the baking, grain, and cereal products it makes, using only the best nutritional whole grains and time-honored stone mill production processes. Bob's Red Mill doesn't sell just plain old flour. It offers "America's Best Baking Flours," nine varieties of differentiated wheat flours, ranging from Unbleached White Fine Pastry Flour and Super-Fine Cake Flour to 100% Whole Grain Organic Ivory Wheat flour. ● The same goes for its oatmeal—billed as the World's Best Oatmeal—with 24 varieties ranging from Extra Thick Rolled Oats to High Fiber Oat Bran hot cereal to Organic Scottish Oatmeal.

Variety-Seeking Buying Behavior

Consumers undertake **variety-seeking buying behavior** in situations characterized by low consumer involvement but significant perceived brand differences. In such cases, consumers often do a lot of brand switching. For example, when buying cookies, a consumer may hold some beliefs, choose a cookie brand without much evaluation, and then evaluate that brand during consumption. But the next time, the consumer might pick another brand out of boredom or simply to try something different. Brand switching occurs for the sake of variety rather than because of dissatisfaction.

In such product categories, the marketing strategy may differ for the market leader and minor brands. The market leader will try to encourage habitual buying behavior by dominating shelf space, keeping shelves fully stocked, and running frequent reminder advertising. Challenger firms will encourage variety seeking by offering lower prices, special deals, coupons, free samples, and advertising that presents reasons for trying something new.

The Buyer Decision Process

Now that we have looked at the influences that affect buyers, we are ready to look at how consumers make buying decisions. ● **Figure 5.5** shows that the buyer decision process consists of five stages: *need recognition, information search, evaluation of alternatives,* the *purchase decision,* and *postpurchase behavior.* Clearly, the buying process starts long before the actual purchase and continues long after. Marketers need to focus on the entire buying process rather than on the purchase decision only.

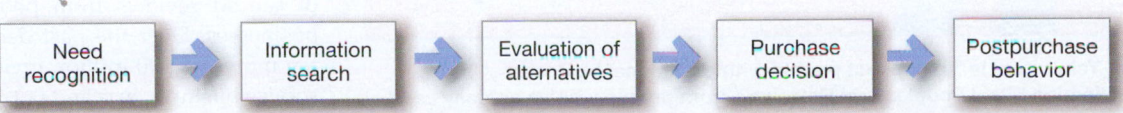

● FIGURE | 5.5
Buyer Decision Process

Figure 5.5 suggests that consumers pass through all five stages with every purchase in a considered way. But buyers may pass quickly or slowly through the buying decision process. And in more routine purchases, consumers often skip or reverse some of the stages. Much depends on the nature of the buyer, the product, and the buying situation. A person buying a regular brand of toothpaste would recognize the need and go right to the purchase decision, skipping information search and evaluation. However, we use the model in Figure 5.5 because it shows all the considerations that arise when a consumer faces a new and complex purchase situation.

Need Recognition

Need recognition
The first stage of the buyer decision process, in which the consumer recognizes a problem or need.

The buying process starts with **need recognition**—the buyer recognizes a problem or need. The need can be triggered by *internal stimuli* when one of the person's normal needs—for example, hunger or thirst—rises to a level high enough to become a drive. A need can also be triggered by *external stimuli*. For example, an advertisement or a discussion with a friend might get you thinking about buying a new car. At this stage, the marketer should research consumers to find out what kinds of needs or problems arise, what brought them about, and how they led the consumer to this particular product.

Information Search

Information search
The stage of the buyer decision process in which the consumer is motivated to search for more information.

An interested consumer may or may not search for more information. If the consumer's drive is strong and a satisfying product is near at hand, he or she is likely to buy it then. If not, the consumer may store the need in memory or undertake an **information search** related to the need. For example, once you've decided you need a new car, at the least, you will probably pay more attention to car ads, cars owned by friends, and car conversations. Or you may actively search online, talk with friends, and gather information in other ways.

Consumers can obtain information from any of several sources. These include *personal sources* (family, friends, neighbors, acquaintances), *commercial sources* (advertising, salespeople, dealer and manufacturer web and mobile sites, packaging, displays), *public sources* (mass media, consumer rating organizations, social media, online searches and peer reviews), and *experiential sources* (examining and using the product). The relative influence of these information sources varies with the product and the buyer.

Traditionally, consumers have received the most information about a product from commercial sources—those controlled by the marketer. The most effective sources, however, tend to be personal. Commercial sources normally *inform* the buyer, but personal sources *legitimize* or *evaluate* products for the buyer. Few advertising campaigns can be as effective as a next-door neighbor leaning over the fence and raving about a wonderful experience with a product you are considering.

Increasingly, that "neighbor's fence" is a digital one. Today, consumers share product opinions, images, and experiences freely across social media. And buyers can find an abundance of user-generated reviews alongside the products they are considering at sites ranging from Amazon.com or BestBuy.com to Yelp, TripAdvisor, and Epicurious. ● For example, Yelp's goal is "to connect people with great local businesses" by maintaining a huge, searchable collection of candid reviews from people who've used those businesses. Over the past decade, Yelpers have written more than 90 million reviews of local restaurants, service business, arts and entertainment activities, and other service in cities across the nation. The site receives some 89 million unique visitors per month

● Yelp's goal is "to connect people with great local businesses" by collecting "Real People. Real Reviews." from people who've actually used those businesses.
Yelp Inc.

seeking reviews and ratings.[29] Although individual user reviews at Yelp and other sites vary widely in quality, an entire body of reviews often provides a reliable product assessment—straight from the fingertips of people like you who've actually purchased and experienced the product.

As more information is obtained, the consumer's awareness and knowledge of the available brands and features increase. In your car information search, you may learn about several brands that are available. The information might also help you to drop certain brands from consideration. A company must design its marketing mix to make prospects aware of and knowledgeable about its brand. It should carefully identify consumers' sources of information and the importance of each source.

Evaluation of Alternatives

Alternative evaluation
The stage of the buyer decision process in which the consumer uses information to evaluate alternative brands in the choice set.

We have seen how consumers use information to arrive at a set of final brand choices. Next, marketers need to know about **alternative evaluation**, that is, how consumers process information to choose among alternative brands. Unfortunately, consumers do not use a simple and single evaluation process in all buying situations. Instead, several evaluation processes are at work.

How consumers go about evaluating purchase alternatives depends on the individual consumer and the specific buying situation. In some cases, consumers use careful calculations and logical thinking. At other times, the same consumers do little or no evaluating. Instead, they buy on impulse and rely on intuition. Sometimes consumers make buying decisions on their own; sometimes they turn to friends, online reviews, or salespeople for buying advice.

Suppose you've narrowed your car choices to three brands. And suppose that you are primarily interested in four attributes—price, style, operating economy, and performance. By this time, you've probably formed beliefs about how each brand rates on each attribute. Clearly, if one car rated best on all the attributes, the marketer could predict that you would choose it. However, the brands will no doubt vary in appeal. You might base your buying decision mostly on one attribute, and your choice would be easy to predict. If you wanted style above everything else, you would buy the car that you think has the most style. But most buyers consider several attributes, each with different importance. By knowing the importance that you assigned to each attribute, the marketer could predict and affect your car choice more reliably.

Marketers should study buyers to find out how they actually evaluate brand alternatives. If marketers know what evaluative processes go on, they can take steps to influence the buyer's decision.

Purchase Decision

Purchase decision
The buyer's decision about which brand to purchase.

In the evaluation stage, the consumer ranks brands and forms purchase intentions. Generally, the consumer's **purchase decision** will be to buy the most preferred brand, but two factors can come between the purchase *intention* and the purchase *decision*. The first factor is the *attitudes of others*. If someone important to you thinks that you should buy the lowest-priced car, then the chances of you buying a more expensive car are reduced.

The second factor is *unexpected situational factors*. The consumer may form a purchase intention based on factors such as expected income, expected price, and expected product benefits. However, unexpected events may change the purchase intention. For example, the economy might take a turn for the worse, a close competitor might drop its price, or a friend might report being disappointed in your preferred car. Thus, preferences and even purchase intentions do not always result in an actual purchase choice.

Postpurchase Behavior

Postpurchase behavior
The stage of the buyer decision process in which consumers take further action after purchase, based on their satisfaction or dissatisfaction.

The marketer's job does not end when the product is bought. After purchasing the product, the consumer will either be satisfied or dissatisfied and will engage in **postpurchase behavior** of interest to the marketer. What determines whether the buyer is satisfied or dissatisfied with a purchase? The answer lies in the relationship between the *consumer's expectations* and the product's *perceived performance*. If the product falls short of expectations, the consumer is disappointed; if it meets expectations,

● Postpurchase cognitive dissonance: Postpurchase customer satisfaction is a key to building profitable customer relationships. Most marketers go beyond merely *meeting* the customer expectations—they aim to *delight* customers.

Dusit/Shutterstock

Cognitive dissonance
Buyer discomfort caused by postpurchase conflict.

the consumer is satisfied; if it exceeds expectations, the consumer is delighted. The larger the negative gap between expectations and performance, the greater the consumer's dissatisfaction. This suggests that sellers should promise only what their brands can deliver so that buyers are satisfied.

Almost all major purchases, however, result in **cognitive dissonance**, or discomfort caused by postpurchase conflict. After the purchase, consumers are satisfied with the benefits of the chosen brand and are glad to avoid the drawbacks of the brands not bought. However, every purchase involves compromise. So consumers feel uneasy about acquiring the drawbacks of the chosen brand and about losing the benefits of the brands not purchased. Thus, consumers feel at least some postpurchase dissonance for every purchase.

Why is it so important to satisfy the customer? Customer satisfaction is a key to building profitable relationships with consumers—to keeping and growing consumers and reaping their customer lifetime value. Satisfied customers buy a product again, talk favorably to others about the product, pay less attention to competing brands and advertising, and buy other products from the company. ● Many marketers go beyond merely *meeting* the expectations of customers—they aim to *delight* customers.

A dissatisfied consumer responds differently. Bad word of mouth often travels farther and faster than good word of mouth. It can quickly damage consumer attitudes about a company and its products. But companies cannot simply wait for dissatisfied customers to volunteer their complaints. Most unhappy customers never tell the company about their problems. Therefore, a company should measure customer satisfaction regularly. It should set up systems that *encourage* customers to complain. In this way, the company can learn how well it is doing and how it can improve.

By studying the overall buyer decision process, marketers may be able to find ways to help consumers move through it. For example, if consumers are not buying a new product because they do not perceive a need for it, marketing might launch advertising messages that trigger the need and show how the product solves customers' problems. If customers know about the product but are not buying because they hold unfavorable attitudes toward it, marketers must find ways to change either the product or consumer perceptions.

Author Comment | Here we look at some special considerations in *new product* buying decisions.

The Buyer Decision Process for New Products

We now look at how buyers approach the purchase of new products. A **new product** is a good, service, or idea that is perceived by some potential customers as new. It may have been around for a while, but our interest is in how consumers learn about products for the first time and make decisions on whether to adopt them. We define the **adoption process** as the mental process through which an individual passes from first learning about an innovation to final adoption. *Adoption* is the decision by an individual to become a regular user of the product.[30]

New product
A good, service, or idea that is perceived by some potential customers as new.

Adoption process
The mental process through which an individual passes from first hearing about an innovation to final adoption.

Stages in the Adoption Process

Consumers go through five stages in the process of adopting a new product:

Awareness. The consumer becomes aware of the new product but lacks information about it.

Interest. The consumer seeks information about the new product.

Evaluation. The consumer considers whether trying the new product makes sense.

Trial. The consumer tries the new product on a small scale to improve his or her estimate of its value.

Adoption. The consumer decides to make full and regular use of the new product.

This model suggests that marketers should think about how to help consumers move through these stages. For example, if a company finds that many consumers are considering its products but are still tentative about buying one, it might offer sales prices or special promotions that help get consumers over the decision hump. To help car buyers past purchase-decision hurdles following the economic meltdown in 2008, Hyundai offered a unique Hyundai Assurance Plan. It promised buyers who financed or leased new Hyundais that they could return them at no cost and with no harm to their credit rating if they lost their jobs or incomes within a year. Sales of the Hyundai Sonata surged 85 percent in the month following the start of the campaign.

Individual Differences in Innovativeness

People differ greatly in their readiness to try new products. In each product area, there are "consumption pioneers" and early adopters. Other individuals adopt new products much later. People can be classified into the adopter categories shown in ● **Figure 5.6**.[31] As shown by the curve, after a slow start, an increasing number of people adopt the new product. As successive groups of consumers adopt the innovation, it eventually reaches its cumulative saturation level. Innovators are defined as the first 2.5 percent of buyers to adopt a new idea (those beyond two standard deviations from mean adoption time); the early adopters are the next 13.5 percent (between one and two standard deviations); and then come early mainstream, late mainstream, and lagging adopters.

The five adopter groups have differing values. *Innovators* are venturesome—they try new ideas at some risk. *Early adopters* are guided by respect—they are opinion leaders in their communities and adopt new ideas early but carefully. *Early mainstream* adopters are deliberate—although they rarely are leaders, they adopt new ideas before the average person. *Late mainstream* adopters are skeptical—they adopt an innovation only after a majority of people have tried it. Finally, *lagging adopters* are tradition bound—they are suspicious of changes and adopt the innovation only when it has become something of a tradition itself.

This adopter classification suggests that an innovating firm should research the characteristics of innovators and early adopters in their product categories and direct initial marketing efforts toward them.

Influence of Product Characteristics on Rate of Adoption

The characteristics of the new product affect its rate of adoption. Some products catch on almost overnight. For example, Apple's iPod, iPhone, and iPad flew off retailers' shelves

● FIGURE 5.6

Adopter Categories Based on
Relative Time of Adoption of
Innovations

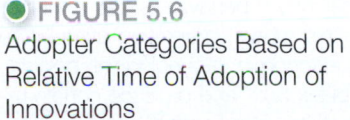

New product marketers often target innovators and early adopters, who in turn influence later adopters.

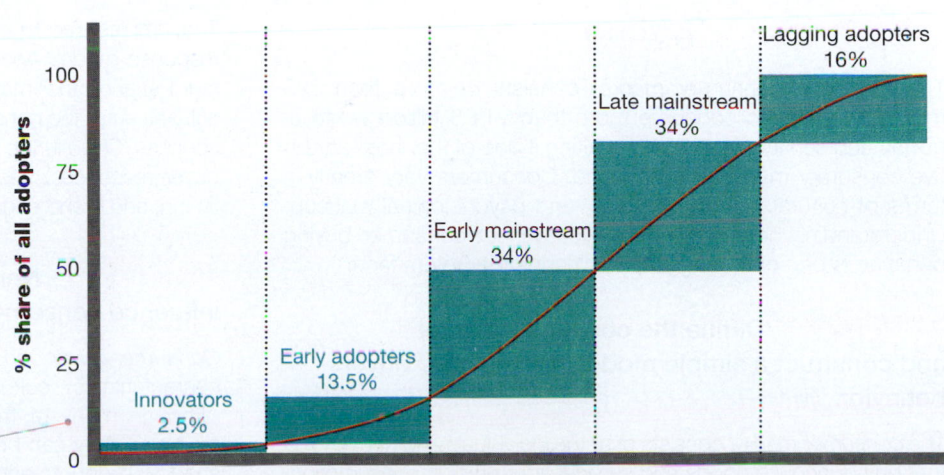

at an astounding rate from the day they were first introduced. Others take a longer time to gain acceptance. For example, all-electric cars were first introduced in the United States in 2010, led by models such as the Nissan Leaf and the Tesla Model S. However, electric vehicles still account for far less than 1 percent of total U.S. automobile sales. It will likely be years or even decades before they replace the gasoline-powered cars.[32]

Five characteristics are especially important in influencing an innovation's rate of adoption. For example, consider the characteristics of all-electric vehicles in relation to their rate of adoption:

Relative advantage. The degree to which the innovation appears superior to existing products. All-electric cars require no gas and use clean, less costly energy. This will accelerate their rate of adoption. However, they have limited driving range before recharging and cost more initially, which will slow the adoption rate.

Compatibility. The degree to which the innovation fits the values and experiences of potential consumers. Electric cars are driven the same way as gas-powered cars. However, they are not compatible with the nation's current refueling network. Plug-in electric charging stations are few and far between. Increased adoption will depend on the development of a national network of recharging stations, which may take considerable time.

Complexity. The degree to which the innovation is difficult to understand or use. Electric cars are not different or complex to drive, which will help to speed up adoption. However, the "conceptual complexity" of the new technologies and concerns about how well they will likely work slow down the adoption rate.

Divisibility. The degree to which the innovation may be tried on a limited basis. Consumers can test-drive electric cars, a positive for the adoption rate. However, current high prices to own and fully experience these new technologies will likely slow adoption.

Communicability. The degree to which the results of using the innovation can be observed or described to others. To the extent that electric cars lend themselves to demonstration and description, their use will spread faster among consumers.

Other characteristics influence the rate of adoption, such as initial and ongoing costs, risk and uncertainty, and social approval. The new product marketer must research all these factors when developing the new product and its marketing program.

5 | Reviewing and Extending the Concepts

OBJECTIVES REVIEW AND KEY TERMS

Objectives Review

The American consumer market consists of more than 323 million people who consume more than $11.8 trillion worth of goods and services each year, making it one of the most attractive consumer markets in the world. Consumers vary greatly in terms of cultural, social, personal, and psychological makeup. Understanding how these differences affect consumer buying behavior is one of the biggest challenges marketers face.

OBJECTIVE 5-1 Define the consumer market and construct a simple model of consumer buyer behavior. (pp 134–135)

The *consumer market* consists of all the individuals and households that buy or acquire goods and services for personal consumption.

The simplest model of consumer buyer behavior is the stimulus-response model. According to this model, marketing stimuli (the four Ps) and other major forces (economic, technological, political, cultural) enter the consumer's "black box" and produce certain responses. Once in the black box, these inputs produce observable buyer responses, such as brand choice, purchase location and timing, and brand engagement and relationship behavior.

OBJECTIVE 5-2 Name the four major factors that influence consumer buyer behavior. (pp 135–149)

Consumer buyer behavior is influenced by four key sets of buyer characteristics: cultural, social, personal, and psychological. Although many of these factors cannot be influenced by the marketer, they can be useful in identifying interested buyers and shaping products and appeals to serve consumer needs better.

Culture is the most basic determinant of a person's wants and behavior. *Subcultures* are "cultures within cultures" that have distinct values and lifestyles and can be based on anything from age to ethnicity. Many companies focus their marketing programs on the special needs of certain cultural and subcultural segments, such as Hispanic American, African American, and Asian American consumers.

Social factors also influence a buyer's behavior. A person's *reference groups*—family, friends, social networks, professional associations—strongly affect product and brand choices. The buyer's age, life-cycle stage, occupation, economic circumstances, personality, and other *personal characteristics* influence his or her buying decisions. Consumer *lifestyles*—the whole pattern of acting and interacting in the world—are also an important influence on purchase decisions. Finally, consumer buying behavior is influenced by four major *psychological factors*: motivation, perception, learning, and beliefs and attitudes. Each of these factors provides a different perspective for understanding the workings of the buyer's black box.

OBJECTIVE 5-3   List and define the major types of buying decision behavior and the stages in the buyer decision process. *(pp 150–154)*

Buying behavior may vary greatly across different types of products and buying decisions. Consumers undertake *complex buying behavior* when they are highly involved in a purchase and perceive significant differences among brands. *Dissonance-reducing behavior* occurs when consumers are highly involved but see little difference among brands. *Habitual buying behavior* occurs under conditions of low involvement and little significant brand difference. In situations characterized by low involvement but significant perceived brand differences, consumers engage in *variety-seeking buying behavior*.

When making a purchase, the buyer goes through a decision process consisting of need recognition, information search, evaluation of alternatives, purchase decision, and postpurchase behavior. The marketer's job is to understand the buyer's behavior at each stage and the influences that are operating. During *need recognition*, the consumer recognizes a problem or need that could be satisfied by a product or service in the market. Once the need is recognized, the consumer is aroused to seek more information and moves into the *information search* stage. With information in hand, the consumer proceeds to *alternative evaluation*, during which the information is used to evaluate brands in the choice set. From there, the consumer makes a *purchase decision* and actually buys the product. In the final stage of the buyer decision process, *postpurchase behavior*, the consumer takes action based on satisfaction or dissatisfaction.

OBJECTIVE 5-4   Describe the adoption and diffusion process for new products. *(pp 154–156)*

The product *adoption process* is made up of five stages: awareness, interest, evaluation, trial, and adoption. New-product marketers must think about how to help consumers move through these stages. With regard to the *diffusion process* for new products, consumers respond at different rates, depending on consumer and product characteristics. Consumers may be innovators, early adopters, early mainstream, late mainstream, or lagging adopters. Each group may require different marketing approaches. Marketers often try to bring their new products to the attention of potential early adopters, especially those who are opinion leaders. Finally, several characteristics influence the rate of adoption: relative advantage, compatibility, complexity, divisibility, and communicability.

Key Terms

OBJECTIVE 5-1

Consumer buyer behavior (p 134)
Consumer market (p 134)

OBJECTIVE 5-2

Culture (p 135)
Subculture (p 136)
Total market strategy (p 137)
Social class (p 138)
Group (p 138)
Word-of-mouth influence (p 139)
Opinion leader (p 139)
Online social networks (p 139)

Lifestyle (p 144)
Personality (p 144)
Motive (drive) (p 145)
Perception (p 148)
Learning (p 149)
Belief (p 149)
Attitude (p 149)

OBJECTIVE 5-3

Complex buying behavior (p 150)
Dissonance-reducing buying behavior (p 150)
Habitual buying behavior (p 150)

Variety-seeking buying behavior (p 151)
Need recognition (p 152)
Information search (p 152)
Alternative evaluation (p 153)
Purchase decision (p 153)
Postpurchase behavior (p 153)
Cognitive dissonance (p 154)

OBJECTIVE 5-4

New product (p 154)
Adoption process (p 154)

DISCUSSION AND CRITICAL THINKING

Discussion Questions

5-1 Define the consumer market and describe the four major sets of factors that influence consumer buyer behavior. Which characteristics influenced your choice when deciding on the school you would attend? Are those the same characteristics that would influence you when deciding what to do on Saturday night? Explain. (AACSB: Communication; Reflective Thinking)

⭐ **5-2** What is a total market strategy, and why do marketers use this approach? Provide a recent example of a product or service that uses the total market strategy approach and discuss the components that make it effective or ineffective. (AACSB: Communication, Diversity, Reflective Thinking)

⭐ **5-3** What is subculture? Describe at least two subcultures to which you belong and identify any reference groups that might influence your consumption behavior. (AACSB: Communication; Diversity; Reflective Thinking)

5-4 Briefly describe the four psychological factors influencing consumer buyer behavior. Explain their importance to marketers. (AACSB: Communication; Reflective Thinking)

⭐ **5-5** Name and describe the stages in the adoption process. How might a student go through the adoption process when choosing a college or university? (AACSB: Communication; Reflective Thinking)

Critical Thinking Exercises

5-6 Researchers study the role of personality on consumer purchase behavior. One research project—Beyond the Purchase—offers a range of surveys consumers can take to learn more about their own personality in general and their consumer personality in particular. Register at http://www.beyondthepurchase.org/ and take the "Spending Habits" surveys along with any of the other surveys that interest you. What do these surveys tell you about your general and consumer personality? Do you agree with the findings? Why or why not? (AACSB: Communication; Use of IT; Diversity; Reflective Thinking)

5-7 Discuss the steps of the consumer buying process for a new product. Next, identify a new product that you have recently adopted into your daily lifestyle. What is the new product that was adopted? As a consumer, did you use the adoption stages as outlined in the chapter? Why or why not? (AACSB: Communication; Reflective Thinking)

5-8 The characteristics of a new product affect its rate of adoption. Identify the five characteristics that influence the rate of adoption and describe how each factor will influence the rate of adoption of the Apple Watch. (AACSB: Communication; Reflective Thinking)

APPLICATIONS AND CASES

Online, Mobile, and Social Media Marketing Digital Influencer Credibility

Fashion and lifestyle bloggers that are multimillionaires? Believe it. Simple fashion blogs have blown up to become huge income sources. Bloggers have integrated affiliate marketing, built their own brands or brand collaborations, and included sponsored content in their blogsites. Companies now see fashion bloggers as increasingly relevant digital influencers. Firms have also found that bloggers can drive more sales volume than celebrity endorsements. Therefore, brands are building more influencer campaigns into their marketing budgets. Ultimately, this means that bloggers can earn significant incomes. For example, the Refinery29 blog started out as a regular fashion blog with its bloggers earning an average income of $55,000 a year. It quickly turned into a fashion and lifestyle empire for Refinery29 founders Justin Stefano and Philippe von Borries. The site now makes $24 million a year, partially from revenue generated when these influencers push sales to affiliates through links embedded in the blog. To learn more about how much money the world's top fashion and lifestyle bloggers earn and about Refinery29's journey, visit www.inc.com/rebecca-borison/refinery29-chat.html and www.whowhatwear.com/how-do-bloggers-make-money.

5-9 Find an example of a blog on a topic that interests you. Are there advertisements on the blog? Does the blogger appear to be sponsored by any companies? Is there information regarding sponsorship? Write a brief report of your observations. (AACSB: Use of IT; Communication; Reflective Thinking)

5-10   Digital influencers can shape consumer product acceptance and adoption. Discuss the process of making a purchase through a podcast, blog, or social media account based on the recommendation of a digital influencer. Are sponsored content, paid advertisements, unpaid advertisements, or product testimonials on blogsites credible information sources? Why or why not? (AACSB: Communication, Reflective Thinking)

Marketing Ethics Ultimate Water

Water is water, right? Not so! Beverly Hills 90H2O claims to be designed "by a world-class team of experts, including a water sommelier." The winner of the World's Best Water Award, this water is sourced in the California mountains. At $72 for a case of 24 bottles, this is not your everyday drinking water. The 7.5 alkalinity "silky" water is loaded with minerals and electrolytes. It is available in fine restaurants, gourmet markets, and luxury hotels but is sold only in California. Beverly Hills 90H2O isn't the only luxury water, and it's actually somewhat of a bargain. Fillico Beverly Hills (from Japan) costs $100 per bottle. That's without the gold or silver crown cap—you can double the price if you want that. Acqua di Cristallo Tributo a Modigliani gold-bottled water tops them all at $60,000 per bottle!

5-11   What buying factors are most likely affecting consumers who purchase luxury bottle water? (AACSB: Communication; Reflective Thinking)

5-12   Discuss the ethical issues surrounding the bottled water industry. (AACSB: Communication; Ethical Reasoning)

Marketing by the Numbers Evaluating Alternatives

One way consumers can evaluate alternatives is to identify important attributes and assess how purchase alternatives perform on those attributes. Consider the purchase of a tablet. Each attribute, such as screen size, is given a weight to reflect its level of importance to that consumer. Then the consumer evaluates each alternative on each attribute. For example, in the following table, price (weighted at 0.5) is the most important attribute for this consumer. The consumer believes that Brand C performs best on price, rating it 7 (higher ratings indicate higher performance). Brand B is perceived as performing the worst on this attribute (rating of 3). Screen size and available apps are the consumer's next most important attributes. Operating system is least important.

A score can be calculated for each brand by multiplying the importance weight for each attribute by the brand's score on that attribute. These weighted scores are then summed to determine the score for that brand. For example, $Score_{Brand A} = (0.2 \times 4) + (0.5 \times 6) + (0.1 \times 5) + (0.2 \times 4) = 0.8 + 3.0 + 0.5 + 0.8 = 5.1$. This consumer will select the brand with the highest score.

5-13   Calculate the scores for brands B and C. Which brand would this consumer likely choose? (AACSB: Communication; Analytic Reasoning)

5-14   Which brand is this consumer least likely to purchase? Discuss two ways the marketer of this brand can enhance consumer attitudes toward purchasing its brand. (AACSB: Communication; Reflective Thinking; Analytic Reasoning)

Attributes	Importance Weight (e)	Alternative Brands		
		A	B	C
Screen size	0.2	4	6	2
Price	0.5	6	3	7
Operating system	0.1	5	5	4
Apps available	0.2	4	6	7

Video Case IMG Worldwide

IMG Worldwide is the world's largest sports entertainment media company. In years past, IMG was all about professional golf and tennis marketing. But today, IMG handles sales and marketing activities for 70 to 80 colleges, making college sports marketing the company's highest-growth business. In short, IMG handles anything and everything that touches the college sports consumer short of actually playing games on the court or field.

Although you might think that all college sports fans are created equal, IMG finds that nothing could be further from the truth. How different fans consume sports and sports-related activities is affected by geographical, generational, and institutional factors. IMG focuses on comprehensively understanding the process that consumers go through to view or attend a sporting event. It then connects with consumers at each and every stage.

After viewing the video featuring IMG Worldwide, answer the following questions:

5-15   What "product" is a college athletics department selling?

5-16   Discuss how a college sports fan might go through the buying decision process, providing examples for each stage.

5-17   Of the four sets of factors affecting consumer behavior, which most strongly affects how college sports fans consume a sport?

Company Case GoldieBlox: Swimming Upstream against Consumer Perceptions

When Debbie Sterling was in high school, her math teacher recognized her quantitative talent and suggested she pursue engineering as a college major. At the time, Sterling couldn't figure out why her teacher thought she should drive trains for a living. But the suggestion was enough to get her started down the right path. After four years at Stanford, Sterling graduated with a degree in mechanical engineering. But throughout the course of her studies, Sterling noticed the lack of women in her engineering program—a characteristic phenomenon in a field where men outnumber women 86 percent to 14 percent. This observation ignited an obsession in Sterling. She set out on a mission to inspire a future generation of female engineers by disrupting the pink aisle in toy stores.

During the past few years, among other accolades, Sterling has been named Time's "Person of the Moment" and one of Business Insider's "30 Women Who Are Changing the World." Why? Because Sterling is the founder and CEO of GoldieBlox, a toy company that is making Sterling's mission a reality.

A Different Kind of Toy Company

After graduating, Sterling started researching everything from childhood development to gender roles. She discovered that in order to gain interest in and pursue a given field, a person must be exposed to the right inputs at an early age. This fact became particularly bothersome as Sterling became more and more familiar with the contents of the average toy aisle in stores. Toys for girls were in the pink aisle, dominated by dolls, stuffed animals, and princesses, whereas toys for boys were found in the blue aisle, filled with macho action figures, various toy weapons, and a huge variety of building block sets. Most experts agree that the toys served up to young girls do little to encourage an interest in STEM subjects (science, technology, engineering, and math). This knowledge led Sterling to develop a plan to create a different kind of toy for girls.

As she began developing ideas for toys, another research finding struck her—girls possess stellar verbal skills and tend to learn better by interacting with stories. That insight was instrumental in the creation of the GoldieBlox line of construction sets. Part erector set and part storybook, the combination was designed to engage girls through their verbal skills and encourage them to build through narratives that feature the adventures of Goldie, a freckled-faced blonde girl donning overalls and a tool belt. Although Goldie comes off as a bit of a tomboy, she's still girlish. Skinny, blonde, and cute, she favors pinks and purples. The toys and stories feature animals and ribbons, and characters are more likely to help others than to succeed on their own.

After her innovative toy sets received little interest at the American International Toy Fair in New York City, Sterling started her own company. That decision sparked more interest than she could have ever imagined. To raise the $150,000 needed for the first round of production, Sterling launched a Kickstarter crowdsourced funding campaign. Her funding goal was reached in just four days, and the funding topped out at $285,000.

With little to spend on traditional advertising, Sterling first promoted her inventive toys with some YouTube ads, including "Princess Machine," featuring young girls who take their stereotypically girly toys and create a sophisticated Rube Goldberg device. That video went viral to the tune of 8 million views in

little more than a week. Shortly thereafter, GoldieBlox's first two products became Amazon's top two selling toys during the industry's busiest month of December. And if all that wasn't enough, GoldieBlox beat out 15,000 contenders in Intuit's "Small Business Big Game" Super Bowl ad contest, winning a $4 million spot during the big game.

Today, only a few years after the launch of its first product, GoldieBlox's toys are sold at Target, Toys"R"Us, Amazon, and 6,000 other retailers worldwide. The brand features dozens of play sets designed for girls ages 3 through 11, the Bloxtown interactive website and app, a collection of original music videos, a Goldie action figure, and a "More Than Just a Princess" line of T-shirts and hoodies. GoldieBlox has won numerous industry awards, and its toys have succeeded in raising awareness about the lack of women in technical and scientific fields as well as the issues associated with the traditional pink aisle.

All That Glitters Is Not Goldie

With all this success, you would think that GoldieBlox would be heralded by anyone and everyone wanting to change gender-based stereotypes in toys. But GoldieBlox has sparked substantial debate over whether it is really helping the cause it claims to be serving. The opposition, led by many feminist voices, claims that GoldieBox's approach is little more than window dressing. The debate got really ugly after the launch of GoldieBlox and the Parade Float, a construction set based on a new challenge faced by Goldie and her friends—to create a float to transport the winner of a beauty pageant. "You cannot create a toy meant to break down stereotypes when you start off with the ideal that 'we know all girls love princesses,'" argues author Melissa Atkins Wardy. Those in the opposition camp call for toys that are gender-neutral. "When we use princess culture, pinkification, and beauty norms to sell STEM toys to girls and fool ourselves that we are amazing and progressive and raising an incredible generation of female engineers, we continue to sell our girls short," says Wardy. Additionally, although the toys are designed to stir interest in girls by having them build and create, critics have raised concerns that GoldieBlox toys are too simplistic.

But Sterling is quick to respond to all such arguments and show that GoldieBlox isn't just trying to hook parents with a gimmick that doesn't deliver. "There's nothing wrong with being a princess," says the 32-year-old entrepreneur. "We just think girls can build their own castles too." This idea is backed by many advocates who recognize that to disrupt the pink aisle, you can't start out by trying to obliterate it.

To influence through play the types of hobbies and academic fields that women pursue, a company first must penetrate a very competitive market. Creating toys that are void of things that girls find appealing will only send girls scrambling for the nearest Bratz or Disney princess doll. GoldieBlox toys may incorporate traditional gender stereotypes, but they tweak and reframe them. GoldieBlox spent years researching gender differences, seeking significant input from Harvard neuroscientists, and observing children's play patterns. "Our stories leverage girls' advanced verbal skills to help develop and build self-confidence in their spatial skills," Sterling asserts.

Besides, Sterling was just getting started. Today, the GoldieBlox portfolio is not only growing in number of play sets, it's becoming more diverse with three new characters who have joined Goldie to create a team to which just about any girl can relate. There's Ruby Rails, a popular African American girl who is a whiz at coding; Valentina Voltz, a Hispanic engineer; and Li Gravity, Goldie's long-time neighbor and best friend who is an expert at physics who knows how to apply the laws of his favorite science, performing stunts with superhero-like precision. Together, these characters take girls on a variety of adventures that go way beyond princess escapades—such as skydiving, ziplining, and auto racing. Then there's the "Invention Mansion," the play set Sterling refers to as the "anti-dollhouse"—a 300-piece play set featuring a "Hacker Hideway" that can be figured and reconfigured into hundreds of different formats.

Whether or not the two sides to the debate will resolve their differences in trying to achieve the same goal, there is no question that GoldieBlox has taken the toy industry by storm. If the most recent annual North American International Toy Fair is any indication, a little GoldieBlox seems to have rubbed off on just about every other toy company. The first year that GoldieBlox set up its booth at the trade show, the tech toy section was a wasteland. Today, nearly every booth features STEM toys, robots, and a lot of not-so-pink products targeted at girls.

Although clearly motivated to put an end to the stereotypes that have long been generated by the toy and entertainment industries, Sterling makes it clear that the goal is to become a multiplatform character brand à la Disney. "We want to be the brand that kids are whining for." If the next few years are anything like GoldieBlox's first few, it's easy to envision a new kind of toy aisle at the local supercenter—one that heavily features GoldieBlox's multiplatform brand.

Questions for Discussion

5-18 Of the factors that influence consumer behavior, which category or categories (cultural, social, personal, or psychological) best explain the existence of a blue toy aisle and a pink toy aisle? Why?

5-19 Choose the specific factor (for example, culture, family, occupation, attitudes) that most accounts for the blue/pink toy aisle phenomenon. Explain the challenges faced by GoldieBlox in attempting to market toys that "swim against the stream" or push back against the forces of that factor.

5-20 To what degree is GoldieBlox bucking the blue/pink toy aisle system?

5-21 If GoldieBlox succeeds at selling lots of its toys, will that accomplish the mission of increasing the presence of females in the field of engineering?

Sources: John Kell, "How Toy Startup GoldieBlox Made Diversity a Priority," *Fortune*, April 1, 2016, www.fortune.com/2016/04/01/goldieblox-toy-startup-diversity/; "Hottest Toys of 2016: On the Ground with GoldieBlox at the Toy Fair," *GeekGirlRising*, www.geekgirlrising.com/hottest-toys-of-2016-focus-on-steam-ggr-and-goldieblox-on-the-ground-at-ny-toy-fair/, accessed June, 2016; Katy Waldman, "GoldieBlox: Great for Girls? Terrible for Girls? Or Just Selling Toys?" *Slate*, November 26, 2013, www.slate.com/blogs/xx_factor/2013/11/26/goldieblox_disrupting_the_pink_aisle_or_just_selling_toys.html; Jennifer Reingold, "Watch Out Disney: This Toy Startup's Coming for You," *Fortune*, November 26, 2014, http://fortune.com/2014/11/26/goldieblox-toy-startup/; and information from www.goldieblox.com, accessed June 2016.

MyMarketingLab

Go to **mymktlab.com** for Auto-graded writing questions as well as the following Assisted-graded writing questions:

5-22 Explain the stages of the consumer buyer decision process and describe how you or your family went through this process to make a recent purchase.

5-23 Discuss how lifestyle influences consumers' buying behavior and how marketers measure lifestyle.

PART 1: Defining Marketing and the Marketing Process (Chapters 1–2)
PART 2: Understanding the Marketplace and Consumer Value (Chapters 3–6)
PART 3: Designing a Customer Value–Driven Strategy and Mix (Chapters 7–17)
PART 4: Extending Marketing (Chapters 18–20)

Business Markets and Business Buyer Behavior

CHAPTER PREVIEW

In the previous chapter, you studied *final consumer* buying behavior and factors that influence it. In this chapter, we'll do the same for *business customers*— those that buy goods and services for use in producing their own products and services or for resale to others. As when selling to final buyers, firms marketing to businesses must engage business customers and build profitable relationships with them by creating superior customer value.

To start, let's look at IBM. Although the IBM brand is very familiar to most final consumers, nearly all of the company's almost $100 billion in annual revenues comes from business and institutional customers. More than just "selling" its products and services to B-to-B customers, IBM succeeds by working closely and deeply with them to develop complete solutions to their information and data analytics problems. From its lofty customer-solutions mission to the "boots on the ground," IBM wants to become a strategic information and insights partner with its business customers.

IBM: The World's Most Valuable Business-to-Business Brand

IBM is a household word to most of us. However, throughout its long history, IBM's fortunes have come not from final consumers but from large business and institutional customers. "Big Blue"—as it's often called—is the quintessential B-to-B brand. In fact, corporate brand tracker Millward Brown recently named IBM the most valuable B-to-B brand in the world. Valued at $94 billion, IBM is worth about 50 percent more than the number-two B-to-B brand, giant GE. Even more impressive, IBM has survived and thrived for more than 100 years, something no other *Fortune* top-25 company has managed.

In some ways, IBM selling B-to-B is like P&G selling to final consumers. It requires a deep-down understanding of customer needs and a customer-driven marketing strategy that engages customers and delivers superior customer value. But that's where most of the similarities end. Rather than selling small-ticket purchases to masses of individual consumers, IBM sells complex big-ticket purchases to a smaller set of much bigger buyers, with each purchase involving perhaps dozens of decision makers. So IBM's B-to-B emphasis is less on selling *to* customers and more on partnering *with* them to help solve their complex information and analytics problems.

> IBM has become the world's most valuable business-to-business brand by solving customer problems and helping them to "outthink" their challenges, competitors, and limits in the new cognitive era.

Solving customer problems has always been a hallmark of IBM's strategy, culture, and success. Over the years, IBM has transformed itself time and again to meet changing customer needs. For example, two decades ago, IBM was known mostly for peddling mainframe computers, PCs, and other basic computer system components. Back then, if you'd asked top managers at Big Blue what their mission was, they'd have answered, "To sell computer hardware and software."

By the early 1990s, however, IBM's sales had plateaued. To learn why, IBM sent its top managers to meet face-to-face with important customers—what it called "bear-hugging customers"—to relearn about their problems and priorities. The managers learned that in the new connected digital age, companies face a perplexing array of data and information technologies. Today's customers don't need just computers and software. Instead, they need total solutions to ever-more-bewildering data, information, and analytics problems.

This realization led to a fundamental transformation of IBM's business. Now, if you ask IBM managers to define the company's mission, they'll tell you, "We deliver *insights* and *solutions* to customers' data and information technology problems." Under this new customer-solutions focus, IBM shifted emphasis away from mainframes and computer hardware. Instead, it added a full slate of integrated information technology, software, and business consulting services. Most recently, to meet customers' ever-changing digital needs, IBM has shifted even more deeply into data analytics, cloud computing, cybersecurity, social networking, and mobile technology solutions.

Thus, customers can still buy mainframe computers from IBM, but they are more likely to buy solutions involving a complex, integrated mix of hardware, software, services, consulting, and advice across collaborative online, mobile, and social networks. The transformed IBM now works arm-in-arm with B-to-B customers on everything from assessing, planning, designing, and implementing their data and analytics systems to actually running those systems for customers.

According to IBM CEO Ginni Rometty, the company's focus on working closely with customers and changing to meet their needs is what makes IBM special. "We're 104 years old," she says. "The reason we're the only tech company still here at 104 is how many times we've transformed." IBM's customer-solutions focus is summed up by its new marketing campaign: "Cognitive Business: Outthink." The campaign positions IBM as a company that helps customers to "outthink your challenges, competitors, and limits" in the new "cognitive era."

But good B-to-B marketing at IBM goes well beyond a high-level customer-solutions mission, sweeping transformations, and imaginative positioning campaigns. At the most basic level, it involves "boots on the ground"—IBM teams and individuals developing close day-in, day-out working relationships with customers.

Consider the classic example of IBMer Vivek Gupta and how he became IBM's top salesperson in its fastest-growing industry (telecommunications) and fastest-growing market (India). When Gupta first joined IBM some years ago, he struggled to gain a foothold in a market where more than 70 percent of corporations are family controlled and where relationships, trust, and family ties trump almost everything else. In addition to his formal IBM training, Gupta launched his own extensive investigative effort, getting to know people, learning about IBM and its customers, and developing a rock-solid knowledge of how the company's products and services fit customer needs.

When Gupta first approached potential customer Vodafone—the dominant firm in India's exploding mobile phone market—the managing director there told him, "I don't do any business with IBM, and I don't intend to." But the quietly determined Gupta kept at it, getting to know Vodafone's key decision makers and patiently listening, observing, and identifying how IBM might be able to help Vodafone succeed in its volatile and competitive markets.

Gupta came to know more about Vodafone than many people who worked there. It took him nearly four years, but

Business-to-business marketing: IBM's "Cognitive Business: Outthink" campaign positions the company as one that works closely with business customers to help them thrive in the new "cognitive era."
NurPhoto/Getty Images

Gupta finally sold Vodafone—the same people who vowed never to do business with IBM—on a gigantic five-year, $600 million turnkey contract to handle everything from Vodafone's customer service to its finances. Gupta became such a well-known figure at Vodafone's offices in Mumbai that many people there were surprised that his badge said "IBM" and not "Vodafone." Gupta thrives on rooting out customer problems to solve. "You have to understand [customers'] pain points," he explains. "And they are not going to spell them out."

Flush with success, Gupta set his sights on still bigger targets. He realized that many big Indian telecoms were so busy simply hammering out their basic back-office operating systems that they had little money and brainpower left for strategy, branding, and marketing. However, IBM had all the technology and expertise required to build and maintain such systems. What if IBM were to take over managing the system innards, freeing the customer to attend to strategy and marketing? Gupta proposed just such a novel solution to Bharti Airtel, then a relative newcomer to India's wireless industry. The result: IBM now runs the bulk of Bharti Airtel's back-office operations, while Bharti Airtel focuses on taking care of its own customers. In the first five years, the deal produced an incredible $1 billion for IBM. Bharti Airtel is now India's wireless industry leader and the deal is a staple "how-to" case study in IBM's emerging markets sales training.

The IBM and Vivek Gupta stories highlight the essentials of B-to-B marketing success. It starts with a customer-focused mission that translates down to individuals working closely with customers to find complete solutions. Gupta doesn't just sell IBM computer hardware, software, and analytics. He works with customers, feels their pain, finds solutions, and sells the IBM systems and people that will deliver results for the customer. "It's at once radically simple and just plain radical," says an analyst. "He wants to convince you that IBM can run your business—your entire business, save for strategy and marketing—better than you can."[1]

OBJECTIVES OUTLINE

IN ONE WAY OR another, most large companies sell to other organizations. Companies such as IBM, Boeing, DuPont, Caterpillar, and countless other firms sell *most* of their products to other businesses. Even large consumer products companies, which make products used by final consumers, must first sell their products to other businesses. For example, General Mills makes many familiar consumer brands—Big G cereals (Cheerios, Wheaties, Trix, Chex, Total, Fiber One), baking products (Pillsbury, Betty Crocker, Bisquick, Gold Medal flour), snacks (Nature Valley, Bugles, Chex Mix), Yoplait yogurt, Häagen-Dazs ice cream, and many others. But to sell these products to consumers, General Mills must first sell them to its wholesaler and retailer customers, who in turn serve the consumer market.

Business buyer behavior refers to the buying behavior of organizations that buy goods and services for use in the production of other products and services that are sold, rented, or supplied to others. It also includes the behavior of retailing and wholesaling firms that acquire goods to resell or rent to others at a profit. In the **business buying process**, business buyers determine which products and services their organizations need to purchase and then find, evaluate, and choose among alternative suppliers and brands. *Business-to-business (B-to-B) marketers* must do their best to understand business markets and business buyer behavior. Then, like businesses that sell to final buyers, they must engage business customers and build profitable relationships with them by creating superior customer value.

Business buyer behavior
The buying behavior of organizations that buy goods and services for use in the production of other products and services that are sold, rented, or supplied to others.

Business buying process
The decision process by which business buyers determine which products and services their organizations need to purchase and then find, evaluate, and choose among alternative suppliers and brands.

Author | Business markets operate
Comment | "behind the scenes" to most consumers. Most of the things you buy involve many sets of business purchases before you ever see them.

Business Markets

The business market is *huge*. In fact, business markets involve far more dollars and items than do consumer markets. For example, think about the large number of business transactions involved in the production and sale of a single set of Goodyear tires. Various suppliers sell Goodyear the rubber, steel, equipment, and other goods that it needs to produce tires. Goodyear then sells the finished tires to retailers, which in turn sell them to consumers. Thus, many sets of *business* purchases were made for only one set of *consumer* purchases. In addition, Goodyear sells tires as original equipment to manufacturers that install them on new vehicles and as replacement tires to companies that maintain their own fleets of company cars, trucks, or other vehicles.

In some ways, business markets are similar to consumer markets. Both involve people who assume buying roles and make purchase decisions to satisfy needs. However, business markets differ in many ways from consumer markets. The main differences are in *market structure and demand*, the *nature of the buying unit*, and the *types of decisions and the decision process* involved.

Market Structure and Demand

The business marketer normally deals with *far fewer but far larger buyers* than the consumer marketer does. Even in large business markets, a few buyers often account for most of the purchasing. For example, when Goodyear sells replacement tires to final consumers, its potential market includes millions of car owners around the world. But its fate in business markets depends on getting orders from only a handful of large automakers.

Further, many business markets have *inelastic and more fluctuating demand*. The total demand for many business products is not much affected by price changes, especially in the short run. A drop in the price of leather will not cause shoe manufacturers to buy much more leather unless it results in lower shoe prices that, in turn, increase consumer demand for shoes. And the demand for many business goods and services tends to change more—and more quickly—than does the demand for consumer goods and services. A small percentage increase in consumer demand can cause large increases in business demand.

Finally, business demand is **derived demand**—it ultimately derives from the demand for consumer goods. For example, demand for Gore-Tex fabrics derives from consumer purchases of outdoor apparel brands made from Gore-Tex. And consumers buy Corning's Gorilla Glass only when they buy laptops, tablets, and smartphones with Gorilla Glass screens from producers such as Apple, Samsung, Lenovo, Dell, HP, Sony, and Microsoft. If consumer demand for these end products increases, so does the demand for the Gore-Tex fabrics or Gorilla Glass they contain.

Therefore, B-to-B marketers sometimes promote their products directly to final consumers to increase business demand. ● For example, Corning's long-running "Tough, yet beautiful" consumer marketing campaign features a family of gorillas who are out to convince final buyers that it makes sense to choose digital devices with screens made of Gorilla Glass rather than a less-tough competitor. Such advertising benefits both Corning and the partner brands that incorporate its durable, scratch-resistant glass. Thanks in part to the consumer marketing campaign, Corning's Gorilla Glass has to date been featured in more than 40 major brands and more than 4.5 billion devices worldwide.[2]

Derived demand
Business demand that ultimately comes from (derives from) the demand for consumer goods.

● **Derived demand: Corning's long-running "Tough, yet beautiful" consumer marketing campaign convinces final users that it makes sense to buy devices with screens made of Gorilla Glass, to the benefit of both Corning and its partner brands.**
Photo courtesy Corning Incorporated.

Nature of the Buying Unit

Compared with consumer purchases, a business purchase usually involves *more decision participants* and a *more professional purchasing effort*. Often, business buying is done by trained purchasing agents who spend their working lives learning how to buy better. The more complex the purchase, the more likely it is that several people will participate in the decision-making process. Buying committees composed of technical experts and top management are common in the buying of major goods. Beyond this, B-to-B marketers now face a new breed of higher-level, better-trained supply managers. Therefore, companies must have well-trained marketers and salespeople to deal with these well-trained buyers.

Types of Decisions and the Decision Process

Business buyers usually face *more complex* buying decisions than do consumer buyers. Business purchases often involve large sums of money, complex technical and economic considerations, and interactions among people at many levels of the buyer's organization. The business buying process also tends to be *longer* and *more formalized*. Large business purchases usually call for detailed product specifications, written purchase orders, careful supplier searches, and formal approval.

Finally, in the business buying process, the buyer and seller are often much *more dependent* on each other. B-to-B marketers may roll up their sleeves and work closely with customers during all stages of the buying process—from helping customers define problems to finding solutions to supporting after-sale operation. In the short run, sales go to suppliers who meet buyers' immediate product and service needs. In the long run, however, business-to-business marketers keep customers by meeting current needs *and* by partnering with them to help solve their problems. For example, consider agricultural and food giant Cargill's Cocoa & Chocolate division:[3]

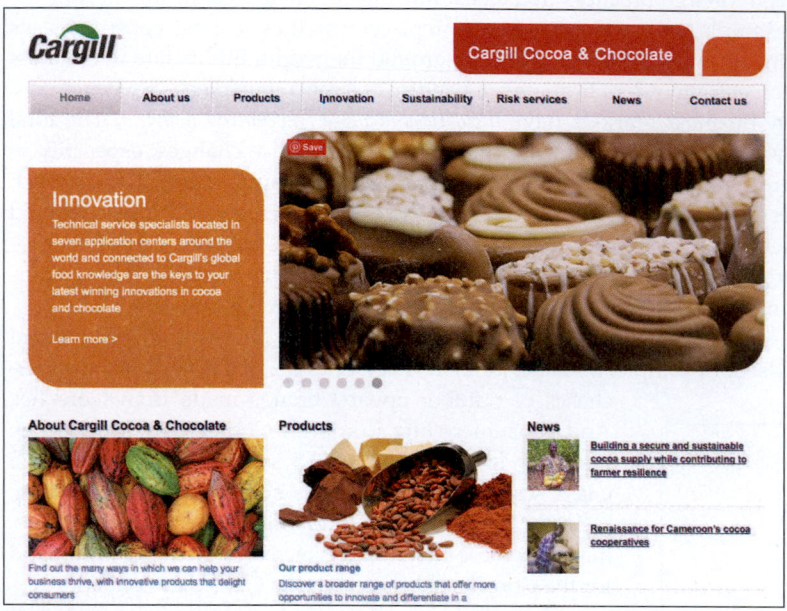

Cargill's Cocoa & Chocolate division sells cocoa and chocolate products to business customers around the world, including giants such as Mars and Mondelēz. But its success lies in doing much more than just selling its products *to* such customers. Instead, Cargill partners closely them, applying its deep expertise to help customers *use* its products to serve their own customers better and more profitably. For example, Cargill's researchers keep customers up to date on the latest global consumer food trends. Its research and development teams give customers personalized product development support. And its technical services specialists provide help in resolving customer ingredient and applications challenges. "Whether you need laboratory or pilot work on finished products or help with production start-up," says the company, "Cargill's applications experts can assist you—from developing new end-product recipes, achieving better pricing for your products, or getting to market more quickly." Thus, more than just selling cocoa and chocolate, Cargill sells customer success in using those products. Its goal is to "[apply] our deep chocolate expertise and broad food knowledge…to provide you with more opportunities to grow your business across a wide range of cocoa and chocolate products and applications…helping you *thrive*, today and into the future."[4]

The business buyer decision process: Cargill's Cocoa & Chocolate division does more than sell it products to consumers. It partners closely with customers to help them use its products to serve their own customers better and more profitably.
Cargill

Supplier development
Systematic development of networks of supplier-partners to ensure an appropriate and dependable supply of products and materials for use in making products or reselling them to others.

As in Cargill's case, in recent years, relationships between most customers and suppliers have been changing from downright adversarial to close and chummy. In fact, many customer companies are now practicing **supplier development**, systematically developing networks of supplier-partners to ensure a dependable supply of the products and materials that they use in making their own products or reselling to others. For example, Walmart doesn't have a "Purchasing Department"; it has a "Supplier Development Department." The giant retailer knows that it can't just rely on spot suppliers who might be available when needed. Instead, Walmart manages a huge network of supplier-partners that help provide the hundreds of billions of dollars of goods that it sells to its customers each year.

Author Comment | Business buying decisions can range from routine to incredibly complex, involving only a few or very many decision makers and buying influences.

Business Buyer Behavior

At the most basic level, marketers want to know how business buyers will respond to various marketing stimuli. **Figure 6.1** shows a model of business buyer behavior. In this model, marketing and other stimuli affect the buying organization and produce certain buyer responses. To design good marketing strategies, marketers must understand what happens within the organization to turn stimuli into purchase responses.

Within the organization, buying activity consists of two major parts: the *buying center*, composed of all the people involved in the buying decision, and the *buying decision process*. The model shows that the buying center and the buying decision process are influenced by internal organizational, interpersonal, and individual factors as well as external environmental factors.

The model in Figure 6.1 suggests four questions about business buyer behavior: What buying decisions do business buyers make? Who participates in the business buying process? What are the major influences on buyers? How do business buyers make their buying decisions?

● FIGURE | 6.1
A Model of Business Buyer Behavior

In some ways, business markets are similar to consumer markets—this model looks a lot like the model of consumer buyer behavior presented in Figure 5.1. But there are some major differences, especially in the nature of the buying unit, the types of decisions made, and the decision process.

The environment		The buying organization	Buyer responses
Marketing stimuli	**Other stimuli**	**The buying center**	Product or service choice
Product	Economic		Supplier choice
Price	Technological	**Buying decision process**	Order quantities
Place	Political		Delivery terms and times
Promotion	Cultural	(Interpersonal and individual influences)	Service terms
	Competitive	(Organizational influences)	Payment

Straight rebuy
A business buying situation in which the buyer routinely reorders something without modifications.

Modified rebuy
A business buying situation in which the buyer wants to modify product specifications, prices, terms, or suppliers.

New task
A business buying situation in which the buyer purchases a product or service for the first time.

Systems selling (or solutions selling)
Buying a packaged solution to a problem from a single seller, thus avoiding all the separate decisions involved in a complex buying situation.

Major Types of Buying Situations

There are three major types of buying situations.[5] In a **straight rebuy**, the buyer reorders something without any modifications. It is usually handled on a routine basis by the purchasing department. To keep the business, "in" suppliers try to maintain customer engagement and product and service quality. "Out" suppliers try to find new ways to add value or exploit dissatisfaction so that the buyer will consider them.

In a **modified rebuy**, the buyer wants to modify product specifications, prices, terms, or suppliers. The "in" suppliers may become nervous and feel pressured to put their best foot forward to protect an account. "Out" suppliers may see the modified rebuy situation as an opportunity to make a better offer and gain new business.

A company buying a product or service for the first time faces a **new task** situation. In such cases, the greater the cost or risk, the larger the number of decision participants and the greater the company's efforts to collect information. The new task situation is the marketer's greatest opportunity and challenge. The marketer not only tries to reach as many key buying influences as possible but also provides help and information. The buyer makes the fewest decisions in the straight rebuy and the most in the new task decision.

Many business buyers prefer to buy a complete solution to a problem from a single seller rather than buying separate products and services from several suppliers and putting them together. The sale often goes to the firm that engages business customers deeply and provides the most complete *system* for meeting a customer's needs and solving its problems. Such **systems selling (or solutions selling)** is often a key business marketing strategy for winning and holding accounts. Consider IBM and its customer Six Flags Entertainment Corporation:[6]

> Six Flags operates 19 regional theme parks across North America featuring exciting rides and water attractions, world-class roller coasters, and special shows and concerts. ● To deliver a fun and safe experience for guests, Six Flags must carefully and effectively manage thousands of park assets—from rides and equipment to buildings and other facilities. Six Flags needed a tool for managing all those assets efficiently and effectively across its far-flung collection of parks. So it turned to IBM, which has software—called Maximo Asset Management software—that handles that very problem well.

But IBM didn't just hand the software over to Six Flags with best wishes for happy implementation. Instead, IBM's Maximo Professional

● Solutions selling: Delivering a fun and safe experience for Six Flags guests requires careful and effective management of thousands of park assets across its 19 regional theme parks. IBM works hand in hand with Six Flags to provide not just software but a complete solution.

Matthew Imaging/Getty Images

Services group combined the software with an entire set of services designed to get and keep the software up and running. IBM worked hand in hand with Six Flags to customize the application and strategically implement and run it across Six Flags's far-flung facilities, along with on-site immersion training and planning workshops. Thus, IBM isn't just selling the software; it's selling a complete solution to Six Flags's complex asset management problem.

Participants in the Business Buying Process

Who does the buying of the trillions of dollars' worth of goods and services needed by business organizations? The decision-making unit of a buying organization is called its **buying center**. It consists of all the individuals and units that play a role in the business purchase decision-making process. This group includes the actual users of the product or service, those who make the buying decision, those who influence the buying decision, those who do the actual buying, and those who control buying information.

The buying center includes all members of the organization who play any of five roles in the purchase decision process.[7]

- **Users** are members of the organization who will use the product or service. In many cases, users initiate the buying proposal and help define product specifications.
- **Influencers** often help define specifications and also provide information for evaluating alternatives. Technical personnel are particularly important influencers.
- **Buyers** have formal authority to select the supplier and arrange terms of purchase. Buyers may help shape product specifications, but their major role is in selecting vendors and negotiating. In more complex purchases, buyers might include high-level officers participating in the negotiations.
- **Deciders** have formal or informal power to select or approve the final suppliers. In routine buying, the buyers are often the deciders, or at least the approvers.
- **Gatekeepers** control the flow of information to others. For example, purchasing agents often have authority to prevent salespersons from seeing users or deciders. Other gatekeepers include technical personnel and even personal secretaries.

The buying center is not a fixed and formally identified unit within the buying organization. It is a set of buying roles assumed by different people for different purchases. Within the organization, the size and makeup of the buying center will vary for different products and for different buying situations. For some routine purchases, one person—say, a purchasing agent—may assume all the buying center roles and serve as the only person involved in the buying decision. For more complex purchases in large companies, the buying center may include 20, 30, or even more people from different levels and departments in the organization.[8]

The buying center concept presents a major marketing challenge. The business marketer must learn who participates in the decision, each participant's relative influence, and what evaluation criteria each decision participant uses. This can be difficult.

The buying center usually includes some obvious participants who are involved formally in the buying decision. For example, the decision to buy a corporate jet will probably involve the company's CEO, the chief pilot, a purchasing agent, some legal staff, a member of top management, and others formally charged with the buying decision. It may also involve less obvious, informal participants, some of whom may actually make or strongly affect the buying decision. Sometimes, even the people in the buying center are not aware of all the buying participants. For example, the decision about which corporate jet to buy may actually be made by a corporate board member who has an interest in flying and who knows a lot about airplanes. This board member may work behind the scenes to sway the decision. Many business buying decisions result from the complex interactions of ever-changing buying center participants.

Major Influences on Business Buyers

Business buyers are subject to many influences when they make their buying decisions. Some marketers assume that the major influences are economic. They think buyers will favor the supplier who offers the lowest price or the best product or the most service. They concentrate on offering strong economic benefits to buyers. Such economic factors are very

---

Buying center
All the individuals and units that play a role in the purchase decision-making process.

Users
Members of the buying organization who will actually use the purchased product or service.

Influencers
People in an organization's buying center who affect the buying decision; they often help define specifications and also provide information for evaluating alternatives.

Buyers
People in an organization's buying center who make an actual purchase.

Deciders
People in an organization's buying center who have formal or informal power to select or approve the final suppliers.

Gatekeepers
People in an organization's buying center who control the flow of information to others.

important to most buyers, especially in a tough economy. However, business buyers actually respond to both economic and personal factors. Far from being cold, calculating, and impersonal, business buyers are human and social as well. They react to both reason and emotion.

Today, most B-to-B marketers recognize that emotion plays an important role in business buying decisions. Consider this example:[9]

● Emotions play a role in business buying. Ads like this one from USG's "It's Your World. Build It." corporate marketing campaign pack a decidedly emotional wallop.

USG

● USG Corporation is a leading manufacturer of gypsum wallboard and other building materials for the construction and remodeling industries. Given its construction contractor, architect, and builder audience, you might expect USG's B-to-B ads to focus heavily on performance features and benefits, such as strength, impact resistance, ease of installation, and costs. USG does promote these benefits. However, its most recent corporate marketing campaign, built around its new "It's Your World. Build It." positioning, packs a decidedly more emotional wallop. The campaign focuses not on how USG's products perform but on what the company and its products stand for and mean. For example, one split-image ad shows excited children building a sand castle on one side and a worker at a construction site, hard hat in hand, on the other. The headline states: "As children we imagine great kingdoms. Build them." As one analyst concludes, "Building materials and emotion aren't something you would link immediately, but the [USG] campaign captures a powerful sentiment about the human need to build."

● **Figure 6.2** lists various groups of influences on business buyers—environmental, organizational, interpersonal, and individual. Business buyers are heavily influenced by factors in the current and expected *economic environment*, such as the level of primary demand, the economic outlook, and the cost of money. Another environmental factor is the *supply* of key materials. Business buyers also are affected by *technological, political*, and *competitive* developments in the environment. Finally, *culture and customs* can strongly influence business buyer reactions to the marketer's behavior and strategies, especially in the international marketing environment (see Real Marketing 6.1). The business buyer must watch these factors, determine how they will affect the buyer, and try to turn these challenges into opportunities.

Organizational factors are also important. Each buying organization has its own objectives, strategies, structure, systems, and procedures, and the business marketer must understand these factors well. Questions such as these arise: How many people are involved in the buying decision? Who are they? What are their evaluative criteria? What are the company's policies and limits on its buyers?

The buying center usually includes many participants who influence each other, so *interpersonal factors* also influence the business buying process. However, it is often difficult to assess such interpersonal factors and group dynamics. Buying center participants do not wear tags that label them as "key decision maker" or "not influential." Nor do buying center participants with the highest rank always have the most influence.

● FIGURE | 6.2
A Model of Business Buyer Behavior

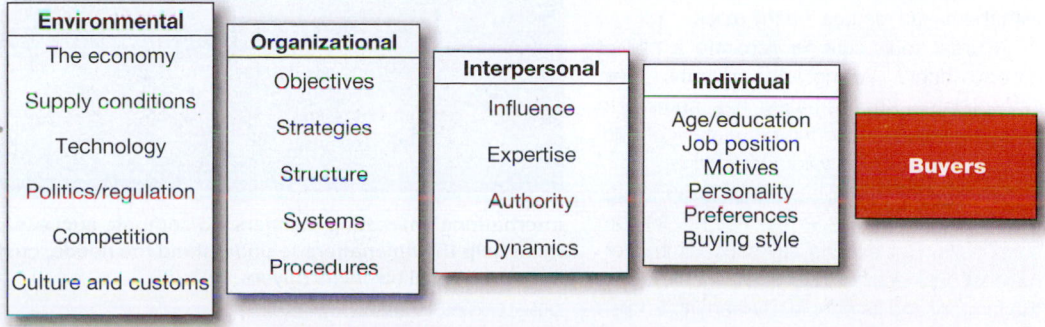

Like consumer buying decisions in Figure 5.2, business buying decisions are affected by an incredibly complex combination of environmental, interpersonal, and individual influences, but with an extra layer of organizational factors thrown into the mix.

Environmental
The economy
Supply conditions
Technology
Politics/regulation
Competition
Culture and customs

Organizational
Objectives
Strategies
Structure
Systems
Procedures

Interpersonal
Influence
Expertise
Authority
Dynamics

Individual
Age/education
Job position
Motives
Personality
Preferences
Buying style

Buyers

Real Marketing

6.1 International Marketing Manners

Picture this: Consolidated Amalgamation Inc. thinks it's time that the rest of the world enjoyed the same fine products it has offered American consumers for two generations. It dispatches Vice President Harry E. Slicksmile to Europe, Asia, and Africa to explore the territory. Mr. Slicksmile stops first in London, where he makes short work of some bankers—he rings them up on the phone. He handles Parisians with similar ease: After securing a table at La Tour d'Argent, he greets his luncheon guest, the director of an industrial engineering firm, with the words, "Just call me Harry, Jacques." In Germany, Mr. Slicksmile is a powerhouse. Whisking through a flashy multimedia presentation on his iPad and an ultra-compact projector, he shows 'em that this Georgia boy knows how to make a buck.

Mr. Slicksmile next swings through Saudi Arabia, where he coolly presents a potential client with a multimillion-dollar proposal in a classy pigskin binder. Heading on to Moscow, Harry strikes up a conversation with the Japanese businessman sitting next to him on the plane. Harry compliments the man's cuff links several times, recognizing him as a man of importance. As the two say good-bye, the man gifts his cuff links to Harry, presents his business card with both hands, and bows at the waist. Harry places his hand firmly on the man's back to express sincere thanks, then slips his own business card into the man's shirt pocket.

Harry takes Russia by storm as he meets with the CEO of a start-up tech firm. Feeling very at ease with the Russia executive, Harry sheds his suit coat, leans back, crosses one foot over the other knee, and slips his hands into his pockets. At his next stop in Beijing, China, Harry talks business over lunch with a group of Chinese executives. After completing the meal, he drops his chopsticks into his bowl of rice and presents each guest with a gift as a gesture of his desire to do business with them—an elegant Tiffany clock.

A great tour, sure to generate a pile of orders, right? Wrong. Six months later, Consolidated Amalgamation has nothing to show for the extended trip but a stack of bills. Abroad, they weren't wild about Harry.

This hypothetical case has been exaggerated for emphasis. Americans are seldom such dolts. But experts say success in international business has a lot to do with knowing the territory and its people. By learning English

and extending themselves in other ways, the world's business leaders have met Americans more than halfway. In contrast, Americans too often do little except assume that others will march to their music. "We want things to be 'American' when we travel. Fast. Convenient. Easy. So we become 'ugly Americans' by demanding that others change," says one American world trade expert. "I think more business would be done if we tried harder."

Poor Harry tried, all right, but in all the wrong ways. The British do not, as a rule, make deals over the phone as much as Americans do. It's not so much a "cultural" difference as a difference in approach. A proper Frenchman neither likes instant familiarity nor refers to strangers by their first names. "That poor fellow, Jacques, probably wouldn't show anything, but he'd not be pleased," explains an expert on French business practices.

Harry's flashy presentation would likely have been a flop with the Germans, who dislike overstatement and showiness. And to the Saudi Arabians, the pigskin binder would have been considered vile. An American salesperson who actually presented such a binder was unceremoniously tossed out of the country and his company was blacklisted from working with Saudi businesses.

Harry also committed numerous faux pas with his new Japanese acquaintance. Because the Japanese strive to please others, especially when someone admires their possessions, the executive likely felt obligated rather than pleased to give up his cuff links. Harry's "hand on the back" probably labeled him as disrespectful and presumptuous. Japan, like many Asian countries, is a "no-contact culture" in which even shaking hands is a strange experience. Harry made matters worse with his casual treatment of the business cards. Japanese people revere the business card as an extension of self and as an indicator of rank. They do not hand it to people; they present it—with both hands.

Things didn't go well in Russia, either. Russian businesspeople maintain a conservative, professional appearance, with dark suits and dress shoes. Taking one's coat off during negotiations of any kind is taken as a sign of weakness. Placing hands in one's pockets is considered rude, and showing the bottoms of one's shoes is a disgusting gesture. Similarly, in China, Harry casually dropping his chopsticks could have been misinterpreted as an act of aggression. Stabbing chopsticks into a bowl of rice and leaving them signifies death to the Chinese.

International marketing manners: To compete successfully in global markets, companies must help their managers to understand the needs, customs, and cultures of international business buyers.

©David Crockett/Shutterstock

The clocks Harry offered as gifts might have confirmed such dark intentions. To "give a clock" in Chinese sounds the same as "seeing someone off to his end."

Thus, to compete successfully in global markets, or even to deal effectively with international firms in their home markets, companies must help their managers to understand the needs, customs, and cultures of international business buyers. Several companies now offer smartphone apps that provide tips to international travelers and help prevent them from making embarrassing mistakes while abroad. Cultures around the world differ greatly, and marketers must dig deeply to make certain they adapt to these differences. "When doing business in a foreign country and a foreign culture...take nothing for granted," advises an international business specialist. "Turn every stone. Ask every question. Dig into every detail."

Sources: Portions adapted from Susan Harte, "When in Rome, You Should Learn to Do What the Romans Do," *The Atlanta Journal-Constitution,* January 22, 1990, pp. D1, D6. Additional information and examples can be found in Susan Adams, "Business Etiquette Tips for International Travel," *Forbes,* June 6, 2012, www.forbes.com/sites/susanadams/2012/06/15/business-etiquette-tips-for-international-travel/; Jeanette S. Martin and Lillian H. Cheney, *Global Business Etiquette* (Santa Barbara, CA: Praeger Publishers, 2013); "A Quick Guide to Business Etiquette around the World," *Business Insider,* May 12, 2015, www.businessinsider.com/a-guide-to-business-etiquette-around-the-world-2015-5; and "International Business Etiquette, Manners, & Culture," www.cyborlink.com, accessed September 2016.

Participants may influence the buying decision because they control rewards and punishments, are well liked, have special expertise, or have a special relationship with other important participants. Interpersonal factors are often very subtle. Whenever possible, business marketers must try to understand these factors and design strategies that take them into account.

Each participant in the business buying decision process brings in personal motives, perceptions, and preferences. These *individual factors* are affected by personal characteristics such as age, income, education, professional identification, personality, and attitudes toward risk. Also, buyers have different buying styles. Some may be technical types who make in-depth analyses of competitive proposals before choosing a supplier. Other buyers may be intuitive negotiators who are adept at pitting the sellers against one another for the best deal.

The Business Buyer Decision Process

● **Figure 6.3** lists the eight stages of the business buyer decision process.[10] Buyers who face a new task buying situation usually go through all stages of the buying process. Buyers making modified or straight rebuys, in contrast, may skip some of the stages. We will examine these steps for the typical new task buying situation.

Problem Recognition

Problem recognition
The first stage of the business buying process in which someone in the company recognizes a problem or need that can be met by acquiring a good or a service.

The buying process begins when someone in the company recognizes a problem or need that can be met by acquiring a specific product or service. **Problem recognition** can result from internal or external stimuli. Internally, the company may decide to launch a new product that requires new production equipment and materials. Or a machine may break down and need new parts. Perhaps a purchasing manager is unhappy with a current supplier's product quality, service, or prices. Externally, the buyer may get some new ideas at a trade show, see an ad or website, or receive a call from a salesperson who offers a better product or a lower price.

● **FIGURE | 6.3**
Stages of the Business Buyer Decision Process

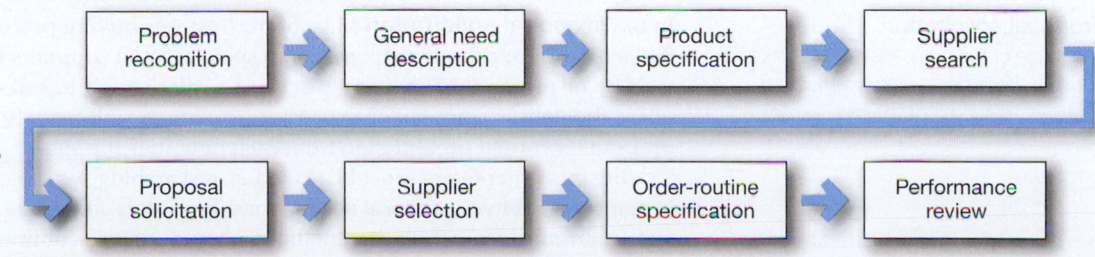

Buyers facing new, complex buying decisions usually go through all of these stages. Those making rebuys often skip some of the stages. Either way, the business buyer decision process is usually much more complicated than this simple flow diagram suggests.

Problem recognition → General need description → Product specification → Supplier search → Proposal solicitation → Supplier selection → Order-routine specification → Performance review

Accenture Digital can help you attract more customers.

Today, technology can transform every aspect of your company. Now every business is a digital business. Our industry expertise, coupled with our integrated digital capabilities across interactive, analytics and mobility, can help you take advantage of the opportunity to innovate and compete. We can also manage your digital processes or take them to the cloud. All so your company will see tangible results from the virtual world. That's high performance, delivered.

High performance. Delivered.

Strategy | Digital | Technology | Operations

accenturedigital

● **Problem recognition:** This Accenture ad alerts customers to the problem of getting up to speed with digital technology, then suggests a solution. It promises "High Performance. Delivered."

Accenture

General need description
The stage in the business buying process in which a buyer describes the general characteristics and quantity of a needed item.

Product specification
The stage of the business buying process in which the buying organization decides on and specifies the best technical product characteristics for a needed item.

Supplier search
The stage of the business buying process in which the buyer tries to find the best vendors.

Proposal solicitation
The stage of the business buying process in which the buyer invites qualified suppliers to submit proposals.

In fact, business marketers often alert customers to potential problems and then show how their products and services provide solutions. ● For example, consulting firm Accenture's award-winning "High Performance. Delivered." B-to-B ads do this. One Accenture ad points to the urgent need for a business to get up to speed with digital technology. "Accenture Digital can help you attract more customers." the ad states, showing moths drawn to a brightly lit smartphone screen. Accenture's solution: "Our industry expertise, coupled with our integrated capabilities across interactive, analytics, and mobility, can help you take advantage of the opportunity to innovate and compete." Other ads in the series tell success stories of how Accenture has helped client companies recognize and solve a variety of other problems.[11]

General Need Description

Having recognized a need, the buyer next prepares a **general need description** that describes the characteristics and quantity of the needed item. For standard items, this process presents few problems. For complex items, however, the buyer may need to work with others—engineers, users, consultants—to define the item. The team may want to rank the importance of reliability, durability, price, and other attributes desired in the item. In this phase, the alert business marketer can help the buyers define their needs and provide information about the value of different product characteristics.

Product Specification

The buying organization next develops the item's technical **product specifications**, often with the help of a value analysis engineering team. *Product value analysis* is an approach to cost reduction in which components are studied carefully to determine if they can be redesigned, standardized, or made by less costly methods of production. The team decides on the best product characteristics and specifies them accordingly. Sellers, too, can use value analysis as a tool to help secure a new account. By showing buyers a better way to make an object, outside sellers can turn straight rebuy situations into new task situations that give them a chance to obtain new business.

Supplier Search

The buyer now conducts a **supplier search** to find the best vendors. The buyer can compile a small list of qualified suppliers by reviewing trade directories, doing online searches, or phoning other companies for recommendations. Today, more and more companies are turning to the internet to find suppliers. For marketers, this has leveled the playing field—the internet gives smaller suppliers many of the same advantages as larger competitors.

The newer the buying task and the more complex and costly the item, the greater the amount of time the buyer will spend searching for suppliers. The supplier's task is to get listed in major directories and build a good reputation in the marketplace. Salespeople should watch for companies in the process of searching for suppliers and make certain that their firm is considered.

Proposal Solicitation

In the **proposal solicitation** stage of the business buying process, the buyer invites qualified suppliers to submit proposals. In response, some suppliers will refer the buyer to their website or promotional materials or send a salesperson to call on the prospect. However, when the item is complex or expensive, the buyer will usually require a detailed written proposal or formal presentation from each potential supplier.

Business marketers must be skilled in researching, writing, and presenting proposals in response to buyer proposal solicitations. Proposals should be marketing documents, not just technical documents. Presentations should inspire confidence and should make the marketer's company stand out from the competition.

Supplier Selection

Supplier selection

The stage of the business buying process in which the buyer reviews proposals and selects a supplier or suppliers.

The members of the buying center now review the proposals and select a supplier or suppliers. During **supplier selection**, the buying center often will draw up a list of the desired supplier attributes and their relative importance. Such attributes include product and service quality, reputation, on-time delivery, ethical corporate behavior, honest communication, and competitive prices. The members of the buying center will rate suppliers against these attributes and identify the best suppliers.

Buyers may attempt to negotiate with preferred suppliers for better prices and terms before making the final selections. In the end, they may select a single supplier or a few suppliers. Many buyers prefer multiple sources of supplies to avoid being totally dependent on one supplier and to allow comparisons of prices and performance of several suppliers over time. Today's supplier development managers want to develop a full network of supplier-partners that can help the company bring more value to its customers.

Order-Routine Specification

Order-routine specification

The stage of the business buying process in which the buyer writes the final order with the chosen supplier(s), listing the technical specifications, quantity needed, expected time of delivery, return policies, and warranties.

The buyer now prepares an **order-routine specification**. It includes the final order with the chosen supplier or suppliers and lists items such as technical specifications, quantity needed, expected delivery time, return policies, and warranties. In the case of maintenance, repair, and operating items, buyers may use blanket contracts rather than periodic purchase orders. A blanket contract creates a long-term relationship in which the supplier promises to resupply the buyer as needed at agreed prices for a set time period.

Many large buyers now practice *vendor-managed inventory*, in which they turn over ordering and inventory responsibilities to their suppliers. Under such systems, buyers share sales and inventory information directly with key suppliers. The suppliers then monitor inventories and replenish stock automatically as needed. For example, most major suppliers to large retailers such as Walmart, Target, Home Depot, and Lowe's assume vendor-managed inventory responsibilities.

Performance Review

Performance review

The stage of the business buying process in which the buyer assesses the performance of the supplier and decides to continue, modify, or drop the arrangement.

In this stage, the buyer reviews supplier performance. The buyer may contact users and ask them to rate their satisfaction. The **performance review** may lead the buyer to continue, modify, or drop the arrangement. The seller's job is to monitor the same factors used by the buyer to make sure that the seller is giving the expected satisfaction.

In all, the eight-stage buying-process model shown in Figure 6.3 provides a simple view of the business buying as it might occur in a new task buying situation. However, the actual process is usually much more complex. In the modified rebuy or straight rebuy situation, some of these stages would be compressed or bypassed. Each organization buys in its own way, and each buying situation has unique requirements.

Different buying center participants may be involved at different stages of the process. Although certain buying-process steps usually do occur, buyers do not always follow them in the same order, and they may add other steps. Often, buyers will repeat certain stages of the process. Finally, a customer relationship might involve many different types of purchases ongoing at a given time, all in different stages of the buying process. The seller must manage the total *customer relationship*, not just individual purchases.

Engaging Business Buyers with Digital and Social Marketing

As in every other area of marketing, the explosion of information technologies and online, mobile, and social media has changed the face of the B-to-B buying and marketing process. In the following sections, we discuss two important technology advancements: *e-procurement and online purchasing* and *B-to-B digital and social media marketing*.

E-procurement and Online Purchasing

E-procurement

Purchasing through electronic connections between buyers and sellers—usually online.

Advances in information technology have dramatically affected the face of the B-to-B buying process. Online purchasing, often called **e-procurement**, has grown rapidly in recent years. Virtually unknown two decades ago, online purchasing is standard procedure for most companies today. In turn, business marketers can connect with customers online to share marketing information, sell products and services, provide customer support services, and maintain ongoing customer relationships.

Companies can do e-procurement in any of several ways. They can conduct *reverse auctions*, in which they put their purchasing requests online and invite suppliers to bid for the business. Or they can engage in online *trading exchanges*, through which companies work collectively to facilitate the trading process. Companies also can conduct e-procurement by setting up their own *company buying sites*. For example, GE operates a company trading site on which it posts its buying needs and invites bids, negotiates terms, and places orders. Or companies can create *extranet links* with key suppliers. For instance, they can create direct procurement accounts with suppliers such as Dell or Staples through which company buyers can purchase equipment, materials, and supplies directly. ● Staples operates a business-to-business procurement division called Staples Business Advantage, which serves the office supplies and services buying needs of businesses of any size, from 10 employees to the *Fortune* 1000.

Business-to-business e-procurement yields many benefits. First, it shaves transaction costs and results in more efficient purchasing for both buyers and suppliers. E-procurement reduces the time between order and delivery. And an online-powered purchasing program eliminates the paperwork associated with traditional requisition and ordering procedures and helps an organization keep better track of all purchases. Finally, beyond the cost and time savings, e-procurement frees purchasing people from a lot of drudgery and paperwork. Instead, they can focus on more-strategic issues, such as finding better supply sources and working with suppliers to reduce costs and develop new products.

The rapidly expanding use of e-procurement, however, also presents some problems. For example, at the same time that the internet makes it possible for suppliers and customers to share business data and even collaborate on product design, it can also erode decades-old customer–supplier relationships. Many buyers now use the power of the internet to pit suppliers against one another and search out better deals, products, and turnaround times on a purchase-by-purchase basis.

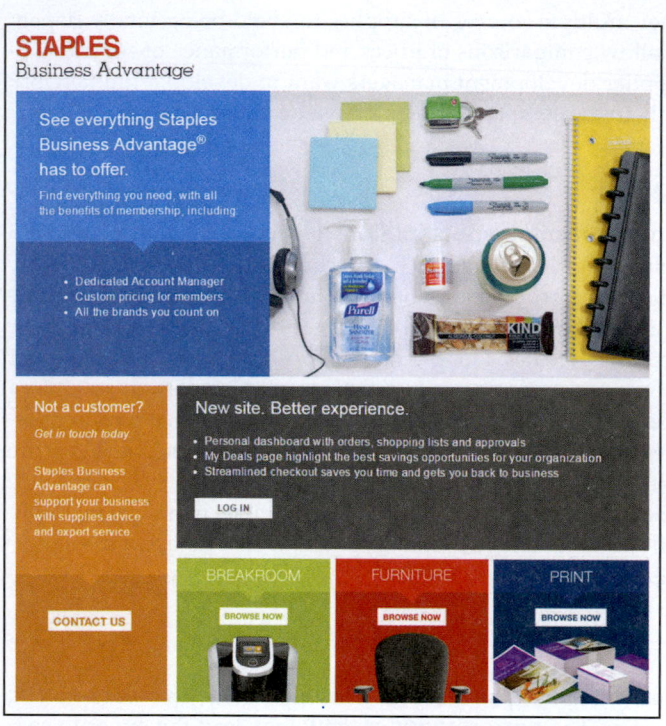

● **Online buying: Staples operates a business-to-business procurement division called Staples Business Advantage, which serves the office supplies and services buying needs of business customers of any size.**

Staples

Business-to-Business Digital and Social Media Marketing

In response to business customers' rapid shift toward online buying, today's B-to-B marketers are now using a wide range of digital and social media marketing approaches—from websites, blogs, mobile apps, e-newsletters, and proprietary online networks to mainstream social media such as Facebook, LinkedIn, YouTube, Google+, and Twitter—to engage business customers and manage customer relationships anywhere, anytime.

B-to-B digital and social media marketing
Using digital and social media marketing approaches to engage business customers and manage customer relationships anywhere, anytime.

B-to-B digital and social media marketing isn't just growing, it's exploding. Digital and social media marketing have rapidly become *the* new space for engaging business customers. Consider Maersk Line, the world's leading container shipping and transport company, serving business customers through 374 offices in 160 countries:[12]

● You might not expect much by way of new-age marketing from an old-line container shipping company, but think again. Maersk Line is one of the most forward-looking and accomplished B-to-B digital and social media marketers in any industry. Maersk Line has sailed full steam ahead into the social media waters with eight global accounts on primary social media networks including Facebook, LinkedIn, Twitter, and YouTube. Maersk Line has more than 1.1 million Facebook followers with an average engagement of 7 percent per post, making Facebook a platform for engaging a broad audience of customers and other stakeholders interested in the brand. On Instagram, the company shares customer and employee images and stories to help visualize the brand. On YouTube it posts informational and educational

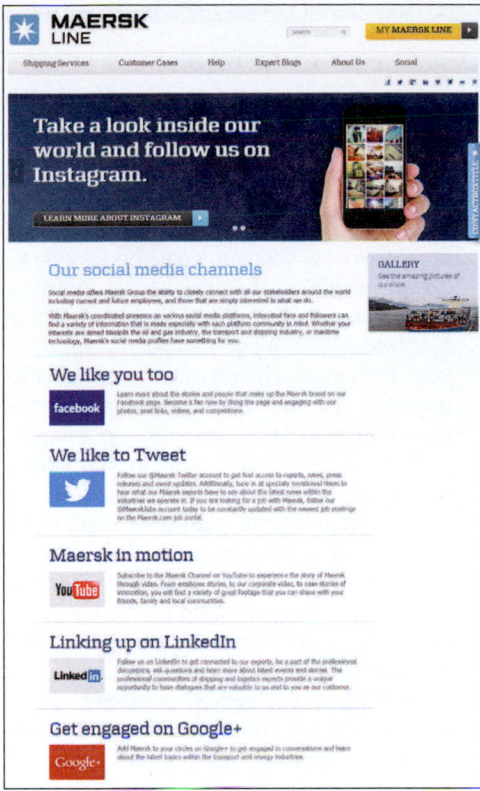

● Container shipping giant Maersk Line engages business customers through a boatload of digital and social media. "The goal is to get closer to our customers."

A.P. Møller-Mærsk A/S

videos detailing Maersk Line's activities, services, and people. Maersk Line's Twitter feed presents the latest news and events, creating conversation and buzz with and among its more than 123,000 Twitter followers. The company's LinkedIn account, with more than 155,500 followers, lets Maersk Line engage customers, opinion leaders, and industry influencers, who share information and discuss industry challenges and opportunities with shipping and logistics experts. Why all this social media? "The goal is to use social media to get closer to our customers," says Maersk Line.

Compared with traditional media and sales approaches, digital and social media can create greater customer engagement and interaction. B-to-B marketers know that they aren't really targeting *businesses,* they are targeting *individuals* in those businesses who affect buying decisions. And today's business buyers are always connected via their digital devices—whether it's PCs, tablets, or smartphones.

Digital and social media play an important role in engaging these always-connected business buyers in a way that personal selling alone cannot. Instead of the old model of sales reps calling on business customers at work or maybe meeting up with them at trade shows, the new digital approaches facilitate anytime, anywhere connections between a wide range of people in the selling and customer organizations. It gives both sellers and buyers more control of and access to important information. B-to-B marketing has always been social network marketing, but today's digital environment offers an exciting array of new networking tools and applications.

Some B-to-B companies mistakenly assume that today's digital and social media are useful primarily to consumer products and services companies. But no matter what the industry, digital platforms can be powerful tools for engaging customers and other important publics. For example, industrial powerhouse GE uses a wide array of digital and social media, not just to engage and support its business customers directly but also to tell the compelling GE brand story more broadly and to keep the company relevant, contemporary, and accessible (see Real Marketing 6.2).

Institutional and Government Markets

So far, our discussion of organizational buying has focused largely on the buying behavior of business buyers. Much of this discussion also applies to the buying practices of institutional and government organizations. However, these two nonbusiness markets have additional characteristics and needs. In this final section, we address the special features of institutional and government markets.

Institutional Markets

Institutional market
Schools, hospitals, nursing homes, prisons, and other institutions that provide goods and services to people in their care.

The **institutional market** consists of schools, hospitals, nursing homes, prisons, and other institutions that provide goods and services to people in their care. Institutions differ from one another in their sponsors and their objectives. For example, Community Health Systems runs 203 for-profit hospitals in 29 states, generating $18 billion in annual revenues. By contrast, the Shriners Hospitals for Children is a nonprofit organization with 21 facilities that provide free specialized health care for children, whereas the government-run Veterans Affairs Medical Centers located across the country provide special services to veterans.[13] Each institution has different buying needs and resources.

Institutional markets can be huge. Consider the massive and expanding U.S. prisons economy:

More than 720 out of every 100,000 people in the United States are in prison—that's 2.2 million people. Criminal correction spending has outpaced budget growth in education, transportation, and public assistance. U.S. prisons spend about $74 billion annually—an average of $31,000 per prisoner—to keep their facilities running, an amount greater than the GDP of 133 nations. The ultimate captive market, it translates into plenty of work for companies looking to break into the prison market. "Our core business touches so many things—security, medicine, education, food service, maintenance, technology—that it presents a unique opportunity for any number of vendors to do business with us," says an executive at Corrections Corporation of America, the largest private prison operator in the country.[14]

Real Marketing

6.2   GE: A Model for B-to-B Digital and Social Media Marketing

Few brands are more familiar than GE. For more than 130 years, we've packed our homes with GE products—from good ol' GE light-bulbs to refrigerators, ranges, clothes washers and dryers, microwave ovens, and hundreds of other products bearing the familiar GE script logo. But here's a fact that might startle you. Less than a meager 8 percent of GE's $117 billion in annual sales comes from consumer products.

The vast majority of the company's sales comes from industrial products and services across a wide range of energy, transportation, and health-care industries. Far beyond lightbulbs and appliances, GE sells everything from jet aircraft engines, giant wind turbines, and diesel locomotives to water processing systems and high-tech medical imaging equipment. GE bills itself as an "industrial infrastructure company," one that's on a mission to "invent the next industrial era, to build, move, power, and cure the world."

Jet engines? Diesel locomotives? Power turbines? Yawn. To many people, "industrial" translates to "dull." It's hardy the fodder for stimulating digital and social media content. But GE doesn't see it that way. GE has a brand story to tell—a story of big, bad machines and innovative technologies that are changing the world and how we live in it. And it sees digital as an ideal platform for sharing that story. As a result, GE has become a model for B-to-B use of digital and social media.

At a core level, GE covers the digital basics well through a wide variety of platforms that inform and engage business customers directly, connect them with GE salespeople, and promote customer purchasing and relationships. For example, GE's various divisions—from GE Aviation to GE Healthcare and GE Energy— offer dozens of industry-specific websites, containing thousands of individual site areas and tens of thousands of pages that provide B-to-B customers with purchasing solutions, product overviews, detailed technical information, online videos and webinars, live chats, and real-time customer support.

GE also helps its sales force engage business customers more deeply through a comprehensive presence in major social media such as Facebook, Twitter, LinkedIn, Google+, Salesforce.com, and even Instagram, Pinterest, and Vine. "We have a core belief that business is social," says GE's chief marketing officer (CMO). "If you're in business you need social because it's going to get you closer to your customers. We want to get our sales team 100 percent digitized."

But GE's most inspired use of digital and social media goes well beyond the basics of engaging and supporting customers directly. GE also uses digital platforms to reach out to other important publics. "The more people know GE, the more they like GE," says the company's director of global media. "So our [digital] content strategy is about uncovering and telling great stories about innovation, technology, big data, developing healthcare, and so on. We want our customers, our shareholders, our employees to know what GE thinks about the world," a task ideally suited to digital and social media. The goal is to make the GE brand relevant, contemporary, and accessible. "No one remembers product specs and features. But a great story well told hits home," says GE's CMO. "Compelling stories bring a brand to life—they make us relevant, poignant, vibrant, droll, and hopefully memorable."

To that end, over the past several years, GE has unleashed a remarkable array of digital content that connects the brand with consumers and positions the 130-year-old company as a youthful, contemporary technology leader in the new digital industrial era. For example, one of GE's first and most successful social media campaigns was #six-secondscience, a program launched on Vine asking people to share their favorite science experiments in video clips of six seconds or less. The campaign drew in 400 videos in a week, including demonstrations of everything from how to make a volcano using a pile of sand, vinegar, and baking soda to a homemade Tesla coil in action. The Vine campaign won awards and accolades. More important, it got people to spend time with the GE brand.

You'll find GE actively engaged on all the major social media. For example, GE's numerous Pinterest, Tumblr, and Instagram sites introduce tech enthusiasts to the raw beauty of the company's innovative industrial products and technologies. "I love our Instagram feed," says the CMO. "It shows the majesty and scale of our big machines. It's GE at our badass best." In fact, the very first board at the GE Pinterest site is "Badass Machines." Others include "From the Factory Floor," "Minds and Machines," and "Brilliant Machines."

Through its inspired use of digital and social media, industrial powerhouse GE engages customers and keeps the GE brand relevant, contemporary, and accessible to important publics in today's digital industrial era.
GE

GE also publishes an innovative daily on-line B-to-B blog, called GE Reports, which features science fiction–like stories on topics such as moon power, digital pathology, and 3D printing done by hand. The blog includes original content from various GE sources, including GE Garages—an initiative designed to reinvigorate innovation and manufacturing by providing a collaborative space where technologists, entrepreneurs, and everyday Americans can engage in hands-on experiences with 3D printers, computer-controlled milling machines, laser cutters, and injection molders. As with GE's other digital content, GE Reports offers easily digestible material that gets people excited about the future of technology and science while positioning GE as a company that is leading them into that future.

GE has also mastered the art of digital video content. An example is the company's recent award-winning "Childlike Imagination" campaign, a series of video ads that show the scope of GE's product lines through the eyes of a little girl whose Mom works at GE. The magical videos bring GE's industrial products—from jet engines, diesel locomotives, and giant wind turbines to hospital diagnostics machines—to life through the eyes of an amazed young girl whose mom works at GE. "My mom? She makes underwater fans that are powered by the moon," declares the girl. "My mom makes airplane engines that can talk." Although these videos can be shown as ads on traditional broadcast TV, they drive substantial online traffic through GE's social media channels.

Thus, in its digital efforts, GE acts less like an advertiser and more like a brand content publisher—creating, curating, and shaping brand content and conversations in real time. "For a brand that has the history that we do, staying modern, contemporary, and relevant is something we think about every single day," says GE's CMO. "We think about who shares our passion and our interest in science, technology, and engineering and we go after that. We do that on platforms as diverse as Instagram, Vine, Snapchat, Yo, and many others." In all, few companies do digital better than GE. "When it comes to innovative social media campaigns," says one analyst, GE is "often light-years ahead of most marketers," regardless of industry.

Sources: Katie Richards, "GE's Chief Marketing Officer on Storytelling in the New Digital Industrial Era," *Adweek,* October 12, 2015, pp. 11–12; Bill Sobel, "GE's Linda Boff: Content Created to Help Is What Sells," *CMSWire,* September 24, 2015, www.cmswire.com/cms/customer-experience/ges-linda-boff-content-created-to-help-is -what-sells-027470.php; Jason Hill, "GE: From an Advertiser to a Publishing Company," in Deborah Malone, *The Reinvention of Marketing* (New York: The Internationalist Press, 2014), Kindle locations 399–400; Anthony Gaenzle, "GE Raises the Bar for B2B Content Marketing," March 2, 2015, http://enveritasgroup.com/2015/03/02/ge-raises -the-bar-for-b2b-content-marketing/; and www.youtube.com/watch?v=Co0qkWRqTdM, www.gereports.com, www.pinterest.com/generalelectric/, www.ge.com, and www.ge.com/investor-relations, accessed September 2016.

● **General Mills Convenience and Foodservice produces, packages, prices, and markets its broad assortment of foods to better serve the specific food service requirements of various institutional markets.**
Justin Sullivan/Getty Images

Many institutional markets are characterized by low budgets and captive patrons. For example, hospital patients have little choice but to eat whatever food the hospital supplies. A hospital purchasing agent has to decide on the quality of food to buy for patients. Because the food is provided as a part of a total service package, the buying objective is not profit. Nor is strict cost minimization the goal—patients receiving poor-quality food will complain to others and damage the hospital's reputation. Thus, the hospital purchasing agent must search for institutional food vendors whose quality meets or exceeds a certain minimum standard and whose prices are low.

Many marketers set up separate divisions to meet the special characteristics and needs of institutional buyers. ● For example General Mills Convenience and Foodservice unit produces, packages, prices, and markets its broad assortment of cereals, cookies, snacks, and other products to better serve the specific food service requirements of hospitals, schools, hotels, and other institutional markets in addition to traditional B-to-B businesses such as convenience stores.[15]

Government Markets

Government market
Governmental units—federal, state, and local—that purchase or rent goods and services for carrying out the main functions of government.

The **government market** offers large opportunities for many companies, both big and small. In most countries, government organizations are major buyers of goods and services. In the United States alone, federal, state, and local governments contain more than 89,000 buying units that purchase more than $3 trillion in goods and services each year.[16] Government buying and business buying are similar in many ways. But there are also differences that must be understood by companies that wish to sell products and services to governments. To succeed in the government market, sellers must locate key decision makers, identify the factors that affect buyer behavior, and understand the buying decision process.

Government organizations typically require suppliers to submit bids, and normally they award the contract to the lowest bidder. In some cases, a governmental unit will make allowances for the supplier's superior quality or reputation for completing contracts on time. Governments will also buy on a negotiated contract basis, primarily in the case of complex projects involving major R&D costs and risks and in cases where there is little competition.

Government organizations tend to favor domestic suppliers over foreign suppliers. A major complaint of multinationals operating in Europe is that each country shows favoritism toward its nationals in spite of superior offers that are made by foreign firms. The European Economic Commission is gradually removing this bias.

Like consumer and business buyers, government buyers are affected by environmental, organizational, interpersonal, and individual factors. One unique thing about government buying is that it is carefully watched by outside publics, ranging from Congress to a variety of private groups interested in how the government spends taxpayers' money. Because their spending decisions are subject to public review, government organizations require considerable documentation from suppliers, who often complain about excessive paperwork, bureaucracy, regulations, decision-making delays, and frequent shifts in procurement personnel.

Given all the red tape, why would any firm want to do business with the U.S. government? The reasons are quite simple: The U.S. government is the world's largest buyer of products and services—about $450 billion last year—and its checks don't bounce. The government buys everything from socks to stealth bombers. For example, this year, the federal government will spend a whopping $80 billion on information technology, $11.4 billion of which is for managing the technology of the Department of Health and Human Services.[17]

Most governments provide would-be suppliers with detailed guides describing how to sell to the government. For example, the U.S. Small Business Administration provides on its website detailed advice for small businesses seeking government contracting opportunities (www.sba.gov/category/navigation-structure/contracting/contracting-opportunities). And the U.S. Commerce Department's website is loaded with information and advice on international trade opportunities (www.commerce.gov/about-commerce/grants-contracting-trade-opportunities).

In several major cities, the General Services Administration operates *Business Service Centers* with staffs to provide a complete education on the way government agencies buy, the steps that suppliers should follow, and the procurement opportunities available. Various trade magazines and associations provide information on how to reach schools, hospitals, highway departments, and other government agencies. And almost all of these government organizations and associations maintain internet sites offering up-to-date information and advice. Still, suppliers have to master the system and find ways to cut through the red tape, especially for large government purchases.

Noneconomic criteria are playing a growing role in government buying. Government buyers are asked to favor depressed business firms and areas; small business firms; minority-owned firms; and business firms that avoid race, gender, or age discrimination. Sellers need to keep these factors in mind when seeking government business.

Many companies that sell to the government have not been very marketing oriented for a number of reasons. Total government spending is determined by elected officials rather than by any marketing effort to develop this market. Government buying has emphasized price, making suppliers invest their effort in technology to bring costs down. When the product's characteristics are specified carefully, product differentiation is not a marketing factor. Nor do advertising or personal selling matter much in winning bids on an open-bid basis.

Several companies, however, have established separate government marketing departments, including GE, Boeing, and Goodyear. Other companies sell primarily to government buyers, such as Lockheed Martin, which makes more than 80 percent of its sales from the U.S. government, either as a prime contractor or a subcontractor. These companies anticipate government needs and projects, participate in the product specification phase, gather competitive intelligence, prepare bids carefully, and produce stronger communications to describe and enhance their companies' reputations.

Other companies have established customized marketing programs for government buyers. For example, Dell has specific business units tailored to meet the needs of federal as well as state and local government buyers. Dell offers its customers tailor-made Premier web pages that include special pricing, online purchasing, and service and support for each city, state, and federal government entity.

During the past decade, a great deal of the government's buying has gone online. The Federal Business Opportunities website (www.fbo.gov) provides a single point of entry through which commercial vendors and government buyers can post, search, monitor, and retrieve opportunities solicited by the entire federal contracting community. The three federal agencies that act as purchasing agents for the rest of government have also launched websites supporting online government purchasing activity. The General Services Administration, which influences more than one-quarter of the federal government's total procurement dollars, has set up a GSA Advantage! website (www.gsaadvantage.gov). The Defense Logistics Agency offers an Internet Bid Board System (www.dibbs.bsm.dla.mil) for purchases by America's military services. And the Department of Veterans Affairs facilitates e-procurement through its VA Advantage! website (https://VAadvantage.gsa.gov).

Such sites allow authorized defense and civilian agencies to buy everything from office supplies, food, and information technology equipment to construction services through online purchasing. The General Services Administration, the Defense Logistics Agency, and the Department of Veterans Affairs not only sell stocked merchandise through their websites but also create direct links between government buyers and contract suppliers. For example, the branch of the Defense Logistics Agency that sells 160,000 types of medical supplies to military forces transmits orders directly to vendors such as Bristol-Myers Squibb. Such online systems promise to eliminate much of the hassle sometimes found in dealing with government purchasing.[18]

6 Reviewing and Extending the Concepts

OBJECTIVES REVIEW AND KEY TERMS

Objectives Review

Business markets and consumer markets are alike in some key ways. For example, both include people in buying roles who make purchase decisions to satisfy needs. But business markets also differ in many ways from consumer markets. For one thing, the business market is *huge*, far larger than the consumer market. Within the United States alone, the business market includes organizations that annually purchase trillions of dollars' worth of goods and services.

OBJECTIVE 6-1 Define the business market and explain how business markets differ from consumer markets. *(pp 164–166)*

The *business market* comprises all organizations that buy goods and services for use in the production of other products and services or for the purpose of reselling or renting them to others at a profit. As compared to consumer markets, business markets usually have fewer but larger buyers. Business demand is derived demand, which tends to be more inelastic and fluctuating than consumer demand. The business buying decision usually involves more, and more professional, buyers. Business buyers usually face more complex buying decisions, and the buying process tends to be more formalized. Finally, business buyers and sellers are often more dependent on each other.

OBJECTIVE 6-2 Identify the major factors that influence business buyer behavior. *(pp 166–171)*

Business buyers make decisions that vary with the three *types of buying* situations: straight rebuys, modified rebuys, and new tasks. The decision-making unit of a buying organization—*the buying center*—can consist of many different persons playing many different roles. The business marketer needs to know the following: Who are the major buying center participants? In what decisions do they exercise influence and to what degree? What evaluation criteria does each decision participant use? The business marketer also needs to understand the major environmental, organizational, interpersonal, and individual influences on the buying process.

OBJECTIVE 6-3 List and define the steps in the business buying decision process. *(pp 171–173)*

The *business buying decision process* itself can be quite involved, with eight basic stages: problem recognition, general need description, product specification, supplier search, proposal solicitation, supplier selection, order-routine specification, and performance review. Buyers who face a new task buying situation usually go through all stages of the buying process.

Buyers making modified or straight rebuys may skip some of the stages. Companies must manage the overall customer relationship, which often includes many different buying decisions in various stages of the buying decision process.

OBJECTIVE 6-4　Discuss how new information technologies and online, mobile, and social media have changed business-to-business marketing.
(pp 173–175)

Recent advances in information and digital technology have given birth to "e-procurement," by which business buyers are purchasing all kinds of products and services online. The internet gives business buyers access to new suppliers, lowers purchasing costs, and hastens order processing and delivery. Business marketers also are increasingly connecting with customers online and through digital, mobile, and social media to engage customers, share marketing information, sell products and services, provide customer support services, and maintain ongoing customer relationships.

OBJECTIVE 6-5　Compare the institutional and government markets and explain how institutional and government buyers make their buying decisions.
(pp 175–179)

The *institutional market* consists of schools, hospitals, prisons, and other institutions that provide goods and services to people in their care. These markets are characterized by low budgets and captive patrons. The *government market*, which is vast, consists of government units—federal, state, and local—that purchase or rent goods and services for carrying out the main functions of government.

Government buyers purchase products and services for defense, education, public welfare, and other public needs. Government buying practices are highly specialized and specified, with open bidding or negotiated contracts characterizing most of the buying. Government buyers operate under the watchful eye of the U.S. Congress and many private watchdog groups. Hence, they tend to require more forms and signatures and respond more slowly and deliberately when placing orders.

Key Terms

OBJECTIVE 6-1
Business buyer behavior (p 164)
Business buying process (p 164)
Derived demand (p 165)
Supplier development (p 166)

OBJECTIVE 6-2
Straight rebuy (p 167)
Modified rebuy (p 167)
New task (p 167)
Systems selling (solutions selling)
　(p 167)

Buying center (p 168)
Users (p 168)
Influencers (p 168)
Buyers (p 168)
Deciders (p 168)
Gatekeepers (p 168)

OBJECTIVE 6-3
Problem recognition (p 171)
General need description (p 172)
Product specification (p 172)
Supplier search (p 172)
Proposal solicitation (p 172)

Supplier selection (p 173)
Order-routine specification (p 173)
Performance review (p 173)

OBJECTIVE 6-4
E-procurement (p 173)
B-to-B digital and social media
　marketing (p 174)

OBJECTIVE 6-5
Institutional market (p 175)
Government market (p 177)

DISCUSSION AND CRITICAL THINKING

MyMarketingLab
Go to **mymktlab.com** to complete the problems marked with this icon ⭐.

Discussion Questions

⭐ **6-1** Explain how the market structure and demand differ for business markets compared with consumer markets. (AACSB: Communication; Reflective Thinking)

⭐ **6-2** Describe the tools B-to-B marketers use to engage customers. What are the challenges with B-to-B social media marketing? (AACSB: Communication; Reflective Thinking)

⭐ **6-3** Briefly discuss the straight rebuy and modified rebuy strategies. What are the similarities and differences? When

might it be beneficial to use one approach over the other? (AACSB: Communication, Reflective Thinking)

6-4 List the participants in the business buying process. What factors influence the buying decision? (AACSB: Communication; Reflective Thinking)

6-5 Compare the institutional and government markets and explain how institutional and government buyers make their buying decisions. (AACSB: Communication)

Critical Thinking Exercises

6-6 Business buying can be a very involved process. Many companies employ procurement or purchasing experts dedicated to managing the firm's buying process. Visit www.glassdoor.com/salaries and www.indeed.com/salary to conduct a search of the salary ranges for "procurement specialists" and similar positions in purchasing. Present your findings. Can e-procurement help to streamline the buying process? Might it eventually replace employees in these careers? Discuss if it is possible for all buying functions to be performed through e-procurement. (AACSB: Communication, Reflective Thinking, Use of IT)

6-7 Interview a businessperson to learn how purchases are made in his or her organization. Ask this person to describe a straight rebuy, a modified rebuy, and a new-task buying situation that took place recently or of which he or she is aware (define them if necessary). Did the buying process differ based on the type of product or purchase situation? Ask the businessperson to explain the role he or she played in a recent purchase and to discuss the factors that influenced the decision. Write a brief report of your interview by applying the concepts you learned in this chapter regarding business buyer behavior. (AACSB: Communication; Reflective Thinking)

6-8 The U.S. government is the world's largest purchaser of goods and services, spending more than $460 billion per year. By law, 23 percent of all government buying must be targeted to small firms. In a small group, visit the Small Business Administration's Government Contracting Classroom at www.sba.gov/content/government-contracting-classroom to learn how small businesses can take advantage of government contracting opportunities. Complete one of the self-paced online courses and develop a brochure explaining the process to small business owners. (AACSB: Communication; Reflective Thinking; Use of IT)

APPLICATIONS AND CASES

Online, Mobile, and Social Media Marketing E-procurement and Mobile Procurement

Gone are the days of tedious, paper-laden, and labor-intensive procurement duties. E-procurement is changing the way buyers and sellers do business, specifically via mobile procurement that offers cloud-based platforms that reduce the search, order, and approval cycle. Most large companies have adopted some form of e-procurement. A recent study found that almost 70 percent of companies utilize some form of e-procurement, mobile procurement, or supply chain management applications. A leading industry platform, Coupa, provides a suite of cloud-based applications for finance, including accounts payable, sourcing, procurement, and expense management that allows customers full functionality from their mobile devices. Employees now enjoy the flexibility and time savings of viewing, approving, or denying requisitions, purchase orders, and invoices. One of Coupa's large retail clients claimed a reduction from 10 days to 5 hours in their requisition-approval-process cycle by implementing Coupa's mobile procurement platform. Talk about savings! Visit www.coupa.com/software/procurement/to learn more about how this company is revolutionizing the e-procurement and mobile procurement environments.

⭐ 6-9 Discuss the advantages of e-procurement to both buyers and sellers. What are the disadvantages? (AACSB: Communication; Reflective Thinking)

6-10 Research mobile procurement and discuss the roles in the buying center that are affected most by this technology. (AACSB: Communication; Reflective Thinking)

Marketing Ethics What Are Our Kids Eating?

Many institutional markets are characterized by low budgets and captive patrons. One institutional food program that has gotten much recent attention is the National School Lunch Program. Although the federal government mandates that schools receiving federal money serve free lunches to children from low-income families, the funds don't cover the entire cost of the meal. The difference comes out of school budgets and that means fewer dollars for the classroom.

According to one study (www.cnn.com/2010/HEALTH/09/29/school.food.investigation/), the number-one meal served to children in U.S. schools is chicken fingers and French fries. Processed food is much cheaper to serve than fresh produce. Another study published in the *Journal of the American Dietetic Association* found that 94 percent of school lunches failed to meet the U.S. Agriculture Department's regulatory standards. Purchasing agents for school systems must search for institutional food vendors whose quality meets or exceeds a minimum standard while offering low prices.

The goal of the federal Healthy, Hunger-Free Kids Act of 2010 is to improve the overall nutritional quality of what students eat at school. The law, which is being implemented over a five-year period, affects several parts of school food. It changes what's in vending machines and how much food students get, rules out fried food, and makes all milk low-fat or fat-free. But it's also changing the way lunches are priced. These changes have dieticians and food service directors facing significant challenges.

6-11 Research what constitutes a healthy lunch in a public school system. Should food companies selling to school systems take responsibility for working with buyers to address this issue? Why or why not?

6-12 How can food marketers go about helping schools to meet the national guidelines for healthy school lunches? What are the benefits of doing so?

Marketing by the Numbers NAICS

The North American Industry Classification System (NAICS) code is very useful for marketers. It replaces the old product-based Standard Industrial Classification (SIC) system introduced in the 1930s. The NAICS system classifies businesses by production processes, better reflecting changes in the global economy, especially in the service and technology industries. It was developed jointly by the United States, Canada, and Mexico in 1997 in concert with the North American Free Trade Agreement (NAFTA), providing a common classification system for the three countries and better compatibility with the International Standard Industrial Classification

(ISIC) system. This six-digit number (in some cases, seven or ten digits) is very useful for understanding business markets.

6-13 What do the six digits of the NAICS code represent? What industry is represented by the NAICS code 721110? How many businesses comprise this code? (AACSB: Communication)

6-14 How can marketers use NAICS codes to better deliver customer satisfaction and value? (AACSB: Communication; Reflective Thinking)

Video Case Eaton

With approximately 70,000 employees in more than 150 countries and annual revenues of nearly $12 billion, Eaton is one of the world's largest suppliers of diversified industrial goods. Eaton has been known for products that make cars peppier and 18-wheelers safer to drive. But a recent restructuring has made Eaton a powerhouse in the growing field of power management. In short, Eaton is making electrical, hydraulic, and mechanical power systems more accessible to and more efficient for its global customers. But Eaton isn't successful only because of the products and services that it sells. It is successful because it works closely with its business customers to help them solve their problems and create better products and services of their own. Eaton is known

for high-quality, dependable customer service and product support. In this manner, Eaton builds strong relationships with its clients.

After viewing the video featuring Eaton, answer the following questions:

6-15 What is Eaton's value proposition?

6-16 Who are Eaton's customers? Describe Eaton's customer relationships.

6-17 Discuss the different ways that Eaton provides value beyond that which customers can provide for themselves.

Company Case Procter & Gamble: Treating Business Customers as Strategic Partners

For decades, Procter & Gamble has been at the top of almost every expert's A list of outstanding marketing companies. The experts point to P&G's stable of top-selling consumer brands or to the fact that year in and year out P&G is the world's largest advertiser. Consumers seem to agree. You'll find at least one of P&G's blockbuster brands in 99 percent of all American households; in many homes, you'll find a dozen or more familiar P&G products. But P&G is also highly respected for something else—maintaining strategic partnerships with business buyers.

P&G recognizes that building enduring relationships between consumers and its category leading brands starts with building enduring relationships with its large retail clients. On the front lines of this effort is P&G's iconic sales force. When it comes to selecting, training, and managing salespeople, P&G sets the gold standard. The company employs a massive sales force of more than 5,000 salespeople worldwide. But at P&G, it isn't just "sales"—it's "Customer Business Development" (CBD). This might seem trivial, but at P&G the distinction goes to the very core of the company's customer relationship strategy.

Developing the Customer's Business

P&G understands that if its business customers don't do well, neither will the company. To grow its own business, therefore, P&G must first grow the business of the retailers that sell its brands to final consumers. In P&G's own words, "CBD is more than mere 'selling'—it's a P&G-specific approach which enables us to grow our business by working as a 'strategic partner' (as opposed to just a supplier) with those who ultimately sell our products to consumers." Says one CBD manager, "We depend on them as much as they depend on us." By partnering with each other, P&G and its customers create "win-win" relationships that help both to prosper.

Most P&G customers are huge and complex businesses—such as Walmart, Walgreens, or Dollar General—with thousands of stores and billions of dollars in revenues. Working with and selling to such customers can be a very complex undertaking, more than any single salesperson or regular sales team could accomplish. Instead, P&G assigns a full CBD team to every large customer account. Each CBD team contains not only salespeople but also a full complement of specialists in every aspect of selling P&G's consumer brands at the retail level.

Teams vary in size depending on the customer. For example, it takes a team of 350 P&G specialists to properly serve Walmart, far and away its biggest customer. By contrast, the P&G Dollar General team consists of about 30 people. Regardless of size, every team constitutes a complete, multifunctional customer service unit. Each team includes a manager and several account executives (each responsible for a specific P&G product category), supported by specialists in marketing strategy, product development, operations, information systems, logistics, finance, and human resources.

To deal effectively with large accounts, P&G salespeople must be smart, well trained, and strategically grounded. They deal daily with high-level retail category buyers who may purchase hundreds of millions of dollars' worth of P&G and competing brands annually. It takes a lot more than a friendly smile and a firm handshake to interact with such buyers. Yet individual P&G salespeople can't know everything. And because of the nature of P&G's B-to-B interactions, they don't have to. Instead, P&G salespeople have at hand all the resources they need to resolve even the most challenging customer problems. "I have everything I need right here," says a household care account executive. "If my customer needs help from us with in-store promotions, I can go right down the hall and talk with someone on my team in marketing about doing some kind of promotional deal. It's that simple."

The multifunctional nature of the CBD team also means that collaboration extends far beyond internal interactions. Each time a team member contacts the customer, he or she represents the entire team. For example, if during a customer call an account executive receives a question about a promotional, logistical, or financial matter, the account executive acts as the liaison with the appropriate specialist. So, although not each CBD member has specialized knowledge in every area, the CBD team as a unit does.

Competitors have attempted to implement some aspects of P&G's multifunctional approach. However, P&G pioneered the CBD structure. And it has built in some unique characteristics that have allowed it to leverage more power from its team structure than its rivals can, giving it real competitive advantage.

A Competitive Edge

One of the things that gives P&G an edge when it comes to maintaining deep relationships with its business customers is a CBD structure that is broader and more comprehensive, making it more multifunctional than similar team structures employed by other companies. But perhaps more important, P&G's structure is designed to accomplish four key objectives. These objectives are so important that they are referred to internally as the "core work" of customer development. These four objectives are:

- *Align strategy*: Create opportunities for both P&G and the customer to benefit by collaborating in strategy development.
- *Create demand*: Build profitable sales volume for P&G and the customer through consumer value and shopper satisfaction.
- *Optimize supply*: Maximize the efficiency of the supply chain from P&G to the point of purchase to optimize cost and responsiveness.
- *Enable the organization*: Develop capabilities to maximize business results by creating the capacity for frequent breakthrough.

More than just corporate catchphrases jotted down in a P&G employee handbook, for sales personnel, these are words to live by. P&G trains sales staff in methods of achieving each objective and evaluates their effectiveness relative to each. In fact, P&G's customer relationship strategy came about through the recognition that to develop true win-win relationships with each customer, P&G would need to accomplish the first objective. As one account executive puts it, "The true competitive advantage is achieved by taking a multi-functional approach from basic selling to strategic customer collaboration!" If the CBD team can effectively accomplish the first objective of aligning strategy and collaborating on strategic development, accomplishing the other three objectives will follow more easily.

Building such strategic partnerships creates shopper value and satisfaction and drives profitable sales at the store level. When it comes to profitably moving Tide, Pampers, Gillette, or other P&G brands off store shelves and into consumers' shopping carts, P&G reps and their teams often know more than the retail buyers they advise. In fact, P&G's retail partners often rely on CBD teams to help them manage not only the P&G brands on their shelves but also entire product categories, including competing brands.

Giving advice on the stocking and placement of competitors' brands as well as its own might seem unwise. But believe it or not, it happens all the time at P&G. In fact, it isn't uncommon for a P&G rep to tell a retail buyer to stock fewer P&G products and more of a competing brand. Although that may seem like retail suicide, keep in mind that a CBD team's primary goal is to help the customer win in each product category. Sometimes, analysis shows that the best solution for the customer is "more of the other guy's product." For P&G, that's OK. The company knows that creating the best situation for the retailer ultimately pulls in more customer traffic, which in turn will likely lead to increased sales for other P&G products in the same category. Because most of P&G's brands are market-share leaders, it stands to benefit more from the increased traffic than competitors do. Again, what's good for the customer is good for P&G—it's a win-win situation.

Honest and open dealings also help to build long-term customer relationships. P&G salespeople become trusted advisors to their retailer-partners, a status they work hard to maintain. "It took me four years to build the trust I now have with my buyer," says a veteran P&G account executive. "If I talk her into buying P&G products that she can't sell or out-of-stocking competing brands that she should be selling, I could lose that trust in a heartbeat."

At P&G, collaboration is usually a two-way street—P&G gives and customers give back in return. "We'll help customers run a set of commercials or do some merchandising events, but there's usually a return-on-investment," explains another CBD manager. "Maybe it's helping us with distribution of a new product or increasing space for fabric care. We're very willing if the effort creates value for us as well as for the customer and the final consumer."

It's Better to Give…*Then* to Receive

As a result of collaborating with customers, P&G receives as much or more than it gives.

For starters, P&G receives information that helps it to remain innovative and create better products. The collaborative nature of its customer relationships also allows for optimizing the product mix, which also optimizes revenue. And the kind of transparency that results from strategic partnerships enables P&G to remain efficient and keep costs low. Indeed, during the first decade of this millennium, P&G was flying high as revenues, profits, and stock price all maintained healthy growth.

But P&G's strong performance flattened out as its vast portfolio of brands began showing a major weakness. Despite holding top positions in many product categories, many of P&G's brands were small, poor performers, or both. This limited the growth and profitability of its stronger brands. So P&G undertook a major restructuring of its product portfolio. Over the past few years, P&G has sold off about 100 brands (including Duracell, Aleve, Noxema, Iams, Clairol, Wella, and Covergirl) in order to focus on the 65 strongest-performing brands (such as Crest, Bounty, Tide, Gillette, and Dawn, to name just a few). Although it may sound like P&G dumped a big chunk of the company, the 65 remaining brands have long been responsible for about 90 percent of total revenues and 95 percent of profits.

The now-leaner brand portfolio is also a much better fit with P&G's approach to strategic customer partnerships. Of the 65 remaining brands, 18 bring in more than $1 billion a year *each*,

whereas another 17 account for at least $500 million annually. Last year, P&G sold more than $10 billion worth of diaper products under the Pampers brand alone. Eliminating the weaker brands not only relieves P&G of a heavy financial burden, but the stronger portfolio also enables P&G to better meet the needs of its customers. The company expects that there will be far fewer occasions where the best solution for the customer will be to recommend a competing brand.

P&G's approach to maintaining customer relationships is much, much more than "selling." "It's a P&G-specific approach [that lets us] grow business by working as a 'strategic partner' with our accounts, focusing on mutually beneficial business-building opportunities," states the CBD website. "All customers want to improve their businesses; it's [our] role to help them identify the biggest opportunities." At P&G, building and maintaining enduring customer relationships involves working with customers to solve their problems for mutual gain. The company knows that if customers succeed, it succeeds.

Questions for Discussion

6-18 Compare and contrast the nature of the business market structure and demand relative to consumer market structure and demand for a specific P&G product.

6-19 For the same product, discuss the differences in the types of decisions and the decision process for business and consumer markets.

6-20 This case covers the various members of a P&G Customer Business Development team. For a P&G corporate client, illustrate how the different roles of the buying center might interact with that CBD team. Be specific.

6-21 Discuss some ways that P&G's CBD structure is more effective than a single sales rep.

6-22 Why have P&G's competitors not been able to duplicate its customer relationship strategy?

6-23 Will P&G's divestment of 100 brands pay off? Why or why not?

Sources: Based on information from numerous P&G managers, with additional information from Demitrios Kalogeropoulos, "The Procter & Gamble Company's Best Product in 2015," *Motley Fool*, December 27, 2015, www.fool.com/investing/general/2015/12/27/the-procter-gamble -companys-best-product-in-2015.aspx; Penny Morgan, "Why Procter & Gamble Is Selling Some of Its Brands," *Market Realist*, March 8, 2016, www.marketrealist.com/2016/03/pgs-sale-brands-johnson-johnson -kimberly-clark/; Phil Whaba, "Procter & Gamble Selling Beauty Brands Like Clairol," *Fortune*, July 9, 2015, www.fortune.com/2015/07/09/ procter-gamble-coty/; and www.us.pgcareers.com/career-areas-find-your -fit/sales/and www.pg.com/vn/careers/our_functions/customer_business _development.shtml, accessed June 2016.

MyMarketingLab

Go to **mymktlab.com** for Auto-graded writing questions as well as the following Assisted-graded writing questions:

6-24   What is supplier development and why are companies practicing it?

6-25   Describe how online purchasing has changed the business-to-business marketing process and discuss the advantages and disadvantages of electronic purchasing.

PART 1: Defining Marketing and the Marketing Process (Chapters 1–2)
PART 2: Understanding the Marketplace and Consumer Value (Chapters 3–6)
PART 3: Designing a Customer Value–Driven Strategy and Mix (Chapters 7–17)
PART 4: Extending Marketing (Chapters 18–20)

7 Customer Value–Driven Marketing Strategy:

Creating Value for Target Customers

CHAPTER PREVIEW So far, you've learned what marketing is and about the importance of understanding consumers and the marketplace. With that as a background, we now delve deeper into marketing strategy and tactics. This chapter looks further into key customer value–driven marketing strategy decisions—dividing up markets into meaningful customer groups (*segmentation*), choosing which customer groups to serve (*targeting*), creating market offerings that best serve targeted customers (*differentiation*), and positioning the offerings in the minds of consumers (*positioning*). The chapters that follow explore the tactical marketing tools—the four Ps—by which marketers bring these strategies to life.

To open our discussion of segmentation, targeting, differentiation, and positioning, let's look at Dunkin' Donuts. Dunkin' has expanded rapidly in recent years into a national powerhouse, on par with Starbucks. But Dunkin' is no Starbucks. In fact, it doesn't want to be. It targets a very different kind of customer with a very different value proposition. Grab yourself a cup of coffee and read on.

DUNKIN' DONUTS: Targeting the Average Joe

A few years back, Dunkin' Donuts paid dozens of faithful customers in cities around the country $100 a week to buy coffee at Starbucks instead. At the same time, the coffee chain paid Starbucks customers to make the opposite switch. When it later debriefed the two groups, Dunkin' says it found them so polarized that company researchers dubbed them "tribes," each of which loathed the very things that made the other tribe loyal to their coffee shop. Dunkin' fans viewed Starbucks as pretentious and trendy, whereas Starbucks loyalists saw Dunkin' as plain and unoriginal. "I don't get it," one Dunkin' regular told researchers after visiting Starbucks. "If I want to sit on a couch, I stay at home."

Dunkin' Donuts has rapidly expanded into a national coffee powerhouse, on par with Starbucks, the nation's largest coffee chain. But the research confirmed a simple fact: Dunkin' is *not* Starbucks. In fact, it doesn't want to be. To prosper, Dunkin' must have its own clear vision of just which customers it wants to serve and how. Dunkin' and Starbucks target very different customers who want very different things from their favorite coffee shops. Starbucks is strongly positioned as a sort of high-brow "third place"—outside the home and office—featuring couches, eclectic music, and art-splashed walls. Dunkin' has a decidedly more low-brow, "everyman" kind of appeal.

Dunkin' Donuts's research showed that its brand fans were largely bewildered and turned off by the atmosphere at Starbucks. They groused that crowds of laptop users made it difficult to find a seat. They didn't like Starbucks's "tall," "grande," and "venti" lingo for small, medium, and large coffees. And they couldn't understand why anyone would pay so much for a cup of coffee. "It was almost as though they were a group of Martians talking about a group of Earthlings," says an executive from Dunkin's advertising agency. The Starbucks customers that Dunkin' paid to switch were equally uneasy in Dunkin' shops. "The Starbucks people couldn't bear that they weren't special any-more," says the ad executive.

Such opposing opinions aren't surprising, given the differences in the two stores' customers. Dunkin's customers include more middle-income

> Dunkin' Donuts targets the "Dunkin' tribe"—not the Starbucks coffee snob but the average Joe. Dunkin' isn't like Starbucks; it doesn't want to be.

blue- and white-collar workers across all age, race, and income demographics. By contrast, Starbucks targets a higher-income, more professional group. But Dunkin' researchers concluded that it was more the ideal, rather than income, that set the two tribes apart: Dunkin's tribe members want to be part of a crowd, whereas members of the Starbucks tribe want to stand out as individuals. "You could open a Dunkin' Donuts right next to Starbucks and get two completely different types of consumers," says one retailing expert.

Dunkin' Donuts built its positioning on serving simple fare at reasonable prices to working-class customers. It gained a reputation as a morning pit stop where everyday folks could get their daily donut and caffeine fix. But in recent years, to broaden its appeal and fuel expansion, the chain has been moving upscale—a bit, but not too far. It has spiffed up its stores and added new menu items, such as lattes and non-breakfast items like a steak wrap and chicken bacon sandwich. Dunkin' has also made dozens of store and atmosphere redesign changes, big and small, ranging from adding free Wi-Fi, digital menu boards, and more electrical outlets for laptops and smartphones to playing relaxing background music. And Dunkin' franchisees can now redecorate their stores in any of four Starbucks-esque color schemes, including "Dark Roast," "Cappuccino Blend," and "Jazz Brew," which features "dark orange and brown cozy booth seating, as well as hanging light fixtures that lend a soft glow to wall murals printed with words such as 'break,' 'fresh' and 'quality.'"

As it inches upscale, however, Dunkin' Donuts is being careful not to alienate its traditional customer base. There are no couches in the remodeled stores. Dunkin' even renamed a new hot sandwich a "stuffed melt" after customers complained that calling it a "panini" was too fancy; it then dropped it altogether when faithful customers thought it was too messy. "We're walking [a fine] line," says the chain's vice president of consumer insights. "The thing about the Dunkin' tribe is, they see through the hype."

Over the past several years, both Dunkin' Donuts and Starbucks have grown rapidly, each targeting its own tribe of customers and riding the wave of America's growing thirst for coffee. Now, both are looking for more growth by convincing "grab-and-go" morning customers to visit later in the day and

Dunkin' Donuts targets everyday Joes who just don't get what Starbucks is all about. Its targeting and positioning are pretty well summed up in its long-running ad slogan "America Runs on Dunkin'."

Getty Images News

stick around longer. Although still smaller than Starbucks—which captures a 36 percent U.S. market share versus Dunkin's roughly 24 percent share—Dunkin' is currently the nation's fastest-growing snack and coffee chain. It hopes that the continuing repositioning and upgrades will help keep that momentum going. Dunkin' plans to add at least 4,000 more U.S. stores by 2020.

Again, however, in refreshing its stores and positioning, Dunkin' Donuts has stayed true to the needs and preferences of the Dunkin' tribe. Dunkin' is "not going after the Starbucks coffee snob," says one analyst, it's "going after the average Joe." So far, so good. For the past nine years, Dunkin' Donuts has topped the coffee category in a leading customer loyalty and engagement survey, ahead of number-two Starbucks. According to the survey, Dunkin' Donuts has been the top brand for consistently meeting or exceeding customer expectations with respect to taste, quality, and customer service.

Dunkin' Donuts' targeting and positioning are pretty well summed up in its long-running ad slogan "America Runs on Dunkin'." No longer just a morning pit stop, Dunkin' now bills itself as America's favorite all-day, everyday stop for coffee and baked goods. "We remain committed to keeping America running with our great coffee, baked goods, and snacks served in a friendly environment at a great value," says Dunkin's chief global marketing officer. Nothing too fancy—just meeting the everyday, all-day needs of the Dunkin' tribe.[1]

OBJECTIVES OUTLINE

OBJECTIVE 7-1	Define the major steps in designing a customer value–driven marketing strategy: market segmentation, targeting, differentiation, and positioning. **Marketing Strategy** *(pp 188–189)*
OBJECTIVE 7-2	List and discuss the major bases for segmenting consumer and business markets. **Market Segmentation** *(pp 189–197)*
OBJECTIVE 7-3	Explain how companies identify attractive market segments and choose a market-targeting strategy. **Market Targeting** *(pp 197–204)*
OBJECTIVE 7-4	Discuss how companies differentiate and position their products for maximum competitive advantage. **Differentiation and Positioning** *(pp 204–212)*

Market segmentation
Dividing a market into distinct groups of buyers who have different needs, characteristics, or behaviors and who might require separate marketing strategies or mixes.

Market targeting (targeting)
Evaluating each market segment's attractiveness and selecting one or more segments to serve.

Differentiation
Actually differentiating the market offering to create superior customer value.

COMPANIES TODAY RECOGNIZE THAT they cannot appeal to all buyers in the marketplace—or at least not to all buyers in the same way. Buyers are too numerous, widely scattered, and varied in their needs and buying practices. Moreover, companies themselves vary widely in their abilities to serve different market segments. Instead, like Dunkin' Donuts, companies must identify the parts of the market they can serve best and most profitably. They must design customer-driven marketing strategies that build the right relationships with the right customers. Thus, most companies have moved away from mass marketing and toward *target marketing*: identifying market segments, selecting one or more of them, and developing products and marketing programs tailored to each.

Marketing Strategy

● **Figure 7.1** shows the four major steps in designing a customer value–driven marketing strategy. In the first two steps, the company selects the customers that it will serve. **Market segmentation** involves dividing a market into distinct groups of buyers who have different needs, characteristics, or behaviors and who might require separate marketing strategies or mixes. The company identifies different ways to segment the market and develops profiles of the resulting market segments. **Market targeting (or targeting)** consists of evaluating each market segment's attractiveness and selecting one or more market segments to enter.

In the final two steps, the company decides on a value proposition—how it will create value for target customers. **Differentiation** involves actually differentiating the

● **FIGURE | 7.1**
Designing a Customer-Driven Marketing Strategy

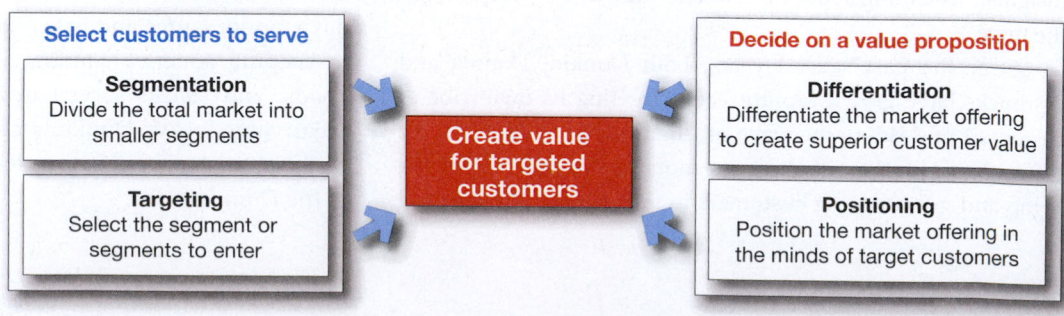

In concept, marketing boils down to two questions: (1) Which customers will we serve? and (2) How will we serve them? Of course, the tough part is coming up with good answers to these simple-sounding yet difficult questions. The goal is to create more value for the customers we serve than competitors do.

Select customers to serve

Segmentation
Divide the total market into smaller segments

Targeting
Select the segment or segments to enter

Create value for targeted customers

Decide on a value proposition

Differentiation
Differentiate the market offering to create superior customer value

Positioning
Position the market offering in the minds of target customers

Positioning
Arranging for a market offering to occupy a clear, distinctive, and desirable place relative to competing products in the minds of target consumers.

Author Comment | Market segmentation addresses the first simple-sounding marketing question: What customers will we serve?

Geographic segmentation
Dividing a market into different geographical units, such as nations, states, regions, counties, cities, or even neighborhoods.

firm's market offering to create superior customer value. **Positioning** consists of arranging for a market offering to occupy a clear, distinctive, and desirable place relative to competing products in the minds of target consumers. We discuss each of these steps in turn.

Market Segmentation

Buyers in any market differ in their wants, resources, locations, buying attitudes, and buying practices. Through market segmentation, companies divide large, diverse markets into smaller segments that can be reached more efficiently and effectively with products and services that match their unique needs. In this section, we discuss four important segmentation topics: segmenting consumer markets, segmenting business markets, segmenting international markets, and the requirements for effective segmentation.

Segmenting Consumer Markets

There is no single way to segment a market. A marketer has to try different segmentation variables, alone and in combination, to find the best way to view market structure. ● **Table 7.1** outlines variables that might be used in segmenting consumer markets. Here we look at the major *geographic, demographic, psychographic,* and *behavioral* variables.

Geographic Segmentation

Geographic segmentation calls for dividing the market into different geographical units, such as nations, regions, states, counties, cities, or even neighborhoods. A company may decide to operate in one or a few geographical areas or operate in all areas but pay attention to geographical differences in needs and wants. Moreover, many companies today are localizing their products, services, advertising, promotion, and sales efforts to fit the needs of individual regions, cities, and other localities.

For example, many large retailers—from Target and Walmart to Kohl's and Staples—are now opening smaller-format stores designed to fit the needs of densely packed urban neighborhoods not suited to their typical large suburban superstores. Target's CityTarget stores average about half the size of a typical Super Target; its TargetExpress stores are even smaller at about one-fifth the size of a big-box outlet. These smaller, conveniently located stores carry a more limited assortment of goods that meet the needs of urban residents and commuters, such as groceries, home essentials, beauty products, and consumer electronics. They also offer pick-up-in-store services and a pharmacy.[2]

Beyond adjusting store size, many retailers also localize product assortments and services. For example, department store chain Macy's has a localization program called MyMacy's in which merchandise is customized under 69 different geographical districts. At stores around the country, Macy's sales clerks record local shopper requests and pass them along to district managers. In turn, blending the customer requests with store

● Table 7.1 | **Major Segmentation Variables for Consumer Markets**

Segmentation Variable	Examples
Geographic	Nations, regions, states, counties, cities, neighborhoods, population density (urban, suburban, rural), climate
Demographic	Age, life-cycle stage, gender, income, occupation, education, religion, ethnicity, generation
Psychographic	Lifestyle, personality
Behavioral	Occasions, benefits, user status, usage rate, loyalty status

transaction data, the district managers customize the mix of merchandise in their stores. So, for instance, Macy's stores in Michigan stock more locally made Sanders chocolate candies. In Orlando, Macy's carries more swimsuits in stores near waterparks and more twin bedding in stores near condominium rentals. The chain stocks extra coffee percolators in its Long Island stores, where it sells more of the 1960s must-haves than anywhere else in the country. In all, the "MyMacy's" strategy is to meet the needs of local markets, making the giant retailer seem smaller and more in touch.[3]

Demographic Segmentation

Demographic segmentation
Dividing the market into segments based on variables such as age, life-cycle stage, gender, income, occupation, education, religion, ethnicity, and generation.

Demographic segmentation divides the market into segments based on variables such as age, life-cycle stage, gender, income, occupation, education, religion, ethnicity, and generation. Demographic factors are the most popular bases for segmenting customer groups. One reason is that consumer needs, wants, and usage rates often vary closely with demographic variables. Another is that demographic variables are easier to measure than most other types of variables. Even when marketers first define segments using other bases, such as benefits sought or behavior, they must know a segment's demographic characteristics to assess the size of the target market and reach it efficiently.

Age and Life-Cycle Stage. Consumer needs and wants change with age. Some companies use **age and life-cycle segmentation**, offering different products or using different marketing approaches for different age and life-cycle groups. For example, Kraft's Oscar Mayer brand markets Lunchables, convenient prepackaged lunches for children. To extend the substantial success of Lunchables, however, Oscar Mayer later introduced Lunchables Uploaded, a version designed to meet the tastes and sensibilities of teenagers. Most recently, the brand launched an adult version, but with the more adult-friendly name P3 (Portable Protein Pack). Now, consumers of all ages can enjoy one of America's favorite noontime meals.

Age and life-cycle segmentation
Dividing a market into different age and life-cycle groups.

Marketers must be careful to guard against stereotypes when using age and life-cycle segmentation. For example, although some 80-year-olds fit the stereotypes of doddering shut-ins with fixed incomes, others ski and play tennis. Similarly, whereas some 40-year-old couples are sending their children off to college, others are just beginning new families. Thus, age is often a poor predictor of a person's life cycle, health, work or family status, needs, and buying power.

Gender segmentation
Dividing a market into different segments based on gender.

Gender. **Gender segmentation** has long been used in marketing clothing, cosmetics, toiletries, toys, and magazines. For example, P&G was among the first to use gender segmentation with Secret, a deodorant brand specially formulated for a woman's chemistry, packaged and advertised to reinforce the female image.

More recently, the men's personal care industry has exploded, and many cosmetics brands that previously catered mostly to women—from L'Oréal, Nivea, and Sephora to Unilever's Dove brand—now successfully market men's lines. For example, Dove's Men+Care line calls itself "The authority on man maintenance." The brand provides a full line of body washes ("skin care built in"), body bars ("fight skin dryness"), antiperspirants ("tough on sweat, not on skin"), face care ("take better care of your face"), and hair care ("3X stronger hair").[4]

NO ONE WILL KNOW IF YOU SKIP THE LAST SET.

WHO WILL YOU BE? DICK'S

● **Gender segmentation: In line with the "athleisure" trend that has more women wearing workout gear as everyday fashion, Dick's Sporting Goods recently launched its first-ever ads aimed directly at fitness-minded women.**
DICK'S Sporting Goods

Going in the other direction, brands that have traditionally targeted men are now targeting women. ● For example, in line with the "athleisure" trend in which more women are wearing workout gear as everyday fashion, sports apparel makers and retailers—from Nike and Under Armour to Dick's Sporting Goods—are boosting their marketing efforts aimed at women buyers. Women now make up half of all sporting good shoppers. Dick's Sporting Goods recently launched its first-ever ads aimed directly at fitness-minded women, as part of its broader "Who Will You Be?" campaign. The ads feature women who must juggle their busy lives to meet their fitness goals. The first ad in the series shows one mom jogging rather than driving to pick up her sons at school. Another mom jogs on a treadmill while listening to her baby monitor. "Who will you be?" asks the ad. "Every run. Every workout. Every day. Every choice. Every season begins with Dick's Sporting Goods." Dick's want women buyers to know that "we understand the choices that they have to make every single day…to fit in fitness," says the retailer's chief marketer.[5]

Income segmentation
Dividing a market into different income segments.

Income. The marketers of products and services such as automobiles, clothing, cosmetics, financial services, and travel have long used **income segmentation**. Many companies target affluent consumers with luxury goods and convenience services. Other marketers use high-touch marketing programs to court the well-to-do. Upscale retailer Saks Fifth Avenue provides exclusive services to its elite clientele of Fifth Avenue Club members, some of whom spend as much as $150,000 to $200,000 a year on clothing and accessories from Saks alone. For example, Fifth Avenue Club members have access to a Saks Personal Stylist. The fashion-savvy, well-connected personal consultant gets to know and helps to shape each client's personal sense of style, then guides him or her "through the maze of fashion must-haves." The personal stylist puts the customer first. For example, if Saks doesn't carry one of those must-haves that the client covets, the personal stylist will find it elsewhere at no added charge.[6]

However, not all companies that use income segmentation target the affluent. For example, many retailers—such as the Dollar General, Family Dollar, and Dollar Tree store chains—successfully target low- and middle-income groups. The core market for such stores is represented by families with incomes under $30,000. When Family Dollar real estate experts scout locations for new stores, they look for lower-middle-class neighborhoods where people wear less-expensive shoes and drive old cars that drip a lot of oil. With their low-income strategies, dollar stores are now the fastest-growing retailers in the nation.

Psychographic Segmentation

Psychographic segmentation
Dividing a market into different segments based on lifestyle or personality characteristics.

Psychographic segmentation divides buyers into different segments based on lifestyle or personality characteristics. People in the same demographic group can have very different psychographic characteristics.

In Chapter 5, we discussed how the products people buy reflect their *lifestyles*. As a result, marketers often segment their markets by consumer lifestyles and base their marketing strategies on lifestyle appeals. For example, retailer Anthropologie, with its whimsical, "French flea market" store atmosphere, sells a Bohemian-chic lifestyle to which its young women customers aspire. And Athleta sells an urban-active lifestyle to women with its yoga, running, and other athletic clothing along with urban-causal, post-workout apparel.

● **Lifestyle segmentation: Panera caters to a healthy-eating lifestyle segment of people who want more than just good-tasting food—they want food that's good for them, too.**

Panera Bread, the Mother Bread logo and Panera Bread Food as it should be are the intellectual property of Panera Bread and are used with permission. Photograph by Brian W. Ferry.

Fast-casual restaurant Panera caters to a lifestyle segment of people who want more than just good-tasting food—they want food that's good for them, too. To better meet the needs of this healthy-living lifestyle segment, Panera recently announced that it would soon banish more than 150 artificial preservatives, sweeteners, colors, and flavors from its food. It then launched a marketing campaign tagged "Food as it should be," showing happy customers eating better at Panera. ● "Eat clean," says one ad, "because clean food just tastes better." According to Panera, food should do more than just fill your stomach. "Food should taste good. It should feel good. It should do good things for you and the world around you. That's food as it should be." If that kind of thinking fits your lifestyle, suggests Panera's head of marketing, "then yeah, come on in…that's why we're here."[7]

Marketers also use *personality* variables to segment markets. For example, ads for Sherwin Williams paint—headlined "Make the most for your color with the very best paint"—seem to appeal to older, more practical do-it-yourself personalities. By contrast, Benjamin Moore's ads and social media pitches appeal to younger, more outgoing fashion individualists. One Benjamin Moore print ad—consisting of a single long line of text in a crazy quilt of fonts—describes Benjamin Moore's Hot Lips paint color this way: "It's somewhere between the color of your lips when you go outside in December with your hair still wet and the color of a puddle left by a melted grape popsicle mixed with the color of that cough syrup that used to make me gag a little. Hot lips. Perfect."

Behavioral segmentation

Dividing a market into segments based on consumer knowledge, attitudes, uses of a product, or responses to a product.

Occasion segmentation

Dividing the market into segments according to occasions when buyers get the idea to buy, actually make their purchase, or use the purchased item.

Benefit segmentation

Dividing the market into segments according to the different benefits that consumers seek from the product.

Behavioral Segmentation

Behavioral segmentation divides buyers into segments based on their knowledge, attitudes, uses, or responses to a product. Many marketers believe that behavior variables are the best starting point for building market segments.

Occasions. Buyers can be grouped according to occasions when they get the idea to buy, actually make their purchases, or use the purchased items. **Occasion segmentation** can help firms build up product usage. Campbell's advertises its soups more heavily in the cold winter months. And for more than a dozen years, Starbucks has welcomed the autumn season with its pumpkin spice latte (PSL). Sold only in the fall, PSLs pull in an estimated $100 million in revenues for Starbucks each year.[8]

Still other companies try to boost consumption by promoting usage during nontraditional occasions. For example, most consumers drink orange juice in the morning, but orange growers have promoted drinking orange juice as a cool, healthful refresher at other times of the day. Similarly, whereas consumers tend to drink soft drinks later in the day, Mountain Dew introduced Mtn Dew A.M. (a mixture of Mountain Dew and orange juice) to increase morning consumption. And Taco Bell's First Meal campaign attempts to build business by promoting Mtn Dew A.M. (available only at Taco Bell) along with the chain's A.M. Crunchwrap and other breakfast items as a great way to start the day.

Benefits Sought. A powerful form of segmentation is grouping buyers according to the different *benefits* that they seek from a product. **Benefit segmentation** requires finding the major benefits people look for in a product class, the kinds of people who look for each benefit, and the major brands that deliver each benefit.

For example, people who buy wearable health and activity trackers are looking for a variety of benefits, everything from counting steps taken and calories burned to heart rate monitoring and high-performance workout tracking and reporting. To meet these varying benefit preferences, Fitbit makes health and fitness tracking devices aimed at buyers in three major benefit segments: Everyday Fitness, Active Fitness, and Performance Fitness:[9]

Everyday Fitness buyers want only very basic fitness tracking. So Fitbit's simplest device, the Fitbit Zip, offers these consumers "A fun, simple way to track your day." It tracks steps taken, distance traveled, calories consumed, and active minutes. The Fitbit One, also aimed at Everyday Fitness buyers, does all that and also monitors how long and well they sleep; the Fitbit Charge adds a wristband and watch. At the other extreme, for the Performance Fitness segment, the high-tech Fitbit Surge helps serious athletes "Train smarter. Go Farther." The Surge is "the ultimate fitness super watch," with GPS tracking, heart rate monitoring, all-day activity tracking, automatic workout tracking and recording, sleep monitoring, text notification, music control, and wireless synching to Fitbit's smartphone and computer app. In all, within Fitbit's family of fitness products, no matter what bundle of benefits one seeks, "There's a Fitbit product for everyone."

User Status. Markets can be segmented into nonusers, ex-users, potential users, first-time users, and regular users of a product. Marketers want to reinforce and retain regular users, attract targeted nonusers, and reinvigorate relationships with ex-users. Included in the potential users group are consumers facing life-stage changes—such as new parents and newlyweds—who can be turned into heavy users. For example, to get new parents off to the right start, P&G makes certain that its Pampers Swaddlers are the diaper most U.S. hospitals provide for newborns and then promotes them as "the #1 choice of hospitals."

● Benefit segmentation: Within Fitbit's family of health and fitness tracking products, no matter what bundle of benefits one seeks, "There's a Fitbit for Everyone."

Paul Marotta/Stringer/Getty Images

Usage Rate. Markets can also be segmented into light, medium, and heavy product users. Heavy users are often a small percentage of the market but account

Targeting heavy users: Sister chains Hardee's and Carl's Jr. use steamy hot-models-in-bikinis commercials to attract an audience of "young, hungry men," who wolf down a lot more of the chains' featured Thickburgers and other indulgent items than consumers in other segments.

CKE Restaurants/Splash News/Newscom

for a high percentage of total consumption. For instance, Carl's Jr. and Hardee's restaurants, both owned by parent company CKE Restaurants, focus on a target of "young, hungry men." These young male customers, ages 18 to 34, fully embrace the chain's "If you're gonna eat, eat like you mean it" positioning. That means they wolf down a lot more Thickburgers and other indulgent items featured on the chains' menus. ● To attract this audience, the company is known for its steamy hot-models-in-bikinis commercials, featuring models such as Kate Upton, Charlotte McKinney, Nina Agdal, and Hannah Ferguson to heat up the brands' images. Such ads clearly show "what our target audience of young, hungry guys like," says CKE's chief executive.[10]

Loyalty Status. A market can also be segmented by consumer loyalty. Consumers can be loyal to brands (Tide), stores (Target), and companies (Apple). Buyers can be divided into groups according to their degree of loyalty. Some consumers are completely loyal—they buy one brand all the time and can't wait to tell others about it. For example, whether they own a MacBook Pro, an iPhone, or an iPad, Apple devotees are granitelike in their devotion to the brand. At one end are the quietly satisfied Apple users, folks who own one or several Apple devices and use them for browsing, texting, email, and social networking. At the other extreme, however, are the Apple zealots—the so-called MacHeads or Macolytes—who can't wait to tell anyone within earshot of their latest Apple gadget. Such loyal Apple devotees helped keep Apple afloat during the lean years a decade ago, and they are now at the forefront of Apple's huge iPhone, iPad, iPod, and iTunes empire.

Other consumers are somewhat loyal—they are loyal to two or three brands of a given product or favor one brand while sometimes buying others. Still other buyers show no loyalty to any brand—they either want something different each time they buy, or they buy whatever's on sale.

A company can learn a lot by analyzing loyalty patterns in its market. It should start by studying its own loyal customers. Highly loyal customers can be a real asset. They often promote the brand through personal word of mouth and social media. Instead of just marketing to loyal customers, companies should engage them fully and make them partners in building the brand and telling the brand story. For example, Mountain Dew has turned its loyal customers into a "Dew Nation" of passionate superfans who have made it the nation's number-three liquid refreshment brand behind only Coca-Cola and Pepsi (see Real Marketing 7.1).

Some companies actually put loyalists to work for the brand. For example, Patagonia relies on its most tried-and-true customers—what it calls Patagonia ambassadors—to field-test products in harsh environments, provide input for "ambassador-driven" lines of apparel and gear, and share their product experiences with others.[11] In contrast, by studying its less-loyal buyers, a company can detect which brands are most competitive with its own. By looking at customers who are shifting away from its brand, the company can learn about its marketing weaknesses and take actions to correct them.

Using Multiple Segmentation Bases

Marketers rarely limit their segmentation analysis to only one or a few variables. Rather, they often use multiple segmentation bases in an effort to identify smaller, better-defined target groups. Several business information services—such as Nielsen, Acxiom, Esri, and Experian—provide multivariable segmentation systems that merge geographic, demographic, lifestyle, and behavioral data to help companies segment their markets down to zip codes, neighborhoods, and even households.

One of the leading consumer segmentation systems is Experian Marketing Services' Mosaic USA system. ● It classifies U.S. households into one of 71 lifestyle segments and 19 overarching groups based on income, age, buying habits, household composition, and life events. Mosaic USA segments carry exotic names such as Birkenstocks and Beemers,

Real Marketing

7.1 Mountain Dew: "Doin' the Dew" with Brand Superfans

Perhaps no brand has built a more passionately loyal and engaged following than PepsiCo's high-flying Mountain Dew. For example, take Jason Hemperly, the shy high school kid who had his grandmother make him a tuxedo for his prom out of flattened Mountain Dew cans. And Chester Atkins and his wife Amy who sport matching Mountain Dew tattoos and who toasted their marriage proposal with champagne flutes filled with the citrusy green drink. Then there's Chris Whitley from Jackson, Mississippi, who drinks some 40 cans of Mountain Dew a week, keeps a copious collection of Mountain Dew T-shirts and hats, and absolutely worships NASCAR driver and Mountain Dew spokesman Dale Earnhardt Jr. "It's pretty much a religious obsession for me, I guess," says Whitley about Mountain Dew. "I just don't drink anything else."

Such fiercely loyal customers—who collectively make up the "Dew Nation"—have made Mountain Dew one of PepsiCo's largest and fastest-growing brands. Mountain Dew's avid superfans make up only 20 percent of its customers but consume a mind-boggling 70 percent of the brand's total volume. Thanks to such fans, even as overall soft drink sales have lost their fizz during the past decade, Mountain Dew's sales are bubbling over. The hugely popular $9 billion brand is now the nation's number-three liquid refreshment, behind only behemoths Coca-Cola and Pepsi.

Such loyalty and sales don't just flow automatically out of bottles and pop-top cans. Mountain Dew markets heavily to its superfans. The brand's long-running "Do the Dew" slogan—what Mountain Dew calls its "iconic rallying cry and brand credo"—headlines the extreme moments and excitement behind the brand's positioning. Mountain Dew spent an estimated $76 million on "Do the Dew" advertising and other brand content last year, 45 percent of it in digital media. One recent action-packed "Do the Dew" ad features professional skateboarder Sean Malto igniting a beach party bonfire by grinding over a line of matches. In another ad, Dale Earnhardt Jr., smokes his tires on a winding, wooded country road to lay down a smoke screen for his paintball team. The "Do the Dew" campaign is loaded with high-octane stunts. However,

according to Mountain Dew's chief marketer, the slogan is "more about enjoying the moment you're in," something highly relevant to the brand's young, largely millennial-male target market.

But marketing to the Dew Nation explains only one part of Mountain Dew's success. The real story revolves around the brand's skill in fueling customer loyalty by actively engaging brand superfans and creating close brand community. Mountain Dew doesn't just market *to* loyal customers; it makes them partners in building the brand and being part of the brand story.

For example, over the years, through several "DEWmocracy" campaigns, the company has involved Mountain Dew lovers in shaping the brand at all levels. Under DEWmocracy, the Dew Nation has participated via online and social media in everything from choosing and naming new flavors and designing the cans to submitting and selecting TV commercials and even picking an ad agency and media. DEWmocracy has produced hit flavors such as Voltage and White Out. More important, DEWmocracy has been a perfect forum for getting youthful, digitally-savvy Dew drinkers engaged with each other and the company, making the brand their own.

In creating engagement and community among loyal brand fans, Mountain Dew views itself as the ultimate lifestyle brand.

Offline, for more than a decade, Mountain Dew has teamed with NBC Sports to sponsor The Dew Tour, a slate of summer and winter action sports events in major cities across the country. At a Dew Tour, superfans can experience the adrenaline-packed Mountain Dew lifestyle firsthand and share their experiences with others in the Dew Nation.

Online, Mountain Dew's dozens of web, mobile, and social media sites provide more by way of entertainment and community building than product information. For example, the main "Do the Dew" website serves as a lifestyle hub where super-passionate fans can check out the latest #dothedew programs, ads, and videos; hang out in the gaming section; and follow the adventures of Mountain Dew's action sports athletes in skateboarding (Paul Rodriguez, Sean Malto, and Trevor Colden), snowboarding (Danny Davis and Scotty Lago), basketball (Russell Westbrook), racing (Dale Earnhardt Jr.), and even fishing (Gerald Swindle).

But the ultimate digital hangout for Mountain Dew superfans is a place called Green Label, a web and social media community created by Mountain Dew as a hub for youth culture, covering Dew-related content on sports, music, art, and style. Green Label "welcomes all kinds: derelict skaters, music nerds, and art doodlers, and focuses

Mountain Dew has turned its loyal customers into a "Dew Nation" of passionate superfans who avidly adhere to the brand's iconic "Do the Dew" rallying cry.
PepsiCo

on the genetically modified cross-pollination that occurs at the intersection of skate, music, and art."

Green Label produces a constant flow of engaging content that gets superfans interacting with the brand. Green Label has also spawned ambitious projects such *Mountain Dew's Green Label Experience*—a cable TV series showcasing action sports from The Dew Tour—and *We Are Blood*—a feature-length film that follows amateur and pro skaters around the world, "celebrating the unconditional bond created by the simple act of skateboarding." The main GreenLabel.com site now draws five times more traffic than MountainDew.com.

In all, few brands can match Mountain Dew when it comes to engaging loyal customers and involving them with the brand. In turn, the cult-like loyalty of the Dew Nation has kept

Mountain Dew flowing even as competitors face declines. "The thing that really makes it different from a lot of other drinks, certainly from a lot of other carbonated soft drinks, is its incredibly loyal and passionate consumer base," says Mountain Dew's top marketer. To such loyal fans, Mountain Dew is more than just a something you drink. In the words of PepsiCo's CEO, to Dew fans, Mountain Dew is "an attitude. It's a fantastic attitude."

Just ask a superfan like 20-year-old Steven Kearney, who's been drinking

Mountain Dew every day since eighth grade. Kearney has a collection of 80 vintage cans and bottles—he collects a new can as a memento every time a new flavor is released. He always starts the show he hosts on his college radio station by popping open a can of Mountain Dew, and he hangs out with a group of friends he calls "The Mountain Dew buddies." Will he ever outgrow his yen to "Do the Dew"? "I feel like it will definitely be something I'm going to drink for the rest of my life," he says.

Sources: Nathalie Tadena, "Mountain Dew Ads Go Global with Return of 'Do The Dew,'" *Wall Street Journal,* March 29, 2015, http://blogs.wsj.com/cmo/2015/03/29/mountain-dew-ads-go-global-with-return-of-do-the-dew/; Jillian Berman, "Here's Why Mountain Dew Will Survive the Death of Soda," *Huffington Post,* January 25, 2015, www.huffingtonpost.com/2015/01/26/mountain-dew-regions_n_6524382.html; Venessa Wong, "Nobody Knows What Mountain Dew Is, and That's the Key to Its Success," *Buzzfeed,* November 1, 2015, www.buzzfeed.com/venessawong/what-is-mountain-dew#.ikdN7aw8X; and www.mountaindew.com and www.greenlabel.com, accessed September 2016.

● **Using Experian's mosaic USA segmentation system, marketers can paint a surprisingly precise picture of who you are and what you might buy. Mosiac USA segments carry colorful names such as Colleges and Cafes, Birkenstocks and Beemers, Bohemian Groove, Hispanic Harmony, Rolling the Dice, Small Town Shallow Pockets, and True Grit Americans that help bring the segments to life.**

zeljkodan/Shutterstock

Bohemian Groove, Sports Utility Families, Colleges and Cafes, Heritage Heights, Small Town Shallow Pockets, and True Grit Americans.[12] Such colorful names help bring the segments to life.

For example, the Birkenstocks and Beemers group is located in the Middle-Class Melting Pot level of affluence and consists of 40- to 65-year-olds who have achieved financial security and left the urban rat race for rustic and artsy communities located near small cities. They find spirituality more important than religion. Colleges and Cafes consumers are part of the Singles and Starters affluence level and are mainly white, under-35 college graduates who are still finding themselves. They are often employed as support or service staff related to a university. They don't make much money and tend to not have any savings.

Mosaic USA and other such systems can help marketers to segment people and locations into marketable groups of like-minded consumers. Each segment has its own pattern of likes, dislikes, lifestyles, and purchase behaviors. For example, Bohemian Groove consumers, part of the Significant Singles group, are urban singles ages 45 to 65 living in apartments in smaller cities such as Sacramento, CA, and Harrisburg, PA. They tend to be laid back, maintain a large circle of friends, and stay active in community groups. They enjoy music, hobbies, and the creative arts. When they go out to eat, they choose places such as the Macaroni Grill or Red Robin. Their favorite TV channels are Bravo, Lifetime, Oxygen, and TNT, and they watch two times more *CSI* than the average American. Using the Mosaic system, marketers can paint a surprisingly precise picture of who you are and what you might buy.

Such rich segmentation provides a powerful tool for marketers of all kinds. It can help companies identify and better understand key customer segments, reach them more efficiently, and tailor market offerings and messages to their specific needs.

Segmenting Business Markets

Consumer and business marketers use many of the same variables to segment their markets. Business buyers can be segmented geographically, demographically (industry, company size), or by benefits sought, user status, usage rate, and loyalty status. Yet business marketers also use some additional variables, such as customer *operating characteristics, purchasing approaches, situational factors*, and *personal characteristics*.

Almost every company serves at least some business markets. For example, Starbucks has developed distinct marketing programs for each of its two business segments: the office coffee segment and the food service segment. In the office coffee and vending segment, Starbucks Office Coffee Solutions markets a variety of workplace coffee services to businesses of any size, helping them to make Starbucks coffee and related products available to their employees in their workplaces. Starbucks helps these business customers design the best office solutions involving its coffees (the Starbucks or Seattle's Best brands), teas (Tazo), syrups, and branded paper products and methods of serving them—portion packs, single cups, or vending. The Starbucks Foodservice division teams up with businesses and other organizations—ranging from airlines, restaurants, colleges, and hospitals to baseball stadiums—to help them serve the well-known Starbucks brand to their own customers. Starbucks provides not only the coffee, tea, and paper products to its food service partners but also equipment, training, and marketing and merchandising support.[13]

Many companies establish separate systems for dealing with larger or multiple-location customers. For example, Steelcase, a major producer of office furniture systems, first divides customers into several segments: health-care, education, hospitality, legal, U.S. and Canadian governments, and state and local governments. Next, company salespeople work with independent Steelcase dealers to handle smaller, local, or regional Steelcase customers in each segment. But many national, multiple-location customers, such as ExxonMobil or IBM, have special needs that may reach beyond the scope of individual dealers. Therefore, Steelcase uses national account managers to help its dealer networks handle national accounts.

Segmenting International Markets

Few companies have either the resources or the will to operate in all, or even most, of the countries that dot the globe. Although some large companies, such as Coca-Cola or Unilever, sell products in more than 200 countries, most international firms focus on a smaller set. Different countries, even those that are close together, can vary greatly in their economic, cultural, and political makeup. Thus, just as they do within their domestic markets, international firms need to group their world markets into segments with distinct buying needs and behaviors.

Companies can segment international markets using one or a combination of several variables. They can segment by *geographic location*, grouping countries by regions such as Western Europe, the Pacific Rim, South Asia, or Africa. Geographic segmentation assumes that nations close to one another will have many common traits and behaviors. Although this is sometimes the case, there are many exceptions. For example, some U.S. marketers lump all Central and South American countries together. However, the Dominican Republic is no more like Brazil than Italy is like Sweden. Many Central and South Americans don't even speak Spanish, including more than 200 million Portuguese-speaking Brazilians and the millions in other countries who speak a variety of Indian dialects.

World markets can also be segmented based on *economic factors*. Countries might be grouped by population income levels or by their overall level of economic development. A country's economic structure shapes its population's product and service needs and therefore the marketing opportunities it offers. For example, many companies are now targeting the BRIC countries—Brazil, Russia, India, and China—which are fast-growing developing economies with rapidly increasing buying power.

Countries can also be segmented by *political and legal factors* such as the type and stability of government, receptivity to foreign firms, monetary regulations, and amount of bureaucracy. *Cultural factors* can also be used, grouping markets according to common languages, religions, values and attitudes, customs, and behavioral patterns.

Segmenting international markets based on geographic, economic, political, cultural, and other factors presumes that segments should consist of clusters of countries. However, as new communications technologies, such as satellite TV and online and social media, connect consumers around the world, marketers can define and reach segments of like-minded consumers no matter where in the world they are. Using **intermarket segmentation** (also called **cross-market segmentation**), they form segments of consumers who have

Intermarket (cross-market) segmentation
Forming segments of consumers who have similar needs and buying behaviors even though they are located in different countries.

● **Intermarket segmentation: Coca-Cola targets teens the world over through universal teen themes, such as music.**

www.lifestylehub.net

similar needs and buying behaviors even though they are located in different countries.

For example, retailer H&M targets fashion-conscious but frugal shoppers in 43 countries with its low-priced, trendy apparel and accessories. And Coca-Cola creates special programs to target teens, core consumers of its soft drinks the world over. By 2020, one-third of the world's population—some 2.5 billion people—will be under 18 years of age. Coca-Cola reaches this important market through the universal teen themes, such as music. ● For example, it joined forces with Spotify to provide a global music network that helps teens discover new music, connect with other music-loving teens, and share their experiences with friends worldwide both online and offline. And it's teen-focused "The Ahh Effect" digital campaign serves up "snackable pieces of content"—games, videos, and music—designed to engage the world's teens with the Coca-Cola brand. "The Aah Effect" is "that multidimensional feeling of happiness, satisfaction and delicious refreshment one experiences after drinking an ice-cold Coke—the sound a smile would make if smiles made sounds."[14]

Requirements for Effective Segmentation

Clearly, there are many ways to segment a market, but not all segmentations are effective. For example, buyers of table salt could be divided into blonde and brunette customers. But hair color obviously does not affect the purchase of salt. Furthermore, if all salt buyers bought the same amount of salt each month, believed that all salt is the same, and wanted to pay the same price, the company would not benefit from segmenting this market.

To be useful, market segments must be

- *Measurable.* The size, purchasing power, and profiles of the segments can be measured.
- *Accessible.* The market segments can be effectively reached and served.
- *Substantial.* The market segments are large or profitable enough to serve. A segment should be the largest possible homogeneous group worth pursuing with a tailored marketing program. It would not pay, for example, for an automobile manufacturer to develop cars especially for people whose height is greater than seven feet.
- *Differentiable.* The segments are conceptually distinguishable and respond differently to different marketing mix elements and programs. If men and women respond similarly to marketing efforts for soft drinks, they do not constitute separate segments.
- *Actionable.* Effective programs can be designed for attracting and serving the segments. For example, although one small airline identified seven market segments, its staff was too small to develop separate marketing programs for each segment.

Author Comment | After dividing the market into segments, it's time to answer that first seemingly simple marketing strategy question we raised in Figure 7.1: Which customers will the company serve?

Market Targeting

Market segmentation reveals the firm's market segment opportunities. The firm now has to evaluate the various segments and decide how many and which segments it can serve best. We now look at how companies evaluate and select target segments.

Evaluating Market Segments

In evaluating different market segments, a firm must look at three factors: segment size and growth, segment structural attractiveness, and company objectives and resources. First, a company wants to select segments that have the right size and growth characteristics. But "right size and growth" is a relative matter. The largest, fastest-growing segments are not always the most attractive ones for every company. Smaller companies may lack the skills and resources needed to serve larger segments. Or they may find these segments too competitive. Such companies may target segments that are smaller and less attractive, in an absolute sense, but that are potentially more profitable for them.

The company also needs to examine major structural factors that affect long-run segment attractiveness.[15] For example, a segment is less attractive if it already contains many strong and aggressive *competitors* or if it is easy for *new entrants* to come into the segment. The existence of many actual or potential *substitute products* may limit prices and the profits that can be earned in a segment. The relative *power of buyers* also affects segment attractiveness. Buyers with strong bargaining power relative to sellers will try to force prices down, demand more services, and set competitors against one another—all at the expense of seller profitability. Finally, a segment may be less attractive if it contains *powerful suppliers* that can control prices or reduce the quality or quantity of ordered goods and services.

Even if a segment has the right size and growth and is structurally attractive, the company must consider its own objectives and resources. Some attractive segments can be dismissed quickly because they do not mesh with the company's long-run objectives. Or the company may lack the skills and resources needed to succeed in an attractive segment. For example, the economy segment of the automobile market is large and growing. But given its objectives and resources, it would make little sense for luxury-performance carmaker Mercedes-Benz to enter this segment. A company should only enter segments in which it can create superior customer value and gain advantages over its competitors.

Selecting Target Market Segments

After evaluating different segments, the company must decide which and how many segments it will target. A **target market** consists of a set of buyers who share common needs or characteristics that a company decides to serve. Market targeting can be carried out at several different levels. ● **Figure 7.2** shows that companies can target very broadly (*undifferentiated marketing*), very narrowly (*micromarketing*), or somewhere in between (*differentiated or concentrated marketing*).

Target market

A set of buyers who share common needs or characteristics that a company decides to serve.

Undifferentiated Marketing

Using an **undifferentiated marketing** (or **mass marketing**) strategy, a firm might decide to ignore market segment differences and target the whole market with one offer. Such a strategy focuses on what is *common* in the needs of consumers rather than on what is *different*. The company designs a product and a marketing program that will appeal to the largest number of buyers.

As noted earlier in the chapter, most modern marketers have strong doubts about this strategy. Difficulties arise in developing a product or brand that will satisfy all consumers. Moreover, mass marketers often have trouble competing with more-focused firms that do a better job of satisfying the needs of specific segments and niches.

Undifferentiated (mass) marketing

A market-coverage strategy in which a firm decides to ignore market segment differences and go after the whole market with one offer.

Differentiated Marketing

Using a **differentiated marketing** (or **segmented marketing**) strategy, a firm decides to target several market segments and designs separate offers for each. For example, P&G

Differentiated (segmented) marketing

A market-coverage strategy in which a firm targets several market segments and designs separate offers for each.

● **FIGURE | 7.2**
Market-Targeting Strategies

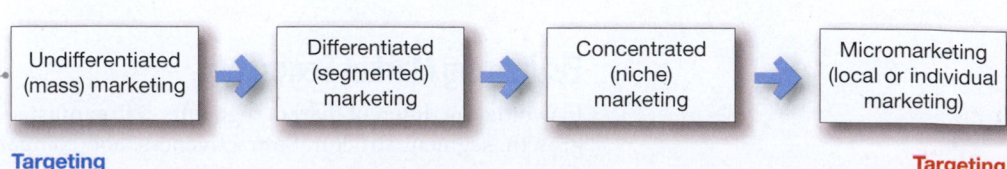

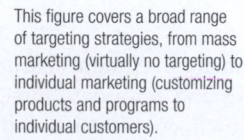

This figure covers a broad range of targeting strategies, from mass marketing (virtually no targeting) to individual marketing (customizing products and programs to individual customers).

Undifferentiated (mass) marketing → Differentiated (segmented) marketing → Concentrated (niche) marketing → Micromarketing (local or individual marketing)

Targeting broadly   **Targeting narrowly**

markets at least six different laundry detergent brands in the United States (Tide, Gain, Cheer, Era, Dreft, and Bold), which compete with each other on supermarket shelves. Then P&G further segments each detergent brand to serve even narrower niches. For example, you can buy any of dozens of versions of Tide—from Tide Original, Tide Coldwater, or Tide Pods to Tide Free & Gentle, Tide Vivid White + Bright, Tide Colorguard, Tide plus Febreze, or Tide with a Touch of Downy.

● **Differentiated marketing: P&G markets multiple laundry detergent brands, then further segments each brand to service even narrower niches. As a result, it's really cleaning up in the U.S. laundry detergent market, with an almost 60 percent market share.**

© Torontonian / Alamy Stock Photo

By offering product and marketing variations to segments, companies hope for higher sales and a stronger position within each market segment. Developing a stronger position within several segments creates more total sales than undifferentiated marketing across all segments. Thanks to its differentiated approach, P&G is really cleaning up in the $15 billion U.S. laundry detergent market. ● Incredibly, by itself, the Tide family of brands captures a 38 percent share of all North American detergent sales; the Gain brand pulls in another 15 percent. Even more incredible, all P&G detergent brands combined capture a 60 percent U.S. market share.[16]

But differentiated marketing also increases the costs of doing business. A firm usually finds it more expensive to develop and produce, say, 10 units of 10 different products than 100 units of a single product. Developing separate marketing plans for separate segments requires extra marketing research, forecasting, sales analysis, promotion planning, and channel management. And trying to reach different market segments with different advertising campaigns increases promotion costs. Thus, the company must weigh increased sales against increased costs when deciding on a differentiated marketing strategy.

Concentrated Marketing

Concentrated (niche) marketing
A market-coverage strategy in which a firm goes after a large share of one or a few segments or niches.

When using a **concentrated marketing** (or **niche marketing**) strategy, instead of going after a small share of a large market, a firm goes after a large share of one or a few smaller segments or niches. ● For example, consider nicher Stance Socks:[17]

"Rihanna designs them, Jay Z sings about them, and the rest of the world can't seem to get enough of Stance socks," says one observer. They've even become the official on-court sock of the NBA and a favorite of many professional players on game day. Nicher Stance sells socks and only socks. Yet it's thriving in the shadows of much larger competitors who sell socks mostly as a sideline. Five years ago, Stance's founders discovered socks as a large but largely overlooked and undervalued market. While walking through the sock section a local Target store, says Stance's CEO and cofounder, Jeff Kearl, "It was like, black, white, brown, and gray—with some argyle—in plastic bags. I thought, we could totally [reinvent] socks, because everyone was ignoring them."

So Stance set out to breathe new life into the sock category by creating technically superior socks that also offered fun, style, and status. Mission accomplished. You'll now find colorful displays of Stance's comfortable but quirky socks in stores in more than 40 countries, from the local surf shop to Foot Locker to Nordstrom, Bloomingdale's, and Macy's. Selling at prices ranging from $10 to $40 a pair, Stance sold an estimated 12 million pairs of socks last year. That's small potatoes for giant competitors such as Hanes or Nike, but it's nicely profitable for nicher Stance. Next up? Another often overlooked niche—Stance men's underwear.

Through concentrated marketing, the firm achieves a strong market position because of its greater knowledge of consumer needs in the niches it serves and the special reputation it acquires. It can market more *effectively* by fine-tuning its products, prices, and programs to the needs of carefully defined segments. It can also market more *efficiently*, targeting its products or services, channels, and communications programs toward only consumers that it can serve best and most profitably.

● **Concentrated marketing: Innovative nicher Stance Socks thrives in the shadows of larger competitors.**

Stance, Inc.

Niching lets smaller companies focus their limited resources on serving niches that may be unimportant to or overlooked by larger competitors. Many companies start as nichers to get a foothold against larger, more resourceful competitors and then grow into broader competitors. For example, Southwest Airlines began by serving intrastate, no-frills commuters in Texas but is now one of the nation's largest airlines. And Enterprise Rent-A-Car began by building a network of neighborhood offices rather than competing with Hertz and Avis in airport locations. Enterprise is now the nation's largest car rental company.

Today, the low cost of setting up shop on the internet makes it even more profitable to serve seemingly small niches. Small businesses, in particular, are realizing riches from serving niches on the web. ● Consider online women's fashion retailer Stitch Fix:[18]

Stitch Fix offers affordable personal styling services online to busy women on the go. It positions itself as "Your partner in personal style." Although "personal service" and "online" might seem a contradiction, Stitch Fix pulls it off with a team of more than 2,000 personal stylists who apply a sophisticated algorithm to determine each customer's unique sense of style. A customer begins by filling out a detailed style profile that goes far beyond the usual sizing charts. It probes personal preferences with questions such as "What do you like to flaunt?" and "How adventurous do you want your Fix selections to be?" (One answer choice: "Frequently: Adventure is my middle name, bring it on!") The customer also rates photo montages of different fashions and can even submit links to her own Pinterest pages or other social media.

Combining the algorithm with large doses of human judgment (the stylist may completely override the algorithm), the personal stylist assembles and ships the customer's first fashion "Fix"—a box containing five clothing or accessory items pegged to the customer's special tastes. "Our professional stylists will pick out items they think you'll love—sometimes a little out of your comfort zone, but that's part of the fun," says the company. The customer keeps what she likes and returns the rest, along with detailed feedback. The first Fix is the hardest because the stylist and algorithm are still learning. But after that, the Stitch Fix experience becomes downright addictive for many shoppers. More than 80 percent of customers visit the site within 90 days for a second order, and one-third spend 50 percent of their clothing budget with Stitch Fix. Thanks to the power and personalization qualities of the internet, Stitch Fix is attracting attention and growing fast. The online nicher has inspired a virtual army of pro–Stitch Fix blog and social media posters, and its revenues have skyrocketed to more than $200 million annually.

● **Online niching:** Thanks to the power and personalization characteristics of online marketing, online women's fashion retailer Stitch Fix is attracting attention and growing fast.

STITCH FIX and FIX are trademarks of Stitch Fix, Inc.

Concentrated marketing can be highly profitable. At the same time, it involves higher-than-normal risks. Companies that rely on one or a few segments for all of their business will suffer greatly if the segment turns sour. Or larger competitors may decide to enter the same segment with greater resources. In fact, many large companies develop or acquire niche brands of their own. For example, Coca-Cola's Venturing and Emerging Brands unit markets a cooler full of niche beverages. Its brands include Honest Tea (the nation's number-one organic bottled tea brand), NOS (an energy drink popular among auto enthusiasts), FUZE (a fusion of tea, fruit, and other flavors), Zico (pure premium coconut water), Odwalla (natural beverages and bars that "bring goodness to your life"), Fairlife (unfiltered milk), and many others. Such brands let Coca-Cola compete effectively in smaller, specialized markets, and some will grow into future powerhouse brands.[19]

Micromarketing

Micromarketing
Tailoring products and marketing programs to the needs and wants of specific individuals and local customer segments; it includes *local marketing* and *individual marketing*.

Differentiated and concentrated marketers tailor their offers and marketing programs to meet the needs of various market segments and niches. At the same time, however, they do not customize their offers to each individual customer. **Micromarketing** is the practice of tailoring products and marketing programs to suit the tastes of specific individuals and local customer segments. Rather than seeing a customer in every individual, micromarketers see the individual in every customer. Micromarketing includes *local marketing* and *individual marketing*.

Local marketing
Tailoring brands and marketing to the needs and wants of local customer segments—cities, neighborhoods, and even specific stores.

Local Marketing. **Local marketing** involves tailoring brands and promotions to the needs and wants of local customers. For example, Marriott's Renaissance Hotels has rolled out its Navigator program, which hyper-localizes guest experiences at each of its 155 lifestyle hotels around the world:[20]

● **Geographic segmentation: Marriott's Renaissance Hotels' Navigators and "Live Life to Discover" program help guests to experience "the hidden gems around the unique neighborhood of each hotel through the eyes of those who know it best."**

Renaissance Hotels, Marriott International, Marriott Rewards. Renaissance is a registered trademark of Marriott International, Inc.

Renaissance Hotels' Navigator program puts a personal and local face on each location by "micro-localizing" recommendations for guests' food, shopping, entertainment, and cultural experiences at each destination. The program is anchored by on-site Renaissance Hotels "Navigators" at each location. Whether it's Omar Bennett, a restaurant-loving Brooklynite at the Renaissance New York Times Square Hotel, or James Elliott at the St. Pancras Renaissance London Hotel, a history buff and local pub expert, Navigators are extensively trained locals who are deeply passionate about the destination and often have a personal connection to the locale. ● Based on 100-plus hours of intense training plus their own personal experiences and ongoing research, they work with guests personally to help them experience "the hidden gems throughout the neighborhood of each hotel through the eyes of those who know it best."

In addition, Renaissance Hotels engages locals in each city to participate by inviting them to follow their local Navigator via social media as well as adding their own favorites to the system, creating each hotel's own version of Yelp. Navigators then cull through submitted tips and feature the best recommendations alongside their own for sharing within the hotel lobby or on its web, mobile, and social media channels. Since introducing the hyper-localized Navigator program as part of Renaissance Hotels' "Live Life to Discover" campaign two years ago, the hotel's website traffic has grown more than 80 percent, Facebook Likes have exploded from 40,000 to more than 900,000, and Twitter followers have surged from 5,000 to 110,000.

Advances in communications technology have given rise to new high-tech versions of location-based marketing. Thanks to the explosion in smartphones and tablets that integrate geolocation technology, companies can now track consumers' whereabouts closely and engage them on the go with localized deals and information fast, wherever they may be. It's called *SoLoMo (social+local+mobile)* marketing. Services such as Foursquare and Shopkick and retailers ranging from REI and Starbucks to Walgreens and Macy's have jumped onto the SoLoMo bandwagon, primarily in the form of smartphone and tablet apps. Mobile app Shopkick excels at SoLoMo:[21]

Shopkick sends special offers and rewards to shoppers simply for checking into client stores such as Target, Macy's, Best Buy, Old Navy, or Crate & Barrel and buying brands from Shopkick partners such as P&G, Unilever, Disney, Kraft, and L'Oréal. When shoppers are near a participating store, the Shopkick app on their phone picks up a signal from the store and spits out store coupons, deal alerts, and product information. When Shopkickers walk into their favorite retail stores, the app automatically checks them in and they rack up rewards points or "kicks." If they buy something or scan product bar codes, they get even more kicks. Users can use their kicks for discounted or free merchandise of their own choosing. Shopkick helps users get the most out of their efforts by mapping out potential kicks in a given geographic area. Shopkick has grown quickly to become one of the nation's top shopping apps, with more 15 million users and 300 brand partners.

Local marketing has some drawbacks, however. It can drive up manufacturing and marketing costs by reducing the economies of scale. It can also create logistics problems as companies try to meet the varied requirements of different local markets. Still, as companies face increasingly fragmented markets and as new supporting digital technologies develop, the advantages of local marketing often outweigh the drawbacks.

Individual marketing
Tailoring products and marketing programs to the needs and preferences of individual customers.

Individual Marketing. In the extreme, micromarketing becomes **individual marketing**—tailoring products and marketing programs to the needs and preferences of individual customers. Individual marketing has also been labeled one-to-one marketing, mass customization, and markets-of-one marketing.

The widespread use of mass marketing has obscured the fact that for centuries consumers were served as individuals: The tailor custom-made a suit, the cobbler designed shoes for an individual, and the cabinetmaker made furniture to order. Today, new technologies are permitting many companies to return to customized marketing. Detailed databases, robotic production and flexible manufacturing, and interactive technologies such as smartphones and online and social media have combined to foster mass customization. *Mass customization* is the process by which firms interact one to one with masses of customers to design products, services, and marketing programs tailor-made to individual needs.

Companies these days are hyper-customizing everything from food, artwork, earphones, and sneakers to high-end luxury products. At one end of the spectrum, candy lovers can go to mymms.com and buy M&Ms with personalized messages or pictures embossed on each little candy. Visit Nike ID or Puma Factory online to design and order your very own personalized sneakers. JH Audio in Orlando makes customized earphones based on molds of customers' ears to provide optimized fit and better and safer sound. The company even laser-prints designs on the tiny ear buds—some people request a kid for each ear; others prefer a dog.

At the other extreme are "bespoke" luxury goods (a fancy word for "custom-made" or "made to order"). For the right price, well-heeled customers can buy custom-designed goods ranging from bespoke fashions and accessories by Hermes and Gucci to bespoke cars from Aston Martin or Rolls-Royce.[22]

● Ninety-five percent of Rolls-Royce buyers customize their cars in some way. Customers can sit down with a Rolls-Royce Bespoke design team—color experts, leather-smiths, master woodworkers—in a lounge filled with images, materials, and other inspirational elements to design their own unique Rolls-Royces. Want to match the exterior paint and interior leather to your favorite pale pink leather gloves? No problem. Want to customize your door handles, have your initials and a meaningful logo stitched into the headrests, or install mother-of-pearl inlays, crocodile skin seating, rabbit-pelt linings, or mahogany trim? Easily done. One customer even wanted his car's interior trim to be made from a favorite tree that had recently fallen on his estate. After analyzing a sample, a Rolls-Royce craftsman deemed the wood acceptable and the customer's tree will now live forever in the dash and door panels of his custom Rolls-Royce. "Outside of compromising the safety of the car—or disfiguring the Spirit of Ecstasy—we won't say no," says a Rolls-Royce executive.

● **Individual marketing: The Rolls-Royce Bespoke design team works closely with individual customers to help them create their own unique Rolls-Royces. "Outside of compromising the safety of the car—or disfiguring the Spirit of Ecstasy—we won't say no."**
Associated Press

Beyond customizing products, marketers also customize their marketing messages to engage customers on a one-to-one basis. For example, Nike collected data on its most enthusiastic customers, those who train using FuelBands and apps such as Nike+ Running. It then used the data to create 100,000 customized animated videos based on each individual's actual workout activities. For example, one video might feature an animation of a person in Los Angeles running past the Hollywood sign; another might show a New Yorker running in the rain along the East River. Nike then emailed the unique customized videos to each of the 100,000 Nike+ users, challenging them to achieve new heights in the coming year. The videos not only engaged Nike's biggest fans, they also spread to the broader Nike community. "These are some of the most social people on the planet," says one campaign manager. "They share like crazy. So that becomes a pretty awesome flagship marketing move for Nike."[23]

Choosing a Targeting Strategy

Companies need to consider many factors when choosing a market-targeting strategy. Which strategy is best depends on the company's resources. When the firm's resources are limited, concentrated marketing makes the most sense. The best strategy also depends on the degree of product variability. Undifferentiated marketing is more suited for uniform products, such as grapefruit or steel. Products that can vary in design, such as cameras and cars, are more suited to differentiation or concentration. The product's life-cycle stage also must be considered. When a firm introduces a new product, it may be practical to launch one version only, and undifferentiated marketing or concentrated marketing may make the most sense. In the mature stage of the product life cycle, however, differentiated marketing often makes more sense.

Another factor is *market variability*. If most buyers have the same tastes, buy the same amounts, and react the same way to marketing efforts, undifferentiated marketing is appropriate. Finally, *competitors' marketing strategies* should be considered. When competitors use differentiated or concentrated marketing, undifferentiated marketing can be suicidal. Conversely, when competitors use undifferentiated marketing, a firm can gain an advantage by using differentiated or concentrated marketing, focusing on the needs of buyers in specific segments.

Socially Responsible Target Marketing

Smart targeting helps companies become more efficient and effective by focusing on the segments that they can satisfy best and most profitably. Targeting also benefits consumers—companies serve specific groups of consumers with offers carefully tailored to their needs. However, target marketing sometimes generates controversy and concern. The biggest issues usually involve the targeting of vulnerable or disadvantaged consumers with controversial or potentially harmful products.

For example, fast-food chains have generated controversy over the years by their attempts to target inner-city minority consumers. They've been accused of pitching their high-fat, salt-laden fare to low-income, urban residents who are much more likely than suburbanites to be heavy consumers. Similarly, big banks and mortgage lenders have been criticized for targeting consumers in poor urban areas with attractive adjustable-rate home mortgages that they can't really afford.

Children are seen as an especially vulnerable audience. Marketers in a wide range of industries—from cereal, soft drinks, and fast food to toys and fashion—have been criticized for their marketing efforts directed toward children. Critics worry that enticing premium offers and high-powered advertising appeals will overwhelm children's defenses. In recent years, for instance, McDonald's has been criticized by various health advocates and parent groups concerned that its popular Happy Meals offers—featuring trinkets and other items tied in with popular children's movies and TV shows—create a too-powerful connection between children and less-healthy eating. McDonald's has responded by putting the Happy Meal on a diet, cutting the overall calorie count by 20 percent, adding fruit to every meal, and promoting Happy Meals only with milk, water, and juice. And for a two-week span each year, McDonald's replaces the toys in its Happy Meals with children's books.[24]

The digital era may make children even more vulnerable to targeted marketing messages. Traditional child-directed TV and print ads usually contain fairly obvious pitches that are easily detected and controlled by parents. However, marketing in digital media may be subtly embedded within the content and viewed by children on personal, small-screen devices that are beyond even the most watchful parent's eye. In digital platforms, the lines between educational, entertainment, and commercial content are often blurred. Thus, as children consume increasing amounts of online and digital content, one expert advises that kids "shouldn't be entirely left to their own devices."[25]

More broadly, the growth of the internet, smartphones, and other carefully targeted direct media has raised fresh concerns about potential targeting abuses. The internet and mobile marketing allow more precise targeting, letting the makers of questionable products or deceptive advertisers zero in on the most vulnerable audiences. Unscrupulous marketers can now send tailor-made, deceptive messages by email directly to millions of unsuspecting consumers. For example, the Federal Bureau of Investigation's Internet Crime Complaint Center website alone received more than 269,000 complaints last year.[26]

Today's marketers are also using sophisticated analytical techniques to track consumers' digital movements and to build amazingly detailed customer profiles containing highly personal information. Such profiles can then be used to hypertarget individual consumers with personalized brand messages and offers. However, with such targeting, marketers often walk a fine line between serving customers better and stalking them:

How well does your smartphone know you? What stories could your laptop tell? In truth, your digital devices probably know more about you than you know about yourself. Smartphones and other digital equipment have become fundamental extensions of our lives. Whatever you do—at work, at play, socializing, shopping—your phone, tablet, laptop, or desktop is almost always a part of the action. These devices go where you go, entertain you, connect you with friends, take you browsing and shopping, feed you news and information, and listen in on even your most intimate voice, text, and email conversations. And more and more, these devices are sharing all that personal information with marketers. Companies have now developed sophisticated new ways that border on wizardry to extract intimate insights about consumers. For brands and marketers, such information is pure gold.

Marketers argue that using all of this up-close-and-personal information better serves both customers and a company. Customers receive tailored, relevant information and offers from brands that really understand and interest them. However, many consumers and privacy advocates are concerned that such intimate information in the hands of unscrupulous marketers could result in more harm than benefit to consumers. ● They often view big data and hypertargeting less as "getting to know consumers better to serve them better" and more as "stalking" consumers and "profiling" them. Although most consumers are willing to share some personal information if it means getting better service or deals, many consumers worry that marketers might go too far.

● **Hypertargeting: Marketers have developed sophisticated new ways to extract intimate insights about consumers that border on wizardry. But hypertargeting walks a fine line between "serving" consumers and "stalking" them.**

Andrew Bret Wallis/Getty Images

Thus, in target marketing, the issue is not really *who* is targeted but rather *how* and for *what*. Controversies arise when marketers attempt to profit at the expense of targeted segments—when they unfairly target vulnerable segments or target them with questionable products or tactics. Socially responsible marketing calls for segmentation and targeting that serve not just the interests of the company but also the interests of those targeted.

Author Comment | At the same time that a company is answering the first simple-sounding question (Which customers will we serve?), it must also be asking the second question (How will we serve them?).

Product position

The way a product is defined by consumers on important attributes—the place it occupies in consumers' minds relative to competing products.

Differentiation and Positioning

Beyond deciding which segments of the market it will target, the company must decide on a *value proposition*—how it will create differentiated value for targeted segments and what positions it wants to occupy in those segments. A **product position** is the way a product is *defined by consumers* on important attributes—the place the product occupies in consumers' minds relative to competing products. Products are made in factories, but brands happen in the minds of consumers.

Method laundry detergent is positioned as a smarter, easier, and greener detergent; Tide is "a washing miracle," an all-purpose, heavy-duty family detergent that gets out grime and tough stains. Your Visa card is "Everywhere you want to be"; with American Express, "The Journey Never Stops." At IHOP, you "Come hungry. Leave happy"; at Buffalo Wild Wings, it's "Wings. Beer. Sports." In the automobile market, the Honda Fit and Nissan Versa are positioned on economy, Mercedes and Cadillac on luxury, and Porsche and BMW on performance. Home-improvement store Lowe's helps you "Never

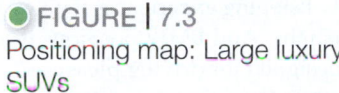 **Positioning: IKEA does more than just sell affordable home furnishings: it's the "Life improvement store."**

Used with the permission of Inter IKEA Systems B.V.

stop improving." ● And IKEA does more than just sell affordable home furnishings; it's the "Life improvement store."

Consumers are overloaded with information about products and services. They cannot reevaluate products every time they make a buying decision. To simplify the buying process, consumers organize products, services, and companies into categories and "position" them in their minds. A product's position is the complex set of perceptions, impressions, and feelings that consumers have for the product compared with competing products.

Consumers position products with or without the help of marketers. But marketers do not want to leave their products' positions to chance. They must *plan* positions that will give their products the greatest advantage in selected target markets, and they must design marketing mixes to create these planned positions.

Positioning Maps

In planning their differentiation and positioning strategies, marketers often prepare *perceptual positioning maps* that show consumer perceptions of their brands versus those of competing products on important buying dimensions. ● **Figure 7.3** shows a positioning map for the U.S. large luxury SUV market.[27] The position of each circle on the map indicates the brand's perceived positioning on two dimensions: price and orientation (luxury versus performance). The size of each circle indicates the brand's relative market share.

Thus, customers view the market-leading Cadillac Escalade as a moderately priced, large, luxury SUV with a balance of luxury and performance. The Escalade is positioned on urban luxury, and in its case, "performance" probably means power and safety performance. You'll find no mention of off-road adventuring in an Escalade ad.

By contrast, the Range Rover and the Land Cruiser are positioned on luxury with nuances of off-road performance. For example, the Toyota Land Cruiser began in 1951 as a four-wheel-drive, jeep-like vehicle designed to conquer the world's most grueling terrains and climates. In recent years, the Land Cruiser has retained this adventure and performance positioning but with luxury added. Its website brags of "legendary off-road capability," with off-road technologies such as an Acoustic Control Induction System to get the most out of the RPMs, "so you can make molehills out of mountains." Despite its ruggedness, however, the company notes that "its Bluetooth hands-free technology, DVD entertainment, and a sumptuous interior have softened its edges."

● **FIGURE | 7.3**

Positioning map: Large luxury SUVs

The location of each circle shows where consumers position a brand on two dimensions: price and luxury-performance orientation. The size of each circle indicates the brand's relative market share in the segment. Thus, Toyota's Land Cruiser is a niche brand that is perceived to be relatively expensive and more performance oriented.

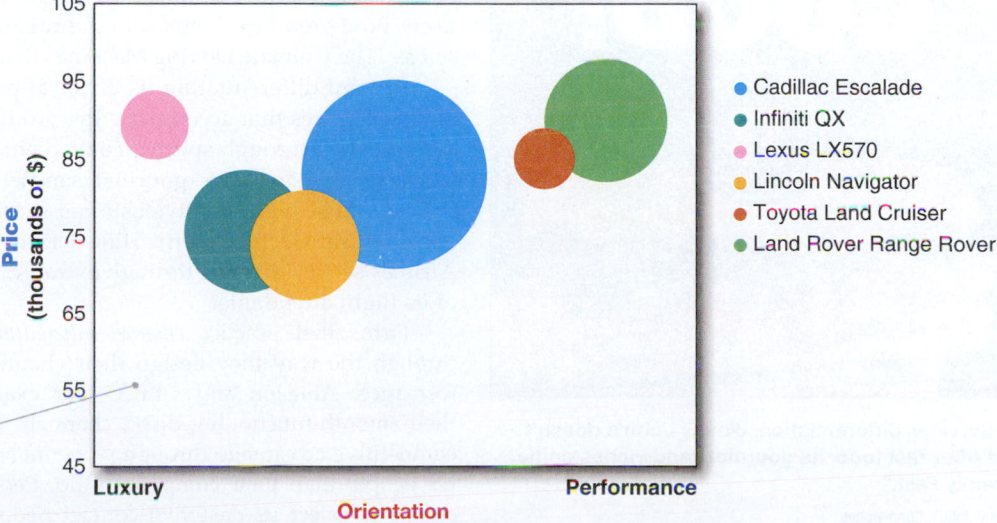

Choosing a Differentiation and Positioning Strategy

Some firms find it easy to choose a differentiation and positioning strategy. For example, a firm well known for quality in certain segments will go after this position in a new segment if there are enough buyers seeking quality. But in many cases, two or more firms will go after the same position. Then each will have to find other ways to set itself apart. Each firm must differentiate its offer by building a unique bundle of benefits that appeal to a substantial group within the segment.

Above all else, a brand's positioning must serve the needs and preferences of well-defined target markets. For example, as discussed in the chapter-opening story, although both Dunkin' Donuts and Starbucks are coffee and snack shops, they target very different customers who want very different things from their favorite coffee seller. Starbucks targets more upscale professionals with more high-brow positioning. In contrast, Dunkin' Donuts targets the "average Joe" with a decidedly more low-brow, "everyman" kind of positioning. Yet each brand succeeds because it creates just the right value proposition for its unique mix of customers.

The differentiation and positioning task consists of three steps: identifying a set of differentiating competitive advantages on which to build a position, choosing the right competitive advantages, and selecting an overall positioning strategy. The company must then effectively communicate and deliver the chosen position to the market.

Identifying Possible Value Differences and Competitive Advantages

To build profitable relationships with target customers, marketers must understand customer needs and deliver more customer value better than competitors do. To the extent that a company can differentiate and position itself as providing superior customer value, it gains **competitive advantage**.

Competitive advantage
An advantage over competitors gained by offering greater customer value either by having lower prices or providing more benefits that justify higher prices.

But solid positions cannot be built on empty promises. If a company positions its product as *offering* the best quality and service, it must actually differentiate the product so that it *delivers* the promised quality and service. Companies must do much more than simply shout out their positions with slogans and taglines. They must first *live* the slogan. For example, online shoes and accessories seller Zappos's "powered by service" positioning would ring hollow if not backed by truly outstanding customer care. Zappos aligns its entire organization and all of its people around providing the best possible customer service. The online seller's number-one core value: "Deliver WOW through service."[28]

To find points of differentiation, marketers must think through the customer's entire experience with the company's product or service. An alert company can find ways to differentiate itself at every customer contact point. In what specific ways can a company differentiate itself or its market offer? It can differentiate along the lines of *product, services, channels, people,* or *image.*

Through *product differentiation,* brands can be differentiated on features, performance, or style and design. Thus, premium audio brand Bose positions its audio products on the innovative, high-quality listening experiences it gives users. Bose promises "better sound through research." And BMW positions itself as "The Ultimate Driving Machine" that's "designed for driving pleasure."

Beyond differentiating its physical product, a firm can also differentiate the services that accompany the product. Some companies gain *services differentiation* through speedy, convenient service. ● Jimmy John's doesn't just offer fast food; its gourmet sandwiches come "Freaky Fast." Other firms promise high-quality customer service. For example, in an age where customer satisfaction with airline service is in constant decline, Singapore Airlines sets itself apart through extraordinary customer care and the grace of its flight attendants.

Firms that practice *channel differentiation* gain competitive advantage through the way they design their channel's coverage, expertise, and performance. Amazon and GEICO, for example, set themselves apart with their smooth-functioning direct channels. Companies can also gain a strong competitive advantage through *people differentiation*—hiring and training better people than their competitors do. People differentiation requires that a company select its customer-contact people carefully and train them well.

● Services differentiation: Jimmy John's doesn't just offer fast food; its gourmet sandwiches come "Freaky Fast."

Jimmy John's Sandwiches

For example, East Coast supermarket chain Wegmans has long been recognized as a customer service champ with a cult-like loyalty among its shoppers. The secret to its extraordinary customer service lies in its carefully selected, superbly trained, happy employees, who personify Wegmans's commitment to customers: "Everyday You Get Your Best." For example, the chain's cashiers aren't allowed to interact with customers until they've had at least 40 hours of training. "Our employees are our number one asset," says the chain's vice president for human resources.[29]

Even when competing offers look the same, buyers may perceive a difference based on company or brand *image differentiation*. A company or brand image should convey a product's distinctive benefits and positioning. Developing a strong and distinctive image calls for creativity and hard work. A company cannot develop an image in the public's mind overnight by using only a few ads. If Ritz-Carlton means quality, this image must be supported by everything the company is, says, and does.

Symbols, such as the McDonald's golden arches, the colorful Google logo, the Twitter bird, the Nike swoosh, or Apple's "bite mark" logo, can provide strong company or brand recognition and image differentiation. The company might build a brand around a famous person, as Nike did with its Michael Jordan, Kobe Bryant, and LeBron James basketball shoe and apparel collections. Some companies even become associated with colors, such as Coca-Cola (red), IBM (blue), or UPS (brown). The chosen symbols, characters, and other image elements must be communicated through advertising that conveys the company's or brand's personality.

Choosing the Right Competitive Advantages

Suppose a company is fortunate enough to discover several potential differentiations that provide competitive advantages. It now must choose the ones on which it will build its positioning strategy. It must decide how many differences to promote and which ones.

How Many Differences to Promote. Many marketers think that companies should aggressively promote only one benefit to the target market. Former advertising executive Rosser Reeves, for example, said a company should develop a *unique selling proposition (USP)* for each brand and stick to it. Each brand should pick an attribute and tout itself as "number one" on that attribute. Buyers tend to remember number one better, especially in this overcommunicated society. Thus, Walmart promotes its unbeatable low prices and Burger King promotes personal choice—"have it your way."

Other marketers think that companies should position themselves on more than one differentiator. This may be necessary if two or more firms are claiming to be best on the same attribute. For example, with its "Expect More. Pay Less." positioning, Targets sets itself apart from Walmart by adding a touch of class to its low prices. And Microsoft differentiates its innovative Surface tablet as being both a laptop and tablet in one. It's the "One device for everything in your life"—lighter and thinner than a laptop but with a click-in keyboard and fuller features than competing tablets. It's "Powerful as a laptop, lighter than Air." Microsoft's challenge is to convince buyers that it's one brand can do it all.

Today, in a time when the mass market is fragmenting into many small segments, companies and brands are trying to broaden their positioning strategies to appeal to more segments.

Which Differences to Promote. Not all brand differences are meaningful or worthwhile, and each difference has the potential to create company costs as well as customer benefits. A difference is worth establishing to the extent that it satisfies the following criteria:

- *Important*. The difference delivers a highly valued benefit to target buyers.
- *Distinctive*. Competitors do not offer the difference, or the company can offer it in a more distinctive way.
- *Superior*. The difference is superior to other ways that customers might obtain the same benefit.
- *Communicable*. The difference is communicable and visible to buyers.
- *Preemptive*. Competitors cannot easily copy the difference.
- *Affordable*. Buyers can afford to pay for the difference.
- *Profitable*. The company can introduce the difference profitably.

Many companies have introduced differentiations that failed one or more of these tests. When the Westin Stamford Hotel in Singapore once advertised itself as the world's tallest hotel, it was a distinction that was not important to most tourists; in fact, it turned many off. Similarly, Coca-Cola's classic product failure—New Coke—failed the superiority and importance tests among core Coca-Cola drinkers:

> Extensive blind taste tests showed that 60 percent of all soft drink consumers chose a new, sweeter Coca-Cola formulation over the original Coke, and 52 percent chose it over Pepsi. So the brand dropped its original-formula Coke and, with much fanfare, replaced it with New Coke, a sweeter, smoother version. However, in its research, Coca-Cola overlooked the many intangibles that have made Coca-Cola so popular for 130 years. To loyal Coke drinkers, the original beverage stands alongside baseball, apple pie, and the Statue of Liberty as an American institution. As it turns out, Coca-Cola differentiates its brand not just by taste but by tradition. By dropping the original formula, Coca-Cola trampled on the sensitivities of the huge core of loyal Coke drinkers who loved Coke just the way it was. After only three months, the company brought the classic Coke back.

Thus, choosing competitive advantages on which to position a product or service can be difficult, yet such choices are crucial to success. Choosing the right differentiators can help a brand stand out from the pack of competitors.

Selecting an Overall Positioning Strategy

Value proposition

The full positioning of a brand—the full mix of benefits on which it is positioned.

The full positioning of a brand is called the brand's **value proposition**—the full mix of benefits on which a brand is differentiated and positioned. It is the answer to the customer's question "Why should I buy your brand?" BMW's "ultimate driving machine/ designed for driving pleasure" value proposition hinges on performance but also includes luxury and styling, all for a price that is higher than average but seems fair for this mix of benefits.

● **Figure 7.4** shows possible value propositions on which a company might position its products. In the figure, the five green cells on the top and right represent winning value propositions—differentiation and positioning that give the company a competitive advantage. The red cells at the lower left, however, represent losing value propositions. The center cell represents at best a marginal proposition. In the following sections, we discuss the five winning value propositions: more for more, more for the same, the same for less, less for much less, and more for less.

More for More. *More-for-more* positioning involves providing the most upscale product or service and charging a higher price to cover the higher costs. A more-for-more market offering not only offers higher quality, it also gives prestige to the buyer. It symbolizes status and a loftier lifestyle. Four Seasons hotels, Patek Philippe watches, Starbucks coffee, Louis Vuitton handbags, Mercedes automobiles, SubZero appliances—each claims superior quality, craftsmanship, durability, performance, or style and therefore charges a higher price.

Similarly, the marketers of Hearts On Fire diamonds have created a more-for-more niche as "The World's Most Perfectly Cut Diamond." ● Hearts On Fire diamonds have a unique "hearts and arrow" design. When viewed under magnification from the bottom, a

● FIGURE | 7.4

Possible value propositions

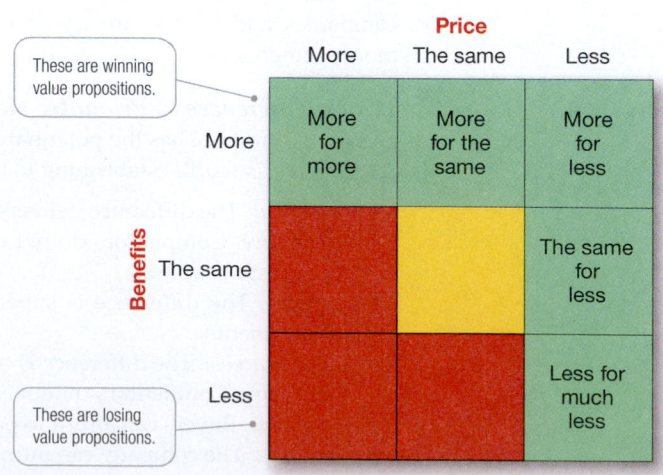

● More-for-more positioning: Hearts On Fire diamonds have created a more-for-more niche as "The World's Most Perfectly Cut Diamond—for those who expect more and give more in return."

Used with permission of Hearts On Fire Company, LLC

perfect ring of eight hearts appears; from the top comes a perfectly formed Fireburst of light. Hearts On Fire diamonds aren't for everyone, says the company. "Hearts On Fire is for those who expect more and give more in return." The brand commands a 15 to 20 percent price premium over comparable competing diamonds.[30]

Although more-for-more can be profitable, this strategy can also be vulnerable. It often invites imitators who claim the same quality but at a lower price. For example, more-for-more brand Starbucks now faces "gourmet" coffee competitors ranging from Dunkin' Donuts to McDonald's. Also, luxury goods that sell well during good times may be at risk during economic downturns when buyers become more cautious in their spending. The recent gloomy economy hit premium brands, such as Starbucks, the hardest.

More for the Same. A company can attack a competitor's value proposition by positioning its brand as offering more for the same price. For example, Target positions itself as the "upscale discounter." It claims to offer more in terms of store atmosphere, service, stylish merchandise, and classy brand image but at prices comparable to those of Walmart, Kohl's, and other discounters.

The Same for Less. Offering *the same for less* can be a powerful value proposition—everyone likes a good deal. Discount stores such as Walmart and "category killers" such as Best Buy, PetSmart, David's Bridal, and DSW Shoes use this positioning. They don't claim to offer different or better products. Instead, they offer many of the same brands as department stores and specialty stores but at deep discounts based on superior purchasing power and lower-cost operations. Other companies develop imitative but lower-priced brands in an effort to lure customers away from the market leader. For example, Amazon offers a line of Kindle Fire tablets, which sell for less than 40 percent of the price of the Apple iPad or Samsung Galaxy tablet. Amazon claims that it offers "Premium products at non-premium prices."

Less for Much Less. A market almost always exists for products that offer less and therefore cost less. Few people need, want, or can afford "the very best" in everything they buy. In many cases, consumers will gladly settle for less-than-optimal performance or give up some of the bells and whistles in exchange for a lower price. For example, many travelers seeking lodgings prefer not to pay for what they consider unnecessary extras, such as a pool, an attached restaurant, or mints on the pillow. Hotel chains such as Ramada Limited, Holiday Inn Express, and Motel 6 suspend some of these amenities and charge less accordingly.

Less-for-much-less positioning involves meeting consumers' lower performance or quality requirements at a much lower price. For example, Costco warehouse stores offer less merchandise selection and consistency and much lower levels of service; as a result, they charge rock-bottom prices. Similarly, at ALDI grocery stores, customers pay super-low prices but must settle for less in terms of the service extras. "You can't eat frills," says ALDI, "so why pay for them?" (See Real Marketing 7.2.)

More for Less. Of course, the winning value proposition would be to offer *more for less*. Many companies claim to do this. And, in the short run, some companies can actually achieve such lofty positions. For example, when it first opened for business, Home Depot had arguably the best product selection, the best service, *and* the lowest prices compared with local hardware stores and other home-improvement chains.

Yet in the long run, companies will no doubt find it very difficult to sustain such best-of-both positioning. Offering more usually costs more, making it difficult to deliver on the "for-less" promise. Companies that try to deliver both may lose out to more focused competitors. For example, facing determined competition from Lowe's stores, Home Depot must now decide whether it wants to compete primarily on superior service or on lower prices.

All said, each brand must adopt a positioning strategy designed to serve the needs and wants of its target markets. *More for more* will draw one target market, *less for much less* will draw another, and so on. In any market, there is usually room for many different

7.2 ALDI's Less-for-Much-Less Value Proposition: You Can't Eat Frills, So Why Pay for Them?

When asked to name the world's largest grocery chains, you'd probably come up with Walmart, the world's largest retailer, and maybe Kroger, the largest U.S. grocery-only merchant. One name that probably wouldn't come to mind is Germany-based discount grocer ALDI. Yet, surprisingly, with more than $81 billion in annual revenues and more than 10,000 stores in 17 countries, ALDI is the world's eighth-largest retailer overall and the second-largest grocery-only retailer behind Kroger. What's more, ALDI is taking the United States and other country markets by storm, growing faster than any of its larger rivals.

How does ALDI do it? With a simple less-for-much-less value proposition. At ALDI you get less, but you pay much less for it. The chain gives customers a basic assortment of good-quality everyday items with no-frills service at everyday extra-low prices. These days, many grocers brag about low prices. But at ALDI, they are an absolute fact. The rapidly expanding chain promises customers "Simply Smarter Shopping," driven by a long list of "ALDI Truths" by which it delivers "impressively high quality at impossibly low prices." (ALDI Truth #1: When deciding between eating well and saving money, always choose both.) ALDI has redesigned the food shopping experience to reduce costs and give customers prices that it claims are up to 50 percent lower than those of rival supermarkets.

To get those super-low prices, however, ALDI customers must settle for less in terms of many of the extras they've come to expect from competitors. For example, they get a smaller selection. To keep costs and prices down, ALDI operates smaller, energy-saving stores (about one-third the size of traditional supermarkets), and each store carries only about 1,800 of the fastest-moving grocery items (the typical supermarket carries about 40,000 items). ALDI also carries fewer national brands; almost 95 percent of its items are ALDI store brands. (ALDI claims customers are paying for the product itself, not national brand advertising and marketing.) ALDI does no promotional pricing or price matching—it just sticks with its efficient everyday very low prices. (ALDI Truth #12: We don't match other stores' prices because that would mean raising ours.)

In trimming costs and passing savings along to customers, ALDI leaves no stone unturned. Even customers themselves help to keep costs low: They bring their own bags (or purchase them from ALDI for a small charge), bag their own groceries (ALDI provides no baggers), return shopping carts on their own (to get back a 25-cent deposit), and pay with cash or a debit card (no credit cards accepted at most ALDI stores). But to ALDI fans, even though they get less in terms of selection and services, the savings make it all worthwhile. (ALDI Truth #14: You can't eat frills, so why pay for them?)

Whereas ALDI cuts operating costs to the bone, it doesn't scrimp on quality. With its preponderance of store brands, ALDI exercises complete control over the quality of the products on its shelves, and the chain promises that everything it sells is certifiably fresh and tasty. ALDI Truth #60—We make delicious cost a lot less—makes it clear that the chain promises more than just low prices. ALDI backs this promise with a Double Guarantee on all items: "If for any reason you are not 100-percent satisfied with any product, we will gladly replace the product AND refund your money."

To improve the quality of its assortment, ALDI has progressively added items that aren't usually associated with "discounted" groceries. Beyond the typical canned, boxed, and frozen food basics, ALDI carries fresh meat, baked goods, and fresh produce. It also carries an assortment of regular and periodic specialty goods, such as Mama Cozzi's Pizza Kitchen Meat Trio Focaccia, Appetitos Spinach Artichoke Dip, and All Natural Mango Salsa. ALDI even offers a selection of gluten-free and organic foods. With such items and with its clean, bright stores, ALDI targets not just low-income customers but frugal middle-class and upper-middle-class customers as well.

None of this is news to German shoppers, who have loved ALDI for decades. In Germany, the chain operates more than 4,200 stores, accounting for more than 28 percent of the market. That might explain why Walmart gave up in Germany just nine years after entering the market. Against competitors like ALDI, Walmart's normally low prices were just too expensive for frugal German consumers.

ALDI's no-frills, less-for-much-less approach isn't for everyone. Whereas some shoppers love the low prices, basic assortments, and simple store atmosphere, others can't imagine life without at least some of the luxuries and amenities offered by rivals. But most people who shop at ALDI quickly become true believers. Testimonials from converts litter the internet. "I just recently switched to ALDI from a 'premium' grocery store … and the savings blow me away!" proclaims one customer. Another fervent fan, a mother shopping on a tight budget for her

Good-value pricing: ALDI keeps costs low so that it can offer customers "impressively high quality at impossibly low prices" every day.

Keri Miksza

family, used to scour the papers for coupons and shop at two or three different stores on a typical grocery trip. Now, she gets everything on her list in a single stop at ALDI, with money left over for extra items not on the list. "I cannot believe how much I saved!" she says. "ALDI is now my immediate go-to grocery store! I'm totally team ALDI."

With tradition behind it and its can't-lose value proposition, ALDI is expanding rapidly in the United States. The company has quickly grown to more than 1,400 stores in 32 states that attract more than a million shoppers a day. That's a huge accomplishment compared with, say, British discount chain Tesco, the world's second-largest retailer, which exited the U.S. market with heavy losses after only seven years. ALDI still has plenty of room for more growth and plans to expand to more than 2,000 stores within the next three years. That's good news for the company but also for customers. When ALDI comes to your neighborhood, "Your wallet and taste buds are in for a treat" (ALDI Truth #34).

Sources: Walter Loeb, "*ALDI Is a Growing Menace to America's Grocery Retailers,*" *Forbes,* April 14, 2015, www.forbes.com/sites/thehartmangroup/2015/04/14/aldi-is-a-growing-menace-to-americas-grocery-retailers/; "Top 250 Global Powers of Retailing 2015," Deloitte, https://nrf.com/2015/global250-table; Craig Rosenblum, "Aldi's Jason Hart: Relentless Focus on Cutting Costs," *Supermarket News,* December 16, 2015, http://supermarketnews.com/limited-assortment/aldis-jason-hart-relentless-focus-cutting-costs#ixzz3wb9dWnMj; and www.aldi.us, www.aldi.us/en/new-to-aldi/aldi-truths/, and www.aldi.us/en/new-to-aldi/switch-save/, accessed September 2016.

companies, each successfully occupying different positions. The important thing is that each company must develop its own winning positioning strategy, one that makes the company special to its target consumers.

Developing a Positioning Statement

Positioning statement

A statement that summarizes company or brand positioning using this form: To (target segment and need) our (brand) is (concept) that (point of difference).

Company and brand positioning should be summed up in a **positioning statement**. The statement should follow the form: To (target segment and need) our (brand) is (concept) that (point of difference).[31] ● Here is an example using the popular digital information management application Evernote: "To busy multitaskers who need help remembering things, Evernote is a digital content management application that makes it easy to capture and remember moments and ideas from your everyday life using your computer, phone, tablet, and the web."

● Positioning statement: Evernote is positioned as a digital content management application that helps busy people to capture and remember moments and ideas and find them fast later.

Evernote Corporation

Note that the positioning statement first states the product's membership in a category (digital content management application) and then shows its point of difference from other members of the category (easily capture moments and ideas and remember them later). Evernote helps you "remember everything" by letting you take notes, capture photos, create to-do lists, and record voice reminders and then makes them easy to find and access using just about any device, anywhere—at home, at work, or on the go.

Placing a brand in a specific category suggests similarities that it might share with other products in the category. But the case for the brand's superiority is made on its points of difference. For example, the U.S. Postal Service ships packages just like UPS and FedEx, but it differentiates its Priority Mail from competitors with convenient, low-price, flat-rate shipping boxes and envelopes. "If it fits, it ships," promises USPS.

Communicating and Delivering the Chosen Position

Once it has chosen a position, the company must take strong steps to deliver and communicate the desired position to its target consumers. All the company's marketing mix efforts must support the positioning strategy.

Positioning the company calls for concrete action, not just talk. If the company decides to build a position on better quality and service, it must first *deliver* that position. Designing the marketing mix—product, price, place, and promotion—involves working out the tactical details of the positioning strategy. Thus, a firm that seizes on a more-for-more position knows that it must produce high-quality products, charge a high price, distribute through high-quality dealers, and advertise in high-quality media. It must hire and train more service people, find retailers that have a good reputation for service, and develop sales and advertising content that supports its superior offer. This is the only way to build a consistent and believable more-for-more position.

Companies often find it easier to come up with a good positioning strategy than to implement it. Establishing a position or changing one usually takes a long time. In contrast, positions that have taken years to build can quickly be lost. Once a company has built the desired position, it must take care to maintain the position through consistent performance and communication. It must closely monitor and adapt the position over time to match changes in consumer needs and competitors' strategies. However, the company should avoid abrupt changes that might confuse consumers. Instead, a product's position should evolve gradually as it adapts to the ever-changing marketing environment.

7 | Reviewing and Extending the Concepts

OBJECTIVES REVIEW AND KEY TERMS

Objectives Review

In this chapter, you learned about the major elements of a customer value–driven marketing strategy: segmentation, targeting, differentiation, and positioning. Marketers know that they cannot appeal to all buyers in their markets—or at least not to all buyers in the same way. Therefore, most companies today practice *target marketing*—identifying market segments, selecting one or more of them, and developing products and marketing mixes tailored to each.

OBJECTIVE 7-1   Define the major steps in designing a customer value–driven marketing strategy: market segmentation, targeting, differentiation, and positioning. (pp 188–189)

A customer value–driven marketing strategy begins with selecting which customers to serve and determining a value proposition that best serves the targeted customers. It consists of four steps. *Market segmentation* is the act of dividing a market into distinct groups of buyers who have different needs, characteristics, or behaviors and who might require separate marketing strategies or mixes. Once the groups have been identified, *market targeting* evaluates each market segment's attractiveness and selects one or more segments to serve. *Differentiation* involves actually differentiating the market offering to create superior customer value. *Positioning* consists of positioning the market offering in the minds of target customers. A customer value–driven marketing strategy seeks to build the *right relationships* with the *right customers*.

OBJECTIVE 7-2   List and discuss the major bases for segmenting consumer and business markets. (pp 189–197)

There is no single way to segment a market. Therefore, the marketer tries different variables to see which give the best

segmentation opportunities. For consumer marketing, the major segmentation variables are geographic, demographic, psychographic, and behavioral. In *geographic segmentation*, the market is divided into different geographical units, such as nations, regions, states, counties, cities, or even neighborhoods. In *demographic segmentation*, the market is divided into groups based on demographic variables, including age, life-cycle stage, gender, income, occupation, education, religion, ethnicity, and generation. In *psychographic segmentation*, the market is divided into different groups based on social class, lifestyle, or personality characteristics. In *behavioral segmentation*, the market is divided into groups based on consumers' knowledge, attitudes, uses, or responses concerning a product.

Business marketers use many of the same variables to segment their markets. But business markets also can be segmented by business *demographics* (industry, company size), *operating characteristics*, *purchasing approaches*, *situational factors*, and *personal characteristics*. The effectiveness of the segmentation analysis depends on finding segments that are *measurable*, *accessible*, *substantial*, *differentiable*, and *actionable*.

OBJECTIVE 7-3   Explain how companies identify attractive market segments and choose a market-targeting strategy. (pp 197–204)

To target the best market segments, the company first evaluates each segment's size and growth characteristics, structural attractiveness, and compatibility with company objectives and resources. It then chooses one of four market-targeting strategies—ranging from very broad to very narrow targeting. The seller can ignore segment differences and target broadly using *undifferentiated* (or *mass*) *marketing*. This involves mass producing, mass distributing, and mass promoting the same product in about the same way to all consumers. Or the seller can adopt *differentiated marketing*—developing different market offers for several segments. *Concentrated marketing* (or *niche marketing*) involves focusing on one or a few market segments only. Finally, *micromarketing* is the practice of tailoring products and marketing programs to suit the tastes of specific individuals and locations. Micromarketing includes *local marketing* and *individual marketing*. Which targeting strategy is best depends on company resources, product variability, product life-cycle stage, market variability, and competitive marketing strategies.

OBJECTIVE 7-4   Discuss how companies differentiate and position their products for maximum competitive advantage. *(pp 204–212)*

Once a company has decided which segments to enter, it must decide on its *differentiation and positioning strategy*. The differentiation and positioning task consists of three steps: identifying a set of possible differentiations that create competitive advantage, choosing advantages on which to build a position, and selecting an overall positioning strategy.

The brand's full positioning is called its *value proposition*—the full mix of benefits on which the brand is positioned. In general, companies can choose from one of five winning value propositions on which to position their products: more for more, more for the same, the same for less, less for much less, or more for less. Company and brand positioning are summarized in positioning statements that state the target segment and need, the positioning concept, and specific points of difference. The company must then effectively communicate and deliver the chosen position to the market.

Key Terms

OBJECTIVE 7-1

Market segmentation (p 188)
Market targeting (targeting) (p 188)
Differentiation (p 188)
Positioning (p 189)

OBJECTIVE 7-2

Geographic segmentation (p 189)
Demographic segmentation (p 190)
Age and life-cycle segmentation (p 190)
Gender segmentation (p 190)

Income segmentation (p 191)
Psychographic segmentation (p 191)
Behavioral segmentation (p 192)
Occasion segmentation (p 192)
Benefit segmentation (p 192)
Intermarket (cross-market) segmentation (p 196)

OBJECTIVE 7-3

Target market (p 198)
Undifferentiated (mass) marketing (p 198)

Differentiated (segmented) marketing (p 198)
Concentrated (niche) marketing (p 199)
Micromarketing (p 200)
Local marketing (p 200)
Individual marketing (p 202)

OBJECTIVE 7-4

Product position (p 204)
Competitive advantage (p 206)
Value proposition (p 208)
Positioning statement (p 211)

DISCUSSION AND CRITICAL THINKING

MyMarketingLab

Go to **mymktlab.com** to complete the problems marked with this icon ✪.

Discussion Questions

✪ **7-1**   Why have companies moved away from mass marketing and toward target marketing? Outline the steps in a customer value-driven strategy. (AACSB: Communication)

7-2   How is demographic segmentation used in consumer markets? Provide an example where marketers have used demographic segmentation. (AACSB: Communication; Reflective Thinking)

7-3   Discuss the challenges marketers face with international market segmentation. (AACSB: Communication)

✪ **7-4**   There are many ways to segment a market, but not all segmentations are effective. Explain the five

requirements for effective market segmentation. (AACSB: Communication)

7-5   Describe micromarketing, local marketing, and individual marketing. When should marketers consider using these segmentation strategies? (AACSB: Communication; Reflective Thinking)

✪ **7-6**   How can a company gain competitive advantage through differentiation? Describe an example of a company that illustrates each type of differentiation discussed in the chapter. (AACSB: Communication)

Critical Thinking Exercises

7-7 Identify a product you use every day. Assume you are the marketer of the product and want to convey the ways your product differs from competing products in the marketplace. Create a differentiation strategy to promote your product and create a competitive advantage. (AACSB: Communication; Reflective Thinking)

7-8 *Manfluencers* is a term that describes a new marketing trend. To what does this term refer? Describe two examples of how marketers have responded to the *manfluencers* trend. (AACSB: Communication; Reflective Thinking)

7-9 In a small group, create an idea for a new business. Using the steps described in the chapter, develop a customer value–driven marketing strategy. Describe your strategy and conclude with a positioning statement for this business. (AACSB: Communication; Reflective Thinking)

APPLICATIONS AND CASES

Online, Mobile, and Social Media Marketing Get Your Groupon

Local marketing is an effective tool used by marketers to reach intended market segments. Groupon has capitalized on this concept by tailoring brands and marketing to the needs and wants of local customer segments—cities, neighborhoods, and even specific stores. According to its website, Groupon "offers a vast mobile and online marketplace where people discover and save on amazing things to do, see, eat, and buy. By enabling real-time commerce across local businesses, travel destinations, consumer products, and live events, shoppers can find the best a city has to offer. Groupon is redefining how small businesses attract and retain customers by providing them with customizable and scalable marketing tools and services to profitably grow their businesses." This concept lies at the heart of Groupon's mission: "to connect local commerce, increasing consumer buying power while driving more business to local merchants through price and discovery." To help consumers make those connections, Groupon offers a mobile app, online marketplace, and social media touchpoints where customers can readily access information on its daily deals.

7-10 How does Groupon use target marketing? Provide examples. Discuss the ways in which small businesses can utilize local social media marketing in your community. (AACSB: Communication; Use of IT; Reflective Thinking)

7-11 Do you use Groupon? Is it effective in helping local businesses to meet the challenges of local marketing? Why or why not? (AACSB: Communication; Reflective Thinking)

Marketing Ethics Targeting to Teens

Discretionary income. It's the amount of money we have left over after paying for life's necessities. And many teens have plenty of it. According to a recent Nielsen survey, 29 percent of teens live in homes where household income is $100,000 or higher. These teens aren't just buying for themselves, either. In addition to having discretionary income, teens have a strong influence on the purchasing decisions of their parents. According to Mary Leigh Bliss, trends editor at youth-focused market research firm YPulse, "Teens are now passing technology down to their parents, not the other way around." This presents significant opportunities for marketers. However, some critics worry that teens may be especially vulnerable to targeted marketing messages and offers from high-powered or unscrupulous marketers.

7-12 Discuss how companies can reach their teen markets using socially responsible target marketing. Cite an example of a company being responsible in targeting teens and another example where a company is not responsible. (AACSB: Communication; Reflective Thinking)

7-13 The bombardment of commercial messages is turning teens into some of the most sophisticated and skeptical consumers in the world, increasing their resistance to conventional advertising tactics. As this highly sought-after teen target market ages, how can marketers prepare to tap into the consumers of the future?

Marketing by the Numbers USAA

USAA is a financial services company formed in 1922 by 25 Army officers who came together to insure each other's automobiles because they were deemed too high-risk to insure. USAA now has almost 25,000 employees and more than 9 million member customers. It consistently ranks in the top 10 automobile insurance companies and offers other types of insurance as well as banking, investment, retirement, and financial planning services. USAA practices a niche marketing strategy—it targets only active and former military personnel and their immediate families. Members earn the right to be customers by serving in the military and can pass that on to their spouses and children. The company was originally even more restrictive, targeting only military officers.

However, in 1996, eligibility was extended to enlisted personnel and is now extended to anyone who served and was honorably discharged from the military and their immediate family members.

7-14 Discuss the factors used to evaluate the usefulness of the military segment. (AACSB: Communication; Reflective Thinking)

7-15 Using the chain ratio method described in Appendix 2: Marketing by the Numbers, estimate the market potential in the military (active duty and veterans) market. Be sure to state any assumptions you make. (AACSB: Communication; Use of IT; Analytical Reasoning)

Video Case Sprout

In the world of children's television programming, Sprout is a relative newcomer. Owned by NBCUniversal, Sprout airs PBS Kids programming as well as additional acquired material. A true multi-platform network, Sprout can be accessed as regular cable programming, as on-demand programming through Comcast, and online through Sproutonline.com.

Sprout does not target only kids, however. It targets preschool families—households that have one or more preschool-age children. Parents need to be involved with their children's viewing of interactive content, multiple access points, and 24-hour programming. For this reason, Sprout's promotional efforts are geared toward parents as well as children.

After viewing the video featuring Sprout, answer the following questions:

7-16 Why does Sprout target preschool families rather than focusing solely on children? Give examples.

7-17 Which target marketing strategy best describes Sprout's efforts? Support your choice.

7-18 How does Sprout use differentiation and positioning to build relationships with target customers?

Company Case Virgin America: Flight Service for the Tech Savvy

After an exceptionally frustrating day at the office, Jessica set out to unwind in one of her favorite third places. The mood lighting immediately brought her blood pressure down as she walked in and took a deep, relaxing breath. She was happy that her favorite spot was available—a comfy leather chair in the back corner of the room, where she used the touchscreen at the table in front of her to order her favorite drink. Then, putting on a set of noise-canceling headphones, Jessica began catching up on her favorite TV show with her own personal entertainment portal.

If this sounds like a local Starbucks or trendy nightclub, think again. Jessica had just boarded a flight on Virgin America, one of the youngest airlines in the United States. It's also the hottest airline, besting all competition in various industry and customer surveys. And after just six years in business, Virgin America also reached profitability faster than any other airline in all of airdom.

How does a startup airline break into one of the most competitive industries in the world, notorious for barriers to entry? For Virgin America, the answer is two-fold—by putting customers first and by targeting the right customer segment.

Targeting the Right Customers

Virgin America first took to the skies in 2007. This wouldn't be the first shot at starting an airline for Richard Branson—founder of parent company Virgin Group. Virgin's international airline, Virgin Atlantic, had been crossing the pond between the United States and Europe since 1984. But Virgin America would be an entirely independent enterprise. And while Branson and other Virgin Group executives make no day-to-day decisions at Virgin America, the unorthodox Virgin culture—fun, creative, even whacky—is unmistakable.

One of Branson's core values that permeates Virgin America is this: Take care of your people first and profits will follow. In an industry characterized by customer complaints about service, it would seem that a customer-centric approach would be enough to gain a foothold in the market. But when Virgin started air service in the United States, at least a few other airlines had already established themselves based on a "customer first" mantra, including industry leader Southwest Airlines. And Virgin America knew that it could not expect to succeed by playing the low-price game. Not only was Southwest the reigning champion on value, but the bulk of airline competitors were already beating each other up for low-price dominance.

Virgin America found a different competitive hook. It targeted a segment of frequent fliers who were young, savvy, influential, and willing to pay just a little bit more for an airline that would take care of them—the Silicon Valley faction. By providing exceptional service and amenities that appeal to this particular slice of airline customers, Virgin America has been able to charge slightly higher fares and still establish a growing base of fiercely loyal patrons.

Homing in on the Details

Offering unique amenities in the airline business is a challenge for any company. But from the beginning, the Virgin America experience was designed with its target customer in mind. Its fleet consists of 61 Airbus A300 series planes, each brand new when it went into service, minimizing the unexpected delays due to maintenance and repairs. Custom-designed leather seats are roomier and more comfortable than average coach seating. And that mood lighting? Not only does it bathe the aircraft cabin in an appealing purplish glow, it automatically adjusts to one of 12 different shades based on outside light.

To appeal to tech gurus, Virgin America focused on equipping its planes with the latest hardware and software. From day one, Virgin was the only domestic carrier to offer fleetwide in-flight Wi-Fi—a distinction that it maintains to this day, even as it has stayed ahead of the competition by upgrading the network to ensure the fastest in-flight speeds available. Every seat has its own power outlet, USB port, and 9-inch video touchscreen with a QWERTY keyboard/remote control.

That touchscreen provides access to the most advanced entertainment and information system in U.S. skies. Virgin America's proprietary Red system allows each guest to choose on-demand movies, TV programs, music, or video games. Red also allows patrons to track their flight on interactive Google Maps, engage in seat-to-seat chat with other customers, and order food and drinks for themselves or anyone else on board. It's a system designed to give passengers a feeling of control during an experience that is otherwise mostly out of their control.

Many of these ideas came by way of Virgin America's techy clientele. It's no accident that the company's headquarters are located in Burlingame, California, just a few short miles from the San Francisco airport. In fact, Virgin America is the only airline based in Silicon Valley. Not only is the company constantly experimenting with every aspect of the business, it has made strong efforts to involve Silicon Valley entrepreneurs and executives in the process, helping Virgin to think like its disruptive clientele. "We see ourselves as more of an incubator," says Luanne Calvert, Virgin America's chief marketing officer.

Take VX Next, for example—a group of 30 or so frequent fliers who act as a brain trust for Virgin America, generating ideas for the company at no charge. Among other winning ideas, this group was instrumental in developing the company's recent interactive promotional campaign. At the center of the campaign is a slick cinematic site that provides viewers with a virtual tour of a Virgin America flight. Demonstrating the airline's in-flight perks are founders and CEOs of companies such as Pandora, Gilt, and Pitchfork. As part of the tour, visitors to the site discover that several of the passengers onboard are Virgin America frequent fliers and Silicon Valley celebrities who have made creative contributions to the airline's services with things such as curating in-flight music and menu items.

Virgin America's home-brewed tech panel was also instrumental in creating the company's latest safety video. When the company started operations, it delighted customers with a safety video like none other—an animated short featuring a techie nun and a matador with his bull. Posted online as well, the video racked up millions of views and cemented Virgin America's image as a company that could find creative alternatives to just about anything, even a federally mandated reminder to wear seatbelts. That image has carried over to Virgin America's new safety video—one created by a top Hollywood director and world-class choreographers that features 10 So You Think You Can Dance alums, two former Olympians, and one American Idol finalist. Debuting in Times Square and getting plenty of coverage from the press, the new safety video racked up 6 million views in less than two weeks.

Above the Clouds

Although there is plenty of anecdotal evidence that Virgin America's customers are thrilled with its service, it's the industry quality ratings that count. Virgin America is coming through with flying colors

there as well. In fact, Virgin America has been number one in the annual Airline Quality Report—a survey that ranks airlines based on mishandled baggage, customer complaints, denied boardings, and on-time percent—for the past three years in a row. In a recent Consumer Reports survey for customer satisfaction in the airline, not only did Virgin America take top honors, it came away with the highest score achieved by any U.S. airline in many years.

Despite all of Virgin America's success, the airline industry is a tough place to survive and thrive. In the United States, just four airlines control more than 80 percent of the market. Virgin America knows that maintaining its high rankings will be a challenge, especially as it expands into new markets—particularly markets with cold climates, a factor that increases the likelihood of canceled or delayed flights. As the number of passengers on flights increases, boarding and deplaning times will also increase, affecting multiple customer service metrics. And with Virgin's techy and connected clientele, any slip-up is likely to be texted, tweeted, or otherwise broadcast for all the world to see. Playing the features and amenities game is also problematic. Things that delight customers today become ho-hum tomorrow, especially when competitors are constantly trying to improve their offerings as well.

To remain competitive as it moves into the future, Virgin America recently announced that it has agreed to be acquired by Alaska Airlines—another small West Coast–based airline known for its high level of service and customer loyalty. With more than 1,200 daily flights and 280 aircraft, the combined airline will provide much stronger competition on the West Coast, even with the largest airlines. This should be a boon for customers of each airline who have been frustrated by limited route options in the past.

But with such a strong and unique positioning targeted toward a specific segment of the industry, many are wondering what effect the union of these two airlines will have on Virgin America's style and quality of service. After all, if "hip" best describes Virgin America's style, Alaska Airlines is best described as "practical." "My hope is that Alaska goes in with an open mind and that they learn some things," says one travel industry analyst. "It's not hip, it's not sexy, but Alaska has a lot going for it."

The deal is still subject to approval by regulators, and airline mergers can take years to complete. But one thing is for sure. Alaska Airlines is not only acquiring an airline with a strong service record, it's taking on an unusually profitable airline. Virgin America achieved an annual profit after just six years. Flying in the face of skeptics, the brash young airline continued on its upward trajectory by posting strong increases in profits in each of the two years since. For the most recent year, Virgin America achieved $201 million in profit on $1.5 billion in revenues—139 percent higher profits than the year before and the highest ever for a young airline. The company also recently went public in the second-largest airline IPO in history. The question is this: Will the new Virgin America continue to do what it has done in the past—wow every customer with exceptional service while giving the tech community a little something extra? Or will that special Virgin America brand personality slowly disappear in the shadow of older, more established Alaska Airlines brand?

Questions for Discussion

7-19 Using the full spectrum of segmentation variables, describe how Virgin America segments and targets the market for airline services.

7-20 Which market targeting strategy is Virgin America following? Justify your answer.

7-21 Write a positioning statement for Virgin America.

7-22 What are the potential issues for Virgin America following the Alaska Airlines acquisition? Will Virgin America continue to appeal to the same types of customers? Why or why not?

Sources: Matt Krupnick, "Virgin America Fans Ask If Alaska Airlines Takeover Will Mean Loss of Cool," *New York Times*, April 11, 2016, www.nytimes.com/2016/04/12/business/virgin-america-fansaskif-alaska-airlines-takeover-will-mean-loss-ofcool.html; Melanie Hanns, "Airline Quality Rating: 2015," *Embry-Riddle Newsroom*, April 4, 2016, www.news.erau.edu/top-news/airline-quality-rating-report-reveal-top-carriers-2015; Lauren Schwartzberg, "Most Innovative Companies: 2015, Virgin America," *Fast Company*, March, 2015, pp. 135–137; Matt Richtel, "At Virgin America, a Fine Line between Pizazz and Profit," *New York Times*, September 8, 2013, p. BU1; Charisse Jones, "Virgin America Posts Record Profit for 2014," *USA Today*, February 18, 2015, www.usatoday.com/story/money/2015/02/18/virgin-america-posts-record-profit/23608205/; and information from www.virginamerica.com/cms/about-our-airline/corporate-facts.html and www.virginamerica.com/cms/news/virgin-america-merger-with-alaska-airlines, accessed June 2016.

MyMarketingLab

Go to **mymktlab.com** for Auto-graded writing questions as well as the following Assisted-graded writing questions:

7-23 Describe how marketers segment international markets. What is intermarket segmentation?

7-24 Describe how marketers manage service differentiation, other than through pricing, and describe an example of a service provider that has successfully differentiated its offering from competitors.

8

Products, Services, and Brands
Building Customer Value

PREVIEWING THE CONCEPTS

After examining customer value–driven marketing strategy, we now take a deeper look at the marketing mix: the tactical tools that marketers use to implement their strategies, engage customers, and deliver superior customer value. In this and the next chapter, we will study how companies develop and manage products, services, and brands. Then, in the chapters that follow, we look at pricing, distribution, and marketing communication tools. The product and brand are usually the first and most basic marketing consideration. We start with a seemingly simple question: What *is* a product? As it turns out, the answer is not so simple.

To dig a little deeper into the question of what is a product, we begin by looking at GoPro. You may never have heard of GoPro, the fast-growing company that makes tiny, wearable HD video cameras. Yet few brands can match the avid enthusiasm and loyalty that GoPro has created in the hearts and minds of its customers. GoPro knows that, deep down, its products are much more than just durable little cameras. More than that, it gives customers a way to share action-charged moments and emotions with friends.

GOPRO: Be a HERO

An ever-growing army of GoPro customers are now strapping amazing little GoPro cameras to their bodies or mounting them on anything from the front bumpers of race cars to the heels of skydiving boots in order to capture the extreme moments of their lives and lifestyles. Then they can't wait to share those emotion-packed GoPro moments with friends. In fact, the chances are good that you've seen many GoPro-created videos on YouTube, Facebook, and Instagram or even on TV.

Maybe it's the video shot by the skier who sets off an avalanche in the Swiss Alps and escapes by parachuting off a cliff—that amateur video received 2.6 million YouTube views in nine months. Or maybe you saw the one where a seagull picks up a tourist's camera and takes off with it, capturing a bird's-eye view of a castle in Cannes, France (3 million views in seven months). Or what about the video of the mountain biker in Africa who is ambushed by a full-grown gazelle (more than 13 million views in four months)? One video in which a tech-challenged Irishman used his son's GoPro to capture his entire Las Vegas vacation with the camera mistakenly pointed at himself instead of the sights snared 6.9 million views in only six days.

> GoPro's success comes from a deep-down understanding that it's selling much more than just tiny, wearable sports-action video cameras. GoPro helps people capture, share, and celebrate with others the most meaningful experiences in their lives.

GoPro's avid customers have become evangelists for the brand. GoPro holds a 47.5 percent share of the action camera market. Its sales soared to more than $1.4 billion last year, a fivefold increase in only four years.

What makes GoPro so successful? Part of the formula is the physical product itself: GoPro cameras are marvels of technology, especially given their affordable starting price of less than $200 for an entry-level model. A GoPro HD video camera looks like little more than a small gray box. But the lightweight, wearable or mountable GoPro is extremely versatile, and it packs amazing power for capturing stunning HD-quality video. A removable housing makes GoPro cameras waterproof to depths of 130 feet. And GoPro cameras are drop-proof from 3,000 feet (so claims one skydiver).

But GoPro knows that it sells much more than just a small metal box that takes action videos. GoPro users—whether extreme sports enthusiasts or just everyday video buffs—don't just want to take videos. More than that, they want to tell the stories and share the emotions and moments in their lives. "Enabling you to share your life through incredible photos and video is what we do," says GoPro. We "help people capture and share their lives' most meaningful experiences with others—to celebrate them together."

When people view a stunning GoPro video clip—like the one of New Zealand's Jed Mildon landing the first-ever BMX triple backflip captured by his helmet camera—to some degree, they experience what the subject experiences. They feel the passion and adrenaline. And when that happens, GoPro creates an emotional connection between the GoPro storyteller and the audience.

Thus, making good cameras is only the start of GoPro's success. GoPro founder Nick Woodman, himself an extreme sports junkie, talks about helping customers through four essential steps in their storytelling and emotion-sharing journeys: capture, creation, broadcast, and recognition. *Capture* is what the cameras do—shooting pictures and videos. *Creation* is the editing and production process that turns raw footage into compelling videos. *Broadcast* involves distributing the video content to an audience. *Recognition* is the payoff for the content creator. Recognition might come in the form of YouTube views or Likes and Shares on Facebook. More probably, it's the enthusiastic oohs and ahhs that their videos evoke from friends and family. The company's slogan sums up what it's really selling: "GoPro: Be a HERO."

Initially, GoPro focused primarily on the capture step of the customer storytelling experience. It offers a seemingly endless supply of rigs, mounts, harnesses, straps, and other accessories that make GoPro cameras wearable or mountable just about anywhere. Users can strap the little cameras to their wrists or mount them on helmets. They can attach them to the tip of a snow ski, the bottom of a skateboard, or the underside of an RC helicopter. In fact, GoPro will soon sell drones—the "ultimate accessory for your GoPro camera"—that will let GoPro enthusiasts take breathtaking videos from on high. The handy little GoPro lets even the rankest video amateur capture some pretty incredible footage.

But to fuel continuing growth, GoPro has broadened its offer to address the full range of customer needs and motivations—not just capture but also creation, broadcast, and recognition. For example, on the creation side, GoPro offers free GoPro Studio software that makes it easier for users to create professional-quality videos from their GoPro content. With the GoPro App, users can "Control. View. Share."—using their phones, tablets, or Apple Watches to control their GoPros remotely, trim and edit images, and share their favorites wirelessly with friends by text or post or on the GoPro Channel, which is already distributed though social media platforms such as YouTube, Facebook, Twitter, Instagram, Vimeo, Pinterest, and GoPro.com/Channels. As for recognition, GoPro now airs TV commercials created from the best videos submitted by customers at its website. GoPro's future lies in enabling and integrating the full user experience, from capturing video to sharing stories and life's emotions with others.

GoPro's amazing little cameras let even the rankest video amateurs take stunning videos, giving them a way to celebrate the action-charged moments and emotions of their lives with others.
Used with permission of Mike Basich

GoPro's rich understanding of what product it's really selling is serving the company well. Its enthusiastic customers are among the most loyal and engaged of any brand. For example, GoPro's Facebook fan base is more than 9.2 million and growing fast. To put that in perspective, much larger Canon USA has only 1.1 million Facebook followers. Beyond uploading nearly half a million videos a year, GoPro fans interact heavily across a broad range of social media. For example, the GoPro hashtag is used more than 45,000 times daily across major social networks. "I think we have the most socially engaged online audience of any consumer brand in the world," claims Woodman.

All that customer engagement and enthusiasm have made GoPro the world's fastest-growing camera company. Today GoPro cameras are available in more than 40,000 stores in more than 100 countries, from small sports-enthusiast shops to REI, Best Buy, and Amazon.com. GoPro's remarkable little cameras have also spread beyond amateurs. They have become standard equipment for many professional filmmakers—whether it's the Discovery Channel or a news show team filming rescues, wildlife, and storms or the production crews of hit reality-TV shows such as *Deadliest Catch* taking pictures of underwater crab pots or the sides of ships in heavy seas. When stuntman Felix Baumgartner made his breathtaking 128,000-foot jump from the edge of space, he was wearing five GoPros. The use of GoPro equipment by professionals lends credibility that fuels even greater consumer demand.

The moral of this story: GoPro knows that it doesn't just sell cameras. More than that, it enables customers to share important moments and emotions. Says Woodman: "We spent a lot of time recently thinking about, What are we really doing here? We know that our cameras are arguably the most socially networked consumer devices of our time, so it's clear we're not just building hardware." The company sums it up this way: "Dream it. Do it. Capture it with your GoPro. Capture and share your world."[1]

OBJECTIVES OUTLINE

OBJECTIVE 8-1	Define *product* and describe the major classifications of products and services. **What Is a Product?** *(pp 220–225)*
OBJECTIVE 8-2	Describe the decisions companies make regarding their individual products and services, product lines, and product mixes. **Product and Service Decisions** *(pp 225–233)*
OBJECTIVE 8-3	Identify the four characteristics that affect the marketing of services and the additional marketing considerations that services require. **Services Marketing** *(pp 234–240)*
OBJECTIVE 8-4	Discuss branding strategy—the decisions companies make in building and managing their brands. **Branding Strategy: Building Strong Brands** *(pp 240–248)*

AS THE GOPRO STORY shows, in their quest to create customer relationships, marketers must build and manage products and brands that connect with customers. This chapter begins with a deceptively simple question: *What is a product?* After addressing this question, we look at ways to classify products in consumer and business markets. Then we discuss the important decisions that marketers make regarding individual products, product lines, and product mixes. Next, we examine the characteristics and marketing requirements of a special form of product—services. Finally, we look into the critically important issue of how marketers build and manage product and service brands.

Author | Comment As you'll see, this deceptively simple question has a very complex answer. For example, think back to the opening GoPro story. What is the GoPro "product"?

What Is a Product?

We define a **product** as anything that can be offered to a market for attention, acquisition, use, or consumption that might satisfy a want or need. Products include more than just tangible objects, such as cars, clothing, or mobile phones. Broadly defined, products also include services, events, persons, places, organizations, and ideas or a mixture of these. Throughout this text, we use the term *product* broadly to include any or all of these entities. Thus, an Apple iPhone, a Toyota Camry, and a Caffé Mocha at Starbucks are products. But so are a trip to Las Vegas, Schwab online investment services, your Instagram account, and advice from your family doctor.

Because of their importance in the world economy, we give special attention to services. **Services** are a form of product that consists of activities, benefits, or satisfactions offered for sale that are essentially intangible and do not result in the ownership of anything. Examples include banking, hotel, airline travel, retail, wireless communication, and home-repair services. We will look at services more closely later in this chapter.

Product
Anything that can be offered to a market for attention, acquisition, use, or consumption that might satisfy a want or need.

Service
An activity, benefit, or satisfaction offered for sale that is essentially intangible and does not result in the ownership of anything.

Products, Services, and Experiences

Products are a key element in the overall *market offering*. Marketing mix planning begins with building an offering that brings value to target customers. This offering becomes the basis on which the company builds profitable customer relationships.

A company's market offering often includes both tangible goods and services. At one extreme, the market offer may consist of a *pure tangible good*, such as soap, toothpaste, or salt; no services accompany the product. At the other extreme are *pure services*, for which the market offer consists primarily of a service. Examples include a doctor's exam and financial services.

● Creating customer experiences: More than just selling products, Apple's highly successful retail stores create engaging life-feels-good brand experiences.

Area 52 Advertising Inc/Getty Images

Between these two extremes, however, many goods-and-services combinations are possible.

Today, as products and services become more commoditized, many companies are moving to a new level in creating value for their customers. To differentiate their offers, beyond simply making products and delivering services, they are creating and managing customer *experiences* with their brands or companies.

Experiences have always been an important part of marketing for some companies. Disney has long manufactured dreams and memories through its movies and theme parks—it wants theme park cast members to deliver a thousand "small wows" to every customer. And Nike has long declared, "It's not so much the shoes but where they take you." Today, however, all kinds of firms are recasting their traditional goods and services to create experiences. ● For example, Apple's highly successful retail stores don't just sell the company's products. They create an engaging Apple brand experience:[2]

Apple's retail stores are very seductive places, where "life-feels-good" experiences abound. The store design is clean, simple, and just oozing with style— much like an Apple iPad or a featherweight MacBook Air. The bustling stores feel more like community centers than retail outlets, with crowds of customers sampling the goods and buzzing excitedly about all things Apple. The stores encourage a lot of purchasing, to be sure. But they also encourage lingering, with tables full of fully functioning Macs, iPods, iPads, and iPhones sitting out for visitors to try and dozens of laid-back Apple employees close at hand to answer questions and cater to every whim. The stores offer expert technical assistance at the Genius Bar and a full schedule of workshops where customers at all experience levels can learn about their Apple devices and explore their creative sides. You don't just visit an Apple store—you experience it in a way that no other consumer electronics company can match. As one Apple retail executive explains, "I don't want to be sold to when I walk into a store. Don't sell! No! Because that's a turn-off. Build an amazing brand experience, and then [sales] will just naturally happen."

Levels of Product and Services

Product planners need to think about products and services on three levels (see ● **Figure 8.1**). Each level adds more customer value. The most basic level is the *core customer value*, which addresses the question: *What is the buyer really buying?* When designing products, marketers must first define the core, problem-solving benefits or services that

● FIGURE | 8.1
Three Levels of Product

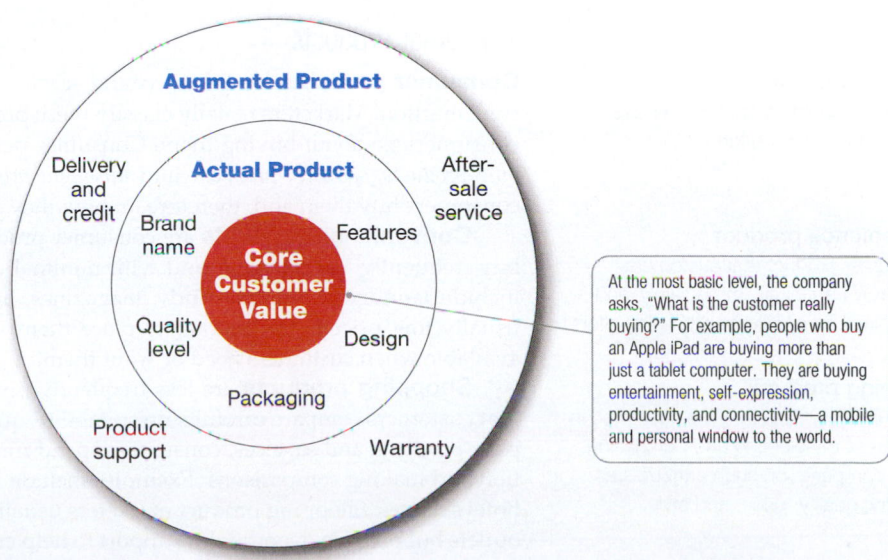

At the most basic level, the company asks, "What is the customer really buying?" For example, people who buy an Apple iPad are buying more than just a tablet computer. They are buying entertainment, self-expression, productivity, and connectivity—a mobile and personal window to the world.

**Core, actual, and augmented product:** People who buy an iPad are buying much more than a tablet computer. They are buying entertainment, self-expression, productivity, and connectivity—a mobile and personal window to the world.

Betsie Van der Meer/Getty Images

consumers seek. A woman buying lipstick buys more than lip color. Charles Revson of Revlon saw this early: "In the factory, we make cosmetics; in the store, we sell hope." And people who buy an Apple iPad are buying much more than just a tablet computer. They are buying entertainment, self-expression, productivity, and connectivity with friends and family—a mobile and personal window to the world.

At the second level, product planners must turn the core benefit into an *actual product*. They need to develop product and service features, a design, a quality level, a brand name, and packaging. For example, the iPad is an actual product. Its name, parts, styling, operating system, features, packaging, and other attributes have all been carefully combined to deliver the core customer value of staying connected.

Finally, product planners must build an *augmented product* around the core benefit and actual product by offering additional consumer services and benefits. The iPad is more than just a digital device. It provides consumers with a complete connectivity solution. Thus, when consumers buy an iPad, Apple and its resellers also might give buyers a warranty on parts and workmanship, quick repair services when needed, and web and mobile sites to use if they have problems or questions. Apple also provides access to a huge assortment of apps and accessories, along with an iCloud service that integrates buyers' photos, music, documents, apps, calendars, contacts, and other content across all of their devices from any location.

Consumers see products as complex bundles of benefits that satisfy their needs. When developing products, marketers first must identify the *core customer value* that consumers seek from the product. They must then design the *actual* product and find ways to *augment* it to create customer value and a full and satisfying brand experience.

Product and Service Classifications

Products and services fall into two broad classes based on the types of consumers who use them: *consumer products* and *industrial products*. Broadly defined, products also include other marketable entities such as experiences, organizations, persons, places, and ideas.

Consumer Products

Consumer product
A product bought by final consumers for personal consumption.

Consumer products are products and services bought by final consumers for personal consumption. Marketers usually classify these products and services further based on how consumers go about buying them. Consumer products include *convenience products, shopping products, specialty products*, and *unsought products*. These products differ in the ways consumers buy them and, therefore, in how they are marketed (see Table 8.1).

Convenience product
A consumer product that customers usually buy frequently, immediately, and with minimal comparison and buying effort.

Convenience products are consumer products and services that customers usually buy frequently, immediately, and with minimal comparison and buying effort. Examples include laundry detergent, candy, magazines, and fast food. Convenience products are usually low priced, and marketers place them in many locations to make them readily available when customers need or want them.

Shopping product
A consumer product that the customer, in the process of selecting and purchasing, usually compares on such attributes as suitability, quality, price, and style.

Shopping products are less frequently purchased consumer products and services that customers compare carefully on suitability, quality, price, and style. When buying shopping products and services, consumers spend much time and effort in gathering information and making comparisons. Examples include furniture, clothing, major appliances, and hotel services. Shopping product marketers usually distribute their products through fewer outlets but provide deeper sales support to help customers in their comparison efforts.

● **Table 8.1** | **Marketing Considerations for Consumer Products**

Marketing Considerations	Type of Consumer Product			
	Convenience	**Shopping**	**Specialty**	**Unsought**
Customer buying behavior	Frequent purchase; little planning, little comparison or shopping effort; low customer involvement	Less frequent purchase; much planning and shopping effort; comparison of brands on price, quality, and style	Strong brand preference and loyalty; special purchase effort; little comparison of brands; low price sensitivity	Little product awareness or knowledge (or, if aware, little or even negative interest)
Price	Low price	Higher price	High price	Varies
Distribution	Widespread distribution; convenient locations	Selective distribution in fewer outlets	Exclusive distribution in only one or a few outlets per market area	Varies
Promotion	Mass promotion by the producer	Advertising and personal selling by both the producer and resellers	More carefully targeted promotion by both the producer and resellers	Aggressive advertising and personal selling by the producer and resellers
Examples	Toothpaste, magazines, and laundry detergent	Major appliances, televisions, furniture, and clothing	Luxury goods, such as Rolex watches or fine crystal	Life insurance and Red Cross blood donations

Specialty product
A consumer product with unique characteristics or brand identification for which a significant group of buyers is willing to make a special purchase effort.

Unsought product
A consumer product that the consumer either does not know about or knows about but does not normally consider buying.

Industrial product
A product bought by individuals and organizations for further processing or for use in conducting a business.

Specialty products are consumer products and services with unique characteristics or brand identifications for which a significant group of buyers is willing to make a special purchase effort. Examples include specific brands of cars, high-priced photography equipment, designer clothes, gourmet foods, and the services of medical or legal specialists. A Lamborghini automobile, for example, is a specialty product because buyers are usually willing to travel great distances to buy one. Buyers normally do not compare specialty products. They invest only the time needed to reach dealers carrying the wanted brands.

Unsought products are consumer products that a consumer either does not know about or knows about but does not normally consider buying. Most major new innovations are unsought until consumers become aware of them through marketing. Classic examples of known but unsought products and services are life insurance, preplanned funeral services, and blood donations to the Red Cross. By their very nature, unsought products require a lot of promoting, personal selling, and other marketing efforts.

Industrial Products

Industrial products are those products purchased for further processing or for use in conducting a business. Thus, the distinction between a consumer product and an industrial product is based on the *purpose* for which the product is purchased. If a consumer buys a lawn mower for use around home, the lawn mower is a consumer product. If the same consumer buys the same lawn mower for use in a landscaping business, the lawn mower is an industrial product.

The three groups of industrial products and services are materials and parts, capital items, and supplies and services. *Materials and parts* include raw materials as well as manufactured materials and parts. Raw materials consist of farm products (wheat, cotton, livestock, fruits, vegetables) and natural products (fish, lumber, crude petroleum, iron ore). Manufactured materials and parts consist of component materials (iron, yarn, cement, wires) and component parts (small motors, tires, castings). Most manufactured materials and parts are sold directly to industrial users. Price and service are the major marketing factors; branding and advertising tend to be less important.

Capital items are industrial products that aid in the buyer's production or operations, including installations and accessory equipment. Installations consist of major purchases such as buildings (factories, offices) and fixed equipment (generators, drill presses, large computer systems, elevators). Accessory equipment includes portable factory equipment and tools (hand tools, lift trucks) and office equipment (computers, fax machines, desks). These types of equipment have shorter lives than do installations and simply aid in the production process.

The final group of industrial products is *supplies and services*. Supplies include operating supplies (lubricants, coal, paper, pencils) and repair and maintenance items (paint, nails, brooms). Supplies are the convenience products of the industrial field because they are usually purchased with a minimum of effort or comparison. Business services include maintenance and repair services (window cleaning, computer repair) and business advisory services (legal, management consulting, advertising). Such services are usually supplied under contract.

Organizations, Persons, Places, and Ideas

In addition to tangible products and services, marketers have broadened the concept of a product to include other market offerings: organizations, persons, places, and ideas.

Organizations often carry out activities to "sell" the organization itself. *Organization marketing* consists of activities undertaken to create, maintain, or change the attitudes and behavior of target consumers toward an organization. Both profit and not-for-profit organizations practice organization marketing.

Business firms sponsor public relations or *corporate image marketing* campaigns to market themselves and polish their images. For example, as noted in Chapter 6, GE's long-running "Imagination at Work" campaign markets the industrial giant as a company whose imaginative products and technologies are making a difference in the world. ● Consider one recent award-winning TV spot, called "Childlike Imagination." The whimsical ad brings GE's products—from jet engines and diesel locomotives to giant wind turbines and hospital diagnostics machines—to life through the eyes of a wide-eyed young girl whose mom works at GE. GE is "Building, powering, moving, and curing the world," says the company. "Not just imagining. Doing. GE works."[3]

People can also be thought of as products. *Person marketing* consists of activities undertaken to create, maintain, or change attitudes or behavior toward particular people. People ranging from presidents, entertainers, and sports figures to professionals such as doctors, lawyers, and architects use person marketing to build their reputations. And businesses, charities, and other organizations use well-known personalities to help sell their products or causes. For example, Nike spends almost $1 billion annually on endorsement deals with a stable of stars spanning almost every conceivable sport worldwide, including headliners such as tennis greats Maria Sharapova and Rodger Federer, world soccer superstars Cristiano Ronaldo and Neymar, and current and former NBA all-stars Michael Jordan, Kobe Bryant, LeBron James, and Kevin Durant.[4]

● Organization marketing: GE's long-running Imagination at Work campaign markets the industrial giant as a company whose imaginative products and technologies are making a difference in the world.
GE

Place marketing involves activities undertaken to create, maintain, or change attitudes or behavior toward particular places. Cities, states, regions, and even entire nations compete to attract tourists, new residents, conventions, and company offices and factories. The New Orleans city website shouts "Go NOLA" and markets annual events such as Mardi Gras festivities and the New Orleans Jazz and Heritage Festival. Tourism Australia advertises that "There's Nothing Like Australia" and provides a website and smartphone app complete with videos, holiday ideas, destination information, and about anything else travelers might need to plan an Australian vacation.[5]

Ideas can also be marketed. In one sense, all marketing is the marketing of an idea, whether it is the general idea of brushing your teeth or the specific idea that Crest toothpastes

Social marketing
The use of traditional business marketing concepts and tools to encourage behaviors that will create individual and societal well-being.

create "healthy, beautiful smiles for life." Here, however, we narrow our focus to the marketing of *social ideas*. This area has been called **social marketing** and consists of using traditional business marketing concepts and tools to encourage behaviors that will create individual and societal well-being.

Social marketing programs cover a wide range of issues. The Ad Council of America (www.adcouncil.org), for example, has developed dozens of social advertising campaigns involving issues ranging from health care, education, and environmental sustainability to human rights and personal safety. But social marketing involves much more than just advertising. It involves a broad range of marketing strategies and marketing mix tools designed to bring about beneficial social change.[6]

Author Comment | Now that we've answered the "What is a product?" question, we dig into the specific decisions that companies must make when designing and marketing products and services.

Product and Service Decisions

Marketers make product and service decisions at three levels: individual product decisions, product line decisions, and product mix decisions. We discuss each in turn.

Individual Product and Service Decisions

● **Figure 8.2** shows the important decisions in the development and marketing of individual products and services. We will focus on decisions about *product attributes, branding, packaging, labeling and logos*, and *product support services*.

Product and Service Attributes

Developing a product or service involves defining the benefits that it will offer. These benefits are communicated and delivered by product attributes such as *quality, features*, and *style and design*.

Product quality
The characteristics of a product or service that bear on its ability to satisfy stated or implied customer needs.

Product Quality. **Product quality** is one of the marketer's major positioning tools. Quality affects product or service performance; thus, it is closely linked to customer value and satisfaction. In the narrowest sense, quality can be defined as "no defects." But most marketers go beyond this narrow definition. Instead, they define quality in terms of creating customer value and satisfaction. The American Society for Quality defines quality as the characteristics of a product or service that bear on its ability to satisfy stated or implied customer needs. Similarly, Siemens defines quality this way: "Quality is when our customers come back and our products don't."[7]

Total quality management (*TQM*) is an approach in which all of the company's people are involved in constantly improving the quality of products, services, and business processes. For most top companies, customer-driven quality has become a way of doing business. Today, companies are taking a *return-on-quality* approach, viewing quality as an investment and holding quality efforts accountable for bottom-line results.

Product quality has two dimensions: level and consistency. In developing a product, the marketer must first choose a *quality level* that will support the product's positioning. Here, product quality means *performance quality*—the product's ability to perform its functions. For example, a Rolls-Royce provides higher performance quality than a Chevrolet: It has a smoother ride, lasts longer, and provides more handcraftsmanship, custom design, luxury, and "creature comforts." Companies rarely try to offer the highest possible performance quality level; few customers want or can afford the high levels of quality offered in products such as a Rolls-Royce automobile, a Viking range, or a Rolex watch. Instead, companies choose a quality level that matches target market needs and the quality levels of competing products.

Beyond quality level, high quality also can mean high levels of quality consistency. Here, product quality means *conformance quality*—freedom from defects and consistency in delivering a targeted level of performance. All companies should strive for high levels

● FIGURE | 8.2
Individual Product Decisions

Don't forget Figure 8.1. The focus of all of these decisions is to create core customer value.

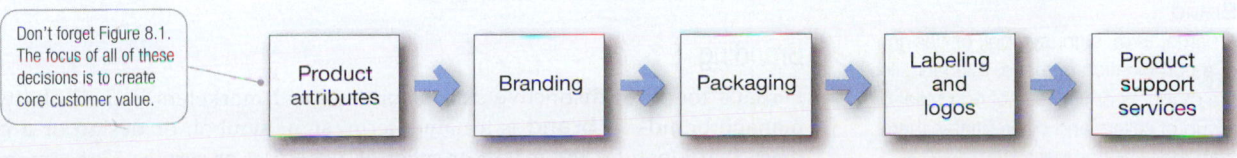

Product attributes → Branding → Packaging → Labeling and logos → Product support services

of conformance quality. In this sense, a Chevrolet can have just as much quality as a Rolls-Royce. Although a Chevy doesn't perform at the same level as a Rolls-Royce, it can just as consistently deliver the quality that customers pay for and expect.

Similarly, the Chick-fil-A fast-food chain doesn't aspire to provide gourmet dining experiences. However, by consistently meeting or exceeding customers' quality expectations, the chain has earned a trophy case full of awards for top food and service quality. Last year, for instance, the chain was the only restaurant named to *24/7 Wall Street's* Customer Service Hall of Fame, based on a survey of 2,500 adults asked about the quality of customer service at 150 of America's best-known companies across 15 industries. Chick-fil-A placed second overall, alongside the likes of Amazon, Marriott, and Apple.[8] Although it doesn't try to be Ritz-Carlton, it does send its managers to the Ritz-Carlton quality training program, where they learn things such as how to greet customers and how to probe for and serve unexpressed needs. Such consistency in meeting quality expectations has helped Chick-fil-A build a following of fiercely loyal customers.

Product Features. A product can be offered with varying features. A stripped-down model, one without any extras, is the starting point. The company can then create higher-level models by adding more features. Features are a competitive tool for differentiating the company's product from competitors' products. Being the first producer to introduce a valued new feature is one of the most effective ways to compete.

How can a company identify new features and decide which ones to add to its product? It should periodically survey buyers who have used the product and ask these questions: How do you like the product? Which specific features of the product do you like most? Which features could we add to improve the product? The answers to these questions provide the company with a rich list of feature ideas. The company can then assess each feature's *value* to customers versus its *cost* to the company. Features that customers value highly in relation to costs should be added.

Product Style and Design. Another way to add customer value is through distinctive *product style and design.* Design is a larger concept than style. *Style* simply describes the appearance of a product. Styles can be eye catching or yawn producing. A sensational style may grab attention and produce pleasing aesthetics, but it does not necessarily make the product *perform* better. Unlike style, *design* is more than skin deep—it goes to the very heart of a product. Good design contributes to a product's usefulness as well as to its looks.

Good design doesn't start with brainstorming new ideas and making prototypes. Design begins with observing customers, understanding their needs, and shaping their product-use experience. Product designers should think less about technical product specifications and more about how customers will use and benefit from the product. For example, using smart design based on consumer needs, Sonos created a wireless, internet-enabled speaker system that's easy to use and fills a whole house with great sound.

> In the past, setting up a whole-house entertainment or sound system required routing wires through walls, floors, and ceilings, creating a big mess and lots of expense. And if you moved, you couldn't take it with you. Enter Sonos, which took home-audio and theater systems to a new level worthy of the digital age. The innovative company created a wireless speaker system that's not just stylish but also easy to set up, easy to use, and easy to move to meet changing needs. With Sonos, you can stream high-quality sound through a variety of stylish speakers anywhere in your home with just an app and a tap on your smartphone. Smart design has paid off handsomely for Sonos. Founded in 2002, over just the past two years the company's sales have nearly tripled to an estimated $1 billion a year.[9]

Brand

A name, term, sign, symbol, or design, or a combination of these, that identifies the products or services of one seller or group of sellers and differentiates them from those of competitors.

Branding

Perhaps the most distinctive skill of professional marketers is their ability to build and manage brands. A **brand** is a name, term, sign, symbol, or design or a combination of these that identifies the maker or seller of a product or service. Consumers view a brand

● The meaning of a strong brand: The "branded" and "unbranded" Joshua Bell. The premier musician packs concert halls at an average of $100 or more a seat but made only $32 as a street musician at a Washington, DC, metro station.

(left) NBC via Getty Images; (right) The Washington Post/Getty Images

as an important part of a product, and branding can add value to a consumer's purchase. Customers attach meanings to brands and develop brand relationships. As a result, brands have meaning well beyond a product's physical attributes. Consider this story:[10]

● One Tuesday evening in January, Joshua Bell, one of the world's finest violinists, played at Boston's stately Symphony Hall before a packed audience who'd paid an average of $100 a seat. Based on the well-earned strength of the "Joshua Bell brand," the talented musician routinely drew standing-room-only audiences at all of his performances around the world. Three days later, however, as part of a *Washington Post* social experiment, Bell found himself standing in a Washington, DC, metro station, dressed in jeans, a T-shirt, and a Washington Nationals baseball cap. As morning commuters streamed by, Bell pulled out his $4 million Stradivarius violin, set the open case at his feet, and began playing the same revered classics he'd played in Boston. During the next 45 minutes, some 1,100 people passed by but few stopped to listen. Bell earned a total of $32. No one recognized the "unbranded" Bell, so few appreciated his artistry. What does that tell you about the meaning of a strong brand?

Branding has become so strong that today hardly anything goes unbranded. Salt is packaged in branded containers, common nuts and bolts are packaged with a distributor's label, and automobile parts—spark plugs, tires, filters—bear brand names that differ from those of the automakers. Even fruits, vegetables, dairy products, and poultry are branded—Cuties mandarin oranges, Dole Classic salads, Horizon Organic milk, Perdue chickens, and Eggland's Best eggs.

Branding helps buyers in many ways. Brand names help consumers identify products that might benefit them. Brands also say something about product quality and consistency—buyers who always buy the same brand know that they will get the same features, benefits, and quality each time they buy. Branding also gives the seller several advantages. The seller's brand name and trademark provide legal protection for unique product features that otherwise might be copied by competitors. Branding helps the seller to segment markets. For example, rather than offering just one general product to all consumers, Toyota can offer the different Lexus, Toyota, and Scion brands, each with numerous sub-brands—such as Avalon, Camry, Corolla, Prius, Yaris, Tundra, and Land Cruiser.

Finally, a brand name becomes the basis on which a whole story can be built about a product's special qualities. For example, the Cuties brand of pint-sized mandarins sets itself apart from ordinary oranges by promising "Kids love Cuties because Cuties are made for kids." They are a healthy snack that's "perfect for little hands": sweet, seedless, kid-sized, and easy to peel.[11] Building and managing brands are perhaps the marketer's most important tasks. We will discuss branding strategy in more detail later in the chapter.

Packaging

Packaging
The activities of designing and producing the container or wrapper for a product.

Packaging involves designing and producing the container or wrapper for a product. Traditionally, the primary function of the package was to hold and protect the product. In recent times, however, packaging has become an important marketing tool as well.

Increased competition and clutter on retail store shelves means that packages must now perform many sales tasks—from attracting buyers to communicating brand positioning to closing the sale. Not every customer will see a brand's advertising, social media pages, or other promotions. However, all consumers who buy and use a product will interact regularly with its packaging. Thus, the humble package represents prime marketing space.

Companies realize the power of good packaging to create immediate consumer recognition of a brand. For example, an average supermarket stocks about 42,000 items; the average Walmart supercenter carries 120,000 items. The typical shopper makes three out of four purchase decisions in stores and passes by some 300 items per minute. In this highly competitive environment, the package may be the seller's best and last chance to influence buyers. So the package itself becomes an important promotional medium.[12]

●**Distinctive packaging may become an important part of a brand's identity. An otherwise plain brown carton imprinted with only the familiar curved arrow from the Amazon.com logo—variously interpreted as "a to z" or even a smiley face—leaves no doubt as to who shipped the package sitting at your doorstep.**

© Lux Igitur/Alamy

Innovative packaging can give a company an advantage over competitors and boost sales. Distinctive packaging may even become an important part of a brand's identity. ● For example, an otherwise plain brown carton imprinted with the familiar curved arrow from the Amazon.com logo—variously interpreted as "a to z" or even a smiley face—leaves no doubt as to who shipped the package sitting at your doorstep. And Tiffany's distinctive blue boxes have come to embody the exclusive jewelry retailer's premium legacy and positioning. As the company puts it, "Glimpsed on a busy street or resting in the palm of a hand, Tiffany Blue Boxes make hearts beat faster and epitomize Tiffany's great heritage of elegance, exclusivity, and flawless craftsmanship."[13]

Poorly designed packages can cause headaches for consumers and lost sales for the company. Think about all those hard-to-open packages, such as DVD cases sealed with impossibly sticky labels, packaging with finger-splitting wire twist-ties, or sealed plastic clamshell containers that cause "wrap rage" and send thousands of people to the hospital each year with lacerations and puncture wounds. Another packaging issue is overpackaging—as when a tiny USB flash drive in an oversized cardboard and plastic display package is delivered in a giant corrugated shipping carton. Overpackaging creates an incredible amount of waste, frustrating those who care about the environment.

Amazon offers Frustration-Free Packaging to alleviate both wrap rage and overpackaging. The online retailer works with more than 2,000 companies, such as Fisher-Price, Mattel, Unilever, Microsoft, and others, to create smaller, easy-to-open, recyclable packages that use less packaging material and no frustrating plastic clamshells or wire ties. It currently offers more than 200,000 such items and to date has shipped more than 75 million of them to 175 countries. In the process, the initiative has eliminated nearly 60 million square feet of cardboard and 25 million pounds of packaging waste.[14]

In recent years, product safety has also become a major packaging concern. We have all learned to deal with hard-to-open "childproof" packaging. Due to the rash of product tampering scares in the 1980s, most drug producers and food makers now put their products in tamper-resistant packages. In making packaging decisions, the company also must heed growing environmental concerns. Fortunately, many companies have gone "green" by reducing their packaging and using environmentally responsible packaging materials.

Labeling and Logos

Labels and logos range from simple tags attached to products to complex graphics that are part of the packaging. They perform several functions. At the very least, the label *identifies* the product or brand, such as the name Sunkist stamped on oranges. The label might also *describe* several things about the product—who made it, where it was made, when it was made, its contents, how it is to be used, and how to use it safely. Finally, the label might help to *promote* the brand and engage customers. For many companies, labels have become an important element in broader marketing campaigns.

Labels and brand logos can support the brand's positioning and add personality to the brand. In fact, they can become a crucial element in the brand-customer connection. Customers often become strongly attached to logos as symbols of the brands they represent. Consider the

● Brand labels and logos: When Gap tried to modernize its familiar old logo, customers went ballistic, highlighting the powerful connection people have to the visual representations of their beloved brands.

Jean Francois FREY/PHOTOPQR/L'ALSACE/Newscom

feelings evoked by the logos of companies such as Google, Coca-Cola, Twitter, Apple, and Nike. Logos must be redesigned from time to time. For example, brands ranging from Yahoo!, eBay, and Southwest Airlines to Wendy's, Pizza Hut, Black+Decker, and Hershey have successfully adapted their logos to keep them contemporary and to meet the needs of new digital devices and interactive platforms such as the mobile apps and social media (see Real Marketing 8.1).

However, companies must take care when changing such important brand symbols. Customers often form strong connections to the visual representations of their brands and may react strongly to changes. ● For example, a few years ago when Gap introduced a more contemporary redesign of its familiar old logo—the well-known white text on a blue square—customers went ballistic and imposed intense online pressure. Gap reinstated the old logo after only one week.

Along with the positives, there has been a long history of legal concerns about labels and packaging. The Federal Trade Commission Act of 1914 held that false, misleading, or deceptive labels or packages constitute unfair competition. Labels can mislead customers, fail to describe important ingredients, or fail to include needed safety warnings. As a result, several federal and state laws regulate labeling. The most prominent is the Fair Packaging and Labeling Act of 1966, which set mandatory labeling requirements, encouraged voluntary industry packaging standards, and allowed federal agencies to set packaging regulations in specific industries. The Nutritional Labeling and Educational Act of 1990 requires sellers to provide detailed nutritional information on food products, and recent sweeping actions by the Food and Drug Administration (FDA) regulate the use of health-related terms such as *low fat, light, high fiber*, and *organic*. Sellers must ensure that their labels contain all the required information.

Product Support Services

Customer service is another element of product strategy. A company's offer usually includes some support services, which can be a minor part or a major part of the total offering. Later in this chapter, we will discuss services as products in themselves. Here, we discuss services that augment actual products.

Support services are an important part of the customer's overall brand experience. Lexus knows that good marketing doesn't end with making a sale. Keeping customers happy *after* the sale is the key to building lasting relationships. Lexus believes that if you delight the customer, and continue to delight the customer, you will have a customer for life. So Lexus dealers across the country will go to almost any lengths to take care of customers and keep them coming back:[15]

The typical Lexus dealership is, well, anything but typical. For example, in addition to its Starbucks coffee shop, one Florida Lexus dealership features four massage chairs, two putting greens, two customer lounges, and a library. At another Lexus dealership in a nearby city, "guests" leave their cars with a valet and are then guided by a concierge to a European-style coffee bar offering complimentary espresso, cappuccino, and a selection of pastries prepared by a chef trained in Rome. But at Lexus, customer service goes much deeper than just dealership amenities. From the very start, Lexus set out to revolutionize the auto ownership experience. Of course, Lexus knows that the best dealership visit is the one you never have to make. So it builds customer-pleasing cars to start with. ● In its "Lexus Covenant," the company vows that it will make "the finest cars ever built"—high-quality cars that need little servicing. However, the covenant also vows to value customers as important individuals and "treat each customer as we would a guest in our own home." So, when a car does need servicing, Lexus goes out of its way to make it easy and painless. Most dealers will even pick up a car and then return it when the maintenance is finished. And the car comes back spotless, thanks to a complimentary cleaning. You might even be surprised to find that they've touched up a door ding to help restore the car to its fresh-from-the-factory luster.

8.1 Brand Logo Makeovers for the Digital Age

It seems like everyone is doing it these days—giving their logos major makeovers. From Google, Hershey, Pizza Hut, and American Airlines to Southwest and IHOP, it's out with the old and in with the new. Such logo redesigns can be risky. Customers often form strong attachments to their favorite brands and the logos that represent them. Brand logos can be like a pair of old shoes—familiar and comforting—and customers often don't take kindly to changes. Given the risks, why are so many companies reworking their logos?

Companies have always taken great care to craft simple, easily recognized logos that quickly identify and position their brands and trigger positive consumer associations. However, in today's digital world, brand logos are being asked to do more than ever. A logo is no longer just a static symbol placed on a printed page, package, TV ad, billboard, or store display. Instead, today's logos must also meet the demands of an ever-more-diverse set of digital devices and media. A brand logo that looks great and communicates well on a package or in a magazine ad might fail miserably in a social media setting on a smartphone screen.

Today's logos must stand out visually on screens of all sizes, from big-screen TVs to tablets, mobile phones, and even smartwatches. Often, they must also function as interactive icons or animated activity indicators on web, mobile, and social media pages. As a result, companies are adapting their logos to keep them in sync with the rapidly evolving digital times.

Most logo modifications focus on creating simpler, brighter, more modern designs that present better on digital screens and platforms. For example, Hershey flipped its colors from light letters on a dark field to dark letters on a white field while also replacing its long-standing image of a Hershey's Kiss wrapped in silver foil with a more contemporary silhouette version. Pizza Hut's new logo consists of a simple pizza-shaped medallion with the brand name and familiar roof symbol reversed out in white. And Southwest went from black all-capital letters beneath a jumbo jet image to bright blue letters in title format accompanied by its signature heart icon in rainbow colors.

Such redesigns have multiple aims, but the primary objective is to make the logos more digital device friendly. For example, the old IHOP logo had white letters placed on a blue field with a downward-curving red banner containing the word *restaurant*. Now, IHOP's letters are blue on a white field, a design that stands out better against the white backgrounds on most web, mobile, and social media sites. The new logo also replaces the old frown-like "restaurant" banner with an upward curving red line under the *o* and the *p*, creating a smiley face that adds a burst of happiness to the brand.

Some logo redesigns go much, much deeper. For example, consider the recent changes to Google's familiar blue, red, green, and yellow logo. At first glance, the changes seem minor—you might not even have noticed them. The letter colors remain largely the same, as does the childlike quality that we've come to associate with the Google brand. The biggest difference is the new typeface—Google changed its old serif typeface (with little lines and squiggles at the ends of letters) to a sans serif typeface (one like this without the added lines and squiggles). The result is a simpler, cleaner, more readable logo. According to Google, the logo change was motivated mostly by mobile usage. The streamlined font shrinks down more legibly than fancier fonts, so it transfers more readily across all kinds of screens. Google claims that its new logo can be read just as well on a 2.5-inch Android Wear watch as it can on a 50-inch TV screen.

But Google didn't just change the logo typeface. It created a full kit of new brand logo tools befitting the digital age. For example, recognizing that six letters are just too many for some uses, Google also created a more compact one-letter version, a *G* in the new sans typeface, partitioned into the four familiar Google colors. It also fashioned a contemporary four-color microphone icon that users can tap to speak into an Android device. Finally, it crafted a set of four animated dots (one in each color) for use during interactive and transitional moments to indicate activities such as waiting, thinking, speaking, and replying.

All of the new Google logo elements work seamlessly together. So, for example, when you pick up your phone and activate the Google microphone icon, "the Google logo will morph from 'Google' into the dots, which undulate like water in anticipation of your query," notes one reporter. "As you talk, the dots will become an equalizer, reacting to the sound of your vocalizations. Then when you're done talking, the waveform becomes dots again, which spin as Google looks up your results. Then once the results are presented, the dots return to good old 'Google' again." Thus, the Google logo is no longer just a static emblem that sits atop an online search bar. It's a full set of dynamic symbols that bring the brand and its many functions to life across today's digital screens and platforms.

Companies need to tread carefully when making changes to their brand logos. Such

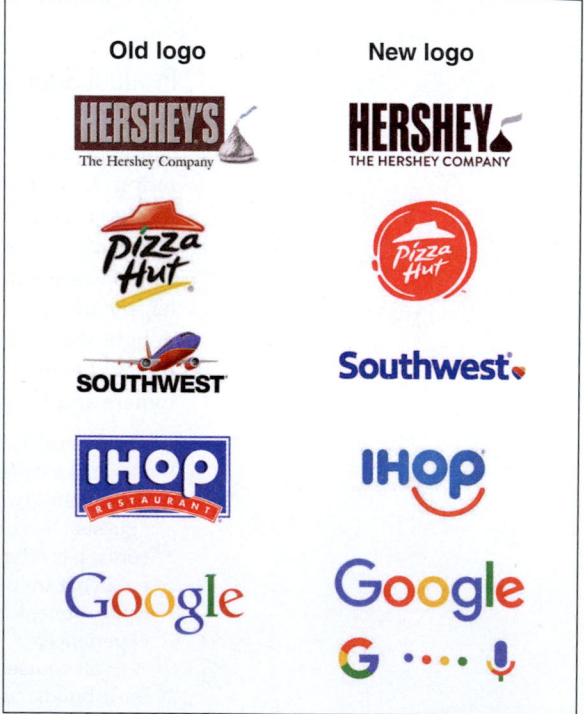

Old logo	New logo

Brand logo makeovers: Many companies are redesigning their logos to keep them in sync with the rapidly evolving digital times.

The Hershey Company; Pizza Hut, Inc.; Southwest Airlines; International House of Pancakes, LLC; Google and the Google logo are registered trademarks of Google Inc., used with permission.

changes often require a huge investment. For example, Southwest's seemingly simple logo redesign requires sweeping changes that touch almost every aspect of the company's operations. Just think of all the places you see Southwest's logo—from its advertising, web, and social media activities to the graphics on its airplanes and the design of its airport gates to its corporate letterhead. Everything must be redone to reflect the new logo look.

Perhaps more important, the old logos closely link brands to the hearts and minds of consumers. Studies show that the stronger their attachments to a brand, the more resistant consumers are to logo changes. For example, although most experts would agree that the new Hershey logo is a vast improvement, some consumers balked, suggesting that the silhouette Kiss resembles a lump of poop. "All I can see is the emoji poo," says one perplexed observer. "With apologies to Hershey: Your new logo kinda stinks." And when American Airlines replaced its familiar 45-year-old "AA eagle" logo with a more modern version, the new logo became a flashpoint for both brand fans and detractors. Although the redesign was probably overdue, fans lamented the loss of the classic design, whereas detractors claimed that the millions spent on repainting all of American's planes should have been invested in improving the airline's customer service.

Such examples highlight the powerful connections people have to the visual representations of their brands. When logo changes are required—as they most certainly will be at some point—the best course is to alert customers to the upcoming changes and to explain why they are needed. Google did that in a widely distributed video showing the evolution of its logo and the reasons behind the most recent redesign. That's one reason that its massive logo makeover went so smoothly. As the video explains, "We think we've taken the best of Google (simple, uncluttered, colorful, friendly), and recast it not just for the Google of today, but for the Google of tomorrow."

Sources: Mark Wilson, "Google's New Logo Is Its Biggest Update in 16 Years," *Fast Company,* September 1, 2015, www.fastcodesign.com/3050613/googles-new-logo-is-its-biggest-update-in-16-years; Richard Feloni, "Did You Notice That These 20 Companies Changed Their Logos This Year?" *Business Insider,* October 27, 2015, www.businessinsider.com/corporate-logo-changes-2015-10; Lauren Entis, "Why We Hate Logo Redesigns," *Entrepreneur,* September 11, 2015, www.entrepreneur.com/article/250559; Traci Cox, "Logo Remixes: Are These Big Brand Logo Changes Hits or Misses?" *Business.com,* September 23, 2015, www.business.com/arts-and-design/are-these-big-brand-logo-changes-hits-or-misses/; "Google, Evolved," www.youtube.com/watch?v=olFEpeMwgHk, accessed June 2016; and www.youtube.com/watch?v=0PU7KX3i2pM and www.usatoday.com/videos/tech/2015/09/01/71532636/, accessed September 2016.

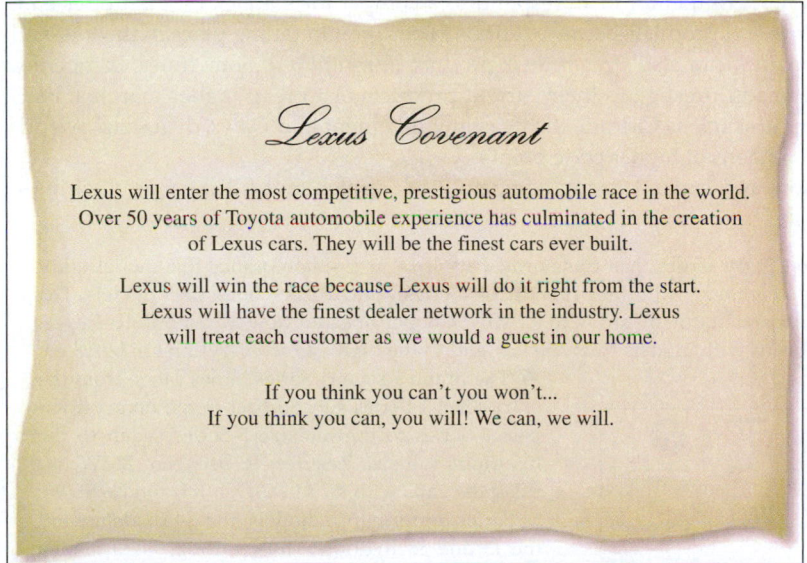

Lexus Covenant

Lexus will enter the most competitive, prestigious automobile race in the world. Over 50 years of Toyota automobile experience has culminated in the creation of Lexus cars. They will be the finest cars ever built.

Lexus will win the race because Lexus will do it right from the start. Lexus will have the finest dealer network in the industry. Lexus will treat each customer as we would a guest in our home.

If you think you can't you won't... If you think you can, you will! We can, we will!

● **Customer service: From the start, under the Lexus Covenant, Lexus's high-quality support services create an unmatched car ownership experience and some of the world's most satisfied car owners.**

Toyota Motor Sales, USA, Inc.

By all accounts, Lexus has lived up to its ambitious customer-satisfaction promise. It has created what appear to be the world's most satisfied car owners. Lexus regularly tops not just the industry quality ratings but also customer-satisfaction ratings in both the United States and globally. "My wife will never buy another car except a Lexus," says one satisfied Lexus owner. "They come to our house, pick up the car, do an oil change, spiff it up, and bring it back. She's sold for life."

The first step in designing support services is to survey customers periodically to assess the value of current services and obtain ideas for new ones. Once the company has assessed the quality of various support services to customers, it can take steps to fix problems and add new services that will both delight customers and yield profits to the company.

Many companies now use a sophisticated mix of phone, email, online, social media, mobile, and interactive voice and data technologies to provide support services that were not possible before. For example, home-improvement store Lowe's offers a vigorous dose of customer service at both its store and online locations that makes shopping easier, answers customer questions, and handles problems. Customers can access Lowe's extensive support by phone, email (CareTW@lowes.com), website, mobile app, and Twitter via @LowesCares. The Lowe's website and mobile app link to a buying guide and how-to library. In its stores, Lowe's has equipped employees with 42,000 iPhones filled with custom apps and add-on hardware, letting them perform service tasks such as checking inventory at nearby stores, looking up specific customer purchase histories, sharing how-to videos, and checking competitor prices—all without leaving the customer's side. Lowe's is even experimenting with putting interactive, talking, moving robots in stores that can greet customers as they enter, answer even their most vexing questions, and guide them to whatever merchandise they are seeking.[16]

Product Line Decisions

Product line

A group of products that are closely related because they function in a similar manner, are sold to the same customer groups, are marketed through the same types of outlets, or fall within given price ranges.

Beyond decisions about individual products and services, product strategy also calls for building a product line. A **product line** is a group of products that are closely related because they function in a similar manner, are sold to the same customer groups, are marketed through the same types of outlets, or fall within given price ranges. For example, Nike produces several lines of athletic shoes and apparel, and Marriott offers several lines of hotels.

The major product line decision involves *product line length*—the number of items in the product line. The line is too short if the manager can increase profits by adding items; the line is too long if the manager can increase profits by dropping items. Managers need to analyze their product lines periodically to assess each item's sales and profits and understand how each item contributes to the line's overall performance.

A company can expand its product line in two ways: by *line filling* or *line stretching*. *Product line filling* involves adding more items within the present range of the line. There are several reasons for product line filling: reaching for extra profits, satisfying dealers, using excess capacity, being the leading full-line company, and plugging holes to keep out competitors. However, line filling is overdone if it results in cannibalization (eating up sales of the company's own existing products) and customer confusion. The company should ensure that new items are noticeably different from existing ones.

Product line stretching occurs when a company lengthens its product line beyond its current range. The company can stretch its line downward, upward, or both ways. Companies located at the upper end of the market can stretch their lines *downward*. For example, Mercedes has stretched downward with the CLA line to draw in younger, first-time buyers. A company may stretch downward to plug a market hole that otherwise would attract a new competitor or to respond to a competitor's attack on the upper end. Or it may add low-end products because it finds faster growth taking place in the low-end segments. Companies can also stretch their product lines *upward*. Sometimes, companies stretch upward to add prestige to their current products or to reap higher margins. P&G did that with brands such as Cascade dishwashing detergent and Dawn dish soap by adding "Platinum" versions at higher price points.

As they grow and expand, many company both stretch and fill their product lines. Consider BMW:[17]

Product mix (or product portfolio)

The set of all product lines and items that a particular seller offers for sale.

Over the years, BMW Group has transformed itself from a single-brand, five-model automaker into a powerhouse with three brands, 14 "Series," and dozens of distinct models. The company has expanded downward with its MINI Cooper line and upward with Rolls-Royce. Its BMW line brims with models from the low end to the high end to everything in between. ● The brand's seven "Series" lines range from the entry-level 1-Series subcompact to the luxury-compact 3-Series to the midsize 5-Series sedan to the luxurious full-size 7-Series. In between, BMW has filled the gaps with its X1, X3, X4, X5, and X6 SUVs; M-Series performance models; the Z4 roadster; and the i3 and i8 hybrids. Thus, through skillful line stretching and filling, while staying within its premium positioning, BMW now has brands and lines that successfully appeal to the rich, the super-rich, and the hope-to-be-rich.

● Product line stretching and filling: Through skillful line stretching and filling, BMW now has brands and lines that successfully appeal to the rich, the super-rich, and the hope-to-be-rich.

BMW of North America

Product Mix Decisions

An organization with several product lines has a product mix. A **product mix** (or **product portfolio**) consists of all the product lines and items that a particular seller offers for sale. For example, Colgate-Palmolive is perhaps best known for its toothpaste and other oral care products. But, in fact, Colgate is a $17.3 billion consumer products company that makes and markets a full product mix

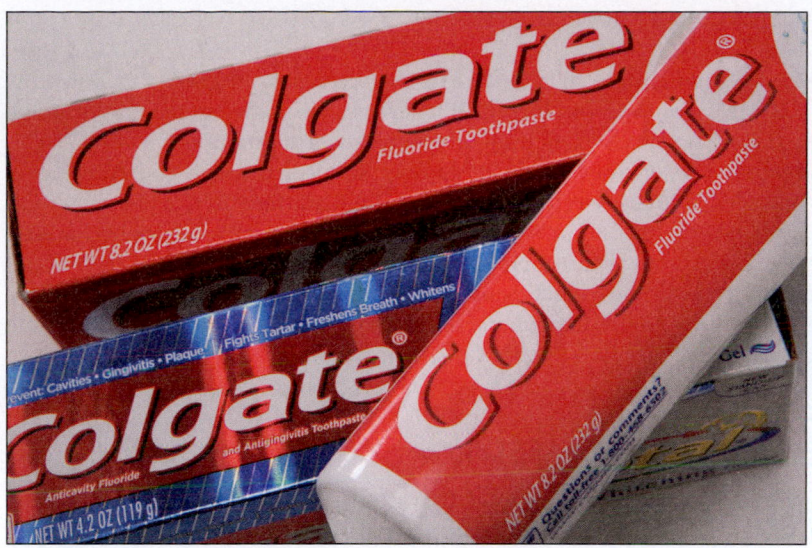

● The product mix: Colgate-Palmolive's nicely consistent product mix contains dozens of brands that constitute the "Colgate World of Care"— products that "every day, people like you trust to care for themselves and the ones they love."

Bloomberg/Getty Images

consisting of dozens of familiar lines and brands. Colgate divides its overall product mix into four major lines: oral care, personal care, home care, and pet nutrition. Each product line consists of many brands and items.[18]

A company's product mix has four important dimensions: width, length, depth, and consistency. Product mix *width* refers to the number of different product lines the company carries. ● For example, Colgate markets a fairly wide product mix, consisting of dozens of brands that constitute the "Colgate World of Care"—products that "every day, people like you trust to care for themselves and the ones they love." By contrast, GE manufactures as many as 250,000 items across a broad range of categories, from lightbulbs to medical equipment, jet engines, and diesel locomotives.

Product mix *length* refers to the total number of items a company carries within its product lines. Colgate carries several brands within each line. For example, its personal care line includes Softsoap liquid soaps and body washes, Irish Spring bar soaps, Speed Stick deodorants, and Skin Bracer, Afta, and Colgate toiletries and shaving products, among others. The Colgate home care line includes Palmolive and AJAX dishwashing products, Suavitel fabric conditioners, and AJAX and Murphy Oil Soap cleaners. The pet nutrition line houses the Hills and Science Diet pet food brands.

Product line *depth* refers to the number of versions offered of each product in the line. Colgate toothpastes come in numerous varieties, ranging from Colgate Total, Colgate Optic White, and Colgate Tartar Protection to Colgate Sensitive, Colgate Enamel Health, Colgate PreviDent, and Colgate Kids. Then each variety comes in its own special forms and formulations. For example, you can buy Colgate Total in regular, clean mint, advanced whitening, deep clean, total daily repair, 2in1 liquid gel, or any of several other versions.

Finally, the *consistency* of the product mix refers to how closely related the various product lines are in end use, production requirements, distribution channels, or some other way. Colgate's product lines are consistent insofar as they are consumer products that go through the same distribution channels. The lines are less consistent insofar as they perform different functions for buyers.

These product mix dimensions provide the handles for defining the company's product strategy. A company can increase its business in four ways. It can add new product lines, widening its product mix. In this way, its new lines build on the company's reputation in its other lines. A company can lengthen its existing product lines to become a more full-line company. It can add more versions of each product and thus deepen its product mix. Finally, a company can pursue more product line consistency— or less—depending on whether it wants to have a strong reputation in a single field or in several fields.

From time to time, a company may also have to streamline its product mix to pare out marginally performing lines and to regain its focus. For example, P&G pursues a megabrand strategy built around 23 billion-dollar-plus brands in the household care and beauty and grooming categories. During the past decade, the consumer products giant has sold off dozens of major brands that no longer fit either its evolving focus or the billion-dollar threshold, ranging from Jif peanut butter, Crisco shortening, Folgers coffee, Pringles snack chips, and Sunny Delight drinks to Noxzema skin care products, Right Guard deodorant, Aleve pain reliever, Duracell batteries, CoverGirl and Max Factor cosmetics, Wella and Clairol hair care products, and Iams and other pet food brands. These divestments allow P&G to focus investment and energy on the 70 to 80 core brands that yield 90 percent of its sales and more than 95 percent of profits. "Less [can] be much more," says P&G's CEO.[19]

Author | As noted at the start of
Comment | this chapter, services are
"products," too—intangible ones. So
all the product topics we've discussed
so far apply to services as well as
to physical products. However, in
this section, we focus on the special
characteristics and marketing needs
that set services apart.

Services Marketing

Services have grown dramatically in recent years. Services now account for almost 80 percent of the U.S. gross domestic product (GDP). Services are growing even faster in the world economy, making up almost 63 percent of the gross world product.[20]

Service industries vary greatly. *Governments* offer services through courts, employment services, hospitals, military services, police and fire departments, the postal service, and schools. *Private not-for-profit organizations* offer services through museums, charities, churches, colleges, foundations, and hospitals. In addition, a large number of *business organizations* offer services—airlines, banks, hotels, insurance companies, consulting firms, medical and legal practices, entertainment and telecommunications companies, real estate firms, retailers, and others.

The Nature and Characteristics of a Service

A company must consider four special service characteristics when designing marketing programs: intangibility, inseparability, variability, and perishability (see ● **Figure 8.3**).

Service intangibility means that services cannot be seen, tasted, felt, heard, or smelled before they are bought. For example, people undergoing cosmetic surgery cannot see the result before the purchase. Airline passengers have nothing but a ticket and a promise that they and their luggage will arrive safely at the intended destination, hopefully at the same time. To reduce uncertainty, buyers look for *signals* of service quality. They draw conclusions about quality from the place, people, price, equipment, and communications that they can see.

Therefore, the service provider's task is to make the service tangible in one or more ways and send the right signals about quality. The Mayo Clinic does this well:[21]

> When it comes to hospitals, most patients can't really judge "product quality." It's a very complex product that's hard to understand, and you can't try it out before buying it. So when considering a hospital, most people unconsciously search for evidence that the facility is caring, competent, and trustworthy. The Mayo Clinic doesn't leave these things to chance. Rather, it offers patients organized and honest evidence of its dedication to "providing the best care to every patient every day."
>
> Inside, staff is trained to act in a way that clearly signals Mayo Clinic's concern for patient well-being. For example, doctors regularly follow up with patients at home to see how they are doing, and they work with patients to smooth out scheduling problems. The clinic's physical facilities also send the right signals. They've been carefully designed to offer a place of refuge, show caring and respect, and signal competence. Looking for external confirmation? Go online and hear directly from those who've been to the clinic or work there. The Mayo Clinic uses social networking—everything from blogs to Facebook, Twitter, YouTube, Instagram, and Pinterest—to enhance the patient experience. ● For example, on the Sharing Mayo Clinic blog (http://sharing.mayoclinic.org), patients and their families retell their Mayo experiences, and Mayo employees offer behind-the-scenes views. The result? Highly loyal customers who willingly spread the good word to others, building one of the most powerful brands in health care.

Service intangibility
Services cannot be seen, tasted, felt, heard, or smelled before they are bought.

● FIGURE | 8.3
Four Service Characteristics

Although services are "products" in a general sense, they have special characteristics and marketing needs. The biggest differences come from the fact that services are essentially intangible and that they are created through direct interactions with customers. Think about your experiences with an airline or Google versus Nike or Apple.

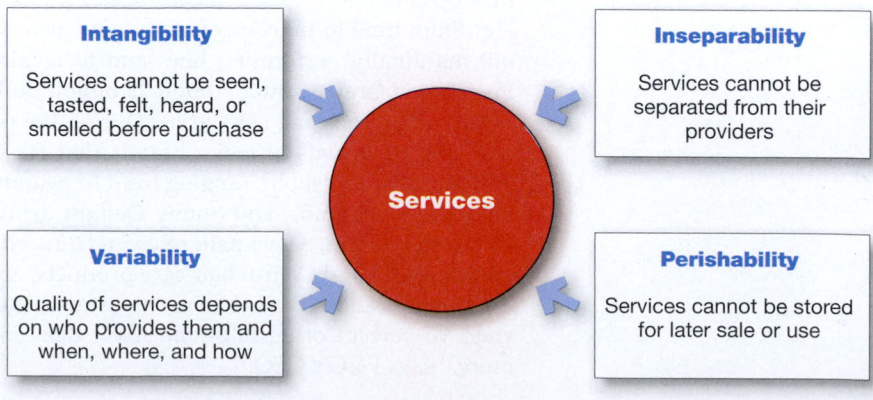

Intangibility
Services cannot be seen, tasted, felt, heard, or smelled before purchase

Inseparability
Services cannot be separated from their providers

Services

Variability
Quality of services depends on who provides them and when, where, and how

Perishability
Services cannot be stored for later sale or use

By providing customers with organized, honest evidence of its capabilities, the Mayo Clinic has built one of the most powerful brands in health care. Its Sharing Mayo Clinic blog lets you hear directly from those who have been to the clinic or who work there.

Mayo Clinic

Service inseparability
Services are produced and consumed at the same time and cannot be separated from their providers.

Service variability
The quality of services may vary greatly depending on who provides them and when, where, and how they are provided.

Service perishability
Services cannot be stored for later sale or use.

Service profit chain
The chain that links service firm profits with employee and customer satisfaction.

Physical goods are produced, then stored, then later sold, and then still later consumed. In contrast, services are first sold and then produced and consumed at the same time. **Service inseparability** means that services cannot be separated from their providers, whether the providers are people or machines. If a service employee provides the service, then the employee becomes a part of the service. And customers don't just buy and use a service; they play an active role in its delivery. Customer coproduction makes *provider–customer interaction* a special feature of services marketing. Both the provider and the customer affect the service outcome.

Service variability means that the quality of services depends on who provides them as well as when, where, and how they are provided. For example, some hotels—say, Marriott—have reputations for providing better service than others. Still, within a given Marriott hotel, one registration-counter employee may be cheerful and efficient, whereas another standing just a few feet away may be grumpy and slow. Even the quality of a single Marriott employee's service varies according to his or her energy and frame of mind at the time of each customer encounter.

Service perishability means that services cannot be stored for later sale or use. Some doctors charge patients for missed appointments because the service value existed only at that point and disappeared when the patient did not show up. The perishability of services is not a problem when demand is steady. However, when demand fluctuates, service firms often have difficult problems. For example, because of rush-hour demand, public transportation companies have to own much more equipment than they would if demand were even throughout the day. Thus, service firms often design strategies for producing a better match between demand and supply. Hotels and resorts charge lower prices in the off-season to attract more guests. And restaurants hire part-time employees to serve during peak periods.

Marketing Strategies for Service Firms

Just like manufacturing businesses, good service firms use marketing to position themselves strongly in chosen target markets. Enterprise Rent-A-Car gives you "Car rental and much more"; Zipcar offers "Wheels when you want them." At CVS Pharmacy, "Expect something extra"; Walgreens meets you "at the corner of happy & healthy." And St. Jude Children's Hospital is "Finding cures. Saving children." These and other service firms establish their positions through traditional marketing mix activities. However, because services differ from tangible products, they often require additional marketing approaches.

The Service Profit Chain

In a service business, the customer and the front-line service employee *interact* to co-create the service. Effective interaction, in turn, depends on the skills of front-line service employees and on the support processes backing these employees. Thus, successful service companies focus their attention on both their customers and their employees. They understand the **service profit chain**, which links service firm profits with employee and customer satisfaction. This chain consists of five links:[22]

- *Internal service quality.* Superior employee selection and training, a quality work environment, and strong support for those dealing with customers, which results in . . .
- *Satisfied and productive service employees.* More satisfied, loyal, and hardworking employees, which results in . . .

- *Greater service value.* More effective and efficient customer value creation, engagement, and service delivery, which results in …
- *Satisfied and loyal customers.* Satisfied customers who remain loyal, make repeat purchases, and refer other customers, which results in …
- *Healthy service profits and growth.* Superior service firm performance.

For example, customer-service all-star Zappos.com—the online shoes, clothing, and accessories retailers—knows that happy customers and profits begin with happy, dedicated, energetic employees (see Real Marketing 8.2). Similarly, at Four Seasons Hotels and Resorts, creating delighted customers involves much more than just crafting a lofty customer-focused marketing strategy and handing it down from the top. At Four Seasons, satisfying customers is everybody's business. And it all starts with satisfied employees:[23]

Four Seasons has perfected the art of high-touch, carefully crafted service. Whether it's at the tropical island paradise at the Four Seasons Resort Mauritius or the luxurious sub-Saharan "camp" at the Four Seasons Safari Lodge Serengeti, guests paying $1,000 or more a night expect to have their minds read. For these guests, Four Seasons doesn't disappoint. As one Four Seasons Maui guest once told a manager, "If there's a heaven, I hope it's run by Four Seasons." What makes Four Seasons so special? It's really no secret. It's the quality of the Four Seasons staff. Four Seasons knows that happy, satisfied employees make for happy, satisfied customers. So just as it does for customers, Four Seasons respects and pampers its employees.

Four Seasons hires the best people, pays them well, orients them carefully, instills in them a sense of pride, and rewards them for outstanding service deeds. It treats employees as it would its most important guests. For example, all employees—from the maids who make up the rooms to the general manager—dine together (free of charge) in the hotel cafeteria. Perhaps best of all, every employee receives free stays at other Four Seasons resorts, six free nights per year after one year with the company. The room stays make employees feel as important and pampered as the guests they serve and motivate employees to achieve even higher levels of service in their own jobs. Says one Four Seasons staffer, "You come back from those trips on fire. You want to do so much for the guests." As a result of such actions, the annual turnover for full-time employees at Four Seasons is only 18 percent, half the industry average. Four Seasons has been included for 18 straight years on *Fortune* magazine's list of 100 Best Companies to Work For. And that's the biggest secret to Four Seasons' success.

Services marketing requires more than just traditional external marketing using the four Ps. ● **Figure 8.4** shows that services marketing also requires *internal marketing* and *interactive marketing*. **Internal marketing** means that the service firm must orient and motivate its customer-contact employees and supporting service people to work as a team to provide customer satisfaction. Marketers must get everyone in the organization to be customer centered. In fact, internal marketing must *precede* external marketing. For example, Zappos starts by hiring the right people and carefully orienting and inspiring them to give unparalleled customer service. The idea is to make certain that employees themselves believe in the brand so that they can authentically deliver the brand's promise to customers.

Interactive marketing means that service quality depends heavily on the quality of the buyer–seller interaction during the service encounter. In product marketing, product quality often depends little on how the product is obtained. But in services marketing, service quality depends on both the service deliverer and the quality of delivery. Service marketers, therefore, have to master interactive marketing skills. Thus, Zappos selects

Internal marketing
Orienting and motivating customer-contact employees and supporting service employees to work as a team to provide customer satisfaction.

Interactive marketing
Training service employees in the fine art of interacting with customers to satisfy their needs.

● FIGURE | 8.4
Three Types of Services Marketing

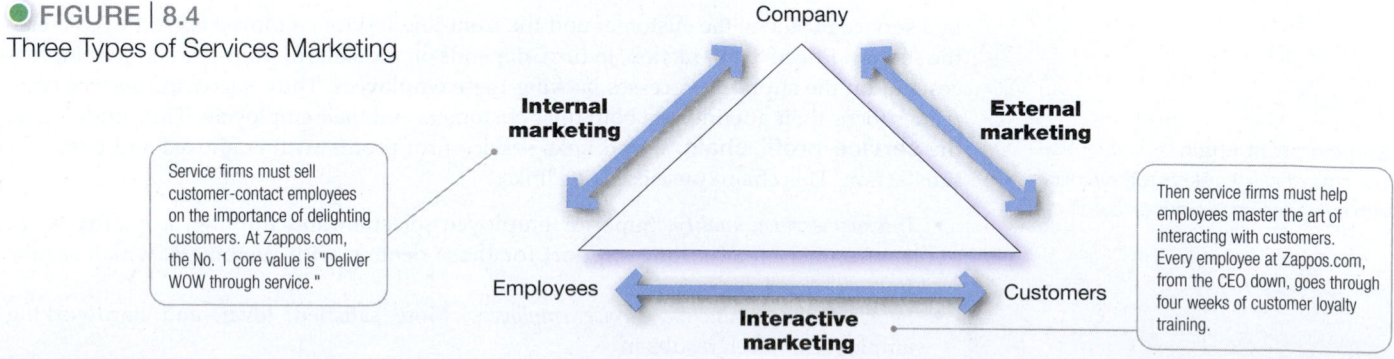

Service firms must sell customer-contact employees on the importance of delighting customers. At Zappos.com, the No. 1 core value is "Deliver WOW through service."

Then service firms must help employees master the art of interacting with customers. Every employee at Zappos.com, from the CEO down, goes through four weeks of customer loyalty training.

Real Marketing

8.2 Zappos.com: Taking Care of Those Who Take Care of Customers

Imagine a retailer with service so good its customers wish it would take over the Internal Revenue Service or start up an airline. It might sound like a marketing fantasy, but this scenario is a reality for customer-service all-star Zappos.com. At Zappos, the customer experience really does come first—it's a daily obsession. Says Zappos's understated CEO Tony Hsieh (pronounced "Shay"), "Our whole goal at Zappos is for the Zappos brand to be about the very best customer service and customer experience." Zappos is "Powered by Service."

From the start, the scrappy online retailer of shoes, clothing, handbags, and accessories made customer service a cornerstone of its marketing. As a result, Zappos grew astronomically. In fact, Zappos's online success and passion for customers made it an ideal match for another highly successful, customer-obsessed online retailer, Amazon.com, which purchased Zappos a few years ago and has allowed it to operate as an independent division.

At Zappos, customer care starts with a deep-down, customer-focused culture. How does Zappos turn this culture into a customer reality? It all starts with the company's customer-service reps—what the company calls its Customer Loyalty Team. Most of Zappos.com's business is driven by word of mouth and customer interactions with company employees. And Zappos knows that happy *customers* begin with happy, dedicated, and energetic *employees*. So the company starts by hiring the right people, training them thoroughly in customer-service basics, and inspiring them to new heights in taking care of customers.

"Getting customers excited about the service they had at Zappos has to come naturally," says one Zappos marketing executive. "You can't teach it; you have to hire for it." Hiring the right people starts with the application process. The invitation to apply on the Zappos website suggests the kind of people Zappos seeks:

Please check out the Zappos Family's 10 Core Values before applying! They are the heart and soul of our culture and central to how we do business. If you are "fun and a little weird"—and think the other 9 Core Values fit you too—please take a look at our openings! PS: At the Zappos Family of Companies, over-sized egos are not welcome. Over-sized Eggos, however, are most welcome and appreciated!

Once hired, to make sure Zappos's customer obsession permeates the entire organization, each new employee—everyone from the CEO and chief financial officer to the children's footwear buyer—is required to go through four weeks of customer loyalty training. In fact, in an effort to weed out the half-hearted, Zappos actually bribes people to quit. During the four weeks of customer-service training, it offers employees a full month's pay in cash plus payment for the time worked if they *leave* the company. The theory goes that those willing to take the money and run aren't right for Zappos's culture anyway.

Once in place, Zappos treats employees as well as it treats customers. "It's not so much about what the company provides externally," says CEO Hsieh. "It's what the employees ultimately feel internally." The Zappos family culture emphasizes "a satisfying and fulfilling job ... and a career you can be proud of. Work hard. Play hard. All the time!" Hsieh continues, "We think it's important for employees to have fun...it drives employee engagement." Zappos creates a relaxed, fun-loving, and close-knit family atmosphere, complete with free meals, a nap room, Nerf gun wars, and Oreo eating contests, not to mention full benefits, a 40 percent employee discount on all Zappos.com merchandise, and even a full-time life coach— all of which make it a great place to work. In fact, Zappos appears annually on *Fortune* magazine's "100 Best Companies to Work For" list.

The result is what one observer calls "1,550 perpetually chipper employees." Every year, the company publishes a "culture book," filled

with unedited, often gushy testimonials from Zapponians about what it's like to work there. "Oh my gosh," says one employee, "this is my home away from home.... It's changed my life.... Our culture is the best reason to work here." Says another, "The most surprising thing about coming to work here is that there are no limits. So pretty much anything you are passionate about is possible." And what are the things about which Zapponians are most passionate? The Zappos family's No. 1 core value: "Deliver WOW through service."

Such enthusiastic employees, in turn, make outstanding brand ambassadors. Whereas many companies bury contact information several links deep on their web and mobile sites because they don't really want to hear from customers, Zappos.com puts the number at the top of every single page and staffs its call center 24/7. Hsieh

Zappos knows that delivering customer happiness begins with happy, dedicated, energetic employees. Zappos is "Powered by Service."
Zappos

sees each customer contact as an opportunity: "We actually want to talk to our customers," he says. "If we handle the call well, we have an opportunity to create an emotional impact and lasting memory." Moreover, the lifetime value of a customer who calls the company for any reason is five to six times as much as the value of a customer who never calls.

Hsieh insists that reps be helpful with anything that customers might call about—and he really means it. One customer called in search of a pizza joint open after midnight in Santa Monica, CA. Two minutes later, the Zappos rep found him one. And Zappos doesn't hold its reps accountable for call times. Its longest phone call lasted 10 hours. Another call, from a customer who wanted the rep's help while she looked at what seemed like thousands of pairs of shoes, lasted almost six hours.

At Zappos, each employee is like a little marketing department. Relationships—inside and outside the company—mean everything at Zappos. Hsieh and many other employees stay in direct touch with customers, with each other, and with just about anyone else interested in the company. They use social networking tools such as Facebook, Twitter, Instagram, and blogs to share information, both good and bad. Such openness might worry some retailers, but Zappos embraces it.

Zappos even features employees in its marketing. For example, it uses associates in short videos to describe and explain its products. In one recent year, it turned out 100,000 such videos of staff—not professional models—showing off shoes, bags, and clothing. Zappos found that when the product includes a personal video explanation, purchases rise and returns decrease.

The moral: Just as the service-profit chain suggests, taking good care of customers begins with taking good care of those who take care of customers. The Zappos customer-driven philosophy is perhaps best summed up by the title of CEO Hsieh's book—*Delivering Happiness: A Path to Profits, Passion, and Purpose*. Zappos's enthusiasm and culture are infectious. Put Zappos happy reps together with happy customers, and good things will result. "We've actually had customers ask us if we would please start an airline or run the IRS," Hsieh says, adding, "30 years from now I wouldn't rule out a Zappos airline that's all about the very best service."

Sources: Portions based on http://about.zappos.com/jobs, accessed June 2016; and Natalie Zmuda, "Zappos: Customer Service First—and a Daily Obsession," *Advertising Age*, October 20, 2008, p. 36; with additional information and quotes from Jim Edwards, "Check Out the Insane Lengths Zappos Customer Service Reps Will Go To," *Business Insider*, January 9, 2012, www.businessinsider.com/zappos-customer-service-crm-2012-1; Tony Hsieh, "Zappos's CEO on Going to Extremes for Customers," *Harvard Business Review*, July–August 2010, pp. 41–44; Christopher Mims, "The Customer-Service Quandary: Touchy Feely or Do It Yourself?" *Wall Street Journal*, November 2, 2015, www.wsj.com/articles/the-customer-service-quandary-touchy-feely-or-do-it-yourself-1446440460; "Zappos Corporate Culture: Innovating for Employees, Clients, and the Ecosystem," *Innovation Is Everywhere*, www.innovationiseverywhere.com/zappos-corporate-culture-innovating-employees-clients-ecosystem/, accessed June 2016; and www.youtube.com/users/zappos and www.zappos.com, accessed September 2016.

only people with an innate "passion to serve" and instructs them carefully in the fine art of interacting with customers to satisfy their every need. All new hires—at all levels of the company—complete a four-week customer-loyalty training regimen.

Today, as competition and costs increase and as productivity and quality decrease, more services marketing sophistication is needed. Service companies face three major marketing tasks: They want to increase their *service differentiation, service quality*, and *service productivity*.

At any of several large REI stores, consumers can get hands-on experience with merchandise before buying it via the store's mountain bike test trail, gear-testing stations, a huge rock climbing wall, or an in-store simulated rain shower.

© Joshua Rainey / Alamy

Managing Service Differentiation

In these days of intense price competition, service marketers often complain about the difficulty of differentiating their services from those of competitors. To the extent that customers view the services of different providers as similar, they care less about the provider than the price. The solution to price competition is to develop a differentiated offer, delivery, and image.

The *offer* can include innovative features that set one company's offer apart from competitors' offers. For example, some retailers differentiate themselves with offerings that take you well beyond the products they stock. Apple's highly successful stores offer a Genius Bar for technical support and a host of free workshops on everything from iPhone, iPad, and Mac basics to the intricacies of using iMovie to turn home movies into blockbusters. ● Similarly, at any of several large REI stores, consumers can get hands-on experience with merchandise before buying it via the store's mountain bike test trail, gear-testing stations, a huge rock climbing wall, or an in-store simulated rain shower.

Service companies can differentiate their service *delivery* by having more able and reliable customer-contact people, developing a superior physical environment in which the service product is delivered, or designing a superior delivery process. For example, many grocery chains now offer online shopping and home delivery as a better way to shop than having to drive, park, wait in line, and tote groceries home. And most banks offer mobile phone apps that allow you to more easily transfer money, check account balances, and make mobile check deposits. "Sign, snap a photo, and submit a check from anywhere," says one Citibank ad. "It's easier than running to the bank."

Finally, service companies also can work on differentiating their *images* through symbols and branding. Aflac adopted the duck as its advertising symbol. Today, the duck is immortalized through stuffed animals, golf club covers, and free ringtones and screensavers. The well-known Aflac duck helped make the big but previously unknown insurance company memorable and approachable. Other well-known service characters and symbols include the GEICO gecko, Progressive Insurance's Flo, McDonald's golden arches, Allstate's "good hands," the Twitter bird, and the freckled, red-haired, pig-tailed Wendy's girl. Progressive's Flo has amassed more the 5 million Facebook Likes.

Managing Service Quality

A service firm can differentiate itself by delivering consistently higher quality than its competitors provide. Like manufacturers before them, most service industries have now joined the customer-driven quality movement. And like product marketers, service providers need to identify what target customers expect in regard to service quality.

Unfortunately, service quality is harder to define and judge than product quality. For instance, it is harder to agree on the quality of a haircut than on the quality of a hair dryer. Customer retention is perhaps the best measure of quality; a service firm's ability to hang onto its customers depends on how consistently it delivers value to them.

Top service companies set high service-quality standards. They watch service performance closely, both their own and that of competitors. They do not settle for merely good service—they strive for 100 percent defect-free service. A 98 percent performance standard may sound good, but using this standard, the U.S. Postal Service would lose or misdirect 356,000 pieces of mail each hour, and U.S. pharmacies would misfill more than 1.5 million prescriptions each week.[24]

Unlike product manufacturers who can adjust their machinery and inputs until everything is perfect, service quality will always vary, depending on the interactions between employees and customers. As hard as they may try, even the best companies will have an occasional late delivery, burned steak, or grumpy employee. However, good *service recovery* can turn angry customers into loyal ones. In fact, good recovery can win more customer purchasing and loyalty than if things had gone well in the first place.

For example, Southwest Airlines has a proactive customer communications team whose job is to find the situations in which something went wrong—a mechanical delay, bad weather, a medical emergency, or a berserk passenger—then remedy the bad experience quickly, within 24 hours if possible.[25] The team's communications to passengers, usually emails or texts these days, have three basic components: a sincere apology, a brief explanation of what happened, and a gift to make it up, usually a voucher in dollars that can be used on their next Southwest flight. Surveys show that when Southwest handles a delay situation well, customers score it 14 to 16 points higher than on regular on-time flights.

These days, social media such as Facebook and Twitter can help companies root out and remedy customer dissatisfaction with service. As discussed in Chapter 4, companies now monitor the digital space to spot customer issues quickly and respond in real time. For example, Southwest has a dedicated team of 29 people who respond to roughly 80,000 Facebook and Twitter posts monthly. A quick and thoughtful response can turn a dissatisfied customer into a brand advocate.[26]

● **Managing service productivity: Companies should be careful not to take things too far. For example, in their attempts to improve productivity, some airlines have mangled customer service.**

DPA/Stringer/Getty Images

Managing Service Productivity

With their costs rising rapidly, service firms are under great pressure to increase service productivity. They can do so in several ways. They can train current employees better or hire new ones who will work harder or more skillfully. Or they can increase the quantity of their service by giving up some quality. Finally, a service provider can harness the power of technology. Although we often think of technology's power to save time and costs in manufacturing companies, it also has great—and often untapped—potential to make service workers more productive.

However, companies must avoid pushing productivity so hard that doing so reduces quality. Attempts to streamline a service or cut costs can make a service company more efficient in the short run. But that can also reduce its longer-run ability to innovate, maintain service quality, or respond to consumer needs and desires. ● For example, some airlines have learned this lesson the hard way as they attempt to economize in the face of rising costs. Passengers on most airlines now encounter "time-saving" check-in kiosks rather than personal counter service. And most airlines have stopped offering even the little things for free—such as in-flight snacks—and now charge extra for everything from checked luggage to aisle seats. The result is a plane full of disgruntled customers. In their attempts to improve productivity, many airlines have mangled customer service.

Thus, in attempting to improve service productivity, companies must be mindful of how they create and deliver customer value. They should be careful not to take *service* out of the service. In fact, a company may purposely lower service productivity in order to improve service quality, in turn allowing it to maintain higher prices and profit margins.

Author Comment | A brand represents everything that a product or service *means* to consumers. As such, brands are valuable assets to a company. For example, when you hear someone say "Coca-Cola," what do you think, feel, or remember? What about "Target"? Or "Google"?

Branding Strategy: Building Strong Brands

Some analysts see brands as *the* major enduring asset of a company, outlasting the company's specific products and facilities. John Stewart, former CEO of Quaker Oats, once said, "If this business were split up, I would give you the land and bricks and mortar, and I would keep the brands and trademarks, and I would fare better than you." A former CEO of McDonald's declared, "If every asset we own, every building, and every piece of equipment were destroyed in a terrible natural disaster, we would be able to borrow all the money to replace it very quickly because of the value of our brand.... The brand is more valuable than the totality of all these assets."[27]

Thus, brands are powerful assets that must be carefully developed and managed. In this section, we examine the key strategies for building and managing product and service brands.

Brand Equity and Brand Value

Brands are more than just names and symbols. They are a key element in the company's relationships with consumers. Brands represent consumers' perceptions and feelings about a product and its performance—everything that the product or the service *means* to consumers. In the final analysis, brands exist in the heads of consumers. As one well-respected marketer once said, "Products are created in the factory, but brands are created in the mind."[28]

A powerful brand has high *brand equity*. **Brand equity** is the differential effect that knowing the brand name has on customer response to the product and its marketing. It's a measure of the brand's ability to capture consumer preference and loyalty. A brand has positive brand equity when consumers react more favorably to it than to a generic or unbranded version of the same product. It has negative brand equity if consumers react less favorably than to an unbranded version.

Brands vary in the amount of power and value they hold in the marketplace. Some brands—such as Coca-Cola, Nike, Disney, GE, McDonald's, Harley-Davidson, and others—become larger-than-life icons that maintain their power in the market for years, even generations. Other brands—such as Google, Zappos, Uber, GoPro, Instagram, and Wikipedia—create fresh consumer excitement and loyalty. These brands win in the marketplace not simply because they deliver unique benefits or reliable service. Rather, they succeed because they forge deep connections with customers. People really do have relationships with brands. ● For example, to devoted Nike fans around the world, the Nike brand stands for much more than just sneakers, apparel, and sports equipment. It stands for gritty sports inspiration, fitness, and achievement—a "Just do it" attitude. As Nike once stated, "It's not so much the shoes but where they take you."

Ad agency Young & Rubicam's BrandAsset Valuator measures brand strength along four consumer perception dimensions: *differentiation* (what makes the brand stand out), *relevance* (how consumers feel it meets their needs), *knowledge* (how much consumers know about the

Brand equity
The differential effect that knowing the brand name has on customer response to the product or its marketing.

● Consumers' relationships with brands: To devoted Nike fans, the brand stands for much more than just sneakers, apparel, and sports equipment. It stands for gritty sports inspiration, fitness, and achievement—a "Just do it" attitude.

© Jon Lord / Alamy

Brand value
The total financial value of a brand.

brand), and *esteem* (how highly consumers regard and respect the brand). Brands with strong brand equity rate high on all four dimensions. The brand must be distinct, or consumers will have no reason to choose it over other brands. However, the fact that a brand is highly differentiated doesn't necessarily mean that consumers will buy it. The brand must stand out in ways that are relevant to consumers' needs. Even a differentiated, relevant brand is far from a shoe-in. Before consumers will respond to the brand, they must first know about and understand it. And that familiarity must lead to a strong, positive consumer-brand connection.[29]

Thus, positive brand equity derives from consumer feelings about and connections with a brand. A brand with high brand equity is a very valuable asset. **Brand value** is the total financial value of a brand. Measuring such value is difficult. However, according to one estimate, the brand value of Apple is a whopping $246 billion, with Google at $174 billion, Microsoft at $115 billion, IBM at $94 billion, AT&T at $92 billion, and Verizon at $86 billion. Other brands rating among the world's most valuable include McDonald's, Facebook, Alibaba, and Amazon.[30]

High brand equity provides a company with many competitive advantages. A powerful brand enjoys a high level of consumer brand awareness and loyalty. Because consumers expect stores to carry the particular brand, the company has more leverage in bargaining with resellers. Because a brand name carries high credibility, the company can more easily launch line and brand extensions. A powerful brand also offers the company some defense against fierce price competition and other competitor marketing actions.

Above all, however, a powerful brand forms the basis for building strong and profitable customer engagement and relationships. The fundamental asset underlying brand equity is *customer equity*—the value of customer relationships that the brand creates. A powerful brand is important, but what it really represents is a profitable set of loyal customers. The proper focus of marketing is building customer equity, with brand management serving as a major marketing tool. Companies need to think of themselves not as portfolios of brands but as portfolios of customers.

Building Strong Brands

Branding poses challenging decisions to the marketer. ● **Figure 8.5** shows that the major brand strategy decisions involve *brand positioning, brand name selection, brand sponsorship,* and *brand development.*

Brand Positioning

Marketers need to position their brands clearly in target customers' minds. They can position brands at any of three levels.[31] At the lowest level, they can position the brand on

Brands are powerful assets that must be carefully developed and managed. As this figure suggests, building strong brands involves many challenging decisions.

Brand positioning	**Brand name selection**	**Brand sponsorship**	**Brand development**
Attributes Benefits Beliefs and values	Selection Protection	Manufacturer's brand Private brand Licensing Co-branding	Line extensions Brand extensions Multibrands New brands

● FIGURE | 8.5 Major Brand Strategy Decisions

product attributes. For example, Whirlpool can position its major home appliance products on attributes such as quality, selection, style, and innovative features. In general, however, attributes are the least desirable level for brand positioning. Competitors can easily copy attributes. More important, customers are not interested in attributes as such—they are interested in what the attributes will do for them.

A brand can be better positioned by associating its name with a desirable *benefit*. Thus, Whirlpool can go beyond technical product attributes and talk about benefits such as taking the hassle out of cooking and cleaning, better energy savings, or more stylish kitchens. For example, for years, Whirlpool positioned its washing machines as having "the power to get more done." Some successful brands positioned on benefits are FedEx (guaranteed on-time delivery), Walmart (save money), and Instagram (capturing and sharing moments).

The strongest brands go beyond attribute or benefit positioning. They are positioned on strong *beliefs and values*, engaging customers on a deep, emotional level. For example, Whirlpool's research showed that home appliances are more than just "cold metal" to customers. They have a deeper meaning connected with the value that they play in customers' lives and relationships. So Whirlpool launched a major positioning campaign—called "Every Day, Care"—based on the warm emotions of taking care of the people you love with Whirlpool appliances. One ad shows a father leaving a note in his son's lunch, accompanied by Johnny Cash singing "You Are My Sunshine" in the background. Another ad centers on a mom's interactions with her daughter around their Whirlpool washer-dryer, and still another shows a couple cooking dinner together with the wish, "May your 'tatoes be fluffy and white." Warming up cold metal worked wonders for Whirlpool. Within just six months, the brand's sales rose 6.6 percent, market share increase 10 percent, and positive social media sentiment surged sixfold.[32]

Advertising agency Saatchi & Saatchi suggests that brands should strive to become *lovemark*s, products or services that "inspire loyalty beyond reason." Brands ranging from Disney, Apple, Nike, and Coca-Cola to Trader Joe's, Google, and Pinterest have achieved this status with many of their customers. Lovemark brands pack an emotional wallop. Customers don't just like these brands; they have strong emotional connections with them and love them unconditionally.[33] ● For example, Disney is a classic lovemark brand. As one Walt Disney World Resort regular affirms: "I have a deep love and bond to all things Disney. Walking down Main Street and seeing Cinderella's castle for the first time always makes my heart jump. It's a moment I can guarantee and rely on. A constant in my life. No matter what I'm going through…suddenly the world is filled with magic and wonder and possibilities all over again and I feel a wave of happiness flow over me and a smile creep back onto my face easily, not forced or painted on. A real, true smile."[34]

When positioning a brand, the marketer should establish a mission for the brand and a vision of what the brand must be and do. A brand is the company's promise to deliver a specific set of features, benefits, services, and experiences consistently to buyers. The brand promise must be clear, simple, and honest. Motel 6, for example, offers clean rooms, low prices, and good service but does not promise expensive furnishings or large bathrooms. In contrast, the Ritz-Carlton offers luxurious rooms and a truly memorable experience but does not promise low prices.

Brand Name Selection

A good name can add greatly to a product's success. However, finding the best brand name is a difficult task. It begins with a careful review of the product and its benefits, the target market, and proposed marketing strategies. After that, naming a brand becomes part science, part art, and a measure of instinct.

● Brand positioning: Some brands—such as Disney—have become lovemarks, products or services that pack an emotional wallop and "inspire loyalty beyond reason."

Art of Drawing / Alamy Stock Photo

Desirable qualities for a brand name include the following: (1) It should suggest something about the product's benefits and qualities: Beautyrest, Slimfast, Snapchat, Pinterest. (2) It should be easy to pronounce, recognize, and remember: iPad, Tide, Jelly Belly, Twitter, JetBlue. (3) The brand name should be distinctive: Panera, Swiffer, Zappos, Nest. (4) It should be extendable—Amazon.com began as an online bookseller but chose a name that would allow expansion into other categories. (5) The name should translate easily into foreign languages. The official name of Microsoft's Bing search engine in China is *bi ying*, which literally means "very certain to respond" in Chinese. (6) It should be capable of registration and legal protection. A brand name cannot be registered if it infringes on existing brand names.

Choosing a new brand name is hard work. After a decade of choosing quirky names (Yahoo!, Google) or trademark-proof made-up names (Novartis, Aventis, Accenture), today's style is to build brands around names that have real meaning. For example, names like Silk (soy milk), Method (home products), Smartwater (beverages), and Snapchat (photo messaging app) are simple and make intuitive sense. But with trademark applications soaring, *available* new names can be hard to find. Try it yourself. Pick a product and see if you can come up with a better name for it. How about Moonshot? Tickle? Vanilla? Treehugger? Simplicity? Mindbender? Google them and you'll find that they are already taken.

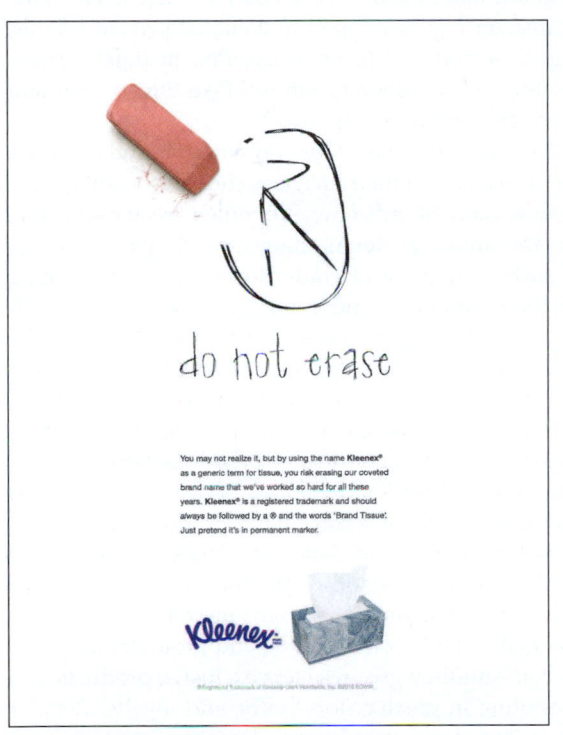

Once chosen, the brand name must be protected. Many firms try to build a brand name that will eventually become identified with the product category. Brand names such as Kleenex, JELL-O, BAND-AID, Scotch Tape, Velcro, Formica, Magic Marker, Post-it Notes, and Ziploc have succeeded in this way. However, their very success may threaten the company's rights to the name. Many originally protected brand names—such as cellophane, aspirin, nylon, kerosene, linoleum, yo-yo, trampoline, escalator, thermos, and shredded wheat—are now generic names that any seller can use.

To protect their brands, marketers present them carefully using the word *brand* and the registered trademark symbol, as in "BAND-AID® Brand Adhesive Bandages." Even the long-standing "I am stuck on BAND-AID 'cause BAND-AID's stuck on me" jingle has now become "I am stuck on BAND-AID brand 'cause BAND-AID's stuck on me." ● Similarly, a recent Kleenex ad advises advertisers and others that the name Kleenex should always be followed by the registered trademark symbol and the words "Brand Tissue." "You may not realize it, but by using the name Kleenex® as a generic term for tissue," says the ad, "you risk erasing our coveted brand name that we've worked so hard for all these years."

Companies often go to great lengths to protect their names and brand symbols. For example, insurance company Travelers zealously pursues companies that infringe in even the slightest way on its familiar trademarked red umbrella symbol. It recently threatened a tiny consulting firm in Anchorage, Alaska—Human Resource Umbrella—with legal action for hanging an umbrella above the two l's in its name. Such actions might seem unneeded, but they are serious business to Travelers. "Mary Poppins might want to consider lawyering up," quips one industry lawyer.[35]

● **Protecting the brand name:** This ad asks advertisers and others to always add the registered trademark symbol and the words "Brand Tissue" to the Kleenex name, helping to keep from "erasing our coveted brand name that we've worked so hard for all these years."

©Kimberly-Clark Worldwide, Inc. Reprinted with permission.

Brand Sponsorship

A manufacturer has four sponsorship options. The product may be launched as a *national brand* (or *manufacturer's brand*), as when Samsung and Kellogg sell their output under their own brand names (the Samsung Galaxy tablet or Kellogg's Frosted Flakes). Or the manufacturer may sell to resellers who give the product a *private brand* (also called a *store brand*). Although most manufacturers create their own brand names, others market licensed brands. Finally, two companies can join forces and *co-brand* a product. We discuss each of these options in turn.

National Brands versus Store Brands. National brands (or manufacturers' brands) have long dominated the retail scene. In recent times, however, increasing numbers of retailers and wholesalers have created their own **store brands** (or **private brands**). Store brands have been gaining strength for more than two decades, but recent tighter economic times have created a store-brand boom. Studies show that consumers are now buying even

Store brand (or private brand)
A brand created and owned by a reseller of a product or service.

more private brands, which on average yield a 25 percent savings.[36] More frugal times give store brands a boost as consumers become more price-conscious and less brand-conscious.

In fact, store brands have grown much faster than national brands in recent years. In a recent survey, 65 percent of consumers indicated that they buy store brands whenever they are available in a supermarket. Similarly, for apparel sales, department store private-label brands have shot up. At Kohl's, for example, private-label sales account for more than half of its annual revenue.[37]

Many large retailers skillfully market a deep assortment of store-brand merchandise. ● For example, Kroger's private brands—the Kroger house brand, Private Selection, Heritage Farm, Simple Truth (natural and organic), Psst and Check This Out (savings), and others—add up to a whopping 25 percent of the giant grocery retailer's sales, nearly $25 billion worth annually. At thrifty grocery chain ALDI, more than 90 percent of sales come from private brands such as Baker's Choice, Friendly Farms, Simply Nature, and Mama Cozzi's Pizza Kitchen. Even online retailer Amazon has developed a stable of private brands, including AmazonBasics (electronics), Pinzon (kitchen gadgets), Strathwood (outdoor furniture), Pike Street (bath and home products), and Denali (tools).[38]

● Store brands: Kroger's store brands—from Private Selection to Simple Truth—account for 25 percent of the grocery retailer's sales.

Associated Press

Once known as "generic" or "no-name" brands, today's store brands have shed their image as cheap knockoffs of national brands. Store brands now offer much greater selection, and they are rapidly achieving name-brand quality. In fact, retailers such as Target and Trader Joe's are out-innovating many of their national-brand competitors. Kroger even offers a Kroger brand guarantee—"Try it, like it, or get the national brand free." As a result, consumers are becoming loyal to store brands for reasons besides price. In some cases, consumers are even willing to pay more for store brands that have been positioned as gourmet or premium items.

In the so-called *battle of the brands* between national and private brands, retailers have many advantages. They control what products they stock, where they go on the shelf, what prices they charge, and which ones they will feature in local promotions. Retailers often price their store brands lower than comparable national brands and feature the price differences in side-by-side comparisons on store shelves. Although store brands can be hard to establish and costly to stock and promote, they also yield higher profit margins for the reseller. And they give resellers exclusive products that cannot be bought from competitors, resulting in greater store traffic and loyalty. Retailer Trader Joe's, which carries approximately 90 percent store brands, largely controls its own brand destiny rather than relying on producers to make and manage the brands it needs to serve its customers best.

To compete with store brands, national brands must sharpen their value propositions, especially when appealing to today's more frugal consumers. Many national brands are fighting back by rolling out more discounts and coupons to defend their market share. In the long run, however, leading brand marketers must compete by investing in new brands, new features, and quality improvements that set them apart. They must design strong advertising programs to maintain high awareness and preference. And they must find ways to partner with major distributors to find distribution economies and improve joint performance.

For example, in response to the surge in private-label sales, consumer product giant Procter & Gamble has redoubled its efforts to develop and promote new and better products, particularly at lower price points. "We invest $2 billion a year in research and development, $400 million on consumer knowledge, and about 10 percent of sales on advertising," says P&G's CEO. "Store brands don't have that capacity." As a result, P&G brands still dominate in their categories. For example, its Tide, Gain, Cheer, and other premium laundry detergent brands capture a combined 60 percent of the $7 billion U.S. detergent market.[39]

Licensing. Most manufacturers take years and spend millions to create their own brand names. However, some companies license names or symbols previously created by other manufacturers, names of well-known celebrities, or characters from popular movies and books. For a fee, any of these can provide an instant and proven brand name. For example, consider the Kodak brand with its familiar red and yellow colors, which has retained its value even after the company went bankrupt and discontinued its consumer products:[40]

> Consumer products carrying the Kodak name are no longer made by Eastman Kodak, which now focuses exclusively on printing-related commercial equipment and technology following its bankruptcy a few years ago. But the Kodak brand name and associated "Kodak moments" still resonate powerfully with consumers. So even though Eastman Kodak has dropped its consumer lines, we'll still be seeing a lot of Kodak-branded consumer products made by other companies under licensing agreements with Eastman Kodak. For example, Sakar International now makes Kodak cameras and accessories, and the Bullitt Group will soon launch a variety of Kodak electronics, including an Android smartphone and a tablet computer. Video monitoring company Seedonk makes and sells a Kodak Baby Monitoring System.
>
> Thus, the venerable old Kodak name still has value to both Eastman Kodak and the licensees who put it on their products. For Kodak, brand licensing agreements earn the company upward of $200 million a year. In turn, licensees get a name that's immediately familiar and trusted—it will be a lot easier to market a Kodak phone than a Bullitt phone or a Kodak baby monitoring system than a Seedonk one. "It was difficult to find a brand that resonated—family values, taking care of loved ones," says a Seedonk executive. "Then the Kodak opportunity came up. Kodak Moments, these are things that are important to our customers."

Apparel and accessories sellers pay large royalties to adorn their products—from blouses to ties and linens to luggage—with the names or initials of well-known fashion innovators such as Calvin Klein, Tommy Hilfiger, Gucci, or Armani. Sellers of children's products attach an almost endless list of character names to clothing, toys, school supplies, linens, dolls, lunch boxes, cereals, and other items. Licensed character names range from classics such as Sesame Street, Disney, Star Wars, Scooby Doo, Hello Kitty, SpongeBob SquarePants, and Dr. Seuss characters to the more recent Doc McStuffins, Monster High, Frozen, and Minions. And currently, numerous top-selling retail toys are products based on television shows and movies.

Name and character licensing has grown rapidly in recent years. Annual retail sales of licensed products worldwide have grown from only $4 billion in 1977 to $55 billion in 1987 and more than $259 billion today. Licensing can be a highly profitable business for many companies. For example, Nickelodeon's hugely popular SpongeBob SquarePants character by itself has generated some $12 billion worth of endorsement deals over the past 15 years. Disney is the world's biggest licensor with a studio full of popular characters, from the Disney Princesses and Disney Fairies to heroes from *Toy Story* and *Star Wars* and classic characters such as Mickey and Minnie Mouse. Disney characters reaped a reported $45 billion in worldwide merchandise sales last year.[41]

● Licensing can be a highly profitable business for companies: Nickelodeon's hugely popular SpongeBob SquarePants character by itself has generated billions of dollars of retail sales over the years.

© AF archive/Alamy

Co-branding

The practice of using the established brand names of two different companies on the same product.

Co-branding. **Co-branding** occurs when two established brand names of different companies are used on the same product. Co-branding offers many advantages. Because each brand operates in a different category, the combined brands create broader consumer appeal and greater brand equity. For example, Benjamin Moore and Pottery Barn joined forces to create a special collection of Benjamin Moore paint colors designed to perfectly coordinate with Pottery Barn's unique furnishings and accents. Taco Bell and Doritos teamed up to create the Doritos Locos Taco. Taco Bell sold more than 100 million of the tacos in just the first 10 weeks and quickly added Cool Ranch and Fiery versions and has since sold more than a billion. More than just co-branding, these companies are "co-making" these products.

Co-branding can take advantage of the complementary strengths of two brands. It also allows a company to expand its existing brand into a category it might otherwise have difficulty entering alone. For example, Nike and Apple co-branded the Nike+iPod Sport Kit, which lets runners link their Nike shoes with their iPods to track and enhance running performance in real time. The Nike+iPod arrangement gave Apple a presence in the sports and fitness market. At the same time, it helps Nike bring new value to its customers.

Co-branding can also have limitations. Such relationships usually involve complex legal contracts and licenses. Co-branding partners must carefully coordinate their advertising, sales promotion, and other marketing efforts. Finally, when co-branding, each partner must trust that the other will take good care of its brand. If something damages the reputation of one brand, it can tarnish the co-brand as well.

Brand Development

A company has four choices when it comes to developing brands (see ● **Figure 8.6**). It can introduce *line extensions, brand extensions, multibrands,* or *new brands.*

Line extension

Extending an existing brand name to new forms, colors, sizes, ingredients, or flavors of an existing product category.

Line Extensions. **Line extensions** occur when a company extends existing brand names to new forms, colors, sizes, ingredients, or flavors of an existing product category. For example, over the years, KFC has extended its "finger lickin' good" chicken lineup well beyond original recipe, bone-in Kentucky fried chicken. It now offers grilled chicken, boneless fried chicken, chicken tenders, hot wings, chicken bites, chicken popcorn nuggets, a Doublicious chicken-bacon-cheese sandwich, and KFC Go Cups—chicken and potato wedges in a handy car-cup holder that lets customers snack on the go.

A company might introduce line extensions as a low-cost, low-risk way to introduce new products. Or it might want to meet consumer desires for variety, use excess capacity, or simply command more shelf space from resellers. However, line extensions involve some risks. An overextended brand name might cause consumer confusion or lose some of its specific meaning.

For example, in its efforts to offer something for everyone—from basic burger buffs to practical parents to health-minded fast-food seekers—McDonald's has created a menu bulging with options. Some customers find the crowded menu a bit overwhelming, and offering so many choices has complicated the chain's food assembly process and slowed service at counters and drive-thrus. In response, McDonald's has recently begun efforts to cut items and simplify its menu, especially at its drive-thrus, which account for 70 percent of sales.[42]

At some point, additional extensions might add little value to a line. For instance, the original Doritos Tortilla Chips have morphed into a U.S. roster of more than 20 different types of chips and flavors, plus dozens more in foreign markets. Flavors include everything from Nacho Cheese and Pizza Supreme to Blazin' Buffalo & Ranch, Fiery Fusion, and Salsa Verde. Or how about duck-flavored Gold Peking Duck Chips or wasabi-flavored Mr. Dragon's Fire Chips (Japan)? Although the line seems to be doing well with U.S. sales of more than $1.3 billion, the original Doritos chips now seem like just another flavor.[43] And how much would adding yet another flavor steal from Doritos' own sales versus those of competitors? A line extension works best when it takes sales away from competing brands, not when it "cannibalizes" the company's other items.

Brand extension

Extending an existing brand name to new product categories.

Brand Extensions. A **brand extension** extends a current brand name to new or modified products in a new category. For example, Nest—the maker of stylish, connected, learning thermostats that can be controlled remotely from a phone—extended its line with an equally smart and stylish Nest Protect home smoke and carbon monoxide alarm. ● It's now extending the Nest line to include "Works with Nest," applications developed with a variety of partners that let its smart devices interact with and control everything from home video monitoring devices, smart door locks, and home lighting systems to home appliances and fitness tracking bands. All of the extensions fit together under Nest's smart homes mission.[44]

These days, a large majority of new products are extensions of already-successful brands. Compared with building new brands, extensions can create immediate new-product

● FIGURE | 8.6
Brand Development Strategies

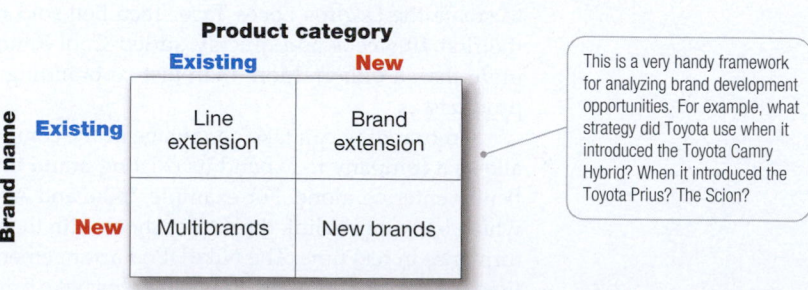

Brand extensions: Nest is now extending its brand to include "Works with Nest," applications developed with a variety of partners that let its smart devices interact with and control everything from video monitoring devices, smart door locks, and home lighting systems to home appliances and fitness tracking bands.

Nest Labs

familiarity and acceptance at lower development costs. For example, it's not just any new wireless charging mat for your mobile devices, it's a Duracell Powermat. And it's not just a new, no-name over-the-counter sleep-aid, it's Vicks ZzzQuil. Extensions such as the Duracell Powermat and Vicks ZzzQuil make good sense—they connect well with the core brand's values and build on its strengths.

At the same time, a brand extension strategy involves some risk. The extension may confuse the image of the main brand—for example, how about Zippo perfume or Fruit of the Loom laundry detergent? Brand extensions such as Cheetos lip balm, Heinz pet food, and Life Savers gum met early deaths.[45] Furthermore, a brand name may not be appropriate to a particular new product, even if it is well made and satisfying—would you consider flying on Hooters Air or wearing an Evian water-filled padded bra (both failed)? And if a brand extension fails, it may harm consumer attitudes toward other products carrying the same brand name. Thus, a company can't just take a familiar brand name and slap it on a product in another category. Instead, a good brand extension should fit the parent brand, and the parent brand should give the extension competitive advantage in its new category.

Multibrands. Companies often market many different brands in a given product category. For example, in the United States, PepsiCo markets at least eight brands of soft drinks (Pepsi, Sierra Mist, Mountain Dew, Manzanita Sol, Mirinda, IZZE, Tropicana Twister, and Mug root beer), three brands of sports and energy drinks (Gatorade, AMP Energy, Starbucks Refreshers), four brands of bottled teas and coffees (Lipton, SoBe, Starbucks, and Tazo), three brands of bottled waters (Aquafina, H2OH!, and SoBe), and nine brands of fruit drinks (Tropicana, Dole, IZZE, Lipton, Looza, Ocean Spray, and others). Each brand includes a long list of sub-brands. For instance, SoBe consists of SoBe Teas & Elixers, SoBe Lifewater, SoBe Lean, and SoBe Lifewater with Coconut Water. Aquafina includes regular Aquafina, Aquafina Flavorsplash, and Aquafina Sparkling.

Multibranding offers a way to establish different features that appeal to different customer segments, lock up more reseller shelf space, and capture a larger market share. For example, although PepsiCo's many brands of beverages compete with one another on supermarket shelves, the combined brands reap a much greater overall market share than any single brand ever could. Similarly, by positioning multiple brands in multiple segments, Pepsi's eight soft drink brands combine to capture much more market share than any single brand could capture by itself.

A major drawback of multibranding is that each brand might obtain only a small market share, and none may be very profitable. The company may end up spreading its resources over many brands instead of building a few brands to a highly profitable level. These companies should reduce the number of brands they sell in a given category and set up tighter screening procedures for new brands. This happened to GM, which in recent years has cut numerous brands from its portfolio, including Saturn, Oldsmobile, Pontiac, Hummer, and Saab. Similarly, as part of its recent turnaround, Ford dropped its Mercury line, sold off Volvo, and pruned the number of Ford nameplates from 97 to fewer than 20.

New Brands. A company might believe that the power of its existing brand name is waning, so a new brand name is needed. Or it may create a new brand name when it enters a new product category for which none of its current brand names is appropriate. For example, Toyota created the separate Lexus brand aimed at luxury car consumers and the Scion brand targeted toward millennial consumers.

As with multibranding, offering too many new brands can result in a company spreading its resources too thin. And in some industries, such as consumer packaged goods, consumers and retailers have become concerned that there are already too many brands with too few differences between them. Thus, P&G, PepsiCo, Kraft, and other large marketers of consumer products are now pursuing megabrand strategies—weeding out weaker or slower-growing brands and focusing their marketing dollars on brands that can achieve the number-one or number-two market share positions with good growth prospects in their categories.

Managing Brands

Companies must manage their brands carefully. First, the brand's positioning must be continuously communicated to consumers. Major brand marketers often spend huge amounts on advertising to create brand awareness and build preference and loyalty. For example, worldwide, Coca-Cola spends more than $3 billion annually to advertise its many brands, GM spends nearly $3.4 billion, Unilever spends $7.9 billion, and P&G spends an astounding $11.5 billion.[46]

Such advertising campaigns can help create name recognition, brand knowledge, and perhaps even some brand preference. However, the fact is that brands are not maintained by advertising but by customers' *engagement* with brands and customers' *brand experiences*. Today, customers come to know a brand through a wide range of contacts and touch points. These include advertising but also personal experience with the brand, word of mouth and social media, company web pages and mobile apps, and many others. The company must put as much care into managing these touch points as it does into producing its ads. As one former Disney top executive put it: "A brand is a living entity, and it is enriched or undermined cumulatively over time, the product of a thousand small gestures."[47]

The brand's positioning will not take hold fully unless everyone in the company lives the brand. Therefore, the company needs to train its people to be customer centered. Even better, the company should carry on internal brand building to help employees understand and be enthusiastic about the brand promise. Many companies go even further by training and encouraging their distributors and dealers to serve their customers well.

Finally, companies need to periodically audit their brands' strengths and weaknesses. They should ask: Does our brand excel at delivering benefits that consumers truly value? Is the brand properly positioned? Do all of our consumer touch points support the brand's positioning? Do the brand's managers understand what the brand means to consumers? Does the brand receive proper, sustained support? The brand audit may turn up brands that need more support, brands that need to be dropped, or brands that must be rebranded or repositioned because of changing customer preferences or new competitors.

8 | Reviewing and Extending the Concepts

OBJECTIVES REVIEW AND KEY TERMS

Objectives Review

A product is more than a simple set of tangible features. Each product or service offered to customers can be viewed on three levels. The *core customer value* consists of the core problem-solving benefits that consumers seek when they buy a product. The *actual product* exists around the core and includes the quality level, features, design, brand name, and packaging. The *augmented product* is the actual product plus the various services and benefits offered with it, such as a warranty, free delivery, installation, and maintenance.

OBJECTIVE 8-1 Define *product* and describe the major classifications of products and services. *(pp 220–225)*

Broadly defined, a *product* is anything that can be offered to a market for attention, acquisition, use, or consumption that might satisfy a want or need. Products include physical objects but also services, events, persons, places, organizations, ideas, or mixtures of these entities. *Services* are products that consist of activities, benefits, or satisfactions offered for sale that are essentially intangible, such as banking, hotel, tax preparation, and home-repair services.

Products and services fall into two broad classes based on the types of consumers who use them. *Consumer products*—those bought by final consumers—are usually classified according to consumer shopping habits (convenience products, shopping products, specialty products, and unsought products). *Industrial products*—those purchased for further processing or for use in conducting a business—include materials and parts, capital items, and supplies and services. Other marketable entities—such as organizations, persons, places, and ideas—can also be thought of as products.

OBJECTIVE 8-2 **Describe the decisions companies make regarding their individual products and services, product lines, and product mixes.** *(pp 225–233)*

Individual product decisions involve product attributes, branding, packaging, labeling, and product support services. *Product attribute* decisions involve product quality, features, and style and design. *Branding* decisions include selecting a brand name and developing a brand strategy. *Packaging* provides many key benefits, such as protection, economy, convenience, and promotion. Package decisions often include designing *labels and logos*, which identify, describe, and possibly promote the product. Companies also develop *product support services* that enhance customer service and satisfaction and safeguard against competitors.

Most companies produce a product line rather than a single product. A *product line* is a group of products that are related in function, customer-purchase needs, or distribution channels. All product lines and items offered to customers by a particular seller make up the *product mix*. The mix can be described by four dimensions: width, length, depth, and consistency. These dimensions are the tools for developing the company's product strategy.

OBJECTIVE 8-3 **Identify the four characteristics that affect the marketing of services and the additional marketing considerations that services require.** *(pp 234–240)*

Services are characterized by four key aspects: they are *intangible, inseparable, variable*, and *perishable*. Each characteristic poses problems and marketing requirements. Marketers work to find ways to make the service more tangible, increase the productivity of providers who are inseparable from their products, standardize quality in the face of variability, and improve demand movements and supply capacities in the face of service perishability.

Good service companies focus attention on *both* customers and employees. They understand the *service profit chain*, which links service firm profits with employee and customer satisfaction. Services marketing strategy calls not only for external marketing but also for *internal marketing* to motivate employees and *interactive marketing* to create service delivery skills among service providers. To succeed, service marketers must create *competitive differentiation*, offer high *service quality*, and find ways to increase *service productivity*.

OBJECTIVE 8-4 **Discuss branding strategy—the decisions companies make in building and managing their brands.** *(pp 240–248)*

Some analysts see brands as *the* major enduring asset of a company. Brands are more than just names and symbols; they embody everything that the product or the service *means* to consumers. *Brand equity* is the positive differential effect that knowing the brand name has on customer response to the product or the service. A brand with strong brand equity is a very valuable asset.

In building brands, companies need to make decisions about brand positioning, brand name selection, brand sponsorship, and brand development. The most powerful *brand positioning* builds around strong consumer beliefs and values. *Brand name selection* involves finding the best brand name based on a careful review of product benefits, the target market, and proposed marketing strategies. A manufacturer has four *brand sponsorship* options: It can launch a *national brand* (or manufacturer's brand), sell to resellers that use a *private brand*, market *licensed brands*, or join forces with another company to *co-brand* a product. A company also has four choices when it comes to developing brands. It can introduce *line extensions, brand extensions, multibrands*, or *new brands*.

Companies must build and manage their brands carefully. The brand's positioning must be continuously communicated to consumers. Advertising can help. However, brands are not maintained by advertising but by customers' *brand experiences*. Customers come to know a brand through a wide range of contacts and interactions. The company must put as much care into managing these touch points as it does into producing its ads. Companies must periodically audit their brands' strengths and weaknesses.

Key Terms

OBJECTIVE 8-1

Product (p 220)
Service (p 220)
Consumer product (p 222)
Convenience product (p 222)
Shopping product (p 222)
Specialty product (p 223)
Unsought product (p 223)
Industrial product (p 223)
Social marketing (p 225)

OBJECTIVE 8-2

Product quality (p 225)
Brand (p 226)
Packaging (p 227)
Product line (p 232)
Product mix (or product portfolio) (p 232)

OBJECTIVE 8-3

Service intangibility (p 234)
Service inseparability (p 235)
Service variability (p 235)
Service perishability (p 235)
Service profit chain (p 235)
Internal marketing (p 236)
Interactive marketing (p 236)

OBJECTIVE 8-4

Brand equity (p 240)
Brand value (p 241)
Store brand (or private brand) (p 243)
Co-branding (p 245)
Line extension (p 246)
Brand extension (p 246)

DISCUSSION AND CRITICAL THINKING

Discussion Questions

✪ **8-1** What is a consumer product? Describe the characteristics of each type of consumer product and give examples of each. (AACSB: Communication; Reflective Thinking)

8-2 Compare and contrast the two dimensions of product quality. (AACSB: Communication)

✪ **8-3** What is a product line? Discuss the various product line decisions marketers make and how a company can expand its product line. (AACSB: Communication)

8-4 Discuss brand equity and brand value. How do marketers use these concepts to build powerful brands? (AACSB: Communication, Reflective Thinking)

✪ **8-5** Explain the four choices companies have when developing brands. Provide an example of each. (AACSB: Communication, Reflective Thinking)

Critical Thinking Exercises

8-6 Walt Disney created the Disney brand from humble beginnings based on his love of drawing and animation. The Walt Disney Company has since expanded successfully into a global entertainment and media brand. Using the internet, research the components that make up the Disney brand and discuss how The Walt Disney Company has expanded its product mix. (AACSB: Communication; Use of IT; Reflective Thinking)

✪ **8-7** Companies must consider four special service characteristics when designing service marketing programs. Discuss a recent service experience using the four characteristics. Compare your service experience with that of a classmate. How do they differ? (AACSB: Communication, Reflective Thinking)

8-8 What is "genericide"? Discuss a recent case and make recommendations regarding how marketers can avoid it. (AACSB: Communication; Reflective Thinking)

APPLICATIONS AND CASES

Online, Mobile, and Social Media Marketing Feeding Pets from Your Smartphone

People lead busy lives, often taking time away from their pets. So Petnet has developed the Smartfeeder, allowing pet owners to schedule feeding times, monitor food intake, and personalize pet nutrition information. The Smartfeeder measures out the appropriate amount of food for a pet based on age, activity, and weight. Additional features include the ability to conveniently store five to seven pounds of pet food in an attached hopper. Petnet has also seamlessly integrated its products with a smartphone app, available with iOS (Apple) products. Pet owners can now control feeding times, portion sizes, and food supply and

even order pet food to be delivered directly to their homes, all from a mobile device.

8-9 What kind of product is Petnet's Smartfeeder? How should this type of product be marketed? (AACSB: Communication; Reflective Thinking)

8-10 What are customers really buying when they purchase a Petnet Smartfeeder? Identify the core, actual, and augmented product levels for this product. (AACSB: Communication; Reflective Thinking)

Marketing Ethics Geographical Indication

Scotch whiskey, Champagne sparkling wine, Parmesan cheese, Dijon mustard—what do all of these have in common? They are not brand names but rather geographical indicators (GIs) of the origin of these foodstuffs. Europe has a long history of gastronomical delicacies that the European Union has been strong to protect for economic reasons. For example, not just any sparkling wine can be labeled "champagne" because only sparkling wine produced in the Champagne region of France

can put that on the label. The British government is launching a registry of Scottish whiskey makers to protect its $4 billion industry from imitators who label their whiskey as Scotch. True Scotch must be aged in oak casks in Scotland for at least three years. Dijon mustard must be produced in Dijon, France, made with chardonnay wine from the Burgundy wine region. Parmesan cheese was developed more than 2,000 years ago in Parma, Italy, which also boasts of Parma ham (Prosciutto di Parma). True Swiss cheeses, such as Emmental, Gruyere, and other varieties, are produced in Switzerland following strict rules to guarantee purity, and the authorities there identify counterfeits with DNA fingerprinting based on the 10,000 strains of milk bacteria that are used for authentic Swiss cheeses. All of these come with a higher price tag for consumers. For example, Portugal Algarve Salt or French Fleur de Sel sea salt cost about $80 per pound compared with 30¢ per pound for regular table salt.

8-11 Are products with geographical indications actually superior to other similar ones not originating from that geographical region? Is it ethical for makers of these products to command higher prices when others can make or grow them just as well? (AACSB: Communication; Reflective Thinking; Ethical Reasoning)

8-12 Do geographical indications (GIs) offer benefits to consumers? Are there disadvantages for sellers? Explain. (AACSB: Communication; Reflective Thinking)

Marketing by the Numbers Pop-Tarts Gone Nutty!

Kellogg, maker of Pop-Tarts, recently introduced Pop-Tarts Nutty! The new product includes flavors such as peanut butter and chocolate peanut butter. Although the new Gone Nutty! product will reap a higher wholesale price for the company ($1.20 per eight-count package of the new product versus $1.00 per package for the original product), it also comes with higher variable costs ($0.55 per eight-count package for the new product versus $0.30 per eight-count package for the original product).

8-13 What brand development strategy is Kellogg undertaking? (AACSB: Communication; Reflective Thinking)

8-14 Assume the company expects to sell 5 million packages of Pop-Tarts Gone Nutty! in the first year after introduction but expects that 80 percent of those sales will come from buyers who would normally purchase existing Pop-Tart flavors (that is, cannibalized sales). Assuming the sales of regular Pop-Tarts are normally 300 million packages per year and that the company will incur an increase in fixed costs of $500,000 during the first year to launch Gone Nutty!, will the new product be profitable for the company? Refer to the discussion of cannibalization in Appendix 2: Marketing by the Numbers for an explanation regarding how to conduct this analysis. (AACSB: Communication; Analytical Reasoning)

Video Case Plymouth Rock Assurance

Plymouth Rock Assurance is an insurance company with a branding tale to tell. What started as a single Massachusetts-based auto insurance company in the early 1980s quickly grew into a group of separate companies that write and manage property and casualty insurance in various states. To streamline operations, cut costs, and better serve customers, the company undertook a rebranding process to combine three distinct auto insurance brands—Plymouth Rock, High Point, and Palisades—into one.

Rather than remaking the brand overnight, the company carried out a gradual transformation that retained existing brand equity and put customers' minds at ease. With Plymouth Rock as the parent brand and High Point and Palisades as sub-brands, the company transitioned the three into a single brand in incremental steps.

After viewing the video featuring Plymouth Rock Assurance, answer the following questions:

8-15 What value proposition lies at the core of Plymouth Rock Assurance?

8-16 What was the reasoning behind the decision to rebrand the three auto insurance brands as one brand?

8-17 Describe the process that Plymouth Rock Assurance used to rebrand the company. How does this process differ from other options it could have pursued?

Company Case Airbnb: Making Hospitality Authentic

Like many services industries, hotel companies have done a tremendous job of ensuring the quality of the customer experience through standardization. People booking rooms through any of the major hotel chains can be pretty much assured of certain basics. They'll enter the 13-by-25-foot room into a short hallway with a bathroom and closet on one side or the other. In the bathroom, they'll find the basics along with a sterile display of soaps, hair care products, and other toiletries. The room features a bed or two flanked on both sides by nightstands with a reading light by each. An upholstered chair and ottoman sit at an angle in the far corner with a desk opposite. A dresser topped with a flat-screen TV sits across from the foot of the bed. Visitors might also discover a mini-fridge and a microwave oven.

The artwork and décor are fairly contemporary although impersonal and nondescript. Other details throughout the hotel property are equally predictable. And although luxury level across these features varies from chain to chain, the vibe is the same. Many travelers count on this standard experience—it assures that their experience will be within a set of narrow, expected boundaries. Minimizing the risk of negative outcomes typically results in a satisfactory lodging experience for most guests most of the time.

But one lodging provider is targeting travelers who have a different set of needs and expectations. Airbnb is turning lodging services upside down by promising a hospitality experience that is the complete opposite of the one provided by major hotel chains. A major player in the new sharing economy, Airbnb is an online community marketplace that connects people who want to rent out space in their homes with those who are looking for accommodations. Like a true online marketplace, Airbnb doesn't own any lodging properties. It just brings buyers and sellers together and facilitates transactions between them. But Airbnb's promise of value is what really sets it apart from the hospitality world's status quo. The new-to-the-game lodging provider pitches an authentic experience—a true sense of what life is like in the place you visit.

Whereas the hotel industry has spent decades sculpting its standardized offering, in just eight years Airbnb has built a global network of more than 2 million listings and 60 million guests throughout 34,000 cities in 191 countries. It has also built a market value of more than $25 billion. Although these numbers may sound impressive on their own, in its brief existence Airbnb has managed to exceed the accomplishments of the largest hotel chain in the world—100-year-old Hilton Worldwide with its 765,000 rooms, 4,660 properties, and a market value of $22 billion.

How did Airbnb pull of this amazing feat? According to Brian Chesky and Joe Gebbia—the start-up's founders—Airbnb simply recognized that the travel industry had lost touch with its customers by offering only one cookie-cutter option—ticky-tack rooms in antiseptic hotels and resorts. This standardized model seemed to dictate an unintended goal for the entire hotel industry—to ensure that nothing remotely interesting happens. Once Chesky and Gebbia recognized this, they set out a strategy to bring authenticity back into the hospitality industry.

Two Million Rooms—No Two Alike

It all started when the founders had a hair-brained thought on how to generate some extra income to help pay the rent on their modest San Francisco loft apartment. During a major convention that had every hotel room in the city booked, they rented out three air mattresses on the floor of their apartment for $40 a night each. In the process, they discovered that the people who booked that real estate got more than just a place to stay at a time when they needed it most—they got a unique networking opportunity. From that moment, Chesky and Gebbia moved quickly to develop and formalize the business concept.

Today, using Airbnb to either list a property or rent one to stay in is relatively simple. For hosts—Airbnb's official term for property owners who want to rent out space—it's a simple matter of registering and being vetted to ensure legitimacy. Listings can be pretty much anything from a couch, a single room, a suite of rooms, or an apartment to a moored yacht, a houseboat, an entire house, or even a castle (Airbnb currently claims more than 1,400 castle listings). Some hosts even rent out space in their yards for guests to pitch a tent. With more than 2 million listed properties for rent, each is as unique as its owner. Because listings are in private homes and apartments, they are typically located in residential neighborhoods rather than commerce centers where national and global hotel brands abound. Bookings can be offered by the day, the week, or the month, and hosts decide on price and the other details of their service and listings. Airbnb keeps only 3 percent of the booking fees and returns the rest to the host within 24 hours.

For guests, the process is about like buying or booking most anything online. Registered users search by city, room type, price range, amenities, host language, or various other options, including entering their own keywords. Most listings provide photos and details that give potential guests a reasonably accurate idea of what their stay will be like. Guests can contact potential hosts with questions before booking. On top of the fee for the property, guests typically lay down a security deposit and pay a 6 to 12 percent service fee to Airbnb. Bookings are made through Airbnb, so money changes hands only through a secure interface. When guests arrive at the chosen property, the host either greets them or arranges for entry.

As the founders were getting Airbnb off the ground, they constantly faced a big challenge. Many people—investors included—were skeptical. In fact, during Airbnb's first year, the founders were turned down by every venture capitalist they approached. "When we started this company, people thought we were crazy," said Chesky. "They said strangers would never stay with strangers, and horrible things are going to happen." They also had a hard time convincing guests; few people were willing to risk staying with someone they'd never met.

But Airbnb overcame these concerns through various means. First, it set up a standard rating system for both hosts and guests, allowing each side to assess the other and reviewing what others have said about prior experiences. A "superhost" status gives an assurance of extensive booking experience and high-quality service. A "business travel ready" badge notes that the host provides specific amenities like Wi-Fi, a desk, and basic toiletries. Airbnb also puts guest and host minds at ease with its verification process, tips for safe and satisfactory bookings, and a 24-hour Trust and Safety hotline. Hosts are further protected by an included insurance policy that protects their property from damages of up to $1 million. Airbnb admits that although these measures do not guarantee that nothing bad will ever happen, the likelihood of a negative outcome is no greater than it is for staying at a chain hotel.

Seeing the World as the Locals Do

From the beginning, Airbnb primarily served budget-minded customers with prices for listings lower than those of comparable hotel rooms. But more and more, Airbnb is seeing a shift toward customers—leisure and business travelers alike—who want more than just low price. This is hardly an accident. Airbnb deliberately positions itself as a provider of unique and authentic experiences through its branding, communications, and other aspects of its business. In doing so, Airbnb has taken the uncertainty of staying in a stranger's house and turned it into an asset. Whereas hotels can compete on price and convenience, they cannot compete when it comes to the relationship between guest and host. "Guests are looking for experiences where they connect with people and connect with culture," says Chesky. "You can't automate hospitality."

Such was the theme of the second-annual Airbnb Open—a motivational event held in Paris, the company's biggest market, and attended by 5,000 hosts from 110 different countries. In his keynote address, Chesky explained that the entire hospitality industry caters to tourists in a way that makes them feel like tourists. But with an Airbnb experience, guests start to feel like they are a part of the neighborhood and the city.

As part of his presentation, Chesky summed up the entire Airbnb philosophy by illustrating the experience his own parents had when they arrived in Paris just days before the event. Pictures of their first day in town—hosted by typical tourist guides—were projected on a big screen. There was a picture of them on a double-decker tour bus, another on a generic boat ride, and a third standing in line at the Louvre. Chesky narrated each image with comical cynicism. "Every year, 30 million people go to Paris. They look at everything and they see nothing. We don't need to go to monuments and landmarks to experience a culture. We can actually stay with people." Then Chesky showed images from his parents' second day in Paris—guided by some of Airbnb's top hosts—where they experienced the city from the perspective of locals. They had coffee at an authentic sidewalk café, took a walk in a garden, and drank and danced at a cozy Parisian boîte. "Maybe we should not travel to Paris," suggested Chesky. "Maybe what we should do is live in Paris."

Executing on the Promise

This ideal—one supported by all Airbnb employees—was the driving force behind a recent and ambitious rebranding effort by the tech start-up. The company tossed out its original straight-forward text logo in favor of something far more abstract—a symbol that resembles a puffy capital letter "A" with the two sides crossing over. Airbnb calls it the "bélo," "the universal symbol of belonging." The new logo communicates a sense of belonging through something that transcends language, culture, and geography. A new slogan accompanies the logo—"Belong Anywhere."

To ensure that the Airbnb guest experience is as authentic and unique as possible, the company focuses first and foremost on its community of hosts. In fact, Airbnb considers its hosts to be its primary customers. As a result, Airbnb has been able to nurture a huge global community of lodging providers who are true believers in the Airbnb vision. Treated as active participants in the business, hosts develop a sense of ownership and devo-tion. In this manner, Airbnb influences hosts to follow certain guidelines toward creating the best guest experience possible. This is by no means intended to create a standardized model. But by urging hosts to offer guest services such as airport pickup and walking tours, Airbnb strengthens the connections formed with guests. "What's special in your world isn't just the home you have," Chesky tells the crowd at the Airbnb Open. "It's your whole life."

The explosive expansion of Airbnb in every world market has certainly caught the attention of the big hotel chains. Developers are beginning to build hotels in places where they normally would not. For example, eight new hotels are going up in Williamsburg,

a Brooklyn neighborhood that is a huge Airbnb market but not a traditional tourist locale. But even as hoteliers attempt to invade Airbnb's turf, they will have a tough time duplicating the Airbnb experience.

Despite its expansion and success, Airbnb still finds itself battling for legitimacy. Some cities do not allow the rental of personal property for any duration less than 30 days. And there are many travelers who might prefer the Airbnb experience but still have concerns about staying with strangers. Airbnb is rising to these challenges with idealistic fervor. In fact, Chesky goes so far as to suggest that Airbnb's mission goes beyond providing an authentic guest experience and into the realm of establishing world peace. He explains that living in close proximity to those from other cultures makes people understand each other a lot more. He concludes, "I think a lot of conflicts in the world are between groups that don't understand each other."

Questions for Discussion

8-18 How do the four characteristics of services apply to Airbnb? How does Airbnb deal with each characteristic?

8-19 Apply the service profit chain concept to Airbnb.

8-20 How does Airbnb differentiate its offer, delivery, and image?

8-21 How much of a threat is competition to Airbnb?

8-22 Will Airbnb last as long as Hilton Worldwide has? Explain.

Sources: Max Chafkin, "Airbnb Opens Up the World?" *Fast Company*, February 2016, pp. 76–95; Marshall Alstyne, Geoffrey Parker, and Sangeet Choudary, "Pipelines, Platforms, and the New Rules of Strategy," *Harvard Business Review*, April, 2016, pp. 54–62; Dan Peltier, "Airbnb's CMO on Authentic Travel Experiences," *Skift*, July 14, 2015, https://skift.com/2015/07/14/skift-global-forum-2015-airbnbs-cmo-on-the-meaning-of-authentic-travel-experiences/; and additional information from www.investopedia.com/articles/personal-finance/032814/pros-and-cons-using-airbnb.asp?performancelayout=true and www.airbnb.com/about/about-us, accessed July, 2016.

MyMarketingLab

Go to **mymktlab.com** for Auto-graded writing questions as well as the following Assisted-graded writing questions:

8-23 Describe the four characteristics of services that marketers must consider when designing marketing programs. How do the services offered by a doctor's office differ from those offered by a bank?

8-24 List the names of the store brands found in the following stores: Walmart, Best Buy, and Whole Foods. Identify the private label brands of another retailer of your choice and compare the price and quality of one of the products to a comparable national brand.

PART 1: Defining Marketing and the Marketing Process (Chapters 1–2)
PART 2: Understanding the Marketplace and Consumer Value (Chapters 3–6)
PART 3: Designing a Customer Value–Driven Strategy and Mix (Chapters 7–17)
PART 4: Extending Marketing (Chapters 18–20)

Developing New Products
and Managing the Product Life Cycle

CHAPTER PREVIEW

In the previous chapter, you learned how marketers manage and develop products and brands. In this chapter, we examine two additional product topics: developing new products and managing products through their life cycles. New products are the lifeblood of an organization. However, new product development is risky, and many new products fail. So, the first part of this chapter lays out a process for finding and growing successful new products. Once introduced, marketers then want their products to enjoy long and happy lives. In the second part of this chapter, you'll see that every product passes through several life-cycle stages, and each stage poses new challenges requiring different marketing strategies and tactics. Finally, we wrap up our product discussion by looking at two additional considerations: social responsibility in product decisions and international product and services marketing.

For openers, consider Samsung, the world's leading consumer electronics maker and one of the world's most innovative companies. Over the past two decades, Samsung has transformed itself by creating a culture of customer-focused innovation and a seemingly endless flow of inspired new products that feature stunning design, innovative technology, life-enriching features, and a big dose of "Wow!"

SAMSUNG: Enriching Customers' Lives through New-Product Innovation

You're probably familiar with the Samsung brand. Maybe you own one of Samsung's hot new Galaxy smartphones that tracks your eye movements to help you navigate the screen, or maybe you've seen one of Samsung's dazzling new Superior 4k Ultra-High-Definition Smart TVs with a fully immersive curved screen and nano-crystal technology. Samsung, the world's largest consumer electronics manufacturer, produces "gotta-have" electronics in just about every category, from TVs and Blu-ray players, tablets and mobile phones, and smartwatches to smart-home devices and even a full range of home appliances.

But little more than 20 years ago, Samsung was barely known, and it was anything but cutting-edge. Back then, Samsung was a Korean copycat brand that you bought off a shipping pallet at Costco if you couldn't afford a Sony, then the world's most coveted consumer electronics brand. However, in 1993 Samsung made an inspired decision. It turned its back on cheap knock-offs and set out to overtake rival Sony. To dethrone the consumer electronics giant, however, Samsung first had to change

> Samsung has become the world's leading consumer electronics company through customer-focused innovation and new products that enrich customers' lives. At Samsung, every new product has to pass the consumer "Wow!" test.

its entire culture, from copycat to leading-edge. To out*sell* Sony, Samsung decided, it first had to out-*innovate* Sony.

Samsung's dramatic shift began with a top-down mandate for reform. Samsung set out to become a premier brand and a trailblazing product leader. It hired a crop of fresh, young designers and managers who unleashed a torrent of new products—not humdrum, me-too products, but sleek, bold, and beautiful products targeted to high-end users. Samsung called them "lifestyle works of art." Every new product had to pass the "Wow!" test: If it didn't get a "Wow!" reaction during market testing, it went straight back to the design studio. Beyond cutting-edge technology and stylish designs, Samsung put the customer at the core of its innovation movement. Its primary innovation goal was to improve the customer experience and bring genuine change to people's lives in everything it did.

With its fresh customer-centered new-product focus, Samsung overtook Sony in less than 10 years. Today, Samsung's annual revenues of $196 billion are more than two and a half times Sony's revenues, placing it at number 13 on *Fortune*'s Global 500—two spots ahead of Apple. But more than just being the biggest, Samsung has also achieved that new-product Wow! factor it sought. For example, Samsung has been dominant in recent years at the International Design Excellence Awards (IDEA) presentations—the Academy Awards of the design world—which judges new products based on appearance, functionality, and inspirational thinking. For the past three years, Samsung has been the top corporate winner, claiming more than twice as many awards as the next runner-up.

In this digital, connected, and mobile era, Samsung now competes less with the Sonys of the world and more with innovation pacesetters like Apple. And against Apple, Samsung is more than holding its own. In mobile devices, for example, Samsung has surged to the top of the market. Just a few years ago, Samsung's goal was to double its market share of smartphones from 5 percent to 10 percent. But the success of its Galaxy line catapulted Samsung's global share to 22 percent, ahead of Apple's 18.5 percent worldwide.

In its favor, Samsung holds a piece of the technology puzzle that Apple doesn't—big screens. In fact, Samsung has been the global leader in television sales for eight straight years. Its Smart TVs not only offer gesture control, voice control, and face recognition but also provide seamless web connectivity that has TV users Facebooking, Skyping, streaming online content, and using their favorite apps with a wave of the hand. Control of so many different kinds of screens gives Samsung a leg up against more-focused competitors in this interconnected age.

But Samsung also realizes that today's "gotta have it" products can be tomorrow's has-beens. Future growth will come not just from bigger TVs and better smartphones. Rather, the electronics powerhouse is constantly on the prowl for the "next big thing," regardless of the product category. To that end, Samsung's market intelligence and product innovation teams around the globe continually research product usage, purchase behavior, and lifestyle trends, looking for consumer insights and innovative new ways to meet consumer needs.

For instance, Samsung is now investing heavily in the "Internet of Things" (IoT), a global environment where everything—from home electronics and appliances to automobiles, buildings, and even clothing—will be digitally connected to everything else. Given that Samsung already makes products in almost every electronics category, IoT provides fertile territory for future innovation and growth. In recent years, Samsung has begun developing a "web of connectivity" that links its products to the rest of the world. The goal is to develop Samsung IoT products and technologies that are "In Sync with Life." The company has already introduced numerous "smart" products—including its entire Smart TV lineup, 16 kitchen appliances, and mobile apps—that connect devices to each other and to those who use them.

Beyond cutting-edge technology and stylish design, Samsung puts the customer at the core of its innovation movement. Its new products "bring genuine change to people's lives."
© Yaacov Dagan / Alamy Stock Photo

Samsung's soon-to-be-released SleepSense device provides just one glimpse into the company's IoT future:

Samsung's SleepSense helps you to better understand and manage your sleep. It's a flat disk that slips under the mattress and provides contactless monitoring of your heart and respiratory rates as well as your movements during sleep. Then, through a smartphone app, SleepSense provides you with daily sleep scores and reports along with expert advice and recommendations based on your own metabolism and other personal characteristics. But here's the best part. SleepSense also connects to Samsung appliances and third-party IoT devices. For example, when it detects that you've fallen asleep during a late-night Netflix binge, it can automatically turn off the television and adjust the air-conditioning for a comfortable sleep environment. In the future, if your Samsung Family Hub Refrigerator detects that you tend to eat dairy before a bad night's sleep, SleepSense might even advise you on better late-night snack alternatives. Wow!

Samsung's current IoT lineup is just the tip of the iceberg. According to one estimate, the number of networked devices will surge from about 1 billion today to 25 billion by 2020, representing a $3 trillion market. By that time, Samsung claims that 100 percent of the products it makes will be internet-connected.

Twenty years ago, few people would have predicted that Samsung could have transformed itself so quickly and completely from a low-cost copycat manufacturer into a world-leading innovator of stylish, high-performing, premium products. But through a dedication to customer-focused new-product innovation, that's exactly what Samsung has done. And even recently, few would have predicted that Samsung would be a driving force behind creating a digitally interconnected world. Yet Samsung seems well on its way to accomplishing that as well. "We have to show consumers what's in it for them and what the Internet of Things can achieve," says Samsung's CEO. "To transform our economy, society, and how we live our lives." Adds another Samsung executive: "We will focus on creating amazing experiences, [on doing] what is right by customers." In short, whatever gets that "Wow!"[1]

OBJECTIVES OUTLINE

AS THE SAMSUNG STORY SUGGESTS, companies that excel at developing and managing new products reap big rewards. Every product seems to go through a life cycle: It is born, goes through several phases, and eventually dies as newer products come along that create new or greater value for customers.

This product life cycle presents two major challenges: First, because all products eventually decline, a firm must be good at developing new products to replace aging ones (the challenge of *new product development*). Second, a firm must be good at adapting its marketing strategies in the face of changing tastes, technologies, and competition as products pass through stages (the challenge of *product life-cycle strategies*). We first look at the problem of finding and developing new products and then at the problem of managing them successfully over their life cycles.

> **Author Comment** | New products are the lifeblood of a company. As old products mature and fade away, companies must develop new ones to take their place. For example, the iPhone and iPad have been around for only about a decade but are now Apple's two top-selling products.

New Product Development Strategy

A firm can obtain new products in two ways. One is through *acquisition*—by buying a whole company, a patent, or a license to produce someone else's product. The other is through the firm's own **new product development** efforts. By *new products* we mean original products, product improvements, product modifications, and new brands that the firm develops through its own product development. In this chapter, we concentrate on new product development.

New products are important to both customers and the marketers who serve them: They bring new solutions and variety to customers' lives, and they are a key source of growth for companies. In today's fast-changing environment, many companies rely on new products for the majority of their growth. For example, new products have almost completely transformed Apple in recent years. The iPhone and iPad—both introduced only within the past decade or so—are now the company's two biggest-selling products, with the iPhone alone bringing in more than 62 percent of Apple's total global revenues and 77 percent of device unit sales.[2]

Yet innovation can be very expensive and very risky. New products face tough odds. For example, by one estimate, 60 percent of all new consumer packaged products introduced by established companies fail; two-thirds of new product concepts are never even launched.[3] Why do so many new products fail? There are several reasons. Although an idea may be good, the company may overestimate market size. The actual product may be poorly designed. Or it might be incorrectly positioned, launched at the wrong time, priced

New product development
The development of original products, product improvements, product modifications, and new brands through the firm's own product development efforts.

too high, or poorly advertised. A high-level executive might push a favorite idea despite poor marketing research findings. Sometimes the costs of product development are higher than expected, and sometimes competitors fight back harder than expected.

So, companies face a problem: They must develop new products, but the odds weigh heavily against success. To create successful new products, a company must understand its consumers, markets, and competitors and develop products that deliver superior value to customers.

The New Product Development Process

> Author | Companies can't just hope
> Comment | that they'll stumble across
> good new products. Instead, they must
> develop a systematic new product
> development process.

Rather than leaving new products to chance, a company must carry out strong new product planning and set up a systematic, customer-driven *new product development process* for finding and growing new products. ● **Figure 9.1** shows the eight major steps in this process.

Idea Generation

Idea generation
The systematic search for new product ideas.

New product development starts with **idea generation**—the systematic search for new product ideas. A company typically generates hundreds—even thousands—of ideas to find a few good ones. Major sources of new product ideas include internal sources and external sources such as customers, competitors, distributors and suppliers, and others.

Internal Idea Sources

Using *internal sources*, the company can find new ideas through formal R&D. For example, Ford operates an innovation and mobility center in Silicon Valley staffed by engineers, app developers, and scientists working on everything from driverless cars to Works with Nest apps that let consumers control home heating, lighting, and appliances from their vehicles. Chick-fil-A set up a large innovation center called Hatch, where its staff and partners explore new ideas in food, design, and service. Hatch is a place to "ideate, explore, and imagine the future," to hatch new food and restaurant ideas and bring them to life.[4]

Beyond its internal R&D process, a company can pick the brains of its own people—from executives to salespeople to scientists, engineers, and manufacturing staff. Many companies have developed successful internal social networks and *intrapreneurial* programs that encourage employees to develop new product ideas. For example, AT&T has set up an internal online innovation community called The Innovation Pipeline (TIP), through which AT&T employees from all areas and levels of the company submit, discuss, and vote on new product and service ideas. Each quarter, the "founders" of top vote-getting ideas pitch them to AT&T senior executives, who select the best three for further funding and development. Since its inception in 2009, AT&T employees have submitted more than 28,000 ideas to the TIP community, and the company has funded more than 75 TIP projects ranging from customer service enhancements to new product offerings.[5]

Tech companies such as Facebook and Twitter sponsor periodic "hackathons," in which employees take a day or a week away from their day-to-day work to develop new ideas. LinkedIn, the 300 million–member professional social media network, holds "hackdays," one Friday each month when it encourages employees to work on whatever

> New product development starts with good new product ideas—lots of them. For example, Cisco's I-Prize crowdsourcing challenge attracted 824 ideas from 2,900 innovators representing more than 156 countries.

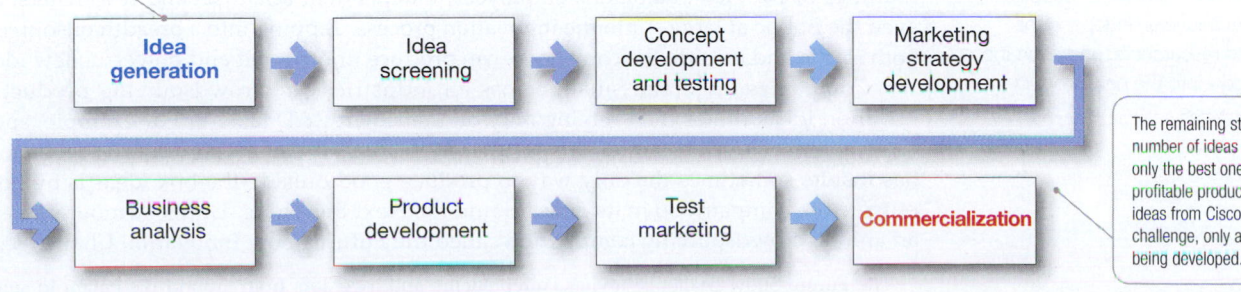

> The remaining steps reduce the number of ideas and develop only the best ones into profitable products. Of the 824 ideas from Cisco's I-Prize challenge, only a handful are being developed.

● FIGURE | 9.1
Major Stages in New Product Development

they want that will benefit the company. LinkedIn takes the process a step further with its InCubator program, under which employees can form teams each quarter that pitch innovative new ideas to LinkedIn executives. If approved, the team gets up to 90 days away from its regular work to develop the idea into reality.[6]

External Idea Sources

Companies can also obtain good new product ideas from any of a number of external sources. For example, *distributors and suppliers* can contribute ideas. Distributors are close to the market and can pass along information about consumer problems and new product possibilities. Suppliers can tell the company about new concepts, techniques, and materials that can be used to develop new products.

Competitors are another important source. Companies watch competitors' ads to get clues about their new products. They buy competing new products, take them apart to see how they work, analyze their sales, and decide whether they should bring out a new product of their own. Other idea sources include trade magazines, shows, websites, and seminars; government agencies; advertising agencies; marketing research firms; university and commercial laboratories; and inventors.

Perhaps the most important sources of new product ideas are *customers* themselves. The company can analyze customer questions and complaints to find new products that better solve consumer problems. Or it can invite customers to share suggestions and ideas. ● For example, The LEGO Group systematically taps users for new product ideas and input via the LEGO Ideas website:[7]

At the LEGO Ideas website, the giant toy maker turns user ideas into new LEGO building sets. The site invites customers to submit their ideas and to evaluate and vote on the ideas of others. Ideas supported by 10,000 votes head to the LEGO Review Board for an internal review by various departments including marketing and design. Ideas passing the review are made into official LEGO products. Customers whose ideas reach production earn 1 percent of total net sales of the product and receive credit as the LEGO Ideas set creator inside every set sold. So far, LEGO Ideas has resulted in 12 major new products, including the likes of LEGO *Doctor Who*, LEGO Birds, LEGO *Big Bang Theory*, LEGO *Ghostbusters*, LEGO WALL•E, LEGO *Back to the Future* DeLorean Time Machine, and the LEGO Labyrinth Marble Maze.

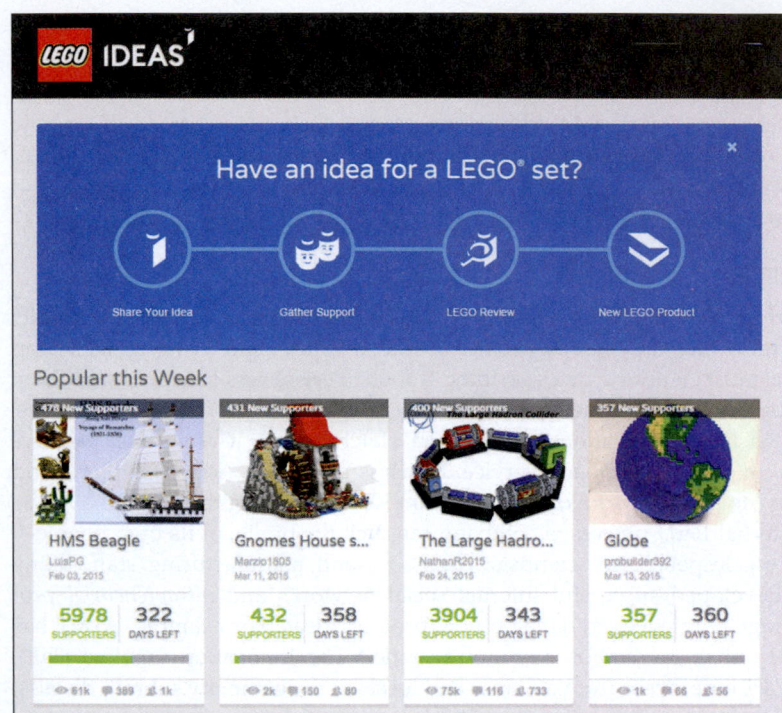

● **New product ideas from customers: The LEGO Ideas website invites customers to submit and vote on new product ideas. So far, LEGO Ideas has resulted in 12 major new products.**

Crowdsourcing

Crowdsourcing
Inviting broad communities of people—customers, employees, independent scientists and researchers, and even the public at large—into the new product innovation process.

More broadly, many companies are now developing crowdsourcing or open-innovation new product idea programs. Through **crowdsourcing**, a company invites broad communities of people—customers, employees, independent scientists and researchers, and even the public at large—into the innovation process. Tapping into a breadth of sources—both inside and outside the company—can produce unexpected and powerful new ideas.

Companies large and small, across all industries, are crowdsourcing product innovation ideas rather than relying only on their own R&D labs. ● For example, sports apparel maker Under Armour knows that no matter how many top-notch developers it has inside, sometimes the only way to produce good outside-the-box ideas is by going outside the company. So in its quest to find the Next Big Thing, Under Armour sponsors an annual crowdsourcing competition called the Future Show Innovation Challenge:[8]

The Future Show challenge invites entrepreneurs and inventors from around the nation to submit new product ideas. Then, from thousands of entries, an Under Armour team culls 12 finalists who go before a panel of seven judges to pitch their products in a splashy, *Shark Tank*–like reality TV setting. The winner earns $50,000 and a contract to work with Under Armour to help develop

● Crowdsourcing: Under Armour sponsors an annual crowdsourcing competition called the Future Show Innovation Challenge, in which it invites outside innovators to pitch new product ideas in a splashy, *Shark Tank*–like reality TV setting.

Thearon W. Henderson / Getty Images

the winning product. The goal of the Future Show Challenge is to "cajole top innovators to come to Under Armour first with gee-whizzers," says CEO Kevin Plank. The first winner, and Plank's favorite so far, is a made-for-athletes zipper—the UA MagZip—that can be zipped easily with only one hand. Under Armour's internal R&D team had been trying to develop a better zipper for two years, but "we couldn't get it to work," says the company's vice president of innovation. That simple zipper is just one of dozens of creative new product ideas from the Future Show. But by itself, it makes the entire crowdsourcing effort worthwhile. "We need to be humble enough to know that the next great thing might come from some kid playing college football who happens to have a better idea," says the Under Armour innovation chief.

Crowdsourcing can produce a flood of innovative ideas. In fact, opening the floodgates to anyone and everyone can overwhelm the company with ideas—some good and some bad. For example, when Cisco Systems sponsored an open-innovation effort called I-Prize, soliciting ideas from external sources, it received more than 820 distinct ideas from more than 2,900 innovators from 156 countries. "The evaluation process was far more labor-intensive than we'd anticipated," says Cisco's chief technology officer. It required "significant investments of time, energy, patience, and imagination . . . to discern the gems hidden within rough stones." In the end, a team of six Cisco people worked full-time for three months to carve out 32 semifinalist ideas as well as nine teams representing 14 countries in six continents for the final phase of the competition.[9]

Thus, truly innovative companies don't rely only on one source or another for new product ideas. Instead, they develop extensive innovation networks that capture ideas and inspiration from every possible source, from employees and customers to outside innovators and multiple points beyond.

Idea Screening

Idea screening

Screening new product ideas to spot good ones and drop poor ones as soon as possible.

The purpose of idea generation is to create a large number of ideas. The purpose of the succeeding stages is to *reduce* that number. The first idea-reducing stage is **idea screening**, which helps spot good ideas and drop poor ones as soon as possible. Product development costs rise greatly in later stages, so the company wants to go ahead only with those product ideas that will turn into profitable products.

Many companies require their executives to write up new product ideas in a standard format that can be reviewed by a new product committee. The write-up describes the product or the service, the proposed customer value proposition, the target market, and the competition. It makes some rough estimates of market size, product price, development time and costs, manufacturing costs, and rate of return. The committee then evaluates the idea against a set of general criteria.

One marketing expert describes an R-W-W ("real, win, worth doing") new product screening framework that asks three questions.[10] First, *Is it real?* Is there a real need and desire for the product, and will customers buy it? Is there a clear product concept, and will such a product satisfy the market? Second, *Can we win?* Does the product offer a sustainable competitive advantage? Does the company have the resources to make such a product a success? Finally, *Is it worth doing?* Does the product fit the company's overall growth strategy? Does it offer sufficient profit potential? The company should be able to answer yes to all three R-W-W questions before developing the new product idea further.

Concept Development and Testing

Product concept

A detailed version of the new product idea stated in meaningful consumer terms.

An attractive idea must then be developed into a **product concept**. It is important to distinguish between a product idea, a product concept, and a product image. A *product idea* is an idea for a possible product that the company can see itself offering to the market.

A *product concept* is a detailed version of the idea stated in meaningful consumer terms. A *product image* is the way consumers perceive an actual or potential product.

Concept Development

Suppose a car manufacturer has developed a practical battery-powered, all-electric car. Its initial models were a sleek, sporty roadster convertible selling for more than $100,000, followed by a full-size sports sedan priced at $71,000.[11] ● However, in the near future it plans to introduce a more-affordable, mass-market compact version that will compete with recently introduced hybrid-electric or all-electric cars such as the Nissan Leaf, Chevy Volt, KIA Soul EV, and Chevy Bolt EV. This 100 percent plug-in electric car will accelerate from 0 to 60 miles per hour in four seconds, travel up to 300 miles on a single charge, recharge in 45 minutes from a normal 120-volt electrical outlet, and cost about one penny per mile to power.

Looking ahead, the marketer's task is to develop this new product into alternative product concepts, find out how attractive each concept is to customers, and choose the best one. It might create the following product concepts for this all-electric car:

● All-electric cars: This is Tesla's initial all-electric full-size sedan. Later, more-affordable compact models will travel more than 300 miles on a single charge, recharge in 45 minutes from a normal 120-volt electrical outlet, and cost about one penny per mile to power.

Tesla

- *Concept 1.* An affordably priced compact car designed as a second family car to be used around town for running errands and visiting friends.
- *Concept 2.* A mid-priced sporty compact appealing to young singles and couples.
- *Concept 3.* A "green" everyday car appealing to environmentally conscious people who want practical, no-polluting transportation.
- *Concept 4.* A compact crossover SUV appealing to those who love the space SUVs provide but lament the poor gas mileage.

Concept Testing

Concept testing

Testing new product concepts with a group of target consumers to find out if the concepts have strong consumer appeal.

Concept testing calls for testing new product concepts with groups of target consumers. The concepts may be presented to consumers symbolically or physically. Here, in more detail, is concept 3:

> An efficient, fun-to-drive, battery-powered compact car that seats four. This 100 percent electric wonder provides practical and reliable transportation with no pollution. It goes 300 miles on a single charge and costs pennies per mile to operate. It's a sensible, responsible alternative to today's pollution-producing gas-guzzlers. Its fully equipped base price is $28,800.

Many firms routinely test new product concepts with consumers before attempting to turn them into actual new products. For some concept tests, a word or picture description might be sufficient. However, a more concrete and physical presentation of the concept will increase the reliability of the concept test. After being exposed to the concept, consumers then may be asked to react to it by answering questions similar to those in ● **Table 9.1**.

The answers to such questions will help the company decide which concept has the strongest appeal. For example, the last question asks about the consumer's intention to buy. Suppose 2 percent of consumers say they "definitely" would buy and another 5 percent say "probably." The company could project these figures to the full population in this target group to estimate sales volume. Even then, however, the estimate is uncertain because people do not always carry out their stated intentions.

Marketing strategy development

Designing an initial marketing strategy for a new product based on the product concept.

Marketing Strategy Development

Suppose the carmaker finds that concept 3 for the new electric car model tests best. The next step is **marketing strategy development**, designing an initial marketing strategy for introducing this car to the market.

● Table 9.1 | Questions for the All-Electric Car Concept Test

1. Do you understand the concept of a battery-powered electric car?
2. Do you believe the claims about the car's performance?
3. What are the major benefits of an all-electric car compared with a conventional car?
4. What are its advantages compared with a hybrid gas-electric car?
5. What improvements in the car's features would you suggest?
6. For what uses would you prefer an all-electric car to a conventional car?
7. What would be a reasonable price to charge for the car?
8. Who would be involved in your decision to buy such a car? Who would drive it?
9. Would you buy such a car (definitely, probably, probably not, definitely not)?

The *marketing strategy statement* consists of three parts. The first part describes the target market; the planned value proposition; and the sales, market-share, and profit goals for the first few years. Thus:

> The target market is younger, well-educated, moderate- to high-income individuals, couples, or small families seeking practical, environmentally responsible transportation. The car will be positioned as more fun to drive and less polluting than today's internal combustion engine or hybrid cars. The company will aim to sell 50,000 cars in the first year, at a loss of not more than $15 million. In the second year, the company will aim for sales of 90,000 cars and a profit of $25 million.

The second part of the marketing strategy statement outlines the product's planned price, distribution, and marketing budget for the first year:

> The battery-powered all-electric car will be offered in three colors—red, white, and blue—and will have a full set of accessories as standard features. It will sell at a base retail price of $28,800, with 15 percent off the list price to dealers. Dealers who sell more than 10 cars per month will get an additional discount of 5 percent on each car sold that month. A marketing budget of $50 million will be split 40-30-30 among a national media campaign, online and social media marketing, and local event marketing. Advertising, the web and mobile sites, and various social media content will emphasize the car's fun spirit and low emissions. During the first year, $100,000 will be spent on marketing research to find out who is buying the car and what their satisfaction levels are.

The third part of the marketing strategy statement describes the planned long-run sales, profit goals, and marketing mix strategy:

> We intend to capture a 3 percent long-run share of the total auto market and realize an after-tax return on investment of 15 percent. To achieve this, product quality will start high and be improved over time. Price will be raised in the second and third years if competition and the economy permit. The total marketing budget will be raised each year by about 10 percent. Marketing research will be reduced to $60,000 per year after the first year.

Business Analysis

Business analysis

A review of the sales, costs, and profit projections for a new product to find out whether these factors satisfy the company's objectives.

Once management has decided on its product concept and marketing strategy, it can evaluate the business attractiveness of the proposal. **Business analysis** involves a review of the sales, costs, and profit projections for a new product to find out whether they satisfy the company's objectives. If they do, the product can move to the product development stage.

To estimate sales, the company might look at the sales history of similar products and conduct market surveys. It can then estimate minimum and maximum sales to assess the range of risk. After preparing the sales forecast, management can estimate the expected costs and profits for the product, including marketing, R&D, operations, accounting, and finance costs. The company then uses the sales and cost figures to analyze the new product's financial attractiveness.

Product Development

Product development

Developing the product concept into a physical product to ensure that the product idea can be turned into a workable market offering.

For many new product concepts, a product may exist only as a word description, a drawing, or perhaps a crude mock-up. If the product concept passes the business test, it moves into **product development**. Here, R&D or engineering develops the product concept into a physical product. The product development step, however, now calls for a huge jump in investment. It will show whether the product idea can be turned into a workable product.

The R&D department will develop and test one or more physical versions of the product concept. R&D hopes to design a prototype that will satisfy and excite consumers and that can be produced quickly and at budgeted costs. Developing a successful prototype can take days, weeks, months, or even years depending on the product and prototype methods.

Often, products undergo rigorous tests to make sure that they perform safely and effectively or that consumers will find value in them. Companies can do their own product testing or outsource testing to other firms that specialize in testing.

Marketers often involve actual customers in product development and testing. ● For example, Carhartt, maker of durable workwear and outerwear, has enlisted an army of Groundbreakers, "hard working men and women to help us create our next generation of products." These volunteers take part in live chats with Carhartt designers, review new product concepts, and field-test products that they helped to create.[12]

A new product must have the required functional features and also convey the intended psychological characteristics. The all-electric car, for example, should strike consumers as being well built, comfortable, and safe. Management must learn what makes consumers decide that a car is well built. To some consumers, this means that the car has "solid-sounding" doors. To others, it means that the car is able to withstand a heavy impact in crash tests. Consumer tests are conducted in which consumers test-drive the car and rate its attributes.

● Product testing: Carhartt has enlisted an army of Groundbreakers, volunteers who take part in live chats with Carhartt designers, review new product concepts, and field-test products that they helped to create.
Carhartt

Test Marketing

Test marketing

The stage of new product development in which the product and its proposed marketing program are tested in realistic market settings.

If the product passes both the concept test and the product test, the next step is **test marketing**, the stage at which the product and its proposed marketing program are tested in realistic market settings. Test marketing gives the marketer experience with marketing a product before going to the great expense of full introduction. It lets the company test the product and its entire marketing program—targeting and positioning strategy, advertising, distribution, pricing, branding and packaging, and budget levels.

The amount of test marketing needed varies with each new product. When introducing a new product requires a big investment, when the risks are high, or when management is not sure of the product or its marketing program, a company may do a lot of test marketing. For instance, Taco Bell took three years and 45 prototypes before introducing Doritos Locos Tacos, now the most successful product launch in the company's history. And Starbucks spent 20 years developing Starbucks VIA instant coffee—one of its most risky product rollouts ever—and several months testing the product in Starbucks shops in Chicago and Seattle before releasing it nationally. The testing paid off. The Starbucks VIA line now accounts for more than $300 million in sales annually.[13]

However, test marketing costs can be high, and testing takes time that may allow market opportunities to slip by or competitors to gain advantages. A company may do little or no test marketing when the costs of developing and introducing a new product are low or when management is already confident about the new product. For example, companies often do not test-market simple line extensions or copies of competitors' successful products.

Companies may also shorten or skip testing in the face of fast-changing market developments. ● For example, to take advantage of digital and mobile trends, Starbucks quickly introduced a less-than-perfect mobile payments app, then worked out the flaws during the six months after launch. The Starbucks app now accounts for 8 million transactions per week. "We don't think it is okay if things aren't perfect," says Starbucks' chief digital officer, "but we're willing to innovate and have speed to market trump a 100 percent guarantee that it'll be perfect."[14]

As an alternative to extensive and costly standard test markets, companies can use controlled test markets or simulated test markets. In *controlled test markets*, new products and tactics are tested among controlled panels of shoppers and stores. By combining information on each test consumer's purchases with consumer demographic and media viewing information, the company assess the impact of in-store and in-home marketing efforts. Using *simulated test markets*, researchers measure consumer responses to new products and marketing tactics in laboratory stores or simulated online shopping environments. Both controlled test markets and simulated test markets reduce the costs of test marketing and speed up the process.

● **Companies sometimes shorten or skip test marketing to take advantage of fast-changing market developments, as Starbucks did with its hugely successful mobile payments app.**

Kevin Schafer/Getty Images

Commercialization
Introducing a new product into the market.

Commercialization

Test marketing gives management the information needed to make a final decision about whether to launch the new product. If the company goes ahead with **commercialization**—introducing the new product into the market—it will face high costs. For example, the company may need to build or rent a manufacturing facility. And, in the case of a major new consumer product, it may spend hundreds of millions of dollars for advertising, sales promotion, and other marketing efforts in the first year. For instance, in a single month surrounding the introduction of the Apple Watch, Apple spent $38 million on TV advertising campaign alone for the new product. Tide spent $150 million on a campaign to launch Tide Pods in the highly competitive U.S. laundry detergent market. And to introduce the original Surface tablet, Microsoft spent close to $400 million on an advertising blitz that spanned TV, print, radio, outdoor, the Internet, events, public relations, and sampling.[15]

A company launching a new product must first decide on introduction *timing*. If the new product will eat into the sales of other company products, the introduction may be delayed. If the product can be improved further or if the economy is down, the company may wait until the following year to launch it. However, if competitors are ready to introduce their own competing products, the company may push to introduce its new product sooner.

Next, the company must decide *where* to launch the new product—in a single location, a region, the national market, or the international market. Some companies may quickly introduce new models into the full national market. Companies with international distribution systems may introduce new products through swift global rollouts. For example, Apple launched its iPhone 6 and iPhone 6 Plus phones in its fastest-ever global rollout, making them available in 115 countries within less than three months of initial introduction.[16]

Author Comment | Above all else, new product development must focus on creating customer value. Says a senior Samsung executive, "We get our ideas from the market. The market is the driver."

Managing New Product Development

The new product development process shown in Figure 9.1 highlights the important activities needed to find, develop, and introduce new products. However, new product development involves more than just going through a set of steps. Companies must take a holistic approach to managing this process. Successful new product development requires a customer-centered, team-based, and systematic effort.

Customer-Centered New Product Development

Above all else, new product development must be customer centered. When looking for and developing new products, companies often rely too heavily on technical research in their R&D laboratories. But like everything else in marketing, successful new product development begins with a thorough understanding of what consumers need and value. **Customer-centered new product development** focuses on finding new ways to solve customer problems and create more customer-satisfying experiences.

One study found that the most successful new products are ones that are differentiated, solve major customer problems, and offer a compelling customer value proposition.

Customer-centered new product development
New product development that focuses on finding new ways to solve customer problems and create more customer-satisfying experiences.

Another study showed that companies that directly engage their customers in the new product innovation process had twice the return on assets and triple the growth in operating income of firms that did not. Thus, customer involvement has a positive effect on the new product development process and product success. "Choosing what kind of value your innovation will create and then sticking to that is critical," says one expert.[17]

Intuit—maker of financial software such as TurboTax, QuickBooks, and Quicken—is a strong proponent of customer-driven new product development:[18]

HOW WE INNOVATE

intuit
simplify the business of life
✓ TurboTax ● QuickBooks Q Quicken ✦ Mint

● **Customer-centered new product development:** Financial software maker Intuit follows a "Design for Delight" philosophy that says products should delight customers by providing experiences that go beyond their expectations.

Reprinted with permission. ©Intuit Inc. All rights reserved.

Intuit follows a "Design for Delight (D4D)" development philosophy that says products should delight customers by providing experiences that go beyond their expectations. ● Design for Delight starts with customer empathy—knowing customers better than they know themselves. To that end, each year, Intuit conducts 10,000 hours of what it calls "follow-me-homes," in which design employees observe firsthand how customers use its products at home and at work. They look to understand problems and needs that even customers themselves might not recognize. Based on customer observations, the next D4D step is to "go broad, go narrow"—developing many customer-driven product ideas, then narrowing them down to one or a few great ideas for products that will solve customer problems. The final D4D step involves turning the great ideas into actual products and services that create customer delight, collecting customer feedback steadily throughout the development process. Intuit works relentlessly to embed Design for Delight concepts deeply into its culture. "You've got to feel it," says the company's vice president of design innovation. "It can't be in your head. It's got to be in your heart. It's got to be in your gut. And we want to put it in our products."

Thus, today's innovative companies get out of the research lab and connect with customers in search of fresh ways to meet customer needs. Customer-centered new product development begins and ends with understanding customers and involving them in the process.

Team-Based New Product Development

Good new product development also requires a total-company, cross-functional effort. Some companies organize their new product development process into the orderly sequence of steps shown in Figure 9.1, starting with idea generation and ending with commercialization. Under this *sequential product development* approach, one company department works individually to complete its stage of the process before passing the new product along to the next department and stage. This orderly, step-by-step process can help bring control to complex and risky projects. But it can also be dangerously slow. In fast-changing, highly competitive markets, such slow-but-sure product development can result in product failures, lost sales and profits, and crumbling market positions.

Team-based new product development
New product development in which various company departments work closely together, overlapping the steps in the product development process to save time and increase effectiveness.

To get their new products to market more quickly, many companies use a **team-based new product development** approach. Under this approach, company departments work closely together in cross-functional teams, overlapping the steps in the product development process to save time and increase effectiveness. Instead of passing the new product from department to department, the company assembles a team of people from various departments that stays with the new product from start to finish. Such teams usually include people from the marketing, finance, design, manufacturing, and legal departments and even supplier and customer companies. In the sequential process, a bottleneck at one phase can seriously slow an entire project. In the team-based approach, however, if one area hits snags, it works to resolve them while the team moves on.

The team-based approach does have some limitations, however. For example, it sometimes creates more organizational tension and confusion than the more orderly sequential approach. However, in rapidly changing industries facing increasingly shorter product life cycles, the rewards of fast and flexible product development far exceed the risks. Companies that combine a customer-centered approach with team-based new product development gain a big competitive edge by getting the right new products to market faster.

Systematic New Product Development

Finally, the new product development process should be holistic and systematic rather than compartmentalized and haphazard. Otherwise, few new ideas will surface, and many good ideas will sputter and die. To avoid these problems, a company can install an *innovation management system* to collect, review, evaluate, and manage new product ideas.

The company can appoint a respected senior person to be its innovation manager. It can set up web-based idea management software and encourage all company stake-holders—employees, suppliers, distributors, dealers—to become involved in finding and developing new products. It can assign a cross-functional innovation management commit-tee to evaluate proposed new product ideas and help bring good ideas to market. It can also create recognition programs to reward those who contribute the best ideas.

The innovation management system approach yields two favorable outcomes. First, it helps create an innovation-oriented company culture. It shows that top management sup-ports, encourages, and rewards innovation. Second, it will yield a larger number of new product ideas, among which will be found some especially good ones. The good new ideas will be more systematically developed, producing more new product successes. No longer will good ideas wither for the lack of a sounding board or a senior product advocate.

Thus, new product success requires more than simply thinking up a few good ideas, turning them into products, and finding customers for them. It requires a holistic approach for finding new ways to create valued customer experiences, from generating and screen-ing new product ideas to creating and rolling out want-satisfying products to customers. More than this, successful new product development requires a whole-company commit-ment. At companies known for their new product prowess, such as Samsung, Google, Apple, 3M, P&G, and GE, the entire culture encourages, supports, and rewards innovation. For example, at Google and its parent company Alphabet, innovation is more just than a process—it's part of the company's DNA (see Real Marketing 9.1).

Author Comment | A company's products are born, grow, mature, and then decline, just as living things do. To remain vital, the firm must continually develop new products and manage them effectively throughout their life cycles.

Product Life-Cycle Strategies

After launching the new product, management wants that product to enjoy a long and happy life. Although it does not expect the product to sell forever, the company wants to earn a decent profit to cover all the effort and risk that went into launching it. Management is aware that each product will have a life cycle, although its exact shape and length is not known in advance.

Product life cycle (PLC)
The course of a product's sales and profits over its lifetime.

● **Figure 9.2** shows a typical **product life cycle (PLC)**, the course that a product's sales and profits take over its lifetime. The PLC has five distinct stages:

1. *Product development* begins when the company finds and develops a new product idea. During product development, sales are zero, and the company's investment costs mount.

● FIGURE | 9.2
Sales and Profits over the Product's Life from Inception to Decline

Some products die quickly; others stay in the mature stage for a long, long time. For example, TABASCO sauce has been around for more than 140 years. Even then, to keep the product young, the company has added a full line of flavors (such as Sweet & Spicy and Chipotle) and a kitchen cabinet full of new TABASCO products (such as salsas, marinades, and a chili mix).

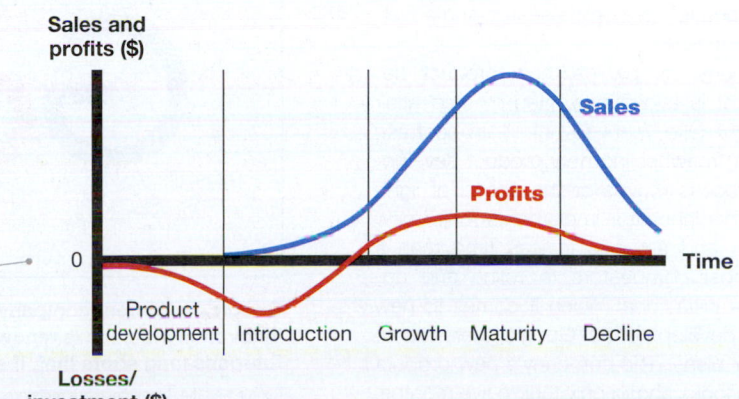

Real Marketing

9.1 Google (...er, Alphabet): The New Product Moonshot Factory

Google is wildly innovative. Over the past decade and a half, it has become a top-five fixture in every list of most-innovative companies. Google simply refuses to get comfortable with the way things are. Instead, it innovates constantly, plunging into new markets and taking on new competitors.

Google began as an online search company with a mission "to organize the world's information and make it universally accessible and useful." In accomplishing that mission, Google has been spectacularly successful. Despite formidable competition from giants such as Microsoft and Yahoo!, Google's U.S. share of online search stands at a decisive 65 percent, more than double the market shares of its next two competitors combined. The company also dominates in paid online and mobile search-related advertising revenue, which accounted for 90 percent of Google's $74.5 billion in revenues last year. And Google is growing at a blistering rate—its revenues have more than doubled in just the past four years.

But Google has rapidly become much more than just an online search and advertising company. In Google's view, information is a kind of natural resource—one to be mined, refined, and universally distributed. That broad mission gives Google's engineers and developers a blank canvas, a broad brush, and plenty of incentive to innovate. For example, Google is famous for its Innovation Time-Off program, which encourages all employees to spend 20 percent of their time—one day a week—developing their own "cool and wacky" new product ideas, no matter what the innovation area. As a result, Google's passion for innovation has taken it well beyond its core online search and advertising businesses.

At many companies, new product development is a cautious, step-by-step affair that might take years to unfold. In contrast, Google's freewheeling new product development process moves at the speed of light. The nimble innovator implements major new products and services in less time than it takes most competitors to refine and approve an initial idea. When it comes to new product development at Google, there are no two-year plans. The company's new product planning looks ahead only four to five months.

Google would rather see projects fail quickly than see a carefully planned, drawn-out project fail. When Google developers face two paths and aren't sure which one to take, they invariably take the quickest one.

Google's famously chaotic innovation process has unleashed a seemingly unending flurry of diverse products, most of which are market leaders in their categories. Although diverse, many of these innovations are tied in one way or another to Google's internet-related information mission. Google's many megahits include an email service (Gmail), a digital media store (Google Play), an online payment service (Google Wallet), a photo sharing service (Google Photos), a mobile operating system (Google Android), an online social network (Google+), a cloud-friendly internet browser (Chrome), affordable laptops with a browser for an operating system (Chromebooks), and even projects for mapping and exploring the world (Google Maps and Google Earth).

But Google's wild-eyed innovation process has also taken the company down paths that are pretty far afield from its main information mission—everything from smart-home systems and self-driving cars to earth-imaging satellites and even a crusade to increase human life span. In fact, Google has innovated into so many diverse new ventures that it recently created a broader organization—a parent holding company called Alphabet—to contain them all. Google is the largest Alphabet company. It continues to house information and internet-related products, anything to do with search, advertising, maps, apps, Android, Chrome, and even YouTube. But along with Google, Alphabet provides an independent home for the company's more far-reaching collection of projects and businesses.

One such business is Nest Labs—a maker of smart thermostats and smoke alarms that Google acquired for an eyeball-bending $3.2 billion. Nest has become Google's (now Alphabet's) doorway into today's Internet of Things (IoT). Fast-growing Nest is moving quickly into the exploding "smart homes" arena with "Works with Nest" applications by which its devices interact with and control everything from basic appliances to state-of-the-art video monitoring devices, smart door locks, and just about anything else around the house. Backed by Alphabet's substantial resources and innovation prowess, Nest may soon be helping you run your entire home, a huge potential market.

If Nest Labs and IoT seem a bit far removed from Google's main mission, they are tame compared with some of the other Google businesses that now fall under Alphabet.

Google and parent company Alphabet are wildly innovative. The company's innovation machine is renowned for producing new product "moonshots," futuristic long shots that, if successful, will profoundly change how people live.

Google and the Google logo are registered trademarks of Google Inc., used with permission.

Google's innovation machine has long been renowned for "moonshots"—futuristic, breathtakingly idealistic long shots that, if successful, will profoundly change how people live. To foster moonshots, Google created Google X—a secretive innovation lab and kind of nerd heaven charged with developing things that seemed audacious, even for Google. Now housed in Alphabet and called simply "X," the innovation lab is Alphabet's incubator for earth-shaking projects that may or may not pay for themselves in the long run. "Anything which is a huge problem for humanity we'll sign up for," says X's director, whose official title is Captain of Moonshots.

X's most notable innovations so far have been in wearable smart devices, such as Glass virtual-reality eyewear, which jumpstarted the wearable technology trend. But behind X's secret curtain are numerous other futuristic projects, such as Project Loon (a Wi-Fi–distributing high-altitude balloons network), Project Titan (like Project Loon only with solar-powered drones), Project Wing (a drone product delivery system), Makani (kite-like wind-energy production), and Replicant (robotics and consumer robot products). X also includes Google's much-publicized self-driving car project, once thought to be pure science fiction but now surprisingly close to reality.

In addition to Nest and X, Alphabet includes Fiber, the ultrafast fiber-optic internet service that is rolling out across the country. Lesser-known Alphabet companies include investment arms Ventures (funding for bold new start-ups) and Capital (funding for long-term tech projects), Verily (health-care projects, such as glucose-monitoring contact lenses), and Calico (research into fighting age-related disease and increasing life span). According to Google co-founder Larry Page, Alphabet's goal is "to keep tremendous focus on the extraordinary opportunities" that exist and will exist within Google and the other companies.

In the end, at Google (and at parent company Alphabet), innovation is more than a process—it's part of the company's DNA. "Where does innovation happen at Google? It happens everywhere," says a Google research scientist.

Talk to Googlers at various levels and departments, and one powerful theme emerges: These people feel that their work can change the world. The marvel of Google is its ability to continue to instill a sense of creative fearlessness and ambition in its employees. Prospective hires are often asked, "If you could change the world using Google's resources, what would you build?" But here, this isn't a goofy or even theoretical question: Google wants to know because thinking—and building—on that scale is what Google does. When it comes to innovation, Google is different. But the difference isn't tangible. It's in the air—in the spirit of the place.

Sources: Rob Price and Mike Nudelman, "Google's Parent Company, Alphabet, Explained in One Chart," *Business Insider,* January 12, 2016, www.businessinsider.com/chart-of-alphabet-google-parent-company-infographic-x-gv-2016-1?r=UK&IR=T; Brad Stone, "Inside the Moonshot Factory," *Bloomberg Businessweek*, May 22, 2013, pp. 56–61; Chuck Salter, "Google: The Faces and Voices of the World's Most Innovative Company," *Fast Company,* March 2008, pp. 74–88; Mark Bergen, "Google X Has a New Logo and New Plan to Turn Moonshots into Actual Businesses," *re/code*, January 13, 2016, http://recode.net/2016/01/13/google-x-has-a-new-logo-and-new-plan-to-turn-moonshots-into-actual-businesses/; and https://abc.xyz/ and http://investor.google.com, accessed September 2016.

100 Years of Keeping Mouths Feeling Fresh

1912   1923   1925
1944   1951
1969   1979   1987
Y2K   2012

LIFE SAVERS MINTS A hole lot of fun.

● **Product life cycle: Some products die quickly; others stay in the mature stage for a long, long time. Life Savers Mints recently celebrated "100 years of keeping mouths feeling fresh."**

The Wrigley Company

2. *Introduction* is a period of slow sales growth as the product is introduced in the market. Profits are nonexistent in this stage because of the heavy expenses of product introduction.
3. *Growth* is a period of rapid market acceptance and increasing profits.
4. *Maturity* is a period of slowdown in sales growth because the product has achieved acceptance by most potential buyers. Profits level off or decline because of increased marketing outlays to defend the product against competition.
5. *Decline* is the period when sales fall off and profits drop.

Not all products follow all five stages of the PLC. Some products are introduced and die quickly; others stay in the mature stage for a long, long time. Some enter the decline stage and are then cycled back into the growth stage through strong promotion or repositioning. It seems that a well-managed brand could live forever. Venerable brands like Coca-Cola, Gillette, Budweiser, Guinness, American Express, Wells Fargo, Heinz, Kikkoman, and TABASCO sauce, for instance, are still going strong after more than 100 years. Guinness beer has been around for more than 250 years, ● Life Savers Mints recently celebrated "100 years of keeping mouths feeling fresh," and 147-year-old TABASCO sauce brags that it's "over 140 years old and still able to totally whup your butt!"

The PLC concept can describe a *product class* (gasoline-powered automobiles), a *product form* (SUVs), or a *brand* (the Ford Escape). The PLC concept applies differently in each case. Product classes have the longest life cycles; the sales of many product classes stay in the mature stage for a long time. Product forms, in contrast, tend to have the standard PLC shape. Product forms such as dial telephones, VHS tapes, and film cameras passed through a regular history of introduction, rapid growth, maturity, and decline.

A specific brand's life cycle can change quickly because of changing competitive attacks and responses. For example, although laundry soaps (product class) and powdered detergents (product form) have enjoyed fairly long life cycles, the life cycles of specific brands have tended to be much shorter. Today's

Style

A basic and distinctive mode of expression.

Fashion

A currently accepted or popular style in a given field.

Fad

A temporary period of unusually high sales driven by consumer enthusiasm and immediate product or brand popularity.

leading U.S. brands of powdered laundry soap are Tide and Gain; the leading brands 100 years ago were Fels-Naptha and Octagon.

The PLC concept also can be applied to what are known as styles, fashions, and fads. Their special life cycles are shown in ● **Figure 9.3**. A **style** is a basic and distinctive mode of expression. For example, styles appear in homes (colonial, ranch, transitional), clothing (formal, casual), and art (realist, surrealist, abstract). Once a style is invented, it may last for generations, passing in and out of vogue. A style has a cycle showing several periods of renewed interest.

A **fashion** is a currently accepted or popular style in a given field. For example, the more formal "business attire" look of corporate dress of the 1980s and 1990s gave way to the "business casual" look of the 2000s and 2010s. Fashions tend to grow slowly, remain popular for a while, and then decline slowly.

Fads are temporary periods of unusually high sales driven by consumer enthusiasm and immediate product or brand popularity.[19] A fad may be part of an otherwise normal life cycle, as in the case of recent surges in the sales of poker chips and accessories. Or the fad may comprise a brand's or product's entire life cycle. Pet Rocks are a classic example. Upon hearing his friends complain about how expensive it was to care for their dogs, advertising copywriter Gary Dahl joked about his pet rock. He soon wrote a spoof of a dog-training manual for it, titled *The Care and Training of Your Pet Rock*. Soon Dahl was selling some 1.5 million ordinary beach pebbles at $4 a pop. Yet the fad, which broke one October, had sunk like a stone by the next February. Dahl's advice to those who want to succeed with a fad: "Enjoy it while it lasts." Other examples of fads include Silly Bandz, Furbies, and selfie sticks.[20]

Marketers can apply the product life-cycle concept as a useful framework for describing how products and markets work. And when used carefully, the PLC concept can help in developing good marketing strategies for the different life-cycle stages. However, using the PLC concept for forecasting product performance or developing marketing strategies presents some practical problems. For example, in practice, it is difficult to forecast the sales level at each PLC stage, the length of each stage, and the shape of the PLC curve. Using the PLC concept to develop marketing strategy also can be difficult because strategy is both a cause and a result of the PLC. The product's current PLC position suggests the best marketing strategies, and the resulting marketing strategies affect product performance in later stages.

Moreover, marketers should not blindly push products through the traditional product life-cycle stages. Instead, marketers often defy the "rules" of the life cycle and position or reposition their products in unexpected ways. By doing this, they can rescue mature or declining products and return them to the growth phase of the life cycle. Or they can leapfrog obstacles that slow consumer acceptance and propel new products forward into the growth phase.

The moral of the product life cycle is that companies must continually innovate; otherwise, they risk extinction. No matter how successful its current product lineup, a company must skillfully manage the life cycles of existing products for future success. And to grow, the company must develop a steady stream of new products that bring new value to customers. Toy maker Mattel is learning this lesson the hard way. It has long dominated the world toy industry with classic brands such as Barbie, Hot Wheels, Fisher-Price, and American Girl. In recent years, however, as its core brands have matured, Mattel's sales have stagnated at the hands of nimbler, more innovative competitors (see Real Marketing 9.2).

We looked at the product development stage of the PLC in the first part of this chapter. We now look at strategies for each of the other life-cycle stages.

● FIGURE | 9.3
Styles, Fashions, and Fads

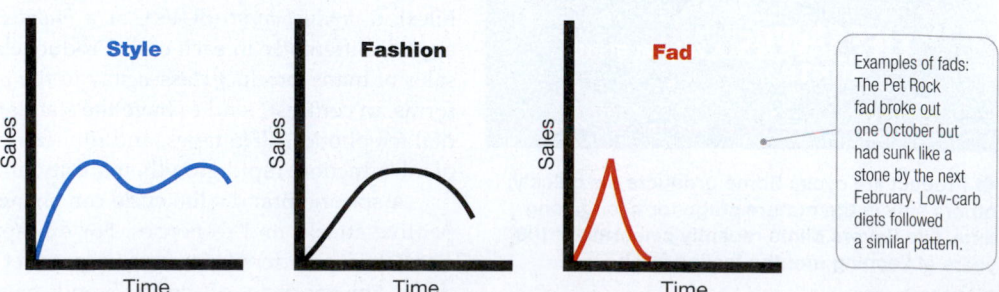

Examples of fads: The Pet Rock fad broke out one October but had sunk like a stone by the next February. Low-carb diets followed a similar pattern.

Real Marketing

9.2 Managing Mattel's Product Life Cycle: More Than Just Fun and Games

Mattel has ruled the toy industry for generations, with classic brands such as Barbie, Hot Wheels, Fisher-Price, American Girl, and a host of others. For more than 50 years, Mattel's toys have topped the wish lists of children across America.

Recently, however, Mattel's sales have fallen off as its core brands have matured. Venerable Barbie, now in her mid-50s, has experienced double-digit sales dips in each of the past three years. Sagging Fisher-Price and American Girl sales suggest that today's toy buyers are less enamored with those storied brands than were previous generations. And Mattel's Hot Wheels brand, while holding its own, now seems coveted more by nostalgic dads than by their young sons.

Mattel could blame its slump on broader toy industry trends—declining birthrates, rising costs, unfavorable economic conditions, and the boom in digital technologies that make many traditional toys now seem like relics from the past. The global toy industry has stagnated in recent years, with market leaders such as Mattel and Hasbro taking the biggest hits. Yet none of that has slowed Mattel's hottest competitor, The LEGO Group. In the past 10 years, despite the toy industry's doldrums, LEGO revenues have quadrupled, up 15 percent last year alone. LEGO recently surged past Mattel and Hasbro to become the world's largest toy maker.

LEGO's success suggests that Mattel's problems go beyond just industry ups and downs. Rather, the company appears to have a product life-cycle problem—lots of good old products but too few good new ones. In an industry facing a barrage of hot new playthings, Mattel has lagged in product development and failed to adapt to rapidly changing toy trends and tastes.

Consider Barbie, Mattel's biggest and oldest brand. Born in 1959, Barbie quickly became a must-have for young girls everywhere. By the late 1970s, 90 percent of U.S. girls between the ages of 5 and 10 owned at least one Barbie. For more than five decades, Barbie has remained Mattel's number-one moneymaker, accounting for as much as 30 percent of its revenues. But during the past few years, Barbie's popularity has spiraled downward. Although still one of the world's largest toy brands, Barbie's current annual revenues of under $1 billion are less than half of what

they were at her peak. Barbie sales dropped a stomach-churning 16 percent last year, prompting one analyst to suggest that "it might be time for Mattel to roll out Retirement Barbie."

That won't happen anytime soon. But like many other Mattel brands, Barbie is showing her age. Designers work tirelessly on new Barbie models and features. An example is Entrepreneur Barbie, the first Barbie with her own smartphone and LinkedIn profile. And Mattel recently introduced Hello Barbie, a talking, interactive, Wi-Fi–connected doll. Still, Barbie continues to lose relevance alongside trendier toy aisle juggernauts like Disney's *Frozen* line of toys and play sets.

Mattel has also misfired in some of its marketing attempts to modernize Barbie. For example, the Barbie "Unapologetic" campaign—with its "If you can dream it, you can be it" slogan—tried to strike a blow for female empowerment. Yet despite the fact that it targeted 3- to 12-year-old girls and even after decades of criticism concerning Barbie's unrealistic figure and the standard of beauty she sets, Mattel kicked the campaign off by featuring Barbie on an advertising wrap on the covers of 1,000 issues of the 50th anniversary *Sports Illustrated* swimsuit edition. That

move incurred the wrath of countless mothers across the nation.

Over the years, as Barbie has aged, Mattel has tried to round out its product portfolio with new, younger lines of dolls. In the late 1990s, the company purchased the wildly popular, premium-priced American Girl line. And more recently, it created runaway hit Monster High—a line of dolls and accessories composed of characters such as Draculaura, Ghoulia Yelps, and Abbey Bominable. However, much like Barbie, both American Girl and Monster High are now maturing and experiencing sales declines. Critics blame Mattel's uninspired designs, conservative innovation mindset, and inability to keep the brands fresh and relevant to the times.

With most of its core brands in mature or declining life-cycle stages, Mattel is fighting an uphill battle. Take Hot Wheels, long the market leader in toy cars. Mattel has had modest success in revitalizing the mature brand by taking it into hot pockets of the market. For example, as the popularity of remote control helicopters and drones has soared in recent years, Hot Wheels launched the Street Hawk, a flying remote control car. Street Hawk became one of the biggest hits during its first

Product life-cycle management: Like many other Mattel brands, Barbie is showing her age. Beyond revitalizing its classic brands, Mattel must create a steady stream of exciting new ones.

REUTERS/Mike Blake

holiday season. Still, the hits have been too few and too far between. Even with its avid cross-generational collector base, the Hot Wheels brand is barely holding its own against the onslaught of new-age products from competitors with more inspired innovation.

As its own core brands have aged, Mattel has injected new life into its product lines by licensing hot characters from popular movies, TV shows, and comic books. Specifically, Mattel made a small fortune with licensed Disney Princesses and *Frozen* dolls and toys. It recently launched a line of Star Wars Hot Wheels cars, and it has partnered with Warner Bros. Entertainment on 10 upcoming films based on DC Comics characters. Although profitable, however, such licensed products can't compensate for Mattel's inability to revitalize its own brands and develop new ones. For example, Mattel recently lost its Disney Princesses and *Frozen* character rights to rival Hasbro, leaving a huge revenue hole to fill.

Thus, to regain its prowess in today's turbulent, fast-changing toy market, Mattel must develop a faster, more nimble, more customer-focused process for developing relevant new products and guiding them profitably through their product life cycles. Beyond reinvigorating its classic brands, Mattel must create a steady stream of exciting new ones that stay ahead of changing consumer trends and tastes. For Mattel, mastering the product life cycle is more than just fun and games. It's a matter of growth, prosperity, and even long-run survival.

Sources: "Mattel Has 20% Upside, Yields 5%," *Barron's*, January 2, 2016, www.barrons.com/articles/mattel-has-20-upside-yields-5-1451704412; Claire Suddath, "The Princess Makeover: How Hasbro Stole Disney's Dolls from Mattel," *Bloomberg Businessweek*, December 17, 2015, pp. 40–45; John Kell, "Mattel's Barbie Sales Down for Third Consecutive Year," *Fortune*, January 30, 2015, http://fortune.com/2015/01/30/mattels-barbie-sales-drop-third-year/; Laura Stampler, "Bye, Bye Barbie: 2015 Is the Year We Abandon Unrealistic Beauty Ideals," *Time*, January 30, 2015, http://time.com/3667580/mattel-barbie-earnings-plus-size-body-image/; Rachel Abrams, "Mattel Aims to Reanimate Sales with Talking Barbie," *New York Times*, October 16, 2015, p. B2; and www.barbie.com and http://corporate.mattel.com, accessed September 2016.

Introduction Stage

Introduction stage
The PLC stage in which a new product is first distributed and made available for purchase.

The **introduction stage** starts when a new product is first launched. Introduction takes time, and sales growth is apt to be slow. Well-known products such as frozen foods and HDTVs lingered for many years before they entered a stage of more rapid growth.

In this stage, as compared to other stages, profits are negative or low because of the low sales and high distribution and promotion expenses. Much money is needed to attract distributors and build their inventories. Promotion spending is relatively high to inform consumers of the new product and get them to try it. Because the market is not generally ready for product refinements at this stage, the company and its few competitors produce basic versions of the product. These firms focus their selling on those buyers who are the most ready to buy.

A company, especially the *market pioneer*, must choose a launch strategy that is consistent with the intended product positioning. It should realize that the initial strategy is just the first step in a grander marketing plan for the product's entire life cycle. If the pioneer chooses its launch strategy to make a "killing," it may be sacrificing long-run revenue for the sake of short-run gain. The pioneer has the best chance of building and retaining market leadership if it plays its cards correctly from the start.

Growth Stage

Growth stage
The PLC stage in which a product's sales start climbing quickly.

If the new product satisfies the market, it will enter a **growth stage** in which sales will start climbing quickly. The early adopters will continue to buy, and later buyers will start following their lead, especially if they hear favorable word of mouth. Attracted by the opportunities for profit, new competitors will enter the market. They will introduce new product features, and the market will expand. The increase in competitors leads to an increase in the number of distribution outlets, and sales jump just to build reseller inventories. Prices remain where they are or decrease only slightly. Companies keep their promotion spending at the same or a slightly higher level. Educating the market remains a goal, but now the company must also meet the competition.

Profits increase during the growth stage as promotion costs are spread over a large volume and as unit manufacturing costs decrease. The firm uses several strategies to sustain rapid market growth as long as possible. It improves product quality and adds new product features and models. It enters new market segments and new distribution channels. It shifts some advertising from building product awareness to building product conviction and purchase, and it lowers prices at the right time to attract more buyers.

In the growth stage, the firm faces a trade-off between high market share and high current profit. By spending a lot of money on product improvement, promotion, and distribution, the company can capture a dominant position. In doing so, however, it gives up maximum current profit, which it hopes to make up in the next stage.

Maturity Stage

Maturity stage
The PLC stage in which a product's sales growth slows or levels off.

At some point, a product's sales growth will slow down, and it will enter the **maturity stage**. This maturity stage normally lasts longer than the previous stages, and it poses strong challenges to marketing management. Most products are in the maturity stage of the life cycle, and therefore most of marketing management deals with the mature product.

The slowdown in sales growth results in many producers with many products to sell. In turn, this overcapacity leads to greater competition. Competitors begin marking down prices, increasing their advertising and sales promotions, and upping their product development budgets to find better versions of the product. These steps lead to a drop in profit. Some of the weaker competitors start dropping out, and the industry eventually contains only well-established competitors.

Although many products in the mature stage appear to remain unchanged for long periods, most successful ones are actually evolving to meet changing consumer needs. Product managers should do more than simply ride along with or defend their mature products—a good offense is the best defense. They should consider modifying the market, product offering, and marketing mix.

In *modifying the market*, the company tries to increase consumption by finding new users and new market segments for its brands. For example, brands such as Harley-Davidson and Axe fragrances, which have typically targeted male buyers, have created products and marketing programs aimed at women. Conversely, Weight Watchers and Bath & Body Works, which have typically targeted women, have created products and programs aimed at men.

The company may also look for ways to increase usage among present customers. For example, 3M recently ran a marketing campaign to inspire more usage of its Post-it products.[21] The Post-it "Go Ahead" campaign aimed to convince customers that the sticky pieces of paper are good for much more than just scribbling temporary notes and reminders. An initial ad showed people on a college campus blanketing a wall outside a building with Post-it Notes answering the question "What inspires you?" "Share on a real wall," the announcer explained. Other scenes showed a young man filling a wall with mosaic artwork created from multiple colors of Post-it Notes, teachers using Post-it Notes to enliven their classrooms, and a man posting a "Morning, beautiful" note on the bathroom mirror as his wife is brushing her teeth. "Go ahead," said the announcer, "keep the honeymoon going." The ad ended with a hand peeling Post-it Notes off a pad one by one to reveal new, unexpected uses: "Go ahead, Connect," "Go ahead, Inspire," and "Go ahead, Explore."

The company might also try *modifying the product*—changing characteristics such as quality, features, style, packaging, or technology platforms to retain current users or attract new ones. Thus, to freshen up their products for today's technology-obsessed children, many classic toy and game makers are creating new digital versions or add-ons for old favorites. For example, the venerable Crayola brand has souped up its product line to meet the technology tastes of the new generation. With the Crayola My Virtual Fashion Show drawing kit and app, for instance, children first design fashions using the provided color pencils and sketchpad. They then take photos of the designs with their smartphones or tablets and watch their original creations magically come to life inside the app on 3D models who walk virtual runways in Milan, New York, and Paris.[22]

Finally, the company can try *modifying the marketing mix*—improving sales by changing one or more marketing mix elements. The company can offer new or improved services to buyers. It can cut prices to attract new users and competitors' customers. It can launch a better advertising campaign or use aggressive sales promotions—trade deals, cents-off, premiums, and contests. In addition to pricing and promotion, the company can also move into new marketing channels to help serve new users.

● PepsiCo used all of these market, product, and marketing mix modification approaches to reinvigorate its 137-year-old Quaker brand

● Managing the product life cycle: Thanks to the "Quaker Up" campaign, 137-year-old Quaker now has a more contemporary appeal as a lifestyle brand that helps give young families the fuel and energy needed to get through the day.
Provided courtesy of The Quaker Oat Company.

and keep it from sinking into decline. To reawaken the brand, Quaker launched a major new "Quaker Up" marketing campaign, supported by an estimated $100 million budget:[23]

> The "Quaker Up" campaign targets a new market of young mothers under 35, positioning Quaker's lines of hot and cold cereals, snack bars, cookies, and other products as healthy lifestyle choices that help give a young family the fuel and energy needed to get through the day. The campaign advises families to "Quaker Up—with Quaker's good energy for the moments that matter." As part of the retargeting and repositioning effort, Quaker has modernized every element of the brand, from products and packaging to in-store displays and ad platforms. To start, it slimmed down the iconic Quaker man by 20 pounds and gave him a facelift to make him look healthier, stronger, and more contemporary. The brand added new energy-packed products, such as Quaker Medleys—a hearty blend of oats and grains with real fruit and nuts; Quaker Soft Baked Bars—high in fiber, protein, and B vitamins; and Quaker Protein—protein-packed instant oatmeal and baked energy bars. Befitting the more mobile and connected lifestyles of today's young parents, the "Quaker Up" campaign also incorporates and healthy dose of digital media, including banner ads, YouTube videos, a Facebook app, a Quaker Up community website, and a full slate of other digital content. In all, despite its age, the reenergized Quaker brand now has a much younger appeal. "People know the brand, people love the brand, but we needed to forge a stronger connection with contemporary moms," says Quaker's chief marketing officer.

Decline Stage

The sales of most product forms and brands eventually dip. The decline may be slow, as in the cases of stamps and oatmeal cereal, or rapid, as in the cases of VHS tapes. Sales may plunge to zero, or they may drop to a low level where they continue for many years. This is the **decline stage**.

Decline stage
The PLC stage in which a product's sales fade away.

Sales decline for many reasons, including technological advances, shifts in consumer tastes, and increased competition. As sales and profits decline, some firms withdraw from the market. Those remaining may prune their product offerings. In addition, they may drop smaller market segments and marginal trade channels, or they may cut the promotion budget and reduce their prices further.

Carrying a weak product can be very costly to a firm, and not just in profit terms. There are many hidden costs. A weak product may take up too much of management's time. It often requires frequent price and inventory adjustments. It requires advertising and sales-force attention that might be better used to make "healthy" products more profitable. A product's failing reputation can cause customer concerns about the company and its other products. The biggest cost may well lie in the future. Keeping weak products delays the search for replacements, creates a lopsided product mix, hurts current profits, and weakens the company's foothold on the future.

For these reasons, companies must identify products in the decline stage and decide whether to maintain, harvest, or drop them. Management may decide to *maintain* its brand, repositioning or reinvigorating it in hopes of moving it back into the growth stage of the product life cycle. P&G has done this with several brands, including Mr. Clean and Old Spice. Over the past decade, P&G has retargeted, repositioned, revitalized, and extended both of these old brands, taking each from near extinction to billion-dollar-brand status.

Management may decide to *harvest* the product, which means reducing various costs (plant and equipment, maintenance, R&D, advertising, sales force), hoping that sales hold up. If successful, harvesting will increase the company's profits in the short run. Finally, management may decide to *drop* the product from its line. The company can sell the product to another firm or simply liquidate it at salvage value. If the company plans to find a buyer, it will not want to run down the product through harvesting. In recent years, P&G has sold off several declining brands and brands that no longer fit strategically, such as Folgers coffee, Crisco oil, Comet cleanser, Sure deodorant, Noxema, Duncan Hines cake mixes, Cover Girl and Max Factor cosmetics, Duracell batteries, Iams pet foods, and others.[24]

● **Table 9.2** summarizes the key characteristics of each stage of the PLC. The table also lists the marketing objectives and strategies for each stage.[25]

● **Table 9.2 | Summary of Product Life-Cycle Characteristics, Objectives, and Strategies**

	Introduction	Growth	Maturity	Decline
Characteristics				
Sales	Low sales	Rapidly rising sales	Peak sales	Declining sales
Costs	High cost per customer	Average cost per customer	Low cost per customer	Low cost per customer
Profits	Negative	Rising profits	High profits	Declining profits
Customers	Innovators	Early adopters	Mainstream adopters	Lagging adopters
Competitors	Few	Growing number	Stable number beginning to decline	Declining number
Marketing objectives				
	Create product engagement and trial	Maximize market share	Maximize profit while defending market share	Reduce expenditure and milk the brand
Strategies				
Product	Offer a basic product	Offer product extensions, service, and warranty	Diversify brand and models	Phase out weak items
Price	Use cost-plus	Price to penetrate market	Price to match or beat competitors	Cut price
Distribution	Build selective distribution	Build intensive distribution	Build more intensive distribution	Go selective: phase out unprofitable outlets
Advertising	Build product awareness among early adopters and dealers	Build engagement and interest in the mass market	Stress brand differences and benefits	Reduce to level needed to retain hard-core loyals
Sales promotion	Use heavy sales promotion to entice trial	Reduce to take advantage of heavy consumer demand	Increase to encourage brand switching	Reduce to minimal level

Source: Based on Philip Kotler and Kevin Lane Keller, *Marketing Management,* 15th ed. (Hoboken, NJ: Pearson Education, 2016), p. 358. © 2016. Printed and electronically reproduced by permission of Pearson Education, Inc., Hoboken, New Jersey.

> Author | Let's look at just a few more
> Comment | product topics, including
> regulatory and social responsibility
> issues and the special challenges of
> marketing products internationally.

Additional Product and Service Considerations

We wrap up our discussion of products and services with two additional considerations: social responsibility in product decisions and issues of international product and services marketing.

Product Decisions and Social Responsibility

Marketers should carefully consider public policy issues and regulations regarding acquiring or dropping products, patent protection, product quality and safety, and product warranties.

Regarding new products, the government may prevent companies from adding products through acquisitions if the effect threatens to lessen competition. Companies dropping products must be aware that they have legal obligations, written or implied, to their suppliers, dealers, and customers who have a stake in the dropped product. Companies must also obey U.S. patent laws when developing new products. A company cannot make its product illegally similar to another company's established product.

Manufacturers must comply with specific laws regarding product quality and safety. The Federal Food, Drug, and Cosmetic Act protects consumers from unsafe and adulterated food, drugs, and cosmetics. Various acts provide for the inspection of sanitary conditions in the meat- and poultry-processing industries. Safety legislation has been passed to regulate fabrics, chemical substances, automobiles, toys, and drugs and poisons. The Consumer Product Safety Act of 1972 established the Consumer Product Safety Commission, which has the authority to ban or seize potentially harmful products and set severe penalties for violation of the law.

If consumers have been injured by a product with a defective design, they can sue manufacturers or dealers. A recent survey of manufacturing companies found that product liability was the second-largest litigation concern, behind only labor and employment matters. Tens of thousands of product liability suits are now tried in U.S. district courts each year. Although manufacturers are found to be at fault in only a small percentage of all product liability cases, when they are found guilty, awards can run into the tens or even hundreds of millions of dollars. Class-action suits can run into the billions. For example, after it recalled 11 million vehicles for acceleration pedal-related issues, Toyota faced more than 100 class-action and individual lawsuits and ended up paying a $1.6 billion settlement to compensate owners for financial losses associated with the defect. And GM has so far paid more than $2 billion in fines and settlements over a faulty ignition switches that caused the deaths of more than 120 drivers.[26]

This litigation phenomenon has resulted in huge increases in product liability insurance premiums, causing big problems in some industries. Some companies pass these higher rates along to consumers by raising prices. Others are forced to discontinue high-risk product lines. Some companies are now appointing *product stewards*, whose job is to protect consumers from harm and the company from liability by proactively ferreting out potential product problems.

International Product and Services Marketing

International product and services marketers face special challenges. First, they must figure out what products and services to introduce and in which countries. Then they must decide how much to standardize or adapt their products and services for world markets.

On the one hand, companies would like to standardize their offerings. Standardization helps a company develop a consistent worldwide image. It also lowers the product design, manufacturing, and marketing costs of offering a large variety of products. On the other hand, markets and consumers around the world differ widely. Companies must usually respond to these differences by adapting their product offerings.

For example, McDonald's operates in more than 100 countries, with sometimes widely varying local food preferences. So although you'll find its signature burgers and fries in most locations around the world, the chain has added menu items that meet the unique taste buds of customers in local markets. McDonald's serves salmon burgers in Norway, mashed-potato burgers in China, shrimp burgers in Japan, a Samurai Pork Burger in Thailand, chicken porridge in Malaysia, and Spam and eggs in Hawaii. In a German McDonald's, you'll find the Nürnburger (three large bratwurst on a soft roll with lots of mustard, of course); in Israel, there's the McFalafel (chickpea fritters, tomatoes, cucumber, and cheese topped with tahini and wrapped in lafa). And menus in Turkey feature a chocolate orange fried pie (Brazil adds banana, Egypt taro, and Hawaii pineapple).

In many major global markets, McDonald's adapts more than just its menu. It also adjusts its restaurant design and operations. ● For example, McDonald's France has redefined itself as a French company that adapts to the needs and preferences of French consumers:[27]

● **Global product adaption:** By adapting its menu and operations to the needs and preferences of French consumers and their culture, McDonald's has turned France into its second-most-profitable world market.

ERIC PIERMONT/AFP/Getty Images/Newscom

"France—the land of haute cuisine, fine wine, and cheese—would be the last place you would expect to find a thriving [McDonald's]," opines one observer. Yet the fast-food giant has turned France into its second-most profitable world market. Although a McDonald's in Paris might at first seem a lot like one in Chicago, McDonald's has carefully adapted its French operations to the preferences of local customers. At the most basic level, although a majority of revenues still come from burgers and fries, McDonald's France has changed its menu to please the French palate. For instance, it offers up burgers with French cheeses such as chevre, cantel, and bleu, topped off with whole-grain French mustard sauce. And French consumers love baguettes, so McDonald's bakes them fresh in its restaurants and sells them in oh-so-French McBaguette sandwiches.

But perhaps the biggest difference isn't in the food, but in the design of the restaurants themselves, which have been adapted to suit French lifestyles. For example, French meal times tend to be longer, with more food consumed per sitting. So McDonald's has refined its restaurant interiors to create a comfortable, welcoming environment where customers want to linger and perhaps order an additional coffee or dessert. McDonald's even provides table-side service. As a result, the average French McDonald's customer spends about four times what an American customer spends per visit.

Service marketers also face special challenges when going global. Some service industries have a long history of international operations. For example, the commercial banking industry was one of the first to grow internationally. Banks had to provide global services to meet the foreign exchange and credit needs of their home-country clients who wanted to sell overseas. In recent years, many banks have become truly global. Germany's Deutsche Bank, for example, serves more than 28 million customers through 2,700 branches in more than 70 countries. For its clients around the world who wish to grow globally, Deutsche Bank can raise money not only in Frankfurt but also in Zurich, London, Paris, Tokyo, and Moscow.[28]

Retailers are among the latest service businesses to go global. As their home markets become saturated, American retailers such as Walmart, Office Depot, and Saks Fifth Avenue are expanding into faster-growing markets abroad. For example, Walmart now serves 260 million customers weekly in 28 countries; its international division's sales account for nearly 29 percent of total sales. Foreign retailers are making similar moves. Asian shoppers can now buy American products in French-owned Carrefour stores. Carrefour—the world's sixth-largest retailer behind the likes of Walmart, Costco, Kroger, Germany's Schwarz, and the UK's Tesco—now operates more than 10,000 stores in 34 countries. It is the leading retailer in Europe, Brazil, and Argentina and the largest foreign retailer in China.[29]

The trend toward growth of global service companies will continue, especially in banking, airlines, telecommunications, and professional services. Today, service firms are no longer simply following their manufacturing customers. Instead, they are taking the lead in international expansion.

9 | Reviewing and Extending the Concepts

OBJECTIVES REVIEW AND KEY TERMS

Objectives Review

A company's current products face limited life spans and must be replaced by newer products. But new products can fail—the risks of innovation are as great as the rewards. The key to successful innovation lies in a customer-focused, holistic, total-company effort; strong planning; and a systematic new product development process.

OBJECTIVE 9-1 Explain how companies find and develop new product ideas. (pp 256–257)

Companies find and develop new product ideas from a variety of sources. Many new product ideas stem from *internal sources*.

Companies conduct formal R&D, or they pick the brains of their employees, urging them to think up and develop new product ideas. Other ideas come from *external sources*. Companies track *competitors'* offerings and obtain ideas from *distributors and suppliers* who are close to the market and can pass along information about consumer problems and new product possibilities.

Perhaps the most important sources of new product ideas are *customers* themselves. Companies observe customers, invite them to submit their ideas and suggestions, or even involve customers in the new product development process. Many companies are now developing *crowdsourcing* or *open-innovation* new product idea programs, which invite broad communities of people—customers, employees, independent scientists and researchers, and even the general public—into the new product innovation process. Truly innovative companies do not rely only on one source for new product ideas.

OBJECTIVE 9-2   **List and define the steps in the new product development process and the major considerations in managing this process.** *(pp 257–265)*

The new product development process consists of eight sequential stages. The process starts with *idea generation*. Next comes *idea screening,* which reduces the number of ideas based on the company's own criteria. Ideas that pass the screening stage continue through *product concept development,* in which a detailed version of the new product idea is stated in meaningful consumer terms. This stage includes *concept testing,* in which new product concepts are tested with a group of target consumers to determine whether the concepts have strong consumer appeal. Strong concepts proceed to *marketing strategy development,* in which an initial marketing strategy for the new product is developed from the product concept. In the *business-analysis* stage, a review of the sales, costs, and profit projections for a new product is conducted to determine whether the new product is likely to satisfy the company's objectives. With positive results here, the ideas become more concrete through *product development* and *test marketing* and finally are launched during *commercialization*.

New product development involves more than just going through a set of steps. Companies must take a systematic, holistic approach to managing this process. Successful new product development requires a customer-centered, team-based, systematic effort.

OBJECTIVE 9-3   **Describe the stages of the product life cycle and how marketing strategies change during a product's life cycle.** *(pp 265–273)*

Each product has a *life cycle* marked by a changing set of problems and opportunities. The sales of the typical product follow an S-shaped curve made up of five stages. The cycle begins with the *product development* stage in which the company finds and develops a new product idea. The *introduction stage* is marked by slow growth and low profits as the product is distributed to the market. If successful, the product enters a *growth stage,* which offers rapid sales growth and increasing profits. Next comes a *maturity stage* in which the product's sales growth slows down and profits stabilize. Finally, the product enters a *decline stage* in which sales and profits dwindle. The company's task during this stage is to recognize the decline and decide whether it should maintain, harvest, or drop the product. The different stages of the PLC require different marketing strategies and tactics.

OBJECTIVE 9-4   **Discuss two additional product issues: socially responsible product decisions and international product and services marketing.** *(pp 273–275)*

Marketers must consider two additional product issues. The first is *social responsibility*. This includes public policy issues and regulations involving acquiring or dropping products, patent protection, product quality and safety, and product warranties. The second involves the special challenges facing international product and services marketers. International marketers must decide how much to standardize or adapt their offerings for world markets.

Key Terms

OBJECTIVE 9-1

New product development (p 256)

OBJECTIVE 9-2

Idea generation (p 257)
Crowdsourcing (p 258)
Idea screening (p 259)
Product concept (p 259)
Concept testing (p 260)

Marketing strategy development (p 260)
Business analysis (p 261)
Product development (p 262)
Test marketing (p 262)
Commercialization (p 263)
Customer-centered new product
   development (p 263)
Team-based new product development
   (p 264)

OBJECTIVE 9-3

Product life cycle (PLC) (p 265)
Style (p 268)
Fashion (p 268)
Fad (p 268)
Introduction stage (p 270)
Growth stage (p 270)
Maturity stage (p 271)
Decline stage (p 272)

DISCUSSION AND CRITICAL THINKING

MyMarketingLab

Go to **mymktlab.com** to complete the problems marked with this icon .

Discussion Questions

9-1   Why do so many new products fail? (AACSB: Communication)

 9-2   What is idea generation? List and explain the sources of new product ideas. (AACSB: Communication; Reflective Thinking)

⭐ **9-3** What actions are performed in the business analysis step of the new product development process? How does a business carry out this step? (AACSB: Communication)

9-4 How can companies adopt a holistic approach to managing new product development? (AACSB: Communication).

⭐ **9-5** Describe the options available to marketers of products in the decline stage of the product life cycle. (AACSB: Communication)

Critical Thinking Exercises

⭐ **9-6** Companies large and small, across all industries, are crowdsourcing product innovation ideas. Research three crowdsourcing campaigns that companies have used within the past two years. Were they successful? Explain. (AACSB: Communication; Use of IT; Reflective Thinking)

9-7 In small groups, research driverless cars. In what stage of the new product development process are driverless cars? What challenges are companies such as Google, Apple, Amazon, and Ford facing in getting this product to the launch stage? (AACSB: Communication; Use of IT; Reflective Thinking)

9-8 Find an example of a company that launched a new consumer product within the past five years. Develop a presentation showing how the company implemented the four Ps in launching the product and report on the product's success since the launch. (AACSB: Communication; Reflective Thinking)

APPLICATIONS AND CASES

Online, Mobile, and Social Media Marketing Telemedicine

With the majority of health-care costs spent for the treatment of chronic diseases and the reason for most emergency room visits being non-emergencies, the time is ripe for telemedicine. Patients are tapping their phones, tablets, and keyboards instead of making an office visit or trip to the emergency room. Technology makes it possible for doctors to consult with patients through Skype or FaceTime on smartphones, access medical tests via electronic medical records, and send a prescription to a patient's local pharmacy—all from miles away. The telemedicine industry is still in its infancy, earning only $200 million in annual revenue, but it is predicted to increase to an almost $2 billion industry in just a few years. Technology isn't the only reason for this industry's growth. The HITECH Act encouraging electronic medical records is also adding fuel to this fire.

9-9 Research the telemedicine industry and describe two companies offering services. What are the pros and cons of offering medical services this way, and is there governmental or industry guidance for this industry? (AACSB: Communications; Reflective Thinking)

9-10 In what stage of the product life cycle is telemedicine? What role has mobile technology played in evolution of this industry? Explain. (AACSB: Communication; Reflective Thinking)

Marketing Ethics Put On Your Thinking Caps!

For years, electrical current has been used to treat brain disorders, such as depression, Parkinson's disease, and epilepsy. Traditional electrical treatment methods are invasive and require sending large currents or implanting devices in users' brains to achieve positive results. Recent studies have shown, however, that sending noninvasive low-dose electric current powered by a nine-volt battery through the brains of adults and children helps them to learn math and languages better. For as little as $55, you can purchase your own transcranial direct-current stimulation (tDCS) device to get better grades in school. The Brain Stimulator tDCS Basic Kit allows users to select between four different current levels and a nice blue headband or cap to hold the electrodes next to your skull. The buyer should beware, however, because these devices have been neither reviewed nor approved by the Food and Drug Administration as medical devices.

9-11 Discuss the ethical issues surrounding this type of product. Is there substantial research to support the claims and safety of these new products? (AACSB: Communication; Ethical Reasoning)

9-12 What is the Food and Drug Administration's stance on these types of devices and other products marketed as cognitive enhancers, such as herbal supplements? (AACSB: Communication; Reflective Thinking)

Marketing by the Numbers Dental House Calls

With the population aging and patients who dread sitting in a sterile dental office, dentists are finding an opportunity in dental house calls. The Blende Dental Group has taken its service on the road in San Francisco and New York City, performing everything from routine exams and cleanings to root canals. Some patients are wealthy and prefer the personal service, whereas others are elderly homebounds who cannot get out to the dentist's office. Recreating a dental office in a home requires additional equipment, such as a portable X-ray machine that looks like a ray gun, sterile water tanks, a dental drill, lights, and a laptop. A portable X-ray machine alone costs $8,000. Refer to Appendix 2: Marketing by the Numbers to answer the following questions.

9-13 What types of fixed costs are associated with this service? Estimate total fixed costs for this additional service, and assuming a contribution margin of 40 percent, determine the amount of sales necessary to break even on this increase in fixed costs to offer this additional service. (AACSB: Communication; Analytical Thinking)

9-14 What other factors must a dentist consider before offering this service in addition to his or her in-office service? (AACSB: Communication; Reflective Thinking)

Video Case Day2Night Convertible Heels

Many women love the fashionable looks and heightening effects of high-heeled shoes. But every woman knows the problems associated with wearing them. For example, they are very uncomfortable for anything more than light walking for short distances. For other activities, you'd better be packing a second pair of shoes.

That's where Day2Night Convertible Heels comes in. Created by a woman who had an epiphany after a hard night of dancing, Day2Night's shoes instantly convert to any one of four heel sizes, from low-heeled pumps to spiked-heeled stilettos. An interchangeable heel makes these high heels a high-tech proposition.

Beyond launching a line of shoes, Day2Night is looking to license the technology to other shoe manufacturers.

After viewing the video featuring Day2Night Convertible Heels, answer the following questions:

9-15 Based on the stages of new product development, discuss how Day2Night was likely developed.

9-16 What stage of the product life cycle best applies to Day2Night's shoe line? As the company attempts to launch the shoes, how should it market them?

9-17 What challenges does Day2Night face?

Company Case Bose: Better Products through Research

In a recent survey by brand strategy firm Lippincott, the most trusted brand in consumer electronics was not Apple. Nor was it Samsung, Sony, or Microsoft. It was Bose, the still relatively small, privately held corporation that has been making innovative audio devices for more than 50 years. Despite putting more than 30 million new sets of headphones alone on or in customers' ears last year, Bose rang up only about $4 billion in revenues versus Apple's $234 billion. But when it comes to the passion customers feel for their brands, the Massachusetts-based technology company outshines even Apple. Bose forges that deep consumer connection based on the brand's design simplicity and brilliant functionality.

Bose adheres religiously to a set of values that have guided the company since its origins. Most companies today focus heavily on building revenues, profits, and stock prices. They try to outdo competitors by differentiating product lines with features and attributes that other companies don't have. Although Bose doesn't ignore such factors, its competitive advantage is rooted in its unique corporate philosophy. "We are not in it strictly to make money," says CEO Bob Maresca. Given the company's focus on research and product innovation, he points out that "the business is almost a secondary consideration."

The Bose Philosophy

To understand Bose the company, you must first look at Bose the man. In the 1950s, founder Amar Bose was working on his third degree at the Massachusetts Institute of Technology. He had a keen interest in research and studied various areas of electrical engineering. He also had a strong interest in music. When he purchased his first hi-fi system—a model that he believed had the best specifications—he was disappointed in the system's ability to reproduce realistic sound. So he began heavily researching the problem to find his own solution. Thus began a stream of research that would ultimately lead to the founding of the Bose Corporation in 1964. It also led to the development of the long-standing Bose slogan "Better Sound Through Research."

From those early days, Amar Bose worked around certain core principles that have guided the philosophy of the company. In conducting his first research on speakers and sound, he did something that has since been repeated time and time again at Bose. He ignored existing technologies and started entirely from scratch, something not common in product development strategies.

In another departure from typical corporate strategies, Amar Bose put all of the privately held company's profits back into research and development, a practice that reflected his avid love of research and his drive to produce the highest-quality products. In doing so, he also bypassed the process of figuring out what customers wanted, instead keeping his research confined to the laboratory and centered on the technical specifications of creating a superior product.

Today, this approach is considered heresy in the innovation world. Amar pursued this approach because he could. He often pointed out that publicly held companies have long lists of constraints that don't apply to privately held companies, noting that "if I worked for another company, I would have been fired a long time ago," For this reason, Bose always vowed that he would never take the company public. "Going public for me would have been the equivalent of losing the company. My real interest is research—that's the excitement—and I wouldn't have been able to do long-term projects with Wall Street breathing down my neck."

Innovating the Bose Way

The company that started so humbly now has a breadth of product lines beyond its core home audio line. Additional lines target a variety of applications that captured Amar Bose's creative attention over the years, including military, automotive, homebuilding/remodeling, aviation, and professional and commercial sound systems. It even has a division that markets testing equipment to research institutions, universities, medical device companies, and engineering companies worldwide. The following are just a few of the products that illustrate the innovative breakthroughs produced by the company.

Speakers. Bose's first product was a speaker introduced in 1965. Expecting to sell $1 million worth of speakers that first year, Bose made 60 but sold only 40. The original Bose speaker evolved into the 901 Direct/Reflecting speaker system launched in 1968. That speaker system was designed around the concept that live sound reaches the human ear via direct as well as reflected channels (off walls, ceilings, and other objects). The speakers featured a completely unorthodox configuration. Shaped like one-eighth of a sphere and mounted facing into a room's corner, the audio waves reflected off the walls and filled the room with sound that seemed to be everywhere but some from nowhere in particular. The speakers had no woofers or tweeters, composed instead of eight four-and-a-half-inch midrange drivers. The speakers were also very small compared with the high-end speakers of the day. The design came much closer to the essence and emotional impact of live music than anything else on the market and won immediate industry acclaim. The reflective approach, although groundbreaking at the time, is commonly found in home theater systems throughout the industry today.

Back then, however, Bose had a hard time convincing customers of the merits of these innovative speakers. At a time when woofers, tweeters, and size meant everything, the 901 series initially flopped. In 1968, a retail salesperson explained to Amar Bose why the speakers weren't selling:

"Look, I love your speaker but I cannot sell it because it makes me lose all my credibility as a salesman. I can't explain to anyone why the 901 doesn't have any woofers or tweeters. A man came in and saw the small size, and he started looking in the drawers for the speaker cabinets. I walked over to him, and he said, 'Where are you hiding the woofer?' I said to him, 'There is no woofer.' So he said, 'You're a liar,' and he walked out."

To resolve this credibility problem, Bose developed another core competency—identifying and targeting the right customer with the products it was confident were superior to even the best offerings. For Bose, this has generally meant targeting higher-income customers who aren't audio buffs but want a good product and are willing to pay a premium price for it. For the 901, this included using innovative display and demonstration tactics. This approach has served Bose well. Although even today hardcore audiophiles scoff at Bose products as little more than smoke and mirrors, customers whose expectations haven't been shaped by preconceived specifications perceive Bose products to be exceptional. So far as the 901 is concerned, the product became so successful that Amar Bose was known for crediting the speaker series with building the company.

The list of major speaker innovations at Bose is a long one. In the 1970s, the company introduced concert-like sound in the bookshelf-size 301 Direct/Reflecting speaker system. Fourteen years of research led to the development of acoustic waveguide speaker technology, a technology today found in the award-winning Wave radio, Wave music system, and Acoustic Wave music system. In the 1980s, the company again changed conventional thinking about the relationship between speaker size and sound. The Acoustimass system enabled palm-size speakers to produce audio quality equivalent to that of high-end systems many times their size—a design so popular it also remains in the current Bose portfolio of speakers. Recently, Bose again introduced the state of the art with the MusicMonitor, a pair of compact computer speakers that rival the sound of three-piece subwoofer systems. And Bose has led the way in developing wireless speaker systems, a move that was quickly followed by all competitors. Not only was each of these speaker systems groundbreaking at the time it was introduced, each was so technologically advanced that Bose still sells it today, even the original 901 series.

Headphones. Maresca recalls that "Bose invested tens of million of dollars over 19 years developing headset technology before making a profit. Now, headsets are a major part of the business." Initially, Bose focused on noise reduction technologies to make headphones for pilots that would block out the high levels of noise interference generated by aircraft. Bose headphones didn't just muffle noise, they electronically canceled ambient noise so that pilots wearing them heard nothing but the intended sound coming through the phones. Bose quickly discovered that airline passengers could benefit as much as pilots from its headphone technology. Today, the Bose QuietComfort series, used in a variety of consumer applications, sets the benchmark in noise-canceling headphones. One journalist considers this product to be so significant that it made his list of "101 gadgets that changed the world"—right up there with aspirin, paper, and the lightbulb.

Automotive suspensions. Since 1980, the inquisitively innovative culture at Bose has even led the company down the path of developing automotive suspensions. Amar Bose's interest in suspensions dates back to the 1950s when he bought both a Citroen and a Pontiac, each riding on unconventional air suspension systems. Thereafter, he was obsessed with the engineering challenge of achieving good cornering capabilities without sacrificing a smooth ride.

The system Bose developed was based on electromagnetic motors installed at each wheel. Based on inputs from road sensing monitors, the motor could retract and extend almost instantaneously. For a bump in the road, the suspension reacted by "jumping" over it. For a pothole, the suspension allowed the wheel to extend downward, retracting it quickly enough that the pothole wouldn't be felt by passengers. In addition to these comfort-producing capabilities, the wheel motors were designed to keep a car completely level during an aggressive maneuver such as cornering or stopping. The system achieved Amar Bose's vision to provide better handling than any sports car while simultaneously giving vehicle occupants the most comfortable ride imaginable.

Bose invested more than $100 million over 30 years in the groundbreaking suspension. In the end, the system was simply too heavy and too expensive for use in passenger cars. Rather than shelf the product, however, Bose did what it has often done—it found a market where the technology could be used to provide genuine customer value. The company now markets a smaller, lighter version of the Bose suspension as the Bose Ride seat system for heavy-duty trucks. Surpassing current air ride and other conventional technologies in performance, its $6,000 price tag also exceeded the going price of a truck seat by five to ten times. Although most companies and drivers were skeptical at first, one Texas driver's reaction drives home the value of this product, even at the substantial price premium: "I had back pains. I used to feel every bump in my back and neck. The truck still bounces down the road, but I don't. It's almost like floating, detached from the truck."

Bose's commitment to research and development has produced state-of-the-art products that have contributed to the trust that Bose customers have in the company. Customers know that the company cares more about their interests—about making the best products—than about maximizing profits. But for a company not driven by the bottom line, Bose does just fine in that department as well. In the personal headphone market, Bose is second only to Beats (Apple) with 11 percent of the market. And with wireless speakers now dominating speaker sales, Bose leads with a decisive 22 percent share, a full six points ahead of number-two Sonos.

Amar Bose passed away a few years ago at the age of 83. With the passion of a genuine scientist, he worked every day well into his 80s. "He's got more energy than an 18-year-old," Maresca once said. "Every one of the naysayers only strengthens his resolve." This work ethic illustrates the passion of the man who shaped one of today's most innovative and most trusted companies. His philosophies have produced Bose's long list of groundbreaking innovations. Even today, the company continues to achieve success by following another one of Amar Bose's basic philosophies: "The potential size of the market? We really have no idea. We just know that we have a technology that's so different and so much better that many people will want it."

Questions for Discussion

9-18 Based on concepts discussed in this chapter, describe the factors that have contributed to Bose's new product success.

9-19 Is Bose's product development process customer centered? Explain.

9-20 How is Bose unique with respect to product life-cycle management?

9-21 With respect to the product life cycle, what challenges does Bose face in managing its product portfolio?

9-22 Can Bose continue to maintain its innovative culture without Amar Bose?

Sources: David Carnoy, "Bose's New Beat," *CNet*, February 3, 2016, www.cnet.com/news/bose-new-beat-ceo-maresca-profile/; Jeff Berman, "Trying to Beat Beats in the Headphone Category Remains a Challenge," *Home Theater Review*, March 21, 2016, www.hometheaterreview.com/trying-to-beat-beats-in-the-headphone-category-remains-a-challenge/; Brian Dumaine, "Amar Bose," *Fortune Small Business*, September 1, 2004, http://money.cnn.com/magazines/fsb/fsb_archive/2004/09/01/8184686/; Olga Kharif, "Selling Sound: Bose Knows," *Bloomberg*, May 14, 2006, www.bloomberg.com/news/articles/2006-05-14/selling-sound-bose-knows; "The Most Trusted Brands Are Like People—Open, Real, and Even Flawed," January 16, 2014, www.lippincott.com/en/news/the-most-trusted-brands-are-like-people-open-real-and-even-flawed/; and www.bose.com/en_us/about_bose.html, accessed July 2016.

MyMarketingLab

Go to **mymktlab.com** for Auto-graded writing questions as well as the following Assisted-graded writing questions:

9-23 Define crowdsourcing and explain why companies use it in new product development. Describe an example of a company using crowdsourcing this way.

9-24 Discuss how a company can maintain success for products in the mature stage of the product life cycle and give examples not already described in the chapter.

10 Pricing
Understanding and Capturing Customer Value

CHAPTER PREVIEW

In this chapter, we look at the second major marketing mix tool—pricing. If effective product development, promotion, and distribution sow the seeds of business success, effective pricing is the harvest. Firms successful at creating customer value with the other marketing mix activities must still capture some of this value in the prices they earn. In this chapter, we discuss the importance of pricing, dig into three major pricing strategies, and look at internal and external considerations that affect pricing decisions. In the next chapter, we examine some additional pricing considerations and approaches.

For openers, let's examine the importance of pricing in online retailing. In case you haven't noticed, there's a war going on—between Walmart, by far the world's largest retailer, and Amazon, the planet's largest online merchant. Each combatant brings an arsenal of potent weapons to the battle. For now, the focus is on price. But in the long run, it'll take much more than low prices to win this war. The spoils will go to the company that delivers the best overall online customer experience and value for the price.

AMAZON VERSUS WALMART: A Price War for Online Supremacy

"Walmart to Amazon: Let's Rumble" read the headline. Ali had Frazier. Coke has Pepsi. The Yankees have the Red Sox. And now, the two retail heavyweights are waging a war all their own. The objective? Online supremacy. The weapon of choice? Prices, at least for now—not surprising, given the two combatants' long-held low-cost positions.

Each side is formidable in its own right. Walmart dominates offline retailing. Its price-driven "Save money. Live better." positioning has made it far and away the world's largest retailer, and the world's largest company to boot. In turn, Amazon is the "Walmart of the Web"—our online general store. Although Walmart's yearly sales total an incredible $482 billion, more than 4.5 times Amazon's $107 billion annually, Amazon's online sales are nearly 8 times greater than Walmart's online sales. By one estimate, Amazon captured nearly 40 percent of all online sales during the most recent year-end holiday season, more than the combined online sales of the next 21 retail competitors.

Why does Walmart worry about Amazon? After all, online sales currently account for only about 7 percent of total U.S. retail sales. Walmart captures most of its business through its 11,000 brick-and-mortar stores—online buying accounts for only a trifling 2.8 percent of its total sales. But this battle isn't about now, it's about the future. Online sales are growing at three times the rate of physical-world sales. Within the next decade, online and mobile buying will capture as much as a third of all retail buying. Because Amazon owns online, its revenues have soared 20 percent or more annually over the past four years. Meanwhile, Walmart's total sales growth has pretty much flatlined during that period. Amazon's revenues reached the $100 billion mark faster than any other company in history.

Amazon has shown a relentless ambition to offer more of almost everything online. It started by selling only books but now sells everything from books, movies, and music to consumer electronics, home and garden products, clothing, jewelry, toys, tools, and even groceries. Thus, Amazon's online prowess now looms as a significant threat to Walmart. If Amazon's expansion continues and online sales spurt as predicted, the digital merchant will eat further and further into Walmart's bread-and-butter store sales.

> Walmart, the world's largest retailer, and Amazon, the world's largest online merchant, are fighting a war for online supremacy. The weapon of choice? Prices, at least for now. But in the long run, winning the war will take much more than low prices.

But Walmart isn't about to let that happen without a fight. Instead, it's taking the battle to Amazon's home territory—the internet and mobile buying. It started with the tactics it knows best—low costs and prices. Through aggressive pricing, Walmart is now fighting for every dollar consumers spend online. If you compare prices at Walmart.com and Amazon.com, you'll find a price war raging across a broad range of products.

In a price war, Walmart would seem to have the edge. Low costs and prices are in the company's DNA. Through the years, Walmart has used its efficient operations and immense buying power to slash prices and thrash one competitor after another. But Amazon is not like most other competitors. Its network is optimized for online shopping, and the internet seller isn't saddled with the costs of running physical stores. As a result, Amazon has been able to match or even beat Walmart at its own pricing game online.

The two giants now seem pretty much stalemated on low prices, giving neither much of an advantage there. In fact, in the long run, reckless price cutting will likely do more damage than good to both Walmart and Amazon. So, although low prices will be crucial, they won't be enough to win over online buyers. Today's online shoppers want it all, low prices *and* selection, speed, convenience, and a satisfying overall shopping experience.

For now, Amazon seems to have the upper hand on most of the important nonprice buying factors. Its made-for-online distribution network speeds orders to buyers' homes quickly and efficiently—including same-day and Sunday delivery in some markets. Amazon's online assortment outstrips even Walmart's, and the online and mobile shopping wizard is now moving into groceries, an area that currently accounts for 56 percent of Walmart's sales. As for Amazon's lack of physical stores—no problem. Amazon's heavily used mobile app lets customers shop Amazon.com even as they are browsing Walmart's stores. Finally, Amazon's unmatched, big data–driven customer interface creates personalized, highly satisfying online buying experiences. Amazon regularly rates among the leaders in customer satisfaction across all industries. According to one analyst, "consumers have said the Amazon shopping experience *is just plain better* than Walmart's. In fact, Amazon arguably offers the best shopping experience, period."

By contrast, Walmart came late to online selling. Although it's now pouring billions of dollars into e-commerce technology, it's still trying to figure out how to efficiently deliver goods into the hands of online shoppers. As its online sales have grown, the store-based giant has patched together a makeshift online distribution network out of unused corners of its store distribution centers. And the still-mostly-store retailer has yet to come close to matching Amazon's online customer buying experience. So even with its impressive low-price legacy, Walmart finds itself playing catch-up online.

To catch up, Walmart is investing heavily to create a next-generation fulfillment network. Importantly, it's taking advantage of a major asset that Amazon can't match—an opportunity

Walmart versus Amazon online: Achieving online supremacy will take more than just waging and winning an online price war. The spoils will go to the company that delivers the best overall online customer experience and value for the price.

(top) © NetPics/Alamy; (bottom) Bloomberg via Getty Images

to integrate online buying with its massive network of brick-and-mortar stores. For example, Walmart now fulfills more than a fifth of Walmart.com orders more quickly and cheaply by having workers in stores pluck and pack items and mail or deliver them to customers' homes. Two-thirds of the U.S. population lives within five miles of a Walmart store, offering the potential for 30-minute delivery.

And by combining its online and offline operations, Walmart can provide some unique services, such as free and convenient pickup and returns of online orders in stores (Walmart.com gives you three buying options: "online," "in-store," and "site-to-store"). Using Walmart's website and mobile app can also smooth in-store shopping. They let customers prepare shopping lists in advance, locate products by aisle to reduce wasted shopping time, and use their smartphones at checkout with preloaded digital coupons applied automatically. Customers who pick up online orders in the store can pay with cash, opening up online shopping to the 20 percent of Walmart customers who don't have bank accounts or credit cards. For customers who do pay online, Walmart is testing in-store lockers where customers can simply go to an assigned locker for pickup.

Who will win the battle for the hearts and dollars of online buyers? Certainly, low prices will continue to be important. But

OBJECTIVES OUTLINE

OBJECTIVE 10-1	Answer the question "What is a price?" and discuss the importance of pricing in today's fast-changing environment. **What Is a Price?** *(pp 284–285)*
OBJECTIVE 10-2	Identify the three major pricing strategies and discuss the importance of understanding customer-value perceptions, company costs, and competitor strategies when setting prices. **Major Pricing Strategies** *(pp 285–293)*
OBJECTIVE 10-3	Identify and define the other important external and internal factors affecting a firm's pricing decisions. **Other Internal and External Considerations Affecting Price Decisions** *(pp 293–299)*

achieving online supremacy will involve much more than just waging and winning an online price war. It will require delivering low prices *plus* selection, convenience, and a world-class online buying experience—something that Amazon perfected long ago. For Walmart, catching and conquering Amazon online will require time, resources, and skills far beyond its trademark everyday low prices. As Walmart's president of global e-commerce puts it, the important task of winning online "will take the rest of our careers and as much as we've got [to invest]. This isn't a project. It's about the future of the company."[1]

● Pricing: No matter what the state of the economy, companies should sell value, not price.

magicoven/Shutterstock.com

Price
The amount of money charged for a product or service, or the sum of the values that customers exchange for the benefits of having or using the product or service.

COMPANIES TODAY FACE A fierce and fast-changing pricing environment. Value-seeking customers have put increased pricing pressure on many companies. Thanks to tight economic times in recent years, the pricing power of the internet, and value-driven retailers such as Walmart and Amazon, today's consumers are pursuing more frugal spending strategies. In response, it seems that almost every company has been looking for ways to cut prices.

● Yet cutting prices is often not the best answer. Reducing prices unnecessarily can lead to lost profits and damaging price wars. It can cheapen a brand by signaling to customers that price is more important than the customer value a brand delivers. Instead, in both good economic times and bad, companies should sell value, not price. In some cases, that means selling lesser products at rock-bottom prices. But in most cases, it means persuading customers that paying a higher price for the company's brand is justified by the greater value they gain.

What Is a Price?

In the narrowest sense, **price** is the amount of money charged for a product or a service. More broadly, price is the sum of all the values that customers give up to gain the benefits of having or using a product or service. Historically, price has been the major factor affecting buyer choice. In recent decades, however, nonprice factors have gained increasing importance. Even so, price remains one of the most important elements that determine a firm's market share and profitability.

Price is the only element in the marketing mix that produces revenue; all other elements represent costs. Price is also one of the most flexible marketing mix elements. Unlike product features and channel commitments, prices can be changed quickly. At the same time, pricing is the number-one problem facing many marketing executives, and many companies do not handle pricing well. Some managers view pricing as a big headache, preferring instead to focus on other marketing mix elements.

However, smart managers treat pricing as a key strategic tool for creating and capturing customer value. Prices have a direct impact on a firm's bottom line. A small percentage improvement in price can generate a large percentage increase in profitability. More important, as part of a company's overall value proposition, price plays a key role in creating customer value and building customer relationships. So, instead of shying away from pricing, smart marketers are embracing it as an important competitive asset.[2]

Major Pricing Strategies

> **Author Comment** | Setting the right price is one of the marketer's most difficult tasks. A host of factors come into play. But as the opening story about Walmart and Amazon illustrates, finding and implementing the right pricing strategy is critical to success.

The price the company charges will fall somewhere between one that is too low to produce a profit and one that is too high to produce any demand. ● **Figure 10.1** summarizes the major considerations in setting prices. Customer perceptions of the product's value set the ceiling for its price. If customers perceive that the product's price is greater than its value, they will not buy the product. Likewise, product costs set the floor for a product's price. If the company prices the product below its costs, the company's profits will suffer. In setting its price between these two extremes, the company must consider several external and internal factors, including competitors' strategies and prices, the overall marketing strategy and mix, and the nature of the market and demand.

Figure 10.1 suggests three major pricing strategies: customer value–based pricing, cost-based pricing, and competition-based pricing.

Customer Value–Based Pricing

> **Author Comment** | Like everything else in marketing, good pricing starts with *customers* and their perceptions of value.

In the end, the customer will decide whether a product's price is right. Pricing decisions, like other marketing mix decisions, must start with customer value. When customers buy a product, they exchange something of value (the price) to get something of value (the benefits of having or using the product). Effective customer-oriented pricing involves understanding how much value consumers place on the benefits they receive from the product and setting a price that captures that value.

Customer value–based pricing
Setting price based on buyers' perceptions of value rather than on the seller's cost.

Customer value–based pricing uses buyers' perceptions of value as the key to pricing. Value-based pricing means that the marketer cannot design a product and marketing program and then set the price. Price is considered along with all other marketing mix variables *before* the marketing program is set.

● **Figure 10.2** compares value-based pricing with cost-based pricing. Although costs are an important consideration in setting prices, cost-based pricing is often product driven. The company designs what it considers to be a good product, adds up the costs of making the product, and sets a price that covers costs plus a target profit. Marketing must then convince buyers that the product's value at that price justifies its purchase. If the price turns out to be too high, the company must settle for lower markups or lower sales, both resulting in disappointing profits.

Value-based pricing reverses this process. The company first assesses customer needs and value perceptions. It then sets its target price based on customer perceptions of value. The targeted value and price drive decisions about what costs can be incurred and the resulting product design. As a result, pricing begins with analyzing consumer needs and value perceptions, and the price is set to match perceived value.

● **FIGURE | 10.1**
Considerations in Setting Price

If customers perceive that a product's price is greater than its value, they won't buy it. If the company prices the product below its costs, profits will suffer. Between the two extremes, the "right" pricing strategy is one that delivers both value to the customer and profits to the company.

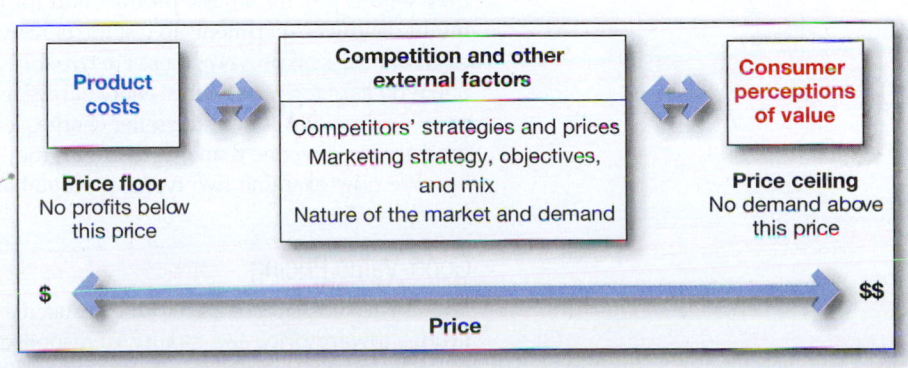

● FIGURE | 10.2
Value-Based Pricing versus Cost-Based Pricing

Cost-based pricing

Design a good product → Determine product costs → Set price based on cost → Convince buyers of product's value

Costs play an important role in setting prices. But like everything else in marketing, good pricing starts with the customer.

Value-based pricing

Assess customer needs and value perceptions → Set target price to match customer-perceived value → Determine costs that can be incurred → Design product to deliver desired value at target price

It's important to remember that "good value" is not the same as "low price." ● For example, some owners consider a luxurious Patek Philippe watch a real bargain, even at eye-popping prices ranging from $20,000 to $500,000:[3]

● **Perceived value: Some owners consider a luxurious Patek Philippe watch a real bargain, even at eye-popping prices ranging from $20,000 to $500,000.**

FABRICE COFFRINI/AFP/Getty Images

Listen up here, because I'm about to tell you why a certain watch costing $20,000, or even $500,000, isn't actually expensive but is in fact a tremendous value. Every Patek Philippe watch is handmade by Swiss watchmakers from the finest materials and can take more than a year to make. Still not convinced? Beyond keeping precise time, Patek Philippe watches are also good investments. They carry high prices but retain or even increase their value over time. Many models achieve a kind of cult status that makes them the most coveted timepieces on the planet. But more important than just a means of telling time or a good investment is the sentimental and emotional value of possessing a Patek Philippe. Says the company's president: "This is about passion. I mean—it really is a dream. Nobody needs a Patek." These watches are unique possessions steeped in precious memories, making them treasured family assets. According to the company, "The purchase of a Patek Philippe is often related to a personal event—a professional success, a marriage, or the birth of a child—and offering it as a gift is the most eloquent expression of love or affection." A Patek Philippe watch is made not to last just one lifetime but many. Says one ad: "You never actually own a Patek Philippe, you merely look after it for the next generation." That makes it a real bargain, even at twice the price.

A company will often find it hard to measure the value customers attach to its product. For example, calculating the cost of ingredients in a meal at a fancy restaurant is relatively easy. But assigning value to other measures of satisfaction such as taste, environment, relaxation, conversation, and status is very hard. Such value is subjective; it varies both for different consumers and different situations.

Still, consumers will use these perceived values to evaluate a product's price, so the company must work to measure them. Sometimes, companies ask consumers how much they would pay for a basic product and for each benefit added to the offer. Or a company might conduct experiments to test the perceived value of different product offers. According to an old Russian proverb, there are two fools in every market—one who asks too much and one who asks too little. If the seller charges more than the buyers' perceived value, the company's sales will suffer. If the seller charges less, its products will sell very well, but they will produce less revenue than they would if they were priced at the level of perceived value.

We now examine two types of value-based pricing: *good-value pricing* and *value-added pricing*.

Good-Value Pricing

The Great Recession of 2008 to 2009 caused a fundamental and lasting shift in consumer attitudes toward price and quality. In response, many companies have changed their pricing

The art of seduction. At a price reduction.

The Concept Style Coupe set the auto show circuit abuzz with its dramatic design and athletic presence. Showgoers had only one request. Build it. The CLA brings an international sensation to life with nothing lost in translation, from its diamond-block grille to its frameless door glass to its sweeping taillamps, all at a down-to-earth price.

● **Good-value pricing: Even premium brands can launch good-value versions. The Mercedes CLA Class gives customers "The Art of Seduction. At a price reduction."**

© Courtesy of Daimler AG

Good-value pricing

Offering just the right combination of quality and good service at a fair price.

Value-added pricing

Attaching value-added features and services to differentiate a company's offers and charging higher prices.

approaches to bring them in line with changing economic conditions and consumer price perceptions. More and more, marketers have adopted the strategy of **good-value pricing**—offering the right combination of quality and good service at a fair price.

In many cases, this has involved introducing less-expensive versions of established brand name products or new lower-price lines. For example, Walmart launched an extreme-value store brand called Price First. Priced even lower than the retailer's already-low-priced Great Value brand, Price First offers thrift-conscious customers rock-bottom prices on grocery staples. Good-value prices are a relative thing—even premium brands can launch value versions. ● Mercedes-Benz recently released its CLA Class, entry-level models starting at $31,500. From its wing-like dash and diamond-block grille to its 208-hp turbo inline-4 engine, the CLA Class gives customers "The Art of Seduction. At a price reduction."[4]

In other cases, good-value pricing involves redesigning existing brands to offer more quality for a given price or the same quality for less. Some companies even succeed by offering less value but at very low prices. For example, Spirit Airlines gives customers "Bare Fare" pricing, by which they get less but don't pay for what they don't get (see Real Marketing 10.1).

An important type of good-value pricing at the retail level is called *everyday low pricing* (*EDLP*). EDLP involves charging a constant, everyday low price with few or no temporary price discounts. The ALDI supermarket chain practices EDLP, with a good-value pricing value proposition that gives customers "more 'mmm' for the dollar" every minute of every day. Perhaps the king of EDLP is Walmart, which practically defined the concept. Except for a few sale items every month, Walmart promises everyday low prices on everything it sells. In contrast, *high-low pricing* involves charging higher prices on an everyday basis but running frequent promotions to lower prices temporarily on selected items. Department stores such as Kohl's and JCPenney practice high-low pricing by having frequent sale days, early-bird savings, and bonus earnings for store credit-card holders.

Value-Added Pricing

Value-based pricing doesn't mean simply charging what customers want to pay or setting low prices to meet competition. Instead, many companies adopt **value-added pricing** strategies. Rather than cutting prices to match competitors, they add quality, services, and value-added features to differentiate their offers and thus support their higher prices.

● For example, premium audio brand Bose doesn't try to beat out its competition by offering discounts or by selling lower-end, more affordable versions of its speakers, headphones, and home theater system products. Instead, for more than 50 years, Bose has poured resources into research and innovation to create high-quality products that merit the premium prices it charges. Bose's goal is to create "better sound through research—an innovative, high-quality listening experience," says the company. "We're passionate engineers, developers, researchers, retailers, marketers … and dreamers. One goal unites us—to create products and experiences our customers simply can't get anywhere else." As a result, Bose has hatched a long list of groundbreaking innovations

● **Value-added pricing: Premium audio brand Bose creates "better sound through research—an innovative, high-quality listening experience," adding value that merits its premium prices.**

Image used with permission of Bose Corporation.

Real Marketing

10.1   Good Value at Spirit Airlines: Getting Less but Paying Much Less for It

"@SpiritAirlines worst, most devious, nickel-and-diming I've ever experienced. I will NEVER fly with you again. #lessonlearned."

This tweet, and a flood of similar social media comments posted regularly by dissatisfied Spirit Airlines customers, isn't the kind of feedback most companies want to hear. What's more, adding to such negative social media testimonials, Spirit Airlines also recently earned the dubious distinction of being *Consumer Reports'* lowest-rated airline for the customer experience, receiving one of the lowest-ever overall scores given by the organization.

So Spirit Airlines must be headed down the path to bankruptcy and ruin, right? To the contrary—Spirit is one of the nation's fastest-growing carriers. It fills almost every available seat on every flight. And it turns a healthy profit every quarter—a difficult feat in the up-and-down airline industry. How does Spirit Airlines do it? By mastering the art and science of extreme good-value pricing. Spirit's value proposition: "Less money. More go."

Spirit Airlines is an unrivaled "ultra low-cost carrier," resulting in prices much lower than those of competitors—up to 90 percent lower in some cases. But to cash in on such rock-bottom fares, customers must accept less in return. Buying a ticket on a Spirit flight gets you one thing and one thing only—a seat on a plane to your destination. If you want more, you pay for it. Under what it calls "Bare Fare" pricing, Spirit charges extra for everything. *Everything.* You get only what you pay for—and not one peanut more.

For example, whereas most airlines provide free beverages, Spirit charges $3 for a bottle of water or can of soda. Want a pillow or a blanket? Glad to oblige—that'll be $7, please. Getting a seat assignment costs $15, and it will cost you $10 extra to have a check-in agent print out your boarding pass. A full-size carry-on bag runs another $55. Adding insult to injury, seats on Spirit flights are crammed much closer together (what Spirit calls "a little cozier seating"), and the seats don't recline. If you do want a little more breathing room—you guessed it—for a fee you can get an exit row or first-class sized front-row seat.

Spirit refers to its pricing practices as "Frill Control," claiming that it gives customers more control over what they pay for and what they don't. It points out that the so-called free sodas and extra legroom on other airlines aren't really free. Customers are forced to pay for them in the all-inclusive ticket price whether they want them or not. On Spirit, passengers have the option. Although this approach sounds refreshing, some customers view it as cheap nickel-and-diming or, worse, as unfair and deceitful. The social media are filled with tales of unwary customers who say they ended up paying more for extras than they saved on the initial ticket.

Spirit Airlines takes a hardline approach in responding to customer complaints. When customers request pricing exceptions, Spirit agents stand their ground. The extra charges are optional, not mandatory, the airline explains. The base ticket price includes everything passengers need to get to their destinations. "We've rejected, for example, charging for bathrooms," says Spirit's CEO. "We're never going to do that. That's not an optional thing."

Rather than hiding from its poor customer service record, Spirit Airlines seems almost to wear it as a badge of honor. When one recent study showed that Spirit ranked dead last in complaints made to the U.S. Department of Transportation, Spirit turned it into bragging rights. Over the five years of the study, the airline averaged only eight complaints per 100,000 customers. Spirit celebrated by offering $24 discounts. "That's right, over 99.99 percent of our customers did not file a complaint with the Department of Transportation," Spirit declared in a press release. "To the 0.01 percent—that's OK, we know we aren't the airline for everyone (though we'd love for you to save by flying with us again!)."

The company further defends its pricing by noting that, for customers who take the time to look, it provides plenty of up-front information about what its fares cover. In fact, Spirit's online site offers "Spirit 101: Your Simple Guide to the Way We Fly," a detailed guide on what you get for what you pay and how to make the Spirit Bare Fare system work to your advantage. Despite the angst of the vocal few who think they are being fleeced, most Spirit customers seem to know exactly what they are getting and are happy with that. When asked if she resented paying $3 for water on a Spirit flight, one passenger replied, "Not at all. They're trying to cover their costs." That attitude is shared by most Spirit customers, who seem more than happy to give up the extras to get the super-cheap fares.

To see what all the fuss was about, one airline analyst put Spirit Airlines to the test, eyes wide open. After paying only $63 for a one-way flight from Detroit to LaGuardia—roughly $300 less than the same fare offered by Delta, American, or United—he reported on his experience. "After we landed I turned to my friend and said, 'I don't get it—what...are people complaining about?'" He concluded

Good-value pricing: Fast-growing Spirit Airlines thrives on giving customers less but charging them less for it. Under its "Bare Fare" pricing, you don't pay for what you don't get.
Associated Press

that most dissatisfaction stems from misconceptions—that if people are aware of Spirit's policies ahead of time, they can avoid unpleasant surprises and add-ons they don't want. If you want entertainment, he suggests, bring along your own on a mobile device. Plan ahead and buy snacks and beverages before boarding. Think ahead and add in the fees for carry-ons or checked bags to calculate the true fare. Or pack light and jam everything into a small carry-on bag or backpack you can take on for free. And prepare yourself mentally that you might "be able to determine the shampoo used by the person in the row ahead of you." For flights no longer than three hours, being a little squished isn't all that bad.

For those customers who complain that the extras add up to more than the savings, official numbers suggest otherwise. Spirit's total flight price (all fees included) is still the lowest in the industry—an average of 40 percent below competitors' prices. Even at those super-low prices, thanks to its industry-lowest cost per seat-mile, Spirit Airlines still reaps industry-leading profit margins. For example, Spirit's

total revenue per passenger is less than half of what United Airlines needs per passenger just to break even. Over the past four years, despite renewed challenges from its large competitors, Spirit's annual revenues shot up more than 80 percent to nearly $2 billion; net income soared almost 200 percent.

Thus, Spirit Airlines is thriving with its less-for-much-less positioning approach. True, you don't get much when you fly Spirit. Then again, you don't pay for what you don't get. And you end up with more money in your

pocket to spend at your destination. If paying for the extras bothers you, don't buy them. Or just fly another airline and pay the full up-front fare. But Spirit won't be giving away those extras for free anytime soon. "[We won't] add costs for things that most customers don't value as much as our low fares just to reduce the complaints of a few customers," says the CEO. "Doing that would raise prices for everyone, compromising our commitment to what our customers have continuously told us they truly value—the lowest possible price."

Sources: Based on information from Shawn Tully, "Behind the Sudden Departure of Spirit Airline's Wildly Unconventional CEO," *Fortune,* January 8, 2016, http://fortune.com/2016/01/08/spirit-airlines-ceo-ouster/; "If Spirit Airlines Is So Unpopular, Why Are Its Flights So Full?" *CBS News,* March 23, 2014, www.cbsnews.com/news/if-spirit-airlines-is-so-unpopular-why-are-its-flights-so-full/; Justin Bachman, "Spirit Airlines Sees All Those Passenger Complaints as Mere Misunderstandings," *Bloomberg Businessweek,* April 18, 2014, www.businessweek.com/articles/2014-04-18/spirit-airlines-passenger-complaints-part-of-its-business-model; Jared Blank, "3 Myths about Spirit Airlines," *Online Travel Review,* September 10, 2012, www.onlinetravelreview.com/2012/09/10/3-myths-about-spirit-airlines-or-rmy-flight-on-spirit-was-perfectly-fine-really/; Adam Levine-Weinberg, "Why Houston Is Spirit Airlines' Next Big Growth Market," *The Motley Fool,* November 20, 2014, www.fool.com/investing/general/2014/11/20/why-houston-is-spirit-airlines-next-big-growth-mar.aspx; "Value Airline of the Year—Spirit Airlines," *ATW,* January 23, 2015, http://atwonline.com/airlines/value-airline-year-spirit-airlines; and http://marketing.spirit.com/how-to-fly-spirit-airlines/en/, http://ir.spirit.com/financials.cfm, and www.spirit.com, accessed September 2016.

and high-quality products that bring added value to its customers. Despite its premium prices, or perhaps because of them, Bose remains a consistent leader in the markets it serves.[5]

Cost-Based Pricing

Author Comment | Costs set the floor for price, but the goal isn't always to *minimize* costs. In fact, many firms invest in higher costs so that they can claim higher prices and margins (think back about Patek Philippe watches). The key is to manage the *spread* between costs and prices—how much the company makes for the customer value it delivers.

Whereas customer value perceptions set the price ceiling, costs set the floor for the price that the company can charge. **Cost-based pricing** involves setting prices based on the costs of producing, distributing, and selling the product plus a fair rate of return for the company's effort and risk. A company's costs may be an important element in its pricing strategy.

Some companies, such as Walmart or Spirit Airlines, work to become the *low-cost producers* in their industries. Companies with lower costs can set lower prices that result in smaller margins but greater sales and profits. However, other companies—such as Apple, BMW, and Steinway—intentionally pay higher costs so that they can add value and claim higher prices and margins. For example, it costs more to make a "handcrafted" Steinway piano than a Yamaha production model. But the higher costs result in higher quality, justifying an average $87,000 price. To those who buy a Steinway, price is nothing; the Steinway experience is everything. The key is to manage the spread between costs and prices—how much the company makes for the customer value it delivers.

Types of Costs

A company's costs take two forms: fixed and variable. **Fixed costs** (also known as **overhead**) are costs that do not vary with production or sales level. For example, a company must pay each month's bills for rent, heat, interest, and executive salaries regardless of the company's level of output. **Variable costs** vary directly with the level of production. Each smartphone or tablet produced by Samsung involves a cost of computer chips, wires, plastic, packaging, and other inputs. Although these costs tend to be the same for each unit produced, they are called variable costs because the total varies with the number of units produced. **Total costs** are the sum of the fixed and variable costs for any given level of production. Management wants to charge a price that will at least cover the total production costs at a given level of production.

The company must watch its costs carefully. If it costs the company more than its competitors to produce and sell a similar product, the company will need to charge a higher price or make less profit, putting it at a competitive disadvantage.

Cost-based pricing
Setting prices based on the costs of producing, distributing, and selling the product plus a fair rate of return for effort and risk.

Fixed costs (overhead)
Costs that do not vary with production or sales level.

Variable costs
Costs that vary directly with the level of production.

Total costs
The sum of the fixed and variable costs for any given level of production.

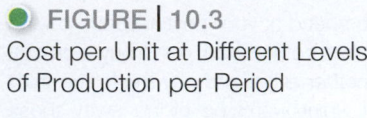

● FIGURE | 10.3

Cost per Unit at Different Levels of Production per Period

What's the point of all the cost curves in this and the next few figures? Costs are an important factor in setting price, and companies must understand them well!

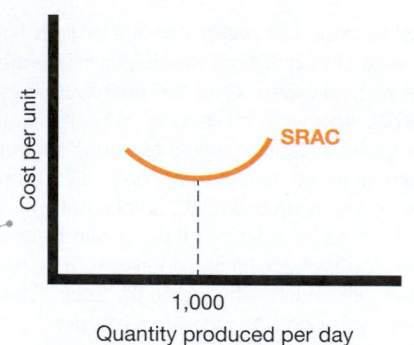

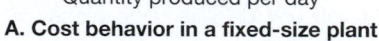

A. Cost behavior in a fixed-size plant

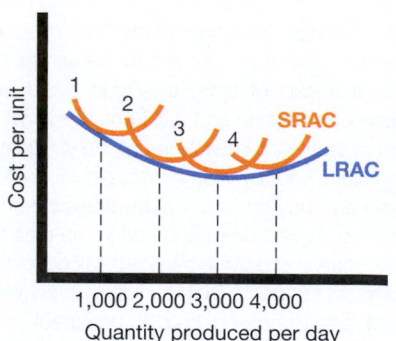

B. Cost behavior over different-size plants

Costs at Different Levels of Production

To price wisely, management needs to know how its costs vary with different levels of production. For example, suppose Lenovo built a plant to produce 1,000 tablet computers per day. ● **Figure 10.3A** shows the typical short-run average cost curve (SRAC). It shows that the cost per tablet is high if Lenovo's factory produces only a few per day. But as production moves up to 1,000 tablets per day, the average cost per unit decreases. This is because fixed costs are spread over more units, with each one bearing a smaller share of the fixed cost. Lenovo can try to produce more than 1,000 tablets per day, but average costs will increase because the plant becomes inefficient. Workers have to wait for machines, the machines break down more often, and workers get in each other's way.

If Lenovo believed it could sell 2,000 tablets a day, it should consider building a larger plant. The plant would use more efficient machinery and work arrangements. Also, the unit cost of producing 2,000 tablets per day would be lower than the unit cost of producing 1,000 units per day, as shown in the long-run average cost (LRAC) curve (● **Figure 10.3B**). In fact, a 3,000-capacity plant would be even more efficient, according to Figure 10.3B. But a 4,000-daily production plant would be less efficient because of increasing diseconomies of scale—too many workers to manage, paperwork slowing things down, and so on. Figure 10.3B shows that a 3,000-daily production plant is the best size to build if demand is strong enough to support this level of production.

Costs as a Function of Production Experience

● FIGURE | 10.4

Cost per Unit as a Function of Accumulated Production: The Experience Curve

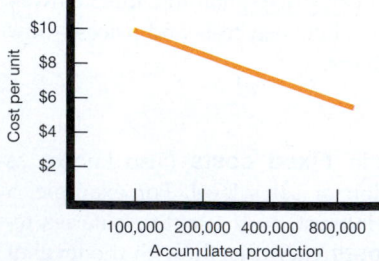

Experience curve (learning curve)
The drop in the average per-unit production cost that comes with accumulated production experience.

Suppose Lenovo runs a plant that produces 3,000 tablets per day. As Lenovo gains experience in producing tablets, it learns how to do it better. Workers learn shortcuts and become more familiar with their equipment. With practice, the work becomes better organized, and Lenovo finds better equipment and production processes. With higher volume, Lenovo becomes more efficient and gains economies of scale. As a result, the average cost tends to decrease with accumulated production experience. This is shown in ● **Figure 10.4**.[6] Thus, the average cost of producing the first 100,000 tablets is $10 per tablet. When the company has produced the first 200,000 tablets, the average cost has fallen to $8.50. After its accumulated production experience doubles again to 400,000, the average cost is $7. This drop in the average cost with accumulated production experience is called the **experience curve** (or the **learning curve**).

If a downward-sloping experience curve exists, this is highly significant for the company. Not only will the company's unit production cost fall, but it will fall faster if the company makes and sells more during a given time period. But the market has to stand ready to buy the higher output. And to take advantage of the experience curve, Lenovo must get a large market share early in the product's life cycle. This suggests the following pricing strategy: Lenovo should price its tablets lower; its sales will then increase, its costs will decrease through gaining more experience, and then it can lower its prices further.

Some companies have built successful strategies around the experience curve. However, a single-minded focus on reducing costs and exploiting the experience curve will not always work. Experience-curve pricing carries some major risks. The aggressive pricing might give the product a cheap image. The strategy also assumes that competitors are weak and not willing to fight it out by meeting the company's price cuts. Finally, while the company is building volume under one technology, a competitor may find a lower-cost technology that lets it start at prices lower than those of the market leader, which still operates on the old experience curve.

Cost-Plus Pricing

Cost-plus pricing (markup pricing)
Adding a standard markup to the cost of the product.

The simplest pricing method is **cost-plus pricing** (or **markup pricing**)—adding a standard markup to the cost of the product. Construction companies, for example, submit job bids by estimating the total project cost and adding a standard markup for profit. Lawyers, accountants, and other professionals typically price by adding a standard markup to their costs. Some sellers tell their customers they will charge cost plus a specified markup; for example, aerospace companies often price this way to the government.

To illustrate markup pricing, suppose a toaster manufacturer had the following costs and expected sales:

Variable cost	$10
Fixed costs	$300,000
Expected unit sales	50,000

Then the manufacturer's cost per toaster is given by the following:

$$\text{unit cost} = \text{variable cost} + \frac{\text{fixed cost}}{\text{unit sales}} = \$10 + \frac{\$300,000}{50,000} = \$16$$

Now suppose the manufacturer wants to earn a 20 percent markup on sales. The manufacturer's markup price is given by the following:[7]

$$\text{markup price} = \frac{\text{unit cost}}{(1 - \text{desired return on sales})} = \frac{\$16}{1 - 0.2} = \$20$$

The manufacturer would charge dealers $20 per toaster and make a profit of $4 per unit. The dealers, in turn, will mark up the toaster. If dealers want to earn 50 percent on the sales price, they will mark up the toaster to $40 ($20 + 50% of $40). This number is equivalent to a *markup on cost* of 100 percent ($20/$20).

Does using standard markups to set prices make sense? Generally, no. Any pricing method that ignores demand and competitor prices is not likely to lead to the best price. Still, markup pricing remains popular for many reasons. First, sellers are more certain about costs than about demand. By tying the price to cost, sellers simplify pricing; they do not need to make frequent adjustments as demand changes. Second, when all firms in the industry use this pricing method, prices tend to be similar, so price competition is minimized. Third, many people feel that cost-plus pricing is fairer to both buyers and sellers. Sellers earn a fair return on their investment but do not take advantage of buyers when buyers' demand becomes great.

Break-Even Analysis and Target Profit Pricing

Break-even pricing (target return pricing)
Setting price to break even on the costs of making and marketing a product or setting price to make a target return.

Another cost-oriented pricing approach is **break-even pricing** (or a variation called **target return pricing**). The firm sets a price at which it will break even or make the target return on the costs of making and marketing a product.

Target return pricing uses the concept of a *break-even chart*, which shows the total cost and total revenue expected at different sales volume levels. ● **Figure 10.5** shows a break-even chart for the toaster manufacturer discussed here. Fixed costs are $300,000 regardless of sales volume. Variable costs are added to fixed costs to form total costs, which rise with volume. The total revenue curve starts at zero and rises with each unit sold. The slope of the total revenue curve reflects the price of $20 per unit.

● **FIGURE** | 10.5
Break-Even Chart for
Determining Target Return
Price and Break-Even
Volume

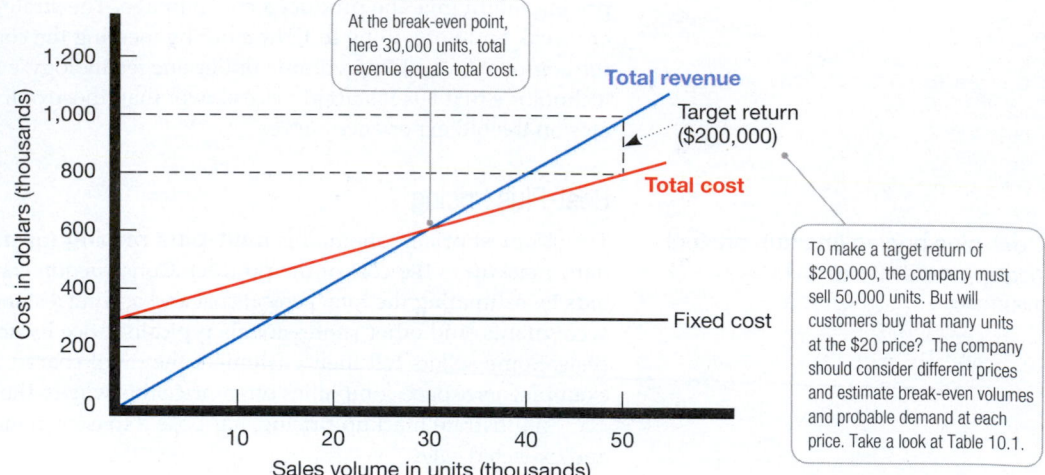

At the break-even point, here 30,000 units, total revenue equals total cost.

Total revenue

Target return ($200,000)

Total cost

Fixed cost

To make a target return of $200,000, the company must sell 50,000 units. But will customers buy that many units at the $20 price? The company should consider different prices and estimate break-even volumes and probable demand at each price. Take a look at Table 10.1.

The total revenue and total cost curves cross at 30,000 units. This is the *break-even volume*. At $20, the company must sell at least 30,000 units to break even, that is, for total revenue to cover total cost. Break-even volume can be calculated using the following formula:

$$\text{break-even volume} = \frac{\text{fixed cost}}{\text{price} - \text{variable cost}} = \frac{\$300,000}{\$20 - \$10} = 30,000$$

If the company wants to make a profit, it must sell more than 30,000 units at $20 each. Suppose the toaster manufacturer has invested $1,000,000 in the business and wants to set a price to earn a 20 percent return, or $200,000. In that case, it must sell at least 50,000 units at $20 each. If the company charges a higher price, it will not need to sell as many toasters to achieve its target return. But the market may not buy even this lower volume at the higher price. Much depends on price elasticity and competitors' prices.

The manufacturer should consider different prices and estimate break-even volumes, probable demand, and profits for each. This is done in ● **Table 10.1**. The table shows that as price increases, the break-even volume drops (column 2). But as price increases, the demand for toasters also decreases (column 3). At the $14 price, because the manufacturer clears only $4 per toaster ($14 less $10 in variable costs), it must sell a very high volume to break even. Even though the low price attracts many buyers, demand still falls below the high break-even point, and the manufacturer loses money. At the other extreme, with a $22 price, the manufacturer clears $12 per toaster and must sell only 25,000 units to break even. But at this high price, consumers buy too few toasters, and profits are negative. The table shows that a price of $18 yields the highest profits. Note that none of the prices produce the manufacturer's target return of $200,000. To achieve this return, the manufacturer will have to search for ways to lower the fixed or variable costs, thus lowering the break-even volume.

● **Table 10.1** | **Break-Even Volume and Profits at Different Prices**

Price	Unit Demand Needed to Break Even	Expected Unit Demand at Given Price	Total Revenue (1) × (3)	Total Costs*	Profit (4) − (5)
$14	75,000	71,000	$994,000	$1,010,000	−$16,000
16	50,000	67,000	1,072,000	970,000	102,000
18	37,500	60,000	1,080,000	900,000	180,000
20	30,000	42,000	840,000	720,000	120,000
22	25,000	23,000	506,000	530,000	−24,000

*Assumes fixed costs of $300,000 and constant unit variable costs of $10.

Competition-based pricing

Setting prices based on competitors'
strategies, prices, costs, and market
offerings.

Competition-Based Pricing

Competition-based pricing involves setting prices based on competitors' strategies, costs, prices, and market offerings. Consumers will base their judgments of a product's value on the prices that competitors charge for similar products.

In assessing competitors' pricing strategies, a company should ask several questions. First, how does the company's market offering compare with competitors' offerings in terms of customer value? If consumers perceive that the company's product or service provides greater value, the company can charge a higher price. If consumers perceive less value relative to competing products, the company must either charge a lower price or change customer perceptions to justify a higher price.

Next, how strong are current competitors, and what are their current pricing strategies? If the company faces a host of smaller competitors charging high prices relative to the value they deliver, it might charge lower prices to drive weaker competitors from the market. If the market is dominated by larger, lower-price competitors, a company may decide to target unserved market niches by offering value-added products and services at higher prices.

Importantly, the goal is not to match or beat competitors' prices. Rather, the goal is to set prices according to the relative value created versus competitors. If a company creates greater value for customers, higher prices are justified. ● For example, Caterpillar makes high-quality, heavy-duty construction and mining equipment. It dominates its industry despite charging higher prices than competitors such as Komatsu. When a commercial customer once asked a Caterpillar dealer why it should pay $500,000 for a big Caterpillar bulldozer when it could get an "equivalent" Komatsu dozer for $420,000, the Caterpillar dealer famously provided an analysis like the following:

$420,000	the Caterpillar's price if equivalent to the competitor's bulldozer
$50,000	the value added by Caterpillar's superior reliability and durability
$40,000	the value added by Caterpillar's lower lifetime operating costs
$40,000	the value added by Caterpillar's superior service
$20,000	the value added by Caterpillar's longer parts warranty
$570,000	the value-added price for Caterpillar's bulldozer
−$70,000	discount
$500,000	final price

● Pricing versus competitors: Caterpillar dominates the heavy equipment industry despite charging premium prices. Customers believe that Caterpillar gives them a lot more value for the price over the lifetime of its machines.

© Kristoffer Tripplaar/Alamy

Thus, although the customer pays an $80,000 price premium for the Caterpillar bulldozer, it's actually getting $150,000 in added value over the product's lifetime. The customer chose the Caterpillar bulldozer.

What principle should guide decisions about prices to charge relative to those of competitors? The answer is simple in concept but often difficult in practice: No matter what price you charge—high, low, or in between—be certain to give customers superior value for that price.

Other Internal and External Considerations Affecting Price Decisions

Beyond customer value perceptions, costs, and competitor strategies, the company must consider several additional internal and external factors. Internal factors affecting pricing include the company's overall marketing strategy, objectives, and marketing mix as well as other organizational considerations. External factors include the nature of the market and demand and other environmental factors.

Overall Marketing Strategy, Objectives, and Mix

Price is only one element of the company's broader marketing strategy. So, before setting price, the company must decide on its overall marketing strategy for the product or service. Sometimes, a company's overall strategy is built around its price and value story. ● For example, grocery retailer Trader Joe's unique price-value positioning has made it one of the nation's fastest-growing, most popular food stores:[8]

Trader Joe's has put its own special twist on the food price-value equation—call it "cheap gourmet." It offers gourmet-caliber, one-of-a-kind products at bargain prices, all served up in a festive,

● Trader Joe's unique price-value strategy has earned it an almost cult-like following of devoted customers who love what they get for the prices they pay.

© Lannis Waters/The Palm Beach Post/ZUMAPRESS.com/Alamy Live News

vacation-like atmosphere that makes shopping fun. Trader Joe's is a gourmet foodie's delight, featuring everything from kettle corn cookies, organic strawberry lemonade, creamy Valencia peanut butter, and fair-trade coffees to kimchi fried rice and triple-ginger ginger snaps. If asked, almost any customer can tick off a ready list of Trader Joe's favorites that he or she just can't live without—a list that quickly grows.

The assortment is uniquely Trader Joe's—90 percent of the store's brands are private labels. The prices aren't all that low in absolute terms, but they're a real bargain compared with what you'd pay for the same quality and coolness elsewhere. "It's not complicated," says Trader Joe's. "We just focus on what matters—great food + great prices = value. So you can afford to be adventurous without breaking the bank." Trader Joe's inventive price-value positioning has earned it an almost cult-like following of devoted customers who love what they get from Trader Joe's for the prices they pay.

Finding that magical price-value trade-off can be very difficult, and pricing strategies often require regular realignment to meet changes in the pricing environment. Just ask Trader Joe's competitor Whole Foods Market, which pretty much invented the upscale organic and natural foods supermarket concept. In recent years Whole Foods Market's pricing strategy has been a constant work in progress as the company struggles to find the right price-value equation (see Real Marketing 10.2).

If a company has selected its target market and positioning carefully, then its marketing mix strategy, including price, will be fairly straightforward. For example, Amazon positions its Kindle Fire tablet as offering the same (or even more) for less and prices it at 40 percent less than Apple's iPads and Samsung's Galaxy tablets. It recently began targeting families with young children, positioning the Kindle Fire as the "perfect family tablet," with models priced as low as $99, bundled with Kindle FreeTime, an all-in-one subscription service starting at $2.99 per month that brings together books, games, educational apps, movies, and TV shows for kids ages 3 through 8. Thus, the Kindle pricing strategy is largely determined by decisions on market positioning.

Pricing may play an important role in helping to accomplish company objectives at many levels. A firm can set prices to attract new customers or profitably retain existing ones. It can set prices low to prevent competition from entering the market or set prices at competitors' levels to stabilize the market. It can price to keep the loyalty and support of resellers or avoid government intervention. Prices can be reduced temporarily to create excitement for a brand. Or one product may be priced to help the sales of other products in the company's line.

Price decisions must be coordinated with product design, distribution, and promotion decisions to form a consistent and effective integrated marketing mix program. Decisions made for other marketing mix variables may affect pricing decisions. For example, a

Real Marketing

10.2 Whole Foods Market: Finding the Right Price-Value Equation

Whole Foods Market practically invented the upscale, socially responsible supermarket concept. Under its "Whole Foods. Whole People. Whole Planet." mission, the chain served up a tantalizing assortment of natural, organic, and gourmet foods at premium prices, all swaddled in Earth Day politics. Its upscale, health-conscious customers were willing and able to pay higher prices for the extra value they got. Throughout the 1990s and 2000s the chain's sales and profits soared.

Then came the Great Recession of 2008. People in all walks of life began rethinking the price-value equation and looking for ways to save. They asked tough questions, such as the following: "I love the wonderful foods and smells in my Whole Foods Market, but is it worth the extra 30 percent versus shopping at Walmart?" Even relatively affluent customers were cutting back and spending less. All of a sudden, Whole Foods Market's seemingly perfect premium marketing strategy looked less like a plum and more like a bruised organic banana. Some customers even amended the company's motto, making it "Whole Foods. Whole Paycheck." For the first time in its history, the company faced declines in same-store sales, and its stock price plunged.

At the same time that its well-heeled customers were cutting back their grocery budgets, Whole Foods Market's early success drew swarms of new, lower-priced competitors—from specialty supermarkets such as Trader Joe's, Sprouts Farmers Market, and ALDI to traditional chains such as Kroger, Walmart, Target, and Costco—that rushed to add organics to their shelves. As Whole Foods Market's CEO noted, "Everyone's jumping on the natural and organic brand wagon and frankly, a lot of that's due to our success." Thus, even as the economy improved, many shoppers continued to spend more of their grocery budgets at lower-priced stores.

Hit hard with these new market realities, Whole Foods Market faced difficult questions. Should it hold the line on the premium positioning that had earned it so much success in the past? Or should it cut prices and reposition itself to fit the leaner, more competitive times? Faced with these alternatives, Whole Foods Market decided to stick with its core upmarket positioning strategy. But it would also subtly realign its value proposition to better meet the needs of more thrift-minded customers. It set out to downplay the gourmet element of its positioning while playing up the real value of the healthy but exciting food it offers.

First, rather than dropping its everyday prices across the board, Whole Foods lowered prices on many basic items that customers demand most and bolstered these savings by offering significant sales on selected other items. It also started emphasizing its private-label brand, 365 Everyday Value. Next, Whole Foods launched a new marketing program aimed at tempering the chain's high-price reputation and convincing customers that Whole Foods Market was, in fact, an affordable place to shop. To help consumers see the value, it beefed up its communications about private-label and sale items using newsletters, coupons, its website, and social media. It assigned workers to serve as "value tour guides" to escort shoppers around stores and point out value items.

New ads featured headlines such as "No wallets were harmed in the buying of our 365 Everyday Value products" and "Sticker shock, but in a good way."

However, in addition to reducing certain prices and subtly increasing its emphasis on affordable options, Whole Foods Market also moved to convince shoppers that its regular products and prices offer good value as well—that when it comes to quality food, price isn't everything. As one tour guide noted, wherever you go, you'll have to pay a premium for organic food. "Value means getting a good exchange for your money." Such conversations helped to shift customers' eyes off of price and back to value.

Whole Foods Market's efforts to shed its "Whole Foods. Whole Paycheck." image have been reasonably successful. Since the down days following the 2008 recession, the chain's sales have almost doubled and profits have increased fivefold. But facing continued price pressures from resourceful competitors, Whole Foods Market has recently seen its growth begin to flag once

Whole Foods Market's "Values Matter" campaign suggests there is more to value than bargain prices. "Value" is inseparable from "values."

NetPhotos/Alamy Stock Photo

again. Its same-store sales and profits have flattened, and its stock price has dipped.

Thus, at Whole Food Market, finding and marketing the right price-value equation is still a work in progress. On the value side, the company's latest marketing campaign—called Values Matter—emphasizes that "value" is inseparable from "values." When shopping at Whole Foods, customers can be confident about "where their food comes from and how it was grown, raised, or made." The retailer's produce is "responsibly grown." The campaign concludes: "Whole Foods Market: America's healthiest grocery store," underscoring the extra value that makes shopping at Whole Foods Market worth the premium prices it charges.

At the same time that it's maintaining a high-end value proposition in its main stores, however, Whole Foods Market is also looking for growth by wooing a new segment of thriftier young consumers. It recently launched a new subchain—called 365 by Whole Foods Market—that targets less affluent but value-savvy, tech-minded millennials. 365 by Whole Foods Market stores are designed to bring "fresh, healthy foods to a broader audience with a streamlined, quality-meets-value shopping experience." The new stores carry Whole Foods' own 365-branded products plus a carefully selected mix of other goods at prices that look more like Trader Joe's than Whole Foods. "We think there are certain customers that the Whole Foods brand is attractive to, but there're others that it's less attractive to," says the Whole Foods CEO. "We think a streamlined, hip, cool, technology-oriented store—a store unlike one anyone's ever seen before…is going to be pretty attractive to that particular generation."

Whole Foods Market's pricing struggles underscore the difficulty many firms face in finding the best balance between price and value. Whole Foods' challenge is to meet the changing demands of today's intensely competitive pricing environment in a way that preserves what has made it special to customers through the years. In all, things aren't really much different inside a local Whole Foods Market these days. There are more sale items, and the private-label 365 Everyday Value brand is more prominently presented, but customers can still find the same alluring assortment of high-quality, flavorful, and natural foods wrapped in Whole Foods, Whole People, Whole Planet values.

But it's a delicate balance. "We have the ability to compete on price and we will do that," says the CEO. "But this is not just a race to the bottom. We are also going to start a new race to the top, with better-quality food, higher standards, richer experiences for our customers, and new levels of transparency and accountability in the marketplace." Even if that means charging a little higher prices.

Sources: Brad Stone, "Whole Foods, Half Off," *Bloomberg Businessweek*, January 25, 2015, pp. 45–49; Alison Griswold, "Whole Foods Wants to Woo Millennials with a 'Hip, Cool, Technology-Oriented Store,'" *Slate*, May 16, 2015, www.slate.com/blogs/moneybox/2015/05/06/whole_foods_q2_2015_earnings_stock_plunges_on_comps_miss.html; "Whole Foods Market Announces Three Additional 365 by Whole Food Market Store Leases," Whole Foods News Room, November 4, 2015, http://media.wholefoodsmarket.com/news/whole-foods-market-announces-three-additional-365-by-whole-foods-market-sto; Palbir Nijjar, "3 Risks Facing Whole Foods Market," *The Motley Fool*, January 31, 2016, www.fool.com/investing/general/2016/01/31/3-risks-facing-whole-foods-market-investors.aspx; and www.wholefoodsmarket.com and www.wholefoodsmarket.com/company-info/investor-relations/annual-reports, accessed September 2016.

decision to position the product on high-performance quality will mean that the seller must charge a higher price to cover higher costs. And producers whose resellers are expected to support and promote their products may have to build larger reseller margins into their prices.

Companies often position their products on price and then tailor other marketing mix decisions to the prices they want to charge. Here, price is a crucial product-positioning factor that defines the product's market, competition, and design. Many firms support such price-positioning strategies with a technique called **target costing**. Target costing reverses the usual process of first designing a new product, determining its cost, and then asking, "Can we sell it for that?" Instead, it starts with an ideal selling price based on customer value considerations and then targets costs that will ensure that the price is met. For example, when Honda initially designed the Honda Fit, it began with a $13,950 starting price point and highway mileage of 33 miles per gallon firmly in mind. It then designed a stylish, peppy little car with costs that allowed it to give target customers those values.

Other companies deemphasize price and use other marketing mix tools to create *nonprice* positions. Often, the best strategy is not to charge the lowest price but rather to differentiate the marketing offer to make it worth a higher price. For example, Sleep Number puts high value into its mattresses and charges a higher price to match that value.

Target costing

Pricing that starts with an ideal selling price, then targets costs that will ensure that the price is met.

At the most basic level, a Sleep Number mattress lets you adjust each side to your ideal level of firmness and support. Add SleepIQ technology and you can track and optimize for the best possible night's sleep. ● Sleep Number lets you "Know. Adjust. Sleep." SleepIQ technology inside the bed monitors restful sleep time, heart rate, breathing rate, movements, and other factors. Then the SleepIQ app reports on your night's SleepIQ score and how you slept. The app even recommends adjustments that will change your sleep for the better. The Sleep Number children's mattress line helps parents track how their kids sleep. It even lets parents know when their kids get out of bed at night and includes a head tilt for stuffy heads, star-based rewards for sleep habits, and a clever "monster detector." Sleep Number beds cost more than a traditional mattresses—models run from $1,000 to more than $7,000 compared with good-quality traditional mattresses at $1,000 or less. But Sleep Number's satisfied

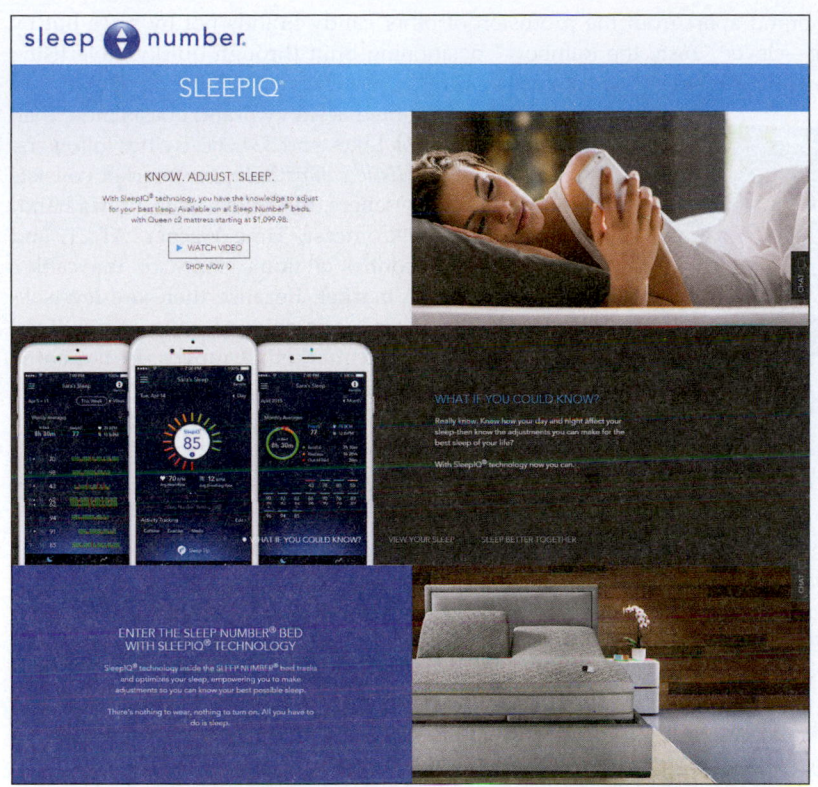

● Nonprice positioning: Sleep Number beds cost more than traditional mattresses, but the brand's highly satisfied customers are willing to pay more to get more. After all, it's hard to put a price on a good night's sleep.

Select Comfort Corporation

customers are willing to pay more to get more. A 2015 J.D. Power Mattress Satisfaction Report rated Sleep Number highest in customer satisfaction with mattresses. After all, it's hard to put a price on a good night's sleep.[9]

Thus, marketers must consider the total marketing strategy and mix when setting prices. But again, even when featuring price, marketers need to remember that customers rarely buy on price alone. Instead, they seek products that give them the best value in terms of benefits received for the prices paid.

Organizational Considerations

Management must decide who within the organization should set prices. Companies handle pricing in a variety of ways. In small companies, prices are often set by top management rather than by the marketing or sales departments. In large companies, pricing is typically handled by divisional or product managers. In industrial markets, salespeople may be allowed to negotiate with customers within certain price ranges. Even so, top management sets the pricing objectives and policies, and it often approves the prices proposed by lower-level management or salespeople.

In industries in which pricing is a key factor (airlines, aerospace, steel, railroads, oil companies), companies often have pricing departments to set the best prices or help others set them. These departments report to the marketing department or top management. Others who have an influence on pricing include sales managers, production managers, finance managers, and accountants.

The Market and Demand

As noted earlier, good pricing starts with understanding how customers' perceptions of value affect the prices they are willing to pay. Both consumer and industrial buyers balance the price of a product or service against the benefits of owning it. Thus, before setting prices, the marketer must understand the relationship between price and demand for the company's product. In this section, we take a deeper look at the price–demand relationship and how it varies for different types of markets. We then discuss methods for analyzing the price–demand relationship.

Pricing in Different Types of Markets

The seller's pricing freedom varies with different types of markets. Economists recognize four types of markets, each presenting a different pricing challenge.

Under *pure competition*, the market consists of many buyers and sellers trading in a uniform commodity, such as wheat, copper, or financial securities. No single buyer or seller has much effect on the going market price. In a purely competitive market, marketing research, product development, pricing, advertising, and sales promotion play little or no role. Thus, sellers in these markets do not spend much time on marketing strategy.

Under *monopolistic competition*, the market consists of many buyers and sellers trading over a range of prices rather than a single market price. A range of prices occurs because sellers can differentiate their offers to buyers. Because there are many competitors, each firm is less affected by competitors' pricing strategies than in oligopolistic markets. Sellers try to develop differentiated offers for different customer segments and, in addition to price, freely use branding, advertising, and personal selling to set their offers apart. Thus, Wrigley sets its

Skittles candy brand apart from the profusion of other candy brands not by price but by brand building—clever "Taste the Rainbow" positioning built through quirky advertising and a heavy presence in social media such as Tumblr, Instagram, YouTube, Facebook, and

Twitter. The social media–savvy brand boasts more than 24 million Facebook Likes and 334,000 Twitter followers.

Under *oligopolistic competition*, the market consists of only a few large sellers. ● For example, only a handful of providers—Comcast, Time Warner, AT&T, and Dish Network—control a lion's share of the cable/satellite television market. Because there are few sellers, each seller is alert and responsive to competitors' pricing strategies and marketing moves. In the battle for subscribers, price becomes a major competitive tool. For example, to woo customers away from Comcast, TimeWarner, and other cable companies, AT&T's DirecTV unit offers low-price "Cable Crusher" offers, lock-in prices, and free HD.

In a *pure monopoly*, the market is dominated by one seller. The seller may be a government monopoly (the U.S. Postal Service), a private regulated monopoly (a power company), or a private unregulated monopoly (De Beers and diamonds). Pricing is handled differently in each case.

● **Pricing in oligopolistic markets: Price is an important competitive tool for AT&T's DirecTV unit. Here, it woos cable customers with low lock-in prices and free HD.**
Bloomberg via Getty Images

Analyzing the Price–Demand Relationship

Each price the company might charge will lead to a different level of demand. The relationship between the price charged and the resulting demand level is shown in the **demand curve** in ● **Figure 10.6**. The demand curve shows the number of units the market will buy in a given time period at different prices that might be charged. In the normal case, demand and price are inversely related—that is, the higher the price, the lower the demand. Thus, the company would sell less if it raised its price from P_1 to P_2. In short, consumers with limited budgets probably will buy less of something if its price is too high.

Understanding a brand's price-demand curve is crucial to good pricing decisions. ConAgra Foods has learned this lesson when pricing its Banquet frozen dinners:[10]

> Banquet has charged about $1 per dinner since its start way back in 1953. And that's what customers still expect. The $1 price is a key component in the brands appeal. Six years ago, when ConAgra tried to cover higher commodity costs by raising the list price of Banquet dinners from $1 to $1.25, consumers turned up their noses to the higher price. Sales dropped sharply, forcing ConAgra to sell off excess dinners at discount prices and drop its prices back to a buck a dinner. To make money at that price, ConAgra tried to do a better job of managing costs by shrinking portions and substituting less expensive ingredients for costlier ones. But as commodity prices continue to rise, Banquet just can't make a decent dinner for a dollar anymore. So it's cautiously raising prices again. Some smaller meals are still priced at $1. For example, the chicken finger meal still comes with macaroni and cheese but no longer includes a brownie. But classic meals such as Salisbury steak are now back up to $1.25, and ConAgra has introduced Banquet Select Recipes meals at a startling $1.50. The brand has seen some initial sales declines since the price increase but not as severe as feared. Banquet is an entry-point brand, notes ConAgra's CEO, but "that doesn't mean it's married to a dollar. It [just] needs to be the best value for our core customer."

Most companies try to measure their demand curves by estimating demand at different prices. The type of market makes a difference. In a monopoly, the demand curve shows the total market demand resulting from different prices. If the company faces competition, its demand at different prices will depend on whether competitors' prices stay constant or change with the company's own prices.

Price Elasticity of Demand

Marketers also need to know **price elasticity**—how responsive demand will be to a change in price. If demand hardly changes with a small change in price, we say demand is *inelastic*. If demand changes greatly, we say the demand is *elastic*.

Demand curve
A curve that shows the number of units the market will buy in a given time period, at different prices that might be charged.

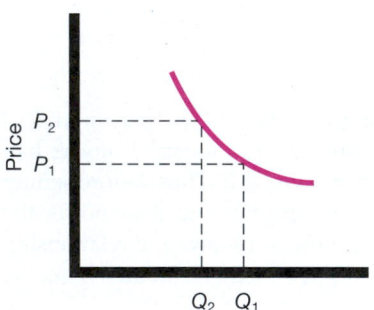

● **FIGURE** | 10.6
Demand Curve

Price elasticity
A measure of the sensitivity of demand to changes in price.

If demand is elastic rather than inelastic, sellers will consider lowering their prices. A lower price will produce more total revenue. This practice makes sense as long as the extra costs of producing and selling more do not exceed the extra revenue. At the same time, most firms want to avoid pricing that turns their products into commodities. In recent years, forces such as deregulation and the instant price comparisons afforded by the internet and other technologies have increased consumer price sensitivity, turning products ranging from phones and computers to new automobiles into commodities in some consumers' eyes.

The Economy

Economic conditions can have a strong impact on the firm's pricing strategies. Economic factors such as a boom or recession, inflation, and interest rates affect pricing decisions because they affect consumer spending, consumer perceptions of the product's price and value, and the company's costs of producing and selling a product.

In the aftermath of the Great Recession of 2008 to 2009, many consumers rethought the price-value equation. They tightened their belts and become more value conscious. Consumers have continued their thriftier ways well beyond the economic recovery. As a result, many marketers have increased their emphasis on value-for-the-money pricing strategies.

The most obvious response to the new economic realities is to cut prices and offer discounts. Thousands of companies have done just that. Lower prices make products more affordable and help spur short-term sales. However, such price cuts can have undesirable long-term consequences. Lower prices mean lower margins. Deep discounts may cheapen a brand in consumers' eyes. And once a company cuts prices, it's difficult to raise them again when the economy recovers.

Rather than cutting prices on their main-market brands, many companies are holding their price positions but redefining the "value" in their value propositions. Other companies have developed "price tiers," adding both more affordable lines and premium lines that span the varied means and preferences of different customer segments.  For example, for cost-conscious customers with tighter budgets, P&G has added lower-price versions of its brands, such as "Basic" versions of Bounty and Charmin and a lower-priced version of Tide called Tide Simply Clean and Fresh. At the same time, at the higher end, P&G has launched upscale versions of some of its brands, such as Bounty DuraTowel and Cascade Platinum dishwasher detergent, which offer superior performance at up to twice the price of the middle-market versions.

Remember, even in tough economic times, consumers do not buy based on prices alone. They balance the price they pay against the value they receive. For example, despite selling its shoes for as much as $150 a pair, Nike commands the highest consumer loyalty of any brand in the footwear segment. Customers perceive the value of Nike's products and the Nike ownership experience to be well worth the price. Thus, no matter what price they charge—low or high—companies need to offer great *value for the money*.

● Pricing and the economy: Many companies have developed "price tiers." For example, P&G offers economically priced versions of many brands—such as Charmin Basic above—but also premium versions that offer superior performance and higher prices.

The Procter & Gamble Company

Other External Factors

Beyond the market and the economy, the company must consider several other factors in its external environment when setting prices. It must know what impact its prices will have on other parties in its environment. How will *resellers* react to various prices? The company should set prices that give resellers a fair profit, encourage their support, and help them to sell the product effectively. The *government* is another important external influence on pricing decisions. Finally, *social concerns* may need to be taken into account. In setting prices, a company's short-term sales, market share, and profit goals may need to be tempered by broader societal considerations. We will examine public policy issues later in Chapter 11.

10 Reviewing and Extending the Concepts

OBJECTIVES REVIEW AND KEY TERMS

Objectives Review

Companies today face a fierce and fast-changing pricing environment. Firms successful at creating customer value with the other marketing mix activities must still capture some of this value in the prices they earn. This chapter examines the importance of pricing, general pricing strategies, and the internal and external considerations that affect pricing decisions.

OBJECTIVE 10-1 Answer the question "What is a price?" and discuss the importance of pricing in today's fast-changing environment. (pp 284–285)

Price can be defined narrowly as the amount of money charged for a product or service. Or it can be defined more broadly as the sum of the values that consumers exchange for the benefits of having and using the product or service. The pricing challenge is to find the price that will let the company make a fair profit by getting paid for the customer value it creates.

Despite the increased role of nonprice factors in the modern marketing process, price remains an important element in the marketing mix. It is the only marketing mix element that produces revenue; all other elements represent costs. More important, as a part of a company's overall value proposition, price plays a key role in creating customer value and building customer relationships. Smart managers treat pricing as a key strategic tool for creating and capturing customer value.

OBJECTIVE 10-2 Identify the three major pricing strategies and discuss the importance of understanding customer-value perceptions, company costs, and competitor strategies when setting prices. (pp 285–293)

Companies can choose from three major pricing strategies: customer value–based pricing, cost-based pricing, and competition-based pricing. *Customer value–based pricing* uses buyers' perceptions of value as the basis for setting price. Good pricing begins with a complete understanding of the value that a product or service creates for customers and setting a price that captures that value. Customer perceptions of the product's value set the ceiling for prices. If customers perceive that a product's price is greater than its value, they will not buy the product.

Companies can pursue either of two types of value-based pricing. *Good-value pricing* involves offering just the right combination of quality and good service at a fair price. EDLP is an example of this strategy. *Value-added pricing* involves attaching value-added features and services to differentiate the company's offers and support charging higher prices.

Cost-based pricing involves setting prices based on the costs for producing, distributing, and selling products plus a fair rate of return for effort and risk. Company and product costs are an important consideration in setting prices. Whereas customer value perceptions set the price ceiling, costs set the floor for

pricing. However, cost-based pricing is product driven rather than customer driven. The company designs what it considers to be a good product and sets a price that covers costs plus a target profit. If the price turns out to be too high, the company must settle for lower markups or lower sales, both resulting in disappointing profits. If the company prices the product below its costs, its profits will also suffer. Cost-based pricing approaches include *cost-plus pricing* and *break-even pricing* (or target profit pricing).

Competition-based pricing involves setting prices based on competitors' strategies, costs, prices, and market offerings. Consumers base their judgments of a product's value on the prices that competitors charge for similar products. If consumers perceive that the company's product or service provides greater value, the company can charge a higher price. If consumers perceive less value relative to competing products, the company must either charge a lower price or change customer perceptions to justify a higher price.

OBJECTIVE 10-3 Identify and define the other important external and internal factors affecting a firm's pricing decisions. (pp 293–299)

Other *internal* factors that influence pricing decisions include the company's overall marketing strategy, objectives, and marketing mix, as well as organizational considerations. Price is only one element of the company's broader marketing strategy. If the company has selected its target market and positioning carefully, then its marketing mix strategy, including price, will be fairly straightforward. Common pricing objectives might include customer retention and building profitable customer relationships, preventing competition, supporting resellers and gaining their support, or avoiding government intervention. Price decisions must be coordinated with product design, distribution, and promotion decisions to form a consistent and effective marketing program. Finally, in order to coordinate pricing goals and decisions, management must decide who within the organization is responsible for setting price.

Other *external* pricing considerations include the nature of the market and demand and environmental factors such as the economy, reseller needs, and government actions. Ultimately, the customer decides whether the company has set the right price. The customer weighs the price against the perceived values of using the product—if the price exceeds the sum of the values, consumers will not buy. So the company must understand such concepts as demand curves (the price–demand relationship) and price elasticity (consumer sensitivity to prices).

Economic conditions can have a major impact on pricing decisions. The Great Recession caused consumers to rethink the price–value equation, and consumers have continued their thriftier ways well beyond the economic recovery. Marketers have responded by increasing their emphasis on value-for-the-money pricing strategies. No matter what the economic times, however, consumers do not buy based on prices alone. Thus, no matter what price they charge—low or high—companies need to offer superior value for the money.

Key Terms

OBJECTIVE 10-1

Price (p 284)

OBJECTIVE 10-2

Customer value–based pricing (p 285)
Good-value pricing (p 287)
Value-added pricing (p 287)
Cost-based pricing (p 289)

Fixed costs (overhead) (p 289)
Variable costs (p 289)
Total costs (p 289)
Experience curve (learning curve) (p 290)
Cost-plus pricing (markup pricing) (p 291)

Break-even pricing (target return pricing) (p 291)
Competition-based pricing (p 293)

OBJECTIVE 10-3

Target costing (p 296)
Demand curve (p 298)
Price elasticity (p 298)

DISCUSSION AND CRITICAL THINKING

MyMarketingLab

Go to **mymktlab.com** to complete the problems marked with this icon ⭐.

Discussion Questions

10-1 Why is finding and implementing the right pricing strategy critical to a company's success? (AACSB: Communication)

⭐ **10-2** Name and describe the two types of value-based pricing methods. (AACSB: Communication)

10-3 What is cost-based pricing? How do companies use fixed and variable costs in cost-based pricing models? (AACSB: Communication)

⭐ **10-4** Explain the price-demand relationship. What factors must sellers consider when setting prices in different types of markets? (AACSB: Communication)

10-5 Define price elasticity and discuss why it is important for marketers to understand this concept. (AACSB: Communication; Reflective Thinking)

Critical Thinking Exercises

⭐ **10-6** Congratulations! You just won your state lottery and will be receiving a check for $1 million. You have always wanted to own your own business and have noticed the increase in the number of food trucks in your local area. A new food truck with a kitchen and related equipment costs about $100,000. Other fixed costs include salaries, gas for the truck, and license fees and are estimated to be about $50,000 per year. You decide to offer traditional Mediterranean cuisine. Variable costs include food and beverages estimated at $6 per platter (meat, rice, vegetable, and pita bread). Meals will be priced at $10. Calculate the break-even for your food truck business. After reviewing your break-even, what changes would you consider? Is this how you want to spend your lottery winnings? (AACSB: Communication; Reflective Thinking)

10-7 In a small group, discuss your perceptions of value and how much you are willing to pay for the following products: automobiles, frozen dinners, jeans, and athletic shoes. Are there differences among members of your group? Explain why those differences exist. Discuss some examples of brands of these products that are positioned to deliver different value to consumers. (AACSB: Communication; Reflective Thinking)

10-8 Your company has developed a new weight-loss breakfast shake that has proven to be successful in the test market phase. Users have experienced an average weight loss of two pounds per week. You hold a patent on the product. The cost to produce the shake is relatively low, with total manufacturing costs running about $0.05 per ounce. Each shake is eight ounces. What pricing strategy do you recommend for this product? (AACSB: Communication; Use of IT; Reflective Thinking)

APPLICATIONS AND CASES

Online, Mobile, and Social Media Marketing Online Price Tracking

Got your eye on a new premium 32-inch Samsung television? Well, you better not purchase it in December—that's when the price was highest on Amazon.com ($500 versus $400 in November or February). Most consumers know that prices fluctuate throughout the year, but did you know they even fluctuate hourly? You probably can't keep up with that, but there's an app that can. Camelcamelcamel is a tool that tracks Amazon's prices for consumers and sends alerts when a price hits the sweet spot. This app allows users to import entire Amazon wish lists and to set desired price levels at which emails or tweets are sent to inform them of the prices. All of this is free. Camel makes its money from an unlikely partner—Amazon—which funnels price data directly to Camel. Camel is a member of Amazon's affiliate program, kicking back 8.5 percent of sales for each customer Camel refers. It would seem that Amazon would want customers to buy when prices are higher, not lower. But the online behemoth sees this as a way to keep the bargain hunters happy while realizing more profitability from less price-sensitive customers. This is an improvement over Amazon's earlier pricing tactics, which charged different customers different prices based on their buying behavior.

10-9   Go to www.camelcamelcamel.com and set up a free account. Track 10 products that interest you. Did any of the products reach your desired price? Write a report on the usefulness of this type of app for consumers. (AACSB: Communication; Use of IT)

10-10   Camel is not the only Amazon tracking or online price-tracking application. Find and describe an example of another online price tracking tool for consumers. (AACSB: Communication; Use of IT)

Marketing Ethics   The Cost of a Life

When loved ones are critically ill, what are families willing to pay to keep them on a path to improved health? In 2015, Turing Pharmaceuticals found itself in the middle of a controversial issue when it purchased an existing drug—Daraprim—from another pharmaceutical company. Daraprim has been around for 62 years and is used to treat life-threatening parasitic infections in AIDS and cancer patients. After acquiring Daraprim, Turing Pharmaceuticals CEO Martin Shkreli quickly raised its price from the previous $13.50 per pill to a whopping $750 per pill. According to CNN Money, CEO Shkreli stated, "We needed to turn a profit on this drug." He added the company would use the profits to research better ways to treat diseases.

10-11   Research the Daraprim pricing issue. Is it wrong for Turing Pharmaceuticals to charge such a high price for this medication? Support your position. (AACSB: Communication; Ethical Reasoning)

10-12   According to one *Harvard Business Review* article (see www.hbr.org/2015/09/its-time-to-rein-in-exorbitant-pharmaceutical-prices), over the past five years returns for the S&P Pharmaceuticals Select Industry Index have been virtually doubled those of the broader S&P 500 (roughly 24 percent versus 12 percent annually). What factors affect profitability in the pharmaceutical industry? Are these high profit levels a good or bad thing? Explain.

Marketing by the Numbers   Pricey Sheets

Many luxury sheets cost less than $200 to make but sell for more than $500 in retail stores. Some cost even more—consumers pay almost $3,000 for Frett'e "Tangeri Pizzo" king-size luxury linens. The creators of a new brand of luxury linens, called Boll & Branch, have entered this market and are determining the price at which to sell their sheets directly to consumers online. They want to price their sheets lower than most brands but still want to earn an adequate margin on sales. The sheets come in a luxurious box that can be reused to store lingerie, jewelry, or other keepsakes. The Boll & Branch brand touts fair-trade practices when sourcing its high-grade long-staple organic cotton from India. Given the cost information below, refer to Appendix 2: Marketing by the Numbers to answer the following questions.

	Cost/King-Size Set
Raw cotton	$28.00
Spinning/weaving/dyeing	$12.00
Cut/sew/finishing	$10.00
Material transportation	$ 3.00
Factory fee	$16.00
Inspection and import fees	$14.00
Ocean freight/insurance	$ 5.00
Warehousing	$ 8.00
Packaging	$15.00
Promotion	$30.00
Customer shipping	$15.00

10-13   Given the cost per king-size sheet set above and assuming the manufacturer has total fixed costs of $500,000 and estimates first year sales will be 50,000 sets, determine the price to consumers if the company desires a 40 percent margin on sales. (AACSB: Communication; Analytical Reasoning)

10-14   If the company decides to sell through retailers instead of directly to consumers online, to maintain the consumer price you calculated in the previous question, at what price must it sell the product to a wholesaler who then sells it to retailers? Assume wholesalers desire a 10 percent margin and retailers get a 20 percent margin, both based on their respective selling prices. (AACSB: Communication; Analytical Reasoning)

Video Case Fast-Food Discount Wars

Fast-food chains are locked in a fierce battle that has them practically giving food away. McDonald's, Wendy's, Burger King, and others are constantly trying to lure customers at the low end of the price spectrum with tempting menu options that can serve as a snack or a meal. Although this technique is nothing new, it's more popular today than ever. The tactic has even found its way into full-service restaurant chains such as Olive Garden.

But are bargain-basement options a sustainable path for restaurant chains? This video takes a look at the various ways discount menus are executed. It also considers the reasons for using discount menu tactics as well as the possible negative outcomes.

After viewing the video featuring restaurant discount menu wars, answer the following questions:

10-15 Can discount menu strategies like those featured in the video be classified as "value pricing"? Explain.

10-16 Discuss why a restaurant chain might employ a discount menu as a pricing option.

10-17 What are the possible negative outcomes of employing a discount menu strategy?

Company Case Trader Joe's: Cheap Gourmet—Putting a Special Twist on the Price-Value Equation

Apple Store openings aren't the only place where long lines form these days. Early on a summer morning, there's a crowd gathered, eagerly awaiting the opening of a Trader Joe's outpost. The waiting shoppers discuss all things Trader Joe's, including their favorite items. One customer suggests the chain will be good for the neighborhood even though there are already plenty of grocery stores around, including various upscale food boutiques.

This is a scene that plays out every time the Southern California–based Trader Joe's opens a new store—something that only happens a handful of times each year. Within moments of a new opening, a deluge of customers makes it almost impossible to navigate the aisles. They line up 10 deep at checkouts with carts full of Trader Joe's exclusive $2.99 Charles Shaw wine—aka "Two-Buck Chuck"—and an assortment of other exclusive gourmet products at impossibly low prices. Amid hanging plastic lobsters and hand-painted signs, a Hawaiian-shirt-clad manager (the "captain") and employees (the "crew") explain to first timers that the prices are not grand opening specials. They are everyday prices.

What is it about Trader Joe's that has consumers everywhere waiting with such anxious anticipation? Trader Joe's seems to have cracked the customer value code by providing the perfect blend of benefits to prices.

High on Benefits

Trader Joe's isn't really a gourmet food store. Then again, it's not a discount food store either. It's actually a bit of both. One of America's hottest retailers, Trader Joe's has put its own special twist on the food price-value equation—call it "cheap gourmet." It offers gourmet-caliber, one-of-a-kind products at bargain prices, all served up in a festive, vacation-like atmosphere that makes shopping fun. Trader Joe's isn't low end, it isn't high end, and it certainly isn't mainstream. "Their mission is to be a nationwide chain of neighborhood specialty grocery stores," said one business professor who does research on the company. However you define it, Trader Joe's inventive price-value positioning has earned it an almost cult-like following of devoted customers who love what they get from Trader Joe's for the prices they pay.

Trader Joe's describes itself as an "island paradise" where "value, adventure, and tasty treasures are discovered, every day." Shoppers bustle and buzz amid cedar-plank-lined walls and fake palm trees as a ship's bell rings out occasionally at checkout, alerting them to special announcements. Unfailingly helpful and cheery associates in aloha shirts chat with customers about everything from the weather to menu suggestions for dinner parties. Customers don't just shop at Trader Joe's; they experience it.

Shelves bristle with an eclectic assortment of gourmet quality grocery items. Trader Joe's stocks only a limited assortment of about 4,000 products (compared with the 45,000 items found in an average supermarket). However, the assortment is uniquely Trader Joe's, including special concoctions of gourmet packaged foods and sauces, ready-to-eat soups, fresh and frozen entrees, snacks, and desserts—all free of artificial colors, flavors, and preservatives.

Trader Joe's is a gourmet foodie's delight, featuring everything from organic broccoli slaw, organic strawberry lemonade, creamy Valencia peanut butter, and fair-trade coffees to corn and chile tomato-less salsa and triple-ginger ginger snaps. Trader Joe's sells various items that are comparable to other stores, like organic vanilla yogurt, almond milk, extra pulp orange juice, smoked gouda cheese, and roasted garlic hummus. But the quirky retailer also maintains pricing power by selling things that are uniquely Trader Joe's. Try finding Ginger Cats cookies, quinoa and black bean tortilla chips, or mango coconut popcorn at any other store.

More than 80 percent of the store's brands are private-label goods, sold exclusively by Trader Joe's. If asked, almost any customer can tick off a ready list of Trader Joe's favorites that they just can't live without—a list that quickly grows. People go into the store intending to buy a few favorites and quickly fill a cart. "I think consumers look at it and think, 'I can go and get things that I can't get elsewhere,'" says one food industry analyst. "They just seem to turn their customers on."

Low on Prices

A special store atmosphere, exclusive gourmet products, helpful and attentive associates—this all sounds like a recipe for high prices. Not so at Trader Joe's. Whereas upscale competitors such as Whole Foods Market charge upscale prices to match their wares ("Whole Foods, Whole Paycheck"), Trader Joe's amazes customers with its relatively frugal prices. The prices aren't all that low in absolute terms but they're a real bargain compared with what you'd pay for the same quality and coolness elsewhere. "At Trader Joe's, we're as much about value as we are about great food," says the company. "So you can afford to be adventurous without breaking the bank."

All that low-price talk along with consumers' perceptions is valid. A recent report from Deutsche Bank compared prices at Trader Joe's with those at Whole Foods for a basket of 77 products—a mix of perishable items, private-label products, and non-food items. Trader Joe's was 21 percent cheaper than Whole Foods and had the lowest price on 78 percent of the items. Even when comparing private-label brands, Trader Joe's was 15 percent cheaper. What's more, Trader Joe's price advantage has been increasing, a point that is particularly telling given that Whole Foods has focused strategically on lowering its prices over the past few years.

How does Trader Joe's keep its gourmet prices so low? By maintaining a sound strategy based on price and adjusting the nonprice elements of the marketing mix accordingly. For starters, Trader Joe's has lean operations and a near-fanatical focus on saving money. To keep costs down, Trader Joe's typically locates its stores in low-rent, out-of-the-way locations, such as suburban strip malls. Notorious for small parking lots that are always packed, Trader Joe's points out that spacious parking lots require more real estate and that costs money. Its small stores with small back rooms and limited product assortment result in reduced facilities and inventory costs. Trader Joe's saves money by eliminating large produce sections and expensive on-site bakery, butcher, deli, and seafood shops. And for its private-label brands, Trader Joe's buys directly from suppliers and negotiates hard on price.

Finally, the frugal retailer saves money by spending almost nothing on advertising. Also, it offers no coupons, discount cards, or special promotions of any kind. Trader Joe's unique combination of quirky products and low prices produces so much word-of-mouth promotion that the company doesn't really need to advertise. The closest thing to an official promotion is the company's website or The Fearless Flyer, a newsletter mailed out monthly to people who opt in.

In the absence of traditional advertising, Trader Joe's most potent promotional weapon is its army of faithful followers. If you doubt the importance and impact of fanatical Trader Joe's fans, just check out the numerous fan sites (such as traderjoesfan.com, whatsgoodattraderjoes.com, clubtraderjoes.com, livingtraderjoes.com, and cooktj.com) where the faithful unite to discuss new products and stores, trade recipes, and swap their favorite Trader Joe's stories.

Something Extra

Although the simple calculation of benefits to prices equates to strong value, there's something bigger that plays in Trader Joe's favor. Beyond all the wonderful and unique products, friendly staff, quirky store design, the combination of all these things produces synergy. It adds up to an atmosphere and kind of trust that eludes most companies. One industry observer who is not a fan of grocery shopping sums it up this way:

> Walking into a Trader Joe's, my demeanor is noticeably different than when I'm shopping anywhere else. Somehow I don't mind going there. At times—and it's still hard for me to believe I'd say this about shopping—I actually look forward to it. Trader Joe's does something pleasant for my brain, as it does for millions of others. There's more transparency in my dealings with TJ's than most other places. Authenticity is something you can feel—it's crucial to the buzz. Trader Joe's proves that even when you get the other elements of the experience right, people still matter most.

Finding the right price-value formula has made Trader Joe's one of the nation's fastest-growing and most popular food stores. Its 482 stores in 45 states now reap annual sales of at least $13 billion by one analyst's estimate (the private company is tight-lipped about its financial results), an amount that has quadrupled in the past decade. Trader Joe's stores pull in an amazing $1,750 per square foot, more than twice the supermarket industry average. In Consumer Reports's "Best Supermarket Chain" review, Trader Joe's has occupied one of the top two spots every year for the past five years.

It's all about value and price—what you get for what you pay. Just ask Trader Joe's regular Chrissi Wright, found early one morning browsing her local Trader Joe's in Bend, Oregon.

> Chrissi expects she'll leave Trader Joe's with eight bottles of the popular Charles Shaw wine priced at $2.99 each tucked under her arms. "I love Trader Joe's because they let me eat like a yuppie without taking all my money," says Wright. "Their products are gourmet, often environmentally conscientious and beautiful … and, of course, there's Two-Buck Chuck—possibly the greatest innovation of our time."

Questions for Discussion

10-18 Under the concept of customer value-based pricing, explain Trader Joe's success.

10-19 Does Trader Joe's employ good-value pricing or value-added pricing? Explain.

10-20 Does Trader Joe's pricing strategy truly differentiate it from the competition?

10-21 Is Trader Joe's pricing strategy sustainable? Explain.

10-22 What changes—if any—would you recommend that Trader Joe's make?

Sources: Kathleen Elkins, "I Compared Prices of Trader Joe's Items to Those of Whole Foods 265 Everyday Value—Here's What I Found," *Business Insider*, February 29, 2016, www.businessinsider.com/i-compared-the-price-of-whole-foods-365-items-to-trader-joes-heres-what-i-found-2016-2; Craig Giammona, "Whole Foods Is Ready to Convince You That It Can Do Cheaper," *Bloomberg*, May 18, 2016, www.bloomberg.com/news/articles/2016-05-18/whole-foods-seeks-to-shed-whole-paycheck-rap-with-new-format; Kathryn Vasel, "Who's Got Better Prices: Whole Foods or Trader Joe's?" *CNNMoney*, March 31, 2016, www.money.cnn.com/2016/03/31/pf/trader-joes-whole-foods-prices/; David DiSalvo, "What Trader Joe's Knows about Making Your Brain Happy," *Forbes*, February 19, 2015, www.forbes.com/sites/daviddisalvo/2015/02/19/what-trader-joes-knows-about-making-your-brain-happy/#27f0f6f41539; Beth Kowitt, "Inside the Secret World of Trader Joe's," *Fortune*, August 23, 2010, accessed at www.fortune.com; and "SN's Top 75 Retailers & Wholesalers 2016," *Supermarket News*, www.supermarketnews.com/rankings-research/top-75-retailers-wholesalers and www.traderjoes.com, accessed June 2016.

MyMarketingLab

Go to **mymktlab.com** for Auto-graded writing questions as well as the following Assisted-graded writing questions:

10-23 Why are consumers so concerned about the price of gas and why are they willing to search out stations with lower prices?

10-24 Describe the cost-plus pricing method and discuss why marketers use it even if it is not the best method for setting prices.

PART 1: Defining Marketing and the Marketing Process (Chapters 1–2)
PART 2: Understanding the Marketplace and Consumer Value (Chapters 3–6)
PART 3: Designing a Customer Value–Driven Strategy and Mix (Chapters 7–17)
PART 4: Extending Marketing (Chapters 18–20)

11 Pricing Strategies
Additional Considerations

CHAPTER PREVIEW In the previous chapter, you learned that price is an important marketing mix tool for both creating and capturing customer value. You explored the three main pricing strategies—customer value–based, cost-based, and competition-based pricing—and the many internal and external factors that affect a firm's pricing decisions. In this chapter, we'll look at some additional pricing considerations: new product pricing, product mix pricing, price adjustments, and initiating and reacting to price changes. We close the chapter with a discussion of public policy and pricing.

For openers, let's examine Apple's premium pricing strategy. Apple sets its prices substantially above those of even its highest-priced competitors. But Apple's appeal to customers has never been about prices. Instead, Apple's vision has always been to provide innovative designs and superior user experiences that make its prices secondary in the minds of customers who covet Apple products.

APPLE: Premium Priced and Worth It

Apple is the prototypical premium pricer. Whether it's an iPhone, iPad, Mac laptop, or Apple Watch, customers pay more for an Apple than for competing devices—a lot more. Apple's iPhone last year sold globally for an average price of $624, compared with $185 for the average Android smartphone. Even compared to Samsung, its closest high-end competitor, the latest iPhone commands a premium of $100 to $200 more than similar Samsung Galaxy models. Similarly, a standard MacBook Pro costs $300 more than a comparable Dell or HP computer.

Yet despite such sky-high prices, Apple's products continue to fly off shelves, as eager customers get in line to snap up the latest models. For example, Apple sold more than 231 million iPhones last year alone. That leaves Apple in an envious position: It charges the highest prices and still captures market-leading shares in most of its product categories. How does Apple pull that off?

For Apple, success has never been about prices. Instead, it's been about the Apple user experience. Many tech companies make products that just occupy space and complete the tasks at hand. By contrast, Apple creates "life-feels-good" experiences.

> Under its premium pricing strategy, Apple sets its prices above those of even its highest-priced competitors. Yet Apple's sales remain hot and its profits even hotter.

Ask Apple users and they'll tell you that their Apple devices simply work better and are easier to use. And they love Apple's clean, simple designs that ooze style.

Apple's obsession with deepening the user experience shows up in everything the company does. From the beginning, Apple has been an innovative leader, churning out one cutting-edge product after another. Making products customers want—usually before consumers themselves even know what they want—has resulted in one Apple-led revolution after another. Apple has always had a genius for wrapping technology beautifully around human needs in a way that puts its customers at the front of the crowd.

In turn, Apple has built a huge corps of avid Apple enthusiasts. For nearly four decades, customers have anointed Apple as the undisputed keeper of all things cool. When you buy an Apple product, you join a whole community of fervent fellow believers. Say the word *Apple* in front of hard-core fans, and they'll go into raptures about the superiority of the brand. Such enthusiasm and support creates demand for Apple products beyond the limits of price. Not only are Apple fans willing to pay more, they believe deep down that the value they receive is well worth the higher price.

One of the best illustrations of Apple's premium pricing power is the Apple Watch. Apple was hardly a pioneer in introducing its smartwatch. Dozens of companies were already selling wearables across a broad range of price points. In the year prior to the launch of the Apple Watch, competitors sold 6.8 million smartwatches at an average price of $189. Apple unveiled its own smartwatch in three versions. The least expensive version, the basic Apple Watch Sport, sold for $349, nearly twice the average industry price. At the other extreme was the ultra-premium Apple Watch Edition, made of solid 18-karat gold with sapphire crystal glass. Fully loaded, it sold for as much as $17,000. Such high prices did anything but scare away buyers. By one estimate, Apple will sell an estimated 21 million Apple Watches a year and now holds a 74 percent share of the greatly expanded smartwatch market.

Apple earns the premium prices it charges. Avid Apple fans have long anointed the brand as the keeper of all things cool.
Thomas Kurmeier/Getting Images

More broadly, Apple's ability to command higher prices and margins has produced stunning sales and profit results. In smartphones, for example, Apple captures an impressive 20 percent share of total global sales. However, it commands an even more impressive 50 percent share of the premium smartphone segment. Most remarkably, thanks to its premium prices, Apple routinely pulls in a lion's share of industry profits. For instance, in one recent quarter, it grabbed a dazzling 92 percent of the total smartphone profits made by the world's top eight smartphone makers. Similarly, Apple captures nearly 50 percent of the profits in the competitively crowded personal computer market.

Overall, in just the past four years, Apple's sales have more than doubled to a record $234 billion, placing the company at number five on the list of Fortune 500 companies, ahead of traditional industrial giants such as GM and GE. Brand tracker Interbrand recently rated Apple as the world's most valuable brand. And the company's soaring stock prices have made Apple one of the world's two most valuable companies, neck and neck with Google parent Alphabet.

Even with all this success, however, Apple's premium pricing strategy does present some risks. For example, in some markets—especially the world's rapidly growing emerging markets—Apple's high prices make it vulnerable to low-price competitors. Consider China, which accounts for a full one-third of all smartphone sales worldwide. In China, Apple now places third in market share behind fast-growing, low-priced local competitors such Xiaomi and Huawei.

Chinese market leader Xiaomi has come from nowhere in just the past three years to become the world's third-largest smartphone producer behind only Apple and Samsung. It produces low-cost smartphones, laptops, and other devices that are modeled closely after Apple devices. It even has a thriving iTunes clone that supplies apps, games, and other content. Xiaomi packs potent technology and stunning design into dirt-cheap phones that sell at a fraction of Apple's prices. For instance, an entry-level iPhone sells in China for $833—that's more than a month's wages for the average Chinese buyer. By contrast, the average Xiaomi smartphone goes for only $149.

With its smart design and low, low prices, Xiaomi is targeting the "technically inclined, geeky, typically younger sort of customer who can't afford a top-of-the-line Apple or Samsung phone," says one tech blogger. Such consumers make up the fastest-rising tech segment not just in China but also in other emerging markets such as India and Brazil. And so far, Apple neither has—nor intends to have—an affordable answer for that type of consumer. Low-end products simply don't fit Apple's operating style or premium positioning.

However, Apple is still thriving in China and other emerging economies by catering to the also-burgeoning numbers of more-affluent consumers in those markets who want and can afford the luxury and status associated with Apple. Just like anywhere else, if you can afford it, an Apple device is well worth the premium price. In China, according to one analyst, "It's a price people have been willing to pay, specifically because it is expensive." For instance, remember that exorbitantly priced Apple Watch Edition? It sold out in China in less than an hour.

Thus, whether here or abroad, Apple's premium pricing strategy will likely remain a winner. "The dominance of Apple is something that is very hard to overcome," says an industry executive. "Apple has to stumble somehow or another, and I don't think that's going to happen." The lesson is simple: Truly premium products earn premium prices.[1]

OBJECTIVES OUTLINE

OBJECTIVE 11-1	Describe the major strategies for pricing new products. New Product Pricing Strategies *(pp 308–309)*
OBJECTIVE 11-2	Explain how companies find a set of prices that maximizes the profits from the total product mix. Product Mix Pricing Strategies *(pp 309–311)*
OBJECTIVE 11-3	Discuss how companies adjust their prices to take into account different types of customers and situations. Price Adjustment Strategies *(pp 311–319)*
OBJECTIVE 11-4	Discuss the key issues related to initiating and responding to price changes. Price Changes *(pp 320–322)*
OBJECTIVE 11-5	Overview the social and legal issues that affect pricing decisions. Public Policy and Pricing *(pp 322–326)*

AS THE APPLE STORY suggests, and as we learned in the previous chapter, pricing decisions are subject to a complex array of company, environmental, and competitive forces. To make things even more complex, a company does not set a single price but rather a *pricing structure* that covers different items in its line. This pricing structure changes over time as products move through their life cycles. The company adjusts its prices to reflect changes in costs and demand and to account for variations in buyers and situations. As the competitive environment changes, the company considers when to initiate price changes and when to respond to them.

This chapter examines additional pricing approaches used in special pricing situations or to adjust prices to meet changing situations. We look in turn at *new product pricing* for products in the introductory stage of the product life cycle, *product mix pricing* for related products in the product mix, *price adjustment tactics* that account for customer differences and changing situations, and strategies for initiating and responding to *price changes*.

> **Author Comment** | Pricing new products can be especially challenging. Just think about all the things you'd need to consider in pricing a new smartphone, say, the first Apple iPhone. Even more, you need to start thinking about the price—along with many other marketing considerations—at the very beginning of the design process.

New Product Pricing Strategies

Pricing strategies usually change as the product passes through its life cycle. The introductory stage is especially challenging. Companies bringing out a new product face the challenge of setting prices for the first time. They can choose between two broad strategies: *market-skimming pricing* and *market-penetration pricing*.

Market-Skimming Pricing

Market-skimming pricing (price skimming)

Setting a high price for a new product to skim maximum revenues layer by layer from the segments willing to pay the high price; the company makes fewer but more profitable sales.

Many companies that invent new products set high initial prices to *skim* revenues layer by layer from the market. Apple frequently uses this strategy, called **market-skimming pricing** (or **price skimming**). With each new generation of Apple iPhone, iPad, or Mac computer, new models start at a high price then work their way down as newer models are introduced. In this way, Apple skims the maximum amount of revenue from the various segments of the market. For example, through smart premium pricing, Apple vacuums up as much as 92 percent of all smartphone profits.[2]

Market skimming makes sense only under certain conditions. First, the product's quality and image must support its higher price, and enough buyers must want the product at that price. Second, the costs of producing a smaller volume cannot be so high that they cancel the advantage of charging more. Finally, competitors should not be able to enter the market easily and undercut the high price.

Market-Penetration Pricing

Rather than setting a high initial price to skim off small but profitable market segments, some companies use **market-penetration pricing**. Companies set a low initial price to *penetrate* the market quickly and deeply—to attract a large number of buyers quickly and win a large market share. The high sales volume results in falling costs, allowing companies to cut their prices even further. For example, AGIT Global used penetration pricing to quickly build demand for its Wavestorm surf boards:[3]

● **Penetration pricing: An entry-level, 8-foot, blue-and-white Wavestorm surfboard at Costco sells for only $99.99.**
AGIT Global North America

> Before Wavestorm, surfers and would-be surfers typically bought custom-made or high-end surfboards at local surf shops, where entry-level boards typically run $300 to $1,000. AGIT Global had a different idea. With a mission to make surfing more accessible for both adults and children, it began 10 years ago mass-producing good quality soft-foam surfboards and selling them through big-box stores at penetration prices. ● For example, it sells an entry-level, 8-foot, blue-and-white Wavestorm board at Costco for only $99.99. Thanks to penetration pricing, Wavestorm is now the market leader, selling an estimated five times more boards than the other largest surfboard brands. The inexpensive boards have even become favorites of advanced surfers, who buy them for their friends or children. "Margins are slim at Costco," says Matt Zilinskas, AGIT's vice president of sales. "But we pump out volume and get paid on time."

Market-penetration pricing
Setting a low price for a new product in order to attract a large number of buyers and a large market share.

Several conditions must be met for this low-price strategy to work. First, the market must be highly price sensitive so that a low price produces more market growth. Second, production and distribution costs must decrease as sales volume increases. Finally, the low price must help keep out the competition, and the penetration pricer must maintain its low-price position. Otherwise, the price advantage may be only temporary.

Author Comment | Most individual products are part of a broader product mix and must be priced accordingly. For example, Gillette prices its Fusion razors low. But once you buy the razor, you're a captive customer for its higher-margin replacement cartridges.

Product Mix Pricing Strategies

The strategy for setting a product's price often has to be changed when the product is part of a product mix. In this case, the firm looks for a set of prices that maximizes its profits on the total product mix. Pricing is difficult because the various products have related demand and costs and face different degrees of competition. We now take a closer look at the five product mix pricing situations summarized in ● **Table 11.1**: *product line pricing*, *optional-product pricing*, *captive-product pricing*, *by-product pricing*, and *product bundle pricing*.

● **Table 11.1** | **Product Mix Pricing**

Pricing Situation	Description
Product line pricing	Setting prices across an entire product line
Optional-product pricing	Pricing optional or accessory products sold with the main product
Captive-product pricing	Pricing products that must be used with the main product
By-product pricing	Pricing low-value by-products to get rid of or make money on them
Product bundle pricing	Pricing bundles of products sold together

Product Line Pricing

Product line pricing

Setting the price steps between various products in a product line based on cost differences between the products, customer evaluations of different features, and competitors' prices.

Companies usually develop product lines rather than single products. In **product line pricing**, management must determine the price steps to set between the various products in a line. The price steps should take into account cost differences between products in the line. More important, they should account for differences in customer perceptions of the value of different features.

For example, Quicken offers an entire line of financial management software, including Starter, Deluxe, Premier, Home & Business, and Rental Property Manager versions priced at $29.99, $64.99, $94.99, $104.99, and $154.99, respectively. Although it costs Quicken no more to produce the Premier version than the Starter version, many buyers happily pay more to obtain additional Premier features, such as financial-planning, retirement, and investment-monitoring tools. Quicken's task is to establish perceived value differences that support the price differences.

Optional-Product Pricing

Optional-product pricing

The pricing of optional or accessory products along with a main product.

Many companies use **optional-product pricing**—pricing optional or accessory products along with the main product. For example, a car buyer may choose to order a navigation system and premium entertainment system. Refrigerators come with optional ice makers. And when you order a new laptop, you can select from a bewildering array of processors, hard drives, docking systems, software options, and service plans. Pricing these options is a sticky problem. Companies must decide which items to include in the base price and which to offer as options.

Captive-Product Pricing

Captive-product pricing

Setting a price for products that must be used along with a main product, such as blades for a razor and games for a video-game console.

Companies that make products that must be used along with a main product are using **captive-product pricing**. Examples of captive products are razor blade cartridges, video games, printer cartridges, single-serve coffee pods, and e-books. Producers of the main products (razors, video-game consoles, printers, single-cup coffee brewing systems, and tablet computers) often price them low and set high markups on the supplies. ● For example, Amazon makes little or no profit on its Kindle readers and tablets. It hopes to more than make up for thin margins through sales of digital books, music, movies, subscription services, and other content for the devices. "We want to make money when people use our devices, not when they buy our devices," declares Amazon CEO Jeff Bezos.[4]

● Captive-product pricing: Amazon makes little profit on its Kindle readers and tablets but makes up for the close-to-cost prices through sales of content for the devices.

Future Publishing/Getty Images

Captive products can account for a substantial portion of a brand's sales and profits. For example, only a relatively small percentage of Keurig's revenues come from the sale of its single-cup brewing systems. The bulk of the brand's revenues—nearly 77 percent—comes from captive sales of its K-Cup portion packs.[5] However, companies that use captive-product pricing must be careful. Finding the right balance between the main-product and captive-product prices can be tricky. Even more, consumers trapped into buying expensive captive products may come to resent the brand that ensnared them.

For example, some customers of single-cup coffee brewing systems may cringe at what they must pay for those handy little coffee portion packs. Although they might seem like a bargain when compared on a cost-per-cup basis versus Starbucks, the pods' prices can seem like highway robbery when broken down by the pound. One investigator calculated the cost of pod coffee at a shocking $50 per pound.[6] At those prices, you'd be better off cost-wise brewing a big pot of premium coffee and pouring out the unused portion. For many buyers, the convenience and selection offered by single-cup brewing systems outweigh the extra costs. However, such captive-product costs might make others avoid buying the device in the first place or cause discomfort during use after purchase.

In the case of services, captive-product pricing is called *two-part pricing*. The price of the service is broken into a *fixed fee* plus a *variable usage rate*. Thus, at Six Flags and other amusement parks, you pay a daily ticket or season pass charge plus additional fees for food and other in-park features.

By-Product Pricing

By-product pricing

Setting a price for by-products to help offset the costs of disposing of them and help make the main product's price more competitive.

Producing products and services often generates by-products. If the by-products have no value and if getting rid of them is costly, this will affect the pricing of the main product. Using **by-product pricing**, the company seeks a market for these by-products to help offset the costs of disposing of them and help make the price of the main product more competitive.

The by-products themselves can even turn out to be profitable—turning trash into cash. For example, cheese makers in Wisconsin have discovered a use for their leftover brine, a salt solution used in the cheese-making process. Instead of paying to have it disposed of, they now sell it to local city and county highway departments, which use it in conjunction with salt to melt icy roads. It doesn't stop there. In New Jersey, pickle makers sell their leftover brine for similar uses. In Tennessee, distilleries sell off potato juice, a by-product of vodka distillation. And on many highways across the nation, highway crews use a product called Beet Heet, which is made from—you guessed it—beet juice brine by-products. The only side effect of these brine solutions is a slight odor. Says one highway department official about cheese brine, "If you were behind a snow plow, you'd immediately smell it."[7]

Product Bundle Pricing

Product bundle pricing

Combining several products and offering the bundle at a reduced price.

Using **product bundle pricing**, sellers often combine several products and offer the bundle at a reduced price. For example, fast-food restaurants bundle a burger, fries, and a soft drink at a "combo" price. Microsoft Office is sold as a bundle of computer software, including Word, Excel, PowerPoint, and Outlook. And Comcast, AT&T, Verizon, and other telecommunications companies bundle TV service, phone service, and high-speed internet connections at a low combined price. Price bundling can promote the sales of products consumers might not otherwise buy, but the combined price must be low enough to get them to buy the bundle.

Author | Comment | Setting the base price for a product is only the start. The company must then adjust the price to account for customer and situational differences. When was the last time you paid the full suggested retail price for something?

Price Adjustment Strategies

Companies usually adjust their basic prices to account for various customer differences and changing situations. Here we examine the seven price adjustment strategies summarized in ● Table 11.2: *discount and allowance pricing, segmented pricing, psychological pricing, promotional pricing, geographical pricing, dynamic pricing,* and *international pricing.*

Discount and Allowance Pricing

Discount

A straight reduction in price on purchases during a stated period of time or of larger quantities.

Most companies adjust their basic price to reward customers for certain responses, such as paying bills early, volume purchases, and off-season buying. These price adjustments—called *discounts* and *allowances*—can take many forms.

One form of **discount** is a *cash discount*, a price reduction to buyers who pay their bills promptly. A typical example is "2/10, net 30," which means that although payment is due within 30 days, the buyer can deduct 2 percent if the bill is paid within 10 days. A *quantity discount* is a price reduction to buyers who buy large volumes. A seller offers a *functional discount* (also called a *trade discount*) to trade-channel members who perform certain functions, such as selling, storing, and record keeping. A *seasonal discount* is a price reduction to buyers who buy merchandise or services out of season.

● **Table 11.2** | **Price Adjustments**

Strategy	Description
Discount and allowance pricing	Reducing prices to reward customer responses such as volume purchases, paying early, or promoting the product
Segmented pricing	Adjusting prices to allow for differences in customers, products, or locations
Psychological pricing	Adjusting prices for psychological effect
Promotional pricing	Temporarily reducing prices to spur short-run sales
Geographical pricing	Adjusting prices to account for the geographic location of customers
Dynamic pricing	Adjusting prices continually to meet the characteristics and needs of individual customers and situations
International pricing	Adjusting prices for international markets

Allowance

Promotional money paid by manufacturers to retailers in return for an agreement to feature the manufacturer's products in some way.

Allowances are another type of reduction from the list price. For example, *trade-in allowances* are price reductions given for turning in an old item when buying a new one. Trade-in allowances are most common in the automobile industry, but they are also given for other durable goods. *Promotional allowances* are payments or price reductions that reward dealers for participating in advertising and sales-support programs.

Segmented Pricing

Segmented pricing

Selling a product or service at two or more prices, where the difference in prices is not based on differences in costs.

Companies will often adjust their basic prices to allow for differences in customers, products, and locations. In **segmented pricing**, the company sells a product or service at two or more prices, even though the difference in prices is not based on differences in costs.

Segmented pricing takes several forms. Under *customer-segment pricing*, different customers pay different prices for the same product or service. For example, museums, movie theaters, and retail stores may charge lower prices for students and senior citizens. Kohl's offers a 15 percent discount every Wednesday to "customers aged 60 or better." ● And Walgreens holds periodic Senior Discount Day events, offering 20 percent price reductions to AARP members and to its Balance Rewards members age 55 and over. "Grab Granny and go shopping!" advises one Walgreens ad.

Under *product form pricing*, different versions of the product are priced differently but not according to differences in their costs. For instance, a round-trip economy seat on a flight from New York to London might cost $1,100, whereas a business-class seat on the same flight might cost $3,400 or more. Although business-class customers receive roomier, more comfortable seats and higher-quality food and service, the differences in costs to the airlines are much less than the additional prices to passengers. However, to passengers who can afford it, the additional comfort and services are worth the extra charge.

Using *location-based pricing*, a company charges different prices for different locations, even though the cost of offering each location is the same. For instance, state universities charge higher tuition for out-of-state students, and theaters vary their seat prices because of audience preferences for certain locations. Finally, using *time-based pricing*, a firm varies its price by the season, the month, the day, and even the hour. For example, movie theaters charge matinee pricing during the daytime, and resorts give weekend and seasonal discounts.

For segmented pricing to be an effective strategy, certain conditions must exist. The market must be segmentable, and segments must show different degrees of demand. The costs of segmenting and reaching the market cannot exceed the extra revenue obtained from the price difference. Of course, the segmented pricing must also be legal.

● **Customer-segment pricing:** Walgreens holds regular Senior Discount Day events, offering 20 percent price reductions to AARP members and to its Balance Rewards members age 55 and over.

Walgreen Co.

Most important, segmented prices should reflect real differences in customers' perceived value. Consumers in higher price tiers must feel that they're getting their extra money's worth for the higher prices paid. Otherwise, segmented pricing practices can cause consumer resentment. For example, buyers reacted negatively when a New York City Department of Consumer Affairs investigation found that women often pay more for female versions of products that are virtually identical to male versions except for gender-specific packaging:[8]

The DCA compared the prices of male and female versions for nearly 800 products—including children's toys and clothing, adult apparel, personal care products, and home goods. It found that items marketed to girls and women cost an average of 7 percent more than similar items aimed at boys and men. In the hair care category, women paid 48 percent more for products such shampoo, conditioner, and gel; razor cartridges cost women 11 percent more. For example, a major drug store chain sold a blue box of Schick Hydro 5 razor cartridges for $14.99; virtually identical cartridges for the Schick Hydro "Silk," a purple-boxed sister brand, sold for $18.49. In another case, Target sold red Radio Flyer scooters for boys at $24.99; the same scooter in pink for girls was priced at $49.99. Target lowered its price for the pink scooter after the DCA report was released, calling the price mismatch a "system error." Although no laws prohibit gender-based pricing differences, such glaring disparities can damage a brand's credibility and reputation.

Companies must also be careful not to treat customers in lower price tiers as second-class citizens. Otherwise, in the long run, the practice will lead to customer resentment and ill will. For example, in recent years, the airlines have incurred the wrath of frustrated customers at both ends of the airplane. Passengers paying full fare for business- or first-class seats often feel that they are being gouged. At the same time, passengers in lower-priced coach seats feel that they're being ignored or treated poorly.

Psychological Pricing

Price says something about the product. For example, many consumers use price to judge quality. A $100 bottle of perfume may contain only $3 worth of scent, but some people are willing to pay the $100 because this price indicates something special.

In using **psychological pricing**, sellers consider the psychology of prices, not simply the economics. For example, consumers usually perceive higher-priced products as having higher quality. When they can judge the quality of a product by examining it or by calling on past experience with it, they use price less to judge quality. But when they cannot judge quality because they lack the information or skill, price becomes an important quality signal. For instance, who's the better lawyer, one who charges $50 per hour or one who charges $500 per hour? You'd have to do a lot of digging into the respective lawyers' credentials to answer this question objectively; even then, you might not be able to judge accurately. Most of us would simply assume that the higher-priced lawyer is better.

Another aspect of psychological pricing is **reference prices**—prices that buyers carry in their minds and refer to when looking at a given product. The reference price might be formed by noting current prices, remembering past prices, or assessing the buying situation. Sellers can influence or use these consumers' reference prices when setting price. For example, a grocery retailer might place its store brand of bran flakes and raisins cereal priced at $2.49 next to Kellogg's Raisin Bran priced at $3.79. Or a company might offer more expensive models that don't sell very well to make its less expensive but still-high-priced models look more affordable by comparison. For example, Williams-Sonoma once offered a fancy bread maker at the steep price of $279. However, it then added a $429 model. The expensive model flopped, but sales of the cheaper model doubled.[9]

For most purchases, consumers don't have all the skill or information they need to figure out whether they are paying a good price. They don't have the time, ability, or inclination to research different brands or stores, compare prices, and get the best deals. Instead, they may rely on certain cues that signal whether a price is high or low. Interestingly, such pricing cues are often provided by sellers, in the form of sales signs, price-matching guarantees, loss-leader pricing, and other helpful hints.

● **Psychological pricing: What do the prices marked on this tag suggest about the product and buying situation?**

© Tetra Images/Alamy

Promotional pricing
Temporarily pricing products below the list price, and sometimes even below cost, to increase short-run sales.

● Even small differences in price can signal product differences. A 9 or 0.99 at the end of a price often signals a bargain. You see such prices everywhere. For example, browse the online sites of top discounters such as Target, Best Buy, or Overstock.com, where almost every price ends in 9. In contrast, high-end retailers might favor prices ending in a whole number (for example, $6, $25, or $200). Others use 00-cent endings on regularly priced items and 99-cent endings on discount merchandise.

Although actual price differences might be small, the impact of such psychological tactics can be big. For example, in one study, people were asked how likely they were to choose among LASIK eye surgery providers based only on the prices they charged: $299 or $300. The actual price difference was only $1, but the study found that the psychological difference was much greater. Preference ratings for the providers charging $300 were much higher. Subjects perceived the $299 price as significantly less, but the lower price also raised stronger concerns about quality and risk. Some psychologists even argue that each digit has symbolic and visual qualities that should be considered in pricing. Thus, eight (8) is round and even and creates a soothing effect, whereas seven (7) is angular and creates a jarring effect.[10]

Promotional Pricing

With **promotional pricing**, companies will temporarily price their products below list price—and sometimes even below cost—to create buying excitement and urgency. Promotional pricing takes several forms. A seller may simply offer *discounts* from normal prices to increase sales and reduce inventories. Sellers also use *special-event pricing* in certain seasons to draw more customers. Thus, TVs and other consumer electronics are promotionally priced in November and December to attract holiday shoppers into the stores. *Limited-time offers*, such as online *flash sales*, can create buying urgency and make buyers feel lucky to have gotten in on the deal.

Manufacturers sometimes offer *cash rebates* to consumers who buy the product from dealers within a specified time; the manufacturer sends the rebate directly to the customer. Rebates have been popular with automakers and producers of mobile phones and small appliances, but they are also used with consumer packaged goods. Some manufacturers offer *low-interest financing, longer warranties*, or *free maintenance* to reduce the consumer's "price." This practice has become another favorite of the auto industry.

Promotional pricing can help move customers over humps in the buying decision process. ● For example, to encourage consumers to convert to its Windows 10 operating system, Microsoft ran an Easy Trade-Up promotion offering buyers $200 trade-ins on their old devices when purchasing new Windows 10 PCs costing $599 or more at the Microsoft Store. It sweetened the deal to $300 for trade-ins of Apple MacBooks or iMacs. In the past, Microsoft has offered customers up to $650 toward the purchase of a Surface Pro when they trade in a MacBook Air. Such aggressive price promotions can provide powerful buying and switching incentives.

Promotional pricing, however, can have adverse effects. During most holiday seasons, for example, it's an all-out bargain war. Marketers carpet-bomb consumers with deals, causing buyer wear-out and pricing confusion. Constantly reduced prices can erode a brand's value in the eyes of customers. And used too frequently, price promotions can create "deal-prone" customers who wait until brands go on sale before buying them. For example, ask most

● **Promotional pricing: To encourage conversions to its Windows 10 operating system, Microsoft ran an Easy Trade-Up promotion offering buyers $200 to $300 trade-ins on their old devices when purchasing new Windows 10 PCs. Such aggressive price promotions can provide powerful buying incentives.**

Microsoft

regular shoppers at home goods retailer Bed Bath & Beyond, and they'll likely tell you that they never shop there without a stack of 20-percent-off or 5-dollar-off coupons in hand. As one reporter put it: "Shopping with a coupon at Bed Bath & Beyond has begun to feel like a given instead of like a special treat, and that's bad news for the chain's bottom line." In fact, greater recent coupon redemption rates have increasingly eaten into the retailer's profit margins.[11]

Geographical Pricing

Geographical pricing

Setting prices for customers located in different parts of the country or world.

A company also must decide how to price its products for customers located in different parts of the United States or the world. Should the company risk losing the business of more-distant customers by charging them higher prices to cover the higher shipping costs? Or should the company charge all customers the same prices regardless of location? We will look at five **geographical pricing** strategies for the following hypothetical situation:

> The Peerless Paper Company is located in Atlanta, Georgia, and sells paper products to customers all over the United States. The cost of freight is high and affects the companies from which customers buy their paper. Peerless wants to establish a geographical pricing policy. It is trying to determine how to price a $10,000 order to three specific customers: Customer A (Atlanta), Customer B (Bloomington, Indiana), and Customer C (Compton, California).

FOB-origin pricing

Pricing in which goods are placed free on board a carrier; the customer pays the freight from the factory to the destination.

One option is for Peerless to ask each customer to pay the shipping cost from the Atlanta factory to the customer's location. All three customers would pay the same factory price of $10,000, with Customer A paying, say, $100 for shipping; Customer B, $150; and Customer C, $250. Called **FOB-origin pricing**, this practice means that the goods are placed *free on board* (hence, *FOB*) a carrier. At that point, the title and responsibility pass to the customer, who pays the freight from the factory to the destination. Because each customer picks up its own cost, supporters of FOB pricing feel that this is the fairest way to assess freight charges. The disadvantage, however, is that Peerless will be a high-cost firm to distant customers.

Uniform-delivered pricing

Pricing in which the company charges the same price plus freight to all customers, regardless of their location.

Uniform-delivered pricing is the opposite of FOB pricing. Here, the company charges the same price plus freight to all customers, regardless of their location. The freight charge is set at the average freight cost. Suppose this is $150. Uniform-delivered pricing therefore results in a higher charge to the Atlanta customer (who pays $150 freight instead of $100) and a lower charge to the Compton customer (who pays $150 instead of $250). Although the Atlanta customer would prefer to buy paper from another local paper company that uses FOB-origin pricing, Peerless has a better chance of capturing the California customer.

Zone pricing

Pricing in which the company sets up two or more zones. All customers within a zone pay the same total price; the more distant the zone, the higher the price.

Zone pricing falls between FOB-origin pricing and uniform-delivered pricing. The company sets up two or more zones. All customers within a given zone pay a single total price; the more distant the zone, the higher the price. For example, Peerless might set up an East Zone and charge $100 freight to all customers in this zone, a Midwest Zone in which it charges $150, and a West Zone in which it charges $250. In this way, the customers within a given price zone receive no price advantage from the company. For example, customers in Atlanta and Boston pay the same total price to Peerless. The complaint, however, is that the Atlanta customer is paying part of the Boston customer's freight cost.

Basing-point pricing

Pricing in which the seller designates some city as a basing point and charges all customers the freight cost from that city to the customer.

Using **basing-point pricing**, the seller selects a given city as a "basing point" and charges all customers the freight cost from that city to the customer location, regardless of the city from which the goods are actually shipped. For example, Peerless might set Chicago as the basing point and charge all customers $10,000 plus the freight from Chicago to their locations. This means that an Atlanta customer pays the freight cost from Chicago to Atlanta, even though the goods may be shipped from Atlanta. If all sellers used the same basing-point city, delivered prices would be the same for all customers, and price competition would be eliminated.

Freight-absorption pricing

Pricing in which the seller absorbs all or part of the freight charges in order to get the desired business.

Finally, the seller who is anxious to do business with a certain customer or geographical area might use **freight-absorption pricing**. Using this strategy, the seller absorbs all or part of the actual freight charges to get the desired business. The seller might reason that if it can get more business, its average costs will decrease and more than compensate for its extra freight cost. Freight-absorption pricing is used for market penetration and to hold on to increasingly competitive markets.

Dynamic and Online Pricing

Dynamic pricing

Adjusting prices continually to meet the characteristics and needs of individual customers and situations.

Throughout most of history, prices were set by negotiation between buyers and sellers. A *fixed-price* policy—setting one price for all buyers—is a relatively modern idea that arose with the development of large-scale retailing at the end of the nineteenth century. Today, most prices are set this way. However, many companies are now reversing the fixed-pricing trend. They are using **dynamic pricing**—adjusting prices continually to meet the characteristics and needs of individual customers and situations.

Dynamic pricing offers many advantages for marketers. For example, online sellers such as Amazon, L.L.Bean, or Apple can mine their databases to gauge a specific shopper's desires, measure his or her means, check out competitors' prices, and instantaneously tailor offers to fit that shopper's situation and behavior, pricing products accordingly.

Services ranging from retailers, airlines, and hotels to sports teams change prices on the fly according to changes in demand, costs, or competitor pricing, adjusting what they charge for specific items on a daily, hourly, or even continuous basis. Done well, dynamic pricing can help sellers to optimize sales and serve customers better. However, done poorly, it can trigger margin-eroding price wars and damage customer relationships and trust. Companies must be careful not to cross the fine line between smart dynamic pricing strategies and damaging ones (see Real Marketing 11.1).

In the extreme, some companies customize their offers and prices based on the specific characteristics and behaviors of individual customers, mined from online browsing and purchasing histories. These days, online offers and prices might well be based on what specific customers search for and buy, how much they pay for other purchases, and whether they might be willing and able to spend more. For example, a consumer who recently went online to purchase a first-class ticket to Paris or customize a new Mercedes coupe might later get a higher quote on a new Bose Wave Radio. By comparison, a friend with a more modest online search and purchase history might receive an offer of 5 percent off and free shipping on the same radio.[12]

Dynamic pricing doesn't happen only online. For example, many store retailers and other organizations now adjust prices by the day, hour, or even minute. For example, Kohl's uses electronic price tags in its stores to adjust prices instantly based on supply, demand, and store traffic factors. It can now stage sales that last only hours instead of days, much as its online competitors do. Ride-sharing services such as Uber and Lyft adjust their fares dynamically during slow or peak times, a practice called "surge pricing." Similarly, supply and demand dictates minute-to-minute price adjustments these days for everything from theater tickets to parking spots and golf course greens fees. One Dallas highway even shifts toll prices every five minutes depending on traffic—the fare for one 7-mile stretch, for example, ranged between 90 cents and $4.50 in one week.[13]

Although such dynamic pricing practices seem legally questionable, they're not. Dynamic pricing is legal as long as companies do not discriminate based on age, gender, location, or other similar characteristics. Dynamic pricing makes sense in many contexts—it adjusts prices according to market forces and consumer preferences. But marketers need to be careful not to use dynamic pricing to take advantage of customers, thereby damaging important customer relationships. Customers may resent what they see as unfair pricing practices or price gouging. For example, consumers reacted badly to reports that Coca-Cola was proposing smart vending machines that would adjust prices depending on outside temperatures. And an Amazon.com dynamic pricing experiment that varied prices by purchase occasion received highly unfavorable headlines.

Just as dynamic and online pricing benefit sellers, however, they also benefit consumers. For example, thanks to the internet, consumers can now get instant product and price comparisons from thousands of vendors at price comparison sites or using mobile apps such as ShopSavvy, Amazon's Price Check, or eBay's RedLaser. For example, the RedLaser mobile app lets customers scan barcodes (or search by voice or image) while shopping in stores. It then searches online and at nearby stores to provide thousands of reviews and comparison prices and even offers buying links for immediate online purchasing.

Such information puts pricing power into the hands of consumers. Alert shoppers take advantage of the constant price skirmishes among sellers, snapping up good deals or leveraging retailer price-matching policies. In fact, many retailers are finding that ready online access to comparison prices is giving consumers *too* much of an edge. Most store retailers

11.1 Dynamic Pricing: The Wonders and Woes of Real-Time Price Adjustments

These days, it seems every seller knows what prices competitors are charging—for anything and everything it sells, minute by minute, and down to the penny. What's more, today's technologies give sellers the flexibility to adjust their own prices on the fly. This often results in some pretty zany pricing dynamics.

For example, during a recent Black Friday weekend, the prices charged for the latest version of one Xbox game experienced some head-spinning dips and dives. The day before Thanksgiving, Amazon marked the game down to $49.96, matching Walmart's price and beating Target's price by three cents. On Thanksgiving Day, Amazon slashed that price in half to just $24.99, matching Best Buy's Thanksgiving Day special. Walmart responded quickly with a rock-bottom price of $15, which Amazon matched immediately. "What kind of pricing lunacy is this?" you ask. Welcome to the wonders and woes of dynamic pricing.

On the plus side, dynamic pricing can help sellers optimize sales and serve customers better by aligning prices with market conditions. For example, airlines routinely use dynamic pricing to constantly adjust fares for specific flights, depending on competitor pricing and anticipated seat availability. As any frequent flyer knows, if you call now to book a seat on a flight to sunny Florida next week, you'll get one price. Try again an hour later and you'll get a different price—maybe higher, maybe lower. Book the same seat a month in advance, and you'll probably pay a lot less.

Dynamic pricing doesn't just happen in the fast-shifting online environment. For example, discount department store Kohl's has replaced static price tags with digital ones. These digital tags can be centrally controlled to change prices dynamically on individual items within a given store or across the entire chain. The technology lets Kohl's apply internet-style dynamic pricing, changing prices by the hour or minute as conditions dictate without the time and costs of changing physical tags.

Beyond using dynamic pricing to match competitors, many sellers use it to adjust prices based on customer characteristics or buying situations. In this age of big data,

sellers can often vary prices they charge different customers based on customer purchase histories or personal data. For example, some online companies offer special discounts to customers with more items in their shopping carts. Others reportedly set higher prices for consumers living in more affluent neighborhoods. And one online travel agent was even reported to charge Mac and iPad users more because Apple fans have higher average household incomes.

Most consumers are surprised to learn that it's perfectly legal under most circumstances to charge different prices to different customers based on their buying behaviors. In fact, one survey found that two-thirds of online shoppers thought the practice was illegal. When they learned that it was not illegal, nearly nine out of ten thought it should be.

Legal or not, dynamic pricing doesn't always sit well with customers. Done poorly, it can cause customer confusion, frustration, or even resentment, damaging hard-won customer relationships. For example, when the fatal derailment of Amtrak Train 188 shut down rail service on the heavily traveled Washington, DC–to–New York City line for nearly a week, demand for airline tickets between the two cities jumped dramatically. As demand surged, the airlines' dynamic pricing bots kicked in to coldly raise fares by as much as five times, infuriating travelers and leading to a Department of Transportation investigation.

More often, however, poorly executed dynamic pricing simply causes shopper confusion or disgruntlement. For example, according to one source, Amazon's automated dynamic pricing system changes the price on as many as 80 million items on its site throughout a given day, based on a host of marketplace factors. Consider this Amazon shopper's experience:

Nancy Plumlee had just taken up mahjong, a Chinese game of tiles similar to rummy. She browsed Amazon.com and,

after sifting through several pages of options, settled on a set for $54.99. She placed it in her [shopping cart] and continued shopping for some scorecards and game accessories. A few minutes later, she scanned the cart and noticed the $54.99 had jumped to $70.99. Plumlee thought she was going crazy. She checked her computer's viewing history and, indeed, the game's original price was listed at $54.99. Determined, she cleared out the cart and tried again. [This time,] the game's price jumped from $54.99 to $59.99. "That just doesn't feel like straight-up business honesty. Shame on Amazon," said Plumlee, who called [Amazon] and persuaded the online retailer to refund her $5.

It is sometimes difficult to locate the fine line between a smart dynamic pricing strategy and one that crosses the line, doing more damage to customer relationships than good to the company's bottom line. Consider Uber, the car-sharing and dispatch service that lets customers summon taxis, cars, or other transportation using the company's phone app:

Uber uses a form of dynamic pricing called "surge pricing." Under normal circumstances, Uber customers pay reasonable fares. However, using Uber in periods of surging demand can result in shocking price escalations. For example, on one recent stormy,

Dynamic pricing: Amazon's automated dynamic pricing system reportedly changes the price on as many as 80 million items on its site in a given day based on a host of marketplace factors.

© webpics/Alamy

holiday-Saturday night in Manhattan, Uber charged—and got—fares that were more than eight times the usual. Although Uber's app warned customers of heightened fares before processing their requests, many customers were outraged. One customer shared an Instagram photo of a taxi receipt for $415. "That is robbery!" tweeted another. However, despite the protests, Uber experienced no subsequent drop in demand in the New York City area. It seems that, to most people who can afford Uber, convenience and prestige are the deciding factors, not price.

Thus, used well, dynamic pricing can help sellers to optimize sales and profits by keeping track of competitor pricing and quickly adjusting to marketplace changes. Used poorly, however, it can trigger margin-eroding price wars and damage customer relationships and trust. Too often, dynamic pricing takes the form of a pricing "arms race" among sellers, putting too much emphasis on prices at the expense of other important customer value–building elements. Pricing—dynamic or otherwise—remains just one part of the buying equation. Companies must be careful to keep pricing in balance with all the other things that matter to customers.

Sources: David Morris, "Are Airline Passengers Getting Ripped Off by Robots?" *Fortune,* August 4, 2015, http://fortune.com/2015/08/04/airline-pricing-algorithms/; David P. Schulz, "Changing Direction," *Stores,* March 2013, p. 30; Laura Gunderson, "Amazon's 'Dynamic' Prices Get Some Static," *The Oregonian,* May 5, 2012, http://blog.oregonlive.com/complaintdesk/2012/05/amazons_dynamic_prices_get_som.html; Jessi Hempel, "Why Surge-Pricing Fiasco Is Great for Uber," *CNNMoney,* December 30, 2013, http://tech.fortune.cnn.com/2013/12/30/why-the-surge-pricing-fiasco-is-great-for-uber/; Greg Petro, "Dynamic Pricing: Which Customers Are Worth the Most?" *Forbes,* April 17, 2015, www.forbes.com/sites/gregpetro/2015/04/17/dynamic-pricing-which-customers-are-worth-the-most-amazon-delta-airlines-and-staples-weigh-in/#5ce4c853b516; and "Flexible Figures," *The Economist,* January 30, 2016, p. 64.

● **Dynamic online pricing benefits both sellers and buyers. Consumers armed with instant access to product and price comparisons can often negotiate better in-store prices.**
© Lev Dolgachov / Alamy

must now devise strategies to deal with the consumer practice of *showrooming*. ● Consumers armed with smartphones now routinely visit stores to see an item, compare prices online while in the store, and then request price matches or simply buy the item online at a lower price. Such behavior is called showrooming because consumers use retailers' stores as de facto "showrooms" for online resellers such as Amazon.com.

Store retailers are now implementing strategies to combat such showrooming and cross-channel shopping or even turn it into an advantage. For example, Best Buy now routinely matches the prices of Amazon and other major online merchants. Once it has neutralized price as a buying factor, Best Buy reasons, it can convert showroomers into in-store buyers with its nonprice advantages, such as immediacy, convenient locations, personal assistance by well-trained associates, and the ability to order goods online and pick up or return them in the store. It has also sharpened its own online and mobile marketing. "Showrooming . . . is not the ideal experience," says a Best Buy marketer, "to do research at home, go to the store, do more research, then…order and hope it arrives on time. There's a better way."[14] We will revisit the subject of showrooming our discussions of retailing in Chapter 13.

International Pricing

Companies that market their products internationally must decide what prices to charge in different countries. In some cases, a company can set a uniform worldwide price. For example, Boeing sells its jetliners at about the same price everywhere, whether the buyer is in the United States, Europe, or a third-world country. However, most companies adjust their prices to reflect local market conditions and cost considerations.

The price that a company should charge in a specific country depends on many factors, including economic conditions, competitive situations, laws and regulations, and the nature of the wholesaling and retailing system. Consumer perceptions and preferences also may vary from country to country, calling for different prices. Or the company may have different marketing objectives in various world markets, which require changes in pricing strategy. For example, Apple uses a premium pricing strategy to introduce sophisticated, feature-rich, premium smartphones in carefully segmented mature markets in developed countries and to affluent consumers in emerging markets. By contrast, it's now under pressure to discount older models and develop cheaper, more basic phone models for sizable but less affluent markets in developing countries, where even discounted older Apple phones sell at prices three to five times those of those of competing low-price models.

Costs play an important role in setting international prices. Travelers abroad are often surprised to find that goods that are relatively inexpensive at home may carry outrageously higher price tags in other countries. A pair of Levi's selling for $30 in the United States might go for $63 in Tokyo and $88 in Paris. A McDonald's Big Mac selling for a modest $4.20 in the United States might cost $7.85 in Norway or $5.65 in Brazil, and an Oral-B toothbrush selling for $2.49 at home may cost $10 in China. Conversely, a Gucci handbag going for only $140 in Milan, Italy, might fetch $240 in the United States.

In some cases, such *price escalation* may result from differences in selling strategies or market conditions. In most instances, however, it is simply a result of the higher costs of selling in another country—the additional costs of operations, product modifications, shipping and insurance, exchange-rate fluctuations, and physical distribution. Import tariffs and taxes can also add to costs. ● For example, China imposes duties as high as 25 percent on imported Western luxury products such as watches, designer dresses, shoes, and leather handbags. It also levies consumption taxes of 30 percent for cosmetics and 20 percent on high-end watches. As a result, Western luxury goods bought in mainland China carry prices as much as 50 percent higher than in Europe.[15]

● International prices: Travelers are often surprised to find that product price tags vary greatly from country to country. For example, thanks to Chinese import tariffs and consumption taxes, Western luxury goods bought in mainland China carry prices as much as 50 percent higher than in Europe.

James McCauley/Harrods via Getty Images

Price has become a key element in the international marketing strategies of companies attempting to enter less affluent emerging markets. Typically, entering such markets has meant targeting the exploding middle classes in developing countries such as China, India, Russia, and Brazil, whose economies have been growing rapidly. More recently, however, as the weakened global economy has slowed growth in both domestic and emerging markets, many companies are shifting their sights to include a new target—the so-called "bottom of the pyramid," the vast untapped market consisting of the world's poorest consumers.

Not long ago, the preferred way for many brands to market their products in developing markets—whether consumer products or cars, computers, and smartphones—was to paste new labels on existing models and sell them at higher prices to the privileged few who could afford them. However, such a pricing approach put many products out of the reach of the tens of millions of poor consumers in emerging markets. As a result, many companies developed smaller, more basic and affordable product versions for these markets. For example, Unilever—the maker of such brands as Dove, Sunsilk, Lipton, and Vaseline—shrunk its packaging and set low prices that even the world's poorest consumers could afford. It developed single-use packages of its shampoo, laundry detergent, face cream, and other products that it could sell profitably for just pennies a pack. As a result, today, 59 percent of Unilever's revenues come from emerging economies.[16]

Although this strategy has been successful for Unilever, most companies are learning that selling profitably to the bottom of the pyramid requires more than just repackaging or stripping down existing products and selling them at low prices. Just like more well-to-do consumers, low-income buyers want products that are both functional *and* aspirational. Thus, companies today are innovating to create products that not only sell at very low prices but also give bottom-of-the-pyramid consumers more for their money, not less.

International pricing presents many special problems and complexities. We discuss international pricing issues in more detail in Chapter 19.

Author | When and how should a
Comment | company change its price?
What if costs rise, putting the squeeze
on profits? What if the economy sags
and customers become more price
sensitive? Or what if a major competitor
raises or drops its prices? As Figure 9.5
suggests, companies face many
price-changing options.

Price Changes

After developing their pricing structures and strategies, companies often face situations in which they must initiate price changes or respond to price changes by competitors.

Initiating Price Changes

In some cases, the company may find it desirable to initiate either a price cut or a price increase. In both cases, it must anticipate possible buyer and competitor reactions.

Initiating Price Cuts

Several situations may lead a firm to consider cutting its price. One such circumstance is excess capacity. Another is falling demand in the face of strong price competition or a weakened economy. In such cases, the firm may aggressively cut prices to boost sales and market share. But as the airline, fast-food, automobile, retailing, and other industries have learned in recent years, cutting prices in an industry loaded with excess capacity may lead to price wars as competitors try to hold on to market share.

A company may also cut prices in a drive to dominate the market through lower costs. Either the company starts with lower costs than its competitors, or it cuts prices in the hope of gaining market share that will further cut costs through larger volume. For example, computer and electronics maker Lenovo uses an aggressive low-cost, low-price strategy to increase its share of the PC market in developing countries. Similarly, Chinese low-price phone maker Xiaomi has now become China's smartphone market leader, and the low-cost producer is making rapid inroads into India and other emerging markets.[17]

Initiating Price Increases

A successful price increase can greatly improve profits. For example, if the company's profit margin is 3 percent of sales, a 1 percent price increase will boost profits by 33 percent if sales volume is unaffected. A major factor in price increases is cost inflation. Rising costs squeeze profit margins and lead companies to pass cost increases along to customers. Another factor leading to price increases is over-demand: When a company cannot supply all that its customers need, it may raise its prices, ration products to customers, or both—consider today's worldwide oil and gas industry.

When raising prices, the company must avoid being perceived as a *price gouger*. For example, when gasoline prices rise rapidly, angry customers often accuse the major oil companies of enriching themselves at the expense of consumers. Customers have long memories, and they will eventually turn away from companies or even whole industries that they perceive as charging excessive prices. In the extreme, claims of price gouging may even bring about increased government regulation.

There are some techniques for avoiding these problems. One is to maintain a sense of fairness surrounding any price increase. Price increases should be supported by company communications telling customers why prices are being raised.

Wherever possible, the company should consider ways to meet higher costs or demand without raising prices. For example, it might consider more cost-effective ways to produce or distribute its products. It can "unbundle" its market offering, removing features, packaging, or services and separately pricing elements that were formerly part of the offer. Or it can shrink the product or substitute less-expensive ingredients instead of raising the price. P&G recently did this with Tide by holding price while shrinking 100-ounce containers to 92 ounces and 50-ounce containers to 46 ounces, creating a more than 8 percent price increase per ounce without changing package prices. Similarly, Kimberly-Clark raised Kleenex prices by "desheeting"—reducing the number of sheets of toilet paper or facial tissues in each package. And a regular Snickers bar now weighs 1.86 ounces, down from 2.07 ounces in the past, effectively increasing prices by 11 percent.[18]

Buyer Reactions to Price Changes

Customers do not always interpret price changes in a straightforward way. A price *increase*, which would normally lower sales, may have some positive meanings for buyers. For example, what would you think if Rolex *raised* the price of its latest watch model? On the one hand,

● Initiating price increases: When gasoline prices rise rapidly, angry consumers often accuse the major oil companies of enriching themselves by gouging customers.

© Jerry and Marcy Monkman/EcoPhotography.com / Alamy

you might think that the watch is even more exclusive or better made. On the other hand, you might think that Rolex is simply being greedy by charging what the traffic will bear.

Similarly, consumers may view a price *cut* in several ways. For example, what would you think if Rolex were to suddenly cut its prices? You might think that you are getting a better deal on an exclusive product. More likely, however, you'd think that quality had been reduced, and the brand's luxury image might be tarnished. A brand's price and image are often closely linked. A price change, especially a drop in price, can adversely affect how consumers view the brand.

Competitor Reactions to Price Changes

A firm considering a price change must worry about the reactions of its competitors as well as those of its customers. Competitors are most likely to react when the number of firms involved is small, when the product is uniform, and when the buyers are well informed about products and prices.

How can the firm anticipate the likely reactions of its competitors? The problem is complex because, like the customer, the competitor can interpret a company price cut in many ways. It might think the company is trying to grab a larger market share or that it's doing poorly and trying to boost its sales. Or it might think that the company wants the whole industry to cut prices to increase total demand.

The company must assess each competitor's likely reaction. If all competitors behave alike, this amounts to analyzing only a typical competitor. In contrast, if the competitors do not behave alike—perhaps because of differences in size, market shares, or policies—then separate analyses are necessary. However, if some competitors will match the price change, there is good reason to expect that the rest will also match it.

Responding to Price Changes

Here we reverse the question and ask how a firm should respond to a price change by a competitor. The firm needs to consider several issues: Why did the competitor change the price? Is the price change temporary or permanent? What will happen to the company's market share and profits if it does not respond? Are other competitors going to respond? Besides these issues, the company must also consider its own situation and strategy and possible customer reactions to price changes.

● **Figure 11.1** shows the ways a company might assess and respond to a competitor's price cut. Suppose a company learns that a competitor has cut its price and decides that this price cut is likely to harm its sales and profits. It might simply decide to hold its current price and profit margin. The company might believe that it will not lose too much market share or that it would lose too much profit if it reduced its own price. Or it might decide that it should wait and respond when it has more information on the effects of the

● **FIGURE | 11.1**
Responding to Competitor Price Changes

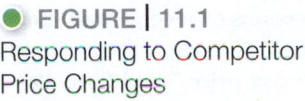

When a competitor cuts prices, a company's first reaction may be to drop its prices as well. But that is often the wrong response. Instead, the firm may want to emphasize the "value" side of the price–value equation.

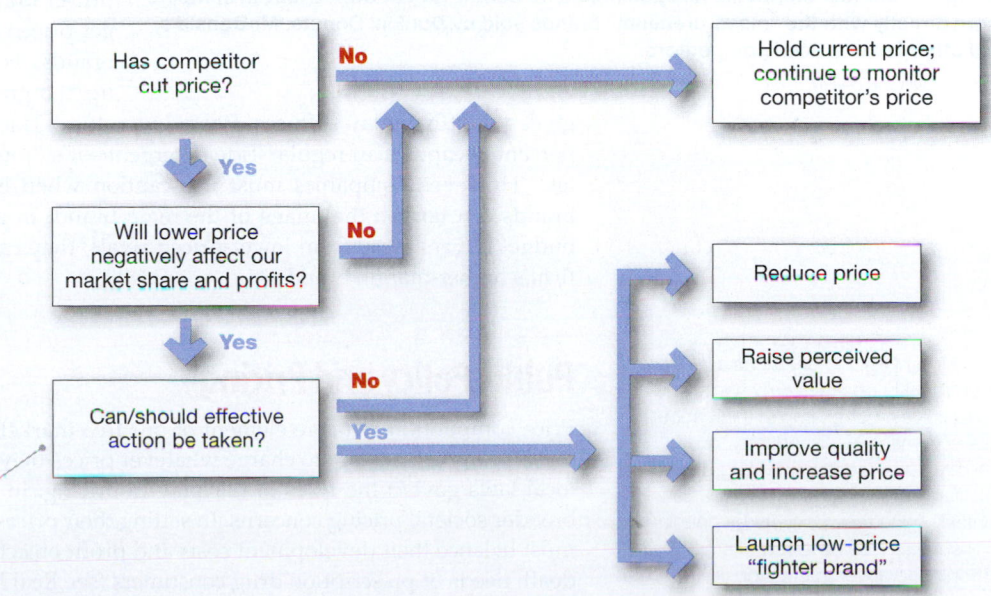

competitor's price change. However, waiting too long to act might let the competitor get stronger and more confident as its sales increase.

If the company decides that effective action can and should be taken, it might make any of four responses. First, it could *reduce its price* to match the competitor's price. It may decide that the market is price sensitive and that it would lose too much market share to the lower-priced competitor. However, cutting the price will reduce the company's profits in the short run. Some companies might also reduce their product quality, services, and marketing communications to retain profit margins, but this will ultimately hurt long-run market share. The company should try to maintain its quality as it cuts prices.

Alternatively, the company might maintain its price but *raise the perceived value* of its offer. It could improve its communications, stressing the relative value of its product over that of the lower-price competitor. The firm may find it cheaper to maintain price and spend money to improve its perceived value than to cut price and operate at a lower margin. Or the company might *improve quality* and *increase price*, moving its brand into a higher price–value position. The higher quality creates greater customer value, which justifies the higher price. In turn, the higher price preserves the company's higher margins.

Finally, the company might launch a *low-price "fighter brand"*—adding a lower-price item to the line or creating a separate lower-price brand. This is necessary if the particular market segment being lost is price sensitive and will not respond to arguments of higher quality. ● Starbucks did this when it acquired Seattle's Best Coffee, a brand positioned with working-class, "approachable-premium" appeal compared to the more professional, full-premium appeal of the main Starbucks brand. Seattle's Best coffee is generally cheaper than the parent Starbucks brand. As such, at retail, it competes more directly with Dunkin' Donuts, McDonald's, and other mass-premium brands through its franchise outlets and through partnerships with Subway, Burger King, Delta, AMC theaters, Royal Caribbean cruise lines, and others. On supermarket shelves, it competes with store brands and other mass-premium coffees such as Folgers Gourmet Selections and Millstone.

● **Fighter brands: Starbucks has positioned its Seattle's Best Coffee unit to compete more directly with the "mass-premium" brands sold by Dunkin' Donuts, McDonald's, and other lower-priced competitors.**

© Curved Light USA / Alamy

To counter store brands and other low-price entrants in a tighter economy, P&G turned a number of its brands into fighter brands. Luvs disposable diapers give parents "premium leakage protection for less than pricier brands." And P&G offers popular budget-priced basic versions of several of its major brands. For example, Charmin Basic "holds up at a great everyday price," and Puffs Basic gives you "Everyday softness. Everyday value." Tide Simply Clean & Fresh is about 35 percent cheaper than regular Tide detergent—it's "tough on odors and easy on your wallet." However, companies must use caution when introducing fighter brands, as such brands can tarnish the image of the main brand. In addition, although they may attract budget buyers away from lower-priced rivals, they can also take business away from the firm's higher-margin brands.

Author Comment | Pricing decisions are often constrained by social and legal issues. For example, think about the pharmaceuticals industry. Are rapidly rising prescription drug prices justified? Or are the drug companies unfairly lining their pockets by gouging consumers who have few alternatives? Should the government step in?

Public Policy and Pricing

Price competition is a core element of our free-market economy. In setting prices, companies usually are not free to charge whatever prices they wish. Many federal, state, and even local laws govern the rules of fair play in pricing. In addition, companies must consider broader societal pricing concerns. In setting their prices, for example, pharmaceutical firms must balance their development costs and profit objectives against the sometimes life-and-death needs of prescription drug consumers (see Real Marketing 11.2)

11.2   Pimeuting: **Pharmaceutical Pricing: No Easy Answers**

Real Marketing

The U.S. pharmaceutical industry has historically been one of the nation's most profitable industries. Over the past five years, returns for the S&P Pharmaceuticals Select Industry Index have doubled those of the broader S&P 500. In most situations, we'd applaud such high-performing companies and industries. However, when it comes to pharmaceutical firms, critics claim, healthy sales and profits may not be so healthy for consumers.

Somehow, learning that major pharmaceutical companies such as Johnson & Johnson, Novartis, Roche, Pfizer, Merck, and GlaxoSmithKline are reaping big profits leaves a bad taste in the mouths of many consumers. It's like learning that the oil companies are profiting when gas prices rocket upward. Although most consumers appreciate the steady stream of beneficial drugs produced by pharmaceutical companies, they worry that the industry's huge success may be coming at their own expense—literally.

Americans spent about $374 billion last year on prescription medications, more than a third of all worldwide spending. Prescription prices have risen rapidly over the years, and health-care costs continue to jump. An AARP study found that the average retail price of a market basket of brand-name drugs widely used by older Americans climbed almost 13 percent higher in 2013 alone, more than eight times the general inflation rate.

The critics claim that competitive forces don't operate well in the pharmaceuticals market, allowing the pharmaceutical companies to charge excessive prices. Unlike purchases of other consumer products, drug purchases cannot be postponed. And consumers don't usually shop for the best deals on medicines—they simply take what the doctor orders. Because physicians who write the prescriptions don't pay for the medicines they recommend, they have little incentive to be price conscious. Moreover, third-party payers—insurance companies, health plans, and government programs—often pay all or part of the bill. Finally, because of patent protection and the huge investment and time needed to develop and test new drugs, there are fewer competing brands to force lower prices.

The critics claim that these market factors leave pharmaceutical companies free to practice monopoly pricing, sometimes resulting in unfair practices or even seemingly outlandish cases of price gouging. One such case made headlines recently when entrepreneur Martin Shkreli and his company Turing Pharmaceuticals acquired Daraprim, a 62-year-old, lifesaving medication used by AIDS patients. Turing immediately jacked up the price of Daraprim from $13.50 per pill to an astounding $750 per pill, a more than 5,000 percent increase. The pill itself costs only about a dollar to produce.

Major drug companies would never commit such atrocities. "He is not us," said Merck's CEO of Turing's Shkreli. Nevertheless, mainstream pharmaceutical makers routinely boost the prices of their cancer, diabetes, MS, and cholesterol-reducing drugs by 10 percent or more per year, much faster than inflation. One study found that the prices for four of the nation's top 10 prescription drugs rose more than 100 percent during the past five years; six others went up more than 50 percent. As just one example, take Gleevec, a drug sold by Novartis to treat blood-based cancer. Gleevec seemed pretty expensive when it first came to market in 2001 at about $30,000 for a year's supply. Yet, for reasons unknown, Novartis has since more than tripled Gleevec's price, leading one industry economist to remark that she could find no economic theory to explain how pharmaceutical companies set or raise their drug prices.

To add insult to injury, the critics say, drug companies pour more than $4.5 billion a year into direct-to-consumer advertising and spend another $24 billion on marketing to physicians. These marketing efforts dictate higher prices at the same time that they build demand for more expensive remedies. Thus, the severest critics say, the big drug companies may be profiting unfairly—or even at the expense of human life—by promoting and pricing products beyond the reach of many people who need them.

The high prices of everyday prescription drugs may be concerning enough. But the costs of some lifesaving specialty medications are outright alarming. According to one cancer doctor at the Mayo Clinic, "The average gross household income in the United States is about $52,000 per year. For an insured patient with cancer who needs a drug that costs $120,000 per year, the out-of-pocket expenses could be as much as $25,000 to $30,000—more than half their average household income." One recent study found that cancer drug prices have gone up an average of $8,500 annually for the past 15 years. The price of one recently developed combination cancer therapy is an astonishing $295,000 per year.

But there's another side to the drug-pricing issue. Industry proponents point out that, over the years, the drug companies have developed a steady stream of medicines that transform people's lives. Developing such

Responsible pharmaceutical pricing: Most consumers understand that they'll have to pay the price for beneficial drugs. They just want to be treated fairly in the process.

Bill/Adobe Stock

new drugs is risky and expensive, involving legions of scientists, expensive technology, and years of effort with no certainty of success. The top 10 pharmaceutical companies combined last year to spend more than $70 billion on R&D, more than 15 percent of sales. On average, it takes 12 to 15 years and costs $1.3 billion to bring a new drug to market. Then 70 percent of new drugs never generate enough revenue to recover the cost of development. Thus, the proponents say, although the prices of new prescription drugs seem high, they're needed to fund the development of important future drugs. As one old ad from pharmaceutical firm GlaxoSmithKline (GSK) concluded: "Inventing new medicines isn't easy, but it's worth it. ...Today's medicines finance tomorrow's miracles."

And so the controversy continues. As drug prices climb, the pharmaceutical companies face pressures from the federal government, insurance companies, managed-care providers, and consumer advocacy groups to exercise restraint in setting prices. However, rather than waiting for tougher legislation on prices—or simply because it's the right thing to do—many of the drug companies are taking action on their own. For example, some companies have committed to keeping their average price hikes at or below inflation. Others employ tiered pricing—selling their medicines in different countries at varying prices based on ability to pay in each country. Most pharmaceutical companies now sponsor patient assistance programs that provide prescription medicines free or at low cost to people who cannot afford them, and they regularly donate free medicines in response to disaster relief efforts around the globe.

In all, pharmaceutical pricing is no easy issue. For the pharmaceutical companies, it's more than a matter of sales and profits. In setting prices, short-term financial goals must be tempered by broader societal considerations. For example, GSK's heartfelt mission is "to improve the quality of human life by enabling people to do more, feel better, and live longer." Accomplishing this mission won't come cheap. Most consumers understand that. One way or another, they know, they'll have to pay the price. All they really ask is that they be treated fairly in the process.

Sources: Peter Jaret, "Prices Spike for Some Generic Drugs," *AARP,* July/August 2015, www.aarp.org/health/drugs-supplements/info-2015/prices-spike-for-generic-drugs.html#slide1; "U.S. Oncologists Decry High Cost of Cancer Drugs," *Health Day,* July 23, 2015, http://consumer.healthday.com/cancer-information-5/mis-cancer-news-102/u-s-oncologists-speak-out-on-high-cost-of-cancer-drugs-701616.html; "Crippling," *The Economist,* June 4, 2015, www.economist.com/blogs/democracyinamerica/2015/06/pharmaceutical-pricing; Alexandra Sifferlin, "Americans Spent a Record Amount on Medicine in 2014," *Time,* http://time.com/3819889/medicine-spending/; John Graham, "Crisis in Pharma R&D," *Forbes,* November 26, 2014, www.forbes.com/sites/theapothecary/2014/11/26/crisis-in-pharma-rd-it-costs-2-6-billion-to-develop-a-new-medicine-2-5-times-more-than-in-2003/print/; Rafi Mohammed, "It's Time to Rein In Exorbitant Pharmaceutical Prices," *Harvard Business Review,* September 22, 2015, https://hbr.org/2015/09/its-time-to-rein-in-exorbitant-pharmaceutical-prices; Benjamin Siegel and Mary Bruce, "Former Pharma Big Martin Shkreli Boasted '$1 Bn Here We Come,' Documents Say," February 2, 2016, http://abcnews.go.com/Politics/pharma-big-martin-shkreli-boasted-bn-documents/story?id=36671216; Carolina Humer, "Exclusive: Makers Took Big Price Increases on Widely Used U.S. Drugs," Reuters, April 5, 2016, http://finance.yahoo.com/news/makers-took-big-price-increases-widely-used-u-141253765–finance.html; and "Our Mission and Strategy," www.gsk.com/en-gb/about-us/our-mission-and-strategy/, accessed October 2016.

The most important pieces of legislation affecting pricing are the Sherman Act, the Clayton Act, and the Robinson-Patman Act, initially adopted to curb the formation of monopolies and regulate business practices that might unfairly restrain trade. Because these federal statutes can be applied only to interstate commerce, some states have adopted similar provisions for companies that operate locally.

● **Figure 11.2** shows the major public policy issues in pricing. These include potentially damaging pricing practices within a given level of the channel (price-fixing and predatory pricing) and across levels of the channel (retail price maintenance, discriminatory pricing, and deceptive pricing).[19]

● **FIGURE** | 11.2
Public Policy Issues in Pricing

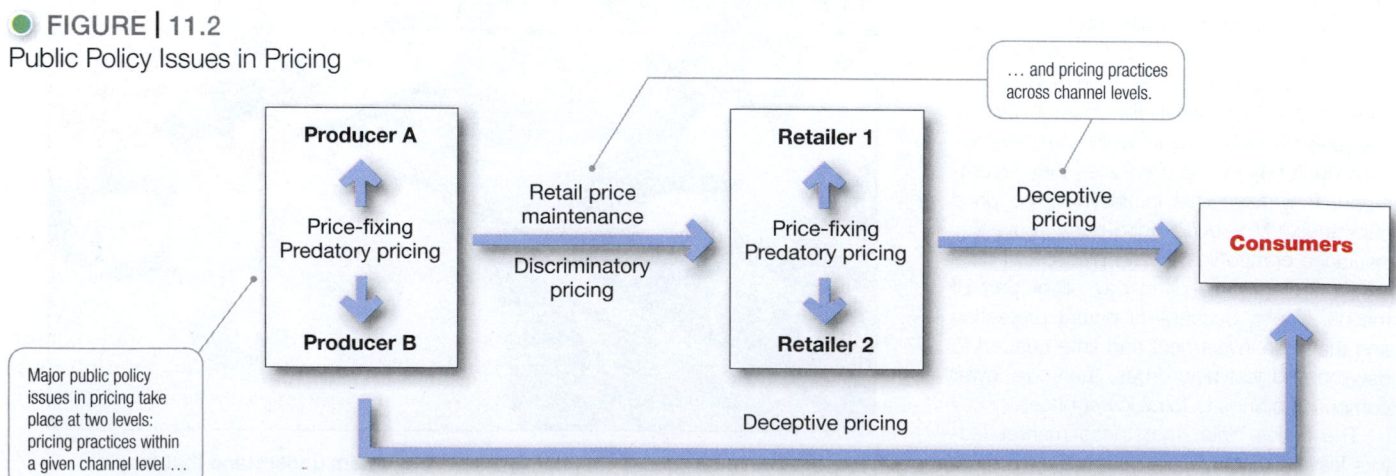

Source: Adapted from Dhruv Grewal and Larry D. Compeau, "Pricing and Public Policy: A Research Agenda and Overview of the Special Issue," *Journal of Public Policy and Marketing,* Spring 1999, pp. 3–10.

Pricing within Channel Levels

Federal legislation on *price-fixing* states that sellers must set prices without talking to competitors. Otherwise, price collusion is suspected. Price-fixing is illegal per se—that is, the government does not accept any excuses for price-fixing. Recently, governments at the state and national levels have been aggressively enforcing price-fixing regulations in industries ranging from gasoline, insurance, and concrete to credit cards, computer chips, and e-books. Companies found guilty of price-fixing practices can pay heavy penalties. For example, Apple recently paid $450 million in fines for conspiring with publishers to fix prices on e-books. And four major U.S. airlines—United, Delta, Southwest, and American—now face a potentially costly class action suit and U.S. Department of Justice investigation for conspiring to artificially inflate air fares to "reap huge profits."[20]

Sellers are also prohibited from using *predatory pricing*—selling below cost with the intention of punishing a competitor or gaining higher long-run profits by putting competitors out of business. This protects small sellers from larger ones that might sell items below cost temporarily or in a specific locale to drive them out of business. The biggest problem is determining just what constitutes predatory pricing behavior. Selling below cost to unload excess inventory is not considered predatory; selling below cost to drive out competitors is. Thus, a given action may or may not be predatory depending on intent, and intent can be very difficult to determine or prove.

In recent years, several large and powerful companies have been accused of predatory pricing. However, turning an accusation into a lawsuit can be difficult. ● For example, many publishers and booksellers have expressed concerns about Amazon.com's predatory practices, especially its book pricing:[21]

● Predatory pricing: Some industry critics have accused Amazon.com of pricing books at fire-sale prices that harm competing booksellers. But is it predatory pricing or just plain good competitive marketing?

© Iain Masterton/Alamy Stock Photo

> Many booksellers and publishers complain that Amazon's book pricing policies are destroying their industry. Amazon routinely sells best-selling hardback books as loss leaders at cut-rate prices. And it peddles e-books at fire-sale prices in order to win customers for its Kindle e-reader and tablets. Such very low book prices have caused considerable damage to competing booksellers, many of whom view Amazon's pricing actions as predatory. According to some industry groups, such practices "harm the interests of America's readers, impoverish the book industry as a whole, and impede the free flow of ideas in our society." Still, no predatory pricing charges have ever been filed against Amazon. It would be extremely difficult to prove that such loss-leader pricing is purposefully predatory as opposed to just plain good competitive marketing. "But wait a minute," states one analyst. "Isn't that what business is supposed to do—compete to lower prices?"

Pricing across Channel Levels

The Robinson-Patman Act seeks to prevent unfair *price discrimination* by ensuring that sellers offer the same price terms to customers at a given level of trade. For example, every retailer is entitled to the same price terms from a given manufacturer, whether the retailer is REI or a local bicycle shop. However, price discrimination is allowed if the seller can prove that its costs are different when selling to different retailers—for example, that it costs less per unit to sell a large volume of bicycles to REI than to sell a few bicycles to the local dealer.

The seller can also discriminate in its pricing if the seller manufactures different qualities of the same product for different retailers. The seller has to prove that these differences are proportional. Price differentials may also be used to "match competition" in "good faith," provided the price discrimination is temporary, localized, and defensive rather than offensive.

Laws also prohibit *retail* (or *resale*) *price maintenance*—a manufacturer cannot require dealers to charge a specified retail price for its product. Although the seller can propose a manufacturer's *suggested* retail price to dealers, it cannot refuse to sell to a dealer that takes independent pricing action, nor can it punish the dealer by shipping late or denying advertising allowances. For example, the Florida attorney general's office investigated Nike for allegedly fixing the retail price of its shoes and clothing. It was concerned that Nike might be withholding items from retailers who were not selling its most expensive shoes at prices the company considered suitable.

Deceptive pricing occurs when a seller states prices or price savings that mislead consumers or are not actually available to consumers. This might involve bogus reference or comparison prices, as when a retailer sets artificially high "regular" prices and then announces "sale" prices close to its previous everyday prices. For example, luxury apparel and accessories retailer Michael Kors recently settled a class action lawsuit alleging that it used deceptive pricing at its outlet stores. The retailer was charged with tagging products with false "manufacturer's suggested retail prices" to make its supposed discounted prices more appealing when, in fact, the products were sold only in the outlet stores. Such artificial comparison pricing is widespread in retailing.[22]

Although comparison pricing claims are legal if they are truthful, the Federal Trade Commission's "Guides against Deceptive Pricing" warn sellers not to advertise (1) a price reduction unless it is a savings from the usual retail price, (2) "factory" or "wholesale" prices unless such prices are what they are claimed to be, and (3) comparable value prices on imperfect goods.[23]

Other deceptive pricing issues include *scanner fraud* and price confusion. The widespread use of scanner-based computer checkouts has led to increasing complaints of retailers overcharging their customers. Most of these overcharges result from poor management, such as a failure to enter current or sale prices into the system. Other cases, however, involve intentional overcharges.

Many federal and state statutes regulate against deceptive pricing practices. For example, the Automobile Information Disclosure Act requires automakers to attach a statement on new vehicle windows stating the manufacturer's suggested retail price, the prices of optional equipment, and the dealer's transportation charges. However, reputable sellers go beyond what is required by law. Treating customers fairly and making certain that they fully understand prices and pricing terms are an important part of building strong and lasting customer relationships.

11 | Reviewing and Extending the Concepts

OBJECTIVES REVIEW AND KEY TERMS

Objectives Review

In this chapter, we examined some additional pricing considerations—new product pricing, product mix pricing, price adjustments, initiating and reacting to prices changes, and pricing and public policy. A company sets not a single price but rather a *pricing structure* that covers its entire mix of products. This pricing structure changes over time as products move through their life cycles. The company adjusts product prices to reflect changes in costs and demand and account for variations in buyers and situations. As the competitive environment changes, the company considers when to initiate price changes and when to respond to them.

OBJECTIVE 11-1 Describe the major strategies for pricing new products. (pp 308–309)

Pricing is a dynamic process, and pricing strategies usually change as the product passes through its life cycle. The introductory stage—setting prices for the first time—is especially challenging. The company can decide on one of several strategies for pricing innovative new products: It can use *market-skimming pricing* by initially setting high prices to "skim" the maximum amount of revenue from various segments of the market. Or it can use *market-penetrating pricing* by setting a low initial price to penetrate the market deeply and win a large market share. Several conditions must be set for either new product pricing strategy to work.

OBJECTIVE 11-2 Explain how companies find a set of prices that maximizes the profits from the total product mix. (pp 309–311)

When the product is part of a product mix, the firm searches for a set of prices that will maximize the profits from the total mix. In *product line pricing*, the company determines the price steps for the entire product line it offers. In addition, the company must set prices for *optional products* (optional or accessory products included with the main product), *captive products* (products that are required for using the main product), *by-products* (waste or residual products produced when making the main product), and *product bundles* (combinations of products at a reduced price).

OBJECTIVE 11-3 Discuss how companies adjust their prices to take into account different types of customers and situations. (pp 311–319)

Companies apply a variety of *price adjustment strategies* to account for differences in consumer segments and situations. One is *discount and allowance pricing*, whereby the company establishes cash, quantity, functional, or seasonal discounts, or varying types of allowances. A second strategy is *segmented pricing,* where the company sells a product at two or more prices to accommodate different customers, product forms, locations, or times. Sometimes companies consider more than economics in their pricing decisions, using *psychological pricing* to better communicate a product's intended position. In *promotional pricing,* a company offers discounts or temporarily sells a product below list price as a special event, sometimes even selling below cost as a loss leader. Another approach is *geographical pricing,* whereby the company decides how to price to distant customers, choosing from such alternatives as FOB-origin pricing, uniform-delivered pricing, zone pricing, basing-point pricing, and freight-absorption pricing. Using *dynamic pricing,* a company can adjust prices continually to meet the characteristics and needs of individual customers and situations. Finally, *international pricing* means that the company adjusts its price to meet different conditions and expectations in different world markets.

OBJECTIVE 11-4 Discuss the key issues related to initiating and responding to price changes. *(pp 320–322)*

When a firm considers initiating a *price change*, it must consider customers' and competitors' reactions. There are different implications to *initiating price cuts* and *initiating price increases.* Buyer reactions to price changes are influenced by the meaning customers see in the price change. Competitors' reactions flow from a set reaction policy or a fresh analysis of each situation.

There are also many factors to consider in responding to a competitor's price changes. The company that faces a price change initiated by a competitor must try to understand the competitor's intent as well as the likely duration and impact of the change. If a swift reaction is desirable, the firm should preplan its reactions to different possible price actions by competitors. When facing a competitor's price change, the company might sit tight, reduce its own price, raise perceived quality, improve quality and raise price, or launch a fighter brand.

OBJECTIVE 11-5 Overview the social and legal issues that affect pricing decisions. *(pp 322–326)*

Many federal, state, and even local laws govern the rules of fair pricing. Also, companies must consider broader societal pricing concerns. The major public policy issues in pricing include potentially damaging pricing practices *within* a given level of the channel, such as price-fixing and predatory pricing. They also include pricing practices *across* channel levels, such as retail price maintenance, discriminatory pricing, and deceptive pricing. Although many federal and state statutes regulate pricing practices, reputable sellers go beyond what is required by law. Treating customers fairly is an important part of building strong and lasting customer relationships.

Key Terms

OBJECTIVE 11-1

Market-skimming pricing (price skimming) (p 308)
Market-penetration pricing (p 309)

OBJECTIVE 11-2

Product line pricing (p 310)
Optional-product pricing (p 310)
Captive-product pricing (p 310)

By-product pricing (p 311)
Product bundle pricing (p 311)

OBJECTIVE 11-3

Discount (p 311)
Allowance (p 312)
Segmented pricing (p 312)
Psychological pricing (p 313)
Reference prices (p 313)

Promotional pricing (p 314)
Geographical pricing (p 315)
FOB-origin pricing (p 315)
Uniform-delivered pricing (p 315)
Zone pricing (p 315)
Basing-point pricing (p 315)
Freight-absorption pricing (p 315)
Dynamic pricing (p 316)

DISCUSSION AND CRITICAL THINKING

MyMarketingLab

Go to **mymktlab.com** to complete the problems marked with this icon ✪.

Discussion Questions

11-1 Name and describe the two broad new-product pricing strategies. When would each be appropriate? (AACSB: Communication)

11-2 Define product bundle pricing. Give examples where companies have used this pricing strategy. (AACSB: Communication; Reflective Thinking)

11-3 What is psychological pricing, and how is it used by sellers? Give an example. (AACSB: Communication)

✪ **11-4** Discuss the decisions companies face when initiating price increases. (AACSB: Communication)

11-5 Discuss the major public policy issues in pricing practices within a given channel level and across channel levels. (AACSB: Communication)

Critical Thinking Exercises

⭐ **11-6** Alicia is a self-employed hair stylist who owns her own salon. She has asked you to consult with her on how to generate more revenue. Using the price adjustment strategies discussed in the chapter, advise Alicia on her options to increase overall sales. (AACSB: Communication; Reflective Thinking)

11-7 Bridgestone Corporation, the world's largest tire and rubber producer, recently agreed to plead guilty to price-fixing along with 25 other automotive suppliers. What is price-fixing? Discuss other recent examples of price-fixing. (AACSB: Communication; Reflective Thinking)

11-8 Identify three online price-comparison shopping sites or apps and shop for a product you are interested in purchasing. Compare the price ranges given at the three sites. Based on your search, determine a "fair" price for the product. (AACSB: Communication; Use of IT; Reflective Thinking)

APPLICATIONS AND CASES

Online, Mobile, and Social Media Marketing Krazy Coupon Lady

Price-conscious consumers are all about finding the best deal. Some even make a sport of it! Krazy couponers, Heather and Joanie, have been showcased on many national television shows and in web and print articles. The two friends run a highly successful company that works tirelessly to uncover the best deals, enabling families to save money. Posted on their website, www.krazycouponlady.com, is the company mantra "You'd be krazy not to be one of us!" The website features promotions and alerts to special pricing on products as well as coupons and discounts to help consumers stretch their dollars. Also featured are retailers with sale-priced merchandise, coupons, and promotions. Community members post their best deals in the brag section.

11-9 Visit www.krazycouponlady.com and browse a deal you would consider purchasing. After identifying the deal, conduct an online price comparison at various retailers to determine the range of prices you would typically pay for the product. Present your conclusions. (AACSB: Communication; Use of IT; Reflective Thinking)

11-10 Using www.krazycouponlady.com, click on Stores, Coupons, and Deals on the navigation bar and make a list of the featured products. Identify the pricing strategy used by the retailer. (AACSB: Communication; Use of IT; Reflective Thinking)

Marketing Ethics Less Bang for Your Buck

Over the past several years, careful shoppers may be spending about the same amount of money at the grocery store but leaving the store with a lighter load in their grocery bags. Food prices on many items have increased, and food manufacturers are facing the same challenges as consumers. With increases in raw materials and transportation, making a profit requires a very sharp pencil. According to Phil Lempert, editor of SupermarketGuru.com, "The reality is, if you look at USDA projections, food is going to get more expensive. And as a result, food companies are going to do one of two or three things: Raise prices and keep packages the same, or reduce the quantity in the package. Or do a little of both."

11-11 Week after week, consumers shop for many of the same groceries. At some point, the product may be priced the same and look the same as before but with less in the package. If consumers are not made aware of the change, is this deception? Is this different from deceptive pricing? Explain. (AACSB: Communication; Ethical Reasoning; Reflective Thinking)

11-12 Develop a list of the products you buy from a grocery store, dollar store, or convenience store where one of two things has occurred: The price has increased or the quantity in the package has decreased. Were you aware of the changes? Explain. (AACSB: Communication; Reflective Thinking)

Marketing by the Numbers Louis Vuitton Price Increase

One way to maintain exclusivity for a brand is to raise its price. That's what luxury fashion and leather goods maker of Louis Vuitton did. The company does not want the brand to become overexposed and too common, so it raised prices 10 percent and is slowing its expansion in China. The Louis Vuitton brand is the largest contributor to the company's $13.3 billion revenue from its fashion and leather division, accounting for $8 billion of those sales. It might seem counterintuitive to want to encourage fewer customers to purchase a company's products, but when price increases, so do the product's contribution margins, making each sale more profitable. Thus, sales can drop and the company can still maintain the same profitability as before the price hike.

11-13 If the company's original contribution margin was 40 percent, calculate the new contribution margin if price is increased 10 percent. Refer to Appendix 2,

Marketing by the Numbers, paying attention to endnote 6 on the price change explanation in which the analysis is done by setting price equal to $1.00. (AACSB: Communications; Analytic Reasoning)

11-14 Determine by how much sales can drop and still let the company maintain the total contribution it had when the contribution margin was 40 percent. (AACSB: Communication; Analytic Reasoning)

Video Case Hammerpress

Printing paper goods may not sound like the best business to get into these days. But Hammerpress is a company that is carving out a niche in this old industry. And Hammerpress is doing it by returning to old technology. Today's printing firms use computer-driven graphic design techniques and printing processes. But Hammerpress creates greeting cards, calendars, and business cards that are hand-crafted by professional artists and printed using traditional letterpress technology.

When it comes to competing, this presents both opportunities and challenges. While Hammerpress's products certainly stand out as works of art, the cost for producing such goods is considerably higher than the industry average. This video illustrates how Hammerpress employs dynamic pricing techniques

in order to meet the needs of various customer segments and thrive in a competitive environment.

After viewing the video featuring Hammerpress, answer the following questions:

11-15 How does Hammerpress employ the concept of dynamic pricing?

11-16 Discuss the three major pricing strategies in relation to Hammerpress. Which of these three do you think is the company's core strategic strategy?

11-17 Does it make sense for Hammerpress to compete in product categories where the market dictates a price that is not profitable for the company? Explain.

Company Case Lululemon: Indulging Customers at a Premium Price

It's a warm summer evening in Brooklyn's Prospect Park. Hundreds of yoga practitioners—commonly known as yogis—have turned out for a free class, arranged on the turf in a perfect grid, mats on the ground. Following the instructions of the class leader, it's one long set of downward-facing dogs, half-moons, and warrior Is, IIs, and IIIs. While these New Yorkers come from various walks of life, most of them have one thing in common. They're wearing outfits by Lululemon—the hottest yoga apparel brand this side of India. The brand's dominance among attendees shouldn't come as a surprise as Lululemon sponsors this free weekly event, providing yoga-appropriate music and teachers from local studios with names like Bend & Bloom, Prana Power Yoga, and Tangerine Hot Yoga. But these Lululemon loyalists have one other thing in common. They paid a premium price for their outfits—and they couldn't be happier.

Vancouver-based Lululemon has quickly risen to the top of a bustling market that it has played a major role in defining. With approximately 400 stores around the world, Lululemon peddles its own brand of yoga-inspired apparel with its instantly recognizable logo—an iridescent lowercase a that resembles an omega. But far more than clothing, this brand perpetuates an image and a lifestyle. The company exudes the philosophy capture by its manifesto: "We are passionate about sweating every day and we want the world to know it. Breathing deeply, drinking water and getting outside also top the list of things we can't live without." In other words, this brand is active, healthy, and back-to-nature and isn't shy about saying so. It's that image complimented by a "no discounts" credo that has a fanatically loyal customer base willing to buy everything Lululemon and not even blink at paying full premium prices.

Riding the Wave

While yoga has been practiced in the United States since the 1960s, over the past 20 years, it has emerged from a niche activity practiced by devout New Agers to become part of the cultural mainstream. Yoga is all the rage now with everyone from students to stressed-out young professionals to retirees among

the devotees of this 5,000-year-old practice. Over the past four years in the United States alone, the largely female population of yogis has increased by 50 percent to more than 36 million. More than twice that many say they want to try it for the first time in the next 12 months. They won't need to go far—there are more than a dozen different types of yoga being taught and practiced through classes in commercial studios, including hatha yoga, acro yoga, iyengar yoga, power yoga, hot yoga, prenatal yoga, and restorative yoga. Spending on classes, clothing, and equipment has also shot up in the past four years, increasing 60 percent to a whopping $16 billion.

As this fitness explosion began to take shape, Lululemon founder Chip Wilson took notice. Having developed a passion for technical athletic fabrics through 20 years in the surf, skate, and snowboarding business, Wilson was no stranger to the apparel industry. But after taking his first yoga class in the mid-1990s, he was hooked. Convinced yoga's time had come, he put his efforts into developing alternatives to the standard cotton yoga clothing of the time—a material that to him seemed completely inappropriate for sweaty, stretchy power yoga.

After establishing the company in 1998, Wilson began selling Lululemon clothing through yoga instructors. In November 2000, the first Lululemon store opened for business in a beach town near Vancouver. The original concept was for the store to sell clothing while also serving as a community hub where the mental and spiritual aspects of living a healthy and powerful life could be taught and discussed. But the popularity of Lululemon's clothing made it impossible for employees to focus on anything other than selling clothing. People were drawn to the fabric, a four-way stretch blend of nylon and lycra. Sub-branded "Luon," the "sweat-wicking and cottony-soft" material is the company's signature fabric.

Since its first products, Lululemon has focused on innovative fabrics for every application, including Luxtreme, a version of Luon designed for the most hardcore workouts; Swift, a strong and lightweight fabric designed for freedom of movement; Boolux, a blend of natural fibers designed for warmth and breathability; Nulu, a buttery-soft and superlight version of Luon designed for a "naked" feel; and Vitasea, an ultrasoft blend of cotton, spandex, and seaweed—yes, seaweed.

In addition to developing fabrics to enhance yoga workouts, Lululemon also focused on style. With unique cuts and colors, Lululemon developed a full line of yoga apparel including full-length and crop pants, tanks, sports bras, underwear, and head-bands. Women couldn't get enough of Lululemon, and the brand became a big driver of "athleisure"—a fashion trend that takes workout-designed clothing outside the workout into casual and social occasions and even into the workplace. Lululemon has ridden this wave, developing lines for running, swimming, and training as well as clothing and accessories for getting to and from "the workout." With a full line for men as well, Lululemon has done a superb job of giving devotees something for every occasion.

Where Price Is No Object

As the brand's popularity skyrocketed, it quickly became a symbol of status and cultural capital as a fixture in the wealthiest counties of the country. Said one Westchester local to a new move-in, "It's fine if you like Lululemon, because that's all women wear up here." A Lululemon employee at its Boulder, Colorado, store reported, "Women would come down from Aspen and Vail in SUV-loads. They would drop $2,000 easy, [saying] 'I like that top, I'll take one in every color.'" And it isn't just the clothes. The company's re-usable shopping bags—plastered with self-improvement quotes like "Do one thing a day that scares you"—are used by women for all kinds of tasks, carried with pride as though they were Gucci. With the brand on display, Luluheads—as they've come to be called and call themselves—are letting people know they are spiritual, healthy, and very flexible and can afford to pay $68 for their T-shirts.

Premium price is typically a hallmark of status brands, and it's no different with Lululemon. Its signature article is the Groove Pant, priced at $98. While all the top athletic apparel brands have now jumped on board with their own lines of yogawear, Lululemon is priced at the top of the heap. Nike sells its most comparable version for $90, while Athleta (Gap), Under Armour, and Reebok sell theirs at $79, $60, and $50, respectively. Pricing for Lululemon's other apparel items compares to competitive offerings in a similar manner. Widening the price gap between Lululemon and the competition even further is the brand's aver-sion to discounts. Products are rarely marked down in stores. Instead, the company sells unsold inventory at modest discounts through only 10 outlet stores or through the company website under the section "We made too much." The fine print stipulates, "No returns, no exchanges."

Expensive—but Worth It

The big question is are Lululemon's products worth the premium price? As with any premium-priced product, numerous individuals have made their own comparisons and have broadcast their opinions via social media. More official inquiries have been made by the business and fashion press. These comparisons reveal differences across the brands. Fabric blends vary a bit, as do styles, fit, and features. But as with most apparel items, perceptions of quality come down to personal preference. Ask Luluheads and they will tell you with conviction that Lululemon's products fit better, feel nicer, last longer, and are more flattering than any competing goods.

On top of perceptions of product quality, the Lulu faithful also point to the shopping experience. Like buying coffee at Starbucks, customers are drawn to the ambience that—when it comes to buying athletic apparel—can only be found in a Lululemon store. Stores are designed to be all at once warm, inviting, eclectic, and accessible. Customers are pampered by "educators" and "key leaders"—Lulu-speak for "sales associ-ates" and "supervisors." And Wilson's original retail vision has come to fruition as community ambassadors—local experts who get a 30 percent discount on Lulu merchandise and exposure for their own businesses—provide in-store workshops and classes on various aspects of healthy living. More Victoria's Secret than Under Armour, Lululemon has full control over its retail experi-ence as the only vertically integrated retailer of athletic wear for women. As one investment banker puts it, "You can go to Sports Authority to get stuff made by Nike for women, but you just don't feel indulgent there."

There are many who have pointed out the irony of a brand that has become an icon of materialism based on selling cloth-ing for yoga—a practice rooted in the philosophy of avoiding all forms of self-indulgence. But the Lululemon faithful either don't get the irony or don't care. Over the past four years, Lululemon's revenues have doubled from $1 billion to $2 billion as it maintains a healthy 13 percent profit margin. And while the company's stock price took a dive a couple of years ago amid various controversies, it has averted the lasting effects of such as the value of its stock has recovered to nearly $10 billion. The company certainly faces challenges as it fends off more and more competition in an already crowded field. Claiming it doesn't want to build more than 400 stores, it may also be reaching its peak. But so long as Luluheads abound, Lululemon will be doing upward-facing dogs all the way to the bank.

Questions for Discussion

11-18 Relative to customer value, explain customers' willing-ness to pay premium prices for Lululemon's products.

11-19 Based on principles from the chapter, explain how price affects customer perceptions of the Lululemon brand.

11-20 Could Lululemon have achieved the same level of suc-cess had it executed an alternative pricing strategy?

11-21 Can Lululemon continue to succeed by employing the same premium-pricing strategy? Explain.

Sources: Based on information from Murray Newlands, "How Lululemon Made Their Brand Iconic," *Forbes*, February 21, 2016, www.forbes.com/sites/mnewlands/2016/02/21/how-lululemon-made-their-brand-iconic-an-interview-with-svp-of-brand-programs-eric-petersen/3/#869e22340aad; "2016 Yoga in America Study Conducted by Yoga Journal and Yoga Alliance Reveals Growth and Benefits of Practice," *PR Newswire*, January 13, 2016, www.prnewswire.com/news-releases/2016-yoga-in-america-study-conducted-by-yoga-journal-and-yoga-alliance-reveals-growth-and-benefits-of-the-practice-300203418.html; Bryant Urstadt, "Lust for Lulu," *New York Magazine*, July 26, 2009, www.nymag.com/shopping/features/58082/; Joe Avella and Sara Silvertein, "Here's How $98 Lululemon Yoga Pants Compare to Cheaper Alternatives," *Business Insider*, January 23, 2015, www.businessinsider.com/yoga-pants-lululemon-reebok-athleta-price-value-2015-1; Brittany McAndrew, "Lululemon Goes Beyond the In-Store Experience," *Alu Mind*, April 15, 2014, www.alumind.com/article/lululemon-goes-beyond-store-experience/; and information from www.info.lululemon.com/about and http://shop.lululemon.com/, accessed June 2016.

MyMarketingLab

Go to **mymktlab.com** for Auto-graded writing questions as well as the following Assisted-graded writing questions:

11-22 Explain how businesses implement segmented pricing and discuss conditions necessary for success.

11-23 Any charge that is not airfare is referred to as ancillary revenue for airlines—and they are cleaning up on it to the tune of $20 billion a year. While consumers can avoid some fees, such as those for food, preferred seating, and wi-fi, the majority can't avoid baggage fees. What type of pricing strategies are airlines using? Is it ethical for airlines to charge baggage fees?

PART 1: Defining Marketing and the Marketing Process (Chapters 1–2)
PART 2: Understanding the Marketplace and Consumer Value (Chapters 3–6)
PART 3: Designing a Customer Value–Driven Strategy and Mix (Chapters 7–17)
PART 4: Extending Marketing (Chapters 18–20)

12 Marketing Channels
Delivering Customer Value

We now look at the third marketing mix tool—distribution. Companies rarely work alone in engaging customers, creating customer value, and building profitable customer relationships. Instead, most are only a single link in a larger supply chain and marketing channel. As such, a firm's success depends not only on how well *it* performs but also on how well its *entire marketing channel* competes with competitors' channels. The first part of this chapter explores the nature of marketing channels and the marketer's channel design and management decisions. We then examine physical distribution—or logistics—an area that has grown dramatically in importance and sophistication. In the next chapter, we'll look more closely at two major channel intermediaries: retailers and wholesalers.

We start by looking at Uber, the fast-growing, app-based car-hailing service that has recently sprouted up in cities around the world. Uber has radically reinvented urban transportation channels, posing a serious threat to conventional taxicab and car service companies. As Uber grows, traditional competitors must innovate or risk being pushed aside.

UBER: Radically Reshaping Urban Transportation Channels

It's rare. But every now and then a company comes along that completely disrupts the traditional ways of distributing a product or service. FedEx revolutionized small package delivery channels, Amazon.com radically transformed online selling, and Apple's iTunes and iPod turned music distribution on its ear. Now comes Uber, the app-based ride service that is revolutionizing urban transportation. Fast-growing Uber is giving conventional taxicab and car services a real ride for their money. In just seven short years, Uber has revved up operations in hundreds of major cities in 67 countries, already booking more than $10 billion in rides annually through its massive network of more than a million drivers.

Why are so many customers around the world bypassing good old taxicabs in favor of newcomer Uber? It's all about convenience and peace of mind. No more stepping out into busy city streets to wave down a passing cab. Instead, Uber's smartphone app lets passengers hail the nearest cab or limo from any location, then track the vehicle on a map as it approaches. The Uber app gives riders an accurate estimate in advance of the fare to their destinations (usually less than that charged by a regular cab),

> Uber—the fast-growing app-based ride service—is revolutionizing urban transportation channels in cities around the globe. As Uber grows, traditional taxicab services must innovate or risk extinction.

eliminating guesswork and uncertainty. After the ride, passengers simply exit and walk away. Uber automatically pays the driver (including tip) from the passenger's prepaid Uber account, eliminating the often-inconvenient and awkward moment of payment. And it's the same process anywhere in the world, from San Francisco, London, Paris, or Abu Dhabi to Ashville, North Carolina, or Athens, Georgia.

Compare the Uber experience to the uncertain and often-unsettling experience of using a standard taxicab. One business reporter describes waiting in line at a taxi stand while a driver tried to convince another would-be passenger—a total stranger—to share the cab, thereby increasing his fare. The cab itself was ancient and filthy, with ripped and worn seats. During the entire ride, the cabbie carried on a phone conversation in a foreign language via his headset, causing safety concerns while distractedly navigating busy city streets. The driver spoke only poor, hard-to-understand English. "That turned out to be a good thing," says the reporter, "because I couldn't understand what he was trying to say when he insulted me for not tipping him enough." The reporter's conclusion: "I stepped out of the taxi in front of my house and realized I just don't have to put up with this garbage anymore. Uber has changed my life, and as God is my witness, [wherever Uber is available] I will never take a taxi again."

Uber drivers range from professional drivers who've switched over from conventional cab and transportation companies to regular people looking for a little adventure and some extra income in their spare time. All Uber drivers go through an orientation that requires proficiency in a market area's dominant language, ensuring that they can communicate effectively with customers. Uber vehicles must be at least 2010-year models or newer, and customers can often choose the type of car they want, from an entry-level Prius to a stretch Mercedes S-Class. A two-way rating system—by which riders rate drivers and drivers rate riders in return—helps keep both sides on their best behavior. Poorly rated drivers risk being rejected by future passengers; poorly rated passengers risk rejection by drivers, who can choose which fares they accept.

Uber lets passengers hail the nearest cab from any location using its smartphone app, then track the vehicle on a map as it approaches.
PAUL J. RICHARDS/AFP/Getty Images

Uber's disruptive innovation has brought a breath of fresh air to an industry begging for change. Urban transportation channels have long been characterized by cartel-like relationships between cab companies and local governments, high fixed fares, poor service, and little accountability. As one economics professor points out, the taxicab industry "was ripe for entry [by start-ups] because everybody hates it."

Like any innovator, upstart Uber faces some significant challenges. For example, Uber has been criticized for exercising too little control over driver quality and security. So far, the company has ridden beneath the radar of industry regulators by not directly employing drivers (all Uber drivers are independent contractors) and not owning any vehicles (all vehicles are driver-owned). However, although some municipalities have passed ordinances favorable to Uber's operations, others are imposing new regulatory restrictions and licensing requirements or even banning ride-hailing services altogether.

Uber has also been criticized for its "surge pricing" practices—a dynamic pricing mechanism that kicks in to raise prices when demand exceeds supply, sometimes resulting in shockingly high fares and accusations of price gouging. Uber justifies surge pricing by pointing that it provides an incentive for more drivers to be available during periods when passengers need them most. According to Uber, if a passenger faces a higher-than-normal fare because of surge pricing, the alternative without Uber would more than likely be no taxi at all. Moreover, Uber informs passengers in advance what the fares will be. If they don't like the fare, they can find another cab, take public transportation, or walk.

Uber's huge success has attracted a garage full of competitors, such as Lyft, Gett, Carma, and Curb. Even Google (itself a

major Uber investor) is reported to be readying the launch of its own ride-hailing service, one that would eventually utilize the driverless vehicles Google is developing. But Uber has a huge first-to-market advantage. Its bookings are 10 times those of nearest competitor Lyft, and Uber is adding new customers at a faster rate.

Moreover, even as competition stiffens, Uber has little to fear from like-minded competitors. In fact, the more competitors adopt the new model, the more the revolutionary channel will grow and thrive versus traditional channels, creating opportunities for all new car-hailing entrants. Instead, the new distribution model poses the biggest threat to traditional taxicab and car-for-hire companies, which are now losing both customers and drivers to Uber and its competitors.

Based on its U.S. success, Uber is now expanding rapidly abroad. Huge markets such as China and India are especially attractive, with their massive populations of people who don't own cars. Uber is already operating in 37 Chinese cities and plans to be shuttling riders around 100 large metro areas in the country within 12 months. In China, however, Uber is playing catch-up to market leader Didi Kuaidi, which already operates in 360 Chinese cities and towns. Similarly, in India, Uber is taking on established market leader Ola.

Despite its explosive growth, Uber—like every other ride-hailing company—has yet to turn a profit. Like Facebook, Amazon, and so many other revolutionary companies in today's internet-driven economy, Uber's start-up model is to build a big user base first, then worry about making money later. Uber keeps 20 to 30 percent of each fare—the rest goes to the driver. But Uber plows back most of its take into expansion and promotional expenses. Investors seem confident. Uber has raised more than $10 billion in venture capital and currently has a valuation of more than $62 billion, making it the world's most valuable privately held technology firm.

OBJECTIVES OUTLINE

OBJECTIVE 12-1	Explain why companies use marketing channels and discuss the functions these channels perform. **Supply Chains and the Value Delivery Network** *(pp 334–337)*
OBJECTIVE 12-2	Discuss how channel members interact and how they organize to perform the work of the channel. **Channel Behavior and Organization** *(pp 338–344)*
OBJECTIVE 12-3	Identify the major channel alternatives open to a company. **Channel Design Decisions** *(pp 344–348)*
OBJECTIVE 12-4	Explain how companies select, motivate, and evaluate channel members. **Channel Management Decisions** *(pp 348–352)*
OBJECTIVE 12-5	Discuss the nature and importance of marketing logistics and integrated supply chain management. **Marketing Logistics and Supply Chain Management** *(pp 352–359)*

Uber-mania is even catching on in other industries. It seems like there's an app-based on-demand "Uber" for almost anything these days—laundry and dry cleaning (Washio), in-home massage (Zeel), 24/7 delivery services (Postmates), and even booze (Minibar). In fact, Uber CEO Travis Kalanick sees no end of future applications for Uber's services, well beyond just delivering people to their destinations. Once Uber has established a dense network of cars in every city, he predicts using the network to deliver everything from packages from retailers to takeout food. As Kalanick puts it, "Once you're delivering cars in five minutes, there are a lot of other things you can deliver in five minutes."[1]

AS THE UBER STORY SHOWS, good distribution strategies can contribute strongly to customer value and create competitive advantage for a firm. But firms cannot bring value to customers by themselves. Instead, they must work closely with other firms in a larger value delivery network.

Supply Chains and the Value Delivery Network

> **Author Comment** | These are pretty hefty terms for a really simple concept: A company can't go it alone in creating customer value. It must work within a broader network of partners to accomplish this task. Individual companies and brands don't compete; their entire value delivery networks do.

Producing a product or service and making it available to buyers requires building relationships not only with customers but also with key suppliers and resellers in the company's *supply chain*. This supply chain consists of upstream and downstream partners. Upstream from the company is the set of firms that supply the raw materials, components, parts, information, finances, and expertise needed to create a product or service. Marketers, however, have traditionally focused on the downstream side of the supply chain—the *marketing channels* (or *distribution channels*) that look toward the customer. Downstream marketing channel partners, such as wholesalers and retailers, form a vital link between the firm and its customers.

The term *supply chain* may be too limited, as it takes a *make-and-sell* view of the business. It suggests that raw materials, productive inputs, and factory capacity should serve as the starting point for market planning. A better term would be *demand chain* because it suggests a *sense-and-respond* view of the market. Under this view, planning starts by identifying the needs of target customers, to which the company responds by organizing a chain of resources and activities with the goal of creating customer value.

Yet even a demand chain view of a business may be too limited because it takes a step-by-step, linear view of purchase-production-consumption activities. Instead, most large companies today are engaged in building and managing a complex, continuously evolving value delivery network. As defined in Chapter 2, a **value delivery network** is made up of the company, suppliers, distributors, and, ultimately, customers who "partner" with each other to improve the performance of the entire system.

Value delivery network

A network composed of the company, suppliers, distributors, and, ultimately, customers who partner with each other to improve the performance of the entire system in delivering customer value.

For example, Pepsi makes great beverages. But to make and market just one of its many lines—say, its classic colas—Pepsi manages a huge network of people within the company, from marketing and sales people to folks in finance and operations. It also coordinates the efforts of thousands of suppliers, bottlers, retailers ranging from Kroger and Walmart to Papa John's Pizza, and advertising agencies and other marketing service firms. The entire network must function together to create customer value and establish the brand's "Pepsi: Live for Now" positioning.

This chapter focuses on marketing channels—on the downstream side of the value delivery network. We examine four major questions concerning marketing channels: What is the nature of marketing channels, and why are they important? How do channel firms interact and organize to do the work of the channel? What problems do companies face in designing and managing their channels? What role do physical distribution and supply chain management play in attracting and satisfying customers? In the next chapter, we will look at marketing channel issues from the viewpoints of retailers and wholesalers.

● **Value delivery network: In making and marketing even just its classic colas, Pepsi manages a huge network of people within the company plus thousands of outside suppliers, bottlers, retailers, and marketing service firms that must work together to create customer value and establish the brand's "Pepsi: Live for Now" positioning.**

AP Images for Pepsi

Author Comment | In this section, we look at the downstream side of the value delivery network—the marketing channel organizations that connect the company and its customers. To understand their value, imagine life without retailers—say, without grocery stores or department stores.

The Nature and Importance of Marketing Channels

Few producers sell their goods directly to final users. Instead, most use intermediaries to bring their products to market. They try to forge a **marketing channel** (or **distribution channel**)—a set of interdependent organizations that help make a product or service available for use or consumption by the consumer or business user.

A company's channel decisions directly affect every other marketing decision. Pricing depends on whether the company works with national discount chains, uses high-quality specialty stores, or sells directly to consumers online. The firm's sales force and communications decisions depend on how much persuasion, training, motivation, and support its channel partners need. Whether a company develops or acquires certain new products may depend on how well those products fit the capabilities of its channel members.

Companies often pay too little attention to their distribution channels—sometimes with damaging results. In contrast, many companies have used imaginative distribution systems to gain a competitive advantage. Enterprise Rent-A-Car revolutionized the car-rental business by setting up off-airport rental offices. Apple turned the retail music business on its head by selling music for the iPod via the internet on iTunes. FedEx's creative and imposing distribution system made it a leader in express package delivery. And Amazon.com forever changed the face of retailing and became the Walmart of the internet by selling anything and everything without using physical stores.

Distribution channel decisions often involve long-term commitments to other firms. For example, companies such as Ford, McDonald's, or Nike can easily change their advertising, pricing, or promotion programs. They can scrap old products and introduce new ones as market tastes demand. But when they set up distribution channels through contracts with franchisees, independent dealers, or large retailers, they cannot readily replace these channels with company-owned stores or internet sites if the conditions change. Therefore, management must design its channels carefully, with an eye on both today's likely selling environment and tomorrow's as well.

Marketing channel (distribution channel)

A set of interdependent organizations that help make a product or service available for use or consumption by the consumer or business user.

How Channel Members Add Value

Why do producers give some of the selling job to channel partners? After all, doing so means giving up some control over how and to whom they sell their products. Producers use intermediaries because they create greater efficiency in making goods available to target markets. Through their contacts, experience, specialization, and scale of operation, intermediaries usually offer the firm more than it can achieve on its own.

● **Figure 12.1** shows how using intermediaries can provide economies. Figure 12.1A shows three manufacturers, each using direct marketing to reach three customers. This system requires nine different contacts. Figure 12.1B shows the three manufacturers working through one distributor, which contacts the three customers. This system requires only six contacts. In this way, intermediaries reduce the amount of work that must be done by both producers and consumers.

From the economic system's point of view, the role of marketing intermediaries is to transform the assortments of products made by producers into the assortments wanted by consumers. Producers make narrow assortments of products in large quantities, but consumers want broad assortments of products in small quantities. Marketing channel members buy large quantities from many producers and break them down into the smaller quantities and broader assortments desired by consumers.

For example, Unilever makes millions of bars of Lever 2000 hand soap each week. However, you most likely want to buy only a few bars at a time. Therefore, big food, drug, and discount retailers, such as Safeway, Walgreens, and Target, buy Lever 2000 by the truckload and stock it on their stores' shelves. In turn, you can buy a single bar of Lever 2000 along with a shopping cart full of small quantities of toothpaste, shampoo, and other related products as you need them. Thus, intermediaries play an important role in matching supply and demand.

In making products and services available to consumers, channel members add value by bridging the major time, place, and possession gaps that separate goods and services from those who use them. Members of the marketing channel perform many key functions. Some help to complete transactions:

- *Information.* Gathering and distributing information about consumers, producers, and other actors and forces in the marketing environment needed for planning and aiding exchange.
- *Promotion.* Developing and spreading persuasive communications about an offer.
- *Contact.* Finding and engaging customers and prospective buyers.
- *Matching.* Shaping offers to meet the buyer's needs, including activities such as manufacturing, grading, assembling, and packaging.
- *Negotiation.* Reaching an agreement on price and other terms so that ownership or possession can be transferred.

Others help to fulfill the completed transactions:

- *Physical distribution.* Transporting and storing goods.
- *Financing.* Acquiring and using funds to cover the costs of the channel work.
- *Risk taking.* Assuming the risks of carrying out the channel work.

● **FIGURE | 12.1**

How a Distributor Reduces the Number of Channel Transactions

Marketing channel intermediaries make buying a lot easier for consumers. Again, think about life without grocery retailers. How would you go about buying that 12-pack of Coke or any of the hundreds of other items that you now routinely drop into your shopping cart?

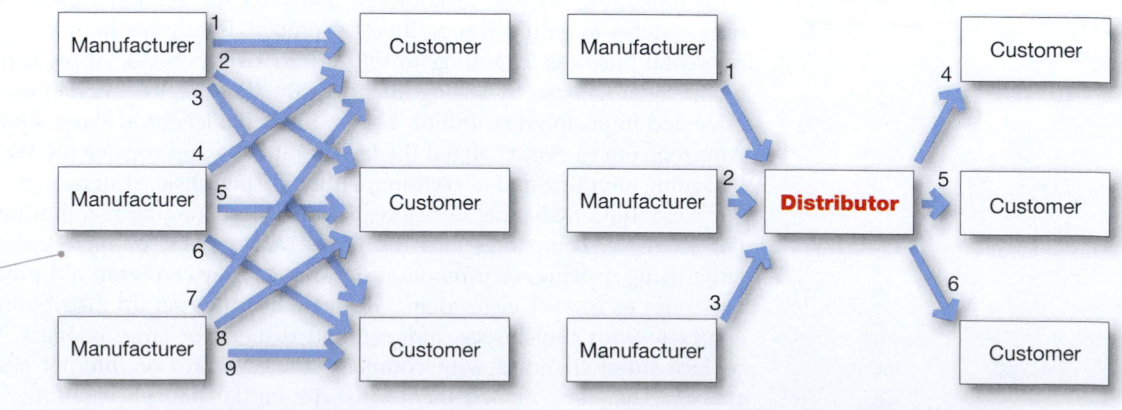

A. Number of contacts without a distributor

B. Number of contacts with a distributor

The question is not *whether* these functions need to be performed—they must be—but rather *who* will perform them. To the extent that the manufacturer performs these functions, its costs go up; therefore, its prices must be higher. When some of these functions are shifted to intermediaries, the producer's costs and prices may be lower, but the intermediaries must charge more to cover the costs of their work. In dividing the work of the channel, the various functions should be assigned to the channel members that can add the most value for the cost.

Number of Channel Levels

Companies can design their distribution channels to make products and services available to customers in different ways. Each layer of marketing intermediaries that performs some work in bringing the product and its ownership closer to the final buyer is a **channel level**. Because both the producer and the final consumer perform some work, they are part of every channel.

The *number of intermediary levels* indicates the *length* of a channel. ● **Figure 12.2** shows both consumer and business channels of different lengths. Figure 12.2A shows several common consumer distribution channels. Channel 1, a **direct marketing channel**, has no intermediary levels—the company sells directly to consumers. For example, Mary Kay Cosmetics and Amway sell their products through home and office sales parties and online websites and social media; companies ranging from GEICO insurance to Omaha Steaks sell directly to customers via internet, mobile, and telephone channels. The remaining channels in Figure 12.2A are **indirect marketing channels**, containing one or more intermediaries.

Figure 12.2B shows some common business distribution channels. The business marketer can use its own sales force to sell directly to business customers. Or it can sell to various types of intermediaries, which in turn sell to these customers. Although consumer and business marketing channels with even more levels can sometimes be found, these are less common. From the producer's point of view, a greater number of levels means less control and greater channel complexity. Moreover, all the institutions in the channel are connected by several types of *flows*. These include the *physical flow* of products, the *flow of ownership*, the *payment flow*, the *information flow*, and the *promotion flow*. These flows can make even channels with only one or a few levels very complex.

Channel level
A layer of intermediaries that performs some work in bringing the product and its ownership closer to the final buyer.

Direct marketing channel
A marketing channel that has no intermediary levels.

Indirect marketing channel
A marketing channel containing one or more intermediary levels.

● **FIGURE | 12.2**
Consumer and Business Marketing Channels

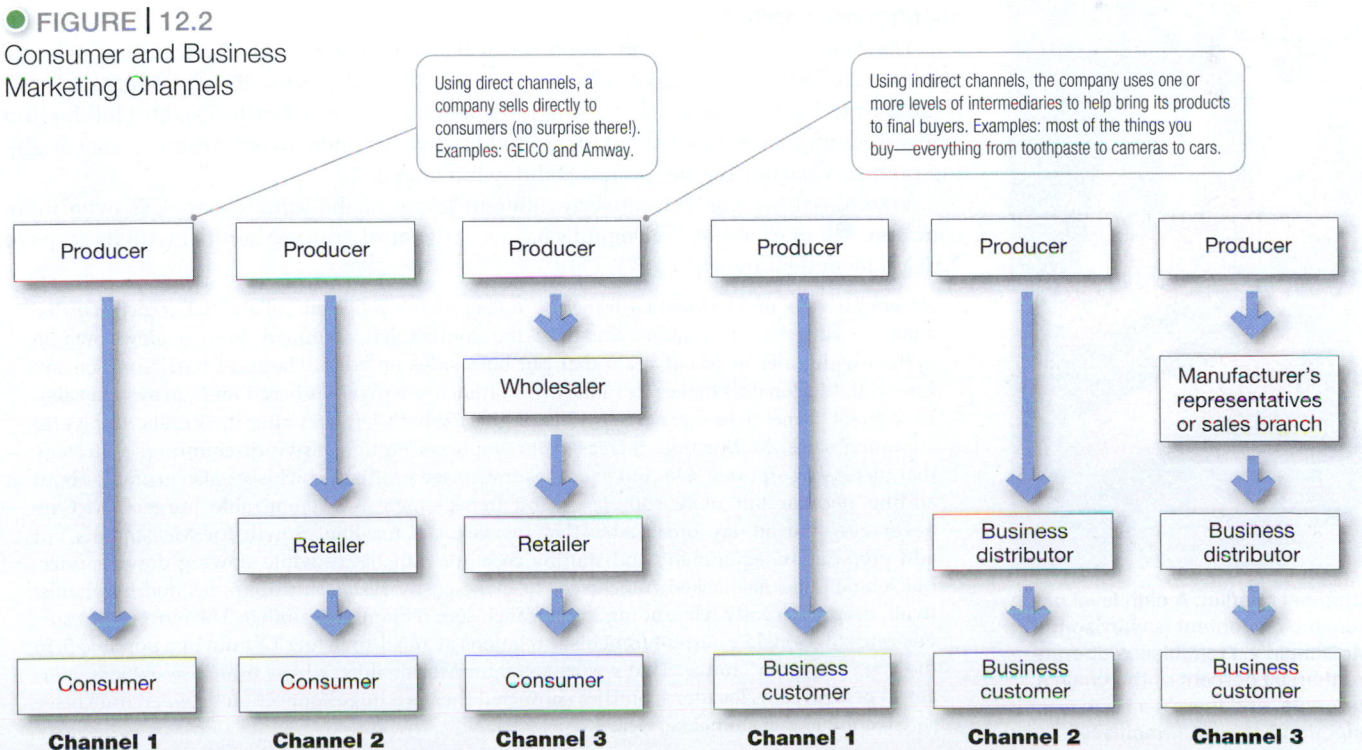

Using direct channels, a company sells directly to consumers (no surprise there!). Examples: GEICO and Amway.

Using indirect channels, the company uses one or more levels of intermediaries to help bring its products to final buyers. Examples: most of the things you buy—everything from toothpaste to cameras to cars.

A. Consumer marketing channels

B. Business marketing channels

Channel Behavior and Organization

Distribution channels are more than simple collections of firms tied together by various flows. They are complex behavioral systems in which people and companies interact to accomplish individual, company, and channel goals. Some channel systems consist of only informal interactions among loosely organized firms. Others consist of formal interactions guided by strong organizational structures. Moreover, channel systems do not stand still—new types of intermediaries emerge and whole new channel systems evolve. Here we look at channel behavior and how members organize to do the work of the channel.

Channel Behavior

A marketing channel consists of firms that have partnered for their common good. Each channel member depends on the others. For example, a Ford dealer depends on Ford to design cars that meet customer needs. In turn, Ford depends on the dealer to engage customers, persuade them to buy Ford cars, and service the cars after the sale. Each Ford dealer also depends on other dealers to provide good sales and service that will uphold the brand's reputation. In fact, the success of individual Ford dealers depends on how well the entire Ford marketing channel competes with the channels of Toyota, GM, Honda, and other auto manufacturers.

Each channel member plays a specialized role in the channel. For example, Samsung's role is to produce electronics products that consumers will covet and create demand through national advertising. Best Buy's role is to display these Samsung products in convenient locations, answer buyers' questions, and complete sales. The channel will be most effective when each member assumes the tasks it can do best.

Ideally, because the success of individual channel members depends on the overall channel's success, all channel firms should work together smoothly. They should understand and accept their roles, coordinate their activities, and cooperate to attain overall channel goals. However, individual channel members rarely take such a broad view. Cooperating to achieve overall channel goals sometimes means giving up individual company goals. Although channel members depend on one another, they often act alone in their own short-run best interests. They often disagree on who should do what and for what rewards. Such disagreements over goals, roles, and rewards generate **channel conflict**.

Horizontal conflict occurs among firms at the same level of the channel. For instance, some Ford dealers in Chicago might complain that other dealers in the city steal sales from them by pricing too low or advertising outside their assigned territories. Or Holiday Inn franchisees might complain about other Holiday Inn operators overcharging guests or giving poor service, hurting the overall Holiday Inn image.

Vertical conflict, conflict between different levels of the same channel, is even more common. ● For example, McDonald's has recently faced growing conflict with its corps of 3,100 independent franchisees:[2]

Recent surveys of McDonald's franchise owners have reflected substantial franchisee discontent with the corporation. Some of the conflict has stemmed from a slowdown in system-wide sales in recent years that put both sides on edge. The most basic conflicts are financial. McDonald's makes its money from franchisee royalties based on total system sales. In contrast, franchisees make money on margins—what's left over after their costs. To reverse slumping sales, McDonald's increased its emphasis on aggressive discounting, a strategy that increases corporate sales but squeezes franchisee profits. Franchisees also grumble about adding popular but more complex menu items—such as customizable burgers, McCafe beverages, and all-day breakfasts—that increase the top-line growth for McDonald's but add preparation, equipment, and staffing costs for franchisees while slowing down service. McDonald's has also asked franchisees to make costly restaurant upgrades and overhauls. In all, despite recently rebounding sales, franchisees remain disgruntled. The most recent survey rates McDonald's current franchisee relations at an all-time low 1.81 out of a possible 5, in the "fair" to "poor" range. That's worrisome for McDonald's, whose franchise owners operate 90 percent of its locations. Studies show that there's a huge connection between franchisee satisfaction and customer service.

Some conflict in the channel takes the form of healthy competition. Such competition can be good for the channel; without it, the channel could become passive and

Channel conflict
Disagreements among marketing channel members on goals, roles, and rewards—who should do what and for what rewards.

● **Channel conflict:** A high level of franchisee discontent is worrisome to McDonald's. Franchisees operate more than 90 percent of the chain's restaurants, and there's a huge connection between franchisee satisfaction and customer service.

© Greg Balfour Evans/Alamy

noninnovative. For example, the McDonald's conflict with its franchisees might represent normal give-and-take over the respective rights of the channel partners. However, severe or prolonged conflict can disrupt channel effectiveness and cause lasting harm to channel relationships. McDonald's should manage the channel conflict carefully to keep it from getting out of hand.

Vertical Marketing Systems

For the channel as a whole to perform well, each channel member's role must be specified, and channel conflict must be managed. The channel will perform better if it includes a firm, agency, or mechanism that provides leadership and has the power to assign roles and manage conflict.

Historically, *conventional distribution channels* have lacked such leadership and power, often resulting in damaging conflict and poor performance. One of the biggest channel developments over the years has been the emergence of *vertical marketing systems* that provide channel leadership. ● **Figure 12.3** contrasts the two types of channel arrangements.

A **conventional distribution channel** consists of one or more independent producers, wholesalers, and retailers. Each is a separate business seeking to maximize its own profits, perhaps even at the expense of the system as a whole. No channel member has much control over the other members, and no formal means exists for assigning roles and resolving channel conflict.

In contrast, a **vertical marketing system (VMS)** consists of producers, wholesalers, and retailers acting as a unified system. One channel member owns the others, has contracts with them, or wields so much power that they must all cooperate. The VMS can be dominated by the producer, the wholesaler, or the retailer.

We look now at three major types of VMSs: *corporate, contractual,* and *administered.* Each uses a different means for setting up leadership and power in the channel.

Corporate VMS

A **corporate VMS** integrates successive stages of production and distribution under single ownership. Coordination and conflict management are attained through regular organizational channels. For example, grocery giant Kroger owns and operates 37 manufacturing plants—17 dairies, 6 bakery plants, 5 grocery plants, 1 deli plant, 2 frozen dough plants, 2 beverage plants, 2 cheese plants, and 2 meat plants. That gives it factory-to-store channel control over 40 percent of the 13,000 private-label items found on its shelves.[3]

Similarly, little-known Italian eyewear maker Luxottica produces many famous eyewear brands—including its own Ray-Ban, Oakley, Persol, and Vogue Eyewear

Conventional distribution channel
A channel consisting of one or more independent producers, wholesalers, and retailers, each a separate business seeking to maximize its own profits, perhaps even at the expense of profits for the system as a whole.

Vertical marketing system (VMS)
A channel structure in which producers, wholesalers, and retailers act as a unified system. One channel member owns the others, has contracts with them, or has so much power that they all cooperate.

Corporate VMS
A vertical marketing system that combines successive stages of production and distribution under single ownership—channel leadership is established through common ownership.

● FIGURE | 12.3
Comparison of Conventional Distribution Channel with Vertical Marketing System

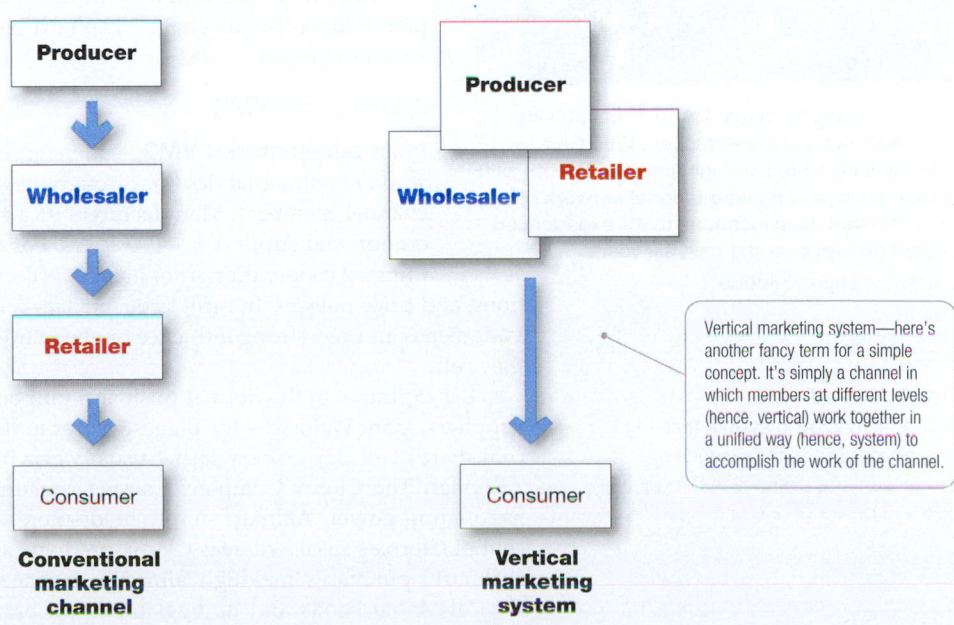

brands and licensed brands such as Burberry, Chanel, Polo Ralph Lauren, Dolce & Gabbana, DKNY, Prada, Versace, and Michael Kors. Luxottica then controls the distribution of these brands through some of the world's largest optical chains—LensCrafters, Pearle Vision, Sunglass Hut, Target Optical, Sears Optical—which it also owns. In all, through vertical integration, Luxottica controls an estimated 60 to 80 percent of the U.S. eyewear market.[4]

Contractual VMS

Contractual VMS
A vertical marketing system in which independent firms at different levels of production and distribution join together through contracts.

A **contractual VMS** consists of independent firms at different levels of production and distribution that join together through contracts to obtain more economies or sales impact than each could achieve alone. Channel members coordinate their activities and manage conflict through contractual agreements.

Franchise organization
A contractual vertical marketing system in which a channel member, called a franchisor, links several stages in the production-distribution process.

The **franchise organization** is the most common type of contractual relationship. In this system, a channel member called a *franchisor* links several stages in the production-distribution process. In the United States alone, almost 800,000 franchise outlets account for $994 billion of economic output. Industry analysts estimate that a new franchise outlet opens somewhere in the United States every eight minutes and that about one out of every 12 retail business outlets is a franchised business.[5]

Almost every kind of business has been franchised—from motels and fast-food restaurants to dental centers and dating services, from wedding consultants and handyman services to funeral homes, fitness centers, and moving services.  For example, through franchising, Two Men and a Truck moving services—"Movers Who Care"—grew quickly from two high school students looking to make extra money with a pickup truck to an international network of over 380 franchise locations that's experienced record growth over the past six years and completed more than 5.5 million moves.[6]

There are three types of franchises. The first type is the *manufacturer-sponsored retailer franchise system*—for example, Ford and its network of independent franchised dealers. The second type is the *manufacturer-sponsored wholesaler franchise system*—Coca-Cola licenses bottlers (wholesalers) in various world markets that buy Coca-Cola syrup concentrate and then bottle and sell the finished product to retailers locally. The third type is the *service-firm-sponsored retailer franchise system*—for example, Burger King and its more than 12,000 franchisee-operated restaurants around the world. Other examples can be found in everything from auto rentals (Hertz, Avis), apparel retailers (The Athlete's Foot, Plato's Closet), and motels (Holiday Inn, Hampton Inn) to supplemental education (Huntington Learning Center, Mathnasium) and personal services (Great Clips, Mr. Handyman, Anytime Fitness).

The fact that most consumers cannot tell the difference between contractual and corporate VMSs shows how successfully the contractual organizations compete with corporate chains. The next chapter presents a fuller discussion of the various contractual VMSs.

Franchising systems: Through franchising, Two Men and a Truck—"Movers Who Care"—grew quickly from two high school students with a pickup truck to an international network of over 380 franchise locations that's experienced record growth over the past six years.
Two Men and a Truck International

Administered VMS

Administered VMS
A vertical marketing system that coordinates successive stages of production and distribution through the size and power of one of the parties.

In an **administered VMS**, leadership is assumed not through common ownership or contractual ties but through the size and power of one or a few dominant channel members. Manufacturers of a top brand can obtain strong trade cooperation and support from resellers. For example, P&G and Apple can command unusual cooperation from many resellers regarding displays, shelf space, promotions, and price policies. In turn, large retailers such as Walmart, Home Depot, Kroger, and Walgreens can exert strong influence on the many manufacturers that supply the products they sell.

For example, in the normal push and pull between Walmart and its consumer goods suppliers, giant Walmart—the biggest grocer in the United States with a more than 25 percent share of all U.S. grocery sales—usually gets its way. Take supplier Clorox, for instance. Although The Clorox Company's strong consumer brand preference gives it significant negotiating power, Walmart simply holds more cards. Sales to Walmart make up 25 percent of Clorox's sales, whereas Clorox products account for only one-third of 1 percent of Walmart's purchases, making Walmart by far the dominant partner. Things get even worse for Cal-Maine Foods and its Eggland's Best brand, which relies on Walmart for nearly one-third of its sales but tallies only about one-tenth of 1 percent of Walmart's volume. For such brands, maintaining a strong relationship with the giant retailer is crucial.[7]

Horizontal Marketing Systems

Horizontal marketing system
A channel arrangement in which two or more companies at one level join together to follow a new marketing opportunity.

Another channel development is the **horizontal marketing system**, in which two or more companies at one level join together to follow a new marketing opportunity. By working together, companies can combine their financial, production, or marketing resources to accomplish more than any one company could alone.

Companies might join forces with competitors or noncompetitors. They might work with each other on a temporary or permanent basis, or they may create a separate company. For example, Walmart partners with noncompetitor McDonald's to place "express" versions of McDonald's restaurants in Walmart stores. McDonald's benefits from Walmart's heavy store traffic, and Walmart keeps hungry shoppers from needing to go elsewhere to eat.

Horizontal channel arrangements also work well globally. ● For example, most of the world's major airlines have joined to together in one of three global alliances: Star Alliance, Skyteam, or Oneworld. Star Alliance consists of 27 airlines "working in harmony," including United, Air Canada, Lufthansa, Air China, Turkish Airlines, and almost two dozen others. It offers more than 18,500 combined daily departures to more than 190 destinations around the world. Such alliances tie the individual carriers into massive worldwide air travel networks with joint branding and marketing, co-locations at airports, interline scheduling and smoother global flight connections, and shared rewards and membership privileges.[8]

● Horizontal marketing systems: Star Alliance consists of 27 airlines "working in harmony" with shared branding and marketing to smooth and extend each member's global air travel capabilities.
Felix Gottwald

Multichannel Distribution Systems

Multichannel distribution system
A distribution system in which a single firm sets up two or more marketing channels to reach one or more customer segments.

In the past, many companies used a single channel to sell to a single market or market segment. Today, with the proliferation of customer segments and channel possibilities, more and more companies have adopted **multichannel distribution systems**. Such multichannel marketing occurs when a single firm sets up two or more marketing channels to reach one or more customer segments.

● Figure 12.4 shows a multichannel marketing system. In the figure, the producer sells directly to consumer segment 1 using catalogs, online, and mobile channels and reaches consumer segment 2 through retailers. It sells indirectly to business segment 1 through distributors and dealers and to business segment 2 through its own sales force.

These days, almost every large company and many small ones distribute through multiple channels. For example, John Deere sells its familiar green-and-yellow lawn and garden tractors, mowers, and outdoor power products to consumers and commercial users through several channels, including John Deere retailers, Lowe's home improvement stores, and online. It sells and services its tractors, combines, planters, and other agricultural equipment through its premium John Deere dealer network. And it sells large construction and forestry equipment through selected large, full-service John Deere dealers and their sales forces.

Multichannel distribution systems offer many advantages to companies facing large and complex markets. With each new channel, the company expands its sales and market coverage and gains opportunities to tailor its products and services to the specific needs of diverse customer segments. But such multichannel systems are harder to control, and they can generate conflict as more channels compete for customers and sales. For example,

● **FIGURE | 12.4**
Multichannel Distribution System

```
                                      Producer
                                         |
         ┌───────────────────────────────┼───────────────────────────────┐
         |                                |                                |
         |                          Distributors                          |
         |                                |                                |
         |                    ┌───────────┴──────────┐                    |
  Catalogs,                   |                      |              Sales
  online,                 Retailers               Dealers           force
  mobile                      |                      |                |
     |                        |                      |                |
  ┌──────────┐         ┌──────────┐          ┌──────────┐      ┌──────────┐
  │ Consumer │         │ Consumer │          │ Business │      │ Business │
  │segment 1 │         │segment 2 │          │segment 1 │      │segment 2 │
  └──────────┘         └──────────┘          └──────────┘      └──────────┘
```

> Most large companies distribute through multiple channels. For example, you could buy a familiar green-and-yellow John Deere lawn tractor from a neighborhood John Deere dealer or from Lowe's. A large farm or forestry business would buy larger John Deere equipment from a premium full-service John Deere dealer and its sales force.

when John Deere first began selling selected consumer products through Lowe's home improvement stores, many of its independent dealers complained loudly. To avoid such conflicts in its online marketing channels, the company routes all of its online sales to John Deere dealers.

Changing Channel Organization

Changes in technology and the explosive growth of direct and online marketing are having a profound impact on the nature and design of marketing channels. One major trend is toward **disintermediation**—a big term with a clear message and important consequences. Disintermediation occurs when product or service producers cut out intermediaries and go directly to final buyers or when radically new types of channel intermediaries displace traditional ones.

Thus, in many industries, traditional intermediaries are dropping by the wayside, as is the case with online marketers taking business from traditional brick-and-mortar retailers. For example, online music download services such as iTunes and Amazon MP3 have pretty much put traditional music-store retailers out of business, with physical CDs sinking fast and now capturing less than a third of the music market. ● In turn, however, streaming music services such as Spotify, Rhapsody, and Apple Music are now disintermediating digital download services—digital downloads peaked last year while music streaming increased 29 percent.[9]

Disintermediation presents both opportunities and problems for producers and resellers. Channel innovators who find new ways to add value in the channel can displace traditional resellers and reap the rewards. In turn, traditional intermediaries must continue to innovate to avoid being swept aside. For example, when Netflix pioneered online DVD-by-mail video rentals, it sent traditional brick-and-mortar video stores such as Blockbuster into ruin. Then Netflix itself faced disintermediation threats from an even hotter channel—video streaming. But instead of simply watching developments, Netflix has led them profitably (see Real Marketing 12.1).

Similarly, superstore booksellers Barnes & Noble and Borders pioneered huge book selections and low prices, shutting down most small independent bookstores. Then along came Amazon.com, which threatened even the largest brick-and-mortar bookstores.

Disintermediation
The cutting out of marketing channel intermediaries by product or service producers or the displacement of traditional resellers by radical new types of intermediaries.

● **Disintermediation: Streaming music services such as Spotify are rapidly disintermediating both traditional music-store retailers and even music download services such as iTunes.**

© DADO RUVIC/Reuters/Corbis

12.1 Netflix: Disintermedi*ate* or Be Disintermediate*d*

Baseball great Yogi Berra, known more for his mangled phrasing than for his baseball prowess, once said, "The future ain't what it used to be." For Netflix, the world's largest video subscription service, no matter how you say it, figuring out the future is challenging and a bit scary. Netflix faces dramatic changes in how video entertainment will be distributed. The question is: Will Netflix be among the disintermediators or among the disintermediated?

Time and again, Netflix has innovated its way to the top in the distribution of video entertainment. In the early 2000s, Netflix's revolutionary DVD-by-mail service put all but the most powerful movie-rental stores out of business. In 2007, Netflix's then-groundbreaking move into digital streaming once again revolutionized how people accessed movies and other video content. Now, with Netflix leading the pack, video distribution has become a roiling pot of emerging technologies and high-tech competitors, one that offers both mind-bending opportunities and stomach-churning risks.

Just ask Blockbuster. Little more than a decade ago, the giant brick-and-mortar movie-rental chain flat-out owned the industry. Then along came Netflix, the fledgling DVD-by-mail service. First thousands, then millions, of subscribers were drawn to Netflix's innovative distribution model. In 2010, as Netflix surged, once-mighty Blockbuster fell into bankruptcy.

The Blockbuster riches-to-rags disintermediation story underscores the turmoil that typifies today's video distribution business. In only the past few years, a glut of video access options has materialized. At the same time that Netflix ascended and Blockbuster plunged, Coinstar's Redbox came out of nowhere to build a novel national network of $1-a-day DVD-rental kiosks. Then high-tech start-ups such as Hulu—with its high-quality, ad-supported free access to movies and current TV shows—began pushing digital streaming via the internet.

All along the way, Netflix has acted boldly to stay ahead of the competition. For example, by 2007, Netflix had mailed out its one billionth DVD. But rather than rest on success, Netflix and its CEO, Reed Hastings, set their sights on a then-revolutionary new video distribution model: Deliver Netflix to any and every internet-connected screen—from laptops to internet-ready TVs to smartphones and other Wi-Fi–enabled devices. Netflix launched a new Watch Instantly service, which let members stream movies to their computers as part of their monthly fee, even if it came at the expense of the company's still-hot DVD-by-mail business.

Although Netflix didn't pioneer digital streaming, it poured resources into improving the technology and building the largest streaming content library. It built a huge subscriber base, and sales and profits soared. With its massive physical DVD library and a streaming library of more than 20,000 high-definition movies accessible via 200 different internet-ready devices, it seemed that nothing could stop Netflix.

But Netflix's stunning success drew a slew of resourceful competitors. Video giants such as Google's YouTube and Apple's iTunes began renting movie downloads, and Hulu introduced subscription-based Hulu Plus. To stay ahead, even to survive, Netflix needed to keep the innovation pedal to the metal. So in the summer of 2011, in an ambitious but risky move, CEO Hastings made an all-in bet on digital streaming. He split off Netflix's still-thriving DVD-by-mail service into a separate business. Although customers can still access Netflix's world's-biggest DVD library, the DVD operation is now called DVD.com, which operates at a separate site.

As it turns out, Hastings made a visionary move. Now more than ever, Netflix's heavy focus is on streaming video. Of the company's current 81.5 million paid subscribers, 69 million are streaming-only customers. Netflix subscribers stream an astounding 3.8 billion hours of movies and TV programs every month. On an average weeknight, Netflix commands more than a third of all internet traffic in North American homes. And the company recently completed an enormous global expansion, taking Netflix's service into more than 190 countries. Streaming now accounts of nearly 90 percent of the company's revenues, which have nearly double in just the past four years.

Despite its continuing success, Netflix knows that it can't rest its innovation machine. Competition continues to move at a blurring rate. For example, Amazon's Prime Instant Video offers streaming of thousands of movies and TV shows to Amazon Prime members at no extra cost. Google has Google Play, an all-media entertainment portal for movies, music, e-books, and apps. Comcast offers Xfinity Streampix, which lets subscribers stream older movies and television programs via their TVs, laptops, tablets, or smartphones. And Apple and Samsung are creating smoother integration with streaming content via smart TVs.

Moving ahead, as the industry settles into streaming as the main delivery model, content—not just delivery—will be a key to distancing Netflix from the rest of the pack.

Netflix's innovative distribution strategy: From DVDs by mail to Watch Instantly to video streaming on almost any device, Netflix has stayed ahead of the howling pack by doing what it does best—revolutionize distribution. What's next?
REUTERS/Mike Blake

Given its head start, Netflix remains well ahead in the content race. However, Amazon, Hulu Plus, and other competitors are working feverishly to sign contracts with big movie and TV content providers. But so is Netflix. It recently scored a big win with a Disney exclusive—soon, Netflix will be the only place viewers can stream Disney's deep catalog and new releases from Walt Disney Animation, Marvel, Pixar, and Lucasfilm.

But as content-licensing deals with movie and television studios become harder to get, in yet another innovative video distribution twist, Netflix and its competitors are now developing their own original content at a torrid pace. Once again, Netflix appears to have the upper hand. For example, it led the way with the smash hit *House of Cards,* a U.S. version of a hit British political drama series produced by Hollywood bigwigs David Fincher and Kevin Spacey. Based on its huge success with *House of Cards,* Netflix developed a number of other original series, including *Master of None, Unbreakable*

Kimmy Schmidt, Daredevil, and *Orange Is the New Black*.

In all, Netflix now broadcasts 39 original series and dozens of documentaries, movies, comedy specials, and other types of shows. Such efforts have left the rest of the video industry scrambling to keep up. And Netflix is just getting started. It plans to more than double its investment in original content for the coming year to an astounding $6 billion. This massive development of original content has taken Netflix beyond just content distribution and into the realm of the largest TV networks.

Thus, from DVDs by mail, to Watch Instantly, to video streaming on almost any device, to developing original content, Netflix has stayed ahead of the howling pack by doing what it does best—innovate and revolutionize distribution. What's next? No one really knows. But one thing seems certain: Whatever's coming, if Netflix doesn't lead the change, it risks being left behind—and quickly. Netflix must continue to disintermediate its own distribution model before competitors can. As Netflix's slower moving competitors have learned the hard way, it's disintermedi*ate* or be disintermediat*ed*.

Sources: See Shalini Ramachandram, "Netflix Drops on Weak-Growth Forecast," *Wall Street Journal*, April 19, 2016, www.wsj.com/articles/netflix-adds-more-users-than-expected-1461010680; Susan Young, "2014 SUCCESS Achiever of the Year: Reed Hastings," *SUCCESS*, February 10, 2015, www.success.achiever-of-the-year-reed-hastings; Cade Metz, "The Counterintuitive Tech behind Netflix's Worldwide Launch," *Wired*, January 7, 2016, www.wired.com/2016/01/the-counterintuitive-tech-behind-netflixs-worldwide-launch/; Craig Smith, "By the Numbers: 50+ Amazing Netflix Statistics and Facts," *Expanded Ramblings*, April 20, 2016, http://expandedramblings.com/index.php/netflix_statistics-facts/; and www.netflix.com, accessed October 2016.

Amazon.com almost single-handedly bankrupted Borders in less than 10 years. Now, both offline and online sellers of physical books are being threatened by digital book downloads and e-readers. Rather than yielding to digital developments, however, Amazon.com is leading them with its highly successful Kindle e-readers and tablets. By contrast, Barnes & Noble—the giant that put so many independent bookstores out of business—was a latecomer with its struggling Nook e-reader and now finds itself locked in a battle for survival.[10]

Like resellers, to remain competitive, product and service producers must develop new channel opportunities, such as the internet and other direct channels. However, developing these new channels often brings them into direct competition with their established channels, resulting in conflict. To ease this problem, companies often look for ways to make going direct a plus for the entire channel.

For example, Volvo Car Group (now owned by Chinese car maker Geeley) recently announced plans to start selling Volvo vehicles online in all of its markets. Some 80 percent of Volvo buyers already shop online for other goods, so cars seem like a natural extension. Few auto makers have tried selling directly, with the exception of Tesla, which sells its all-electric cars online, bypassing dealers altogether. Other car companies worry that selling directly would alienate their independent dealer networks. "If you say e-commerce, initially dealers get nervous," says Volvo's head of marketing. So, to avoid channel conflicts, Volvo will pass all online sales through established dealers for delivery. In that way, boosting sales through direct marketing will benefit both Volvo and its channel partners.[11]

Author Comment | Like everything else in marketing, good channel design begins with analyzing customer needs. Remember, marketing channels are really *customer value delivery networks*.

Channel Design Decisions

We now look at several channel design decisions manufacturers face. In designing marketing channels, manufacturers struggle between what is ideal and what is practical. A new firm with limited capital usually starts by selling in a limited market area. In this case, deciding on the best channels might not be a problem: The problem might simply be how to convince one or a few good intermediaries to handle the line.

If successful, the new firm can branch out to new markets through existing intermediaries. In smaller markets, the firm might sell directly to retailers; in larger markets, it might sell through distributors. In one part of the country, it might grant exclusive franchises; in another, it might sell through all available outlets. Then it might add an online store that sells directly to hard-to-reach customers. In this way, channel systems often evolve to meet market opportunities and conditions.

For maximum effectiveness, however, channel analysis and decision making should be more purposeful. **Marketing channel design** calls for analyzing consumer needs, setting channel objectives, identifying major channel alternatives, and evaluating the alternatives.

Marketing channel design

Designing effective marketing channels by analyzing customer needs, setting channel objectives, identifying major channel alternatives, and evaluating those alternatives.

Analyzing Consumer Needs

As noted previously, marketing channels are part of the overall *customer value delivery network*. Each channel member and level adds value for the customer. Thus, designing the marketing channel starts with finding out what target consumers want from the channel. Do consumers want to buy nearby, or are they willing to travel to more centralized locations? Would customers rather buy in person, by phone, or online? Do they value breadth of assortment, or do they prefer specialization? Do consumers want many add-on services (delivery, installation, repairs), or will they obtain these services elsewhere? The faster the delivery, the greater the assortment provided, and the more add-on services supplied, the greater the channel's service level.

Providing the fastest delivery, the greatest assortment, and the most services, however, may not be possible, practical, or desired. The company and its channel members may not have the resources or skills needed to provide all the desired services. Also, higher levels of service result in higher costs for the channel and higher prices for consumers. The success of modern discount retailing shows that consumers often accept lower service levels in exchange for lower prices. For example, Walmart typically rates dead last in *Consumer Reports* rankings of grocery retailers on customer shopping experience and satisfaction compared to the likes of Wegmans, Publix, Kroger, Whole Foods, or about any other grocery retailer. Yet it captures a 25 percent share of the U.S. grocery market.[12]

Many companies, however, position themselves on higher service levels, and customers willingly pay the higher prices. For example, whereas Walmart typically rates last in *Consumers Reports* rankings of grocery retailer customer satisfaction, East Coast supermarket chain Wegmans consistently ranks first:[13]

● Wegmans prides itself on its broad and deep selection, clean stores, very high service levels, and well-trained and friendly employees. "Best supermarket around, hands down," says one customer in a Yelp review. "The knowledge and helpfulness of the workers is beyond amazing." Says another, "Aside from the overwhelming options of everything on the planet to choose from, it's an amazing place. I walk around thinking...ok, I'm impressed!" The result is avidly loyal customers. Actor Alec Baldwin's mother reportedly refused to move from New York to Los Angeles because she didn't want to abandon her favorite Wegmans store. So even though they could probably save money by shopping at Walmart, to devoted Wegmans shoppers, the higher quality and extraordinary service are well worth the somewhat-higher prices.

● Meeting customers' channel service needs: Wegmans is the "best supermarket around, hands down." To devoted Wegmans shoppers, retailer's extraordinary people and service are well worth its somewhat higher prices.

Associated Press

Thus, companies must balance consumer needs not only against the feasibility and costs of meeting these needs but also against customer price preferences.

Setting Channel Objectives

Companies should state their marketing channel objectives in terms of targeted levels of customer service. Usually, a company can identify several segments wanting different levels of service. The company should decide which segments to serve and the best channels to use in each case. In each segment, the company wants to minimize the total channel cost of meeting customer service requirements.

The company's channel objectives are also influenced by the nature of the company, its products, its marketing intermediaries, its competitors, and the environment. For example, the company's size and financial situation determine which marketing functions it can handle itself and which it must give to intermediaries. Companies selling perishable products, for example, may require more direct marketing to avoid delays and too much handling.

In some cases, a company may want to compete in or near the same outlets that carry competitors' products. For example, Maytag and other appliance makers want their products displayed alongside competing brands to facilitate comparison shopping. In other cases, companies may avoid the channels used by competitors. The Pampered Chef, for instance, sells high-quality kitchen tools directly to consumers through its corps of more than 60,000 consultants worldwide rather than going head-to-head with other kitchen tool makers for scarce positions in retail stores. And Stella & Dot sells quality jewelry through more than 30,000 independent reps—called stylists—who hold Tupperware-like in-home "trunk shows."[14] GEICO and USAA primarily market insurance and banking products to consumers via phone and internet channels rather than through agents.

Finally, environmental factors such as economic conditions and legal constraints may affect channel objectives and design. For example, in a depressed economy, producers will want to distribute their goods in the most economical way, using shorter channels and dropping unneeded services that add to the final price of the goods.

Identifying Major Alternatives

When the company has defined its channel objectives, it should next identify its major channel alternatives in terms of the *types* of intermediaries, the *number* of intermediaries, and the *responsibilities* of each channel member.

Types of Intermediaries

A firm should identify the types of channel members available to carry out its channel work. Most companies face many channel member choices. For example, Dell initially sold directly to final consumers and business buyers only through its sophisticated phone and online marketing channel. It also sold directly to large corporate, institutional, and government buyers using its direct sales force. However, to reach more consumers and match competitors such as Samsung and Apple, Dell now sells indirectly through retailers such as Best Buy, Staples, and Walmart. It also sells indirectly through *value-added resellers*, independent distributors and dealers that develop computer systems and applications tailored to the special needs of small and medium-sized business customers.

Using many types of resellers in a channel provides both benefits and drawbacks. For example, by selling through retailers and value-added resellers in addition to its own direct channels, Dell can reach more and different kinds of buyers. However, these are more difficult to manage and control. In addition, the direct and indirect channels compete with each other for many of the same customers, causing potential conflict. In fact, Dell often finds itself "stuck in the middle," with its direct sales reps complaining about competition from retail stores, whereas its value-added resellers complain that the direct sales reps are undercutting their business.

Number of Marketing Intermediaries

Intensive distribution
Stocking the product in as many outlets as possible.

Companies must also determine the number of channel members to use at each level. Three strategies are available: intensive distribution, exclusive distribution, and selective distribution. Producers of convenience products and common raw materials typically seek **intensive distribution**—a strategy in which they stock their products in as many outlets as possible. These products must be available where and when consumers want them. For example, toothpaste, candy, and other similar items are sold in millions of outlets to provide maximum brand exposure and consumer convenience. Kraft, Coca-Cola, Kimberly-Clark, and other consumer goods companies distribute their products in this way.

Why is the world's number one selling brand of chain saw not sold at Lowe's or The Home Depot?

We can give you 8,000 reasons, our legion of independent STIHL dealers nationwide. We count on them every day and so can you. To give you a product demonstration, straight talk and genuine advice about STIHL products. To offer fast and expert on-site service. And to stand behind every product they carry, always fully assembled. You see, we won't sell you a chain saw in a box, not even in a big one. **Are you ready for a STIHL?**

To find a dealer: stihlusa.com or call 1-800 GO STIHL

STIHL

● **Selective distribution: STIHL sells its chain saws, blowers, hedge trimmers, and other products through a select corps of independent hardware and lawn and garden retailers. "We count on them every day and so can you."**

STIHL Incorporated

Exclusive distribution
Giving a limited number of dealers the exclusive right to distribute the company's products in their territories.

Selective distribution
The use of more than one but fewer than all of the intermediaries that are willing to carry the company's products.

By contrast, some producers purposely limit the number of intermediaries handling their products. The extreme form of this practice is **exclusive distribution**, in which the producer gives only a limited number of dealers the exclusive right to distribute its products in their territories. Exclusive distribution is often found in the distribution of luxury brands. Breitling watches—positioned as "Instruments for Professionals" and selling at prices from $5,000 to more than $100,000—are sold by only a few authorized dealers in any given market area. For example, the brand sells through only one jeweler in Chicago and only six jewelers in the entire state of Illinois. Exclusive distribution enhances Breitling's distinctive positioning and earns greater dealer support and customer service.

Between intensive and exclusive distribution lies **selective distribution**—the use of more than one but fewer than all of the intermediaries who are willing to carry a company's products. Most consumer electronics, furniture, and home appliance brands are distributed in this manner. ● For example, outdoor power equipment maker STIHL doesn't sell its chain saws, blowers, hedge trimmers, and other products through mass merchandisers such as Lowe's, Home Depot, or Sears. Instead, it sells through a select corps of independent hardware and lawn and garden dealers. By using selective distribution, STIHL can develop good working relationships with dealers and expect a better-than-average selling effort. Selective distribution also enhances the STIHL brand's image and allows for higher markups resulting from greater value-added dealer service. "We count on our select dealers every day and so can you," says one STIHL ad.

Responsibilities of Channel Members

The producer and intermediaries need to agree on the terms and responsibilities of each channel member. They should agree on price policies, conditions of sale, territory rights, and the specific services to be performed by each party. The producer should establish a list price and a fair set of discounts for the intermediaries. It must define each channel member's territory, and it should be careful about where it places new resellers.

Mutual services and duties need to be spelled out carefully, especially in franchise and exclusive distribution channels. For example, McDonald's provides franchisees with promotional support, a record-keeping system, training at Hamburger University, and general management assistance. In turn, franchisees must meet company standards for physical facilities and food quality, cooperate with new promotion programs, provide requested information, and buy specified food products.

Evaluating the Major Alternatives

Suppose a company has identified several channel alternatives and wants to select the one that will best satisfy its long-run objectives. Each alternative should be evaluated against economic, control, and adaptability criteria.

Using *economic criteria*, a company compares the likely sales, costs, and profitability of different channel alternatives. What will be the investment required by each channel alternative, and what returns will result? The company must also consider *control issues*. Using intermediaries usually means giving them some control over the marketing of the product, and some intermediaries take more control than others. Other things being equal, the company prefers to keep as much control as possible. Finally, the company must apply *adaptability criteria*. Channels often involve long-term commitments, yet the company wants to keep the channel flexible so that it can adapt to environmental changes. Thus, to be considered, a channel involving long-term commitments should be greatly superior on economic and control grounds.

Designing International Distribution Channels

International marketers face many additional complexities in designing their channels. Each country has its own unique distribution system that has evolved over time and changes very slowly. These channel systems can vary widely from country to country.

Thus, global marketers must usually adapt their channel strategies to the existing structures within each country.

In some markets, the distribution system is complex, competitive, and hard to penetrate. For example, many Western companies find India's distribution system difficult to navigate. Large discount, department store, and supermarket retailers still account for only a small portion of the huge Indian market. Instead, most shopping is done in small neighborhood stores called *kirana* shops, run by their owners and popular because they offer personal service and credit. In addition, large Western retailers have difficulty dealing with India's complex government regulations and poor infrastructure.

Distribution systems in developing countries may be scattered, inefficient, or altogether lacking. For example, China's rural markets are highly decentralized, made of many distinct submarkets, each with its own subculture. And, because of inadequate distribution systems, most companies can profitably access only a small portion of China's massive population located in affluent cities. China's distribution system is so fragmented that logistics costs to wrap, bundle, load, unload, sort, reload, and transport goods amount to 16 percent of the nation's GDP, far higher than in most other countries. (In comparison, U.S. logistics costs account for about 8.3 percent of the nation's GDP.) After years of effort, even Walmart executives admit that they have been unable to assemble an efficient supply chain in China.[15]

Sometimes local conditions can greatly influence how a company distributes products in global markets. For example, in low-income neighborhoods in Brazil where consumers have limited access to supermarkets, Nestlé supplements its distribution with thousands of self-employed salespeople who sell Nestlé products from refrigerated carts door to door. And in big cities in Asia and Africa, where crowded streets and high real estate costs make drive-thrus impractical, fast-food restaurants such as McDonald's and KFC offer delivery. Legions of motorbike delivery drivers in colorful uniforms dispense Big Macs and buckets of chicken to customers who call in. More than 30 percent of McDonald's total sales in Egypt and 12 percent of its Singapore sales come from delivery. Similarly, for KFC, delivery accounts for nearly half of all sales in Kuwait and a third of sales in Egypt.[16]

● **KFC delivers: Delivery accounts for large chunks of KFC sales in many crowded Asian and African cities.**

© FogStock / Alamy Stock Photo

Thus, international marketers face a wide range of channel alternatives. Designing efficient and effective channel systems between and within various country markets poses a difficult challenge. We discuss international distribution decisions further in Chapter 15.

Author Comment │ Now it's time to implement the chosen channel design and work with selected channel members to manage and motivate them.

Channel Management Decisions

Once the company has reviewed its channel alternatives and determined the best channel design, it must implement and manage the chosen channel. **Marketing channel management** calls for selecting, managing, and motivating individual channel members and evaluating their performance over time.

Marketing channel management
Selecting, managing, and motivating individual channel members and evaluating their performance over time.

Selecting Channel Members

Producers vary in their ability to attract qualified marketing intermediaries. Some producers have no trouble signing up channel members. For example, when Toyota first introduced its Lexus line in the United States, it had no trouble attracting new dealers. In fact, it had to turn down many would-be resellers.

At the other extreme are producers that have to work hard to line up enough qualified intermediaries. For example, when Timex first tried to sell its inexpensive watches through regular jewelry stores, most jewelry stores refused to carry them. The company then

CVSquitsforgood

This is the right thing to do.

● Selecting channels: Even established brands may have difficulty keeping desired channels. CVS Health's decision to stop selling cigarettes has left tobacco companies seeking new sales channels.

CVS Health

managed to get its watches into mass-merchandise outlets. This turned out to be a wise decision because of the rapid growth of mass merchandising.

Even established brands may have difficulty gaining and keeping their desired distribution, especially when dealing with powerful resellers. For example, you won't find Marlboro, Winston, Camel, or any other cigarette brand at your local CVS pharmacy store. ● CVS Health recently announced that it will no longer sell cigarettes in its stores, despite the resulting loss of more than $2 billion in annual sales. "This is the right thing to do," says the company. "We came to the decision that cigarettes and providing healthcare just don't go together in the same setting." Target dropped cigarettes nearly 20 years ago, and public advocates are pressuring Walmart to do the same. If the major discount stores and other drugstore chains such as Walgreens and Rite Aid follow suit, Philip Morris, R.J. Reynolds, and other tobacco companies will have to seek new channels for selling their brands.[17]

When selecting intermediaries, the company should determine what characteristics distinguish the better ones. It will want to evaluate each channel member's years in business, other lines carried, location, growth and profit record, cooperativeness, and reputation.

Managing and Motivating Channel Members

Once selected, channel members must be continuously managed and motivated to do their best. The company must sell not only *through* the intermediaries but also *to* and *with* them. Most companies see their intermediaries as first-line customers and partners. They practice strong *partner relationship management* to forge long-term partnerships with channel members. This creates a value delivery system that meets the needs of both the company *and* its marketing partners.

In managing its channels, a company must convince suppliers and distributors that they can succeed better by working together as a part of a cohesive value delivery system. Companies must work in close harmony with others in the channel to find better ways to bring value to customers. Thus, Amazon and P&G work closely to accomplish their joint goal of selling consumer package goods profitably online. And companies ranging from automaker Toyota to cosmetics maker L'Oréal forge beneficial relationships with their large networks of suppliers to gain mutual competitive advantage (see Real Marketing 12.2).

For example, heavy-equipment manufacturer Caterpillar works hand-in-hand with its superb dealer network—together they dominate the world's construction, mining, and logging equipment business:

> Heavy-equipment manufacturer Caterpillar produces innovative, high-quality industrial equipment products. But ask anyone at Caterpillar, and they'll tell you that the most important reason for Caterpillar's dominance is its outstanding distribution network of 189 independent dealers in more than 180 countries. Dealers are the ones on the front line. Once the product leaves the factory, the dealers take over. They're the ones that customers see. So rather than selling to or through its dealers, Caterpillar treats dealers as inside partners. When a big piece of Caterpillar equipment breaks down, customers know that they can count on both Caterpillar and its dealer network for support. A strong dealer network makes for a strong Caterpillar, and the other way around. On a deeper level, dealers play a vital role in almost every aspect of Caterpillar's operations, from product design and delivery to service and support. As a result of its close partnership with dealers, Caterpillar dominates the world's markets for heavy construction, mining, and logging equipment. Its familiar yellow tractors, crawlers, loaders, bulldozers, and trucks capture a commanding share of the worldwide heavy-equipment business, nearly twice that of number-two Komatsu.

Many companies are now installing integrated high-tech partnership relationship management (PRM) systems to coordinate their whole-channel marketing efforts. Just as they use customer relationship management (CRM) software systems to help manage

Real Marketing

12.2 Working with Channel Partners to Create Value for Customers

Today's successful companies know that they can't go it alone in creating value for customers. Instead they must create effective value delivery systems, consisting of suppliers, producers, and distributors who work together to get the job done. Partnering with suppliers and distributors can yield big competitive advantages. Consider these examples.

Toyota

Achieving satisfying supplier relationships has been a cornerstone of Toyota's stunning success. Historically, Toyota's U.S. competitors often alienated their suppliers through self-serving, heavy-handed dealings. "The [U. S. automakers] set annual cost-reduction targets [for the parts they buy]," said one supplier. "To realize those targets, they'll do anything. [They've unleashed] a reign of terror, and it gets worse every year." Says another, "[One automaker] seems to send its people to 'hate school' so that they learn how to hate suppliers."

By contrast, Toyota has long known the importance of building close relationships with suppliers. Rather than bullying them, Toyota partners with suppliers and helps them to meet its very high expectations. It learns about their businesses, conducts joint improvement activities, helps train supplier employees, gives daily performance feedback, and actively seeks out supplier concerns. It even recognizes top suppliers with annual performance awards.

As a result, for 13 of the past 15 years, Toyota has received the top supplier relations score in the respected North American Automotive Supplier Working Relations Index Study. The study rates companies on financial dealings with suppliers, valuing suppliers and treating them fairly, open and honest communication, and providing opportunities to make profits. The study suggests that Toyota suppliers consider themselves true partners with the automotive giant.

Such high supplier satisfaction means that Toyota can rely on suppliers to help it improve its own quality, reduce costs, and develop new products quickly. For example, when Toyota recently launched a program to reduce prices by 30 percent on 170 parts that it would buy for its next generation of cars, suppliers didn't complain. Instead, they pitched

in, trusting that Toyota will help them achieve the targeted reductions, in turn making them more competitive and profitable in the future. In all, creating satisfied suppliers helps Toyota produce lower-cost, higher-quality cars, which in turn results in more satisfied customers.

L'Oréal

L'Oréal is the world's largest cosmetics maker, with 23 global brands ranging from Maybelline and Kiehl's to Lancôme and Redken. Like Toyota, L'Oréal's extensive supplier network—which supplies everything from polymers and fats to spray cans and packaging to production equipment and office supplies—is crucial to its success.

As a result, L'Oréal treats suppliers as respected partners. On the one hand, it expects a lot from suppliers in terms of design innovation, quality, and socially responsible actions. The company carefully screens new suppliers and regularly assesses the performance of current suppliers. On the other hand, L'Oréal works closely with suppliers to help them meet its exacting standards. Whereas some companies make unreasonable demands of their suppliers and "squeeze" them for short-term gains, L'Oréal builds long-term supplier relationships based on mutual benefit and growth.

According to the company's supplier website, it treats suppliers with "fundamental respect for their business, their culture, their growth, and the individuals who work there." Each relationship is based on "dialogue and

joint efforts. L'Oréal seeks not only to help its suppliers meet its expectations but also to contribute to their growth through opportunities for innovation and competitiveness." As a result, more than 75 percent of L'Oréal's supplier partners have been working with the company for 10 years or more and the majority of them for several decades. Says the company's head of purchasing, "The CEO wants to make L'Oréal a top performer and one of the world's most respected companies. Being respected also means being respected by our suppliers."

Amazon–P&G

Until recently, if you ordered Bounty paper towels, Pampers diapers, Charmin toilet paper, or any of the dozens of other P&G consumer products from Amazon.com, they probably came to your doorstep by a circuitous distribution route. The paper towels, for example, might well have been produced in P&G's large northeastern Pennsylvania factory and shipped by the trailer-truck load to its nearby Tunkhannock warehouse, where they were unloaded and repacked with other P&G goods and shipped to Amazon's Dinwiddie, Virginia, fulfillment center. At the fulfillment center, they were unloaded and shelved and then finally picked and packed by Amazon employees for shipment to you via UPS, FedEx, or the USPS.

But these days, Amazon and P&G have partnered to blaze a new, simpler, lower-cost distribution trail for such goods. Now, for example, at the Pennsylvania warehouse, rather

Partnering in the distribution channel: Under Amazon's Vendor Flex program, P&G and Amazon share warehouse facilities, creating distribution cost and delivery advantages for both partners.
© raywoo/Fotolia; © grzegorz knec/Alamy; E.G. Pors/Shutterstock.com; © Sergio Azenha /Alamy

than reloading truckloads of P&G products and shipping them to Amazon fulfillment centers, P&G employees simply cart the goods to a fenced-off area inside their own warehouse. The fenced-in area is run by Amazon. From there, Amazon employees pack, label, and ship items directly to customers who've ordered them online. Amazon calls this venture Vendor Flex—and it's revolutionizing how people buy low-priced, low-margin everyday household products.

Amazon's Vendor Flex program takes channel partnering to an entirely new level. Co-locating "in the same tent" creates advantages for both partners. For Amazon, Vendor Flex reduces the costs of storing bulky items in its own distribution centers, and it frees up space for more higher-margin goods. The sharing arrangement lets Amazon extend its consumer package goods selection without building more distribution center space. For example, the P&G warehouse also stocks other popular P&G household brands, from Gillette razors to Pantene shampoo to

Tide laundry detergent. Finally, locating at the source guarantees Amazon immediate availability and facilitates quick delivery of P&G products to customers.

P&G also benefits from the Vendor Flex partnership. It saves money by cutting out the costs of transporting goods to Amazon's fulfillment centers, which in turn lets it charge more competitive prices to the e-commerce giant. And although P&G is a superb in-store brand marketer, it is still a relative newcomer to online selling, one of the company's top priorities. By partnering more closely with Amazon, P&G gets Amazon's expert help in moving its brands online.

So the Amazon–P&G Vendor Flex partnership looks like an ideal match for both companies. If P&G wants to be more effective in selling its brands online, what better partner could it have than Amazon, the undisputed master of online retailing? If Amazon wants to be more effective in selling household staples, what better partner could it have than P&G, the acknowledged master of consumer package goods marketing? Together, under Amazon's Vendor Flex, these respective industry leaders can flex their distribution muscles to their own benefit, and to the benefit of the consumers they jointly serve.

Sources: Alex Short, "Amazon and P&G Blow Business Collaboration Wide Open!" *Vizibl,* July 21, 2015, http://blog.vizibl.co/amazon-pg-blow-business-collaboration-wide-open/; Serena Ng, "Soap Opera: Amazon Moves In with P&G," *Wall Street Journal*, October 15, 2013, p. A1; Jeffery K. Liker and Thomas Y. Choi, "Building Deep Supplier Relationships," *Harvard Business Review,* 2004, pp.104–113; "OEM-Supplier Relations Study Shows Strong Gains for Toyota and Honda, with Ford, Nissan, FCA and GM Falling Well Behind," *PR Newswire,* May 8, 2015, www.prnewswire.com/news-releases/oem-supplier-relations-study-shows-strong-gains-for-toyota-and-honda-with-ford-nissan-fca-and-gm-falling-well-behind-300084605.html; and www.toyotasupplier.com and www.loreal.com/_en/_ww/html/suppliers/, accessed October, 2016.

relationships with important customers, companies can now use PRM and supply chain management (SCM) software to help recruit, train, organize, manage, motivate, and evaluate relationships with channel partners.

Evaluating Channel Members

The company must regularly check channel member performance against standards such as sales quotas, average inventory levels, customer delivery time, treatment of damaged and lost goods, cooperation in company promotion and training programs, and services to the customer. The company should recognize and reward intermediaries that are performing well and adding good value for consumers. Those that are performing poorly should be assisted or, as a last resort, replaced.

Finally, companies need to be sensitive to the needs of their channel partners. Those that treat their partners poorly risk not only losing their support but also causing some legal problems. The next section describes various rights and duties pertaining to companies and other channel members.

Public Policy and Distribution Decisions

For the most part, companies are legally free to develop whatever channel arrangements suit them. In fact, the laws affecting channels seek to prevent the exclusionary tactics of some companies that might keep another company from using a desired channel. Most channel law deals with the mutual rights and duties of channel members once they have formed a relationship.

Many producers and wholesalers like to develop exclusive channels for their products. When the seller allows only certain outlets to carry its products, this strategy is called *exclusive distribution*. When the seller requires that these dealers not handle competitors' products, its strategy is called *exclusive dealing*. Both parties can benefit from exclusive arrangements: The seller obtains more loyal and dependable outlets, and the dealers obtain a steady source of supply and stronger seller support. But exclusive arrangements also exclude other producers from selling to these dealers. This situation brings exclusive dealing contracts under the scope of the Clayton Act of 1914. They are legal as long as they do not substantially lessen competition or tend to create a monopoly and as long as both parties enter into the agreement voluntarily.

Exclusive dealing often includes *exclusive territorial agreements*. The producer may agree not to sell to other dealers in a given area, or the buyer may agree to sell only in its own territory. The first practice is normal under franchise systems as a way to increase dealer enthusiasm and commitment. It is also perfectly legal—a seller has no legal obligation to sell through more outlets than it wishes. The second practice, whereby the producer tries to keep a dealer from selling outside its territory, has become a major legal issue.

Producers of a strong brand sometimes sell it to dealers only if the dealers will take some or all of the rest of its line. This is called *full-line forcing*. Such *tying agreements* are not necessarily illegal, but they violate the Clayton Act if they tend to lessen competition substantially. The practice may prevent consumers from freely choosing among competing suppliers of these other brands.

Finally, producers are free to select their dealers, but their right to terminate dealers is somewhat restricted. In general, sellers can drop dealers "for cause." However, they cannot drop dealers if, for example, the dealers refuse to cooperate in a doubtful legal arrangement, such as exclusive dealing or tying agreements.

Marketing Logistics and Supply Chain Management

Author Comment | Marketers used to call this plain-old "physical distribution." But as these titles suggest, the topic has grown in importance, complexity, and sophistication.

In today's global marketplace, selling a product is sometimes easier than getting it to customers. Companies must decide on the best way to store, handle, and move their products and services so that they are available to customers in the right assortments, at the right time, and in the right place. Logistics effectiveness has a major impact on both customer satisfaction and company costs. Here we consider the nature and importance of logistics management in the supply chain, the goals of the logistics system, major logistics functions, and the need for integrated supply chain management.

Nature and Importance of Marketing Logistics

Marketing logistics (physical distribution)

Planning, implementing, and controlling the physical flow of materials, final goods, and related information from points of origin to points of consumption to meet customer requirements at a profit.

To some managers, marketing logistics means only trucks and warehouses. But modern logistics is much more than this. **Marketing logistics**—also called **physical distribution**—involves planning, implementing, and controlling the physical flow of goods, services, and related information from points of origin to points of consumption to meet customer requirements at a profit. In short, it involves getting the right product to the right customer in the right place at the right time profitably.

In the past, physical distribution planners typically started with products at the plant and then tried to find low-cost solutions to get them to customers. However, today's *customer-centered* logistics starts with the marketplace and works backward to the factory or even to sources of supply. Marketing logistics involves not only *outbound logistics* (moving products from the factory to resellers and ultimately to customers) but also *inbound logistics* (moving products and materials from suppliers to the factory) and *reverse logistics* (reusing, recycling, refurbishing, or disposing of broken, unwanted, or excess products returned by consumers or resellers). That is, it involves the entirety of **supply chain management**—managing upstream and downstream value-added flows of materials, final goods, and related information among suppliers, the company, resellers, and final consumers, as shown in ● **Figure 12.5**.

Supply chain management

Managing upstream and downstream value-added flows of materials, final goods, and related information among suppliers, the company, resellers, and final consumers.

The logistics manager's task is to coordinate the activities of suppliers, purchasing agents, marketers,

● FIGURE | 12.5
Supply Chain Management

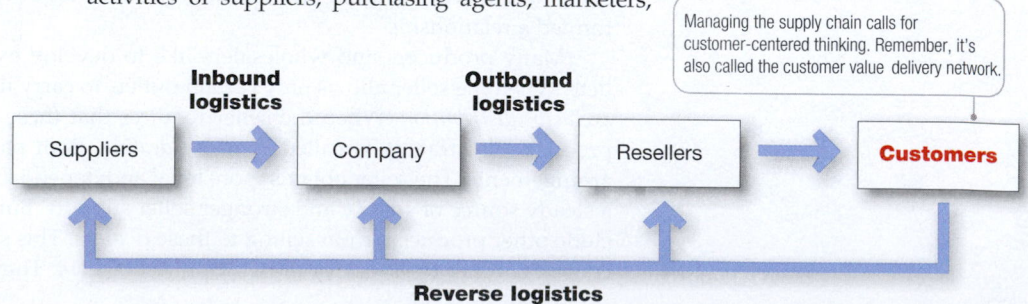

Managing the supply chain calls for customer-centered thinking. Remember, it's also called the customer value delivery network.

Inbound logistics → Outbound logistics

Suppliers → Company → Resellers → **Customers**

Reverse logistics

channel members, and customers. These activities include forecasting, information systems, purchasing, production planning, order processing, inventory, warehousing, and transportation planning.

Companies today are placing greater emphasis on logistics for several reasons. First, companies can gain a powerful competitive advantage by using improved logistics to give customers better service or lower prices.

Second, improved logistics can yield tremendous cost savings to both a company and its customers. As much as 20 percent of an average product's price is accounted for by shipping and transport alone. American companies spend $1.45 trillion each year—about 8.3 percent of GDP—to wrap, bundle, load, unload, sort, reload, and transport goods.

● The importance or logistics: At any given time, GM has hundreds of millions of tons of finished vehicles and parts in transit, running up an annual logistics bill of about $8 billion. Even small savings can be substantial.

Bloomberg/Getty Images

That's more than the total national GDPs of all but 12 countries worldwide. ● By itself, General Motors has hundreds of millions of tons of finished vehicles, production parts, and aftermarket parts in transit at any given time, running up an annual logistics bill of around $8 billion dollars. Shaving off even a small fraction of logistics costs can mean substantial savings. For example, GM recently announced a logistical overhaul that would save nearly $2 billion over two years in North America alone.[18]

Third, the explosion in product variety has created a need for improved logistics management. For example, in 1916 the typical Piggly Wiggly grocery store carried only 605 items. Today, a Piggly Wiggly carries a bewildering stock of between 20,000 and 35,000 items, depending on store size. A Walmart Supercenter store carries more than 140,000 products, 30,000 of which are grocery products.[19] Ordering, shipping, stocking, and controlling such a variety of products presents a sizable logistics challenge.

Improvements in information technology have also created opportunities for major gains in distribution efficiency. Today's companies are using sophisticated supply chain management software, internet-based logistics systems, point-of-sale scanners, RFID tags, satellite tracking, and electronic transfer of order and payment data. Such technology lets them quickly and efficiently manage the flow of goods, information, and finances through the supply chain.

Finally, more than almost any other marketing function, logistics affects the environment and a firm's environmental sustainability efforts. Transportation, warehousing, packaging, and other logistics functions are typically the biggest supply chain contributors to the company's environmental footprint. Therefore, many companies are now developing *green supply chains*.

Sustainable Supply Chains

Companies have many reasons for reducing the environmental impact of their supply chains. For one thing, if they don't green up voluntarily, a host of sustainability regulations enacted around the world will soon require them to. For another, many large customers—from Walmart and Nike to the federal government—are demanding it. Even consumers are demanding it: According to one survey, 50 percent of millennials are willing to pay more for sustainable products and 39 percent do research into the sustainability practices of companies before making a purchase.[20] Thus, environmental sustainability has become an important factor in supplier selection and performance evaluation. But perhaps even more important than *having* to do it, designing sustainable supply chains is simply the *right* thing to do. It's one more way that companies can contribute to saving our world for future generations.

But that's all pretty heady stuff. As it turns out, companies have a more immediate and practical reason for turning their supply chains green. Not only are sustainable channels good for the world, they're also good for a company's bottom line. The very logistics activities that create the biggest environmental footprint—such as transportation, warehousing, and packaging—also account for a lion's share of logistics costs. Companies green up their supply chains through greater efficiency, and greater efficiency means lower costs and higher profits. In other words, developing a sustainable supply chain is not only environmentally responsible, it can also be profitable. Consider Nike:[21]

Nike, the iconic sports shoe and apparel company, has developed a sweeping strategy for greening every phase of its supply chain. 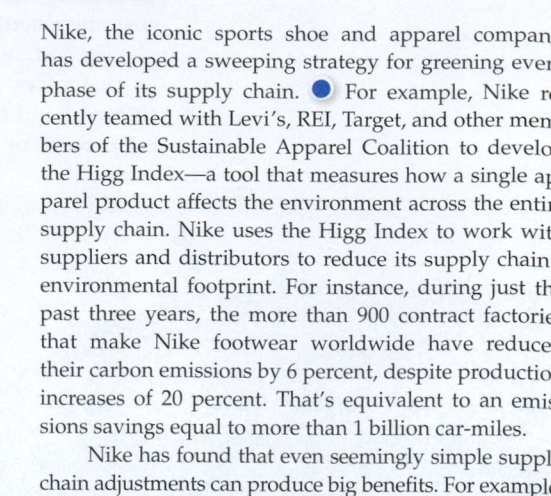 For example, Nike recently teamed with Levi's, REI, Target, and other members of the Sustainable Apparel Coalition to develop the Higg Index—a tool that measures how a single apparel product affects the environment across the entire supply chain. Nike uses the Higg Index to work with suppliers and distributors to reduce its supply chain's environmental footprint. For instance, during just the past three years, the more than 900 contract factories that make Nike footwear worldwide have reduced their carbon emissions by 6 percent, despite production increases of 20 percent. That's equivalent to an emissions savings equal to more than 1 billion car-miles.

Nike has found that even seemingly simple supply chain adjustments can produce big benefits. For example, the company sources its shoes in Asia, but most are sold in North America. Until about a decade ago, the shoes were shipped from factory to store by airfreight. After analyzing distribution costs more carefully, Nike shifted a sizable portion of its cargo to ocean freight. That simple shoes-to-ships shift reduced emissions per product by 4 percent, making environmentalists smile. But it also put a smile on the faces of Nike's accountants by saving the company some $8 million a year in shipping costs.

● **Green supply chains: Nike has developed a sweeping strategy for greening its supply chain. The Higg Index lets Nike work with suppliers and distributors to reduce the supply chain's environmental footprint while at the same time reducing its logistics costs.**

Thanapun/Shutterstock

Goals of the Logistics System

Some companies state their logistics objective as providing maximum customer service at the least cost. Unfortunately, as nice as this sounds, no logistics system can *both* maximize customer service *and* minimize distribution costs. Maximum customer service implies rapid delivery, large inventories, flexible assortments, liberal returns policies, and other services—all of which raise distribution costs. In contrast, minimum distribution costs imply slower delivery, smaller inventories, and larger shipping lots—which represent a lower level of overall customer service.

The goal of marketing logistics should be to provide a *targeted* level of customer service at the least cost. A company must first research the importance of various distribution services to customers and then set desired service levels for each segment. The objective is to maximize *profits*, not sales. Therefore, the company must weigh the benefits of providing higher levels of service against the costs. Some companies offer less service than their competitors and charge a lower price. Other companies offer more service and charge higher prices to cover higher costs.

Major Logistics Functions

Given a set of logistics objectives, the company designs a logistics system that will minimize the cost of attaining these objectives. The major logistics functions are *warehousing, inventory management, transportation*, and *logistics information management*.

Warehousing

Production and consumption cycles rarely match, so most companies must store their goods while they wait to be sold. For example, Snapper, Toro, and other lawn mower manufacturers run their factories all year long and store up products for the heavy spring and summer buying seasons. The storage function overcomes differences in needed quantities and timing, ensuring that products are available when customers are ready to buy them.

A company must decide on *how many* and *what types* of warehouses it needs and *where* they will be located. The company might use either *storage warehouses* or *distribution centers*. Storage warehouses store goods for moderate to long periods. In contrast, **distribution centers** are designed to move goods rather than just store them. They are large and highly automated warehouses designed to receive goods from various plants and suppliers, take orders, fill them efficiently, and deliver goods to customers as quickly as possible.

For example, Amazon operates more than 100 giant distribution centers, called fulfillment centers, which fill online orders and handle returns. These centers are huge and highly automated. For example, the Amazon fulfillment center in Tracy, California, covers 1.2 million square feet (equivalent to 27 football fields). At the center, 4,000 employees control an inventory of 21 million items and ship out up to 700,000 packages a day to Amazon customers in Northern California and parts of the Pacific Northwest. During last year's Cyber Monday, Amazon's fulfillment center network filled customer orders at a rate of more than 500 items per second globally.[22]

Like almost everything else these days, warehousing has seen dramatic changes in technology in recent years. Outdated materials-handling methods are steadily being replaced by newer, computer-controlled systems requiring fewer employees. Computers and scanners read orders and direct lift trucks, electric hoists, or robots to gather goods, move them to loading docks, and issue invoices. For example, to improve efficiency in its massive fulfillment centers, Amazon recently purchased robot maker Kiva Systems:[23]

When you buy from Amazon, the chances are still good that your order will be plucked and packed by human hands. However, the humans in Amazon's fulfillment centers are increasingly being assisted by an army of squat, ottoman-size, day-glo orange robots. Amazon now has more than 30,000 of them in 13 fulfillment centers, double the number from a year ago. The robots bring racks of merchandise to workers, who in turn fill boxes. Dubbed the "magic shelf," racks of items simply materialize in front of workers, with red lasers pointing to items to be picked. The robots then drive off and new shelves appear. The super-efficient robots work tirelessly 16 hours a day, seven days a week. They never complain about the workload or ask for pay raises, and they are pretty much maintenance free. "When they run low on power, they head to battery-charging terminals," notes one observer, "or, as warehouse personnel say, 'They get themselves a drink of water.'"

Distribution center

A large, highly automated warehouse designed to receive goods from various plants and suppliers, take orders, fill them efficiently, and deliver goods to customers as quickly as possible.

● **High-tech distribution centers: Amazon employs teams of super-retrievers—day-glo orange Kiva robots—to keep its fulfillment centers humming.**

Bloomberg via Getty Images

Inventory Management

Inventory management also affects customer satisfaction. Here, managers must maintain the delicate balance between carrying too little inventory and carrying too much. With too little stock, the firm risks not having products when customers want to buy. To remedy this, the firm may need costly emergency shipments or production. Carrying too much inventory results in higher-than-necessary inventory-carrying costs and stock obsolescence. Thus, in managing inventory, firms must balance the costs of carrying larger inventories against resulting sales and profits.

Many companies have greatly reduced their inventories and related costs through *just-in-time* logistics systems. With such systems, producers and retailers carry only small inventories of parts or merchandise, often enough for only a few days of operations. New stock arrives exactly when needed rather than being stored in inventory until being used. Just-in-time systems require accurate forecasting along with fast, frequent, and flexible delivery so that new supplies will be available when needed. However, these systems result in substantial savings in inventory-carrying and inventory-handling costs.

Marketers are always looking for new ways to make inventory management more efficient. In the not-too-distant future, handling inventory might even become fully automated. For example, many companies now use some form of RFID or "smart tag" technology, by which small transmitter chips are embedded in or placed on products and packaging for everything from flowers and razors to tires. Such "smart" products could make the entire supply chain—which accounts for up to 75 percent of a product's cost—intelligent and automated.

Companies using RFID know, at any time, exactly where a product is located physically within the supply chain. "Smart shelves" would not only tell them when it's time to reorder but also place the order automatically with their suppliers. Such exciting new information technology is revolutionizing distribution as we know it. Many large and resourceful marketing companies, such as Walmart, Macy's, P&G, Kraft, and IBM, are investing heavily to make the full use of RFID technology a reality.

Transportation

The choice of transportation carriers affects the pricing of products, delivery performance, and the condition of goods when they arrive—all of which will affect customer satisfaction. • In shipping goods to its warehouses, dealers, and customers, the company can choose among five main transportation modes: truck, rail, water, pipeline, and air along with an alternative mode for digital products—the internet.

● Transportation: In shipping goods to their warehouses, dealers, and customers, companies can choose among many transportation modes, including truck, rail, water, pipeline, and air. Much of today's shipping requires multiple modes.

Thanapun/Shutterstock

Trucks have increased their share of transportation steadily and now account for 40 percent of total cargo ton-miles (a ton of freight moved one mile) transported in the United States. Trucks are highly flexible in their routing and time schedules, and they can usually offer faster service than railroads. They are efficient for short hauls of high-value merchandise. Trucking firms have evolved in recent years to become full-service providers of global transportation services. For example, large trucking firms now offer everything from satellite tracking, internet-based shipment management, and logistics planning software to cross-border shipping operations.[24]

Railroads account for 26 percent of the total cargo ton-miles moved. They are one of the most cost-effective modes for shipping large amounts of bulk products—coal, sand, minerals, and farm and forest products—over long distances. In recent years, railroads have increased their customer services by designing new equipment to handle special categories of goods, providing flatcars for carrying truck trailers by rail (piggyback), and providing in-transit services such as the diversion of shipped goods to other destinations en route and the processing of goods en route.

Water carriers, which account for 7 percent of the cargo ton-miles, transport large amounts of goods by ships and barges on U.S. coastal and inland waterways. Although the cost of water transportation is very low for shipping bulky, low-value, nonperishable products such as sand, coal, grain, oil, and metallic ores, water transportation is the slowest mode and may be affected by the weather. *Pipelines*, which account for 17 percent of the cargo ton-miles, are a specialized means of shipping petroleum, natural gas, and chemicals from sources to markets. Most pipelines are used by their owners to ship their own products.

Although *air* carriers transport less than 1 percent of the cargo ton-miles of the nation's goods, they are an important transportation mode. Airfreight rates are much higher than rail or truck rates, but airfreight is ideal when speed is needed or distant markets have to be reached. Among the most frequently airfreighted products are perishables (such as fresh fish, cut flowers) and high-value, low-bulk items (technical instruments, jewelry). Companies find that airfreight also reduces inventory levels, packaging costs, and the number of warehouses needed.

The *internet* carries digital products from producer to customer via satellite, cable, phone wire, or wireless signal. Software firms, the media, music and video companies, and education all make use of the internet to deliver digital content. The internet holds the potential for lower product distribution costs. Whereas planes, trucks, and trains move freight and packages, digital technology moves information bits.

Shippers also use **multimodal transportation**—combining two or more modes of transportation. Eight percent of the total cargo ton-miles are moved via multiple modes.

Multimodal transportation

Combining two or more modes of transportation.

Piggyback describes the use of rail and trucks; *fishyback*, water and trucks; *trainship*, water and rail; and *airtruck*, air and trucks. Combining modes provides advantages that no single mode can deliver. Each combination offers advantages to the shipper. For example, not only is piggyback cheaper than trucking alone, but it also provides flexibility and convenience. Numerous logistics companies provide single-source multimodal transportation solutions.

Logistics Information Management

Companies manage their supply chains through information. Channel partners often link up to share information and make better joint logistics decisions. From a logistics perspective, flows of information, such as customer transactions, billing, shipment and inventory levels, and even customer data, are closely linked to channel performance. Companies need simple, accessible, fast, and accurate processes for capturing, processing, and sharing channel information.

Information can be shared and managed in many ways, but most sharing takes place through *electronic data interchange* (*EDI*), the digital exchange of data between organizations, which primarily is transmitted via the internet. Walmart, for example, requires EDI links with its more than 100,000 suppliers through its Retail Link sales data system. If new suppliers don't have the required EDI capability, Walmart will work with them to find and implement the needed tools.[25]

In some cases, suppliers might actually be asked to generate orders and arrange deliveries for their customers. Many large retailers—such as Walmart and Home Depot—work closely with major suppliers such as P&G or Moen to set up *vendor-managed inventory* (*VMI*) systems or *continuous inventory replenishment* systems. Using VMI, the customer shares real-time data on sales and current inventory levels with the supplier. The supplier then takes full responsibility for managing inventories and deliveries. Some retailers even go so far as to shift inventory and delivery costs to the supplier. Such systems require close cooperation between the buyer and seller.

Integrated Logistics Management

Integrated logistics management
The logistics concept that emphasizes teamwork—both inside the company and among all the marketing channel organizations—to maximize the performance of the entire distribution system.

Today, more and more companies are adopting the concept of **integrated logistics management**. This concept recognizes that providing better customer service and trimming distribution costs require *teamwork*, both inside the company and among all the marketing channel organizations. Inside, the company's various departments must work closely together to maximize its own logistics performance. Outside, the company must integrate its logistics system with those of its suppliers and customers to maximize the performance of the entire distribution network.

Cross-Functional Teamwork Inside the Company

Most companies assign responsibility for various logistics activities to many different departments—marketing, sales, finance, operations, and purchasing. Too often, each function tries to optimize its own logistics performance without regard for the activities of the other functions. However, transportation, inventory, warehousing, and information management activities interact, often in an inverse way. Lower inventory levels reduce inventory-carrying costs. But they may also reduce customer service and increase costs from stockouts, backorders, special production runs, and costly fast-freight shipments. Because distribution activities involve strong trade-offs, decisions by different functions must be coordinated to achieve better overall logistics performance.

The goal of integrated supply chain management is to harmonize all of the company's logistics decisions. Close working relationships among departments can be achieved in several ways. Some companies have created permanent logistics committees composed of managers responsible for different physical distribution activities. Companies can also create supply chain manager positions that link the logistics activities of functional areas. For example, P&G has created product supply managers who manage all the supply chain activities for each product category. Many companies have a vice president of logistics or a supply chain VP with cross-functional authority.

Finally, companies can employ sophisticated, system-wide supply chain management software, now available from a wide range of software enterprises large and small, from

 Integrated logistics management: Oracle's supply chain management software solutions help companies to "gain sustainable advantage and drive innovation by transforming their traditional supply chains into integrated value chains."

Oracle Corporation

Oracle and SAP to Infor and Logility.  For example, Oracle's supply chain management software solutions help companies to "gain sustainable advantage and drive innovation by transforming their traditional supply chains into integrated value chains."[26] It coordinates every aspect of the supply chain, from value chain collaboration to inventory optimization to transportation and logistics management. The important thing is that the company must coordinate its logistics, inventory investments, demand forecasting, and marketing activities to create high market satisfaction at a reasonable cost.

Building Logistics Partnerships

Companies must do more than improve their own logistics. They must also work with other channel partners to improve whole-channel distribution. The members of a marketing channel are linked closely in creating customer value and building customer relationships. One company's distribution system is another company's supply system. The success of each channel member depends on the performance of the entire supply chain. For example, furniture retailer IKEA can create its stylish but affordable furniture and deliver the "IKEA lifestyle" only if its entire supply chain—consisting of thousands of merchandise designers and suppliers, transport companies, warehouses, and service providers—operates at maximum efficiency and with customer-focused effectiveness.

Smart companies coordinate their logistics strategies and forge strong partnerships with suppliers and customers to improve customer service and reduce channel costs. Many companies have created *cross-functional, cross-company teams*. For example, Nestlé's Purina pet food unit has a team of dozens of people working in Bentonville, Arkansas, the home base of Walmart. The Purina Walmart team members work jointly with their counterparts at Walmart to find ways to squeeze costs out of their distribution system. Working together benefits not only Purina and Walmart but also their shared, final consumers.

Other companies partner through *shared projects*. For example, many large retailers conduct joint in-store programs with suppliers. Home Depot allows key suppliers to use its stores as a testing ground for new merchandising programs. The suppliers spend time at Home Depot stores watching how their product sells and how customers relate to it. They then create programs specially tailored to Home Depot and its customers. Clearly, both the supplier and the customer benefit from such partnerships. The point is that all supply chain members must work together in the cause of bringing value to final consumers.

Third-Party Logistics

Third-party logistics (3PL) provider
An independent logistics provider that performs any or all of the functions required to get a client's product to market.

Although most big companies love to make and sell their products, many loathe the associated logistics "grunt work." They detest the bundling, loading, unloading, sorting, storing, reloading, transporting, customs clearing, and tracking required to supply their factories and get products to their customers. They hate it so much that many firms outsource some or all of their logistics to **third-party logistics (3PL) providers** such as Ryder, Penske Logistics, BAX Global, DHL Logistics, FedEx Logistics, and UPS Business Solutions.

For example, UPS knows that, for many companies, logistics can be a real nightmare. But logistics is exactly what UPS does best. To UPS, logistics is today's most powerful force for creating competitive advantage. "We ❤ logistics," proclaims UPS. "It makes running your business easier. It can make your customers happier. It's a whole new way of thinking." As one UPS ad concludes: "We love logistics. Put UPS to work for you and you'll love logistics too."

At one level, UPS can simply handle a company's package shipments. But on a deeper level, UPS can help businesses sharpen their own logistics systems to cut costs and serve customers better. At a still deeper level, companies can let UPS take over and manage part or all of their logistics operations. For example, consumer electronics maker Toshiba lets UPS handle its entire laptop PC repair process—lock, stock, and barrel. And UPS not only delivers packages for online shoe and accessories marketer Zappos, it also manages Zappos's important and complex order returns process in an efficient, customer-pleasing way.[27]

3PL providers like UPS can help clients tighten up sluggish, overstuffed supply chains; slash inventories; and get products to customers more quickly and reliably. According to one report, 86 percent of *Fortune* 500 companies use 3PL (also called *outsourced logistics* or *contract logistics*) services. General Motors, P&G, and Walmart each use 50 or more 3PLs.[28]

Companies use third-party logistics providers for several reasons. First, because getting the product to market is their main focus, using these providers makes the most sense, as they can often do it more efficiently and at lower cost. Outsourcing logistics typically results in a 10 to 25 percent cost savings.[29] Second, outsourcing logistics frees a company to focus more intensely on its core business. Finally, integrated logistics companies understand increasingly complex logistics environments.

12 | Reviewing and Extending the Concepts

OBJECTIVES REVIEW AND KEY TERMS

Objectives Review

Some companies pay too little attention to their distribution channels; others, however, have used imaginative distribution systems to gain a competitive advantage. A company's channel decisions directly affect every other marketing decision. Management must make channel decisions carefully, incorporating today's needs with tomorrow's likely selling environment.

OBJECTIVE 12-1 Explain why companies use marketing channels and discuss the functions these channels perform. *(pp 334–337)*

In creating customer engagement and value, a company can't go it alone. It must work within an entire network of partners—a value delivery network—to accomplish this task. Individual companies and brands don't compete; their entire value delivery networks do.

Most producers use intermediaries to bring their products to market. They forge a *marketing channel* (or *distribution channel*)—a set of interdependent organizations involved in the process of making a product or service available for use or consumption by the consumer or business user. Through their contacts, experience, specialization, and scale of operation, intermediaries usually offer the firm more than it can achieve on its own.

Marketing channels perform many key functions. Some help *complete transactions* by gathering and distributing *information* needed for planning and aiding exchange, developing and spreading persuasive *communications* about an offer, performing *contact* work (finding and communicating with prospective buyers), *matching* (shaping and fitting the offer to the buyer's needs), and entering into *negotiation* to reach an agreement on price and other terms of the offer so that ownership can be transferred. Other functions help to *fulfill* the completed

transactions by offering *physical distribution* (transporting and storing goods), *financing* (acquiring and using funds to cover the costs of the channel work), and *risk taking* (assuming the risks of carrying out the channel work.

OBJECTIVE 12-2 Discuss how channel members interact and how they organize to perform the work of the channel. *(pp 338–344)*

The channel will be most effective when each member assumes the tasks it can do best. Ideally, because the success of individual channel members depends on overall channel success, all channel firms should work together smoothly. They should understand and accept their roles, coordinate their goals and activities, and cooperate to attain overall channel goals. By cooperating, they can more effectively sense, serve, and satisfy the target market.

In a large company, the formal organization structure assigns roles and provides needed leadership. But in a distribution channel composed of independent firms, leadership and power are not formally set. Traditionally, distribution channels have lacked the leadership needed to assign roles and manage conflict. In recent years, however, new types of channel organizations have appeared that provide stronger leadership and improved performance.

OBJECTIVE 12-3 Identify the major channel alternatives open to a company. *(pp 344–348)*

Channel alternatives vary from direct selling to using one, two, three, or more intermediary *channel levels*. Marketing channels face continuous and sometimes dramatic change. Three of the most important trends are the growth of *vertical, horizontal,* and *multichannel marketing systems*. These trends affect channel cooperation, conflict, and competition.

Channel design begins with assessing customer channel service needs and company channel objectives and constraints. The company then identifies the major channel alternatives in terms of the *types* of intermediaries, the *number* of intermediaries, and the *channel responsibilities* of each. Each channel alternative must be evaluated according to economic, control, and adaptive criteria. *Channel management* calls for selecting qualified intermediaries and motivating them. Individual channel members must be evaluated regularly.

OBJECTIVE 12-4 Explain how companies select, motivate, and evaluate channel members. *(pp 348–352)*

Producers vary in their ability to attract qualified marketing intermediaries. Some producers have no trouble signing up channel members, whereas others have to work hard to line up enough qualified intermediaries. When selecting intermediaries, the company should evaluate each channel member's qualifications and select those that best fit its channel objectives.

Once selected, channel members must be continuously motivated to do their best. The company must sell not only *through* the intermediaries but also *with* them. It should forge strong partnerships with channel members to create a marketing system that meets the needs of both the manufacturer *and* the partners.

OBJECTIVE 12-5 Discuss the nature and importance of marketing logistics and integrated supply chain management. *(pp 352–359)*

Marketing logistics (or *physical distribution*) is an area of potentially high cost savings and improved customer satisfaction. Marketing logistics addresses not only *outbound logistics* but also *inbound logistics* and *reverse logistics*. That is, it involves the entire *supply chain management*—managing value-added flows between suppliers, the company, resellers, and final users. No logistics system can both maximize customer service and minimize distribution costs. Instead, the goal of logistics management is to provide a *targeted* level of service at the least cost. The major logistics functions are *warehousing, inventory management, transportation*, and *logistics information management*.

The *integrated supply chain management concept* recognizes that improved logistics requires teamwork in the form of close working relationships across functional areas inside the company and across various organizations in the supply chain. Companies can achieve logistics harmony among functions by creating cross-functional logistics teams, integrative supply manager positions, and senior-level logistics executive positions with cross-functional authority. Channel partnerships can take the form of cross-company teams, shared projects, and information-sharing systems. Today, some companies are outsourcing their logistics functions to third-party logistics (3PL) providers to save costs, increase efficiency, and gain faster and more effective access to global markets.

Key Terms

OBJECTIVE 12-1

Value delivery network (p 335)
Marketing channel (distribution channel) (p 335)
Channel level (p 337)
Direct marketing channel (p 337)
Indirect marketing channel (p 337)

OBJECTIVE 12-2

Channel conflict (p 338)
Conventional distribution channel (p 339)
Vertical marketing system (VMS) (p 339)

Corporate VMS (p 339)
Contractual VMS (p 340)
Franchise organization (p 340)
Administered VMS (p 340)
Horizontal marketing system (p 341)
Multichannel distribution system (p 341)
Disintermediation (p 342)

OBJECTIVE 12-3

Marketing channel design (p 345)
Intensive distribution (p 346)
Exclusive distribution (p 347)
Selective distribution (p 347)

OBJECTIVE 12-4

Marketing channel management (p 348)

OBJECTIVE 12-5

Marketing logistics (physical distribution) (p 352)
Supply chain management (p 352)
Distribution center (p 355)
Multimodal transportation (p 356)
Integrated logistics management (p 357)
Third-party logistics (3PL) provider (p 358)

DISCUSSION AND CRITICAL THINKING

MyMarketingLab

Go to **mymktlab.com** to complete the problems marked with this icon ⭐.

Discussion Questions

12-1 Compare and contrast upstream and downstream partners in a company's supply chain. Explain why *value delivery network* might be a better term to use than *supply chain*. (AACSB: Communication)

12-2 Discuss direct marketing channels and indirect marketing channels. Provide examples of each type of marketing channel. (AACSB: Communication; Reflective Thinking)

12-3 What channel design decisions do manufacturers face for maximum effectiveness?

⭐ **12-4** Name and describe the three strategies available when determining the number of marketing intermediaries. (AACSB: Communication; Reflective Thinking)

12-5 List and briefly describe the major logistics functions. Provide an example of a decision a logistics manager would make for each major function. (AACSB: Communication; Reflective Thinking)

Critical Thinking Exercises

12-6 Form a small group and research the distribution challenges faced by companies expanding into emerging international markets such as China, Africa, and India. Develop a multimedia presentation on how one company overcame these challenges. (AACSB: Communication; Reflective Thinking; Use of IT)

12-7 The term *last mile* is often used in the telecommunications industry. Research what is going on in this industry and how the *last mile* has evolved in recent years, and then predict where it is heading in the future.

What companies are major players in the last mile, and how does the concept of net neutrality fit in? (AACSB: Communication; Reflective Thinking)

12-8 Multimodal transportation is a crucial component of the logistics industry. Search the internet to find the largest multimodal facilities in the United States. Review the key features offered at these terminals and report your findings on their similarities and differences. (AACSB: Communication; Use of IT; Reflective Thinking)

APPLICATIONS AND CASES

Online, Mobile, and Social Media Marketing Fabletics Changing Channels

According to Fabletics company website, www.fabletics.com, "JustFab Inc. co-CEOs, Don Ressler and Adam Goldenberg, launched Fabletics with Kate Hudson after they saw a gap in the activewear marketplace. There were plenty of luxury brands, but none that offered stylish and high-quality gear at an accessible price point. These three unstoppable innovators joined forces to create the Fabletics brand in 2013." Fabletics, a division of Just-Fab, offers affordable, high-quality, and stylish workout clothes including yoga pants, leggings, joggers, tops, tees, and more for women and men at every fitness level. After being in business just a few short years, the company ranked number 98 in the Internet Retailer 2015 Top 500 Guide with revenues of

$150 million. Although initially internet-based, Fabletics moved into brick-and-mortar retailing in 2015. It plans to open 75 to 100 stores by 2020. (AACSB: Communication; Reflective Thinking; Use of IT)

12-9 Conduct your own research to learn more about Fabletics. Discuss how Fabletics is meeting customer needs through its value delivery network. What controversy surrounds the company?

⭐ **12-10** What type of marketing channel is Fabletics using? What is its distribution strategy? Does opening brick-and-mortar stores make sense for Fabletics? Explain.

Marketing Ethics Trucker Rest Rules

Large trucks are an important piece of the logistics chain. However, there were 333,000 large truck crashes in 2012, resulting in almost 3,800 fatalities, the majority being drivers or passengers of other vehicles, not the truck driver. One accident in 2014 caused a public uproar when a Walmart truck driver fell asleep at the wheel after being awake for 24 hours and crashed into another car, killing one person and critically injuring others, including a well-known comedian. The U.S. Department of Transportation's Federal Motor Carrier Safety Administration enacted tougher hours-of-service rules that went into effect in July 2013. However, the new rules have caused considerable controversy and have caused hardships for truck drivers. As one driver put it, "If the wheels aren't turning, you're not earning." One report claimed that the trucking industry would lose $1 billion in lost productivity as a result of these rules. But another analysis concluded that the industry would realize almost $500 million in benefits from reduced driver mortality.

12-11 Research the DOT's trucker hours-of-service rules and write a brief report outlining the rules. What is the current status of the 2013 rules? (AACSB: Communication; Reflective Thinking)

12-12 Is it ethical that the trucking industry wants the hours-of-service rules repealed? Why or why not? (AACSB: Communication; Reflective Thinking; Ethical Reasoning)

Marketing by the Numbers Tyson Expanding Distribution

Tyson Foods is the largest U.S. beef and chicken supplier, processing more than 100,000 head of cattle and 40-plus million chickens weekly. Primary distribution channels are supermarket meat departments. However, the company is now expanding distribution into convenience stores. There are almost 150,000 gas stations and convenience stores where the company would like to sell hot buffalo chicken bites near the checkout. This is a promising channel, as sales are growing considerably at these retail outlets and profit margins on prepared foods are higher than selling raw meat to grocery stores. Tyson will have to hire 10 more sales representatives at a salary of $45,000 each to expand into this distribution channel because many of these types of stores are independently owned. Each convenience store is expected to generate an average of $50,000 in revenue for Tyson. Refer to Appendix 2: Marketing by the Numbers to answer the following questions.

12-13 If Tyson's contribution margin is 30 percent on this product, what increase in sales will it need to break even on the increase in fixed costs to hire the new sales reps? (AACSB: Communication; Analytical Reasoning)

12-14 How many new retail accounts must the company acquire to break even on this tactic? What average number of accounts must each new rep acquire? (AACSB: Communication; Analytical Reasoning)

Video Case Progressive

Progressive has attained top-tier status in the insurance industry by focusing on innovation. Progressive was the first company to offer drive-in claims service, installment payment of premiums, and 24/7 customer service. But perhaps Progressive's most innovative moves involve its channels of distribution. Whereas most insurance companies distribute via intermediary agents or direct-to-consumer methods, Progressive was one of the first to see value in doing both. In the late 1980s, it augmented its agency distribution with a direct 800-number channel.

Two decades ago, Progressive moved into the digital future by becoming the first major insurer to launch a website. Soon after, it allowed customers to buy auto insurance policies online in real time. Today, customers can use Progressive's website to do everything from managing their own account information to reporting claims directly. Progressive even offers one-stop concierge claim service.

After viewing the Progressive video segment, answer the following questions about marketing channels.

12-15 Apply the concept of the supply chain to Progressive.

12-16 Using the model of consumer and business channels found in the chapter, sketch out as many channels for Progressive as you can. How does each of these channels meet distinct customer needs?

12-17 Discuss the various ways that Progressive has had an impact on the insurance industry.

Company Case Apple Pay: Taking Mobile Payments Mainstream

After leaving his office in Manhattan, Tag stopped at a nearby Panera to grab a Frontega Chicken Panini and Green Passion Power Smoothie as a quick dinner on his way to see some friends in Soho. Upon ordering, he held his Apple Watch to the contactless reader near the register, gently pressed his finger to the TouchID fingerprint sensor on the small screen, and let Apple Pay do the rest.

Wanting to get across town as soon as possible, Tag used his Uber app to summon an UberX car. During the car ride, he remembered that he needed a couple of new dress shirts. With a few quick clicks on his watch, he selected the shirts through his Macy's app. With a simple tap, he used Apple Pay to seamlessly complete the transaction. As he neared his destination, Tag added a tip to the bill for the ride through the Uber app, which he'd already configured to use Apple Pay as the default. With one simple press of his finger to TouchID on his watch, he exited the cab.

Three purchases—offline, online, and, well, sort of in between—no wallet required. No traditional wallet, that is. This new reality—one that many early adopters are already living—is rapidly expanding toward what some experts predict will become the future for everyone. Folks like Tag don't even carry traditional wallets anymore, only their mobile devices and perhaps an ID and a backup credit card for retailers that don't accept mobile payments—yet. After years of predictions that mobile payments would replace cash and credit cards, there are finally signs that it might actually be happening. And Apple is leading the way.

Hardly New

The ability to pay for transactions with a mobile device is hardly new. In fact, the first technology for mobile payments was invented by Sony way back in 1989. It was first put into use in Hong Kong's subway system in 1997 and began taking root in Japan in 2001. The tech-savvy Japanese warmed to the idea quickly, and mobile wallet apps were being used on mobile phones throughout Japan by 2004. Ever since, more than 245 million Japanese mobile phones have been equipped with the capability to make mobile payments, and Japanese consumers use mobile payments for everything from transportation to food and household purchases.

So it seems odd that a similar system has not taken root in the United States, although it has not been for lack of trying. Companies have been experimenting with different approaches for years. PayPal was the first to take advantage of the smartphone revolution by creating a payment app that gave just about every smartphone the potential for mobile payments. About a year later, Google entered the mobile payment game with the launch of Google Wallet. In the past six years, numerous other companies—from small start-ups to retailing giants—have tried to gain market acceptance in mobile payments. They include the likes of Samsung, Square, and CurrentC—a failed mobile wallet

app backed by Walmart and a consortium of U.S. retailers in hopes of cutting credit card companies and their fees out of the buying loop.

But none of these players—individually or together—has made much of a dent in replacing traditional credit cards and cash as a form of payment in the multitrillion-dollar U.S. retail market. Although the mobile payments concept may seem like a no-brainer for convenience-loving American consumers, numerous barriers on both the buyer and seller sides have kept the concept from gaining momentum. Late to the game with Apple Pay, Apple is clearly a market follower. But it's a feat that the innovative company has performed to perfection time and again—take a new technology, make it better than any of the initial offerings, then watch the market explode as the Apple version becomes the runaway market leader.

Overcoming Negative Consumer Perceptions

As with every new technology that involves paying for things, consumers have concerns about the security of mobile payments. PayPal, Google, and the others took significant measures to design secure systems. However, most consumers just weren't comfortable with the idea that their phone might be used as a portal to their credit cards and bank accounts if it fell into the wrong hands. Never mind that the same could be said of a wallet or handbag, "devices" that are far less secure.

Recognizing consumer reluctance to place digital versions of their financial devices in one app, Apple took security to a higher level. Requiring a fingerprint makes the process much more secure than the more common safeguard of entering a passcode. And if a mobile device is ever lost or stolen, the owner can use its Find My iPhone feature to immediately lock down Apple Pay or even wipe the device completely clean.

Additionally, every compatible Apple device is assigned a unique device account number. This is encrypted and securely stored in a dedicated security chip on the device. It and a transaction-specific security code are the only numbers that Apple transmits to merchants. In fact, the merchant doesn't even need to know the customer's name. Credit and debit card numbers are stored only on the local device, not on Apple servers. This makes Apple Pay even more secure and more private than paying by credit card.

Beyond consumer security concerns, previous adoption of mobile payment apps has been slowed by perceptions of a clunky user experience. If convenience is the biggest draw for consumers, then anything more arduous than the already-convenient swipe of a credit card simply won't cut it. Setting up any of the existing mobile payment apps takes time and effort. Using such apps at the point of purchase is far from seamless, especially if the technology isn't working quite right. "I don't want to be that guy holding up the line while we fumble around to get it all to work," says one business columnist, "just like I don't want to be the guy who holds up the line boarding an airplane because his mobile boarding pass can't be read." Mobile apps that hit the market prior to Apple Pay required entering a passcode and—in some cases—hitting multiple buttons. That took longer than the traditional swipe of the card, even if everything worked as intended.

With Apple Pay, users still need to configure the app. But Apple entered the digital wallet business with 800 million credit cards already on file within its existing iTunes store. Not only can this facilitate a setup that is already streamlined compared with existing apps, it's a sign that iTunes users may be more comfortable with using the app given that they have already given their credit card information to Apple. And with the TouchID sensor, Apple has the transaction down to a one-touch process. That's quicker than swiping a card and going through the typical menu, not to mention quicker than inputting a passcode.

Establishing Points of Acceptance

For mobile payments to penetrate the market, consumer acceptance is necessary. But companies face a twofold challenge in making such a technology successful. Consumers won't adopt it if retailers don't accept it, and retailers won't invest the resources necessary to accept it unless there is sufficient consumer demand. And the lack of consumer demand is the biggest factor that has kept retailers from jumping onto the mobile payments bandwagon. As a result, having too few retailers accept mobile payments was a barrier to convincing people to leave their credit cards at home.

But thanks to Apple that situation is changing rapidly. It may be because of Apple's clout or because of its massive and loyal user base. But in less than a year, Apple signed up far more retailers than all the previous mobile payment providers combined. Today, more than 2.5 million contactless-enabled terminals in the United States accept Apple Pay, a level that demonstrates the type of momentum that will keep Apple on a growth trajectory. "You need so many points of acceptance to make mobile payments work," says a mobile payments analyst for Forrester Research. "Apple has made that happen, striking partnerships with top national brands across a variety of categories that will give consumers plenty of opportunity to use the service." Apple has also signed up enough credit card–issuing banks and credit unions to cover the vast majority of charge volume.

Given the tremendous potential for this market, the competition has been very active. Google has pulled back on Google Wallet, even as it has released a more user-friendly and more widely accepted Android Pay. PayPal has the advantage of its massive online payments network as well as the first-mover advantage. Samsung intends for Samsung Pay to be a fluid component for its foray into the Internet of Things. Banks such as Capital One, JPMorgan Chase, and Wells Fargo are intent on keeping payment transactions in the banking business with apps of their own. And numerous startups are pushing digital wallet apps, including Coin, eWallet, Gyft, KeyRing, and

LevelUp. What's more, most of these digital wallets utilize the contactless-reader technologies that are already part of existing point-of-sale terminals, eliminating retailer acceptance as a barrier to entry.

In addition to the competition, Apple still faces other challenges. For starters, while Apple's market penetration far exceeds that of the competition and continues to grow by a million new users each week, the mobile payments leader has a long way to go before reaching critical mass as digital wallets are still being used for only a sliver of all retail transactions. Additionally, the complexity of the payments industry has required Apple and other companies to focus on developing one system. And with everything from smartwatches to refrigerators now featuring payment capabilities, changes in consumer payment behaviors are inevitable. In an environment as volatile as this one, an alternative technology could certainly upset the apple cart.

Still, Apple remains confident. With in-browser and peer-to-peer payments on the horizon, there is more potential than ever to boost transactions. And don't count out an Apple Pay app for Android devices. In short, experts predict that this year will be a watershed one for the payments industry. Although there are still plenty of doubters that mobile payments will replace plastic as the go-to method for purchasing goods and services, there are also plenty of believers. And although Apple is clearly ahead at this point, its success also bodes well for the competition. As the concept catches on and technologies become more compatible, demand among non-Apple users will increase as well.

Questions for Discussion

12-18 As completely as possible, sketch the value delivery network for Apple Pay.

12-19 With respect to Apple Pay, is Apple a producer, a consumer, or an intermediary? Explain.

12-20 Identify all the reasons why Apple's partnerships are essential to the success of Apple Pay.

12-21 With respect to marketing channels, what are some threats to Apple Pay's future?

Sources: Andrew Meola, "Apple Pay Is Showing Promising Growth," *Business Insider*, April 28, 2016, www.businessinsider.com/apple-pay-is-showing-promising-growth-2016-4; Jason Del Rey, "Apple Pay Coming to Mobile Websites before Holiday Shopping Season," *Recode*, March 23, 2016, www.recode.net/2016/3/23/11587214/apple-pay-coming-to-mobile-websites-before-holiday-shopping-season; Robert Hof, "Apple Pay Starts to Take Off, Leaving Competition in the Dust," *Forbes*, January 27, 2015, www.forbes.com/sites/roberthof/2015/01/27/apple-pay-starts-to-take-off-leaving-competition-in-the-dust/; Robert Hof, "Apple Pay Momentum Keeps Growing Despite Challenges in Stores," *Forbes*, April 27, 2015, www.forbes.com/sites/roberthof/2015/04/27/apple-pay-momentum-keeps-growing-despite-challenges-in-stores/; and information from www.apple.com/apple-pay/, accessed June 2016.

MyMarketingLab

Go to **mymktlab.com** for Auto-graded writing questions as well as the following Assisted-graded writing questions:

12-22 Describe multichannel distribution systems and the advantages and disadvantages of using them.

12-23 Why does channel conflict occur? Name and describe the various types of channel conflict.

13 Retailing and Wholesaling

CHAPTER PREVIEW

We now look more deeply into the two major intermediary marketing channel functions: retailing and wholesaling. You already know something about retailing—retailers of all shapes and sizes serve you every day, both in stores and online. However, you probably know much less about the hoard of wholesalers working behind the scenes. In this chapter, we examine the characteristics of different kinds of retailers and wholesalers, the marketing decisions they make, and trends for the future.

When it comes to retailers, you have to start with Walmart. This megaretailer's phenomenal success has resulted from an unrelenting focus on bringing value to its customers. Day in and day out, Walmart lives up to its promise: "Save money. Live better." That focus on customer value has made Walmart the world's largest retailer, the world's largest company. Yet, despite its huge success, Walmart still faces plenty of fresh opportunities and some daunting challenges as well.

WALMART: The World's Largest *Retailer*—the World's Largest *Company*

Walmart is almost unimaginably big. It's the world's largest retailer—the world's largest *company*. It rang up an incredible $482 billion in sales last year—more than double the sales of competitors Costco, Target, Macy's, Sears, Kmart, JCPenney, and Kohl's *combined*. If Walmart were a country, its sales would rate it 28th in the world in GDP, just behind Norway and ahead of Austria.

Walmart is the number-one seller in many consumer product categories, including groceries, clothing, toys, and pet care products. Walmart sells nearly twice as many groceries as Kroger, the leading grocery-only food retailer. Its apparel sales alone are 20 percent greater than the total revenues of Macy's Inc., parent of both Macy's and Bloomingdale's department stores. And it captures an estimated twice the toy market share of competitors Target and Toys"R"Us.

On average, worldwide, Walmart serves more than 260 million customers per week through more than 11,500 stores in 28 countries and online in 11 countries. It's also hard to fathom Walmart's impact on the U.S. economy. It's the nation's largest employer—one out of every 231 men, women, and children in the United States is a Walmart associate.

> Day in and day out, giant Walmart lives up to its promise: "Save money. Live better." Its obsession with customer value has made Walmart not only the world's largest retailer but also the world's largest *company*.

What's behind this spectacular success? First and foremost, Walmart is passionately dedicated to its long-time, low-price value proposition and what its low prices mean to customers: "Save money. Live better." To accomplish this mission, Walmart offers a broad selection of goods at "unbeatable low prices," day in and day out. No other retailer has come nearly so close to mastering the concepts of everyday low prices and one-stop shopping. Sam Walton himself summed up Walmart's mission best when he said, "If we work together, we'll lower the cost of living for everyone…we'll give the world an opportunity to see what it's like to save and have a better life."

How does Walmart make money with such low prices? Walmart is a lean, mean distribution machine—it has the lowest cost structure in the industry. Low costs let the giant retailer charge lower prices while remaining profitable. Lower prices attract more shoppers, producing more sales, making the company more efficient, and enabling it to lower prices even more.

Walmart's low costs result from superior operations management, sophisticated information technology, and good-old "tough buying." Its huge, fully automated distribution centers supply stores efficiently. It employs an information technology system that the U.S. Department of Defense would envy, giving managers around the world instant access to sales and operating information. And Walmart is known for using its massive scale to wring low prices from suppliers. "Don't expect a greeter and don't expect friendly," said one supplier's sales executive after a visit to Walmart's buying offices. "Once you are ushered into one of the spartan little buyers' rooms, expect a steely eye across the table and be prepared to cut your price. They are very, very focused people, and they use their buying power more forcefully than anyone else in America."

Despite its incredible success over the past five decades, mighty Walmart faces some weighty challenges ahead. Having grown so big, the maturing giant is having difficulty maintaining the rapid growth rates of its youth. Its same-store sales growth has stagnated over the past few years. Think about this: To grow just 6 percent next year, Walmart will have to add more than $29 billion in new sales. That's a sales *increase* greater than the *total* sales of all but the top 100 or so companies on the *Fortune* 500, including companies such as McDonald's, Macy's, American Express, Xerox, Goodyear, Nike, or more than two Whole Foods. The bigger and more mature Walmart gets, the harder it is to maintain a high rate of growth, especially facing challenges from online juggernaut Amazon and hot discount formats such as dollar stores.

To regain growth, Walmart has pushed into new, faster-growing product and service lines, including organic foods, store brands, in-store health clinics, and consumer financial services. To combat trendier competitors such as Target, Walmart even gave itself a modest image face-lift. It spruced up its stores with a cleaner, brighter, more open look and less clutter to make them more shopper friendly. To broaden its appeal to middle and higher income consumers, it has added new, higher-quality products. Walmart stores now carry a selection of higher-end consumer electronics products, from Samsung ultra-thin televisions to Dell and Toshiba laptops to Apple iPhones and iPads. And the retailer is now upgrading

At Walmart: "Save money. Live better." Says Walmart's CEO, "We're obsessed with delivering value to customers."
Bloomberg via Getty Images

its grocery offerings, both in its big-box stores and its smaller Neighborhood Market stores.

Despite its massive presence, Walmart still has room to expand. In recent years, the giant retailer has grown rapidly into international markets, which now account for 28 percent of its total revenues. Walmart is also investing heavily in online, mobile, and social media commerce and building its omni-channel distribution capabilities. Although it remains a distant also-ran next to Amazon in e-commerce, Walmart is now the nation's fourth-largest online merchant, and its online sales grew 12 percent last year (see the Chapter 10 opening story on Walmart versus Amazon). Walmart lists "winning in global e-commerce" as one of its top priorities for the future.

As Walmart continues to adapt and grow, however, one thing seems certain. The giant retailer may add new product lines and services. It might go digital and global. It might brush up its look and image. But Walmart has no intention of ever giving up its core low-price value proposition. After all, Walmart is and always will be a discounter. "I don't think Walmart's...ever going to be edgy," says a Walmart marketer. "I don't think that fits our brand. Our brand is about saving people money" so that they can live better.[1]

THE WALMART STORY SETS the stage for examining the fast-changing world of today's resellers. This chapter looks at *retailing* and *wholesaling*. In the first section, we look at the nature and importance of retailing, the major types of store and nonstore retailers, the decisions retailers make, and the future of retailing. In the second section, we discuss these same topics as they apply to wholesalers.

OBJECTIVES OUTLINE

OBJECTIVE 13-1	Explain the role of retailers in the distribution channel and describe the major types of retailers. **Retailing** *(pp 368–375)*
OBJECTIVE 13-2	Describe the major retailer marketing decisions. **Retailer Marketing Decisions** *(pp 376–381)*
OBJECTIVE 13-3	Discuss the major trends and developments in retailing. **Retailing Trends and Developments** *(pp 381–387)*
OBJECTIVE 13-4	Explain the major types of wholesalers and their marketing decisions. **Wholesaling** *(pp 387–392)*

Author | Comment You already know a lot about retailers. You deal with them every day—store retailers, service retailers, online and mobile retailers, and others.

Retailing

All the activities involved in selling goods or services directly to final consumers for their personal, nonbusiness use.

Retailer

A business whose sales come *primarily* from retailing.

Shopper marketing

Focusing the entire marketing process on turning shoppers into buyers as they approach the point of sale, whether during in-store, online, or mobile shopping.

Retailing

What is retailing? We all know that Costco, Home Depot, Macy's, and Whole Foods Market are retailers, but so are Amazon.com, the local Hampton Inn, and a doctor seeing patients. **Retailing** includes all the activities involved in selling products or services directly to final consumers for their personal, nonbusiness use. Many institutions—manufacturers, wholesalers, and retailers—do retailing. But most retailing is done by **retailers**, businesses whose sales come *primarily* from retailing. Retailing plays a very important role in most marketing channels. Last year, retailers accounted for more than $5.3 trillion of sales to final consumers.[2]

Retailing: Connecting Brands with Consumers

Retailers connect brands with consumers in the final phases of the buying process and at the point of purchase. In fact, many marketers are now embracing the concept of **shopper marketing**, focusing the entire marketing process—from product and brand development to logistics, promotion, and merchandising—toward turning shoppers into buyers as they approach the point of sale. Of course, every well-designed marketing effort focuses on customer buying behavior. What differentiates the concept of shopper marketing is the suggestion that these efforts should be coordinated around the shopping process itself.

Shopper marketing builds around what P&G calls the "First Moment of Truth"—the critical three to seven seconds that a shopper considers a product on a store shelf. However, the dramatic growth of online and mobile shopping has added new dimensions to shopper marketing. The retailing "moment of truth" no longer takes place only in stores. Instead, Google defines a "zero moment of truth," when consumers begin the buying process by searching for and learning about products online.[3]

Today's consumers are increasingly *omni-channel buyers*, who make little distinction between in-store and online shopping and for whom the path to a retail purchase runs across multiple channels. For these buyers, a particular purchase might consist of researching a product online and buying it from an online retailer without ever setting foot in a retail store. Alternatively, they might use a smartphone to research a purchase on the fly or even while in retail store aisles. For example, it's common to see a consumer examining an item on a shelf at Target while at the same time using a mobile app to look for coupons or check product reviews and prices at Amazon.com.

Thus, these days, shopper marketing and the "point of purchase" go well beyond in-store buying. ● They involve consumers working across multiple channels as they

● **Shopper marketing: The dramatic growth in online and mobile shopping has added new dimensions to "point of purchase." Influencing consumers' buying decisions as they shop now involves omni-channel efforts aimed at integrating in-store, online, and mobile shopping.**

Betsie Van der Meer/Getty Images

Omni-channel retailing
Creating a seamless cross-channel buying experience that integrates in-store, online, and mobile shopping.

shop. Influencing consumers' buying decisions calls for **omni-channel retailing**, creating a seamless cross-channel buying experience that integrates in-store, online, and mobile shopping.[4]

Although most retailing is still done in retail stores, in recent years direct and online retailing have been growing much faster than store retailing. We discuss direct, online, and omni-channel retailing in detail later in this chapter and in Chapter 17. For now, we will focus on store retailing.

Types of Retailers

Retail stores come in all shapes and sizes—from your local hairstyling salon or family-owned restaurant to national specialty chain retailers such as REI or Williams-Sonoma to megadiscounters such as Costco or Walmart. The most important types of retail stores are described in ● Table 13.1 and discussed in the following sections. They can be classified in terms of several characteristics, including the *amount of service* they offer, the breadth and depth of their *product lines*, the *relative prices* they charge, and how they are *organized*.

Amount of Service

Different types of customers and products require different amounts of service. To meet these varying service needs, retailers may offer one of three service levels: self-service, limited service, and full service.

Self-service retailers serve customers who are willing to perform their own *locate-compare-select* process to save time or money. Self-service is the basis of all discount operations and is typically used by retailers selling convenience goods (such as supermarkets) and nationally branded, fast-moving shopping goods (such as Target or Kohl's). *Limited-service retailers*, such as Sears or JCPenney, provide more sales assistance because they carry more shopping goods about which customers need information. Their increased operating costs result in higher prices.

Full-service retailers, such as high-end specialty stores (for example, Tiffany or Williams-Sonoma) and first-class department stores (such as Nordstrom or Neiman Marcus), assist customers in every phase of the shopping process. Full-service stores usually carry more specialty goods for which customers need or want assistance or advice. They provide more services, which results in much higher operating costs. These higher costs are passed along to customers as higher prices.

Product Line

Retailers can also be classified by the length and breadth of their product assortments. Some retailers, such as **specialty stores**, carry narrow product lines with deep assortments within those lines. Today, specialty stores are flourishing. The increasing use of market segmentation, market targeting, and product specialization has resulted in a greater need for stores that focus on specific products and segments.

By contrast, **department stores** carry a wide variety of product lines. In recent years, middle-market department stores have been squeezed between more focused and flexible specialty stores on the one hand and more efficient, lower-priced discounters on the other. In response, many have added promotional pricing to meet the discount threat. Others have stepped up the use of store brands and single-brand *shop-in-shop* concepts to compete with specialty stores. Still others are trying direct and online selling. Service remains the key differentiating factor. Retailers such as Nordstrom, Saks, Neiman Marcus, and other high-end department stores are doing well by emphasizing exclusive merchandise and high-quality service.

Specialty store
A retail store that carries a narrow product line with a deep assortment within that line.

Department store
A retail store that carries a wide variety of product lines, each operated as a separate department managed by specialist buyers or merchandisers.

● **Table 13.1** | **Major Store Retailer Types**

Type	Description	Examples
Specialty store	A store that carries a narrow product line with a deep assortment, such as apparel stores, sporting-goods stores, furniture stores, florists, and bookstores.	REI, Sunglass Hut, Sephora, Williams-Sonoma
Department store	A store that carries several product lines—typically clothing, home furnishings, and household goods—with each line operated as a separate department managed by specialist buyers or merchandisers.	Macy's, Sears, Neiman Marcus
Supermarket	A relatively large, low-cost, low-margin, high-volume, self-service operation designed to serve the consumer's total needs for grocery and household products.	Kroger, Publix, Safeway, SuperValu
Convenience store	A relatively small store located near residential areas, open 24/7, and carrying a limited line of high-turnover convenience products at slightly higher prices.	7-Eleven, Circle K, Speedway, Sheetz
Discount store	A store that carries standard merchandise sold at lower prices with lower margins and higher volumes.	Walmart, Target, Kohl's
Off-price retailer	A store that sells merchandise bought at less-than-regular wholesale prices and sold at less than retail. These include *factory outlets* owned and operated by manufacturers; *independent off-price retailers* owned and run by entrepreneurs or by divisions of larger retail corporations; and *warehouse (or wholesale) clubs* selling a limited selection of goods at deep discounts to consumers who pay membership fees.	Mikasa (factory outlet); TJ Maxx (independent off-price retailer); Costco, Sam's Club, BJ's (warehouse clubs)
Superstore	A very large store that meets consumers' total needs for routinely purchased food and nonfood items. This includes *supercenters*, combined supermarket and discount stores, and *category killers*, which carry a deep assortment in a particular category.	Walmart Supercenter, SuperTarget, Meijer (discount stores); Best Buy, Petco, Staples, Bed Bath & Beyond (category killers)

Supermarket
A large, low-cost, low-margin, high-volume, self-service store that carries a wide variety of grocery and household products.

Supermarkets are the most frequently visited type of retail store. Today, however, they are facing slow sales growth because of slower population growth and an increase in competition from discounters (Walmart, Costco, and Dollar General) on the one hand and specialty food stores (Whole Foods Market, Trader Joe's, ALDI, Sprouts) on the other. Supermarkets' share of U.S. packaged foods sales slipped from 53 percent in 1998 to 37 percent in 2012.[5] Supermarkets also have been hit hard by the rapid growth of out-of-home eating over the past two decades.

In the battle for "share of stomachs," some supermarkets are competing head-on with large discounters such as Costco and Walmart by cutting costs, establishing more-efficient operations, and lowering prices. An example is WinCo, the fast-growing regional discount-grocery chain in the western United States that positions itself directly against mighty Walmart as "The Supermarket Low Price Leader." WinCo's large, efficient, no-frills stores carry a limited assortment of basic fast-moving merchandise, and customers help to keep costs down by bagging their own groceries and paying cash (no credit cards accepted). As a result, WinCo doesn't just match Walmart's prices; it often undercuts them.

Other supermarkets have moved upscale, providing improved store environments and higher-quality food offerings, such as from-scratch bakeries, gourmet deli counters, natural foods, and fresh seafood departments. Still others are introducing their own smaller, fresh-format stores that compete with higher-end specialty grocers such as Whole Foods Market, Sprouts, or Fresh Thyme. These fresh-format stores cater to customers seeking health and wellness and the ease of shopping in smaller, warmer environments.

They specialize in fresh produce and high-quality prepared foods—all at affordable prices. An example is Kroger's Main & Vine stores, "where eating is healthy, affordable, and fun."[6] According to its online site, "Main & Vine is an awesome new market (really, it's awesome!) where fresh food comes first and flavor brings people together. You'll find groceries you can feel good about, friendly advice, and a whole lot more…right where you live, work and play."

Convenience stores are small stores that carry a limited line of high-turnover convenience goods. After several years of stagnant sales, these stores are now experiencing growth. Many convenience store chains have tried to expand beyond their primary market of young, blue-collar men by redesigning their stores to attract female shoppers. They are shedding the image of a "truck stop" where men go to buy gas, beer, cigarettes, or shriveled hot dogs on a roller grill and are instead offering freshly prepared foods and cleaner, safer, more-upscale environments.

Many convenience stores are expanding their offerings to attract "fill-in" shoppers—people looking to pick up a few items between major grocery store trips. For example, in addition to supermarkets, Kroger operates almost 800 convenience stores. It is currently testing the fill-in concept in its Loaf 'N Jug chain:[7]

> Loaf 'N Jug convenience stores offer gas and an expanded selection of fresh produce, meats, frozen foods, and dairy items along with a wide variety of snacks, beverages, groceries, and other convenience products. They offer a range of healthier options as well, such as fresh fruit, salads, and nuts and dried fruit. Loaf 'N Jug stores also carry Kroger's affordable Simple Truth store brand of natural and organic foods. "We're trying to provide that one-stop shop for the customer who's looking for a place for that fill-in shop: fresh produce, meat, meal solutions, whether it be hot meal solutions or expanded grocery, expanded frozen," says the president of Loaf 'N Jug. "It's the place where variety meets convenience."

Superstores are much larger than regular supermarkets and offer a large assortment of routinely purchased food products, nonfood items, and services. Walmart, Target, Meijer, and other discount retailers offer *supercenters*, very large combination food and discount stores. Whereas a traditional grocery store brings in about $517,000 a week in sales, a supercenter brings in about $1.4 million a week.[8]

Recent years have also seen the rapid growth of superstores that are actually giant specialty stores, the so-called **category killers** (for example, Best Buy, Home Depot, Petco, and Bed Bath & Beyond). They feature stores the size of airplane hangars that carry a very deep assortment of a particular line. Category killers are found in a wide range of categories, including electronics, home-improvement products, books, baby gear, toys, home goods, party goods, sporting goods, and even pet supplies.

Finally, for many retailers, the product line is actually a service. **Service retailers** include hotels and motels, banks, airlines, restaurants, colleges, hospitals, movie theaters, tennis clubs, bowling alleys, repair services, hair salons, and dry cleaners. Service retailers in the United States are growing faster than product retailers.

Relative Prices

Retailers can also be classified according to the prices they charge (see Table 13.1). Most retailers charge regular prices and offer normal-quality goods and customer service. Others offer higher-quality goods and service at higher prices. Retailers that feature low prices are discount stores and "off-price" retailers.

Discount Stores. A **discount store** (for example, Target, Kohl's, or Walmart) sells standard merchandise at lower prices by accepting lower margins and selling higher volume. The early discount stores cut expenses by offering few services and operating in warehouse-like facilities in low-rent, heavily traveled districts. Today's discounters have improved their store environments and increased their services while at the same time keeping prices low through lean, efficient operations.

Leading "big-box" discounters, such as Walmart and Target, now dominate the retail scene. However, even "small-box" discounters are thriving in the current economic environment. For example, dollar stores are now today's fastest-growing retail format. Back in the day, dollar stores sold mostly odd-lot assortments of novelties, factory overruns, closeouts, and outdated merchandise—most priced at $1. Not anymore. Dollar General, the

Convenience store
A small store, located near a residential area, that is open long hours seven days a week and carries a limited line of high-turnover convenience goods.

Superstore
A store much larger than a regular supermarket that offers a large assortment of routinely purchased food products, nonfood items, and services.

Category killer
A giant specialty store that carries a very deep assortment of a particular line.

Service retailer
A retailer whose product line is actually a service; examples include hotels, airlines, banks, colleges, and many others.

Discount store
A retail operation that sells standard merchandise at lower prices by accepting lower margins and selling at higher volume.

● Discounter Dollar General, the nation's largest small-box discount retailer, makes a powerful value promise for the times: "Save time. Save money. Every day!"

Bloomberg via Getty Images

nation's largest small-box discount retailer, makes a powerful value promise for the times: "Save time. Save money. Every day":[9]

● Dollar General's slogan isn't just for show. It's a careful statement of the store's value promise. The retailer's goal is to keep shopping simple by offering only a selected assortment of popular brands at everyday low prices in small and convenient locations. Dollar General's slimmed-down product line and smaller stores (you could fit more than 25 Dollar General stores inside the average Walmart supercenter) add up to a quick trip—the average customer is in and out of the store in less than 10 minutes. And its prices on the popular brand name products it carries are an estimated 20 to 40 percent lower than grocery store prices and on par with Walmart. Put it all together, and performance is strong at Dollar General. Moreover, the fast-growing retailer is well positioned for the future. We "see signs of a new consumerism," says Dollar General's CEO, "as people shift where they shop, switch to lower-cost brands, and stay generally more frugal." Convenience and low prices, it seems, never go out of style.

Off-price retailer

A retailer that buys at less-than-regular wholesale prices and sells at less than retail.

Off-Price Retailers. As the major discount stores traded up, a new wave of **off-price retailers** moved in to fill the ultralow-price, high-volume gap. Ordinary discounters buy at regular wholesale prices and accept lower margins to keep prices down. By contrast, off-price retailers buy at less-than-regular wholesale prices and charge consumers less than retail. Off-price retailers can be found in all areas, from food, clothing, and electronics to no-frills banking and discount brokerages.

Independent off-price retailer

An off-price retailer that is independently owned and operated or a division of a larger retail corporation.

The three main types of off-price retailers are *independents, factory outlets,* and *warehouse clubs.* **Independent off-price retailers** either are independently owned and run or are divisions of larger retail corporations. Although many off-price operations are run by smaller independents, most large off-price retailer operations are owned by bigger retail chains. Examples include store retailers such as TJ Maxx, Marshalls, and HomeGoods, all owned by TJX Companies, and online sellers such as Overstock.com. TJ Maxx promises brand name and designer fashions for 20 to 60 percent off department store prices. How does it fulfill this promise? Its buyers are constantly on the lookout for deals. "So when a designer overproduces and department stores overbuy," says the company, "we swoop in, negotiate the lowest possible price, and pass the savings on."[10]

Factory outlet

An off-price retailing operation that is owned and operated by a manufacturer and normally carries the manufacturer's surplus, discontinued, or irregular goods.

Factory outlets—manufacturer-owned and operated stores by firms such as J.Crew, Gap, Levi Strauss, and others—sometimes group together in *factory outlet malls* and *value-retail centers.* At these centers, dozens of outlet stores offer prices as much as 50 percent below retail on a wide range of mostly surplus, discounted, or irregular goods. Whereas outlet malls consist primarily of manufacturers' outlets, value-retail centers combine manufacturers' outlets with off-price retail stores and department store clearance outlets.

These malls in general are now moving upscale—and even dropping *factory* from their descriptions. A growing number of outlet malls now feature luxury brands such as Coach, Polo Ralph Lauren, Dolce & Gabbana, Giorgio Armani, Burberry, and Versace. As consumers become more value-minded, even upper-end retailers are accelerating their factory outlet strategies, placing more emphasis on outlets such as Nordstrom Rack, Neiman Marcus Last Call, Bloomingdale's Outlets, and Saks Off 5th. Many companies now regard outlets not simply as a way of disposing of problem merchandise but as an additional way of gaining business for fresh merchandise. For example, 90 percent of the merchandise sold in Neiman Marcus's Last Call outlets is made specifically for those stores.[11] The combination of highbrow brands and lowbrow prices found at outlets provides powerful shopper appeal, especially in thriftier times.

Warehouse club

An off-price retailer that sells a limited selection of brand name grocery items, appliances, clothing, and other goods at deep discounts to members who pay annual membership fees.

Warehouse clubs (also known as *wholesale clubs* or *membership warehouses*), such as Costco, Sam's Club, and BJ's, operate in huge, warehouse-like facilities and offer few frills.

In exchange for the bare-bones environment, they offer ultralow prices and surprise deals on selected branded merchandise. Warehouse clubs have grown rapidly in recent years. These retailers appeal not only to low-income consumers seeking bargains on bare-bones products but also to all kinds of customers shopping for a wide range of goods, from necessities to extravagances.

Consider Costco, now the world's second-largest retailer behind only Walmart. Low price is an important part of Costco's equation, but what really sets Costco apart is the products it carries and the sense of urgency that it builds into the Costco shopper's store experience (see Real Marketing 13.1).

Organizational Approach

Although many retail stores are independently owned, others band together under some form of corporate or contractual organization. ●**Table 13.2** describes four major types of retail organizations—*corporate chains, voluntary chains, retailer cooperatives,* and *franchise organizations.*

Corporate chains
Two or more outlets that are commonly owned and controlled.

Corporate chains are two or more outlets that are commonly owned and controlled. They have many advantages over independents. Their size allows them to buy in large quantities at lower prices and gain promotional economies. They can hire specialists to deal with areas such as pricing, promotion, merchandising, inventory control, and sales forecasting.

The great success of corporate chains caused many independents to band together in one of two forms of contractual associations. One is the *voluntary chain*—a wholesaler-sponsored group of independent retailers that engages in group buying and common merchandising. Examples include the Independent Grocers Alliance (IGA), Western Auto, and True Value hardware stores. The other type of contractual association is the *retailer cooperative*—a group of independent retailers that bands together to set up a jointly owned, central wholesale operation and conduct joint merchandising and promotion efforts. Examples are Associated Grocers and Ace Hardware. These organizations give independents the buying and promotion economies they need to meet the prices of corporate chains.

Franchise
A contractual association between a manufacturer, wholesaler, or service organization (a franchisor) and independent businesspeople (franchisees) who buy the right to own and operate one or more units in the franchise system.

Another form of contractual retail organization is a **franchise**. The main difference between franchise organizations and other contractual systems (voluntary chains and retail cooperatives) is that franchise systems are normally based on some unique product or service; a method of doing business; or the trade name, goodwill, or patent that the franchisor has developed. Franchising has been prominent in fast-food restaurants, motels, health and fitness centers, auto sales and service dealerships, and real estate agencies.

●**Table 13.2** | **Major Types of Retail Organizations**

Type	Description	Examples
Corporate chain	Two or more outlets that are commonly owned and controlled. Corporate chains appear in all types of retailing but they are strongest in department stores, discount stores, food stores, drugstores, and restaurants.	Macy's (department stores), Target (discount stores), Kroger (grocery stores), CVS (drugstores)
Voluntary chain	Wholesaler-sponsored group of independent retailers engaged in group buying and merchandising.	Independent Grocers Alliance (IGA), Western Auto (auto supply), True Value (hardware)
Retailer cooperative	Group of independent retailers who jointly establish a central buying organization and conduct joint promotion efforts.	Associated Grocers (groceries), Ace Hardware (hardware)
Franchise organization	Contractual association between a franchisor (a manufacturer, wholesaler, or service organization) and franchisees (independent businesspeople who buy the right to own and operate one or more units in the franchise system).	McDonald's, Subway, Pizza Hut, Jiffy Lube, Meineke Mufflers, 7-Eleven

Real Marketing

13.1 Costco: Merchandising Magic That Competitors Can't Match

Giant Walmart is used to beating up on competitors. It outsells Toys"R"Us in toys, gives Best Buy migraines in consumer electronics, sells more dog food than PetSmart or Petco, and dresses more people than Gap, American Eagle Outfitters, and Abercrombie & Fitch combined. With 24 percent of the grocery market, it sells far more groceries than leading grocery-only retailer Kroger. Almost every retailer, no matter what the category, has its hands full devising strategies by which it can compete with Walmart and survive.

But this isn't a story about Walmart. It's about Costco, the red-hot warehouse retailer that competes head-on with Walmart's Sam's Club—and wins. Sam's Club is huge. With 652 stores and $57 billion in revenues, if Sam's Club were a separate company, it would be the eighth-largest U.S. retailer. But when it comes to warehouse retailing, it's Costco that's the bully, not the other way around.

With only about 60 more stores than Sam's Club, Costco has more than twice the revenues, and the revenue gap grows bigger every year. Costco's $116 billion in sales makes it the world's second-largest retailer, behind only Walmart. This year Costco moved up to number 18 among *Fortune* 500 companies. And unlike Sam's Club, whose revenues are flat or falling, Costco's sales are growing rapidly. In just the past four years, Costco's revenues have surged 30 percent; profits are up 50 percent. How is Costco beating Sam's Club at its own low-price game? The two retailers are very similar in many ways. But inside the store, Costco adds a certain merchandising magic that Sam's Club just can't match.

Let's start with the similarities. Both Costco and Sam's Club are warehouse retailers. They offer a limited selection of nationally branded and private-label products in a wide range of categories at very low prices to shoppers who pay an annual membership fee. Both retailers stock about 4,000 items, often only jumbo sizes (a typical supermarket stocks 40,000 items; a Walmart supercenter about 150,000). And to keep costs and prices low, both operate out of big, drafty, bare-bones stores and use their substantial buying power to wring low prices from suppliers.

Price is an important part of the equation, and both Costco and Sam's Club seem addicted to selling every item at the lowest possible price. But more than just focusing on low discount prices, Costco focuses on high value through low mark-ups, regardless of the ultimate price. From the beginning, *discount* has been a bad word at Costco—it denotes "cheap." Instead, Costco's strategy is to give customers the best value through low margins, whether it's on a pantry staple or a high-priced wine. Costco's operating profit margins average a razor-thin 3.1 percent. Then again, Sam's Club's margins are only 3.5 percent.

Thus, both Costco and Sam's Club excel at low-cost operations and low prices. What is it, then, that really sets Costco apart? It has to do with Costco's differentiated value proposition—with the products it carries and sense of urgency that it builds into the shopping experience. Whereas Sam's Club and other wholesale retailers stand for low prices, Costco is a retail treasure hunt where both low-end and high-end products meet deep-discount prices. Alongside the gallon jars of peanut butter, four packs of toothpaste, and 2,250-count packs of Q-Tips that make other warehouse clubs popular, Costco offers an ever-changing assortment of high-quality products—even luxuries—all at tantalizingly low margins.

Last year, Costco sold more than 110 million hot dog–soda combos (still only $1.50, as they have been for more than three decades). At the same time, it sold more than 100,000 carats of diamonds at up to $100,000 per item. Costco is the nation's biggest baster of poultry (nearly 70,000 rotisserie chickens a day at $4.99 and a million whole turkeys during a holiday season), but it's also the country's biggest seller of fine wines (including the likes of a Chateau Cheval Blanc Premier Grand Cru Classe at $1,750 a bottle). Just for the fun of it, a Costco in Arizona once sold an extremely limited-edition bottle of Macallan Lalique single-malt scotch for $17,000 (actually a $6,000 discount). And Costco.com once offered a Pablo Picasso drawing at only $129,999.99!

Costco brings flair to an otherwise-dreary setting. Mixed in with its regular stock of staples, Costco features a glittering, constantly shifting array of one-time specials on brands such as Andrew Marc, Calvin Klein, Chanel, Prada, and Breitling—deals you just won't get anywhere else. It finds the best deals on premium electronics and appliances, then sells them at rock-bottom prices. In fact, 25 percent of the items that Costco carries are designated as "treasure items" (Costco's words). The deals come and go quickly, and the changing assortment and great prices keep people coming back, wallets in hand.

Warehouse clubs: Costco is a retail treasure hunt, where both low-end and high-end products meet deep-discount prices.
Bloomberg/Getty Images

Once inside, many customers fall prey to "the Costco effect"—spending more than they'd planned to. Some even become "Costcoholics," as one reporter's story illustrates:

A good friend of mine was raving about Costco recently, going on about how she couldn't resist shopping there at least two to three times a week. She said sometimes she doesn't even plan on buying anything. She just loves wandering around in the enormous, double-football-field-sized warehouse, hunting for what's new. She is also obsessed by what the big luxury "surprise" of the week might be—stuff like Waterford Crystal, Coach handbags, or Omega watches, to name a few, all selling out quickly at shock-and-awe low prices. And even though she may have shopped with no intention of purchasing, she says she always finds something that seduces her to buy.

There was a time when only the great unwashed masses shopped at off-price retailers. But Costco has changed all that. Even people who don't have to pinch pennies shop there. Not by accident, Costco's stores tend to be located in more affluent locations than Sam's Clubs. The average Costco member has a household income of nearly $100,000.

Costco's flair even extends to its store brand—Kirkland Signature. Whereas the Sam's Club Member's Mark store brand covers a limited assortment of generic-priced food, household, and apparel lines, Costco puts the Kirkland Signature brand on a much wider range of goods. Customers seek out Kirkland Signature products not just for price but also for quality. Costco customers can buy anything from a $19 bottle of Kirkland Signature Series Mendoza Malbec red wine to a $2,299 Kirkland Signature Braeburn five-piece woven fire pit patio set to a $3,799-per-person, seven-day Kirkland Signature river cruise package in France.

So, in its own warehouse club retailing backyard, it's Costco, not Walmart, that's beating up on competitors. In fact, mighty but frustrated Walmart has spent years trying to make Sam's Club more Costco-like. Costco is much more than a big-box store that "stacks 'em high and sells 'em cheap"—more than just a place to load up on large sizes of consumer staples. Each Costco store is a theater of retail that creates buying urgency and excitement for customers.

In many ways, retailing boils down to the unglamorous art of getting the right product in the right place at the right time at the right price. But there's a lot more than that to Costco's value proposition. Says Costco founder and former CEO Jim Sinegal: "Do that without being boring. That's the trick."

Sources: Robin Lewis, "'Costoholics': Costco's $113.7 Billion Addicts," *Forbes*, February 16, 2016, www.forbes.com/sites/robinlewis/2016/02/16/costcoholics-costcos-113-7-billion-addicts/#179cdc9b5f73; "Top 250 Global Retailers," *National Retail Federation*, https://nrf.com/2016/global250-table, accessed July 2016; "The Sorry State of Sam's Club, and Why Walmart Stores, Inc. Can't Give Up on the Warehouse," *The Motley Fool*, January 1, 2015, www.fool.com/investing/general/2015/01/25/sams-clubs-sorry-story-and-why-wal-mart-cannot-giv.aspx; Matthew Boyle, "Why Costco Is So Addictive," *Fortune*, October 25, 2006, pp. 126–132; Stan Laegreid, "The Choreography of Design, Treasure Hunts, and Hot Dogs That Have Made Costco So Successful," *Fast Company*, January 24, 2014, www.fastcompany.com/3025312; John Kell, "Dancing in the Aisles," *Fortune,* December 15, 2015, p. 26; Phalguni Soni, "Analyzing Walmart—The World's Largest Retailer," *Market Realist*, February 18, 2015, http://marketrealist.com/2015/02/analyzing-walmart-worlds-largest-retailer/; "Costco Wholesale Corporation: Key Statistics," *Yahoo! Finance*, https://finance.yahoo.com/q/ks?s=COST, accessed March 2016; and information from www.corporate.walmart.com, www.costco.com, http://phx.corporate-ir.net/Phoenix.zhtml?c=83830&p=irol-news, and www.costco.com/insider-guide-amazing-facts.html, accessed October 2016.

However, franchising covers a lot more than just burger joints and fitness centers. Franchises have sprung up to meet just about any need. For example, Mad Science Group franchisees put on science programs for schools, scout troops, and birthday parties. Soccer Shots offers programs that give kids ages two to eight an introduction to basic soccer skills at daycare centers, schools, and parks. Mr. Handyman provides repair services for homeowners, while Merry Maids tidies up their houses. Supercuts offers affordable, anytime, walk-in haircuts, and H&R Block provides tax-preparation services. ● More than one-third of H&R Block's 12,000 retail offices are owned and operated by franchisees.[12]

Franchises now command about 45 percent of all retail sales in the United States. These days, it's nearly impossible to stroll down a city block or drive on a city street without seeing a McDonald's, Subway, Jiffy Lube, or Hampton Inn. One of the best-known and most successful franchisers, McDonald's, now has more than 36,000 stores in more than 100 countries, including more than 14,000 in the United States. It serves 69 million customers a day and racks up more than $98 billion in annual system-wide sales. More than 80 percent of McDonald's restaurants worldwide are owned and operated by franchisees.[13]

● **Franchising covers a lot more than just burger joints and fitness centers. More than one-third of H&R Block's 12,000 retail offices are owned and operated by franchisees.**

Bloomberg/Getty Images

Retailer Marketing Decisions

Retailers are always searching for new marketing strategies to attract and hold customers. In the past, retailers attracted customers with unique product assortments and more or better services. Today, the assortments and services of various retailers are looking more and more alike. You can find most consumer brands not only in department stores but also in mass-merchandise discount stores, off-price discount stores, and all over the internet. Thus, it's now more difficult for any one retailer to offer exclusive merchandise.

Service differentiation among retailers has also eroded. Many department stores have trimmed their services, whereas discounters have increased theirs. In addition, customers have become smarter and more price sensitive. They see no reason to pay more for identical brands, especially when service differences are shrinking. For all these reasons, many retailers today are rethinking their marketing strategies.

As shown in ● **Figure 13.1**, retailers face major marketing decisions about *segmentation and targeting, store differentiation and positioning*, and the *retail marketing mix*.

Segmentation, Targeting, Differentiation, and Positioning Decisions

Retailers must first segment and define their target markets and then decide how they will differentiate and position themselves in these markets. Should they focus on upscale, midscale, or downscale shoppers? Do target shoppers want variety, depth of assortment, convenience, or low prices? Until they define and profile their markets, retailers cannot make consistent decisions about product assortment, services, pricing, advertising, store décor, online and mobile site design, or any of the other decisions that must support their positions.

Too many retailers, even big ones, fail to clearly define their target markets and positions. For example, what market does clothing chain Gap target? What is Gap's value proposition? If you're having trouble answering those questions, you're not alone—so is Gap's management.[14]

In its heyday, Gap was solidly positioned on "effortless cool"—the then-fashionable preppy look focused on comfortable, casual clothes and easy shopping. But as its core Generation X customers aged and moved on, Gap stores didn't. Moving into the 2000s, Gap catered to short-lived fashion trends that alienated its loyal customer base. At the same time, it has struggled unsuccessfully to define new positioning that works with today's younger shoppers. And more-contemporary fast-fashion retailers such as H&M, Forever 21, Zara, and Uniqlo have moved in aggressively on Gap's turf. Whereas these brands are clearly targeted and positioned, Gap's identity has become muddled. As a result, the chain's sales have flattened for fallen off, and last year it closed 175 of its 675 North American stores. "Neither they nor their consumer know exactly who they are targeting," says one retail analyst. Gap "hasn't got a story," says another. Is it "trying to sell to my wife or my teenage daughter or both? I don't think you can do both." To rekindle the brand, Gap needs to "define who the brand's core customers are and be exceptional to them."

● FIGURE | 13.1
Retailer Marketing Strategies

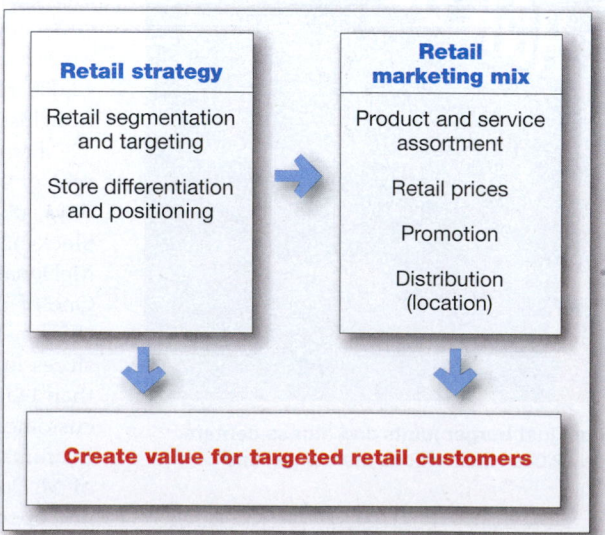

By contrast, successful retailers define their target markets well and position themselves strongly. For example, Trader Joe's has established its "cheap gourmet" value proposition. Walmart is powerfully positioned on low prices and what those always-low prices mean to its customers. And highly successful outdoor products retailer Bass Pro Shops positions itself strongly as being "as close to the Great Outdoors as you can get indoors!"

With solid targeting and positioning, a retailer can compete effectively against even the largest and strongest competitors. ● For example, compare small In-N-Out Burger to giant McDonald's. In-N-Out now has only about 300 stores in five states, with estimated sales of $750 million. McDonald's has 36,000 stores in more than 100 countries, racking up more than $98 *billion* of annual system-wide sales. How does In-N-Out compete with the world's largest fast-food chain? It doesn't—at least not directly. In-N-Out succeeds by carefully positioning itself *away* from McDonald's:[15]

In-N-Out has never wanted to be like McDonald's, growing rapidly and expanding both its menu and locations. Instead, In-N-Out thrives by doing the unthinkable: growing slowly and not changing. From the start, In-N-Out's slogan has been, "Quality you can taste." Burgers are made from 100 percent pure beef—no additives, fillers, or preservatives—and they're always fresh, not frozen. Fries are made from whole potatoes, and, yes, milkshakes are made from real ice cream. You won't find a freezer, heating lamp, or microwave oven in an In-N-Out restaurant. And unlike McDonald's unending stream of new menu items, In-N-Out stays with what the chain has always done well: making really good hamburgers, really good fries, and really good shakes—that's it.

Moreover, far from standardized fare, In-N-Out gladly customizes any menu item. Menu modifications have become so common at In-N-Out that a "secret" ordering code has emerged that isn't posted on menu boards. Customers in the know can order their burgers "animal style" (pickles, extra spread, grilled onions, and a mustard-fried patty). And whereas the "Double-Double" (double meat, double cheese) is on the menu, burgers can also be ordered 3×3 or 4×4. Fries can also be ordered animal style (two slices of cheese, grilled onions, and spread), well-done, or light. This secret menu makes customers feel special. Another thing that makes them feel special is In-N-Out's outgoing, enthusiastic, and capable employees who deliver unexpectedly friendly service. You won't find that at McDonald's. Finally, in contrast to McDonald's obsession to grow, grow, grow; In-N-Out's slow-and-steady growth means that you won't find one on every corner. The scarcity of In-N-Out stores only adds to its allure. Customers regularly go out of their way and drive long distances to get their In-N-Out fix.

● Retail targeting and positioning: In-N-Out Burger thrives by positioning itself *away* from McDonald's. The chain stays with what it does best: making really good hamburgers, really good fries, and really good shakes—that's it.
© E.J. Baumeister Jr. / Alamy

So, In-N-Out can't match McDonald's massive economies of scale, incredible volume purchasing power, ultra-efficient logistics, and low prices. Then again, it doesn't even try. By positioning itself away from McDonald's and other large competitors, In-N-Out has developed a cult-like following. When it comes to customer satisfaction, In-N-Out regularly posts the highest customer satisfaction scores of any fast-food restaurant in its markets. Long lines snake out the door of any location at lunchtime and In-N-Out's average per-store sales are double the industry average.

Product Assortment and Services Decision

Retailers must decide on three major product variables: product assortment, services mix, and store atmosphere.

The retailer's *product assortment* should differentiate it while matching target shoppers' expectations. One strategy is to offer a highly targeted product assortment: Lane Bryant carries plus-size clothing, Brookstone offers an unusual assortment of gadgets and gifts, and BatteryDepot.com offers about every imaginable kind of replacement battery. Alternatively, a retailer can differentiate itself by offering merchandise that no other competitor carries, such as store brands or national brands on which it holds exclusive rights. For example, Kohl's gets exclusive rights to carry well-known labels such as Simply Vera by Vera Wang and a Food Network-branded line of kitchen tools, utensils, and appliances. Kohl's also offers its own private-label lines, such as Sonoma, Croft & Barrow, Candies, and Apt. 9.

The *services mix* can also help set one retailer apart from another. For example, some retailers invite customers to ask questions or consult service representatives in person or via phone or tablet. Home Depot offers a diverse mix of services to do-it-yourselfers, from "how-to" classes and "do-it-herself" and kid workshops to a proprietary credit card. Nordstrom delivers top-notch service and promises to "take care of the customer, no matter what it takes."

The *store's atmosphere* is another important element in the reseller's product arsenal. Retailers want to create a unique store experience, one that suits the target market and moves customers to buy. Many retailers practice *experiential retailing*. For example, L.L.Bean has turned its flagship Freeport store and campus into a full-fledged outdoor adventure center, where customers can hike, bike, golf, kayak, or even go seal watching or fishing at nearby Cisco Bay. Along with selling outdoor apparel and gear, L.L.Bean offers a slate of free in-store, hands-on clinics along with Outdoor Discovery Schools programs in snowshoeing, cross-country skiing, stand-up paddleboarding, fly fishing, biking, birdwatching, canoeing, hunting, or any of a dozen other outdoor activities.

● **Experiential retailing: Furnishings retailer Restoration Hardware has unleashed a new generation of furniture galleries that are part store, part interior design studio, and part restaurant. In these new stores, you don't just see the furnishings, you *experience* them.**

Mike Dupre / Stringer / Getty Images

● Similarly, up-scale home furnishings retailer Restoration Hardware has unleashed a new generation of furniture galleries in Chicago, Atlanta, Denver, Tampa, and Hollywood that are part store, part interior design studio, part restaurant, and part home:[16]

Picture this: You're sipping a glass of good wine, surrounded by plush furnishings and crystal chandeliers with soothing music playing in the background. You're not sure whether to order another glass of wine, a light lunch, or both. Instead, you decide to buy the furniture you're upon which you are sitting. You're not in a fancy restaurant; you're in RH Chicago, a new retail concept by Restoration Hardware. Most retail furniture stores do little more than display their wares in functional fashion. Not so at RH galleries. "We wanted to blur the lines between residential and retail, and create a sense of place that is more home than store," says Restoration Hardware's CEO. The RH Atlanta gallery is a massive 70,000-square-foot, six-story estate on two acres, complete with a 40-foot-tall entry rotunda flanked by a double staircase, gardens, terraces, a 50-foot-long reflecting pool, and a rooftop park. Its rooms and outdoor places serve as showrooms for the goods that Restoration Hardware sells, from glasses to furniture to rugs to items for the garden. But it feels more like a grand home. You don't just see the furnishings, you *experience* them. "We created spaces where guests who visit our new homes are saying 'I want to live here,'" says the CEO. "I've been in retail almost 40 years and I've never heard anyone say they wanted to live in a retail store, until now."

Successful retailers carefully orchestrate virtually every aspect of the consumer store experience. The next time you step into a retail store—whether it sells consumer electronics, hardware, food, or high fashion—stop and carefully consider your surroundings. Think about the store's layout and displays. Listen to the background music. Check out the colors. Smell the smells. Chances are good that everything in the store, from the layout and lighting to the music and even the colors and smells, has been carefully orchestrated to help shape the customers' shopping experiences—and open their wallets.

For example, retailers choose the colors in their logos and interiors carefully: Black suggests sophistication, orange is associated with fairness and affordability, white signifies simplicity and purity (think Apple stores), and blue connotes trust and dependability (financial institutions use it a lot). And most large retailers have developed signature scents that you smell only in their stores:[17]

Anytime Fitness pipes in "Inspire," a eucalyptus-mint fragrance to create a uniform scent from store to store and mask that "gym" smell. Bloomingdale's uses different essences in different departments: the soft scent of baby powder in the baby store, coconut in the swimsuit area, lilacs in intimate apparel, and sugar cookies and evergreen scent during the holiday season. Luxury men's fashion brand Hugo Boss chose a signature smooth, musky scent for all of its stores. "We wanted it to feel like coming home," says a Hugo Boss marketer. Scents can subtly reinforce a brand's imagery and positioning. For example, the Hard Rock Café Hotel in Orlando added a scent of the ocean in its lobby to help guests imagine checking into a seaside resort (even though the hotel is located an hour from the coast). To draw customers into the hotel's often-overlooked downstairs ice cream shop, the hotel put a sugar cookie aroma at the top of the stairs and a whiff of waffle cone at the bottom. Ice cream sales jumped 45 percent in the following six months.

Such experiential retailing confirms that retail stores are much more than simply assortments of goods. They are environments to be experienced by the people who shop in them.

Price Decision

A retailer's price policy must fit its target market and positioning, product and service assortment, the competition, and economic factors. All retailers would like to charge high markups and achieve high volume, but the two seldom go together. Most retailers seek *either* high markups on lower volume (most specialty stores) *or* low markups on higher volume (mass merchandisers and discount stores).

Thus, 110-year-old Bergdorf Goodman caters to the upper crust by selling apparel, shoes, and jewelry created by designers such as Chanel, Prada, Hermes, and Jimmy Choo. The upmarket retailer pampers its customers with services such as a personal shopper and in-store showings of the upcoming season's trends with cocktails and hors d'oeuvres. By contrast, TJ Maxx sells brand name clothing at discount prices aimed at middle-class Americans. As it stocks new products each week, the discounter provides a treasure hunt for bargain shoppers. "No sales. No gimmicks." says the retailer. "Just brand name and designer fashions for you…for up to 60 percent off department store prices."

Retailers must also decide on the extent to which they will use sales and other price promotions. Some retailers use no price promotions at all, competing instead on product and service quality rather than on price. For example, it's difficult to imagine Bergdorf Goodman holding a two-for-the-price-of-one sale on Chanel handbags, even in a tight economy. Other retailers—such as Walmart, Costco, ALDI, and Family Dollar—practice *everyday low pricing (EDLP)*, charging constant, everyday low prices with few sales or discounts.

Still other retailers practice *high-low pricing*—charging higher prices on an everyday basis coupled with frequent sales and other price promotions to increase store traffic, create a low-price image, or attract customers who will buy other goods at full prices. Recent tighter economic times caused a rash of high-low pricing, as retailers poured on price cuts and promotions to coax bargain-hunting customers into their stores. Which pricing strategy is best depends on the retailer's overall marketing strategy, the pricing approaches of its competitors, and the economic environment.

Promotion Decision

Retailers use various combinations of the five promotion tools—advertising, personal selling, sales promotion, public relations, and direct and social media marketing—to reach consumers. They advertise in newspapers and magazines and on radio and television. Advertising may be supported by newspaper inserts and catalogs. Store salespeople greet customers, meet their needs, and build relationships. Sales promotions may include in-store demonstrations, displays, sales, and loyalty programs. PR activities, such as new-store openings, special events, newsletters and blogs, store magazines, and public service activities, are also available to retailers.

Most retailers also interact digitally with customers using websites and digital catalogs, online ads and video, social media, mobile ads and apps, blogs, and email. Almost every retailer, large or small, maintains a full social media presence. For example, giant Walmart leads the way with a whopping 33 million Facebook Likes, 66,000 Pinterest followers, 754,000 Twitter followers, and 109,000 YouTube subscribers. By contrast, Fairway Market, the small but fast-growing metropolitan New York grocery chain that carries a huge product assortment—from "sky-high piles" of produce to overflowing bins of fresh seafood to hand-roasted coffee—has only 118,000 Facebook Likes. But Fairway isn't complaining—that's twice as many Facebook Likes per million dollars of sales as mighty Walmart.[18]

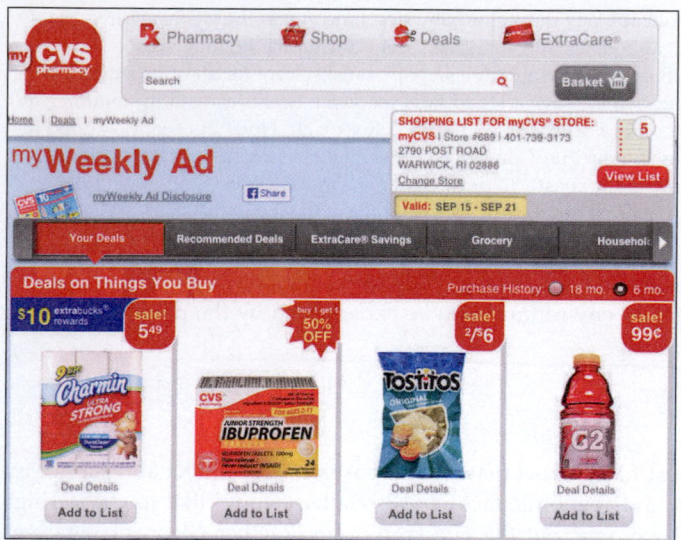

Retailer promotion: Most retailers interact digitally with customers using websites and digital catalogs, mobile and social media, and other digital platforms. CVS's myWeekly Ad program distributes personalized versions of its weekly circulars to the chain's ExtraCare loyalty program members.

CVS Health

Shopping center

A group of retail businesses built on a site that is planned, developed, owned, and managed as a unit.

Digital promotions let retailers reach individual customers with carefully targeted messages. For example, to compete more effectively against rivals online, CVS distributes personalized versions of its weekly circulars to the chain's ExtraCare loyalty program members. Called myWeekly Ad, customers can view their circulars by logging into their personal accounts at CVS.com on computers, tablets, or smartphones. Based on ExtraCare members' characteristics and previous purchases, the personalized promotions highlight sales items and special offers of special interest to each specific customer. With the myWeekly Ad program, "We're trying to get people to change their behavior," says the CVS marketer heading up the effort, "going online for a much more personalized experience" rather than checking weekly circulars.[19]

Place Decision

Retailers often point to three critical factors in retailing success: location, location, and location! It's very important that retailers select locations that are accessible to the target market in areas that are consistent with the retailer's positioning. For example, Apple locates its stores in high-end malls and trendy shopping districts—such as the Magnificent Mile on Chicago's Michigan Avenue or Fifth Avenue in Manhattan—not low-rent strip malls on the edge of town. By contrast, to keep costs down and support its "cheap gourmet" positioning, Trader Joe's places its stores in lower-rent, out-of-the-way locations. Small retailers may have to settle for whatever locations they can find or afford. Large retailers, however, usually employ specialists who use advanced methods to select store locations.

Most stores today cluster together to increase their customer pulling power and give consumers the convenience of one-stop shopping. Central business districts were the main form of retail cluster until the 1950s. Every large city and town had a central business district with department stores, specialty stores, banks, and movie theaters. When people began moving to the suburbs, however, many of these central business districts, with their traffic, parking, and crime problems, began to lose business. In recent years, many cities have joined with merchants to revive downtown shopping areas, generally with only mixed success.

A **shopping center** is a group of retail businesses built on a site that is planned, developed, owned, and managed as a unit. A *regional shopping center*, or *regional shopping mall*, the largest and most dramatic shopping center, has from 50 to more than 100 stores, including two or more full-line department stores. It is like a covered mini-downtown and attracts customers from a wide area. A *community shopping center* contains between 15 and 50 retail stores. It normally contains a branch of a department store or variety store, a supermarket, specialty stores, professional offices, and sometimes a bank. Most shopping centers are *neighborhood shopping centers* or *strip malls* that generally contain between 5 and 15 stores. These centers, which are close and convenient for consumers, usually contain a supermarket, perhaps a discount store, and several service stores—dry cleaner, drugstore, hardware store, local restaurant, or other stores.[20]

A newer form of shopping center is the so-called power center. *Power centers* are huge unenclosed shopping centers consisting of a long strip of retail stores, including large, free-standing anchors such as Walmart, Home Depot, Costco, Best Buy, Michaels, PetSmart, and Office Depot. Each store has its own entrance with parking directly in front for shoppers who wish to visit only one store.

In contrast, *lifestyle centers* are smaller, open-air malls with upscale stores, convenient locations, and nonretail activities, such as a playground, skating rink, hotel, dining establishments, and a movie theater complex. The most recent lifestyle centers often consist of *mixed-use* developments, with ground-floor retail establishments and apartments or condominiums above, combining shopping convenience with the community feel of a neighborhood center. Meanwhile, traditional regional shopping malls are adding lifestyle elements—such as fitness centers, children's play areas, common areas, and multiplex theaters—to make themselves more social and welcoming. In all, today's centers are more like places to hang out rather than just places to shop.

The past few years have brought hard times for shopping centers. Many experts suggest that the country has long been "overmalled." Not surprisingly, the Great Recession and its aftermath hit shopping malls hard. Consumer spending cutbacks forced many retailers—small and large—out of business, and vacancy rates at the nation's enclosed malls soared.[21] Power centers were also hard hit as their big-box retailer tenants such as Circuit City, Borders, Mervyns, and Linens N Things went out of business and others such as Best Buy, Barnes & Noble, and Office Depot reduced the number or size of their stores. Some of the pizzazz has also gone out of lifestyle centers, whose upper-middle-class shoppers suffered most during the recession.

As the economy has improved, however, malls of all types have rebounded a bit. Many power centers, for example, are filling their empty space with a broader range of retailers, from the likes of Ross Dress for Less, Boot Barn, Nordstrom Rack, and other off-price retailers to dollar stores, warehouse grocers, and traditional discounters like Walmart and Target.

Retailing Trends and Developments

Author Comment | Retailers must constantly adapt their marketing strategies and mixes to today's challenging, fast-changing retail environment.

Retailers operate in a harsh and fast-changing environment, which offers threats as well as opportunities. Consumer demographics, lifestyles, and spending patterns are changing rapidly, as are retailing technologies. To be successful, retailers need to choose target segments carefully and position themselves strongly. They need to take the following retailing developments into account as they plan and execute their competitive strategies.

Tighter Consumer Spending

Following many years of good economic times for retailers, the Great Recession of 2008–2009 turned many retailers' fortunes from boom to bust. Even as the economy has recovered, retailers will feel the effects of changed consumer spending patterns well into the future.

Some retailers actually benefit from a down economy. For example, as consumers cut back and looked for ways to spend less on what they bought, big discounters such as Costco scooped up new business from bargain-hungry shoppers. And price-oriented and off-price retailers such as ALDI, Dollar General, and TJ Maxx have attracted greater shares of more frugal buyers.

For other retailers, however, tighter consumer spending meant tough times. During and following the recession, several large and familiar retailers declared bankruptcy or closed their doors completely—including household names such as Linens N Things, Circuit City, KB Toys, Borders Books, and The Sharper Image, to name a few. Other retailers, from Macy's and Home Depot to Starbucks, laid off employees, cut their costs, and offered deep price discounts and promotions aimed at luring cash-strapped customers back into their stores.

As the economy has improved and as consumers have retained their more frugal spending ways, many retailers have added new value pitches to their positioning. For example, Home Depot replaced its older "You can do it. We can help." theme with a thriftier one: "More saving. More doing." Retailers ranging from Walmart to Macy's to Kroger and Whole Foods Market have boosted their emphasis on more economical private-label brands. And to compete with the boom in fast-casual restaurants such as Panera Bread and Chipotle, traditional sit-down restaurants have added value offerings of their own. For example, Applebee's has a 2 for $20 menu—two meals and one appetizer, all for just $20. ● TGI Fridays offers The 474 "Where less is more" menu, featuring right-sized portions of its signature dishes with appetizers at $4, main dishes at $7, and desserts at $4.

When reacting to economic difficulties, retailers must be careful that their short-run actions don't damage their long-run images and positions. For example, drastic price discounting can increase immediate sales but damage brand loyalty. One analyst calls this "death by discount" and suggests that "virtually every retailer—at both the high and

● **Value positioning:** To attract today's more value-oriented consumers, TGI Friday's offers The 474 "Where less is more" menu, featuring right-sized appetizers at $4, main dishes at $7, and desserts at $4.

the low end—has fallen so deeply into the trap that discounting has become an expectation of customers rather than a bonus."[22] A stroll through your local shopping mall confirms this assessment. However, instead of relying on cost-cutting and price reductions, retailers should focus on building greater customer value within their long-term store positioning strategies.

New Retail Forms, Shortening Retail Life Cycles, and Retail Convergence

New retail forms continue to emerge to meet new situations and consumer needs, but the life cycle of new retail forms is getting shorter. Department stores took about 100 years to reach the mature stage of the life cycle; more recent forms, such as warehouse stores, reached maturity in about 10 years. In such an environment, seemingly solid retail positions can crumble quickly. Of the top 10 discount retailers in 1962 (the year that the first Walmart, Kmart, Target, and Kohl's stores opened), not one still exists today. Even the most successful retailers can't sit back with a winning formula. To remain successful, they must keep adapting.

New retail forms are always emerging. One of the most recent blockbuster retailing trend is the advent of online retailing, by both online-only and store retailers, via websites, mobile apps, and social media. But lesser innovations occur regularly. For example, many retailers are now using limited-time *pop-up stores* that let them promote their brands to seasonal shoppers and create buzz in busy, high-rent areas. As an example, during an NBA All-Star weekend at the Barclays Center in Brooklyn, New York, Nike opened a Jordan-themed pop-up shop across the street. 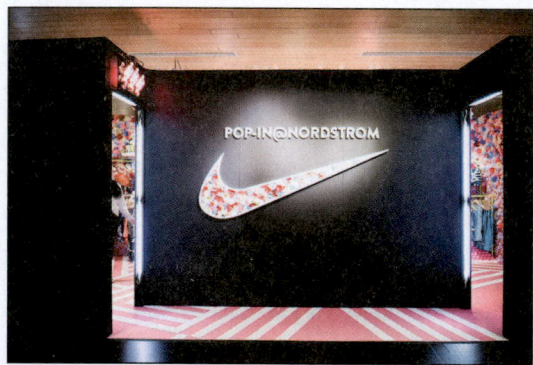 And Nordstrom offers monthly The Pop-In@ Nordstrom shops, specially designed in-store pop-up shops featuring rotating themes, new and exclusive products, and brand partnerships meant to create experiences that excite and intrigue customers. "I love the frenzy that's created from a pop-up shop concept—that spontaneity and emotion is one of my favorite things about working in retail," says Nordstrom's director of creative projects.[23]

The online and mobile equivalent is *flash sales* sites, such as Nordstrom's HauteLook and Amazon's MyHabit, which host time-limited sales events on top fashion and lifestyle brands. Similarly, Gilt.com flashes member-only, 70 percent discounts on designer-label clothing, and Groupon offers flash deals on travel through Groupon Getaways. Zulily flashes sales on products for moms, babies, and kids, offering limited-time sales "events" that quickly "scoot away to make room for new events." Flash sales add excitement and urgency to buying. Says Zulily, "Shopping here is like opening a new treasure chest every day. You never know exactly what you'll uncover, but you know gems are waiting."[24]

Today's retail forms appear to be converging. Increasingly, different types of retailers now sell the same products at the same prices to the same consumers thanks in part to the price transparency the internet provides. For example, you can buy brand name home appliances at department stores, discount stores, home-improvement stores, off-price retailers, electronics superstores, and a slew of online sites that all compete for the same customers. If you can't find the microwave oven you want at Sears or Lowe's, you can step across the street and find one for a better price at Target or Best Buy—or just order one online from Amazon.com. This merging of consumers, products, prices, and retailers is called *retail convergence*. Such convergence means greater competition for retailers and greater difficulty in differentiating the product assortments of different types of retailers.

● **New retail forms: Nordstrom's Pop-In@ Nordstrom shops feature rotating themes, new and exclusive products, and brand partnerships that excite and intrigue customers.**

Nordstrom

The Rise of Megaretailers

The rise of huge mass merchandisers and specialty superstores, the formation of vertical marketing systems, and a rash of retail mergers and acquisitions have created a core of superpower megaretailers. With their size and buying power, these giant retailers can offer better merchandise selections, good service, and strong price savings to consumers. As a result, they grow even larger by squeezing out their smaller, weaker competitors.

The megaretailers have shifted the balance of power between retailers and producers. A small handful of retailers now controls access to enormous numbers of consumers, giving them the upper hand in their dealings with manufacturers. For example, you may never have heard of specialty coatings and sealants manufacturer RPM International, but you've probably used one or more of its many familiar do-it-yourself brands—such as

Rust-Oleum paints, Plastic Wood and Dap fillers, Mohawk and Watco finishes, and Testors hobby cements and paints—all of which you can buy at your local Home Depot store. Home Depot is a very important customer to RPM, accounting for a significant share of its consumer sales. However, Home Depot's sales of $83 billion are 18 times RPM's sales of $4.6 billion. As a result, the giant retailer can, and often does, use this power to wring concessions from RPM and thousands of other smaller suppliers.[25]

Growth of Direct, Online, Mobile, and Social Media Retailing

Most consumers still make a majority of their purchases the old-fashioned way: They go to a store, find what they want, plunk down their cash or credit cards, and bring home the goods. However, consumers now have a broad array of nonstore alternatives, including direct and digital shopping via websites, mobiles apps, and social media. As we'll discuss in Chapter 17, direct and digital marketing are currently the fastest-growing forms of marketing.

Today, thanks to advanced technologies, easier-to-use and enticing online sites and mobile apps, improved online services, and the increasing sophistication of search technologies, online retailing is thriving. In fact, although it currently accounts for only about 8 percent of total U.S. retail sales, online buying is growing at a much brisker pace than retail buying as a whole. Last year's U.S. online retail sales grew 14 percent over the previous year versus a 2.2 percent increase in overall retail sales.[26]

Retailer online sites, mobile apps, and social media also influence a large amount of in-store buying. It's estimated that more than half of total U.S. retail sales are either transacted directly or influenced by online research. And an estimated 15 percent of all online sales now take place on mobile devices. Retailers of all kinds rely on social media to engage their buyer communities. For example, whereas McDonald's leads among retailers in Facebook Likes, Nordstrom is tops in Pinterest followers. Starbucks leads in Twitter followers. And Victoria's Secret has the most YouTube subscribers and Instagram followers.[27]

> ● **Showrooming: The now-common practice of viewing products in stores but buying them online presents serious challenges to store retailers. But rather than fighting showrooming, retailers are now embracing it as a way to showcase their omni-channel strengths.**
> © Kumar Sriskandan/Alamy

Showrooming
The shopping practice of coming into retail store showrooms to check out merchandise and prices but instead buying from an online-only rival, sometimes while in the store.

The spurt in online, mobile, and social media retailing is both a blessing and a curse to store retailers. Although it gives them new channels for engaging and selling to customers, it also creates more competition from online-only retailers. Many shoppers now check out merchandise at physical-store showrooms but then buy it online using a computer or mobile device, sometimes while in the store—a process called **showrooming**. ● These days, 90 percent of smartphone-carrying shoppers use their phones while shopping in stores. And as many as half of all shoppers who buy products online check them out first at a traditional store.[28] Store retailers such as Target, Walmart, Best Buy, Bed Bath & Beyond, and Toys"R"Us have been hit hard by showrooming.

Today, however, many store retailers are developing effective strategies to counter showrooming. Others are even embracing it as an opportunity to highlight the advantages of shopping in stores versus online-only retailers. The flip side of showrooming is *webrooming*, by which consumers first check out merchandise online, then buy it in a store. The key for store retailers is to convert showrooming shoppers into buyers when they visit the store.

The Need for Omni-Channel Retailing

The boundaries between in-store and online retailing are rapidly blurring. For most customers, it's no longer a matter of deciding whether to shop in a store *or* to shop online. The internet and digital devices have spawned a whole new breed of shopper and way of shopping. Today's omni-channel buyers shift seamlessly across online and in-store channels throughout the buying process. They've gotten used to researching and buying anywhere, anytime—whether it's in the store, online, on the go, or even online while in the store. To meet the needs of these omni-channel buyers, store retailers must master *omni-channel retailing*, integrating store and online channels into a single shopper experience (see Real Marketing 13.2).

13.2   Omni-Channel Retailing: Creating a Seamless Shopping Experience

The shopping process has changed radically in recent years. Not all that long ago, shopping consisted mostly of going store to store—or perhaps flipping through catalogs—to gather product information, make price comparisons, and purchase goods. That was then. Now—in this age of the internet, computers, smartphones, and other digital devices—shopping typically involves a dazzling array of channels and platforms.

Today's omni-channel consumers readily research products and prices online, shopping digitally from home, from work, in stores, or anywhere in between. They scour retailer websites and social media for buying ideas, inspiration, and advice. They might see products in stores and order them online, see products online then buy them in stores, or even buy goods online for in-store pickup. This massive shift in how people shop calls for massive changes in how store retailers operate. Omni-channel *buying* calls for omni-channel *retailing*, integrating all available shopping channels and devices into a seamless customer shopping experience.

At first, as online and mobile shopping caught fire, store retailers worried about *showrooming*—smartphone-wielding customers researching products online while examining them in stores, then jumping ship to catch lower online prices. But most store retailers have now adjusted to the showrooming threat with price-matching and other in-store tactics. In fact, smart retailers now see phone-toting customers not as a threat but as an opportunity.

For example, Best Buy has found that omni-channel shoppers have a higher-than-average propensity to purchase. One study showed that shoppers who use mobile devices in stores are almost twice as likely to purchase from the same retailer in-store or online than to buy elsewhere. "We love being used as the internet's showroom," says Best Buy's CEO. Where Best Buy once fought showrooming, the chain now facilitates the process, converting showroomers into buyers. Best Buy sales associates are trained to proactively cross-check prices against both their own and other retailer's online offers, including online retailers like Amazon. Employees can then price-match competitors, putting the price question to rest and letting associates focus on areas where Best Buy has the advantage—such as personal advice and service, immediacy, convenient locations, and easy returns. Best Buy's new tagline highlights this strategy: "Best Buy: Expert Service. Unbeatable Prices."

Retailers have learned that shoppers with smartphones are doing far more than just checking online prices. More often, they are filling in the information gap. "The consumer has never been more informed, and that information comes from their phone," says a senior marketer at outdoor-gear retailer REI. "We love when someone enters the store holding their phone saying, 'I want this tent. I want this bike. Help me find this.'" This type of activity shows how digital and store retailing can come together to make a sale, even without cutting price.

But omni-channel retailing goes way beyond just helping in-store customers as they cross-shop on digital devices. It requires carefully integrating the entire range of available shopping channels, both in-store and out, from discovery to purchase in the buying process. For example, most large retailers are now boosting their own online and digital selling options and linking them with stores. One popular way to do that is by letting customers order online and pick up in the store. The "click-and-collect" experience merges the attractions of digital and in-store shopping. For example, Walmart has upped its emphasis on in-store pickups. It tells customers that they can order from its Walmart.com site, often pick up items on the same day, avoid shipping fees, and easily return items to the store if not satisfied. Customers now pick up half of all Walmart.com purchases in stores, often buying additional merchandise during the visit.

Some customers even use mobile to place online orders with a given retailer while visiting that retailer's store. Ten percent of Walmart purchases via mobile devices are made from inside a Walmart store. GAP Inc.—which operates the GAP, Old Navy, and Banana Republic chains—actively promotes in-store online ordering. Sales associates with tablets help customers search company-wide store and online inventories to find out-of-stock items. "It gives the team in the store the full capability to...meet your needs without you having to go home and do it yourself," says a Banana Republic marketer.

In addition to websites, omni-channel retailers are integrating other digital shopping channels. Walmart, Target, Macy's, and other major retailers offer handy mobile apps that pull customers to both their websites and stores, let them prepare shopping lists, help them locate merchandise inside stores, and, in Target's case, send daily alerts and exclusive

Athletic footwear and apparel giant Foot Locker has mastered omni-channel retailing. It skillfully integrates its in-store environment, high-powered websites, and extensive social media presence to create the seamless, anytime, anywhere, omni-channel shopping experience that today's customers seek.

Luke Sharrett/Bloomberg/Getty Images; Image Source

discounts to their phones. Macy's uses beacon technology, by which in-store sensors detect opted-in customers as they enter a Macy's store, welcome them via the Macy's app on their phones, and pass along personalized shopping information and "only-for-you" deals.

Social media also play an important part in omni-channel retailing. Thirty percent of shoppers made purchases via social media last year, 44 percent discovered new products via social networks, and 49 percent made purchases based on referrals from social media. In turn, most large store retailers now use social media extensively to engage customers, build community, and link buyers to their websites and stores.

But simply creating a digital-friendly store, high-powered website, and extensive social media presence doesn't constitute good omni-channel retailing. The key is to integrate these elements to create that critical seamless, anywhere, anytime, omni-channel shopping experience that today's customers seek. Consider athletic footwear and apparel giant Foot Locker, which operates several chains, including Foot Locker and Champs Sports:

Foot Locker has mastered omni-channel retailing. It now gets 12 percent of its sales online, half of that from mobile buying, and its online sales are growing at an eye-popping 40 percent annually. Its online and mobile efforts link seamlessly with store operations, offering options such as "buy online, ship from store" and "buy online, reserve in store" for pickup. And you'll find Foot Locker everywhere in social media, with more than 150 million total followers across Instagram, Facebook, Snapchat, Twitter, YouTube, and Pinterest, where it builds customer community and pulls customers to its online and store locations.

Foot Locker's omni-channel prowess comes to life inside its Foot Locker, Champs Sports, and other stores. The chain gives sales associates the same mobile research capabilities that customers have. Tablets in hand, using online information about products and competitor offers, associates work with and educate customers. Foot Locker trains store employees to go beyond prices and engage customers in ways that add value through personal touches. With 3,500 stores and Foot Locker's own substantial online presence, the store retailer can help customers to shape almost any kind of shopping experience, including a broad choice of service, payment, and delivery options not available from online-only retailers. Thanks to its omni-channel mastery, whereas other shoe and apparel retailers have had trouble fending off web-only sellers like online star Zappos, Foot Locker is thriving in the new omni-channel shopping environment. Over the past five years, the retailer's sales have zoomed 47 percent and profits have more than tripled.

Sources: "Total Retail 2015: Retailers and the Age of Disruption," *PwC*, February 2015, accessed at www.pwc.com/gx/en/retail-consumer/retail-consumer-publications/global-multi-channel-consumer-survey/assets/pdf/total-retail-2015.pdf; Sarah Halzack, "Online or In-Store? How about a Little of Both?" *Washington Post*, November 28, 2014, p. A01; Christine Birkner, "Good Tidings for Retail," *Marketing News*, December 2014, p. 14; Laura Heller, "How Foot Locker Is Using Mobile to Reach Millennials," *FierceMobileRetail*, August 4, 2014, www.fierceretail.com/mobileretail/story/how-foot-locker-using-mobile-reach-millennials/2014-08-04; Brian Sozzi, "Foot Locker Transforming Its Stores as It Seeks to Keep Sales on Fire," *TheStreet*, March 17, 2015, www.thestreet.com/story/13081277/1/foot-locker-transforming-its-stores-as-it-seeks-to-keep-sales-on-fire.html; Matt Lindner, "Foot Locker Races to Over 40% Domestic Online Sales Growth in Q2," *Internet Retailer*, August 21, 2015, www.internetretailer.com/2015/08/21/foot-locker-races-over-40-domestic-online-sales-growth-q2; and www.footlocker-inc.com and www.footlocker.com, accessed October 2016.

An increasing share of the growth in online sales is being captured by omni-channel retailers who successfully merge the virtual and physical worlds. Physical store operators are experiencing considerable digital success, while online merchants—including Amazon—are expanding with showrooms, pop-up shops, and other ways of meeting shoppers face-to-face. "Omnichannel is the new reality for all retailers whether they engage or not. If you're available where and when consumers look for you, great. If not, you lose to someone who is," says an analyst. "Online-only retailers lack the high engagement that only the in-store experience can deliver. Offline-only retailers don't deliver the comfortable and information-browsing experience that consumers utilize to make their shopping itineraries."[29]

For example, Macy's found that customers who shop across channels are eight times more valuable than those who shop in a single channel. Macy's has become so committed to pushing beyond bricks-and-mortar—where it lately has been downsizing—that it opened an Idea Lab in San Francisco to produce new ideas on online shopping technology. And it has opened a giant 1.3 million-square-foot fulfillment center in Tulsa, Oklahoma, that can ship 325,000 orders a day. Macy's also recently introduced an image-search extension to its mobile application, and the retailer's 300,000 followers can shop directly via Instagram. Macy's even offers same-day delivery in 17 markets nationwide. Says the Chief Omnichannel Officer for Macy's, "Our goal is to provide our shopper with the best experience in whatever way she chooses to interact with us: mobile, desktop, store, or all of them together."[30]

Growing Importance of Retail Technology

As omni-channel shopping becomes the norm, retail technologies have become critically important as competitive tools. Progressive retailers are using advanced information technology and software systems to produce better forecasts, control inventory costs, interact electronically with suppliers, send information between stores, and even sell to customers within stores. They have adopted sophisticated systems for checkout scanning, RFID inventory tracking, merchandise handling, information sharing, and customer interactions.

Perhaps the most startling advances in retail technology concern the ways in which retailers are connecting with consumers. As the surge in online and mobile shopping has changed retail customer behaviors and expectations, a wide range of store retailers are merging the physical and digital worlds to create new-age experiential retailing environments. For example, at AT&T's new flagship store in Chicago, customers can sit at any of dozens of stations, sampling the latest phone apps and electronic gadgetry. Enthusiastic, iPad-wielding associates mingle with customers, talking tech and dispensing hands-on help and advice. With 130 digital screens and an 18-foot video wall, every aspect of the open space is designed to engage customers about future wireless technologies and services and let them experience the impact of AT&T's devices and services on their lives. It's "like walking into a website," says AT&T's president of retail.[31]

Many other advanced technologies are finding their way into retail showrooms. One is beacon technology, Bluetooth connections that greet and engage customers via their smartphones as they shop around in stores. For example, when opted-in customers enter a Macy's store, a beacon signal wakes up an app on their smartphone or tablet, which welcomes them and alerts them to location-specific rewards, deals, discounts, and personalized product recommendations within the store. The technology can also link in-store and at-home browsing; if the customer "likes" a specific product online, the app can remind them where to find it in the store, pop up a brief product video, and maybe pass along a for-you-only deal. The goal is to engage Macy's tech-savvy and social customers as a trusted companion and to personalize their in-store shopping experience.[32]

● **Retail technology: Retailers are experimenting with virtual reality to enhance the in-store shopping experience. At North Face's Manhattan store, customers can don virtual-reality headsets that transport them to remote outdoor experiences, such as a gutsy jump off a 420-foot cliff.**

The Washington Post / Contributor

Other retailers are experimenting with *virtual reality* to enhance the in-store shopping experience. ● For example, customers at North Face's Manhattan store can don virtual-reality headsets that transport them to remote hiking, climbing, or even base-jumping locations where they can experience gutsy jumps off a 420-foot cliff, all while using North Face gear. Marriott guests can put on virtual-reality goggles for up-close tours of destinations such as Hawaii or London. Intel has developed a "smart" dressing room in which shoppers can change outfits and colors with a wave of the hand. And automaker Audi is testing a virtual reality in dealer showrooms. Customers use iPads to select any Audi model and then customize each element, from engine type and wheels to paint color and interior seats. They then put on a headset and earphones to experience the sights and sounds of their customized car in virtual reality. They can move around the outside of the car, open the trunk and doors, check under the hood, and even sit in the driver's seat. Although virtual reality technologies are difficult and expensive to implement now, they hold interesting promise for the future.[33]

Green Retailing

Today's retailers are increasingly adopting environmentally sustainable practices. They are greening up their stores and operations, promoting more environmentally responsible products, launching programs to help customers be more responsible, and working with channel partners to reduce their environmental impact.

At the most basic level, most large retailers are making their stores more environmentally friendly through sustainable building design, construction, and operations. ● For example, under its "People & Planet Positive" sustainability strategy, home furnishings retailer IKEA's long-term goal is to become 100 percent sustainable:[34]

The "People & Planet Positive" strategy begins with making IKEA's 328 giant stores in 28 countries more energy independent and efficient. To power its stores, IKEA has committed to owning and operating 224 wind turbines and has installed 700,000 solar panels—90 percent of its U.S. stores have solar panels. By 2020, IKEA will generate as much energy as it uses from renewable sources. Inside its stores, IKEA uses only energy-efficient LED lighting. Most stores also sort food waste from in-store customer restaurants for composting or send it to treatment centers where it is turned into animal feed or biogas to fuel cars and buses. Some IKEAs offer customer recycling centers for products such as plastic, paper, CFL lightbulbs, batteries, and even end-of-life appliances.

● **Green retailing: Under its "People & Planet Positive" sustainability strategy, home furnishings retailer IKEA's long-term goal is to become 100% sustainable, both in its operations and in the products it sells.**

Used with the permission of Inter IKEA Systems B.V.

Retailers are also greening up their product assortments. For example, IKEA now sells only LED lighting products in its stores, and a growing proportion of the home furnishing products it sells are made from sustainable and renewable cotton, wood, and other resources. IKEA suppliers must adhere to the retailer's IWAY supplier code of conduct sustainability standards. IKEA's goal is have all of its home furnishings made from renewable, recyclable, or recycled materials. "At IKEA, sustainability is central to our business," says the company, "to ensure that we have a positive impact on people and the planet."

Many retailers have also launched programs that help consumers make more environmentally responsible decisions. Staples's Easy on the Planet program "makes it easier to make a difference" by helping customers to identify green products sold in its stores and to recycle printer cartridges, mobile phones, computers, and other office technology products. Staples recycles some 30 million printer cartridges and 10 million pounds of old technology each year.[35]

Finally, many large retailers are joining forces with suppliers and distributors to create more sustainable products, packaging, and distribution systems. For example, Amazon.com works closely with the producers of many of the products it sells to reduce and simplify their packaging. And beyond its own substantial sustainability initiatives, Walmart wields its huge buying power to urge its army of suppliers to improve their environmental impact and practices. The retailer has even developed a worldwide Sustainable Product Index by which it rates suppliers. It plans to translate the index into a simple rating for consumers to help them make more sustainable buying choices.

Green retailing yields both top- and bottom-line benefits. Sustainable practices lift a retailer's top line by attracting consumers looking to support environmentally friendly sellers and products. They also help the bottom line by reducing costs. For example, Amazon.com's reduced-packaging efforts increase customer convenience and eliminate "wrap rage" while at the same time saving packaging costs. And IKEA's more energy-efficient buildings not only appeal to customers and help save the planet but also cost less to operate.

Global Expansion of Major Retailers

Retailers with unique formats and strong brand positions are increasingly moving into other countries. Many are expanding internationally to escape saturated home markets. Over the years, some giant U.S. retailers, such as McDonald's and Walmart, have become globally prominent as a result of their marketing prowess.

However, some U.S. retailers are still significantly behind Europe and Asia when it comes to global expansion. Although nine of the world's top 20 retailers are U.S. companies, only six of these retailers have set up operations outside North America (Walmart, Home Depot, Walgreens, Amazon, Costco, and Best Buy). Of the 11 non-U.S. retailers in the world's top 20, 10 have stores in at least 10 countries. Foreign retailers that have gone global include France's Carrefour, Groupe Casino, and Groupe Auchan; Germany's Metro, Lidl, and ALDI chains; Britain's Tesco; and Japan's Seven & I.[36]

International retailing presents challenges as well as opportunities. Retailers can face dramatically different retail environments when crossing countries, continents, and cultures. Simply adapting the operations that work well in the home country is usually not enough to create success abroad. Instead, when going global, retailers must understand and meet the needs of local markets.

Wholesaling
All the activities involved in selling goods and services to those buying for resale or business use.

Wholesaler
A firm engaged *primarily* in wholesaling activities.

Author Comment | Whereas retailers primarily sell goods and services directly to final consumers for personal use, wholesalers sell primarily to those buying for resale or business use. Because wholesalers operate behind the scenes, they are largely unknown to final consumers. But they are very important to their business customers.

Wholesaling

Wholesaling includes all the activities involved in selling goods and services to those buying them for resale or business use. Firms engaged *primarily* in wholesaling activities are called **wholesalers**.

Wholesalers buy mostly from producers and sell mostly to retailers, industrial consumers, and other wholesalers. As a result, many of the nation's largest and most important wholesalers are largely unknown to final consumers. For example, how much do you know about McKesson, the huge $179 billion diversified health-care-services provider and the nation's leading wholesaler of pharmaceutical, health and beauty care, home health-care, and medical supply and equipment products? Or how about wholesaler Arrow Electronics, which supplies $23 billion worth of computer chips, capacitors, and other electronics and computer components annually to more than 100,000 original equipment manufacturers and commercial customers through a global network of more than 460 locations in 56 countries? ● And you may never have heard of a company called Grainger, even though it is very well known and much valued by its more than 2 million business and institutional customers in more than 150 countries:[37]

Grainger may be the biggest market leader you've never heard of. It's a $10 billion business that offers more than 1.5 million maintenance, repair, and operating (MRO) products from 4,800 manufacturers to more than 2 million active customers. Through its branch network, service centers, sales reps, catalog, and online and social media sites, Grainger links customers with the supplies they need to keep their facilities running smoothly—everything from lightbulbs, cleaners, and display cases to nuts and bolts, motors, valves, power tools, test equipment, and safety supplies. Grainger's nearly 670 branches, 34 strategically located distribution centers, more than 25,000 employees, and innovative web and mobile sites handle more than 140,000 transactions a day. Grainger's customers include organizations ranging from factories, garages, and grocers to schools and military bases.

Grainger operates on a simple value proposition: to make it easier and less costly for customers to find and buy MRO supplies. It starts by acting as a one-stop shop for products needed to maintain facilities. On a broader level, it builds lasting relationships with customers by helping them find *solutions* to their overall MRO problems. Acting as consultants, Grainger sales reps help buyers with everything from improving their supply chain management to reducing inventories and streamlining warehousing operations.

So, how come you've never heard of Grainger? Perhaps it's because the company operates in the not-so-glamorous world of MRO supplies, which are important to every business but not so important to consumers. More likely, it's because Grainger is a wholesaler. And like most wholesalers, it operates behind the scenes, selling mostly to other businesses.

● **Wholesaling: Many of the nation's largest and most important wholesalers—like Grainger—are largely unknown to final consumers. But they are very well known and much valued by the business customers they serve.**

TJP / Alamy Stock Photo

Why are wholesalers important to sellers? For example, why would a producer use wholesalers rather than selling directly to retailers or consumers? Simply put, wholesalers add value by performing one or more of the following channel functions:

- *Selling and promoting.* Wholesalers' sales forces help manufacturers reach many small customers at a low cost. The wholesaler has more contacts and is often more trusted by the buyer than the distant manufacturer.
- *Buying and assortment building.* Wholesalers can select items and build assortments needed by their customers, thereby saving much work.
- *Bulk breaking.* Wholesalers save their customers money by buying in carload lots and breaking bulk (breaking large lots into small quantities).
- *Warehousing.* Wholesalers hold inventories, thereby reducing the inventory costs and risks of suppliers and customers.
- *Transportation.* Wholesalers can provide quicker delivery to buyers because they are closer to buyers than are producers.
- *Financing.* Wholesalers finance their customers by giving credit, and they finance their suppliers by ordering early and paying bills on time.
- *Risk bearing.* Wholesalers absorb risk by taking title and bearing the cost of theft, damage, spoilage, and obsolescence.
- *Market information.* Wholesalers give information to suppliers and customers about competitors, new products, and price developments.
- *Management services and advice.* Wholesalers often help retailers train their salesclerks, improve store layouts and displays, and set up accounting and inventory control systems.

Types of Wholesalers

Merchant wholesaler

An independently owned wholesale business that takes title to the merchandise it handles.

Wholesalers fall into three major groups (see ● **Table 13.3**): *merchant wholesalers, brokers and agents*, and *manufacturers' and retailers' branches and offices*. **Merchant wholesalers** are the largest single group of wholesalers, accounting for roughly 50 percent of all

● Table 13.3 | Major Types of Wholesalers

Type	Description
Merchant wholesalers	Independently owned businesses that take title to all merchandise handled. There are full-service wholesalers and limited-service wholesalers.
Full-service wholesalers	Provide a full line of services: carrying stock, maintaining a sales force, offering credit, making deliveries, and providing management assistance. Full-service wholesalers include wholesale merchants and industrial distributors.
Wholesale merchants	Sell primarily to retailers and provide a full range of services. General merchandise wholesalers carry several merchandise lines, whereas general line wholesalers carry one or two lines in great depth. Specialty wholesalers specialize in carrying only part of a line.
Industrial distributors	Sell to manufacturers rather than to retailers. Provide several services, such as carrying stock, offering credit, and providing delivery. May carry a broad range of merchandise, a general line, or a specialty line.
Limited-service wholesalers	Offer fewer services than full-service wholesalers. Limited-service wholesalers are of several types:
Cash-and-carry wholesalers	Carry a limited line of fast-moving goods and sell to small retailers for cash. Normally do not deliver.
Truck wholesalers (or truck jobbers)	Perform primarily a selling and delivery function. Carry a limited line of semiperishable merchandise (such as milk, bread, snack foods), which is sold for cash as deliveries are made to supermarkets, small groceries, hospitals, restaurants, factory cafeterias, and hotels.
Drop shippers	Do not carry inventory or handle the product. On receiving an order, drop shippers select a manufacturer, who then ships the merchandise directly to the customer. Drop shippers operate in bulk industries, such as coal, lumber, and heavy equipment.
Rack jobbers	Serve grocery and drug retailers, mostly in nonfood items. Rack jobbers send delivery trucks to stores, where the delivery people set up toys, paperbacks, hardware items, health and beauty aids, or other items. Rack jobbers price the goods, keep them fresh, set up point-of-purchase displays, and keep inventory records.
Producers' cooperatives	Farmer-owned members that assemble farm produce for sale in local markets. Producers' cooperatives often attempt to improve product quality and promote a co-op brand name, such as Sun-Maid raisins, Sunkist oranges, or Diamond nuts.
Mail-order or web wholesalers	Send catalogs to or maintain websites for retail, industrial, and institutional customers featuring jewelry, cosmetics, specialty foods, and other small items. Its primary customers are businesses in small outlying areas.
Brokers and agents	Do not take title to goods. The main function is to facilitate buying and selling, for which they earn a commission on the selling price. Generally specialize by product line or customer type.
Brokers	Bring buyers and sellers together and assist in negotiation. Brokers are paid by the party who hired the broker and do not carry inventory, get involved in financing, or assume risk. Examples include food brokers, real estate brokers, insurance brokers, and security brokers.
Agents	Represent either buyers or sellers on a more permanent basis than brokers do. There are four types:
Manufacturers' agents	Represent two or more manufacturers of complementary lines. Often used in such lines as apparel, furniture, and electrical goods. A manufacturer's agent is hired by small manufacturers who cannot afford their own field sales forces and by large manufacturers who use agents to open new territories or cover territories that cannot support full-time salespeople.
Selling agents	Have contractual authority to sell a manufacturer's entire output. The selling agent serves as a sales department and has significant influence over prices, terms, and conditions of sale. Found in product areas such as textiles, industrial machinery and equipment, coal and coke, chemicals, and metals.

(Continued)

● **Table 13.3** | **Major Types of Wholesalers (Continued)**

Type	Description
Purchasing agents	Generally have a long-term relationship with buyers and make purchases for them, often receiving, inspecting, warehousing, and shipping the merchandise to buyers. Purchasing agents help clients obtain the best goods and prices available.
Commission merchants	Take physical possession of products and negotiate sales. Used most often in agricultural marketing by farmers who do not want to sell their own output. Take a truckload of commodities to a central market, sell it for the best price, deduct a commission and expenses, and remit the balance to the producers.
Manufacturers' and retailers' branches and offices	Wholesaling operations conducted by sellers or buyers themselves rather than operating through independent wholesalers. Separate branches and offices can be dedicated to either sales or purchasing.
Sales branches and offices	Set up by manufacturers to improve inventory control, selling, and promotion. Sales branches carry inventory and are found in industries such as lumber and automotive equipment and parts. Sales offices do not carry inventory and are most prominent in the dry goods and notions industries.
Purchasing offices	Perform a role similar to that of brokers or agents but are part of the buyer's organization. Many retailers set up purchasing offices in major market centers, such as New York and Chicago.

wholesaling. Merchant wholesalers include two broad types: full-service wholesalers and limited-service wholesalers. *Full-service wholesalers* provide a full set of services, whereas the various *limited-service wholesalers* offer fewer services to their suppliers and customers. The different types of limited-service wholesalers perform varied specialized functions in the distribution channel.

Brokers and *agents* differ from merchant wholesalers in two ways: They do not take title to goods, and they perform only a few functions. Like merchant wholesalers, they generally specialize by product line or customer type. A **broker** brings buyers and sellers together and assists in negotiation. **Agents** represent buyers or sellers on a more permanent basis. *Manufacturers' agents* (also called *manufacturers' representatives*) are the most common type of agent wholesaler. The third major type of wholesaling is that done in **manufacturers' and retailers' branches and offices** by sellers or buyers themselves rather than through independent wholesalers.

Wholesaler Marketing Decisions

Wholesalers now face growing competitive pressures, more-demanding customers, new technologies, and more direct-buying programs on the part of large industrial, institutional, and retail buyers. As a result, they have taken a fresh look at their marketing strategies. As with retailers, their marketing decisions include choices of segmentation and targeting, differentiation and positioning, and the marketing mix—product and service assortments, price, promotion, and distribution (see ● **Figure 13.2**).

Segmentation, Targeting, Differentiation, and Positioning Decisions

Like retailers, wholesalers must segment and define their target markets and differentiate and position themselves effectively—they cannot serve everyone. They can choose a target group by size of customer (for example, large retailers only), type of customer (convenience stores only), the need for service (customers who need credit), or other factors. Within the target group, they can identify the more profitable customers, design stronger offers, and build better relationships with them. They can propose automatic reordering systems, establish management-training and advisory systems, or even sponsor a voluntary chain. They can discourage less-profitable customers by requiring larger orders or adding service charges to smaller ones.

Broker
A wholesaler who does not take title to goods and whose function is to bring buyers and sellers together and assist in negotiation.

Agent
A wholesaler who represents buyers or sellers on a relatively permanent basis, performs only a few functions, and does not take title to goods.

Manufacturers' and retailers' branches and offices
Wholesaling by sellers or buyers themselves rather than through independent wholesalers.

● **FIGURE** | 13.2
Wholesaler Marketing Strategies

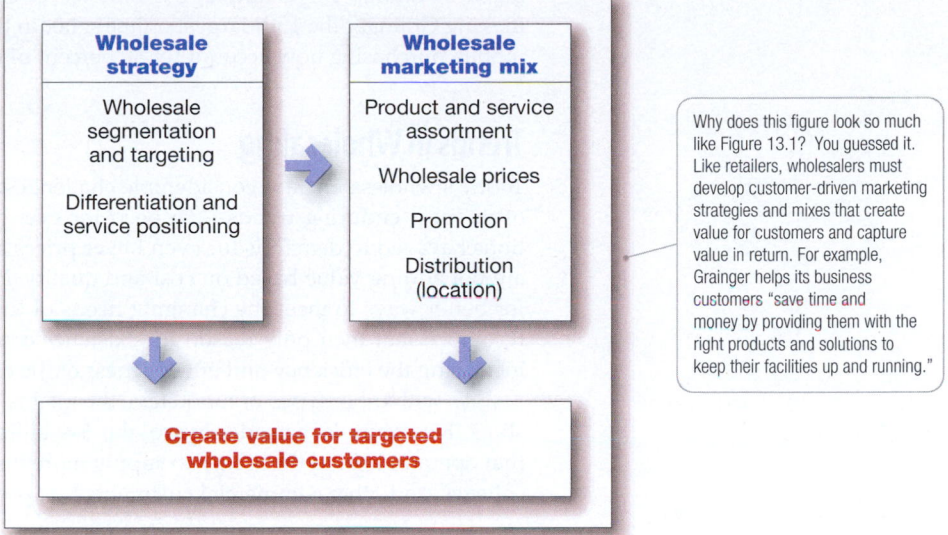

Why does this figure look so much like Figure 13.1? You guessed it. Like retailers, wholesalers must develop customer-driven marketing strategies and mixes that create value for customers and capture value in return. For example, Grainger helps its business customers "save time and money by providing them with the right products and solutions to keep their facilities up and running."

Marketing Mix Decisions

Like retailers, wholesalers must decide on product and service assortments, prices, promotion, and place. Wholesalers add customer value though the *products and services* they offer. They are often under great pressure to carry a full line and stock enough for immediate delivery. But this practice can damage profits. Wholesalers today are cutting down on the number of lines they carry, choosing to carry only the more profitable ones. They are also rethinking which services count most in building strong customer relationships and which should be dropped or paid for by the customer. The key for companies is to find the mix of services most valued by their target customers.

Price is also an important wholesaler decision. Wholesalers usually mark up the cost of goods by a standard percentage and operate on small margins. As retail and industrial customers face increasing costs and margins pressures, they turn to wholesalers, looking for lower prices. Wholesalers may, in turn, cut their margins on some lines to keep important customers. They may also ask suppliers for special price breaks in cases when they can turn them into an increase in the supplier's sales.

Although *promotion* can be critical to wholesaler success, most wholesalers are not promotion minded. They have historically used largely scattered and unplanned trade advertising, sales promotion, personal selling, and public relations. Like other business-to-business marketers, wholesalers need to make a team effort to sell, build, and service major accounts. Wholesalers also need to adopt some of the nonpersonal promotion techniques used by retailers. They need to develop an overall promotion strategy and make greater use of supplier promotion materials and programs.

Digital and social media are playing an increasingly important role in wholesaler promotion. For example, Grainger maintains an active presence on Facebook, YouTube, Twitter, LinkedIn, and Google+. It also provides a feature-rich mobile app. On its YouTube channel, Grainger lists more than 500 videos on topics ranging from the company and its products and services to keeping down inventory costs.

Finally, *distribution* (location) is important. Wholesalers must choose their locations, facilities, and other locations carefully. There was a time when wholesalers could locate in low-rent, low-tax areas and invest little money in their buildings, equipment, and systems. Today, however, as technology zooms forward, such behavior results in outdated systems for material handling, order processing, and delivery.

Instead, today's large and progressive wholesalers have reacted to rising costs by investing in automated warehouses and IT systems. Orders are fed from the retailer's information system directly into the wholesaler's, and the items are picked up by mechanical devices and automatically taken to a shipping platform where they are assembled. Most large wholesalers use technology to carry out accounting, billing, inventory control, and forecasting. Modern wholesalers are adapting their services to the needs of target customers and finding cost-reducing methods of doing business. They are also transacting more business online. For example, e-commerce is Grainger's fastest-growing sales channel, making Grainger the 13th-largest online seller in the United States and Canada. Online and mobile purchasing now account for 40 percent of the wholesaler's total sales.[38]

Trends in Wholesaling

Today's wholesalers face considerable challenges. The industry remains vulnerable to one of its most enduring trends—the need for ever-greater efficiency. Tight economic conditions have led to demands for even lower prices and the winnowing out of suppliers who are not adding value based on cost and quality. Progressive wholesalers constantly watch for better ways to meet the changing needs of their suppliers and target customers. They recognize that their only reason for existence comes from adding value, which occurs by increasing the efficiency and effectiveness of the entire marketing channel.

As with other types of marketers, the goal is to build value-adding customer relationships. For example, consider Sysco, the $49 billion wholesale food distribution company that operates behind the scenes to supply more than 425,000 restaurants, schools, hospitals, colleges, and other commercial customers that prepare meals away from home.[39]

● **Giant food distribution wholesaler Sysco lives up to its "Good things come from Sysco" motto by procuring and delivering food and food service supplies more dependably, efficiently, and cheaply than customers could ever hope to do on their own.**

Sysco Corporation

● Whether it's a hot dog from Reliant Stadium in Houston, the original Italian sub from Jersey Mike's, crab cakes from a Hilton Hotel, or a ham and cheese sandwich at the local hospital cafeteria, the chances are good that the ingredients were supplied by Sysco, the nation's top food supplier. Sysco supplies anything and everything needed to run an eating establishment, from boxes of seafood, chicken, and beef to 25-pound bags of rice or pasta to gallon jars of ketchup or salsa to boxes of plastic gloves and jugs of dishwashing detergent. What makes Sysco so valuable to its customers is that it procures and delivers these supplies more dependably, efficiently, and cheaply than customers could ever hope to do on their own.

For example, Lowell's, the iconic restaurant in Seattle's Pike Place Market, procures almost all of its products conveniently through the Sysco Market online ordering system. Its orders are processed quickly and accurately at Sysco's automated distribution center. Then, Lowell's—by itself or with the help of Sysco sales associates and dispatchers—can track the location of individual deliveries via the My Sysco Truck program. Sysco constantly seeks new ways to add more value and build trust, from product traceability for safety to sourcing products from local, small-to mid-sized farms, ranches, and processors to serve the needs of customers whose businesses are positioned on sustainability and community. In short, Sysco more than lives up to its motto: "Good things come from Sysco."

The distinction between large retailers and large wholesalers continues to blur. Many retailers now operate formats such as wholesale clubs and supercenters that perform many wholesale functions. In return, some large wholesalers are setting up their own retailing operations. For example, SuperValu is the nation's largest food wholesaler, and it's also one of the country's largest food retailers. About half of the company's sales come from its Cub Foods, Save-A-Lot, Farm Fresh, Hornbacher's, Shop 'n Save, and Shoppers stores.[40]

Wholesalers will continue to increase the services they provide to retailers—retail pricing, cooperative advertising, marketing and management information services, accounting services, online transactions, and others. However, both the more value-focused environment and the demand for increased services have put the squeeze on wholesaler profits. Wholesalers that do not find efficient ways to deliver value to their customers will soon drop by the wayside. Fortunately, the increased use of computerized, automated, and internet-based systems will help wholesalers contain the costs of ordering, shipping, and inventory holding, thus boosting their productivity.

13 | Reviewing and Extending the Concepts

OBJECTIVES REVIEW AND KEY TERMS

Objectives Review

Retailing and wholesaling consist of many organizations bringing goods and services from the point of production to the point of use. In this chapter, we examined the nature and importance of retailing, the major types of retailers, the decisions retailers make, and the future of retailing. We then examined these same topics for wholesalers.

OBJECTIVE 13-1 Explain the role of retailers in the distribution channel and describe the major types of retailers. *(pp 368–375)*

Retailing includes all the activities involved in selling goods or services directly to final consumers for their personal, nonbusiness use. Retailers play an important role in connecting brands to consumers in the final phases of the buying process. *Shopper marketing* involves focusing the entire marketing process on turning shoppers into buyers as they approach the point of sale. These days, shopper marketing and the "point of purchase" go well beyond in-store buying. Today's buyers are omni-channel consumers who work across multiple channels as they shop. Thus, influencing consumers' buying decisions calls for *omni-channel retailing*, creating a seamless cross-channel buying experience that integrates in-store, online, and mobile shopping.

Retail stores come in all shapes and sizes, and new retail types keep emerging. Store retailers can be classified by the *amount of service* they provide (self-service, limited service, or full service), *product line sold* (specialty stores, department stores, supermarkets, convenience stores, superstores, and service businesses), and *relative prices* (discount stores and off-price retailers). Today, many retailers are banding together in corporate and contractual *retail organizations* (corporate chains, voluntary chains, retailer cooperatives, and franchise organizations).

OBJECTIVE 13-2 Describe the major retailer marketing decisions. *(pp 376–381)*

Retailers are always searching for new marketing strategies to attract and hold customers. They face major marketing decisions about segmentation and targeting, store differentiation and positioning, and the retail marketing mix.

Retailers must first segment and define their target markets and then decide how they will differentiate and position themselves in these markets. Those that try to offer "something for everyone" end up satisfying no market well. By contrast, successful retailers define their target markets well and position themselves strongly.

Guided by strong targeting and positioning, retailers must decide on a retail marketing mix—product and services assortment, price, promotion, and place. Retail stores are much more than simply an assortment of goods. Beyond the products and services they offer, today's successful retailers carefully orchestrate virtually every aspect of the consumer store experience.

A retailer's price policy must fit its target market and positioning, products and services assortment, and competition. Retailers use various combinations of the five promotion tools—advertising, personal selling, sales promotion, PR, and direct marketing—to reach consumers. Online, mobile, and social media tools are playing an ever-increasing role in helping retailers to engage customers. Finally, it's very important that retailers select locations that are accessible to the target market in areas that are consistent with the retailer's positioning.

OBJECTIVE 13-3 Discuss the major trends and developments in retailing. *(pp 381–387)*

Retailers operate in a harsh and fast-changing environment, which offers threats as well as opportunities. Following years of good economic times, retailers have now adjusted to the new economic realities and more thrift-minded consumers. New retail forms continue to emerge. At the same time, however, different types of retailers are increasingly serving similar customers with the same products and prices (retail convergence), making differentiation more difficult. Other trends in retailing include the rise of megaretailers; the rapid growth of direct, online, mobile, and social media retailing; the need for omni-channel retailing; the growing importance of retail technology; a surge in green retailing; and the global expansion of major retailers.

OBJECTIVE 13-4 Explain the major types of wholesalers and their marketing decisions. *(pp 387–392)*

Wholesaling includes all the activities involved in selling goods or services to those who are buying for the purpose of resale or business use. Wholesalers fall into three groups. First, *merchant wholesalers* take possession of the goods. They include *full-service wholesalers* (wholesale merchants and industrial distributors) and *limited-service wholesalers* (cash-and-carry wholesalers, truck wholesalers, drop shippers, rack jobbers, producers' cooperatives, and mail-order wholesalers). Second, *brokers* and *agents* do not take possession of the goods but are paid a commission for aiding companies in buying and selling. Finally, *manufacturers' and retailers' branches and offices* are wholesaling operations conducted by non-wholesalers to bypass the wholesalers.

Like retailers, wholesalers must target carefully and position themselves strongly. And, like retailers, wholesalers must decide on product and service assortments, prices, promotion, and place. Progressive wholesalers constantly watch for better ways to meet the changing needs of their suppliers and target customers. They recognize that, in the long run, their only reason for existence comes from adding value, which occurs by increasing the efficiency and effectiveness of the entire marketing channel. As with other types of marketers, the goal is to build value-adding customer relationships.

Key Terms

OBJECTIVE 13-1

Retailing (p 368)
Retailer (p 368)
Shopper marketing (p 368)
Omni-channel retailing (p 369)
Specialty store (p 369)
Department store (p 369)
Supermarket (p 370)
Convenience store (p 371)
Superstore (p 371)
Category killer (p 371)

Service retailer (p 371)
Discount store (p 371)
Off-price retailer (p 372)
Independent off-price retailer (p 372)
Factory outlet (p 372)
Warehouse club (p 372)
Corporate chains (p 373)
Franchise (p 373)

OBJECTIVE 13-2

Shopping center (p 380)

OBJECTIVE 13-3

Showrooming (p 383)

OBJECTIVE 13-4

Wholesaling (p 387)
Wholesaler (p 387)
Merchant wholesaler (p 388)
Broker (p 390)
Agent (p 390)
Manufacturers' and retailers' branches
    and offices (p 390)

DISCUSSION AND CRITICAL THINKING

MyMarketingLab

Go to **mymktlab.com** to complete the problems marked with this icon ⭐.

Discussion Questions

13-1 Define *omni-channel retailing* and explain its connection to *shopper marketing*. (AACSB: Communication)

⭐ **13-2** Explain the various marketing decisions retailers must consider in designing strategies to attract and hold customers. (AACSB: Communication)

⭐ **13-3** Name and describe the three types of off-price retailers. How do off-price retailers differ from discount stores? (AACSB: Communication)

⭐ **13-4** Name and describe the three major groups of wholesalers. (AACSB: Communication; Reflective Thinking)

⭐ **13-5** Discuss the marketing mix decisions faced by wholesalers. What current challenges do wholesalers face? (AACSB: Communication; Reflective Thinking)

Critical Thinking Exercises

⭐ **13-6** You need a new pair of jeans, and you have several retail options. From Table 13.1, choose three different major store retailer types and select a specific store for each type chosen. Visit each store and describe each store's segmentation and positioning strategy and retail marketing mix—product, price, place, and promotion. How do the product assortments differ? What is each store's pricing approach? What promotional tools are used? Discuss store locations. (AACSB: Communication; Reflective Thinking; Use of IT)

13-7 In a small group, present a plan for a new retail store. Who is the target market? Describe the merchandise, atmospherics, price points, services provided, location, and how you would promote your retail store. Describe how you will differentiate your store from competitors. (AACSB: Communication; Reflective Thinking)

13-8 Identify a retailer that is currently struggling. Discuss why it is having difficulties and suggest ways to turn things around. (AACSB: Communication; Reflective Thinking)

APPLICATIONS AND CASES

Online, Mobile, and Social Media Marketing   Skipping the Checkout Line

The convenience of running to the store for a few grocery items can be hampered by long checkout lines. The creative geniuses at Selfycart solved this issue by developing an app that allows shoppers to browse, scan, and pay for products in participating stores using their mobile devices without waiting in line. Selfycart's technology continues to change, including a virtual shopping cart, shopping lists, historical purchase information, list sharing, and a coupon portal that virtually clips coupons. Selfycart also developed a daily deal section that offers discounts and special offers specific to each store. Selfycart will eventually introduce online ordering so consumers can add products to a virtual shopping cart, pay, and arrange store pickup at a specified time. Selfycart continues to discover new ways to create value for its users. Suddenly, skipping the line is an extremely appealing prospect!

13-9 Investigate the Selfycart app. What benefits and challenges will stores face in introducing Selfycart or any other mobile checkout app? (AACSB: Communication; Use of IT; Reflective Thinking)

13-10 If Selfycart or a similar mobile checkout app was available at your grocery store, would you use it? What benefits would you gain by using this new technology? Discuss the challenges you would face. (AACSB: Communication; Reflective Thinking)

Marketing Ethics Lilly for Target

The Lilly Pulitzer brand of brightly colored dresses and resort-themed designer items is the uniform of the preppy, Palm Beach set. Indeed, only select young women belonging to certain sororities in certain communities are allowed discounts on the $100 to $500 items. But Target created a buying frenzy by debuting its Lilly for Target collection in April 2015. Target's Pulitzer line comprised 250 items, such as Lilly dresses at $40, which sold out within minutes of launch, crashed the store's website, and created a firestorm of negative online comments from customers. The long lines outside stores caused one manager to name the event "Preppy Black Friday," likening it to the frenzied shopping day after Thanksgiving known as Black Friday. Most shoppers went home empty-handed because others scooped up as much as they could, emptying the racks within minutes. Items then sold on eBay for much higher prices. This type of launch is not new for Target. In 2011, the retailer launched a line of Missoni items

priced at $30 to $40. Missoni's distinctive zigzag- and geometric-patterned knitwear, shoes, and houseware items normally sell for hundreds of dollars at retailers such as Bloomingdale's and Saks Fifth Avenue. During the Missoni event, shoppers grabbed goods by the armload, even poaching items from other shoppers' carts. While some shoppers went away happy, many more were not. In both merchandise promotions, Target officials announced the sold-out items would not be replenished.

13-11 Is it ethical for retailers to create a promotion but not have sufficient merchandise for all shoppers who want to buy the items? (AACSB: Communication; Ethical Reasoning)

13-12 Is it smart for Target to create such shopping frenzies even though some customers are dissatisfied? Explain why or why not. (AACSB: Communication; Reflective Thinking)

Marketing by the Numbers Stockturn Rate

Retailers need merchandise to make sales. In fact, a retailer's inventory is its biggest asset. Not stocking enough merchandise can result in lost sales, but carrying too much inventory increases costs and lowers margins. Both circumstances reduce profits. One measure of a reseller's inventory management effectiveness is its *stockturn rate* (also called *inventory turnover rate* for manufacturers). The key to success in retailing is realizing a large volume of sales on as little inventory as possible while maintaining enough stock to meet customer demands.

13-13 Refer to Appendix 2: Marketing by the Numbers, and determine the stockturn rate of a retailer carrying an average inventory at cost of $350,000, with a cost of goods sold of $800,000. (AACSB: Communication; Analytical Reasoning)

13-14 If this company's stockturn rate was 3.5 last year, is the stockturn rate calculated above better or worse? Explain. (AACSB: Communication; Reflective Thinking)

Video Case Kmart

Once the leader in discount retailing, Kmart long ago took a back seat to Walmart, Target, and others discount chains. But recent efforts to provide value to customers through innovation show that the veteran retailer may still have its edge. To gain a competitive one-up, Kmart started a unique program that combined the benefits of online and brick-and-mortar shopping. When an item that customers wanted to purchase was not in stock at one of its stores, Kmart would ship the item to the customer's home for free.

To launch this program, Kmart unveiled an ad campaign that illustrated an uncharacteristic relevance to younger, tech-savvy customers. With the slight-of-mouth message that customers could "ship their pants" (or any of the other 65 million items in Kmart's inventory) for free, the ad went viral. As a result, Kmart

got its message out in spades, entertaining many while offending a few along the way.

After viewing the video featuring Kmart, answer the following questions:

13-15 Consider the retail marketing mix. How did Kmart differentiate itself from other retailers with its free shipping program?

13-16 What kind of customer does the "Ship My Pants" campaign target? How is this significant?

13-17 Discuss what will be the ultimate effects of this Kmart campaign.

Company Case Bass Pro Shops: Creating Nature's Theme Park for People Who Hate to Shop

Outdoor-products megaretailer Bass Pro Shops has seemingly been breaking the rules of retail for more than 40 years, basking in the spoils as a result. With more than 90 retail stores throughout the United States and Canada, the privately held Springfield, Missouri–based company reeled in $4.3 billion in revenues last year—nearly $50 million per store—making it the nation's number-one outdoor-products retailer. Going against common retail wisdom, Bass Pro Shops stores are enormous and are packed to the rafters with overhead. Even more daring, the chain has achieved retail success by targeting customers who hate to shop. The typical Bass Pro Shops customer is a reclusive male outdoorsman who yearns for the great outdoors but detests jostling crowds and shopping.

Over the past few decades, Bass Pro Shops has evolved from a popular mail-order catalog business into one of the nation's hottest store retailers. Despite Bass Pro Shops often-remote locations, customers flock to its superstores to buy hunting, fishing, and outdoor gear. Nearly 200 million people visited a Bass Pro Shops store last year—almost double the number that attended games put on by the NFL, NBA, and MLB combined. In a true display of "destination retail," customers drive an average of more than 50 miles to get to a Bass Pro Shops store (some drive hundreds of miles) and stay an average of 2 hours. Schools, churches, and senior centers even send people in by the busload.

Filling a Gap in the Market

So what explains Bass Pro Shops's climb to the top? Bass Pro Shops's ability to reel in hordes of otherwise reluctant shoppers to its stores is part of a double-hook strategy that dates back to the company's beginning. First, each store guarantees a product assortment as wide as the Mississippi River and as deep as the Mariana Trench. In 1971, Johnny Morris—a tournament fisherman and avid outdoorsman—was frustrated by the lack of decent fishing tackle in sporting goods stores. With the ink on his college diploma barely dry, he rented a U-Haul trailer and headed out on a cross-country road trip, filling the trailer with the latest and greatest in premium fishing tackle. Returning to Springfield, he set up shop in his father's liquor store near Table Rock Lake. With that, Bass Pro Shops was born.

That first Bass Pro Shops store quickly outgrew his dad's liquor store, and within a few years, Morris's vision for what he wanted Bass Pro Shops to become began to take shape. At the time, the sporting goods retail sector was fragmented with lots of independent retail shops catering to different outdoor activities. To meet the needs of customers across the country, Bass Pro Shops printed its first catalog in 1974. The company's catalog business has been a mainstay ever since.

At the same time, the company moved to fill a gap in brick-and-mortar retail. With no national chain that could serve the outdoor-loving masses, Bass Pro Shops quickly moved beyond fishing, adding hunting, camping, outdoor cooking gear, outdoor footwear and apparel, and nature-themed gifts. During this expansion, Bass Pro Shops not only carried the leading national brands, it also developed a portfolio of store brands, including its first brand, Bass Tracker—the first and still-market-leading dedicated bass boat. By manufacturing and selling direct, Bass Pro Shops could not only pass on huge savings to customers, it could compete on price with just about any company.

As Bass Pro Shops grew rapidly throughout the 1970s, the second hook of its strategy solidified with the opening of the first Outdoor World showroom adjacent to its headquarters. From that day on, Bass Pro Shops became more than a chain of stores that sells lots of cool outdoors stuff—it became a place that provided engaging customer *experiences* for all who visited. Bass Pro Shops has now created what amounts to a natural history theme park for outdoor enthusiasts—the "Walt Disney World" of sporting goods.

Nature's Theme Park

Take the store in Memphis, Tennessee, for example—Bass Pro Shops at the Pyramid. Former home of the Memphis Grizzlies, the 535,000-square-foot, 32-story glass-and-steel Pyramid now houses the largest Bass Pro Shops store. The store is dominated by various representations of wildlife, from the deer, duck, turkey, bear, bobcat, and wolf tracks imprinted in the concrete floors to the hand-painted murals from renowned artists depicting nature scenes reflecting local geography.

But the Pyramid brings wildlife to life in three dimensions. Each store features lifelike, museum-quality taxidermy animals in action poses—everything from prairie dogs, deer, elk, and caribou to brown bears, polar bears, musk oxen, and mountain goats—set in natural dioramas that make customers feel as though they're on location in striking outdoor landscapes. And although the animals are stuffed, the Pyramid store boasts 600,000 gallons of water features stocked with live fish and other wildlife. Features include the cypress swamp with an 84,000-gallon alligator habitat (live feedings every Saturday) surrounded by 100-foot-tall trees and the Live Duck Aviary with a four-pond multi-habitat home to five species of ducks.

The carefully orchestrated wildlife displays set the structure for what amounts to one of the most dynamic and captivating retail adventures in the world. Visitors can ride the nation's tallest freestanding glass elevator to the Lookout, a breathtaking glass-floored cantilevered observation deck at the top of the Pyramid. From there, they can survey the view outside the store as well as inside. And there is plenty to see inside, including the arcade shooting gallery, archery and pistol ranges, Beretta Fine Gun Center, interactive Ducks Unlimited Waterfowling Heritage Center, and the 103-room Big Cypress Lodge.

Because visitors to Bass Pro Shops at the Pyramid often make a day of it, the store has two full-service restaurants on site, including Uncle Buck's Fishbowl & Grill, one of six company-owned restaurant chains. Uncle Buck's offers a nautical-themed dining experience with a saltwater aquarium that weaves in and around the restaurant, offering diners full views of exotic and tropical fish. And before or after the meal, diners can work up an appetite or work off calories in the Fishbowl's 13-lane ocean-themed bowling alley where the balls are returned through a shark's gaping jaws.

Half the Size—All the Fun

Bass Pro Shops at the Pyramid is larger and more fantastic than any of the chain's other stores. But each Outdoor World store is designed to shower shoppers with the same captivating experience. Most stores are just under 200,000 square feet—about the size of the average Walmart Supercenter—with only one restaurant and no hotel. But the rest of the Bass Pro Shops formula plays out in magnificent splendor across its many North American outlets. One mother sums up the Bass Pro Shops experience this way:

> We recently had a visiting family group that included two 5-year-olds. They thoroughly enjoyed our trip to Bass Pro Shops! It's half retail store and half wildlife museum. There was plenty to see for any outdoor sports enthusiast. The kids loved seeing real fish and ducks, as well as plenty of inanimate displays. There were boats they could sit on and "trees" they could hide in. The store includes a restaurant. They offer plenty of merchandise for every budget, but you don't really have to spend money to enjoy the visit. Highly recommended!

With its retail design that builds theater and entertainment into every store, Bass Pro Shops is not only a haven for the reluctant male outdoorsman, it's enjoyable for everyone else. "First off, I am not an outdoor person so Bass Pro isn't a shop for me," says a recent store visitor. "That being said, I loved this store. I felt like I was in a museum and aquarium."

Bass Pro Shops provides even more reasons to visit, with various special events such as Family Summer Camp, Professional Bull Riders Event, Fall Hunting Classic, and Halloween Bass Pro Style. Each event is filled with demonstrations and activities, including fishing and hunting seminars featuring national and local experts. But no other Bass Pro Shops event compares to Santa's Wonderland, a six-week extravaganza that transforms each Bass Pro Shops outlet into a veritable Christmas village featuring rustic cabins, moving model trains, animated Christmas characters, interactive talking caribou, and live elves set among snow-covered hills and illuminated Christmas trees. Kids can hang out in the play zone and get their hands on old-time model trains, RC trucks, slot cars, and both laser and foam-dart guns. Families can spend time at various activity tables and make decorations and crafts to take home. They can also enjoy one of various seasonal goodies. And, of course, Santa's Wonderland wouldn't be complete without a visit from the jolly old elf himself, the event's main feature that includes a free studio-quality photo.

As amazing as Bass Pro Shops's retail design is, the company is not alone in its approach to marketing the great outdoors. Nebraska-based Cabela's started its own operations just before Bass Pro Shops. Cabela's has almost as many stores and pulls in nearly as much revenue. The Cabela's retail experience is nearly identical to that of Bass Pro Shops, down to the aquariums, animal-filled dioramas, and shooting galleries.

However, the two chains have at least one major difference: Whereas Bass Pro Shops is thriving, Cabela's long and successful run has been dogged in recent years by declining sales and losses. Falling victim to the intense competition from online vendors, Cabela's was recently ranked by *Forbes* as the nation's second-most troubled retail chain, trailing only the now-defunct Radio Shack. As Cabela's has explored options to escape bankruptcy, the most prominent option at this point appears to be selling the company—to Bass Pro Shops. That's right. The number-two outdoor retailer is currently entertaining an offer from number one. And if it goes through, Bass Pro Shops would not only double in size (the two chains rarely have stores in the same market), it would gain economy-of-scale advantages including cost savings and greater leverage with manufacturers.

But even if the acquisition of Cabela's doesn't pan out, Bass Pro Shops will keep doing what it has been doing for decades—wowing customers with the unsurpassed retail experience of its nature theme parks. "People spend time there when they go," Morris says of Bass Pro Shops stores. "They can't wait to see what's around the next aisle. It's an experience. It's about creating memories. It's about being with friends and family. It's about having fun."

Questions for Discussion

13-18 Define Bass Pro Shops's targeting strategy. Does the chain provide a truly differentiated experience?

13-19 Describe how Bass Pro Shops became the nation's leading outdoor retailer based on the retail marketing mix.

13-20 In terms of the major types of retailers, how would you classify Bass Pro Shops?

13-21 Why is Bass Pro Shops succeeding while Cabela's is floundering?

13-22 Is it a good idea for Bass Pro Shops to acquire Cabela's? Explain.

Sources: Sean McCoy, "Mega-Outdoors? Bass Pro, Cabela's Merger May Be on Horizon," *Gear Junkie*, May 31, 2016, https://gearjunkie.com/bass-pro-shops-cabelas-acquisition; Liyan Chen, "Next RadioShack? Here Are the Most Troubled Retails Stores," *Forbes*, February 10, 2015, www.forbes.com/sites/liyanchen/2015/02/10/next-radioshack-here-are-the-most-troubled-retail-stocks/#7d35e34dbc44; "Cabela's May Have a New Suitor," *Fortune*, April 20, 2016, www.fortune.com/2016/04/20/cabelas-suitor-goldman-sachs/; Lee Tolliver, "Money Hasn't Changed Humble Bass Pro Founder," *The Virginian-Pilot*, January 16, 2011, www.pilotonline.com/sports/outdoors/money-hasn-t-changed-humble-bass-pro-founder/article_939a1378-026d-517b-9875-dd01ddc69b8e.html; and www.basspro.com/webapp/wcs/stores/servlet/CFPageC?appID=94&storeId=10151&catalogId=10051&langId=-1&tab=3, www.tripadvisor.com, and www.basspro.com, accessed September 2016.

MyMarketingLab

Go to **mymktlab.com** for Auto-graded writing questions as well as the following Assisted-graded writing questions:

13-23 What is retail convergence? Has it helped or harmed small retailers?

13-24 Describe the types of shopping centers and identify specific examples in your community or a nearby city.

14 Engaging Consumers and Communicating Customer Value
Integrated Marketing Communication Strategy

CHAPTER PREVIEW In this and the next three chapters, we'll examine the last of the marketing mix tools—promotion. Companies must do more than just create customer value. They must also clearly and persuasively communicate that value. Promotion is not a single tool but rather a mix of several tools. Ideally, under the concept of *integrated marketing communications,* a company will carefully coordinate these promotion elements to engage customers and build a clear, consistent, and compelling message about an organization and its products.

We'll begin by introducing the various promotion mix tools. Next, we'll examine the rapidly changing communications environment—especially the addition of digital, mobile, and social media—and the need for integrated marketing communications. Finally, we discuss the steps in developing marketing communications and the promotion budgeting process. In the next three chapters, we'll present the specific marketing communications tools: advertising and public relations (Chapter 15); personal selling and sales promotion (Chapter 16); and direct, online, mobile, and social media marketing (Chapter 17).

Let's start by looking at a good integrated marketing communications campaign. In the fiercely competitive snack and candy industry, where well-established brands are fighting for survival, the inspired-yet-durable Snickers "You're not you when you're hungry" campaign has given the iconic brand new life. No matter where you see the message—on TV, on a mobile screen, in a friend's post, or even on a Snickers candy bar wrapper—the imaginative campaign clearly and consistently drives home the brand's "Snickers satisfies" and "You're not you when you're hungry" positioning in an engaging and memorable way. It has also made Snickers the world's leading sweet snack.

SNICKERS: "You're Not You When You're Hungry"

It all started with a now-classic Snickers ad in the 2010 Super Bowl. In the ad, during a neighborhood pickup football game, octogenarian Golden Girl Betty White appeared as a football player who was "playing like Betty White"—that is, very poorly. But after biting into a Snickers bar, she morphed back into a young, athletic footballer who played more like his usual self. The ad ended with the now-familiar slogan "You're not you when you're hungry" followed by the tagline "Snickers satisfies."

The Betty White ad generated tremendous buzz, reinvigorating the then-stagnant Snickers candy bar brand. According to Nielsen, it was the "best-liked spot" of that year's Super Bowl, and it achieved the highest score on the *USA Today* Ad Meter rankings. The ad went viral, racking up tens of millions of views online and earning seemingly endless media attention. The "You're not you when you're hungry" slogan went on to become the cornerstone

> The enduring Snickers "You're not you when you're hungry" integrated marketing communications campaign clearly and consistently drives the brand's "Snickers satisfies" positioning in an engaging and memorable way, helping to make Snickers the world's leading sweet snack.

for of a long-running, highly successful integrated marketing communications campaign that has propelled Snickers to the top of the global confectionary market.

Every great marketing communications campaign starts with a unique brand message, something that sets the brand apart. For decades, Mars has positioned Snickers on one overriding brand attribute: Snickers is satisfying. Heartier than most candy bars, Snickers combines ingredients like chocolate, nougat, and caramel with the protein power of peanuts. The "Snickers satisfies" tagline emphasizes the bar's stomach-filling properties. Before the current campaign, Snickers pitched the bar to young athletic males as a meal alternative. One classic print ad, for example, showed an approving mother sending her son off to football practice with a Snickers bar.

But by the early 2000s, Snickers was in a rut. Its positioning had grown stale; its sales and market share had flattened.

The brand needed a new creative concept—something that would rejuvenate Snickers and broaden its market appeal. Rather than abandoning its established positioning, however, Mars extended it with the fresh new "You're not you when you're hungry" theme. So while "Snickers satisfies" remains the brand's baseline positioning, "You're not you" is the creative "big idea" that now brings the positioning to life in a clever and engaging way.

"You're not you when you're hungry" taps into a powerful and universal emotional appeal—hunger. It reaches a broad market. Almost everyone can relate to how being hungry changes who you are. The positioning is as powerful for women as for men; for older generations as for younger ones; for office workers, factory workers, or students. It works across global cultural lines. Finally, the "You're not you" theme lends itself to no end of imaginative and entertaining ads and executions across varied media platforms.

The Snickers "You're not you when you're hungry" mantra taps into a powerful and universal emotional appeal—hunger. Everyone can relate to how being hungry changes who you are.

Judy Unger/Alamy Stock Photo

From that first Betty White Super Bowl ad, the "You're not you" campaign has spawned a host of creative ads in more than 80 countries. One memorable TV ad featured the late Robin Williams as a football coach instructing his team to "kill them—with kindness" by making balloon animals and tea cosies. Then there was the Snickers *Brady Bunch* ad for Super Bowl XLIX in which roughneck Danny Trejo portrayed a snarling Marcia and quirky Steve Buscemi played a disgruntled Jan. That ad ranked third-highest among that year's Super Bowl ads in terms of earned impressions and went on to win a first-ever Super Clio (the Academy Awards of advertising). During Super Bowl 50, another Snickers ad mimicked the iconic photo shoot featuring Marilyn Monroe in a white dress standing over a breezy subway grate—only this time, the updraft revealed grumpy-faced Willem Dafoe's bony legs and tighty-whiteys. That ad pulled in more than 11 million views on the Snickers YouTube channel alone.

The "You're not you" campaign also works well in print. One print ad shows three sprinters in start position on a track, one of them facing the wrong direction. Another shows four soccer players in position to block a free kick, all with their cupped hands protecting important body parts save one who is unguarded, hands above his head with his jersey pulled over his face. Still another ad gets the point across without using humans at all. In a reversal of roles, it shows a zebra in hot pursuit of a lion. Each simple visual is accompanied by a cross-section of a Snickers bar and the phrase "You're not you when you're hungry. Snickers satisfies."

Beyond TV and print ads, the "You're not you" campaign is fully integrated across a range of digital, mobile, positional, and other media, even packaging. Snickers's current "Hunger Bar" wrappers directly reinforce the campaign message, with labels containing mood descriptors such as Cranky, Loopy, Spacey, Whiny, Snippy, Curmudgeon, Goofball, and Drama Mama. Snickers urges customers to call out contrarian-acting friends with an appropriately labeled Snickers bar. Mars even created a clever two-minute mini-reality show video highlighting a Snickers hotline operator who dispatches bike messengers to deliver the wrappers to deserving candidates.

The Snickers "You're not you when you're hungry" campaign's numerous digital elements are designed to engage customers and trigger consumer-generated content. For example, a recent "Snap a Selfie with your Snickers Bar" contest invites the brand's more than 11 million Facebook followers to share photos of "who R U when U R hungry"—the winner will receive $100,000 and his or her own personalized Snickers bars. A Snickers "You're Not YouTube" campaign signed up 13 influential YouTubers, with a combined following of 7 million subscribers, to illustrate their own "You're not you" moments. Snickers also ran a YouTube contest inviting fans to submit their own photos, videos, or memes and to share them socially with #EatASnickers.

In yet another digital campaign, this one in the United Kingdom, British celebrities posted four "out-of-character" tweets—such as professional soccer player Rio Ferdinand tweeting "Really getting into knitting!!!" or glamor model Katie Price tweeting "Large scale quantitative easing could distort liquidity of government bond market"—followed by a fifth tweet promoting Snickers bars and quoting the campaign slogan #yourenotyouwhenyourehungry. Such digital efforts effectively engage and entertain the brand's digitally savvy fans while reinforcing the Snickers mantra.

OBJECTIVES OUTLINE

OBJECTIVE 14-1	Define the five promotion mix tools for communicating customer value.
	The Promotion Mix (pp 400–401)
OBJECTIVE 14-2	Discuss the changing communications landscape and the need for integrated marketing communications.
	Integrated Marketing Communications (pp 401–406)
OBJECTIVE 14-3	Outline the communication process and the steps in developing effective marketing communications.
	Developing Effective Marketing Communication (pp 406–413)
OBJECTIVE 14-4	Explain the methods for setting the promotion budget and factors that affect the design of the promotion mix.
	Setting the Total Promotion Budget and Mix (pp 413–420)

Despite its diversity, no matter what the platform—whether print or packaging or TV, laptop, and mobile screens or something else—the Snickers campaign is much more than just a scattered collection of clever content. What makes the campaign so powerful is that all its pieces are carefully integrated under the brand's "Snickers satisfies" and "You're not you when you're hungry" positioning. The message strikes a core human emotion—that you're likely to get a little out of sorts when you haven't eaten for a while—in an engaging and memorable way. No matter where you are in the world or how you receive the message, the campaign delivers a clear and consistent brand message.

Thus, after more than six years, the popular Snickers "You're not you" campaign is still packing energy. Prior to the campaign, Snickers was losing market share. However, not long after Betty White made her Super Bowl debut, Snickers surpassed Mars's own M&Ms to become the planet's best-selling candy, a position it still holds today. With an expanded lineup that now includes Snickers Almond, Snickers Peanut Butter Squared, Snickers Bites, and Snickers Ice Cream bars, the $3.5 billion Snickers brand now contributes more than 10 percent of giant Mars, Inc.'s total annual revenues. Thanks in large part to the innovative "You're not you when you're hungry" integrated marketing communications campaign, the brand's long-standing claim holds truer than ever for both the company and its customers: "Snickers satisfies."[1]

Promotion mix (marketing communications mix)
The specific blend of promotion tools that the company uses to persuasively communicate customer value and build customer relationships.

BUILDING GOOD CUSTOMER RELATIONSHIPS calls for more than just developing a good product, pricing it attractively, and making it available to target customers. Companies must also *engage* consumers and *communicate* their value propositions to customers, and what they communicate should not be left to chance. All communications must be planned and blended into carefully integrated programs. Just as good communication is important in building and maintaining any other kind of relationship, it is a crucial element in a company's efforts to engage customers and build profitable customer relationships.

Author Comment | The promotion mix is the marketer's bag of tools for engaging and communicating with customers and other stakeholders. To deliver a clear and compelling message, each tool must be carefully coordinated under the concept of integrated marketing communications (IMC).

The Promotion Mix

A company's total **promotion mix**—also called its **marketing communications mix**—consists of the specific blend of advertising, public relations, personal selling, sales promotion, and direct marketing tools that the company uses to engage consumers, persuasively

Advertising
Any paid form of nonpersonal presentation and promotion of ideas, goods, or services by an identified sponsor.

Sales promotion
Short-term incentives to encourage the purchase or sale of a product or a service.

Personal selling
Personal presentation by the firm's sales force for the purpose of engaging customers, making sales, and building customer relationships.

Public relations (PR)
Building good relations with the company's various publics by obtaining favorable publicity, building up a good corporate image, and handling or heading off unfavorable rumors, stories, and events.

Direct and digital marketing
Engaging directly with carefully targeted individual consumers and customer communities to both obtain an immediate response and build lasting customer relationships.

communicate customer value, and build customer relationships. The five major promotion tools are defined as follows:[2]

- **Advertising**. Any paid form of nonpersonal presentation and promotion of ideas, goods, or services by an identified sponsor.
- **Sales promotion**. Short-term incentives to encourage the purchase or sale of a product or service.
- **Personal selling**. Personal customer interactions by the firm's sales force for the purpose of engaging customers, making sales, and building customer relationships.
- **Public relations (PR)**. Building good relations with the company's various publics by obtaining favorable publicity, building up a good corporate image, and handling or heading off unfavorable rumors, stories, and events.
- **Direct and digital marketing**. Engaging directly with carefully targeted individual consumers and customer communities to both obtain an immediate response and build lasting customer relationships.

Each category involves specific promotional tools that are used to communicate with customers. For example, *advertising* includes broadcast, print, online, mobile, outdoor, and other forms. *Sales promotion* includes discounts, coupons, displays, demonstrations, and events. *Personal selling* includes sales presentations, trade shows, and incentive programs. *Public relations* includes press releases, sponsorships, events, and webpages. And *direct and digital marketing* includes direct mail, email, catalogs, online and social media, mobile marketing, and more.

At the same time, marketing communication goes beyond these specific promotion tools. The product's design, its price, the shape and color of its package, and the stores that sell it—*all* communicate something to buyers. Thus, although the promotion mix is the company's primary engagement and communications activity, the entire marketing mix—promotion *and* product, price, and place—must be coordinated for greatest impact.

Author | Integrated marketing
Comment | communications—IMC—is a really hot topic these days. No other area of marketing is changing so quickly and profoundly. A big part of the reason is the huge surge in customer engagement through digital media—online, mobile, and social media marketing.

Integrated Marketing Communications

In past decades, marketers perfected the art of mass marketing: selling highly standardized products to masses of customers. In the process, they developed effective mass-media communication techniques to support these strategies. Large companies now routinely invest millions or even billions of dollars in television, magazine, or other mass-media advertising, reaching tens of millions of customers with a single ad. Today, however, marketing managers face some new marketing communications realities. Perhaps no other area of marketing is changing so profoundly as marketing communications, creating both exciting and challenging times for marketing communicators.

The New Marketing Communications Model

Several major factors are changing the face of today's marketing communications. First, *consumers* are changing. In this digital, wireless age, consumers are better informed and more communications empowered. Rather than relying on marketer-supplied information, they can use the internet, social media, and other technologies to find information on their own. They can connect easily with other consumers to exchange brand-related information or even create their own brand messages and experiences.

Second, *marketing strategies* are changing. As mass markets have fragmented, marketers are shifting away from mass marketing. More and more, they are developing focused marketing programs designed to engage customers and build customer relationships in more narrowly defined micromarkets.

Finally, sweeping advances in *digital technology* are causing remarkable changes in the ways companies and customers communicate with each other. The digital age has spawned a host of new information and communication tools—from satellite and cable television systems to smartphones and tablets to the many faces of the internet (brand websites, email, blogs, social media and online communities, the mobile web, and so much more). Just as mass marketing once gave rise to a new generation of mass-media communications, the new digital and social media have given birth to a more targeted, social, and engaging marketing communications model.

Although network television, magazines, newspapers, and other traditional mass media remain very important, their dominance is declining. In their place, advertisers are now adding a broad selection of more-specialized and highly targeted media to engage smaller customer communities with more personalized, interactive content. The new media range from specialty cable television channels and made-for-the-web videos to online ads, email and texting, blogs, mobile catalogs and coupons, and a burgeoning list of social media. Such new media have taken marketing by storm.

Some advertising industry experts even predict that the old mass-media communications model will eventually become obsolete. Mass-media costs are rising, audiences are shrinking, ad clutter is increasing, and viewers are gaining control of message exposure through technologies such as video streaming or DVRs that let them skip disruptive television commercials. As a result, the skeptics suggest, marketers are shifting ever-larger portions of their marketing budgets away from old-media mainstays and moving them to online, social, mobile, and other new-age media.

In recent years, although TV remains a potent advertising medium that captures a third or more of total advertising spending, its growth has slowed or declined. Ad spending in magazines, newspapers, and radio has also lost ground. Meanwhile, spending in digital media has surged. Growing at a rate of 15 percent a year, total digital ad spending is expected to pass TV spending this year. By 2020, digital media will capture an estimated 45 percent of all ad spending compared with TV's 33 percent. By far the fastest-growing digital category is mobile, which grew 38 percent last year and will account for an estimated 74 percent of all digital ad spending by 2020.

More and more, large advertisers—from Nike and P&G to Unilever—are moving toward a "digital-first" approach to building their brands. For example, Unilever, one of the world's largest advertisers, now spends as much as one-quarter of its $8 billion global marketing budget on digital media. In countries such as the United States and China, digital media account for closer to 50 percent of its marketing budget.[3]

Some marketers now rely almost entirely on digital and social media. ● For example, eco-friendly household products maker Method employs a full but mostly digital promotional campaign themed "Clean happy":[4]

Method is known for offbeat campaigns using slogans like "People against dirty" and "For the love of clean." But the most notable thing about the "Clean happy" campaign is that it at first used zero ads in traditional media like TV or magazines. Instead, the centerpiece of the campaign was brand videos aired only on YouTube and on the Method Facebook page. The campaign also employed online media ads as well as a major presence in social media that included, in addition to YouTube and Facebook, the Method Twitter feed and blogs. The "Clean happy" campaign fit both Method's personality and its budget. Method is the kind of grassroots brand that benefits from social media–type word of mouth. Moreover, "Clean happy" ran a first-year budget of only about $3.5 million, compared with the whopping $150 million or so that rival P&G might spend just to bring out a single new product, such as Tide Pods detergent packets.

Method ran the digital-only campaign for a full year before beginning to bring it to TV. Even now, the "Clean happy" campaign relies heavily on digital and social media, supported only by carefully targeted regional cable TV in selected markets. More recent campaign installments include "Life's Messy Moments," a romantic comedy–style series of TV and online ads and other social media content that follow a young couple and their relatable messes from their first kiss to first kid to a clean, happy ending. To kick off the campaign on Facebook, Method hosted a photo contest called Clean Happy Awards, asking fans to submit their best pet, kid, and party messes. "We're embracing this grassroots movement," says a Method ad executive. "When you don't have 150 million bucks, that's what you have to do."

● The new marketing communications model: Method's successful and long-running "Clean happy" campaign began as an online-only effort and still relies heavily on digital and social media, supported only by carefully targeted regional cable TV ads in selected markets.

Method Products PBC

In the new marketing communications world, rather than using old approaches that interrupt customers and force-feed them mass messages, new media formats let marketers reach smaller communities of consumers in more engaging ways. For example, think about television viewing these days. Consumers can now watch their favorite programs on just about anything with a screen—on televisions but also laptops, smartphones, or tablets. And they can choose to watch programs whenever and wherever they wish, often without commercials. Increasingly, some programs, ads, and videos are being produced only for online viewing.

Despite the shift toward digital media, however, traditional mass media still capture a sizable share of the promotion budgets of most major marketing firms, a fact that probably won't change quickly. Thus, rather than the old-media model collapsing completely, most marketers foresee a shifting mix of both traditional mass media and online, mobile, and social media that engage more-targeted consumer communities in a more personalized way. In the end, regardless of the communications channel, the key is to integrate all of these media in a way that best engages customers, communicates the brand message, and enhances the customer's brand experiences.

As the marketing communications environment shifts, so will the role of marketing communicators. Rather than just creating and placing "TV ads" or "print ads" or "Snapchat branded story ads," many marketers now view themselves more broadly as **content marketing** managers. As such, they create, inspire, and share brand messages and conversations with and among customers across a fluid mix of *paid, owned, earned,* and *shared* communication channels. These channels include media that are both traditional and new as well as controlled and not controlled. It's not just advertising anymore, notes one ad agency executive. "It's about [communications] context and channels now, rather than just the message itself. It's about mapping the customer journey to start a conversation with consumers, one that leads to engagement, purchase, loyalty, and advocacy at different touchpoints against this integrated journey" (see Real Marketing 14.1).[5]

Content marketing
Creating, inspiring, and sharing brand messages and conversations with and among consumers across a fluid mix of paid, owned, earned, and shared channels.

The Need for Integrated Marketing Communications

The shift toward a richer mix of media and content approaches poses a problem for marketers. Consumers today are bombarded by brand messages from a broad range of sources. But all too often, companies fail to integrate their various communication channels. Mass-media ads say one thing, whereas company's internet site, emails, social media pages, or videos posted on YouTube say something altogether different.

One problem is that marketing content often comes from different parts of the company. Advertising messages are prepared by the advertising department or an ad agency. Other company departments or agencies prepare public relations messages, sales promotion events, and online or social media content. However, consumers don't distinguish between content sources the way marketers do. In the consumer's mind, brand-related content from different sources—whether it's a Super Bowl ad, in-store display, mobile app, or friend's social media post—all merge into a single message about the brand or company. Conflicting content from these different sources can result in confused company images, brand positions, and customer relationships.

Thus, the explosion of online, mobile, and social media marketing presents tremendous opportunities but also big challenges. It gives marketers rich new tools for understanding and engaging customers. At the same time, it complicates and fragments overall marketing communications. The challenge is to bring it all together in an organized way. To that end, most companies practice the concept of **integrated marketing communications (IMC)**. Under this concept, as illustrated in ● **Figure 14.1**, the company carefully integrates its many communication channels to deliver a clear, consistent, and compelling message about the organization and its brands.

Integrated marketing communications (IMC)
Carefully integrating and coordinating the company's many communications channels to deliver a clear, consistent, and compelling message about the organization and its products.

Often, different media play unique roles in engaging, informing, and persuading consumers. For example, a recent study showed that more than two-thirds of advertisers and their agencies are planning video ad campaigns that stretch across multiple viewing platforms, such as traditional TV and digital, mobile, and social media. Such *video convergence,* as it's called, combines TV's core strength—vast reach—with digital's better targeting,

14.1 Just Don't Call It Advertising: It's Content Marketing

In the good old days, life seemed so simple for advertisers. When a brand needed an advertising campaign, everybody knew what that meant. The brand team and ad agency came up with a creative strategy, developed a media plan, produced and placed a set of TV commercials and magazine or newspaper ads, and maybe issued a press release to stir up some news. But in these digital times, the old practice of placing "advertisements" in well-defined "media" within the tidy framework of a carefully managed "advertising campaign" just doesn't work anymore.

Instead, the lines are rapidly blurring between traditional advertising and new digital content. To be relevant, today's brand messages must be social, mobile, interactively engaging, and multi-platformed. Says one industry insider: "Today's media landscape keeps getting more diverse—it's broadcast, cable, and streaming; it's online, tablet, and smartphone; it's video, rich media, social media, branded content, banners, apps, in-app advertising, and interactive technology products."

The new digital landscape has called into question the very definition of advertising. "What Is Advertising Anyway?" asks one provocative headline. Call it whatever you want, admonishes another, but "Just *Don't* Call It Advertising." Instead, according to many marketers these days, it's "content marketing," creating and distributing a broad mix of compelling content that engages customers, builds relationships with and among them, and moves them to act and advocate the brand to others. To feed today's digital and social media machinery, and to sustain "always-on" consumer conversations, brands need a constant supply of fresh content across a breadth of traditional and digital platforms.

Many advertisers and marketers now view themselves more broadly as *content marketing managers* who create, inspire, share, and curate marketing content—both their own content and that created by consumers and others. Rather than using traditional media breakdowns, they subscribe to a new framework that builds on how and by whom marketing content is created, controlled, and distributed. The new classification identifies four major types of media: paid, owned, earned, and shared (POES):

Paid media—promotional channels paid for by the marketer, including traditional media (such as TV, radio, print, or outdoor) and online and digital media (paid search ads, web and social media display ads, mobile ads, or email marketing).

Owned media—promotional channels owned and controlled by the company, including company websites, corporate blogs, owned social media pages, proprietary brand communities, sales forces, and events.

Earned media—PR media channels, such as television, newspapers, blogs, online video sites, and other media not directly paid for or controlled by the marketer but that include the content because of viewer, reader, or user interest.

Shared media—media shared by consumers with other consumers, such as social media, blogs, mobile media, and viral channels as well as traditional word-of-mouth.

In the past, advertisers have focused on traditional paid (broadcast, print) or earned (public relations) media. Now, however, content marketers have rapidly added the new digital generation of owned (websites, blogs, brand communities) and shared (online social, mobile, email) media. Whereas a successful paid ad used to be an end in itself, marketers are now developing integrated marketing content that leverages the combined power of all the POES channels. Thus, many TV ads often aren't just TV ads any more. They're "video content" you might see anywhere—on a TV screen but also on a tablet or phone. Other video content looks a lot like TV advertising but was never intended for TV, such as made-for-online videos posted on websites or social media. Similarly, printed brand messages and pictures no longer appear only in carefully crafted magazine ads or catalogs. Instead, such content, created by a variety of sources, pops up in anything from formal ads and online brand pages to mobile and social media and independent blogs.

Content marketing: Tecate's content-rich, skillfully integrated "Soccer Gentleman" campaign produced striking results across POES media by helping men to balance the two true loves of their lives: women and World Cup soccer.

Cervecería Cuauhtémoc Moctezuma, SA de CV

The new "content marketing" campaigns look a lot different from the old "advertising" campaigns. For example, consider Tecate—Heineken-Mexico's leading beer brand. In Mexico, Tecate stands for all things male, including soccer, Mexico's favorite sport. But Tecate faced a tough creative challenge during the recent Soccer World Cup. It wanted to tap into the fan fever surrounding the tournament but couldn't directly mention either the World Cup or the Mexican national team, both sponsored by competitor Corona. So instead of just running big-budget TV ads filled with the usual clichés, Tecate launched a novel, content-rich "Soccer Gentleman" campaign that went well beyond traditional media:

Tecate's "Soccer Gentleman" campaign recognized that during the World Cup a real Tecate man must balance the two true loves of his life: women and soccer. So the campaign set out to help men successfully juggle their love lives and watching soccer nonstop by being "perfect gentlemen." The campaign was built around a beautifully penned, 185-page love letter that took 90 minutes to read (which just happens to be the length of a soccer match).

In an opening TV spot aired a minute before a big match, a man touchingly presents the lengthy letter to his beloved and implores her to read it right away. Enchanted by his romantic gesture, she settles in to read his heartfelt words, so enrapt that she fails to notice as he races off to watch the World Cup match with his friends without interruption. During the match, five more TV spots, a campaign website, and 47 Facebook posts follow the reading of the letter in real time, with updates such as "She is now halfway through your 90-minute letter." A final post-game ad shows the man racing home just in time to greet his love as she emerges from her rapture and falls into his arms. Men could then download the entire letter for the next match and customize it by changing the woman's name; 16,000 people did so and lived the experience of reading the actual letter.

In another part of the campaign, a Tecate man refuses his new girlfriend's invitation to come inside after a first date, proclaiming his deep affection for her and his honorable intentions to be a perfect gentleman by defying the "macho culture" and the temptations of a one-night stand. As she swoons, he races off to catch the next game. "Watching World Cup soccer and being loved for it?" concludes Tecate. "Life doesn't get much better than that."

Skillfully integrated across POES channels, the "Soccer Gentleman" content campaign produced striking results. Tecate sales increased 11 percent during the World Cup period. During the four-month campaign, the brand saw a 228 percent increase in YouTube followers, added 1.2 million Facebook fans, and generated a flurry of media coverage and social media buzz. The campaign's ads and videos garnered 17 million YouTube views and accounted for two of YouTube's 10 most-watched ads during the World Cup. "Soccer Gentleman" was named by ad industry publication *Advertising Age* as the year's best integrated marketing communications campaign. "Soccer Gentleman" has "become a cultural phenomenon in Mexico," says a Tecate marketer. "The phrase is part of the popular culture; with memes, videos, and T-shirts. You hear it in restaurants and taxis. During the World Cup, without being able to say anything, we took everything!"

So, we can't just call it "advertising" anymore. Today's shifting and sometimes chaotic marketing communications environment calls for more than just creating and placing ads in well-defined and controlled media spaces. Rather, today's marketing communicators must be marketing content strategists, creators, connectors, and catalysts who manage brand conversations with and among customers and help those conversations catch fire across a fluid mix of channels. That's a tall order, but with today's new thinking, anything is POES–ible!

Sources: "How PESO Makes Sense in Influencer Marketing," *PR Week*, June 8, 2015, www.prweek.com/article/1350303/peso-makes-sense-influencer-marketing; Randall Rothenberg, "What Is Advertising Anyway?" *Ad Week*, September 16, 2013, p. 15; Paul Nolan, "The C Word: What Is Content Marketing," *Sales & Marketing Management*, January/February 2014; Peter Himler, "Paid, Earned & Owned: Revisited," *The Flack*, June 21, 2011, http://flatironcomm.com/2011/06/paid-earned-owned-revisited/; Laurel Wentz, "Integrated Campaign of the Year: 'Soccer Gentleman' for Tecate," *Advertising Age*, August 3, 2015, http://adage.com/article/print/299755; "Soccer Gentlemen," *Facebook Studio*, www.facebook-studio.com/gallery/submission/soccer-gentlemen-4, accessed October 2016.

interaction, and engagement.[6] These varied media and roles must be carefully coordinated under the overall integrated marketing communications plan.

One good example of a well-integrated marketing communications effort is home-improvement retailer Lowe's "Never Stop Improving" campaign, which integrates the

FIGURE | 14.1
Integrated Marketing Communications

Today's customers are bombarded by brand content from all directions. For example, think about all the ways you interact with companies such as Nike, Apple, or Coca-Cola. Integrated marketing communications means that companies must carefully coordinate all of these customer touch points to ensure clear brand messages.

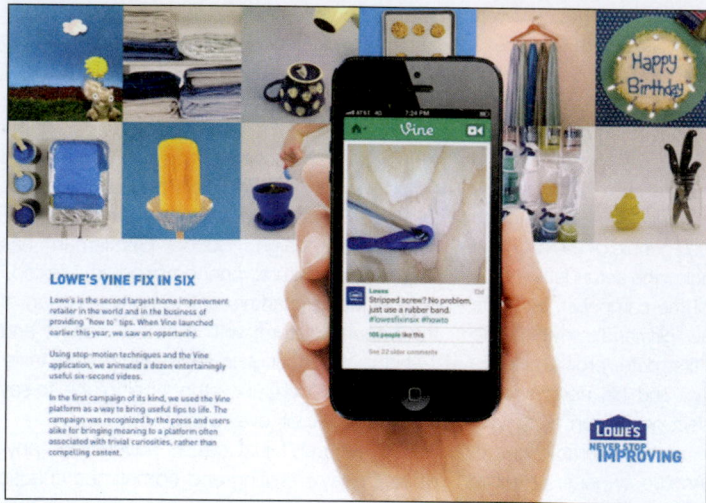

LOWE'S VINE FIX IN SIX

Lowe's is the second largest home improvement retailer in the world and in the business of providing 'how to' tips. When Vine launched earlier this year, we saw an opportunity.

Using stop-motion techniques and the Vine application, we animated a dozen entertainingly useful six-second videos.

In the first campaign of its kind, we used the Vine platform as a way to bring useful tips to life. The campaign was recognized by the press and users alike for bringing meaning to a platform often associated with trivial curiosities, rather than compelling content.

● **Integrated marketing communications: The Lowe's "Never Stop Improving" campaign integrates the clout of big-budget traditional media with the power of social media to create personalized, real-time customer engagement.**

LOWE'S, the Gable Mansard Design, and NEVER STOP IMPROVING are trademarks or registered trademarks of LF, LLC

clout of big-budget traditional media with the power of social media to create personalized, real-time customer engagement:[7]

To be sure, Lowe's runs a full slate of big-budget television spots and other traditional media ads that drive home its "Never Stop Improving" positioning. But in recent years, the company has added a rich flow of engaging, carefully integrated social media content that personalizes and enriches the Lowe's customer experience in ways that traditional media can't. Just one example is the Lowe's "Fix in Six" Vine video campaign. ● "Fix in Six" features dozens of clever six-second looping videos showing quick-fix solutions to home-improvement problems—everything from removing stripped screws to keeping squirrels away from plants. The award-winning series was a huge success from the start, generating 28,000 social media mentions within just the first week and earning millions of total campaign impressions to date.

Beyond Vine, the Lowe's "Never Stop Improving" campaign integrates a broad mix of social media, each playing its own unique role. Lowe's uses its heavily subscribed YouTube channel for longer DIY video tips and tutorials to supplement the quick hits on Vine. It uses Pinterest and Instagram to bring customers' projects to life through high-impact imagery. Facebook provides a platform for engaging customers in dialogue—every Facebook comment gets an answer. Twitter serves for posting short comments or spreading the word about special offers. No matter what the platform, all content—from television spots to online videos to Facebook posts—is carefully coordinated under Lowe's "Never Stop Improving" mantra and its mission of helping customers find home-improvement solutions. According to one Lowe's marketer, the integrated marketing campaign is less about making the cash register ring and more about "making sure that customers . . . know that Lowe's is offering them value and [about keeping them] engaged with the brand."

In the past, no one person or department was responsible for thinking through the communication roles of the various promotion tools and coordinating the promotion mix. To help implement integrated marketing communications, some companies have appointed a marketing communications director who has overall responsibility for the company's communications efforts. This helps to produce better communications consistency and greater sales impact. It places the responsibility in someone's hands—where none existed before—to unify the company's image as it is shaped by thousands of company activities.

Developing Effective Marketing Communication

A View of the Communication Process

Author Comment | To develop effective marketing communications, you must first understand the general communication process.

Integrated marketing communications involves identifying the target audience and shaping a well-coordinated promotional program to obtain the desired audience response. Too often, marketing communications focus on immediate awareness, image, or preference goals in the target market. But this approach to communication is too shortsighted. Today, marketers are moving toward viewing communications as managing ongoing customer engagement and relationships with the company and its brands.

Because customers differ, communications programs need to be developed for specific segments, niches, and even individuals. And, given today's interactive communications technologies, companies must ask not only "How can we engage our customers?" but also "How can we let our customers engage us?"

Thus, the communications process should start with an audit of all the potential touch points that target customers may have with the company and its brands. For example, someone purchasing a new wireless phone plan may talk to others, see television or magazine ads, visit various online sites for prices and reviews, and check out plans at Best Buy, Walmart, or a wireless provider's kiosk or store. The marketer needs to assess what influence each communication experience will have at different stages of the buying process. This understanding helps marketers allocate their communication dollars more efficiently and effectively.

To communicate effectively, marketers need to understand how communication works. Communication involves the nine elements shown in ● Figure 14.2. Two of these elements are the major parties in a communication—the *sender* and the *receiver*. Another two are the major communication tools—the *message* and the *media*. Four more are major communication functions—*encoding, decoding, response,* and *feedback*. The last element is *noise* in the system. Definitions of these elements follow and are applied to a McDonald's "i'm lovin' it" television commercial.

- *Sender.* The *party sending the message* to another party—here, McDonald's.
- *Encoding.* The process of *putting thought into symbolic form*—for example, McDonald's ad agency assembles words, sounds, and illustrations into a TV advertisement that will convey the intended message.
- *Message.* The *set of symbols* that the sender transmits—the actual McDonald's ad.
- *Media.* The *communication channels* through which the message moves from the sender to the receiver—in this case, television and the specific television programs that McDonald's selects.
- *Decoding.* The process by which the receiver *assigns meaning to the symbols* encoded by the sender—a consumer watches the McDonald's commercial and interprets the words and images it contains.
- *Receiver.* The *party receiving the message* sent by another party—the customer who watches the McDonald's ad.
- *Response.* The *reactions of the receiver* after being exposed to the message—any of hundreds of possible responses, such as the consumer likes McDonald's better, is more likely to eat at McDonald's next time, hums the "i'm lovin' it" jingle, or does nothing.
- *Feedback.* The part of the *receiver's response communicated back to the sender*—McDonald's research shows that consumers are either struck by and remember the ad or they email or call McDonald's, praising or criticizing the ad or its products.
- *Noise.* The *unplanned static or distortion* during the communication process, which results in the receiver getting a different message than the one the sender sent—the consumer is distracted while watching the commercial and misses its key points.

For a message to be effective, the sender's encoding process must mesh with the receiver's decoding process. The best messages consist of words and other symbols that are familiar to the receiver. The more the sender's field of experience overlaps

● FIGURE | 14.2

Elements in the
Communication Process

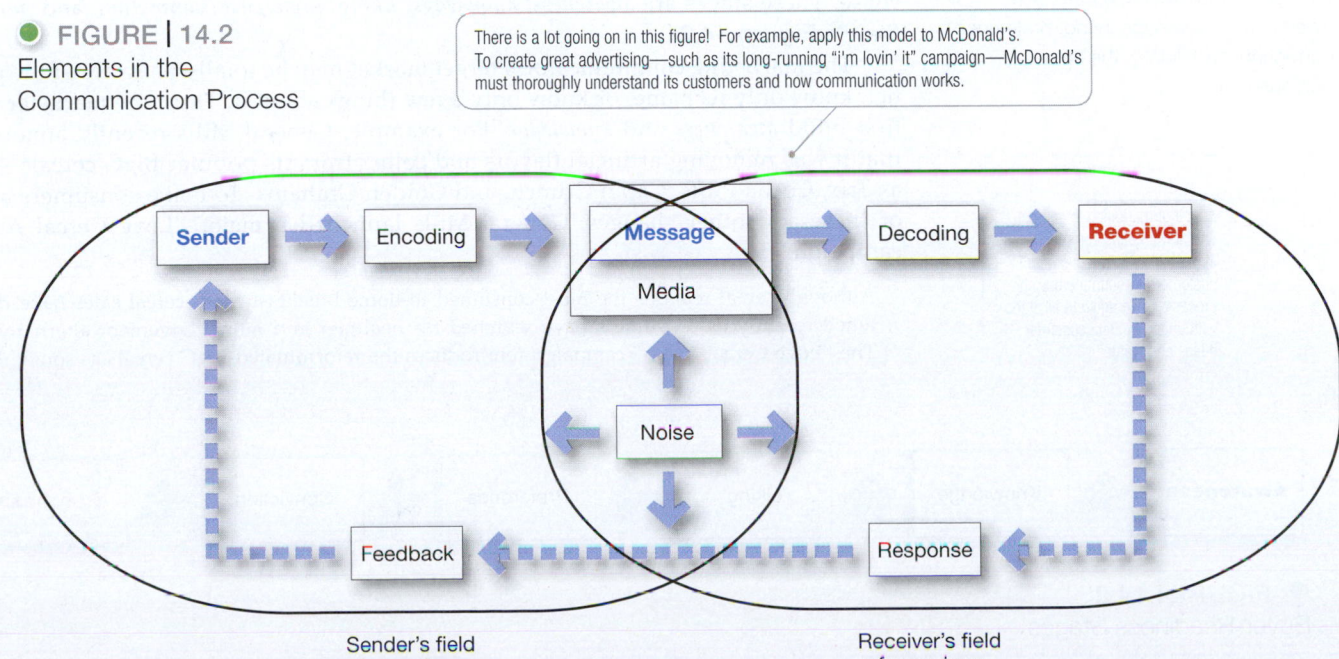

There is a lot going on in this figure! For example, apply this model to McDonald's. To create great advertising—such as its long-running "i'm lovin' it" campaign—McDonald's must thoroughly understand its customers and how communication works.

Sender → Encoding → Message / Media → Decoding → Receiver

Noise

Feedback ← Response

Sender's field of experience   Receiver's field of experience

with that of the receiver, the more effective the message is likely to be. Marketing communicators may not always *share* the customer's field of experience. For example, an advertising copywriter from one socioeconomic level might create ads for customers from another level—say, wealthy business owners. However, to communicate effectively, the marketing communicator must *understand* the customer's field of experience.

This model points out several key factors in good communication. Senders need to know what audiences they wish to reach and what responses they want. They must be good at encoding messages that take into account how the target audience decodes them. They must send messages through media that reach target audiences, and they must develop feedback channels so that they can assess an audience's response to the message. Also, in today's interactive media environment, companies must be prepared to "flip" the communications process—to become good receivers of and responders to messages sent by consumers.

Author Comment | Now that we understand how communication works, it's time to turn all of those promotion mix elements into an actual marketing communications program.

Steps in Developing Effective Marketing Communication

We now examine the steps in developing an effective integrated communications and promotion program. Marketers must do the following: identify the target audience, determine the communication objectives, design a message, choose the media through which to send the message, select the message source, and collect feedback.

Identifying the Target Audience

A marketing communicator starts with a clear target audience in mind. The audience may be current users or potential buyers, those who make the buying decision or those who influence it. The audience may be individuals, groups, special publics, or the general public. The target audience will heavily affect the communicator's decisions on *what* will be said, *how* it will be said, *when* it will be said, *where* it will be said, and *who* will say it.

Determining the Communication Objectives

Once the target audience has been defined, marketers must determine the desired response. Of course, in many cases, they will seek a *purchase* response. But purchase may result only after a lengthy consumer decision-making process. The marketing communicator needs to know where the target audience now stands and to what stage it needs to be moved. The target audience may be in any of six **buyer-readiness stages**, the stages consumers normally pass through on their way to making a purchase. These stages are *awareness, knowledge, liking, preference, conviction,* and *purchase* (see ● **Figure 14.3**).

Buyer-readiness stages
The stages consumers normally pass through on their way to a purchase: awareness, knowledge, liking, preference, conviction, and, finally, the actual purchase.

The marketing communicator's target market may be totally unaware of the product, know only its name, or know only a few things about it. Thus, the marketer must first build *awareness* and *knowledge*. For example, General Mills recently announced that it was removing artificial flavors and colors from its popular BigG cereals—such as Trix, Cocoa Puffs, Cap'n Crunch, and Golden Grahams. To make consumers aware of these and other changes, General Mills launched a major "Love Cereal Again" campaign:

A goal of marketing in general, and of marketing communications in particular, is to move target customers through the buying process. Once again, it all starts with understanding customer needs and wants.

Although cereal remains the most-consumed in-home breakfast food, cereal sales have flattened recently as consumers have searched for healthier and more convenient alternatives. The "Love Cereal Again" campaign reintroduces the reformulated BigG cereals as something

● FIGURE | 14.3
Buyer-Readiness Stages

● **Moving customers through the buyer-readiness stages:** To create awareness, knowledge, preference, and purchase for its newly reformulated BigG cereals, General Mills launched a major "Love Cereal Again" campaign.

Used with permission of General Mills Marketing, Inc., Tupelo Penningroth (talent) and Eric Fell (talent).

that parents can once again love. ● One 30-second TV ad shows variations on a familiar family scene—a young child asking a parent to do something again—"Do it again! Again!" It finishes with a father throwing a handful of Trix in the air and catching the cereal in his mouth as his daughter enthusiastically urges him to do it again. The extensive "Love Cereal Again" campaign, wrapped in the nostalgia of childhood breakfast, uses a broad range of traditional, digital, mobile, social, and in-store media to quickly create awareness and knowledge across the entire market.[8]

Assuming that target consumers *know* about a product, how do they *feel* about it? Almost all American consumers know about Trix, Cocoa Puffs, and other BigG cereals. These brands have been around since the late 1950s. General Mills wants to move buyers through successively stronger stages of feelings toward the revamped cereals. These stages include *liking* (feeling favorable about BigG cereals), *preference* (preferring the BigG cereals to competing brands), and *conviction* (believing that BigG cereals are the best cereals for them).

General Mills marketers use a combination of promotion mix tools to create positive feelings and conviction. Initial TV commercials help build anticipation and an emotional brand connection. Images, text, and videos on General Mills' social media sites engage, entertain, and educate potential buyers on the reformulation of the cereal products. Press releases and other PR activities help keep the buzz going about the products. A packed microsite (www.generalmills.com/cereal) provides additional information and buying opportunities.

Finally, some members of the target market might be convinced about the product but not quite get around to making the *purchase*. The communicator must lead these consumers to take the final step. To help reluctant consumers over such hurdles, General Mills might offer buyers special promotional prices (coupons, in-store discounts, and special offers) and support the product with comments and reviews from customers at its web and social media sites and elsewhere.

Of course, marketing communications alone cannot create positive feelings and purchases for BigG cereals. The cereal itself must provide superior value for customers. In fact, outstanding marketing communications can actually speed the demise of a poor product. The more quickly potential buyers learn about a poor product, the more quickly they become aware of its faults. Thus, good marketing communications call for "good deeds followed by good words." For example, to ensure that the healthier versions of its old BigG favorites would succeed, before introducing the reformulated versions, General Mills researched 69 colors and 86 flavors, did 98 consumer tastings, completed 301 recipe experiments, and spent 140 hours listening to customers about the products.

Designing a Message

Having defined the desired audience response, the communicator then turns to developing an effective message. Ideally, the message should get *attention*, hold *interest*, arouse *desire*, and obtain *action* (a framework known as the *AIDA model*). In practice, few messages take the consumer all the way from awareness to purchase, but the AIDA framework suggests the desirable qualities of a good message.

When putting a message together, the marketing communicator must decide what to say (*message content*) and how to say it (*message structure* and *format*).

Message Content. The marketer has to figure out an appeal or theme that will produce the desired response. There are three types of appeals: rational, emotional, and moral. *Rational appeals* relate to the audience's self-interest. They show that the product will produce the desired benefits. Examples are messages showing a product's quality, economy, value, or performance. Thus, an ad for Aleve makes this matter-of-fact claim: "More pills doesn't mean more pain relief. Aleve has the strength to keep back, body, and arthritis pain away all day with fewer pills than Tylenol." And a Weight Watchers' ad states this simple fact: "The diet secret to end all diet secrets is that there is no diet secret."

Emotional appeals attempt to stir up either negative or positive emotions that can motivate purchase. Communicators may use emotional appeals ranging from love, joy, and humor to fear and guilt. Advocates of emotional messages claim that they attract more attention and create more belief in the sponsor and the brand. The idea is that consumers often feel before they think, and persuasion is emotional in nature.

Good storytelling in a commercial often strikes an emotional chord. For example, rather than focusing only on the nuts and bolts and mileage information found in many car ads, an Audi Super Bowl 50 ad, called "The Commander," played to consumer's emotions: [9]

> "The Commander" draws on nostalgia, sentiment, and father-and-son relationships. It opens with depressed former astronaut whose life has seemingly passed him by. His son drops in to check on him, then takes him outside and offers him the keys to his Audi R8 V10 Plus—Audi's highest-performing car—which can reach speeds of 205 miles per hour. As he drives the Audi, the father is transported back to the best moments of his life, launching once again into the unknown, all to the soundtrack of David Bowie's "Starman." The commercial effectively tugged at the human spirit while reinforcing the Audi's extreme performance credentials. According to one journalist, the commercial created "the melancholy that comes from watching a man whose best days in life have already passed by, and a resolution in watching him be his younger, courageous self." By pinging viewer emotions, "The Commander" placed in the top 10 on the *USA Today* Ad Meter and received more than 8 million views on YouTube in less than one month.

Moral appeals are directed to an audience's sense of what is "right" and "proper." They are often used to urge people to support social causes, such as a cleaner environment or aid to the disadvantaged. For example, a Colgate ad campaign urges people to "Close the tap while brushing" their teeth to conserve water. One ad shows a young boy in a developing economy with a water bucket atop his head, noting, "What you waste in two minutes is all his family needs for a day."

Message Structure. Marketers must also decide how to handle three message structure issues. The first is whether to draw a conclusion or leave it to the audience. Research suggests that, in many cases, rather than drawing a conclusion, the advertiser is better off asking questions and letting buyers come to their own conclusions.

The second message structure issue is whether to present the strongest arguments first or last. Presenting them first gets strong attention but may lead to an anticlimactic ending.

The third message structure issue is whether to present a one-sided argument (mentioning only the product's strengths) or a two-sided argument (touting the product's strengths while also admitting its shortcomings). Usually, a one-sided argument is more effective in sales presentations—except when audiences are highly educated or likely to hear opposing claims or when the communicator has a negative association to overcome. In this spirit, Heinz once ran the message "Heinz Ketchup is slow good," and Listerine ran the message "Listerine tastes bad twice a day." In such cases, two-sided messages can enhance an advertiser's credibility and make buyers more resistant to competitor attacks.

Message Format. The marketing communicator also needs a strong *format* for the message. In a print ad, the communicator has to decide on the headline, copy, illustration, and colors. To attract attention, advertisers can use novelty and contrast; eye-catching pictures and headlines; distinctive formats; message size and position; and color, shape, and movement. For example, Reese's Peanut Butter Cup ads are bold and simple. They feature the brand's familiar orange, yellow, and brown colors with text overlaying images of the classic candy. ● They feature clever headlines that unite the candy's two distinctive

Message format: To attract attention, advertisers can use novelty and contrast, eye-catching images and headlines, and distinctive formats, as in this Reese's ad.

The Hershey Company

Personal communication channels
Channels through which two or more people communicate directly with each other, including face-to-face, on the phone, via mail or email, or even through an internet "chat."

Word-of-mouth influence
The impact of the personal words and recommendations of trusted friends, family, associates, and other consumers on buying behavior.

Buzz marketing
Cultivating opinion leaders and getting them to spread information about a product or a service to others in their communities.

ingredients, such as "Chocolate and peanut butter walked into a bar. The rest is history." and "Ever since peanut butter hooked up with chocolate, peanut butter still talks to jelly, but the relationship is very strained."

Presenters plan every detail carefully, from start to finish. If the message is to be communicated by television or video, the communicator must incorporate motion, pace, and sound. If the message is carried on the product or its package, the communicator must watch texture, scent, color, size, and shape. For example, color alone can significantly enhance message recognition for a brand—think about Target (red), McDonald's (yellow and red), John Deere (green and yellow), Twitter (blue), or UPS (brown). Thus, in designing effective marketing communications, marketers must consider color and other seemingly unimportant details carefully.

Choosing Communication Channels and Media

The communicator must now select the *channels of communication*. There are two broad types of communication channels: *personal* and *nonpersonal*.

Personal Communication Channels. In **personal communication channels**, two or more people communicate directly with each other. They might communicate face-to-face, on the phone, via mail or email, or even through texting or an internet chat. Personal communication channels are effective because they allow for personal addressing and feedback.

Some personal communication channels are controlled directly by the company. For example, company salespeople contact business buyers. But other personal communications about the product may reach buyers through channels not directly controlled by the company. These channels might include independent experts—consumer advocates, bloggers, and others—making statements to buyers. Or they might be neighbors, friends, family members, associates, or other consumers talking to target buyers, in person or via social media or other interactive media. This last channel, **word-of-mouth influence**, has considerable effect in many product areas.

Personal influence carries great weight, especially for products that are expensive, risky, or highly visible. One survey found that recommendations from friends and family are far and away the most powerful influence on consumers worldwide: More than 80 percent of consumers said friends and family are the number-one influence on their awareness and purchase. Another study found that 72 percent of consumers cited online reviews and trusted sources of buying information. Trust in ads ran from about 63 percent to only 36 percent, depending on the medium.[10] Is it any wonder, then, that few consumers buy a big-ticket item before checking out what existing users have to say about the product at a site such as Amazon.com? Who hasn't made an Amazon purchase based on another customer's review or the "Customers who bought this also bought …" section or decided against purchase because of negative customer reviews?

Companies can take steps to put personal communication channels to work for them. For example, as we discussed in Chapter 5, they can create *opinion leaders* for their brands—people whose opinions are sought by others—by supplying influencers with the product on attractive terms or by educating them so that they can inform others. **Buzz marketing** involves cultivating opinion leaders and getting them to spread information about a product or a service to others in their communities. For example, Netflix recruits "Grammasters," influencers who have large Instagram followings. The Grammasters travel around the world taking photos and creating video content of familiar sets and scenes from popular original Netflix shows and posting them to Instagram, letting Netflix bingers engage even more deeply with their favorite Netflix series.[11]

● Social marketing firm BzzAgent takes a different approach to creating buzz. It creates customers for a client brand, then turns them into influential brand advocates:[12]

BzzAgent has assembled a volunteer army of natural-born buzzers, millions of actual shoppers around the world who are highly active in social media and who love to talk about and recommend products. Once a client signs on, BzzAgent searches its database and selects "agents" that fit the profiles of the product's target customers. Selected volunteers receive product samples, creating a personal brand experience. BzzAgent then urges the agents to share their honest opinions of the product through face-to-face conversations and via tweets, Facebook posts, online photo and video sharing, blogs, and other social sharing venues. If the product is good, the positive word of mouth spreads quickly. If the product is iffy—well, that's worth learning quickly as well. BzzAgent advocates have successfully buzzed the brands of hundreds of top marketing companies, from P&G, Nestle, Coca-Cola, and Estee Lauder to Kroger, Disney, and Dunkin' Donuts. BzzAgent's appeal is its authenticity. The agents aren't scripted. Instead, the company tells its advocates, "Here's the product; if you believe in it, say whatever you think. Bzz is no place for excessive, repetitive, or unauthentic posts."

● **Buzz marketing: Social marketing firm BzzAgent turns a brand's actual users into influential brand advocates.**

dunnhumby

Nonpersonal communication channels

Media that carry messages without personal contact or feedback, including major media, atmospheres, and events.

Nonpersonal Communication Channels. **Nonpersonal communication channels** are media that carry messages without personal contact or feedback. They include major media, atmospheres, and events. Major *media* include print media (newspapers, magazines, direct mail), broadcast media (television, radio), display media (billboards, signs, posters), and online media (email, company websites, and brand mobile and social media sites). *Atmospheres* are designed environments that create or reinforce the buyer's leanings toward buying a product. Thus, lawyers' offices and banks are designed to communicate confidence and other qualities that might be valued by clients. *Events* are staged occurrences that communicate messages to target audiences. For example, public relations departments arrange grand openings, shows and exhibits, public tours, and other events.

Nonpersonal communication affects buyers directly. In addition, using mass media often affects buyers indirectly by causing more personal communication. For example, communications might first flow from television, magazines, and other mass media to opinion leaders and then from these opinion leaders to others. Thus, opinion leaders step between the mass media and their audiences and carry messages to people who are less exposed to media. Interestingly, marketers often use nonpersonal communication channels to replace or stimulate personal communications by embedding consumer endorsements or word-of-mouth testimonials in their ads and other promotions.

Selecting the Message Source

In either personal or nonpersonal communication, the message's impact also depends on how the target audience views the communicator. Messages delivered by highly credible or popular sources are more persuasive. Thus, many food companies promote to doctors, dentists, and other health-care providers to motivate these professionals to recommend specific food products to their patients. And marketers hire celebrity endorsers—well-known athletes, actors, musicians, and even cartoon characters—to deliver their messages. A host of NBA superstars lend their images to brands such as Nike, McDonald's, and Coca-Cola. Actress Sophia Vergara speaks for CoverGirl, State Farm, Comcast, Rooms to Go, and other brands and has her own Kmart clothing line. Actor George Clooney loves his Nestle Nespresso expresso machine, and tennis great Serena Williams endorses Gatorade, Nike, and Beats By Dre.

But companies must be careful when selecting celebrities to represent their brands. Picking the wrong spokesperson can result in embarrassment and a tarnished image. For example, a dozen or more big brands—including Nike, Anheuser-Busch, Radio Shack, Oakley, Trek bikes, and Giro helmets—faced embarrassment when pro cyclist Lance Armstrong was stripped of his Tour de France titles and banned for life from competitive cycling for illegal use of performance-enhancing drugs. Previously considered a model brand spokesman, Armstrong once earned nearly $20 million in endorsement income in a single year. "Arranged marriages between brands and celebrities are inherently risky," notes one expert. "Ninety-nine percent of celebrities do a strong job for their brand partners," says another, "and 1 percent goes off the rails."[13] More than ever, it's important to pick the right celebrity for the brand.

Collecting Feedback

After sending the message or other brand content, the communicator must research its effect on the target audience. This involves asking target audience members whether they remember the content, how many times they saw it, what points they recall, how they felt about the content, and their past and present attitudes toward the brand and company. The communicator would also like to measure behavior resulting from the content—how many people bought the product, talked to others about it, or visited the store.

Feedback on marketing communications may suggest changes in the promotion program or in the product offer itself. For example, Macy's uses television and newspaper advertising to inform area consumers about its stores, services, and merchandising events. Suppose feedback research shows that 80 percent of all shoppers in an area recall seeing the store's ads and are aware of its merchandise and sales. Sixty percent of these aware shoppers have visited a Macy's store in the past month, but only 20 percent of those who visited were satisfied with the shopping experience.

These results suggest that although promotion is creating *awareness*, Macy's stores aren't giving consumers the *satisfaction* they expect. Therefore, Macy's needs to improve the shopping experience while staying with the successful communications program. In contrast, suppose research shows that only 40 percent of area consumers are aware of the store's merchandise and events, only 30 percent of those aware have shopped recently, but 80 percent of those who have shopped return soon to shop again. In this case, Macy's needs to strengthen its promotion program to take advantage of its power to create customer satisfaction in the store.

Author Comment In this section, we'll look at the promotion budget-setting process and at how marketers blend the various marketing communication tools into a smooth-functioning integrated promotion mix.

Setting the Total Promotion Budget and Mix

We have looked at the steps in planning and sending communications to a target audience. But how does the company determine its total *promotion budget* and the division among the major promotional tools to create the *promotion mix*? By what process does it blend the tools to create integrated marketing communications? We now look at these questions.

Setting the Total Promotion Budget

One of the hardest marketing decisions facing a company is how much to spend on promotion. John Wanamaker, the department store mogul, once said, "I know that half of my advertising is wasted, but I don't know which half. I spent $2 million for advertising, and I don't know if that is half enough or twice too much." ● For example, Coca-Cola spends hundreds of millions of dollars annually on advertising, but is that too little, just right, or too much? Thus, it is not surprising that industries and companies vary widely in how much they spend on promotion. Promotion spending may be 10–12 percent of sales for consumer packaged goods, 20 percent for cosmetics, and only 1.9 percent for household appliances. Within a given industry, both low and high spenders can be found.[14]

How does a company determine its promotion budget? Here, we look at four common methods used to set the total budget for advertising: the *affordable method*, the *percentage-of-sales method*, the *competitive-parity method*, and the *objective-and-task method*.

Affordable method
Setting the promotion budget at the level management thinks the company can afford.

Affordable Method

Some companies use the **affordable method**: They set the promotion budget at the level they think the company can afford. Small businesses often use this method, reasoning that

● Setting the promotion budget is one of the hardest decisions facing a company. Coca-Cola spends hundreds of millions of dollars annually, but is that too little, just right, or too much?

migstock / Alamy Stock Photo

Percentage-of-sales method
Setting the promotion budget at a certain percentage of current or forecasted sales or as a percentage of the unit sales price.

Competitive-parity method
Setting the promotion budget to match competitors' outlays.

Objective-and-task method
Developing the promotion budget by (1) defining specific promotion objectives, (2) determining the tasks needed to achieve these objectives, and (3) estimating the costs of performing these tasks. The sum of these costs is the proposed promotion budget.

the company cannot spend more on advertising than it has. They start with total revenues, deduct operating expenses and capital outlays, and then devote some portion of the remaining funds to advertising.

Unfortunately, this method of setting budgets completely ignores the effects of promotion on sales. It tends to place promotion last among spending priorities, even in situations in which advertising is critical to the firm's success. It leads to an uncertain annual promotion budget, which makes long-range market planning difficult. Although the affordable method can result in overspending on advertising, it more often results in underspending.

Percentage-of-Sales Method

Other companies use the **percentage-of-sales method**, setting their promotion budget at a certain percentage of current or forecasted sales. Or they budget a percentage of the unit sales price. The percentage-of-sales method is simple to use and helps management think about the relationships between promotion spending, selling price, and profit per unit.

Despite these claimed advantages, however, the percentage-of-sales method has little to justify it. It wrongly views sales as the *cause* of promotion rather than as the *result*. Although studies have found a positive correlation between promotional spending and brand strength, this relationship often turns out to be effect and cause, not cause and effect. Stronger brands with higher sales can afford the biggest ad budgets.

Thus, the percentage-of-sales budget is based on the availability of funds rather than on opportunities. It may prevent the increased spending sometimes needed to turn around falling sales. Because the budget varies with year-to-year sales, long-range planning is difficult. Finally, the method does not provide any basis for choosing a *specific* percentage, except what has been done in the past or what competitors are doing.

Competitive-Parity Method

Still other companies use the **competitive-parity method**, setting their promotion budgets to match competitors' outlays. They monitor competitors' advertising or get industry promotion spending estimates from publications or trade associations and then set their budgets based on the industry average.

Two arguments support this method. First, competitors' budgets represent the collective wisdom of the industry. Second, spending what competitors spend helps prevent promotion wars. Unfortunately, neither argument is valid. There are no grounds for believing that the competition has a better idea of what a company should be spending on promotion than does the company itself. Companies differ greatly, and each has its own special promotion needs. Finally, there is no evidence that budgets based on competitive parity prevent promotion wars.

Objective-and-Task Method

The most logical budget-setting method is the **objective-and-task method**, whereby the company sets its promotion budget based on what it wants to accomplish with promotion. This budgeting method entails (1) defining specific promotion objectives, (2) determining the tasks needed to achieve these objectives, and (3) estimating the costs of performing these tasks. The sum of these costs is the proposed promotion budget.

The advantage of the objective-and-task method is that it forces management to spell out its assumptions about the relationship between dollars spent and promotion results. But it is also the most difficult method to use. Often, it is hard to figure out which specific tasks will achieve the stated objectives. For example, suppose Samsung wants a 95-percent-awareness level for its latest smartphone model during the six-month introductory period. What specific advertising messages, marketing content, and media schedules should Samsung use to attain this objective? How much would this content and media cost? Samsung management must consider such questions, even though they are hard to answer.

Shaping the Overall Promotion Mix

The concept of integrated marketing communications suggests that the company must blend the promotion tools carefully into a coordinated *promotion mix*. But how does it determine what mix of promotion tools to use? Companies within the same industry differ greatly in the design of their promotion mixes. For example, cosmetics maker Mary Kay spends most of its promotion funds on personal selling and direct marketing, whereas competitor CoverGirl spends heavily on consumer advertising. We now look at factors that influence the marketer's choice of promotion tools.

> **Author Comment** | In this section, we'll look at how marketers blend the various marketing communication tools into a smooth-functioning, integrated, and engaging promotion mix.

The Nature of Each Promotion Tool

Each promotion tool has unique characteristics and costs. Marketers must understand these characteristics in shaping the promotion mix.

Advertising. Advertising can reach masses of geographically dispersed buyers at a low cost per exposure, and it enables the seller to repeat a message many times. Television advertising can reach huge audiences. For example, more than 111 million Americans watched the most recent Super Bowl, and as many as 18 million avid fans tuned in each week for the latest season of *NCIS*. What's more, a popular TV ad's reach can be extended through online and social media. ● For example, consider the commercial for Supercell's popular mobile game "Clash of Clans: Revenge" starring Liam Neeson, which aired during Super Bowl XLIX. In addition to the more than 100-plus million TV viewers, it became the most-viewed Super Bowl ad on YouTube for the year, capturing a stunning 82 million YouTube views by year's end. Thus, for companies that want to reach a mass audience, TV is the place to be.[15]

Beyond its reach, large-scale advertising says something positive about the seller's size, popularity, and success. Because of advertising's public nature, consumers tend to view advertised products as more legitimate. Advertising is also very expressive; it allows the company to dramatize its products through the artful use of visuals, print, sound, and color. On the one hand, advertising can be used to build up a long-term image for a product (such as Coca-Cola ads). On the other hand, advertising can trigger quick sales (as when Kohl's advertises weekend specials).

Advertising also has some shortcomings. Although it reaches many people quickly, mass-media advertising is impersonal and lacks the direct persuasiveness of company salespeople. For the most part, advertising can carry on only a one-way communication with an audience, and the audience does not feel that it has to pay attention or respond. In addition, advertising can be very costly. Although some advertising forms—such as newspaper, radio, or online advertising—can be done on smaller budgets, other forms, such as network TV advertising, require very large budgets. For example, the one-minute "Clash of Clans: Revenge" Super Bowl ad cost $9 million for media time alone, not counting the costs of producing the ad. That's $150,000 per tick of the clock.

● TV has vast reach: Supercell's "Clash of Clans: Revenge" ad during Super Bowl XLIX drew 100-plus million TV viewers and triggered tens of millions of online views and shares.

IanDagnall Computing / Alamy Stock Photo

Personal Selling. Personal selling is the most effective tool at certain stages of the buying process, particularly in building up buyers' preferences, convictions, and actions. It involves personal interaction between two or more people, so each person can observe the other's needs and characteristics and make quick adjustments. Personal selling also allows all kinds of customer relationships to spring up, ranging from matter-of-fact selling relationships to personal friendships. An effective salesperson keeps the customer's interests at heart to build a long-term relationship by solving a customer's problems. Finally, with personal selling, the buyer usually feels a greater need to listen and respond, even if the response is a polite "No, thank you."

These unique qualities come at a cost, however. A sales force requires a longer-term commitment than does advertising—advertising can be turned up or down, but the size of a sales force is harder to change. Personal selling is also the company's most expensive promotion tool, costing companies on average $600 or more per sales call, depending on the industry.[16] U.S. firms spend up to three times as much on personal selling as they do on advertising.

Sales Promotion. Sales promotion includes a wide assortment of tools—coupons, contests, discounts, premiums, and others—all of which have many unique qualities. They attract consumer attention, engage consumers, offer strong incentives to purchase, and can be used to dramatize product offers and boost sagging sales. Sales promotions invite and reward quick response. Whereas advertising says, "Buy our product," sales promotion says, "Buy it now." Sales promotion effects can be short lived, however, and often are not as effective as advertising or personal selling in building long-run brand preference and customer relationships.

Public Relations. Public relations is very believable—news stories, features, sponsorships, and events seem more real and believable to readers than ads do. PR can also reach many prospects who avoid salespeople and advertisements—the message gets to buyers as "news and events" rather than as a sales-directed communication. And, as with advertising, public relations can dramatize a company or product. Marketers tend to underuse public relations or use it as an afterthought. Yet a well-thought-out public relations campaign used with other promotion mix elements can be very effective and economical.

Direct and Digital Marketing. The many forms of direct and digital marketing—from direct mail, catalogs, and telephone marketing to online, mobile, and social media—all share some distinctive characteristics. Direct marketing is more targeted: It's usually directed to a specific customer or customer community. Direct marketing is immediate and personalized: Messages can be prepared quickly—even in real time—and tailored to appeal to individual consumers or brand groups. Finally, direct marketing is interactive: It allows a dialogue between the marketing team and the consumer, and messages can be altered depending on the consumer's response. Thus, direct and digital marketing are well suited to highly targeted marketing efforts, creating customer engagement, and building one-to-one customer relationships.

Promotion Mix Strategies

Marketers can choose from two basic promotion mix strategies: *push* promotion or *pull* promotion. ● **Figure 14.4** contrasts the two strategies. The relative emphasis given to the specific promotion tools differs for push and pull strategies. A **push strategy** involves "pushing" the product through marketing channels to final consumers. The producer directs its marketing activities (primarily personal selling and trade promotion) toward channel members to induce them to carry the product and promote it to final consumers. For example, John Deere does very little promoting of its lawn mowers, garden tractors, and other residential consumer products to final consumers. Instead, John Deere's sales force works with Lowe's, The Home Depot, independent dealers, and other channel members, who in turn push John Deere products to final consumers.

Using a **pull strategy**, the producer directs its marketing activities (primarily advertising, consumer promotion, and direct and digital media) toward final consumers to induce them to buy the product. For example, Unilever promotes its Axe grooming products directly to its young male target market using TV and print ads, web and social media brand sites, and other channels. If the pull strategy is effective, consumers will then demand the brand from retailers such as CVS, Walgreens, or Walmart, which will in turn demand it from Unilever. Thus, under a pull strategy, consumer demand "pulls" the product through the channels.

Push strategy
A promotion strategy that calls for using the sales force and trade promotion to push the product through channels. The producer promotes the product to channel members who in turn promote it to final consumers.

Pull strategy
A promotion strategy that calls for spending a lot on consumer advertising and promotion to induce final consumers to buy the product, creating a demand vacuum that "pulls" the product through the channel.

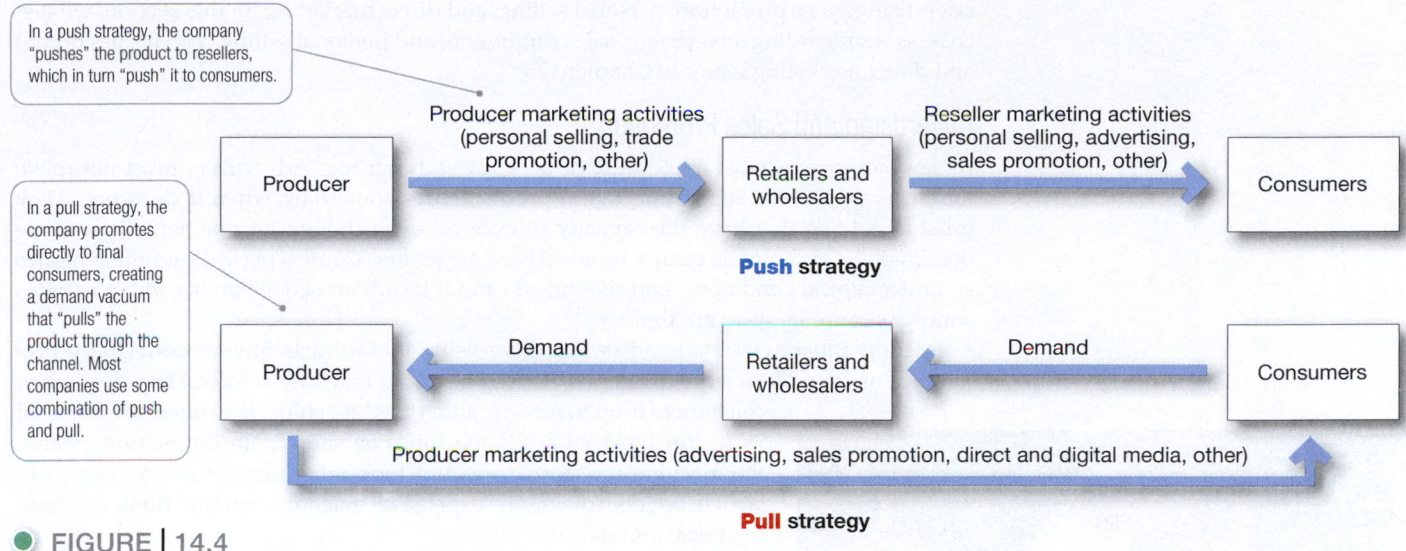

In a push strategy, the company "pushes" the product to resellers, which in turn "push" it to consumers.

In a pull strategy, the company promotes directly to final consumers, creating a demand vacuum that "pulls" the product through the channel. Most companies use some combination of push and pull.

Producer marketing activities (personal selling, trade promotion, other)

Producer → Retailers and wholesalers

Reseller marketing activities (personal selling, advertising, sales promotion, other)

Retailers and wholesalers → Consumers

Push strategy

Producer ← Demand ← Retailers and wholesalers ← Demand ← Consumers

Producer marketing activities (advertising, sales promotion, direct and digital media, other)

Pull strategy

● FIGURE | 14.4
Push versus Pull Promotion Strategy

Some industrial-goods companies use only push strategies; likewise, some direct marketing companies use only pull strategies. However, most large companies use some combination of both. For example, Unilever spends $8 billion worldwide each year on consumer marketing and sales promotions to create brand preference and pull customers into stores that carry its products.[17] At the same time, it uses its own and distributors' sales forces and trade promotions to push its brands through the channels so that they will be available on store shelves when consumers come calling.

Companies consider many factors when designing their promotion mix strategies, including the type of product and market. For example, the importance of different promotion tools varies between consumer and business markets. Business-to-consumer companies usually pull more, putting more of their funds into advertising, followed by sales promotion, personal selling, and then public relations. In contrast, business-to-business marketers tend to push more, putting more of their funds into personal selling, followed by sales promotion, advertising, and public relations.

Integrating the Promotion Mix

Having set the promotion budget and mix, the company must now take steps to see that each promotion mix element is smoothly integrated. Guided by the company's overall communications strategy, the various promotion elements should work together to carry the firm's unique brand messages and selling points. Integrating the promotion mix starts with customers. Whether it's advertising, personal selling, sales promotion, public relations, or digital and direct marketing, communications at each customer touch point must deliver consistent marketing content and positioning. An integrated promotion mix ensures that communications efforts occur when, where, and how *customers* need them.

To achieve an integrated promotion mix, all of the firm's functions must cooperate to jointly plan communications efforts. Many companies even include customers, suppliers, and other stakeholders at various stages of communications planning. Scattered or disjointed promotional activities across the company can result in diluted marketing communications impact and confused positioning. By contrast, an integrated promotion mix maximizes the combined effects of all a firm's promotional efforts.

Socially Responsible Marketing Communication

In shaping its promotion mix, a company must be aware of the many legal and ethical issues surrounding marketing communications. Most marketers work hard to communicate openly and honestly with consumers and resellers. Still, abuses may occur, and public policy makers have developed a substantial body of laws and regulations to govern advertising, sales promotion, personal selling, and direct marketing. In this section, we discuss issues regarding advertising, sales promotion, and personal selling. We discuss digital and direct marketing issues in Chapter 17.

Advertising and Sales Promotion

By law, companies must avoid false or deceptive advertising. Advertisers must not make false claims, such as suggesting that a product cures something when it does not. They must avoid ads that have the capacity to deceive, even though no one actually may be deceived. An automobile cannot be advertised as getting 32 miles per gallon unless it does so under typical conditions, and diet bread cannot be advertised as having fewer calories simply because its slices are thinner.

Sellers must avoid bait-and-switch advertising that attracts buyers under false pretenses. For example, a large retailer advertised a sewing machine at $179. However, when consumers tried to buy the advertised machine, the seller downplayed its features, placed faulty machines on showroom floors, understated the machine's performance, and took other actions in an attempt to switch buyers to a more expensive machine. Such actions are both unethical and illegal.

A company's trade promotion activities also are closely regulated. For example, under the Robinson-Patman Act, sellers cannot favor certain customers through their use of trade promotions. They must make promotional allowances and services available to all resellers on proportionately equal terms.

Beyond simply avoiding legal pitfalls, such as deceptive or bait-and-switch advertising, companies can use advertising and other forms of promotion to encourage and promote socially responsible programs, actions, and ideas. Companies in almost every industry now promote a wide range of social and environmental causes related to their brands (see Real Marketing 14.2). For example, Google recently launched a $50 million "Made with Code" marketing and advertising campaign that encourages young girls to pursue science and technology careers. The company found that 74 percent of middle school girls express interest in science, technology, engineering, and math (STEM), but by high school, less than 1 percent of girls plan to major in computer science. Through ads, dedicated digital and social media sites, events, and partnerships with not-for-profit organizations, Google's campaign promotes the idea that the things young girls love, from their smartphone apps to fashions to their favorite movies, are "made with code." "Simply put, code is a tool that lets you write your story with technology," says Google. "Girls start out with a love of science and technology, but lose it somewhere along the way. Let's help encourage that passion."[18]

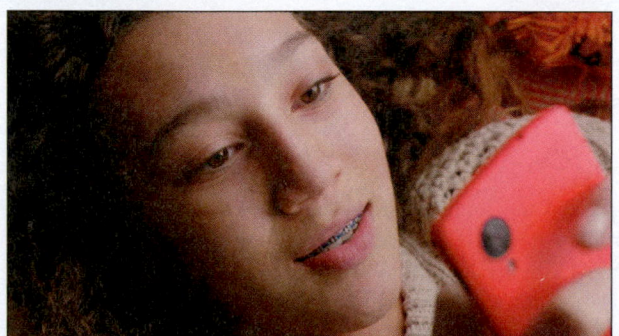

● **Promoting socially responsible programs and actions:** Google's broad-based "Made with Code" marketing and advertising campaign encourages young girls to pursue science and technology careers.

Google and the Google logo are registered trademarks of Google Inc., used with permission.

Personal Selling

A company's salespeople must follow the rules of "fair competition." Most states have enacted deceptive sales acts that spell out what is not allowed. For example, salespeople may not lie to consumers or mislead them about the advantages of buying a particular product. To avoid bait-and-switch practices, salespeople's statements must match advertising claims.

Different rules apply to consumers who are called on at home or who buy at a location that is not the seller's permanent place of business versus those who go to a store in search of a product. Because people who are called on may be taken by surprise and may be especially vulnerable to high-pressure selling techniques, the Federal Trade Commission (FTC) has adopted a *three-day cooling-off rule* to give special protection to customers who are not seeking products. Under this rule, customers who agree in their own homes, workplace, dormitory, or facilities rented by the seller on a temporary basis—such as hotel rooms, convention centers, and restaurants—to buy something costing more than $25 have 72 hours in which to cancel a contract or return merchandise and get their money back—no questions asked.

14.2 Doing Good with Advertising and Marketing

Real Marketing

Most companies today have built social responsibility into their corporate missions, and they use advertising and marketing to promote socially responsible programs, actions, and ideas. Rather than focusing only on profits, they recognize that company success is inexorably linked to the welfare of their customers and the world around them.

An all-time classic example is the long-running "Dove Campaign for Real Beauty," which set out to change stereotypical definitions of beauty with ads featuring candid and confident images of real women with all sorts of body types (not glamorous actresses or skinny models). "Our mission is to make more women feel beautiful every day by broadening the definition of beauty," says Dove. Over the years, the constantly evolving "Campaign for Real Beauty"—consisting of ads, heavily viewed digital videos, and other content—has done much to serve the cause of lifting women's self-esteem. And although the campaign has noble motives beyond sales and profits, it has also contributed greatly to Dove's success. During the first decade of the campaign, the brand's annual revenues grew from $2.5 billion to more than $4 billion.

Companies in almost every industry now support and promote a wide range of social and environmental causes. Chipotle's "Food with Integrity" campaign challenges factory farming and promotes organic, local, and family-farmed ingredients. Intel's "Girl Rising" campaign promotes education for girls around the world; Google's "Made with Code" campaign encourages young girls to pursue science and technology careers. And Apple's "Better" campaign raises awareness of important environmental issues because "it's our responsibility to make sure that while creating beautiful products, we're also caring for our beautiful planet."

Thus, more and more, companies are using advertising and marketing to take a stand on relevant social and environmental issues, not just to make a buck but because it's the right thing to do. Let's look more deeply into three successful campaigns promoting social responsibility.

AT&T: "It Can Wait"

As the texting-while-driving epidemic has worsened, AT&T—one of the nation's largest voice and data services providers—has stepped in with its "It Can Wait" campaign, which urges people to put away their phones while driving.

At the heart of the campaign is a slate of TV and digital ads that depict the horrific potential outcomes of using a phone while driving. One recent three-minute digital ad, "Close to Home," shows different people going about their day. One is a young mother out running errands with her daughter securely seat-belted in the back seat. She looks down briefly to check a social media post on her phone, inadvertently crosses the center line, and causes a head-on collision with an oncoming car. The ad is graphic and difficult to watch, but the message is clear: Even a quick glance at your phone while driving can have disastrous consequences. "It can wait," admonishes the ad.

Ads are just the beginning of the extensive "It Can Wait" campaign. AT&T also offers a DriveMode app that kicks in automatically while the car is rolling to silence texts and alerts and to notify senders that the user is behind the wheel. The campaign promotes the It Can Wait Pledge, by which people commit to keeping their eyes on the road and not their phones—almost 8 million people have taken the pledge so far. There's even an It Can Wait virtual reality simulator that puts people behind the wheel to experience smartphone-induced crashes. Other efforts include celebrity tweets and outreach sessions at schools.

With the help of dozens of partnering companies and media organizations, "It Can Wait" has garnered hundreds of millions of impressions. Now in its seventh year, the campaign appears to be helping. "We do surveys [that show] we are making a difference," says an AT&T marketer. "About a third of people say our no-texting-while-driving message has changed their behavior."

The Rainforest Alliance: "Follow the Frog"

Nonprofit organizations also rely heavily on advertising and promotion to market their social and environmental missions. Since 1987, the Rainforest Alliance—an international nonprofit conservation organization—has promoted the cause of minimizing harmful human impact on the environment. Companies committed to sustainable sourcing from farms and forests can earn the right to display the Rainforest Alliance Certified logo—with its signature green tree frog symbol—on their packages and promotional materials. The organization also offers sourcing assistance and training to help businesses improve their sustainability efforts.

In 2012, to boost awareness of pressing ecological challenges—such as deforestation, climate change, and water quality—the Rainforest Alliance launched an encompassing and clever promotional campaign called "Follow the Frog." The campaign began with an award-winning three-minute web video comically illustrating what people *don't* have to do to help the environment. The video features a young professional who goes to ecological extremes. He quits his job, leaves his wife and young child, and heads to the heart of the Amazon jungle, where he joins in a crusade against evil factions that are

YOU DON'T HAVE TO GO TO THE ENDS OF THE EARTH TO PROTECT THE PLANET

JUST FOLLOW THE FROG

By choosing products with the Rainforest Alliance Certified™ seal, you're supporting a sustainable future. Scan the QR code for an adventure-packed video to learn more.

Promoting social responsibility: The Rainforest Alliance's "Follow the Frog" promotional campaign boosts awareness of pressing ecological challenges and promotes the cause of minimizing harmful human impact on the environment.

Used with permission of the Rainforest Alliance. The Rainforest Alliance Certified™ seal is a trademark of the Rainforest Alliance.

destroying the environment. The video concludes that there's an easier way: "You don't have to go to the ends of the Earth to protect the planet. Just follow the frog" by choosing products that display the Rainforest Alliance Certified seal.

The "Follow the Frog" campaign now encompasses a wide range of marketing content and activities, from print ads, retail promotional materials, Follow the Frog events, and a Frog Blog to alliances with nearly 6,000 companies that display and promote the Rainforest Alliance Certified seal. The campaign has been effective. The initial video quickly captured more than 5 million YouTube views and 32,000 shares, was nominated for a Webby award for online video excellence, and won a TED award as the top Ad Worth Spreading in the social causes category. The overall campaign has increased consumer awareness and boosted the number of companies committing to sourcing from Rainforest Alliance Certified operations, including major brands such as Lipton, Mars, and McDonald's.

Always: "Like a Girl"

P&G's Always feminine hygiene brand is on a mission. Based on research showing that a girl's confidence plummets at puberty, Always launched a big-budget ad campaign aimed at changing the meaning of doing something "like a girl." The first "Like a Girl" ad used a reality show format, asking young women, men, boys, and girls to "show me what it looks like to run like a girl" or "fight like a girl" or "throw like a girl." The women, men, and boys portrayed the classic "feminine" stereotypes. Young girls, however, attacked the tasks with gusto, devoid of any negative connotations. "When did doing something 'like a girl' become an insult?" the ad asked. "Always wants to change that." The ad closed with inspirational images of girls running, throwing, and kicking with skill and confidence. "Let's make #RunLikeAGirl mean amazing things," concluded the ad.

When the "Like a Girl" ad ran during Super Bowl XLIX, viewer reaction was nothing short of spectacular. The ad placed first or second in virtually every major ad-rating poll, and it topped all other Super Bowl ads by a wide margin in social media mentions and sharing. Later in the year, "Like a Girl" took home an Emmy for most outstanding commercial and a Grand Prix award for best PR campaign at the Cannes international ad festival. In its first year, "Like a Girl" racked up an amazing 85 million views and more than a billion global impressions.

The Always "Like a Girl" effort has now expanded into a full-blown, ongoing educational and support campaign. "When you have a message that really addresses such an important and a real issue and it's done in a way that is very consistent with who you are as a brand, I think consumers want to engage with that," says P&G's vice president of global feminine care. "We have started an epic battle to show the world that doing things like a girl is downright amazing."

Sources: Ann-Christine Diaz, "The Story behind AT&T's Disturbing Phone Safety Ad," *Advertising Age*, July 27, 2015, http://adage.com/print/299678/; John McDermott, "AT&T's Anti-Texting Campaign: Lots of Impressions, Zero Success," *Digiday*, August 14, 2014, http://digiday.com/platforms/att-asks-twitter-whether-anti-texting-driving-campaign-working/; Paul Polizzotto, "Millennials Are Embracing Corporate Social Responsibility Campaigns," *Advertising Age*, December 18, 2015, http://adage.com/print/301796/; "Why That 'Like A Girl' Super Bowl Ad Was So Groundbreaking," *Huffington Post*, February 2, 2015, www.huffingtonpost.com/2015/02/02/always-super-bowl-ad_n_6598328.html; Sheila Shayon, "How P&G Is Making the Always #LikeAGirl Movement Unstoppable," *Brandchannel*, July 8, 2015, www.brandchannel.com/2015/07/08/pg-always-like-a-girl-070815/; and information from www.apple.com/environment/; www.itcanwait.com/all, www.rainforest-alliance.org/about; www.rainforest-alliance.org/followthefrog, and http://always.com/en-us, accessed October, 2016.

Much personal selling involves business-to-business trade. In selling to businesses, salespeople may not offer bribes to purchasing agents or others who can influence a sale. They may not obtain or use technical or trade secrets of competitors through bribery or industrial espionage. Finally, salespeople must not disparage competitors or competing products by suggesting things that are not true.

14 | Reviewing and Extending the Concepts

OBJECTIVES REVIEW AND KEY TERMS

Objectives Review

In this chapter, you learned how companies use integrated marketing communications (IMC) to communicate customer value. Modern marketing calls for more than just creating customer value by developing a good product, pricing it attractively, and making it available to target customers. Companies also must clearly and persuasively engage current and prospective consumers and *communicate* that value to them. To do this, they must blend five promotion mix tools, guided by a well-designed and implemented IMC strategy.

OBJECTIVE 14-1 Define the five promotion mix tools for communicating customer value. *(pp 400–401)*

A company's total *promotion mix*—also called its *marketing communications mix*—consists of the specific blend of *advertising, personal selling, sales promotion, public relations,* and *direct and digital marketing* tools that the company uses to engage consumers, persuasively communicate customer value, and build customer relationships. *Advertising* includes any paid form of nonpersonal presentation and promotion of ideas, goods, or services by an identified sponsor. In contrast, *public relations* focuses on building good relations with the company's various publics. *Personal selling* is personal presentation by the firm's sales force for the purpose of making sales and building customer relationships. Firms use *sales promotion* to provide short-term incentives to encourage the purchase or sale of a product or service. Finally, firms seeking immediate response from targeted individual customers use *direct and digital marketing* tools to engage directly with customers and cultivate relationships with them.

OBJECTIVE 14-2 Discuss the changing communications landscape and the need for integrated marketing communications. *(pp 401–406)*

The explosive developments in communications technology and changes in marketer and customer communication strategies have had a dramatic impact on marketing communications. Advertisers are now adding a broad selection of more-specialized and highly targeted media and content—including online, mobile, and social media—to reach smaller customer segments with more-personalized, interactive messages. As they adopt richer but more fragmented media and promotion mixes to reach their diverse markets, they risk creating a communications hodgepodge for consumers. To prevent this, companies have adopted the concept of *integrated marketing communications (IMC)*. Guided by an overall IMC strategy, the company works out the roles that the various promotional tools and marketing content will play and the extent to which each will be used. It carefully coordinates the promotional activities and the timing of when major campaigns take place.

OBJECTIVE 14-3 Outline the communication process and the steps in developing effective marketing communications. *(pp 406–413)*

The communication process involves nine elements: two major parties (sender, receiver), two communication tools (message,

media), four communication functions (encoding, decoding, response, and feedback), and noise. To communicate effectively, marketers must understand how these elements combine to communicate value to target customers.

In preparing marketing communications, the communicator's first task is to *identify the target audience* and its characteristics. Next, the communicator has to determine the *communication objectives* and define the response sought, whether it be *awareness, knowledge, liking, preference, conviction*, or *purchase*. Then a *message* should be constructed with an effective content and structure. *Media* must be selected, both for personal and nonpersonal communication. The communicator must find highly credible sources to deliver messages. Finally, the communicator must collect *feedback* by watching how much of the market becomes aware, tries the product, and is satisfied in the process.

OBJECTIVE 14-4 Explain the methods for setting the promotion budget and factors that affect the design of the promotion mix. *(pp 413–420)*

The company must determine how much to spend for promotion. The most popular approaches are to spend what the company can afford, use a percentage of sales, base promotion on competitors' spending, or base it on an analysis and costing of the communication objectives and tasks. The company has to divide the *promotion budget* among the major tools to create the *promotion mix*. Companies can pursue a *push* or a *pull* promotional strategy—or a combination of the two. People at all levels of the organization must be aware of the many legal and ethical issues surrounding marketing communications. Companies must work hard and proactively at communicating openly, honestly, and agreeably with their customers and resellers.

Key Terms

OBJECTIVE 14-1

Promotion mix (or marketing communications mix) (p 400)
Advertising (p 401)
Sales promotion (p 401)
Personal selling (p 401)
Public relations (PR) (p 401)
Direct and digital marketing (p 401)

OBJECTIVE 14-2

Content marketing (p 403)
Integrated marketing communications (IMC) (p 403)

OBJECTIVE 14-3

Buyer-readiness stages (p 408)
Personal communication channels (p 411)
Word-of-mouth influence (p 411)
Buzz marketing (p 411)
Nonpersonal communication channels (p 412)

OBJECTIVE 14-4

Affordable method (p 413)
Percentage-of-sales method (p 414)

Competitive-parity method (p 414)
Objective-and-task method (p 414)
Push strategy (p 416)
Pull strategy (p 416)

DISCUSSION AND CRITICAL THINKING

MyMarketingLab
Go to **mymktlab.com** to complete the problems marked with this icon ✪.

Discussion Questions

14-1 Name and describe the five major promotion tools used in a company's marketing communications mix. (AASCB: Communication)

✪ **14-2** Discuss content marketing and how marketers are using a new framework that builds on how and by whom marketing content is created, controlled, and distributed. (AACSB: Communication)

14-3 What is integrated marketing communications (IMC), and how does a company go about implementing it? (AACSB: Communication)

✪ **14-4** Discuss the two broad types of communication channels used by marketing communicators to distribute messages. (AACSB: Communication)

14-5 How does a company determine its promotional budget? (AACSB: Communication)

Critical Thinking Exercises

✪ **14-6** Identify a new consumer food or beverage product. Using the major promotion tools, design a promotion campaign for the product. Identify how you are using both push and pull strategies. (AACSB: Communication; Use of IT; Reflective Thinking)

14-7 In a small group, select an advertisement that appropriately addresses each aspect of the communication process shown in Figure 14.2. Illustrate how each element is represented in the company's advertisement. Discuss how the advertisement, by itself, does or does not constitute effective marketing communication for the product. (AACSB: Communication; Reflective Thinking)

14-8 According to a Nielsen Global Survey, consumers are more likely to support companies that they perceive as socially responsible. Find three examples of advertisements that incorporate socially responsible marketing messages. Do these advertisements increase your likelihood of buying from the company sponsoring them? Explain. (AACSB: Communication; Ethical Reasoning; Reflective Thinking)

APPLICATIONS AND CASES

Online, Mobile, and Social Media Marketing #withoutshoes

Blake Mycoskie launched TOMS with a commitment to donate one pair of shoes for every pair sold. In May 2015, TOMS took to the social media with a campaign to extend its philanthropic mission. For each Instagram post showing bare feet and using the hashtag #withoutshoes, TOMS donated a pair of shoes to a child in need. The campaign demonstrated the company's commitment to its cause while expertly piggybacking on a common Instagram trend. The #withoutshoes campaign resulted in the donation of 296,243 pairs of shoes and won a Silver Anvil Award of Excellence from the Public Relations Society of America. TOMS's many one-for-one programs for shoes and now necessities such as eyewear, water, and even "kindness" (anti-bullying training) help build strong customer relationships and brand community.

14-9 Explain how TOMS used public relations for the #withoutshoes campaign as part of the company's promotion mix. It what ways did this tool helped promote TOMS? (AACSB: Communication, Reflective Thinking)

14-10 Research the internet for more information on how TOMS engages consumers using promotion tools. Choose two specific campaigns and evaluate TOMS's promotion strategies for both. (AACSB: Communication, Reflective Thinking, Use of IT)

Marketing Ethics An Ethical Promotion?

A Unilever brand in Thailand ran into some problems with one of its promotion campaigns, the "Citra 3D Brightening Girls Search." Citra Pearly White UV Body Lotion is marketed as a skin-whitening product. Skin whitening is popular in many Asian countries because lighter skin color is associated with higher economic status. However, this belief is not created by marketers. Anthropologists point out that Asian cultures, and Thailand in particular, have long histories of associating darker skin tones with outdoor peasants and field workers and lighter skin tones with higher socioeconomic status. Citra's advertising was criticized because it showed two female students—one lighter-skinned than the other—and asked them what would make them "outstanding in uniform." The darker girl seemed confused and didn't answer, while the lighter girl answered with Citra's product slogan. After considerable social media outcry, Citra pulled the ad, but it did not stop a related scholarship competition. The competition offered a 100,000 baht ($3,200) prize for the college student best demonstrating "product efficacy" – that is, the whitest skin. The company claims its products help people feel good about themselves and enhance their self-esteem.

14-11 Because lighter skin and skin whitening are popular in Thailand, is it wrong for marketers to offer and promote products that encourage this belief and behavior? Explain why or why not. (AACSB: Communication; Reflective Thinking; Ethical Reasoning)

14-12 Find other examples of marketers creating controversy by promoting culture-based products that could be viewed as inappropriate by others outside of that culture. (AACSB: Communication; Reflective Thinking)

Marketing by the Numbers Advertising-to-Sales Ratios

Using the percent of sales method, an advertiser sets its budget at a certain percentage of current or forecasted sales. However, determining what percentage to use is not always clear. Many marketers look at industry averages and competitor spending for comparisons. Websites and trade publications publish data regarding industry averages to guide marketers in setting the percentage to use.

14-13 Find industry advertising-to-sales ratio data. Why do some industries have higher advertising-to-sales ratios than others? (AACSB: Communication; Use of IT; Reflective Thinking)

14-14 Determine the advertising-to-sales ratios for two competing companies and compare them to the industry advertising-to-sales ratio found above. Why do you think there is a difference between competitors and the industry average? (AACSB: Communication; Use of IT; Analytical Reasoning; Reflective Thinking)

Video Case OXO

You might know OXO for its well-designed, ergonomic kitchen gadgets. But OXO's expertise at creating handheld tools that look great *and* work well has led it to expand into products for bathrooms, garages, offices, babies' rooms, and even medicine cabinets. In the past, this award-winning manufacturer has managed to move its products into almost every home in the United States by relying on a consistent and in some cases nontraditional marketing strategy.

But in a highly competitive and turbulent market, OXO has focused on evaluating and modifying its marketing strategy in order to grow the brand. This video demonstrates how OXO is using strategic planning to ensure that its marketing strategy results in the best marketing mix for the best and most profitable customers.

After viewing the video featuring OXO, answer the following questions:

14-15 What is OXO's mission?

14-16 What are some of the market conditions that have led OXO to reevaluate its marketing strategy?

14-17 How has OXO modified its marketing mix? Are these changes in line with its mission?

Company Case Volvo Trucks: Integrated Marketing Communications of Epic Proportions

When you think of Volvo, you probably think of the boxy and sedate, practical and safe automobiles made in Sweden—the ones professors and young, married couples with children use to cart their groceries home. This story is about another Volvo—the Volvo Group, maker of trucks. And not just SUVs or pickups, mind you. We're talking about full-sized, heavy-duty semi-trucks and trailers, mining and construction vehicles, and buses. Once one and the same with Volvo cars. the Volvo Group is now a separate company and one of the largest producers of commercial trucks in the world under various brands including Renault Trucks, Mack Trucks, UD Trucks, and its largest, Volvo Trucks.

A few years ago, Volvo Trucks faced a big challenge. It was preparing for its first major product launch in 20 years—five new truck models in one year. With that launch, Volvo Trucks needed an integrated communication strategy that would achieve a lofty goal—to get people worldwide to talk about its commercial trucks. Volvo Trucks wasn't just interested in creating buzz among its normal target set of corporate truck buyers. It wanted to appeal to regular folks in a way that would heighten their awareness of the brand, elevate the brand's cool factor, and get people talking, sharing, and supporting the brand from Singapore to Swaziland. How it accomplished this—and how Volvo Trucks keeps the brand in the public eye today—is an advertising coup of epic proportions.

A Consumer Approach

Typically, when a B-to-B company wants to promote a new product, it goes through an agency that specializes in its industry. That's what Volvo Trucks did previously, working with various agencies through different types of traditional media including print advertising, PR, and direct mail. But as it prepared to unleash its all-new line of heavy-duty trucks, the Swedish trucking firm realized that the media landscape had fundamentally changed since its last major launch. And the new media world called for a different approach to broadcasting the brand's message—something unique that would outsmart competitors.

Rather than go through a B-to-B agency with experience in commercial trucks, Volvo Trucks enlisted Forsman & Bodenfors—one of Sweden's leading creative agencies with a history of groundbreaking consumer campaigns for the likes of IKEA, UNICEF, and Volvo Cars. As Forsman & Bodenfors developed the campaign, its research revealed two important insights about commercial trucks. First, long-haul truckers love their trucks, forming an emotional connection with them that resembles the relationship between regular drivers and their daily rides. Second, a large volume of influencers have an impact on truck-buying decisions—a set that includes friends, family members, colleagues, bosses, and even the clients and businesses whose products the trucks carry.

Armed with these insights, the team set out to create an integrated campaign that would amaze experienced truckers by showcasing the new trucks' features while simultaneously captivating the general public with breathtaking demonstrations. Traditional television advertising was out of reach budgetwise. It was also not a good fit for the kinds of messages the campaign needed to communicate or the types of buzz the agency hoped to create. So Forsman & Bodenfors turned to social media. The result was a campaign dubbed "Live Tests," a fully integrated promotional effort rooted in a series of documentary-style films designed to have impact on a Hollywood scale.

Appealing to the Masses with "Live Tests"

The first film to go up on Volvo Trucks' YouTube channel was "The Ballerina," a three-minute "making of"–style video in which world record–holding highliner Faith Dickey walked a wire between two speeding Volvo trucks, completing the run just in time to duck as the trucks entered two opposing sides of a tunnel, violently snapping the tight wire. The video was designed to demonstrate the tremendous steering precision of the new Volvo trucks. Although the "Live Tests" campaign eventually panned out into a multi-feature, long-running campaign, it was only after "The Ballerina" was posted that the campaign's strategy began to take shape. "When you create for YouTube, you can't plan too much in advance because you really don't know how… popular an idea or piece of film will be," recounts Bjorn Engström, senior partner with the ad agency.

After that first successful effort, Volvo Trucks and the agency created a set of five more films. In "The Technician," a Volvo semi roars over the head of an engineer buried up to his neck in sand, demonstrating the truck's 12-inch ground clearance. "The Hook" provides a dramatic testimonial of the strength of Volvo truck tow hooks, given by Volvo Trucks president Claes Nilsson as he stands perched atop a Volvo truck with trailer suspended high above a harbor. "Hamster" demonstrates "ease of steering," with a tiny hamster named Charlie steering a huge mining dump truck by running on an exercise wheel attached to the truck's steering wheel. And in an interactive 360-degree experience illustrating maneuverability, "The Chase" provides the point of view of a Volvo truck as it runs from bulls through the tight streets of a Spanish town.

The timed release of each of these videos was accompanied by various supporting promotional efforts designed to extend the campaign's message and drive traffic to YouTube. Volvo Truck sponsored print ads in the trucking press as well as interviews with Volvo engineers, released in both print and video. The videos had another purpose—to increase the social media fan base for Volvo Trucks, building toward the campaign's grand finale. In little more than a year and on the eve of the debut of the campaign's dramatic video climax, the number of Volvo Trucks YouTube subscribers had increased 2,300 percent to 85,000 while the Volvo Trucks Facebook page experienced a 1,700 percent increase in fans to 290,000.

But it was the final installment in the first round of the "Live Tests" campaign that hit the ball out of the park. In "Epic Split," martial arts superstar Jean-Claude Van Damme stood with one foot on the mirrors of two side-by-side shiny new gold Volvo trucks as they moved progressively farther apart in reverse, stabilizing their distance at the point where the Muscles from Brussels is poised in full and perfect splits. The dramatic video highlighted Volvo Dynamic Steering—an electronically controlled mechanism that adjusts 2,000 times per second for unsurpassed precision. Within a month, the video had drawn 60 million YouTube hits, going on to become the most viral non–Super Bowl automotive ad of all time. Also by the end of the month, Volvo Trucks delivered 31 percent more trucks to dealers than it had for the same month the previous year.

The Synergy of IMC

Although each piece of the "Live Tests" campaign was laudable in itself, the sum of the parts produced a result more impressive than any of the stunts performed in the campaign videos. According to Forsman & Bodenfors, the campaign produced more than 100 million video views, 8 million social media shares, and more than 20,000 editorial features. It also produced thousands of video spoofs good for another 50 million views, including "Greetings from Chuck," a video for the holidays featuring a CGI Chuck Norris performing splits on the wings of two Lockheed C-5s while a lit-up, tree-shaped pyramid of military paratroopers stood on his head. In all, the media impact of the campaign was valued at more than $170 million. The campaign received so many awards—including the Creative Effectiveness Grand Prix at Cannes—that *Advertising Age* dubbed Volvo Trucks the "Most Awarded Advertiser of the Year."

The campaign also produced measurable behaviors among target customers. In a survey of 2,200 commercial truck owners, half of those who saw the videos indicated they were more likely to choose Volvo for their next purchase, while a third of respondents had either contacted a dealer or visited a Volvo Trucks website. "If we talk to our salespeople in our 140 markets all over the world," said Anders Vilhelmsson, PR director for Volvo Trucks, "they tell us very often one of the first things prospective customers bring up in conversation is the viral film."

With all this success achieved on a shoestring budget, it's no surprise that Volvo Trucks extended the "Live Tests" campaign. Following the same model set by the first six videos, the team produced some unlikely pieces, including a race between a Volvo tractor and a supercar as well as a hidden-camera exposé showing the reaction of a valet as a Volvo truck pulls up in front of a black-tie casino. But the most recent video became one of the most successful entries of the campaign to date. "Look Who's Driving" puts a darling British four-year-old behind the remote controls of the Volvo FMX—a dump truck that the ad proclaims is "the toughest truck we ever built."

Rather than just a clever series of stunts for the sake of stunts, "Live Tests" pulled off a monumental task. By selecting features with high relevance to both its new models and the target audience, Volvo communicated those features through stories that captivated viewers everywhere. The campaign achieved the goal of successfully launching five new trucks, with phase two ultimately producing a social media fan base double the size of the one Volvo Trucks had achieved following the first phase of the campaign. The campaign has also helped Volvo Trucks to achieve record sales and market share worldwide. Even more amazing, Volvo Trucks did all that on a shoestring budget. In the world of integrated marketing communications, "Live Tests" is truly an epic.

Questions for Discussion

14-18 Which promotional mix elements does Volvo Trucks use?

14-19 How does the "Live Tests" campaign demonstrate the characteristic of integrated marketing communication? What grade would you give "Live Tests" on integration effectiveness?

14-20 Is the consumer marketing approach taken by "Live Tests" appropriate for all B-to-B marketers? Explain.

14-21 What challenges does Volvo Trucks face in maintaining the success it has achieved with this campaign?

Sources: Steve Skinner, "Sweden's Secrets to Success with Trucks," *Owner Driver*, June 22, 2016, www.ownerdriver.com.au/industry-news/1606/swedens-secrets-to-success-with-trucks/; Tessa Wegert, "How Volvo Trucks Turned B2B Video into a Viral Art Form," *Contently*, March 18, 2016, https://contently.com/strategist/2016/03/08/volvo-trucks-turned-b2b-video-viral-artform/; David Griner, "A 4-Year-Old Pilots a Volvo Truck in Rollicking Follow-Up to 'Epic Split,'" *Adweek*, December 3, 2015, www.adweek.com/print/168418; Meg Carter, "How Volvo Trucks Pulled Off an Epic Split and Game-Changing Campaign," *Fast Company*, June 18, 2016, www.fastcocreate.com/3031654/cannes/how-volvo-trucks-pulled-off-an-epic-split-and-a-game-changing-campaign; David Griner, "Undivided Attention: How 'Epic Split' Became the Buzziest Ad at Cannes," *Adweek*, June 16, 2014, www.adweek.com/print/158248; and "Six Years of Ambitious Integrated Campaigns," www.dandad.org/en/d-ad-integrated-marketing-campaigns/, accessed July 2016.

MyMarketingLab

Go to **mymktlab.com** for Auto-graded writing questions as well as the following Assisted-graded writing questions:

14-22 Name and describe the types of appeals marketers use when designing marketing communication messages. What message structure issues must be considered when creating messages?

14-23 Select an advertisement for a national brand. What type of appeal is the advertiser using? Describe the message structure used. Create an advertisement for the brand that communicates the same information but uses a different type of appeal and message structure.

15 Advertising and Public Relations

CHAPTER PREVIEW

After an analysis of overall integrated marketing communications (IMC) planning, we dig more deeply into the specific marketing communication tools. In this chapter, we explore advertising and public relations (PR). Advertising involves communicating the company's or brand's value proposition by using paid media to inform, persuade, and remind consumers. PR involves building good relations with various company publics—from consumers and the general public to the media, investor, donor, and government publics. As with all the promotion mix tools, advertising and PR must be blended into the overall IMC program.

In Chapters 16 and 17, we will discuss the remaining promotion mix tools: personal selling, sales promotion, and direct and digital marketing.

Let's start by looking at an outstanding advertising campaign. Two decades ago, GEICO was a little-known nicher in the U.S. auto-insurance industry. But now, thanks in large part to an industry-changing, big-budget advertising program featuring an enduring tagline and a likeable but unlikely spokes-lizard, GEICO has muscled its way to the number-two position in its ultra-competitive industry. The message: Good advertising really does matter. Here's the story.

GEICO: From Bit Player to Behemoth through Good Advertising

Founded in 1936, GEICO initially targeted a select customer group of government employees and non-commissioned military officers with exceptional driving records. Unlike its competitors, GEICO had no agents. Instead, the auto insurer marketed directly to customers, keeping its costs low and passing on the savings in the form of lower premiums. For nearly 60 years, GEICO's marketing relied almost entirely on direct mail and telephone advertising.

In 1994, however, when GEICO decided to expand its customer base, it knew that it must also expand its marketing. So it entered the world of mass media, a shift that would dramatically change the face of insurance advertising. GEICO started slowly, spending a paltry $10 million to launch its first national TV, radio, and print ads. Then, in 1996, billionaire investor Warren Buffett bought the company and famously told the marketing group "money is no object" when it comes to growing the business, so "speed things up." Did it ever. Over the next 10 years, GEICO's ad spending jumped 50-fold, to more than $500 million a year.

> Thanks in large part to an industry-changing, big-budget advertising program featuring an enduring tagline and a likeable but unlikely spokes-lizard, GEICO has muscled its way to the number-two position in its ultra-competitive industry.

By now, you know a lot about GEICO and its smooth-talking gecko. But at the start, the insurer faced a tough task—introducing a little-known brand with a funny name to a national audience. Like all good advertising, the GEICO campaign began with a simple but compelling theme, one that highlights the convenience and savings advantages of GEICO's direct-to-customers system. To this day, every single one of the hundreds of ads and other content pieces in the GEICO campaign has driven home the now-familiar pitch: "15 minutes could save you 15 percent or more on car insurance."

But what really set GEICO's advertising apart was the inspired way the company chose to bring its value proposition to life. At the time, competitors were using serious and sentimental pitches—"You're in good hands with Allstate" or "Like a good neighbor, State Farm is there." To make its advertising stand out, GEICO decided to deliver its punch line with humor. The creative approach worked, and sales began to climb.

In trying to grow the brand, it become apparent that customers had difficulty pronouncing the GEICO name (which stands for Government Employees Insurance Company). Too often, *GEICO* became "gecko." Enter the charismatic green lizard. In 1999, GEICO ran a 15-second spot in which the now-famous, British-accented gecko calls a press conference and pleads: "I am a gecko, not to be confused with GEICO, which could save you hundreds on car insurance. So stop calling me." The ad was supposed to be a one-time "throwaway," but consumers quickly flooded the company with calls and letters begging to see more of the gecko. The rest, as they say, is history.

Although the gecko remains GEICO's iconic spokesman, one lizard could take the company only so far. So over the years, to keep its pitch fresh and entertaining, GEICO has supplemented the gecko ads with a continuous flow of clever, buzzworthy new executions telling the brand's value story. Early on, when GEICO first went online, the campaign employed a clutch of cultured cavemen, insulted by the company's advertising slogan "It's so easy to use GEICO.com, even a caveman could do it." Later, in response to the question "Can switching to GEICO really save you 15 percent or more on car insurance?," the "Rhetorical Questions" campaign responded, "Is Ed 'Too Tall' Jones too tall?," "Was Abe Lincoln honest?," and "Did the little piggy cry 'wee wee wee' all the way home?" That last ad introduced the world to Maxwell, the talking pig who went on to star in his own GEICO campaign, emphasizing GEICO's growing digital, social, and mobile advances. The brand's later "Happier than..." campaign introduced yet another talking animal, the popular Caleb the Camel, who proclaimed that GEICO customers are "Happier than a camel on hump day."

In its more recent "It's what you do..." installment of the campaign, GEICO found yet another way to underline its value proposition in an entertaining and memorable way. In one ad, an immature Peter Pan annoyingly disrupts a staid convention luncheon because when you're Peter Pan, "you stay young forever. It's what you do." Another ad featured a mom who calls her son while he's in the midst of a dramatic James Bond–style exploit to vent about his dad's refusal to call exterminators to handle a backyard squirrel problem because if you're a mom, "you always call at the worst possible time. It's what you do." Each ad in the series concluded: "If you want to save money on car insurance, you switch to GEICO. It's what you do."

GEICO's award-winning "Unskippable" campaign offered hilarious online video ads that viewers simply couldn't skip. Each video featured a seemingly boring, everyday scene, such as a family eating a spaghetti dinner. The ads opened with an unabashedly huge GEICO logo in the middle of the screen and the line, "You can't skip this ad because it's already over. Fifteen minutes could save you 15 percent or more on car insurance." But that's when the fun kicked in. For example, in the family dinner video, the family freezes while their dog leaps onto the table, methodically and comically scarfing up everyone's spaghetti (you have to see the video to appreciate

For more than 20 years, GEICO's advertising and charismatic gecko have creatively and relentlessly driven home the brand's value proposition: "15 minutes could save you 15 percent or more on car insurance."

All text and images are copy written with permission from GEICO.

it—it's truly unskippable). The "Unskippable" campaign won the Film Grand Prix award at the Cannes international ad festival and received *Advertising Age*'s first-ever Campaign of the Year award.

"No matter how many GEICO ads you've seen over the years—and it's a bunch—they never seem to grow stale," observes one expert. The company's chief marketing officer explains, "We're trying to stay ever-present in the consumer's mind but not bore them and have them just tune out yet another GEICO ad." However, no matter how varied, each mini-campaign has a distinctly GEICO flavor, and every single ad closes strongly with the crucial "15 minutes could save you 15 percent" tagline.

GEICO continues to invest heavily in advertising and content marketing, outspending every other insurance company in measured media by a nearly two-to-one margin. Its annual advertising budget, now more than $1.1 billion, makes GEICO the third-most-advertised U.S. megabrand. However, the brand's creative and relentless advertising messaging plus its heavy investment have paid big dividends. The once little-known GEICO brand now enjoys well over 90 percent awareness among insurance shoppers. And after years of double-digit market share gains, GEICO now occupies second place in the ultra-competitive U.S. car-insurance market.

Moreover, beyond spurring GEICO's spectacular growth, the brand's advertising has changed the way the entire insurance industry markets its products. In what was once a yawn-provoking category, competitors ranging from Allstate (with "Mayhem") to Progressive (with "Flo") are now injecting humor and interest in their own advertising campaigns. "This strategy is absolutely working for GEICO," asserts one analyst. It's "a testament to how GEICO has used advertising to evolve from a bit player to a behemoth," says another.[1]

OBJECTIVES OUTLINE

OBJECTIVE 15-1	Define the role of advertising in the promotion mix. Advertising *(p 428)*
OBJECTIVE 15-2	Describe the major decisions involved in developing an advertising program. Major Advertising Decisions *(pp 429–446)*
OBJECTIVE 15-3	Define the role of public relations in the promotion mix. Public Relations *(pp 446–448)*
OBJECTIVE 15-4	Explain how companies use PR to communicate with their publics. Major Public Relations Tools *(p 448)*

COMPANIES MUST DO MORE than simply create customer value. They must also engage target customers and clearly and persuasively communicate that value to them. In this chapter, we take a closer look at two marketing communications tools: *advertising* and *public relations*.

Author Comment | You already know a lot about advertising—you are exposed to it every day. But here we'll look behind the scenes at how companies make advertising decisions.

Advertising

Advertising
Any paid form of nonpersonal presentation and promotion of ideas, goods, or services by an identified sponsor.

Advertising can be traced back to the very beginnings of recorded history. Archaeologists working in countries around the Mediterranean Sea have dug up signs announcing various events and offers. The Romans painted walls to announce gladiator fights, and the Phoenicians painted pictures on large rocks to promote their wares along parade routes. During the golden age in Greece, town criers announced the sale of cattle, crafted items, and even cosmetics. An early "singing commercial" went as follows: "For eyes that are shining, for cheeks like the dawn/For beauty that lasts after girlhood is gone/For prices in reason, the woman who knows/Will buy her cosmetics from Aesclyptos."

Modern advertising, however, is a far cry from these early efforts. U.S. advertisers now run up an estimated annual bill of nearly $190 billion on measured advertising media; worldwide ad spending is an estimated $545 billion. P&G, the world's largest advertiser, spent more than $4.6 billion on U.S. advertising and $11.5 billion worldwide.[2]

Although advertising is used mostly by business firms, a wide range of not-for-profit organizations, professionals, and social agencies also use advertising to promote their causes to various target publics. In fact, the 39th-largest U.S. advertising spender is a not-for-profit organization—the U.S. government, which advertises in many ways. For example, its Centers for Disease Control and Prevention spent $70 million on the fourth year of an anti-smoking advertising campaign titled "Tips from a Former Smoker," showing people who have paid dearly due to smoking-related diseases.[3] Advertising is a good way to engage, inform, and persuade, whether the purpose is to sell Coca-Cola worldwide, help smokers kick the habit, or educate people in developing nations on how to lead healthier lives.

Marketing management must make four important decisions when developing an advertising program (see **Figure 15.1**): *setting advertising objectives, setting the advertising budget, developing advertising strategy (message decisions and media decisions),* and *evaluating advertising effectiveness.*

● FIGURE | 15.1
Major Advertising Decisions

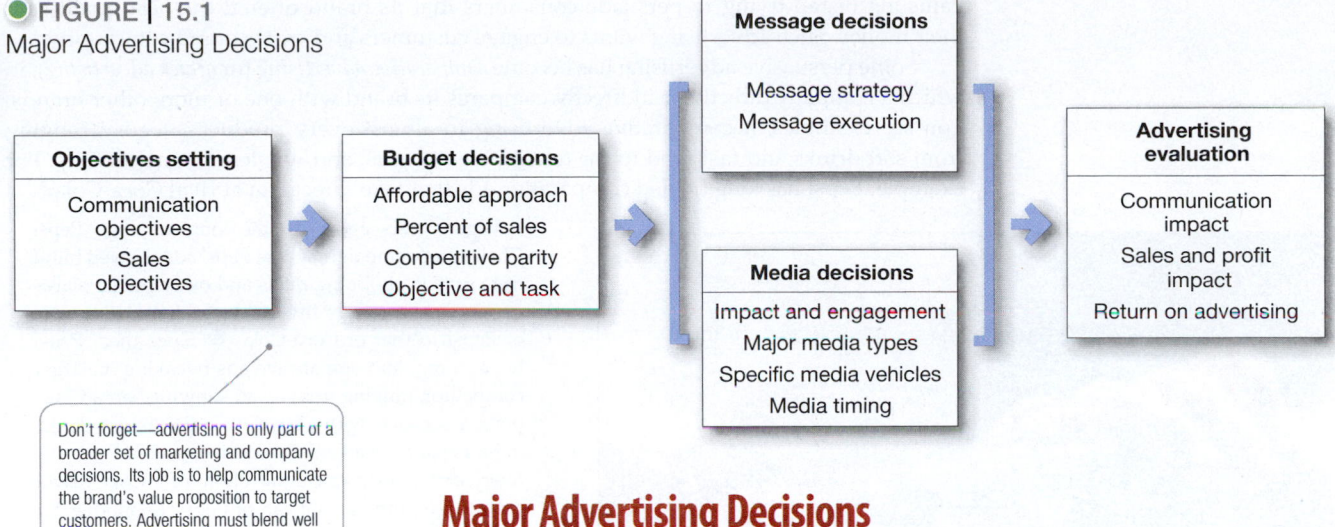

Don't forget—advertising is only part of a broader set of marketing and company decisions. Its job is to help communicate the brand's value proposition to target customers. Advertising must blend well with other promotion and marketing mix decisions.

Major Advertising Decisions

Setting Advertising Objectives

The first step is to set *advertising objectives*. These objectives should be based on past decisions about the target market, positioning, and the marketing mix, which define the job that advertising must do in the total marketing program. The overall advertising objective is to help engage customers and build customer relationships by communicating customer value. Here, we discuss specific advertising objectives.

Advertising objective

A specific communication *task* to be accomplished with a specific *target* audience during a specific period of *time*.

An **advertising objective** is a specific communication *task* to be accomplished with a specific *target* audience during a specific period of *time*. Advertising objectives can be classified by their primary purpose—to *inform*, *persuade*, or *remind*. ● **Table 15.1** lists examples of each of these specific objectives.

Informative advertising is used heavily when introducing a new product category. In this case, the objective is to build primary demand. Thus, early producers of big-screen HDTVs first had to inform consumers of the image quality and size benefits of the new product. *Persuasive advertising* becomes more important as competition increases. Here, the company's objective is to build selective demand. For example, once HDTVs became established,

● **Table 15.1** | **Possible Advertising Objectives**

Informative Advertising

Communicating customer value	Suggesting new uses for a product
Building a brand and company image	Informing the market of a price change
Telling the market about a new product	Describing available services and support
Explaining how a product works	Correcting false impressions

Persuasive Advertising

Building brand preference	Persuading customers to purchase now
Encouraging switching to a brand	Creating customer engagement
Changing customer perceptions of product value	Building brand community

Reminder Advertising

Maintaining customer relationships	Reminding consumers where to buy the product
Reminding consumers that the product may be needed in the near future	Keeping the brand in a customer's mind during off-seasons

Samsung began trying to persuade consumers that *its* brand offered the best quality for their money. Such advertising wants to engage customers and create brand community.

Some persuasive advertising has become *comparative advertising* (or *attack advertising*), in which a company directly or indirectly compares its brand with one or more other brands. You see examples of comparative advertising in almost every product category, ranging from soft drinks and fast food to car rentals, credit cards, and wireless phone services. For example, Pepsi has long fielded comparative ads that take direct aim at rival Coca-Cola:[4]

● Comparative advertising: Pepsi has long taken direct aim at rival Coca-Cola with comparative ads. "There are few things that grab our fans' attention as much as seeing our beloved blue and that red next to each other," says a Pepsi marketer.

PepsiCo

It began years ago with the long-running "Pepsi Challenge" campaign, where Pepsi ads showed blind taste tests in shopping malls and other public places in which consumers invariably preferred the taste of Pepsi to that of Coca-Cola. ● Since then, Pepsi has run regular comparative ads tweaking its larger competitor, ranging from an ad showing Santa Claus (long associated with Coca-Cola advertising) choosing a Pepsi over a Coke to one in which a Pepsi delivery driver snaps a candid photo of a Coke driver covertly draining a cold can of Pepsi. In another ad, a happy Pepsi drinker mocks a Coke buyer by telling him, "You've still got the polar bear" (another Coca-Cola ad symbol). A scraggly polar bear then sadly pets the Coke drinker. Such comparison ads have been popular with Pepsi fans. "There are few things that grab our fans' attention as much as seeing our beloved blue and that red next to each other," says Pepsi's brand marketing and digital director. "It's done well for us in the past, and it's just something that we know works and that they love to see."

Comparative advertising campaigns often create controversy. Many times, that's the point of using them. Whereas established market leaders want to exclude other brands from the consumer's choice set, challengers want to shake things up, inject their brands into the consumer conversation, and put themselves on equal footing with the leader. For example, Microsoft has a long history of successful comparative advertising, both in initiating challenges against market-leading rivals and fending off attacks by challengers (see Real Marketing 15.1).

Still, advertisers should use comparative advertising with caution. All too often, such ads invite competitor responses, resulting in an advertising war that neither competitor can win. Upset competitors might also take more drastic action, such as filing complaints with the self-regulatory National Advertising Division of the Council of Better Business Bureaus or even filing false-advertising lawsuits. Consider the reactions of competitors to recent comparative ads by Chobani:

One Chobani Simply 100 yogurt ad shows a woman scrutinizing the label on a container of Yoplait Greek 100 yogurt and promptly discarding it as the ad voiceover says, "Potassium sorbate? Really? That stuff is used to kill bugs." The ad concludes by noting that Chobani Simply 100 Greek yogurt contains zero preservatives. Another ad portrays a woman sitting poolside tossing a container of Dannon Light and Fit into the trash as a voiceover declares, "Sucralose, why? That stuff has chlorine added to it. Chobani Simply 100 is the only 100-calorie yogurt sweetened naturally." Competitors didn't take kindly to the jabs. Yoplait maker General Mills filed a lawsuit against Chobani for misleading advertising. And Dannon's lawyers sent Chobani a cease-and-desist letter asking it to discontinue the campaign. In turn, Chobani sued Dannon asking the courts to confirm that Chobani's advertising is not misleading. Only time will tell how it all turns out. But the skirmishes aren't likely to benefit any of the competitors.[5]

Reminder advertising is important for mature products; it helps to maintain customer relationships and keep consumers thinking about the product. For example, a recent ad campaign for Silk soymilk tells consumers to "Fall back in love with Soymilk," reminding them of the many reasons that "Silk helps you bloom." Expensive Coca-Cola television ads primarily build and maintain the Coca-Cola brand relationship rather than inform consumers or persuade them to buy it in the short run.

Real Marketing

15.1 Microsoft's Comparative Advertising: "I Couldn't Do That on My Mac"

For as long as there's been advertising, challenger brands have squared off against market leaders with comparative ads. There was Avis versus Hertz ("We're #2 so we try harder"); Pepsi versus Coke (The Pepsi Challenge), Dunkin' Donuts versus Starbucks ("Friends don't let friends drink Starbucks"); T-Mobile versus Verizon (#BallBusterChallenge), and countless more. But few companies have made more or better use of challenge campaigns than Microsoft, which has gone toe to toe time and again over the past decade with worthy rivals such as Apple and Google.

It all started a decade ago when Apple set out to loosen Microsoft's iron grip on the personal computer market. Microsoft-powered PCs had long dominated the market, with Apple's Macs competing for niche segments. So Apple fired the first direct salvo at Microsoft by launching the now-classic "Get a Mac" comparative campaign.

"Get a Mac" ads featured two characters—"Mac" and "PC"—sparring over the relative advantages of the Apple Mac versus Microsoft Windows-based PCs. The ads portrayed Mac as a young, hip, laid-back guy in a hoodie, whereas PC was a stodgy, befuddled, error-prone, middle-aged nerd in baggie khakis, a brown sport coat, and unfashionable glasses. Not surprisingly, Mac always got the best of outdated and inflexible PC. Over the next few years, Apple unleashed a nonstop barrage of Mac versus PC ads that bashed Windows-based machines—and their owners—as outmoded and dysfunctional.

The smug "Get a Mac" ads hit their mark. Within two years, the Mac's share of the U.S. personal computer market had doubled and consumer value perceptions of Apple computers skyrocketed. Even though its computers were viewed as more expensive, at one point Apple scored a whopping 70 on the BrandIndex (which tracks consumer perceptions of brand value on a scale of −100 to +100). Microsoft, meanwhile, floundered below zero.

Microsoft needed to do something dramatic. So two years after the Apple "Get a Mac" onslaught began, Microsoft counterpunched with its own cheeky "I'm a PC" campaign, featuring a dead-on look-alike of Apple's PC character. In the first ad, dressed in PC's dorky outfit, Microsoft's character opened with "I'm a

PC. And I've been made into a stereotype." He was followed by a parade of everyday PC users—from environmentalists, political bloggers, mixed martial arts fighters, and mash-up DJs to budget-conscious laptop shoppers and remarkably tech-savvy preschoolers—each proclaiming, "I'm a PC."

The Microsoft "I'm a PC" campaign struck a chord with Windows users, who no longer had to sit back and take Apple's jibes. Microsoft quickly extended the "I'm a PC" campaign with a new pitch, one more in tune with the then-troubled economy. Part advertising and part reality TV, the new comparative campaign—called "Laptop Hunters"—tagged along with real consumers as they shopped for computers. The task? Find a laptop with everything a person could want for under $1,000. Shopper after shopper visited PC and Apple retailers, only to find that getting a decent Mac for that price was impossible, whereas fully loaded Windows-driven laptops came in well under the mark.

If previous "I'm a PC" ads started a shift in perceptions, the "Laptop Hunters" series really moved the needle. The ads spoke volumes in a difficult economy, portraying Apple as too expensive, "too cool," and out of touch with mainstream consumers. The provocative ads bumped Microsoft's BrandIndex score from less than zero to 46, while Apple's score dropped from its previous high of 70 to only 12. Apple struck back with one of its most negative comparative Mac versus PC ads yet. Called "Broken Promises," it featured a skeptical Mac attacking PC about whether the newest Windows version would eliminate problems associated with previous Window's versions. Many analysts thought that the biting tone of the ad suggested that Apple was feeling the heat and getting defensive. Uncharacteristically, Mac seemed to be losing his cool.

The Microsoft–Apple ad skirmish continued for another two years, with neither combatant gaining much new headway. In

Microsoft has a long history of successful comparative advertising. Says the happy user in this video ad for the Microsoft Surface Pro, "I couldn't do that on my Mac." The Surface Pro 4 does more.

Microsoft

fact, the constant bickering seemed to wear thin with consumers of both brands. So both companies eventually turned down the comparative advertising heat, instead fielding ads that focused on their own positives rather than the rival's negatives.

A few years later, however, when it introduced its Bing search engine, Microsoft once again turned to comparative advertising, this time as the attacker rather than the attacked. To get Bing—a distant also-ran to search leader Google—into consumers' choice sets, Microsoft launched an aggressive campaign called "Bing It On." The campaign challenged users to make direct side-by-side comparisons of Bing search results to Google search results without knowing which results were from which search engine. According to Microsoft, to the surprise of many people, those making the comparison chose Bing over Google by a two-to-one margin.

Microsoft pressed on against Google with an even more aggressive "Scroogled" campaign, which attacked Google's search engine for "Scroogling" users by exploiting their personal data with everything from invasive ads in Gmail to sharing data with app developers to maximize advertising profits. "For an honest search engine," said the Scroogled ads, "try Bing." Although controversial, the Scroogled campaign got many consumers to look at Bing and other Microsoft products in a new light versus Google. Research showed that following a visit to Scroogled.com, Google's favorability gap over Bing faded from 45 points to just 5. And after watching a Scroogled ad,

the chance of a viewer recommending Bing to a friend rose 7 percent.

In a more recent comparative campaign, this one for Microsoft's Surface tablet, Microsoft once again turned its sights on Apple, which dominates the high-end tablet market. But rather than going after Apple's wildly successful iPad, the Surface campaign directly challenged Apple's MacBook Air laptop, positioning the Surface Pro as a laptop alternative rather than an iPad killer. For example, one online video ad made a direct and convincing side-by-side comparison of the Microsoft Surface Pro with the Apple MacBook Air, concluding that the Surface is "the tablet that can replace your laptop." A Surface Pro print ad proclaimed, "Powerful as a laptop, lighter than Air." And in a Surface Pro TV ad, reminiscent of the original Mac versus PC ads, a MacBook Air owner at first gloats over his Apple. But after watching one after another Surface Pro user, the dejected MacBook owner confesses, "I like your Surface Pro. No, seriously, where can I get one?"

Although the Bing It On, Scroogled, and Surface Pro comparative campaigns have now faded into history, each accomplished its

purpose—to bring a new Microsoft product, whether Bing or the Surface Pro or something else, into the competitive set against established rivals. The comparative campaigns have created controversy along with heated debate about the relative merits of, say, Bing versus Google or the Surface Pro versus the MacBook Air. But that's the point. Whereas established market leaders want to maintain the status quo and monopolize the conversation, market challengers want to shake things up and put their products on equal footing with the leader. That's what a good comparative advertising campaign does.

Comparative advertising must be working for Microsoft. New ads and videos for its Microsoft Surface Pro 4 and kick-off content for its new Microsoft Surface Book hybrid laptop/tablet—which features "the power of touch"—have taken up where previous comparative campaigns left off. They take direct aim at competing Apple models, positioning the Surface line as equipment that "does more. Just like you." One online video shows a happy user working magic on her Microsoft Surface Pro touchscreen, concluding, "I couldn't do that on my Mac."

Sources: Mitchel Broussard, "Microsoft's Surface Book Ads Borrow Music from Apple to Focus on Things a Mac 'Just Can't Do,'" *MacRumors*, March 9, 2016, www.macrumors.com/2016/03/09/microsoft-surface-book-ads/; Alex Wilhelm, "Microsoft's Scroogled Ad Campaign Appears to Be Working," *TechCrunch*, October 15, 2013, http://techcrunch.com/2013/10/15/microsofts-scroogled-ad-campaign-appears-to-be-working/; Tom Spring, "Microsoft Amps Up Apple Attack with Switch to Surface Campaign," *CRN*, December 20, 2014, www.crn.com/news/mobility/300075218/microsoft-amps-up-apple-attack-with-switch-to-surface-campaign.htm; Brian Fagioli, "Microsoft Acting Like Donald Trump by Attacking Apple MacBook in New Surface Book Videos," *betanews*, March 3, 2016, http://betanews.com/2016/03/07/microsoft-donald-trump-attack-apple-macbook-pro-surface-videos/; and www.microsoft.com/en-us/switch/mac-surface and www.whymicrosoft.com/, accessed October 2016.

Advertising's goal is to help move consumers through the buying process. Some advertising is designed to move people to immediate action. For example, a direct-response television ad by Weight Watchers urges consumers to go online and sign up right away, and a Best Buy newspaper insert for a weekend sale encourages immediate store visits. However, many ads focus on building or strengthening long-term customer relationships. For example, a Nike television ad in which well-known athletes work through extreme challenges in their Nike gear never directly asks for a sale. Instead, the goal is to engage customers and somehow change the way they think or feel about the brand.

Setting the Advertising Budget

Advertising budget

The dollars and other resources allocated to a product or a company advertising program.

After determining its advertising objectives, the company next sets its **advertising budget** for each product. Four commonly used methods for setting promotion budgets are discussed in Chapter 14. Here we discuss some specific factors that should be considered when setting the advertising budget.

A brand's advertising budget often depends on its stage in the product life cycle. For example, new products typically need relatively large advertising budgets to build awareness and to gain consumer trial. In contrast, mature brands usually require lower budgets as a ratio to sales. Also, brands in a market with many competitors and high advertising clutter must be advertised more heavily to be noticed above the noise in the marketplace.

Undifferentiated brands—those that closely resemble other brands in their product class (soft drinks, laundry detergents)—may require heavy advertising to set them apart. When the product differs greatly from those of competitors, advertising can be used to point out the differences to consumers.

No matter what method is used, setting the advertising budget is no easy task. How does a company know if it is spending the right amount? Companies such as Coca-Cola and Kraft have built sophisticated statistical models to determine the relationship between promotional spending and brand sales and to help determine the "optimal investment" across various media. Still, because so many factors affect advertising effectiveness, some controllable and others not, measuring the results of advertising spending remains an inexact science. In most cases, managers must rely on large doses of judgment along with more quantitative analysis when setting advertising budgets.

As a result of such thinking, advertising is one of the easiest budget items to cut when economic times get tough. Cuts in brand-building advertising appear to do little short-term harm to sales. In the long run, however, slashing ad spending may cause long-term damage to a brand's image and market share. In fact, companies that can maintain or even increase their advertising spending while competitors are decreasing theirs can gain competitive advantage.

For example, during the Great Recession, while competitors were cutting back, car maker Audi actually increased its marketing and advertising spending. Audi "kept its foot on the pedal while everyone else [was] pulling back," said an Audi ad executive. "Why would we go backwards now when the industry is generally locking the brakes and cutting spending?" As a result, Audi's brand awareness and buyer consideration reached record levels during the recession, outstripping those of BMW, Mercedes, and Lexus and positioning Audi strongly for the post-recession era. Audi is now one of the hottest auto brands on the market, neck and neck with BMW and Mercedes in global luxury car sales.[6]

Developing Advertising Strategy

Advertising strategy
The strategy by which the company accomplishes its advertising objectives. It consists of two major elements: creating advertising messages and selecting advertising media.

Advertising strategy consists of two major elements: creating advertising *messages* and selecting advertising *media*. In the past, companies often viewed media planning as secondary to the message-creation process. After the creative department created good advertisements, the media department then selected and purchased the best media for carrying those advertisements to the desired target audiences. This often caused friction between creatives and media planners.

Today, however, soaring media costs, more-focused target marketing strategies, and the blizzard of new online, mobile, and social media have promoted the importance of the media-planning function. The decision about which media to use for an ad campaign—television, newspapers, magazines, video, a website, social media, mobile devices, or email—is now sometimes more critical than the creative elements of the campaign. Also, brand content is now often co-created through interactions with and among consumers. As a result, more and more advertisers are orchestrating a closer harmony between their messages and the media that deliver them. As discussed in the previous chapter, the goal is to create and manage brand content across a full range of media, whether they are paid, owned, earned, or shared.

Creating the Advertising Message and Brand Content

No matter how big the budget, advertising can succeed only if it engages consumers and communicates well. Good advertising messages and content are especially important in today's costly and cluttered advertising environment.

Today, the average U.S. household receives about 190 TV channels and consumers have more than 7,200 magazines from which to choose.[7] Add in the countless radio stations and a continuous barrage of catalogs, direct mail, out-of-home media, email, and online, mobile, and social media exposures, and consumers are being bombarded with ads and brand content at home, work, and all points in between. For example, Americans are exposed to a cumulative 5.3 trillion online ad impressions each year and a daily diet of 500 million tweets, 4 billion YouTube videos, 58 million photos shared on Instagram, 5 million article pins on Pinterest, and 4.75 billion pieces of shared content on Facebook.[8]

● **Advertising clutter:** Today's consumers, armed with an arsenal of technologies, can choose what they watch and don't watch. Increasingly, they are choosing not to watch ads.

Piotr Marcinski/Shutterstock

Madison & Vine
A term that has come to represent the merging of advertising and entertainment in an effort to break through the clutter and create new avenues for reaching customers with more engaging messages.

Breaking Through the Clutter. If all this clutter bothers some consumers, it also causes huge headaches for marketers. Take the situation facing network television advertisers. They pay an average of $342,000 to produce a single 30-second commercial. Then each time they show it, they pay an average of $112,100 for 30 seconds of advertising time during a popular primetime program. They pay even more if it's an especially popular program, such as *Sunday Night Football* ($803,000), *Empire* ($497,000), *Big Bang Theory* ($348,000), or a mega-event such as the Super Bowl (averaging $5 million per 30 seconds!). Then their ads are sandwiched in with a clutter of other commercials, network promotions, and other nonprogram material totaling as much as 20 minutes per primetime hour, with long commercial breaks coming every six minutes on average. Such clutter in television and other ad media has created an increasingly hostile advertising environment.[9]

It used to be that television viewers were pretty much a captive audience for advertisers. But today's digital wizardry has given viewers a rich new set of information and entertainment options—the internet, video streaming, social and mobile media, tablets and smartphones, and others. ● Digital technology has also armed consumers with an arsenal of technologies for choosing what they watch or don't watch and when. Increasingly, thanks to the growth of DVR systems and digital streaming, consumers are choosing *not* to watch ads.

Thus, advertisers can no longer force-feed the same old cookie-cutter messages and content to captive consumers through traditional media. Simply interrupting or disrupting consumers no longer works. Unless ads provide content that is engaging, useful, or entertaining, many consumers will simply ignore or skip them.

Merging Advertising and Entertainment. To break through the clutter, many marketers have subscribed to a new merging of advertising and entertainment, dubbed "**Madison & Vine**." You've probably heard of Madison Avenue, the New York City street that houses the headquarters of many of the nation's largest advertising agencies. You may also have heard of Hollywood & Vine, the intersection of Hollywood Avenue and Vine Street in Hollywood, California, long the symbolic heart of the U.S. entertainment industry. Now, Madison Avenue and Hollywood & Vine have come together to form a new intersection—Madison & Vine—that represents the merging of advertising and entertainment in an effort to create new avenues for reaching consumers with more engaging messages.

This merging of advertising and entertainment takes one of two forms: advertainment or brand integrations. The aim of *advertainment* is to make ads and brand content themselves so entertaining or so useful that people *want* to watch them. There's no chance that you'd watch ads on purpose, you say? Think again. For example, the Super Bowl has become an annual advertainment showcase. Tens of millions of people tune in to the Super Bowl each year, as much to watch the entertaining ads as to see the game. And ads and related content posted online before and after the big game draw tens of millions of views. These days, it's common to see an entertaining ad on YouTube long before you see it on TV.

Advertisers are also creating content forms that look less like ads and more like short films or shows. A range of brand messaging platforms—from webisodes and blogs to online videos and social media posts—now blur the line between ads and other consumer content. For example, as part of its long-running, highly successful Campaign for Real Beauty, Unilever's Dove brand has created numerous long-form ad videos about how women of all ages view themselves. Its "Real Beauty Sketches" video compared images of women drawn by an FBI-trained sketch artist based on their self-descriptions versus strangers' descriptions of them. Side-by-side comparisons show that the stranger-described images are invariably more accurate and more flattering, creating strong reactions from the women. The tagline concludes, "You're more beautiful than you think." Although the award-winning video was never shown on TV, it drew more than 163 million global YouTube views within just two months, making it the most-watched video ever. Other blockbuster Dove Real Beauty videos—with titles such as "Evolution" and "Change One Thing"—have met with similar receptions.[10]

Marketers have tested all kinds of novel ways to break through today's clutter and engage consumers. For example, Hostess Brands—maker of those yummy Twinkies,

Ho Hos, Ding Dongs, and cream-filled cupcakes—recently shared a tweet celebrating the opening day of the Major League Baseball season. The tweet contained a picture of baseball-decorated cupcakes but also the bold headline TOUCHDOWN. As expected, the tweet grabbed plenty of attention, as droves of Twitter followers pounced to point out the mistake, just the reaction Hostess intended. "The 'touchdown' line was intentional," says the marketing director of Hostess Brands. "It's fun and aimed at young audiences who are in on the running joke."

Other brands have also "tested the stupid waters," as one analyst puts it. For example, JCPenney once posted incoherent tweets, grabbing widespread attention and leading to speculation that the retailer's social media person was either drunk or had been hacked. Instead, says JCPenney, the person was tweeting with mittens on to promote its winter merchandise. P&G's Charmin brand's #tweetfromtheseat Twitter campaign uses irreverent humor to create engagement and drive buzz, with questions such as "Charmin asks: What are your thoughts on streaming while streaming?" and "There's no toilet paper left on the roll, do you yell for help, wiggle and air dry, text someone for help?"[11]

Brand integrations (or *branded entertainment*) involve making the brand an inseparable part of some other form of entertainment or content. The most common form of brand integration is product placements—embedding brands as props within other programming. It might be a brief glimpse of Starbucks coffee products on *Morning Joe* on MSNBC or of Microsoft's Surface tablet and Bing search engine in episodes of *Elementary* or *Arrow*. It could be scenes from *Avengers: Age of Ultron* in which Black Widow rides a Harley-Davidson Livewire.

Or the product placement might be scripted into a movie or an episode of a TV show. For example, a GoPro camera played a starring role opposite Matt Damon in the movie *The Martian*. And a three-episode story on the hit TV show *Empire* was built entirely around the making of a Pepsi commercial in which the character of Jamal, a rising singer, becomes the new face of Pepsi. Then Pepsi ran the actual ad during commercial breaks in subsequent episodes of the show. The *Empire* brand integration cost Pepsi an estimated $20 million.[12]

● Branded integration: A three-episode story on the hit **TV** show *Empire* was built around the making of a Pepsi commercial in which one of the show's characters becomes the new face of **Pepsi**.

Ron Batzdorff/Getty Images

● Similarly, a storyline in one episode of *Black-ish* was built around a Buick Encore, which characters Dre and Bow purchased for their daughter, Zoey. Dre lists all of the great features of the Enclave. However, after his work colleagues remind him of the riskier things teenagers do to and in cars, Dre has second thoughts about whether Zoey is really ready for a car. Dre's mother, Ruby, feeds his concerns so that she can claim the car for her own. Ruby even posts a selfie with the car on her Facebook page, proclaiming, "Praise Jesus. That son of mine finally got his mother a Buick." By the end of the episode, Zoey gets the car. Other *Black-ish* episodes feature storylines built around brands ranging State Farm to Chipotle.

Originally created with TV in mind, brand integration has spread quickly into other sectors of the entertainment industry. If you look carefully, you'll see product placements in movies, video games, comic books, Broadway musicals, and even pop music. For example, last year's top 31 movies contained 430 identifiable brand placements.[13] The highly acclaimed film *The LEGO Movie* was pretty much a 100-minute product placement for iconic LEGO construction bricks. According to one writer, "The audience happily sits through a cinematic sales pitch...that shows off the immense versatility of the product while placing it in a deeply personal context. The majority of the film is a breathtaking display of what LEGO bricks are capable of as creative tools, but the personal element is what really elevates this film to product-placement perfection." *The LEGO Movie* boosted The LEGO Group's sales by 13 percent the year after it opened.[14]

A related form of brand integration is so-called **native advertising** (also called *sponsored content*), advertising or other brand-produced online content that appears to be

Native advertising
Advertising or other brand-produced online content that looks in form and function like the other natural content surrounding it on a web or social media platform.

"native to" the web or social media site in which it is placed. That is, the brand content looks in form and function like the other natural content surrounding it on a web or social media platform. It might be an article on a website such as *The Huffington Post, BuzzFeed, Mashable,* or even *The New York Times* or *The Wall Street Journal* that is paid for, written by, and placed by an advertiser but uses the same format as articles written by the editorial staff. Or it might be brand-prepared videos, pictures, posts, or pages integrated into social media such as Facebook, YouTube, Instagram, Pinterest, or Twitter that match the form and feel of native content on those media. Examples include Twitter's promoted tweets, Facebook's promoted stories, *BuzzFeed*'s sponsored posts, or Snapchat's "brand story" ads, branded posts that appear in the app's "Stories" feed. Native advertising is an increasingly popular form of brand content. It lets advertisers create relevant associations between brand and consumer content. According to a recent study by the Association of National Advertisers, "given today's media landscape, where consumers can avoid ads more than ever, advertisers are looking for new ways to get their messages noticed and acted upon."[15]

Thus, Madison & Vine is now the meeting place for advertising, brand content, and entertainment. The goal is to make brand messages a part of the broader flow of consumer content and conversation rather than an intrusion or interruption of it. As advertising agency JWT puts it, "We believe advertising needs to stop *interrupting* what people are interested in and *be* what people are interested in." However, advertisers must be careful that the new intersection itself doesn't become too congested. With all the new brand content formats and integration, Madison & Vine threatens to create even more of the very clutter that it was designed to break through. At that point, consumers might decide to take yet a different route.

Creative concept

The compelling "big idea" that will bring an advertising message strategy to life in a distinctive and memorable way.

Message and Content Strategy. The first step in creating effective advertising content is to plan a *message strategy*—the general message that will be communicated to consumers. The purpose of advertising is to get consumers to engage with or react to the product or company in a certain way. People will engage and react only if they believe they will benefit from doing so. Thus, developing an effective message strategy begins with identifying customer *benefits* that can be used as advertising appeals. Ideally, the message strategy will follow directly from the company's broader positioning and customer value–creation strategies.

Message strategy statements tend to be plain, straightforward outlines of benefits and positioning points that the advertiser wants to stress. The advertiser must next develop a compelling **creative concept**—or *big idea*—that will bring the message strategy to life in a distinctive and memorable way. At this stage, simple message ideas become great ad campaigns. Usually, a copywriter and an art director will team up to generate many creative concepts, hoping that one of these concepts will turn out to be the big idea. The creative concept may emerge as a visualization, a phrase, or a combination of the two.

The creative concept will guide the choice of specific appeals to be used in an advertising campaign. *Advertising appeals* should have three characteristics. First, they should be *meaningful*, pointing out benefits that make the product more desirable or interesting to consumers. Second, appeals must be *believable*. Consumers must believe that the product or service will deliver the promised benefits.

However, the most meaningful and believable benefits may not be the best ones to feature. Appeals should also be *distinctive*. They should tell how the product is better than competing brands. For example, the most meaningful benefit of a refrigerator is that it keeps foods cold. ● But GE sets its Café refrigerator apart as one that gives users an in-the-door filtered hot water dispenser and a Keurig® K-Cup® single-serve brewing system for making cups of coffee, tea, and other hot beverages at the fridge. It's "a new way to brew." Similarly, the most meaningful benefit of owning a wristwatch is that it keeps accurate time, yet few watch ads feature this benefit. Instead, watch advertisers might select any of a number of advertising themes. For years, Timex has been the affordable watch that "takes a licking and keeps on ticking." In contrast, Rolex ads talk about the brand's "obsession with perfection" and the fact that "Rolex has been the preeminent symbol of performance and prestige for more than a century."

● Distinctive advertising appeals: GE sets its Café refrigerator apart as one that gives users an in-the-door filtered hot water dispenser and Keurig® K-Cup® single-serve brewing system. It's creating "a new way to brew."

Courtesy of Haier US Appliance Solutions, Inc and Keurig Green Mountain Inc.

Execution style

The approach, style, tone, words, and format used for executing an advertising message.

Message Execution. The advertiser now must turn the big idea into an actual ad execution that will capture the target market's attention and interest. The creative team must find the best approach, style, tone, words, and format for executing the message. The message can be presented in various **execution styles**, such as the following:

- *Slice of life.* This style shows one or more "typical" people using the product in a normal setting. For example, IKEA content—from microsites and Instagram posts to print ads and television commercials—features people living in rooms furnished with IKEA furniture and household goods.
- *Lifestyle.* This style shows how a product fits in with a particular lifestyle. For example, an ad for Athleta activewear shows a woman in a complex yoga pose and states: "If your body is your temple, build it one piece at a time."
- *Fantasy.* This style creates a fantasy around the product or its use. For example, a Calvin Klein "Drive in to Fantasy" ad shows a woman floating blissfully above a surf-strewn beach at sunset in her Calvin Klein Nightwear.
- *Mood or image.* This style builds a mood or image around the product or service, such as beauty, love, intrigue, serenity, or pride. Few claims are made about the product or service except through suggestion. For example, a tear-inducing Budweiser "Lost Dog" commercial portrayed a little lost puppy that was rescued from a hungry wolf by his pals the Budweiser Clydesdales. The ad tugged effectively at heartstrings and topped the ad charts during Super Bowl XLIX while saying nothing about the taste or other qualities of Budweiser beer.
- *Musical.* This style shows people or cartoon characters singing about the product. For example, the M&M's "Love Ballad" ad, part of the Better with M campaign, featured Red singing Meat Loaf's "I'd Do Anything for Love," showcasing his commitment to actress Naya Rivera. Red has second thoughts, however, when Rivera can't resist adding Red to some of her favorite treats, including cookies, cake, and ice cream. To all of that, Red answers with the lyric, "But I won't do that…or that…or that…or that."

● **Novel formats can make an advertisement stand out: In this Sherwin-Williams ad, the eye-catching illustration delivers the bulk of the "Where will color take you?" message.**

The Sherwin-Williams Company

- *Personality symbol.* This style creates a character that represents the product. The character might be animated (Mr. Clean, the GEICO Gecko, or the Pillsbury Doughboy) or real (perky Progressive Insurance spokeswoman Flo, Dos Equis beer's "The Most Interesting Man in the World," or Ronald McDonald).
- *Technical expertise.* This style shows the company's expertise in making the product. Thus, Jim Koch of the Boston Beer Company tells about his many years of experience in brewing Samuel Adams beer.
- *Scientific evidence.* This style presents survey or scientific evidence that the brand is better or better liked than one or more other brands. For years, Crest toothpaste has used scientific evidence to convince buyers that Crest is better than other brands at fighting cavities.
- *Testimonial evidence or endorsement.* This style features a highly believable or likable source endorsing the product. It could be ordinary people saying how much they like a given product. For example, Whole Foods features a variety of real customers in its Values Matter marketing campaign. Or it might be a celebrity presenting the product, such as Taylor Swift for Diet Coke or NBA star Stephen Curry for Under Armour.

The advertiser also must choose a *tone* for the ad. For example, P&G always uses a positive tone: Its ads say something very positive about its products. Other advertisers now use edgy humor to break through the commercial clutter. Doritos commercials are famous for this.

The advertiser must use memorable and attention-getting *words* in the ad. For example, rather than just saying that its prescription sunglass lenses protect your eyes and look good at the same time, a LensCrafters ad announces, "Sunblock Never Looked So Good." Rather than claiming that "a BMW is a well-engineered automobile," BMW uses more creative and higher-impact phrasing: "The ultimate driving machine." And instead of stating plainly that Hanes socks last longer than less expensive ones, Hanes suggests, "Buy cheap socks and you'll pay through the toes."

Finally, *format* elements make a difference in an ad's impact as well as in its cost. A small change in an ad's design can make a big difference in its effect. In a print or display ad, the *illustration* is the first thing the reader notices—it must be strong enough to draw attention. Next, the *headline* must effectively entice the right people to read the copy. Finally, the *copy*—the main block of text in the ad—must be simple but strong and convincing. Moreover, these three elements must effectively work *together* to engage customers and persuasively present customer value. However, novel formats can help an ad stand out from the clutter. ● For example, in recent ads for Sherwin-Williams paint, eye-catching illustrations—featuring dazzling colors and unique designs—capture attention and deliver the bulk of the message. Once the illustrations engage the reader, small-print headlines ask, "Where will color take you?" while a familiar Sherwin-Williams "Cover the Earth" logo identifies the brand.

Consumer-Generated Content. Taking advantage of today's digital and social media technologies, many companies are now tapping consumers for marketing content, message ideas, or even actual ads and videos. Sometimes the results are outstanding; sometimes they are forgettable. If done well, however, user-generated content can incorporate the voice of the customer into brand messages and generate greater customer engagement.

Perhaps the best-known consumer-generated content effort is the former "Crash the Super Bowl Challenge" held annually by PepsiCo's Doritos brand. For more than a decade, Doritos invited consumers to create their own 30-second video ads, with winners receiving cash awards and having their ads run during the Super Bowl. Based on the success of the "Crash the Super Bowl" contest, Doritos now runs new campaigns that create fun fan-made ads and other content throughout the year.[16]

Brands across a wide range of industries—from automakers and fast-food chains to home furnishings brands and pet food marketers—now routinely incorporate user-generated social media content into their own traditional and social media marketing campaigns. For example, trendy home furnishings maker West Elm runs a campaign called #MyWestElm. The campaign collects user-generated photos of West Elm products shared online and uses them in promotional posts on its web, Facebook, and Pinterest sites along with links to similar products on the company's online store. So far, some 18,000 photos have been uploaded, and the MyWestElm website attracts 2 million monthly users. Moreover, 40 percent of West Elm's product webpages now also contain user-generated photos showing buyers how fellow customers use the products in the real world.[17]

Consumer-generated content can make customers an everyday part of the brand. For example, rather than relying on high-powered advertising, shoe brand Converse steps aside and lets customers themselves co-create the brand and co-author the brand story (see Real Marketing 15.2). And action-camera maker GoPro has long featured consumer-made videos on its web and social media sites as a means of letting customers share their high-octane experiences with others. Such videos have attracted a huge following, creating an engaged GoPro customer community that helps shape and share GoPro usage and lore. The collection of high-quality user-made GoPro content contains truly spellbinding scenes captured by adventure-seeking amateurs and professionals. ● Some of content is so good that the company has set up a GoPro Licensing division that licenses the best user-generated GoPro content to other brands for use in their own promotional campaigns, inviting them to "use the best of GoPro to tell your story."[18]

Not all consumer-generated content efforts, however, are so successful. As many

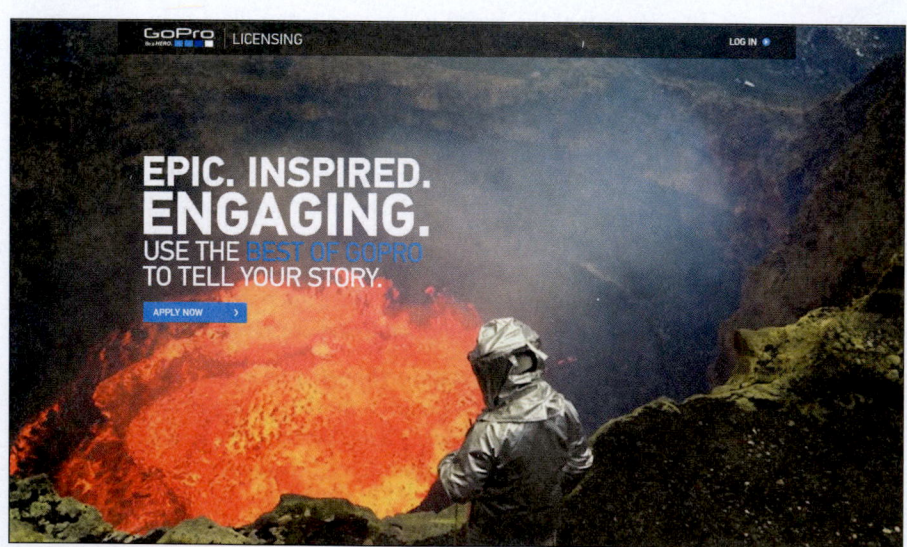

● Consumer-generated content: Some of GoPro's user-made content is so good that the company's GoPro Licensing division now licenses it to other brands for use in their own promotional campaigns, inviting them to "use the best of GoPro to tell your story."
GoPro

Real Marketing

15.2 Converse: Letting Customers Co-author the Brand Story

The iconic Converse brand has a long, storied history. The story began in 1923 when Converse introduced the first pair of Chuck Taylor All Star basketball shoes—known around the world as Cons, Connies, Convics, Verses, or just plain Chucks. Throughout the '30s, '40s, '50s, and '60s, Chucks were *the* shoes to have. The first Olympic basketball team wore them, and they dominated basketball courts—amateur and professional—for more than 50 years. By the mid-1970s, 70 to 80 percent of basketball players still wore Converse.

However, the Converse brand story almost came to an end little more than a decade ago. As the sneaker market exploded in the 1980s and 1990s, Converse failed to keep up with the times. Aggressive new competitors like Nike, Adidas, and Reebok took the market by storm with new high-performance shoes and even higher-performing marketing schemes. By 2001, Converse's market share had dwindled to only 1 percent and the once-dominant brand declared Chapter 11 bankruptcy.

The Converse story would likely have ended right there if not for the foresight of an unlikely suitor. Following the bankruptcy, market leader Nike stepped in and quietly bought Converse on the cheap. Nike still saw promise in the venerable-though-depleted old brand. But Nike faced a perplexing question: How does a mega-marketer like Nike bring a fading icon like Converse back to life? The answer: Let customers do it. Rather than following the Nike model of using high-powered marketing to shape the brand's image and positioning, Converse invited customers themselves to help co-create the Converse brand and co-author a new Converse story.

That's something that Converse customers had long had been doing anyway. Converse discovered that, despite its dwindling market share, the brand had acquired a small but fiercely loyal following. And despite the fact that Converse had never promoted the brand as anything but basketball shoes, avid brand fans were defining Converse in an entirely different way. During the 1990s, street kids had begun wearing affordable Converse shoes as an expression of individuality. Soon to follow were emerging artists, designers, and musicians who wore Chucks because of their simplicity and classic looks. Converse became a favorite of the anti-establishment,

anti-corporate crowd, those tired of trendy fashions. Individualistic Converse fans would take a pair of cheap but comfy All Stars, trash them, scribble on them, and customize them as a canvas for personal expression.

Converse recognized that today's young consumers don't want a brand that's neatly defined, packaged, and handed to them; they want to experience a brand, help shape it, and share it with other like-minded people. So rather than forcing a new brand story onto the market, Converse decided to turn the brand over to consumers themselves and let them write the next chapter. At the heart of the rekindled Converse brand is the philosophy that, these days, customers control brands, not companies. In the eyes of consumers, Converse today is less about the shoes and more about self-expression. Converse sees its role simply as making great products that customers want to wear. Beyond that, it participates in the brand story rather than dictating it.

Thus, today's Converse is built less on big-budget marketing campaigns and more on consumer-generated content by which customers express themselves and share their brand experiences. Converse has fully embraced social media, an ideal forum for engaging young consumers and letting them share content that helps to define the brand. Converse now spends more than 90 percent of its marketing dollars on digital media. Consider this: Converse has become the most popular sneaker brand on Facebook, with more than 37 million Facebook fans, 50 percent more than parent company and market leader Nike. Converse also has more than a million Twitter followers and 3.6 million followers on Instagram. That's amazing social sharing for a niche brand that still captures only 3 percent of the U.S. market.

The latest example of how Converse inspires consumer-generated content is its recently launched "Made By You" campaign. The campaign celebrates individuality and self-expression

by inviting people to share photos of their uniquely customized Converse All Stars along with backstories on their Converse experiences. "Made By You" was inspired by the reality that consumers by the thousands are already sharing pictures, videos, and other content of themselves in their Chucks via social media. "It's an idea that is already sort of happening," says a Converse marketer. "People are taking pics of their Chucks on the weekend, vacation, whatever it may be. We see 13,000 to 15,000 [Converse] tags a day."

The "Made By You" campaign helps inspire and organize the consumer-generated content process. It assembles photos of customized Converse sneakers submitted by fans from around the world and makes them available in a curated online collection, all presented and signed by the people who created them. The collection includes photos from notable celebrities such as Patti Smith and Andy Warhol. But the bulk of the creative images come

The Chuck Taylor All Star

Made by Joel Sussman

CONVERSE
Made by you

Today's Converse brand is built less on big-budget marketing campaigns and more on consumer-generated content by which customers express themselves and share their brand experiences. The Converse brand is "Made By You."

Courtesy of Converse Inc., Anomaly, and Joel Sussman

from ordinary but impassioned Converse consumers. "This is just a general celebration of people who love to wear Chuck Taylors," says Converse's VP of global marketing.

"Made By You" also uses real exhibitions designed to both showcase fans' creations and encourage them to share their Chuck experiences. For example, Converse took over window and store displays in retail locations of partners such as Foot Locker, Nordstrom, and Journeys. Some locations provided portable portrait studios that let people become part of the campaign on the spot. And at a Converse location in New York's Flatiron district and through a mobile app, a "Made By You" virtual reality experience let consumers walk in the shoes of artist Ron English, actress Joanna DeLane, musician King Tuff, and urban explorer Thomas Midlane.

The "Made By You" campaign is part and parcel of Converse's philosophy of letting consumers define the brand and share brand experiences. Converse sums up "Made By You" this way: "We made them to sink jump

shots on the court. You, however, saw them as something more…and started wearing our sneakers to do whatever you wanted. You played music, made art, skated the streets, and kicked back. You wore them as fashion. You wore them to work. You customized them with your personal style. You did everything to them, and in them. To this day, this spirit continues. As soon as you put them on and start doing your thing, their true life begins. You define them. You determine their journey. They become a one-of-a-kind celebration of your individuality and self-expression. They become a part of you. They're Made By You."

Converse's approach of stepping aside to let customers themselves talk about the brand and share their "Made By You" brand experiences has paid off handsomely. Since Nike acquired Converse, the brand's sales have soared 10-fold, from $200 million to almost $2 billion. Whereas Nike's sales have grown in recent years at an impressive 10 percent annually, Converse's sales have grown at twice that rate. And all that success comes despite the fact that Converse spends less than 1 percent of its revenues on promotion versus Nike's 10 percent. That's just one more benefit of letting customers do the talking.

Sources: Ashley Rodrigues, "Converse Breaks 'Made By You' Campaign for Chuck Taylors," *Advertising Age*, March 2, 2015, http://adage.com/print/297320; Jennifer Rooney, "With 'Made By You,' Converse Lets Wearers' Portraits Sell Chucks," *Forbes*, March 2, 2015, www.forbes.com/sites/jenniferrooney/2015/03/02/with-made-by-you-converse-lets-wearers-portraits-sell-chucks/#115405b11f5f; Jennifer Rooney, "Geoff Cottrill Departs as CMO of Converse," *Forbes*, February 5, 2016, www.forbes.com/sites/jenniferrooney/2016/02/05/geoff-cottrill-departs-as-cmo-of-converse/#c3e37865d992; "How Does Converse Remain Relevant after All These Years?" *Copernicus Marketing*, http://copernicusmarketing.com/copernican-news/building-your-brand/how-does-converse-remain-relevant-after-all-these-years/, accessed October 2016; and www.converse.com and www.converse.com/us/en/about/about-us.html, accessed October 2016.

big companies have learned, ads and other content made by amateurs can be…well, pretty amateurish. If done well, however, consumer-generated content efforts can produce new creative ideas and fresh perspectives on the brand from consumers who actually experience it. Such campaigns can boost consumer engagement and get customers talking and thinking about a brand and its value to them.

Selecting Advertising Media

Advertising media

The vehicles through which advertising messages are delivered to their intended audiences.

The major steps in **advertising media** selection are (1) determining *reach, frequency, impact,* and *engagement*; (2) choosing among major *media types*; (3) selecting specific *media vehicles*; and (4) choosing *media timing*.

Determining Reach, Frequency, Impact, and Engagement. To select media, the advertiser must determine the reach and frequency needed to achieve the advertising objectives. *Reach* is a measure of the *percentage* of people in the target market who are exposed to an ad campaign during a given period of time. For example, the advertiser might try to reach 70 percent of the target market during the first three months of a campaign. *Frequency* is a measure of how many *times* the average person in the target market is exposed to a message. For example, the advertiser might want an average exposure frequency of three.

But advertisers want to do more than just reach a given number of consumers a specific number of times. The advertiser also must determine the desired *media impact*—the *qualitative value* of message exposure through a given medium. For example, the same message in one magazine (say, *Time*) may be more believable than in another (say, the *National Enquirer*). For products that need to be demonstrated, television ads or online videos may have more impact than radio messages because they use sight, motion, *and* sound. Products for which consumers provide input on design or features might be better promoted at an interactive website or social media page than in a direct mailing.

More generally, an advertiser wants to choose media that will *engage* consumers rather than simply reach them. Using any medium, the relevance of ad content for its audience is often much more important than how many people it reaches. ● For example, when Mazda wanted to preannounce the sale of 100 25th-anniversary models of its iconic Mazda MX-5 Miata car at the New York International Auto show, it didn't use big-budget, high-reach media. Instead, it began

OUR TRIBUTE TO MX-5 LOVERS WORLDWIDE.

In celebration of a quarter century of pure fun to drive, Mazda is proud to unveil the Mazda MX-5 Miata 25th anniversary edition. Since the ground-breaking first generation we have continued building the MX-5 Miata to be an exuberant partner with unmatched driving pleasure, stimulating and exciting for both drivers and onlookers alike. In February 2011 total production surpassed 900,000 vehicles, earning the MX-5 Miata certification from Guinness World Records as the world's best selling two-seater sports car. All of us at Mazda deeply appreciate the enthusiastic support our lightweight roadster has received from around the world since its debut. And so, to express our gratitude we crafted this 25th anniversary edition, equipping it with special, carefully-selected parts. Now we invite you to experience this anniversary celebration of the unique Jinba Ittai driving performance — and just plain fun — that have always been hallmarks of the MX-5 Miata.

n. yamamoto

Nobuhiro Yamamoto
Mazda MX-5 Miata Program Manager

● **Engaging the right consumers with the right media worked well for Mazda. Using a highly targeted digital campaign, it sold out 100 25th-anniversary models of its iconic Mazda MX-5 Miata car in only 10 minutes.**

Special thanks to those at Mazda North America Operations. Here's to 26 years of the MX-5 Miata and beyond. Long live the roadster.

churning out Facebook, Twitter, and Google+ posts directly to its large MX-5 Miata fan base, directing them to a microsite where they could preorder the sporty little car. Engaging the right audience in the right media worked well for Mazda. The microsite opened a month later to a flood of responses, and the limited-edition Miata model sold out within only 10 minutes.[19]

Although Nielsen is beginning to measure *media engagement* levels for some television, radio, and social media, such measures are still hard to find in most cases. Current media measures are things such as ratings, readership, listenership, and click-through rates. However, engagement happens inside the head of the consumer. It's hard enough to measure how many people are exposed to a given television ad, video, or social media post, let alone measure the depth of engagement with that content. Still, marketers need to know how customers connect with an ad and brand idea as a part of the broader brand relationship.

Engaged consumers are more likely to act upon brand messages and even share them with others. Thus, rather than simply tracking *consumer impressions* for a media placement—how many people see, hear, or read an ad—Coca-Cola now also tracks the *consumer expressions* that result, such as a comment, a "Like," uploading a photo or video, or sharing brand content on social networks. Today's empowered consumers often generate more messages about a brand than a company can.

For example, Coca-Cola estimates that of the hundreds of millions of views of Coca-Cola–related content on YouTube each year, only about 18 percent are of content created by Coca-Cola. The other 82 percent are of content created by engaged consumers. So, many Coca-Cola marketing campaigns are aimed at sparking brand-related consumer expressions rather than just impressions. For instance, the brand's recent "Share a Coke" summer campaign—in which it swapped out the company's iconic logo on 20-ounce Coke bottles for one of more than 1,000 of the nation's most popular names—encouraged Coca-Cola fans to share the bottles with friends and family. Consumers could also share their Coca-Cola photos, stories, and experiences online using the hashtag #ShareaCoke, with selected posts featured on the brand's website and across company billboards. The "Share a Coke" campaign resulted in more than 500,000 photos and 6 million virtual Coke bottles shared online along with a boost of almost 25 million Coca-Cola Facebook followers.[20]

Choosing among Major Media Types. As summarized in ● **Table 15.2**, the major media types are television; digital, mobile, and social media; newspapers; direct mail; magazines; radio; and outdoor. Each medium has its advantages and its limitations. Media planners want to choose a mix of media that will effectively and efficiently present the advertising message to target customers. Thus, they must consider each medium's impact, message effectiveness, and cost.

As discussed earlier in the chapter, traditional mass media still make up a majority of today's media mixes. However, as mass-media costs rise and audiences shrink, companies have now added digital, mobile, and social media that cost less, target more effectively, and engage consumers more fully. Today's marketers are assembling a full mix of *paid, owned, earned, and shared media* that create and deliver engaging brand content to target consumers.

In addition to the explosion of online, mobile, and social media, cable and satellite television systems are thriving. Such systems allow narrow programming formats, such as all sports, all news, nutrition, arts, home improvement and gardening, cooking, travel, history, finance, and others that target select groups. Comcast and other cable operators are even testing systems that will let them target specific types of ads to TVs in specific neighborhoods or individually to specific types of customers. For example, ads for a Spanish-language channel would run in only Hispanic neighborhoods, or only pet owners would see ads from pet food companies.

● **Table 15.2 | Profiles of Major Media Types**

Medium	Advantages	Limitations
Television	Good mass-marketing coverage; low cost per exposure; combines sight, sound, and motion; appealing to the senses	High absolute costs; high clutter; fleeting exposure; less audience selectivity
Digital, mobile, and social media	High selectivity; low cost; immediacy; engagement capabilities	Potentially low impact; high audience control of content and exposure
Newspapers	Flexibility; timeliness; good local market coverage; broad acceptability; high believability	Short life; poor reproduction quality; small pass-along audience
Direct mail	High audience selectivity; flexibility; no ad competition within the same medium; allows personalization	Relatively high cost per exposure; "junk mail" image
Magazines	High geographic and demographic selectivity; credibility and prestige; high-quality reproduction; long life and good pass-along readership	Long ad purchase lead time; high cost; no guarantee of position
Radio	Good local acceptance; high geographic and demographic selectivity; low cost	Audio only; fleeting exposure; low attention ("the half-heard" medium); fragmented audiences
Outdoor	Flexibility; high repeat exposure; low cost; low message competition; good positional selectivity	Little audience selectivity; creative limitations

Finally, in their efforts to find less costly and more highly targeted ways to reach consumers, advertisers have discovered a dazzling collection of *alternative media*. These days, no matter where you go or what you do, you will probably run into some new form of advertising:

Tiny billboards attached to shopping carts urge you to buy Pampers while ads roll by on the store's checkout conveyor touting your local Chevy dealer. Step outside and there goes a city trash truck sporting an ad for Glad trash bags or a school bus displaying a Little Caesar's pizza ad. A nearby fire hydrant is emblazoned with advertising for KFC's "fiery" chicken wings. You escape to the ballpark, only to find billboard-size video screens running Budweiser ads while a blimp with an electronic message board circles lazily overhead. ● In midwinter, you wait in a city bus shelter that looks like an oven—with heat coming from the coils—shouting out Caribou Coffee's lineup of hot breakfast sandwiches.

These days, you're likely to find ads—well—anywhere. Taxi cabs sport electronic messaging signs tied to GPS location sensors that can pitch local stores and restaurants wherever they roam. Ad space is being sold on parking-lot tickets, airline boarding passes, subway turnstiles, highway toll booth gates, ATMs, municipal garbage cans, and even police cars, doctors' examining tables, and church bulletins. One company even sells space on toilet paper furnished free to restaurants, stadiums, and malls—the paper carries advertiser logos, coupons, and codes you can scan with your smartphone to download digital coupons or link to advertisers' social media pages. Now that's a captive audience.

Such alternative media seem a bit far-fetched, and they sometimes irritate consumers who resent it all as "ad nauseam." But for many marketers, these media can save money and provide a way to hit selected consumers where they live, shop, work, and play.

Another important trend affecting media selection is the rapid growth in the number of *media multitaskers,* people who absorb more than one medium at a time. For

● Marketers have discovered a dazzling array of alternative media, like this heated Caribou Coffee bus shelter.
Caribou Coffee

example, it's not uncommon to find someone watching TV with a smartphone in hand, tweeting, Snapchatting with friends, and chasing down product information on Google. One recent survey found that 90 percent of consumers now multitask while watching TV and that millennials and Gen X consumers engage in an average of three additional media activities while watching television, including internet browsing, text messaging, and reading email. Although some of this multitasking is related to TV viewing—such as looking up related product and program information—most multitasking involves tasks unrelated to the shows or ads being watched. Marketers need to take such media interactions into account when selecting the types of media they will use.[21]

Selecting Specific Media Vehicles. Media planners must also choose the best media vehicles—specific media within each general media type. For example, television vehicles include *Modern Family* and *ABC World News Tonight*. Magazine vehicles include *Time, Real Simple*, and *ESPN The Magazine*. Online and mobile vehicles include Twitter, Facebook, Instagram, and YouTube.

Media planners must compute the cost per 1,000 persons reached by a vehicle. For example, if a full-page, four-color advertisement in the U.S. national edition of *Forbes* costs $163,413 and *Forbes*'s readership is 900,000 people, the cost of reaching each group of 1,000 persons is about $181. The same advertisement in *Bloomberg Businessweek*'s Northeast U.S. regional edition may cost only $48,100 but reach only 155,000 people—at a cost per 1,000 of about $310.[22] The media planner ranks each magazine by cost per 1,000 and favors those magazines with the lower cost per 1,000 for reaching target consumers. In the previous case, if a marketer is targeting Northeast business managers, *Bloomberg Businessweek* might be the more cost-effective buy, even at a higher cost per thousand.

Media planners must also consider the costs of producing ads for different media. Whereas newspaper ads may cost very little to produce, flashy television ads can be very costly. Many online and social media ads cost little to produce, but costs can climb when producing made-for-the-web video and ad series.

In selecting specific media vehicles, media planners must balance media costs against several media effectiveness factors. First, the planner should evaluate the media vehicle's audience quality. For a Huggies disposable diapers ad, for example, *Parents* magazine would have a high exposure value; men's lifestyle magazine *Maxim* would have a low exposure value. Second, the media planner should consider audience engagement. Readers of *Vogue*, for example, typically pay more attention to ads than do *Time* readers. Third, the planner should assess the vehicle's editorial quality. *Time* and *The Wall Street Journal* are more believable and prestigious than *Star* or the *National Enquirer*.

● Media timing: Peeps' "Every Day Is a Holiday" campaign promotes the favorite marshmallow chicks and bunnies candies at holiday seasons other than just Easter, here Halloween.

Richard Levine / Alamy Stock Photo

Deciding on Media Timing. An advertiser must also decide how to schedule the advertising over time. Suppose sales of a product peak in December and drop in March (for winter outdoor gear, for instance). The firm can vary its advertising to follow the seasonal pattern, oppose the seasonal pattern, or be the same all year. Most firms do some seasonal advertising. For example, weight-loss product and service marketers tend to heavy up after the first of the year, targeting consumers who let their appetites get the better of them over the holiday season. Weight Watchers, for instance, spends more than a quarter of its annual advertising budget in January. ● By contrast, Peeps, the perennial Easter favorite marshmallow chicks and bunnies candies, launched an "Every Day Is a Holiday" campaign to broaden demand beyond Easter, which accounts for an estimated 70 percent of the brand's business. The campaign now promotes Peeps at Valentine's Day, Halloween, Thanksgiving, Christmas, and other holiday seasons. Some marketers do *only* seasonal advertising: For instance, P&G advertises its Vicks NyQuil only during the cold and flu season.[23]

Today's online and social media let advertisers create ads that respond to events in real time. For example, Lexus recently introduced a new model through live streaming from the North American International Auto Show via Facebook's News Feed. Some 100,000 people watched the introduction live in only the first 10 minutes; another 600,000 viewed it online within the next few days. Oreos reacted in a timely way to a power outage during Super Bowl XLVII with an outage-related "You can still dunk in the dark" tweet ad. The fast-reaction ad was re-tweeted and Favorited thousands of times in only 15 minutes. Similarly, Arby's created big buzz during a recent Grammy Awards show with a real-time tweet responding to Pharrell Williams's infamous Vivienne Westwood hat, which looks a bit like the hat in the familiar Arby's logo. The tweet "Hey @Pharrell, can we have our hat back?" earned more than 80,000 re-tweets and 45,000 Favorites.[24]

Evaluating Advertising Effectiveness and the Return on Advertising Investment

Return on advertising investment
The net return on advertising investment divided by the costs of the advertising investment.

Measuring advertising effectiveness and the **return on advertising investment** has become a hot issue for most companies. Top management at many companies is asking marketing managers, "How do we know that we're spending the right amount on advertising?" and "What return are we getting on our advertising investment?"

Advertisers should regularly evaluate two types of advertising results: the communication effects and the sales and profit effects. Measuring the *communication effects* of an ad or ad campaign tells whether the ads and media are communicating the ad message well. Individual ads can be tested before or after they are run. Before an ad is placed, the advertiser can show it to consumers, ask how they like it, and measure message recall or attitude changes resulting from it. After an ad is run, the advertiser can measure how the ad affected consumer recall or product awareness, engagement, knowledge, and preference. Pre- and post-evaluations of communication effects can be made for entire advertising campaigns as well.

Advertisers have gotten pretty good at measuring the communication effects of their ads and ad campaigns. However, *sales and profit* effects of advertising and other content are often much harder to measure. For example, what sales and profits are produced by an ad campaign that increases brand awareness by 20 percent and brand preference by 10 percent? Sales and profits are affected by many factors other than advertising—such as product features, price, and availability.

One way to measure the sales and profit effects of advertising is to compare past sales and profits with past advertising expenditures. Another way is through experiments. For example, to test the effects of different advertising spending levels, Coca-Cola could vary the amount it spends on advertising in different market areas and measure the differences in the resulting sales and profit levels. More complex experiments could be designed to include other variables, such as differences in the ads or media used.

However, because so many factors affect advertising effectiveness, some controllable and others not, pretesting ads and measuring the results of advertising spending remains an inexact science. Managers often must rely on large doses of judgment along with quantitative analysis when assessing content and advertising performance. That's especially true in this content-hungry digital age, where large quantities of ads and other content are produced and run on a virtual real-time basis. Thus, whereas companies tend to carefully pretest traditional big-budget media ads before running them, digital marketing content usually goes untested. For digital and social media campaigns, says one chief marketing officer, "it's very tough to test [and measure] just because of the volume [and timing] of the content we are putting out."[25]

Other Advertising Considerations

In developing advertising strategies and programs, the company must address two additional questions. First, how will the company organize its advertising and content function—who will perform which advertising tasks? Second, how will the company adapt its advertising strategies and programs to the complexities of international markets?

Organizing for Advertising

Different companies organize in different ways to handle advertising. In small companies, advertising might be handled by someone in the sales department. Large companies have advertising departments whose job it is to set the advertising budget, work with ad agencies, and handle other advertising not done by an agency. However, most large companies use outside advertising agencies because they offer several advantages.

Advertising agency
A marketing services firm that assists companies in planning, preparing, implementing, and evaluating all or portions of their advertising programs.

How does an **advertising agency** work? Advertising agencies originated in the mid- to late 1800s from salespeople and brokers who worked for the media and received a commission for selling advertising space to companies. As time passed, the salespeople began to help customers prepare their ads. Eventually, they formed agencies and grew closer to the advertisers than to the media.

Today's agencies employ specialists who can often perform advertising and brand content tasks better than the company's own staff can. Agencies also bring an outside point of view to solving the company's problems along with lots of experience from working with different clients and situations. So, today, even companies with strong advertising departments of their own use advertising agencies.

Some ad agencies are huge; the largest U.S. agency group, Y&R, has annual gross U.S. revenues of $3.7 billion. In recent years, many agencies have grown by gobbling up other agencies, thus creating huge agency holding companies. The largest of these megagroups, WPP, includes several large advertising, PR, digital, and promotion agencies with combined worldwide revenues of more than $19 billion.[26]

Most large advertising agencies have the staff and resources to handle all phases of an advertising campaign for their clients, from creating a marketing plan to developing ad and content campaigns and preparing, placing, and evaluating ads and content. Large brands commonly employ several agencies that handle everything from mass-media advertising campaigns to shopper marketing to social media content.

International Advertising Decisions

International advertisers face many complexities not encountered by domestic advertisers. The most basic issue concerns the degree to which global advertising should be adapted to the unique characteristics of various country markets.

Some advertisers have attempted to support their global brands with highly standardized worldwide advertising, with campaigns that work as well in Bangkok as they do in Baltimore. ● For example, McDonald's unifies its creative elements and brand presentation under the familiar "i'm lovin' it" theme in all its 100-plus markets worldwide. Oreo's latest "Open Up with Oreo" runs in 50 global with a simple universal message—"Open your heart to people who are different and you will discover similarities."[27] And Snickers runs similar versions of its "You're not you when you're hungry" ads in 80 different countries, from the United States and the United Kingdom to Mexico, Australia, and even Russia. No matter what the country, as noted in the Chapter 14 opening story, the ads strike a common human emotion that everyone can relate to—people get out of sorts and do uncharacteristic things when they need nutrition. A Snickers bar can help them get back to being their real selves. Snickers lets local markets make adjustments for local languages and personalities. Otherwise, the ads are similar worldwide.

In recent years, the increased popularity of online marketing and social media sharing has boosted the need for advertising standardization for global brands. Most big marketing and advertising campaigns include a large online presence. Connected consumers can now zip easily across borders via the internet and social media, making it difficult for advertisers to roll out adapted

● **International advertising: McDonald's unifies its global advertising under the familiar "i'm lovin' it" theme in all its 100-plus markets worldwide, here China.**

TED ALJIBE/AFP/GettyImages

campaigns in a controlled, orderly fashion. As a result, at the very least, most global consumer brands coordinate their digital sites internationally. For example, Coca-Cola web and social media sites around the world, from Australia and Argentina to France, Romania, and Russia, are surprisingly uniform. All feature splashes of familiar Coke red, iconic Coke bottle shapes, and Coca-Cola's music and "Taste the Feeling" themes.

Standardization produces many benefits—lower advertising costs, greater global advertising coordination, and a more consistent worldwide image. But it also has drawbacks. Most important, it ignores the fact that country markets differ greatly in their cultures, demographics, and economic conditions. Thus, most international advertisers "think globally but act locally." They develop global advertising *strategies* that make their worldwide efforts more efficient and consistent. Then they adapt their advertising *programs* to make them more responsive to consumer needs and expectations within local markets. For example, although Visa employs its "Everywhere you want to be" theme globally, ads in specific locales employ local language and inspiring local imagery that make the theme relevant to the local markets in which they appear.

Global advertisers face several special problems. For instance, advertising media costs and availability differ vastly from country to country. Countries also differ in the extent to which they regulate advertising practices. Many countries have extensive systems of laws restricting how much a company can spend on advertising, the media used, the nature of advertising claims, and other aspects of the advertising program. Such restrictions often require advertisers to adapt their campaigns from country to country.

Thus, although advertisers may develop global strategies to guide their overall advertising efforts, specific advertising programs must usually be adapted to meet local cultures and customs, media characteristics, and regulations.

Public Relations

Author Comment | Not long ago, public relations was considered a marketing stepchild because of its limited marketing use. That situation is changing fast, however, as more marketers recognize PR's brand building, customer engagement, and social power.

Another major promotion tool, **public relations**, consists of activities designed to engage and build good relations with the company's various publics. PR may include any or all of the following functions:[28]

Public relations (PR)
Building good relations with the company's various publics by obtaining favorable publicity; building up a good corporate image; and handling or heading off unfavorable rumors, stories, and events.

- *Press relations or press agency.* Creating and placing newsworthy information in the news media to attract attention to a person, product, or service.
- *Product and brand publicity.* Publicizing specific products and brands.
- *Public affairs.* Building and maintaining national or local community relationships.
- *Lobbying.* Building and maintaining relationships with legislators and government officials to influence legislation and regulation.
- *Investor relations.* Maintaining relationships with shareholders and others in the financial community.
- *Development.* Working with donors or members of nonprofit organizations to gain financial or volunteer support.

Public relations is used to promote products, people, places, ideas, activities, organizations, and even nations. Companies use PR to build good relations with consumers, investors, the media, and their communities. PR is often used to build support for newsworthy company events and actions. For example, a few years ago when CVS Health announced its bold decision to stop selling cigarettes and tobacco products in its stores, even though it meant sacrificing $2 billion in tobacco-related revenues, it knew that the decision would make headlines. But it left little to chance about how the full story would be told. Instead, CVS crafted a comprehensive "CVS Quits for Good" public relations campaign to tell consumers, Wall Street, and the health-care community that the decision would benefit both customers and the company:[29]

The "CVS Quits" PR campaign kicked off with full-page ads in *The New York Times*, *The Wall Street Journal*, the *Boston Globe*, and other major newspapers along with multimedia news releases featuring video announcements from CVS's president and other company leaders. The ads and releases explained that dropping tobacco products "is simply the right thing to do for the good of our customers and our company," consistent "with our purpose—helping people on their path to better health." CVS also created an information-packed cvs-quits.com microsite along with a #cvsquits hashtag and banners announcing the decision on the company's many web and social media sites. The "CVS Quits" story was snapped up by major print and broadcast media, creating some 2,557 broadcast mentions and more than 218 million total media impressions. The news also went viral online, becoming a top trending topic on both Facebook and Twitter and generating 200,000 social media mentions and 152,000 shares.

On the day the decision was activated, CVS's CEO rang the New York Stock Exchange bell and CVS Health executives snuffed out a 50-foot high cigarette at an event in New York City's Bryant Park. Both events received substantial media coverage. Finally, at the same time that it nixed tobacco products, CVS launched a nationwide campaign to help smokers kick the habit, cementing the company's message of "helping people on their path to better health" and generating even more positive news.

The "CVS Quits" PR campaign achieved impressive results. On Capitol Hill, eight US senators, 12 House members, and other influential leaders released statements urging other retailers to follow in CVS's footsteps. CVS's stock price jumped 9.2 percent in the three weeks following the announcement. And a survey showed that one in four consumers not currently shopping at CVS pharmacies said they would switch their prescriptions there after it quit tobacco. "CVS Quits" was named *PR Week*'s campaign of the year. "This is a new standard in PR," said one judge. "Great business decision that led to amazing PR results [that had] a real business impact on stock value, consumer behavior, and brand reputation."

The Role and Impact of PR

Like other promotional forms, public relations has the power to engage consumers and make a brand part of their lives and conversations. However, public relations can have a strong impact at a much lower cost than advertising can. Interesting brand stories, events, videos, or other content can be picked up by different media or shared virally by consumers, giving it the same or even greater impact than advertising that would cost millions of dollars. Consider recent PR moves by Burger King:[30]

Last year's Floyd Mayweather–Manny Pacquiao fight in Las Vegas was a commercial-free pay-per-view event. ● So when "The King"—Burger King's quirky, ceramic-headed robed mascot—appeared as part of Mayweather's entourage during the walkout prior the "Fight of the Century," it caused quite a stir. Beyond the 4.4 million viewers who watch the fight live worldwide, The King's appearance was all over Facebook and Twitter, generating big-time buzz for the burger chain. Burger King paid Mayweather an estimated $1 million, but that was a small fraction of the $5 million companies spend for a single 30-second Super Bowl ad. A month later, the bearded mascot popped up at the Belmont Stakes in an owner's box behind trainer Bob Baffert, whose horse American Pharoah ran for the coveted Triple Crown that day. As TV cameras panned Baffert before the race, The King stole the show, once again sparking a social media frenzy. The Belmont appearance reportedly cost Burger King only a $200,000 donation to a racing-related charity.

In yet another clever PR move, Burger King recently issued an invitation to rival McDonald's to call a cease-fire on Peace Day. In a full slate of online content, as well as full-page ads in *The New York Times* and the *Chicago Tribune*, Burger King publicly proposed that the chains jointly develop and sell a McWhopper, containing "all the tastiest bits of your Big Mac and our Whopper, united in one delicious, peace-loving burger," with all the proceeds benefiting the Peace One Day organization. McDonald's refused, but the gesture generated hugely positive PR for Burger King. Through these and other PR moves, Burger King has found a way to inject itself into daily social media conversations. "Burger King has really found a way to get attention by doing the unexpected and somewhat irreverent," says one expert. "They're generating an enormous amount of publicity at a very modest cost." Says another expert, "If you have the right spark, it will generate more buzz than paid media."

● **Public relations moves: Burger King's quirky, ceramic-headed "The King" mascot pops up in unexpected places—here in American Pharoah's owner's box at the Belmont Stakes—sparking media attention and big-time social media buzz.**

Gary Gershoff / Stringer/Getty Images

Despite its potential strengths, public relations is occasionally described as a marketing stepchild because of its sometimes limited and scattered use. The PR department is often located at corporate headquarters or handled by a third-party agency. Its staff is so busy dealing with various publics—stockholders, employees, legislators, and the press—that PR programs to support product marketing objectives may be ignored. Moreover, marketing managers and PR practitioners do not always speak the same language. Whereas many PR practitioners see their jobs as simply communicating, marketing managers tend to be much more interested in how advertising and PR affect brand building, sales and profits, and customer engagement and relationships.

This situation is changing, however. Although public relations still captures only a modest portion of the overall marketing budgets of many firms, PR can be a powerful brand-building tool. Especially in this digital age, the lines between advertising, PR, and other content are becoming more and more blurred. For example, are brand websites, blogs, brand videos, and social media activities advertising, PR, or something else? All are marketing content. And as the use of earned and shared digital content grows rapidly, PR is playing a bigger role in marketing content management.

More than any other department, PR has always been responsible for creating relevant marketing content that draws consumers to a brand rather than pushing messages out. "PR pros are an organization's master storytellers. In a word, they *do* content," says one expert. "The rise of social media [is] moving public relations professionals from the backroom, crafting press releases and organizing events, to the forefront of brand development and customer engagement," says another.[31] The point is that PR should work hand in hand with advertising within an integrated marketing communications program to help build customer engagement and relationships.

Major Public Relations Tools

Public relations uses several tools. One of the major tools is *news*. PR professionals find or create favorable news about the company and its products or people. Sometimes news stories occur naturally; sometimes the PR person can suggest events or activities that would create news. Another common PR tool is *special events*, ranging from news conferences and speeches, brand tours, and sponsorships to multimedia presentations or educational programs designed to reach and interest target publics.

Public relations people also prepare *written materials* to reach and influence their target markets. These materials include annual reports, brochures, articles, and company newsletters and magazines. *Audiovisual materials*, such as videos, are being used increasingly as communication tools. *Corporate identity materials* can also help create a corporate identity that the public immediately recognizes. Logos, stationery, brochures, signs, business forms, business cards, buildings, uniforms, and company cars and trucks all become marketing tools when they are attractive, distinctive, and memorable. Finally, companies can improve public goodwill by contributing money and time to *public service activities*.

As previously discussed, the web and social media are also important PR channels. Websites, blogs, and social media such as YouTube, Facebook, Instagram, Snapchat, Pinterest, and Twitter are providing new ways to reach and engage people. As noted, storytelling and engagement are core PR strengths, and that plays well into the use of online, mobile, and social media.

As with the other promotion tools, in considering when and how to use product public relations, management should set PR objectives, choose the PR messages and vehicles, implement the PR plan, and evaluate the results. The firm's PR should be blended smoothly with other promotion activities within the company's overall integrated marketing communications effort.

15 Reviewing and Extending the Concepts

OBJECTIVES REVIEW AND KEY TERMS

Objectives Review

Companies must do more than make good products; they have to engage consumers, inform them persuasively about product benefits, and carefully position products in consumers' minds. To do this, they must master *advertising* and *public relations*.

OBJECTIVE 15-1 Define the role of advertising in the promotion mix. *(p 428)*

Advertising—the use of paid media by a seller to inform, persuade, and remind buyers about its products or its organization—is an important promotion tool for engaging customers and communicating the value that marketers create for customers. American marketers spend more than $190 billion each year on advertising; worldwide spending exceeds $545 billion. Advertising takes many forms and has many uses. Although advertising is employed mostly by business firms, a wide range of not-for-profit organizations, professionals, and social agencies also employ advertising to promote their causes to various target publics. *Public relations*—gaining favorable publicity and creating a favorable company image—is the least used of the major promotion tools, although it has great potential for building consumer awareness and preference.

OBJECTIVE 15-2 Describe the major decisions involved in developing an advertising program. *(pp 429–446)*

Advertising decision making involves making decisions about the advertising objectives, budget, messages and media, and evaluation of the results. Advertisers should set clear target, task, and timing *objectives*, whether the aim is to inform, engage, persuade, or remind buyers. Advertising's goal is to move consumers through the buyer-readiness stages discussed in Chapter 14. Some advertising is designed to move people to immediate action. However, many of the ads you see today focus on building or strengthening long-term customer engagement and relationships. The advertising *budget* depends on many factors. No matter what method is used, setting the advertising budget is no easy task.

Advertising strategy consists of two major elements: creating advertising *messages and content* and selecting advertising *media*. The *message decision* calls for planning a message strategy and executing it effectively. Good messages and other content are especially important in today's costly and cluttered advertising environment. Just to gain and hold attention, today's messages must be better planned, more imaginative, more entertaining, and more rewarding to consumers. In fact, many marketers are now subscribing to a new merging of advertising and entertainment, dubbed *Madison & Vine*. The *media decision* involves defining reach, frequency, impact, and engagement goals; choosing major media types; selecting media vehicles; and choosing media timing. Message and media decisions must be closely coordinated for maximum campaign effectiveness.

Finally, *evaluation* calls for evaluating the communication and sales effects of advertising before, during, and after ads are placed. Advertising accountability has become a hot issue for most companies. Increasingly, top management is asking: "What return are we getting on our advertising investment?" and "How do we know that we're spending the right amount?" Other important advertising issues involve *organizing* for advertising and dealing with the complexities of international advertising.

OBJECTIVE 15-3 Define the role of public relations in the promotion mix. *(pp 446–448)*

Public relations, or *PR,* is used to promote products, people, places, ideas, activities, organizations, and even nations. Companies use PR to build good relationships with consumers, investors, the media, and their communities. PR can have a strong impact on public awareness at a much lower cost than advertising can, and PR results can sometimes be spectacular. Although PR still captures only a modest portion of the overall marketing budgets of many firms, it is playing an increasingly important brand-building role. In the digital, mobile, and social media age, the lines between advertising and PR are becoming more and more blurred.

OBJECTIVE 15-4 Explain how companies use public relations to communicate with their publics. *(p 448)*

Companies use PR to communicate with their publics by setting PR objectives, choosing PR messages and vehicles, implementing the PR plan, and evaluating PR results. To accomplish these goals, PR professionals use several tools, such as news and special events. They also prepare written, audiovisual, and corporate identity materials and contribute money and time to public service activities. The internet has also become an increasingly important PR channel, as websites, blogs, and social media are providing interesting new ways to reach more people.

Key Terms

OBJECTIVE 15-1

Advertising (p 428)

OBJECTIVE 15-2

Advertising objective (p 429)
Advertising budget (p 432)

Advertising strategy (p 433)
Madison & Vine (p 434)
Native advertising (p 435)
Creative concept (p 436)
Execution style (p 437)
Advertising media (p 440)

Return on advertising
investment (p 444)
Advertising agency (p 445)

OBJECTIVE 15-3

Public relations (PR) (p 446)

DISCUSSION AND CRITICAL THINKING

Discussion Questions

⭐ **15-1** Explain the decisions marketing managers make when developing an advertising program. (AACSB: Communication)

15-2 By what primary purposes are advertising objectives classified? Explain. Provide two examples of each. (AASCB: Communication; Reflective Thinking)

15-3 Discuss how marketers can break through the cluttered advertising environment. (AACSB: Communication)

15-4 What is an advertising agency? Discuss the changes in advertising agencies today compared with how they operated in the past. (AACSB: Communication)

⭐ **15-5** Define *public relations* and explain the many public relations functions. (AACSB: Communication)

Critical Thinking Exercises

15-6 Search YouTube for three of your favorite television commercials, each using a different execution style. For each ad, identify the execution style used and the audience targeted. Is it a good ad? Be prepared to present the commercials and support your conclusions. (AACSB: Communication; Use of IT; Reflective Thinking)

⭐ **15-7** Advertising objectives can be classified by their primary purpose—to *inform, persuade,* or *remind*. In a small group, locate one advertisement that primarily informs, one that persuades, and one that reminds. Explain how each ad meets the desired objective. (AACSB: Communication; Use of IT; Reflective Thinking)

15-8 In early 2016, the Wounded Warrior Project suffered a major blow to its fundraising when reports surfaced suggesting that the nonprofit organization spent too much of its money on travel, conferences, and high-end events rather than direct assistance to wounded veterans. Research this case. Was the Wounded Warrior Project's public relations response to the alleged misspending accusations effective in reaching out to its donors and other audiences? Why or why not? How is social media changing the public relations process? (AACSB: Communication; Use of IT; Reflective Thinking)

APPLICATIONS AND CASES

Online, Mobile, and Social Media Marketing Facebook Audience Network

Facebook has 1.44 billion monthly users and a large proportion of users typically visits the site daily on a mobile device. What started as an online social network that let people connect with each other has transformed into a behemoth media platform that promises to be a game-changer in mobile advertising. Facebook announced its new mobile ad platform called Audience Network to deliver targeted mobile ads for advertisers. While there are other mobile ad platforms (Google is the dominant player), Facebook has a treasure trove of data that is useful for advertisers. Google is strong in search data, but Facebook is part of our lives. Facebook has been placing ads on its site for advertisers, but now Facebook will be pushing those ads to third-party apps. This is a win-win-win situation for advertisers, app developers, and Facebook because advertisers get their mobile ads to people based on very personal information, app developers get ad revenue, and Facebook gets a cut of the ad revenue for placing the ad. And it's no small cut—in just the last quarter of 2015, Facebook earned $5.6 billion in mobile ad revenue. That's 80 percent of Facebook's overall ad revenue.

15-9 Compare and contrast Facebook's, Google's, and Twitter's ad networks. Which is most effective for advertisers? (AACSB: Communication; Reflective Thinking)

15-10 Mobile advertising is one of the fastest-growing sectors of digital advertising, but how is mobile advertising effectiveness measured? Research this issue and create a report of your findings. (AACSB: Communication; Reflective Thinking)

Marketing Ethics Native Advertising

Native advertising—articles paid for and/or written by a brand that appear on a publisher's site—has emerged as a powerful and popular new marketing content tool over the past few years. Media companies such as *BuzzFeed, The New York Times,* *The Wall Street Journal,* and *The Atlantic* have all invested heavily in the creation and distribution of native advertisements (also called *sponsored content*) on behalf of brands, with many charging more than $100,000 for a native advertising campaign.

Such sponsored content is designed to blend with the look and feel of the other content on a site, and written disclosures such as "Sponsored" or "Advertisement" are often hard to see even if consumers are looking for them. So it's no surprise that consumers often can't tell the difference between paid brand content and regular articles. Marketing content agency Contently recently surveyed adult consumers, showing them one brand-sponsored online content piece from *The New York Times, The Wall Street Journal, The Atlantic, The Onion, BuzzFeed,* or *Forbes* or an actual article on Whole Foods in *Fortune*. In four out of the six groups shown a native advertisement, a strong majority said they thought the ad was an article.

15-11 Search the internet to find examples of native advertising or other sponsored content. Could such content mislead consumers? Are companies responsible for ensuring consumers understand can distinguish between sponsored content and other content? Explain. (AACSB: Reflective Thinking, Communication; Use of IT)

15-12 Are the FTC's current regulations and guidelines regarding online advertising adequate for regulating native advertising and sponsored content? Is it likely that the FTC will issue new guidelines or regulations? Explain. (AACSB Communication; Reflective Thinking)

Marketing by the Numbers C3, CPM, and CPP

Nielsen ratings are very important to both advertisers and television programmers because the cost of television advertising time is based on these ratings. A show's *rating* is the number of households in Nielsen's sample that are tuned to that show divided by the number of television-owning households—115.6 million in the United States. One rating point represents 1 percent of the households (HHS) in the TV market. Nielsen's TV ratings are referred to as C3 and measure viewers who watch commercials live or watch recorded commercials up to three days later. A common measure of advertising efficiency is cost per thousand (CPM), which is the ad cost per thousand potential audience contacts. Advertisers also assess the cost per rating point by dividing the ad cost by the rating. These numbers are used to assess the efficiency of a media buy. Use the following average price and rating information for programs that are shown at the 8 p.m. hour on network television to answer the questions:

Program	Cost per 30-Second Spot	C3 Rating
Sunday Night Football	$594,000	7.9
Big Bang Theory	$317,000	5.1
The Voice	$264,575	3.9
How I Met Your Mother	$168,435	3.2
Agents of S.H.I.E.L.D.	$169,730	3.1

15-13 How many households are expected to watch each program? (AACSB: Communication; Analytical Reasoning)

15-14 Calculate the cost per thousand (CPM) and cost per point (CPP) for each program. How should advertisers use these measures when planning a television media buy? (AACSB: Communication; Analytical Reasoning; Reflective Thinking)

Video Case Kmart

On the heels of its wildly popular "Ship My Pants" ads, Kmart struck again with an ad that was considered hilarious by some, offensive by others, and a stroke of genius by advertising critics. Its latest ad, "Big Gas Savings," was launched on YouTube prior to airing on television. And like its "Ship My Pants" predecessor, the ad also went viral.

In addition to relying on potty humor to pull its sales out of the toilet, Kmart struck a very timely note in the tune of customer value—saving money on gasoline. Customers could save 30 cents a gallon on gas by spending $50 or more in its stores.

Millions of customers took advantage of the offer, driving traffic into Kmart stores.

After viewing the video featuring Kmart, answer the following questions:

15-15 What is the advertising message in the Kmart "Big Gas Savings" ad?

15-16 Why did Kmart choose to air this video on YouTube?

15-17 Is this Kmart ad effective? Explain.

Company Case Allstate: Bringing Mayhem to the Auto Insurance Advertising Wars

In the spring of 1950, the teenage daughter of Allstate general sales manager Davis Ellis was stricken with hepatitis shortly before she was to graduate from high school. The worried executive arrived home from work one evening just as his wife returned from the hospital where their daughter was admitted. As he met her at the front door, his wife reported, "The hospital said not to worry. . .we're in good hands with the doctor."

Later that year, Ellis became part of a team charged with developing the first major national advertising campaign for the Allstate Insurance Company. As the team discussed the message

they wanted the brand to convey, Ellis recalled his wife's "we're in good hands" remark and how good it made him feel. The phrase projected security, reassurance, and responsibility, exactly the traits the team wanted customers to associate with Allstate. Thus was born the slogan, "You're in Good Hands with Allstate."

By the early 2000s, a study by Northwestern University found that the long-standing Allstate catchphrase was the most recognized slogan in the United States. For years, Allstate held the position as the second-largest personal lines insurer, trailing only State Farm. Shortly thereafter, Allstate hired actor Dennis

Haysbert as the brand's spokesperson. After starring in dozens of Allstate commercials—each culminating with the question "Are you in good hands?"—Haysbert's deep voice became a comforting familiarity to television viewers. Today, the "Good Hands" slogan is the oldest surviving slogan for a paid campaign.

An Advertising Shakeup

Although Allstate's advertising served it well for decades, the company eventually fell into the same routine as the rest of the insurance industry. Big auto insurance companies were spending modestly on sleepy ad campaigns featuring touchy-feely, reassuring messages such as Allstate's "You're in good hands," or State Farm's "Like a good neighbor." In an industry characterized by low budgets and even lower-key ads, no brand's marketing stood out.

However, the advertising serenity ended with the first appearance of the now-iconic GEICO Gecko, backed by a big budget, pitching direct sales and low prices. That single GEICO ad campaign sparked a frenzy of ad spending and creativity in the insurance industry that quickly escalated into a full-scale advertising war. Once-conservative car insurance ads became creative showstoppers, as edgy and creative as ads found in any industry. Here are a few highlights:

- **GEICO:** GEICO got the auto insurance advertising wars rolling when it was acquired by billionaire Warren Buffet's Berkshire Hathaway company and given a blank check to aggressively increase market share. That led to an onslaught of advertising the likes of which the auto insurance industry had never seen. A string of creative GEICO campaigns featured everything from civilized cavemen to a stack of cash with googly eyes. But it was the GEICO Gecko that had the biggest impact. With his signature English accent, the Gecko made GEICO's simple message clear—"15 minutes can save you 15 percent or more on car insurance." More than any other industry spokesperson, the Gecko lent personality and pizzazz to the previously sleepy insurance industry and its staid brands.
- **Progressive:** Following GEICO's lead, Progressive created its own perky and endearing personality—Flo. Progressive created the ever-upbeat, ruby-lipped sales clerk to help convince consumers who are already in the market that they can get an even better price deal from Progressive. Flo helped put Progressive hot on the heels of rising GEICO as the fourth-largest auto insurer. Flo assists people when they are ready to shop. Progressive later introduced a complementary campaign featuring the Messenger—the mustachioed, leather-jacket-wearing stranger—and Brad—the easy-going, self-assured man with an absurdly funny sense of self-esteem who refers to himself only in the third person. Like the GEICO Gecko, Flo, the Messenger, and Brad have pitched price savings as their primary appeal.
- **State Farm:** As GEICO and Progressive shook up the industry with their direct, low-price, high-profile selling models, conventional agent-based auto insurers were forced to respond. Ninety-year-old State Farm, the long-time industry leader, was hardly a stranger to advertising. Like Allstate, State Farm had a long-standing, widely recognized slogan—"Like a good neighbor, State Farm is there"—a jingle written by pop music icon Barry Manilow way back in 1971. Sensing the threat from the rising newcomers, State Farm fought back vigorously with a new campaign centered on its enduring jingle. In its "magic jingle" campaign, State Farm agents magically appear when summoned with the jingle by young drivers in trouble—including the likes of LeBron James. The campaign's goal—to convince consumers that they still need the services of one of State Farms' 18,000 agents. To help make the point more forcefully, State Farm doubled its ad budget.

"Good Hands" Meets Mayhem

Amid this surge in competition and advertising creativity, Allstate struggled just to hold its own, let alone to grow. In the wake of the Gecko and Flo, Allstate had lost market share for two years running, even with Haysbert's presence as company pitchman. The brand needed its own over-the-top personality. So Allstate tapped ad agency Leo Burnett to bring mayhem to life—literally. With the new creepy Mayhem character played by actor Dean Winters, Allstate created a villainous counterpart to Haysbert's soothing hero. The campaign's goal: to convince consumers that there is more to buying car insurance than just price. "We knew we needed . . . a loud thunderclap to tell people that we cared about them," said Lisa Cochrane, senior VP of marketing at Allstate. "Mayhem is there to change the conversation, to disrupt the commoditization of insurance, and to provide you with something to think about to make sure that you have the right coverage." A Leo Burnett executive put it more bluntly—"We wanted to kick Flo's ass."

Mayhem portrays all of the unlikely events that can lead to a major auto insurance claim. He first appeared as a tree branch falling on a car, then as an emotionally compromised teenager ramming her pink SUV into an unsuspecting vehicle. According to Cochrane, after only these two early ads, "it made an impression." The possible situations for Mayhem are endless. As a deer, Mayhem jumps into the path of a moving car at night, "because that's what we deer do." As a torrential downpour, he loves leaky sunroofs. As a malfunctioning GPS, he sends a driver swerving into another car. As snow, he weighs down the roof of a garage until it collapses, smashing the car within. Each quirky ad ends with the statement and question "If you have cut-rate insurance, you could be paying for this yourself. Are you in good hands?"

Through such clever ads, Allstate's creative "Mayhem. It's Everywhere." campaign has put a contemporary, attention-grabbing twist on the company's long-standing "You're in good hands with Allstate" slogan, helping to position the brand as a superior alternative to price-oriented competitors. Even with its long-standing "Good Hands" campaign, Allstate needed something unconventional. In fact, mayhem didn't just describe the Allstate campaign—it characterized the entire world of auto insurance advertising.

The Mayhem campaign was not only well-received by consumers, it earned critical acclaim, winning approximately 80 advertising awards in the first year. But perhaps a bigger indication of the campaign's impact is the extent to which the character has become ingrained in pop culture. Although Mayhem has only a little more than a third of Flo's 4.9 million Facebook fans, he commands an engagement score roughly five times that of Progressive's perky spokeswoman. And when the character's creator recently saw a Mayhem-costumed trick-or-treater walking down her street, she called it "a career highlight that gave her chills."

More than just popular, Mayhem is right on message. At the end of each ad, he warns, "If you've got cut-rate insurance, you could be paying for this yourself." Then the reassuring voice of Haysbert provides the solution: "Are you in good hands?" he asks. "Get Allstate. You can save money and be better protected from Mayhem." This "worth-paying-a-little-more" message puts Allstate back at the top in terms of customer value.

Mayhem Redux

Allstate's ads were not only creative, they were effective. After a few years of Mayhem ads complementing Haysbert's Good Hands ads, Allstate's unaided brand awareness of 74 percent trailed State Farm's by only a slight margin, despite State Farm's 60 percent greater ad spending. And for a time, the Mayhem campaign halted Allstate's market share slide. According to Allstate CEO Thomas Wilson, "It's working. If you look at our quotes and our new business, it's way up." All this prompted Allstate to extend the campaign, including the introduction of Mayhem's Hispanic cousin, Mala Suerte (bad luck), aimed at Hispanic consumers. Mayhem has now been causing mayhem in the advertising industry for the past six years via more than 25 TV ads as well as numerous radio spots, billboard placements, and internet banner ads.

To extend the campaign, Allstate took Mayhem to the next level, giving the character his own Twitter account. Seemingly late to the Twitter party, Allstate executives indicated that the delay was intentional. "We've been very careful about not overdoing Mayhem and not overexposing [him]," said Jennifer Egeland, Allstate's director of advertising. "[We wanted] the right idea for launching him in the Twitter space."

The right idea was to conform to Mayhem's persona. As a recent football season dawned, Mayhem polled followers about what he should portray in the next ad—a charcoal grill or a cheap bungee cord. Consumers voted for the cord. Mayhem disobeyed, tweeting: "Too bad I'm a tailgate grill. Who's got a light?" He followed that up with Vine videos of a car set on fire from a grill mishap. Allstate then released two new Mayhem ads—"Tailgate Grill Fire" and "Cheap Bungee Cord"—making everyone happy. Also driving traffic to its social media sites was the "#MayhemSale" installment, a spot in which unsuspecting football fans Matt and Shannon had their house raided by a social media–savvy burglar. The spot drove significant web traffic and won a gold ADDY.

With all this activity and positive public response, Allstate seems to have found a weapon for maintaining its market position. But the all-out auto insurance advertising war illustrates just how critical it is to stay one step ahead of the competition. For the most recent year, Allstate increased its ad budget to $887 million, outdoing even market leader State Farm's $802 million effort. However, both companies were eclipsed by GEICO's eye-popping $1.1 billion advertising spending. Today, no less than 11 car insurance brands are running national TV advertising campaigns. Combined, the auto insurers now spend more than $6 billion each year to get their messages out. That makes things confusing for consumers, who struggle under the deluge of clever ads for the respective brands. It also creates mayhem for the insurers.

The intense competition, big budgets, and focus on consumer advertising have kept industry market share dynamic. In fact, during the past last year, GEICO moved into the number-two spot behind State Farm and is pulling away with a 10.8 percent share of the auto insurance market to Allstate's 10.0 percent. Although Allstate has grown its auto insurance business in recent years, GEICO's growth has been consistently stronger. With that development, Allstate is left to reconsider the value that it is getting out of its advertising investments and just how it might slow down GEICO and retake its number-two market position.

Questions for Discussion

15-18 Why has Allstate's "good hands" slogan withstood the test of time to become advertising's longest-running slogan?

15-19 Analyze Allstate's Mayhem ads based on the process of creating an advertising message as outlined in the text (for the latest Mayhem ads, check www.allstate.com/mayhem-is-everywhere.aspx).

15-20 Discuss issues of selecting advertising media for the Mayhem campaign. How might this process differ from that of campaigns for other companies?

15-21 Based on the information in this case, how might Allstate measure the effectiveness of the Mayhem campaign?

15-22 Has the Mayhem campaign been effective? Support your answer.

Sources: Victoria Moran, "Leo Burnett Chicago Wins Best of Show Gold ADDY Award for Allstate's #MayhemSale Campaign," *Advertising Age*, June 8, 2016, www.adage.com/print/304370; Ashley Rodriguez, "How Allstate's Mayhem Disrupted the Chatter around Insurance," *Advertising Age*, June 10, 2015, www.adage.com/print/298779; Steve Daniels, "GEICO Overtakes Allstate as No. 2 Auto Insurer," *Advertising Age*, March 3, 2014, www.adage.com/print/291947; E.J. Schultz, "Allstate's Mayhem Joins Twitter…Now What," *Advertising Age*, October 14, 2013, p. 28; Anthony Crup, "Allstate's Marketing Boss Talks Up 'March Mayhem,'" *Adweek*, March 25, 2014, www.adweek.com/print/156471; and advertisements and other information accessed at www.allstatenewsroom.com and www.allstate.com/mayhem-is-every-where.aspx, June 2015.

MyMarketingLab

Go to **mymktlab.com** for Auto-graded writing questions as well as the following Assisted-graded writing questions:

15-23 Discuss the characteristics advertising appeals should possess to be effective.

15-24 Name and describe the various execution styles for presenting messages and provide an example of each style different from the ones in the chapter.

PART 1: Defining Marketing and the Marketing Process (Chapters 1–2)
PART 2: Understanding the Marketplace and Consumer Value (Chapters 3–6)
PART 3: Designing a Customer Value–Driven Strategy and Mix (Chapters 7–17)
PART 4: Extending Marketing (Chapters 18–20)

16 | Personal Selling and Sales Promotion

In the previous two chapters, you learned about engaging customers and communicating customer value through integrated marketing communications (IMC) and two elements of the promotion mix: advertising and public relations. In this chapter, we examine two more IMC elements: personal selling and sales promotion. Personal selling is the interpersonal arm of marketing communications, in which the sales force engages customers and prospects to build relationships and make sales. Sales promotion consists of short-term incentives to encourage the purchase or sale of a product or service. Although this chapter presents personal selling and sales promotion as separate tools, they must be carefully integrated with the other elements of the promotion mix.

First, let's look at a real-life sales force. When you think of salespeople, perhaps you think of pushy retail sales clerks, "yell and sell" TV pitchmen, or the stereotypical glad-handing "used-car salesman." But such stereotypes don't fit the reality of most of today's salespeople—sales professionals who succeed not by taking advantage of customers but by listening to their needs and helping to forge solutions. Consider Salesforce—the industry leader in customer relationship management solutions. Salesforce not only produces market-leading sales management software, it also excels at practicing what it preaches—effective personal selling.

SALESFORCE: You Need a Great Sales Force to Sell Salesforce

Salesforce is way out in front of the $20 billion market for customer relationship management (CRM) solutions. The Salesforce logo, set inside the image of a puffy cloud, underscores Salesforce's highly successful cloud-based computing model (no software to install or own). Cloud-based systems are common today, but they were state-of-the-art when Salesforce pioneered the concept more than 15 years ago. Since then, the company has established itself as a leading innovator, constantly finding new ways to help client companies connect with customers and achieve greater sales force effectiveness using the latest online, mobile, social, and cloud technologies.

Salesforce helps businesses to "supercharge their sales." It supplies what it calls a "Customer Success Platform," a wide array of cloud-based sales force automation and customer relationship management tools that gather, organize, analyze, and disseminate in-depth data about a company's customers, sales, and individual sales rep and overall sales force performance. From its home in the cloud, Salesforce makes all these data and analyses readily available anytime, from anywhere, on any device with online access—desktops, laptops, tablets, or smartphones. Salesforce also integrates with major social media, providing tools for social media monitoring and real-time customer engagement and collaboration on its Salesforce Chatter platform, a kind of Facebook for enterprises.

Salesforce's innovative products have made it the world's number-one and fastest-growing CRM platform, ahead of blue-chip competitors such as Microsoft, Oracle, SAP, and IBM. The company's revenues hit $6.2 billion last year, up an impressive 24 percent over the previous year and more than four times what they were just five years ago. Salesforce has placed first or second on *Forbes* World's Most Innovative Company in any industry list for six straight years.

Innovative products and platforms have played a major role in Salesforce's stunning success. But even the best products don't sell themselves. You need a great sales force to sell Salesforce, and the company excels at practicing what it preaches—effective personal selling. Like the companies that buy its services, Salesforce has its own army of experienced, well-trained, highly motivated sales reps who take the company's products

> Salesforce leads the market in sales force automation and customer relationship management solutions. But even Salesforce's innovative products won't sell themselves. The company knows that it needs a great sales force to sell Salesforce.

to customers. In many respects, Salesforce's own sales force serves as a model for the products and services it sells—not just for using the Salesforce cloud but more generally for achieving the "supercharged" sales force results that the company promises its clients.

At Salesforce, developing an outstanding sales force starts with recruiting and hiring top-notch salespeople. Salesforce's aggressive but highly selective recruiting program skims the cream off the top of the global sales rep candidate pool. Each year on average, Salesforce hires only 4.5 percent of the more than 100,000 candidates who applied. Experience counts. Salesforce expects a minimum of two years of prior sales experience for small-business sales reps and up to two decades of experience for sales execs assigned to major accounts. To find such experienced candidates, Salesforce freely raids rival companies for new hires, counting on its high-energy culture and strong compensation packages to lure successful salespeople into the Salesforce fold.

Once hired, as you might expect, Salesforce salespeople have access to all the latest high-tech selling tools. In fact, the first major assignment of new hires is to study 20 hours of at-home video that teaches them the ins and outs of the Salesforce technologies that they won't be just selling but also using. But Salesforce would be the first to tell you that, although its cloud wizardry can help to optimize customer contact and the selling process, it doesn't take the place of good personal selling skills. So in training and fine-tuning its own sales force, the company starts by preaching tried-and-true selling fundamentals, tempered by its own modern twists.

The first fundamental of good selling at Salesforce is to *listen and learn*. As new recruits go through Salesforce's weeklong selling boot camp, taught at the company's Salesforce U, they learn that they should begin building customer relationships by asking probing questions and getting customers to talk, seeking to understand everything they can about a customer's situation and needs. "Eighty-five percent of salespeople don't slow down enough to really understand their customer's business," says a senior Salesforce sales executive.

Understanding the customer leads to a second selling fundamental: *empathize*—let customers know that you understand their issues and feel their pain. Empathy builds rapport and trust, an important step toward closing sales and building long-term customer relationships. Listening, learning, and empathizing are important first steps, but more is needed. "If all you are is responsive and helpful, then all you are is an administrative assistant," says the Salesforce sales executive.

So the next important step is to *offer solutions*—to show how Salesforce's cloud-based solutions will help clients make their sales forces more effective and productive in connecting with and selling to customers. Salesforce believes that the best

Salesforce's cloud-based "Customer Success Platform" provides a wide array of customer relationship management tools that help its customers "supercharge their sales."
Bloomberg/Getty Images

way to offer solutions is by telling good stories that highlight other customers' successes with its products. "Storytelling is very, very important," says Salesforce's sales productivity manager. "It can be the foundation of things like the corporate pitch and your interactions with your customers and prospects." When it comes to handling objections—such as "I don't trust putting our data in the cloud," "My current system is working fine," or "It costs too much"—Salesforce tells its salespeople that stories can be the most powerful tools they have. "When faced with objections, we always relate it back to a customer story," says a Salesforce marketing manager. "We're not the hero in our customer's stories," says another manager. "It's how the customer succeeded, not how we saved them."

When it comes to competitors, Salesforce's salespeople are ferocious. But Salesforce reps are trained to take the high road—to sell Salesforce's strengths, not competitors' weaknesses. "Internally, we have these posters: Crush Microsoft and Obliterate Oracle," says the Salesforce marketing manager. But, he adds, "when you go out to your customers, you have to be careful that you're guiding them and not just stepping on Microsoft. Even though we all want to."

Thus, effective professional selling is about much more than glad-handing and back-slapping on the one hand or plying high-tech CRM tools and data analytics on the other. Even though Salesforce boasts the best sales and customer connection tools in the business, backed by big data and combined with plenty of new-school techniques, its sales reps stay focused on old-school selling principles. At Salesforce—or anywhere else—good selling starts with the fundamentals of engaging and listening to customers, understanding and empathizing with their problems, and building relationships by offering meaningful solutions for mutual gain. That's how you build an incredibly successful sales force and Salesforce.[1]

OBJECTIVES OUTLINE

OBJECTIVE 16-1	Discuss the role of a company's salespeople in creating value for customers and building customer relationships. **Personal Selling** *(pp 456–458)*
OBJECTIVE 16-2	Identify and explain the six major sales force management steps. **Managing the Sales Force** *(pp 458–469)*
OBJECTIVE 16-3	Discuss the personal selling process, distinguishing between transaction-oriented marketing and relationship marketing. **The Personal Selling Process** *(pp 469–472)*
OBJECTIVE 16-4	Explain how sales promotion campaigns are developed and implemented. **Sales Promotion** *(pp 472–479)*

IN THIS CHAPTER, we examine two more promotion mix tools: *personal selling* and *sales promotion*. Personal selling consists of interpersonal interactions with customers and prospects to make sales and maintain customer relationships. Sales promotion involves using short-term incentives to encourage customer purchasing, reseller support, and sales force efforts.

Author Comment | Personal selling is the interpersonal arm of the promotion mix. A company's sales force creates and communicates customer value by personally engaging customers and building customer relationships.

Personal Selling

Robert Louis Stevenson once noted, "Everyone lives by selling something." Companies around the world use sales forces to sell products and services to business customers and final consumers. But sales forces are also found in many other kinds of organizations. For example, colleges use recruiters to attract new students. Museums and fine arts organizations use fundraisers to contact donors and raise money. Even governments use sales forces. The U.S. Postal Service, for instance, uses a sales force to sell Express Mail and other shipping and mailing solutions to corporate customers. In the first part of this chapter, we examine personal selling's role in the organization, sales force management decisions, and the personal selling process.

The Nature of Personal Selling

Personal selling
Personal presentations by the firm's sales force for the purpose of engaging customers, making sales, and building customer relationships.

Personal selling is one of the oldest professions in the world. The people who do the selling go by many names, including salespeople, sales representatives, agents, district managers, account executives, sales consultants, and sales engineers.

People hold many stereotypes of salespeople—including some unfavorable ones. *Salesman* may bring to mind the image of Dwight Schrute, the opinionated Dunder Mifflin paper salesman from the old TV show *The Office*, who lacks both common sense and social skills. Or you may think of the real-life "yell-and-sell" TV pitchmen, who hawk everything from the Flex Seal to the FOCUS T25 Workout and the Ove Glove in infomercials. However, the majority of salespeople are a far cry from these unfortunate stereotypes.

As the opening Salesforce story shows, most salespeople are well-educated and well-trained professionals who add value for customers and maintain long-term customer relationships. They listen to their customers, assess customer needs, and organize the company's efforts to solve customer problems. The best salespeople are the ones who work

● **Professional selling: It takes more than fast talk and a warm smile to sell expensive GE locomotives. GE's real challenge is to win and keep business by building day-in, day-out, year-in, year-out partnerships with customers.**

GE

Salesperson

An individual who represents a company to customers by performing one or more of the following activities: prospecting, communicating, selling, servicing, information gathering, and relationship building.

closely with customers for mutual gain. ● Consider GE's diesel locomotive business:

It takes more than fast talk and a warm smile to sell a batch of $2-million high-tech locomotives. A single big sale can easily run into the hundreds of millions of dollars. GE salespeople head up an extensive team of company specialists, all dedicated to finding ways to satisfy the needs of large customers. The selling process can be nerve-rackingly slow, involving dozens or even hundreds of decision makers from all levels of the buying organization and layer upon layer of subtle and not-so-subtle buying influences. A major sale can take years from the first sales presentation to the day the sale is announced. After getting the order, salespeople then must stay in almost constant touch to keep track of the account's equipment needs and to make certain the customer stays satisfied. The real challenge is to win and keep buyers' business by building day-in, day-out, year-in, year-out partnerships with them based on superior products and close collaboration.

The term **salesperson** covers a wide range of positions. At one extreme, a salesperson might be largely an *order taker*, such as the department store salesperson standing behind the counter. At the other extreme are *order getters*, whose positions demand *creative selling, social selling*, and *relationship building* for products and services ranging from appliances, industrial equipment, and airplanes to insurance and IT services. In this chapter, we focus on the more creative types of selling and the process of building and managing an effective sales force.

The Role of the Sales Force

Personal selling is the interpersonal arm of the promotion mix. It involves interpersonal interactions and engagement between salespeople and individual customers—whether face-to-face, by phone, via email or social media, through video or online conferences, or by other means. Personal selling can be very effective in complex selling situations. Salespeople can probe customers to learn more about their problems and then adjust the marketing offer and presentation to fit each customer's special needs.

The role of personal selling varies from company to company. Some firms have no salespeople at all—for example, companies that sell only online or companies that sell through manufacturers' reps, sales agents, or brokers. In most firms, however, the sales force plays a major role. In companies that sell business products and services, such as IBM, DuPont, or GE, salespeople work directly with customers. In consumer product companies such as P&G or Nike, the sales force plays an important behind-the-scenes role. It works with wholesalers and retailers to gain their support and help them be more effective in selling the company's products to final buyers.

Linking the Company with Its Customers

The sales force serves as a critical link between a company and its customers. In many cases, salespeople serve two masters—the seller and the buyer. First, they *represent the company to customers*. They find and develop new customers and communicate information about the company's products and services. They sell products by engaging customers and learning about their needs, presenting solutions, answering objections, negotiating prices and terms, closing sales, servicing accounts, and maintaining account relationships.

At the same time, salespeople *represent customers to the company*, acting inside the firm as "champions" of customers' interests and managing the buyer–seller relationship. Salespeople relay customer concerns about company products and actions back inside to those who can handle them. They learn about customer needs and work with other marketing and nonmarketing people in the company to develop greater customer value.

● In fact, to many customers, the salesperson *is* the company—the only tangible manifestation of the company that they see. Hence, customers may become loyal to salespeople as well as to the companies and products they represent. This concept of *salesperson-owned loyalty* lends even more importance to the salesperson's customer-relationship-building abilities. Strong relationships with the salesperson will result in strong relationships with

● Salespeople link the company with its customers. To many customers, the salesperson is the company.

Hero Images/Getty Images

the company and its products. Conversely, poor salesperson relationships will probably result in poor company and product relationships.

Coordinating Marketing and Sales

Ideally, the sales force and other marketing functions (marketing planners, brand managers, marketing content managers, and researchers) should work together closely to jointly create value for customers. Unfortunately, however, some companies still treat sales and marketing as separate functions. When this happens, the separate sales and marketing groups may not get along well. When things go wrong, marketers blame the sales force for its poor execution of what they see as an otherwise splendid strategy. In turn, the sales team blames the marketers for being out of touch with what's really going on with customers. Neither group fully values the other's contributions. However, if not repaired, such disconnects between marketing and sales can damage customer relationships and company performance.

A company can take several actions to help bring its marketing and sales functions closer together. At the most basic level, it can increase communications between the two groups by arranging joint meetings and spelling out communication channels. It can create opportunities for salespeople and marketers to work together. Brand managers and researchers can tag along on sales calls or sit in on sales planning sessions. In turn, salespeople can sit in on marketing planning sessions and share their firsthand customer knowledge.

A company can also create joint objectives and reward systems for sales and marketing teams or appoint marketing–sales liaisons—people from marketing who "live with the sales force" and help coordinate marketing and sales force programs and efforts. Finally, it can appoint a high-level marketing executive to oversee both marketing and sales. Such a person can help infuse marketing and sales with the common goal of creating value for customers to capture value in return.[2]

> **Author Comment** | Here's another definition of sales force management: "planning, organizing, leading, and controlling personal contact programs designed to achieve profitable customer relationships." Once again, the goal of every marketing activity is to create customer value, engage customers, and build profitable customer relationships.

Sales force management
Analyzing, planning, implementing, and controlling sales force activities.

Managing the Sales Force

We define **sales force management** as analyzing, planning, implementing, and controlling sales force activities. It includes designing sales force strategy and structure as well as recruiting, selecting, training, compensating, supervising, and evaluating the firm's salespeople. These major sales force management decisions are shown in ● **Figure 16.1** and discussed in the following sections.

Designing the Sales Force Strategy and Structure

Marketing managers face several sales force strategy and design questions. How should salespeople and their tasks be structured? How big should the sales force be? Should salespeople sell alone or work in teams with other people in the company? Should they sell in the field, by phone, or using online and social media? We address these issues next.

● FIGURE | 16.1
Major Steps in Sales Force Management

> The goal of this process? You guessed it! The company wants to build a skilled and motivated sales team that will help to engage customers, create customer value, and build strong customer relationships.

| Designing sales force strategy and structure | ➤ | Recruiting and selecting salespeople | ➤ | Training salespeople | ➤ | Compensating salespeople | ➤ | Supervising salespeople | ➤ | Evaluating salespeople |

The Sales Force Structure

A company can divide sales responsibilities along any of several lines. The structure decision is simple if the company sells only one product line to one industry with customers in many locations. In that case the company would use a *territorial sales force structure*. However, if the company sells many products to many types of customers, it might need a *product sales force structure*, a *customer sales force structure*, or a combination of the two.

In the **territorial sales force structure**, each salesperson is assigned to an exclusive geographic area and sells the company's full line of products or services to all customers in that territory. This organization clearly defines each salesperson's job and fixes accountability. It also increases the salesperson's desire to build local customer relationships that, in turn, improve selling effectiveness. Finally, because each salesperson travels within a limited geographic area, travel expenses are relatively small. A territorial sales organization is often supported by many levels of sales management positions. For example, individual territory sales reps may report to area managers, who in turn report to regional managers who report to a director of sales.

If a company has numerous and complex products, it can adopt a **product sales force structure**, in which the sales force specializes along product lines. For example, GE employs different sales forces within different product and service divisions of its major businesses. Within GE Infrastructure, for instance, the company has separate sales forces for aviation, energy, transportation, and water processing products and technologies. No single salesperson can become expert in all of these product categories, so product specialization is required. Similarly, GE Healthcare employs different sales forces for diagnostic imaging, life sciences, and integrated IT products and services. In all, a company as large and complex as GE might have dozens of separate sales forces serving its diverse product and service portfolio.

Using a **customer (or market) sales force structure**, a company organizes its sales force along customer or industry lines. Separate sales forces may be set up for different industries, serving current customers versus finding new ones, and serving major accounts versus regular accounts. Organizing the sales force around customers can help a company build closer relationships with important customers. Many companies even have special sales forces to handle the needs of individual large customers. For example, GE Aviation has a special Boeing sales team. And P&G sales reps are integrated into Customer Business Development (CBD) teams. Each CBD team is assigned to a major P&G customer, such as Walmart, Safeway, or CVS Health. ● For example, P&G's Walmart CBD team consists of hundreds of P&Gers who partner with Walmart buyers in Walmart's hometown of Bentonville, Arkansas. The CBD organization places the focus on serving the complete needs of each major customer. It lets P&G "grow business by working as a 'strategic partner' with our accounts," not just as a supplier.[3]

When a company sells a wide variety of products to many types of customers over a broad geographic area, it often employs a *complex sales force structure*, which combines several types of organization. Salespeople can be specialized by customer and territory; product and territory; product and customer; or territory, product, and customer. For example, P&G specializes its sales force by customer (with different sales teams for Safeway, CVS Health, or other large customers) *and* by territory for each key customer group (territory CBD representatives, territory managers, regional managers, and so on). No single structure is best for all companies and situations. Each company should select a sales force structure that best serves the needs of its customers and fits its overall marketing strategy.

Territorial sales force structure
A sales force organization that assigns each salesperson to an exclusive geographic territory in which that salesperson sells the company's full line.

Product sales force structure
A sales force organization in which salespeople specialize in selling only a portion of the company's products or lines.

Customer (or market) sales force structure
A sales force organization in which salespeople specialize in selling only to certain customers or industries.

● **Customer sales force structure:** P&G's Walmart Customer Business Development sales team consists of hundreds of P&Gers who work closely with Walmart buyers in Walmart's hometown of Bentonville, Arkansas.
© grzegorz knec/Alamy

Sales Force Size

Once the company has set its structure, it is ready to consider *sales force size*. Sales forces may range in size from only a few salespeople to tens of thousands. Some sales forces are huge—for example, in the United States, PepsiCo employs 36,000 salespeople; American Express, 23,400; GE, 16,400; and Cisco Systems, 14,000.[4] Salespeople constitute one of the company's most productive—and most expensive—assets. Therefore, increasing their numbers will increase both sales and costs.

A company might use some form of *workload approach* to set sales force size. Using this approach, a company first groups accounts into different classes according to size, account status, or other factors related to the amount of effort required to maintain the account. It then determines the number of salespeople needed to call on each class of accounts the desired number of times.

The company might think as follows: Suppose we have 1,000 A-level accounts and 2,000 B-level accounts. A-level accounts require 36 calls per year, and B-level accounts require 12 calls per year. In this case, the sales force's *workload*—the number of calls it must make per year—is 60,000 calls [$(1,000 \times 36) + (2,000 \times 12) = 36,000 + 24,000 = 60,000$]. Suppose our average salesperson can make 1,000 calls a year. Thus, we need 60 salespeople ($60,000 \div 1,000$).

Other Sales Force Strategy and Structure Issues

Sales management must also determine who will be involved in the selling effort and how various sales and sales-support people will work together.

Outside sales force (or field sales force)
Salespeople who travel to call on customers in the field.

Inside sales force
Salespeople who conduct business from their offices via telephone, online and social media interactions, or visits from prospective buyers.

Outside and Inside Sales Forces. A company may have an **outside sales force (or field sales force)**, an **inside sales force**, or both. Outside salespeople travel to call on customers in the field. In contrast, inside salespeople conduct business from their offices via telephone, online and social media interactions, or visits from buyers. The use of inside sales has grown in recent years as a result of increased outside selling costs and the surge in online, mobile, and social media technologies.

Some inside salespeople provide support for the outside sales force, freeing them to spend more time selling to major accounts and finding new prospects. For example, *technical sales-support people* provide technical information and answers to customers' questions. *Sales assistants* provide research and administrative backup for outside salespeople. They track down sales leads, call ahead and confirm appointments, follow up on deliveries, and answer customers' questions when outside salespeople cannot be reached. Using such combinations of inside and outside salespeople can help serve important customers better. The inside rep provides daily access and support, whereas the outside rep provides face-to-face collaboration and relationship building.

Other inside salespeople do more than just provide support. *Telemarketers* and *online sellers* use the phone, internet, and social media to find new leads, learn about customers and their business, or sell and service accounts directly. Telemarketing and online selling can be very effective, less costly ways to sell to smaller, harder-to-reach customers. Depending on the complexity of the product and customer, for example, a telemarketer can make from 20 to 33 decision-maker contacts a day compared with the average of four that an outside salesperson can make. In addition, whereas the cost of a business-to-business (B-to-B) field sales call can average close to $600, a routine industrial telemarketing or online contact might average only $25 to $75.[5]

Although the federal government's Do Not Call Registry put a dent in telephone sales to consumers, telemarketing remains a vital tool for most B-to-B marketers. For some smaller companies, telephone and online selling may be the primary sales approaches. However, most of the larger companies also use these tactics extensively, either to sell directly to small and midsize customers or to assist their sales forces in selling to larger ones.

● In addition to costs savings, in today's digital, mobile, and social media environments, many buyers are more receptive to—or even prefer—phone and online contact versus the high level of face-to-face contact once required. Today's customers are more inclined to gather their own information online—one study showed that a typical buyer reports contacting a sales rep only after independently completing about 60 percent of the buying

● Outside and inside sales: In in today's digital, mobile, and social media environment, inside selling is growing much faster than in-person selling. And a growing proportion of outside selling is now done over a phone or mobile device.

LDProd/Shutterstock

process. Then buyers routinely use the phone, online meetings, and social media interactions to engage sellers and close deals. "With virtual meeting software such as GoToMeeting.com and WebEx, communications tools such as Skype, and social media sites such as Twitter, Facebook, and LinkedIn, it's become easier to sell with few if any face-to-face meetings," says an inside sales consultant.[6]

As a result of these trends, telephone and online selling are growing much faster than in-person selling. One recent study found that inside sales positions are growing 300 times faster than outside sales positions. Another study also notes the emergence of the "hybrid sales rep," a modern cross between a field sales rep and an inside rep who often works from a remote location. Some 41 percent of outside sales activity is now done over the phone or a mobile device, from a home office or a company office or on the go.[7] For many types of products and selling situations, phone or online selling can be as effective as a personal sales call.

Team selling

Using teams of people from sales, marketing, engineering, finance, technical support, and even upper management to service large, complex accounts.

Team Selling. As products become more complex and as customers grow larger and more demanding, a single salesperson simply can't handle all of a large customer's needs. Instead, most companies now use **team selling** to service large, complex accounts. Sales teams can unearth problems, solutions, and sales opportunities that no individual salesperson could. Such teams might include experts from any area or level of the selling firm—sales, marketing, technical and support services, research and development, engineering, operations, finance, and others.

In many cases, the move to team selling mirrors similar changes in customers' buying organizations. Many large customer companies have implemented team-based purchasing, requiring marketers to employ equivalent team-based selling. When dealing with large, complex accounts, one salesperson can't be an expert in everything the customer needs. Instead, selling is done by strategic account teams, quarterbacked by senior account managers or customer business managers.

For example, the P&G Walmart Customer Business Development team is a complete, multifunctional customer service unit consisting of more than 300 people. The team includes a CBD manager and several CBD account executives (each responsible for a specific P&G product category), supported by specialists in marketing strategy, product development, operations, information systems, logistics, finance, and human resources.

Team selling does have some pitfalls, however. For example, salespeople are by nature competitive and have often been trained and rewarded for outstanding individual performance. Salespeople who are used to having customers all to themselves may have trouble learning to work with and trust others on a team. In addition, selling teams can confuse or overwhelm customers who are used to working with only one salesperson. Finally, difficulties in evaluating individual contributions to the team-selling effort can create some sticky compensation issues.

Recruiting and Selecting Salespeople

At the heart of any successful sales force operation is the recruitment and selection of good salespeople. The performance difference between an average salesperson and a top salesperson can be substantial. In a typical sales force, the top 30 percent of the salespeople might bring in 60 percent of the sales. Thus, careful salesperson selection can greatly increase overall sales force performance.

Beyond the differences in sales performance, poor selection results in costly turnover. When a salesperson quits, the costs of finding and training a new salesperson—plus the costs of lost sales—can be very high. One sales consulting firm calculates the total costs of a bad sales hire at a whopping $616,000.[8] Also, a sales force with many new people is less productive, and turnover disrupts important customer relationships and sales team morale.

What sets great salespeople apart from all the rest? In an effort to profile top sales performers, Gallup Consulting, a division of the well-known Gallup polling organization, has interviewed hundreds of thousands of salespeople. Its research suggests that the best salespeople possess four key talents: intrinsic motivation, a disciplined work style, the ability to close a sale, and, perhaps most important, the ability to build relationships with customers.[9]

Super salespeople are motivated from within—they have an unrelenting drive to excel. Some salespeople are driven by money, a desire for recognition, or the satisfaction of competing and winning. Others are driven by the desire to provide service and build relationships. The best salespeople possess some of each of these motivations. However, another analysis found that the best salespeople are driven by a strong sense of purpose: "The salespeople who sold with noble purpose, who truly want to make a difference to customers, consistently outsold the salespeople focused on sales goals and money." Selling with such a sense of customer-related purpose is not only more successful, it's also more profitable and more satisfying to salespeople.[10]

● Great salespeople: The best salespeople possess intrinsic motivation, a disciplined work style, the ability to close a sale, and, perhaps most important, the ability to build relationships with customers.

© Mint Images Limited/Alamy Stock Photo

Super salespeople also have a disciplined work style. They lay out detailed, organized plans and then follow through in a timely way. But motivation and discipline mean little unless they result in closing more sales and building better customer relationships. Super salespeople build the skills and knowledge they need to get the job done. ● Perhaps most important, top salespeople are excellent customer problem solvers and relationship builders. They understand their customers' needs. Talk to sales executives and they'll describe top performers in these terms: good listeners, empathetic, patient, caring, and responsive. Top performers can put themselves on the buyer's side of the desk and see the world through their customers' eyes. They don't want just to be liked; they want to add value for their customers.

That said, there is no one right way to sell. Each successful salesperson uses a different approach, one that best applies his or her unique strengths and talents. For example, some salespeople enjoy the thrill of a harder sell in confronting challenges and winning people over. Others might apply "softer" talents to reach the same goal. "The truth is, no two great sales reps are alike," says one sales consultant. "You might thrive on fierce competition, while a colleague wins by being a super-analytical problem solver. Or maybe you have a tremendous talent for building relationships, while your fellow top performer is a brilliant strategist. What's most important is that you win business your way."[11]

When recruiting, a company should analyze the sales job itself and the characteristics of its most successful salespeople to identify the traits needed by a successful salesperson in its industry. Then it must recruit the right salespeople. The human resources department looks for applicants by getting names from current salespeople, using employment agencies, searching the internet and online social media, posting ads and notices on its website and industry media, and working through college placement services. Another source is to attract top salespeople from other companies. Proven salespeople need less training and can be productive immediately.

Recruiting will attract many applicants from which the company must select the best. The selection procedure can vary from a single informal interview to lengthy testing and interviewing. Many companies give formal tests to sales applicants. Tests typically measure sales aptitude, analytical and organizational skills, personality traits, and other characteristics. But test scores provide only one piece of information in a set that includes personal characteristics, references, past employment history, and interviewer reactions.

Training Salespeople

New salespeople may spend anywhere from a few weeks or months to a year or more in training. After the initial training ends, most companies provide continuing sales training via seminars, sales meetings, and online learning throughout the salesperson's career. According to one source, American firms spend approximately $20 billion on sales training each year. Although training can be expensive, it can also yield dramatic returns. For instance, one recent study showed that sales training conducted by ADP, an administrative services firm, resulted in a return on investment of nearly 340 percent in only 90 days.[12]

Training programs have several goals. First, salespeople need to know about customers and how to build relationships with them. Therefore, the training program must teach them about different types of customers and their needs, buying motives, and buying habits. It must also teach them how to sell effectively and train them in the basics of the selling process. Salespeople also need to know and identify with the company, its products, and its competitors. Therefore, an effective training program teaches them about the company's objectives, organization, products, and the strategies of major competitors.

Today, many companies are adding digital e-learning components to their sales training programs. Online training may range from simple self-paced text- and video-based product training and internet-based sales exercises that build sales skills to sophisticated simulations that re-create the dynamics of real-life sales calls. One of the most basic forms is virtual instructor-led training (VILT). Using this method, a small group of salespeople at remote locations logs on to an online conferencing site, where a sales instructor leads training sessions using online video, audio, and interactive learning tools.[13]

Training online instead of on-site can cut travel and other training costs, and it takes up less of a salesperson's selling time. It also makes on-demand training available to salespeople, letting them train as little or as much as needed, whenever and wherever needed. Although most e-learning is web-based, companies can offer on-demand training from anywhere via almost any mobile device.

Many companies are now using imaginative new e-learning techniques to make sales training more efficient and effective—and sometimes even more fun. For example, learning solutions company Bottom-Line Performance has developed a digital game-based sales-training tool called Knowledge Guru, which helps salespeople learn and remember key product, company, and customer facts as well as selling skills and processes.[14]

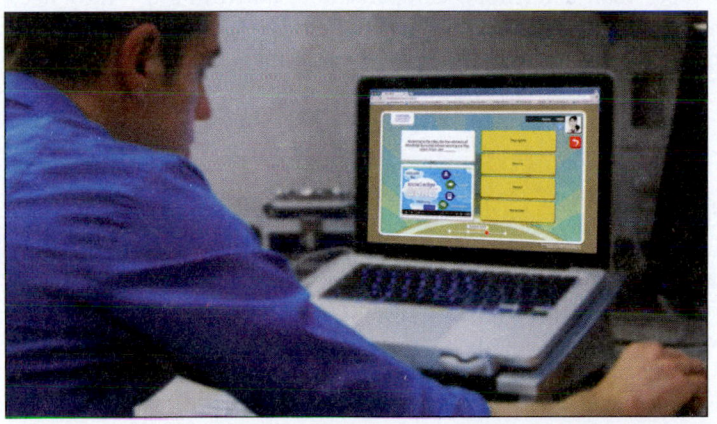

● **E-training can make sales training more effective—and more engaging. BLP's game-based sales-training tool—called Knowledge Guru—helps sales people learn key product, company, and customer facts as well as selling skills and processes.**

Bottom-Line Performance

Using Knowledge Guru, companies can create single-pass games that teach foundational knowledge to new salespeople or for new products or extended-play games with performance challenges for teaching new selling skills. ● Salespeople can play the learning games alone or in competition with others, offline or online on a smartphone, tablet, or desktop. All the while, sales trainers can track individual salesperson learning performance. Several Fortune 500 companies use Knowledge Guru to add fun and engagement to training tasks that can sometimes be dull or intimidating. For example, IT networking company Cisco Systems uses Knowledge Guru as part of each module within its certified sales associate program. According to a Cisco program manager who helped introduce Knowledge Guru into the program, "Before they can work with customers, new [sales] associates must obtain a deep knowledge of our architectures and technologies. Knowledge Guru is essential to reinforcing this technical knowledge, and participants have rated Knowledge Guru highly as a learning tool." Most important, the game really works, helping salespeople achieve an average retention rate of 87 percent against training objectives across all Cisco users.

Compensating Salespeople

To attract good salespeople, a company must have an appealing compensation plan. Compensation consists of four elements: a fixed amount, a variable amount, expenses, and fringe benefits. The fixed amount, usually a salary, gives the salesperson some stable income. The variable amount, which might be commissions or bonuses based on sales performance, rewards the salesperson for greater effort and success.

● A sales force compensation plan can both motivate salespeople and direct their activities. Compensation should direct salespeople toward activities that are consistent with the overall sales force and marketing objectives.[15] For example, if the strategy is to acquire new business, grow rapidly, and gain market share, the compensation plan might include a larger commission component, coupled with a new account bonus to encourage high sales performance and new account development. In contrast, if the goal is to maximize current account profitability, the compensation plan might contain a larger base-salary component with additional incentives for current account sales or customer satisfaction.

In fact, more and more companies are moving away from high-commission plans that may drive salespeople to make short-term grabs for business. They worry that a

● **Sales force compensation: A good compensation plan both motivates salespeople and directs their activities.**

Amble Design/Shutterstock

salesperson who is pushing too hard to close a deal may ruin the customer relationship. Instead, companies are designing compensation plans that reward salespeople for building customer relationships and growing the long-run value of each customer.

When times get tough economically, some companies are tempted to cut costs by reducing sales compensation. However, although some cost-cutting measures make sense when business is sluggish, cutting sales force compensation across the board is usually an action of last resort. Top salespeople are always in demand, and paying them less might mean losing them at a time when they are needed most. Thus, short-changing key salespeople can result in short-changing important customer relationships. If the company must reduce its compensation expenses, rather than making across-the-board cuts, companies should continue to pay top performers well while turning loose low performers.

Supervising and Motivating Salespeople

New salespeople need more than a territory, compensation, and training—they need supervision and motivation. The goal of *supervision* is to help salespeople "work smart" by doing the right things in the right ways. The goal of *motivation* is to encourage salespeople to "work hard" and energetically toward sales force goals. If salespeople work smart and work hard, they will realize their full potential—to their own and the company's benefit.

Supervising Salespeople

Companies vary in how closely they supervise their salespeople. Many help salespeople identify target customers and set call objectives. Some may also specify how much time the sales force should spend prospecting for new accounts and set other time management priorities. One tool is the weekly, monthly, or annual *call plan* that shows which customers and prospects to call on and which activities to carry out. Another tool is *time-and-duty analysis*. In addition to time spent selling, the salesperson spends time traveling, waiting, taking breaks, and doing administrative chores.

● **Figure 16.2** shows how salespeople spend their time. On average, active selling time accounts for only 37 percent of total working time.[16] Companies are always looking for ways to save time—simplifying administrative duties, developing better sales-call and routing plans, supplying more and better customer information, and using phone, email, online, or mobile conferencing instead of traveling.

● **FIGURE | 16.2**

How Salespeople Spend Their Time

Source: "2014 Performance Optimization Study," *CSO Insights*, www.csoinsights. com. Used with permission.

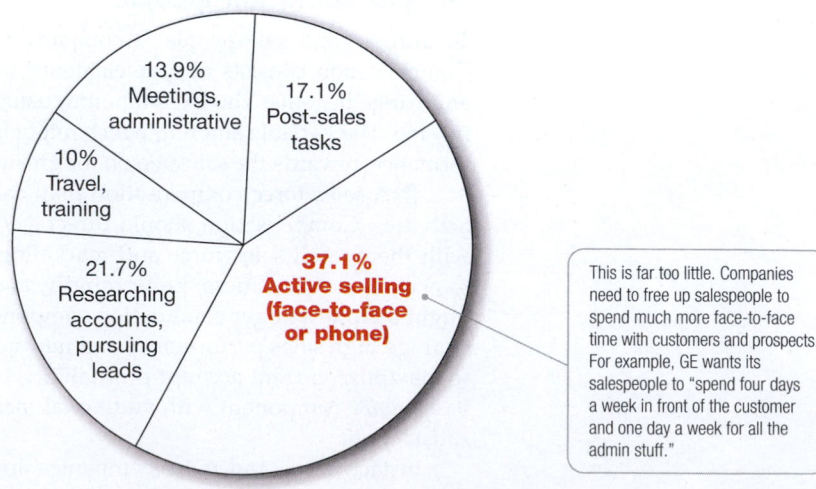

Many firms have adopted *sales force automation systems*: computerized, digitized sales force operations that let salespeople work more effectively anytime, anywhere. Companies now routinely equip their salespeople with laptops or tablets, smartphones, wireless connections, videoconferencing technologies, and customer-contact and relationship management software. Armed with these technologies, salespeople can more effectively and efficiently profile customers and prospects, analyze and forecast sales, engage customers, make presentations, prepare sales and expense reports, and manage account relationships. The result is better time management, improved customer service, lower sales costs, and higher sales performance. In all, technology has reshaped the ways in which salespeople carry out their duties and engage customers.

Motivating Salespeople

Beyond directing salespeople, sales managers must also motivate them. Some salespeople will do their best without any special urging from management. To them, selling may be the most fascinating job in the world. But selling can also be frustrating. Salespeople often work alone, and they must sometimes travel away from home. They may also face aggressive competing salespeople and difficult customers. Therefore, salespeople often need special encouragement to do their best.

Management can boost sales force morale and performance through its organizational climate, sales quotas, and positive incentives. *Organizational climate* describes the feeling that salespeople have about their opportunities, value, and rewards for a good performance. Some companies treat salespeople as if they are not very important, so performance suffers accordingly. Other companies treat their salespeople as valued contributors and allow virtually unlimited opportunity for income and promotion. Not surprisingly, these companies enjoy higher sales force performance and less turnover.

Sales quota

A standard that states the amount a salesperson should sell and how sales should be divided among the company's products.

Many companies motivate their salespeople by setting **sales quotas**—standards stating the amount they should sell and how sales should be divided among the company's products. Compensation is often related to how well salespeople meet their quotas. Companies also use various *positive incentives* to increase the sales force effort. *Sales meetings* provide social occasions, breaks from the routine, chances to meet and talk with "company brass," and opportunities to air feelings and identify with a larger group. Companies also sponsor *sales contests* to spur the sales force to make a selling effort above and beyond what is normally expected. Other incentives include honors, merchandise and cash awards, trips, and profit-sharing plans.

Evaluating Salespeople and Sales Force Performance

We have thus far described how management communicates what salespeople should be doing and how it motivates them to do it. This process requires good feedback, which means getting regular information about salespeople to evaluate their performance.

Management gets information about its salespeople in several ways. The most important source is *sales reports*, including weekly or monthly work plans and longer-term territory marketing plans. Salespeople also write up their completed activities on *call reports* and turn in *expense reports* for which they are partly or wholly reimbursed. The company can also monitor the sales and profit performance data in the salesperson's territory. Additional information comes from personal observation, customer surveys, and talks with other salespeople.

Using various sales force reports and other information, sales management evaluates the members of the sales force. It evaluates salespeople on their ability to "plan their work and work their plan." Formal evaluation forces management to develop and communicate clear standards for judging performance. It also provides salespeople with constructive feedback and motivates them to perform well.

On a broader level, management should evaluate the performance of the sales force as a whole. Is the sales force accomplishing its customer relationship, sales, and profit objectives? Is it working well with other areas of the marketing and company organization? Are sales force costs in line with outcomes? As with other marketing activities, the company wants to measure its *return on sales investment*.

Author | Like just about everything
Comment | else these days, digital
technologies have affected selling
big time. Today's sales forces
are mastering the use of online,
mobile, and social media tools to
engage business customers, build
relationships, and make sales.

Social selling

Using online, mobile, and social media
to engage customers, build stronger
customer relationships, and augment
sales performance.

Social Selling: Online, Mobile, and Social Media Tools

The fastest-growing sales trend is the explosion in **social selling**—the use of online, mobile, and social media to engage customers, build stronger customer relationships, and augment sales performance. Digital sales force technologies are creating exciting new avenues for connecting with and engaging customers in the digital and social media age. Some analysts even predict that the internet will mean the death of person-to-person selling, as salespeople are ultimately replaced by websites, online social media, mobile apps, video and conferencing technologies, and other tools that allow direct customer contact. "Don't believe it," says one sales expert. "There may be less face-to-face selling," says another. "But on the seller's side, there needs to be someone in charge of that (customer) interaction. That will remain the role of the salesperson" (see Real Marketing 16.1).[17] Thus, online and social media technologies won't likely make salespeople obsolete. Used properly, however, they will make salespeople more productive and effective.

The new digital technologies are providing salespeople with powerful tools for identifying and learning about prospects, engaging customers, creating customer value, closing sales, and nurturing customer relationships. Social selling technologies can produce big organizational benefits for sales forces. They help conserve salespeople's valuable time, save travel dollars, and give salespeople new vehicles for selling and servicing accounts.

Social selling hasn't really changed the fundamentals of selling. Sales forces have always taken the primary responsibility for reaching out to and engaging customers and managing customer relationships. Now, more of that is being done digitally. However, online and social media are dramatically changing the customer buying process. As a result, they are also changing the selling process. In today's digital world, many customers no longer rely as much as they once did on information and assistance provided by salespeople. Instead, they carry out more of the buying process on their own—especially the early stages. Increasingly, they use online and social media resources to analyze their own problems, research solutions, get advice from colleagues, and rank buying options before ever speaking to a salesperson. One study of business buyers found that 92 percent of buyers start their searches online and that, on average, buyers completed nearly 60 percent of the buying process before contacting a supplier.[18]

Thus, today's customers have much more control over the sales process than they had in the days when brochures, pricing, and product advice were available only from a sales rep. Customers can now browse corporate websites, blogs, and YouTube videos to identify and qualify sellers. They can hobnob with other buyers on social media such as LinkedIn, Google+, Twitter, or Facebook to share experiences, identify solutions, and evaluate products they are considering. As a result, if and when salespeople do enter the buying process, customers often know almost as much about a company's products as the salespeople do. And when customers do call in salespeople, they are more often doing it digitally, with the expectation of real-time engagement.

In response to this new digital buying environment, sellers are reorienting their selling processes around the new customer buying process. They are "going where customers are"—social media, web forums, online communities, blogs—in order to engage customers earlier. They are engaging customers not just where and when they are buying but also where and when they are learning about and evaluating what they will buy.

Salespeople now routinely use digital tools that monitor customer social media exchanges to spot trends, identify prospects, and learn what customers would like to buy, how they feel about a vendor, and what it would take to make a sale. They generate lists of prospective customers from online databases and social networking sites, such as InsideView, Hoovers, and LinkedIn. They create dialogues when prospective customers visit their web and social media sites through live chats with the sales team. They use internet conferencing tools such as WebEx, Zoom, GoToMeeting, or TelePresence to talk live with customers about products and services. They provide videos and other information on their YouTube channels and Facebook pages.

Today's sales forces are also ramping up their own use of digital content and social media to engage customers throughout the buying process. A recent survey of business-to-business marketers found that, although they have recently cut back on traditional media and event spending, they are investing more in social media, ranging from proprietary

16.1 B-to-B Salespeople: In This Digital and Social Media Age, Who Needs Them Anymore?

It's hard to imagine a world without salespeople. But according to some analysts, there will be a lot fewer of them a decade from now. With the explosion of the internet, mobile devices, social media, and other technologies that link customers directly with companies, they reason, who needs face-to-face selling anymore? According to the doubters, salespeople are rapidly being replaced by websites, email, blogs, mobile apps, video sharing, virtual trade shows, social media such as LinkedIn and Facebook, and a host of other digital-age interaction tools.

Research firm Forrester has predicted a 22 percent decline in the number of B-to-B sales reps in the United States over the next five years. That means that one in five sales reps will be out of a job. "The world no longer needs salespeople," one doomsayer boldly proclaims. "Sales is a dying profession and soon will be as outmoded as oil lamps and the rotary phone."

So, is business-to-business selling really dying? Will the internet, mobile technologies, and social media replace the age-old art of selling face-to-face? To answer these questions, *SellingPower* magazine called together a panel of sales experts and asked them to weigh in on the future of B-to-B sales. The panel members agreed that technology is radically transforming the selling profession. Today's revolutionary changes in how people communicate are affecting every aspect of business, and selling is no exception.

But is B-to-B selling dead in this digital and social media age? Don't believe it, says the *SellingPower* panel. Technology and the internet won't soon be replacing person-to-person buying and selling. Selling has changed, agrees the panel, and the technology can greatly enhance the selling process. But it can't replace many of the functions that salespeople perform. "The internet can take orders and disseminate content, but what it can't do is discover customer needs," says one panelist. "It can't build relationships, and it can't prospect on its own." Adds another panelist, "Someone must define the company's value proposition and unique message and communicate it to the market, and that person is the sales rep."

What is dying, however, is what one panelist calls the account-maintenance role—the order taker who stops by the customer's office on Friday and says, "Hey, got anything for me?" Likewise, there's not much of a future for explainers, reps who simply convey product and service information that can be obtained more quickly and easily online. Such salespeople are not creating value and can easily be replaced by automation. However, salespeople who excel at new customer acquisition, relationship management, problem solving, and account growth with existing customers will always be in high demand. "People who do that kind of selling are only going to get more valuable," says another sales force expert. "That's not going to go away."

There's no doubt about it—technology is transforming the selling profession. Instead of relying on salespeople for basic information and education, customers can now do much of their own prepurchase research via websites, online searches, phone apps, social media contacts, and other venues. Many customers now start the sales process online and do their homework about problems, competing products, and suppliers before the first sales meeting ever takes place. They don't need basic information or product education; they need solutions and new insights. According to one survey, business buyers are at least 57 percent of the way through the buying process by the time they reach out to a vendor. So today's salespeople need "to move into the discovery and relationship-building phase, uncovering pain points and focusing on the prospect's business," says a panelist. In fact, jobs for such consultant-type sales reps are expected to grow at a healthy clip during the next five years.

Rather than replacing salespeople, technology is augmenting them. Today's salespeople aren't really doing anything fundamentally new. They've always done customer research and social networking. Today, however, they are doing it on steroids, using a new kit of high-tech digital tools and applications.

For example, many companies have moved rapidly into online-community-based

Online selling tools, such as SAP's EcoHub and SAP Store online community-based marketplaces, can help to build customer engagement and generate buying interest and sales. But rather than replacing salespeople, such efforts extend their reach and effectiveness.

©2015 SAP SE or an SAP Affiliate Company

selling. Case in point: Enterprise-software company SAP, which six years ago set up EcoHub, its own online, community-powered social media and mobile marketplace consisting of customers, SAP software experts, partners, and almost anyone else who wanted to join. The EcoHub community grew quickly to more than 2 million users in 200 countries, extending across a broad online spectrum—a dedicated website, mobile apps, Twitter channels, LinkedIn groups, Facebook and Google+ pages, YouTube channels, and more. EcoHub grew to more than 600 "solution storefronts," where visitors could "discover, evaluate, and buy" software solutions and services from SAP and its partners. EcoHub also let users rate and share the solutions and advice they got from other community members.

SAP was surprised to learn that what it had originally seen as a place for customers to discuss issues, problems, and solutions turned into a significant point of sale. The information, give-and-take discussions, and conversations at the site drew in customers, even for big-ticket sales of $20 to $30 million or more. In fact, EcoHub has now

evolved into SAP Store, a gigantic SAP marketplace where customers can engage with SAP, its partners, and each other to share information, post comments and reviews, discover problems, and evaluate and buy SAP solutions.

However, although the SAP Store draws in new potential customers and takes them through many of the initial stages of product discovery and evaluation, it doesn't replace SAP's or its partners' salespeople. Instead, it extends their reach and effectiveness. Its real value is the flood of sales leads it creates for the SAP and partner sales forces. Once prospective customers have discovered, discussed, and evaluated SAP solutions online, SAP invites them to initiate contact, request a proposal, or start the negotiation process.

That's where the person-to-person selling begins.

All this suggests that B-to-B selling isn't dying, it's just changing. The tools and techniques may be different as sales forces leverage and adapt to selling in the digital and social media age. But the panelists agree strongly that B-to-B marketers will never be able to do without strong sales teams. Salespeople who can engage customers, discover customer needs, solve customer problems, and build relationships will be needed and successful, regardless of what else changes. Especially for those big-ticket B-to-B sales, "all the new technology may make it easier to sell by building strong ties to customers even before the first sit-down, but when the signature hits the dotted line, there will be a sales rep there."

Sources: Based on information from Andy Hoar, "Death of a (B2B) Salesman," *Forbes,* April 15, 2015, www.forbes.com/sites/forrester/2015/04/15/death-of-a-b2b-salesman/#2bfaac2539be; "Robots Can't Close," *Sales & Marketing Management,*" November 13, 2015, https://salesandmarketing.com/content/robots-can't-close; Lain Chroust Ehmann, "Sales Up!" *SellingPower,* January/February 2011, p. 40; Paul Nolan, "Mapping the Buyer's Journey," *Sales and Marketing Management,* March 27, 2015, www.salesandmarketing.com/content/mapping-buyer's-journey; John Ellett, "SAP's Success Formula for B2B Social Selling," *Forbes,* April 1, 2016, www.forbes.com/sites/johnellett/2016/04/01/saps-success-formula-for-btob-social-selling/#1ecd7ec213cb; and https://store.sap.com/ and https://scn.sap.com, accessed October 2016.

online customer communities to webinars and social media and mobile applications. Consider Makino, a leading manufacturer of metal cutting and machining technology:[19]

> There's a hot new video on YouTube these days, featured at the Makino Machine Tools YouTube channel. It shows a Makino five-axis vertical machining center in action, with metal chips flying as the machinery mills a new industrial part. Sound exciting? Probably not to you. But to the right industrial customer, the video is downright spellbinding. YouTube is just one of a wide variety of social media initiatives that Makino uses to complement its salespeople in their efforts to engage and inform customers and enhance customer relationships. For example, Makino hosts an ongoing series of industry-specific webinars that position the company as an industry thought leader. Makino produced and archived hundreds webinars on topics ranging from how to get the most out of your machine tools to how metal-cutting processes are done. Webinar content is tailored to specific industries, such as aerospace or medical, and is promoted through carefully targeted online ads and email invitations. The webinars help to build Makino's customer database, generate sales leads, build customer relationships, and prepare the way for salespeople by serving up relevant information and educating customers online. Makino also uses Facebook, YouTube, and Twitter to inform customers and prospects about the latest Makino innovations and events and to demonstrate the company's machines in action. Such digital content and social media don't replace salespeople. Instead, they help salespeople build

Social selling: Machine tool manufacturer Makino engages customers through extensive digital content and social media, which complement sales force efforts to engage customers and build product–customer relationships.
Courtesy of Makino

even more fruitful customer relationships. When it comes to B-to-B selling these days, Makino has learned, social marketing is *the* space to be.

Ultimately, social selling technologies are helping to make sales forces more efficient, cost-effective, and productive. The technologies help salespeople do what good salespeople have always done—build customer relationships by solving customer problems—but do it better, faster, and cheaper.

However, social selling also has some drawbacks. For starters, it's not cheap. But even more, there are some things you just can't present or teach via the internet—things that require personal engagement and interaction. For these reasons, some high-tech experts recommend that sales executives use online and social media technologies to spot opportunities, provide information, maintain customer contact, and make preliminary client sales presentations but resort to old-fashioned, face-to-face meetings when the time draws near to close a big deal.

The Personal Selling Process

> **Author Comment** | So far, we've examined how sales management develops and implements overall sales force strategies and programs. In this section, we'll look at how individual salespeople and sales teams sell to customers and build relationships with them.

We now turn from designing and managing a sales force to the personal selling process. The **selling process** consists of several steps that salespeople must master. These steps focus on the goal of getting new customers and obtaining orders from them. However, most salespeople spend much of their time maintaining existing accounts and building long-term customer relationships. We will discuss the relationship aspect of the personal selling process in a later section.

Steps in the Selling Process

Selling process
The steps that salespeople follow when selling, which include prospecting and qualifying, preapproach, approach, presentation and demonstration, handling objections, closing, and follow-up.

As shown in ● **Figure 16.3**, the selling process consists of seven steps: prospecting and qualifying, preapproach, approach, presentation and demonstration, handling objections, closing, and follow-up.

Prospecting and Qualifying

Prospecting
The sales step in which a salesperson or company identifies qualified potential customers.

The first step in the selling process is **prospecting**—identifying qualified potential customers. Approaching the right customers is crucial to selling success. Salespeople don't want to call on just any potential customers. They want to call on those who are most likely to appreciate and respond to the company's value proposition—those the company can serve well and profitably.

A salesperson must often approach many prospects to get only a few sales. Although the company supplies some leads, salespeople need skill in finding their own. The best source is referrals. Salespeople can ask current customers for referrals and cultivate other referral sources, such as suppliers, dealers, noncompeting salespeople, and online or social media contacts. They can also search for prospects in directories or on the internet and track down leads using the telephone, email, and social media. Or, as a last resort, they can drop in unannounced on various offices (a practice known as *cold calling*).

● FIGURE | 16.3
Steps in the Selling Process

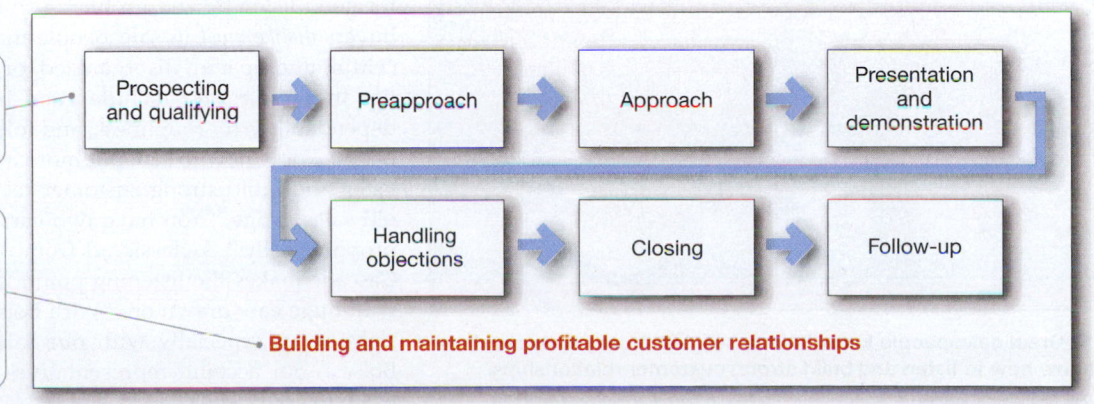

As shown here, these steps are transaction-oriented—aimed at closing a specific sale with the customer...

...but remember that in the long run, a single sale is only one element of a long-term customer relationship. So the selling process steps must be understood in the broader context of maintaining profitable customer relationships.

Prospecting and qualifying → Preapproach → Approach → Presentation and demonstration → Handling objections → Closing → Follow-up

Building and maintaining profitable customer relationships

Salespeople also need to know how to *qualify* leads—that is, how to identify the good ones and screen out the poor ones. Prospects can be qualified by looking at their financial ability, volume of business, special needs, location, and possibilities for growth.

Preapproach

Preapproach
The sales step in which a salesperson learns as much as possible about a prospective customer before making a sales call.

Before calling on a prospect, the salesperson should learn as much as possible about the organization (what it needs, who is involved in the buying) and its buyers (their characteristics and buying styles). This step is known as **preapproach**. A successful sale begins long before the salesperson makes initial contact with a prospect. Preapproach begins with good research and preparation. The salesperson can consult standard industry and online sources, acquaintances, and others to learn about the company. He or she can scour the prospect's web and social media sites for information about its products, buyers, and buying processes. Then the salesperson must apply the research gathered to develop a customer strategy.

The salesperson should set *call objectives*, which may be to qualify the prospect, gather information, or make an immediate sale. Another task is to determine the best approach, which might be a personal visit, a phone call, an email, or a text or tweet. The ideal timing should be considered carefully because many prospects are busiest at certain times of the day or week. Finally, the salesperson should give thought to an overall sales strategy for the account.

Approach

Approach
The sales step in which a salesperson meets the customer for the first time.

During the **approach** step, the salesperson should know how to meet and greet the buyer and get the relationship off to a good start. The approach might take place offline or online, in-person or via digital conferencing or social media. This step involves the salesperson's appearance, opening lines, and follow-up remarks. The opening lines should be positive to build goodwill from the outset. This opening might be followed by some key questions to learn more about the customer's needs or by showing a display or sample to attract the buyer's attention and curiosity. As in all stages of the selling process, listening to the customer is crucial.

Presentation and Demonstration

Presentation
The sales step in which a salesperson tells the "value story" to the buyer, showing how the company's offer solves the customer's problems.

During the **presentation** step of the selling process, the salesperson tells the "value story" to the buyer, showing how the company's offer solves the customer's problems. The *customer-solution approach* fits better with today's relationship marketing focus than does a hard sell or glad-handing approach.

The goal should be to show how the company's products and services fit the customer's needs. Buyers today want insights and solutions, not smiles; results, not razzle-dazzle. Moreover, buyers don't want just products; they want to know how those products will add value to their businesses. They want salespeople who listen to their concerns, understand their needs, and respond with the right products and services.

But before salespeople can *present* customer solutions, they must *develop* solutions to present. The solutions approach calls for good listening and problem-solving skills. The qualities that buyers *dislike most* in salespeople include being pushy, late, deceitful, unprepared, disorganized, or overly talkative. The qualities they *value most* include good listening, empathy, honesty, dependability, thoroughness, and follow-through. ● Great salespeople know how to sell, but more important, they know how to listen and build strong customer relationships. According to an old sales adage, "You have two ears and one mouth. Use them proportionally." A classic ad from office products maker Boise Cascade makes the listening point. It shows a Boise salesperson with huge ears drawn on. "With Boise, you'll notice a difference right away, especially with our sales force," says the ad. "At Boise... our account representatives have the unique ability to listen to your needs."

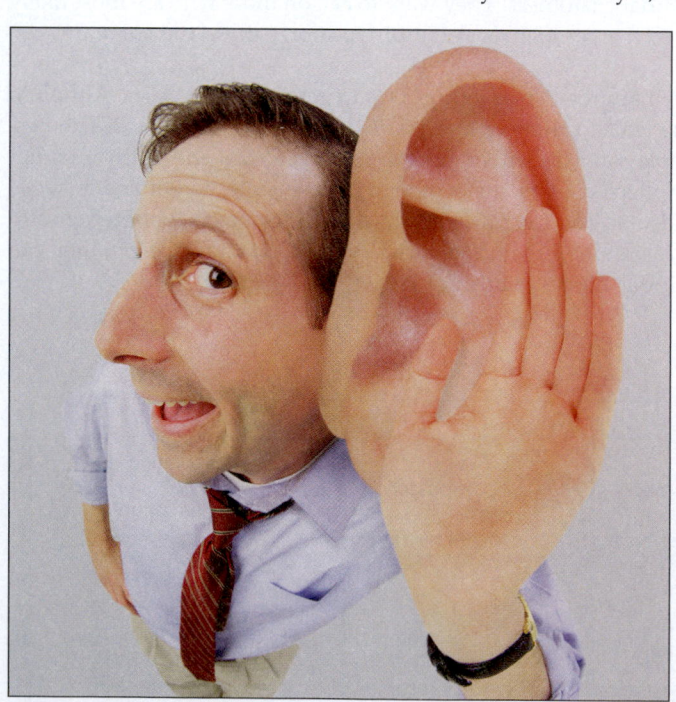

● **Great salespeople know how to sell, but more important, they know how to listen and build strong customer relationships.**

Tony Garcia/Getty Images

Finally, salespeople must also plan their presentation methods. Good interpersonal communication skills count when it comes to engaging customers and making effective sales presentations. However, the current media-rich and cluttered communications environment presents many new challenges for sales presenters. Today's information-overloaded customers demand richer presentation experiences. For their part, presenters now face multiple distractions during presentations from mobile phones, text messages, and other digital competition. As a result, salespeople must deliver their messages in more engaging and compelling ways.

Thus, today's salespeople are employing advanced presentation technologies that allow for full multimedia presentations to only one or a few people. The venerable old sales presentation flip chart has been replaced with tablets, sophisticated presentation software, online presentation technologies, interactive whiteboards, and digital projectors.

Handling Objections

Handling objections
The sales step in which a salesperson seeks out, clarifies, and overcomes any customer objections to buying.

Customers almost always have objections during the presentation or when asked to place an order. The objections can be either logical or psychological, and they are often unspoken. In **handling objections**, the salesperson should use a positive approach, seek out hidden objections, ask the buyer to clarify any objections, take objections as opportunities to provide more information, and turn the objections into reasons for buying. Every salesperson needs training in the skills of handling objections.

Closing

Closing
The sales step in which a salesperson asks the customer for an order.

After handling the prospect's objections, the salesperson next tries to close the sale. However, some salespeople do not get around to **closing** or don't handle it well. They may lack confidence, feel guilty about asking for the order, or fail to recognize the right moment to close the sale. Salespeople should know how to recognize closing signals from the buyer, including physical actions, comments, and questions. For example, the customer might sit forward and nod approvingly or ask about prices and credit terms.

Salespeople can use any of several closing techniques. They can ask for the order, review points of agreement, offer to help write up the order, ask whether the buyer wants this model or that one, or note that the buyer will lose out if the order is not placed now. The salesperson may offer the buyer special reasons to close, such as a lower price, an extra quantity at no charge, or additional services.

Follow-Up

Follow-up
The sales step in which a salesperson follows up after the sale to ensure customer satisfaction and repeat business.

The last step in the selling process—**follow-up**—is necessary if the salesperson wants to ensure customer satisfaction and repeat business. Right after closing, the salesperson should complete any details on delivery time, purchase terms, and other matters. The salesperson then should schedule a follow-up call after the buyer receives the initial order to make sure proper installation, instruction, and servicing occur. This visit would reveal any problems, assure the buyer of the salesperson's interest, and reduce any buyer concerns that might have arisen since the sale.

Personal Selling and Managing Customer Relationships

The steps in the just-described selling process are *transaction oriented*—their aim is to help salespeople close a specific sale with a customer. But in most cases, the company is not simply seeking a sale. Rather, it wants to engage the customer over the long haul in a mutually profitable *relationship*. The sales force usually plays an important role in customer relationship building. Thus, as shown in Figure 16.3, the selling process must be understood in the context of building and maintaining profitable customer relationships. Moreover, as discussed in a previous section, today's buyers are increasingly moving through the early stages of the buying process themselves, before ever engaging sellers. Salespeople must adapt their selling process to match the new buying process. That means discovering and engaging customers on a relationship basis rather than a transaction basis.

Successful sales organizations recognize that winning and keeping accounts requires more than making good products and directing the sales force to close lots of sales. If the

● **Value selling: Sales management's challenge is to transform salespeople from customer advocates for price cuts into company advocates for value.**

© almagami/123rf.com

company wishes only to close sales and capture short-term business, it can do this by simply slashing its prices to meet or beat those of competitors. Instead, most companies want their salespeople to practice *value selling*—demonstrating and delivering superior customer value and capturing a return on that value that is fair for both the customer and the company.

Unfortunately, in the heat of closing sales, salespeople too often take the easy way out by cutting prices rather than selling value. ● Sales management's challenge is to transform salespeople from customer advocates for price cuts into company advocates for value. Here's how Rockwell Automation sells value and relationships rather than price:[20]

> Under pressure from Walmart to lower its prices, a condiment producer asked several competing supplier representatives—including Rockwell Automation sales rep Jeff Policicchio—to help it find ways to reduce its operating costs. After spending a day in the customer's plant, Policicchio quickly put his finger on the major problem: Production was suffering because of downtime due to poorly performing pumps on the customer's 32 large condiment tanks. Quickly gathering cost and usage data, Policicchio used his Rockwell Automation laptop value-assessment tool to develop an effective solution for the customer's pump problem.
>
> The next day, as he and competing reps presented their cost-reduction proposals to plant management, Policicchio offered the following value proposition: "With this Rockwell Automation pump solution, through less downtime, reduced administrative costs in procurement, and lower spending on repair parts, your company will save at least $16,268 per pump—on up to 32 pumps—relative to our best competitor's solution." Compared with competitors' proposals, Policicchio's solution carried a higher initial price. However, no competing rep offered more than fuzzy promises about possible cost savings. Most simply lowered their prices.
>
> Impressed by Policicchio's value proposition—despite its higher initial price—the plant managers opted to buy and try one Rockwell Automation pump. When the pump performed even better than predicted, the customer ordered all of the remaining pumps. By demonstrating tangible value rather than simply selling on price, Policicchio not only landed the initial sale but also earned a loyal future customer.

Thus, value selling requires listening to customers, understanding their needs, and carefully coordinating the whole company's efforts to create lasting relationships based on customer value.

Sales Promotion

Personal selling and advertising often work closely with another promotion tool: sales promotion. **Sales promotion** consists of short-term incentives to encourage the purchase or sales of a product or service. Whereas advertising offers reasons to buy a product or service, sales promotion offers reasons to buy *now*.

Examples of sales promotions are found everywhere. A freestanding insert in the Sunday newspaper contains a coupon offering $2 off Seventh Generation laundry detergent. ● A Sunday newspaper ad from your local Orange Leaf frozen yogurt store offers "Buy 1 Get 1 Free" and "20% off your next purchase." The end-of-the-aisle display in the local supermarket tempts impulse buyers with a wall of Coca-Cola cases—four 12-packs for $12. Buy a new Samsung tablet and get a free memory upgrade. A hardware store chain receives a 10 percent discount on selected Stihl power lawn and garden tools if it agrees to advertise them in local newspapers. Sales promotion includes a wide variety of promotion tools designed to stimulate earlier or stronger market response.

Sales promotion
Short-term incentives to encourage the purchase or sale of a product or a service.

The Rapid Growth of Sales Promotion

Sales promotion tools are used by most organizations, including manufacturers, distributors, retailers, and not-for-profit institutions. They are targeted toward final buyers (*consumer promotions*), retailers and wholesalers (*trade promotions*), business customers

Sales promotions are found everywhere. For example, your Sunday newspaper or favorite magazine is loaded with offers like this one that promote a strong and immediate response.

Orange Leaf Frozen Yogurt

(*business promotions*), and members of the sales force (*sales force promotions*). Today, in the average consumer packaged-goods company, sales promotion accounts for 60 percent of all marketing budgets.[21]

Several factors have contributed to the rapid growth of sales promotion, particularly in consumer markets. First, inside the company, product managers face greater pressures to increase current sales, and they view promotion as an effective short-run sales tool. Second, externally, the company faces more competition, and competing brands are less differentiated. Increasingly, competitors are using sales promotion to help differentiate their offers. Third, advertising efficiency has declined because of rising costs, media clutter, and legal restraints. Finally, consumers have become more deal oriented. In the current economy, consumers are demanding lower prices and better deals. Sales promotions can help attract today's more thrift-oriented consumers.

The growing use of sales promotion has resulted in *promotion clutter*, which is similar to advertising clutter. With so many products being sold on deal these days, a given promotion runs the risk of being lost in a sea of other promotions, weakening its ability to trigger an immediate purchase. Manufacturers are now searching for ways to rise above the clutter, such as offering larger coupon values, creating more dramatic point-of-purchase displays, or delivering promotions through new digital media—such as the internet or mobile phones. According to one study, 90 percent of the top 100 retailers use digital promotions—such as mobile coupons. Digital promotions can help drive both in-store and online sales.[22]

In developing a sales promotion program, a company must first set sales promotion objectives and then select the best tools for accomplishing these objectives.

Sales Promotion Objectives

Sales promotion objectives vary widely. Sellers may use *consumer promotions* to urge short-term customer buying or boost customer–brand engagement. Objectives for *trade promotions* include getting retailers to carry new items and more inventory, buy ahead, or promote the company's products and give them more shelf space. *Business promotions* are used to generate business leads, stimulate purchases, reward customers, and motivate salespeople. For the sales force, objectives include getting more sales force support for current or new products and getting salespeople to sign up new accounts.

Sales promotions are usually used together with advertising, personal selling, direct and digital marketing, or other promotion mix tools. Consumer promotions must usually be advertised and can add excitement and pulling power to ads and other marketing content. Trade and business sales promotions support the firm's personal selling process.

When the economy tightens and sales lag, it's tempting to offer deep promotional discounts to spur consumer spending. In general, however, rather than creating only short-term sales or temporary brand switching, sales promotions should help to reinforce the product's position and build long-term customer relationships. If properly designed, every sales promotion tool has the potential to build both short-term excitement and long-term consumer engagement and relationships. Marketers should avoid "quick fix," price-only promotions in favor of promotions that are designed to build brand equity. Examples include the various *frequency marketing programs* and loyalty cards. Most hotels, supermarkets, and airlines offer frequent-guest/buyer/flier programs that give rewards to regular customers to keep them coming back. Such promotional programs can build loyalty through added value rather than discounted prices.

● Customer loyalty programs: An REI membership gives customers exclusive access to deals and limited-edition products and events. More important, it makes them feel like a genuine part of the REI outdoor adventure community.

Keri Miksza

Consumer promotions
Sales promotion tools used to boost short-term customer buying and engagement or enhance long-term customer relationships.

For example, at outdoor outfitter REI, customers can pay a $20 one-time fee to become a lifetime member. ● Once members, they receive members-only coupons and deals, access to exclusive limited-edition products and events, and special pricing on certain REI-sponsored travel, services, and classes. Another membership perk is the REI Dividend—an annual year-end 10 percent back on all their eligible purchases. Beyond the perks, the success of REI's membership program lies in its ability to make members feel like a genuine part of the REI outdoor adventure community.

Major Sales Promotion Tools

Many tools can be used to accomplish sales promotion objectives. Descriptions of the main consumer, trade, and business promotion tools follow.

Consumer Promotions

Consumer promotions include a wide range of tools—from samples, coupons, refunds, premiums, and point-of-purchase displays to contests, sweepstakes, and event sponsorships.

Samples are offers of a trial amount of a product. Sampling is the most effective—but most expensive—way to introduce a new product or create new excitement for an existing one. Some samples are free; for others, the company charges a small amount to offset its cost. The sample might be sent by mail, handed out in a store or at a kiosk, attached to another product, or featured in an ad, email, or mobile offer. Samples are sometimes combined into sample packs, which can then be used to promote other products and services. Sampling can be a powerful promotional tool. ● For example, for the past 37 years, Ben & Jerry's has set aside one day each year as Free Cone Day, on which it invites customers to stop by its scoop shops to sample any of a variety of the brand's classic ice cream flavors for free. Around the country, the unique sampling promotion is a huge success, with lines stretching out the doors and around the block at most shops. Officially, Ben & Jerry's uses Free Cone Day to thank its customers for being "so uniquely awesome." But the sampling program also generates tons of buzz and draws new customers into its shops, something that Ben & Jerrys hopes will turn into a habit.

Coupons are certificates that save buyers money when they purchase specified products. Most consumers love coupons. U.S. consumer packaged goods companies distributed 321 billion coupons with an average face value of $1.68 last year. Consumers redeemed more than 2.5 billion of them for a total savings of more than $3 billion.[23] Coupons can promote early trial of a new brand or stimulate sales of a mature brand. However, to combat the increase in coupon clutter, most major consumer goods companies are issuing fewer coupons and targeting them more carefully.

Marketers are also cultivating new outlets for distributing coupons, such as supermarket shelf dispensers, electronic point-of-sale coupon printers, and online and mobile coupon programs. Digital coupons represent today's fastest-growing coupon segment. Digital coupons can be individually targeted and personalized in ways that print coupons can't. Whether printed at home or redeemed via smartphone or other mobile devices, digital coupon redemptions are growing much more rapidly the traditional coupon redemptions. According to one study, an estimate 40 percent of smartphone users will redeem a mobile coupon this year.[24]

As mobile phones become appendages that many people can't live without, businesses are increasingly eyeing them as prime real estate for coupons, offers, and other marketing

● Consumer samples can be a powerful promotion tool. Ben & Jerry's annual Free Cone Day thanks customers for being "so uniquely awesome" and also generates tons of buzz and draws new customer into its scoop shops

Helen H. Richardson/Denver Post/Getty Images

messages. For example, drugstore chain Walgreens makes coupons available to its customers through several mobile channels:[25]

> Using the Walgreens smartphone app, customers can instantly download coupons ranging in value from 50 cents to $5, good toward anything from health and beauty products to everyday essentials such as diapers. The coupons are conveniently scannable—no clipping or printing required. Customers simply pull up the coupons on the Walgreens app and cashiers scan them straight from the customer's phone. Walgreens also tweets mobile coupons to customers who check in to any of its 8,100 stores nationwide using check-in apps such as Foursquare, Yelp, or Shopkick. Walgreens has mobile scanning capabilities available at all of its stores, giving it the nation's largest retail mobile coupon program. Through its mobile app, "Walgreens is using technology to go above and beyond," says one analyst. "They're thinking about the customer."

Rebates (or *cash refunds*) are like coupons except that the price reduction occurs after the purchase rather than at the retail outlet. The customer sends proof of purchase to the manufacturer, which then refunds part of the purchase price by mail. For example, Toro ran a clever preseason promotion on some of its snowblower models, offering a rebate if the snowfall in the buyer's market area turned out to be below average. Competitors were not able to match this offer on such short notice, and the promotion was very successful.

Price packs (also called *cents-off deals*) offer consumers savings off the regular price of a product. The producer marks the reduced prices directly on the label or package. Price packs can be single packages sold at a reduced price (such as two for the price of one) or two related products banded together (such as a toothbrush and toothpaste). Price packs are very effective—even more so than coupons—in stimulating short-term sales.

Premiums are goods offered either free or at low cost as an incentive to buy a product, ranging from toys included with kids' products to phone cards and DVDs. A premium may come inside the package (in-pack), outside the package (on-pack), or through the mail. For example, over the years, McDonald's has offered a variety of premiums in its Happy Meals—from *My Little Pony* characters to Beanie Boos and LEGO hologram drink cups. Customers can visit www.happymeal.com to play games, read e-books, and watch commercials associated with the current Happy Meal sponsor.[26]

Advertising specialties, also called *promotional products*, are useful articles imprinted with an advertiser's name, logo, or message that are given as gifts to consumers. Typical items include T-shirts and other apparel, pens, coffee mugs, calendars, key rings, tote bags, coolers, golf balls, and caps. U.S. marketers spent more than $20 billion on advertising specialties last year. Such items can be very effective. The "best of them stick around for months, subtly burning a brand name into a user's brain," notes a promotional products expert.[27]

Point-of-purchase (POP) promotions include displays and demonstrations that take place at the point of sale. Think of your last visit to the local Costco, Walmart, or Bed Bath & Beyond. Chances are good that you were tripping over aisle displays, promotional signs, "shelf talkers," or demonstrators offering free tastes of featured food products. Unfortunately, many retailers do not like to handle the hundreds of displays, signs, and posters they receive from manufacturers each year. Manufacturers have therefore responded by offering better POP materials, offering to set them up, and tying them in with television, print, or online messages.

Contests, sweepstakes, and *games* give consumers the chance to win something, such as cash, trips, or goods, by luck or through extra effort. A *contest* calls for consumers to submit an entry—a jingle, guess, suggestion—to be judged by a panel that will select the best entries. A *sweepstakes* calls for consumers to submit their names for a drawing. A *game* presents consumers with something—bingo numbers, missing letters—every time they buy, which may or may not help them win a prize.

All kinds of companies use sweepstakes and contests to create brand attention and boost consumer involvement. For example, Google's "Doodle 4 Google" contest invited kids to design a Google logo based on the theme "If I could invent one thing to make the world a better place…," with prizes ranging from T-shirts and tablets to a $30,000 college scholarship. Kellogg's Eggo brand hosted a Great Eggo Waffle Off! contest on Facebook, with entrants submitting their best recipes for waffles—winners received $5,000. And Dove ran a "Real Beauty Should Be Shared" contest asking its Facebook fans to name a friend and say why that friend "represents Real Beauty." The winners became the next faces of Dove.

Event marketing (or event sponsorships)
Creating a brand-marketing event or serving as a sole or participating sponsor of events created by others.

Finally, marketers can promote their brands through **event marketing (or event sponsorships)**. They can create their own brand-marketing events or serve as sole or participating sponsors of events created by others. The events might include anything from mobile brand tours to festivals, reunions, marathons, concerts, or other sponsored gatherings. Event marketing is huge, and it may be the fastest-growing area of promotion. Effective event marketing links events and sponsorships to a brand's value proposition. And with the social sharing power of today's digital media, even local events can have far-reaching impact. For example, Delta Faucet used an imaginative event to promote its H2Okinetic low-flow showerheads—which use 40 percent less water but work just as well as competing higher-flow models—to its fitness and family-oriented target audience.[28]

● **Event marketing:** As part of its **#HappyMess campaign**, Delta Faucet used an imaginative event to show target consumers firsthand how well its low-flow showerheads worked under really tough conditions—following a 5K mud run race.
AP Images for Delta Faucet Company

Delta's #HappiMess promotion campaign is based on the insight that some of its customers' happiest moments came from making and overcoming big messes. To show target consumers first-hand how well its low-flow showerheads work under really tough conditions, Delta partnered with Warrior Dash, which sponsored several 5K mud run races around the country over the summer. ● At each event, Delta built a huge custom shower station, complete with 184 Delta showerheads, where mud-soaked competitors could meet and wash off after the race. "Warrior Dash is a great example of a place where people are having fun getting messy," says a senior Delta Faucet senior brand manager. "We want people to celebrate those fun moments having confidence that we have products that will help transform them back to clean." At one event in Indiana, 331 people gathered to shower, setting a Guinness World Record for most people showering simultaneously. After experiencing the showerheads, 75 percent of runners surveyed said they'd consider buying one. The shower stations also included a selfie station. As a result, the event boosted social media activity around Delta's #HappiMess campaign by 85 percent and gave the brand a 50 percent sales lift.

All kinds of brands now hold events. But one-time events are rarely as effective as well-planned event campaigns that tie into a brand's broader promotions and positioning. Consider energy drink maker Red Bull. Called by one business reporter the "mother of all event marketers," Red Bull holds hundreds of events around the globe each year designed to bring the high-octane world of Red Bull to its community of enthusiasts (see Real Marketing 16.2).

Trade Promotions

Trade promotions
Sales promotion tools used to persuade resellers to carry a brand, give it shelf space, and promote it in advertising.

Manufacturers direct more sales promotion dollars toward retailers and wholesalers (79 percent of all promotions dollars) than to final consumers (21 percent).[29] **Trade promotions** can persuade resellers to carry a brand, give it shelf space, promote it in advertising, and push it to consumers. Shelf space is so scarce these days that manufacturers often have to offer price-offs, allowances, buy-back guarantees, or free goods to retailers and wholesalers to get products on the shelf and, once there, to keep them on it.

Manufacturers use several trade promotion tools. Many of the tools used for consumer promotions—contests, premiums, displays—can also be used as trade promotions. Or the manufacturer may offer a straight *discount* off the list price on each case purchased during a stated period of time (also called a *price-off, off-invoice,* or *off-list*). Manufacturers also may offer an *allowance* (usually so much off per case) in return for the retailer's agreement to feature the manufacturer's products in some way. For example, an advertising allowance compensates retailers for advertising the product, whereas a display allowance compensates them for using special displays.

Manufacturers may offer *free goods*, which are extra cases of merchandise, to resellers who buy a certain quantity or who feature a certain flavor or size. They may also offer *push money*—cash or gifts to dealers or their sales forces to "push" the manufacturer's goods. Manufacturers may give retailers free *specialty advertising items* that carry the company's name, such as pens, calendars, memo pads, flashlights, and tote bags.

Real Marketing

16.2   Red Bull: The Mother of All Event Marketers

There's no question: Coca-Cola and PepsiCo dominate the global beverage industry. Each boasts leading brands in almost every category, from carbonated soft drinks to enhanced juice drinks to bottled waters. Last year, Coca-Cola sold more than $44 billion worth of beverages worldwide; PepsiCo was a solid runner-up at nearly $30 billion. Both companies spend hundreds of millions of dollars annually on sophisticated marketing and advertising programs. So how does a smaller company compete effectively with such global powerhouses? The best answer: It doesn't—at least not directly. Instead, it uses a unique marketing approach and runs where the big dogs don't.

That's what Red Bull does. When Red Bull first introduced its energy drink more than 28 years ago, few imagined that it would become the $6.5 billion-a-year success that it is today. Red Bull has succeeded by avoiding head-to-head promotional battles with giants like Coca-Cola and Pepsi. Instead, it has energized brand fans with a unique product, brand personality, and event-marketing approach.

Back in 1987, energy drinks simply didn't exist. If you wanted a quick pick-me-up, about the only options were caffeinated soft drinks or a good old cup of coffee. But Red Bull formulated a new beverage containing a hefty dose of caffeine along with little-known ingredients such as taurine and glucuronolactone. It tasted terrible. But it packed the right punch, producing unique physical-energy and mental-clarity benefits. To make the new beverage even more distinctive, the founders gave it a unique name (Red Bull) and packaged it in a slim 8.3-ounce blue-and-silver can with a distinct red-and-yellow logo. Thus was born a whole new energy drink category, with Red Bull as its only player.

The unique Red Bull product demanded equally unique brand positioning and personality, a declaration that this was no ordinary beverage. Red Bull's marketing didn't disappoint. The brand's first and still-only slogan—"Red Bull Gives You Wings"—communicated the product's energy-inducing benefits. More important, it tapped into the forces that moved the brand's narrow target segment—customers seeking to live life in the adrenaline-stoked fast lane.

To reinforce the "Gives You Wings" brand promise and in line with the new brand's meager early finances, Red Bull shunned the big-budget, mass-media advertising common in the beverage industry at the time. Instead, it relied on grassroots, high-octane sports and event marketing. It sponsored extreme sports events and athletes who were overlooked by big beverage competitors but were spiking in popularity with Red Bull's target customers, events such as snowboarding and freestyle motocross and athletes like Shawn White and Travis Pastrana.

In the years since, Red Bull has turned event marketing into a science. Today, the brand holds hundreds of events each year in dozens of sports around the world. Each event features off-the-grid experiences designed to bring the high-octane world of Red Bull to its impassioned community of enthusiasts. Red Bull owns Formula 1 car racing teams and soccer clubs. Its name is plastered all over events such as the Red Bull Crashed Ice World Championship and the annual Red Bull Rampage freeride mountain bike competition.

Red Bull even hosts a "Holy S**t" tab on its website, featuring videos of everything from 27-meter ocean cliff dives at its Cliff Diving Series event in Grimstad, Norway, to daredevil freeskiing feats at its Red Bull Cold Rush event in the Colorado mountain peaks to absolutely breathtaking wing suit flights at Red Bull events staged in exotic locations from Monterrey, Mexico, to Hunan Province, China. The Red Bull Final Descent series is a mountain biking challenge that pushes riders to the brink and back over some of the most technically challenging terrain in North America.

Just one classic example of Red Bull's event marketing genius is the Red Bull Stratos project, in which extreme skydiver Felix Baumgartner jumped from a helium balloon 128,000 feet (more than 24 miles) above the earth, breaking the sound barrier and numerous other records in the process. The jump also set records for consumer brand engagement. Baumgartner diving into space fit perfectly with Red Bull's "Gives You Wings" brand message. And both Baumgartner's capsule and his space-age jumpsuit were emblazoned with the Red Bull name and logo. More than 8 million people watched the event live on 40 TV stations and 130 digital channels. For months before and after the event, you couldn't see or hear anything about Baumgartner without thinking about Red Bull.

Red Bull's event marketing engages customers in a way that big-budget traditional marketing by competitors like Coca-Cola or Pepsi can't. For example, within 40 minutes of posting photos of Baumgartner's jump, Red Bull's Facebook page gained almost 216,000 Likes, 10,000 comments, and more than 29,000 shares. On Twitter, literally half of the worldwide trending topics were related to Red Bull Stratos. And by one estimate, 90 million people worldwide followed the campaign on

Event marketing: Red Bull has turned event marketing into a science. It hosts hundreds of event each year designed to bring the high-octane world of Red Bull to its community of enthusiasts.
Max Rossi/Reuters

social media, creating 60 million trusted brand impressions. You just can't buy that kind of consumer engagement in traditional media.

More than just a beverage company, Red Bull today has become a close-knit brand community. Red Bull events have produced a steady stream of absorbing brand content that engages and entertains brand fans in relevant ways. During the past few years, Red Bull's Media House unit has filmed movies, signed a deal with NBC for a show called *Red Bull Signature Series*, developed reality-TV ideas with big-name producers, become one of YouTube's biggest partners in publishing original content, and loaded its own web and mobile sites with unique content features. "Whenever we [have done] any event, or signed an athlete or executed a project, everything has been put on film or photographed. Stories have been told," says the head of the Red Bull Media House unit. "It's part of the DNA of the brand."

Thus, Red Bull can't compete directly across the board with big-budget brands like Coca-Cola and PepsiCo—it doesn't even try. Then again, given the depth of consumer engagement and loyalty that Red Bull engenders in its own corner of the beverage world, Coke and Pepsi have found it even more difficult to compete with Red Bull in the energy drink segment. Red Bull still owns 43 percent of the energy drink category it created, with other independents Monster and Rockstar holding strong second- and third-place positions. By contrast, despite hefty promotion budgets, Coca-Cola and PepsiCo have yet to put much of a dent in the category. Coca-Cola's NOS and Full Throttle brands capture only about a 4 percent combined market share; Pepsi's Amp and Kickstart brands have suffered the same dismal fate.

In the end, although Red Bull events draw large crowds and plenty of media coverage, it's about more than just the events—it's about customer engagement. Event marketing is about creating tactile engagements where people can feel, touch, taste, and live the brand face-to-face rather than simply reading about or watching it. Red Bull doesn't just sponsor an event—it *is* the event. The brand experience is often as much of the story as the event itself. Through smart event marketing, Red Bull has given its customers—and itself—new wings and a big shot of energy. As one observer puts it, Red Bull is the "mother of all event marketers."

Sources: Christian Kresse, "Brands in eSports—Red Bull: King of Content Marketing," *eSports,* March 14, 2016, http://esports-marketing-blog.com/red-bull-esports-marketing/#.VwVVoelrJhE; Janean Chun, "Bull Stratos May Change Future of Marketing," *Huffington Post,* October 15, 2012, www.huffingtonpost.com/2012/10/15/red-bull-stratos-marketing_n_1966852.html; Brian Kotlyar, "7 Social Campaign Insights from Red Bull Stratos," *DG Blog,* October 23, 2012, http://dachisgroup.com/2012/10/7-social-campaign-insights-from-redbull-stratos//; "Top Selling Energy Drink Brands," *Caffeine Informer,* www.caffeineinformer.com/the-15-top-energy-drink-brands, accessed September 2016; and www.coca-colacompany.com/investors; www.pepsico.com/investors; www.redbull.com/us/en and www.redbull.com/us/en/events, accessed October 2016.

Business Promotions

Companies spend billions of dollars each year on promotion geared toward industrial customers. **Business promotions** are used to generate business leads, stimulate purchases, reward customers, and motivate salespeople. Business promotions include many of the same tools used for consumer or trade promotions. Here, we focus on two additional major business promotion tools: conventions and trade shows and sales contests.

Many companies and trade associations organize *conventions and trade shows* to promote their products. Firms selling to the industry show their products at the trade show. Vendors at these shows receive many benefits, such as opportunities to find new sales leads, contact customers, introduce new products, meet new customers, sell more to present customers, and educate customers with publications and audiovisual materials. Trade shows also help companies reach many prospects that are not reached through their sales forces.

Some trade shows are huge. For example, at this year's International Consumer Electronics Show, more than 3,600 exhibitors attracted some 170,000 professional visitors. ● Even more impressive, at the Bauma mining and construction equipment trade show in Munich, Germany, more than 3,400 exhibitors from 57 countries presented their latest product innovations to more than 530,000 attendees from more than 200 countries. Total exhibition space equaled about 6.1 million square feet (more than 127 football fields).[30]

A *sales contest* is a contest for salespeople or dealers to motivate them to increase their sales performance over a given period. Sales contests motivate and recognize good company performers, who may receive trips, cash prizes, or other gifts. Some companies award points for performance, which the receiver can turn in for any of a variety of prizes. Sales contests work best when they are tied to measurable and achievable sales objectives (such as finding new accounts, reviving old accounts, or increasing account profitability).

● **Some trade shows are huge. At this year's Bauma mining and construction equipment trade show, more than 3,400 exhibitors from 57 countries presented their latest product innovations to more than 530,000 attendees from more than 200 countries.**

Messe München

Developing the Sales Promotion Program

Beyond selecting the types of promotions to use, marketers must make several other decisions in designing the full sales promotion program. First, they must determine the *size of the incentive*. A certain minimum incentive

Business promotions
Sales promotion tools used to generate business leads, stimulate purchases, reward customers, and motivate salespeople.

is necessary if the promotion is to succeed; a larger incentive will produce more sales response. The marketer also must set *conditions for participation*. Incentives might be offered to everyone or only to select groups.

Marketers must determine how to *promote and distribute the promotion* program itself. For example, a $2-off coupon could be given out in a package, in an advertisement, at the store, via the internet, or in a mobile download. Each distribution method involves a different level of reach and cost. Increasingly, marketers are blending several media into a total campaign concept. The *length of the promotion* is also important. If the sales promotion period is too short, many prospects (who may not be buying during that time) will miss it. If the promotion runs too long, the deal will lose some of its "act now" force.

Evaluation is also very important. Marketers should work to measure the returns on their sales promotion investments, just as they should seek to assess the returns on other marketing activities. The most common evaluation method is to compare sales before, during, and after a promotion. Marketers should ask: Did the promotion attract new customers or more purchasing from current customers? Can we hold onto these new customers and purchases? Will the long-run customer relationship and sales gains from the promotion justify its costs?

Clearly, sales promotion plays an important role in the total promotion mix. To use it well, the marketer must define the sales promotion objectives, select the best tools, design the sales promotion program, implement the program, and evaluate the results. Moreover, sales promotion must be coordinated carefully with other promotion mix elements within the overall IMC program.

16 Reviewing and Extending the Concepts

OBJECTIVES REVIEW AND KEY TERMS

Objectives Review

This chapter is the third of four chapters covering the final marketing mix element—promotion. The previous two chapters dealt with overall integrated marketing communications and with advertising and public relations. This chapter investigated personal selling and sales promotion. Personal selling is the interpersonal arm of the communications mix. Sales promotion consists of short-term incentives to encourage the purchase or sale of a product or service.

As an element of the promotion mix, the sales force is very effective in achieving certain marketing objectives and carrying out such activities as prospecting, communicating, selling and servicing, and information gathering. But with companies becoming more market oriented, a customer-focused sales force also works to produce both customer satisfaction and company profit. The sales force plays a key role in engaging customers and developing and managing profitable customer relationships.

OBJECTIVE 16-1 Discuss the role of a company's salespeople in creating value for customers and building customer relationships. (pp 456–458)

Most companies use salespeople, and many companies assign them an important role in the marketing mix. For companies selling business products, the firm's sales force works directly with customers. Often, the sales force is the customer's only direct contact with the company and therefore may be viewed by customers as representing the company itself. In contrast, for consumer product companies that sell through intermediaries, consumers usually do not meet salespeople or even know about them. The sales force works behind the scenes, dealing with wholesalers and retailers to obtain their support and helping them become more effective in selling the firm's products.

OBJECTIVE 16-2 Identify and explain the six major sales force management steps. (pp 458–469)

High sales force costs necessitate an effective sales management process consisting of six steps: designing sales force strategy and structure, recruiting and selecting, training, compensating, supervising, and evaluating salespeople and sales force performance.

In designing a sales force, sales management must address various issues, including what type of sales force structure will work best (territorial, product, customer, or complex structure), sales force size, who will be involved in selling, and how various salespeople and sales-support people will work together (inside or outside sales forces and team selling).

Salespeople must be recruited and selected carefully. In recruiting salespeople, a company may look to the job duties and the characteristics of its most successful salespeople to suggest the traits it wants in new salespeople. It must then look for applicants through recommendations of current salespeople, ads, and the internet and social media as well as college recruitment/placement centers. After the selection process is complete, training programs familiarize new salespeople not only with the art of selling but also with the company's history, its products and policies, and the characteristics of its customers and competitors.

The sales force compensation system helps to reward, motivate, and direct salespeople. In addition to compensation, all salespeople need supervision, and many need continuous encouragement because they must make many decisions and face many frustrations. Periodically, the company must evaluate their performance to help them do a better job. In evaluating salespeople, the company relies on information gathered from sales reports, personal observations, customer surveys, and conversations with other salespeople.

The fastest-growing sales trend is the explosion in social selling—using online, mobile, and social media in selling. The new digital technologies are providing salespeople with powerful tools for identifying and learning about prospects, engaging customers, creating customer value, closing sales, and nurturing customer relationships. Many of today's customers no longer rely as much on assistance provided by salespeople. Instead, increasingly, they use online and social media resources to analyze their own problems, research solutions, get advice from colleagues, and rank buying options before ever speaking to a salesperson. In response, sellers are reorienting their selling processes around the new customer buying process. They are using social media, mobile devices, web forums, online communities, blogs, and other digital tools to engage customers earlier and more fully. Ultimately, online, mobile, and social media

technologies are helping to make sales forces more efficient, cost-effective, and productive.

OBJECTIVE 16-3 **Discuss the personal selling process, distinguishing between transaction-oriented marketing and relationship marketing.** *(pp 469–472)*

Selling involves a seven-step process: prospecting and qualifying, preapproach, approach, presentation and demonstration, handling objections, closing, and follow-up. These steps help marketers close a specific sale and, as such, are transaction oriented. However, a seller's dealings with customers should be guided by the larger concept of relationship marketing. The company's sales force should help to orchestrate a whole-company effort to develop profitable long-term relationships with key customers based on superior customer value and satisfaction.

OBJECTIVE 16-4 **Explain how sales promotion campaigns are developed and implemented.** *(pp 472–479)*

Sales promotion campaigns call for setting sales promotion objectives (in general, sales promotions should be *consumer relationship building*); selecting tools; and developing and implementing the sales promotion program by using *consumer promotion tools* (from coupons, refunds, premiums, and point-of-purchase promotions to contests, sweepstakes, and events), *trade promotion tools* (from discounts and allowances to free goods and push money), and *business promotion tools* (conventions, trade shows, and sales contests) as well as determining such things as the size of the incentive, the conditions for participation, how to promote and distribute the promotion package, and the length of the promotion. After this process is completed, the company must evaluate its sales promotion results.

Key Terms

OBJECTIVE 16-1

Personal selling (p 456)
Salesperson (p 457)

OBJECTIVE 16-2

Sales force management (p 458)
Territorial sales force
   structure (p 459)
Product sales force
   structure (p 459)
Customer (or market) sales force
   structure (p 459)

Outside sales force (or field sales force)
   (p 460)
Inside sales force (p 460)
Team selling (p 461)
Sales quota (p 465)
Social selling (p 466)

OBJECTIVE 16-3

Selling process (p 469)
Prospecting (p 469)
Preapproach (p 470)
Approach (p 470)

Presentation (p 470)
Handling objections (p 471)
Closing (p 471)
Follow-up (p 471)

OBJECTIVE 16-4

Sales promotion (p 472)
Consumer promotions (p 474)
Event marketing (or event
   sponsorships) (p 476)
Trade promotions (p 476)
Business promotions (p 478)

DISCUSSION AND CRITICAL THINKING

MyMarketingLab

Go to **mymktlab.com** to complete the problems marked with this icon ⭐.

Discussion Questions

⭐ **16-1** Define *personal selling* and discuss its role in a company's promotion mix. (AASCB: Communication; Reflective Thinking)

16-2 Name and describe the four sales compensation elements. What are the various compensation combinations, and how can they be used to achieve the company's marketing objectives? (AACSB: Communication; Reflective Thinking)

16-3 What is social selling, and how is it affecting the sales function in organizations? (AACSB: Communication; Reflective Thinking)

⭐ **16-4** Name and explain the steps in the selling process. (AACSB: Communication)

16-5 What is sales promotion? Discuss its growth as a short-term consumer promotion tool. (AACSB: Communication)

Critical Thinking Exercises

16-6 There are considerable free sales training resources available on the internet. Search "free sales training" to find some of these resources and access one of them. Create a presentation highlighting what you learned. (AACSB: Communication; Use of IT; Reflective Thinking)

⭐ **16-7** You are the district manager for Pureation Beverage Group, a beer and wine distributor. The company has experienced rapid growth and needs to add additional salespeople to its team. Using the sales force management steps in Figure 16.1, discuss what needs to be

done to effectively manage your sales force. Support your position. (AACSB: Communication; Reflective Thinking)

16-8 In a small group, design a sales promotion campaign using online, social media, and mobile marketing for a small business or organization in your community. Develop a presentation to pitch your campaign to the business or organization and incorporate what you've learned about the selling process. (AACSB: Communication; Reflective Thinking)

APPLICATIONS AND CASES

Online, Mobile, and Social Media Marketing Snap It and Redeem It!

More than 320 billion coupons are distributed each year, with more than 90 percent of them printed on paper. Consumers redeem only about 1 percent of coupons distributed, often because they clip them but forget to use them in the store. SnipSnap has a solution for consumers. Hailed as the Best Shopping App by About.com and winning Media Post's Apply Awards for Best Finance App, this app has mobilized those paper coupons for consumers. SnipSnap now boasts 4 million users and more than 50 national retail partners. The app allows consumers to snap a photo of retailers' paper coupons and redeem them at the store. Users can share with friends on Facebook and Twitter and follow others' couponing. SnipSnap is the first mobile app that scans the text, images, logos, and barcodes in printed coupons and creates a mobile coupon. It also sends expiration date reminders and location-based notifications. Retailer Lord & Taylor installed iBeacon technology and partnered with SnipSnap to send shoppers targeted coupons based on where they are in the store. So if you want a good deal on a Michael Kors purse, it knows you are looking at the item and might send you a coupon through

the app. SnipSnap employees noticed consumers were snapping pictures of "coupons" they created to send to friends and family that were good for some special treatment, so the company created a spinoff app called GoodFor. Now, if you want to send a special someone a coupon good for a 30-minute massage or your kid a "get out of chores free" coupon, GoodFor allows you to do it!

16-9 Research other types of apps that rely on smartphone cameras to redeem a sales promotion offer. Explain how they work and how they are similar to and different from SnipSnap. (AACSB: Communication; Use of IT; Reflective Thinking)

16-10 The profitable growth potential for SnipSnap is in the enterprise market where it provides mobile promotion services to retailers. SnipSnap is working with retailers to create and manage geo-conquesting campaigns. Research what this is and create a presentation explaining how it works. (AACSB: Communication; Use of IT; Reflective Thinking)

Marketing Ethics Walking the Customer

Employees at Staples face a challenging work environment. According to *The New York Times*, Staples maintains an internal reporting system nicknamed "Market Basket" that carefully tracks all equipment and protection plan add-ons that each sales staff member sells. Staples expects that each salesperson will upsell each transaction by $200 with additional merchandise and warranty contracts. Staples salespeople have been trained to push until they get at least three objections. This is a classic hard-sell technique. Sales staff who do not meet their goals are coached. If that doesn't work, the underperforming employees face disciplinary action that can lead to more night and weekend shifts, reduced work hours, or even termination.

Store managers also face intense scrutiny. They have received a clear message that to avoid bringing down a store's Market Basket averages, salespeople should "walk the customer" if they cannot be successfully upsold. The customer is informed that the merchandise is not in stock and then leave the store empty-handed. Salespeople have another option: They can escort customers to an in-store kiosk to place an online order. Online orders are not subject to Staples's key performance indicators (KPI) and are not reported to a store's Market Basket. (For more reading, see David Haggler, "Selling It with Extras, or Not at All," www.nytimes.com/2012/09/09/your-money/sales-incentives-at-staples-draw-complaints-the-haggler.html?smid=pl-share.)

16-11 A company's sales force creates and communicates customer value by personally engaging customers and building customer relationships. With its Market Basket approach, was Staples focusing on building customer value and relationships? Explain.

16-12 Read Staples's code of ethics at www.staples.com/sbd/cre/marketing/staples_soul/documents/staples-code-of-ethics_english.pdf. Is the situation outlined above consistent with Staples's ethics policies? Is "walking the customer" a violation of the ethics code? Provide specific examples.

Marketing by the Numbers Sales Force Analysis

Wheels, Inc. is a manufacturer of bicycles sold through retail bicycle shops in the southeastern United States. The company has two salespeople that do more than just sell the products—they manage relationships with the bicycle shops to enable them to better meet consumers' needs. The company's sales reps visit the shops several times per year, often for hours at a time. The owner of Wheels is considering expanding to the rest of the country and would like to have distribution through 1,000 bicycle shops. To do so, however, the company would have to hire more salespeople. Each salesperson earns $40,000 plus 2 percent commission on all sales. Another alternative is to use the services of sales agents instead of its own sales force. Sales agents would be paid 5 percent of sales.

16-13 Refer to Appendix 2 to answer this question. Determine the number of salespeople Wheels needs if it has 1,000 bicycle shop accounts that need to be called on four times per year. Each sales call lasts approximately 2.5 hours, and each sales rep has approximately 1,250 hours per year to devote to customers. (AACSB: Communication; Analytical Reasoning)

16-14 At what level of sales would it be more cost efficient for Wheels to use to sales agents compared with its own sales force? To determine this, consider the fixed and variable costs for each alternative. What are the pros and cons of using a company's own sales force over independent sales agents? (AACSB: Communication; Analytical Reasoning; Reflective Thinking)

Video Case First Flavor

First Flavor is a start-up company with a unique product. It manufactures great-tasting edible film that can replicate the flavor of just about anything, from an eight-topping pizza to an alcoholic beverage. If you're wondering why a company would make such a product, think of the endless possibilities it allows for consumers to sample the taste of a food or beverage before purchasing it.

Although First Flavor first replicated flavors on thin film in order to market the product as a new method for product sampling, the company is now evaluating many other applications of the technology. This video demonstrates how one product can be marketed in multiple ways.

After viewing the video featuring First Flavor, answer the following questions:

16-15 Classify First Flavor's core business as a sales promotion element.

16-16 Brainstorm a list of the ways that First Flavor's edible film might be used to sample products.

16-17 Can First Flavor successfully in pursue consumer product opportunities in addition to its promotional services? Explain.

Company Case SunGard: Building Sustained Growth by Selling the SunGard Way

If asked what company topped the most recent *Selling Power* magazine list of 50 Best Companies to Sell For, you'd probably guess IBM, P&G, or maybe Xerox, companies long known for their outstanding sales forces. But number one on this year's list is a company you probably know less about—software and technology services company SunGard.

What makes SunGard such a good place to work as a salesperson? For starters, SunGard has strong name recognition and a solid reputation in its industry. SunGard has long provided excellent compensation and training to its salespeople. And the company has consistently delivered strong customer growth and retention. However, although SunGard has long been good in these areas, what has made it outstanding and put it at the top of *Selling Power*'s list is a recent complete transformation of SunGard's sales force model.

Pioneering a New Industry

In the late 1970s, the computer services division of the Sun Oil Company (today Sunoco) pioneered a service now considered indispensable by virtually every company in the world. Sun and 20 other Philadelphia-area companies entered an agreement to act as backups for each other's data systems. To create the needed capacity, the group developed a designated disaster recovery backup center. But when member companies were slow to pay their shares of the expenses, Sun Oil took over the backup operation and began selling computer services. In 1983, Sun Oil spun off the computer division and SunGard was born.

Since then, with the help of a few acquisitions, SunGard has grown steadily. It's now one of the world's leading software and technology services companies, with nearly $3 billion in annual revenues. SunGard now provides processing solutions for the financial services industry, K–12 education, and public sector organizations. It serves 16,000 customers in more than 70 countries. As a business-to-business service provider, that requires a substantial sales force.

Good, but Not Great

When Russell Fradin took over as the CEO of SunGard, business was good. But the company faced some issues of concern. For starters, the internet increasingly provided SunGard clients and potential clients with the information they needed to solve their own problems. For both its private and public sector businesses, compliance with government regulations was also increasing. And increasing globalization made it more and more challenging for SunGard's sales reps to meet client needs. SunGard was not alone in facing these issues. But that just added to the pressure—any company finding effective ways to meet these challenges would gain considerable strategic advantage.

SunGard also faced plenty of internal issues. The company sold multiple product lines, and Fradin felt that the SunGard sales force wasn't achieving its potential in terms of selling the optimal mix of products. The company's thousands of sales reps spent most of their time and effort selling licensed software rather than developing broader solutions to customer problems. Moreover, with multiple divisions and product lines and a fragmented go-to-market approach, SunGard often had multiple sales reps pursuing the same clients, sapping productivity and even driving some customers away.

Based on these assessments, Fradin asked himself, "How can SunGard make its sales force—one of the company's biggest and most important investments—perform more effectively?" SunGard had decent systems in place for recruiting, hiring, and training its salespeople. And SunGard's sales executives did a reasonable job of making incremental changes. But Fradin felt that the company needed to do more in order to improve its growth and performance. If more drastic changes weren't made, the mounting challenges would likely limit future sales and profits. To Fradin's thinking, SunGard needed a complete sales force transformation.

According to a report by global sales consulting firm ZA Associates, companies that move sales force effectiveness from good to excellent by virtue of a sales force transformation can increase profitable growth by as much as 20 percent. But that kind of transformation would require a major effort, many months

to plan and execute, and even longer to take hold. It would demand nothing less than a total commitment from everyone in the organization—those at the lowest rung on the corporate ladder up to senior management and executives. It would also require that everyone have a clear vision of the benefits, both for themselves and for the organization as a whole. Disruptions from implementing such a sweeping change would likely mean losing good people and clients. It might also result in a short-term dip in performance before the benefits began to kick in.

Setting Transformation in Motion

All challenges considered, Fradin hired Jim Neve and Ken Powell to head up SunGard's global sales efforts. The two-person team had worked on other successful large-scale sales force transformations and planned to carry out the same process at SunGard. "We needed to maximize our channels, sell the broadest set of solutions possible, and go to market in a coordinated manner," said Powell. "We needed to build a sustainable growth engine."

Neve and Powell branded the sales force transformation initiative as "Selling the SunGard Way." More than just a fancy title, "Selling the SunGard Way" was a philosophy defined by specific goals and characteristics. First and foremost, the transformation would shift the basic sales approach from selling based on meeting customer needs to selling based on insights. SunGard reps needed to thoroughly understand the client buying decision process, anticipate needs before even customers themselves were aware of them, and tailor the client relationship to meet shifting concerns. Focusing on product functionality and price just wouldn't cut it anymore. And sales interactions would need to draw from technology and services across all SunGard business units, not just within specific divisions or product lines. In order to achieve these skills, SunGard's sales personnel would need greater knowledge and expertise of the full line of company products as well as the nature of each client's business.

After thoroughly surveying the needs of SunGard sales associates, Neve and Powell drafted a detailed transformation plan. Sales reps needed better training, detailed competitive analyses, and more effective sales campaigns. They needed better data, fewer administrative tasks, and a simplified interface for the company's Salesforce CRM sales management tool. To achieve such goals, Neve and Powell set out to overhaul SunGard's core sales functions, including recruiting, training, managing, and compensating sales force personnel.

This transformation would take time and effort, and it would cost millions. But by the time the plan was revealed, there was support throughout the company. "The whole organization gravitated toward change," said Powell. "[Everyone] knew it had to happen." To help cover costs, the company shifted budgets, reallocating funds from ineffective programs to the transformation project.

On the recruiting front, SunGard adopted a new talent-assessment tool that defined ideal job profiles and evaluated skills and performance patterns of potential hires. The company also hired a team of sales development managers, charged with increasing the productivity of first-year sales reps. It was their job to make sure that new sales reps received all the training and exposure necessary to understand the company's structure, strategic plans, products, and sales tools. That relieved front-line sales managers of these tasks, letting them focus more on selling. Sales development manager compensation hinged on the performance of first-year sales reps.

For existing sales personnel, SunGard revised procedures, metrics, training, and tools to make them consistent across the organization. It also made major revisions to its Salesforce CRM and sales management tool with an eye toward providing salespeople with all the information they needed for every aspect of the sales process. The important tool now provided easy and immediate access to content such as case studies, customer information, and market data. Additional tools were made available to guide people through the necessary steps of effectively closing a sale.

But to improve effectiveness for both new and existing sales personnel, SunGard needed to make even more changes in how it measured and tracked performance. For example, prior to the transformation, the company tracked incentives and commissions manually, and they were not readily accessible by relevant stakeholders. Under the new scheme, metrics such as individual goals and forecasts, as well as how often sales were made or lost, became part of an automated system, accessible by sales reps and managers via mobile interface at any time. They could even run "what-if" scenarios to determine potential earnings of different situations. This capability motivated sales reps by increasing accountability and promoting a competitive spirit.

From Transformation to Results

As the new sales structure and tools took root, it wasn't long before they began to bear fruit. "There was a tremendous product suite that had yet to capture its full market share," says Todd Albright, who joined SunGard as senior vice president of sales for the Americas after the transformation was under way. That market share will soon be achieved. "There were tremendous assets locked up at SunGard," Neve summarizes. "We put a road map in place to unlock those assets, translating them into new sales and revenue growth."

With its billion-dollar sales plan now in place, SunGard is on target. As one example, consider the productivity improvements for first-year reps. Prior to the transformation, about 75 percent of new reps booked their first sale before the end of their first year at an average of about $400,000. Through the new policies, that sales productivity has doubled, adding an incremental $30 to $40 million to annual sales.

If boosting sales force effectiveness was easy, every company would achieve optimal sales force productivity. SunGard was willing to pay the price. In the first year following the implementation of the transformation, as expected, SunGard revenues decreased over the previous year—down by about 16 percent. However, profits rose by nearly 35 percent, thanks in part to reduced costs from more efficient operations. By the end of the second year, revenues were back on the rise. Fradin was notably pleased. "Clients are responding positively to these initiatives, knowing that our offerings help their businesses be more competitive. We [are] particularly pleased with our sales momentum and our organic revenue growth."

Importantly, SunGard's sales force is now much more coordinated and collaborative. It's better trained and equipped to sell based on insights. Its products and services are bundled across product lines rather than within lines. And reps are developing partnerships with customers, assisting them in streamlining operations, accelerating growth, and complying with regulations. By transforming its sales force to "Selling the SunGard Way," SunGard is on a path to sustainable, organic growth for years to come.

Questions for Discussion

16-18 Compare SunGard's sales force structure before and after the transformation.

16-19 What are the positive and negative aspects of SunGard's new sales force structure?

16-20 How would the challenges faced by SunGard have affected sales productivity had the company not initiated its transformational plan?

16-21 Identify specific ways SunGard's transformational plan addresses the different steps of managing the sales force.

16-22 Will "Selling the SunGard Way" really work? Why or why not?

Sources: Henry Canaday, "Selling the New SunGard Way," *Selling Power*, www.sellingpower.com/content/article/?a=10217/selling-the-new-sungard-way&page=1, accessed June 2016; "50 Best Companies to Sell for in 2015," *Selling Power*, www.sellingpower.com/2015/50-best-companies-to-sell-for/, accessed June 2016; Andris Zoltners, P. K. Sinha, and Sally Lorimer, "Improving Your Sales Force: Fine-tune or Transform?" *Harvard Business Review*, November 13, 2012, http://blogs.hbr.org/2012/11/improving-your-sales-force-fin/; and information from www.sungard.com/about-us and www.sungard.com/financials, accessed June 2016.

MyMarketingLab

Go to **mymktlab.com** for Auto-graded writing questions as well as the following Assisted-graded writing questions:

16-23 Describe the roles a salesperson and the sales force perform in marketing.

16-24 What is team selling, and why has it become more important? Are there any pitfalls to this approach?

17 Direct, Online, Social Media, and Mobile Marketing

CHAPTER PREVIEW

In the previous three chapters, you learned about engaging consumers and communicating customer value through integrated marketing communication and about four elements of the marketing communications mix: advertising, publicity, personal selling, and sales promotion. In this chapter, we examine direct marketing and its fastest-growing form: digital marketing (online, social media, and mobile marketing). Today, spurred by the surge in internet usage and buying as well as rapid advances in digital technologies—from smartphones, tablets, and other digital devices to the spate of online mobile and social media—direct marketing has undergone a dramatic transformation. As you read this chapter, remember that although direct and digital marketing are presented as separate tools, they must be carefully integrated with each other and with other elements of the promotion and marketing mixes.

Let's start by looking at Amazon, a company that markets *only* directly and digitally. In little more than 20 years, Amazon has blossomed from an obscure dot-com upstart into one of the most powerful names on the internet. According to one survey, an amazing 40 percent of people turn to Amazon.com first when searching for or buying products online. How has Amazon become such an incredibly successful direct and online marketer in such a short time? It's all about creating customer engagement, value, and relationships through personal and satisfying online customer experiences. Few online marketers do that as well as Amazon.com.

AMAZON.COM: The Poster Child for Direct and Digital Marketing

When you think of shopping online, chances are good that you think first of Amazon. The online pioneer first opened its virtual doors in 1995, selling books out of founder Jeff Bezos's garage in suburban Seattle. Amazon still sells books—lots and lots of books. But it now sells just about everything else as well, from music, electronics, tools, housewares, apparel, and groceries to fashions, loose diamonds, and Maine lobsters. Most analysts view Amazon as *the* model for direct marketing in the digital age.

From the start, Amazon has grown explosively. Its annual sales have rocketed from a modest $150 million in 1997 to $107 billion today. During just the past five years, Amazon's revenues have more than tripled. On last year's Cyber Monday alone, Amazon.com sold approximately 52 million items to its 300 million active customers worldwide—that's more than 600 items per second. Currently, Amazon is the nation's second-largest retailer, trailing only Walmart.

What has made Amazon such an amazing success story? Founder and CEO Bezos puts it in three simple words: "Obsess over customers." To its core, the company is relentlessly customer driven. "The thing that drives everything is creating genuine value for customers," says Bezos. Amazon believes that if it does what's good for customers, profits will follow. So the company starts with the customer and works backward. Rather than asking what it can do with its current capabilities, Amazon first asks: Who are our customers? What do they need? Then it develops whatever capabilities are required to meet those customer needs.

At Amazon, every decision is made with an eye toward improving the Amazon.com customer experience. In fact, at many Amazon meetings, the most influential figure in the room is "the empty chair"—literally an empty chair at the table that represents the all-important customer. At times, the empty chair isn't empty but is occupied by a "Customer Experience Bar Raiser," an employee who is specially trained to represent customers' interests.

Amazon's obsession with serving the needs of its customers drives the company to take risks and innovate in ways that other companies don't. For example, when it noted that its book-buying customers needed better access to e-books

> Amazon's deep-down passion for creating superb online customer experiences has made it one of the most powerful names on the internet. Amazon is *the* model for successful direct and digital marketing.

and other digital content, Amazon developed the Kindle e-reader, its first-ever original product. The Kindle took more than four years and a whole new set of skills to develop. But Amazon's start-with-the-customer thinking paid off handsomely. The Kindle is one of the company's best-selling products, and Amazon.com now sells more e-books than hardcovers and paperbacks combined. What's more, the company's growing line of Kindle Fire tablets now leads the market for low-priced tablet computers. Thus, what started as an effort to improve the customer experience now gives Amazon a powerful presence in the burgeoning world of digital, mobile, and social media. Not only does the Kindle allow access to e-books, music, videos, and apps sold by Amazon, it makes interacting online with the digital giant easier than ever. Customers use their Kindle tablets to shop at Amazon.com and interact with the company on its blogs and social media pages.

Amazon does much more than just sell goods online. It engages customers and creates direct, personalized, and highly satisfying customer online buying experiences.
AFP/Getty Images

Amazon wants to deliver a special online experience to every customer. Most Amazon.com regulars feel a surprisingly strong relationship with the company, especially given the almost complete lack of actual human interaction. Amazon obsesses over making each customer's experience uniquely personal. For example, the Amazon.com site greets customers with their very own home pages, complete with personalized recommendations. Amazon was the first company to sift through each customer's past purchases and browsing histories and the purchasing patterns of customers with similar profiles to come up with personalized site content. Amazon wants to personalize the shopping experience for each individual customer. If it has 300 million customers, it reasons, it should have 300 million stores.

Visitors to Amazon.com receive a unique blend of benefits: huge selection, good value, low prices, and convenience. But it's the "discovery" factor that makes the buying experience really special. Once on the Amazon.com site, you're compelled to stay for a while—looking, learning, and discovering. To create even greater selection and discovery for customers, Amazon allows competing retailers—from mom-and-pop operations to Marks & Spencer—to sell their products on Amazon.com through the Amazon Marketplace, creating a virtual shopping mall of incredible proportions. The broader selection attracts more customers, and everyone benefits. Last year, Amazon customers bought billions of items from tens of thousands of third-party Amazon Marketplace sellers worldwide, accounting for close to 50 percent of Amazon's unit sales.

Amazon also makes the order delivery experience a whiz with its Amazon Prime service. For $99 a year, Prime members can receive free two-day shipping for all eligible purchases plus unlimited streaming of movies and TV shows with Prime Instant Video and access to borrowing e-books from the Kindle Owners' Lending Library. Amazon is moving rapidly toward same-day delivery. It recently launched Prime Now, which offers speedy two-hour free delivery of tens of thousands of items in several

large metropolitan areas (or one-hour delivery for a $7.99 fee). "In the past six weeks my husband and I have made an embarrassing number of orders through Amazon Prime Now," says one excited customer. "It's cheap, easy, and insanely fast."

More than just a place to buy things, Amazon.com has become a kind of online community in which customers can browse for products, research purchase alternatives, share opinions and reviews with other visitors, and chat online with authors and experts. In this way, Amazon does much more than just sell goods online. It engages customers and creates direct, personalized customer relationships and satisfying online experiences. Year after year, Amazon places at or near the top of almost every customer satisfaction ranking, regardless of industry.

Based on its powerful growth, many analysts have speculated that Amazon will become the Walmart of the web. In fact, some argue, it already is. Although Walmart's total sales of $482 billion dwarf Amazon's $107 billion in sales, Amazon's online sales are nearly eight times greater than Walmart's. And Amazon's e-commerce revenue is growing at a faster rate than Walmart's. So online, it's Walmart that's chasing Amazon. Put another way, Walmart wants to become the Amazon of the web, not the other way around. However, despite its mammoth proportions, to catch Amazon online, Walmart will have to match the superb Amazon.com online customer experience, and that won't be easy.

Thus, Amazon has become the poster child for direct and digital marketing. "The reason I'm so obsessed with … the customer experience is that I believe [our success] has been driven exclusively by that experience," says Jeff Bezos. It all starts with customer value. If Amazon creates superior value for customers, it will earn their business and loyalty, and success will follow in terms of company sales and returns. As Bezos puts it, "When things get complicated, we simplify them by asking, 'What's best for the customer?' We believe that if we do that, things will work out in the long term."[1]

OBJECTIVES OUTLINE

MANY OF THE MARKETING and promotion tools that we've examined in previous chapters were developed in the context of *mass marketing*: targeting broad markets with standardized messages and offers distributed through intermediaries. Today, however, with the trend toward narrower targeting and the surge in digital and social media technologies, many companies are adopting *direct marketing*, either as a primary marketing approach or as a supplement to other approaches. In this section, we explore the exploding world of direct marketing and its fastest-growing form—digital marketing using online, social media, and mobile marketing channels.

> Author | For most companies, direct
> Comment | and digital marketing are
> supplemental channels or media. But
> for many other companies today—such
> as Amazon, GEICO, or Priceline—direct
> marketing is a complete way of doing
> business.

Direct and Digital Marketing

Direct and digital marketing involve engaging directly with carefully targeted individual consumers and customer communities to both obtain an immediate response and build lasting customer relationships. Companies use direct marketing to tailor their offers and content to the needs and interests of narrowly defined segments or individual buyers. In this way, they build customer engagement, brand community, and sales.

Direct and digital marketing
Engaging directly with carefully targeted individual consumers and customer communities to both obtain an immediate response and build lasting customer relationships.

For example, Amazon.com interacts directly with customers via its website or mobile app to help them discover and buy almost anything and everything online. Similarly, GEICO interacts directly with customers—by telephone, through its website or smartphone app, or on its Facebook, Twitter, and YouTube pages—to build individual brand relationships, give insurance quotes, sell policies, or service customer accounts.

The New Direct Marketing Model

Early direct marketers—catalog companies, direct mailers, and telemarketers—gathered customer names and sold goods mainly by mail and telephone. Today, however, spurred by the surge in internet usage and buying and by rapid advances in digital technologies—from smartphones, tablets, and other digital devices to the spate of online social and mobile media—direct marketing has undergone a dramatic transformation.

In previous chapters, we discussed direct marketing as direct distribution—as marketing channels that contain no intermediaries. We also included direct and digital marketing elements of the promotion mix—as an approach for engaging consumers directly and creating brand community. In actuality, direct marketing is both of these things and much more.

Most companies still use direct marketing as a supplementary channel or medium. Thus, most department stores, such as Sears or Macy's, sell the majority of their merchandise off their store shelves, but they also sell through direct mail, online catalogs, and social media pages. Pepsi's Mountain Dew brand markets heavily through mass-media advertising and its retail partners' channels. However, it also supplements these channels with a heavy dose of direct marketing. Mountain Dew's marketing mix consists of 55 percent television advertising and 45 percent digital. It uses its several brand websites and a long list of social media to engage its digitally connected customer community in everything from designing their own Mountain Dew lifestyle pages to deciding which limited-edition flavors should be launched or retired. Through such direct interactions, Mountain Dew has created one of the most passionately loyal fan bases of any brand, which in turn has made it the nation's fourth-largest soft drink brand.[2]

However, for many companies today, direct and digital marketing are more than just supplementary channels or advertising media—they constitute a complete model for doing business. Firms employing this direct model use it as the only approach. Companies such as Amazon, Google, Facebook, eBay, Netflix, GEICO, and Priceline.com have successfully built their entire approach to the marketplace around direct and digital marketing. For example, Priceline.com, the online travel company, sells its services exclusively through online, mobile, and social media channels. Priceline.com and other online travel agency competitors such as Expedia and Orbitz have pretty much driven traditional offline travel agencies to extinction.[3]

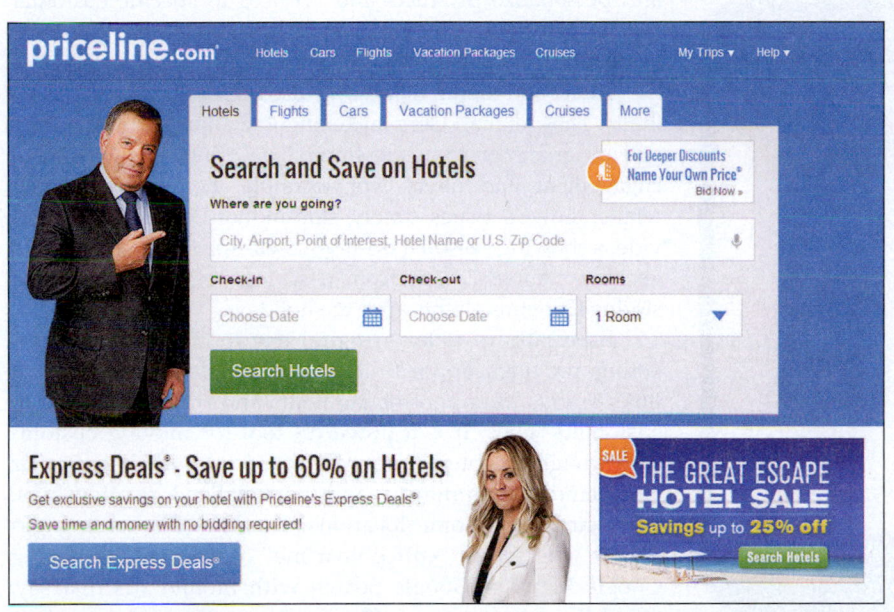

● The new direct marketing model: Online travel agency Priceline.com sells its services exclusively through online, mobile, and social media channels. Along with other online competitors, Priceline.com has pretty much driven traditional offline travel agencies to extinction.

priceline.com

Rapid Growth of Direct and Digital Marketing

Direct and digital marketing have become the fastest-growing form of marketing. According to one source, U.S. companies will spend an estimated $163 billion on direct and digital marketing this year, up more than 6 percent over the previous year. Direct marketing continues to become more internet-based, and digital direct marketing is claiming a surging share of marketing spending and sales. For example, U.S. marketers will spend an estimated $60 billion on digital advertising last year, up 20 percent over the previous year. Total digital advertising spending—including online display and search advertising, social media, mobile, video, email, and other—now accounts for the largest share of media spending, overtaking even television spending. And as consumers spend more and more time on their tablets and smartphones, ad spending on mobile advertising is exploding. Last year alone, mobile ad spending grew by 66 percent, and by 2019 it will account for an expected 29 percent of total U.S. ad spending.[4]

Benefits of Direct and Digital Marketing to Buyers and Sellers

For buyers, direct and digital marketing are convenient, easy, and private. They give buyers anywhere, anytime access to an almost unlimited assortment of goods and a wealth of product and buying information. For example, on its website and mobile app, Amazon.com offers more information than most of us can digest, ranging from top 10 product lists, extensive product descriptions, and expert and user product reviews to recommendations based on customers' previous searches and purchases.

Through direct marketing, buyers can interact with sellers by phone or on the seller's website or mobile app to create exactly the configuration of information, products, or services they want and then order them on the spot. Finally, for consumers who want it, digital marketing through online, mobile, and social media provides a sense of brand engagement and community—a place to share brand information and experiences with other brand fans.

For sellers, direct marketing often provides a low-cost, efficient, speedy alternative for reaching their markets. Today's direct marketers can target small groups or individual customers. Because of the one-to-one nature of direct marketing, companies can interact with customers by phone or online, learn more about their needs, and personalize products and services to specific customer tastes. In turn, customers can ask questions and volunteer feedback.

Direct and digital marketing also offer sellers greater flexibility. They let marketers make ongoing adjustments to prices and programs or to create immediate, timely, and personal engagement and offers. For example, home-improvement retailer Lowe's issues timely stop-motion Vine "Fix in Six" videos showing seasonal do-it-yourself tips for anything from keeping squirrels away from a spring vegetable garden to storing Christmas lights after the holidays.

Especially in today's digital environment, direct marketing provides opportunities for *real-time marketing* that links brands to important moments and trending events in customers' lives. It is a powerful tool for moving customers through the buying process and for building customer engagement, community, and personalized relationships. For example, in some locations, Dunkin' Donuts engages people who search "coffee near me" on their phones using Google Maps or Google Search with mobile ads that say, "Find the fastest coffee." ● Clicking on the ad brings up a map and wait times at nearby Dunkin' Donuts locations. And brands ranging from Chipotle or Starbucks to the Red Cross use Twitter to communicate with consumers in real time about important promotions, events, and other news and announcements.

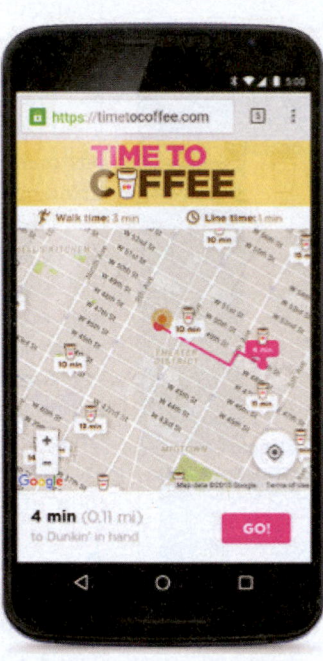

● Direct and digital marketing lets brands create immediate and timely customer engagement, as when Dunkin' Donuts beams maps and wait times for nearby locations to people who search "coffee near me" on their phones.

Courtesy of Dunkin' Donuts

Author Comment | Direct marketing is rich in tools, from traditional favorites such as direct mail and catalogs to dazzling new digital tools—online, mobile, and social media.

Forms of Direct and Digital Marketing

The major forms of direct and digital marketing are shown in ● **Figure 17.1**. Traditional direct marketing tools include face-to-face selling, direct-mail marketing, catalog marketing, telemarketing, direct-response television marketing, and kiosk marketing. In recent years, however, a dazzling new set of digital direct marketing tools has burst onto the marketing scene, including online marketing (websites, online ads and promotions, email, online videos, and blogs), social media marketing, and mobile marketing.

We'll begin by examining the new direct digital and social media marketing tools that have received so much attention lately. Then we'll look at the still heavily used and very important traditional direct marketing tools. As always, however, it's important to remember that all of these tools—both the new digital and the more traditional forms—must be blended into a fully integrated marketing communications program.

● FIGURE | 17.1

Forms of Direct and Digital Marketing

We'll begin with the fast-growing digital forms of direct marketing. But remember that the traditional forms are still heavily used and that the new and old must be integrated for maximum impact.

Digital and social media marketing
Online marketing
(Websites, online advertising, email, online videos, blogs)
Social media marketing
Mobile marketing

Build direct customer engagement and community

Traditional direct marketing
Face-to-face selling
Direct-mail marketing
Catalog marketing
Telemarketing
Direct-response TV marketing
Kiosk marketing

As noted earlier, **digital and social media marketing** is the fastest-growing form of direct marketing. It uses digital marketing tools such as websites, online video, email, blogs, social media, mobile ads and apps, and other digital platforms to directly engage consumers anywhere, anytime via their computers, smartphones, tablets, internet-ready TVs, and other digital devices. The widespread use of the internet and digital technologies is having a dramatic impact on both buyers and the marketers who serve them.

Author | Direct digital and social
Comment | media marketing is surging and grabbing all the headlines these days, so we'll start with it. But the traditional direct marketing tools are still heavily used. We'll dig into them later in the chapter.

Digital and social media marketing
Using digital marketing tools such as websites, social media, mobile apps and ads, online video, email, and blogs that engage consumers anywhere, anytime via their digital devices.

Marketing, the Internet, and the Digital Age

Much of the world's business today is carried out over digital networks that connect people and companies. These days, people connect digitally with information, brands, and each other at almost any time and from almost anywhere. In the age of the "Internet of Things" (IoT), it seems that everything and everyone will soon be connected digitally to everything and everyone else. The digital age has fundamentally changed customers' notions of convenience, speed, price, product information, service, and brand interactions. As a result, it has given marketers a whole new way to create customer value, engage customers, and build customer relationships.

Digital usage and impact continues to grow steadily. More than 87 percent of all U.S. adults use the internet, and the average U.S. internet user spends almost six hours a day using digital media, primarily via mobile devices. Worldwide, more than 46 percent of the population has internet access. And 30 percent has access to the mobile internet, a number that's expected to double by 2020 as mobile becomes an ever-more-popular way to get online.[5]

As a result, more than half of all U.S. households now regularly shop online, and digital buying continues to grow at a healthy double-digit rate. U.S. online retail sales were an estimated $350 billion last year, about 7.1 percent of total retail sales. By 2020, as consumers continue to shift their spending from physical to digital stores, that number is expected to grow to more than $520 billion (8.9 percent of total retail sales). Perhaps even more important, it's estimated that more than half of all U.S. retail sales were either transacted directly online or influenced by internet research.[6] As today's omni-channel consumers become more and more adept at blending online and in-store shopping, digital channels will come into play for an ever-larger proportion of their purchases.

To reach this burgeoning market, most companies now market online. Some companies operate *only* online. They include a wide array of firms, from *e-tailers* such as Amazon, Overstock.com, and Expedia.com that sell products and services directly to final buyers via the internet to *search engines and portals* (such as Google, Bing, Yahoo!, and DuckDuckGo), *transaction sites* (eBay, Craigslist), *content sites* (the *New York Times* on the web, ESPN.com, and *Encyclopædia Britannica*), and *online social media* (Facebook, Twitter, YouTube, Instragram, and Snapchat).

Today, however, it's hard to find a company that doesn't have a substantial online presence. Even companies that have traditionally operated offline have now created their own online sales, marketing, and brand community channels. Traditional store retailers are reaping increasingly larger proportions of their sales online. For example, Macy's is now the world's seventh-largest e-tailer, with almost 20 percent of its revenues coming from online. Staples captures about 22 percent of its sales online; at Williams-Sonoma, it's more than 50 percent.[7]

Omni-channel retailing
Creating a seamless cross-channel buying experience that integrates in-store, online, and mobile shopping.

In fact, **omni-channel retailing** companies are having as much online success as their online-only competitors. For example, home-improvement retailer Home Depot has nearly 2,000 U.S. stores. But its hottest growth area in recent years has been online sales, which have grown at nearly 40 percent annually over the past five years:[8]

Although it might be hard to imagine selling sheets of plywood, pre-hung doors, dishwashers, or vinyl siding online, Home Depot does that and much more these days. Last year, Home Depot sold some $4.7 billion worth of goods online, an amount equal to the total retail revenues of retailers such as Neiman-Marcus, Barnes & Noble, Tiffany, or Abercrombie & Fitch. Home Depot is now one of the world's top 10 online merchants. Its online inventory exceeds 1 million products, compared with only about 35,000 in a typical Home Depot store.

The home-improvement retailer now offers its customers multiple contact points and delivery modes. Of course, customers can buy products off the shelf in Home Depot stores. ● But they can also order online from home, a job site, or anywhere in between on their computers, tablets, or smartphones and then have goods shipped or pick them up at a store. More than 40 percent of online orders are now picked up inside a Home Depot store. Finally, in the store, associates armed with tablets can help customers order out-of-stock items for later pickup or delivery. In all, Home Depot uses online as a sales channel to drive both online and in-store sales and as a way to improve the customer experience by providing product, project, and other information. "Our customers are changing the way they shop and how they engage with us," says Home Depot. The goal is to provide "a seamless and frictionless experience no matter where our customers shop, be it in the digital world, our brick-and-mortar stores, at home, or on the job site. Anywhere the customer is, we need to be there."

● **Omni-channel retailing: Home Depot's goal is to provide "a seamless and frictionless experience no matter where our customers shop, be it in the digital world, our brick and mortar stores, at home, or on the job site. Anywhere the customer is, we need to be there."**

THE HOME DEPOT name and logo are trademarks of Home Depot Product Authority, LLC, used under license.

Direct digital and social media marketing takes any of the several forms shown in Figure 17.1. These forms include online marketing, social media marketing, and mobile marketing. We discuss each in turn, starting with online marketing.

Online Marketing

Online marketing
Marketing via the internet using company websites, online ads and promotions, email, online video, and blogs.

Online marketing refers to marketing via the internet using company websites, online advertising and promotions, email marketing, online video, and blogs. Social media and mobile marketing also take place online and must be closely coordinated with other forms of digital marketing. However, because of their special characteristics, we discuss the fast-growing social media and mobile marketing approaches in separate sections.

Websites and Branded Web Communities

Marketing website
A website that engages consumers to move them closer to a direct purchase or other marketing outcome.

For most companies, the first step in conducting online marketing is to create a website. Websites vary greatly in purpose and content. Some websites are primarily **marketing websites**, designed to engage customers and move them closer to a direct purchase or other marketing outcome.

For example, car companies like Hyundai operate marketing websites. Once a potential customer clicks in to Hyundai's site, the carmaker wastes no time trying to turn the inquiry into a sale and then into a long-term relationship. The site opens with a promotional message, then offers a garage full of useful information and interactive selling features, including detailed descriptions of current Hyundai models, tools for designing your own Hyundai, an area to calculate the trade-in value of your current car, information on dealer locations and services, and even a place to request a quote online. Inventory search and schedule a test drive features encourage customers to take the plunge and visit a Hyundai dealership.

Brand community website
A website that presents brand content that engages consumers and creates customer community around a brand.

In contrast, **brand community websites** do much more than just sell products. Instead, their primary purpose is to present brand content that engages consumers and creates customer–brand community. Such sites typically offer a rich variety of brand information, videos, blogs, activities, and other features that build closer customer relationships and generate engagement with and between the brand and its customers. For example, at Sephora's Beauty Talk site, visitors can interact with like-minded people to explore and

discover beauty products, post photo and links, and ask other members to weigh in with information and advice ("all the things marketers dreamed would happen on Facebook, but didn't," notes one observer). ● And you can't buy anything at ESPN.com. Instead, the site creates a vast branded sports community:[9]

> At ESPN.com, sports fans can access an almost overwhelming repository of sports information, statistics, and game updates. They can customize site content by sport, team, players, and authors to match their own special sports interests and team preferences. The site engages fans in contests and fantasy games (everything from fantasy football, baseball, basketball, and hockey to poker). Sports fans from around the world can participate in discussions with other fans and celebrities before, during, and after sporting events. They can friend and message other users and post comments on message boards and blogs. By downloading various widgets and apps, fans can customize their ESPN experience and carry it with them wherever they go. In all, ESPN's website creates a virtual brand community without walls, a must-have experience that keeps fans coming back again and again.

● **Brand community websites: You can't buy anything at ESPN.com. Instead, the site creates a vast branded sports community.**
© NetPhotos / Alamy

Creating a website is one thing; getting people to *visit* the site is another. To attract visitors, companies aggressively promote their websites in offline print and broadcast advertising and through ads and links on other sites. But today's web users are quick to abandon any website that doesn't measure up. The key is to create enough engaging and valued content to get consumers to come to the site, stick around, and come back again.

At the very least, a website should be easy to use and visually appealing. Ultimately, however, websites must also be *useful*. When it comes to online browsing and shopping, most people prefer substance over style and function over flash. For example, ESPN's site isn't all that flashy, and it's pretty heavily packed and congested. But it connects customers quickly and effectively to all the sports information and involvement they are seeking. Thus, effective websites contain deep and useful information, interactive tools that help find and evaluate content of interest, links to other related sites, changing promotional offers, and entertaining features that lend relevant excitement.

Online advertising

Advertising that appears while consumers are browsing online, including display ads, search-related ads, online classifieds, and other forms.

Online Advertising

As consumers spend more and more time online, companies are shifting more of their marketing dollars to **online advertising** to build brand sales or attract visitors to their internet, mobile, and social media sites. Online advertising has become a major promotional medium. The main forms of online advertising are display ads and search-related ads. Together, display and search-related ads account for the largest portion of firms' digital marketing budgets.

Online display ads might appear anywhere on an internet user's screen and are often related to the information being viewed. Such display ads have come a long way in recent years in terms of engaging consumers and moving them along the path to purchase. Today's *rich media* ads incorporate animation, video, sound, and interactivity. ● For example, while browsing sports-related content on your laptop, tablet, or phone, you might see a bright blue and green banner ad for Gillette Fusion PROGLIDE razors floating at the bottom of the page, with the provocative headline "Our Gentlest Shave." A click on the banner

● **Online display advertising: Today's dynamic rich media ads incorporate animation, video, sound, and interactivity, engaging consumers and moving them along the path to purchase.**
The Procter & Gamble Company

expands it into a full interactive display ad, complete with an embedded 15-second demonstration video plus click-throughs to the Gillette Fusion PROGLIDE microsite and a buy-now link. Similarly, while perusing your favorite backpacking site, you might see an attention-grabbing video ad from The North Face. Roll over the brand logo and up pops an interactive ad panel, with the video continuing in the upper-right corner alongside information on featured products and real-time links to The North Face website and a store locator. Such dynamic ads can engage consumers and deliver substantial impact.[10]

Using *search-related ads* (or *contextual advertising*), text- and image-based ads and links appear atop or alongside search engine results on sites such as Google, Yahoo!, and Bing. For example, search Google for "LED TVs." At the top and side of the resulting search list, you'll see inconspicuous ads for 10 or more advertisers, ranging from Samsung and Panasonic to Best Buy, Amazon.com, Walmart.com, Crutchfield, and CDW. Almost 90 percent of Google's $74.5 billion in revenues last year came from ad sales. Search is an always-on kind of medium, and the results are easily measured.[11]

A search advertiser buys search terms from the search site and pays only if consumers click through to its site. For instance, enter "Coke" or "Coca-Cola" or even just "soft drinks" or "rewards" into your search engine and almost without fail "My Coke Rewards" comes up as one of the top options, perhaps along with a display ad and link to Coca-Cola's official Google+ page. This is no coincidence. Coca-Cola supports its popular online loyalty program largely through search buys. The soft drink giant started first with traditional TV and print advertising but quickly learned that search was the most effective way to bring consumers to its www.mycokerewards.com web or mobile site to register. Now, any of dozens of purchased search terms will return mycokerewards.com at or near the top of the search list.

Email marketing
Sending highly targeted, highly personalized, relationship-building marketing messages via email.

WARBY PARKER

YOU'VE HAD YOUR WARBY PARKER
FRAMES FOR ONE YEAR NOW.

TELL 'EM WE SAID

Happy Birthday!

WE HOPE THE PAST 365 DAYS
HAVE BEEN JOYFUL.

HERE'S TO MANY MORE.

(WANT TO START MORE TRADITIONS?
WE'VE GOT SOME GOOD CANDIDATES...)

● **Email marketing:** Eyewear brand Warby Parker sends personalized emails to home try-on customers throughout the purchase and after-purchase process. "You've had your Warby Parker frames for one year now. Tell 'em we said Happy Birthday!"

Courtesy of Warby Parker

Email Marketing

Email marketing remains an important and growing digital marketing tool. "Social media is the hot new thing," says one observer, "but email is still the king."[12] Around the world, more than 200 million emails are sent out every minute of every day. According to one account, 72 percent of adults prefer that companies communicate with them via email, and 91 percent say they like receiving promotional emails from companies with which they do business. What's more, email is no longer limited to PCs; 66 percent of all emails are now opened on mobile devices. Not surprisingly, 25 percent of companies in one survey say that email is their top channel in terms of return on investment.[13]

When used properly, email can be the ultimate direct marketing medium. Today's emails are anything but the staid, text-only messages of the past. Instead, they are colorful, inviting, and interactive. Email lets marketers send highly targeted, tightly personalized, relationship-building messages. For example, toymaker Fisher-Price uses email to send timely check-ins, updates, and birthday wishes to subscribers. A mother might receive a colorful, personalized "happy birthday to your baby" email on her child's first birthday that contains links to age-related playtime ideas, parenting tips, and product information.[14]

Similarly, eyewear brand Warby Parker sends a sequence of nine informational and promotional emails to home try-on customers. Each is personally addressed and keyed to steps in the trial process, from initial registration and order confirmation to offers of selection assistance and instructions for returning frames. "The magical part was feeling like Warby Parker was right there with me throughout the process," says one customer. Warby Parker also sends cheerful after-purchase follow-up and announcement emails. ● For example, it sends personalized emails to customers on the first anniversary of their purchase, with the message "You've had your Warby Parker frames for one year now. Tell 'em we said Happy Birthday! We hope the first 365 days have been joyful." And just in case the customer wants "to start more traditions," the email also includes a link to Warby Parker's website.[15]

But there's a dark side to the growing use of email marketing. The explosion of **spam**—unsolicited, unwanted commercial email messages that clog up our email boxes—has produced consumer irritation and frustration. According to one source, spam now accounts for about half of the billions of emails sent worldwide each day. Workers in American businesses send and receive nearly 109 billion emails per day and spend nearly one-third of their workweek managing email.[16] Email marketers walk a fine line between adding value for consumers and being intrusive and annoying.

To address these concerns, most legitimate marketers now practice *permission-based email marketing*, sending email pitches only to customers who "opt in." Many companies use configurable email systems that let customers choose what they want to get. Amazon targets opt-in customers with a limited number of helpful "we thought you'd like to know" messages based on their expressed preferences and previous purchases. Few customers object, and many actually welcome such promotional messages. Amazon benefits through higher return rates and by avoiding alienating customers with emails they don't want. In fact, in the recent SPAMMY awards, which each year recognize the worst email abusers but also the most liked, Amazon topped the most-popular email subscriptions list for the second year in a row.[17]

Online Videos

Another form of online marketing is posting digital video content on brand websites or on social media sites such as YouTube, Facebook, Vine, and others. Some videos are made specifically for the web and social media. Such videos range from "how-to" instructional videos and public relations pieces to brand promotions and brand-related entertainment. Other videos are ads that a company makes primarily for TV and other media but posts online before or after an advertising campaign to extend their reach and impact.

Good online videos can engage consumers by the tens of millions. The online video audience is soaring. Almost 75 percent of the U.S. population has viewed online videos. YouTube users now upload more than 500 hours of video every minute. Facebook alone generates 8 billion video views per day worldwide; Snapchat adds another 6 billion views.[18]

Marketers hope that some of their videos will go viral. **Viral marketing**, the digital version of word-of-mouth marketing, involves creating videos, ads, and other marketing content that are so infectious that customers will seek them out or pass them along to their friends. Because customers find and pass along the content, viral marketing can be very inexpensive. And when content comes from a friend, the recipient is much more likely to view or read it.

All kinds of videos can go viral, producing engagement and positive exposure for a brand. ● For example, Google Android launched a compellingly sharable video called "Friends Furever," which featured unlikely pairings of animals—an orangutan and a dog, a bear and a tiger, a cat and a duckling—being pals and enjoying life together. The video was the latest installment in Android's two-year-old "Be together. Not the same." marketing campaign. The campaign highlights how people can be different and still be stronger together, in line with Android's core competency of running on diverse devices, each with its own design and features. The heartwarming "Friends Furever" video went viral in a big way. It captured more than 24 million YouTube views and was shared more than 6.4 million times across Facebook, Twitter, and the blogosphere in its first nine months, making it the most-shared video of all time.[19]

Many brands produce multi-platform video campaigns that bridge traditional TV, online, and mobile media. For example, Adidas's recent "Take It" campaign—a series of action-packed 60-second video ads featuring famous Adidas

Spam
Unsolicited, unwanted commercial email messages.

Viral marketing
The digital version of word-of-mouth marketing: videos, ads, and other marketing content that is so infectious that customers will seek it out or pass it along to friends.

● Viral marketing: Google Android's "Friends Furever" video went viral in a big way. It was shared more than 6.4 million times across Facebook, Twitter, and the blogosphere in its first nine months, making it the most-shared video of all time.

Google and the Google logo are registered trademarks of Google Inc., used with permission.

athletes gutting it out in practice and on game day—began on TV but quickly zoomed to the top of the viral charts. The campaign drove home a captivating motivational message: "Do something and be remembered. Or do nothing and be forgotten. No one owns today. Take it." The initial "Take It" ad broke during NBA All-Star Weekend, but that was only the beginning. The video ad went on to capture a whopping 21 million YouTube views in just the first week and 40 million in the first two months. Additional videos in the ad series grabbed millions more views, making "Take It" one of the most successful viral campaigns of the decade.[20]

Despite these viral successes, it's important to note that marketers usually have little control over where their viral messages end up. They can seed content online, but that does little good unless the message itself strikes a chord with consumers. Says one creative director, "You hope that the creative is at a high enough mark where the seeds grow into mighty oaks. If they don't like it, it ain't gonna move. If they like it, it'll move a little bit; and if they love it, it's gonna move like a fast-burning fire through the Hollywood hills."[21]

Blogs and Other Online Forums

Brands also conduct online marketing through various digital forums that appeal to specific special-interest groups and brand communities. **Blogs** (or web logs) are online forums where people and companies post their thoughts and other content, usually related to narrowly defined topics. Blogs can be about anything, from politics or baseball to haiku, car repair, brands, or the latest television series. Many bloggers use social networks such as Twitter, Facebook, Tumblr, and Instagram to promote their blogs, giving them huge reach. Such reach can give blogs—especially those with large and devoted followings—substantial influence.

Most marketers are now tapping into the blogosphere with their own brand-related blogs that reach customer communities. For example, on the Coca-Cola Unbottled blog, Coke fans and company insiders can "look at what's beyond the bottle," sharing posts on everything from new products and sustainability initiatives to fun and inspiring "what's bubbling" fan stories about "spreading happiness." On the Netflix Blog, members of the Netflix team (themselves rabid movie fans) tell about the latest Netflix features, share tricks for getting the most out of the Netflix experience, and collect feedback from subscribers. ● And the creative Nuts About Southwest blog, written by Southwest Airline employees, fosters a two-way dialogue that gives customers a look inside the company's culture and operations. At the same time, it lets Southwest engage customers directly and get feedback from them.

Beyond their own brand blogs, many marketers use third-party blogs to help get their messages out. For example, some fashion bloggers have amassed millions of followers, with fan bases larger even than the blogs and social media accounts of major fashion magazines. For example, 23-year-old Danielle Bernstein started the We Wore What fashion blog as an undergraduate at the Fashion Institute of Technology in New York City. The blog is now a source of daily outfit inspiration to a fan base of more than 1.4 million. Because of such large followings, brands flock to Bernstein and other fashion blog influencers such as BryanBoy, The Blonde Salad, Song of Style, and Gal Meets Glam, paying them $15,000 or more to post and tag product images in their blog, Facebook, and Instagram sites. Bernstein posts images that contain sponsored products from small brands such as Schultz Shoes and Revolve Clothing to large brands such as Nike, Lancôme, and Nordstrom.[22]

Blogs
Online forums where people and companies post their thoughts and other content, usually related to narrowly defined topics.

● **Tapping into blogs: The creative Nuts About Southwest blog, written by Southwest employees, fosters a two-way dialogue that gives customers a look inside the company's culture and operations.**

Southwest Airlines Co.

As a marketing tool, blogs offer some advantages. They can offer a fresh, original, personal, and cheap way to enter into consumer online and social media conversations. However, the blogosphere is cluttered and difficult to control. And although companies can sometimes leverage blogs to engage customers in meaningful relationships, blogs remain largely a consumer-controlled medium. Whether or not they actively participate in the blogs, companies should monitor and listen to them. Marketers can use insights from consumer online conversations to improve their marketing programs.

Social Media and Mobile Marketing

Social Media Marketing

Author Comment | As in about every other area of our lives, digital media and mobile technologies have taken the marketing world by storm. They offer some amazing marketing possibilities. But truth be told, many marketers are still sweating over how to use them most effectively.

As we've discussed throughout the text, the surge in internet usage and digital technologies and devices has spawned a dazzling array of online **social media** and other digital communities. Countless independent and commercial social networks have arisen where people congregate to socialize and share messages, opinions, pictures, videos, and other content. These days, it seems, almost everyone is buddying up on Facebook or Google+, checking in with Twitter, tuning into the day's hottest videos at YouTube, pinning images on social scrapbooking site Pinterest, or sharing photos with Instagram and Snapchat. And, of course, wherever consumers congregate, marketers will surely follow.

Social media
Independent and commercial online social networks where people congregate to socialize and share messages, opinions, pictures, videos, and other content.

Most marketers are now riding the huge social media wave. According to one survey, 92 percent of U.S. companies now claim that social media marketing is important for their businesses.[23] Interestingly, just as marketers are now learning how to use social media to engage customers, the social media themselves are learning how to make their communities a suitable platform for marketing content, in a way that benefits both social media users and brands. Most social media, even the most successful ones, still face a monetization issue: How can they profitably tap the marketing potential of their massive communities to make money without driving off loyal users (see Real Marketing 17.1)?

Using Social Media

Marketers can engage in social media in two ways: They can use existing social media or they can set up their own. Using existing social media seems the easiest. Thus, most brands—large and small—have set up shop on a host of social media sites. Check the websites of brands ranging from Coca-Cola, Nike, and Victoria's Secret to the Chicago Bulls or even the U.S. Forest Service and you'll find links to each brand's Facebook, Google+, Twitter, YouTube, Flickr, Instagram, or other social media pages. Such social media can create substantial brand communities. For example, the Chicago Bulls have more the 18 million Facebook fans; Coca-Cola has an eye-popping 97 million Facebook fans.

Some of the major social networks are huge. Nearly 1.6 billion people access Facebook every month, almost five times the population of the United States. Twitter has more than 305 million active monthly users. And YouTube's more than 1 billion users upload 500 hours of video every minute of every day. The list goes on: Google+ has 359 million active users, Instagram 400 million, LinkedIn 100 million, and Pinterest 100 million.[24]

Although these large, general-interest social media networks grab most of the headlines, countless niche and interest-based social media have also emerged. These online social networks cater to the needs of smaller communities of like-minded people, making them ideal vehicles for marketers who want to target special-interest groups. There's at least one social media network for just about every interest, hobby, or group. ● Goodreads is a social network where 55 million avid readers can "Meet your next favorite book" and discuss it with friends, whereas moms share advice and commiseration at CafeMom.com. FarmersOnly.com provides online dating for down-to-earth "country folks" who enjoy "blue skies, living free and at peace in wide open spaces, raising animals, and appreciating nature"—"because city folks just don't get it." At Birdpost.com, avid bird

● Countless niche and special-interest social media have emerged, catering to communities of like-minded people. Goodreads is a place where you can "Meet your next favorite book" and discuss it with others.
Goodreads, LLC

17.1   Social Media Monetization: Making Money without Driving Fans Away

As the world has rapidly gone social and mobile, social media have played a huge role. Whether it's on massive networks such as Facebook, Twitter, YouTube, Instagram, and Snapchat or lesser-known niche sites such as Blurty, Dogster, and Reddit, it's common to see people everywhere these days, heads down with devices in hand, connecting, posting, messaging, and sharing. On Facebook alone, every day, a mind-blowing 1 billion of the network's 1.6 billion active users worldwide upload 350 million photos, generate 4.5 billion Likes, and share 4.75 billion pieces of content.

However, even as social media networks have achieved incredible success in terms of numbers of users, sheer volume of content and activity, and company valuations, a nagging problem still plagues them. It's called *monetization*. How can social media profitably tap the marketing potential of their massive communities to make money without driving off their legions of loyal users? Most social media still struggle to make a profit, and even the most popular ones are only beginning to tap their full financial potential.

The first and best bet for converting the social-sharing potential of a social network's gigantic user community into real dollars is online advertising. For marketers, the targeting and customer engagement potential of social media is a dream come true, and advertisers willingly pay for access via ads and other paid brand content. But successfully injecting brand content alongside user content can be tricky and risky. Social media users often cherish the free (and commercial-free) sharing cultures of their online communities. If not well conceived, commercial content becomes an unwelcome intrusion that can alienate users and potentially drive them away.

Thus, although social media have exploded in popularity, most are still having trouble making money. Even Facebook—far and away the most financially successful social network, which earned $3.7 billion in profits on $18 billion in revenues last year—has little more than scratched the surface of its vast financial potential.

To illustrate the monetization difficulties that social media face, let's dig deeper into one of today's most successful ones, Snapchat, the wildly popular messaging app. Snapchat serves a fast-growing community of approximately 200 million users, heavily weighted toward young millennials and GenZ. Snapchat started as a messaging app for sharing pictures and videos—known as Snaps—that disappear without a trace after a few seconds. But it has now morphed into a full and vibrant communication platform. Snapchatters can choose from a full menu of options, including text, photos, drawings, video notes, audio notes, video calls, and audio calls, all in full-screen glory. Snapchat also offers up a variety of news and entertainment content.

Snapchat exploded onto the scene only five years ago. By the end of its first year, 1 billion photos had been shared through Snapchat's servers; today more than 100 million daily Snapchat users share some 10 billion daily video views. As Snapchat's popularity soared, so did its valuation. Two years in, Facebook made Snapchat's founders a then-startling $3 billion buyout offer; the founders politely declined. Today, Snapchat has raised more than $1.1 billion in venture capital funding and is valued at $16 billion. Yet in its rise to glory, Snapchat only recently started to generate revenue of any kind and has yet to make even a dime of profits.

Snapchat's financial story is typical for successful social media: modest beginnings as a start-up followed by meteoric growth in popularity and use leading to outrageously high valuation—all with little or no income. Then comes that difficult question: How can they monetize their massive user bases to make profits and sustain themselves? For Snapchat, that's especially difficult. The very feature that makes Snapchat unique and so popular—content lasting only seconds—makes it difficult to track and analyze users for targeting purposes, a turnoff to marketers. In this era of big data, how can Snapchat, which collects no user data, attract marketers? Snapchat's challenge is to persuade marketers that the benefits of reaching its young millennials and GenZ community outweigh user anonymity and lack of pinpoint targeting potential.

Careful not to ruffle its community's sensitivities or disrupt the user experience, Snapchat didn't introduce its first advertising opportunities until October 2014. However, it now offers several ad platforms. At the most basic level, Snapchat sells traditional paid video ad placements alongside other site content. Next, it offers a magazine-like platform called "Discover." Discover is a Snapchat content area where publishers ranging from ESPN, CNN, Comedy Central, and Food Channel to *Cosmopolitan,*

Wildly popular messaging app Snapchat and other social media face a nagging *monetization* issue: How can they profitably tap the marketing potential of their massive communities to make money without driving off their legions of loyal users?

Thomas Trutschel/Getty Images

National Geographic, and *People* post daily collections of their best content. Snapchat users can share Discover news stories and video with personalized comments or emoji. Advertisers pay a minimum of $50,000 a day to advertise alongside the Discover content, and Snapchat has hinted that it will soon offer brand-owned Discover stories.

Snapchat also offers advertisers a sponsored feeds platform called "Live Story." These feeds are TV-like streams of an event such as New Year's Eve, March Madness, an important football game, or the Macy's Thanksgiving Parade, featuring user-generated content curated by Snapchat. Advertisers can buy sponsorship rights for a Live Story feed starting at $250,000, which includes a brand mention in the opening title as well as branded snaps interspersed throughout the feed. For example, Macy's sponsors the Macy's Thanksgiving Parade feed, weaving its own brand content in with user content. Advertisers can also pay for a single 10-second brand snap woven into a feed. Live Stories feeds garner an estimated 20 million daily views within the Snapchat community.

In addition to the Discover and Live Story platforms, Snapchat continues to tinker with other advertising products and rates to find the best monetization formula. Although it now generates only a trickle of ad revenue compared with Facebook—a meager $50 million last year—the brash young social network projects that ad revenues will be six to seven times that amount this year.

In its quest to monetize, Snapchat has a lot at stake. Will increased advertising and brand content alienate avid Snapchat fans? If done right, probably not. Studies show that social media users readily accept—even welcome—well-targeted brand content. A recent Snapchat survey found that 60 percent of Snapchat users actually like its Live Story ads.

But that's the catch—doing it right. Like its own disappearing photo feature, Snapchat's soaring popularity could vanish quickly if overly aggressive monetization causes resentment within its highly mobile and typically fickle fan base. Snapchat must move forward carefully. As one Snapchat marketer concludes, "We're always fine tuning to ensure we deliver the best possible experience for our community."

Sources: Kimberlee Morrison, "If You Really Want to Reach GenZ, Snapchat Is the Way," *Adweek,* March 23, 2016, www.adweek.com/socialtimes/print/636450; Garrett Sloane, "Snapchat Persuades Brands to Go Vertical with Their Video," *Adweek,* April 27, 2015, pp. 20–22; Tim Peterson, "With Snapchat's First Ad Format on Hold, Focus Shifts to Live Event Feeds," *Advertising Age,* April 16, 2015, www.adage.com/print/298082; Austin Carr, "I Ain't Afraid of No Ghosts," *Fast Company,* November 2015, pp. 100–104; Kia Kokalitcheva, "Snapchat Reportedly Targets at Least $300 Million in 2016 Revenue," *Fortune,* March 7, 2016, http://fortune.com/2016/03/07/snapchat-revenue-target/; and Sarah Frier, "Snapchat User 'Stories' Fuel 10 Billion Daily Video Views," *Bloomberg Technology,* April 28, 2016, www.bloomberg.com/news/articles/2016-04-28/snapchat-user-content-fuels-jump-to-10-billion-daily-video-views.

watchers can keep an online list of birds they've seen and share bird sightings with other members using modern satellite maps.[25]

Social Media Marketing Advantages and Challenges

Using social media presents both advantages and challenges. On the plus side, social media are *targeted* and *personal*—they allow marketers to create and share tailored brand content with individual consumers and customer communities. Social media are *interactive*, making them ideal for starting and participating in customer conversations and listening to customer feedback. For example, TOMS shoes—which gives a free pair of shoes to a child in need for every shoe purchased, one for one—recently ran a two-week #withoutshoes campaign in which it donated one pair of shoes for every person who snapped a picture of their bare feet, shared it on Instagram, and urged others to do the same. The campaign resulted in more than 296,000 pairs of shoes donated, engaging customers in spreading the brand's philanthropic message to millions around the world.[26]

Social media are also *immediate* and *timely*. They can be used to reach customers anytime, anywhere with timely and relevant marketing content regarding brand happenings and activities. As discussed earlier in the chapter, the rapid growth in social media usage has caused a surge in *real-time marketing,* allowing marketers to create and join consumer conversations around situations and events as they occur. Marketers can now watch what's trending and create content to match.

Social media can be very *cost-effective*. Although creating and administering social media content can be costly, many social media are free or inexpensive to use. Thus, returns on social media investments are often high compared with those of expensive traditional media such as television or print. The low cost of social media puts them within easy reach of even small businesses and brands that can't afford the high costs of big-budget marketing campaigns.

Perhaps the biggest advantage of social media is their *engagement and social sharing capabilities.* Social media are especially well suited to creating customer engagement and community—for getting customers involved with the brand and with each other. More than any other channels, social media can involve customers in shaping and sharing brand content, experiences, information, and ideas.

For example, consider Etsy—the online craft marketplace that's "Your place to buy and sell all things handmade." ● Etsy uses its web and mobile sites and a host of social media to create an Etsy lifestyle community, where buyers congregate to learn about, explore, exchange,

● **Through its extensive online and social media presence, Etsy has created an active and engaged brand community of buyers and sellers in a "marketplace we make together."**

Daniel Acker/Bloomberg via Getty Images

and share ideas about handmade and vintage products and related topics. In addition to its active Facebook, Twitter, and YouTube pages, Etsy engages 780,000 brand followers on photo-sharing site Instagram, where the Etsy community shares photos of creative ideas and projects. It also engages almost a million followers on social scrapbooking site Pinterest, with 120 boards on topics ranging from "DIY Projects," "Entertaining," and "Stuff We Love" to "Etsy Weddings" and even "Yum! Recipes to Share," where the community posts favorite recipes. Etsy sells few of the ingredients that go into the recipes, but it's all part of the Etsy lifestyle. Through its extensive online and social media presence, Etsy has created an active and engaged worldwide community of 24 million shoppers and 1.6 million sellers worldwide in what it calls "The marketplace we make together."[27]

Social media marketing also presents challenges. First, many companies are still experimenting with how to use them effectively and results are hard to measure. Second, such social networks are largely user controlled. The company's goal in using social media is to make the brand a part of consumers' conversations and their lives. However, marketers can't simply muscle their way into consumers' digital interactions—they need to earn the right to be there. Rather than intruding, marketers must become a valued part of the online experience by developing a steady flow of engaging content.

Because consumers have so much control over social media content, even a seemingly harmless social media campaign can backfire. That's what happened when Sea World launched a "Sea World Cares" marketing campaign to educate the public about its work to protect killer whales and other aquatic species in captivity and in the wild:

> As part of the broader campaign, recognizing that "some people have questions about the welfare of killer whales in human care," Sea World invited Twitter users to pose their questions to the company directly using the hashtag #AskSeaWorld. But rather than the constructive Q&A exchange that Sea World intended, the hashtag turned into a bashtag nightmare. Angry Twitter users used the hashtag to jump all over Sea World for what they saw as animal abuse practices. Some typical responses: "#AtSeaWorld how do you sleep knowing you imprison innocent animals, abuse them for entertainment, lie to the public, and make millions?" and "#AskSeaWorld do you think it's morally okay to take a child away from its mother? #EmptyTheTanks."[28]

There's a clear message. With social media, "you're going into the consumer's backyard. This is their place," warns one social marketer. "Social media is a pressure cooker," says another. "The hundreds of thousands, or millions, of people out there are going to take your idea, and they're going to try to shred it or tear it apart and find what's weak or stupid in it."[29]

Integrated Social Media Marketing

Using social media might be as simple as posting some messages and promotions on a brand's Facebook or Twitter pages or creating brand buzz with videos or images on YouTube, Instagram, or Pinterest. However, most large companies are now designing full-scale social media efforts that blend with and support other elements of a brand's marketing content strategy and tactics. More than making scattered efforts and chasing "Likes" and tweets, companies that use social media successfully are integrating a broad range of diverse media to create brand-related social sharing, engagement, and customer community.

Managing a brand's social media efforts can be a major undertaking. For example, Starbucks is one of the most successful social media marketers. Its core social media team connects with its fans through 30 accounts on 12 different social platforms. Frappuccino alone has more than 11 million followers on Facebook, Twitter, Instagram, and We Heart It. Managing and integrating all that social media content is challenging, but the results are worth the investment. Customers can and do engage with Starbucks by the tens of millions digitally, without ever setting foot in a store.[30]

But more than just creating online engagement and community, Starbucks' social media presence also drives customers into its stores. For example, in its first big social media promotion six years ago, Starbucks offered a free pastry with a morning drink purchase. A million people showed up. A more recent "Tweet-a-Coffee" promotion, which let customers give a $5 gift card to a friend by putting both #tweetacoffee and the friend's handle in a tweet, resulted in $180,000 in purchases within little more than one month. Social media "are not just about engaging and telling a story and connecting," says Starbucks's head of global digital marketing. "They can have a material impact on the business."[31]

Mobile Marketing

Mobile marketing
Marketing messages, promotions, and other content delivered to on-the-go consumers through their mobile devices.

Mobile marketing features marketing messages, promotions, and other marketing content delivered to on-the-go consumers through their mobile devices. Marketers use mobile marketing to engage customers anywhere, anytime during the buying and relationship-building processes. The widespread adoption of mobile devices and the surge in mobile web traffic have made mobile marketing a must for most brands.

With the recent proliferation of mobile phones, smartphones, and tablets, mobile device penetration is now greater than 100 percent in the United States (many people possess more than one mobile device). Almost 70 percent of people in the United States own a smartphone and nearly half of all U.S. households are currently mobile-only households with no landline phone. The mobile apps market has exploded globally: There are more than 3 million apps available, and the average smartphone has 11 to 20 apps installed on it.[32]

Most people love their phones and rely heavily on them. According to one study, nearly 90 percent of consumers who own smartphones, tablets, computers, and TVs would give up all of those other screens before giving up their phones. On average, Americans check their phones 46 times a day—74 times a day for 18- to 24-year-olds—and spend three hours and 40 minutes a day using apps, talking, texting, and browsing the web. Thus, although TV is still a big part of people's lives, mobile is rapidly becoming their "first screen." Away from home, it's their only screen.[33]

For consumers, a smartphone or tablet can be a handy shopping companion. It can provide on-the-go product information, price comparisons, advice and reviews from other consumers, and access to instant deals and digital coupons. One recent study found that 90 percent of smartphone-toting shoppers have used their phone while shopping. Not surprisingly, then, more than 42 percent of all e-commerce purchases are made on mobile devices.[34] Mobile provides a rich platform for engaging consumers more deeply as they move through the buying process with tools ranging from mobile ads, coupons, and texts to apps and mobile websites.

Mobile advertising spending in the United States is surging. It grew 66 percent last year alone and will more than double during the next four years.[35] Mobile ad spending is expected to overtake TV ad spending by 2020. Almost every major marketer—from Nike, P&G, and Macy's to your local supermarket to nonprofits such as the Red Cross—is now integrating mobile marketing into its direct marketing programs.

Companies use mobile marketing to stimulate immediate buying, make shopping easier, enrich the brand experience, or all of these (see Real Marketing 17.2). It lets marketers provide consumers with information, incentives, and choices at the moment they are expressing an interest or when they are most likely to make a buying choice. For example, Taco Bell uses mobile advertising to reach consumers at what it calls mobile "moments that matter."[36]

As part of its ongoing push to promote Taco Bell for breakfast, the chain uses carefully targeted mobile advertising to reach consumers just as they are starting their day. It targets mobile ads based on specific behaviors such as which apps consumers use first in the morning, their favorite news apps, or what time of day they've looked at a breakfast recipe. "We're weaving into morning behaviors," says a Taco Bell marketer. ● Taco Bell also targets mobile ads geographically using navigation and traffic apps such as Google's Waze to zero in on specific customer locations, even providing step-by-step directions to nearby stores. In these ways, Taco Bell can customize mobile ads according to each customer's actions, experiences, and environment. In marketing its breakfasts, says the marketer, mobile lets Taco Bell be "present on experiences that consumers turn to when they first open their eyes in the morning."

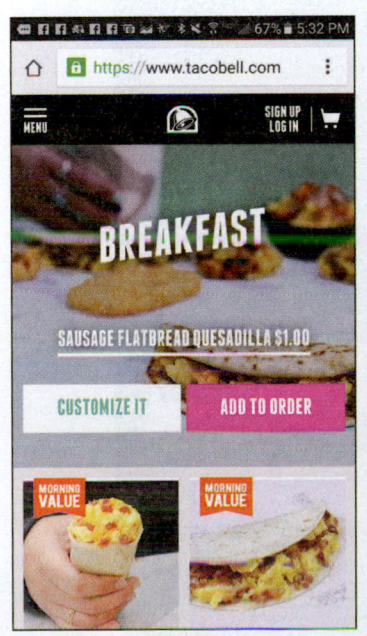 

● **Mobile marketing: Carefully-targeted mobile advertising lets Taco Bell reach breakfast customers at "moments that matter"—such as when they first open their eyes in the morning.**

Taco Bell Corp.

17.2 Mobile Marketing: Engaging Customers Anywhere, Anytime

Armed only with a smartphone or other mobile device, you can learn, do, or buy almost anything these days, from anywhere, and at any time. Google's Waze app does more than just help you navigate—it pinpoints traffic jams, accidents, speed traps, and gas prices in real time, faithfully updated by members of the Waze community. Is that Redbox kiosk too slow? Download the Redbox app—it lets you find and reserve a DVD using your mobile device and have it waiting for you at the kiosk.

REI's Powder Project app gives you "backcountry, sidecountry, and secret stashes" ski slope information for locations throughout the United States and Canada. Beyond just the basics like snow conditions, number of open lifts, and trail maps, the app offers webcam views, GPS routing, elevation profiles, forums, and a host of interactive features plus links to REI for times when you decide you can't live without a new set of K2 skis or a two-man Hubba Hubba tent.

Welcome to the world of mobile marketing. Today's smartphones and other mobile devices are changing how people live, becoming indispensable hubs for communication, information, and entertainment. They are also revolutionizing the way people shop and buy, giving marketers new opportunities to engage customers in more effective and satisfying ways.

Marketers are responding to the huge growth in mobile access and use. Mobile ad spending skyrocketed 66 percent last year and is expected to more than double in the next four. And the mobile app market has outright exploded. Just seven years ago, Apple's App Store had a then-astounding 10,000 apps. But by last year, it boasted 1.5 million apps; Android's Google Play now has the lead with more than 1.6 million apps. Mobile has become today's brave new marketing frontier, especially for brands courting younger consumers. Mobile devices are very personal, ever-present, and always on. That makes them an ideal medium for obtaining quick responses to individualized, time-sensitive offers.

Successful mobile marketing goes beyond just giving people a coupon and a link to buy. Instead, it enhances brand engagement and creates a "frictionless" buying experience. For example, with Amazon's mobile app—thanks to "1-click" purchasing, Prime membership, and other features—customers located anywhere, anytime can have products delivered to practically any location in less than 24 hours with nothing more than a smartphone, a simple search or scan, and the click of a button.

Consumers have come to expect such frictionless mobile buying experiences from marketing giants like Amazon. But with recent rapid advances in mobile capabilities, from location-based technologies to mobile payment systems, more and more companies are becoming the Amazons of their industries. Consider mobile app-based car-sharing service Getaround.

In the United States alone, personal cars sit idle for 6 billion car-hours every day. Peer-to-peer car-sharing service Getaround lets car owners earn money by sharing those unused hours with others in the Getaround community for a fee. The young company has already developed a fast-growing base of 300,000 members, who receive 60 percent of the rental fees—an average of $500 to $1,000 per month depending on the car. Getaround takes care of everything—customer contact and support, insurance, roadside assistance, and payment. To use Getaround, you just download the mobile app and supply credit card and driver's license information. Then you can use the app to search among and view thousands of cars available in the neighborhood and rent one by the hour or day, right when you need it. You locate the car with your phone's GPS, unlock it with the app, and get in and drive it away. Pay with a credit card on file or using Apple Pay with a single tap. It's that simple. The Getaround app even provides trip management tools for planning getaways on the go.

Mobile marketing can do much more than simply ease the buying process. It can also take ads, coupons, and other promotions to new levels. Mobile marketers can personalize promotions and weave them into relevant everyday customer experiences. For example, Kiip, a mobile reward network, specializes in helping brands provide customers with just the right reward at just the right time based on their everyday activities. The agency started by embedding its technology into video game apps such as Zombie Farm and Mega Jump. Gamers who reach a new game level or meet some other goal get a coupon to one of their favorite retailers, such as American Apparel.

Mobile marketing: Mobile promotions company Kiip helps client brands link mobile offers to relevant customer experiences and positive moments. "We want to capitalize on happiness," says Kiip's CEO.

Kiip, Inc.

Kiip now boasts a network of 2,500 apps and 60 million users across games, fitness, productivity, music, and cooking categories. It showcases more than 500 million reward moments every month for clients like McDonald's, Propel, Sour Patch Kids, P&G, and MasterCard. For fitness apps like MapMyRun and productivity apps like Any.do, Kiip ties rewards to real-life achievements. When users cross things off their to-do lists or achieve a running goal, they get a reward from a relevant brand. For example, P&G's Secret deodorant recently rewarded female MapMyRun users with free song downloads for their workout playlists. And snack giant Mondelēz rewarded Any.do users with free packs of Trident when they set new personal records.

Kiip helps marketers reach targeted users at positive moments with rewards relevant to their real-time doings and accomplishments. Readers who finish a certain number of pages in a reading app receive a free magazine subscription. People using a couple's app to stay in touch receive credits toward a purchase from 1-800-Flowers. Kiip is even working with connected-car company Mojio, whose 4G telematic device plugs into a car's diagnostic port, tracks information about the car's status, and keeps the owner connected to favorite people, places, and things. Through Mojio, Kiip helps clients—from insurance companies and car repair shops to parking meter and garage operators—provide rewards tied to specific driver locations and behaviors.

Unlike typical banner ads, pop-ups, or emails, Kiip offers enhance a user's regular activities rather than interrupting them. According to Kiip's founder and CEO, Kiip "is less about real-time marketing and more about real-time-needs addressing." In fact, he asserts, Kiip isn't really in the mobile ad business at all—it's in the happiness business. "We want to capitalize on happiness," he says. "Everything's better when you're happy." Mobile timeliness, relevance, and happiness pay off in terms of consumer response. Users redeem Kiip's mobile promotions at a 22-percent clip compared with the 0.3 percent for typical app ad engagement. Kiip's offers also increase mobile app revisits by 30 percent and more than double average app length of use.

Many consumers are initially skeptical about mobile marketing. But they often change their minds if mobile offers deliver useful brand and shopping information, entertaining content, or timely coupons and discounted prices. Most mobile efforts target only consumers who voluntarily opt in or download apps. In the increasingly cluttered mobile marketing space, customers just won't do that unless they see real value in it. The challenge for marketers: develop valued mobile offers, ads, and apps that make customers come calling.

Sources: Denise Restauri, "With the Getaround App, Your Idle Car Can Pay for Itself," *Forbes,* February 25, 2016, www.forbes.com/sites/deniserestauri/2016/02/25/this-millennial-is-upending-the-transportation-industry-and-she-needs-your-car/#616b02e843f4; Lindsay Harrison, "Kiip: For Making Mobile Ads That People Want," *Fast Company,* February 11, 2013, www.fastcompany.com/most-innovative-companies/2013/kiip; Christina Chaey, "How Kiip Ties Brand Rewards to Game and Life Achievements to Make Mobile Ads Engaging," *Fast Company,* July 23, 2012, www.fastcocreate.com/1681287; Neil Undgerleider, "Advertisers Are about to Enter Your Connected Car," *Fast Company,* April 11, 2014, www.fastcompany.com/3028744/most-innovative-companies/advertisers-are-about-to-enter-your-connected-car; Katherine Dunkin, "Building a Peer-to-Peer Car Sharing Network at Age 27," *Entrepreneur,* August 20, 2014, www.entrepreneur.com/article/236473; "Digital Ad Spending to Surpass TV Next Year," *eMarketer,* March 8, 2016, www.emarketer.com/Article/Digital-Ad-Spending-Surpass-TV-Next-Year/1013671; and www.powderproject.com/, www.kiip.com/me, www.getaround.com/mobile, www.getaround.com/tour, and www.getaround.com/tour/benefits, accessed October 2016.

Today's rich-media mobile ads can create substantial engagement and impact. For example, Macy's built a recent "Brasil: A Magical Journey" promotion around a popular and imaginative smartphone app. The campaign featured apparel from Brazilian designers and in-store experiences celebrating Brazilian culture. By using their smartphones to scan codes throughout the store, shoppers could learn about featured fashions and experience Brazilian culture through virtual tours, such as a trip to the Amazon, a visit to Rio de Janeiro during Carnival, or attending a Brazilian soccer match.

Most marketers have created their own mobile online sites, optimized for specific phones and mobile service providers. Others have created useful or entertaining mobile apps to engage customers with their brands and help them shop. For example, the Benjamin Moore Color Capture app lets customers take photos of colorful objects, then match them to any of 3,500 Benjamin Moore paint colors. Starbucks's mobile app lets customers use their phones as a Starbucks card to make fast and easy purchases. And Charles Schwab's mobile apps let customers get up-to-the-minute investment news, monitor their accounts, and make trades at any time from any location—it helps you "stay connected with your money."

As with other forms of direct marketing, however, companies must use mobile marketing responsibly or risk angering already ad-weary consumers. Most people don't want to be interrupted regularly by advertising, so marketers must be smart about how they engage people on mobile devices. The key is to provide genuinely useful information and offers that will make consumers want to engage. And many marketers target mobile ads on an opt-in-only basis.

In all, digital direct marketing—online, social media, and mobile marketing—offers both great promise and many challenges for the future. Its most ardent apostles still envision a time when the internet and digital marketing will replace magazines, newspapers, and even stores as sources for information, engagement, and buying. Most marketers, however, hold a more realistic view. For most companies, digital and social media marketing will remain just one important approach to the marketplace that works alongside other approaches in a fully integrated marketing mix.

Author | Although online, social
Comment | media, and mobile direct
marketing seem to be getting much
of the attention these days, traditional
direct media still carry a lot of the direct
marketing freight. Just think about your
often overstuffed mailbox.

Traditional Direct Marketing Forms

Although the fast-growing digital marketing tools have grabbed most of the headlines lately, traditional direct marketing tools are very much alive and still heavily used. We now examine the traditional direct marketing approaches shown on the right side of Figure 17.1.

The major traditional forms of direct marketing are face-to-face or personal selling, direct-mail marketing, catalog marketing, telemarketing, direct-response television (DRTV) marketing, and kiosk marketing. We examined personal selling in depth in Chapter 16. Here, we look into the other forms of traditional direct marketing.

Direct-Mail Marketing

Direct-mail marketing
Marketing that occurs by sending an offer, announcement, reminder, or other item directly to a person at a particular address.

Direct-mail marketing involves sending an offer, announcement, reminder, or other item to a person at a particular address. Using highly selective mailing lists, direct marketers send out millions of mail pieces each year—letters, catalogs, ads, brochures, samples, videos, and other "salespeople with wings." U.S. marketers spend an estimated $47 billion annually on direct mail (including both catalog and noncatalog mail), which accounts for 30 percent of all direct marketing spending.[37]

Direct mail is well suited to direct, one-to-one communication. It permits high target-market selectivity, can be personalized, is flexible, and allows the easy measurement of results. Although direct mail costs more per thousand people reached than mass media such as television or magazines, the people it reaches are much better prospects. Direct mail has proved successful in promoting all kinds of products, from books, insurance, travel, gift items, gourmet foods, clothing, and other consumer goods to industrial products of all kinds. Charities also use direct mail heavily to raise billions of dollars each year.

Some analysts predict a decline in the use of traditional forms of direct mail in the coming years as marketers switch to newer digital forms, such as email and online, social media, and mobile marketing. The newer digital direct marketing approaches deliver messages at incredible speeds and lower costs compared to the U.S. Post Office's "snail mail" pace.

However, even though new digital forms of direct marketing are bursting onto the scene, traditional direct mail is still heavily used by most marketers. Mail marketing offers some distinct advantages over digital forms. It provides something tangible for people to hold and keep, and it can be used to send samples. "Mail makes it real," says one analyst. It "creates an emotional connection with customers that digital cannot. They hold it, view it, and engage with it in a manner entirely different from their [digital] experiences." According to the U.S. Postal Service, 98 percent of people check their physical mailboxes every day. In contrast, email and other digital forms are easily ignored, filtered, or trashed. With spam filters and ad blockers filtering out email and mobile ads these days, says a direct marketer, "sometimes you have to lick a few stamps."[38]

Traditional direct mail can be an effective component of a broader integrated marketing campaign. For example, GEICO relies heavily on TV advertising to establish broad customer awareness and positioning. However, it also uses lots of good old direct mail to break through the glut of insurance advertising clutter on TV. GEICO uses direct mail offers that invite carefully targeted customers act immediately to save money on their auto insurance by visiting geico.com, calling 1-800-947-AUTO, or contacting a local GEICO agent. GEICO makes its direct mailers as unskippable as its TV and digital ads. ● For example, potential customers might receive a personally addressed mail piece with a "save money" message and scannable code on the front of the envelope, inviting them to look inside or simply scan the code with their smartphone. Scanning the code takes them directly to GEICO's mobile site where they received additional information and calls to action.

Direct mail may be resented as *junk mail* if sent to people who have no interest in it. For this reason, smart marketers are targeting their direct mail carefully so as not to waste their money and recipients' time. They are designing permission-based programs that send direct mail only to those who want to receive it.

● **Direct-mail marketing: GEICO uses lots of good old direct mail to break through the glut of insurance advertising clutter.**

All text and images are copywritten with permission from GEICO.

Catalog Marketing

Catalog marketing

Direct marketing through print, video, or digital catalogs that are mailed to select customers, made available in stores, or presented online.

Advances in technology, along with the move toward personalized, one-to-one marketing, have resulted in exciting changes in **catalog marketing**. *Catalog Age* magazine used to define a *catalog* as "a printed, bound piece of at least eight pages, selling multiple products, and offering a direct ordering mechanism." Today, the definition must be revamped to meet the changing times.

With the stampede to the internet and digital marketing, more and more catalogs are going digital. A variety of online-only catalogers have emerged, and most print catalogers have added web-based catalogs and mobile catalog shopping apps to their marketing mixes. For example, catalogs from retailers such as Macy's, Anthropologie, L.L. Bean, Hammacher Schlemmer, or West Elm are only a swipe of the finger away on a smartphone or tablet. And days before the latest Eddie Bauer catalog arrives in the mail, customers can access it digitally on a laptop or mobile device at eddiebauer.com or catch highlights via social media outlets such as Pinterest. Eddie Bauer's mobile catalog gives customers the convenience of on-the-go browsing and purchasing.

Digital catalogs eliminate printing and mailing costs. They also allow real-time merchandising: Products and features can be added or removed as needed and prices can be adjusted instantly to match demand. And whereas space is limited in a print catalog, online catalogs can offer an almost unlimited amount of merchandise. Customers can carry digital catalogs anywhere they go, even when shopping at physical stores. Online catalogs also offer a broader assortment of presentation formats, including search and video. Finally, digital catalogs can be interactive. For example, IKEA's catalog app allows customers to experiment with room designs and colors schemes to see how an IKEA product might look in their own space and to share product and design ideas with others via social media.

Telemarketing

Using the telephone to sell directly to customers.

Despite the advantages of digital catalogs, however, as your overstuffed mailbox may suggest, printed catalogs are still thriving. U.S. direct marketers mailed out some 12 billion catalogs last year—more than 97 per American household.[39] Why aren't companies ditching their old-fashioned paper catalogs in this new digital era? For one thing, printed catalogs are one of the best ways to drive online and mobile sales, making them more important than ever in digital time. For example, one survey found that 75 percent of Lands' End shoppers say they look at a catalog before heading to the retailer's online or mobile site to buy. And menswear company Bonobos discovered that 30 percent of its first-time online customers are inspired to shop there after receiving a catalog, and these buyers spend 50 percent more than catalog-free Bonobos shoppers.[40]

But beyond their ability to drive immediate sales, paper catalogs create emotional connections with customers. Somehow, turning actual catalog pages engages consumers in a way that digital images simply can't. And many sellers are revamping their catalogs, making them much more than just big books full of product pictures and prices. For example, Anthropologie calls its catalogs "journals" and fills them with lifestyle images. "Of course we're trying to sell clothes and accessories," says Anthropologie's CMO, "but it's more to inspire and engage."

Similarly, in addition to the 10 or so traditional catalogs that it publishes each year, Patagonia sends out other catalogs built around themes.  One recent catalog featured falconry, with images of children with condors in Chile and wildlife volunteers in California releasing rehabilitated red-tailed hawks. The catalog included only a handful of products, placed on the last four pages of the 43-page book. Such catalogs are "a way we're speaking to our closest friends and people who know the brand really well," says a Patagonia marketer. "Years ago, [a catalog] was a selling tool, and now it's become an inspirational source," says another direct marketer. "We know our customers love a tactile experience."[41]

 **Catalogs: Even in the digital era, printed catalogs are still thriving. In addition to its traditional catalogs, Patagonia sends out catalogs built around lifestyle themes, as "a way we're speaking to our closest friends and people who know the brand really well."**

Patagonia

Telemarketing

Telemarketing involves using the telephone to sell directly to consumers and business customers. U.S. marketers will spend an estimated $44 billion on telemarketing this year, almost as much as on direct mail.[42] We're all familiar with telephone marketing directed toward consumers, but business-to-business (B-to-B) marketers also use telemarketing extensively. Marketers use *outbound* telephone marketing to sell directly to consumers and businesses. They also use *inbound* toll-free numbers to receive orders from television and print ads, direct mail, or catalogs.

Properly designed and targeted telemarketing provides many benefits, including purchasing convenience and increased product and service information. However, the explosion in unsolicited outbound telephone marketing over the years annoyed many consumers, who objected to the almost daily "junk phone calls." In 2003, U.S. lawmakers responded with the National Do Not Call Registry, which is managed by the Federal Trade Commission (FTC). The legislation bans most telemarketing calls to registered phone numbers (although people can still receive calls from nonprofit groups, politicians, and companies with which they have recently done business). Consumers responded enthusiastically. To date, more than 222 million home and mobile phone numbers have been registered at www.donotcall.gov or by calling 888-382-1222.[43] Businesses that break do-not-call laws can be fined up to $16,482 per violation. As a result, the program has been very successful.

Do-not-call legislation has hurt parts of the consumer telemarketing industry. However, two major forms of telemarketing—inbound consumer telemarketing and outbound B-to-B telemarketing—remain strong and growing. Telemarketing also remains a major fundraising tool for nonprofit and political groups. Interestingly, do-not-call regulations appear to be helping some direct marketers more than they're hurting them. Rather than making unwanted calls, many of these marketers are developing "opt-in" calling systems, in which they provide useful information and offers to customers who have invited the company to contact them by phone or email. The opt-in model provides better returns for marketers than the formerly invasive one.

Direct-Response Television Marketing

Direct-response television (DRTV)
marketing

Direct marketing via television, including direct-response television advertising (or infomercials) and interactive television (iTV) advertising.

Direct-response television (DRTV) marketing takes one of two major forms: direct-response television advertising and interactive TV (iTV) advertising. Using *direct-response television advertising*, direct marketers air television spots, often 60 or 120 seconds in length, which persuasively describe a product and give customers a toll-free number or an online site for ordering. It also includes full 30-minute or longer advertising programs, called *infomercials*, for a single product.

Successful direct-response television advertising campaigns can ring up big sales. For example, little-known infomercial maker Guthy-Renker has helped propel its Proactiv Solution acne treatment and other "transformational" products into power brands that pull in $1.8 billion in sales annually to 5 million active customers (compare that to only about $150 million in annual drugstore sales of acne products in the United States). Guthy-Renker now combines DRTV with social media campaigns using Facebook, Pinterest, Google+, Twitter, and YouTube to create a powerful integrated direct marketing channel that builds consumer involvement and buying.[44]

DRTV ads are often associated with somewhat loud or questionable pitches for cleaners, stain removers, kitchen gadgets, and nifty ways to stay in shape without working very hard at it. For example, over the past few years yell-and-sell TV pitchmen like Anthony Sullivan (Swivel Sweeper, Awesome Auger) and Vince Offer (ShamWow, SlapChop) have racked up billions of dollars in sales of "As Seen on TV" products. Brands like OxiClean, ShamWow, and the Snuggie (a blanket with sleeves) have become DRTV cult classics. And direct marketer Beachbody brings in more than $570 million annually via an army of workout videos—from P90X and T-25 to Insanity and Hip Hop Abs—that it advertises on TV using before-and-after stories, clips of the workout, and words of encouragement from the creators.[45]

In recent years, however, a number of large companies—from P&G, Disney, Revlon, and Apple to Toyota, Coca-Cola, Sears, Home Depot, and even the U.S. Navy—have begun using infomercials to sell their wares, refer customers to retailers, recruit members, or attract buyers to their online, mobile, and social media sites.

A more recent form of direct-response television marketing is *interactive TV (iTV)*, which lets viewers interact with television programming and advertising. Thanks to technologies such as interactive cable systems, internet-ready smart TVs, and smartphones and tablets, consumers can now use their TV remotes, phones, or other devices to obtain more information or make purchases directly from TV ads. For example, fashion retailer H&M recently ran ads that let viewers with certain Samsung smart TVs use their remotes to interact directly with the commercials. A small pop-up menu, shown as the ads ran, offered product information, the ability to send that information to another device, and the option to buy directly.[46]

Also, increasingly, as the lines continue to blur between TV and other screens, interactive ads and infomercials are appearing not just on TV, but also on mobile, online, and social media platforms, adding even more TV-like interactive direct marketing venues. Also, most TV ads these days routinely feature web, mobile, and social media links that let multiscreen consumers connect in real time to obtain and share more information about advertised brands.

Kiosk Marketing

As consumers become more and more comfortable with digital and touchscreen technologies, many companies are placing information and ordering machines—called *kiosks* (good old-fashioned vending machines but so much more)—in stores, airports, hotels, college campuses, and other locations. Kiosks are everywhere these days, from self-service hotel and airline check-in devices, to unmanned product and information kiosks in malls, to in-store ordering devices that let you order merchandise not carried in the store. Many modern "smart kiosks" are now wireless-enabled. And some machines can even use facial recognition software that lets them guess gender and age and make product recommendations based on those data.

● **Kiosk marketing: Redbox operates more than 42,000 DVD rental kiosks in supermarkets, fast-food restaurants, and other retail outlets.**

© Images-USA/Alamy Stock Photo

In-store Kodak, Fuji, and HP kiosks let customers transfer pictures from memory cards, mobile phones, and other digital storage devices; edit them; and make high-quality color prints. Seattle's Best kiosks in grocery, drug, and mass merchandise stores grind and brew fresh coffee beans and serve coffee, mochas, and lattes to on-the-go customers around the clock. ● Redbox operates more than 42,000 DVD rental kiosks in McDonald's, Walmart, Walgreens, CVS, Family Dollar, and other retail outlets—customers make their selections on a touchscreen, then swipe a credit or debit card to rent DVDs for less than $2 a day.

ZoomSystems creates small, freestanding kiosks called ZoomShops for retailers ranging from Apple, Sephora, and The Body Shop to Macy's and Best Buy. For example, 100 Best Buy Express ZoomShop kiosks across the country—conveniently located in airports, busy malls, military bases, retail stores, and resorts—automatically dispense an assortment of portable media players, digital cameras, gaming consoles, headphones, phone chargers, travel gadgets, and other popular products. According to ZoomSystems, today's automated retailing "offers [consumers] the convenience of online shopping with the immediate gratification of traditional retail."[47]

Author Comment | Although we mostly benefit from direct and digital marketing, like most other things in life, they have a dark side as well. Marketers and customers alike must guard against irritating or harmful direct and digital marketing practices.

Public Policy Issues in Direct and Digital Marketing

Direct marketers and their customers usually enjoy mutually rewarding relationships. Occasionally, however, a darker side emerges. The aggressive and sometimes shady tactics of a few direct marketers can bother or harm consumers, giving the entire industry a black eye. Abuses range from simple excesses that irritate consumers to instances of unfair practices or even outright deception and fraud. The direct marketing industry has also faced growing privacy concerns, and online marketers must deal with internet and mobile security issues.

Irritation, Unfairness, Deception, and Fraud

Direct marketing excesses sometimes annoy or offend consumers. For example, most of us dislike direct-response TV commercials that are too loud, long, and insistent. Our mailboxes fill up with unwanted junk mail, our email inboxes bulge with unwanted spam, and our computer, phone, and tablet screens flash with unwanted online or mobile display ads, pop-ups, or pop-unders.

● **Internet fraud has multiplied in recent years. The FBI's Internet Crime Complaint Center provides consumers with a convenient way to alert authorities to suspected violations.**

FBI

Beyond irritating consumers, some direct marketers have been accused of taking unfair advantage of impulsive or less-sophisticated buyers. Television shopping channels, enticing websites, and program-long infomercials targeting television-addicted shoppers seem to be the worst culprits. They feature smooth-talking hosts, elaborately staged demonstrations, claims of drastic price reductions, "while they last" time limitations, and unequaled ease of purchase to inflame buyers who have low sales resistance.

Fraudulent schemes, such as investment scams or phony collections for charity, have also multiplied in recent years. *Internet fraud*, including identity theft and financial scams, has become a serious problem. ● According to the Internet Crime Complaint Center, since 2005, internet scam complaints have more than tripled to almost 275,000 per year. Last year, the monetary loss of scam complaints exceeded $800 million.[48]

One common form of internet fraud is *phishing*, a type of identity theft that uses deceptive emails and fraudulent online sites to fool users into divulging their personal data. For example, consumers may receive an email, supposedly from their bank or credit card company, saying that their account's security has been compromised. The sender asks them to log on to a provided web address and confirm their account number, password, and perhaps even their Social Security number. If they follow the instructions, users are actually turning this sensitive information over to scam artists. Although many consumers are now aware of such schemes, phishing can be extremely costly to those caught in the net. It also damages the brand identities of legitimate online marketers who have worked to build user confidence in web, email, and other digital transactions.

Many consumers also worry about *online and digital security*. They fear that unscrupulous snoopers will eavesdrop on their online transactions and social media postings, picking up personal information or intercepting credit and debit card numbers. Although online shopping is now commonplace, one recent study indicated that 70 percent of participants were still concerned about identity theft. Such concerns are often justified in this age of mass consumer data breaches by organizations ranging from retailers, telecommunications services, and banks to health-care providers and the government. According to one source, there were 781 major data security breaches in the United States last year alone.[49]

Another internet marketing concern is that of *access by vulnerable or unauthorized groups*. For example, marketers of adult-oriented materials and sites have found it difficult to restrict access by minors. Although Facebook, Snapchat, Twitter, Instagram, and other social networks allow no children under age 13 to have profiles, all have significant numbers of underage users. Young social media users can be especially vulnerable to identity theft schemes, revealing personal information, negative experiences, and other online dangers. Concerned state and national lawmakers are currently debating bills that would help better protect children online. Unfortunately, this requires the development of technology solutions, and as Facebook puts it, "That's not so easy."[50]

Consumer Privacy

Invasion of privacy is perhaps the toughest public policy issue now confronting the direct marketing industry. Consumers often benefit from database marketing; they receive more offers that are closely matched to their interests. However, many critics worry that marketers may know *too* much about consumers' lives and that they may use this knowledge to take unfair advantage of consumers. At some point, they claim, the extensive use of databases intrudes on consumer privacy. Consumers, too, worry about their privacy. Although they are now much more willing to share personal information and preferences with marketers via digital and social media, they are still nervous about it. One recent survey found that 92 percent of U.S. internet users worry about their privacy online. Another found that more than 90 percent of Americans feel they have lost control over the collection and use by companies of their personal data and information they share on social media sites.[51]

In these days of "big data," it seems that almost every time consumers post something on social media or send a tweet, visit a website, enter a sweepstakes, apply for a credit card, or order products by phone or online, their names are entered into some company's already bulging database. Using sophisticated big data analytics, direct marketers can mine these databases to "microtarget" their selling efforts. Most marketers have become highly skilled at collecting and analyzing detailed consumer information both online and offline. Even the experts are sometimes surprised by how much marketers can learn. Consider this account by one *Advertising Age* reporter:[52]

> I'm no neophyte when it comes to targeting—not only do I work at *Ad Age*, but I cover direct marketing. Yet even I was taken aback when, as an experiment, we asked the database-marketing company to come up with a demographic and psychographic profile of me. Was it ever spot-on. Using only publicly available information, it concluded my date of birth, home phone number, and political-party affiliation. It gleamed that I was a college graduate, that I was married, and that one of my parents had passed away. It found that I have several bank, credit, and retail cards at "low-end" department stores. It knew not just how long I've lived at my house but how much it cost, how much it was worth, the type of mortgage that's on it, and—within a really close ballpark guess—how much is left to pay on it. It estimated my household income—again nearly perfectly—and determined that I am of British descent.
>
> But that was just the beginning. The company also nailed my psychographic profile. It correctly placed me into various groupings such as: someone who relies more on their own opinions than the recommendations of others when making a purchase; someone who is turned off by loud and aggressive advertising; someone who is family-oriented and has an interest in music, running, sports, computers, and is an avid concert-goer; someone who is never far from an internet connection, generally used to peruse sports and general news updates; and someone who sees health as a core value. Scary? Certainly.

Some consumers and policy makers worry that the ready availability of information may leave consumers open to abuse. For example, they ask, should credit card companies be allowed to make data on their millions of cardholders worldwide available to merchants who accept their cards? Is it right for states to sell the names and addresses of driver's license holders, along with height, weight, and gender information, allowing apparel retailers to target tall or overweight people with special clothing offers? Or is it right for telecommunications companies to make mobile phone usage data available to data analytics firms that then sell customer insights to marketers? For example, SAP's Consumer Insight 365 unit gleans and sells customer insights from up to 300 mobile call, web surfing, and text messaging events per day for each of 20 million to 25 million mobile subscribers from data supplied by mobile operators.[53]

A Need for Action

To curb direct marketing excesses, various government agencies are investigating not only do-not-call lists but also do-not-mail lists, do-not-track-online lists, and Can Spam legislation. In response to online privacy and security concerns, the federal government has considered numerous legislative actions to regulate how online, social media, and mobile operators obtain and use consumer information. For example, Congress is drafting legislation that would give consumers more control over how online information is used. In addition, the FTC is taking a more active role in policing online privacy.

All of these concerns call for strong actions by marketers to monitor and prevent privacy abuses before legislators step in to do it for them. For example, to head off increased government regulation, six advertiser groups—the American Association of Advertising Agencies, the American Advertising Federation, the Association of National Advertisers, the Direct Marketing Association, the Interactive Advertising Bureau, and the Network Advertising Initiative—issued a set of online advertising principles through the Digital Advertising Alliance. Among other measures, the self-regulatory principles call for online and mobile marketers to provide transparency and choice to consumers if online viewing data are collected or used for targeting interest-based advertising. ● The ad industry uses an *advertising option icon*—a little "i" inside a triangle—that it adds to behaviorally targeted online ads to tell consumers why they are seeing a particular ad and allowing them to opt out.[54]

Of special concern are the privacy rights of children. In 2000, Congress passed the Children's Online Privacy Protection Act (COPPA), which requires online operators targeting children to post privacy policies on their sites. They must also notify parents about any information they're gathering and obtain parental consent before collecting personal information from children under age 13. With the subsequent advent of online

● Consumer privacy: The ad industry has agreed on an *advertising option icon* that will tell consumers why they are seeing a particular ad and allow them to opt out.

Digital Advertising Alliance

social media, mobile phones, and other digital technologies, Congress in 2013 extended COPPA to include "identifiers such as cookies that track a child's activity online, as well as geolocation information, photos, videos, and audio recordings." The main concern is the amount of data mined by third parties from social media as well as social media's own hazy privacy policies.[55]

Many companies have responded to consumer privacy and security concerns with actions of their own. Still others are taking an industry-wide approach. For example, TRUSTe, a nonprofit self-regulatory organization, works with many large corporate sponsors, including Microsoft, Yahoo!, AT&T, Facebook, Disney, and Apple, to audit privacy and security measures and help consumers navigate the internet safely. According to the company's website, "TRUSTe believes that an environment of mutual trust and openness will help make and keep the internet a free, comfortable, and richly diverse community for everyone." To reassure consumers, the company lends its TRUSTe privacy seal to websites, mobile apps, email marketing, and other online and social media channels that meet its privacy and security standards.[56]

The direct marketing industry as a whole is also addressing public policy issues. For example, in an effort to build consumer confidence in shopping direct, the Direct Marketing Association—the largest association for businesses practicing direct, database, and interactive marketing, including nearly half of the *Fortune* 100 companies—launched a "Privacy Promise to American Consumers." The Privacy Promise requires that all DMA members adhere to a carefully developed set of consumer privacy rules. Members must agree to notify customers when any personal information is rented, sold, or exchanged with others. They must also honor consumer requests to opt out of receiving further solicitations or having their contact information transferred to other marketers. Finally, they must abide by the DMA's Preference Service by removing the names of consumers who do not wish to receive mail, phone, or email offers.[57]

Direct marketers know that, if left untended, such direct marketing abuses will lead to increasingly negative consumer attitudes, lower response and engagement rates, and calls for more restrictive state and federal legislation. Most direct marketers want the same things that consumers want: honest and well-designed marketing offers targeted only toward consumers who will appreciate and respond to them. Direct marketing is just too expensive to waste on consumers who don't want it.

17 Reviewing and Extending the Concepts

OBJECTIVES REVIEW AND KEY TERMS

Objectives Review

This chapter is the last of four chapters covering the final marketing mix element—promotion. The previous chapters dealt with advertising, public relations, personal selling, and sales promotion. This one investigates the burgeoning field of direct and digital marketing, including online, social media, and mobile marketing.

OBJECTIVE 17-1 Define *direct and digital marketing* and discuss their rapid growth and benefits to customers and companies. (pp 488–490)

Direct and digital marketing involve engaging directly with carefully targeted individual consumers and customer communities to both obtain an immediate response and build lasting customer relationships. Companies use direct marketing to tailor their offers and content to the needs and interests of narrowly defined segments or individual buyers to build direct customer engagement, brand community, and sales. Today, spurred by the surge in internet usage and buying and by rapid advances in digital technologies—from smartphones, tablets, and other digital devices to the spate of online social and mobile media—direct marketing has undergone a dramatic transformation.

For buyers, direct and digital marketing are convenient, easy to use, and private. They give buyers anywhere, anytime access to an almost unlimited assortment of products and buying information. Direct marketing is also immediate and interactive, allowing buyers to create exactly the configuration of information, products, or services they desire and then order them on the spot. Finally, for consumers who want it, digital marketing through online, mobile, and social media provides a sense of brand engagement and community—a place to share brand information and experiences with other brand fans. For sellers, direct and digital marketing are powerful tools for building customer engagement and close, personalized, interactive customer relationships. They also offer greater flexibility, letting marketers make ongoing adjustments to prices and programs or make immediate, timely, and personal announcements and offers.

OBJECTIVE 17-2 Identify and discuss the major forms of direct and digital marketing. *(pp 490–491)*

The main forms of direct and digital marketing include traditional direct marketing tools and the new digital marketing tools. Traditional direct approaches are face-to-face personal selling, direct-mail marketing, catalog marketing, telemarketing, DRTV marketing, and kiosk marketing. These traditional tools are still heavily used and very important in most firms' direct marketing efforts. In recent years, however, a dazzling new set of direct digital marketing tools has burst onto the marketing scene, including online marketing (websites, online ads and promotions, email, online videos, and blogs), social media marketing, and mobile marketing. The chapter first discusses the fast-growing new digital direct marketing tools and then examines the traditional tools.

OBJECTIVE 17-3 Explain how companies have responded to the internet and the digital age with various online marketing strategies. *(pp 491–497)*

The internet and digital age have fundamentally changed customers' notions of convenience, speed, price, product information, service, and brand interactions. As a result, they have given marketers a whole new way to create customer value, engage customers, and build customer relationships. The internet now influences a large proportion of total sales—including sales transacted online plus those made in stores but encouraged by online research. To reach this burgeoning market, most companies now market online.

Online marketing takes several forms, including company websites, online advertising and promotions, email marketing, online video, and blogs. Social media and mobile marketing also take place online. But because of their special characteristics, we discuss these fast-growing digital marketing approaches in separate sections. For most companies, the first step in conducting online marketing is to create a website. The key to a successful website is to create enough value and engagement to get consumers to come to the site, stick around, and come back again.

Online advertising has become a major promotional medium. The main forms of online advertising are display ads and search-related ads. Email marketing is also an important form of digital marketing. Used properly, email lets marketers send highly targeted, tightly personalized, relationship-building messages. Another important form of online marketing is posting digital video content on brand websites or social media. Marketers hope that some of their videos will go viral, engaging consumers by the tens of millions. Finally, companies can use blogs as effective means of reaching customer communities. They can create their own blogs and advertise on existing blogs or influence content there.

OBJECTIVE 17-4 Discuss how companies use social media and mobile marketing to engage consumers and create brand community. *(pp 497–503)*

In the digital age, countless independent and commercial social media have arisen that give consumers online places to congregate, socialize, and exchange views and information. Most marketers are now riding this huge social media wave. Brands can use existing social media or they can set up their own. Using existing social media seems the easiest. Thus, most brands—large and small—have set up shop on a host of social media sites. Some of the major social networks are huge; other niche social media cater to the needs of smaller communities of like-minded people. Beyond these independent social media, many companies have created their own online brand communities. More than making just scattered efforts and chasing "Likes" and tweets, most companies are integrating a broad range of diverse media to create brand-related social sharing, engagement, and customer community.

Using social media presents both advantages and challenges. On the plus side, social media are targeted and personal, interactive, immediate and timely, and cost-effective. Perhaps the biggest advantage is their engagement and social sharing capabilities, making them ideal for creating customer community. On the down side, consumers' control over social media content makes social media difficult to control.

Mobile marketing features marketing messages, promotions, and other content delivered to on-the-go consumers through their mobile devices. Marketers use mobile marketing to engage customers anywhere, anytime during the buying and relationship-building processes. The widespread adoption of mobile devices and the surge in mobile web traffic have made mobile marketing a must for most brands, and almost every major marketer is now integrating mobile marketing into its direct marketing programs. Many marketers have created their own mobile online sites. Others have created useful or entertaining mobile apps to engage customers with their brands and help them shop.

OBJECTIVE 17-5 Identify and discuss the traditional direct marketing forms and overview the public policy and ethical issues presented by direct marketing. *(pp 504–510)*

Although the fast-growing digital marketing tools have grabbed most of the headlines lately, traditional direct marketing tools are very much alive and still heavily used. The major forms are face-to-face or personal selling, direct-mail marketing, catalog marketing, telemarketing, direct-response television (DRTV) marketing, and kiosk marketing.

Direct-mail marketing consists of the company sending an offer, announcement, reminder, or other item to a person at a specific address. Some marketers rely on catalog marketing—selling through catalogs mailed to a select list of customers, made available in stores, or accessed online. Telemarketing consists of using the telephone to sell directly to consumers. DRTV marketing has two forms: direct-response advertising (or infomercials) and interactive television (iTV) marketing. Kiosks are information and ordering machines that direct marketers place in stores, airports, hotels, and other locations.

Direct marketers and their customers usually enjoy mutually rewarding relationships. Sometimes, however, direct marketing presents a darker side. The aggressive and sometimes shady tactics of a few direct marketers can bother or harm consumers, giving the entire industry a black eye. Abuses range from simple excesses that irritate consumers to instances of unfair practices or even outright deception and fraud. The direct marketing industry has also faced growing concerns about invasion-of-privacy and internet security issues. Such concerns call for strong action by marketers and public policy makers to curb direct marketing abuses. In the end, most direct marketers want the same things that consumers want: honest and well-designed marketing offers targeted only toward consumers who will appreciate and respond to them.

Key Terms

OBJECTIVE 17-1

Direct and digital
   marketing (p 488)

OBJECTIVE 17-2

Digital and social media
   marketing (p 491)

OBJECTIVE 17-3

Omni-channel retailing (p 492)

Online marketing (p 492)
Marketing website (p 492)
Branded community
   website (p 492)
Online advertising (p 493)
Email marketing (p 494)
Spam (p 495)
Viral marketing (p 495)
Blogs (p 496)

OBJECTIVE 17-4

Social media (p 497)
Mobile marketing (p 501)

OBJECTIVE 17-5

Direct-mail marketing (p 504)
Catalog marketing (p 505)
Telemarketing (p 505)
Direct-response television (DRTV) mar-
   keting (p 506)

DISCUSSION AND CRITICAL THINKING

> MyMarketingLab
>
> Go to **mymktlab.com** to complete the problems marked with this icon ⭐.

Discussion Questions

17-1   Discuss the benefits of direct and digital marketing to buyers and sellers. (AACSB: Communication)

⭐ **17-2**   Define *omni-channel retailing*. How are retailers responding to the omni-channel consumer? (AACSB: Communication)

⭐ **17-3**   What are blogs, and how are marketers using them to market their products and services? What advantages and disadvantages do blogs pose for marketers? (AACSB: Communication)

⭐ **17-4**   Discuss how the traditional forms of direct marketing continue to be important promotion tools. (AACSB: Communication)

17-5   What is phishing, and how does it affect internet marketing? (AACSB: Communication; Reflective Thinking)

Critical Thinking Exercises

17-6   In a small group, search the internet to locate a controversial or failed social media campaign. Present an analysis of the failed campaign. Make a recommendation on how to address the controversy. (AACSB: Use of IT; Communication; Reflective Thinking)

⭐ **17-7**   Review the Telephone Consumer Protection Act and discuss a recent case in which a marketer was fined for violating the act. (AACSB: Communication; Use of IT; Reflective Thinking)

17-8   Although mobile advertising makes up a small percentage of online advertising, it is one of the fastest-growing advertising channels. But one obstacle is measuring return on investment in mobile. How are marketers measuring the return on investment in mobile advertising? Develop a presentation suggesting metrics marketers should use to measure effectiveness of mobile advertising. (AACSB: Communication; Use of IT; Reflective Thinking)

APPLICATIONS AND CASES

Online, Mobile, and Social Media Marketing   "Buy" Buttons

Amazon is the big gun in e-commerce that has disrupted traditional retailing. But now, it seems, Amazon is in for some disruptive competition itself. With global e-commerce sales expected to reach almost $2 trillion a year, Google and social media sites such as Facebook, Twitter, Pinterest, and Instagram want to get in on the action. Several social media sites are experimenting with "Buy" buttons on their sites that let consumers purchase directly through the social medium. Google is experimenting with "Buy" buttons on search results to counter the almost 40 percent of consumers who now start their shopping searches on Amazon instead of search engines like Google. The biggest game changer, however, might be Pinterest. Pinterest started in 1999 as a sharable bulletin board where participants "pin" pictures of things they like. It is now a multibillion-dollar company with 70 million monthly visitors who have saved more than 50 billion objects on a billion Pinterest bulletin boards. Lots of people would like to be able to buy some of those pinned objects, so Pinterest has added a "Buy" button to its mobile app. Users had already been able to click through to a marketer's website, but now they can purchase any of more than 2 million products from retailers such as Macy's, Bloomingdales, and Nordstrom directly through Pinterest without leaving the site. Payments are processed through Pinterest's partners Stripe, Brainstorm, or Apply Pay, but the seller provides the order fulfillment. In the future, Pinterest users may see an appetizing recipe, click the "Buy" button to order the ingredients from Fresh Direct, and have them delivered to their homes in less than an hour.

17-9 What competitive advantage does Pinterest (www.pinterest.com) have over other social media that might make its "Buy" button more successful? (AACSB: Communication; Reflective Thinking)

17-10 Discuss advantages and disadvantages of "Buy" buttons for social media sites like Pinterest and search engines like Google. What are the advantages and disadvantages for marketers making their goods available through "Buy" buttons on these sites? (AACSB Communication; Reflective Thinking)

Marketing Ethics #Fail

According to one survey, 92 percent of U.S. companies now claim that social media marketing is important for their businesses. Fashion designer Kenneth Cole took advantage of the trend in 2011 by posting the following tweet: "Millions are in uproar in #Cairo. Rumor is they heard our new spring collection is now available online at http://bit.ly/KCairo -KC." Kenneth Cole was criticized on social media for capitalizing on the strife of the Egyptian revolution to promote his website. The offensive tweet was deleted, and Cole apologized by tweeting: "Re Egypt tweet: we weren't intending to make light of a serious situation. We understand the sensitivity of this historic moment -KC."

Most marketers would not make the same mistake twice. However, in September 2013, as the United States deliberated military action in Syria, Cole tweeted the following: "'Boots on the ground' or not, let's not forget about sandals, pumps and loafers. #Footwear." To justify this action, Cole told *Details* magazine, "Billions of people read my inappropriate, self-promoting tweet. I got a lot of harsh responses, and we hired a crisis management firm. If you look at lists of the biggest Twitter gaffes ever, we're always one through five. But our stock went up that day, our e-commerce business was better, the business at every one of our stores improved, and I picked up 3,000 new followers on Twitter. So on what criteria is this a gaffe? Within hours, I tweeted an explanation, which had to be vetted by lawyers. I'm not even sure I used the words I'm sorry—because I wasn't sorry."

17-11 Kenneth Cole believes that his controversial tweets improve business and provoke conversation and awareness. Is this an effective use of social media to engage customers with the brand? Why or why not? (AACSB: Communication, Reflective Thinking)

17-12 Many marketers are still learning how to use social media platforms effectively to engage customers in meaningful relationships. Locate three social media platforms used by the Kenneth Cole brand to engage customers. Is the brand's marketing message consistent across all platforms? Explain. (AACSB: Communication; Use of IT; Reflective Thinking)

Marketing by the Numbers   Field Sales versus Telemarketing

Many companies are realizing the efficiency of telemarketing in the face of soaring sales force costs. Whereas an average business-to-business sales call by an outside salesperson costs $600, the cost of a telemarketing sales call can be as little as $20 to $30. And telemarketers can make 20 to 33 decision-maker contacts per day to a salesperson's four per day. This has gotten the attention of many business-to-business marketers, where telemarketing can be very effective.

17-13 Refer to Appendix 2, Marketing by the Numbers, to determine the marketing return on sales (marketing ROS) and return on marketing investment (marketing ROI) for Company A and Company B in the chart at right. Which company is performing better? Explain. (AACSB: Communication; Analytical Reasoning; Reflective Thinking)

	Company A (sales force only)	Company B (telemarketing only)
Net sales	$1,000,000	$850,000
Cost of goods sold	$ 500,000	$425,000
Sales expenses	$ 300,000	$100,000

17-14 Should all companies consider reducing their sales forces in favor of telemarketing? Discuss the pros and cons of this action. (AACSB: Communication; Reflective Thinking)

Video Case   Nutrisystem

You've probably heard of Nutrisystem, a company that produced $800 million in revenues last year by selling weight-loss products. What started as a small effort based on an e-commerce marketing plan has evolved into a multipronged marketing campaign that not only has expanded the business but also provides substantial return-on-investment potential.

The key to Nutrisystem's efforts is its direct-to-consumer platform. Using various advertising outlets, from magazines to television, Nutrisystem's promotions all have one thing in common—they let customers make direct contact with the company. Inserting a unique URL or 800 number in every ad also lets Nutrisystem track the success of each and every effort.

After viewing the video featuring Nutrisystem, answer the following questions:

17-15 In what different ways does Nutrisystem engage in direct marketing?

17-16 What advantages does Nutrisystem's marketing campaign have over selling through intermediary channels?

17-17 In addition to its direct-to-consumer distribution and promotional efforts, what is essential to the success of Nutrisystem?

Company Case   Alibaba: The World's Largest E-tailer Is Not Amazon

There's a new king of e-commerce, and it dwarfs Amazon. Introducing Alibaba, the China-based behemoth that sold more than $485 billion worth of goods and services last year and is rapidly building an online empire that will include businesses ranging from a traditional online marketplace to online investment services. As successful as Amazon has been, its annual sales of $107 billion are but a fraction of what Alibaba pulled in. In fact, with last year's take, Alibaba surpassed Walmart to become the largest company on the planet. How is this Chinese upstart pulling off such a startling internet and retailing feat? Let's start by looking at Alibaba's founder, Jack Ma.

Unlikely Beginnings

Jack Ma is an unlikely figure to be atop of one of the world's most powerful companies. Time and again, U.S. tech start-ups have emerged from California garages. However, perhaps none of those start-ups were founded by individuals as seemingly unprepared as Ma. Growing up in Shanghai, Ma did poorly in school. He failed the college entrance exam twice before getting in and completing a teaching degree. He learned to speak English by hanging out around tourists and listening to radio broadcasts. Ma was rejected for a number of jobs—including being a manager for KFC—before finally landing a job teaching English for $12 a month.

But Ma was animated and energetic, and he had lofty goals and ambitions, a combination that earned him the nickname "Crazy Jack." During China's export boom in the 1990s, Ma started a translation company. On a business trip to the United States, he was exposed to the World Wide Web and was surprised to find almost no Chinese content. After a failed attempt at starting an internet company in China, Ma corralled 17 friends in his apartment in 1999 and set out to build an online marketplace. Substituting vision and charisma for coding skills, Ma started Alibaba.com only a few years after legendary e-commerce marketers Amazon and eBay got their starts.

Feeding the Masses

It's difficult to examine Alibaba without making comparisons to the more globally familiar online sellers. In fact, Alibaba is often referred to as the "Amazon of China." But it's the differences between Alibaba and the Amazons, eBays, Googles, Walmarts, Costcos, Sears, and thousands of other successful e-tailers that explain how the Chinese company has grown so big and will grow so much bigger in the future.

For starters, consider the respective domestic markets. Amazon and the others got their starts in the United States, home to roughly 320 million people. This market serves up the most developed retail industry and the highest standard of living in the world. As the tech boom took off, numerous ambitious upstarts competed fiercely to transfer America's retail businesses into the quickly developing space. Tech-savvy U.S. consumers scrambled to convert some of their buying from brick-and-mortar stores to online purchases.

Contrast this with China. With 1.3 billion people and the fastest-growing economy in the world, the Chinese market has tremendous power and potential. But perhaps more important, China's retail sector was still in the Dark Ages when Alibaba got its start. "E-commerce in the United States is like a dessert. It's just supplementary to your main business," Ma said recently. "In China, because the infrastructure of [traditional retail] commerce is [so] bad, e-commerce becomes the main course."

As many Chinese moved from poverty to middle-class status, their exposure to buying online coincided with their exposure to any kind of buying. Relative to the U.S. market, there were relatively few competitors. The size and nature of China's market have Alibaba boasting more than 420 million active users, a base that comfortably exceeds the size of the entire population of the United States. And internet penetration in China is still only 52 percent compared with the much more saturated 88 percent in the United States, providing enormous growth potential.

In adapting traditional retail to an online environment, Amazon and the other U.S. e-tailers operate a "managed marketplace"—they own their own distribution centers, sell a majority of their products directly, and even market their own brands, all characteristics that mimic traditional retail structures. This allows U.S. e-tailers to benefit from established distribution channels and to maintain a great deal of control over their operations. But it also requires massive investments in infrastructure and armies of employees, both of which result in wafer-thin profit margins. In fact, for two of the past four years, Amazon has lost money. For the other two years, the biggest profit it could muster was only 0.5 percent of sales. Walmart's profit margin percentages for both online and offline sales are typically in the low single digits.

But Alibaba does not own or operate massive distribution centers. It doesn't own the items sold on its sites. And it only employs about 36,000 people, a fraction of Amazon's 230,000 employees. Instead, Alibaba's open market platform simply connects buyers with sellers. That might sound like an eBay approach, but Ma insists that it is not. "Amazon and eBay are e-commerce companies, and Alibaba is not an e-commerce company," Ma said recently. "Alibaba helps others to do e-commerce. We do not sell things." While this gives Alibaba less control over the customer experience, Ma sleeps easier at night without the burden of obsessing over keeping prices low. As market forces work to set price points, Alibaba sits back and watches the cash pour in. Its profit margin over the past three years averaged about 40 percent.

A Little of Everything

The continuous influx of cash has allowed Alibaba to invest in just about every kind of business imaginable. In its infancy, Alibaba.com primarily matched Chinese exporters with businesses throughout the rest of the world. But the company quickly shifted focus, catering to the growing purchasing power of its domestic market. Unlike its Western counterparts, Alibaba developed and acquired different online sites and established major divisions. For example, Taobao.com is a site that helps small businesses and private parties sell merchandise to customers. But unlike eBay's commission structure, Taobao sellers pay only for the advertised promotion. From a shopping standpoint, Alibaba's Tmall.com is more similar to Amazon, pairing customers with big corporations, including many global corporations such as Nike, P&G, Apple, and even retailers like Costco.

But Alibaba's development has taken it down numerous other paths as well. And although it may seem that the surging Chinese conglomerate is simply playing copycat, Ma's vision plays out creatively in every case. For example, Alipay is similar to PayPal. But starved for investment opportunities in an environment dominated by state-run banks, Alipay customers have access to financial products that pay attractive returns. In the first year of making such options available, Alipay customers tucked away $82 billion.

In another example of "follow the Silicon Valley guru," the soon-to-be-launched Tmall Box Office—or TBO—"aims to become [the equivalent] of Netflix in the U.S.," including plans to run original content produced by Alibaba's own Alibaba Pictures. But in an environment where TV viewers aren't accustomed to the pay-to-watch model, Alibaba is a true pioneer. And that pioneering effort extends to a crowdsourced film investment fund, a model that threatens to upend traditional film financing in China by allowing regular folks to become producers with less risk.

Alibaba has spent billions investing in start-up firms. Today, the Alibaba Group spreads out over a constellation of services and technologies, including music, gaming, blogs, social networks, event ticket sales, shipping, ridesharing, wearables, and smartphones. On well-known U.S. interests, Alibaba has invested $200 million in Snapchat and $1 billion in Lyft, and it recently bought up 5.6 percent of languishing Groupon. Apparently, Mr. Ma sees something in the daily deals market that others don't.

As Alibaba's list of businesses grows, Ma's vision and innovation seem unbounded. After all, how many U.S. internet veterans can say they started their own holiday? Just seven years ago, Ma enthusiastically launched Singles Day on November 11. What started as a sort of anti-Valentine's Day for single people is now one of the biggest blockbuster sales holidays in the world. Last year, it resulted in $14.3 billion in sales in a 24-hour period, almost five times what fanatical U.S. residents spent on Cyber Monday across all ecommerce companies combined.

With a goal of doubling its current revenues by 2020, one frontier looms large for Alibaba—global expansion. Although China's biggest dot.com success certainly has global ambitions, it has so far chosen to focus on the massive potential of its home market. That will change. "We plan to invest more in [the U.S. and U.K. markets] to get more traffic and…build brand awareness," says Joe Yan, director of international B2C at Alibaba's export division. "Our biggest advantage is abundance—with 100 million products, we have more options for customers who can buy our products cheaper and at high quality." And while it remains to be seen how Alibaba will attack global markets, one analyst recently predicted a future marriage down the road of Alibaba and eBay.

At the same time, U.S. companies such as Netflix and Amazon are exploring ways to expand their small presence in China. However, although the massive markets on both sides of the pond represent opportunities too tempting to pass up, only time will tell whether any of these U.S. companies can export the models they have applied so successfully in their home markets.

As U.S. competitors try to counter Alibaba, they will face one more big hurdle. The Chinese love Jack Ma. For their own part, U.S. tech founders such as Bezos, Zuckerberg, Brin and Page, and the late Steve Jobs are considered visionaries who have shaped the world's digital ecosystem. But the Chinese revere Mr. Ma, the man who turned a local underdog into a dominant giant with revenues bigger than Amazon, Facebook, Google, and Apple combined. Those kinds of patriotic emotions will be tough to crack.

Questions for Discussion

17-18 As a digital retailer, how does Alibaba provide value to Chinese consumers? What sets of values are unique to the Chinese market?

17-19 Given that Alibaba does not own or distribute any of the merchandise exchanged on its sites, describe what factors had to develop for the company to succeed.

17-20 Analyze Alibaba's business model relative to all the different forms of digital and online marketing covered in this chapter.

17-21 Can Alibaba succeed in countries outside of China? Why or why not?

Sources: Melanie Lee, "Alibaba Breaks 3 Trillion RMB Milestone," *Forbes*, March 21, 2016, www.forbes.com/sites/melanieleest/2016/03/21/alibaba-groups-3-trillion-rmb-breakthrough/#78cf4ba22a43; Jason Lim, "Alibaba Group FY2016 Revenue Jumps 33%," *Forbes*, May 5, 2016, www.forbes.com/sites/jlim/2016/05/05/alibaba-fy2016-revenue-jumps-33-ebitda-up-28/#25890c0e61a9; Kathy Chu and Sarah Nassauer, "Alibaba Acknowledges Looming Challenges," *Wall Street Journal*, March 21, 2016, www.wsj.com/articles/alibaba-to-announce-transaction-volume-milestone-3-trillion-yuan-1458539799; Aaron Back, "Alibaba Dreams of E-commerce Globally but Acts Locally," *Wall Street Journal (Eastern Edition)*, June 24, 2015, p. C12; Jillian D'Onfro, "How Jack Ma Went from Being a Poor School Teacher to Turning Alibaba into a $160 Billion Behemoth," *Business Insider*, September 14, 2014, www.businessinsider.com/the-story-of-jack-ma-founder-of-alibaba-2014-9#ixzz3dqFm4M9B; Charles Riley, "Alibaba Is Not the Amazon of China," *CNNMoney*, September 16, 2014, http://money.cnn.com/2014/09/15/investing/alibaba-amazon-china/; Mohanbir Sawhney and Sanjay Khosla, "Alibaba vs. Amazon: Who Will Win the Global E-Commerce War?" *Forbes*, September 22, 2014, www.forbes.com/sites/forbesleadershipforum/2014/09/22/alibaba-vs-amazon-who-will-win-the-global-e-commerce-war/; and Paul Carsten, "Alibaba's Singles' Day Sales Surge 60 Percent to $14.3 Billion," *Reuters*, November 11, 2015, www.reuters.com/article/us-alibaba-singles-day-idUSKCN0SZ34J20151112.

MyMarketingLab

Go to **mymktlab.com** for Auto-graded writing questions as well as the following Assisted-graded writing questions:

17-22 What public policy issues are related to direct and digital marketing?

17-23 Compare and contrast a marketing website and a branded community website.

PART 1: Defining Marketing and the Marketing Process (Chapters 1–2)
PART 2: Understanding the Marketplace and Consumer Value (Chapters 3–6)
PART 3: Designing a Customer Value–Driven Strategy and Mix (Chapters 7–17)
PART 4: Extending Marketing (Chapters 18–20)

18 | Creating Competitive Advantage

CHAPTER PREVIEW

In previous chapters, you explored the basics of marketing. You learned that the aim of marketing is to engage customers and to create value *for* them in order to capture value *from* them in return. Good marketing companies win, keep, and grow customers by understanding customer needs, designing customer-driven marketing strategies, constructing value-delivering marketing programs, engaging customers, and building customer and marketing partner relationships. In the final three chapters, we'll extend this concept to three special areas: creating competitive advantage, global marketing, and social and environmental marketing sustainability.

To start, let's dig into the competitive strategy of Microsoft, the technology giant that dominated the computer software world throughout the 1990s and much of the 2000s. Its Windows and Office products have long been must-haves in the PC market. But with the decline in standalone personal computers and the surge in digitally connected devices—everything from smartphones and tablets to internet-connected TVs—mighty Microsoft recently found itself struggling to revamp its competitive marketing strategy in a fast-changing digital environment. The tech giant is now reinventing itself as a relevant brand that consumers can't live without in the post-PC era.

MICROSOFT: A New Competitive Marketing Strategy for the Post-PC Era

Fifteen years ago, talking high-tech meant talking about the almighty personal computer. Intel provided the PC microprocessors, and manufacturers such as Dell and HP built and marketed the machines. But it was Microsoft that really drove the PC industry—it made the operating systems that made most PCs go. As the dominant software developer, Microsoft put its Windows operating system and Office productivity suite on almost every computer sold.

The huge success of Windows drove Microsoft's revenues, profits, and stock price to dizzying heights. By the start of 2000, the total value of Microsoft's stock had hit a record $619 billion, making it the most valuable company in history. In those heady days, no company was more relevant than Microsoft. And from a competitive standpoint, no company was more powerful.

But moving through the first decade of the new millennium, PC sales growth flattened as the world fell in love with a rush of alluring new digital devices and technologies. It started with iPods and smartphones and evolved rapidly into a full complement of digital devices—from e-readers, tablets, and sleek new laptops to internet-connected TVs and game consoles. These devices are connected and mobile, not stationary standalones like the old PCs. They link users to an ever-on, head-spinning new world of information, entertainment, and socialization options. And, for the most part, these new devices were coming to market without the need for Microsoft's tried-and-true products. Increasingly, even the trusty old PC became a digital-connection device—a gateway to the web, social media, and cloud computing. And much of that could be done without once-indispensable Microsoft software.

In this new digitally connected world, Microsoft found itself lagging behind new, more-glamorous competitors such as Google, Apple, Samsung, and even Amazon and Facebook, which seemed to provide all things digital—the smart devices, the connecting technologies, and even the digital destinations. In the new competitive environment, although still financially strong and still the world's

> Microsoft is undergoing dramatic transformation in its competitive marketing strategy to align itself better with the new digital world order in the post-PC era. More than just making the software that makes PCs run, Microsoft now wants to be a full-line digital devices and services company that connects people to communication, productivity, entertainment, and one another.

dominant PC software maker, Microsoft lost some of its luster. In the year 2000—due largely to the collapse of the stock market technology bubble—Microsoft's value plummeted by 60 percent. And whereas other tech stocks recovered, Microsoft's share price and profits languished at early 2000's levels for a dozen years or more.

Over the past few years, however, in an attempt to align itself better with the new digital world order and the host of new competitors, Microsoft has undergone a dramatic transformation in its vision and competitive strategy. Microsoft now wants to be a full-line digital devices and services company that delivers "delightful, seamless technology experiences" that connect people to communication, productivity, entertainment, and one another.

Under this new competitive strategy, Microsoft has unleashed a flurry of new, improved, or acquired digital products and services. Over the past few years, it has introduced new versions of Windows and Office that serve not just computers but also tablets and smartphones, a next-generation Xbox console that doubles as a TV, a music and movie service to rival iTunes and Google Play, an upgraded version of Skype, the OneDrive cloud storage solution, and even innovative new digital hardware—the Microsoft Surface tablet and Microsoft Surface Book laptop—that it hopes will lead the way to even more innovative Windows devices.

But these new individual offerings don't begin to tell the full story of Microsoft's transformation. More important is the way that these software, hardware, and service offerings work together to deliver a full digital experience. It all revolves around Windows 10, a dramatic digital-age metamorphosis from previous Windows versions. Windows 10 employs colorful, interactive tiles and touchscreen navigation, with interactive features that compete head-on with the systems of rivals Apple, Google, and Amazon. Best of all, Windows 10 works seamlessly across desktops and laptops, tablets, phones, and even the company's own Xbox, providing the cloud-based connectivity that today's users covet.

Using Windows 10 software and apps with Windows-based devices and cloud computing services, you can select a movie from a tablet, start playing it on the TV or Xbox, and finish watching it on your phone, pausing to call or text a friend using Skype. What you do on one Windows device is automatically updated on other devices. Playlists created or songs and TV programs purchased from a mobile device will be waiting for you on your home PC or laptop. And Windows 10 is a social creature; for example, it updates contacts automatically with tweets and photos from friends. The new Windows seems to be pushing all the right digital buttons for customers. In its first eight months, it was placed on 270 million active devices, making it the most successful launch in Windows's nearly 30-year history.

The latest version of Microsoft Office—Office 365—has also been transformed for the connected age. Office 365 positions Microsoft's venerable productivity suite as a service, not just

In the fast-changing digital environment, Microsoft is revamping its competitive strategy to make itself a brand that consumers can't live without in the post-PC world.
VESA MOILANEN/Stringer/Getty Images

standalone software. With an annual subscription, you get the latest version of Office, a terabyte of cloud storage on OneDrive, 60 minutes of Skype calls per month, free updates and new features, and free tech support by phone or chat through the Microsoft Answer Desk. Microsoft also released an Office version for Apple devices. So Office now works across devices, operating systems, and the cloud, making it easier than ever to stay connected with others and to create and share documents on the go.

Perhaps Microsoft's biggest about-face is the development of its own hardware devices. In the past, the company has relied on partners like Dell, HP, and Nokia to develop the PCs, tablets, and phones that run its software. But to gain better control in today's superheated digital and mobile markets, Microsoft is now doing its own development of Windows-enabled devices.

For starters, Microsoft developed the cutting-edge Surface tablet, a unique combination of tablet and mini-laptop. More recently, it released its first dedicated laptop, the Surface Book, which goes head-to-head with the Apple MacBook Pro. Microsoft is also dabbling seriously with mobile phones, first buying then selling phone maker Nokia and now rumored to soon be introducing a Windows-based Surface phone of its own. The Surface line, along with Xbox, will give Microsoft better control of access to three important digital screens beyond the PC—tablets, TVs, and phones.

Microsoft's revamped competitive strategy also plays to the company's long-held competitive advantage in business markets as the company plunges headlong into new business products and services. In addition to flexible bundling of its Windows, Office, and Enterprise Mobility Suite for business customers, Microsoft now offers Azure, a "cloud for modern business." And it recently acquired Yammer, a web-services provider and hip maker of business social networking tools—a sort of Facebook for businesses. Finally, Microsoft is now exploring a wide range of futuristic digital technologies, from intelligent chatbots, machine learning, and augmented/virtual reality to Internet of Things applications.

OBJECTIVES OUTLINE

OBJECTIVE 18-1	Discuss the need to understand competitors as well as customers through competitor analysis. **Competitor Analysis** *(pp 518–525)*
OBJECTIVE 18-2	Explain the fundamentals of competitive marketing strategies based on creating value for customers. **Competitive Strategies** *(pp 525–535)*
OBJECTIVE 18-3	Illustrate the need for balancing customer and competitor orientations in becoming a truly market-centered organization. **Balancing Customer and Competitor Orientations** *(pp 535–536)*

Thus, Microsoft's sweeping competitive strategy transformation is well under way and the company seems to be making the right moves to stay ahead of the times. The company's sales have trended strongly upward over the past few years, and Microsoft is confident that it's now on the right track. Still, continued success will depend on the Microsoft's ability to effectively adapt to—or even lead—the lightning-quick changes occurring in the marketing environment. "The opportunity ahead for Microsoft is vast," says Microsoft's CEO, "but to seize it, we must focus clearly, move faster, and continue to transform."[1]

Competitive advantage
An advantage over competitors gained by offering consumers greater value.

Competitor analysis
Identifying key competitors; assessing their objectives, strategies, strengths and weaknesses, and reaction patterns; and selecting which competitors to attack or avoid.

Competitive marketing strategies
Strategies that strongly position the company against competitors and give it the greatest possible competitive advantage.

TODAY'S COMPANIES FACE THEIR toughest competition ever. In previous chapters, we argued that to succeed in today's fiercely competitive marketplace, companies must move from a product-and-selling philosophy to a customer-and-marketing philosophy.

This chapter spells out in more detail how companies can go about outperforming competitors to win, keep, and grow customers. To win in today's marketplace, companies must become adept not only in managing products but also in managing customer relationships in the face of determined competition and a difficult marketing environment. Understanding customers is crucial, but it's not enough. Building profitable customer relationships and gaining **competitive advantage** require delivering more value and satisfaction to target customers than competitors do. Customers will see competitive advantages as customer advantages, giving the company an edge over its competitors.

In this chapter, we examine competitive marketing strategies—how companies analyze their competitors and develop successful, customer value–based strategies for engaging customers and building profitable customer relationships. The first step is **competitor analysis**, the process of identifying, assessing, and selecting key competitors. The second step is developing **competitive marketing strategies** that strongly position the company against competitors and give the company the strongest possible strategic advantage.

> **Author** | Creating competitive
> **Comment** | advantage begins with a
> thorough understanding of competitors'
> strategies. But before a company can
> analyze its competitors, it must first
> identify them—a task that's not as
> simple as it seems.

Competitor Analysis

To plan effective marketing strategies, a company needs to find out all it can about its competitors. It must constantly compare its marketing strategies, products, prices, channels, and promotions with those of close competitors. In this way, the company can find areas of potential competitive advantage and disadvantage. As shown in ● **Figure 18.1**, competitor analysis involves first identifying and assessing competitors and then selecting which competitors to attack or avoid.

Identifying Competitors

Normally, identifying competitors would seem to be a simple task. At the narrowest level, a company can define its competitors as other companies offering similar products and

● **FIGURE | 18.1**
Steps in Analyzing Competitors

Identifying competitors isn't as easy as it seems. For example, Kodak saw other camera film makers as its major competitors. But its real competitors turned out to be the makers of digital cameras that used no film at all. Kodak fell behind in digital technologies and ended up declaring bankruptcy.

Identifying the company's competitors → **Assessing** competitors' objectives, strategies, strengths and weaknesses, and reaction patterns → **Selecting** which competitors to attack or avoid

services to the same customers at similar prices. Thus, Forever 21 might see H&M as a major competitor, but not Nordstrom or Target. The Ritz-Carlton might see the Four Seasons hotels as a major competitor, but not Holiday Inn, Hampton Inn, or any of the thousands of bed-and-breakfasts that dot the nation.

However, companies actually face a much wider range of competitors. The company might define its competitors as all firms with the same product or class of products. Thus, the Ritz-Carlton would see itself as competing against all other hotels. Even more broadly, competitors might include all companies making products that supply the same service. Here the Ritz-Carlton would see itself competing not only against other hotels but also against anyone who supplies rooms for busy travelers. Finally, and still more broadly, competitors might include all companies that compete for the same consumer dollars. Here the Ritz-Carlton would see itself competing with travel and leisure products and services, from cruises and summer homes to vacations abroad.

Companies must avoid "competitor myopia." A company is more likely to be "buried" by its latent competitors than its current ones. For example, Kodak didn't lose out to competing film makers such as Fuji; it fell to the makers of digital cameras that use no film at all (see Real Marketing 18.1). And once-blazing-hot video-rental superstore Blockbuster didn't go bankrupt at the hands of other traditional brick-and-mortar retailers. It fell victim first to unexpected competitors such as direct marketer Netflix and kiosk marketer Redbox and then to a host of new digital video streaming services and technologies. By the time Blockbuster recognized and reacted to these unforeseen competitors, it was too late.

Companies can identify their competitors from an *industry* point of view. They might see themselves as being in the oil industry, the pharmaceutical industry, or the beverage industry. A company must understand the competitive patterns in its industry if it hopes to be an effective player in that industry. Companies can also identify competitors from a *market* point of view. Here they define competitors as companies that are trying to satisfy the same customer need or build relationships with the same customer group.

From an industry point of view, Google once defined its competitors as other search engine providers such as Yahoo! or Microsoft's Bing. Now, Google takes a broader view of serving market needs for online and mobile access to the digital world. Under this market definition, Google squares off against once-unlikely competitors such as Apple, Samsung, Microsoft, and even Amazon and Facebook.

In general, the market concept of competition opens the company's eyes to a broader set of actual and potential competitors. ● For example, from an industry view, Cinnabon long defined itself as a mall- and airport-based fresh baked goods chain. Adopting a market view, however, let the brand grow into a much broader competitive arena against consumer packaged goods competitors:[2]

Cinnabon has long been known for its ginormous "World Famous Cinnamon Rolls," creations that radiate that enticing Cinnabon aroma at your local mall or airport. But from a broader market view, Cinnabon realized that it doesn't just sell cinnamon rolls in malls. Instead, it sells "irresistible indulgence," with attributes such as "aroma," "soft," "moist," and "indulgent." Cinnabon fans "wanted the flavors of Cinnabon in other sorts of occasions where they indulge," says the brand's CEO. This realization led to an expansion

● **Market-based competitive definition: By changing to a market concept of competition—selling "irresistible indulgence"—Cinnabon has grown into a much broader competitive arena. Some 75 percent of the brand's total revenues now come from licensed consumer packaged goods.**

FOCUS Brands

Real Marketing

18.1 Kodak: The Competitor It Didn't See Soon Enough—No Film

Kodak. That venerable brand name has been a household word for generations worldwide. For more than a century, people relied on Kodak for products to help them capture "Kodak moments"—important personal and family events to be shared and recorded for posterity. The Hollywood movie industry evolved around Kodak technology. In 1972, Paul Simon even had a number-two hit single called "Kodachrome," a song that put into words the emotional role that Kodak products played in people's lives.

In 2012, however, Kodak fell into bankruptcy. Today, the brand that once monopolized the consumer photography industry, capturing 85 percent of all camera sales and 90 percent of a huge film market, doesn't even sell consumer cameras and film anymore. Once among the bluest of blue chips and rolling in cash, a completely transformed Kodak now struggles with declining sales and year-after-year losses. Of the roughly 200 buildings that once stood on Kodak's sprawling business park in Rochester, New York, 109 have been demolished or sold off.

How could such a storied brand—as mighty in its day as Apple or Microsoft today—fall so far so fast? Kodak fell victim to marketing and competitor myopia—focusing on a narrow set of current products and competitors rather than on underlying customer needs and emerging market dynamics. It wasn't competing film makers that brought Kodak down. It was the competitor Kodak didn't see soon enough—digital photography and cameras that used no film at all. All along, Kodak continued to make the very best film. But in an increasingly digital world, customers no longer needed film. Clinging to its legacy products, Kodak lagged behind competitors in making the shift to digital.

In 1880, George Eastman founded Kodak based on a method for dry-plate photography. In 1888, he introduced the Kodak camera, which used glass plates for capturing images. Looking to expand the market, Eastman next developed film and the innovative little Kodak Brownie film camera. He sold the camera for only $1 but reaped massive profits from the sale of film, along with the chemicals and paper required to produce photographs. Although Kodak also developed innovative imaging technologies for industries ranging from health care to publishing, throughout the twentieth century, cameras and film remained the company's massive cash cow.

Interestingly, way back in 1975, Kodak engineers invented the first digital camera—a toaster-sized image sensor that captured rough hues of black and white. However, failing to recognize the mass-market potential of digital photography and fearing that digital technology would cannibalize its precious film business, Kodak shelved the digital project. Company managers simply could not envision a filmless world. So Kodak held fast to film and focused its innovation and competitive energies on making better film and out-innovating other film producers. When the company later realized its mistake, it was too late.

Blinded by its film fixation, Kodak failed to see emerging competitive trends associated with capturing and sharing images. Kodak's culture became bound up in its history and the nostalgia that accompanied it. "They were a company stuck in time," says one analyst. "Their history was so important to them—this rich century-old history when they made a lot of amazing things and a lot of money along the way. [Then,] their history [became] a liability."

By the time Kodak finally introduced a line of pocket-sized digital cameras in the late 1990s, the market was already crowded with digital products from Sony, Canon, Nikon, Samsung, and a dozen other camera makers. That was soon followed by a completely new category of competitors, as more and more people began pointing and clicking their phones and other mobile devices and sharing photos instantly via texting, email, and online photo-sharing social networks. Late to the digital game, Kodak became a relic of the past and an also-ran to a host of new-age digital competitors that hadn't even existed a decade or two earlier.

Somewhere along the way, swelled with success, once-mighty Kodak lost sight of founder George Eastman's visionary knack for defining customer needs and competitor dynamics. According to one biographer, Eastman's legacy was not film; it was innovation. "George Eastman never looked back. He always looked forward to doing something better than what he had done, even if he had the best on the market at the time." If it had retained Eastman's philosophy, Kodak

Competitor myopia: It wasn't competing film makers that brought Kodak down. It was the competitor Kodak didn't see soon enough—digital photography and cameras that used no film at all.

© Finnbarr Webster/Alamy

might well have been the market leader in digital technologies. We might all still be capturing "Kodak moments" on Kodak digital cameras and smartphones and sharing them on social media and Kodak-run online sites.

As Kodak emerged from bankruptcy, it stopped making cameras and discontinued its famous Kodachrome color film. Instead, it now licenses its name to other manufacturers that will make cameras under the Kodak brand. Almost all of its revenues now come from commercial imaging and printing products and services for business customers in

graphic arts, commercial print, publishing, packaging, electronic displays, and entertainment and commercial films. So, along with

Kodak's illustrious fortunes, it looks as though the famed "Kodak moment" has now passed into history.

Sources: Questin Hardy, "At Kodak, Clinging to a Future beyond Film," *New York Times*, March 22, 2015, p. BU1; Ernest Scheyder, "Focus on Past Glory Kept Kodak from Digital Win," *Reuters*, January 19, 2012, www.reuters.com/article/2012/01/19/us-kodak-bankruptcy-idUSTRE80I1N020120119; Dawn McCarty and Beth Jink, "Kodak Files for Bankruptcy as Digital Era Spells End to Film," *Bloomberg Businessweek*, January 25, 2012, www.businessweek.com/news/2012-01-25/kodak-files-for-bankruptcy-as-digital-era-spells-end-to-film.html; Michael Hiltzik, "Kodak's Long Fade to Black," *Los Angeles Times*, December 4, 2011; "Kodak to Stop Making Digital Cameras," *Digital Photography Review*, February 9, 2012, www.dpreview.com/news/2012/02/09/Kodak_exits_camera_business; and www.kodak.com/ek/us/en/corp/aboutus/heritage/milestones/default.htm, http://investor.kodak.com/annuals.cfm, and www.kodak.com, accessed October 2016.

into consumer products through licensing partnerships with companies ranging from Pillsbury and Green Mountain Coffee to Taco Bell, Air Wick, and even Pinnacle vodka. Each partner now makes products that capture the irresistible Cinnabon taste and smell. Cinnabon now captures more than $1 billion annually in consumer packaged goods sales, accounting for 75 percent of the brand's total revenues.

Assessing Competitors

Having identified the main competitors, marketing management now asks: What are the competitors' objectives? What does each seek in the marketplace? What is each competitor's strategy? What are various competitors' strengths and weaknesses, and how will each react to actions the company might take?

Determining Competitors' Objectives

Each competitor has a mix of objectives. The company wants to know the relative importance that a competitor places on current profitability, market share growth, cash flow, technological leadership, service leadership, and other goals. Knowing a competitor's mix of objectives reveals whether the competitor is satisfied with its current situation and how it might react to different competitive actions. For example, a company that pursues low-cost leadership will react much more strongly to a competitor's cost-reducing manufacturing breakthrough than to the same competitor's increase in advertising.

A company also must monitor its competitors' objectives for various segments. If the company finds that a competitor has discovered a new segment, this might be an opportunity. If it finds that competitors plan new moves into segments now served by the company, it will be forewarned and, hopefully, forearmed.

Identifying Competitors' Strategies

Strategic group
A group of firms in an industry following the same or a similar strategy.

The more that one firm's strategy resembles another firm's strategy, the more the two firms compete. In most industries, the competitors can be sorted into groups that pursue different strategies. A **strategic group** is a group of firms in an industry following the same or a similar strategy in a given target market. For example, in the auto industry, Ford and Toyota belong to the same strategic group. Each produces a full line of low- to medium-price mainstream vehicles supported by great warranties and broad dealership networks. BMW, Audi, and Mercedes belong to a different strategic group that focuses more on luxury performance. In contrast, Ferrari, Lamborghini, and McLaren produce narrower lines of very high-performance, premium-priced sports cars through a highly exclusive distribution and support network.

Some important insights emerge from identifying strategic groups. For example, if a company enters a strategic group, the members of that group become its key competitors. Thus, if the company enters a group against Ford and Toyota, it can succeed only if it develops strategic advantages over these two companies. Tesla is doing this by introducing more mainstream all-electric cars such as the Tesla Model 3. Tesla can succeed only if its models outperform and outclass the hybrid and electric models of the major automakers.

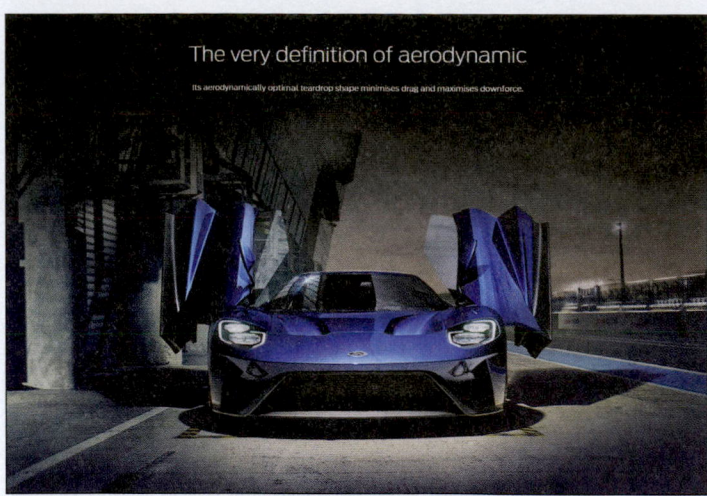

The very definition of aerodynamic

Its aerodynamically optimal teardrop shape minimises drag and maximises downforce.

● **Strategic groups: Brands sometimes cross strategic groups. For example, Ford sells a limited-production, ultra-high performance, $400,000 Ford GT road car that showcases its innovation and technological prowess. The Ford GT is "The very definition of aerodynamic."**

Ford Motor Company

Although competition is most intense within a strategic group, there is also rivalry among groups. First, some strategic groups may appeal to overlapping customer segments. For example, no matter what their strategy, most automobile manufacturers offer high-performance vehicle models. Second, customers may not see much difference in the offerings of different groups; they may see little difference in quality between a high-end Ford and a Mercedes. Finally, members of one strategic group might expand into new strategy segments. Thus, Toyota's Lexus division offered a bespoke Lexus LFA "Supercar" model that rivals a Ferrari or Lamborghini, with a starting price of $375,000. ● And Ford returns to that segment with a limited-production, ultra-high performance, $400,000 Ford GT road car developed alongside a successful racing program to showcase its innovation and technological prowess.[3]

The company needs to look at all the dimensions that identify strategic groups within the industry. It must understand how each competitor delivers value to its customers. It needs to know each competitor's product quality, features, and mix; customer services; pricing policy; distribution coverage; sales force strategy; and advertising, sales promotion, and online and social media programs. And it must study the details of each competitor's research and development (R&D), manufacturing, purchasing, financial, and other strategies.

Assessing Competitors' Strengths and Weaknesses

Marketers need to carefully assess each competitor's strengths and weaknesses to answer a critical question: What *can* our competitors do? As a first step, companies can gather data on each competitor's goals, strategies, and performance over the past few years. Admittedly, some of this information will be hard to obtain. For example, business-to-business (B-to-B) marketers find it hard to estimate competitors' market shares because they do not have the same syndicated data services that are available to consumer packaged-goods companies.

Companies normally learn about their competitors' strengths and weaknesses through secondary data, personal experience, and word of mouth. They can also conduct primary marketing research with customers, suppliers, and dealers. They can check competitors' online and social media sites. Or they can try **benchmarking** themselves against other firms, comparing the company's products and processes to those of competitors or leading firms in other industries to identify best practices and find ways to improve quality and performance. Benchmarking is a powerful tool for increasing a company's competitiveness.

Benchmarking

Comparing the company's products and processes to those of competitors or leading firms in other industries to identify best practices and find ways to improve quality and performance.

Estimating Competitors' Reactions

Next, the company wants to know: What *will* our competitors do? A competitor's objectives, strategies, and strengths and weaknesses go a long way toward explaining its likely actions. They also suggest its likely reactions to company moves, such as price cuts, promotion increases, or new product introductions. In addition, each competitor has a certain philosophy of doing business, a certain internal culture and guiding beliefs. Marketing managers need a deep understanding of a competitor's mentality if they want to anticipate how that competitor will act or react.

Each competitor reacts differently. Some do not react quickly or strongly to a competitor's move. They may feel their customers are loyal, they may be slow in noticing the move, or they may lack the funds to react. Some competitors react only to certain types of moves and not to others. Other competitors react swiftly and strongly to any action. Thus, P&G does not allow a competitor's new product to come easily into the market. Many firms avoid direct competition with P&G and look for easier prey, knowing that P&G will react fiercely if it is challenged. Knowing how major competitors react gives the company clues on how best to attack competitors or how best to defend its current positions.

In some industries, competitors live in relative harmony; in others, competitors are more openly combative. For example, competitors in the U.S. wireless industry have been at each other's throats for years. Verizon Wireless, AT&T, and T-Mobile have aggressively attacked each other in comparative ads:

> Verizon started the most recent round of attacks with TV ads using colorful balls to illustrate its supposed network dominance over specifically named competitors. AT&T, T-Mobile, and Sprint responded with vigorous counterattacks debunking Verizon's claims. For example, T-Mobile launched a #BallBusterChallenge campaign inviting consumers and media to make side-by-side comparisons of T-Mobile's full network against Verizon's, claiming that its LTE network is not just the nation's fastest, it's also the nation's fastest growing. The challenge traveled across the country, urging Verizon users to match T-Mobile's network head-on, testing data speeds, texting, and calls. If a customer's Verizon network beat out T-Mobile's two out of three times, the customer received $100.  When customers lost, they posed for a photo with sign such as "T-Mobile's network was just as good as Verizon's #BallBusterChallenge" or "Verizon's network just got spanked by T-Mobile #BallBusterChallenge." At the same time, T-Mobile ran its own "balls" ad on the Super Bowl correcting Verizon's dated facts, complete with a #Ballogize hashtag.[4]

In some cases, such competitive exchanges can provide useful information to consumers and advantages for brands. In other cases, they can reflect unfavorably on the entire industry.

● **Competitor reactions: In the U.S. wireless industry, T-Mobile, AT&T, and Verizon Wireless have attacked each other aggressively in comparative ads, as in T-Mobile's recent #BallBusterChallenge campaign.**

T-Mobile, USA Inc.

Customer value analysis

An analysis conducted to determine what benefits target customers value and how they rate the relative value of various competitors' offers.

Selecting Competitors to Attack and Avoid

A company has already largely selected its major competitors through prior decisions on customer targets, positioning, and its marketing mix strategy. Management now must decide which competitors to compete against most vigorously.

Strong or Weak Competitors

A company can focus on one of several classes of competitors. Most companies prefer to compete against weak competitors. This requires fewer resources and less time. But in the process, the firm may gain little. You could argue that a firm also should compete with strong competitors to sharpen its abilities. And sometimes, a company can't avoid its largest competitors, as in the case of T-Mobile, Verizon, and AT&T. But even strong competitors have some weaknesses, and succeeding against them often provides greater returns.

A useful tool for assessing competitor strengths and weaknesses is **customer value analysis**. The aim of customer value analysis is to determine the benefits that target customers value and how customers rate the relative value of various competitors' offers. In conducting a customer value analysis, the company first identifies the major attributes that customers value and the importance customers place on these attributes. Next, it assesses its performance against competitors on those valued attributes.

The key to gaining competitive advantage is to examine how a company's offer compares to that of its major competitors in each customer segment. The company wants to find the place in the market where it meets customers' needs in a way rivals can't. If the company's offer delivers greater value than the competitor's offer on important attributes, it can charge a higher price and earn higher profits, or it can charge the same price and gain more market share. But if the company is seen as performing at a lower level than its major competitors on some important attributes, it must invest in strengthening those attributes or finding other important attributes where it can build a lead.

Good or Bad Competitors

A company really needs and benefits from competitors. The existence of competitors results in several strategic benefits. Competitors may share the costs of market and product development and help legitimize new technologies. They may serve less-attractive segments or lead to more product differentiation. Finally, competitors may help increase total demand.

For example, you might think that Apple's introduction of its iPad tablet would have spelled trouble for Amazon's smaller, dowdier Kindle e-reader, which had been on the market for three years prior to the iPad's debut. Many analysts thought that Apple had created the "Kindle killer." However, as it turns out, the competing iPad created a stunning surge in tablet demand that benefited both companies. Kindle e-reader sales increased sharply with the iPad introduction, and new tablet demand spurred Amazon to introduce its own full line of Kindle tablets. As an added bonus, the surge

in iPad usage increased Amazon's sales of e-books and other digital content, which can be read on the iPad using a free Kindle for iPad app. Burgeoning tablet demand following the iPad introduction also opened the market to a host of new competitors, such as Samsung, Google, and Microsoft.

However, a company may not view all its competitors as beneficial. An industry often contains *good competitors* and *bad competitors*. Good competitors play by the rules of the industry. Bad competitors, in contrast, break the rules. They try to buy share rather than earn it, take large risks, and play by their own rules.

● For example, the nation's traditional newspapers face a lot of bad competitors these days. Digital services that overlap with traditional newspaper content are bad competitors because they offer for free real-time content that subscription-based newspapers printed once a day can't match. An example is the *Huffington Post*, the Pulitzer Prize–winning online newspaper started in 2005 by Arianna Huffington as an outlet for liberal commentary. The publication has since expanded and is now owned by AOL, which is in turn owned by Verizon. The site offers news, blogs, and original content and covers politics, business, entertainment, technology, popular media, lifestyle, culture, comedy, healthy living, women's interest, and local news. The ad-supported site is free to users versus the subscription rates charged by traditional newspapers, and that's about as bad as a competitor can get. HuffingtonPost.com is currently the 38th most visited site in the United States.[5] Such digital competitors have helped to drive many traditional newspapers into bankruptcy in recent years.

Finding Uncontested Market Spaces

Rather than competing head-to-head with established competitors, many companies seek out unoccupied positions in uncontested market spaces. They try to create products and services for which there are no direct competitors. Called a "blue-ocean strategy," the goal is to make competition irrelevant.[6]

Companies have long engaged in head-to-head competition in search of profitable growth. They have fought for competitive advantage, battled over market share, and struggled for differentiation. Yet in today's overcrowded industries, competing head-on results in nothing but a bloody "red ocean" of rivals fighting over a shrinking profit pool. In their book *Blue Ocean Strategy,* two strategy professors contend that although most companies compete within such red oceans, the strategy isn't likely to create profitable growth in the future. Tomorrow's leading companies will succeed not by battling competitors but by creating "blue oceans" of uncontested market space. Such strategic moves—termed *value innovation*—create powerful leaps in value for both the firm and its buyers, creating all-new demand and rendering rivals obsolete. By creating and capturing blue oceans, companies can largely take rivals out of the picture.

● Good and bad competitors: Rather than spelling trouble for Amazon's Kindle, Apple's iPad introduction created a surge in tablet demand that benefited not only Amazon but other tablet competitors as well.

Victor J. Blue/Bloomberg via Getty Images

Apple has long practiced this strategy, introducing product firsts such as the iPod, iTunes, iPhone, App Store, and iPad that created whole new categories. Similarly, Redbox reinvented the DVD-rental category via kiosks in convenient locations. And rather than competing against traditional coffee maker brands such as Hamilton Beach and Mr. Coffee that brew coffee by the pot, Keurig reinvented the process with innovative cup-at-a-time, pod-based coffee makers. As a result, Keurig has achieved annual sales of coffee makers and pods exceeding $4.5 billion and captures 60 percent of the U.S. single-serve market.[7]

● Another example is Cirque du Soleil, which reinvented the circus as a higher form of modern entertainment targeting adults rather than children. At a time when the circus industry was declining, Cirque du Soleil innovated by eliminating high-cost and controversial elements such as animal acts and bearded ladies, instead focusing on artistic theatrical experiences. Cirque du Soleil did not compete with then–market leader Ringling Bros. and Barnum & Bailey; it was altogether different from anything that preceded it. Instead, it created an uncontested new market space that

● Blue-ocean strategy: Cirque du Soleil reinvented the circus, finding uncontested new market space that made existing competitors irrelevant.

Paul Marotta/Getty Images

made existing competitors irrelevant. The results have been spectacular. Thanks to its blue-ocean strategy, Cirque du Soleil is now the undisputed leader in the redefined circus industry. In only its first 20 years, the company achieved more revenues than Ringling Brothers and Barnum & Bailey achieved in its first 100 years. Recently, however, as traditional circuses have updated their acts and smaller Cirque-like rivals have emerged, Cirque du Soleil's blue ocean "is now full of sharks," says a company executive. Cirque du Soleil must continue to find innovative new ways to separate itself from competitors in bringing value to customers.[8]

Designing a Competitive Intelligence System

We have described the main types of information that companies need about their competitors. This information must be collected, interpreted, distributed, and used. Gathering competitive intelligence can cost much money and time, so the company must design a cost-effective competitive intelligence system.

The competitive intelligence system first identifies the vital types of competitive information needed and the best sources of this information. Then the system continuously collects information from the field (sales force, channels, suppliers, market research firms, internet and social media sites, online monitoring, and trade associations) and published data (government publications, speeches, and online databases). Next the system checks the information for validity and reliability, interprets it, and organizes it in an appropriate way. Finally, it sends relevant information to decision makers and responds to inquiries from managers about competitors.

With this system, company managers receive timely intelligence about competitors in the form of reports and assessments, posted bulletins, newsletters, and email and mobile alerts. Managers can also connect when they need to interpret a competitor's sudden move, know a competitor's weaknesses and strengths, or assess how a competitor will respond to a planned company move.

> **Author Comment** | Now that we've identified competitors and know all about them, it's time to design a strategy for gaining competitive advantage.

Competitive Strategies

Having identified and evaluated its major competitors, a company now must design broad marketing strategies by which it can gain competitive advantage. But what broad competitive marketing strategies might the company use? Which ones are best for a particular company or for the company's different divisions and products?

Approaches to Marketing Strategy

No one strategy is best for all companies. Each company must determine what makes the most sense given its position in the industry and its objectives, opportunities, and resources. Even within a company, different strategies may be required for different businesses or products. Johnson & Johnson uses one marketing strategy for its leading brands in stable consumer markets, such as BAND-AID, Tylenol, Listerine, or J&J's baby products, and a different marketing strategy for its high-tech health-care businesses and products, such as Monocryl surgical sutures or NeuFlex finger joint implants.

Companies also differ in how they approach the strategy-planning process. Many large firms develop formal competitive marketing strategies and implement them religiously. However, other companies develop strategy in a less formal and orderly fashion. Some companies, such as Harley-Davidson, Red Bull, and Shinola, succeed by breaking many of the rules of marketing strategy. Such companies don't operate large marketing departments, conduct expensive marketing research, spell out elaborate competitive strategies, and spend huge sums on advertising. Instead, they sketch out strategies on the fly, stretch their limited resources, live close to their customers, and create more satisfying solutions to customer needs. They form buyers' clubs, use buzz marketing, engage customers up close, and focus on winning customer loyalty. It seems that not all marketing must follow in the footsteps of marketing giants such as P&G, McDonald's, and Microsoft.

● **Entrepreneurial marketing: Boston Beer Company founder Jim Koch first marketed his Samuel Adams beer by carrying bottles in a suitcase from bar to bar, telling his story, educating consumers, getting people to taste the beer, and persuading bartenders to carry it. The company is now the leading craft brewery in America.**

Bloomberg/Getty Images

In fact, approaches to marketing strategy and practice often pass through three stages—entrepreneurial marketing, formulated marketing, and intrapreneurial marketing:

- *Entrepreneurial marketing.* Most companies are started by individuals who live by their wits. They visualize an opportunity, construct flexible strategies on the backs of envelopes, and knock on every door to gain attention. ● Jim Koch, founder of Boston Beer Company, whose Samuel Adams Boston Lager beer has become the top-selling craft beer in America, started out in 1984 brewing a cherished family beer recipe in his kitchen. For marketing, Koch carried bottles of Samuel Adams in a suitcase from bar to bar, telling his story, educating consumers about brewing quality and ingredients, getting people to taste the beer, and persuading bartenders to carry it. For 10 years, he couldn't afford advertising; he sold his beer through direct selling and grassroots public relations. "It was all guerilla marketing," says Koch. "The big guys were so big, we had to do innovative things like that." Today, however, his business pulls in more than $1 billion a year, making it the leader over more than 1,000 competitors in the craft brewery market.[9]

- *Formulated marketing.* As small companies achieve success, they inevitably move toward more-formulated marketing. They develop formal marketing strategies and adhere to them closely. Boston Beer now employs a large sales force and has a marketing department that carries out market research and plans strategy. Although Boston Beer is far less formal and sophisticated in its strategy than $43-billion mega-competitor Anheuser-Busch Inbev, it has adopted some of the tools used in professionally run marketing companies.

- *Intrapreneurial marketing.* Many large and mature companies get stuck in formulated marketing. They pore over the latest Nielsen numbers, scan market research reports, and try to fine-tune their competitive strategies and programs. These companies sometimes lose the marketing creativity and passion they had at the start. They now need to build more marketing initiative and "intrapreneurship"—encouraging employees to be more entrepreneurial within the larger corporation—recapturing some of the spirit and action that made them successful in the first place.

Some companies build intrapreneurship into their core marketing operations. For example, IBM encourages employees at all levels to interact on their own with customers through blogs, social media, and other platforms. Google's Innovation Time-Off program encourages all of its engineers and developers to spend 20 percent of their time developing "cool and wacky" new product ideas—blockbusters such as Google News, Gmail, Google Maps, and AdSense are just a few of the resulting products. And Facebook sponsors regular "hackathons," during which it encourages internal teams to come up with and present intrapreneurial ideas. One of the most important innovations in the company's history—the "Like button"—resulted from such a hackathon.[10]

The bottom line is that there are many approaches to developing effective competitive marketing strategies. There will be a constant tension between the formulated side of marketing and the creative side. It is easier to learn the formulated side of marketing, which has occupied most of our attention in this book. But we have also seen how marketing creativity and passion in the strategies of many of the companies studied—whether small or large, new or mature—have helped to build and maintain success in the marketplace. With this in mind, we now look at the broad competitive marketing strategies companies can use.

Basic Competitive Strategies

More than three decades ago, Michael Porter suggested four basic competitive positioning strategies that companies can follow—three winning strategies and one losing one.[11] The three winning strategies are as follows:

- *Overall cost leadership.* Here the company works hard to achieve the lowest production and distribution costs. Low costs let the company price lower than its competitors and win a large market share. Walmart, Lenovo, and Spirit Airlines are leading practitioners of this strategy.

- *Differentiation.* Here the company concentrates on creating a highly differentiated product line and marketing program so that it comes across as the class leader in the industry. Most customers would prefer to own this brand if its price is not too high. Nike and Caterpillar follow this strategy in apparel and heavy construction equipment, respectively.
- *Focus.* Here the company focuses its effort on serving a few market segments well rather than going after the whole market. For example, Ritz-Carlton focuses on the top 5 percent of corporate and leisure travelers. Bose concentrates on very high-quality electronics products that produce better sound. Hohner owns a stunning 85 percent of the harmonica market.

Companies that pursue a clear strategy—one of the above—will likely perform well. The firm that carries out that strategy best will make the most profits. But firms that do not pursue a clear strategy—*middle-of-the-roaders*—do the worst. Sears, Levi-Strauss, and Holiday Inn encountered difficult times because they did not stand out as the lowest in cost, highest in perceived value, or best in serving some market segment. Middle-of-the-roaders try to be good on all strategic counts but end up being not very good at anything.

Two marketing consultants, Michael Treacy and Fred Wiersema, offer a more customer-centered classification of competitive marketing strategies.[12] They suggest that companies gain leadership positions by delivering superior value to their customers. Companies can pursue any of three strategies—called *value disciplines*—for delivering superior customer value:

- *Operational excellence.* The company provides superior value by leading its industry in price and convenience. It works to reduce costs and create a lean and efficient value delivery system. It serves customers who want reliable, good-quality products or services but want them cheaply and easily. Examples include Walmart, IKEA, Zara, and Southwest Airlines.
- *Customer intimacy.* The company provides superior value by precisely segmenting its markets and tailoring its products or services to exactly match the needs of targeted customers. It specializes in satisfying unique customer needs through a close relationship with and intimate knowledge of the customer. It empowers its people to respond quickly to customer needs. Customer-intimate companies serve customers who are willing to pay a premium to get precisely what they want. They will do almost anything to build long-term customer loyalty and to capture customer lifetime value. For example, retailer Nordstrom is a customer-intimacy all-star that's obsessed with "Taking care of customers no matter what it takes" (see Real Marketing 18.2). Other companies that practice customer intimacy include Lexus, Zappos, L.L. Bean, and Ritz-Carlton hotels.
- *Product leadership.* The company provides superior value by offering a continuous stream of leading-edge products or services. It aims to make its own and competing products obsolete. Product leaders are open to new ideas, relentlessly pursue new solutions, and work to get new products to market quickly. They serve customers who want state-of-the-art products and services regardless of the costs in terms of price or inconvenience. One example of a product leader is Tesla Motors:[13]

● **Product leadership: Tesla makes the ultimate in cutting-edge electric vehicles, here the Tesla Model X crossover SUV with futuristic falcon-wing doors.**

© Bai Xuefei/Xinhua/Alamy Live News

A Tesla automobile—any model—doesn't come cheap, and you'll have to wait a while to get one. But it's the ultimate in cutting-edge electric vehicles. The Tesla Model S goes from 0 to 60 in under 3 seconds when driven in "Ludicrous Mode" and offers a host of innovative features, such as retractable door handles, a 17-inch touchscreen, a sound system that rivals a recording studio, and a host of safety features. Best of all: It needs no oil changes and has no gas tank to fill. ● The Tesla Model X crossover SUV even features futuristic falcon-wing doors.

Tesla's product leadership has sparked the imaginations of people who want to stay ahead of the curve in auto ownership. For example, within only days of unveiling the more affordable yet still incredibly stylish $35,000 Tesla Model 3, Tesla was swamped with 400,000 reservation deposits of $1,000, even though the cars wouldn't be delivered for a year or more. Auto research site Edwards sums it up this way: "Tesla has found success not because they built an electric vehicle, but because they built a sports car that happens to have an innovative electric powertrain. It is a vehicle that customers love."

18.2   Nordstrom: Taking Care of Customers No Matter What It Takes

Nordstrom is legendary for outstanding customer service. The upscale department store chain thrives on stories about its service heroics, such as employees dropping off orders at customers' homes or warming up their cars on a cold day while customers spend a little more time shopping. Then there's the one about the Nordstrom employee who split pairs of shoes in order to fit a man with different-sized feet or the sales clerk who ironed a new shirt for a customer who needed it for a meeting that afternoon. In another case, a man reportedly walked into Nordstrom to return a set of tires that he insisted he'd bought there. Nordstrom doesn't sell tires. But without hesitation, even though his receipt clearly indicated a different store, the Nordstrom clerk refunded the man's money out of her own pocket. Later, on her lunch hour, she took the tires and receipt to the store where they'd been purchased and got her money back.

Whether factual or fictional, such stories are rooted in actual customer experiences at Nordstrom. It seems that almost everyone who shops regularly at Nordstrom has a favorite story to tell. As one journalist noted after seeing the chain near the top of yet another Customer Service Hall of Fame list, "It almost gets old: Nordstrom and its legendarily good customer service." But such stories never get old at Nordstrom. "Nordstrom just goes above and beyond in a way that customers never forget," says a retailing expert.

Superb customer service is deeply rooted in the 100-year-old Nordstrom's DNA, as summarized in its staunchly held mantra: Take care of customers no matter what it takes. Although many companies pay homage to similar pronouncements hidden away in their mission statements, Nordstrom really means it—and really makes it happen. Consider these customer delight–inducing stories:

- One man tells a story about his wife, a loyal Nordstrom customer, who died with $1,000 owing on her Nordstrom account. Not only did Nordstrom settle the account, it also sent flowers to the funeral.
- A woman had been shopping with her daughter at San Diego's ritzy Horton Plaza. After browsing in Nordstrom for a while and believing nobody was around,

she said with an exhausted sigh, as if thinking out loud to herself, "I could sure use a Dr Pepper." Sure enough, within only a few short minutes, a Nordstrom employee appeared out of nowhere with an ice-cold can of Dr Pepper.

- One late November, a woman buying a sweater as a Christmas present for her husband found just the one she wanted at Nordstrom, but not in the right color or size. No worries, said the Nordstrom manager. He'd find her one in plenty of time for the holidays. A week before Christmas, just as the woman was beginning to worry, the manager called ahead and delivered the sweater to her home, already beautifully gift-wrapped. That's amazing enough, but here's the back story: The manager hadn't been able to find the right sweater after all. But while discussing the problem with his wife, he learned that she'd already bought that very sweater for *him* for Christmas and that it was already wrapped and under their tree. The manager and his wife quickly agreed to pass his sweater along to the customer.

How does Nordstrom consistently exceed customer expectations? For starters, it hires people who truly enjoy serving other people. Then it trains them thoroughly on the intricacies of providing customer care and turns them loose. Nordstrom trusts its employees to make the right judgments without bogging them down with procedures and policies. The famous Nordstrom employee

"handbook" consists of a single two-sided card containing only 74 words, among them: "Rule #1: Use good judgment in all situations. There will be no additional rules." As a result, at Nordstrom, customer service doesn't come across as sales clerks reciting rehearsed scripts. Rather, it's about Nordstrom people genuinely connecting with and serving customers. "What it boils down to is we give employees complete freedom to take care of the customer," says a Nordstrom executive. "And we say, if you're going to make a mistake, let's make sure you make it in the customer's favor."

To motivate its employees even more, Nordstrom collects and recycles stories of customer service heroics. Every Nordstrom register supplies pens and paper with which customers can share their good experiences. Every morning, in the main lobby of each store, managers share some of the best customer stories from the previous day and reward the employees involved for their good deeds. In turn, the feel-good stories inspire everyone in the store to continue the cycle of pampering customers and making them feel special.

Founded in 1901 by Swedish immigrant John W. Nordstrom, the company is now run by the fourth generation of Nordstroms—brothers Blake, Pete, and Erik (co-presidents) and second-cousin Jamie Nordstrom—in a way that would make their great-great-grandfather proud. This team of young executives has given Nordstrom's ageless philosophy a dose of modern technology. For example, they completely restructured the chain's entire

Customer intimacy: Taking care of customers no matter what it takes is deeply rooted in Nordstrom's DNA. "Our one rule: Use good judgment in all situations."
Nordstrom, Inc.

purchasing and inventory management system, making it easier for tablet-toting front-line employees to quickly find and obtain items that customers want. When the system went live, sales immediately surged. But more important, customer service improved dramatically.

Nordstrom is also blurring the line between the digital world and its brick-and-mortar stores. For example, shoppers can buy items they see on Pinterest or Instagram with just a couple of taps on their smartphones via apps such as Like2Buy. The upscale retailer is investing heavily in its own online shopping platforms, updating its web and mobile sites and offering faster delivery. "Our goal is to build a seamless 'One Nordstrom' customer experience…no matter how they choose to shop," says Nordstrom. Each contact—in-store or online—"represents an opportunity for us to connect with customers on their terms, which means an experience that is increasingly relevant, convenient, and personalized."

Creating customer delight has been good for Nordstrom's top and bottom lines over the years. During just the past four years, Nordstrom's sales have grown almost 35 percent to a record $14.1 billion. And whereas many rival department stores have grown little or not at all, Nordstrom has continued to gain market share with six straight years of growth.

As Erik Nordstrom shared these and other good tidings with shareholders at a recent Nordstrom annual meeting, he also shared yet another story of customer delight. He told of a woman in North Carolina who recently lost the diamond from her wedding ring while trying on clothes at a Nordstrom store. A store security worker saw her crawling on the sales floor under the racks and joined the search. When they came up empty, the security employee enlisted the help of two building-services workers, who vacuumed the area and then opened the vacuum cleaner bags and painstakingly searched the contents, where they recovered the sparkling gem.

After showing a video clip featuring the delighted shopper, to thunderous applause, Erik Nordstrom introduced the three employees to the shareholders. Extending his hand to the three, Nordstrom proclaimed that when it comes to taking care of customers no matter what it takes, "this raises the bar."

Sources: Stacy Conradt, "21 of the Best Customer Service Stories Ever," *Mental Floss,* January 12, 2016, http://mentalfloss.com/article/73540/21-best-customer-service-stories-ever; Carol Toller, "How Nordstrom Built the World's Best Customer-Service Machine," *Canadian Business,* March 5, 2015, www.canadianbusiness.com/innovation/secrets-of-nordstrom-customer-service/; Amy Martinez, "Tale of Lost Diamond Adds Glitter to Nordstrom's Customer Service," *Seattle Times,* May 11, 2011; Garrett Pierson and Scott Brandley, *The Trust Factor* (eBookit.com, 2013), Chapter 7; Micah Solomon, "What Any Business Can Learn from Nordstrom Customer Service," *Forbes,* January 26, 2016, www.forbes.com/sites/micahsolomon/2016/01/26/what-any-business-can-learn-from-the-way-nordstrom-handles-customer-service/#14ba40644d45; and http://shop.nordstrom.com/c/company-history and www.investor.nordstrom.com, accessed October 2016.

Some companies successfully pursue more than one value discipline at the same time. For example, FedEx excels at both operational excellence and customer intimacy. However, such companies are rare; few firms can be the best at more than one of these disciplines. By trying to be *good at all* value disciplines, a company usually ends up being *best at none.*

Thus, most excellent companies focus on and excel at a single value discipline while meeting industry standards on the other two. Such companies design their entire value delivery network to single-mindedly support the chosen discipline. For example, Walmart knows that customer intimacy and product leadership are important. Compared with other discounters, it offers good customer service and an excellent product assortment. Still, it purposely offers less customer service and less product depth than does Nordstrom or Williams-Sonoma, which pursue customer intimacy. Instead, Walmart focuses obsessively on operational excellence—on reducing costs and streamlining its order-to-delivery process to make it convenient for customers to buy just the right products at the lowest prices.

By the same token, Equinox Fitness Clubs wants to be efficient and employ the latest operations technologies. But what really sets the luxury gym apart is its customer intimacy. Equinox coddles its customers with an app to sign up for classes ahead of time, refrigerated eucalyptus towels, and Kiehl's products in the locker rooms. In addition, each location has a spa and snack bar filled with organic selections. "Epic workouts demand unexpected luxuries. Exclusive Kiehl's products. Eco-chic amenities. Spaces that inspire and ignite," says Equinox. "Equinox isn't just a fitness club, it's a temple of well-being. It's not fitness. It's life."

Classifying competitive strategies as value disciplines is appealing. It defines marketing strategy in terms of the single-minded pursuit of delivering superior value to customers. Each value discipline defines a specific way to build lasting customer relationships.

Competitive Positions

Firms competing in a given target market at any point in time differ in their objectives and resources. Some firms are large; others are small. Some have many resources; others are strapped for funds. Some are mature and established; others new and fresh. Some strive for rapid market share growth; others for long-term profits. And these firms occupy different competitive positions in the target market.

We now examine competitive strategies based on the roles firms play in the target market—leader, challenger, follower, or nicher. Suppose that an industry contains the firms shown in ● **Figure 18.2**. As you can see, 40 percent of the market is in the hands of the **market leader**, the firm with the largest market share. Another 30 percent is in the hands of **market challengers**, runner-up firms that are fighting hard to increase their market share. Another 20 percent is in the hands of **market followers**, other runner-up firms that want to hold their share without rocking the boat. The remaining 10 percent is in the hands of **market nichers**, firms that serve small segments not being pursued by other firms.

● **Table 18.1** shows specific marketing strategies that are available to market leaders, challengers, followers, and nichers.[14] Remember, however, that these classifications often do not apply to a whole company but only to its position in a specific industry. Large companies such as GE, Microsoft, Google, P&G, or Disney might be leaders in some markets and nichers in others. For example, Amazon leads the online retailing market but challenges Apple and Samsung in smartphones and tablets. P&G leads in many segments, such as laundry detergents and shampoo, but it challenges Unilever in hand soaps and Kimberly-Clark in facial tissues. Such companies often use different strategies for different business units or products, depending on the competitive situations of each.

Market Leader Strategies

Most industries contain an acknowledged market leader. The leader has the largest market share and usually leads the other firms in price changes, new product introductions, distribution coverage, and promotion spending. The leader may or may not be admired or respected, but other firms concede its dominance. Competitors focus on the leader as a company to challenge, imitate, or avoid. Some of the best-known market leaders are Walmart (retailing), Amazon (online retailing), McDonald's (fast food), Verizon (wireless), Coca-Cola (beverages), Caterpillar (earth-moving equipment), Nike (athletic footwear and apparel), Facebook (social media), and Google (internet search).

A leader's life is not easy. It must maintain a constant watch. Other firms keep challenging its strengths or trying to take advantage of its weaknesses. The market leader can easily miss a turn in the market and plunge into second or third place. A product innovation may come along and hurt the leader (as when Netflix's direct marketing and video streaming unseated then-market leader Blockbuster or when Apple developed the iPod and iTunes and took the market lead from Sony's Walkman portable audio devices). The leader might grow arrogant or complacent and misjudge the competition (as when Sears lost its lead to Walmart). Or the leader might look old-fashioned against new and peppier rivals (as when Abercrombie & Fitch lost ground to stylish or lower-cost brands such as Zara, H&M, and Forever 21).

To remain number one, leading firms can take any of three actions. First, they can find ways to expand total demand. Second, they can protect their current market share through good defensive and offensive actions. Third, they can try to expand their market share further, even if market size remains constant.

Expanding Total Demand

The leading firm normally gains the most when the total market expands. If Americans eat more fast food, McDonald's stands to gain the most because it holds a much larger fast-food market share than competitors such as Subway, Burger King, or Taco Bell. If

Market leader
The firm in an industry with the largest market share.

Market challenger
A runner-up firm that is fighting hard to increase its market share in an industry.

Market follower
A runner-up firm that wants to hold its share in an industry without rocking the boat.

Market nicher
A firm that serves small segments that the other firms in an industry overlook or ignore.

● **FIGURE | 18.2**
Competitive Market Positions and Roles

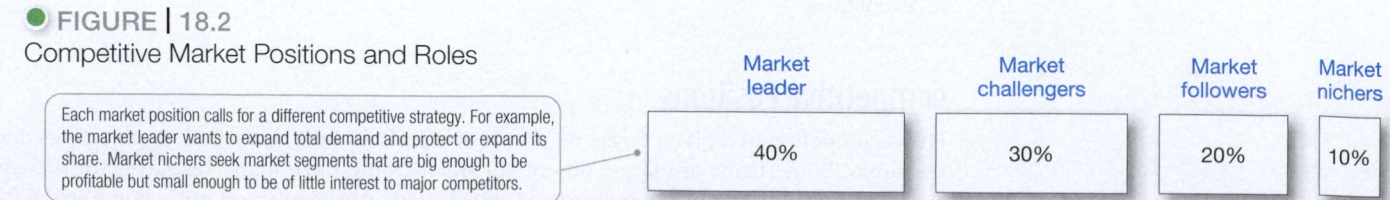

Each market position calls for a different competitive strategy. For example, the market leader wants to expand total demand and protect or expand its share. Market nichers seek market segments that are big enough to be profitable but small enough to be of little interest to major competitors.

Market leader	Market challengers	Market followers	Market nichers
40%	30%	20%	10%

● **Table 18.1** | **Strategies for Market Leaders, Challengers, Followers, and Nichers**

Market Leader Strategies	Market Challenger Strategies	Market Follower Strategies	Market Nicher Strategies
Expand total market	Full frontal attack	Follow closely	By customer, market, quality, price, service
Protect market share	Indirect attack	Follow at a distance	
Expand market share			Multiple niching

McDonald's can convince more Americans that fast food is the best eating-out choice, it will benefit more than its competitors.

Market leaders can expand the market by developing new users, new uses, and more usage of its products. They usually can find *new users* or untapped market segments in many places. For example, traditionally boy-focused LEGOs—the world's biggest toymaker—now successfully targets girls. Based on extensive research into differences between how boys and girls play, in 2011 the company introduced the LEGO Friends line for girls. The line features pastel color bricks and construction sets that encourage girls to build everything from Olivia's House or Emma's Pet Salon to Andrea's City Park Café. LEGO Friends has become one of the most successful lines in LEGO history, helping to triple LEGO's sales to girls within only one year. Last year alone, sales of the Friends line were up 30 percent over the previous year.[15]

Marketers can expand markets by discovering and promoting *new uses* for the product. For example, The WD-40 Company's knack for expanding the market by finding new uses has made this popular substance one of the truly essential survival items in most American homes:[16]

Some years ago, the company launched a search to uncover 2,000 unique uses for WD-40. After receiving 300,000 individual submissions, it narrowed the list to the best 2,000, which are now posted on the company's website. Some consumers suggested simple and practical uses, such as keeping wicker chairs from squeaking, freeing stuck LEGO bricks, or cleaning crayon marks from just about anywhere. ● And, it seems, lots of people use WD-40 to make squirrels slide off birdfeeder poles. Others, however, reported some pretty unusual applications. One man uses WD-40 to polish his glass eye; another uses it to remove a prosthetic leg. A bus driver in Asia used WD-40 to remove a python that had coiled itself around the undercarriage of his vehicle. And did you hear about the nude burglary suspect who had wedged himself in a vent at a café in Denver? The fire department extracted him with a large dose of WD-40. Or how about the Mississippi naval officer who used WD-40 to repel an angry bear? Then there's the college student who wrote to say that a friend's nightly amorous activities in the next room were causing everyone in his dorm to lose sleep—he solved the problem by treating the squeaky bedsprings with WD-40. As the company concludes: "You often hear it said, 'You only need two things in life: duct tape and WD-40. If it moves and shouldn't, use duct tape. If it doesn't move and should, use WD-40.' Surely there's a reason for that."

Finally, market leaders can encourage *more usage* by convincing people to use the product more often or use more per occasion. For example, Campbell's urges people to eat soup and other Campbell's products more often by running ads containing new recipes. At the Campbell's Kitchen website (www.campbellskitchen.com), visitors can search for or exchange recipes, create their own personal recipe box, learn ways to eat healthier, and sign up for a daily or weekly Meal Mail program. At the Campbell's Facebook, Pinterest, and Twitter sites, consumers can join in and share on Campbell's Kitchen Community conversations.

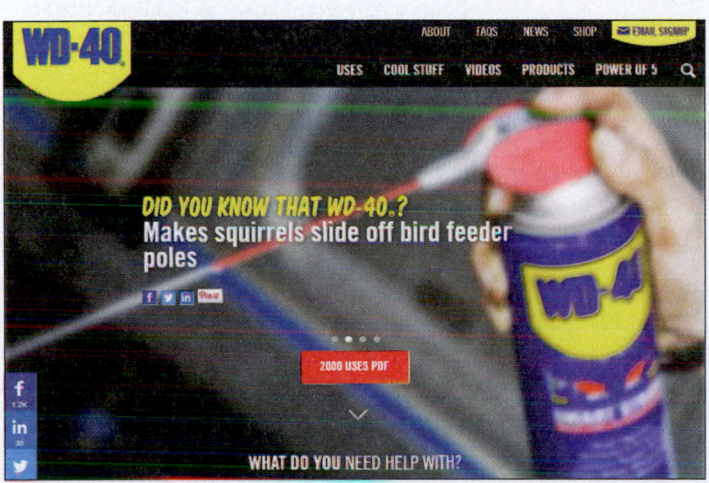

● Promoting new uses: The WD-40 Company's knack for finding new uses has made this popular substance one of the truly essential survival items in most American homes.

WD-40® is a registered trademark of WD-40 Company.

Protecting Market Share

While trying to expand total market size, the leading firm also must protect its current business against competitors' attacks. Walmart must constantly guard against Target and Costco; Caterpillar against Komatsu; Apple's iPad and iPhone against Samsung; and McDonald's against Wendy's and Burger King.

What can the market leader do to protect its position? First, it must prevent or fix weaknesses that provide opportunities for competitors. It must always fulfill its value promise and work tirelessly to engage valued customers in strong relationships. Its prices must remain consistent with the value that customers see in the brand. The leader should "plug holes" so that competitors do not jump in.

But the best defense is a good offense, and the best response is *continuous innovation*. The market leader refuses to be content with the way things are and leads the industry in new products, customer services, distribution effectiveness, promotion, and cost cutting. It keeps increasing its competitive effectiveness and value to customers. And when attacked by challengers, the market leader reacts decisively. For example, in the $53 billion global disposable diaper market, market leader P&G—with its Pampers and Luvs brands—has been relentless in its offense against challengers such as Kimberly-Clark's Huggies:[17]

P&G invests huge resources in disposable diaper and baby-care R&D, seeking to build the ultimate diaper that yields "zero leakage, ultimate dryness, ultimate comfort, with an under-wear-like fit," says a P&G baby-care research manager. ● At five baby-care centers around the globe, P&G's researchers push the boundaries of science and style to keep a technological edge over challengers. P&G's baby-care division now has more than 5,000 diaper patents granted or pending. For instance, in 2010 P&G introduced Dry Max Pampers, perhaps the biggest diaper innovation in 25 years—20 percent thinner yet twice as absorbent as before. More recently, it introduced Pamper Premium Care Pants, diapers with all-around elastic that can be pulled on like underwear. Next up in diaper innovation: smart diapers with imbedded sensors that alert parents through smartphone apps when their babies wet a diaper or even notify parents if they detect the wearer catching a disease. Beyond its push for technological superiority, P&G employs its hefty marketing clout to engage consumers and persuade them that its diapers are best for their babies. In all, thanks to its relentless innovation and brand building, in the United States P&G holds a 42.9-percent-and-growing market share versus challenger Kimberly-Clark's 37 percent. In the huge Chinese diaper market, it holds a 42 percent share to Kimberly Clark's 11 percent.

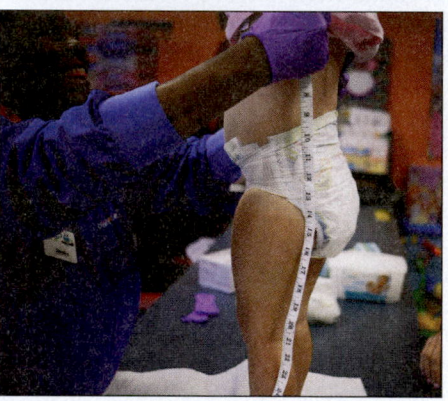

● **Protecting market share:** P&G's researchers push the boundaries of science and style to keep a technological edge over disposable diaper challengers. Thanks to relentless innovation and brand building, P&G maintains a commanding market share lead.

Bloomberg via Getty Images

Expanding Market Share

Market leaders also can grow by increasing their market shares further. In many markets, small market share increases mean very large sales increases. For example, in the U.S. shampoo market, a 1 percent increase in market share is worth $70 million in annual sales; in carbonated soft drinks, almost $1 billion![18]

Studies have shown that, on average, profitability rises with increasing market share. Because of these findings, many companies have sought expanded market shares to improve profitability. GE, for example, declared that it wants to be at least number one or two in each of its markets or else get out. GE shed its computer, air-conditioning, small appliances, and television businesses because it could not achieve top-dog position in those industries.

However, some studies have found that many industries contain one or a few highly profitable large firms, several profitable and more focused firms, and a large number of medium-sized firms with poorer profit performance. It appears that profitability increases as a business gains share relative to competitors in its *served market*. For example, Lexus holds only a small share of the total car market, but it earns a high profit because it is a leading brand in the luxury-performance car segment. And it has achieved this high share in its served market because it does other things right, such as producing high-quality products, creating outstanding service experiences, and building close customer relationships.

Companies must not think, however, that gaining increased market share will automatically improve profitability. Much depends on their strategy for gaining increased share. There are many high-share companies with low profitability and many low-share companies with high profitability. The cost of buying higher market share may far exceed the returns. Higher shares tend to produce higher profits only when unit costs fall with increased market share or when the company offers a superior-quality product and charges a premium price that more than covers the cost of offering higher quality.

Market Challenger Strategies

Firms that are second, third, or lower in an industry are sometimes quite large, such as PepsiCo, Ford, Lowe's, Hertz, Target, and AT&T. These runner-up firms can adopt one of two competitive strategies: They can challenge the market leader and other competitors in an aggressive bid for more market share (market challengers), or they can play along with competitors and not rock the boat (market followers).

A market challenger must first define which competitors to challenge and its strategic objective. The challenger can attack the market leader, a high-risk but potentially high-gain strategy. Its goal might be to take over market leadership. Or the challenger's objective may simply be to wrest more market share.

Although it might seem that the market leader has the most going for it, challengers often have what some strategists call a "second-mover advantage." The challenger observes what has made the market leader successful and improves on it. For example, The Home Depot invented the home-improvement superstore. However, after observing The Home Depot's success, number-two Lowe's, with its brighter stores, wider aisles, and arguably more helpful salespeople, has positioned itself as the friendly alternative to Big Bad Orange. Over the past decade, follower Lowe's has substantially closed the gap in sales and market share with The Home Depot.

In fact, challengers often become market leaders by imitating and improving on the ideas of pioneering processors. For example, McDonald's first imitated and then mastered the fast-food system first pioneered by White Castle. And founder Sam Walton admitted that Walmart borrowed most of its practices from discount pioneer Sol Price's FedMart and Price Club chains and then perfected them to become today's dominant retailer.

Alternatively, the challenger can avoid the leader and instead challenge firms its own size or smaller local and regional firms. These smaller firms may be underfinanced and not serving their customers well. Several of the major beer companies grew to their present size not by challenging large competitors but by gobbling up small local or regional competitors. For example, SABMiller became the world's number-two brewer by acquiring brands such as Miller, Molson, Coors, and dozens of others. If the challenger goes after a small local company, its objective may be to put that company out of business. The important point remains: The challenger must choose its opponents carefully and have a clearly defined and attainable objective.

How can the market challenger best attack the chosen competitor and achieve its strategic objectives? It may launch a full *frontal attack*, matching the competitor's product, advertising, price, and distribution efforts. It attacks the competitor's strengths rather than its weaknesses. The outcome depends on who has the greater strength and endurance. PepsiCo challenges Coca-Cola in this way, and Ford challenges Toyota frontally.

If the market challenger has fewer resources than the competitor, however, a frontal attack makes little sense. Thus, many new market entrants avoid frontal attacks, knowing that market leaders can head them off with ad blitzes, price wars, and other retaliations. Rather than challenging head-on, the challenger can make an *indirect attack* on the competitor's weaknesses or on gaps in the competitor's market coverage. It can carve out toeholds using tactics that established leaders have trouble responding to or choose to ignore.

For example, consider how challenger Red Bull first entered the U.S. soft drink market against market leaders Coca-Cola and PepsiCo. Red Bull tackled the leaders indirectly by selling a high-priced niche product in nontraditional distribution points. It began by selling Red Bull via unconventional outlets that were under the radar of the market leaders, such as nightclubs and bars where young revelers gulped down their caffeine fix so they could go all night. Once it had built a core customer base, the brand expanded into more traditional outlets, where it now sits within arm's length of Coke and Pepsi. Finally, Red Bull used a collection of guerilla marketing tactics rather than the high-cost traditional media used by the market leaders. The indirect approach worked for Red Bull. Despite ever-intensifying competition in the United States, Red Bull is now a $6.5 billion brand that captures a 43 percent share of the energy drink market versus a combined energy drink share of about 4 percent for Coca-Cola and Pepsi.[19]

Market Follower Strategies

Not all runner-up companies want to challenge the market leader. The leader never takes challenges lightly. If the challenger's lure is lower prices, improved service, or additional product features, the market leader can quickly match these to defuse the attack. The leader probably has more staying power in an all-out battle for customers. For example, a few years ago, when Kmart launched its renewed low-price "bluelight special" campaign, directly challenging Walmart's everyday low prices, it started a price war that it couldn't win. Walmart had little trouble fending off Kmart's challenge, leaving Kmart worse off for the attempt. Thus, many firms prefer to follow rather than challenge the market leader.

A follower can gain many advantages. The market leader often bears the huge expenses of developing new products and markets, expanding distribution, and educating the market. By contrast, as with challengers, the market follower can learn from the market leader's experience. It can copy or improve on the leader's products and programs, usually with much less investment. Although the follower will probably not overtake the leader, it often can be as profitable.

Following is not the same as being passive or a carbon copy of the market leader. A follower must know how to hold current customers and win a fair share of new ones. It must find the right balance between following closely enough to win customers from the market leader and following at enough of a distance to avoid retaliation. Each follower tries to bring distinctive advantages to its target market—location, services, financing. A follower is often a major target of attack by challengers. Therefore, the market follower must keep its manufacturing costs and prices low or its product quality and services high. It must also enter new markets as they open up.

Market Nicher Strategies

Almost every industry includes firms that specialize in serving market niches. Instead of pursuing the whole market or even large segments, these firms target subsegments. Nichers are often smaller firms with limited resources. But smaller divisions of larger firms also may pursue niching strategies. Firms with low shares of the total market can be highly successful and profitable through smart niching.

Why is niching profitable? The main reason is that the market nicher ends up knowing the target customer group so well that it meets their needs better than other firms that casually sell to that niche. As a result, the nicher can charge a substantial markup over costs because of the added value. Whereas the mass marketer achieves high volume, the nicher achieves high margins.

Nichers try to find one or more market niches that are safe and profitable. An ideal market niche is big enough to be profitable and has growth potential. It is one that the firm can serve effectively. Perhaps most important, the niche is of little interest to major competitors. And the firm can build the skills and customer goodwill to defend itself against a major competitor as the niche grows and becomes more attractive.

The key idea in niching is specialization. Nichers thrive by meeting in depth the special needs of well-targeted customer groups. For example, when it comes to online dating sites, general sites such as eHarmony.com and Match.com get the most notice. But recently, there's been an explosion of niche dating sites that focus on the narrower preferences of small but well-defined audiences:[20]

PURRsonals.com pairs cat lovers—it's where "cat lovers meet and greet." SeaCaptainDate.com helps lovers of the ocean "find your first mate." Faith-focused ChristianMingle.com is "where good people find great relationships." And TallFriends.com brings tall people nose to nose (there's even a choice for people taller than 6'11"!). If that's not nichie enough for you, maybe you need a super-nicher such as GlutenfreeSingles. com, with 4,000 love-seeking gluten-free users. There's even a dating site for mustache wearers and people who love them (StachePassions.com).

Although some of these niche sites seem a bit extreme, they can be ideal for people who think they know precisely what kind of person they want. ● For example, FarmersOnly.com serves hundreds of thousands of country-folk members every day seeking like-minded mates with rural persuasions. Farmers Only founder Jerry Miller started the dating site after noticing that the isolated and demanding farming lifestyle makes it hard to find understanding partners. He cites an example in which a country girl and her city boyfriend discussed marriage. Their relationship went to seed when she said that she wanted to raise horses; he said they could keep the horses in the garage. At that point, says Miller, "She knew they were not compatible." Hence the dating service's popular tagline: FarmersOnly.com, because "City folks just don't get it."

● **Market nichers: FarmersOnly.com pairs country folk with like-minded others because "City folks just don't get it."**

FarmersOnly Media Inc. Photo: Caiaimage/Agnieszka Olek/Getty Images.

A market nicher can specialize along any of several market, customer, product, or marketing mix lines. For example, it can specialize in serving one type of *end user*, as when a law firm specializes in the criminal, civil, or business law markets. The nicher can specialize in serving a given *customer-size* group. Many nichers specialize in serving small and midsize customers who are neglected by the majors.

Some nichers focus on one or a few *specific customers*, selling their entire output to a single company, such as Walmart or General Motors. Still other nichers specialize by *geographic market*, selling only in a certain locality, region, or area of the world. For example, Vegemite is primarily sold and consumed in Australia. *Quality-price* nichers operate at the low or high end of the market. For example, Manolo Blahnik specializes in the high-quality, high-priced women's shoes. Finally, *service nichers* offer services not available from other firms. For example, LendingTree provides online lending and realty services, connecting homebuyers and sellers with national networks of mortgage lenders and realtors who compete for the customer's business. "When lenders compete," it proclaims, "you win."

Niching carries some major risks. For example, the market niche may dry up, or it might grow to the point that it attracts larger competitors. That is why many companies practice *multiple niching*. By developing two or more niches, a company increases its chances for survival. Even some large firms prefer a multiple niche strategy to serving the total market. For example, apparel maker VF Corporation markets more than 30 premium lifestyle brands in niche markets ranging from jeanswear, sportswear, and contemporary styles to outdoor gear and imagewear (workwear). For example, VF's Vans unit creates footwear, apparel, and accessories for skate-, surf-, and snowboarders. Its 7 for All Mankind brand offers premium denim and accessories sold in boutiques and high-end department stores. The North Face and Timberland brands offer top-of-the-line gear and apparel for outdoor enthusiasts. In contrast, the company's Red Kap, Bulwark, and Chef Designs workwear brands provide an array of uniforms and protective apparel for businesses and public agencies, whether it's outfitting a police force or a chef's crew. Together, these separate niche brands combine to make VF a $12.4-billion apparel powerhouse. No matter who you are, says the company, "We fit your life."[21]

Balancing Customer and Competitor Orientations

Whether a company is the market leader, challenger, follower, or nicher, it must watch its competitors closely and find the competitive marketing strategy that positions it most effectively. And it must continually adapt its strategies to the fast-changing competitive

● FIGURE | 18.3
Evolving Company Orientations

Market-centered companies understand both customers and competitors. They build profitable customer relationships by delivering more customer value than competitors do.

environment. This question now arises: Can the company spend *too* much time and energy tracking competitors, damaging its customer orientation? The answer is yes. A company can become so competitor centered that it loses its even more important focus on maintaining profitable customer relationships.

A **competitor-centered company** is one that spends most of its time tracking competitors' moves and market shares and trying to find strategies to counter them. This approach has some pluses and minuses. On the positive side, the company develops a fighter orientation, watches for weaknesses in its own position, and searches out competitors' weaknesses. On the negative side, the company becomes too reactive. Rather than carrying out its own customer relationship strategy, it bases its own moves on competitors' moves. As a result, it may end up simply matching or extending industry practices rather than seeking innovative new ways to create more value for customers.

A **customer-centered company**, by contrast, focuses more on customer developments in designing its strategies. Clearly, the customer-centered company is in a better position to identify new opportunities and set long-run strategies that make sense. By watching customer needs evolve, it can decide what customer groups and what emerging needs are the most important to serve. Then it can concentrate its resources on delivering superior value to target customers.

In practice, today's companies must be **market-centered companies**, watching both their customers and their competitors. But they must not let competitor watching blind them to customer focusing.

● **Figure 18.3** shows that companies might have any of four orientations. First, they might be product oriented, paying little attention to either customers or competitors. Next, they might be customer oriented, paying attention to customers. In the third orientation, when a company starts to pay attention to competitors, it becomes competitor oriented. Today, however, companies need to be market oriented, paying balanced attention to both customers and competitors. Rather than simply watching competitors and trying to beat them on current ways of doing business, they need to watch customers and find innovative ways to build profitable customer relationships by delivering more customer value than competitors do.

Competitor-centered company
A company whose moves are mainly based on competitors' actions and reactions.

Customer-centered company
A company that focuses on customer developments in designing its marketing strategies and delivering superior value to its target customers.

Market-centered company
A company that pays balanced attention to both customers and competitors in designing its marketing strategies.

18 Reviewing and Extending the Concepts

OBJECTIVES REVIEW AND KEY TERMS

Objectives Review

Today's companies face their toughest competition ever. Understanding customers is an important first step in developing strong customer relationships, but it's not enough. To gain competitive advantage, companies must use this understanding to design market offers that deliver more value than the offers of competitors seeking to win over the same customers. This chapter examines how firms analyze their competitors and design effective competitive marketing strategies.

OBJECTIVE 18-1 Discuss the need to understand competitors as well as customers through competitor analysis. (pp 518–525)

To prepare an effective marketing strategy, a company must consider its competitors as well as its customers. Building profitable customer relationships requires satisfying target consumer needs better than competitors do. A company must continuously analyze competitors and develop competitive marketing strategies that position it effectively against competitors and give it the strongest possible competitive advantage.

Competitor analysis first involves identifying the company's major competitors, using both an industry-based and a market-based analysis. The company then gathers information on competitors' objectives, strategies, strengths and weaknesses, and reaction patterns. With this information in hand, it can select competitors to attack or avoid. Competitive intelligence must be collected, interpreted, and distributed continuously. Company marketing managers should be able to obtain full and reliable information about any competitor affecting their decisions.

OBJECTIVE 18-2 Explain the fundamentals of competitive marketing strategies based on creating value for customers. *(pp 525–535)*

Which competitive marketing strategy makes the most sense depends on the company's industry and on whether it is the market leader, challenger, follower, or nicher. The market leader has to mount strategies to expand the total market, protect market share, and expand market share. A market challenger is a firm that tries aggressively to expand its market share by attacking the leader, other runner-up companies, or smaller firms in the industry. The challenger can select from a variety of direct or indirect attack strategies.

A market follower is a runner-up firm that chooses not to rock the boat, usually from fear that it stands to lose more than it might gain. But the follower is not without a strategy and seeks to use its particular skills to gain market growth. Some followers enjoy a higher rate of return than the leaders in their industry. A *market nicher* is a smaller firm that is unlikely to attract the attention of larger firms. Market nichers often become specialists in some end use, customer size category, specific customer group, geographic area, or service.

OBJECTIVE 18-3 Illustrate the need for balancing customer and competitor orientations in becoming a truly market-centered organization. *(pp 535–536)*

A competitive orientation is important in today's markets, but companies should not overdo their focus on competitors. Companies are more likely to be hurt by emerging consumer needs and new competitors than by existing competitors. Market-centered companies that balance customer and competitor considerations are practicing a true market orientation.

Key Terms

OBJECTIVE 18-1

Competitive advantage
  (p 518)
Competitor analysis (p 518)
Competitive marketing strategies
  (p 518)
Strategic group (p 521)

Benchmarking (p 522)
Customer value analysis
  (p 523)

OBJECTIVE 18-2

Market leader (p 530)
Market challenger (p 530)

Market follower (p 530)
Market nicher (p 530)

OBJECTIVE 18-3

Competitor-centered company (p 536)
Customer-centered company (p 536)
Market-centered company (p 536)

DISCUSSION AND CRITICAL THINKING

MyMarketingLab

Go to **mymktlab.com** to complete the problems marked with this icon ⭐.

Discussion Questions

18-1 Define competitive advantage. How do companies go about finding their competitive advantage? (AASCB: Communication)

⭐ **18-2** How does a company identify its competitors? What do marketing managers want to know about the companies identified as competitors? (AACSB: Communication; Reflective Thinking)

18-3 Describe the strategies market challengers can adopt and explain why challengers might have an advantage over market leaders. (AACSB: Communication)

⭐ **18-4** What is a market nicher? Discuss the strategies and risks associated with this competitive position. (AACSB: Communication)

18-5 Compare the evolving company orientations used to adapt to the fast-changing competitive environment. Is there one orientation that companies should be following? (AACSB: Communication; Reflective Thinking)

Critical Thinking Exercises

18-6 Form a small group and conduct a customer value analysis for your college or university. What are the strong and weak competitors? For the strong competitors, what are their vulnerabilities? (AACSB: Communication; Reflective Thinking)

18-7 Using the internet, find one company market nicher in each of three different industries. Identify the competitive strategy each one uses. (AACSB: Communication; Reflective Thinking)

⭐ **18-8** The chapter describes Apple, Redbox, and Keurig as examples of companies that have been successful with a Blue Ocean strategy. Find another example of a company that has successfully pursued a blue ocean strategy. Explain. (AACSB: Communication; Reflective Thinking)

APPLICATIONS AND CASES

Online, Mobile, and Social Media Marketing Social Logins

How many times have you left a website or app because of the hassle of setting up a login account or because you forgot your username or password for one you had already set up? If you are like the 90 percent of users bothered by having to log in, you probably just leave the site and never return. Social networks are helping with that problem by offering social logins on third-party sites and applications. With more than 1.6 billion monthly active users, 1.44 billion of whom are monthly mobile users, Facebook is the largest social network. The company is using that power to become even more valuable to both users and businesses. Facebook Login allows website visitors and app users to use their Facebook login credentials to log in to other sites and apps instead of establishing a separate login for each one. Google+, Twitter, LinkedIn, and other social networks also offer social login capabilities, but Facebook is the leader, powering more than half of all social logins online and more than 60 percent of mobile logins. This seems to be a winning arrangement for all parties—users conveniently log in to multiple sites with one username and password, third-party sites and apps gain access to Facebook users' demographic data, and Facebook gathers useful information on users' behavior to better sell advertising.

18-9 How is Facebook Login expanding the total demand for social networks? (AACSB: Communication; Reflective Thinking)

18-10 A major criticism of social logins is consumer privacy. How has Facebook addressed this issue? Do you think it will hurt the company's competitive advantage in this area? (AACSB: Communication; Reflective Thinking)

Marketing Ethics Creating Competitive Advantage … to What End?

In late September 2015, Volkswagen found itself in the midst of a firestorm. The company, which captures 70 percent of the U.S. diesel-powered passenger-car market, was caught cheating on diesel emissions tests. Over the past many years, Volkswagen had installed software on more than half a million diesel cars in the United States—and roughly 10.5 million more worldwide—that detected when the cars were undergoing emissions tests and triggered so-called "defeat devices" that temporarily switched operating modes and allowed them to pass the tests. VW diesel autos were found to actually be emitting up to 40 times the allowable levels of nitrogen oxide pollutants.

Volkswagen has long pitched its diesel cars as efficient, non-polluting vehicles. But in 2008, when U.S. rules on diesel exhaust became stricter, VW faced difficulties meeting the new standards and living up to its "clean diesel" advertising promises and image. So, under competitive pressures, it covertly installed the secret "defeat devices." When the scandal broke, Volkswagen's global sales plunged along with its reputation. The company halted sales of affected diesel models and suspended all of its "clean diesel" marketing and advertising. To mitigate the damage, Volkswagen created a "Customer Goodwill Package" in which it doled out $1,000 in cash and dealership purchases to VW diesel owners along with access to free 24-hour roadside assistance for three years. It also reached a more than $15 billion settlement with U.S. regulators to cover the costs of possible vehicle buybacks and other remedial actions. The full long-run harm to VW's reputation and market performance remains to be seen.

18-11 Is Volkswagen a competitor-centered company, customer-centered company, or market-centered company? Explain your answer. (AACSB: Communication, Reflective Thinking)

18-12 What competitive thinking moved Volkswagen, one of the world's major automakers, to cheat on emission standards rather than comply with them? How could Volkswagen have prevented this scandal, and what are the lessons for other firms? (AACSB: Ethical Reasoning, Communication)

Marketing by the Numbers Market Share

Bottled water is a hot industry with sales of $11.8 billion in the United States. Big players in this industry include Nestlé, PepsiCo, and Coca-Cola. Nestlé is the market leader with four brands in the top 10 leading brands. Nestlé's Pure Life brand was the top-selling brand with sales of $1.18 billion, but the company's other brands make up an additional $1.6 billion, giving the company total overall sales of almost $3 billion. Nestlé saw opportunity in this market and launched a new brand called Resource, targeted to affluent women. Resource is fortified with electrolytes and is promoted as "more than hydration, it's total electrolytenment." Nestlé is attempting to take market share away from Glaceau's Vitaminwater and Smartwater. If Resource attains just 3 percent market share, it will be in the top 10 selling brands.

18-13 Refer to Appendix 2, Marketing by the Numbers, and calculate Nestlé's Pure Life and the company's overall market share in the bottled water industry. (AACSB: Communication; Analytical Reasoning)

18-14 How much revenue does one market share point represent in this industry? Assuming total market sales remain the same, what sales must Resource attain to be in the top 10 selling brands? (AACSB: Communication; Reflective Thinking)

Video Case Umpqua Bank

The retail banking industry has become very competitive. And with a few powerhouses that dominate the market, how is a small bank to thrive? By differentiating itself through a competitive advantage that the big guys can't touch.

That's exactly what Umpqua has done. One step inside a branch of this Oregon-based community bank and it is immediately apparent that this is not your typical Christmas club savings account/free toaster bank. Umpqua has created a business model that has transformed banking from retail drudgery to a holistic experience. Umpqua has created an environment where people just love to hang out. It not only has its own music download service featuring local artists, it even has its own blend of coffee.

But under all these bells and whistles lies the core of what makes Umpqua so different: a rigorous service culture where every branch and each employee gets measured on how well they serve customers. That's why every customer feels like he or she gets the help and attention needed from employees.

After viewing the video featuring Umpqua Bank, answer the following questions about creating competitive advantage:

18-15 With what companies does Umpqua compete?

18-16 What is Umpqua's competitive advantage?

18-17 Do you think that Umpqua will be able to maintain this advantage in the long run? Why or why not?

Company Case YouTube: Google's Quest for Video Dominance

There's no doubt about it. Google—now part of holding company Alphabet—is an unquestioned success. With annual revenues of $71.5 billion last year, only 35 U.S. companies were bigger—and Google is younger than every one of them. But even its rapid rise in revenues doesn't capture the power and influence of this brash, young company. After all, Google powers a whopping 70 percent of all desktop internet searches, a statistic that balloons to 95 percent on mobile devices.

But when it comes to defining its competition, the picture isn't cut so clear for the undisputed sultan of search. Certainly, Microsoft (Bing) and Yahoo! are in Google's crosshairs when it comes to search. But when it comes to keeping an eye on competitors, Google is likely more concerned about Apple, Amazon, Facebook, and Samsung. In fact, not one of these companies makes a move that Google doesn't notice and evaluate.

How do such seemingly diverse companies end up competing so fiercely with one another? It turns out that these companies really aren't so different when it comes to their ultimate goal—to meet the digital needs of consumers everywhere, a need set that is rapidly evolving and tricky to define. But as consumers have turned more and more of their time and attention to the connected devices they hold in their hands, Google has realized that capturing the biggest possible share of "time spent" in the digital space is what it really seeks. And although Google and competitors Apple, Amazon, Facebook, Microsoft, and Samsung each started out focusing on specific product categories, the quest for online dominance has blurred those market borders and placed the companies in direct competition with each other.

Consider Google's portfolio of internet-oriented products—Gmail, Chrome, Google Maps, Google Earth, Google Drive, Google Docs, and Google Photos. Throw in Android, Google Wallet, Chromebooks, and Google+ and suddenly Google and its competitors lock horns in more ways than one. Expand even further to the "moonshot" projects that fall under Google parent Alphabet's umbrella—the Internet of Things (IoT), drones, robots, alternative energy production, and autonomous vehicles—and Google and its competitors become so intertwined that its hard to tease things apart.

Google knows that to be as competitive as possible, it isn't enough to diversify into various businesses and product lines. Rather than being disjointed pieces, every piece must fit neatly into a holistic pie. For Google, all those projects may center around internet search and organizing the world's information. But ultimately, Google wants a big piece of consumers' digital world. And perhaps nowhere is this more apparent than in Google's efforts to be the leading source of streaming video programming, with its YouTube unit at the heart of those efforts.

"I Want My TV!"

When it comes to how people carve up their days, working and sleeping occupy the most ticks of the clock. But according to one recent study, leisure activities take a strong third place. Americans average 5.3 hours each day of leisure time, including activities such as socializing, playing games, reading, recreation and exercise, and relaxing. But a whopping half of all leisure time is spent watching TV. Nowadays, that includes any and all video programing on any and all devices. And although traditional television is still king, the average person now consumes 70 minutes of online video each day, a number that is growing rapidly. Most of that viewing time is spent on mobile devices over traditional computers. In fact, video will account for 80 percent of all mobile traffic within the next few years.

The compelling new viewing outlets brought to us by mobile, on-demand, and digital technologies are part and parcel to the slow but inevitable fraying of traditional primetime lineups and cable TV bundles. All of this has sparked an intense battle to capture viewing audiences that have never before been more in play. Content that was once only consumed via long-standing broadcast and cable networks such as NBC, ABC, CBS, HBO, MTV, TNT, TBS, and ESPN is now being gobbled up through new venues.

The most dominant new player is Netflix. The company that once established itself as the leading distributor of rented DVDs by mail is now the leading source of streaming television and movie programming. More than 75 million paying Netflix subscribers in 190 countries have their eyes glued to 3.8 billion ad-free hours of streaming content every month. In the United States, Netflix commands more than one-third of all internet traffic on any given weeknight. And although most of its content originates from outside sources, Netflix is fast becoming a force as a producer of original content. In fact, with hit series such as *House of Cards, Orange Is The New Black, Jessica Jones*, and *The Unbreakable Kimmy Schmidt*, Netflix is winning Golden Globes and Emmys, not to mention adding millions of new subscribers to its massive user base each month. And with the soon-to-be-released talk show starring comedian Chelsea Handler, Netflix is making its first move into live television. With annual revenues of $6.7 billion and most of that being spent on content, Netflix is keeping television and cable network executives awake at night.

But Google is no shrinking violet when it comes to internet video. Through its Google Play media store, it rents and sells movies and TV programs à la iTunes. More important, its own YouTube unit is still far and away the leading source for streaming video with a whopping 77 percent share of all video site visits. YouTube has always generated revenue for Google, with advertising accounting for the vast majority of that income—a model that has set a standard for internet video. In addition, YouTube provides viewers with a second Google option to rent or purchase movies and TV programs as well as a selection of pay-per-view subscription channels. By itself, YouTube generated an estimated $9 billion in revenue for Google last year.

Making more money on internet video than even Netflix, you might think Google would be satisfied with its offerings. But Google has never been satisfied with the status quo. It knows that it must keep doing more if it wants to remain on top of the online video heap.

The Competition Intensifies

As online video explodes, Netflix is hardly Google's only concern. Other premium viewing sites such as Hulu and Crackle are also of concern. But perhaps even more pressing, every one of Google's formidable competitors poses a credible threat with its own online video portals. When it comes to subscription services, Amazon Prime is second only to Netflix with about one-third the number of paying subscribers. Hulu Plus is close behind. Apple invented the online media store with iTunes. And with more than a billion users, Apple certainly has a captive audience for its video portal through the most coveted devices in the world.

Facebook now boasts 8 billion video views a day and growing—a statistic that some suggest makes the world's largest social network YouTube's biggest threat. And with its Surface and Xbox interfaces, even Microsoft has a foot in the door for its Windows media store. Even Twitter recently signed a deal

with the NFL to live-stream Thursday night games. With Verizon, Yahoo!, and even Alibaba vying for the attention of eyeballs worldwide with their video content, the industry is red hot.

Lately, each of these players has poured money into building a video empire. And these days it's all about original content. In that arena, Netflix is leading the way and has completely shaken up the competitive landscape. Many Hollywood actors, directors, and producers have jumped ship to Netflix not only for the money but for the lure of artistic freedom that traditional channels simply cannot provide. "[Competitors are] in awe of the clout Netflix carries with both consumers and media companies," says Blair Westlake, former chairman of Universal Television and head of media and entertainment for Microsoft. And although they may not walk with Netflix's swagger, Amazon, Hulu, and Crackle each hold a hand at the table of original content.

At the most recent Sundance Film Festival, it was "invitation only" at the iTunes Lounge, the Apple-hosted revolving door of A-listers at the Imperial Hotel on Park City's main drag. Apple's presence at the high-profile festival was part of its current plan to develop a roster of exclusive content intended to rival the options on Netflix—content that will be available only through iTunes and apps on Apple devices.

Apple is pursuing a "two-lane" approach to content development. The first is a collection of short films, music videos, and documentaries built around associates of Dr. Dre and Jimmy Iovine—the founders of Beats Electronics, which Apple purchased for $3 billion and rebranded as Apple Music, its answer to Spotify. In a holistic fashion, this content not only will attract viewers but will serve to promote Apple Music. The second lane is to develop original TV-style programming in the vein of Netflix, Amazon, and Hulu. With a stockpile of cash that exceeds $200 billion, Apple has the funds to pave both lanes with gold.

While Apple is putting together deals behind closed doors, Facebook is pursuing its own path. Rumor has it that Facebook's Mark Zuckerberg is obsessed with video. In fact, Facebook is predicting the end of the written word on its platform. In five years' time, Facebook "will be definitely mobile, it will be probably all video," says Nicola Mendelsohn, head of Facebook for Europe, the Middle East, and Africa. "The best way to tell stories in this world, where so much information is coming at us, actually is video."

With its unparalleled reach, analytics, and targeting capabilities, Facebook has been very successful in getting studios to use the social network as a platform for trailers and sneak peeks. But Facebook is currently pushing hard with its money and other resources to move beyond promotional partnerships with Hollywood. It aims to be a serious option for destination viewing of original content. Enter Facebook Live, a live streaming platform designed to house just about anything. For example, Whoopi Goldberg provided a behind-the-scenes play-by-play of the most recent Academy Awards in a series of video diaries that received millions of hits. But that's just the tip of the iceberg. Facebook is in talks with everyone from TV producers, comedians, and musicians to athletes, chefs, politicians, and journalists to stream live shows, including exclusives.

Doing Video Its Own Way

So what is Google doing to surpass competitors in this very crowded field? You might think that it would turn Google Play into a Netflix or Hulu clone. Indeed, some analysts have suggested that Google simply purchase one of the proven video portals, pointing to the $75 billion pile of cash it's sitting on. But Google doesn't want to be Netflix. Rather, Google is out to fortify its position as the online video leader based on its own strengths—and that means YouTube. Last year, YouTube launched its own paid subscription service, Red. For $9.99 a month, viewers receive ad-free access to all YouTube content across all YouTube interfaces. Subscribers can save videos and playlists on devices to be viewed offline. There is even a "music only" setting for music videos, integrating with YouTube Music and Google Play Music to make Red a commercial-free streaming music service.

Although such features are nice, YouTube Red's biggest draw will likely be its recently launched Originals—original programming available exclusively to Red subscribers. But unlike Netflix, Amazon, and even Apple, YouTube is developing content with its own twist. First and foremost, it's capitalizing on the personalities made famous at home. There's *Scare PewDiePie*, a scripted reality horror show from the producers of *The Walking Dead* and starring YouTube's biggest celebrity, Felix Kjellberg. There's *A Trip to Unicorn Island*, a documentary focusing on Lilly "Superwoman" Singh. And there's *Fight of the Living Dead*, which puts YouTube talent in a fight to survive a zombie apocalypse.

But even as YouTube signs its own celebrities to star in top-quality programs, it doesn't have a lock on these stars. In a first-ever competitive move, Netflix recently signed YouTube sensation Miranda Sings to star in an original comedy series, *Haters Back Off!* Although YouTube has plenty of homegrown personalities to choose from, it must now add them to the list of possible competitive threats.

YouTube Red currently has 10 programs available. And with many more in the works, including more high-profile shows featuring high-profile industry talent, YouTube Originals is off and running. Offering very competitive compensation for personalities, directors, and producers, Hollywood insiders as well as Google's competitors have gotten the message—YouTube means business.

Questions for Discussion

18-18 Define YouTube in terms of competitive advantage.

18-19 Of all Google's competitors, which ones should it attack? Which ones should it avoid?

18-20 Which basic competitive strategy does Google follow?

18-21 How would you classify Google in terms of competitive position? Why?

18-22 Is Google a market-centered company? Support your answer.

Sources: Nicole LaPorte, "Apple, Facebook, Google, and Alibaba Take Hollywood," *Fast Company*, May, 2016, pp. 68–96; Sarah Mitroff, "Everything You Need to Know about YouTube Red," *Cnet*, February 17, 2016, www.cnet.com/how-to/youtube-red-details/; Cassie Werber, "Facebook Is Predicting the End of the Written Word," *Quartz*, June 14, 2016, www.qz.com/706461/facebook-is-predicting-the-end-of-the-written-word/; "Mobile Spearheads Digital Video Advertising's Growth," *eMarketer*, February 22, 2016, www.emarketer.com/Article/Mobile-Spearheads-Digital-Video-Advertisings-Growth/1013611; Leah Libresco, "Here's How Americans Spend Their Working, Relaxing, and Parenting Time," *FiveThirtyEight*, June 24, 2015, http://fivethirtyeight.com/data-lab/heres-how-americans-spend-their-working-relaxing-and-parenting-time/; Farhad Manjoo, "The Great Tech War of 2012," *Fast Company*, November, 2011, pp. 106–146; and www.youtube.com/red, accessed July 2016.

MyMarketingLab

Go to **mymktlab.com** for Auto-graded writing questions as well as the following Assisted-graded writing questions:

18-23 Explain the difference between a good and a bad competitor.

18-24 Discuss the similarities and differences between Michael Porter's competitive strategies and the Treacy and Wiersema "value disciplines." Which classification of competitive strategies has more appeal for marketers and why?

PART 1: Defining Marketing and the Marketing Process (Chapters 1–2)
PART 2: Understanding the Marketplace and Consumer Value (Chapters 3–6)
PART 3: Designing a Customer Value–Driven Strategy and Mix (Chapters 7–17)
PART 4: Extending Marketing (Chapters 18–20)

19

The Global Marketplace

You've now learned the fundamentals of how companies develop competitive marketing strategies to engage customers, create customer value, and build lasting customer relationships. In this chapter, we extend these fundamentals to global marketing. Although we've discussed global topics in each previous chapter—it's difficult to find an area of marketing that doesn't contain at least some international elements—here we'll focus on special considerations that companies face when they market their brands globally. Advances in communication, transportation, and digital technologies have made the world a much smaller place. Today,

almost every firm, large or small, faces international marketing issues. In this chapter, we will examine six major decisions marketers make in going global.

To start our exploration of global marketing, let's look at Scandinavian furniture and housewares retailer IKEA. IKEA operates successfully in 51 countries, engaging consumers across vastly different means, languages, and cultures. IKEA follows a highly standardized international operating model designed to create good-quality, functional furniture at low prices that everyday people can afford. However, IKEA has learned that, when it comes to global markets, one size rarely fits all.

IKEA: Just the Right Balance between Global Standardization and Local Adaptation

IKEA, the world's largest furniture retailer, is the quintessential global cult brand. Last year, more than 771 million shoppers flocked to the Scandinavian retailer's 368 huge stores in 51 countries, generating revenues of more than $37 billion. That's an average of about $100 million per store annually, more than double Walmart's average per-store sales. IKEA is big and getting bigger—its revenues have doubled during the past decade.

IKEA offers a classic model for how to do business in a global environment. Far more than just a big furniture merchant, IKEA has achieved global success by engaging consumers of all nationalities and cultures. From Beijing to Moscow to Middletown, Ohio, customers are drawn to the IKEA lifestyle, one built around trendy but simple and practical furniture at affordable prices. IKEA's mission worldwide is to "create a better everyday life for the many people … by offering a wide range of well-designed, functional home furnishing products at prices so low that as many people as possible will be able to afford them."

IKEA succeeds globally by striking just the right balance between global standardization and local market adaptation. No

> IKEA, the world's largest furniture retailer, is the quintessential global brand. Operating in more countries than Walmart, IKEA is a model for global standardization versus local adaptation in international markets.

matter where in the world you shop at IKEA, you'll find huge stores, the familiar blue-and-yellow brand logo and signage, large selections of contemporary Scandinavian-design furnishings, and affordable prices. At the same time, IKEA carefully adapts its merchandise assortments, store operations, and marketing to cater to the unique needs of customers in different global markets characterized by vastly different means, languages, and cultures.

Many aspects of IKEA's strategy are standard worldwide. For starters, all of its products are rooted in Swedish, contemporary design. Its classic, simple designs have a timeless, near-universal appeal. Low prices are another constant in IKEA's global formula. As a benchmark, every IKEA product is designed to sell for half the price of similar competing products. IKEA keeps its prices low through a relentless focus on cost cutting. Selling largely standardized products worldwide helps keep costs down. So does IKEA's space-saving "flat pack" approach—selling furniture in pieces to be assembled by customers at home.

IKEA's stores around the world share a standardized design. All are gigantic. At an average size of 300,000 square feet, the average IKEA store is 50 percent larger than an average Walmart

Supercenter. To offset such massive size, IKEA stores everywhere are divided into three main sections: *Showrooms* display furnishings in real-room settings, the *marketplace* houses small items, and the *warehouse* makes it easy for customers to pull their own furniture items in flat-pack boxes and cart them to checkout. At any IKEA in the world, parents can drop off their children in the IKEA Småland play area and feed the entire family in the snack bar or the three-meal-a-day restaurant, making it easy to hang around and shop for hours.

Although IKEA tries to standardize its operations as much as possible, however, it has learned that, in global marketing, one size rarely fits all. IKEA found this out the hard way in the early 1980s when it opened its first U.S. store in Philadelphia and stocked it by importing the same goods it sold in Europe. Americans weren't much impressed. For example, IKEA carried beds that were too small and too firm for American tastes. Sales suffered, and IKEA considered pulling out of the U.S. market altogether.

Instead, the company made a decision that would become the cornerstone for its expansions into all-new international markets—study the market intensely and adapt accordingly. "The more far away we go from our culture, the more we need to understand, learn, and adapt," says IKEA's head of research. Fueled by a better understanding of U.S. consumers, IKEA changed the composition of its mattresses and added king-size beds. After similar changes storewide, sales took off. The United States is now IKEA's second-largest market behind only Germany.

IKEA now routinely adjusts its product designs and assortments worldwide to meet the distinct needs and tastes of local consumers. For example, although IKEA stores in China carry many of the same items found in other parts of the world, they also heavy up on rice cookers and chopsticks. The Chinese love a good, hard mattress, so IKEA sells mostly firmer ones there. And because the average living space in China's crowded cities is much smaller than in Europe and the United States, Chinese IKEAs stock smaller appliances and products geared toward saving space and organizing a household.

But there are limits to how much IKEA can adapt product designs and assortments without increasing costs. Says one analyst, "The IKEA model, remember, is volume, volume, volume: It needs vast economies of scale to keep costs low, and that means creating one-size-fits-all solutions as often as possible." So instead of making wholesale product changes around the globe, IKEA often simply adapts its marketing and merchandising to show locals how IKEA's standard products fit with their lives and cultures. "IKEA has gotten awfully good at showing how the same product can mesh with different regional habitats," says the analyst.

For example, showrooms in Japan and the Netherlands may feature the same beds and cabinets, but the Japanese display

No matter where in the world you shop at IKEA, you'll find the huge and familiar blue-and-yellow stores and large selections of Scandinavian-design furnishings at affordable prices. At the same time, IKEA carefully adapts its merchandise and marketing to the unique needs of customers in specific global markets.
LIU JIN/Stringer/Getty Images

might show tatami mats while the Dutch room incorporates slanted ceilings. In the United States, those same beds will be covered with decorative pillows. Similarly, the heavily circulated IKEA catalog (more than 217 million printed each year) is customized to show standard IKEA products in localized settings. IKEA publishes 67 versions of the catalog in 32 languages, each one carefully prepared to reflect local tastes and preferences.

Beyond adapting designs, assortments, and merchandising, IKEA often adjusts its basic store operations to turn local cultural nuances into competitive advantages. For example, IKEA's Chinese stores are a big draw for up-and-coming Chinese consumers. But IKEA customers in China want a lot more from its stores then just affordable Scandinavian-designed furniture.

In Chinese, IKEA is known as Yi Jia. Translated, it means "comfortable home," a concept taken literally by the millions of consumers who visit one of IKEA's 20 huge Chinese stores each year. "Customers come on family outings, hop into display beds and nap, pose for snapshots with the décor, and hang out for hours to enjoy the air conditioning and free soda refills," notes one observer. On a typical Saturday afternoon, for example, display beds and other furniture in a huge Chinese IKEA store are occupied, with customers of all ages lounging or even fast asleep. One Chinese IKEA has even hosted several weddings.

Whereas this might be considered as unwanted loitering in the United States or other Western markets, IKEA managers in China encourage such behavior, figuring that familiarity with the store will result in later purchasing when shoppers' incomes eventually rise to match their aspirations. "Maybe if you've been visiting IKEA, eating meatballs, hot dogs, or ice cream for 10 years, then maybe you will consider IKEA when you get yourself a sofa," says the company's Asia-Pacific president.

OBJECTIVES OUTLINE

In fact, that seems to be the case. Thanks to such cultural understandings coupled with competitively low prices, China is now IKEA's fastest-growing market. Eight of the world's 10 biggest IKEA stores are in China. What do Chinese consumers think of Swedish meatballs? "They love them," says IKEA China's marketing director.[1]

IN THE PAST, U.S. COMPANIES paid little attention to international trade. If they could pick up some extra sales via exports, that was fine. But the big market was at home, and it teemed with opportunities. The home market was also much safer. Managers did not need to learn other languages, deal with strange and changing currencies, face political and legal uncertainties, or adapt their products to different customer needs and expectations. Today, however, the situation is much different. Organizations of all kinds, from Coca-Cola and Nike to Google, Facebook, and even the NBA, have gone global.

Author Comment | The rapidly changing global environment provides both opportunities and threats. It's difficult to find a marketer today that isn't affected in some way by global developments.

Global Marketing Today

The world is shrinking rapidly with the advent of faster digital communication, transportation, and financial flows. Products developed in one country— McDonald's hamburgers, Netflix video service, Samsung electronics, Zara fashions, Caterpillar construction equipment, German BMWs, Facebook social networking—have found enthusiastic acceptance in other countries. It would not be surprising to hear about a German businessman wearing an Italian suit meeting an English friend at a Japanese restaurant who later returns home to drink Russian vodka while watching *The Big Bang Theory* on TV and checking Facebook posts from friends around the world.

International trade has boomed over the past three decades. Since 1990, the number of multinational corporations in the world has more than doubled to more than 65,000. Some of these multinationals are true giants. In fact, of the largest 150 economies in the world, only 88 are countries. The remaining 62 are multinational corporations. Walmart, the world's largest company (based on a weighted average of sales, profits, assets, and market value), has annual revenues greater than the gross domestic product (GDP) of all but the world's 26 largest countries.[2] Despite a dip in world trade caused by the recent worldwide recession, the global trade of products and services last year was valued at $16.5 trillion, about 22 percent of GDP worldwide.[3]

● Many U.S. companies have long been successful at international marketing: Coca-Cola, McDonald's, Starbucks, Nike, GE, IBM, Apple, Google, Colgate, Caterpillar, Boeing, and dozens of other American firms have made the world their market. In the United States,

● **Many American companies have now made the world their market.**

Prakash Singh/AFP/Getty Images

non-American brands such as Toyota, Samsung, Nestlé, IKEA, Canon, and adidas have become household words. Other products and services that appear to be American are, in fact, produced or owned by foreign companies, such as Ben & Jerry's ice cream, Budweiser beer, Purina pet foods, 7-Eleven, GE and RCA televisions, Carnation milk, Universal Studios, and Motel 6. Michelin, the oh-so-French tire manufacturer, now does 39 percent of its business in the United States; J&J, the maker of quintessentially all-American products such as BAND-AIDs and Johnson's Baby Shampoo, does half of its business abroad. America's own Caterpillar belongs more to the wider world, with 62 percent of its sales coming from outside the United States. Once all-American McDonald's captures nearly two-thirds of its revenues in foreign markets. And with more than 3,500 products worldwide, American favorite Coca-Cola now lets consumers "taste the feeling" more than 1.9 billion times a day in more than 200 countries.[4]

But as global trade grows, global competition is also intensifying. Foreign firms are expanding aggressively into new international markets, and home markets are no longer as rich in opportunity. Few industries are currently safe from foreign competition. If companies delay taking steps toward internationalizing, they risk being shut out of growing markets in Western and Eastern Europe, China and the Pacific Rim, Russia, India, Brazil, and elsewhere. Firms that stay at home to play it safe might not only lose their chances to enter other markets but also risk losing their home markets. Domestic companies that never thought about foreign competitors suddenly find these competitors in their own backyards.

Ironically, although the need for companies to go abroad is greater today than in the past, so are the risks. Companies that go global may face highly unstable governments and currencies, restrictive government policies and regulations, and high trade barriers. The recently dampened global economic environment has also created big global challenges. In addition, corruption is an increasing problem; officials in several countries often award business not to the best bidder but to the highest briber.

A **global firm** is one that, by operating in more than one country, gains marketing, production, research and development (R&D), and financial advantages that are not available to purely domestic competitors. Because the global company sees the world as one market, it minimizes the importance of national boundaries and develops global brands. The global company raises capital, obtains materials and components, and manufactures and markets its goods wherever it can do the best job.

For example, U.S.-based Otis Elevator, the world's largest elevator maker, is headquartered in Farmington, Connecticut. However, it sells and maintains elevators and escalators in more than 200 countries and achieves more than 80 percent of its sales from outside the United States. It gets elevator door systems from France, small-geared parts from Spain, electronics from Germany, and special motor drives from Japan. It operates manufacturing facilities in the Americas, Europe, and Asia and engineering and test centers in the United States, Austria, Brazil, China, Czech Republic, France, Germany, India, Italy, Japan, Korea, and Spain. In turn, Otis Elevator is a wholly owned subsidiary of global commercial and aerospace giant United Technologies Corporation.[5] Many of today's global corporations—both large and small—have become truly borderless.

This does not mean, however, that every firm must operate in dozens of countries to succeed. Smaller firms can practice global niching. But the world is becoming smaller, and every company operating in a global industry—whether large or small—must assess and establish its place in world markets.

The rapid move toward globalization means that all companies will have to answer some basic questions: What market position should we try to establish in our country, in our economic region, and globally? Who will our global competitors be, and what are their

Global firm
A firm that, by operating in more than one country, gains R&D, production, marketing, and financial advantages in its costs and reputation that are not available to purely domestic competitors.

● FIGURE | 19.1

Major International Marketing Decisions

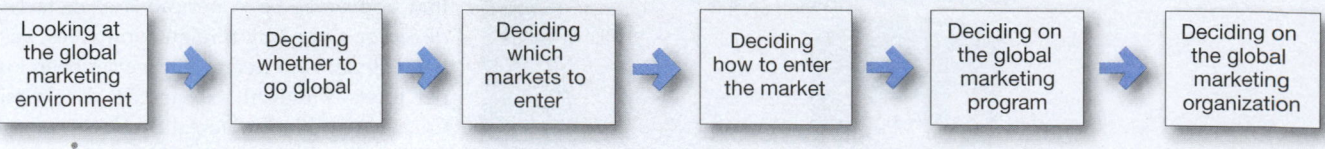

| Looking at the global marketing environment | → | Deciding whether to go global | → | Deciding which markets to enter | → | Deciding how to enter the market | → | Deciding on the global marketing program | → | Deciding on the global marketing organization |

It's a big and beautiful but threatening world out there for marketers! Most large American firms have made the world their market. For example, once all-American McDonald's now captures 66 percent of its sales from outside the United States.

strategies and resources? Where should we produce or source our products? What strategic alliances should we form with other firms around the world?

As shown in ● **Figure 19.1**, a company faces six major decisions in international marketing. We discuss each decision in detail in this chapter.

Author Comment | As if operating within a company's own borders wasn't difficult enough, going global adds many layers of complexities. For example, Coca-Cola markets its products in hundreds of countries around the globe. It must understand the varying trade, economic, cultural, and political environments in each market.

Elements of the Global Marketing Environment

Before deciding whether to operate internationally, a company must understand the international marketing environment. That environment has changed a great deal in recent decades, creating both new opportunities and new problems.

The International Trade System

U.S. companies looking abroad must start by understanding the international *trade system*. When selling to another country, a firm may face restrictions on trade between nations. Governments may charge *tariffs* or *duties*, taxes on certain imported products designed to raise revenue or protect domestic firms. Tariffs and duties are often used to force favorable trade behaviors from other nations.

For example, the European Union (EU) recently placed import duties on Chinese solar panels after determining that Chinese companies were selling the panels in EU countries at under-market prices. To retaliate, the very next day, the Chinese government placed duties on EU wine exports to China. The duties targeted the wines of Spain, France, and Italy but spared Germany, which had taken China's side in the solar panel dispute. The disputes were resolved when Chinese solar panel producers agreed to a minimum price in Europe and Europe agreed to help China develop its own wine industry in return for promoting European wines there.[6]

Countries may set *quotas*, limits on the amount of foreign imports that they will accept in certain product categories. The purpose of a quota is to conserve on foreign exchange and protect local industry and employment. Firms may also encounter *exchange controls*, which limit the amount of foreign exchange and the exchange rate against other currencies.

A company also may face *nontariff trade barriers*, such as biases against its bids, restrictive product standards, or excessive host-country regulations or enforcement. ● For example, Walmart recently scaled down its once-ambitious plans to expand into India's huge but fragmented retail market by opening hundreds of Walmart superstores there. Beyond difficult market conditions, such as spotty electricity and poor roads, India is notorious for throwing up nontariff obstacles to protect the nation's own predominately mom-and-pop retailers, which control 96 percent of India's $500 billion in retail sales. One such obstacle is a government regulation requiring foreign retailers in India to buy 30 percent of the merchandise they sell from local small businesses. Such a requirement is nearly impossible for

● **Nontariff trade barriers: Because of nontariff obstacles, Walmart recently scaled down its once-ambitious plans to expand in India's huge but fragmented retail market.**

Bloomberg via Getty Images

Walmart because small suppliers can't produce the quantities of goods needed by the giant retailer. Further, India's few large domestic retailers are not bound by the same rule, making it difficult for Walmart to compete profitably. Walmart is now looking for a domestic partner that can help it crack the mammoth Indian market.[7]

At the same time, certain other forces can *help* trade between nations. Examples include the World Trade Organization (WTO) and various regional free trade agreements.

● **The WTO promotes trade by reducing tariffs and other international trade barriers. It also imposes international trade sanctions and mediates global trade disputes.**

(left) Corbis Images; (right) Donald Stampfli/Associated Press

The World Trade Organization. The General Agreement on Tariffs and Trade (GATT), established in 1947 and modified in 1994, was designed to promote world trade by reducing tariffs and other international trade barriers. ● It established the World Trade Organization (WTO), which replaced GATT in 1995 and now oversees the original GATT provisions. WTO and GATT member nations (currently numbering 162) have met in eight rounds of negotiations to reassess trade barriers and establish new rules for international trade. The WTO also imposes international trade sanctions and mediates global trade disputes. Its actions have been productive. The first seven rounds of negotiations reduced the average worldwide tariffs on manufactured goods from 45 percent to just 5 percent.[8]

The most recently completed negotiations, dubbed the Uruguay Round, took a long seven years before concluding in 1994. The benefits of the Uruguay Round will be felt for many years, as the accord promoted long-term global trade growth, reduced the world's remaining merchandise tariffs by 30 percent, extended the WTO to cover trade in agriculture and a wide range of services, and toughened the international protection of copyrights, patents, trademarks, and other intellectual property. A new round of global WTO trade talks, the Doha Round, began in Doha, Qatar, in late 2001 and was set to conclude in 2005; however, the discussions still continued through 2016. The Doha round covers a gamut of trade issues from intellectual property to agriculture.[9]

Economic community

A group of nations organized to work toward common goals in the regulation of international trade.

Regional Free Trade Zones. Certain countries have formed *free trade zones* or **economic communities**. These are groups of nations organized to work toward common goals in the regulation of international trade. One such community is the *European Union (EU)*. Formed in 1957, the EU set out to create a single European market by reducing barriers to the free flow of products, services, finances, and labor among member countries and developing policies on trade with nonmember nations. Today, the EU represents one of the world's largest single markets. ● Currently, it has 28 member countries containing more than half a billion consumers and accounting for almost 16 percent of the world's imports and exports.[10] The EU offers tremendous trade opportunities for U.S. and other non-European firms.

Over the past decade and a half, 19 EU member nations have adopted the euro as a common currency. Widespread adoption of the euro decreased much of the currency risk associated with doing business in Europe, making member countries with previously weak currencies more attractive markets. However, the adoption of a common currency has also caused problems, as European economic powers such as Germany and France have had to step in recently to prop up weaker economies such as those of Greece, Portugal, and Cyprus. This recent ongoing "euro crisis" has led some analysts to predict the possible breakup of the euro zone as it is now set up.[11]

It is unlikely that the EU will ever go against 2,000 years of tradition and become the "United States of Europe." A community with more than two dozen different languages and cultures and a history of sometimes strained relationships will always have

● **Economic communities: The European Union represents one of the world's largest single markets. It contains more than half a billion consumers and accounts for almost 16 percent of the world's imports and exports.**

© European Union, 2016

difficulty coming together and acting as a single entity. For example, in a 2016 national referendum, the people of the United Kingdom voted to exit the European Union. Although actual British separation from the EU could take many forms and require years of negotiations, the "Brexit" vote sent aftershocks across Europe and the world, raising substantial concerns about the future of European economic and political unity. Still, with a combined annual GDP approaching $20 trillion, the EU remains a potent economic force.[12]

In 1994, the *North American Free Trade Agreement (NAFTA)* established a free trade zone among the United States, Mexico, and Canada. The agreement created a single market of 478 million people who produce and consume $20.75 trillion worth of goods and services annually. Over the past 20 years, NAFTA has eliminated trade barriers and investment restrictions among the three countries. Total trade among the NAFTA countries nearly tripled from $288 billion in 1993 to more than $1.1 trillion a year.[13]

Following the apparent success of NAFTA, in 2005 the Central American Free Trade Agreement (CAFTA-DR) established a free trade zone between the United States and Costa Rica, the Dominican Republic, El Salvador, Guatemala, Honduras, and Nicaragua. Other free trade areas have formed in Latin America and South America. For example, the Union of South American Nations (UNASUR), modeled after the EU, was formed in 2004 and formalized by a constitutional treaty in 2008. Consisting of 12 countries, UNASUR makes up the largest trading bloc after NAFTA and the EU, with a population of more than 418 million and a combined economy of more than $4.1 trillion. Similar to NAFTA and the EU, UNASUR aims to eliminate all tariffs between nations by 2019.[14]

Two other major world trade agreements are the Trans-Pacific Partnership (TPP) and the Transatlantic Trade and Investment Partnership (TTIP). The recently signed TPP promises to lower trade barrier and increase economic cooperation among twelve Pacific Rim countries: the United States, Australia, Brunei, Canada, Chile, Japan, Malaysia, Mexico, New Zealand, Peru, Singapore, and Vietnam. The companion TTIP agreement between the United States and the European Union is still under negotiation. These major trade agreements will have a significant and sometimes controversial economic and political impact. For example, the 12 TPP countries have a collective population of 800 million people, nearly double that of the EU, and account for 40 percent of all world trade.[15]

Each nation has unique features that must be understood. A nation's readiness for different products and services and its attractiveness as a market to foreign firms depend on its economic, political-legal, and cultural environments.

Economic Environment

The international marketer must study each country's economy. Two economic factors reflect the country's attractiveness as a market: its industrial structure and its income distribution.

The country's *industrial structure* shapes its product and service needs, income levels, and employment levels. For example, in *subsistence economies,* most people engage in simple agriculture, consume most of their output, and barter the rest for simple goods and services. These economies offer few market opportunities. Many African countries fall into this category. At the other extreme, *industrial economies* are major importers and exporters of manufactured goods and services. Their varied manufacturing activities and large middle classes make them rich markets for all sorts of goods. The United States, Japan, and the Western European countries are examples.

Emerging economies are those experiencing rapid economic growth and industrialization. Examples include the BRIC countries—Brazil, Russia, India, and China. Other hot emerging markets include Colombia, Indonesia, Vietnam, Egypt, Turkey, and South Africa (CIVETS). Industrialization typically creates a new rich class and a growing middle class, both demanding new types of goods and services. As more-developed markets stagnate and become increasingly competitive, many marketers are now targeting growth opportunities in emerging markets.

The second economic factor is the country's *income distribution.* Industrialized nations may have low-, medium-, and high-income households. In contrast, countries with subsistence economies consist mostly of households with very low family incomes. Still other countries may have households with either very low or very high incomes. Even poor or emerging economies may be attractive markets for all kinds of goods. In recent years, as the weakened global economy has slowed growth in both domestic and emerging markets, many companies are shifting their sights to include a new target—the so-called "bottom of the economic pyramid," the vast untapped market consisting of the world's poorest consumers (see Real Marketing 19.1).

These days, companies in a wide range of industries—from cars to computers to soft drinks—are increasingly targeting middle-income or low-income consumers in subsistence and emerging economies. For example, as soft drink sales growth has lost its fizz in North America and Europe, Coca-Cola has had to look elsewhere to meet its ambitious growth goals. So the company has set its sights on Africa, with its promising though challenging long-term growth opportunities. Many Western companies view Africa as an untamed final frontier, plagued by poverty, political instability, unreliable transportation, and shortages of fresh water and other essential resources. But Coca-Cola sees plenty of opportunity to justify the risks. The African continent has a growing population of more than 1.1 billion people, a just-emerging middle class, and $2.4 trillion of GDP and spending power. Six of the world's 10 fastest-growing markets are in Africa:[16]

Coca-Cola has operated in Africa since 1929 and holds a dominant 29 percent market share in Africa and the Middle East, compared with Pepsi's 15 percent share. However, there's still plenty of room for Coca-Cola to grow there. For example, annual per capita consumption of Coke and other soft drinks is about 13 times less in Africa than in North America. Still, marketing in Africa is very different from marketing in more developed regions. Beyond just marketing through traditional channels in larger African cities, Coca-Cola is now invading smaller communities with more grassroots tactics.

Small stores play a big role in helping Coca-Cola to grow in Africa. ● In countless poor neighborhoods across the continent, crowded streets are lined with shops painted Coke red, selling low-priced Coca-Cola products by the bottle out of Coke-provided, refrigerated coolers. Such shops are supplied by a rudimentary but effective network of Coca-Cola distributors, whose crews often deliver crates of Coke products by hand-pulled trolleys or even a crate at a time carried on their heads. Because of the poor roads crowded with traffic, moving drinks by hand is often the best method. The company's first rule is to get its products "cold and close." "If they don't have roads to move products long distances on trucks, we will use boats, canoes, or trolleys," says the president of Coca-Cola South Africa. For example, in Nigeria's Makako district—a maze of stilt houses on the Lagos lagoon—women crisscross the waterways in canoes selling Coca-Cola directly to residents.

● With sales stagnating in its mature markets, Coca-Cola is looking to emerging markets—such as Africa—to meet its ambitious growth goals. Its African distribution network is rudimentary but effective.

Getty Images

Political-Legal Environment

Nations differ greatly in their political-legal environments. In considering whether to do business in a given country, a company should consider factors such as the country's attitudes toward international buying, government bureaucracy, political stability, and monetary regulations.

Some nations are very receptive to foreign firms; others are less accommodating. For example, India has tended to bother foreign businesses with import quotas, currency restrictions, and other limitations that make operating there a challenge. In contrast, neighboring Asian countries such as Singapore, Vietnam, and Thailand court foreign investors and shower them with incentives and favorable operating conditions. Political and regulatory stability is another issue. For example, Russia is consumed by corruption and governmental red tape, which the government finds difficult to control. The country's recent geopolitical conflicts with Europe, the United States, and other countries have made doing business in Russia difficult and risky.[17]

Companies must also consider a country's monetary regulations. Sellers want to take their profits in a currency of value to them. Ideally, the buyer can pay in the seller's currency or in other world currencies. Short of this, sellers might accept a blocked currency—one whose removal from the country is restricted by the buyer's government—if

19.1 International Marketing: Targeting the Bottom of the Economic Pyramid

Many companies are now waking up to a shocking statistic. Of the more than 7 billion people on this planet, 4 billion of them (that's 57 percent) live in poverty. Known as the "bottom of the pyramid," the world's poor might not seem like a promising market. However, despite their paltry incomes, as a group, these consumers represent an eye-popping $5 trillion in annual purchasing power. Moreover, this vast segment is largely untapped. The world's poor often have little or no access to even the most basic products and services taken for granted by more affluent consumers. As the weakened global economy has flattened domestic markets and slowed the growth of emerging middle-class markets, companies are increasingly looking to the bottom of the pyramid for fresh growth opportunities.

But how can a company sell profitably to consumers with incomes below the poverty level? For starters, the *price* has got to be right. And in this case, says one analyst, "right" means "lower than you can imagine." With this in mind, many companies have made their products more affordable simply by offering smaller package sizes or lower-tech versions of current products. For example, in Nigeria, P&G sells a Gillette razor for 23 cents, a 1-ounce package of Ariel detergent for about 10 cents, and a 10-count pack of one-diaper-a-night Pampers for $2.30. Although there isn't much margin on products selling for pennies apiece, P&G is succeeding through massive volume.

Consider Pampers: Nigeria alone produces some 6 million newborns each year, almost 50 percent more than the United States, a country with twice the population. Nigeria's astounding birthrate creates a huge, untapped market for Pampers diapers, P&G's top-selling brand. However, the typical Nigerian mother spends only about 5,000 naira a month, about $30, on all household purchases. P&G's task is to make Pampers affordable to this mother and to convince her that Pampers are worth some of her scarce spending. To keep costs and prices low in markets like Nigeria, P&G invented an absorbent diaper with fewer features. Although much less expensive, the diaper still functions at a high level. When creating such affordable new products, says

an R&D manager at P&G, "Delight, don't dilute." That is, the diaper needs to be priced low, but it also has to do what other cheap diapers don't—keep a baby comfortable and dry for 12 hours.

Even with the right diaper at the right price, selling Pampers in Nigeria presents a challenge. In the West, babies typically go through numerous disposable diapers a day. In Nigeria, however, most babies are in cloth diapers. To make Pampers more acceptable and even more affordable for Nigerians, P&G markets the diapers as a one-a-day item. According to company ads, "One Pampers equals one dry night." The campaign tells mothers that keeping babies dry at night helps them to get a good night's sleep, which in turn helps them to grow and achieve. The message taps into a deep sentiment among Nigerians, unearthed by P&G researchers, that their children will have a better life than they do. Thus, thanks to affordable pricing, a product that meets customers' needs, and relevant positioning, Pampers sales are booming. In Nigeria, the name Pampers is now synonymous with diapers.

As P&G has learned, in most cases, selling profitably to the bottom of the pyramid

takes much more than just developing single-use packets and pennies-apiece pricing. It requires broad-based innovation that produces not just lower prices but also new products that give people in poverty more for their money, not less. As another example, consider how Indian appliance company Godrej & Boyce used customer-driven innovation to successfully tap the market for low-priced refrigerators in India:

Because of their high cost to both buy and operate, traditional compressor-driven refrigerators had penetrated only 18 percent of the Indian market. But rather than just produce a cheaper, stripped-down version of its higher-end refrigerators, Godrej assigned a team to study the needs of Indian consumers with poor or no refrigeration. The semi-urban and rural people the team observed typically earned 5,000 to 8,000 rupees (about $125 to $200) a month, lived in single-room dwellings with four or five family members, and changed residences frequently. Unable to afford conventional refrigerators, these consumers were making do with communal, usually second-hand ones. But even the shared fridges usually contained only a few items. Their users tended to shop daily and buy only small quantities of vegetables and

Selling to the world's poor: At only $69, Godrej's ChotuKool ("little cool") does a better job of meeting the needs of low-end Indian consumers at half the price of even the most basic conventional refrigerator.

Courtesy Godrej & Boyce Mfg. Co. Ltd.

milk. Moreover, electricity was unreliable, putting even the little food they wanted to keep cool at risk.

Godrej concluded that the low-end segment had little need for a conventional high-end refrigerator; it needed a fundamentally new product. So Godrej invented the ChotuKool ("little cool"), a candy red, top-opening, highly portable, dorm-size unit that has room for the few items users want to keep fresh for a day or two. Rather than a compressor and refrigerant, the miserly little unit uses a chip that cools when current is applied, and its top-opening design keeps cold air inside when the lid is opened. In all, the ChotuKool uses less than half the energy of a conventional refrigerator and can run on a battery during the power outages common in rural villages. The best part: At only $69, "little cool" does a better job of meeting the needs of low-end consumers

at half the price of even the most basic traditional refrigerator.

Thus, the bottom of the pyramid offers huge untapped opportunities to companies that can develop the right products at the right prices. And companies such as P&G are moving aggressively to capture these opportunities. P&G has set lofty goals for acquiring new customers, moving the company's emphasis from the developed West, where it

currently gets most of its revenue, to the developing economies of Asia and Africa.

But successfully tapping these new developing markets will require more than just shipping out cheaper versions of existing products. "Our innovation strategy is not just diluting the top-tier product for the lower-end consumer," says P&G's CEO. "You have to discretely innovate for every one of those consumers on that economic curve, and if you don't do that, you'll fail."

Sources: See Erik Simanis and Duncan Duke, "Profits at the Bottom of the Pyramid," *Harvard Business Review,* October 2014, pp. 87–93; Matthew J. Eyring, Mark W. Johnson, and Hari Nair, "New Business Models in Emerging Markets," *Harvard Business Review,* January–February 2011, pp. 89–95; Mya Frazier, "How P&G Brought the Diaper Revolution to China," *CBS News,* January 7, 2010, www.cbsnews.com/8301-505125_162-51379838/; David Holthaus, "Health Talk First, Then a Sales Pitch," April 17, 2011, *Cincinnati.com,* http://news.cincinnati.com/article/20110417/BIZ01/104170344/; "Godrej & Boyce Is Getting Sexier in a Hurry," *The Economic Times,* October 7, 2015, http://economictimes.indiatimes.com/magazines/brand-equity/godrej-boyce-is-getting-sexier-in-a-hurry/articleshow/49241727.cms; and "The State of Consumption Today," *Worldwatch Institute,* www.worldwatch.org/node/810, accessed October 2016.

they can buy other goods in that country that they need or can sell elsewhere for a needed currency. In addition to currency limits, a changing exchange rate also creates high risks for the seller.

Most international trade involves cash transactions. Yet many nations have too little hard currency to pay for their purchases from other countries. They may want to pay with other items instead of cash. *Barter* involves the direct exchange of goods or services. For example, Venezuela regularly barters oil, which it produces in surplus quantities, for food on the international market—rice from Guyana; coffee from El Salvador; cattle, sugar, coffee, meat, and more from Nicaragua; and beans and pasta from the Dominican Republic. Venezuela has even struck a deal to supply oil to Cuba in exchange for Cuban doctors and medical care for Venezuelans.[18]

Cultural Environment

Each country has its own folkways, norms, and taboos. When designing global marketing strategies, companies must understand how culture affects consumer reactions in each of its world markets. In turn, they must also understand how their strategies affect local cultures.

The Impact of Culture on Marketing Strategy. Sellers must understand the ways that consumers in different countries think about and use certain products before planning a marketing program. There are often surprises. For example, the average French man uses almost twice as many cosmetics and grooming aids as his wife. The Germans and the French eat more packaged, branded spaghetti than Italians do. Some 49 percent of Chinese eat on the way to work. Most American women let down their hair and take off makeup at bedtime, whereas 15 percent of Chinese women style their hair at bedtime and 11 percent put *on* makeup.[19]

Companies that violate cultural norms and differences can make some very expensive and embarrassing mistakes. Here are just two examples:[20]

Nike inadvertently offended Chinese officials when it ran an ad featuring LeBron James crushing a number of culturally revered Chinese figures in a kung fu–themed television ad. The Chinese government found that the ad violated regulations to uphold national dignity and respect the "motherland's culture" and yanked the multimillion-dollar campaign. With egg on its face, Nike released a formal apology.

Coca-Cola recently stumbled with a Christmas ad posted on Russia's most popular social media site showing a map of Russia decorated with Christmas trees, snowflakes, and wrapped Christmas presents and the message "Ring in the New Year Together with Coca-Cola." However, the map didn't at first include Crimea, which Russia annexed controversially from Ukraine in

2014. When the ad drew strong criticism from Russians, Coca-Cola quickly redrew the map to include the disputed territory, saying, "We apologize … the map is fixed." The new map, of course, set off a new flurry of protest in neighboring Ukraine, where lawmakers called for a boycott of Coke. Coca-Cola finally pulled the offending ad altogether.

Business norms and behaviors also vary from country to country. For example, American executives like to get right down to business and engage in fast and tough face-to-face bargaining. However, Japanese and other Asian businesspeople often find this behavior offensive. They prefer to start with polite conversation, and they rarely say no in face-to-face conversations. As another example, firm handshakes are a common and expected greeting in most Western countries; in some Middle Eastern countries, however, handshakes might be refused if offered. Microsoft founder Bill Gates once set off a flurry of international controversy when he shook the hand of South Korea's president with his right hand while keeping his left hand in his pocket, something that Koreans consider highly disrespectful. In some countries, when being entertained at a meal, not finishing all the food implies that it was somehow substandard. In other countries, in contrast, wolfing down every last bite might be taken as a mild insult, suggesting that the host didn't supply enough quantity.[21] American business executives need to understand these kinds of cultural nuances before conducting business in another country.

By the same token, companies that understand cultural nuances can use them to their advantage in global markets. For example, when British clothing retailer Marks & Spencer decided to open its first standalone lingerie and beauty store, to the surprise of many it bypassed Paris, London, and New York and instead chose Saudi Arabia. Operating in Saudi Arabia requires some significant but worthwhile cultural adjustments:[22]

The Saudi retail market is booming, and the country has a fast-growing and affluent consumer class. However, the conservative Islamic kingdom has no end of restrictive cultural and religious rules, especially when it involves retailing to women. In Saudi Arabia, women cover themselves in full-length black cloaks—called *abaya*—when they go out in public and must have a male chaperone, usually a relative. However, because they typically wear Western clothes at home or when traveling abroad, Western-style fashion stores are still very popular.

● When selling to Saudi women, Marks & Spencer must adhere to rigorously enforced religious and cultural strictures. For example, by government decree, its lingerie stores must employ an exclusively female sales staff. Because women's faces can't be shown and certain public dress is prohibited, Marks & Spencer uses tamer in-store marketing photos and video displays requiring separate photo shoots. Music is forbidden in Saudi malls and stores, so Marks & Spencer has eliminated the usual background compositions. Thanks to these and many other cultural adaptations, Saudi Arabia has become one of Marks & Spencer's highest-grossing emerging markets, well worth the additional costs of operating there. Marks & Spencer now has six lingerie and beauty stores in Saudi Arabia along with 16 full department stores. It has even gone so far as to use headless female mannequins to display its lingerie. "Unfortunately," says one Marks & Spencer marketer, "even the mannequins are not allowed to show faces."

● **Culture and marketing strategy: Mark & Spencer's stores in Saudi Arabia require significant but worthwhile adjustments to meet the Islamic kingdom's strict religious rules. Notice the headless female mannequin?**

© 2016 Marks and Spencer plc

Thus, understanding cultural traditions, preferences, and behaviors can help companies not only avoid embarrassing mistakes but also take advantage of cross-cultural opportunities.

The Impact of Marketing Strategy on Cultures. Whereas marketers worry about the impact of global cultures on their marketing strategies, others may worry about the impact of marketing strategies on global cultures. For example, social critics contend that large American multinationals, such as McDonald's, Coca-Cola, Starbucks, Nike, Google, Disney, and Facebook, aren't just globalizing their brands; they are Americanizing the world's cultures. Other elements of American culture have become pervasive worldwide. For instance, more people now study English in China than speak it in the United States. If you assemble businesspeople from Brazil, Germany, and China, they'll likely transact in

English. And the thing that binds the world's teens together in a kind of global community, notes one observer, "is American culture—the music, the Hollywood fare, the electronic games, Google, Facebook, American consumer brands. The ... rest of the world is becoming [evermore] like us—in ways good and bad."[23]

"Today, globalization often wears Mickey Mouse ears, eats Big Macs, drinks Coke or Pepsi, and does its computing with Windows," says Thomas Friedman in his book *The Lexus and the Olive Tree: Understanding Globalization*. "Some Chinese kids' first English word [is] Mickey," notes another writer.[24]

Critics worry that, under such "McDomination," countries around the globe are losing their individual cultural identities. Teens in Turkey watch MTV, connect with others globally through Facebook and Twitter, and ask their parents for more Westernized clothes and other symbols of American pop culture and values. Grandmothers in small European villas no longer spend each morning visiting local meat, bread, and produce markets to gather the ingredients for dinner. Instead, they now shop at Walmart. Women in Saudi Arabia see American films, question their societal roles, and shop at any of the country's growing number of Victoria's Secret boutiques. In China, most people never drank coffee before Starbucks entered the market. Now Chinese consumers rush to Starbucks stores because it symbolizes a new kind of lifestyle. Similarly, in China, where McDonald's operates more than 80 restaurants in Beijing alone, nearly half of all children identify the chain as a domestic brand.

Such concerns have sometimes led to a backlash against American globalization. Well-known U.S. brands have become the targets of boycotts and protests in some international markets. As symbols of American capitalism, companies such as Coca-Cola, McDonald's, Nike, and KFC have been singled out by protestors and governments in hot spots around the world, especially when anti-American sentiment peaks. For example, following Russia's annexation of Crimea and the resulting sanctions by the West, Russian authorities initiated a crackdown on McDonald's franchises (even though most were Russian-owned), forcing some to close for uncertain reasons. McDonald's flagship store in Moscow was shut down for several weeks by the Russian Food Safety Authority. And the three McDonald's in Crimea were permanently shuttered, with at least one becoming a nationalist chain outlet called Rusburger, serving "Czar Cheeseburgers" where Quarter Pounders once flowed.[25]

Despite such problems, defenders of globalization argue that concerns of Americanization and the potential damage to American brands are overblown. U.S. brands are doing very well internationally. In the most recent Millward Brown BrandZ brand value survey of global consumer brands, 19 of the top 25 global brands were American owned, including megabrands such as Google, Apple, IBM, Microsoft, McDonald's, Coca-Cola, GE, Amazon.com, and Walmart.[26]

Many iconic American brands are soaring globally. For example, most international markets covet American fast food. Consider KFC in Japan. On the day that KFC introduced its outrageous Double Down sandwich—bacon, melted cheese, and a "secret sauce" between two deep-fried chicken patties—in one of its restaurants in Japan, fans formed long lines and slept on the sidewalks outside to get a taste. "It was like the iPhone," says the CMO of KFC International, "people [were] crazy." The U.S. limited-time item has since become a runaway success worldwide, from Canada to Australia, the Philippines, and Malaysia. More broadly, KFC has become its own cultural institution in Japan. ● For instance, the brand has long been one of Japan's leading Christmas dining traditions, with the iconic Colonel Sanders standing in as a kind of Japanese Father Christmas:[27]

Japan's KFC Christmas tradition began more than 40 years ago when the company unleashed a "Kentucky for Christmas" advertising campaign in Japan to help the brand get off the ground. Now, eating Kentucky Fried Chicken has become one of the country's most popular holiday traditions. Each KFC store displays a life-size Colonel Sanders statue, adorned in a traditional fur-trimmed red suit and Santa hat. A month in advance, Japanese customers order their special Christmas meal—a special bucket of fried chicken with wine and cake for about

● American brands in other cultures: KFC has become one of Japan's leading Christmas dining traditions, with the iconic Colonel Sanders standing in as a kind of Japanese Father Christmas.

Anthea Freshwater

$40. Some 3.6 million Japanese households had a KFC Christmas feast last year. Those who don't preorder risk standing in lines that snake around the block or having to go without KFC's coveted blend of 11 herbs and spices altogether. Christmas Eve is KFC's most successful sales day of the year in Japan, and December monthly sales run as much as 10 times greater than sales in other months.

More fundamentally, the cultural exchange goes both ways: America gets as well as gives cultural influence. True, Hollywood dominates the global movie market, but British TV originated the programming that was Americanized into such hits as *House of Cards, Dancing with the Stars,* and *Hell's Kitchen*. Although Chinese and Russian youth are donning NBA superstar jerseys, the increasing popularity of soccer in America has deep international roots.

Even American childhood has been increasingly influenced by European and Asian cultural imports. Most kids know all about imports such as Hello Kitty, Pokemon, or any of a host of Nintendo or Sega game characters. And J. K. Rowling's so-very-British Harry Potter books shaped the thinking of a generation of American youngsters, not to mention the millions of American oldsters who fell under their spell as well. For the moment, English remains the dominant language of the internet, and having web and mobile access often means that third-world youth have greater exposure to American popular culture. Yet these same technologies let Eastern European students studying in the United States hear webcast news and music from Poland, Romania, or Belarus.

Thus, globalization is a two-way street. If globalization has Mickey Mouse ears, it is also talking on a Samsung smartphone, buying furniture at IKEA, driving a Toyota Camry, and watching a British-inspired show on a Panasonic OLED TV.

Deciding Whether to Go Global

Not all companies need to venture into international markets to survive. For example, most local businesses need to market well only in their local marketplaces. Operating domestically is easier and safer. Managers don't need to learn another country's language and laws. They don't have to deal with unstable currencies, face political and legal uncertainties, or redesign their products to suit different customer expectations. However, companies that operate in global industries, where their strategic positions in specific markets are affected strongly by their overall global positions, must compete on a regional or worldwide basis to succeed.

Any of several factors might draw a company into the international arena. For example, global competitors might attack the company's home market by offering better products or lower prices. The company might want to counterattack these competitors in their home markets to tie up their resources. The company's customers might be expanding abroad and require international servicing. Or, most likely, international markets might simply provide better opportunities for growth. For example, as noted previously, Coca-Cola has emphasized international growth in recent years to offset stagnant or declining U.S. soft drink sales. Today, non–North America markets account for 80 percent of Coca-Cola's unit case volume, and the company is making major pushes into 90 emerging markets, such as China, India, and the entire African continent.[28]

Before going abroad, the company must weigh several risks and answer many questions about its ability to operate globally. Can the company learn to understand the preferences and buyer behavior of consumers in other countries? Can it offer competitively attractive products? Will it be able to adapt to other countries' business cultures and deal effectively with foreign nationals? Do the company's managers have the necessary international experience? Has management considered the impact of regulations and the political environments of other countries?

Deciding Which Markets to Enter

Before going abroad, a company should try to define its international *marketing objectives and policies*. It should decide what *volume* of foreign sales it wants. Most companies start small when they go abroad. Some plan to stay small, seeing international sales as a small part of their business. Other companies have bigger plans, however, seeing international business as equal to—or even more important than—their domestic business.

The company also needs to choose in *how many* countries it wants to market. Companies must be careful not to spread themselves too thin or expand beyond their capabilities by operating in too many countries too soon. Next, the company needs to decide on the *types* of countries to enter. A country's attractiveness depends on the product, geographical factors, income and population, political climate, and other considerations. In recent years, many major new markets have emerged, offering both substantial opportunities and daunting challenges.

After listing possible international markets, the company must carefully evaluate each one. It must consider many factors. For example, Amazon's decision to expand into India seems like a no-brainer. The online merchant is already doing well in such global markets as Germany, Japan, and the United Kingdom, which combined with the United States produce 95 percent of Amazon's profits. India is now the world's fastest-growing economy, with a population of 1.25 billion people, four times the U.S. population and double Europe's. What's more, only one-quarter of India's population now has access to the internet and only a small proportion of Indians have ever shopped online, leaving explosive room for growth in online shopping.

However, as Amazon considers expanding into new markets such as India, it must ask some important questions. Can it compete effectively with local competitors? Can it master the varied cultural and buying differences of Indian consumers? Will it be able to meet environmental and regulatory hurdles in each country? Can it overcome some daunting infrastructure problems?

In entering India, Amazon faces many challenges. For example, it must confront two established local competitors there—Flipkart and Snapdeal—plus a slew of smaller Indian start-ups. Flipkart, by itself, currently captures 44 percent of India's e-commerce compared with Amazon's 15 percent. Amazon also faces a tangle of Indian regulations, including a law that forbids foreign companies from selling directly to Indians. Thus, rather than buying goods and reselling them as it does in the United States, Amazon in India will be only a platform for vendors, similar to its "fulfillment by Amazon" operations in the West.

Package delivery is another major obstacle. India is characterized by muddy, potholed rural roads or congested city streets with arcane address systems, and there are no reliable delivery services such as FedEx, UPS, or the postal service. To make speedy deliveries, Amazon has had to set up its own motorcycle delivery service, consisting of thousands of motorbike riders with large black backpacks who race around the country delivering packages. Still another concern is payment. Only 60 percent of Indians have bank accounts, and only a small fraction of those have credit cards. Most customers pay cash for home-delivered purchases or when they collect their packages from local shops across the country that serve as pick-up and payment points. ● The small local shops also serve as online ordering spots for the majority of Indian consumers who have no internet connections. Store owners guide customers through Amazon's site, write down their orders, and collect the cash when orders are picked up from the shop.

● Entering new global markets: Amazon's entry into India seems like a no-brainer. But it's also a very large and complex undertaking. The challenge is summed up by this slogan: "Transforming the way India sells, transforming the way India buys."
Mint/Getty Images

Thus, Amazon's decision to enter India is, in fact, a no-brainer. "The size of the opportunity is so large it will be measured in trillions, not billions—trillions of dollars, that is, not rupees," says Amazon's senior vice president for international retail. But it's also a very large and complex undertaking. A slogan posted on the wall in Amazon's Hyderabad warehouse sums up the challenge: "Transforming the way India sells, transforming the way India buys."[29]

Possible global markets should be ranked on several factors, including market size, market growth, the cost of doing business, competitive advantage, and risk level. The goal is to determine the potential of each market, using indicators such as those shown in ● Table 19.1. Then the marketer must decide which markets offer the greatest long-run return on investment.

Table 19.1 | Indicators of Market Potential

Demographic Characteristics	Sociocultural Factors
Education	Consumer lifestyles, beliefs, and values
Population size and growth	Business norms and approaches
Population age composition	Cultural and social norms
	Languages

Geographic Characteristics	Political and Legal Factors
Climate	National priorities
Country size	Political stability
Population density—urban, rural	Government attitudes toward global trade
Transportation structure and market accessibility	Government bureaucracy
	Monetary and trade regulations

Economic Factors

GDP size and growth
Income distribution
Industrial infrastructure
Natural resources
Financial and human resources

> **Author Comment** | A company has many options for entering an international market, from simply exporting its products to working jointly with foreign companies to setting up its own foreign-based operations.

Deciding How to Enter the Market

Once a company has decided to sell in a foreign country, it must determine the best mode of entry. Its choices are *exporting, joint venturing,* and *direct investment.* ● **Figure 19.2** shows the three market entry strategies along with the options each one offers. As the figure shows, each succeeding strategy involves more commitment and risk but also more control and potential profits.

Exporting

Exporting
Entering foreign markets by selling goods produced in the company's home country, often with little modification.

The simplest way to enter a foreign market is through **exporting**. The company may passively export its surpluses from time to time, or it may make an active commitment to expand exports to a particular market. In either case, the company produces all its goods in its home country. It may or may not modify them for the export market. Exporting involves the least change in the company's product lines, organization, investments, or mission.

Companies typically start with *indirect exporting,* working through independent international marketing intermediaries. Indirect exporting involves less investment because the firm does not require an overseas marketing organization or network. It also involves less risk. International marketing intermediaries bring know-how and services to the

● **FIGURE | 19.2**
Market Entry Strategies

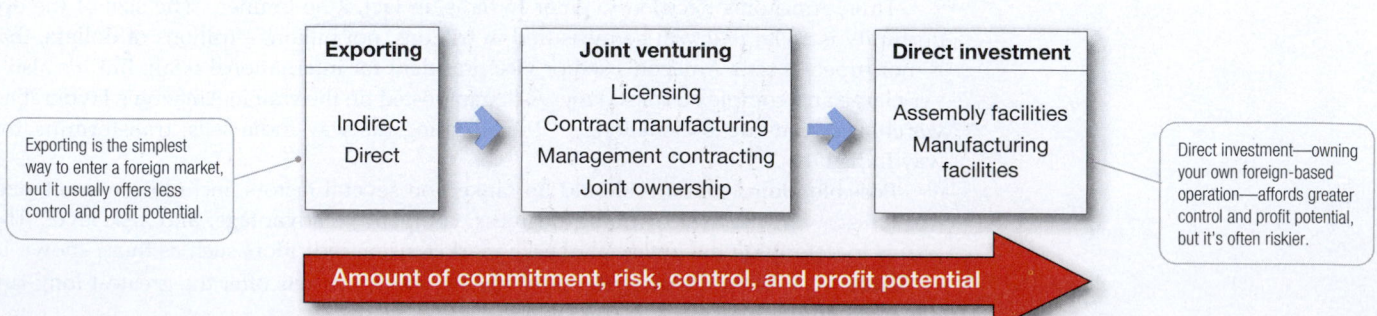

relationship, so the seller normally makes fewer mistakes. Sellers may eventually move into *direct exporting*, whereby they handle their own exports. The investment and risk are somewhat greater in this strategy, but so is the potential return.

Joint Venturing

Joint venturing
Entering foreign markets by joining with foreign companies to produce or market a product or service.

A second method of entering a foreign market is by **joint venturing**—joining with foreign companies to produce or market products or services. Joint venturing differs from exporting in that the company joins with a host country partner to sell or market abroad. It differs from direct investment in that an association is formed with someone in the foreign country. There are four types of joint ventures: *licensing, contract manufacturing, management contracting,* and *joint ownership.*

Licensing

Licensing
Entering foreign markets through developing an agreement with a licensee in the foreign market.

Licensing is a simple way for a manufacturer to enter international marketing. The company enters into an agreement with a licensee in the foreign market. For a fee or royalty payments, the licensee buys the right to use the company's manufacturing process, trademark, patent, trade secret, or other item of value. The company thus gains entry into a foreign market at little risk; at the same time, the licensee gains production expertise or a well-known product or name without having to start from scratch.

In Japan, Budweiser beer flows from Kirin breweries, and Mizkan produces Sunkist lemon juice, drinks, and dessert items. ● Tokyo Disney Resort is owned and operated by Oriental Land Company under license from The Walt Disney Company. The 45-year license gives Disney licensing fees plus a percentage of admissions and food and merchandise sales. And Coca-Cola markets internationally by licensing bottlers around the world and supplying them with the syrup needed to produce the product. Its global bottling partners range from the Coca-Cola Bottling Company of Saudi Arabia to beer maker SABMiller in Africa to Europe-based Coca-Cola Hellenic, which bottles and markets 136 Coca-Cola brands to 593 million people in 28 countries, from Italy and Greece to Nigeria and Russia.[30]

● International licensing: The Tokyo Disney Resort is owned and operated by Oriental Land Company (a Japanese development company) under license from The Walt Disney Company.
Yuriko Nakao/Reuters

Licensing has potential disadvantages, however. The firm has less control over the licensee than it would over its own operations. Furthermore, if the licensee is very successful, the firm has given up these profits, and if and when the contract ends, it may find it has created a competitor.

Contract Manufacturing

Contract manufacturing
A joint venture in which a company contracts with manufacturers in a foreign market to produce its product or provide its service.

Another option is **contract manufacturing**, in which the company makes agreements with manufacturers in the foreign market to produce its product or provide its service. For example, P&G serves 650 million consumers across India with the help of nine contract manufacturing sites there. And Volkswagen contracts with Russia's largest auto manufacturer, GAZ Group, to make Volkswagen Jettas for the Russian market as well as its Škoda (VW's Czech Republic subsidiary) Octavia and Yeti models sold there.[31] The drawbacks of contract manufacturing are decreased control over the manufacturing process and loss of potential profits on manufacturing. The benefits are the chance to start faster with less risk and the later opportunity either to form a partnership with or buy out the local manufacturer. Contract manufacturing can also reduce plant investment, transportation, and tariff costs while at the same time helping to meet the host country's local manufacturing requirements.

Management Contracting

Management contracting
A joint venture in which the domestic firm supplies the management know-how to a foreign company that supplies the capital; the domestic firm exports management services rather than products.

Under **management contracting**, the domestic firm provides the management know-how to a foreign company that supplies the capital. In other words, the domestic firm exports management services rather than products. Hilton uses this arrangement in managing hotels around the world. For example, the hotel chain operates DoubleTree by Hilton hotels in countries ranging from the UK and Italy to Peru and Costa Rica to China, Russia, and Tanzania. The properties are locally owned, but Hilton manages the hotels with its world-renowned hospitality expertise.[32]

Management contracting is a low-risk method of getting into a foreign market, and it yields income from the beginning. The arrangement is even more attractive if the contracting firm has an option to buy some share in the managed company later on. The arrangement is not sensible, however, if the company can put its scarce management talent to better uses or if it can make greater profits by undertaking the whole venture. Management contracting also prevents the company from setting up its own operations for a period of time.

Joint Ownership

Joint ownership

A cooperative venture in which a company creates a local business with investors in a foreign market who share ownership and control.

Joint ownership ventures consist of one company joining forces with foreign investors to create a local business in which they share possession and control. A company may buy an interest in a local firm, or the two parties may form a new business venture. Joint ownership may be needed for economic or political reasons. For example, the firm may lack the financial, physical, or managerial resources to undertake the venture alone. Alternatively, a foreign government may require joint ownership as a condition for entry. Disney's Hong Kong Disneyland and Shanghai Disneyland are both joint ownership ventures with the Chinese government-owned Shanghai Shendi Group. Disney owns 43 percent of the Shanghai resort; the Shanghai Shendi Group owns 57 percent.[33]

● Joint ownership and direct investment: To increase its understanding and influence in China's huge mobile device market, Intel has invested heavily there in joint ownership ventures and its own manufacturing facilities.
ICHPL Imaginechina

Often, companies form joint ownership ventures to merge their complementary strengths in developing a global marketing opportunity. ● For example, to increase its presence and local influence in China's mobile phone and tablets markets, chipmaker Intel recently paid $1.5 billion for 20 percent ownership in China's state-run Tsinghua Unigroup, which controls two domestic mobile chipmakers. The joint ownership investment will help Intel to better understand Chinese consumers. It may also help to earn more favorable treatment from Chinese regulators. So far, Intel has gone untouched by China's recent crackdown on foreign technology companies such as competitor Qualcomm and software makers Microsoft and Symantec.[34]

Joint ownership has certain drawbacks, however. The partners may disagree over investment, marketing, or other policies. Whereas many U.S. firms like to reinvest earnings for growth, local firms often prefer to take out these earnings; whereas U.S. firms emphasize the role of marketing, local investors may rely on selling.

Direct Investment

Direct investment

Entering a foreign market by developing foreign-based assembly or manufacturing facilities.

The biggest involvement in a foreign market comes through **direct investment**—the development of foreign-based assembly or manufacturing facilities. For example, in addition to joint ownership ventures in China, Intel has also made substantial investments in its own manufacturing and research facilities there. It recently spent $1.6 billion upgrading its decade-old chip factory in the central Chinese city of Chengdu and another $2.5 billion to build a shiny new fabrication plant in Dalian, a port city in China's northeast. "China is our fastest-growing major market," says Intel's CEO, "and we believe it's critical that we invest in markets that will provide for future growth to better serve our customers." [35]

If a company has gained experience in exporting and if the foreign market is large enough, foreign production facilities offer many advantages. The firm may have lower costs in the form of cheaper labor or raw materials, foreign government investment incentives, and freight savings. The firm may also improve its image in the host country because it creates jobs. Generally, a firm develops a deeper relationship with the government, customers, local suppliers, and distributors, allowing it to adapt its products to the local market better. Finally, the firm keeps full control over the investment and therefore can develop manufacturing and marketing policies that serve its long-term international objectives.

The main disadvantage of direct investment is that the firm faces many risks, such as restricted or devalued currencies, falling markets, or government changes. In some cases, a firm has no choice but to accept these risks if it wants to operate in the host country.

Author | The major global marketing
Comment | decision usually boils down
to this: How much, if at all, should a
company adapt its marketing strategy
and programs to local markets? How
might the answer differ for Boeing
versus McDonald's?

Standardized global marketing
A global marketing strategy that basically
uses the same marketing strategy and
mix in all of the company's international
markets.

Adapted global marketing
A global marketing approach that
adjusts the marketing strategy and mix
elements to each international target
market, which creates more costs but
hopefully produces a larger market share
and return.

Deciding on the Global Marketing Program

Companies that operate in one or more foreign markets must decide how much, if at all,
to adapt their marketing strategies and programs to local conditions. At one extreme are
global companies that use **standardized global marketing**, essentially using the same
marketing strategy approaches and marketing mix worldwide. At the other extreme is
adapted global marketing. In this case, the producer adjusts the marketing strategy
and mix elements to each target market, resulting in more costs but hopefully producing a
larger market share and return.

The question of whether to adapt or standardize the marketing strategy and program
has been much debated over the years. On the one hand, some global marketers believe
that technology is making the world a smaller place, and consumer needs around the
world are becoming more similar. This paves the way for global brands and standardized
global marketing. Global branding and standardization, in turn, result in greater brand
power and reduced costs from economies of scale.

On the other hand, the marketing concept holds that marketing programs will be more
engaging if tailored to the unique needs of each targeted customer group. If this concept
applies within a country, it should apply even more across international markets. Despite
global convergence, consumers in different countries still have widely varied cultural
backgrounds. They still differ significantly in their needs and wants, spending power,
product preferences, and shopping patterns. Because these differences are hard to change,
most marketers today adapt their products, prices, channels, and promotions to fit consumer desires in each country.

However, global standardization is not an all-or-nothing proposition. It's a matter of degree. Most international marketers suggest that companies should "think globally but act locally." They should seek a balance between standardization and adaptation, leveraging global
brand recognition but adapting their marketing, products, and operations to specific markets.

● Consider L'Oréal, the world's biggest cosmetics
maker. L'Oréal and its brands are truly global in scope and appeal. The company's well-known brands originated in a half-
dozen or more different cultures, including French (L'Oréal
Paris, Garnier, Lancôme), American (Maybelline, Kiehl's,
SoftSheen-Carson, Ralph Lauren, Urban Decay, Clarisonic,
Redken), British (The Body Shop), Italian (Giorgio Armani),
and Japanese (Shu Uemura). But the company's outstanding
international success comes from achieving a global–local balance, one that adapts and differentiates L'Oréal's well-known
brands to meet local needs while also integrating them across
world markets to optimize their global impact:[36]

● Global–local balance: Cosmetics and beauty care giant L'Oréal
balances local brand responsiveness and global brand impact, making
it "The United Nations of Beauty."

Marc Piasecki/Stringer/Getty images

L'Oréal digs deep to understand what beauty means to consumers in different parts of the world, with research insights
gained through everything from in-home visits to observations made in "bathroom laboratories" equipped with high-
tech gadgetry. How many minutes does a Chinese woman
devote to her morning beauty routine? How do people wash
their hair in Bangkok? How many brush strokes does a
Japanese woman or a French woman use to apply mascara?
L'Oréal then uses such detailed insights to create products
and positioning for brands in local markets. For example,
more than 260 scientists work in L'Oréal's Shanghai research center, tailoring products ranging
from lipstick to herbal cleaners to cucumber toners for Chinese tastes.

L'Oréal also adapts brand positioning and marketing to international needs and expectations. For example, more than 20 years ago, the company bought stodgy American makeup
producer Maybelline. To reinvigorate and globalize the brand, it moved the unit's headquarters
from Tennessee to New York City and added "New York" to the label. The resulting urban,
street-smart, Big Apple image played well with the midprice positioning of the workaday
makeup brand globally. The makeover soon earned Maybelline a 20 percent market share in its
category in Western Europe. The young urban positioning also hit the mark in Asia, where few
women realized that the trendy "New York" Maybelline brand belonged to a French cosmetics
giant. L'Oréal's CEO sums up the company's global approach this way: "We have global brands,
but we need to adapt them to local needs." When a former CEO once addressed a UNESCO conference, nobody batted an eyelid when he described L'Oréal as "The United Nations of Beauty."

19.2   7-Eleven: Making Life a Little Easier for People around the Globe

Americans love convenience stores. There's one just around the corner, and they're open long hours, seven days a week. Whether it's big chains like 7-Eleven and Circle K or more-local favorites like Illinois-based Moto-Mart, Nebraska's Bucky's, or Minnesota's own Pump 'N Munch, convenience stores have become an American mainstay for buying snacks, gas, or a few fill-in items between major grocery store trips. It's hard to imagine a convenience store being anything else.

But as it turns out, the convenience store concept doesn't translate in a standard way across international borders. Just ask 7-Eleven, a chain that's sweeping the planet. 7-Eleven is America's largest convenience store chain, with more than 10,000 U.S. stores in 34 states. But it's also the world's biggest convenience chain, with more than 56,000 stores in 16 countries generating nearly $85 billion in annual worldwide sales. 7-Eleven's global success results from carefully adapting its overall convenience format to unique market-by-market needs.

7-Eleven began in 1927 when "Uncle Johnny" Jefferson Green started selling milk, bread, and eggs from the dock of the Southland Ice Company where he worked, often on Sundays and evenings when regular grocery stores were closed. Within 10 years, Southland Ice Company had opened 60 such outlets selling basic staples—everything from canned goods to cold watermelon. As the chain grew, the convenience store concept took root—small stores in convenient locations, a limited line of high-demand products, speedy transactions, and friendly service.

In 1946, the fast-growing chain boldly established longer store hours—you guessed it, 7 a.m. to 11 p.m.—a practice unheard of at the time. And to cement its convenience positioning, it changed its name to 7-Eleven. To support its breakneck expansion, 7-Eleven also adopted a franchise model by which franchisees shared some of the financial and operational burdens of growth. In return, 7-Eleven granted franchisees lots of flexibility in catering to local tastes in their stores. The company calls this "retailer initiative" and considers it a key competitive advantage. Catering to local tastes would later become the cornerstone of 7-Eleven's international expansion.

In 1969, 7-Eleven became the first convenience chain to go global, first in Canada, then Mexico, and soon Japan and other Asian markets. In each global market, the chain has retained its key strategy elements—the small-store format, convenience positioning, and global brand identity—you'll see the familiar 7-Eleven logo and orange, red, white, and green stripes on every 7-Eleven store anywhere in the world. At first glance, a 7-Eleven in Tokyo looks pretty like one in Teaneck, New Jersey. But true to its "retailer initiative" philosophy, 7-Eleven skillfully adapts its operations in each global market to match widely differing local definitions of just what "convenience" means.

Consider Japan, one of 7-Eleven's first international ventures. 7-Elevens are everywhere in Japan, more the 17,000 of them—2,300 in Tokyo alone. Japan is now by far the company's largest market. Once you get past the familiar signage on the outside of a Japanese 7-Eleven, you'll find some pretty stark contrasts on the inside. More than just a place to grab a loaf of bread or a Slurpee, Big Gulp, or Big Bite, 7-Eleven in Japan has become the country's most popular eatery.

Around mealtime, the aisles at every Japanese 7-Eleven are packed with long lines of patrons who are treated to some of the finest prepared foods in the world. Typical offerings include salmon on rice with butter and soy sauce, hashed beef doria in a red wine demi-glace, and ground chicken with ginger and a side of spinach coleslaw. Fresh sushi abounds, and the ongiri (rice balls with seaweed) is wrapped in a way that keeps the seaweed crispy and the rice moist. 7-Eleven in Japan also offers a wide selection of beverages, including soft drinks, beer, sake, Champagne, single-malt scotch, wine, and more than 20 varieties of iced coffee.

This is not your typical American 7-Eleven. Stores receive several food deliveries each day, keeping shelves well stocked with fresh goods and ensuring that everything is locally made. Food is served in open display cases in a manner that's more Trader Joe's than convenience store. Japanese customers can even order food and groceries online and have them delivered at work or home. The chain also meets other customer service needs. At 7-Eleven, customers can pay their phone or utility bills, pick up their mail and parcel deliveries, and even buy baseball tickets from the copy machine.

For 7-Eleven, Japan now represents far more than just a booming international market. Since the early 1990s, Japan has become 7-Eleven's home market. When Dallas-based 7-Eleven encountered financial difficulties in 1991, its own highly successful

● **Global–local balance: At first glance, a 7-Eleven in Tokyo looks pretty much like one in Teaneck, New Jersey. However, 7-Eleven skillfully adapts its operations in each global market to match widely differing local definitions of just what "convenience" means.**

Rodrigo Reyes Marin/AFLO/Alamy Live News

Japanese subsidiary bailed it out, buying a majority stake. In 2005, 7-Eleven Japan created Tokyo-based Seven & I Holdings, which acquired the remaining shares of 7-Eleven. Then, in a case of the student becoming the teacher, the new parent corporation applied its well-honed "retailer initiative" skills to strengthen the U.S. division.

Wherever it operates, 7-Eleven seeks to become a part of the local culture. Nowhere is that more apparent than in Indonesia, one of 7-Eleven's newest markets. On a typical Saturday night, thousands of young Indonesians gather at one of the country's 200 7-Eleven's to sip coffee or beer at outdoor café tables, listen to live music, and engage in their newest passion—the internet. Sounds more like Starbucks? That's no accident. As Seven & I Holdings analyzed the Indonesian market, it learned that hanging out and doing nothing—something the locals refer to as "nongkrong"—is a favorite pastime. People gather at street markets, roadside food stalls, and Western fast-food outlets simply to pass the time and share stories. However, when 7-Eleven entered Indonesia, such hangouts were in short supply and few hangouts provided wireless connectivity. So 7-Eleven Indonesia adopted the Starbucks-like concept of a "third place"—somewhere to go that's away from home and work.

7-Eleven Indonesia still offers basic convenience store products, such as inexpensive readymade food, snacks, and a variety of popular beverages. And its 24-hour operations are perfect for an Indonesian culture not bound by time. But to appeal more strongly to plugged-in 18- to 35-year-old customers, 7-Eleven Indonesia also provides hassle-free parking (a premium convenience in the traffic-choked island nation), a venue for local bands, air-conditioning, free wireless connectivity, and lots and lots of space to hang out. More than a no-frills store where customers can grab snacks and everyday products, 7-Eleven Indonesia has become a trendy place where young people spend time, surf the internet, and meet friends.

Thus, 7-Eleven's fine-tuned global marketing strategy has made it the world's largest convenience store chain. Wherever 7-Eleven operates, its overall brand identity and convenience positioning remain constant: "At 7-Eleven, our purpose and mission is to make life a little easier for our guests," says the company, by "giving customers what they want, when and where they want it." But 7-Eleven knows that those whats, whens, and wheres can shift dramatically from market to market. The real secret is to weave the global 7-Eleven strategy into the fabric of each local culture.

Sources: See Marleen Dieleman, Ishtiaq Mahmood, and Peter Darmawan, "7-Eleven Indonesia Innovating in Emerging Markets," Ivey Publishing, September 15, 2015, www.iveycases.com/ProductView.aspx?id=73622; Taryn Stenvei, "What 7-Elevens in Tokyo Taught Me about Japan," *AWOL,* September 11, 2014, http://awol.com.au/what-7-elevens-in-tokyo-taught-me-about-japan/98; Justin Moyer, "In Honor of 7/11: How Japan Slurped Up 7-Eleven," *Washington Post,* July 11, 2014, www.washingtonpost.com/news/morning-mix/wp/2014/07/11/in-honor-of-711-how-japan-slurped-up-7-eleven/; Margot Huber, "Hangout Haven," *Business Today,* May 26, 2013, http://businesstoday.intoday.in/story/london-business-school-case-study-on-7-eleven/1/194769.html; George Martin Sirait and Michele Ford, "Revolutionizing Retail," *Inside Indonesia,* April–June 2014, www.insideindonesia.org/revolutionising-retail; and http://corp.7-eleven.com/corp/7-eleven-profile and http://franchise.7-eleven.com/franchise/our-iconic-brand, accessed October 2016.

Collectively, local brands still account for the overwhelming majority of consumer purchases. Most consumers, wherever they live, lead very local lives. So a global brand must engage consumers at a local level, respecting the culture and becoming a part of it. For example, 7-Eleven has become the world's largest convenience store chain by skillfully adapting its operations in each global market to match widely differing local definitions of just what "convenience" means (see Real Marketing 19.2).

Product

Five strategies are used for adapting product and marketing communication strategies to a global market (see ● Figure 19.3).[37] We first discuss the three product strategies and then turn to the two communication strategies.

Straight product extension
Marketing a product in a foreign market without making any changes to the product.

Straight product extension means marketing a product in a foreign market without making significant changes to the product. Top management tells its marketing people, "Take the product as is and find customers for it." The first step, however, should be to find out whether foreign consumers use that product and what form they prefer.

Straight extension has been successful in some cases and disastrous in others. Apple iPads, Gillette razors, and Black & Decker tools are all sold successfully in about the same form around the world. But when General Foods introduced its standard powdered JELL-O in the British market, it discovered that British consumers prefer a solid wafer or

● FIGURE | 19.3
Five Global Product and
Communications Strategies

The real question buried in this figure is this: How much should a company standardize or adapt its products and marketing across global markets?

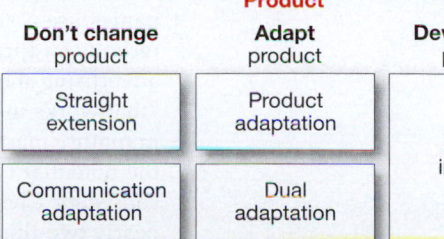

		Product	
	Don't change product	**Adapt** product	**Develop new** product
Don't change communications	Straight extension	Product adaptation	Product invention
Adapt communications	Communication adaptation	Dual adaptation	

● **Product adaptation: In India, Dunkin' Donuts serves up a full selection of India-inspired doughnuts. But more, the company has adjusted its full menu, operations, and even its name—Dunkin' Donuts & More—to suit the local culture.**

Bloomberg via Getty Images

Product adaptation

Adapting a product to meet local conditions or wants in foreign markets.

Product invention

Creating new products or services for foreign markets.

cake form. Likewise, Philips began to make a profit in Japan only after it reduced the size of its coffeemakers to fit into smaller Japanese kitchens and its shavers to fit smaller Japanese hands. And Panasonic's refrigerator sales in China surged 10-fold in a single year after it shaved the width of its appliances by 15 percent to fit smaller Chinese kitchens.[38] Straight extension is tempting because it involves no additional product development costs, manufacturing changes, or new promotion. But it can be costly in the long run if products fail to satisfy consumers in specific global markets.

Product adaptation involves changing the product to meet local requirements, conditions, or wants. For example, in the United States, Dunkin' Donuts sells good old glazed, powdered sugar, jelly, cream-filled, and chocolate-covered doughnuts to on-the-go customers in the morning. In South Korea, however, you'll find an olive oil and tapioca starch donut called a Chewisty. In China, Dunkin' serves doughnuts covered in mango pudding or green tea; in Russia, it dishes up doughnuts filled with scalded cream. And in many major global markets, Dunkin' Donuts adjusts more than just the doughnuts. ● In India, for example, the company has also adjusted its full menu, its operations, and even its name to suit the local culture:[39]

"My grandmother only recently found out what a doughnut is," says a 20-something Indian business professional as she wraps her mouth around a Dunkin' Donuts Original Tough Guy Chicken Burger. "I don't think anyone would come [here] just for a doughnut." As it turns out, Indian consumers don't start their day with frosted sweets or even with an early breakfast on the go. People usually eat breakfast at home with their families. And unlike Americans, they'll maybe eat a doughnut for dessert, but they want a meal first.

So Dunkin' Donuts has reworked its strategy for India, making a drastic shift from a predominantly "a.m. brand" to more of a "p.m. brand." For starters, it changed its store hours, opening later in the morning and staying open later at night. It even changed its name, to "Dunkin' Donuts & More." To be sure, the chain serves a full selection of India-inspired doughnuts—stuffed, topped, and glazed with everything from rice pudding to saffron to crushed pistachios. (Top sellers in India include "It's a Mistake," a white chocolate doughnut topped with guava and chili.) But Dunkin' features the doughnuts more as after-meal desserts. Befitting its new "& More" name, Dunkin's all-day menu includes a hefty lineup of savory sandwiches, wraps, and eight varieties of burgers (all beef-free), such as the Brute Tough Guy Veg Burger. The adapted format is working well for Dunkin' Donuts, which plans to have more than 100 outlets in India by next year.

Product invention consists of creating something new to meet the needs of consumers in a given country. As markets have gone global, companies ranging from appliance manufacturers and carmakers to candy and soft drink producers have developed products that meet the special purchasing needs of low-income consumers in developing economies.

For example, Chinese appliance producer Haier developed sturdier washing machines for rural users in emerging markets, where it found that lighter-duty machines often became clogged with mud when farmers used them to clean vegetables as well as clothes. And solar lighting manufacturer d.light Solar has developed affordable solar-powered home lighting systems for the hundreds of millions of people in the developing world who don't have access to reliable power. d.light's hanging lamps and portable lanterns require no energy source other than the sun and can last up to 15 hours on one charge. The company has already reached 51 million users, is adding 1 million users per month, and plans to reach 100 million users by 2020.[40]

Promotion

Companies can either adopt the same communication strategy they use in the home market or change it for each local market. Consider advertising messages. Some global companies use a standardized advertising theme around the world. For example, Chevrolet recently swapped out its previous, American-focused "Chevy Runs Deep" positioning and advertising theme with a more global "Find New Roads" theme. The new theme is one "that works in all markets," says a GM marketing executive. ● "The theme has meaning in mature markets like the U.S. as well as emerging markets like Russia and India, where the potential for continued growth is the greatest." The time is right for a more globally consistent Chevy brand message. Chevrolet sells cars in more than 140 countries, and nearly two-thirds of its sales are now outside the United States, compared with only about one-third a decade ago.[41]

● **Communication standardization: With nearly two-thirds of its sales now outside the United States, Chevy recently switched to a new, more global "Find New Roads" positioning and advertising theme that has meaning in all markets worldwide, here Russia.**

General Motors, LLC 2011

Communication adaptation

A global communication strategy of fully adapting advertising messages to local markets.

Of course, even in highly standardized communications campaigns, some adjustments might be required for language and cultural differences. For example, ads for Pepsi's youthful "Live for Now" campaign have a similar look worldwide but are adapted in different global markets to feature local consumers, languages, and events. Similarly, in Western markets, fast-casual clothing retailer H&M runs fashion ads with models showing liberal amounts of bare skin. But in the Middle East, where attitudes toward public nudity are more conservative, the retailer runs the same ads digitally adapted to better cover its models.

Global companies often have difficulty crossing the language barrier, with results ranging from mild embarrassment to outright failure. Seemingly innocuous brand names and advertising phrases can take on unintended or hidden meanings when translated into other languages. For example, Interbrand of London, the firm that created household names such as Prozac and Acura, recently developed a brand name "hall of shame" list, which contained these and other foreign brand names you're never likely to see inside the local Kroger supermarket: Krapp toilet paper (Denmark), Plopp chocolate (Scandinavia), Crapsy Fruit cereal (France), Poo curry powder (Argentina), and Pschitt lemonade (France). Similarly, advertising themes often lose—or gain—something in the translation. In Chinese, the KFC slogan "finger-lickin' good" came out as "eat your fingers off." And Motorola's Hellomoto ringtone sounds like "Hello, Fatty" in India.

Marketers must be watchful to avoid such mistakes, taking great care when localizing their brand names and messages to specific global markets. In important but culturally different markets such as China, finding just the right name can make or break a brand:

After a long day's work, an average upscale Beijinger can't wait to dash home, lace on a comfortable pair of Enduring and Persevering, pop the top on a refreshing can of Tasty Fun, then hop into his Dashing Speed and head to the local tavern for a frosty glass of Happiness Power with friends. Translation? In China, those are the brand name meanings for Nike, Coca-Cola, Mercedes, and Heineken, respectively. To Westerners, such names sound pretty silly, but to brands doing business in China, they are no laughing matter. Perhaps more than anywhere else in the world, brand names in China take on deep significance.

Ideally, to maintain global consistency, the Chinese name should sound similar to the original while at the same time conveying the brand's benefits in meaningful symbolic terms. Nike's Chinese brand name, Nai ke, does this well. Not only does it sound the same when pronounced in Chinese, its "enduring and persevering" meaning powerfully encapsulates the "Just Do It" essence of the Nike brand the world over. Similarly, P&G's Tide is Taizi in China, which translates to "gets out the dirt," a perfect moniker for a tough-acting detergent. Other names that wear well on Chinese ears while also conveying a brand's essence include Lay's snack foods—Le shi ("happy things"); Reebok—Rui bu ("quick steps"); and Colgate—Gau lu jie ("revealing superior cleanliness").[42]

Rather than standardizing their advertising globally, other companies follow a strategy of **communication adaptation**, fully adapting their advertising messages to local markets. For example, in the United States and most Western countries, where running is accepted as a positive, healthful activity, Nike advertising focuses on products and personal performance. In China, however, running is viewed as a boring sport or even a punishment—something rigorous and painful. It's not something that most people in Asia's polluted cities choose to do, especially on streets jammed with pedestrians, bicycles, cars, and even rickshaws. "The joke is that when there's a person running in the city (and it's often a Westerner), people turn to see who's chasing him," quips one observer.

However, China is the largest footwear market in the world, offering huge untapped potential for Nike. So, in China, rather than pushing products and performance, Nike's advertising focuses on just trying to get more Chinese to put on running shoes. Ads and social media feature ordinary people who choose to run on city streets, letting them relate their reasons in their own words. "I run to make the hidden visible," says one young woman. "I run to get lost," says another. Salad—a stressed-out office worker who lives and runs in Shanghai—relates: "The city is always noisy and busy. This adds even more pressure to my day. I guess for me, running is about shutting down the noise." To make running a more social activity, Nike also sponsors nighttime "Lunar Runs" in big cities like Beijing and marathons in Shanghai, featuring fitness instructors, live music, and celebrities to introduce Chinese students and young professionals to running as a fun and rewarding after-class or after-work activity. The goal is to get more people to at least give running a try. But changing basic perceptions of the sport won't be easy. "It's a very long road for us," says a Nike China marketer.[43]

Media also need to be adapted internationally because media availability and regulations vary from country to country. TV advertising time is very limited in Europe, for instance, ranging from four hours a day in France to none in Scandinavian countries. Advertisers must buy time months in advance, and they have little control over airtimes. However, mobile phone ads are much more widely accepted in Europe and Asia than in the United States. Magazines also vary in effectiveness. For example, magazines are a major medium in Italy but a minor one in Austria. Newspapers are national in the United Kingdom but only local in Spain.[44]

Price

Companies also face many considerations in setting their international prices. For example, how might Makita price its power tools globally? It could set a uniform price globally, but this amount would be too high of a price in poor countries and not high enough in rich ones. It could charge what consumers in each country would bear, but this strategy ignores differences in the actual costs from country to country. Finally, the company could use a standard markup of its costs everywhere, but this approach might price Makita out of the market in some countries where costs are high.

Regardless of how companies go about pricing their products, their foreign prices probably will be higher than their domestic prices for comparable products. An Apple iPad Pro that sells for $799 in the United States goes for $993 in the United Kingdom. Why? Apple faces a *price escalation* problem. It must add the cost of transportation, tariffs, importer margin, wholesaler margin, and retailer margin to its factory price. Depending on these added costs, a product may have to sell for two to five times as much in another country to make the same profit.

To overcome this problem when selling to less-affluent consumers in developing countries, many companies make simpler or smaller versions of their products that can be sold at lower prices. Others have introduced new, more affordable brands for global markets. ● For example, Lenovo's Motorola division developed the modestly priced Moto G smartphone. Although not a flashy, high-tech gadget, the latest full-function version of the device sells for as little as $179.99 in the United States with no contract. Motorola first introduced the phone in Brazil, one of the largest and fastest-growing emerging markets, then in other parts of South America, the Middle East, India, and more of Asia. Intended primarily for emerging markets where consumers want low-cost phones, the Moto G may also sell well to cost-conscious consumers in major developed markets, such as the United States and Europe.

The Moto G phone puts pressure on Apple, which has focused on selling older models at reduced prices rather than developing cheaper models. The extremely affordable Moto G is now the most popular smartphone in Brazil, where it is priced at $260 versus iPhones starting at $1,080. The low-end phone also helped

● **International pricing:** Lenovo's Motorola division developed the ultra-cheap Moto G smartphone intended primarily for emerging markets where consumers want low-cost phones.

Photo by ChinaFotoPress/ChinaFotoPress via Getty Images

● FIGURE | 19.4

Whole-Channel Concept for International Marketing

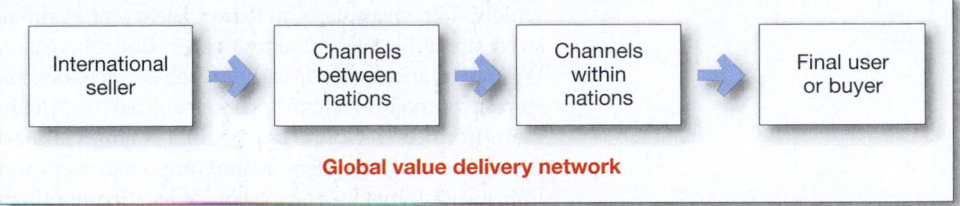

Distribution channels can vary dramatically around the world. For example, in the U.S., Coca-Cola distributes products through sophisticated retail channels. In less-developed countries, it delivers Coke using everything from push carts to delivery donkeys

| International seller | → | Channels between nations | → | Channels within nations | → | Final user or buyer |

Global value delivery network

catapult a then-flagging Motorola into the number-four position in the huge Indian smart-phone market.[45]

Recent economic and technological forces have had an impact on global pricing. For example, the internet is making global price differences more obvious. When firms sell their wares over the internet, customers can see how much products sell for in different countries. They can even order a given product directly from the company location or dealer offering the lowest price. This is forcing companies toward more standardized international pricing.

Distribution Channels

Whole-channel view

Designing international channels that take into account the entire global supply chain and marketing channel, forging an effective global value delivery network.

An international company must take a **whole-channel view** of the problem of distributing products to final consumers. ● **Figure 19.4** shows the two major links between the seller and the final buyer. The first link, *channels between nations*, moves company products from points of production to the borders of countries within which they are sold. The second link, *channels within nations*, moves products from their market entry points to the final consumers. The whole-channel view takes into account the entire global supply chain and marketing channel. It recognizes that to compete well internationally, the company must effectively design and manage an entire *global value delivery network*.

Channels of distribution within countries vary greatly from nation to nation. There are large differences in the numbers and types of intermediaries serving each country market and in the transportation infrastructure serving these intermediaries. For example, whereas large-scale retail chains dominate the U.S. scene, most of the retailing in other countries is done by small, independent retailers. In India or Indonesia, millions of retailers operate tiny shops or sell in open markets.

When selling in emerging markets, companies must often overcome distribution infrastructure and supply challenges. For example, in Nigeria, Domino's Pizza has had to dig wells and install water-treatment plants behind many of its restaurants to obtain clean water. Similarly, after having difficulty sourcing quality beef in South Africa, rather than buying scarce beef from scrawny cattle raised by local herdsmen, Burger King finally invested $5 million in its own local cattle ranch.[46] ● And to serve northeast Brazil's Amazon River basin, which lacks a solid network of good roads, Nestlé has even launched a floating supermarket that takes goods directly to customers. The boat serves 1.5 million consumers

● **Marketing in emerging markets: To tap the growing potential in Brazil's less developed regions, Nestlé's "Ate Voce" ("Reaching You") program includes innovative distribution approaches, such as this floating supermarket that serves customers in the country's Amazon River basin.**

Bloomberg via Getty Images

in 27 riverside towns with 300 different Nestlé products, spending one day at each stop. Customers can check the floating store's schedule at nestleatevoce.com.br, call a toll-free number, or text for more information and plan their shopping accordingly.[47]

Even in world markets containing similar types of sellers, retailing practices can vary widely. For example, you'll find plenty of Walmarts, Carrefours, Tescos, and other retail superstores in major Chinese cities. But whereas consumer brands sold in such stores in Western markets rely largely on self-service, brands in China hire armies of uniformed in-store promoters—called "promoter girls" or "push girls"—to dispense samples and pitch their products person to person. In a Beijing Walmart, on any given weekend, you'll find 100 or more such promoters acquainting customers with products from Kraft, Unilever, P&G, Johnson & Johnson, and a slew of local competitors. "Chinese consumers know the brand name through media," says the director of a Chinese retail marketing service, "but they want to feel the product and get a detailed understanding before they make a purchase."[48]

Deciding on the Global Marketing Organization

Author | **Comment** | Many large companies, regardless of their "home country," now think of themselves as truly *global* organizations. They view the entire world as a single borderless market. For example, although headquartered in Chicago, Boeing is as comfortable selling planes to Lufthansa or Air China as to American Airlines.

Companies manage their international marketing activities in at least three different ways: Most companies first organize an export department, then create an international division, and finally become a global organization.

A firm normally gets into international marketing by simply shipping out its goods. If its international sales expand, the company will establish an *export department* with a sales manager and a few assistants. As sales increase, the export department can expand to include various marketing services so that it can actively go after business. If the firm moves into joint ventures or direct investment, the export department will no longer be adequate.

Many companies get involved in several international markets and ventures. A company may export to one country, license to another, have a joint ownership venture in a third, and own a subsidiary in a fourth. Sooner or later it will create *international divisions* or subsidiaries to handle all its international activity.

International divisions are organized in a variety of ways. An international division's corporate staff consists of marketing, manufacturing, research, finance, planning, and personnel specialists. It plans for and provides services to various operating units, which can be organized in one of three ways. They can be *geographical organizations*, with country managers who are responsible for salespeople, sales branches, distributors, and licensees in their respective countries. Or the operating units can be *world product groups*, each responsible for worldwide sales of different product groups. Finally, operating units can be *international subsidiaries*, each responsible for their own sales and profits.

Many firms have passed beyond the international division stage and are truly global organizations. For example, as discussed previously, despite its French origins, L'Oréal no longer has a clearly defined home market. Nor does it have a home-office staff. Instead, the company is famous for building global brand teams around managers who have deep backgrounds in several cultures. L'Oréal managers around the world bring diverse cultural perspectives to their brands as if they were, say, German or American or Chinese—or all three at once. As explained by one Indian-American-French manager of a team that launched a men's skin care line in Southeast Asia: "I cannot think about things one way. I have a stock of references in different languages: English, Hindi, and French. I read books in three different languages, meet people from different countries, eat food from different [cultures], and so on."[49]

Global organizations don't think of themselves as national marketers that sell abroad but as global marketers. The top corporate management and staff plan worldwide manufacturing facilities, marketing policies, financial flows, and logistical systems. The global operating units report directly to the chief executive or the executive committee of the organization, not to the head of an international division. Executives are trained in worldwide operations, not just domestic *or* international operations. Global companies recruit management from many countries, buy components and supplies where they cost the least, and invest where the expected returns are greatest.

Today, major companies must become more global if they hope to compete. As foreign companies successfully invade their domestic markets, companies must move more aggressively into foreign markets. They will have to change from companies that treat their international operations as secondary to companies that view the entire world as a single borderless market.

19 Reviewing and Extending the Concepts

OBJECTIVES REVIEW AND KEY TERMS

Objectives Review

Companies today can no longer afford to pay attention only to their domestic market, regardless of its size. Many industries are global industries, and firms that operate globally achieve lower costs and higher brand awareness. At the same time, global marketing is risky because of variable exchange rates, unstable governments, tariffs and trade barriers, and several other factors. Given the potential gains and risks of international marketing, companies need a systematic way to make their global marketing decisions.

OBJECTIVE 19-1 Discuss how the international trade system and the economic, political-legal, and cultural environments affect a company's international marketing decisions. (pp 544–556)

A company must understand the *global marketing environment*, especially the international trade system. It should assess each foreign market's *economic, political-legal*, and *cultural characteristics*. The company can then decide whether it wants to go abroad and consider the potential risks and benefits. It must decide on the volume of international sales it wants, how many countries it wants to market in, and which specific markets it wants to enter. These decisions call for weighing the probable returns against the level of risk.

OBJECTIVE 19-2 Describe three key approaches to entering international markets. (pp 556–558)

The company must decide how to enter each chosen market—whether through *exporting, joint venturing*, or *direct investment*. Many companies start as exporters, move to joint ventures, and finally make a direct investment in foreign markets. In *exporting*, the company enters a foreign market by sending and selling products through international marketing intermediaries (indirect exporting) or the company's own department, branch, or sales representatives or agents (direct exporting). When establishing a *joint venture*, a company enters foreign markets by joining with foreign companies to produce or market a product or service. In *licensing*, the company enters a foreign market by contracting with a licensee in the foreign market and offering the right to use a manufacturing process, trademark, patent, trade secret, or other item of value for a fee or royalty.

OBJECTIVE 19-3 Explain how companies adapt their marketing strategies and mixes for international markets. (pp 559–566)

Companies must also decide how much their marketing strategies and their products, promotion, price, and channels should be adapted for each foreign market. At one extreme, global companies use *standardized global marketing* worldwide. Others use *adapted global marketing*, in which they adjust the marketing strategy and mix to each target market, bearing more costs but hoping for a larger market share and return. However, global standardization is not an all-or-nothing proposition. It's a matter of degree. Most international marketers suggest that companies should "think globally but act locally"—that they should seek a balance between globally standardized strategies and locally adapted marketing mix tactics.

OBJECTIVE 19-4 Identify the three major forms of international marketing organization. (p 566)

The company must develop an effective organization for international marketing. Most firms start with an *export department* and graduate to an *international division*. Large companies eventually become *global organizations*, with worldwide marketing planned and managed by the top officers of the company. Global organizations view the entire world as a single, borderless market.

Key Terms

OBJECTIVE 19-1
Global firm (p 545)
Economic community (p 547)

OBJECTIVE 19-2
Exporting (p 556)
Joint venturing (p 557)
Licensing (p 557)

Contract manufacturing (p 557)
Management contracting (p 557)
Joint ownership (p 558)
Direct investment (p 558)

OBJECTIVE 19-3
Standardized global marketing (p 559)
Adapted global marketing (p 559)

Straight product
  extension (p 561)
Product adaptation (p 562)
Product invention (p 562)
Communication
  adaptation (p 563)
Whole-channel
  view (p 565)

DISCUSSION AND CRITICAL THINKING

MyMarketingLab

Go to **mymktlab.com** to complete the problems marked with this icon ✪.

Discussion Questions

✪ **19-1** What environmental factors must international marketers consider when enter foreign markets? (AACSB: Communication)

✪ **19-2** Name and explain a company's market entry options for international markets. (AACSB: Communication)

19-3 Name and describe the four types of joint ventures as methods for entering another country. How does joint venturing differ from other methods of entering a foreign market? (AACSB: Communication; Reflective Thinking)

19-4 Briefly outline the strategies used for adapting products to a global market. Provide an example for each strategy. (AACSB: Communication)

✪ **19-5** Explain what is meant by a whole-channel view and why it is important in international marketing. (AACSB: Communication; Reflective Thinking)

Critical Thinking Exercises

✪ **19-6** Visit www.transparency.org and find the most recent Corruption Perceptions Index (CPI) report. What is the most recent CPI for the following countries: Argentina, Denmark, Jamaica, Myanmar, New Zealand, Somalia, and the United States? What are the implications of this index for U.S.-based companies doing business in these countries? (AACSB: Communication; Use of IT; Reflective Thinking)

19-7 In a small group, identify and research an environmental threat—such as a regulatory threat, a cultural threat, or an economic threat—posed to global marketers. Analyze the issues related to this threat, discuss how affected companies are reacting, and make recommendations regarding how these companies should address the threat. (AACSB: Communication; Reflective Thinking)

19-8 You have been asked to consult with a small business owner who wants to expand her company overseas. She has asked you to develop a global marketing strategy. You are not certain if the owner thoroughly understands the international expansion process and the challenges involved. Prior to meeting with the owner next week, create a presentation listing the factors she will need to consider prior to her company going global. (AACSB: Communication; Use of IT; Reflective Thinking)

APPLICATIONS AND CASES

Online, Mobile, and Social Media Marketing China's Great Firewall

China has emerged as an enormous social media market. With more than 1.35 billion people and 635 million internet users, internet usage in China is growing explosively at about 30 percent annually. That makes it an extremely attractive market for Western social media companies such as Facebook, Google, Twitter, and YouTube. However, under what has come to be called the "Great Firewall of China"—an extensive level of control and censorship of websites and internet activities by the Chinese government—many such Western social media and other online marketers have been largely blocked from operating in China. According to *The Diplomat*, eight of the top 25 most-visited global sites are now blocked in China. However, even with constant government monitoring of internet activities, China has become one of the world's most active social media environments. Chinese consumers can connect through carefully controlled local social networking platforms such as Ren-ren (everyone's website), Baidu (Google-like search engine), Youku (China's answer to YouTube), WeChat (Tencent's instant messaging app), Jiepang (similar to Foursquare), microblogging sites such as Sina Weibo (like Twitter), and Dianping (similar to Yelp).

As more marketers enter the social media landscape in China, strategies to reach consumers must be carefully shaped to the country's culture, consumers, content, platforms, and regulations. Online marketers must understand Chinese culture, translations, and etiquette to help craft better messages and marketing content that will resonate with Chinese consumers. At the same time, they must navigate under the watchful eye of the Chinese government.

19-9 Research the Great Firewall of China. How will such government control affect social media marketing in China? Report on a Western online company now operating in China. How is it able to work within and around Chinese regulations? (AACSB: Communication; Reflective Thinking)

19-10 Suppose that your company is preparing to enter the Chinese market with a product line that you believe will have great success. What is the best mode of entry for your company? Review the economic and political climates. Is the timing right for entering China? (AACSB: Communication; Use of IT; Reflective Thinking)

Marketing Ethics Global Safety Standards

India is home to some of the world's deadliest roads. However, international automobile makers do not provide standard safety features in entry-level cars sold in India that are required in other developed countries. India's death toll on the roads has ranked top in the world for eight straight years, exceeding 130,000 fatalities a year. Despite this, automakers strip safety features such as air bags and antilock brakes out of the cars most people in India drive. They argue that Indian consumers cannot afford or are not willing to pay for safety features that could increase the cost of the car by 30 percent or more. Some manufacturers have begun to offer more safety features as standard in their models. But other producers are offering them only as an option, and some are not offering them at all to maintain price competitiveness.

19-11 Is it right for manufacturers to include product safety features that are known to save lives in countries that require them but to exclude such features in one country where they are not specifically required? (AACSB: Communication; Ethical Reasoning)

19-12 Discuss world organizations that assist companies in developing and abiding by global standards to protect consumers worldwide. (AACSB: Communication; Reflective Thinking)

Marketing by the Numbers Netflix's Global Expansion

Video streaming service Netflix is expanding rapidly around the globe. It is currently available in 50 countries with the goal of expanding to 200 countries by the end of 2016. Netflix's international slogan is "Have content, will travel." There are challenges to international expansion for this type of service, such as inadequate disposable household income and a low percentage of households with high-speed internet needed to stream videos. And even though almost half of France's TV-owning households have internet-connected TVs, cultural restrictions limit English-language program content, requiring Netflix to invest in local content for French customers. The next countries to get Netflix are Italy, Spain, and Portugal. Similar to Netflix's other European offerings, service will be offered at a price of €7.99 per month, which converts to U.S. $8.97 during the time of expansion.

19-13 Refer to Appendix 2, Marketing by the Numbers, to calculate the annual market sales potential for Spain

in euros and U.S. dollars. There are 18,217,300 television households in Spain, with 75 percent having high-speed internet. Assume 50 percent of the households are willing and able to purchase the service and would purchase one subscription at an average price of €7.99 per month ($8.97). (AACSB: Communication; Analytical Reasoning; Reflective Thinking)

19-14 Calculate the market sales potential using the current exchange rate between euros and U.S. dollars (see www.xe.com/currencyconverter/). Is the dollar currently strong or weak compared to the euro? Why are U.S.-based international companies concerned when the U.S. dollar is strong compared to other currencies? (AACSB: Communication; Analytic Reasoning; Reflective Thinking)

Video Case Monster

Monster.com is one of the most visited employment sites in the United States and one of the largest in the world. Now a part of parent company Monster Worldwide, Monster.com pioneered job recruiting on the internet. Today, it is the only online recruitment provider that can service job seekers and job posters on a truly global basis. With a presence in 50 countries around the world, Monster has unparalleled international reach. Even through tough economic times, Monster continued to invest heavily in order to maintain and expand its global presence.

Monster's international expansion included the purchase of ChinaHR.com, giving it a strong presence in the world's largest country. Monster already gets about 45 percent of its annual

revenue of $1.3 billion from outside the United States. But it expects to become even more global in the coming years. To back that geographic expansion, Monster is also investing heavily in search technologies and web design in order to appeal to clients everywhere.

After viewing the video featuring Monster Worldwide, answer the following questions:

19-15 Which of the five strategies for adapting products and promotion for global markets does Monster employ?

19-16 Which factors in the global marketing environment have challenged Monster's global marketing activities most? How has Monster met those challenges?

Company Case L'Oréal: The United Nations of Beauty

How does a French company successfully market an American version of a Korean skin beautifier under a French brand name in Australia? Ask L'Oréal, which sells more than $28 billion worth of cosmetics, hair care products, skin care concoctions, and fra-

grances each year in 130 countries, making it the world's biggest cosmetics marketer. L'Oréal's success is based on a concept it calls "universalisation." It sells its brands globally by understanding how they appeal to varied cultural nuances of beauty in specific local markets. Then it finds the best balance between standardizing its brands for global impact and adapting them to meet local needs and desires.

L'Oréal is as global as a company gets. With offices spread across 130 nations and more than half of its sales coming from markets outside Europe and North America, the company no longer has a clearly defined home market. L'Oréal's well-known brands originated in a half-dozen or more different cultures, including French (L'Oréal Paris, Garnier, Lancôme), American (Maybelline, Kiehl's, SoftSheen-Carson, Ralph Lauren, Urban Decay, Clarisonic, Redken), British (The Body Shop), Italian (Giorgio Armani), and Japanese (Shu Uemura). With these and many other well-known brands, the master global marketer is the uncontested world leader in makeup, skin care, and hair coloring and second only to P&G in hair care.

Because I'm Worth It

L'Oréal's strategy of universalisation is tied to its mission— "beauty for all." If there is one thing that L'Oréal has discovered about women worldwide, it is that they want to feel good about themselves. And how they feel is inherently connected to how they care for themselves and their appearance. This universal characteristic holds true regardless of ethnicity, culture, age, or socioeconomic status. For this reason, "beauty for all" has L'Oréal focused on providing the ultimate in luxury beauty for the masses.

While the Paris-based giant has been peddling cosmetics for more than a century, the relevance of its mission became more apparent than ever in the 1970s. The company launched Superior Preference hair color with an advertisement that presented a woman's point of view and ended with four words— "Because I'm Worth It." From the moment the ad hit, those words struck a chord with women. Here was a brand with a message about what a woman thought—about her self-confidence, her decisions, her style.

Originally just a tagline, those four words have transcended their intended purpose and have even become part of the social fabric. They have been written into global language, used by a woman for any situation where she wants to stand up for herself and proclaim her self-worth. Today, 80 percent of women worldwide recognize and respond to this phrase in a positive and powerful way. And today, "Because I'm Worth It" is translated into action every day by L'Oréal.

Beauty from Multiple Perspectives

To achieve "beauty for all" globally, L'Oréal's starts with a corps of highly multicultural managers. The company is famous for building global brand teams around managers who have deep backgrounds in several cultures. Unlike many global corporations that set up an international structure composed of autonomous subsidiaries, divisions, and management teams in different parts of the world, L'Oréal knew that such a structure would not provide the balance between standardization and adaptation that is critical in today's cosmetics industry. Instead, the company built global teams around individual managers with deep backgrounds in multiple cultures, allowing them to switch easily among them.

Able to see things from multiple perspectives, a truly multicultural manager can think at any moment as if he or she were German, American, or Chinese—or all three at once. The Indian-American-French manager of a team that launched a men's skin care line in Southeast Asia explains: "I have a stock of references in different languages: English, Hindi, and French. I read books in three different languages, meet people from different countries, eat food from different [cultures], and so on. I cannot think about things one way."

For example, a French-Irish-Cambodian manager working on skin care noticed that, in Europe, face creams tended to be either "tinted" (and considered as makeup) or "lifting" (and considered as skin care). But in Asia, many face creams combined the two traits. Recognizing the growing popularity of Asian beauty trends in Europe, this manager guided his team in developing a tinted cream with lifting effects for the French market, a product that proved to be highly successful. As the global environment has created a greater need for this type of knowledge integration across cultures, L'Oréal's strategic use of multicultural managers provides built-in shortcuts. This management structure has given L'Oréal a critical competitive advantage in new product development.

Diving Deep for Beauty

L'Oréal digs deep to understand what beauty means to consumers in different parts of the world. It outspends all major competitors on R&D, painstakingly researching beauty and personal care behaviors unique to specific locales. One of the goals of its global R&D efforts is to gain an in-depth understanding of the behaviors of women and men around the world with respect to beautifying and taking care of themselves. L'Oréal explains the need for this worldwide approach to beauty rituals:

> How many minutes does a Chinese woman devote to her morning beauty routine? How do people wash their hair in Bangkok? How many brush strokes does a Japanese woman or a French woman use to apply mascara? These beauty rituals, repeated thousands of times, are inherently cultural. Passed on by tradition, influenced by climate and by local living conditions, they strive to achieve an ideal of perfection that is different from one country and from one continent to the next. They provide an incredibly rich source of information for L'Oréal Research. Behind these rituals, there are physiological realities: fine, straight and short eyelashes cannot be made up the same way as thick, curled, and long lashes.

To facilitate this major R&D effort, L'Oréal has set up centers all over the world, developing a science of local observation it calls "geocosmetics." This science is fueled with insight gained through in-home visits as well as observations made in "bathroom laboratories." Equipped with high-tech gadgetry, these labs enable teams to study consumer behavior around the world.

L'Oréal's R&D program produces very precise information about regional rituals of hygiene and beauty as well as local conditions and constraints that affect the use of products, such as humidity and temperature. These insights feed R&D teams in the process of creating products for local markets. Combined with insights from global locations, such products can be adapted for multiple markets.

For example, consider Elséve Total Reparação, a hair care line initially developed at L'Oréal's labs in Rio de Janeiro to address specific hair problems described by Brazilian women. In Brazil, more than half of all women have long, dry, dull, and very curly hair, resulting from the humid Brazilian climate, exposure to the sun, frequent washing, and smoothing and straightening treatments. Elséve Total Reparação was an immediate hit in Brazil, and L'Oréal quickly rolled it out to other South American and Latin American markets. The company then tracked down other global locales with climate characteristics and hair care rituals similar to those faced by Brazilian women. Subsequently, L'Oréal launched the brand as Elséve Total Repair in numerous

European, Indian, and other South East Asian markets, where consumers greeted it with similar enthusiasm.

Such adaptation often plays out across multiple L'Oréal brands—which takes us back to that Korean skin beautifier sold under a French brand in Australia mentioned in the opening paragraph. Blemish balm cream (BB cream) was originally created by dermatologists in Korea to soothe skin and hide minor blemishes. It quickly became a high-flying Korean brand. However, applying their deep knowledge of skin colors, treatments, and makeup worldwide, L'Oréal researchers developed a successful new-generation BB cream adapted to conditions and skin colors in U.S. markets (where *BB* stands for "beauty balm") and launched it under the Maybelline New York brand. Still not finished, L'Oréal created yet another local version for Europe under the Garnier brand, which it also introduced in other world markets, including Australia.

L'Oréal's global R&D efforts have produced a "geography of skin colors"—a proprietary mapping of the world that makes it possible to adapt cosmetic products to the needs of women around the world. In a similar manner, the company has expanded the traditional classification of three hair types (African, Asian, and European) to eight different categories, based on a scientific measurement of curl characteristics that includes the diameter of the curvature, the curl index, the number of waves, and tendrils.

L'Oréal doesn't just adapt its product formulations globally. It also adapts brand positioning and marketing to international needs and expectations. For example, more than 20 years ago, the company bought stodgy American makeup producer Maybelline. To reinvigorate and globalize the brand, it moved the unit's headquarters from Tennessee to New York City and added "New York" to the label. The resulting urban, street-smart, Big Apple image played well globally with the midprice positioning of the workaday makeup brand. The makeover soon earned Maybelline a 20 percent market share in its category in Western Europe. The young urban positioning also hit the mark in Asia, where few women realized that the trendy "New York" Maybelline brand belonged to French cosmetics giant L'Oréal.

By acquiring brands such as Maybelline, L'Oréal also gains brands that have immediate recognition and products already made for a given market. This gives the company an immediate point of entry to a market at a cost that is lower than building a brand from scratch. Such is the case with Yue-Sai Cosmetics, a Chinese company that uses herbs in its creams. L'Oréal bought it a decade ago. Sales of Yue-Sai products increased by 20 percent last year.

L'Oréal and its brands are truly global, and its approach to providing luxury beauty for the masses is working. Total revenues have grown by 30 percent over the past four years. Even as the Western European market growth has slowed and Brazil is in a slump, L'Oréal's revenues climbed by 12 percent in the past year alone. In the United States, L'Oréal is growing even as key rival Unilever has seen its revenue decline and is losing market share.

L'Oréal's huge international success comes from achieving a global–local balance that adapts and differentiates brands in local markets while optimizing their impact across global markets. L'Oréal is one of few companies that has achieved both local brand responsiveness and global brand integration. "We respect the differences among our consumers around the world," says L'Oréal's CEO. "We have global brands, but we need to adapt them to local needs." When a former CEO once addressed a UNESCO conference, nobody batted an eyelid when he described L'Oréal as "The United Nations of Beauty."

Questions for Discussion

19-17 Of the five global product and communications strategies, which best describes L'Oréal's approach?

19-18 On a scale of 1 to 5, to what degree does L'Oréal adapt its offering in each global market? Support your answer.

19-19 What are the disadvantages to L'Oréal's global approach?

19-20 Which strategy does L'Oréal employ for entering a new market? How does the company benefit from this approach?

19-21 Will L'Oréal continue to succeed at such a high level? Why or why not?

Sources: Based on information from Andrew Roberts, "L'Oréal Sales Beat Estimates on Accelerating Luxury Growth," *Bloomberg Businessweek*, February 11, 2016, www.bloomberg.com/news/articles/2016-02-11/l-oreal-sales-beat-estimates-on-accelerating-growth-in-luxury; "Leading Global Cosmetics Company L'Oréal Saw Its Sales Grow 12 Percent Last Year," *US News*, February 11, 2016, www.usnews.com/news/business/articles/2016-02-11/loreal-2015-sales-up-across-markets-net-profit-down; "Our Mission Is 'Beauty for All,' Says L'Oréal Global CEO Jean-Paul," *The Economic Times,* January 30, 2015, http://articles.economictimes.indiatimes.com/2015-01-30/news/58625572_1_l-oreal-loreal-jean-paul-agon; Hae-Jung Hong and Yves Doz, "L'Oréal Masters Multiculturalism," *Harvard Business Review*, June, 2013, pp. 114–119; Liza Lin, "L'Oréal Puts on a Happy Face in China," *Bloomberg Businessweek*, April 1–7, 2013, pp. 25–26; "A Worldwide Approach to Beauty Rituals," www.loreal.com/research-innovation/when-the-diversity-of-types-of-beauty-inspires-science/a-world-wide-approach-to-beauty-rituals.aspx, accessed June 2016; and additional information and quotes from www.lorealparisusa.com/en/about-loreal-paris/overview.aspx, accessed June, 2016.

MyMarketingLab

Go to **mymktlab.com** for Auto-graded writing questions as well as the following Assisted-graded writing questions:

19-22 Discuss the strategies used for adapting products to a global market. Which strategy is best?

19-23 Name and describe the advantages and disadvantages of the different types of joint venturing when entering a foreign market.

PART 1: Defining Marketing and the Marketing Process (Chapters 1–2)
PART 2: Understanding the Marketplace and Consumer Value (Chapters 3–6)
PART 3: Designing a Customer Value–Driven Strategy and Mix (Chapters 7–17)
PART 4: Extending Marketing (Chapters 18–20)

20

Sustainable Marketing
Social Responsibility and Ethics

In this final chapter, we'll examine the concept of sustainable marketing, meeting the needs of consumers, businesses, and society—now and in the future—through socially and environmentally responsible marketing actions. We'll start by defining sustainable marketing and then look at some common criticisms of marketing as it affects individual consumers as well as public actions that promote sustainable marketing. Finally, we'll see how companies themselves can benefit from proactively pursuing sustainable marketing practices that bring value to not only individual customers but also society as a whole. Sustainable marketing

actions are more than just the right thing to do; they're also good for business.

First, let's look at an example of sustainable marketing in action at Unilever, the world's third-largest consumer products company. For 17 years running, Unilever has been named sustainability leader in the food and beverage industry by the Dow Jones Sustainability Indexes. The company recently launched its Sustainable Living Plan, by which it intends to double its size by 2020 while at the same time reducing its impact on the planet and increasing the social benefits arising from its activities. That's an ambitious goal.

SUSTAINABILITY AT UNILEVER: Creating a Better Future Every Day

When Paul Polman took over as CEO of Unilever a half-dozen years ago, the foods, home, and personal care products company was a slumbering giant. Despite its stable of star-studded brands—including the likes of Dove, Axe, Noxzema, Sunsilk, OMO, Hellmann's, Knorr, Lipton, and Ben & Jerry's—Unilever had experienced a decade of stagnant sales and profits. The company needed renewed energy and purpose. "To drag the world back to sanity, we need to know why we are here," said Polman.

To answer the "why are we here" question and find a more energizing mission, Polman looked beyond the usual corporate goals of growing sales, profits, and shareholder value. Instead, he asserted, growth results from accomplishing a broader social and environmental mission. Unilever exists "for consumers, not shareholders," he said. "If we are in sync with consumer needs and the environment in which we operate, and take responsibility for our [societal impact], then the shareholder will also be rewarded."

Evaluating and working on sustainability impact is nothing new at Unilever. Prior to Polman taking the reins, the company

already had multiple programs in place to manage the impact of its products and operations. But the existing programs and results—while good—simply didn't go far enough for Polman. So in late 2010 Unilever launched its Sustainable Living Plan—an aggressive long-term plan that takes capitalism to the next level. Under the plan, the company set out to "create a better future every day for people around the world: the people who work for us, those we do business with, the billions of people who use our products, and future generations whose quality of life

> Under Unilever's Sustainable Living Plan, the consumer goods giant has set out to "create a better future every day for people around the world." Unilever's long-run commercial success depends on how well it manages the social and environmental impact of its actions.

depends on the way we protect the environment today." According to Polman, Unilever's long-run commercial success depends on how well it manages the social and environmental impact of its actions.

The Sustainable Living Plan sets out three major social and environmental objectives to be accomplished by 2020: "(1) To help more than one billion people take action to improve their health and well-being; (2) to halve the environmental footprint of the making and use of our products; and (3) to enhance the livelihoods of millions of people as we grow our business." The Sustainable Living Plan pulls together all of the work Unilever had already been doing and sets ambitious new sustainability goals. These goals span the entire value chain, from how the company sources raw materials to how consumers use and dispose of its products. "Our aim is to make our activities more sustainable and also encourage our customers, suppliers, and others to do the same," says the company.

On the "upstream supply side," more than half of Unilever's raw materials come from agriculture, so the company is helping suppliers develop sustainable farming practices that meet its own high expectations for environmental and social impact. Unilever assesses suppliers against two sets of standards. The first is the Unilever Supplier Code, which calls for socially responsible actions regarding human rights, labor practices, product safety, and care for the environment. Second, specifically for agricultural suppliers, the Unilever Sustainable Agriculture Code details Unilever's expectations for sustainable agriculture practices so that it and its suppliers "can commit to the sustainability journey together."

But Unilever's Sustainable Living Plan goes far beyond simply creating more responsible supply and distribution chains. Approximately 68 percent of the total greenhouse gas footprint of Unilever's products and 50 percent of the water footprint occur during consumer use. So Unilever is also working with its customers to improve the environmental impact of its products in use. About 2 billion people in 190 markets worldwide use a Unilever product on any given day. Therefore, small everyday consumer actions can add up to a big difference. Unilever sums it up with this equation: "Unilever brands × small everyday actions × billions of consumers = big difference."

For example, almost one-third of households worldwide use Unilever laundry products to do their washing—approximately 125 billion washes every year. Therefore, under its Sustainable Living Plan, Unilever is both creating more eco-friendly laundry products and motivating consumers to improve their laundry habits.

Around the world, for instance, Unilever is encouraging consumers to wash clothes at lower temperatures and use the correct dosage of detergent. Unilever products such as OMO and Persil Small & Mighty concentrated laundry detergents use less packaging, making them cheaper and less polluting to transport. More important, they've been reformulated to wash efficiently at lower temperatures, using less energy and water. Unilever estimates that these changes have achieved a 15 percent reduction in greenhouse gas emissions. Another Unilever product, Comfort One Rinse fabric conditioner, was created for hand-washing clothes in developing and emerging markets where water is often in short supply. The innovative product requires only one bucket of water for rinsing rather than three, saving consumers time, effort, and 30 liters of water per wash.

Such energy and water savings don't show up on Unilever's income statement, but they will be extremely important to the people and the planet. "Ultimately," says the company, "we will only succeed if we inspire people around the world to take small, everyday actions that can add up to a big difference for the world." To meet this objective, Unilever has

Under its Sustainable Living Plan, Unilever is working with billions of customers worldwide to improve the social and environmental impact of its products. "Small actions. Big difference."

Reproduced with kind permission of Unilever PLC and group companies

identified "Five Levers for Change"—things that its marketers can do to inspire people to adopt specific sustainable behaviors. The model helps marketers identify the barriers and triggers for change. The levers for change are: make it understood, make it easy, make it desirable, make it rewarding, and make it a habit.

Will Unilever's Sustainable Living Plan produce results for the company? So far, so good. Unilever is making excellent progress on its overall mission of "making sustainable living commonplace" and on its 79 aggressive Sustainable Living Plan goals. The company has already achieved 13 specific targets, is right on pace with 57 more, and is making good progress on the other nine. And despite volatility in its global markets, Unilever's profits continue to grow.

The sustainability plan is not just the right thing to do for people and the environment, claims Polman, it's also right for Unilever. The quest for sustainability saves money by reducing energy use and minimizing waste. It fuels innovation, resulting in new products and new consumer benefits. And it creates new market opportunities: More than half of Unilever's sales are from developing countries, the very places that face the greatest sustainability challenges.

OBJECTIVES OUTLINE

OBJECTIVE 20-1	Define *sustainable marketing* and discuss its importance. Sustainable Marketing *(pp 574–576)*
OBJECTIVE 20-2	Identify the major social criticisms of marketing. Social Criticisms of Marketing *(pp 576–583)*
OBJECTIVE 20-3	Define *consumerism* and *environmentalism* and explain how they affect marketing strategies. Consumer Actions to Promote Sustainable Marketing *(pp 583–589)*
OBJECTIVE 20-4	Describe the principles of sustainable marketing. Business Actions Toward Sustainable Marketing *(pp 589–593)*
OBJECTIVE 20-5	Explain the role of ethics in marketing. Marketing Ethics and the Sustainable Company *(pp 593–596)*

In all, Polman predicts, the sustainability plan will help Unilever double in size while also creating a better future for billions of people without increasing the environmental footprint. "We do not believe there is a conflict between sustainability and profitable growth," he concludes. "The daily act of making and selling consumer goods drives economic and social progress. There are billions of people around the world who deserve the better quality of life that everyday products like soap, shampoo, and tea can provide. Sustainable living is not a pipedream. It can be done, and there is very little downside."[1]

RESPONSIBLE MARKETERS DISCOVER WHAT consumers want and respond with market offerings that create value for buyers and capture value in return. The *marketing concept* is a philosophy of customer value and mutual gain. Its practice leads the economy by an invisible hand to satisfy the many and changing needs of consumers.

Not all marketers follow the marketing concept, however. In fact, some companies use questionable marketing practices that serve their own rather than consumers' interests. Moreover, even well-intentioned marketing actions that meet the current needs of some consumers may cause immediate or future harm to other consumers or the larger society. Responsible marketers must consider whether their actions are sustainable in the longer run.

Sustainable marketing
Socially and environmentally responsible marketing that meets the present needs of consumers and businesses while also preserving or enhancing the ability of future generations to meet their needs.

This chapter examines sustainable marketing and the social and environmental effects of private marketing practices. First, we address the question: What is sustainable marketing, and why is it important?

Author Comment | Marketers must think beyond immediate customer satisfaction and business performance toward sustainable strategies that preserve the world for future generations.

Sustainable Marketing

Sustainable marketing calls for socially and environmentally responsible actions that meet the present needs of consumers and businesses while also preserving or enhancing the ability of future generations to meet their needs. **Figure 20.1** compares the sustainable marketing concept with marketing concepts we studied in earlier chapters.

The *marketing concept* recognizes that organizations thrive by determining the current needs and wants of target customers and fulfilling them more effectively and efficiently

● **FIGURE | 20.1**
Sustainable Marketing

The marketing concept means meeting the current needs of both customers and the company. But that can sometimes mean compromising the future of both.

	Now	**Future**
Now (Needs of Consumers)	Marketing concept	Strategic planning concept
Future	Societal marketing concept	**Sustainable marketing concept**

Needs of Business

Sustainable marketing means meeting current needs in a way that preserves the rights and options of future generations of consumers and businesses.

than competitors do. It focuses on meeting the company's short-term sales, growth, and profit needs by engaging customers and giving them what they want now. However, satisfying consumers' immediate needs and desires doesn't always serve the future best interests of either customers or the business.

For example, McDonald's early decisions to market tasty but fat- and salt-laden fast foods created immediate satisfaction for customers as well as sales and profits for the company. However, critics assert that McDonald's and other fast-food chains contributed to a longer-term national obesity epidemic, damaging consumer health and burdening the national health system. In turn, many consumers began looking for healthier eating options, causing a slump in the sales and profits of the fast-food industry. Beyond issues of ethical behavior and social welfare, McDonald's was also criticized for the sizable environmental footprint of its vast global operations, everything from wasteful packaging and solid waste creation to inefficient energy use in its stores. Thus, McDonald's strategy was not sustainable in the long run in terms of either consumer or company benefit.

Whereas the *societal marketing concept* identified in Figure 20.1 considers the future welfare of consumers and the *strategic planning concept* considers future company needs, the *sustainable marketing concept* considers both. Sustainable marketing calls for socially and environmentally responsible actions that meet both the immediate and future needs of customers and the company.

For example, for more than a decade, McDonald's has responded to these challenges with a more sustainable strategy of diversifying into salads, fruits, grilled chicken, low-fat milk, and other healthy fare. The company has also sponsored major education campaigns—such as one called "it's what i eat and what i do … i'm lovin' it"—to help consumers better understand the keys to living balanced, active lifestyles. And it has announced a list of "Commitments to Offer Improved Nutrition Choices," including a continuing commitment to children's well-being, expanded and improved nutritionally balanced menu choices, and increased consumer and employee access to nutrition information. ● McDonald's points out that 80 percent of the items on its national menu fall into its "favorites under 400 calories" category—from a basic cheeseburger to products such as Fruit & Maple Oatmeal and the Egg White Delight McMuffin, made with eight grams of whole grain, 100 percent egg whites, and extra-lean Canadian bacon.[2]

McDonald's sustainability initiatives also address environmental issues. For example, it calls for food-supply sustainability, reduced and environmentally sustainable packaging, reuse and recycling, and more responsible store designs. McDonald's has even developed an environmental scorecard that rates its suppliers' performance in areas such as water use, energy use, and solid waste management. Thus, McDonald's is now well positioned for a sustainably profitable future.

● **Responding to sustainability challenges:** Eighty percent of McDonald's menu is now under 400 calories, including this Egg White Delight McMuffin, which weighs in at eight grams of whole grain against only 250 calories and five grams of fat.
© Michael Neelon(misc)/Alamy

Truly sustainable marketing requires a smooth-functioning marketing system in which consumers, companies, public policy makers, and others work together to ensure socially and environmentally responsible marketing actions. Unfortunately, however, the marketing system doesn't always work smoothly. The following sections examine several sustainability questions: What are the most frequent social criticisms of marketing? What steps have private citizens taken to curb marketing ills? What steps have legislators and government agencies taken to promote sustainable marketing? What steps have enlightened companies taken to carry out socially responsible and ethical marketing that creates sustainable value for both individual customers and society as a whole?

> **Author Comment** | In most ways, we all benefit greatly from marketing activities. However, like most other human endeavors, marketing has its flaws. Here we present both sides of some of the most common criticisms of marketing.

Social Criticisms of Marketing

Marketing receives much criticism. Some of this criticism is justified; much is not. Social critics claim that certain marketing practices hurt individual consumers, society as a whole, and other business firms.

Marketing's Impact on Individual Consumers

Consumers have many concerns about how well the American marketing system serves their interests. Surveys usually show that consumers hold mixed or even slightly unfavorable attitudes toward marketing practices. Consumer advocates, government agencies, and other critics have accused marketing of harming consumers through high prices, deceptive practices, high-pressure selling, shoddy or unsafe products, planned obsolescence, and poor service to disadvantaged consumers. Such questionable marketing practices are not sustainable in terms of long-term consumer or business welfare.

High Prices

Many critics charge that the American marketing system causes prices to be higher than they would be under more "sensible" systems. Such high prices are hard to swallow, especially when the economy gets tight. Critics point to three factors—*high costs of distribution, high advertising and promotion costs*, and *excessive markups*.

A long-standing charge is that greedy marketing channel members mark up prices beyond the value of their services. As a result, distribution costs too much and consumers pay for these excessive costs in the form of higher prices. Resellers respond that intermediaries do work that would otherwise have to be done by manufacturers or consumers. Their prices reflect services that consumers want—more convenience, larger stores and assortments, more service, longer store hours, return privileges, and others. In fact, they argue, retail competition is so intense that margins are actually quite low. And discounters such as Walmart, Costco, and others pressure their competitors to operate efficiently and keep their prices down.

Modern marketing is also accused of pushing up prices to finance unneeded advertising, sales promotion, and packaging. ● For example, a heavily promoted national brand sells for much more than a virtually identical store-branded product. Critics charge that much of this promotion and packaging adds only psychological, not functional, value. Marketers respond that although advertising adds to product costs, it also adds value by informing potential buyers of the availability and merits of a brand. Brand name products may cost more, but branding assures buyers of consistent quality. Moreover, although consumers can usually buy functional versions of products at lower prices, they *want* and are willing to pay more for products that also provide psychological benefits—that make them feel wealthy, attractive, or special.

Critics also charge that some companies mark up goods excessively. They point to the drug industry, where a

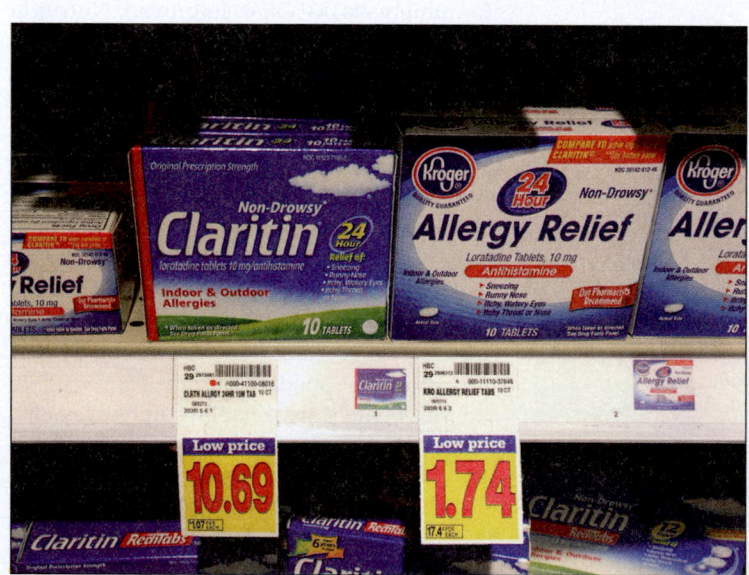

● A heavily promoted national brand sells for much more than a virtually identical non-branded or store-branded product. Critics charge that promotion adds only psychological value to the product rather than functional value.

Keri Miksza

pill costing five cents to make may cost the consumer $2 to buy, and to the high charges for auto repairs and other services. Marketers respond that most businesses try to price fairly to consumers because they want to build customer relationships and repeat business. Also, they assert, consumers often don't understand the reasons for high markups. For example, pharmaceutical markups help cover the costs of making and distributing existing medicines plus the high costs of developing and testing new medicines. As pharmaceuticals company GlaxoSmithKline has stated in its ads, "Today's medicines finance tomorrow's miracles."

Deceptive Practices

Marketers are sometimes accused of deceptive practices that lead consumers to believe they will get more value than they actually do. Deceptive practices fall into three groups: promotion, packaging, and pricing. *Deceptive promotion* includes practices such as misrepresenting the product's features or performance or luring customers to the store for a bargain that is out of stock. *Deceptive packaging* includes exaggerating package contents through subtle design, using misleading labeling, or describing size in misleading terms.

Deceptive pricing includes practices such as falsely advertising "factory" or "wholesale" prices or a large price reduction from a phony high retail "list price." For example, retailers the likes of JCPenney and Kohl's were hit with lawsuits last year alleging that they used inflated original prices. A class-action suit against Macy's accused the retailer of duping customers with a "phantom markdown scheme" and of "purporting to offer steep discounts off of fabricated, arbitrary, and false former or purported original, regular or 'compare at' prices."[3] And Overstock.com was recently fined $6.8 million by a California court as a result of a fraudulent pricing lawsuit filed by the attorneys general of eight California counties. The suit charged that the online giant routinely advertised its prices as lower than fabricated "list prices." It recites one example in which Overstock sold a patio set for $449 while claiming that the list price was $999. When the item was delivered, the customer found that it had a Walmart sticker stating a price of $247.[4]

Deceptive practices have led to legislation and other consumer protection actions. For example, in 1938 Congress enacted the Wheeler-Lea Act, which gave the Federal Trade Commission (FTC) power to regulate "unfair or deceptive acts or practices." The FTC has since published several guidelines listing deceptive practices. Despite regulations, however, some critics argue that deceptive claims are still common, even for well-known brands. ● For example, Luminosity recently agreed to pay $2 million to settle FTC charges that it deceived consumers with unsupported claims that its "brain training" games would protect them against cognitive decline. "Lumosity preyed on consumers' fears about age-related cognitive decline, suggesting their games could stave off memory loss, dementia, and even Alzheimer's disease," said the director of the FTC's Bureau of Consumer Protection. "But Lumosity simply did not have the science to back up its ads."[5]

The toughest problem often is defining what is "deceptive." For instance, an advertiser's claim that its chewing gum will "rock your world" isn't intended to be taken literally. Instead, the advertiser might claim, it is "puffery"—innocent exaggeration for effect. However, others claim that puffery and alluring imagery can harm consumers in subtle ways. Think about the popular and long-running MasterCard Priceless commercials that once painted pictures of consumers fulfilling their priceless dreams despite the costs. The ads suggested that your credit card could make it happen. But critics charge that such imagery by credit card companies encouraged a spend-now-pay-later attitude that caused many consumers to *over*use their cards.

● **Deceptive advertising: Luminosity recently settled with the FTC on charges that it deceived consumers with unsupported claims that its "brain training" games would protect them against cognitive decline. "Lumosity simply did not have the science to back up its ads," said the FTC.**

Westend61/Getty Images

Marketers argue that most companies avoid deceptive practices. Because such practices harm a company's business in the long run, they simply aren't sustainable. Profitable customer relationships are built on a foundation of value and trust. If consumers do not get what they expect, they will switch to more reliable products. In addition, consumers usually protect themselves from deception. Most consumers recognize a marketer's selling intent and are careful when they buy, sometimes even to the point of not believing completely true product claims.

High-Pressure Selling

Salespeople are sometimes accused of high-pressure selling that persuades people to buy goods they had no thought of buying. It is often said that insurance, real estate, and used cars are *sold*, not *bought*. Salespeople are trained to deliver smooth, canned talks to entice purchases. They sell hard because sales contests promise big prizes to those who sell the most. Similarly, TV infomercial pitchmen use "yell and sell" presentations that create a sense of consumer urgency that only those with strong willpower can resist.

But in most cases, marketers have little to gain from high-pressure selling. Although such tactics may work in one-time selling situations for short-term gain, most selling involves building long-term relationships with valued customers. High-pressure or deceptive selling can seriously damage such relationships. For example, imagine a P&G account manager trying to pressure a Walmart buyer or an IBM salesperson trying to browbeat an information technology manager at GE. It simply wouldn't work.

Shoddy, Harmful, or Unsafe Products

Another criticism concerns poor product quality or function. One complaint is that, too often, products and services are not made well or do not perform well. A second complaint concerns product safety. Product safety has been a problem for several reasons, including company indifference, increased product complexity, and poor quality control. A third complaint is that many products deliver little benefit or may even be harmful.

For example, think about the soft drink industry. For years, industry critics have blamed the plentiful supply of sugar-laden, high-calorie soft drinks for the obesity epidemic and other health issues in the United States. They are quick to fault what they see as greedy beverage marketers for cashing in on vulnerable consumers, turning us into a nation of Big Gulpers. Although U.S. consumption of soft drinks has dropped in recent years, beverage companies are now looking to emerging markets for growth. ● According to a report by the Center for Science in the Public Interest (CSPI) titled "Carbonating the World," in 2008 emerging markets such as China, India, and Mexico accounted for just over half of global soft drink consumption. But by 2018 nearly 70 percent of soft drinks will be sold in such markets. The CPSI accuses beverage companies of behaving much like the tobacco industry, marketing their harmful products to countries already struggling to provide health care to their citizens.[6]

Is the soft drink industry being socially irresponsible by aggressively promoting overindulgence to ill-informed or unwary consumers in emerging markets? Or is it simply serving the wants of customers by offering products that ping consumer taste buds while letting consumers make their own consumption choices? Is it the industry's job to police public tastes? As in many matters of social responsibility, what's right and wrong may be a matter of opinion. Whereas some analysts criticize the industry, others suggest that responsibility lies with consumers. Maybe companies shouldn't sell Big Gulps. Then again, nobody is forced to buy and drink one.

Most manufacturers *want* to produce quality goods. After all, the way a company deals with product quality and safety problems can harm or help its reputation. Companies selling poor-quality or unsafe products risk damaging conflicts with consumer groups and regulators. Unsafe products can result in product liability suits and large awards for damages. More fundamentally, consumers who are unhappy with a firm's products may avoid future purchases and talk other consumers into doing the same. In today's social media and online review environment, word of poor quality can spread like wildfire. Thus, quality missteps are not consistent with sustainable marketing. Today's marketers know that good quality results in customer value and satisfaction, which in turn create sustainable customer relationships.

● Harmful products: Is the soft drink industry being irresponsible by promoting harmful products in emerging markets, or is it simply serving the wants of consumers while letting them make their own consumption choices?

Center for Science in the Public Interest

Planned Obsolescence

Critics also have charged that some companies practice *planned obsolescence*, causing their products to become obsolete before they actually should need replacement. They accuse some producers of using materials and components that will break, wear, rust, or rot sooner than they should. And if the products themselves don't wear out fast enough, other companies are charged with *perceived obsolescence*—continually changing consumer concepts of acceptable styles to encourage more and earlier buying. An obvious example is the fast-fashion industry with its constantly changing clothing fashions, which some critics claim creates a wasteful disposable clothing culture. "Too many garments end up in landfill sites," bemoans one designer. "They are deemed aesthetically redundant and get discarded at the end of the season when there are often years of wear left."[7]

Still others are accused of introducing planned streams of new products that make older models obsolete, turning consumers into "serial replacers." Critics claim that this occurs in the consumer electronics industries. If you're like most people, you probably have a drawer full of yesterday's hottest technological gadgets—from mobile phones and cameras to iPods and flash drives—now reduced to the status of fossils. It seems that anything more than a year or two old is hopelessly out of date.

Marketers respond that consumers *like* style changes; they get tired of the old goods and want a new look in fashion. Or they *want* the latest high-tech innovations, even if older models still work. No one has to buy a new product, and if too few people like it, it will simply fail. Finally, most companies do not design their products to break down earlier because they do not want to lose customers to other brands. Instead, they seek constant improvement to ensure that products will consistently meet or exceed customer expectations.

Much of the so-called planned obsolescence is the working of the competitive and technological forces in a free society—forces that lead to ever-improving goods and services. For example, if Apple produced a new iPhone or iPad that would last 10 years, few consumers would want it. Instead, buyers want the latest technological innovations. "Obsolescence isn't something companies are forcing on us," confirms one analyst. "It's progress, and it's something we pretty much demand. As usual, the market gives us exactly what we want."[8]

Poor Service to Disadvantaged Consumers

Finally, the American marketing system has been accused of poorly serving disadvantaged consumers. For example, critics claim that the urban poor often have to shop in smaller stores that carry inferior goods and charge higher prices. The presence of large national chain stores in low-income neighborhoods would help to keep prices down. However, the critics accuse major chain retailers of *redlining*, drawing a red line around disadvantaged neighborhoods and avoiding placing stores there.

For example, the nation's poor areas have 30 percent fewer supermarkets than affluent areas do. As a result, many low-income consumers find themselves in *food deserts*, which are awash with small markets offering frozen pizzas, Cheetos, Moon Pies, and Cokes but where fruits and vegetables or fresh fish and chicken are out of reach. The U.S. Department of Agriculture has identified more than 6,500 food deserts in rural and urban areas of the United States. Currently, some 23.5 million Americans—including 6.5 million children—live in low-income areas that lack stores selling affordable and nutritious foods. In turn, the lack of access to healthy, affordable fresh foods has a negative impact on the health of underserved consumers in these areas.[9]

Many national chains, such as Walmart, Walgreens, SuperValu, and even Whole Foods Market have recently agreed to open or expand more stores that bring nutritious and fresh foods to underserved communities. Other retailers have found that they can operate profitably by focusing on low-income areas ignored by other companies. Consider Brown's Super Stores, Inc., in Philadelphia:[10]

● Serving underserved consumers: Jeff Brown's seven ShopRite stores operate profitably in low-income Philadelphia neighborhoods by becoming a part of the communities they serve.

Steven M. Falk/Philadelphia Inquirer

● When Jeff Brown opened his first grocery store in a low-income Southwest Philly neighborhood, most people thought he was crazy. How could he make money in a food desert? But Brown now operates seven profitable ShopRite stores in low-income areas in and around Philadelphia. Brown knows that serving consumers in low-income areas takes more than just opening a store and stocking it with healthy foods. Prices have to be low. At the same time, food quality and service have to be good. So Brown takes cues from high-end grocers by doing things like hand-stacking fresh fruits and produce to avoid bruising and make it more eye-catching. His ShopRite stores also hire skilled butchers, fishmongers, and in-store chefs to entice shoppers to choose healthier options, such as "fire-grilled chicken," cooked right in the store.

Perhaps most important, Brown's ShopRite stores have become parts of the communities in which they operate. Brown and his associates work with local leaders even before a store opens to learn exactly what they seek in a neighborhood grocery store. They research neighborhood demographics and tailor offerings to community preferences. Brown's ShopRite stores are also community gathering places, providing community center space in stores for local meetings and events. The company even works with local nonprofits to provide free services such as credit unions, social workers, and health clinics. Such services help the community but also help Brown's ShopRites by building a more frequent and loyal customer base. "In the end, it's really about putting the supermarket at the center of the community," concludes one food retailing expert.

Clearly, better marketing systems must be built to service disadvantaged consumers. In fact, like Brown's, marketers in many industries profitably target such consumers with legitimate goods and services that create real value. In cases where marketers do not step in to fill the void, the government likely will. For example, the FTC has taken action against sellers that advertise false values, wrongfully deny services, or charge disadvantaged customers too much.

Marketing's Impact on Society as a Whole

The American marketing system has been accused of adding to several "evils" in American society at large, such as creating too much materialism, too few social goods, and a glut of cultural pollution.

False Wants and Too Much Materialism

Critics have charged that the marketing system urges too much interest in material possessions, and that America's love affair with worldly possessions is not sustainable. Too often, people are judged by what they *own* rather than by who they *are*. The critics do not view this interest in material things as a natural state of mind but rather as a matter of false wants created by marketing. Marketers, they claim, stimulate people's desires for goods and create materialistic models of the good life. Thus, marketers have created an endless cycle of mass consumption based on a distorted interpretation of the "American Dream."

● Materialism: A marketing campaign by the Center for a New American Dream urges people to reject "buy more" messages and instead say "More fun! Less stuff!"

Center for the New American Dream

In this view, marketing's purpose is to promote consumption, and the inevitable outcome of successful marketing is unsustainable *over*consumption. According to the critics, more is not always better. Some groups have taken their concerns straight to the public. For example, the Center for a New American Dream is a nonprofit organization founded on a mission to "help Americans to reduce and shift their consumption to improve quality of life, protect the environment, and promote social justice." ● Through educational videos and marketing campaigns such as "More fun! Less stuff!" the organization works with individuals, institutions, communities, and businesses to help conserve natural resources, counter the commercialization of culture, and promote positive changes in the way goods are produced and consumed.[11]

Marketers respond that such criticisms overstate the power of business to create needs. They claim people have strong defenses against advertising and other marketing tools. Marketers are most effective when they appeal to existing wants rather than when they attempt to create new ones. Furthermore, people seek information when making important purchases and often do not rely on single sources. Even minor purchases that may be affected by advertising messages lead to repeat purchases only if the product delivers the promised customer value. Finally, the high failure rate of new products shows that companies are not able to control demand.

On a deeper level, our wants and values are influenced not only by marketers but also by family, peer groups, religion, cultural background, and education. If Americans are highly materialistic, these values arose out of basic socialization processes that go much deeper than business and marketing could produce alone. Consumption patterns and attitudes are also subject to larger forces, such as the economy. As discussed in Chapter 1, the recent Great Recession put a damper on materialism and conspicuous spending.

These days consumers are also more supportive of environmental and social sustainability efforts by companies. As a result, instead of encouraging today's more sensible and conscientious consumers to overspend or spend wastefully, many marketers are working to help them find greater value with less. For example, Patagonia's recent "conscious consumption" campaign actually urges its customers to buy less, telling them "Don't buy what you don't need." and "Think twice before you buy anything." Similarly, L.L Bean's "When" campaign encourages customers to buy and hang onto products that last rather than always buying new ones. It asks, "When did disposable become our default?" The answer: "At L.L. Bean, it never did. When you buy something from us, we want you to like it for a long time #llasting."[12]

Too Few Social Goods

Business has been accused of overselling private goods at the expense of public goods. As private goods increase, they require more public services that are usually not forthcoming. For example, private automobile ownership (private good) requires highways, traffic control, parking spaces, and police services (public goods). The overselling of private goods results in social costs. For cars, some of the social costs include traffic congestion, gasoline shortages, and air pollution. For example, American travelers lose, on average, 42 hours a year in traffic jams, costing the United States more than $160 billion a year—$960 per commuter. In the process, they waste 3.1 billion gallons of fuel (enough to fill the New Orleans Superdome more than four times).[13]

A way must be found to restore a balance between private and public goods. One option is to make producers bear the full social costs of their operations. For example, the government is requiring automobile manufacturers to build cars with more efficient engines and better pollution-control systems. Automakers will then raise their prices to cover the extra costs. If buyers find the price of some car models too high, these models will disappear. Demand will then move to those producers that can support the sum of the private and social costs.

A second option is to make consumers pay the social costs. For example, many cities around the world are now levying congestion tolls and other charges in an effort to reduce traffic congestion. The island nation of Singapore—about the size of three and a half Washington, DCs—has taken such measures to extremes:

> To control traffic congestion and pollution, Singapore's government makes car ownership very expensive. New car purchases are taxed at 100 percent or more of their market value and buyers must purchase a "certificate of entitlement," which costs tens of thousands of dollars. As a result, a Toyota Corolla purchased in Singapore runs close to $96,000; a Toyota Prius goes for about $154,000. That plus the high cost of gas and "Electronic Road Pricing" tolls collected automatically as cars are driven around the country makes car ownership prohibitively expensive for most Singaporeans. Only about 15 percent of the population owns a car, keeping congestion, pollution, and other auto evils to a minimum and making Singapore one of the greenest urban areas in Asia.[14]

Cultural Pollution

Critics charge the marketing system with creating *cultural pollution*. They feel our senses are being constantly assaulted by marketing and advertising. ● Commercials interrupt serious programs; pages of ads obscure magazines; billboards mar beautiful scenery; spam fills our email inboxes; flashing display ads intrude on our online and mobile screens. What's more, the critics claim, these interruptions continually pollute people's minds with messages of materialism, sex, power, or status. Some critics call for sweeping changes.

● **Cultural pollution: People's senses are sometimes assaulted by a clutter of commercial messages and noise.**

Christian Science Monitor/Getty Images

Marketers answer the charges of commercial noise with these arguments: First, they hope that their ads primarily reach the target audience. But because of mass-communication channels, some ads are bound to reach people who have no interest in the product and are therefore bored or annoyed. People who buy magazines they like or who opt in to email, social media, or mobile marketing programs rarely complain about the ads because they involve products and services of interest.

Second, because of ads, many television, radio, online, and social media sites are free to users. Ads also help keep down the costs of magazines and newspapers. Many people think viewing ads is a small price to pay for these benefits. In addition, consumers find many television commercials entertaining and seek them out; for example, ad viewership during the Super Bowl usually equals or exceeds game viewership. Finally, today's consumers have alternatives. For example, they can zip or zap TV commercials on recorded programs or avoid them altogether on many paid cable, satellite, and online streaming channels. Thus, to hold consumer attention, advertisers are making their ads more entertaining and informative.

Marketing's Impact on Other Businesses

Critics also charge that a company's marketing practices can harm other companies and reduce competition. They identify three problems: acquisitions of competitors, marketing practices that create barriers to entry, and unfair competitive marketing practices.

Critics claim that firms are harmed and competition is reduced when companies expand by acquiring competitors rather than by developing their own new products. The large number of acquisitions and the rapid pace of industry consolidation over the past several decades have caused concern that vigorous young competitors will be absorbed, thereby reducing competition. In virtually every major industry—retailing, entertainment, financial services, utilities, transportation, automobiles, telecommunications, health care—the number of major competitors is shrinking.

Acquisition is a complex subject. In some cases, acquisitions can be good for society. The acquiring company may gain economies of scale that lead to lower costs and lower prices. In addition, a well-managed company may take over a poorly managed company and improve its efficiency. An industry that was not very competitive might become more competitive after the acquisition. But acquisitions can also be harmful and therefore are closely regulated by the government.

Critics have also charged that marketing practices bar new companies from entering an industry. Large marketing companies can use patents and heavy promotion spending or tie up suppliers or dealers to keep out or drive out competitors. Those concerned with antitrust regulation recognize that some barriers are the natural result of the economic advantages of doing business on a large scale. Existing and new laws can challenge other barriers. For example, some critics have proposed a progressive tax on advertising spending to reduce the role of selling costs as a major barrier to entry.

Finally, some firms have, in fact, used unfair competitive marketing practices with the intention of hurting or destroying other firms. They may set their prices below costs, threaten to cut off business with suppliers, discourage the buying of a competitor's products, or use their size and market dominance to unfairly damage rivals. Although various laws work to prevent such predatory competition, it is often difficult to prove that the intent or action was really predatory. It's often difficult to differentiate predatory practices from effective competitive strategy and tactics.

In recent years, search giant Google has been accused of using predatory practices at the expense of smaller competitors. ● For example, the European Commission recently accused Google of abusing its web-search dominance, harming both competitors and consumers in European Union markets.[15] The commission also began investigating antitrust issues related to Google's Android mobile operating system. Google's web-search engine

claims a commanding 92 percent European market share; the Android operating system dominates with a 71 percent share.

The European Commission formally accused Google of manipulating its search-engine results to favor its own shopping services at the expense of rivals. According to the commission, such "conduct may therefore artificially divert traffic from rival comparison shopping services and hinder their ability to compete, to the detriment of consumers, as well as stifling innovation." The commission's future antitrust investigations could expand beyond Google's shopping services into areas such as online and mobile searches for travel services and restaurants. For its part, however, Google contends that its web-search and mobile operations constitute fair and effective competition that serves the best interests of consumers. If the antitrust charges stand, the European Commission could hit Google with billions of dollars in fines.

● **Competitive marketing practices: The European Commission recently accused Google of abusing its web-search dominance, harming both competitors and consumers in European Union markets. Google claims that its practices constitute fair and effective competition.**
Associated Press

Author Comment | Sustainable marketing isn't something that only businesses and governments do. Through consumerism and environmentalism, consumers themselves can play an important role.

Consumer Actions to Promote Sustainable Marketing

Sustainable marketing calls for more responsible actions by both businesses and consumers. Because some people view businesses as the cause of many economic and social ills, grassroots movements have arisen from time to time to keep businesses in line. Two major movements have been *consumerism* and *environmentalism*.

Consumerism

Consumerism
An organized movement of citizens and government agencies designed to improve the rights and power of buyers in relation to sellers.

Consumerism is an organized movement of citizens and government agencies to improve the rights and power of buyers in relation to sellers. Traditional *sellers' rights* include the following:

- The right to introduce any product in any size and style, provided it is not hazardous to personal health or safety, or, if it is, to include proper warnings and controls
- The right to charge any price for the product, provided no discrimination exists among similar kinds of buyers
- The right to spend any amount to promote the product, provided it is not defined as unfair competition
- The right to use any product message, provided it is not misleading or dishonest in content or execution
- The right to use buying incentive programs, provided they are not unfair or misleading

Traditional *buyers' rights* include the following:

- The right not to buy a product that is offered for sale
- The right to expect the product to be safe
- The right to expect the product to perform as claimed

In comparing these rights, many believe that the balance of power lies on the seller's side. True, the buyer can refuse to buy. But critics feel that the buyer has too little information, education, and protection to make wise decisions when facing sophisticated sellers. Consumer advocates call for the following additional consumer rights:

- The right to be well informed about important aspects of the product
- The right to be protected against questionable products and marketing practices
- The right to influence products and marketing practices in ways that will improve "quality of life"
- The right to consume now in a way that will preserve the world for future generations of consumers

● **Consumer desire for more information led to package labels with useful facts, from ingredients and nutrition facts to recycling and country of origin information.**

E+/Getty Images

Each proposed right has led to more specific proposals by consumerists and consumer protection actions by the government. ● The right to be informed includes the right to know the true interest on a loan (truth in lending), the true cost per unit of a brand (unit pricing), the ingredients in a product (ingredient labeling), the nutritional value of foods (nutritional labeling), product freshness (open dating), and the true benefits of a product (truth in advertising).

Proposals related to consumer protection include strengthening consumer rights in cases of business fraud and financial protection, requiring greater product safety, ensuring information privacy, and giving more power to government agencies. Proposals relating to quality of life include controlling the ingredients that go into certain products and packaging and reducing the level of advertising "noise." Proposals for preserving the world for future consumption include promoting the use of sustainable ingredients, recycling and reducing solid wastes, and managing energy consumption.

Sustainable marketing applies not only to businesses and governments but also to consumers. Consumers have not only the *right* but also the *responsibility* to protect themselves instead of leaving this function to the government or someone else. Consumers who believe they got a bad deal have several remedies available, including contacting the company; making their case through the media or social media; contacting federal, state, or local agencies; and going to small-claims courts. Consumers should also make good consumption choices, rewarding companies that act responsibly while punishing those that don't. Ultimately, the move from irresponsible consumption to sustainable consumption is in the hands of consumers.

Environmentalism

Environmentalism

An organized movement of concerned citizens, businesses, and government agencies designed to protect and improve people's current and future living environment.

Whereas consumerists consider whether the marketing system is efficiently serving consumer wants, environmentalists are concerned with marketing's effects on the environment and the environmental costs of serving consumer needs and wants. **Environmentalism** is an organized movement of concerned citizens, businesses, and government agencies designed to protect and improve people's current and future living environment.

Environmentalists are not against marketing and consumption; they simply want people and organizations to operate with more care for the environment. They call for doing away with what sustainability advocate and Unilever CEO Paul Polman calls "mindless consumption." According to Polman, "The road to well-being doesn't go via reduced consumption. It has to be done via more responsible consumption."[16] The marketing system's goal, environmentalists assert, should not be to maximize consumption, consumer choice, or consumer satisfaction but rather to maximize life quality. Life quality means not only the quantity and quality of consumer goods and services but also the quality of the environment, now and for future generations.

Environmentalism is concerned with damage to the ecosystem caused by global warming, resource depletion, toxic and solid wastes, litter, the availability of fresh water, and other problems. Other issues include the loss of recreational areas and the increase in health problems caused by bad air, polluted water, and chemically treated food.

Over the past several decades, such concerns have resulted in federal and state laws and regulations governing industrial commercial practices affecting the environment. Some companies have strongly resented and resisted such environmental regulations, claiming that they are too costly and have made their industries less competitive. These companies responded to consumer environmental concerns by doing only what was required to avert new regulations or keep environmentalists quiet.

Environmental sustainability

A management approach that involves developing strategies that both sustain the environment and produce profits for the company.

In recent years, however, most companies have accepted responsibility for doing no harm to the environment. They have shifted from protest to prevention and from regulation to responsibility. More and more companies are now adopting policies of **environmental sustainability**. Simply put, environmental sustainability is about generating profits while helping to save the planet. Today's enlightened companies are taking action not because someone is forcing them to or to reap short-run profits but because it's the right thing to do—because it's for their customers' well-being, the company's well-being, and the planet's environmental future. For example, fast-food chain Chipotle has successfully built its core mission around environmental sustainability—its aim is to serve "Food With Integrity" (see Real Marketing 20.1).

● **Figure 20.2** shows a grid that companies can use to gauge their progress toward environmental sustainability. It includes both internal and external *greening* activities that will pay off for the firm and environment in the short run and *beyond greening* activities that will pay off in the longer term.

At the most basic level, a company can practice *pollution prevention*. This involves more than pollution control—cleaning up waste after it has been created. Pollution prevention means eliminating or minimizing waste *before* it is created. Companies emphasizing prevention have responded with internal green marketing programs—designing and developing ecologically safer products, recyclable and biodegradable packaging, better pollution controls, and more energy-efficient operations.

● For example, in creating new products, athletic shoe and apparel maker adidas considers their environmental impact before ever producing them. This results in low-waste footwear and apparel, such as Element Soul shoes, which yield both performance and sustainability benefits. With their simplified design—only 12 parts instead of the typical 50—the lightweight shoes give athletes a more natural run while at the same time cutting down on materials, waste, and energy use in production. On a broader scale, adidas has developed a restricted substances list for product design and manufacturing: no PVCs, no materials from endangered or threatened species, and less and less materials from non-sustainable sources. adidas has also set ambitious internal goals for reducing greenhouse emissions and energy, water, and paper consumption in its operations. And it has set up Green Teams at locations around the world whose members promote adidas's environmental programs internally and urge their colleagues to "think green," such as reducing office waste going to landfills.[17]

At the next level, companies can practice *product stewardship*—minimizing not only pollution from production and product design but also all environmental impacts throughout the full product life cycle while at the same time reducing costs. Many companies have adopted *design for environment (DFE)* and *cradle-to-cradle* practices. This involves thinking ahead to design products that are easier to recover, reuse, recycle, or safely return to nature after usage, thus becoming part of the ecological cycle. DFE and cradle-to-cradle practices not only help to sustain the environment, but they can also be highly profitable for the company.

For example, more than a decade ago, IBM started a business—IBM Global Asset Recovery Services—designed to reuse and recycle parts from returned mainframe computers and other equipment. Last year, IBM processed more than 54.3 million pounds of end-of-life products and product waste worldwide, stripping down old equipment to recover chips and valuable metals. Since 2002 it has processed more than 1.09 billion pounds of machines, parts, and material. IBM Global Asset Recovery Services finds uses for more than 99 percent of what

● Environmental sustainability: adidas sets ambitious goals for sustainable products and operations. In creating new products, the company considers their environmental impact before ever producing them.

adidas

● **FIGURE** | 20.2

Environmental Sustainability and Sustainable Value

Source: Based on Stuart L. Hart, "Sustainable Value," www.stuartlhart.com/sustainablevalue.html, October 2016.

	Today: **Greening**	**Tomorrow:** **Beyond Greening**
Internal	**Pollution prevention** Eliminating or reducing waste before it is created	**New clean technology** Developing new sets of environmental skills and capabilities
External	**Product stewardship** Minimizing environmental impact throughout the entire product life cycle	**Sustainability vision** Developing a strategy framework for creating sustainable value

This framework addresses more than just natural environmental challenges. It also points to opportunities for creating sustainable value for markets and the firm through environmentally sustainable strategies and practices.

20.1   Chipotle's Environmental Sustainability Mission: "Food With Integrity"

Envision this. You're sitting in a restaurant where the people—from the CEO on down to the kitchen crew—obsess over using only the finest ingredients. They come to work each morning inspired by all the "fresh produce and meats they have to marinate, rice they have to cook, and fresh herbs they have to chop," says the CEO. The restaurant prefers to use sustainable, naturally raised ingredients sourced from local family farms. It's on a mission not just to serve its customers good food but to change the way its entire industry produces food.

This sounds like one of those high-falutin', gourmet specialty restaurants, right? Wrong. It's your neighborhood Chipotle Mexican Grill. That's right, it's a fast-food restaurant. In an age when many fast-feeders seem to be using ever-cheaper ingredients and centralization of food preparation to cut costs and keep prices low, Chipotle is doing just the opposite. The chain's core sustainable mission is to serve "Food With Integrity." What does that mean? The company explains it this way:

Day after day we're committed to sourcing the very best ingredients we can find and preparing them by hand. To vegetables grown in the healthy soil and pork from pigs allowed to freely root and roam outdoors or in deeply bedded barns. We're committed because we understand the connection between how food is raised and prepared and how it tastes. We do it for farmers, animals, the environment, dentists, crane operators, ribbon dancers, magicians, cartographers, and you. While industrial farming practices have evolved to maximize profits and production, we make an extra effort to partner with farmers, ranchers, and other suppliers whose practices emphasize quality and responsibility. With every burrito we roll or bowl we fill, we're working to cultivate a better world. In other words, "integrity" is kind of a funny word for "good."

When founder and CEO Steve Ells opened the first Chipotle in Denver in 1993, his primary goal was to make the best gourmet burrito around. However, as the chain grew, Ells found that he didn't like the way the ingredients Chipotle used were raised and processed. So, in 2000, Chipotle began developing a supply chain with the goal of producing and using naturally raised, organic, hormone-free, non–genetically modified ingredients. Pursuing this healthy-food mission

was no easy task. As the fast-food industry increasingly moved toward low-cost, efficient food processing, factory farms were booming, whereas independent farms producing naturally raised and organic foods were in decline.

To obtain the ingredients it needed, Chipotle had to develop many new sources by supporting family farming and encouraging sustainable farming practices. Such efforts have paid off. Today, 100 percent of Chipotle's pork and beef comes from producers that meet or exceed its "naturally raised" standards (the animals are raised in a humane way, fed a vegetarian diet, never given hormones or subtherapeutic antibiotics, and allowed to display their natural tendencies). Chipotle's goal is to meet that same 100 percent mark for its chicken, its dairy, and even its produce. It then plans to tighten its standards even more.

Sourcing such natural and organic ingredients not only serves Chipotle's sustainability mission, it results in one of the most nutritious, best-tasting fast-food burritos on the market—something the company can brag about to customers. Whereas some fast-food companies intentionally obscure the sometimes less-than-appetizing truths about their ingredients, Chipotle doesn't play that game. Instead, it commits fast-food heresy:

Proudly telling customers what's really inside its burritos.

Chipotle chose the "Food With Integrity" slogan because it sends the right message in an appetizing way. "Saying that we don't buy dairy from cows that are given the hormone rBGH is not an appetizing message," says Ells. So the company built its marketing campaign around the more positive message that food production should be healthier and more ethical.

Chipotle doesn't spend much on traditional media advertising. "We deliberately spend less on our marketing so we can afford these higher-quality ingredients," says Chipotle's chief marketing officer. That's not to say the company is a stranger to mass-media advertising. Chipotle made a big splash a few years ago during the broadcast for the Grammy Awards with its first-ever national television ad, "Back to the Start"—a two-and-a-half-minute stop-motion animation film showing the negative effects of industrialized farming. The ad received critical acclaim and racked up millions of views online.

As a follow-up, Chipotle released "The Scarecrow," another animated video indicting the industrial food industry. Accompanied by Fiona Apple's cover of "Pure Imagination," the star character leaves his job at a factory farm

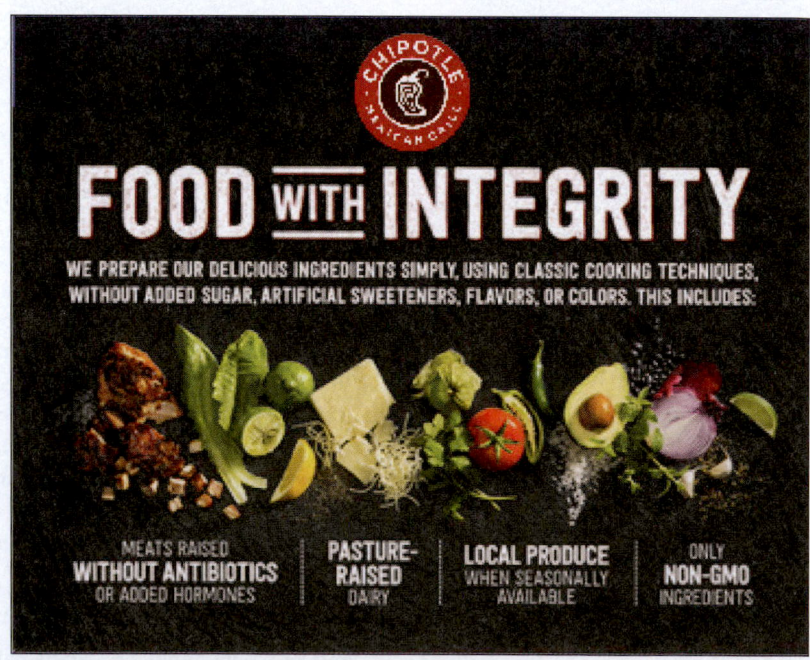

Fast-food chain Chipotle Mexican Grill has successfully built its core mission around environmental sustainability—its aim is to serve "Food With Integrity."

and opens his own little shop selling freshly prepared food under the banner "Cultivate a better world." The online ad directed people to the campaign's centerpiece—an arcade-style game app that racked up millions of downloads, even as the ad itself scored over 15 million views on YouTube.

Chipotle's strongest promotional efforts center on social media, with a strong and steady presence across Facebook, Twitter, YouTube, Pinterest, LinkedIn, and Instagram. It uses quirky digital content, strong brand images, and special promotions to get out the word on food sustainability. Chipotle has launched numerous efforts to engage and educate customers, such as posting links to Taste Invaders, an old-style video game billed as "a galactic battle against artificial ingredients." And there's Chipotle's annual Cultivate Festival—a free event held in multiple cities where brand fans come together to enjoy food, music, and ideas focusing on sustainable food practices. Whether it's an award-winning ad, a quirky game, or a food and music festival, Chipotle keeps its both its food and its sustainability story fresh.

Companies with socially responsible business models often struggle to grow and make profits. But Chipotle is proving that a company can do both. Last year, its 59,000 employees chopped, sliced, diced, and grilled

their way to $4.5 billion in revenues and $475 million in profits at Chipotle's almost 2,000 U.S. restaurants. And the chain is growing fast, opening a new restaurant about every two days. Over the past five years, Chipotle's revenues and profits have surged by more than 250 percent.

Chipotle has recently faced some challenges in carrying out its mission. The most serious were incidents of *E. coli*, norovirus, and salmonella contamination traced to Chipotle restaurants in multiple states, striking at the heart of the chain's Food With Integrity promise and causing sales to slump. Chipotle has since retrained employees, made adjustments in it supply chain and food processing procedures, and redoubled its focus on transparency and food safety.

Although the incidents temporarily turned down the heat on Chipotle's short-term sales and profits growth, the company hasn't cooled off on its Food With Integrity mission. Founder and CEO Ells wants Chipotle to grow and make money. But ultimately, on a larger stage, he wants to change the way fast food is produced and sold—not just by Chipotle but by the entire industry. "We think the more people understand where their food comes from and the impact that has on independent family farmers [and] animal welfare, the more they're going to ask for better ingredients," says Ells. Whether customers stop by Chipotle's restaurants to support the cause, gobble down the tasty food, or both, it all suits Ells just fine. Chipotle's sustainability mission isn't an add-on, created just to position the company as "socially responsible." To hear Chipotle tell it, doing good "is the company's ethos and ingrained in everything we do."

Sources: See Denise Lee Yohn, "How Chipotle Changed American Fast Food Forever," *Fast Company,* March 14, 2014, www.fastcompany.com/3027647/lessons-learned/how-chipotle-changed-american-fast-food-forever; David Alba, "Chipotle's Health Crisis Shows Fresh Food Comes at a Price," *Wired,* January 15, 2016, www.wired.com/2016/01/chipotles-health-crisis-shows-fresh-food-comes-at-a-price/; Jessica Wohl, "Chipotle Deliberately Spends Less on Marketing to Afford Higher-Quality Ingredients," *Advertising Age,* October 20, 2015, http://adage.com/print/300998/; Emily Bryson York, "Chipotle Ups the Ante on Its Marketing," *Chicago Tribune,* September 30, 2011, http://articles.chicagotribune.com/2011-09-30/business/ct-biz-chipotle-profile-20110930_1_chipotle-plans-executive-steve-ells-chipotle-founder; "5 Ways Chipotle Creates an Awesome Social Media Strategy," *Unmetric Blog,* January 21, 2016, http://blog.unmetric.com/5-ways-chipotle-creates-an-awesome-social-media-strategy; and information from www.chipotle.com and www.chipotle.com/food-with-integrity, accessed October, 2016.

it takes in, sending less than 1 percent to landfills and incineration facilities. What started out as an environmental effort has now grown into a multibillion-dollar IBM business that profitably recycles electronic equipment at 22 sites worldwide.[18]

Today's *greening* activities focus on improving what companies already do to protect the environment. The *beyond greening* activities identified in Figure 20.2 look to the future. First, internally, companies can plan for *new clean technology*. Many organizations that have made good sustainability headway are still limited by existing technologies. To create fully sustainable strategies, they will need to develop innovative new technologies.

For example, by 2020, Coca-Cola has committed to reclaiming and recycling the equivalent of all the packaging it uses around the world. It has also pledged to dramatically reduce its overall environmental footprint. To accomplish these goals, the company invests heavily in new clean technologies that address a host of environmental issues, such as recycling, resource usage, and distribution:[19]

First, to attack the solid waste problem caused by its plastic bottles, Coca-Cola invested heavily to build the world's largest state-of-the-art plastic-bottle-to-bottle recycling plant. As a more permanent solution, Coke is researching and testing new bottles made from aluminum, corn, or bioplastics. It has been steadily replacing its PET plastic bottles with PlantBottle packaging, which incorporates 30 percent plant-based materials. The company is also designing more eco-friendly distribution alternatives. Currently, some 10 million vending machines and refrigerated coolers gobble up energy and use potent greenhouse gases called hydrofluorocarbons (HFCs) to keep Cokes cold. To eliminate them, the company has been installing sleek new HFC-free coolers that use 30 to 40 percent less energy—so far more than 1.4 million have been installed. Coca-Cola has even developed a line of "eKOCool" solar-powered coolers that not only conserve energy resources but are also functional in rural areas of emerging economies such as India, where conventional power sources are often unreliable. And Coca-Cola is now almost 100 percent "water neutral," adding back to communities and nature the equivalent of all the fresh water that its bottlers use in the production of Coca-Cola beverages.

Finally, companies can develop a *sustainability vision*, which serves as a guide to the future. It shows how the company's products and services, processes, and policies must evolve and what new technologies must be developed to get there. This vision of sustainability provides a framework for pollution control, product stewardship, and new environmental technology for the company and others to follow. It addresses not just challenges in the natural environment but also strategic opportunities for using environmental strategies to create sustainable value for the firm and its markets.

Most companies today focus on the upper-left quadrant of the grid in Figure 20.2, investing most heavily in pollution prevention. Some forward-looking companies practice product stewardship and are developing new environmental technologies. However, emphasizing only one or two quadrants in the environmental sustainability grid can be shortsighted. Investing only in the left half of the grid puts a company in a good position today but leaves it vulnerable in the future. In contrast, a heavy emphasis on the right half suggests that a company has good environmental vision but lacks the skills needed to implement it. Thus, companies should work at developing all four dimensions of environmental sustainability.

The North Face, for example, is doing just that through its own environmental sustainability actions and its impact on the actions of suppliers and consumers:[20]

The North Face's new headquarters building in Alameda, California, comes complete with solar panels and wind turbines that generate more electricity than the building uses. The building employs an evaporating cooling system that eliminates the need for emissions-heavy coolants. The company's other regional headquarters and distribution centers also incorporate solar or water-saving features. In manufacturing, The North Face works closely with suppliers to achieve its goal to use polyester—which makes up 80 percent of its clothing lines—from 100 percent recycled content. The North Face also partners with suppliers to reduce waste and chemical, water, and energy usage in their mills. Since 2010, The North Face's suppliers have removed more than 100 tanker trucks of chemicals and more than 230 Olympic swimming pools of water from their manufacturing processes.

In addition, The North Face has dedicated itself to inspiring customers to reduce the waste generated by today's fast-fashion era. The company's lifetime apparel and gear warranty results in the return and repair of more than 80,000 products annually. ● The North Face also runs a program called "Clothes the Loop," by which it collects worn-out or unwanted used clothing of any brand from customers for recycling or renewal. Items dropped in its collection bins are sent to a recycling center where they are carefully sorted, then repurposed for reuse to extend their life or recycled into raw materials for use in making other products. Proceeds from the program benefit the Conservation Alliance, which funds community-based campaigns to protect shared wilderness and recreation areas.

PROTECT OUR PLAYGROUND

RECYCLE RENEW REWARD

Recycle your used apparel and footwear at any The North Face retail store or outlet. Receive a reward for your efforts and help preserve our outdoor playground.

● **Sustainability vision: At The North Face, sustainability is about more than just doing the right thing—it also makes good business sense. Sustainability efforts such as its "Clothes the Loop" program are good for the company, its customers, *and* the planet.**

VF Corporation

For The North Face, being environmentally sustainable is about more than just doing the right thing. It also makes good business sense. More efficient operations and less wasteful products not only are good for the environment but also save The North Face money, helping it to deliver more value to customers. It's a winning combination. "At the heart of The North Face is a mission to inspire a global movement of outdoor exploration and conservation," says The North Face's president. "We believe the success of our business is fundamentally linked to having a healthy planet."[21]

Public Actions to Regulate Marketing

Citizen concerns about marketing practices will usually lead to public attention and legislative proposals. Many of the laws that affect marketing were identified in Chapter 3. The task is to translate these laws into a language that marketing executives understand as they make decisions about competitive relations, products, price, promotion, and distribution channels. ● **Figure 20.3** illustrates the major legal issues facing marketing management.

● **FIGURE | 20.3**
Major Marketing Decision Areas That May Be Called into Question under the Law
Wavebreakmedia/Shutterstock (photo)

Selling decisions
Bribing?
Stealing trade secrets?
Disparaging customers?
Misrepresenting?
Disclosure of customer rights?
Unfair discrimination?

Product decisions
Product additions and deletions?
Patent protection?
Product quality and safety?
Product warranty?

Advertising decisions
False advertising?
Deceptive advertising?
Bait-and-switch advertising?
Promotional allowances and services?

Packaging decisions
Fair packaging and labeling?
Excessive cost?
Scarce resources?
Pollution?

Channel decisions
Exclusive dealing?
Exclusive territorial distributorship?
Tying agreements?
Dealer's rights?

Price decisions
Price fixing?
Predatory pricing?
Price discrimination?
Minimum pricing?
Price increases?
Deceptive pricing?

Competitive relations decisions
Anticompetitive acquisition?
Barriers to entry?
Predatory competition?

Author Comment | In the end, marketers themselves must take responsibility for sustainable marketing. That means operating in a responsible and ethical way to bring both immediate and future value to customers.

Business Actions Toward Sustainable Marketing

At first, many companies opposed consumerism, environmentalism, and other elements of sustainable marketing. They thought the criticisms were either unfair or unimportant. But by now, most companies have grown to embrace sustainability principles as a way to create both immediate and future customer value and strengthen customer relationships.

Sustainable Marketing Principles

Under the sustainable marketing concept, a company's marketing should support the best long-run performance of the marketing system. It should be guided by five sustainable marketing principles: *consumer-oriented marketing, customer value marketing, innovative marketing, sense-of-mission marketing,* and *societal marketing*.

Consumer-Oriented Marketing

Consumer-oriented marketing
A company should view and organize its marketing activities from the consumer's point of view.

Consumer-oriented marketing means that the company should view and organize its marketing activities from the consumer's point of view. It should work hard to sense, serve, and satisfy the needs of a defined group of customers—both now and in the future. The good marketing companies that we've discussed throughout this text have had this in common: an all-consuming passion for delivering superior value to carefully chosen customers. Only by seeing the world through its customers' eyes can the company build sustainable and profitable customer relationships.

Customer Value Marketing

Customer value marketing
A company should put most of its resources into customer value–building marketing investments.

According to the principle of **customer value marketing**, the company should put most of its resources into customer value–building marketing investments. Many things marketers do—one-shot sales promotions, cosmetic product changes, direct-response advertising—may raise sales in the short run but add less *value* than would actual improvements in the product's quality, features, or convenience. Enlightened marketing calls for building long-run consumer engagement, loyalty, and relationships by continually improving the value consumers receive from the firm's market offering. By creating value *for* consumers, the company can capture value *from* consumers in return.

Innovative Marketing

The principle of **innovative marketing** requires that the company continuously seek real product and marketing improvements. The company that overlooks new and better ways to do things will eventually lose customers to another company that has found a better way.

Innovative marketers never stop looking for new and better ways to create customer value. For example, fast and dependable delivery is highly important to online shoppers. So Amazon delighted customers by being the first to innovate with free shipping on orders over $50. But Amazon didn't stop there. It next introduced Amazon Prime, by which customers could receive their packages within only two days for no extra charge or in one day for a small additional fee. ● Still not satisfied, Amazon innovated with Amazon Prime Now, which offers super-fast same-day delivery—or even one-hour delivery—on tens of thousands of items in major metropolitan areas. In its never-ending quest to shorten delivery times, Amazon has even invested heavily in research on drones, driverless vehicles, and robots. This and a seemingly endless list of other innovations over the years—from Recommendations for You, Customer Reviews, and 1-Click Ordering features to the Amazon Marketplace, Kindle e-readers, and Amazon Cloud services—have helped Amazon to enhance the shopping customer experience and dominate online retailing.

● **Innovative marketing: Amazon never stops looking for new ways to create customer value, such as Amazon Prime Now, which gives same-day—or even one-hour—delivery of customer orders.**

creativep/Alamy Stock Photo

Innovative marketing
A company should seek real product and marketing improvements.

Sense-of-mission marketing
A company should define its mission in broad social terms rather than narrow product terms.

Sense-of-Mission Marketing

Sense-of-mission marketing means that the company should define its mission in broad *social* terms rather than narrow *product* terms. When a company defines a social mission, employees feel better about their work and have a clearer sense of direction. Brands linked with broader missions can serve the best long-run interests of both the brand and consumers.

For example, successful home furnishings retailer IKEA has a deeply ingrained sense of mission—called The IKEA Way—to create a better everyday life for people by "offering well-designed, functional home furnishing products at prices so low that as many people as possible will be able to afford them." Johnson & Johnson's flagship Johnson's Baby brand dedicates itself to a mission of understanding babies and the special nurturing they require, then uses that knowledge to provide parents with safe and effective baby-care products. The company's recently launched "Our Promise" advertising and social media campaign—which will include some 40 videos featuring and shared by Johnson's Baby brand employees—assures parents that "It's a responsibility we take seriously as we continue to apply our knowledge and research to bring you safe, innovative products that live up to our pure, mild, and gentle promise." The first "Our Promise" video states that "We are moms and dads just like you. We'll always listen and be here for you. Promise." Sense-of-mission marketing has made Johnson's Baby the world's leading baby-care brand, with a nearly 25 percent worldwide market share.[22]

Some companies define their overall corporate missions in broad societal terms. For example, under its buy-one-give-one model, shoe maker TOMS seeks both profits and to make the world a better place. Thus, at TOMS, "doing good" and "doing well" go hand in hand. To achieve its social-change mission, TOMS has to make money. At the same time, the brand's social mission gives customers a powerful reason to buy.

However, having a *double bottom line* of values and profits isn't easy. Over the years, brands such as Ben & Jerry's, Timberland, The Body Shop, and Burt's Bees—all known and respected for putting "principles before profits"—have at times struggled with less-than-stellar financial returns. In recent years, however, a new generation of social entrepreneurs has emerged, well-trained business managers who know that to *do good*, they must first *do well* in terms of profitable business operations.

Moreover, today, socially responsible business is no longer the sole province of small, socially conscious entrepreneurs. Many large, established companies and brands—from Walmart and Nike to Starbucks, Coca-Cola, and CVS Health—have

●FIGURE | 20.4
Societal Classification of Products

Immediate Satisfaction

	Low	High	
High	Salutary products	**Desirable products**	
Low	Deficient products	Pleasing products	

Long-run Consumer Benefit

The goal? Create desirable products—those that create both immediate customer satisfaction and long-run benefit. For example, Method home and personal cleaning products "put the hurt on dirt without doing harm to people, creatures, or the planet."

Societal marketing
A company should make marketing decisions by considering consumers' wants, the company's requirements, consumers' long-run interests, and society's long-run interests.

Deficient products
Products that have neither immediate appeal nor long-run benefits.

Pleasing products
Products that give high immediate satisfaction but may hurt consumers in the long run.

Salutary products
Products that have low immediate appeal but may benefit consumers in the long run.

Desirable products
Products that give both high immediate satisfaction and high long-run benefits.

adopted substantial social and environmental responsibility missions. Rather than being at odds with revenues and profits, purpose-driven missions can drive them. For example, sense-of-mission marketing and doing what's right for customers has helped transform CVS into the nation's largest health-care company (see Real Marketing 20.2).

Societal Marketing

Following the principle of **societal marketing**, a company makes marketing decisions by considering consumers' wants, the company's requirements, consumers' long-run interests, and society's long-run interests. Companies should be aware that neglecting consumer and societal long-run interests is a disservice to consumers and society. Alert companies view societal problems as opportunities.

Sustainable marketing calls for products that are not only pleasing but also beneficial. The difference is shown in ● **Figure 20.4**. Products can be classified according to their degree of immediate consumer satisfaction and long-run consumer benefit. **Deficient products**, such as bad-tasting and ineffective medicine, have neither immediate appeal nor long-run benefits. **Pleasing products** give high immediate satisfaction but may hurt consumers in the long run. Examples include cigarettes and junk food. **Salutary products** have low immediate appeal but may benefit consumers in the long run, for instance, bicycle helmets or some insurance products. **Desirable products** give both high immediate satisfaction and high long-run benefits, such as a tasty *and* nutritious breakfast food.

Companies should try to turn all of their products into desirable products. The challenge posed by pleasing products is that they sell very well but may end up hurting the consumer. The product opportunity, therefore, is to add long-run benefits without reducing the product's pleasing qualities. The challenge posed by salutary products is to add some pleasing qualities so that they will become more desirable in consumers' minds.

● Consider method, the "people against dirty" brand of household and personal cleaning products. Many effective household cleaning products contain chemicals or even toxic ingredients that can be harmful to people and the environment. But method products are formulated with naturally derived, biodegradable ingredients, nontoxic ingredients. "We prefer ingredients that come from plants, not chemical plants," says the brand. Method also uses recycled and recyclable packaging, and it works with suppliers to reduce the carbon intensity of producing its products. Method uses renewable energy sources such as wind turbines and solar trees to help power its Chicago manufacturing facility. In all, "method cleaners put the hurt on dirt without doing harm to people, creatures, or the planet," says the company. As method cofounder and "chief greenskeeper" puts it: "Beautiful design and environmental responsibility are equally important when creating a product and we shouldn't have to trade functionality for sustainability."

● **Desirable products: method's cleaning products are both effective and beneficial. "method cleaners put the hurt on dirt without doing harm to people, creatures, or the planet," so you can "fear no mess."**
Method Products, PBC

20.2   CVS Health: Balancing Purpose with Profit

In 2014, CVS made the bold decision to stop selling cigarettes and other tobacco products. It was a risky decision. Although it won high praise from health advocates and public officials, stubbing out cigarettes resulted in the immediate loss of $2 billion in annual tobacco sales, and it risked driving a significant portion of CVS's smoking customers to competitors such as Walgreens, Rite-Aid, Walmart, or Kroger, all of which continued to sell cigarettes.

But to CVS, dropping tobacco was pretty much a no-brainer. CVS is on an important mission: "Millions of times a day, close to home and across the country, we're helping people on their path to better health," says CVS. Selling cigarettes *and* helping people on their path to better health? The two simply didn't jibe with one another. So CVS pulled tobacco products from its shelves. "CVS quits for good," the company announced. "This is the right thing to do."

Stopping tobacco sales was a landmark moment for CVS. And it was the event that received most of the headlines. However, the ban on tobacco was only one step in a more sweeping purpose-driven transformation. Consistent with its broader mission, CVS has been on a decade-long shift from being the traditional "drug store on the corner" to becoming a "multi-spectrum health care company." In fact, CVS no longer considers itself just a retail pharmacy. Rather, it sees itself as a pharmacy innovation company. "We're reinventing pharmacy to have a more active, supportive role in each person's unique health experience and in the greater health care environment," says the company.

Underscoring this commitment, at the same time that CVS suspended tobacco sales, it changed its name from CVS Caremark to CVS Health. And true to its mission and new name, CVS Health now offers a full range of products and services that help people on their path to better health. It all starts, of course, with CVS Health's network of 9,600 retail pharmacies, which sell an extensive assortment of prescription and nonprescription pharmaceuticals, personal care products, health and beauty aids, and general merchandise. CVS/pharmacy dispenses more prescriptions than any other drugstore chain, and

prescriptions account for 71 percent of the chain's retail sales. More than 1,100 CVS locations also house a CVS MinuteClinic, where medical professionals treat minor health conditions, give vaccinations, and provide other walk-in care.

CVS Health's pursuit of its "path to better health" mission extends well beyond retail pharmacies. For example, the company's CVS Caremark division provides Pharmacy Benefits Management (PBM) services that help big companies and insurers manage their prescription-drug programs. CVS Caremark helps clients to manage costs while improving health outcomes for 75 million Caremark members. CVS Health recently acquired Coram, which provides home infusion services to homebound patients, and Omnicare, a distributor of prescription drugs to nursing home and assisted-living facilities. The company has also broadened its range of customer contact activities to include tailored in-store and phone advising to customers managing chronic and specialty health conditions. In all, these days, CVS likes to think of itself as a kind of one-stop shop for health care.

Beyond these products and services, CVS Health also takes an active role in health-care management through research, consumer outreach and education, and support of health-related programs and organizations. For example, it has joined forces with a variety of organizations in efforts to curb tobacco use in the United States. It has partnered with the American Cancer Society and the National Urban League to lobby for anti-tobacco legislation, and with the American Academy of Pediatrics, the Campaign for Tobacco-Free Kids, and Scholastic, Inc. on tobacco-related education.

CVS recently launched a five-year, $50 million "Be the First" campaign by which it will work with national health organizations and youth groups to combat smoking through education, advocacy, tobacco control, and healthy behavior programming. "We are at a critical moment in our nation's efforts to end the

epidemic of tobacco use that ... threatens the health and well-being of our next generation," says CVS Health's chief medical officer. "We're partnering with experts across the public health community ... to move us one step closer to delivering the first tobacco-free generation."

So how is sense-of-mission marketing working for CVS Health? An interesting thing happened after the company stopped selling tobacco products in 2014. Although front-of-store sales dropped that year, overall CVS revenues increased by nearly 10 percent. And in the following year, revenues jumped another 10 percent. It appears that the loss of revenues from tobacco products has been more than offset by revenues from new sources, including those resulting from the decision to quit selling cigarettes.

Strange as it sounds, one source of new sales is smokers themselves. In turns out that 70 percent of smokers want to quit. At the same time that CVS Health pulled cigarettes off its shelves, it launched a "Let's

Sense-of-mission marketing: CVS Health is on a mission of helping people on their path to better health. It succeeds by "delivering what's right for people every day in a way that creates economic value for the business."

CVS Health

Quit Together" assistance program to help smokers kick the habit, complete with an information-packed website offering tips, testimonials, and other resources. In stores, racks once filled with cartons of cigarettes now displayed signs urging customers, "We quit tobacco. Ask a trained pharmacist or [MinuteClinic] nurse practitioner to help you quit, too." CVS is now poised to become the retailer of choice for those seeking smoking cessation products and services. By the end of the first year, CVS prescriptions for smoking cessation products grew by 63 percent and CVS Smoking Cessation Hubs received nearly one million visits.

Probably more significant, however, CVS's decision to purge tobacco products gave its reputation a boost, earning new business from non-smoking consumers on the one hand and PBM partners and clients on the other. Although it's difficult to track benefits from such sources, in the months following the elimination of tobacco from its shelves, revenues from CVS's pharmacy benefits services rose by 12 percent and the company lined up $11 billion worth of new contracts for its PBM business.

The decision to quit tobacco may have led to another important opportunity for CVS. About a year later, when Target went looking for a partner to buy and operate the pharmacies in 1,700 of its stores, CVS was a natural choice. Target had stopped selling cigarettes and tobacco products almost a decade earlier. CVS's new image and sense-of-mission strategy fit perfectly with the like-minded "no tobacco" mentality of Target and its customers.

Thus, CVS Health is on a mission. Its genuine concern for "helping people on their path to better health" reaches far beyond just revenues and profits. But as it turns out, doing good and doing well are not at odds. To the contrary, rather than stunting sales, CVS's lofty mission is driving new growth and profits. No longer just the "drugstore on the corner," CVS Health is now a $153 billion health-care giant, number 10 among the *Fortune* 500 and the nation's largest health care–related company. Eighty-five percent of CVS's revenues now come from health care.

As for that decision to quit tobacco? "I cannot think of another example in corporate America where a company sacrificed $2 billion of revenue for what they felt was the right thing to do," says CVS's chief marketer. "It's a stunning thing, [and] it proved out for us in [so may] ways." For CVS Health, he says, success means "delivering what's right for people every day in a way that creates economic value for the business."

Sources: Bruce Japsen, "CVS Kicks In Another $50 Million for Anti-Tobacco Push," *Forbes*, March 10, 2016, www.forbes.com/sites/brucejapsen/2016/03/10/cvs-kicks-in-another-50m-to-anti-tobacco-push/#41c6eb5f11f3; Phil Wahba, "She Thanks You for Not Smoking," *Fortune*, September 11, 2015, fortune.com/2015/09/11/cvs-health-helena-foulkes/; "Golden Halo Winner (Business): CVS Health," *Adweek*, May 25, 2015, www.adweek.com/print/164911; Kristina Monllos, "CVS Health's Marketing Chief on Turning the Pharmacy Brand into a Healthcare Player," *Adweek*, March 28, 2016, www.adweek.com/print/170437; and information from cvshealth.com/about/facts-and-company-information, http://investors.cvshealth.com, and https://cvshealth.com/about/purpose-statement, accessed October, 2016.

Marketing Ethics and the Sustainable Company

Marketing Ethics

Good ethics are a cornerstone of sustainable marketing. In the long run, unethical marketing harms customers and society as a whole. Further, it eventually damages a company's reputation and effectiveness, jeopardizing its very survival. Thus, the sustainable marketing goals of long-term consumer and business welfare can be achieved only through ethical marketing conduct.

Conscientious marketers face many moral dilemmas. The best thing to do is often unclear. Because not all managers have fine moral sensitivity, companies need to develop *corporate marketing ethics policies*—broad guidelines that everyone in the organization must follow. These policies should cover distributor relations, advertising standards, customer service, pricing, product development, and general ethical standards.

The finest guidelines cannot resolve all the difficult ethical situations the marketer faces. ● **Table 20.1** lists some difficult ethical issues marketers could face during their careers. If marketers choose immediate-sales-producing actions in all of these cases, their marketing behavior might well be described as immoral or even amoral. If they refuse to go along with *any* of the actions, they might be ineffective as marketing managers and unhappy because of the constant moral tension. Managers need a set of principles that will help them figure out the moral importance of each situation and decide how far they can go in good conscience.

But *what* principle should guide companies and marketing managers on issues of ethics and social responsibility? One philosophy is that the free market and the legal system should decide such issues. Under this principle, companies and their managers are not responsible for making moral judgments. Companies can in good conscience do whatever the market and legal systems allow. However, history provides an endless list of examples of company actions that were legal but highly irresponsible.

A second philosophy puts responsibility not on the system but in the hands of individual companies and managers. This more enlightened philosophy suggests that a company should have a social conscience. Companies and managers should apply high standards of ethics and morality when making corporate decisions, regardless of "what the system allows."

● Table 20.1 | Some Morally Difficult Situations in Marketing

1. Your R&D department has changed one of your company's products slightly. It is not really "new and improved," but you know that putting this statement on the package and in advertising will increase sales. What would you do?

2. You have been asked to add a stripped-down model to your line that could be advertised to pull customers into the store. The product won't be very good but salespeople will be able to switch buyers who come into the store up to higher-priced units. You are asked to give the green light for the stripped-down version. What would you do?

3. You are thinking of hiring a product manager who has just left a competitor's company. She would be more than happy to tell you all the competitor's plans for the coming year. What would you do?

4. One of your top dealers in an important territory recently has had family troubles and his sales have slipped. It looks like it will take him a while to straighten out his family problems. Meanwhile, you are losing many sales. Legally, on performance grounds, you can terminate the dealer's franchise and replace him. What would you do?

5. You have a chance to win a big account in another country that will mean a lot to you and your company. The purchasing agent hints that a "gift" would influence the decision. Such gifts are common in that country and some of your competitors will probably make one. What would you do?

6. You have heard that a competitor has a new product feature that will make a big difference in sales. The competitor will demonstrate the feature in a private dealer meeting at the annual trade show. You can easily send a snooper to this meeting to learn about the new feature. What would you do?

7. You have to choose between three advertising and social media campaigns outlined by your agency. The first (a) is a soft-sell, honest, straight-information campaign. The second (b) uses sex-loaded emotional appeals and exaggerates the product's benefits. The third (c) involves a noisy, somewhat irritating commercial that is sure to gain audience attention. Pretests show that the campaigns are effective in the following order: c, b, and a. What would you do?

8. You are interviewing a capable female applicant for a job as salesperson. She is better qualified than the men who have been interviewed. Nevertheless, you know that in your industry some important customers prefer dealing with men and you will lose some sales if you hire her. What would you do?

Each company and marketing manager must work out a philosophy of socially responsible and ethical behavior. Under the societal marketing concept, each manager must look beyond what is legal and allowed and develop standards based on personal integrity, corporate conscience, and long-run consumer welfare.

Dealing with issues of ethics and social responsibility in a proactive, open, and forthright way helps to build and maintain strong customer relationships based on honesty and trust. For example, think about SC Johnson, maker of familiar home-products brands such as Pledge, Shout, Windex, Ziploc, and Saran Wrap. SC Johnson believes deeply that "Integrity is part of our DNA. It's been our family way since 1886." Based on that belief, the company has a long tradition of doing what's right, even at the expense of sales. Just one example involves Saran Wrap, a longtime market leader and one of SC Johnson's best-known and biggest brands:[23]

For more than 50 years, Saran Wrap was made with polyvinylidene chloride (PVDC), an ingredient responsible for the product's two major differentiating features: impenetrable odor barrier qualities and superior microwavability. Without PVDC, Saran Wrap would have been no better than competing wraps by Glad and Reynolds, which did not contain PVDC. In the early 2000s, however, regulators, environmentalists, and consumers began to voice concerns about materials containing chlorine, specifically polyvinyl chloride (PVC). In fact, SC Johnson's own Greenlist analysis—by which it rates product ingredients based on their impact on environmental and human health—confirmed the hazards of PVCs, and the company quickly pledged to eliminate them from its products and packaging.

But SC Johnson took things a step further. In 2004, it also eliminated PVDCs, even though that important ingredient had not yet come under scrutiny. The company developed a PVDC-free polyethylene version of Saran Wrap, an admittedly less effective product. Sure enough, Saran Wrap's market share dropped from 18 percent in 2004 to only 11 percent today. Over the years, however, even though such decisions have sometimes hurt sales, they have helped

SC Johnson to earn and keep the trust of customers. "I don't regret the decision," says SC Johnson's CEO. "Despite the cost, it was the right thing to do, and...I sleep better at night because of it. We gained a surer sense of who we are as a company and what we want SC Johnson to represent."

As with environmentalism, the issue of ethics presents special challenges for international marketers. Business standards and practices vary a great deal from one country to the next. For example, bribes and kickbacks are illegal for U.S. firms, and various treaties against bribery and corruption have been signed and ratified by more than 60 countries. Yet these are still standard business practices in many countries. The World Bank estimates that bribes totaling more than $1 trillion per year are paid out worldwide. One study showed that the most flagrant bribe-paying firms were from Indonesia, Mexico, China, and Russia. Other countries where corruption is common include Sierra Leone, Kenya, and Yemen. The least corrupt were companies from Australia, Denmark, Finland, and Japan.[24] The question arises as to whether a company must lower its ethical standards to compete effectively in countries with lower standards. The answer is no. Companies should make a commitment to a common set of shared standards worldwide.

Many industrial and professional associations have suggested codes of ethics, and many companies are now adopting their own codes. For example, the American Marketing Association, an international association of marketing managers and scholars, developed a code of ethics that calls on marketers to adopt the following ethical norms:[25]

- *Do no harm.* This means consciously avoiding harmful actions or omissions by embodying high ethical standards and adhering to all applicable laws and regulations in the choices we make.
- *Foster trust in the marketing system.* This means striving for good faith and fair dealing so as to contribute toward the efficacy of the exchange process as well as avoiding deception in product design, pricing, communication, and delivery or distribution.
- *Embrace ethical values.* This means building relationships and enhancing consumer confidence in the integrity of marketing by affirming these core values: honesty, responsibility, fairness, respect, transparency, and citizenship.

Companies are also developing programs to teach managers about important ethical issues and help them find the proper responses. They hold ethics workshops and seminars and create ethics committees. Furthermore, most major U.S. companies have appointed high-level ethics officers to champion ethical issues and help resolve ethics problems and concerns facing employees. And most companies have established their own codes of ethical conduct.

Google is a good example.  Its official Google Code of Conduct is the mechanism by which the company puts its well-known "Don't be evil" motto into practice. The detailed code's core message is simple: Google employees (known inside as "Googlers") must earn users' faith and trust by holding themselves to the highest possible standards of ethical business conduct. The Google Code of Conduct is "about providing our users unbiased access to information, focusing on their needs, and giving them the best products and services that we can. But it's also about doing the right thing more generally—following the law, acting honorably, and treating each other with respect."

Google requires all Googlers—from board members to the newest employee—to take personal responsibility for practicing both the spirit and letter of the code and encouraging other Googlers to do the same. It urges employees to report violations to their managers, to human resources representatives, or using an Ethics & Compliance hotline. "If you have a question or ever think that one of your fellow Googlers or the

● **Marketing ethics:** Google's Code of Conduct is the mechanism by which the company puts its well-known "Don't be evil—do the right thing" motto into practice.

company as a whole may be falling short of our commitment, don't be silent," states the code. "We want—and need—to hear from you."[26]

Still, written codes and ethics programs do not ensure ethical behavior. Ethics and social responsibility require a total corporate commitment. They must be a component of the overall corporate culture. As the Google Code of Conduct concludes: "It's impossible to spell out every possible ethical scenario we might face. Instead, we rely on one another's good judgment to uphold a high standard of integrity for ourselves and our company. Remember … don't be evil. If you see something that isn't right, speak up!"

The Sustainable Company

At the foundation of marketing is the belief that companies that fulfill the needs and wants of customers will thrive. Companies that fail to meet customer needs or that intentionally or unintentionally harm customers, others in society, or future generations will decline.

Says one observer, "Sustainability is an emerging business megatrend, like electrification and mass production, that will profoundly affect companies' competitiveness and even their survival." Says another, "increasingly, companies and leaders will be assessed not only on immediate results but also on … the ultimate effects their actions have on societal well-being. This trend has been coming in small ways for years but now is surging. So pick up your recycled cup of fair-trade coffee, and get ready."[27]

Sustainable companies are those that create value for customers through socially, environmentally, and ethically responsible actions. Sustainable marketing goes beyond caring for the needs and wants of today's customers. It means having concern for tomorrow's customers in ensuring the survival and success of the business, shareholders, employees, and the broader world in which they all live. It means pursuing the mission of shared value and a triple bottom line: people, planet, profits. Sustainable marketing provides the context in which companies can engage customers and build profitable relationships with them by creating value *for* customers in order to capture value *from* customers in return—now and in the future.

20 | Reviewing and Extending the Concepts

OBJECTIVES REVIEW AND KEY TERMS

Objectives Review

In this chapter, we addressed many of the important *sustainable marketing* concepts related to marketing's sweeping impact on individual consumers, other businesses, and society as a whole. Sustainable marketing requires socially, environmentally, and ethically responsible actions that bring value to not only present-day consumers and businesses but also future generations and society as a whole. Sustainable companies are those that act responsibly to create value for customers in order to capture value from customers in return—now and in the future.

OBJECTIVE 20-1 Define *sustainable marketing* and discuss its importance. *(pp 574–576)*

Sustainable marketing calls for meeting the present needs of consumers and businesses while preserving or enhancing the ability of future generations to meet their needs. Whereas the marketing concept recognizes that companies thrive by fulfilling the day-to-day needs of customers, sustainable marketing calls

for socially and environmentally responsible actions that meet both the immediate and future needs of customers and the company. Truly sustainable marketing requires a smooth-functioning marketing system in which consumers, companies, public policy makers, and others work together to ensure responsible marketing actions.

OBJECTIVE 20-2 Identify the major social criticisms of marketing. *(pp 576–583)*

Marketing's *impact on individual consumer welfare* has been criticized for its high prices, deceptive practices, high-pressure selling, shoddy or unsafe products, planned obsolescence, and poor service to disadvantaged consumers. Marketing's *impact on society* has been criticized for creating false wants and too much materialism, too few social goods, and cultural pollution. Critics have also denounced marketing's *impact on other businesses* for harming competitors and reducing competition through acquisitions, practices that create barriers to entry, and unfair competitive marketing practices. Some of these concerns are justified; some are not.

OBJECTIVE 20-3 Define *consumerism* and *environmentalism* and explain how they affect marketing strategies. *(pp 583–589)*

Concerns about the marketing system have led to citizen action movements. *Consumerism* is an organized social movement intended to strengthen the rights and power of consumers relative to sellers. Alert marketers view it as an opportunity to serve consumers better by providing more consumer information, education, and protection. *Environmentalism* is an organized social movement seeking to minimize the harm done to the environment and quality of life by marketing practices. Most companies are now accepting responsibility for doing no environmental harm. They are adopting policies of *environmental sustainability*—developing strategies that both sustain the environment and produce profits for the company. Both consumerism and environmentalism are important components of sustainable marketing.

OBJECTIVE 20-4 Describe the principles of sustainable marketing. *(pp 589–593)*

Many companies originally resisted these social movements and laws, but most now recognize a need for positive consumer information, education, and protection. Under the sustainable marketing concept, a company's marketing should support the best long-run performance of the marketing system. It should be guided by five sustainable marketing principles: *consumer-oriented marketing, customer value marketing, innovative marketing, sense-of-mission marketing*, and *societal marketing*.

OBJECTIVE 20-5 Explain the role of ethics in marketing. *(pp 593–596)*

Increasingly, companies are responding to the need to provide company policies and guidelines to help their managers deal with questions of *marketing ethics*. Of course, even the best guidelines cannot resolve all the difficult ethical decisions that individuals and firms must make. But there are some principles from which marketers can choose. One principle states that the free market and the legal system should decide such issues. A second and more enlightened principle puts responsibility not on the system but in the hands of individual companies and managers. Each firm and marketing manager must work out a philosophy of socially responsible and ethical behavior. Under the sustainable marketing concept, managers must look beyond what is legal and allowable and develop standards based on personal integrity, corporate conscience, and long-term consumer welfare.

Key Terms

OBJECTIVE 20-1

Sustainable
  marketing (p 574)

OBJECTIVE 20-3

Consumerism (p 583)
Environmentalism (p 584)

Environmental
  sustainability (p 584)

OBJECTIVE 20-4

Consumer-oriented
  marketing (p 589)
Customer value
  marketing (p 589)

Innovative marketing (p 590)
Sense-of-mission
  marketing (p 590)
Societal marketing (p 591)
Deficient products (p 591)
Pleasing products (p 591)
Salutary products (p 591)
Desirable products (p 591)

DISCUSSION AND CRITICAL THINKING

MyMarketingLab

Go to **mymktlab.com** to complete the problems marked with this icon ⭐.

Discussion Questions

⭐ **20-1** Compare and contrast how the marketing concept, the societal marketing concept, and the sustainable marketing concept meet the needs of consumers and companies. (AASCB: Communication)

20-2 What are the major social criticisms of marketing? How do marketers respond to these criticisms? (AACSB: Communication; Reflective Thinking)

⭐ **20-3** Discuss the two major grassroots movements that work to keep companies' sustainability efforts in line. (AACSB: Communication)

20-4 What is environmental sustainability? How should companies gauge their progress toward achieving it? (AACSB: Communication)

20-5 Describe the sustainability principles marketers can use to operate in a responsible and ethical manner? (AACSB: Communication)

Critical Thinking Exercises

⭐ **20-6** Figure 20.4 outlines a societal classification of products. Identify two products for each of the four categories and explain why they are deficient, pleasing, salutary, or desirable products. (AACSB: Communication; Reflective Thinking)

20-7 Suppose that you are leading PepsiCo's environmental sustainability efforts. How would you gauge the effectiveness of these programs? How would you communicate your efforts to loyal consumers of your brand? (AACSB: Communication, Use of IT, Reflective Thinking)

20-8 In a small group, discuss each of the morally difficult situations in marketing presented in Table 20.1. Which ethics philosophy is guiding your decision in each situation? (AACSB: Communication; Ethical Reasoning)

APPLICATIONS AND CASES

Online, Mobile, and Social Media Marketing   Teens and Social Media

Facebook recently announced that it will let teens' posts become public. Before the change, Facebook would only allow 13- to 17-year-old users' posts to be seen by their "friends" and "friends of friends." Now, however, their posts can be seen by anyone on the network if they choose to make their posts "public." Twitter, another social medium gaining popularity with teens, has always let users, including teens, share tweets publicly. But because of Facebook's vast reach, privacy advocates are very concerned about this latest development, particularly when it comes to children's safety. Online predators and bullying are real safety issues facing youth. Other criticisms of Facebook's decision boil down to money—some argue that this is just about monetizing kids. Facebook will be able to offer a younger demographic to advertisers wanting to reach them. Facebook defends its actions, saying the change in policy is due to teenagers wanting the ability to post publicly, primarily for fundraising and promoting extracurricular activities such as sports and other school student organizations. Facebook has added precautions, such as a pop-up warning before teens can post publicly and setting "seen only by friends" as the default that must be changed if the teen desires posts to be public.

20-9 Is Facebook acting responsibly or merely trying to monetize kids as critics claim? (AACSB: Communication; Ethical Reasoning)

20-10 Come up with creative ways marketers can reach this demographic on Facebook without alienating their parents. (AACSB: Communication; Reflective Thinking)

Marketing Ethics   Milking the International Market

Since the 1970s, Nestlé and other companies have faced criticism about their marketing of infant formula to families in underdeveloped countries. Their marketing has positioned formula as superior to breast milk and as a more modern way of feeding babies despite emerging research findings that breast milk usually led to healthier outcomes for babies. Third-world women grew dependent on infant formula to feed their babies but began watering it down to make it last longer and save money, often with contaminated water. This too often resulted in child malnourishment and other serious health problems and even death in some cases.

Nestlé has been accused by some child watchdog groups of using overly aggressive marketing tactics to sell its infant formula products. Nestlé targeted many new mothers with tactics such as providing samples, promoting products directly in hospitals and communities, and giving gifts to health-care workers and new moms. Other infant formula companies even hired salesgirls in nurses' uniforms to drop by homes unannounced and sell potential customers on using baby formula rather than breastfeeding.

In April 2012, Nestlé acquired Pfizer's infant nutrition unit, making it the biggest player in the infant formula market. According to *The Guardian*, this business unit generates approximately 85 percent of its revenues from emerging markets, demonstrating that Nestlé and other infant formula companies are still capitalizing on consumers in emerging economies. An International Nestlé Boycott Committee was started in 1984 to address this global issue and is still active today.

20-11 In a small group, conduct research on this topic and formulate a sustainable, responsible marketing plan for marketing infant formula across the globe. Present your plan. (AACSB: Communication, Use of IT, Ethical Reasoning)

20-12 Is it wrong for marketers to create wants where none exist in the marketplace in order to make profits? Support your answer. (AACSB: Communication, Ethical Reasoning)

Marketing by the Numbers   The Cost of Sustainability

Kroger, the country's leading grocery-only chain, added a line of private-label organic and natural foods call Simple Truth to its stores. If you've priced organic foods, you know they are more expensive. For example, a dozen conventionally farmed grade-A eggs at Kroger costs consumers $1.70, whereas Simple Truth eggs are priced at $3.50 per dozen. One study found that, overall, the average price of organic foods is 85 percent more than conventional foods. However, if prices get too high, consumers will not purchase the organic options. One element of sustainability is organic farming, which costs much more than conventional farming, and those higher costs are passed on to consumers. Suppose that a conventional egg farmer's average fixed costs per year for conventionally farmed eggs are $1 million per year, but an organic egg farmer's fixed costs are three times that amount. The organic farmer's variable costs of $1.80 per dozen are twice as much as conventional farmer's variable costs. Refer to Appendix 2, Marketing by the Numbers, to answer the following questions.

20-13 Most large egg farmers sell eggs directly to retailers. Using Kroger's prices, what is the farmer's price per dozen to the retailer for conventional and organic eggs if Kroger's margin is 20 percent based on its retail price? (AACSB: Communication; Analytical Reasoning)

20-14 How many dozen eggs does a conventional farmer need to sell to break even? How many does an organic farmer need to sell to break even? (AACSB: Communication; Analytical Reasoning)

Video Case Honest Tea

Honest Tea, the Coca-Cola brand that produced $130 million in global revenues last year, got its start because cofounder Seth Goldman didn't like the options in the beverage coolers at convenience stores. So with the help of a former professor, he launched Honest Tea—the nation's first fully organic bottled tea.

But the company's drive for success was not based not as much on profits as on a desire to change the world. With social responsibility steeped deep into its business model, Honest Tea set out to help develop the economic structure of impoverished nations. Honest Tea purchased raw ingredients from Native American and South African farmers and invested in its supplier-farmers to help them become self-reliant. Although Honest Tea

has been a wholly owned subsidiary of the Coca-Cola Company since 2011, it continues to operate on the principles of social responsibility established by its founders.

After viewing the video featuring Honest Tea, answer the following questions:

20-15 List as many examples as you can showing how Honest Tea defies the common social criticisms of marketing.

20-16 How does Honest Tea practice sustainable marketing?

20-17 With all its efforts to do good, can Honest Tea continue to do well? Explain.

Company Case adidas: Athletic Apparel with Purpose

As CEO of the adidas Group for the past 15 years, Herbert Hainer has made quite a mark. Although the global athletic footwear and apparel giant has established itself as a leader in just about every sport, Hainer's legacy might stand in an area that has little to do with basketball, baseball, or even soccer. Under Hainer's influence, adidas has emerged as one of the global leaders in sustainable practices. Last year, the Germany-based sports giant ranked fifth among the Global 100 Most Sustainable Corporations.

A Marathon, Not a Sprint

Some companies have sustainability built in to their DNA. Companies such as Patagonia, Ben & Jerry's, and Method were founded by folks who were more driven to create socially responsible products, companies, and business practices than to make money. But companies such as Unilever, BMW, and adidas—all current sustainability leaders—discovered over time that they could succeed financially in their respective industries while at the same time being kind to the environment and providing better working conditions. In fact, these companies contend that a sound strategic plan built on sustainable practices makes them better financial performers than they might be otherwise.

adidas came to that realization nearly 20 years ago. In 1998, the company issued its first official environmental statement. In the years that followed, it tracked its performance against social and environmental goals and made its progress transparent in an annual report. But in 2008, the company revised its sustainability strategy, making it more comprehensive and ambitious than ever before.

These days just about every company makes claims about reducing its carbon footprint. But adidas's sustainability path stands as a model to any company that truly wants to make a difference. In short, making a difference when it comes to the health and well-being of the planet and its inhabitants takes more than just lip service. For a company to make an impact, sustainability must be ingrained in its organizational culture.

At adidas, such a cultural commitment is apparent in the degree to which the company has woven sustainability into its core business. Using a sports analogy, adidas's sustainability statement describes its efforts to become more sustainable and socially responsible as a marathon, not a sprint. "It's about preparedness and setting the right pace, having both the drive and the stamina to make it the distance. And most of all, it is about endurance: overcoming setbacks and difficulties, keeping the finishing line always in the forefront of our minds."

Some time ago, adidas established a set of core values that have shaped its corporate culture: performance, passion, integrity, and diversity. If these were just words on the wall at corporate headquarters, they wouldn't amount to much. But at adidas, these values "commit us to playing by the rules that society expects of a responsible company." Such values create the cultural infrastructure that drives "designing products that are environmentally sound...reducing the environmental impacts of our day-to-day operations and in our supply chain...setting workplace standards for our suppliers to meet...looking after the well-being and careers of our employees...and making a positive contribution to the communities where we operate."

The Four Ps of Sustainability

To translate this culture into action, adidas sticks to the four Ps—but not the same four Ps that make up the marketing mix. Rather, adidas frames and reviews its sustainability goals and performance within the context of four pillars—people, product, planet, and partnership. It's what adidas calls its "Fair Play Framework."

People. "We positively influence the lives of our employees, factory workers, and people living in the communities where we have a business presence." To achieve a more positive impact on the lives of people, adidas involves itself in hundreds of community projects with either financial support or providing employees as volunteers. But the "people" pillar also teaches common sense in doing the right thing.

When the owners of an apparel factory in Indonesia promptly closed and abandoned a factory just six months after being unable to resolve differences with adidas regarding its operations, hundreds of workers were left without jobs. adidas was there to ensure the workers were taken care of. This included millions of dollars in humanitarian aid, placement services, and direct advocacy with the Indonesian government to improve workers' rights. These efforts had a direct and positive impact on the lives of people who had been working to make adidas products.

Product. "We find better ways to create our products—mainly through efficiencies, increased use of more sustainable materials, and innovation." Among the product targets are specific goals, such as reducing the number of colors used in products by 50 percent, reducing product samples to intermediaries through virtualization, and increasing the use of sustainable materials in footwear and apparel. As the company focuses on these and other initiatives, compliance can be tracked, as can the impact on such factors as water usage, carbon emissions, and volume of product being disposed of in landfills.

For example, the adidas's virtualization project has reduced the demand for samples by 2.4 million items over a four-year period. Its initiative to source 100 percent of its cotton as "sustainable cotton" takes into account the use of water, health of the soil, and quality of the fiber. adidas is 43 percent of the way to its goal and ahead of schedule. And increasing the use of innovative fabrics has saved 50 million liters of water by reducing the amount needed to launder such items.

Planet. "We reduce the environmental footprint of both our own operations and our suppliers' factories." In addition to product actions that reduce environmental impact, adidas also sets goals targeting operational facilities and human behavior. One of the main initiatives for this pillar is the ISO 14001 certification of company and supplier facilities. To move office buildings, factories, and distribution plants toward the international standards for certification, adidas sets specific goals and provides employees with specific directives.

For example, the company has a goal to reduce energy consumption by 15 percent. Some directives include turning off computers when they are not in use and turning off lights when people leave a room or their office. To achieve a goal of 50 percent reduction in paper use, employees are encouraged to "think before printing" and "reuse paper for notes." adidas has almost fulfilled each of these goals.

Partnership. "We engage with critical stakeholders and collaborate with partners to improve our industry." The partnership pillar provides direction and motivation to seek out supplier, distributor, and relationships with other organizations that are trying to achieve the same sustainability goals as adidas. This includes working with partners to help them develop strategies whereby they can get on track and make progress. As one example, the adidas Group is an active participant of the Sustainable Apparel Coalition, a trade association that has worked to develop an index for measuring and tracking the comprehensive environmental and social impact of products across the value chain.

Doing Well by Doing Good?

These are just a few examples of how adidas is putting sustainable concepts into action and achieving sustainability results. Not only is adidas achieving results, it is being recognized for them. Its recent fifth-place ranking is not its first time on the Global 100 Index list—it the company's 11th appearance. adidas has also garnered Gold Class status and Sector Leader awards from RobecoSam—a well-known investment firm that focuses on sustainability investing. And adidas has been included in the Dow Jones Sustainability Indexes for each of the past 15 years.

Although adidas is clearly succeeding at implementing sustainable practices, one big question remains: Does all this do-gooding translate into sound financial performance as many companies claim? Many adidas stakeholders have asked that question. During Hainer's watch, superstar Nike has risen to such global dominance that adidas's financial performance is suffering. While Nike's revenues have shown strong gains year over year, adidas's have flattened. Not only has Nike been outperforming adidas in the United States, but Nike is getting the best of adidas in sales growth on its home turf in Europe. Nike is even stealing adidas's thunder in soccer, a sport where the German company has long been the global leader.

But adidas continues to press forward in its efforts to make the company and the world better places. In Hainer's own words, "We are not perfect and we do not always get it right. But as we go about our work, we aim to honor the spirit of 'fair play' in everything we do. Therefore, let me assure you that we continue to take serious responsibility for our actions. And we continue to integrate sustainability into our business strategy."

Questions for Discussion

20-18 Give as many examples as you can for how adidas defies the common social criticisms of marketing.

20-19 Of the five sustainable marketing principles discussed in the text, which one best describes adidas's approach?

20-20 Analyze adidas's business according to the Societal Classification of Products (Figure 20.4).

20-21 Would adidas be more financially successful if it were not so focused on social responsibility? Explain.

Sources: Margaret Ekblom, "Adidas's Version of Sustainability Ethics—The World Is Flat," *Stakeholderorgwed*, April 14, 2016, https://stakeholderorgwed.wordpress.com/2016/04/14/adidas-and-the-4ps-to-achieving-sustainable-ethics/; "Spotlight on the 2016 Global 100," *Corporate Knights*, January 20, 2016, www.corporateknights.com/reports/global-100/spotlight-on-the-2016-global-100-14533333/; and information from www.adidas-group.com/en/sustainability/managing-sustainability/general-approach/#/our-sustainability-strategy/and www.adidas-group.com/en/sustainability/reporting-policies-and-data/sustainability-reports/, accessed June 2016.

MyMarketingLab

Go to **mymktlab.com** for Auto-graded writing questions as well as the following Assisted-graded writing questions:

20-22 How can marketing practices create barriers to entry that potentially harm other firms? Are these barriers helpful or harmful to consumers?

20-23 Discuss the principles that will guide marketing managers to determine the moral importance of each situation they face.

Marketing Plan

The Marketing Plan: An Introduction

As a marketer, you will need a good marketing plan to provide direction and focus for your brand, product, or company. With a detailed plan, any business will be better prepared to launch a new product or build sales for existing products. Nonprofit organizations also use marketing plans to guide their fundraising and outreach efforts. Even government agencies put together marketing plans for initiatives such as building public awareness of proper nutrition and stimulating area tourism.

The Purpose and Content of a Marketing Plan

Unlike a business plan, which offers a broad overview of the entire organization's mission, objectives, strategy, and resource allocation, a marketing plan has a more limited scope. It serves to document how the organization's strategic objectives will be achieved through specific marketing strategies and tactics, with the customer as the starting point. It is also linked to the plans of other departments within the organization. Suppose, for example, a marketing plan calls for selling 200,000 units annually. The production department must gear up to make that many units, the finance department must arrange funding to cover the expenses, the human resources department must be ready to hire and train staff, and so on. Without the appropriate level of organizational support and resources, no marketing plan can succeed.

Although the exact length and layout will vary from company to company, a marketing plan usually contains the sections described in Chapter 2. Smaller businesses may create shorter or less formal marketing plans, whereas corporations frequently require highly structured marketing plans. To guide implementation effectively, every part of the plan must be described in considerable detail. Sometimes a company will post its marketing plans on an intranet site, which allows managers and employees in different locations to consult specific sections and collaborate on additions or changes.

The Role of Research

Marketing plans are not created in a vacuum. To develop successful strategies and action programs, marketers need up-to-date information about the environment, the competition, and the market segments to be served. Often, analysis of internal data is the starting point for assessing the current marketing situation, supplemented by marketing intelligence and research investigating the overall market, the competition, key issues, and threats and opportunities. As the plan is put into effect, marketers use a variety of research techniques to measure progress toward objectives and identify areas for improvement if results fall short of projections.

Finally, marketing research helps marketers learn more about their customers' requirements, expectations, perceptions, and satisfaction levels. This deeper understanding provides a foundation for building competitive advantage through well-informed segmenting, targeting, differentiating, and positioning decisions. Thus, the marketing plan should outline what marketing research will be conducted and how the findings will be applied.

The Role of Relationships

The marketing plan shows how the company will establish and maintain profitable customer relationships. In the process, however, it also shapes a number of internal and external relationships. First, it affects how marketing personnel work with each other and with other departments to deliver value and satisfy customers. Second, it affects how the company works with suppliers, distributors, and strategic alliance partners to achieve the objectives listed in the plan. Third, it influences the company's dealings with other stakeholders, including government regulators, the media, and the community at large. All of these relationships are important to the organization's success, so they should be considered when a marketing plan is being developed.

From Marketing Plan to Marketing Action

Companies generally create yearly marketing plans, although some plans cover a longer period. Marketers start planning well in advance of the implementation date to allow time for marketing research, thorough analysis, management review, and coordination between departments. Then, after each action program begins, marketers monitor ongoing results, compare them with projections, analyze any differences, and take corrective steps as needed. Some marketers also prepare contingency plans for implementation if certain conditions emerge. Because of inevitable and sometimes unpredictable environmental changes, marketers must be ready to update and adapt marketing plans at any time.

For effective implementation and control, the marketing plan should define how progress toward objectives will be measured. Managers typically use budgets, schedules, and performance standards for monitoring and evaluating results. With budgets, they can compare planned expenditures with actual expenditures for a given week, month, or other period. Schedules allow management to see when tasks were supposed to be completed— and when they were actually completed. Performance standards track the outcomes of marketing programs to see whether the company is moving toward its objectives. Some examples of performance standards are market share, sales volume, product profitability, and customer satisfaction.

Sample Marketing Plan: Chill Beverage Company

Executive Summary

The Chill Beverage Company is preparing to launch a new line of vitamin-enhanced water called NutriWater. Although the bottled water market is maturing, the functional water category—and more specifically the vitamin-enhanced water category—is still growing. NutriWater will be positioned by the slogan "Expect more"—indicating that the brand offers more in the way of desirable product features and benefits at a competitive price. Chill Beverage is taking advantage of its existing experience and brand equity among its loyal current customer base of millennials who consume its Chill Soda soft drink. NutriWater will target similar millennials who are maturing and looking for an alternative to soft drinks and high-calorie sugared beverages.

The primary marketing objective is to achieve first-year U.S. sales of $50 million, roughly 2 percent of the functional water market. Based on this market share goal, the company expects to sell more than 26 million units the first year and break even in the final quarter of the year.

Current Marketing Situation

The Chill Beverage Company—founded in 2010—markets niche and emerging products in the beverage industry. Rather than directly challenging established beverage giants like the Coca-Cola Company and PepsiCo, the Chill Beverage Company has focused on the fringes of the industry. Its Chill Soda soft drink brand hit the market with six unique flavors in glass bottles. The company now markets dozens of Chill Soda flavors, many unique to the brand. Over the past few years, Chill has successfully introduced new lines including energy drinks, natural juice drinks, and iced teas. Chill Beverage has grown its business every year since it was founded. In the most recent year, it achieved $230 million in revenue and net profits of $18.6 million. As part of its future growth strategy, Chill Beverage has plans to introduce new lines of beverages to continue to take advantage of emerging trends in the industry. Currently, it is preparing to launch a line of vitamin-enhanced waters.

For years, U.S. consumers have imbibed more carbonated soft drinks than any other bottled beverage. But concerns over health and obesity have taken the fizz out of the soda market—sales have declined for the past 11 years in a row. Meanwhile, bottled water consumption is on a growth trajectory that shows no sign of slowing down. Currently, the average person in the United States consumes more than 36.5 gallons of bottled water every year (compared with 42 gallons for carbonated soft drinks), a 7 percent year-over-year increase and more than double the figure just 15 years ago. A $15 billion market, bottled water sales in the U.S. are expected to increase by 35 percent over the next four years. Already ahead of milk, beer, and coffee, experts predict that bottled water sales will surpass carbonated soft drink sales within the next year.

Competition is more intense now than ever as the industry consolidates and new types of bottled water emerge. The U.S. market is dominated by three global corporations. With a global portfolio of more than 50 brands (including Poland Spring, Nestlé Pure Life, Arrowhead, Deer Park, and Ice Mountain), Nestlé leads the market for "plain" bottled water. However, when all subcategories of bottled water are included (sparkling, functional water, flavored water, and so on), Coca-Cola leads the U.S. market with a 22.9 percent share. Nestlé is number two at 21.5 percent of the total bottled water market followed by PepsiCo with 16.2 percent.

While bottled water as a whole is strong, the market for the subcategory of functional waters is even stronger, growing by 12 percent for the most recent year. In the current market environment, functional waters have thrived based on the promise of incremental benefits for health-conscious consumers based on the infusion of ingredients such as vitamins, minerals (including electrolytes), herbs, and other additives. Functional waters, therefore, carry the standard benefits of taste and convenience with an increased appeal to lifestyle and well-being. Most functional waters are sweetened and flavored and are distinguished from sports drinks that have the primary purpose of maximizing hydration by replenishing electrolytes.

To break into this market, dominated by huge global corporations and littered with dozens of other small players, Chill Beverage must carefully target specific segments with features and benefits valued by those segments.

Market Description

The bottled water market consists of many different types of water. Varieties of plain water include spring, purified, mineral, and distilled. Although these different types of water are sold as consumer products, they also serve as the core ingredient for the various types of functional waters. The flexibility of bottled water as a category seems to be endless.

Although some consumers may not perceive much of a difference between brands, others are drawn to specific product features and benefits provided by different brands. For example, some consumers may perceive spring water as healthier than other types of water. Some may look for water that is optimized for hydration. Others seek additional nutritional benefits claimed by bottlers that enhance their brands with vitamins, minerals, herbs, and other additives. Still other consumers make selections based on flavor. The industry as a whole has positioned bottled water of all kinds as a low-calorie, healthy alternative to soft drinks, sports drinks, energy drinks, and other types of beverages.

Bottled water brands also distinguish themselves by size and type of container, multipacks, and refrigeration at point of sale. Chill Beverage's market for NutriWater consists of consumers of single-serving-sized bottled beverages who are looking for a healthy yet flavorful alternative. *Healthy* in this context means both low-calorie and enhanced nutritional content. This market includes traditional soft drink consumers who want to improve their health as well as non–soft drink consumers who want an option other than plain bottled water. Specific segments that Chill Beverage will target during the first year include athletes, the health conscious, the socially responsible, and millennials who favor independent corporations. The Chill Soda brand has established a strong base of loyal customers, primarily among millennials. This generational segment is becoming a prime target as it matures and seeks alternatives to full-calorie soft drinks. ● **Table A1.1** shows how NutriWater addresses the needs of targeted consumer segments.

Product Review

Chill Beverage's new line of NutriWater vitamin-enhanced water offers the following features:

- Six new-age flavors: peach mango, berry pomegranate, kiwi dragonfruit, mandarin orange, blueberry grape, and Key lime.
- Single-serving size, 20-ounce, PET-recyclable bottles.

● **Table A1.1** | **Segment Needs and Corresponding Features/Benefits of NutriWater**

Targeted Segment	Customer Need	Corresponding Features/Benefits
Athletes	• Hydration and replenishment of essential minerals • Energy to maximize performance	• Electrolytes and carbohydrates • B vitamins, carbohydrates
Health conscious	• Maintain optimum weight • Optimize nutrition levels • Avoid harmful chemicals and additives • Desire to consume a tastier beverage than water	• Half the calories of fully sugared beverages • Higher levels of vitamins A, B, C, E, zinc, chromium, and folic acid than other products; vitamins unavailable in other products • All natural ingredients • Six new-age flavors
Socially conscious	• Support causes that help solve world's social problems	• 25-cent donation from each purchase to Vitamin Angels
Millennials	• Aversion to mass-media advertising/technologically savvy • Counterculture attitude • Diet enhancement due to fast-paced lifestyle	• Less-invasive online and social networking promotional tactics • Small, privately held company • Full RDA levels of essential vitamins and minerals

- Formulated for wellness, replenishment, and optimum energy.
- Full recommended daily allowance (RDA) of essential vitamins and minerals (including electrolytes).
- Higher vitamin concentration—vitamin levels are 2 to 10 times higher than market-leading products, with more vitamins and minerals than any other brand.
- Additional vitamins—vitamins include A, E, and B_2 as well as folic acid—none of which are contained in the market-leading products.
- All natural—no artificial flavors, colors, or preservatives.
- Sweetened with pure cane sugar and Stevia, a natural zero-calorie sweetener.
- Twenty-five cents from each purchase will be donated to Vitamin Angels, a nonprofit organization with a mission to prevent vitamin deficiency in at-risk children.

Competitive Review

As sales of bottled waters entered a strong growth phase in the 1990s, the category began to expand. In addition to the various types of plain water, new categories emerged. These included flavored waters—such as Aquafina's Flavorsplash—as well as functional waters. Functional waters emerged to bridge the gap between soft drinks and waters, appealing to people who knew they should drink more water and less soft drinks but still wanted flavor. Initially, development of brands for this product variation occurred in start-up and boutique beverage companies like SoBe and Glacéau, creator of Vitaminwater. In the 2000s, major beverage corporations acquired the most successful smaller brands, providing the bigger firms with a solid market position in this category and diversification in bottled waters in general. Backed by the marketing expertise and budgets of the leading beverage companies, functional water grew at a rate exceeding that of plain water.

At one point, Coca-Cola's Vitaminwater was the fourth-largest bottled water brand, behind Nestlé Pure Life, Coca-Cola's Dasani, and Pepsi's Aquafina. After taking a hit in the press for the low amount of vitamins and high amount of sugar contained in most brands of vitamin-enhanced waters, sales for vitamin water brands temporarily slipped. But Coca-Cola lost no ground as sales for Smartwater—Vitaminwater's non-flavored sibling—rose to the fourth largest brand. Currently, functional water sales account for approximately 20 percent of the total bottled water market, and industry insiders expect sales to outpace nonfunctional waters in the coming years.

The fragmentation of this category, combined with domination by the market leaders, has created a severely competitive environment. Although there is indirect competition posed by all types of bottled waters and even other types of beverages (soft drinks, energy drinks, juices, teas, and flavor drops), this competitive analysis focuses on direct competition from leading functional water brands. Functional water brands are either sweetened and flavored, just flavored, or neither sweetened nor flavored. Sweetened varieties blend traditional sugars with zero-calorie sweeteners. The types of sweeteners used create a point of differentiation. The result is a range of sugar content, carbohydrates, and calories as high as half that of regular soft drinks and other sweetened beverages and as low as zero.

Pricing for this product is consistent across brands and varies by type of retail outlet, with convenience stores typically charging more than grocery stores. The price for a 20-ounce bottle ranges from $1.00 to $1.89, with some niche brands costing slightly more. While Smartwater is the leading functional water brand, it is a plain still water enhanced with electrolytes. Chill Beverage's NutriWater will focus on competition posed by flavored and enhanced water brands, include the following:

- *Vitaminwater:* Created in 2000 as a new product for Energy Brands' Glacéau, which was also the developer of Smartwater (distilled water with electrolytes). Coca-Cola purchased Energy Brands for $4.1 billion in 2007. Vitaminwater is sold in regular and zero-calorie versions. With 18 bottled varieties—9 regular and 9 zero-calorie—as well as availability in fountain form and drops, Vitaminwater offers more options than any brand on the market. Whereas Vitaminwater varieties are distinguished by flavor, they are named to invoke perceptions of benefits such as Refresh, Power-C, Focus, and Revive. The brand's current slogan is "Hydrate the Hustle." Vitaminwater is vapor distilled, de-ionized, and/or filtered and is sweetened with crystalline fructose (corn syrup) and cane sugar or erythritol and stevia. Vitaminwater exceeds $700 million in annual sales and commands 34 percent of the functional water market.
- *Propel:* Gatorade created Propel in 2000, just one year prior to PepsiCo's purchase of this leading sports drink marketer. Marketed as "The Workout Water," Propel was originally available in regular and zero-calorie varieties. However, it is now available only as a zero-calorie beverage. Propel comes in 10 varieties, each containing the same blend of B vitamins, vitamin C, vitamin E, antioxidants, and electrolytes. It is sweetened with sucralose. Propel is available in a wide variety of sizes, with 16.9-, 20-, and 24-ounce PET bottles and multipacks. Propel is also marketed in powder form and as a liquid enhancer to be added to bottled water. With $183 million in revenues, Propel is the number-three functional water brand with approximately 9 percent of the functional water market.
- *SoBe Lifewater:* PepsiCo bought SoBe in 2000. SoBe introduced Lifewater in 2008 with a hit Super Bowl ad as an answer to Coca-Cola's Vitaminwater. The Lifewater line includes six zero-calorie varieties. Each variety is infused with a formulation of vitamins, minerals, and herbs designed to provide a claimed benefit. Sweetened with Stevia-based PureVia, Lifewater makes the claim to be "all natural." It contains no artificial flavors or colors. Lifewater is sold in 20-ounce PET bottles and multipacks. With $144 million in annual revenues, Lifewater is the fourth-largest functional water brand with a 7 percent share.
- *Niche brands:* The market for functional waters includes companies that market their wares on a small scale through independent retailers: Assure, Ex Aqua Vitamins, Ayala Herbal Water, and Skinny Water. Some brands feature exotic additives and/or artistic glass bottles.

Despite the strong competition, NutriWater believes it can create a relevant brand image and gain recognition among the targeted segments. The brand offers strong points of differentiation with higher and unique vitamin content, all-natural ingredients, and support for a relevant social cause. With other strategic assets, Chill Beverage is confident that it can establish a competitive advantage that will allow NutriWater to grow in the market. ● **Table A1.2** shows a sample of competing products.

Channels and Logistics Review

With the three main brands now owned by Coca-Cola and PepsiCo, there is a huge hole in the independent distributor system. NutriWater will be distributed through an independent distributor to a network of retailers in the United States. This strategy will avoid some of the head-on competition for shelf space with the Coca-Cola and PepsiCo brands and will also directly target likely NutriWater customers. As with the rollout of the core Chill Soda

Table A1.2 | Sample of Competitive Products

Competitor	Brand	Features
Coca-Cola	Vitaminwater	Regular and zero-calorie versions; 18 varieties; each flavor provides a different function based on blend of vitamins and minerals; vapor distilled, de-ionized, and/or filtered; sweetened with crystalline fructose and cane sugar; 20-ounce single-serve or multipack, fountain, and drops.
PepsiCo	Propel	Zero-calorie only; 10 flavors; fitness positioning based on "Replenish + Energize + Protect"; B vitamins, vitamin C, vitamin E, antioxidants, and electrolytes; sweetened with sucralose; 16.9-ounce, 20-ounce PET bottles and multipacks; powdered packets; liquid enhancer.
PepsiCo	SoBe Lifewater	Six zero-calorie versions; vitamins, minerals, and herbs; Pure—mildly flavored, sweetened with Stevia; "all natural"; 20-ounce single-serve and multipacks.

brand, this strategy will focus on placing coolers in retail locations that will exclusively hold NutriWater. These retailers include:

- *Grocery chains:* Regional grocery chains such as HyVee in the Midwest, Wegman's in the East, and WinCo in the West.
- *Health and natural food stores:* Chains such as Whole Foods as well as local health food co-ops.
- *Fitness centers:* National fitness center chains such as 24 Hour Fitness, Gold's Gym, and other regional chains.

As the brand gains acceptance, channels will expand into larger grocery chains, convenience stores, and unique locations relevant to the target customer segment.

Strengths, Weaknesses, Opportunities, and Threat Analysis

NutriWater has several powerful strengths on which to build, but its major weakness is lack of brand awareness and image. Major opportunities include a growing market and consumer trends targeted by NutriWater's product traits. Threats include barriers to entry posed by limited retail space, as well as image issues for the bottled water industry. Table A1.3 summarizes NutriWater's main strengths, weaknesses, opportunities, and threats.

Table A1.3 | NutriWater's Strengths, Weaknesses, Opportunities, and Threats

Strengths	Weaknesses
• Superior quality • Expertise in alternative beverage marketing • Social responsibility • Antiestablishment image	• Lack of brand awareness • Limited budget

Opportunities	Threats
• Market growth • Gap in the distribution network • Health trends • Antiestablishment image	• Limited shelf space • Image of enhanced waters • Environmental issues

Strengths

NutriWater can rely on the following important strengths:

1. *Superior quality:* NutriWater boasts the highest levels of added vitamins of any enhanced water, including full RDA levels of many vitamins. It is all natural with no artificial flavors, colors, or preservatives. It is sweetened with both pure cane sugar and the natural zero-calorie sweetener Stevia.
2. *Expertise in alternative beverage marketing:* The Chill Soda brand went from nothing to a successful and rapidly growing soft drink brand with fiercely loyal customers in a matter of only one decade. This success was achieved by starting small and focusing on gaps in the marketplace.
3. *Social responsibility:* Every customer will have the added benefit of helping malnourished children throughout the world. Although the price of NutriWater is in line with other competitors, low promotional costs allow for the substantial charitable donation of 25 cents per bottle while maintaining profitability.
4. *Antiestablishment image:* The big brands have decent products and strong distribution relationships. But they also carry the image of the large, corporate establishments. Chill Beverage has achieved success with an underdog image while remaining privately held. Vitaminwater, Propel, and SoBe were built on this same image but are now owned by major multinational corporations.

Weaknesses

1. *Lack of brand awareness:* As an entirely new brand, NutriWater will enter the market with limited or no brand awareness. The affiliation with Chill Soda will be kept at a minimum in order to prevent associations between NutriWater and soft drinks. This issue will be addressed through promotion and distribution strategies.
2. *Limited budget:* As a smaller company, Chill Beverage has much smaller funds available for promotional and research activities.

Opportunities

1. *Market growth:* Functional water as a category is growing at a rate of about 12 percent annually. Of the top six beverage categories, soft drinks, beer, milk, and fruit drinks experienced declines. The growth for coffee was less than 1 percent.
2. *Gap in the distribution network:* The market leaders distribute directly to retailers. This gives them an advantage in large national chains. However, no major enhanced water brands are currently being sold through independent distributors.
3. *Health trends:* Weight and nutrition continue to be issues for consumers in the United States. The country has the highest obesity rate for developed countries at 34 percent, with well over 60 percent of the population officially "overweight." Those numbers continue to rise. Additionally, Americans get 21 percent of their daily calories from beverages, a number that has tripled in the past three decades. Consumers still desire flavored beverages but look for lower-calorie alternatives.
4. *Antiestablishment image.* Millennials (born between 1977 and 2000) maintain a higher aversion to mass marketing messages and global corporations than do Gen Xers and baby boomers.

Threats

1. *Limited shelf space:* Whereas competition is generally a threat for any type of product, competition in retail beverages is particularly high because of limited retail space. Carrying a new beverage product requires retailers to reduce shelf or cooler space already occupied by other brands.
2. *Image of enhanced waters:* The image of enhanced waters took a hit as Coca-Cola recently fought a class-action lawsuit accusing it of violating FDA regulations by promoting the health benefits of Vitaminwater. The lawsuit exposed the number-one functional water brand as basically sugar water with minimal nutritional value. Each of the major brands is strengthening its zero-calorie lines. They no longer promote health benefits on the labels. While this is potentially a threat, it is also an opportunity for Chill to exploit.
3. *Environmental issues:* Environmental groups continue to educate the public on the environmental costs of bottled water, including landfill waste, carbon emissions from production and transportation, and harmful effects of chemicals in plastics.

Objectives and Issues

Chill Beverage has set aggressive but achievable objectives for NutriWater for the first and second years of market entry.

First-Year Objectives

During the initial year on the market, Chill Beverage aims for NutriWater to achieve a 2 percent share of the functional water market, or approximately $50 million in sales, with break-even achieved in the final quarter of the year. With an average retail price of $1.89, that equates with a sales goal of 26,455,026 bottles.

Second-Year Objectives

During the second year, Chill Beverage will unveil additional NutriWater flavors, including zero-calorie varieties. The second-year objective is to double sales from the first year, to $100 million.

Issues

In launching this new brand, the main issue is the ability to establish brand awareness and a meaningful brand image based on positioning that is relevant to target customer segments. Chill Beverage will invest in nontraditional means of promotion to accomplish these goals and to spark word of mouth. Establishing distributor and retailer relationships will also be critical in order to make the product available and provide point-of-purchase communications. Brand awareness and knowledge will be measured in order to adjust marketing efforts as necessary.

Marketing Strategy

NutriWater's marketing strategy will involve developing a "more for the same" positioning based on extra benefits for the price. The brand will also establish channel differentiation, as it will be available in locations where major competing brands are not. NutriWater will focus on a primary target segment of millennials, specifically young adults aged 16 to 39. Subsets of this generational segment include athletes, the health conscious, and the socially responsible.

Positioning

NutriWater will be positioned on an "Expect more" value proposition. This will allow for differentiating the brand based on product features (expect more vitamin content and all natural ingredients), desirable benefits (expect greater nutritional benefits), and values (do more for a social cause). Marketing will focus on conveying that NutriWater is more than just a beverage: It gives customers much more for their money in a variety of ways.

Product Strategy

NutriWater will be sold with all the features described in the Product Review section. As awareness takes hold and retail availability increases, more varieties will be made available. A zero-calorie version will be added to the product line, providing a solid fit with the health benefits sought by consumers. Chill Beverage's considerable experience in brand building will be applied as an integral part of the product strategy for NutriWater. All aspects of the marketing mix will be consistent with the brand.

Pricing

There is little price variation in the enhanced waters category, particularly among leading brands. For this reason, NutriWater will follow a competition-based pricing strategy. Given that NutriWater claims superior quality, it must be careful not to position itself as a lower-cost alternative. Manufacturers do not quote list prices on this type of beverage, and prices vary considerably based on type of retail outlet and whether the product is refrigerated. Regular prices for single 20-ounce bottles of competing products are as low as $1.00 in discount-retailer stores and as high as $1.89 in convenience stores. Because NutriWater will not be targeting discount retailers and convenience stores initially, this will allow Chill Beverage to set prices at the average to higher end of the range for similar products in the same outlets. For grocery chains, this should be approximately $1.59 per bottle, with that price rising to $1.99 at health food stores and fitness centers, where prices tend to be higher.

Distribution Strategy

NutriWater will employ a selective distribution strategy with well-known regional grocers, health and natural food stores, and fitness centers. This distribution strategy will be executed through a network of independent beverage distributors, as there are no other major brands of enhanced water following this strategy. Chill Beverage gained success for its core Chill Soda soft drink line using this method. It also placed coolers with the brand logo in truly unique venues such as skate, surf, and snowboarding shops; tattoo and piercing parlors; fashion stores; and music stores—places that would expose the brand to target customers. Then the soft drink brand expanded by getting contracts with retailers such as Panera, Barnes & Noble, Target, and Starbucks. This same approach will be taken with NutriWater by starting small, then expanding into larger chains. NutriWater will not target all the same stores used originally by Chill Soda, as many of those outlets were unique to the positioning and target customer for the Chill Soda soft drink brand.

Marketing Communication Strategy

As with the core Chill Soda brand, the marketing communication strategy for NutriWater will not follow a strategy based on traditional mass-communication advertising. Initially, there will be no broadcast or print advertising. Promotional resources for NutriWater will focus on three areas:

- *Online and mobile marketing:* The typical target customer for NutriWater spends more time online than with traditional media channels. A core component for this strategy will be building web and mobile brand sites and driving traffic to those sites by creating a presence on social networks, including Facebook, Twitter, Instagram, and Snapchat. The NutriWater brand will also incorporate location-based services by Foursquare and Facebook to help drive traffic to retail locations. A mobile phone ad campaign will provide additional support to the online efforts.
- *Trade promotions:* Like the core Chill Soda brand, NutriWater's success will rely on relationships with retailers to create product availability. Primary incentives to retailers will include point-of-purchase displays, branded coolers, and volume incentives and contests. This push marketing strategy will combine with the other pull strategies.
- *Event marketing:* NutriWater will deploy teams in brand-labeled RVs to distribute product samples at events such as skiing and snowboarding competitions, golf tournaments, and concerts.

Marketing Research

To remain consistent with the online promotional approach, as well as using research methods that will effectively reach target customers, Chill Beverage will monitor online discussions. In this manner, the company will gauge customer perceptions of the brand, the products, and general satisfaction. For future development of the product and new distribution outlets, crowdsourcing methods will be utilized.

Action Programs

NutriWater will be introduced in February. The following are summaries of action programs that will be used during the first six months of the year to achieve the stated objectives.

January: Chill Beverage representatives will work with both independent distributors and retailers to educate them on the trade promotional campaign, incentives, and advantages for selling NutriWater. Representatives will also ensure that distributors and retailers are educated on product features and benefits as well as instructions for displaying point-of-purchase materials and coolers. The brand website and other sites such as Facebook will present teaser information about the product as well as availability dates and locations. Buzz will be enhanced by providing product samples to selected product reviewers, opinion leaders, influential bloggers, and celebrities.

February: On the date of availability, product coolers and point-of-purchase displays will be placed in retail locations. The full brand website and social network campaign will launch with full efforts on Facebook, Twitter, Instagram, and Snapchat. This campaign will drive the "Expect more" slogan as well as illustrate the ways that Nutri-Water delivers more than expected on product features, desirable benefits, and values by donating to Vitamin Angels and the social cause of battling vitamin deficiency in children.

March: To enhance the online and social marketing campaign, location-based services Foursquare and Facebook Location Services will be employed to drive traffic to retailers. Point-of-purchase displays and signage will be updated to support these efforts and to continue supporting retailers. The message of this campaign will focus on all aspects of "Expect more."

April: A mobile ad campaign will provide additional support, driving traffic to the brand website and social network sites as well as driving traffic to retailers.

May: A trade sales contest will offer additional incentives and prizes to the distributors and retailers that sell the most NutriWater during a four-week period.

June: An event marketing campaign will mobilize a team of NutriWater representatives in NutriWater RVs to concerts and sports events. This will provide additional visibility for the brand as well as giving customers and potential customers the opportunity to sample products.

Budgets

Chill Beverage has set a first-year retail sales goal of $50 million with a projected average retail price of $1.89 per unit for a total of 26,455,026 units sold. With an average wholesale price of 95 cents per unit, this provides revenues of $25.1 million. Chill Beverage expects to break even during the final quarter of the first year. A break-even analysis assumes per-unit wholesale revenue of 95 cents per unit, a variable cost per unit of 22 cents, and estimated first-year fixed costs of $12,500,000. Based on these assumptions, the break-even calculation is:

$$\frac{\$12,500,000}{\$0.95/\text{unit} - \$0.22/\text{unit}} = 17,123,287$$

Controls

Chill Beverage is planning tight control measures to closely monitor product quality, brand awareness, brand image, and customer satisfaction. This will enable the company to react quickly in correcting any problems that may occur. Other early warning signals that will be monitored for signs of deviation from the plan include monthly sales (by segment and channel) and monthly expenses. Given the market's volatility, contingency plans are also in place to address fast-moving environmental changes such as shifting consumer preferences, new products, and new competition.

Sources: Hadley Malcolm, "Bottled Water about to Beat Soda as Most Consumed Beverage," *USA Today*, June 8, 2016, www.usatoday.com/story/money/2016/06/08/americans-cut-calories-drinking-more-bottled-water/85554612/; Elizabeth Crawford, "Functional and Sparkling Bottled Water Sales Are 'Very Hot in the US,' Analyst Says," *Food Navigator-USA*, May 23, 2016, www.foodnavigator-usa.com/Manufacturers/Functional-sparking-bottled-water-sales-are-very-hot-in-the-US; "Channel Check," *Bevnet*, June 2016, p. 26; "2016 State of the Industry: Bottle Water Market Has Potential to Surpass CSDs," *Beverage Industry*, July 11, 2016, www.bevindustry.com/articles/89424-state-of-the-industry-bottled-water-market-has-potential-to-surpass-csds; "U.S. Bottled Water Market Grows by 6.4 Percent in 2015," *Beverage Industry*, February 26, 2016, www.bevindustry.com/articles/89123-us-bottled-water-market-grows-64-percent-in-2015; and product and market information obtained from www.sobe.com, www.vitaminwater.com, www.propelwater.com, and www.nestle-waters.com, accessed July 2016.

Marketing by the Numbers

Marketing managers are facing increased accountability for the financial implications of their actions. This appendix provides a basic introduction to measuring marketing financial performance. Such financial analysis guides marketers in making sound marketing decisions and in assessing the outcomes of those decisions.

The appendix is built around a hypothetical manufacturer of consumer electronics products—HD. The company is introducing a device that plays videos and television programming streamed over the internet on multiple devices in a home, including high-definition televisions, tablets, and mobile phones. In this appendix, we will analyze the various decisions HD's marketing managers must make before and after the new-product launch.

The appendix is organized into *three sections*. The *first section* introduces pricing, break-even, and margin analysis assessments that will guide the introduction of HD's new product. The *second section* discusses demand estimates, the marketing budget, and marketing performance measures. It begins with a discussion of estimating market potential and company sales. It then introduces the marketing budget, as illustrated through a *pro forma* profit-and-loss statement followed by the actual profit-and-loss statement. Next, we discuss marketing performance measures, with a focus on helping marketing managers to better defend their decisions from a financial perspective. In the *third section*, we analyze the financial implications of various marketing tactics.

Each of the three sections ends with a set of quantitative exercises that provide you with an opportunity to apply the concepts you learned to situations beyond HD.

Pricing, Break-Even, and Margin Analysis

Pricing Considerations

Determining price is one of the most important marketing-mix decisions. The limiting factors are demand and costs. Demand factors, such as buyer-perceived value, set the price ceiling. The company's costs set the price floor. In between these two factors, marketers must consider competitors' prices and other factors such as reseller requirements, government regulations, and company objectives.

Most current competing internet streaming products sell at retail prices between $100 and $500. We first consider HD's pricing decision from a cost perspective. Then, we consider consumer value, the competitive environment, and reseller requirements.

Determining Costs

Fixed costs
Costs that do not vary with production or sales level.

Variable costs
Costs that vary directly with the level of production.

Total costs
The sum of the fixed and variable costs for any given level of production.

Recall from Chapter 10 that there are different types of costs. **Fixed costs** do not vary with production or sales level and include costs such as rent, interest, depreciation, and clerical and management salaries. Regardless of the level of output, the company must pay these costs. Whereas total fixed costs remain constant as output increases, the fixed cost per unit (or average fixed cost) will decrease as output increases because the total fixed costs are spread across more units of output. **Variable costs** vary directly with the level of production and include costs related to the direct production of the product (such as costs of goods sold—COGS) and many of the marketing costs associated with selling it. Although these costs tend to be uniform for each unit produced, they are called variable because their total varies with the number of units produced. **Total costs** are the sum of the fixed and variable costs for any given level of production.

HD has invested $10 million in refurbishing an existing facility to manufacture the new video streaming product. Once production begins, the company estimates that it will incur fixed costs of $20 million per year. The variable cost to produce each device is estimated to be $125 and is expected to remain at that level for the output capacity of the facility.

Setting Price Based on Costs

Cost-plus pricing (or markup pricing)
A standard markup to the cost of the product.

HD starts with the cost-based approach to pricing discussed in Chapter 10. Recall that the simplest method, **cost-plus pricing** (or **markup pricing**), simply adds a standard markup to the cost of the product. To use this method, however, HD must specify expected unit sales so that total unit costs can be determined. Unit variable costs will remain constant regardless of the output, but *average unit fixed costs* will decrease as output increases.

To illustrate this method, suppose HD has fixed costs of $20 million, and variable costs of $125 per unit and expects unit sales of 1 million players. Thus, the cost per unit is given by:

$$\text{Unit cost} = \text{variable cost} + \frac{\text{fixed costs}}{\text{unit sales}} = \$125 + \frac{\$20,000,000}{1,000,000} = \$145$$

Relevant costs
Costs that will occur in the future and that will vary across the alternatives being considered.

Note that we do *not* include the initial investment of $10 million in the total fixed cost figure. It is not considered a fixed cost because it is not a *relevant* cost. **Relevant costs** are those that will occur in the future and that will vary across the alternatives being considered. HD's investment to refurbish the manufacturing facility was a one-time cost that will not reoccur in the future. Such past costs are *sunk costs* and should not be considered in future analyses.

Break-even price
The price at which total revenue equals total cost and profit is zero.

Also notice that if HD sells its product for $145, the price is equal to the total cost per unit. This is the **break-even price**—the price at which unit revenue (price) equals unit cost and profit is zero.

Suppose HD does not want to merely break even but rather wants to earn a 25% markup on sales. HD's markup price is:[i]

$$\text{Markup price} = \frac{\text{unit cost}}{(1 - \text{desired return on sales})} = \frac{\$145}{1 - 0.25} = \$193.33$$

This is the price at which HD would sell the product to resellers such as wholesalers or retailers to earn a 25% profit on sales.

Return on investment (ROI) pricing (or target-return pricing)
A cost-based pricing method that determines price based on a specified rate of return on investment.

Another approach HD could use is called **return on investment (ROI) pricing** (or **target-return pricing**). In this case, the company *would* consider the initial $10 million investment, but only to determine the dollar profit goal. Suppose the company wants a 30% return on its investment. The price necessary to satisfy this requirement can be determined by:

$$\text{ROI price} = \text{unit cost} + \frac{\text{ROI} \times \text{investment}}{\text{unit sales}} = \$145 + \frac{0.3 \times \$10,000,000}{1,000,000} = \$148$$

That is, if HD sells its product for $148, it will realize a 30% return on its initial investment of $10 million.

In these pricing calculations, unit cost is a function of the expected sales, which were estimated to be 1 million units. But what if actual sales were lower? Then the unit cost would be higher because the fixed costs would be spread over fewer units, and the realized percentage markup on sales or ROI would be lower. Alternatively, if sales are higher than the estimated 1 million units, unit cost would be lower than $145, so a lower price would produce the desired markup on sales or ROI. It's important to note that these cost-based pricing methods are *internally* focused and do not consider demand, competitors' prices, or reseller requirements. Because HD will be selling this product to consumers through wholesalers and retailers offering competing brands, the company must consider markup pricing from this perspective.

Setting Price Based on External Factors

Whereas costs determine the price floor, HD also must consider external factors when setting price. HD does not have the final say concerning the final price of its product to consumers—retailers do. So it must start with its suggested retail price and work back. In doing so, HD must consider the markups required by resellers that sell the product to consumers.

Markup
The difference between a company's selling price for a product and its cost to manufacture or purchase it.

In general, a dollar **markup** is the difference between a company's selling price for a product and its cost to manufacture or purchase it. For a retailer, then, the markup is the difference between the price it charges consumers and the cost the retailer must pay for the product. Thus, for any level of reseller:

$$\text{Dollar markup} = \text{selling price} - \text{cost}$$

Markups are usually expressed as a percentage, and there are two different ways to compute markups—on *cost* or on *selling price*:

$$\text{Markup percentage on cost} = \frac{\text{dollar markup}}{\text{cost}}$$

$$\text{Markup percentage on selling price} = \frac{\text{dollar markup}}{\text{selling price}}$$

To apply reseller margin analysis, HD must first set the suggested retail price and then work back to the price at which it must sell the product to a wholesaler. Suppose retailers expect a 30% margin and wholesalers want a 20% margin based on their respective selling prices. And suppose that HD sets a manufacturer's suggested retail price (MSRP) of $299.99 for its product.

HD selected the $299.99 MSRP because it is lower than most competitors' prices but is not so low that consumers might perceive it to be of poor quality. And the company's research shows that it is below the threshold at which more consumers are willing to purchase the product. By using buyers' perceptions of value and not the seller's cost to determine the MSRP, HD is using **value-based pricing**. For simplicity, we will use an MSRP of $300 in further analyses.

Value-based pricing
Offering just the right combination of quality and good service at a fair price.

To determine the price HD will charge wholesalers, we must first subtract the retailer's margin from the retail price to determine the retailer's cost ($300 − ($300 × 0.30) = $210). The retailer's cost is the wholesaler's price, so HD next subtracts the wholesaler's margin ($210 − ($210 × 0.20) = $168). Thus, the **markup chain** representing the sequence of markups used by firms at each level in a channel for HD's new product is:

Markup chain
The sequence of markups used by firms at each level in a channel.

Suggested retail price:	$300
minus retail margin (30%):	−$90
Retailer's cost/wholesaler's price:	$210
minus wholesaler's margin (20%):	−$42
Wholesaler's cost/HD's price:	$168

By deducting the markups for each level in the markup chain, HD arrives at a price for the product to wholesalers of $168.

Break-Even and Margin Analysis

The previous analyses derived a value-based price of $168 for HD's product. Although this price is higher than the break-even price of $145 and covers costs, that price assumed a demand of 1 million units. But how many units and what level of dollar sales must HD achieve to break even at the $168 price? And what level of sales must be achieved to realize various profit goals? These questions can be answered through break-even and margin analysis.

Determining Break-Even Unit Volume and Dollar Sales

Based on an understanding of costs, consumer value, the competitive environment, and reseller requirements, HD has decided to set its price to wholesalers at $168. At that price, what sales level will be needed for HD to break even or make a profit on its product? **Break-even analysis** determines the unit volume and dollar sales needed to be profitable given a particular price and cost structure. At the break-even point, total revenue equals total costs and profit is zero. Above this point, the company will make a profit; below it, the company will lose money. HD can calculate break-even volume using the following formula:

Break-even analysis
Analysis to determine the unit volume and dollar sales needed to be profitable given a particular price and cost structure.

$$\text{Break-even volume} = \frac{\text{fixed costs}}{\text{price} - \text{unit variable cost}}$$

Unit contribution
The amount that each unit contributes to covering fixed costs—the difference between price and variable costs.

The denominator (price − unit variable cost) is called **unit contribution** (sometimes called contribution margin). It represents the amount that each unit contributes to covering fixed costs. Break-even volume represents the level of output at which all (variable and fixed) costs are covered. In HD's case, break-even unit volume is:

$$\text{Break-even volume} = \frac{\text{fixed cost}}{\text{price} - \text{variable cost}} = \frac{\$20,000,000}{\$168 - \$125} = 465,116.2 \text{ units}$$

Thus, at the given cost and pricing structure, HD will break even at 465,117 units.

To determine the break-even dollar sales, simply multiply unit break-even volume by the selling price:

$$\text{BE sales} = \text{BE}_{\text{vol}} \times \text{price} = 465,117 \times \$168 = \$78,139,656$$

Contribution margin

The unit contribution divided by the selling price.

Another way to calculate dollar break-even sales is to use the percentage contribution margin (hereafter referred to as **contribution margin**), which is the unit contribution divided by the selling price:

$$\text{Contribution margin} = \frac{\text{price} - \text{variable cost}}{\text{price}} = \frac{\$168 - \$125}{\$168} = 0.256 \text{ or } 25.6\%$$

Then,

$$\text{Break-even sales} = \frac{\text{fixed costs}}{\text{contribution margin}} = \frac{\$20,000,000}{0.256} = \$78,125,000$$

Note that the difference between the two break-even sales calculations is due to rounding.

Such break-even analysis helps HD by showing the unit volume needed to cover costs. If production capacity cannot attain this level of output, then the company should not launch this product. However, the unit break-even volume is well within HD's capacity. Of course, the bigger question concerns whether HD can sell this volume at the $168 price. We'll address that issue a little later.

Understanding contribution margin is useful in other types of analyses as well, particularly if unit prices and unit variable costs are unknown or if a company (say, a retailer) sells many products at different prices and knows the percentage of total sales variable costs represent. Whereas unit contribution is the difference between unit price and unit variable costs, total contribution is the difference between total sales and total variable costs. The overall contribution margin can be calculated by:

$$\text{Contribution margin} = \frac{\text{total sales} - \text{total variable costs}}{\text{total sales}}$$

Regardless of the actual level of sales, if the company knows what percentage of sales is represented by variable costs, it can calculate contribution margin. For example, HD's unit variable cost is $125, or 74% of the selling price ($125 ÷ $168 = 0.74). That means for every $1 of sales revenue for HD, $0.74 represents variable costs, and the difference ($0.26) represents contribution to fixed costs. But even if the company doesn't know its unit price and unit variable cost, it can calculate the contribution margin from total sales and total variable costs or from knowledge of the total cost structure. It can set total sales equal to 100% regardless of the actual absolute amount and determine the contribution margin:

$$\text{Contribution margin} = \frac{100\% - 74\%}{100\%} = \frac{1 - 0.74}{1} = 1 - 0.74 = 0.26 \text{ or } 26\%$$

Note that this matches the percentage calculated from the unit price and unit variable cost information. This alternative calculation will be very useful later when analyzing various marketing decisions.

Determining "Breakeven" for Profit Goals

Although it is useful to know the break-even point, most companies are more interested in making a profit. Assume HD would like to realize a $5 million profit in the first year. How many must it sell at the $168 price to cover fixed costs and produce this profit? To determine this, HD can simply add the profit figure to fixed costs and again divide by the unit contribution to determine unit sales:

$$\text{Unit volume} = \frac{\text{fixed cost} + \text{profit goal}}{\text{price} - \text{variable cost}} = \frac{\$20,000,000 + \$5,000,000}{\$168 - \$125} = 581,395.3 \text{ units}$$

Thus, to earn a $5 million profit, HD must sell 581,396 units. Multiply by price to determine dollar sales needed to achieve a $5 million profit:

$$\text{Dollar sales} = 581{,}396 \text{ units} \times \$168 = \$97{,}674{,}528$$

Or use the contribution margin:

$$\text{Sales} = \frac{\text{fixed cost} + \text{profit goal}}{\text{contribution margin}} = \frac{\$20{,}000{,}000 + \$5{,}000{,}000}{0.256} = \$97{,}656{,}250$$

Again, note that the difference between the two break-even sales calculations is due to rounding.

As we saw previously, a profit goal can also be stated as a return on investment goal. For example, recall that HD wants a 30% return on its $10 million investment. Thus, its absolute profit goal is $3 million ($10,000,000 × 0.30). This profit goal is treated the same way as in the previous example:[ii]

$$\text{Unit volume} = \frac{\text{fixed cost} + \text{profit goal}}{\text{price} - \text{variable cost}} = \frac{\$20{,}000{,}000 + \$3{,}000{,}000}{\$168 - \$125} = 534{,}884 \text{ units}$$

$$\text{Dollar sales} = 534{,}884 \text{ units} \times \$168 = \$89{,}860{,}512$$

Or

$$\text{Dollar sales} = \frac{\text{fixed cost} + \text{profit goal}}{\text{contribution margin}} = \frac{\$20{,}000{,}000 + \$3{,}000{,}000}{0.256} = \$89{,}843{,}750$$

Finally, HD can express its profit goal as a percentage of sales, which we also saw in previous pricing analyses. Assume HD desires a 25% return on sales. To determine the unit and sales volume necessary to achieve this goal, the calculation is a little different from the previous two examples. In this case, we incorporate the profit goal into the unit contribution as an additional variable cost. Look at it this way: If 25% of each sale must go toward profits, that leaves only 75% of the selling price to cover fixed costs. Thus, the equation becomes:

$$\text{Unit volume} = \frac{\text{fixed cost}}{\text{price} - \text{variable cost} - (0.25 \times \text{price})} \text{ or } \frac{\text{fixed cost}}{(0.75 \times \text{price}) - \text{variable cost}}$$

So,

$$\text{Unit volume} = \frac{\$20{,}000{,}000}{(0.75 \times \$168) - \$125} = 20{,}000{,}000 \text{ units}$$

$$\text{Dollar sales necessary} = 20{,}000{,}000 \text{ units} \times \$168 = \$3{,}360{,}000{,}000$$

Thus, HD would need more than $3 billion in sales to realize a 25% return on sales given its current price and cost structure! Could it possibly achieve this level of sales? The major point is this: Although break-even analysis can be useful in determining the level of sales needed to cover costs or to achieve a stated profit goal, it does not tell the company whether it is *possible* to achieve that level of sales at the specified price. To address this issue, HD needs to estimate demand for this product.

Before moving on, however, let's stop here and practice applying the concepts covered so far. Now that you have seen pricing and break-even concepts in action as they relate to HD's new product, here are several exercises for you to apply what you have learned in other contexts.

Marketing by the Numbers Exercise Set One

Now that you've studied pricing, break-even, and margin analysis as they relate to HD's new product launch, use the following exercises to apply these concepts in other contexts.

1.1 Elkins, a manufacturer of ice makers, realizes a cost of $250 for every unit it produces. Its total fixed costs equal $5 million. If the company manufactures 500,000 units, compute the following:

a. unit cost
b. markup price if the company desires a 10% return on sales
c. ROI price if the company desires a 25% return on an investment of $1 million

1.2 A gift shop owner purchases items to sell in her store. She purchases a chair for $125 and sells it for $275. Determine the following:
  a. dollar markup
  b. markup percentage on cost
  c. markup percentage on selling price

1.3 A consumer purchases a coffee maker from a retailer for $90. The retailer's markup is 30%, and the wholesaler's markup is 10%, both based on selling price. For what price does the manufacturer sell the product to the wholesaler?

1.4 A lawn mower manufacturer has a unit cost of $140 and wishes to achieve a margin of 30% based on selling price. If the manufacturer sells directly to a retailer who then adds a set margin of 40% based on selling price, determine the retail price charged to consumers.

1.5 Advanced Electronics manufactures DVDs and sells them directly to retailers who typically sell them for $20. Retailers take a 40% margin based on the retail selling price. Advanced's cost information is as follows:

DVD package and disc	$2.50/DVD
Royalties	$2.25/DVD
Advertising and promotion	$500,000
Overhead	$200,000

Calculate the following:
  a. contribution per unit and contribution margin
  b. break-even volume in DVD units and dollars
  c. volume in DVD units and dollar sales necessary if Advanced's profit goal is 20% profit on sales
  d. net profit if 5 million DVDs are sold

Demand Estimates, the Marketing Budget, and Marketing Performance Measures

Market Potential and Sales Estimates

HD has now calculated the sales needed to break even and to attain various profit goals on its new product. However, the company needs more information regarding demand in order to assess the feasibility of attaining the needed sales levels. This information is also needed for production and other decisions. For example, production schedules need to be developed and marketing tactics need to be planned.

Total market demand

The total volume that would be bought by a defined consumer group in a defined geographic area in a defined time period in a defined marketing environment under a defined level and mix of industry marketing effort.

The **total market demand** for a product or service is the total volume that would be bought by a defined consumer group in a defined geographic area in a defined time period in a defined marketing environment under a defined level and mix of industry marketing effort. Total market demand is not a fixed number but a function of the stated conditions. For example, next year's total market demand for this type of product will depend on how much other producers spend on marketing their brands. It also depends on many environmental factors, such as government regulations, economic conditions, and the level of consumer confidence in a given market. The upper limit of market demand is called **market potential**.

Market potential

The upper limit of market demand.

One general but practical method that HD might use for estimating total market demand uses three variables: (1) the number of prospective buyers, (2) the quantity purchased by an average buyer per year, and (3) the price of an average unit. Using these numbers, HD can estimate total market demand as follows:

$$Q = n \times q \times p$$

where

Q = total market demand
n = number of buyers in the market
q = quantity purchased by an average buyer per year
p = price of an average unit

Chain ratio method

Estimating market demand by multiplying a base number by a chain of adjusting percentages.

A variation of this approach is the **chain ratio method**. This method involves multiplying a base number by a chain of adjusting percentages. For example, HD's product is designed to stream high-definition video on high-definition televisions as well as play other video content streamed from the internet to multiple devices in a home. Thus, consumers who do not own a high-definition television will not likely purchase this player. Additionally, only households with broadband internet access will be able to use the product. Finally, not all HDTV-owning internet households will be willing and able to purchase this product. HD can estimate U.S. demand using a chain of calculations like the following:

Total number of U.S. households ×
The percentage of HDTV-owning U.S. households with broadband internet access ×
The percentage of these households willing and able to buy this device

The U.S. Census Bureau estimates that there are approximately 115 million households in the United States.[iii] HD's research indicates that 60 percent of U.S. households own at least one HDTV and have broadband internet access. Finally, the company's research also revealed that 30 percent of households possess the discretionary income needed and are willing to buy a product such as this. Then the total number of households willing and able to purchase this product is:

115 million households × 0.60 × 0.30 = 20.7 million households

Households only need to purchase one device because it can stream content to other devices throughout the household. Assuming the average retail price across all brands is $350 for this product, the estimate of total market demand is as follows:

20.7 million households × 1 device per household × $350 = $7,245,000,000

This simple chain of calculations gives HD only a rough estimate of potential demand. However, more detailed chains involving additional segments and other qualifying factors would yield more accurate and refined estimates. Still, these are only *estimates* of market potential. They rely heavily on assumptions regarding adjusting percentages, average quantity, and average price. Thus, HD must make certain that its assumptions are reasonable and defendable. As can be seen, the overall market potential in dollar sales can vary widely given the average price used. For this reason, HD will use unit sales potential to determine its sales estimate for next year. Market potential in terms of units is 20.7 million (20.7 million households × 1 device per household).

Assuming that HD forecasts it will have a 3.6% market share in the first year after launching this product, then it can forecast unit sales at 20.7 million units × 0.036 = 745,200 units. At a selling price of $168 per unit, this translates into sales of $125,193,600 (745,200 units × $168 per unit). For simplicity, further analyses will use forecasted sales of $125 million.

This unit volume estimate is well within HD's production capacity and exceeds not only the break-even estimate (465,117 units) calculated earlier but also the volume necessary to realize a $5 million profit (581,396 units) or a 30% return on investment (534,884 units). However, this forecast falls well short of the volume necessary to realize a 25% return on sales (20 million units!) and may require that HD revise expectations.

To assess expected profits, we must now look at the budgeted expenses for launching this product. To do this, we will construct a pro forma profit-and-loss statement.

The Profit-and-Loss Statement and Marketing Budget

Pro forma (or projected) profit-and-loss statement (or income statement or operating statement)

A statement that shows projected revenues less budgeted expenses and estimates the projected net profit for an organization, product, or brand during a specific planning period, typically a year.

All marketing managers must account for the profit impact of their marketing strategies. A major tool for projecting such profit impact is a **pro forma** (or **projected**) **profit-and-loss statement** (also called an **income statement** or **operating statement**). A pro forma statement shows projected revenues less budgeted expenses and estimates the projected net profit for an organization, product, or brand during a specific planning period, typically a year. It includes direct product production costs, marketing expenses budgeted to attain a given sales forecast, and overhead expenses assigned to the organization or product. A profit-and-loss statement typically consists of several major components (see ● **Table A2.1**):

- *Net sales*—gross sales revenue minus returns and allowances (for example, trade, cash, quantity, and promotion allowances). HD's net sales for 2017 are estimated to be $125 million, as determined in the previous analysis.

● **Table A2.1** | **Pro Forma Profit-and-Loss Statement for the 12-Month Period Ended December 31, 2017**

			% of Sales
Net Sales		$125,000,000	100%
Cost of Goods Sold		62,500,000	50%
Gross Margin		$62,500,000	50%
Marketing Expenses			
Sales expenses	$17,500,000		
Promotion expenses	15,000,000		
Freight	12,500,000	45,000,000	36%
General and Administrative Expenses			
Managerial salaries and expenses	$2,000,000		
Indirect overhead	3,000,000	5,000,000	4%
Net Profit Before Income Tax		$12,500,000	10%

- *Cost of goods sold*—(sometimes called *cost of sales*)—the actual cost of the merchandise sold by a manufacturer or reseller. It includes the cost of inventory, purchases, and other costs associated with making the goods. HD's cost of goods sold is estimated to be 50% of net sales, or $62.5 million.
- *Gross margin (or gross profit)*—the difference between net sales and cost of goods sold. HD's gross margin is estimated to be $62.5 million.
- *Operating expenses*—the expenses incurred while doing business. These include all other expenses beyond the cost of goods sold that are necessary to conduct business. Operating expenses can be presented in total or broken down in detail. Here, HD's estimated operating expenses include *marketing expenses* and *general and administrative expenses*.

Marketing expenses include sales expenses, promotion expenses, and distribution expenses. The new product will be sold through HD's sales force, so the company budgets $5 million for sales salaries. However, because sales representatives earn a 10% commission on sales, HD must also add a variable component to sales expenses of $12.5 million (10% of $125 million net sales), for a total budgeted sales expense of $17.5 million. HD sets its advertising and promotion to launch this product at $10 million. However, the company also budgets 4% of sales, or $5 million, for cooperative advertising allowances to retailers who promote HD's new product in their advertising. Thus, the total budgeted advertising and promotion expenses are $15 million ($10 million for advertising plus $5 million in co-op allowances). Finally, HD budgets 10% of net sales, or $12.5 million, for freight and delivery charges. In all, total marketing expenses are estimated to be $17.5 million + $15 million + $12.5 million = $45 million.

General and administrative expenses are estimated at $5 million, broken down into $2 million for managerial salaries and expenses for the marketing function and $3 million of indirect overhead allocated to this product by the corporate accountants (such as depreciation, interest, maintenance, and insurance). Total expenses for the year, then, are estimated to be $50 million ($45 million marketing expenses + $5 million in general and administrative expenses).

- *Net profit before taxes*—profit earned after all costs are deducted. HD's estimated net profit before taxes is $12.5 million.

In all, as Table A2.1 shows, HD expects to earn a profit on its new product of $12.5 million in 2017. Also note that the percentage of sales that each component of the profit-and-loss statement represents is given in the right-hand column. These percentages are determined by dividing the cost figure by net sales (that is, marketing expenses represent 36% of net sales determined by $45 million ÷ $125 million). As can be seen, HD projects a net profit return on sales of 10% in the first year after launching this product.

Marketing Performance Measures

Now let's fast-forward a year. HD's product has been on the market for one year and management wants to assess its sales and profit performance. One way to assess this performance is to compute performance ratios derived from HD's **profit-and-loss statement** (or **income statement** or **operating statement**).

Profit-and-loss statement (or income statement or operating statement)

A statement that shows actual revenues less expenses and net profit for an organization, product, or brand during a specific planning period, typically a year.

Whereas the pro forma profit-and-loss statement shows *projected* financial performance, the statement given in ● **Table A2.2** shows HD's *actual* financial performance based on actual sales, cost of goods sold, and expenses during the past year. By comparing the profit-and-loss statement from one period to the next, HD can gauge performance against goals, spot favorable or unfavorable trends, and take appropriate corrective action.

The profit-and-loss statement shows that HD lost $1 million rather than making the $12.5 million profit projected in the pro forma statement. Why? One obvious reason is that net sales fell $25 million short of estimated sales. Lower sales translated into lower variable costs associated with marketing the product. However, both fixed costs and the cost of goods sold as a percentage of sales exceeded expectations. Hence, the product's contribution margin was 21% rather than the estimated 26%. That is, variable costs represented 79% of sales (55% for cost of goods sold, 10% for sales commissions, 10% for freight, and 4% for co-op allowances). Recall that contribution margin can be calculated by subtracting that fraction from one (1 − 0.79 = 0.21). Total fixed costs were $22 million, $2 million more than estimated. Thus, the sales that HD needed to break even given this cost structure can be calculated as:

$$\text{Break-even sales} = \frac{\text{fixed costs}}{\text{contribution margin}} = \frac{\$22,000,000}{0.21} = \$104,761,905$$

If HD had achieved another $5 million in sales, it would have earned a profit.

Although HD's sales fell short of the forecasted sales, so did overall industry sales for this product. Overall industry sales were only $2.5 billion. That means that HD's **market share** was 4% ($100 million ÷ $2.5 billion = 0.04 = 4%), which was higher than forecasted.

Market share

Company sales divided by market sales.

● **Table A2.2** | **Profit-and-Loss Statement for the 12-Month Period Ended December 31, 2017**

			% of Sales
Net Sales		$100,000,000	100%
Cost of Goods Sold		55,000,000	55%
Gross Margin		$45,000,000	45%
Marketing Expenses			
Sales expenses	$15,000,000		
Promotion expenses	14,000,000		
Freight	10,000,000	39,000,000	39%
General and Administrative Expenses			
Managerial salaries and expenses	$2,000,000		
Indirect overhead	5,000,000	7,000,000	7%
Net Profit Before Income Tax		−$1,000,000	−1%

Thus, HD attained a higher-than-expected market share but the overall market sales were not as high as estimated.

Analytic Ratios

Operating ratios

The ratios of selected operating statement items to net sales.

The profit-and-loss statement provides the figures needed to compute some crucial **operating ratios**—the ratios of selected operating statement items to net sales. These ratios let marketers compare the firm's performance in one year to that in previous years (or with industry standards and competitors' performance in that year). The most commonly used operating ratios are the gross margin percentage, the net profit percentage, and the operating expense percentage. The inventory turnover rate and return on investment (ROI) are often used to measure managerial effectiveness and efficiency.

Gross margin percentage

The percentage of net sales remaining after cost of goods sold—calculated by dividing gross margin by net sales.

The **gross margin percentage** indicates the percentage of net sales remaining after cost of goods sold that can contribute to operating expenses and net profit before taxes. The higher this ratio, the more a firm has left to cover expenses and generate profit. HD's gross margin ratio was 45%:

$$\text{Gross margin percentage} = \frac{\text{gross margin}}{\text{net sales}} = \frac{\$45,000,000}{\$100,000,000} = 0.45 = 45\%$$

Note that this percentage is lower than estimated, and this ratio is seen easily in the percentage of sales column in Table A2.2. Stating items in the profit-and-loss statement as a percent of sales allows managers to quickly spot abnormal changes in costs over time. If there was previous history for this product and this ratio was declining, management should examine it more closely to determine why it has decreased (that is, because of a decrease in sales volume or price, an increase in costs, or a combination of these). In HD's case, net sales were $25 million lower than estimated, and cost of goods sold was higher than estimated (55% rather than the estimated 50%).

Net profit percentage

The percentage of each sales dollar going to profit—calculated by dividing net profits by net sales.

The **net profit percentage** shows the percentage of each sales dollar going to profit. It is calculated by dividing net profits by net sales:

$$\text{Net profit percentage} = \frac{\text{net profit}}{\text{net sales}} = \frac{-\$1,000,000}{\$100,000,000} = -0.01 = -1.0\%$$

This ratio is easily seen in the percent of sales column. HD's new product generated negative profits in the first year, not a good situation given that before the product launch net profits before taxes were estimated at more than $12 million. Later in this appendix, we will discuss further analyses the marketing manager should conduct to defend the product.

Operating expense percentage

The portion of net sales going to operating expenses—calculated by dividing total expenses by net sales.

The **operating expense percentage** indicates the portion of net sales going to operating expenses. Operating expenses include marketing and other expenses not directly related to marketing the product, such as indirect overhead assigned to this product. It is calculated by:

$$\text{Operating expense percentage} = \frac{\text{total expenses}}{\text{net sales}} = \frac{\$46,000,000}{\$100,000,000} = 0.46 = 46\%$$

This ratio can also be quickly determined from the percent of sales column in the profit-and-loss statement by adding the percentages for marketing expenses and general and administrative expenses (39% + 7%). Thus, 46 cents of every sales dollar went for operations. Although HD wants this ratio to be as low as possible, and 46% is not an alarming amount, it is of concern if it is increasing over time or if a loss is realized.

Inventory turnover rate (or stock-turn rate)

The number of times an inventory turns over or is sold during a specified time period (often one year)—calculated based on costs, selling price, or units.

Another useful ratio is the **inventory turnover rate** (also called **stockturn rate** for resellers). The inventory turnover rate is the number of times an inventory turns over or is sold during a specified time period (often one year). This rate tells how quickly a business is moving inventory through the organization. Higher rates indicate that lower investments in inventory are made, thus freeing up funds for other investments. It may be computed on a cost, selling price, or unit basis. The formula based on cost is:

$$\text{Inventory turnover rate} = \frac{\text{cost of goods sold}}{\text{average inventory at cost}}$$

Assuming HD's beginning and ending inventories were $30 million and $20 million, respectively, the inventory turnover rate is:

$$\text{Inventory turnover rate} = \frac{\$55,000,000}{(\$30,000,000 + \$20,000,000)/2} = \frac{\$55,000,000}{\$25,000,000} = 2.2$$

That is, HD's inventory turned over 2.2 times in 2017. Normally, the higher the turnover rate, the higher the management efficiency and company profitability. However, this rate should be compared to industry averages, competitors' rates, and past performance to determine if HD is doing well. A competitor with similar sales but a higher inventory turnover rate will have fewer resources tied up in inventory, allowing it to invest in other areas of the business.

Return on investment (ROI)
A measure of managerial effectiveness and efficiency—net profit before taxes divided by total investment.

Companies frequently use **return on investment (ROI)** to measure managerial effectiveness and efficiency. For HD, ROI is the ratio of net profits to total investment required to manufacture the new product. This investment includes capital investments in land, buildings, and equipment (here, the initial $10 million to refurbish the manufacturing facility) plus inventory costs (HD's average inventory totaled $25 million), for a total of $35 million. Thus, HD's ROI for this product is:

$$\text{Return on investment} = \frac{\text{net profit before taxes}}{\text{investment}} = \frac{-\$1,000,000}{\$35,000,000} = -.0286 = -2.86\%$$

ROI is often used to compare alternatives, and a positive ROI is desired. The alternative with the highest ROI is preferred to other alternatives. HD needs to be concerned with the ROI realized. One obvious way HD can increase ROI is to increase net profit by reducing expenses. Another way is to reduce its investment, perhaps by investing less in inventory and turning it over more frequently.

Marketing Profitability Metrics

Given the above financial results, you may be thinking that HD should drop this new product. But what arguments can marketers make for keeping or dropping this product? The obvious arguments for dropping the product are that first-year sales were well below expected levels and the product lost money, resulting in a negative return on investment.

So what would happen if HD did drop this product? Surprisingly, if the company drops the product, the profits for the total organization will decrease by $4 million! How can that be? Marketing managers need to look closely at the numbers in the profit-and-loss statement to determine the *net marketing contribution* for this product. In HD's case, the net marketing contribution for the product is $4 million, and if the company drops this product, that contribution will disappear as well. Let's look more closely at this concept to illustrate how marketing managers can better assess and defend their marketing strategies and programs.

Net Marketing Contribution

Net marketing contribution (NMC)
A measure of marketing profitability that includes only components of profitability controlled by marketing.

Net marketing contribution (NMC), along with other marketing metrics derived from it, measures *marketing* profitability. It includes only components of profitability that are controlled by marketing. Whereas the previous calculation of net profit before taxes from the profit-and-loss statement includes operating expenses not under marketing's control, NMC does not. Referring back to HD's profit-and-loss statement given in Table A2.2, we can calculate net marketing contribution for the product as:

$$\text{NMC} = \text{net sales} - \text{cost of goods sold} - \text{marketing expenses}$$

$$= \$4 \text{ million} = \$100 \text{ million} - \$55 \text{ million} - \$41 \text{ million}$$

The marketing expenses include sales expenses ($15 million), promotion expenses ($14 million), freight expenses ($10 million), and the managerial salaries and expenses of the marketing function ($2 million), which total $41 million.

Thus, the product actually contributed $4 million to HD's profits. It was the $5 million of indirect overhead allocated to this product that caused the negative profit. Further, the amount allocated was $2 million more than estimated in the pro forma profit-and-loss statement. Indeed, if only the estimated amount had been allocated, the product would have earned a *profit* of $1 million rather than losing $1 million. If HD drops the product, the $5 million in fixed overhead expenses will not disappear—it will simply have to be allocated elsewhere. However, the $4 million in net marketing contribution *will* disappear.

Marketing Return on Sales and Investment

To get an even deeper understanding of the profit impact of marketing strategy, we'll now examine two measures of marketing efficiency—*marketing return on sales* (marketing ROS) and *marketing return on investment* (marketing ROI).[iv]

Marketing return on sales (or **marketing ROS**) shows the percent of net sales attributable to the net marketing contribution. For our product, ROS is:

$$\text{Marketing ROS} = \frac{\text{net marketing contribution}}{\text{net sales}} = \frac{\$4,000,000}{\$100,000,000} = 0.04 = 4\%$$

Marketing return on sales (or marketing ROS)

The percent of net sales attributable to the net marketing contribution—calculated by dividing net marketing contribution by net sales.

Thus, out of every $100 of sales, the product returns $4 to HD's bottom line. A high marketing ROS is desirable. But to assess whether this is a good level of performance, HD must compare this figure to previous marketing ROS levels for the product, the ROSs of other products in the company's portfolio, and the ROSs of competing products.

Marketing return on investment (or **marketing ROI**) measures the marketing productivity of a marketing investment. In HD's case, the marketing investment is represented by $41 million of the total expenses. Thus, marketing ROI is:

$$\text{Marketing ROI} = \frac{\text{net marketing contribution}}{\text{marketing expenses}} = \frac{\$4,000,000}{\$41,000,000} = 0.0976 = 9.76\%$$

Marketing return on investment (or marketing ROI)

A measure of the marketing productivity of a marketing investment—calculated by dividing net marketing contribution by marketing expenses.

As with marketing ROS, a high value is desirable, but this figure should be compared with previous levels for the given product and with the marketing ROIs of competitors' products. Note from this equation that marketing ROI could be greater than 100%. This can be achieved by attaining a higher net marketing contribution and/or a lower total marketing expense.

In this section, we estimated market potential and sales, developed profit-and-loss statements, and examined financial measures of performance. In the next section, we discuss methods for analyzing the impact of various marketing tactics. However, before moving on to those analyses, here's another set of quantitative exercises to help you apply what you've learned to other situations.

Marketing by the Numbers Exercise Set Two

2.1 Determine the market potential for a product that has 20 million prospective buyers who purchase an average of 2 per year and price averages $50. How many units must a company sell if it desires a 10% share of this market?

2.2 Develop a profit-and-loss statement for the Westgate division of North Industries. This division manufactures light fixtures sold to consumers through home-improvement and hardware stores. Cost of goods sold represents 40% of net sales. Marketing expenses include selling expenses, promotion expenses, and freight. Selling expenses include sales salaries totaling $3 million per year and sales commissions (5% of sales). The company spent $3 million on advertising last year, and freight costs were 10% of sales. Other costs include $2 million for managerial salaries and expenses for the marketing function and another $3 million for indirect overhead allocated to the division.
   a. Develop the profit-and-loss statement if net sales were $20 million last year.
   b. Develop the profit-and-loss statement if net sales were $40 million last year.
   c. Calculate Westgate's break-even sales.

2.3 Using the profit-and-loss statement you developed in question 2.2b, and assuming that Westgate's beginning inventory was $11 million, ending inventory was $7 million, and total investment was $20 million including inventory, determine the following:
   a. gross margin percentage
   b. net profit percentage
   c. operating expense percentage
   d. inventory turnover rate
   e. return on investment (ROI)
   f. net marketing contribution
   g. marketing return on sales (marketing ROS)
   h. marketing return on investment (marketing ROI)
   i. Is the Westgate division doing well? Explain your answer.

Financial Analysis of Marketing Tactics

Although the first-year profit performance for HD's new product was less than desired, management feels that this attractive market has excellent growth opportunities. Although the sales of HD's product were lower than initially projected, they were not unreasonable given the size of the current market. Thus, HD wants to explore new marketing tactics to help grow the market for this product and increase sales for the company.

For example, the company could increase advertising to promote more awareness of the new product and its category. It could add salespeople to secure greater product distribution. HD could decrease prices so that more consumers could afford its product. Finally, to expand the market, HD could introduce a lower-priced model in addition to the higher-priced original offering. Before pursuing any of these tactics, HD must analyze the financial implications of each.

Increase Advertising Expenditures

HD is considering boosting its advertising to make more people aware of the benefits of this device in general and of its own brand in particular. What if HD's marketers recommend increasing national advertising by 50% to $15 million (assume no change in the variable cooperative component of promotional expenditures)? This represents an increase in fixed costs of $5 million. What increase in sales will be needed to break even on this $5 million increase in fixed costs?

A quick way to answer this question is to divide the increase in fixed cost by the contribution margin, which we found in a previous analysis to be 21%:

$$\text{Increase in sales} = \frac{\text{increase in fixed cost}}{\text{contribution margin}} = \frac{\$5{,}000{,}000}{0.21} = \$23{,}809{,}524$$

Thus, a 50% increase in advertising expenditures must produce a sales increase of almost $24 million to just break even. That $24 million sales increase translates into an almost 1 percentage point increase in market share (1% of the $2.5 billion overall market equals $25 million). That is, to break even on the increased advertising expenditure, HD would have to increase its market share from 4% to 4.95% ($123,809,524 ÷ $2.5 billion = 0.0495 or 4.95% market share). All of this assumes that the total market will not grow, which might or might not be a reasonable assumption.

Increase Distribution Coverage

HD also wants to consider hiring more salespeople in order to call on new retailer accounts and increase distribution through more outlets. Even though HD sells directly to wholesalers, its sales representatives call on retail accounts to perform other functions in addition to selling, such as training retail salespeople. Currently, HD employs 60 sales reps who earn an average of $50,000 in salary plus 10% commission on sales. The product is currently sold to consumers through 1,875 retail outlets. Suppose HD wants to increase that number of outlets to 2,500, an increase of 625 retail outlets. How many additional salespeople will HD need, and what sales will be necessary to break even on the increased cost?

One method for determining what size sales force HD will need is the **workload method**. The workload method uses the following formula to determine the sales-force size:

Workload method
An approach to determining sales force size based on the workload required and the time available for selling.

$$NS = \frac{NC \times FC \times LC}{TA}$$

where

NS = number of salespeople
NC = number of customers
FC = average frequency of customer calls per customer
LC = average length of customer call
TA = time an average salesperson has available for selling per year

HD's sales reps typically call on accounts an average of 20 times per year for about 2 hours per call. Although each sales rep works 2,000 hours per year (50 weeks per year × 40 hours per week), they spent about 15 hours per week on nonselling activities such as administrative duties and travel. Thus, the average annual available selling time per sales rep per year is 1,250 hours (50 weeks × 25 hours per week). We can now calculate how many sales reps HD will need to cover the anticipated 2,500 retail outlets:

$$NS = \frac{2{,}500 \times 20 \times 2}{1{,}250} = 80 \text{ salespeople}$$

Therefore, HD will need to hire 20 more salespeople. The cost to hire these reps will be $1 million (20 salespeople × $50,000 salary per sales person).

What increase in sales will be required to break even on this increase in fixed costs? The 10% commission is already accounted for in the contribution margin, so the contribution margin remains unchanged at 21%. Thus, the increase in sales needed to cover this increase in fixed costs can be calculated by:

$$\text{Increase in sales} = \frac{\text{increase in fixed cost}}{\text{contribution margin}} = \frac{\$1{,}000{,}000}{0.21} = \$4{,}761{,}905$$

That is, HD's sales must increase almost $5 million to break even on this tactic. So, how many new retail outlets will the company need to secure to achieve this sales increase? The average revenue generated per current outlet is $53,333 ($100 million in sales divided by 1,875 outlets). To achieve the nearly $5 million sales increase needed to break even, HD would need about 90 new outlets ($4,761,905 ÷ $53,333 = 89.3 outlets), or about 4.5 outlets per new rep. Given that current reps cover about 31 outlets apiece (1,875 outlets ÷ 60 reps), this seems very reasonable.

Decrease Price

HD is also considering lowering its price to increase sales revenue through increased volume. The company's research has shown that demand for most types of consumer electronics products is elastic—that is, the percentage increase in the quantity demanded is greater than the percentage decrease in price.

What increase in sales would be necessary to break even on a 10% decrease in price? That is, what increase in sales will be needed to maintain the total contribution that HD realized at the higher price? The current total contribution can be determined by multiplying the contribution margin by total sales:[v]

$$\text{Current total contribution} = \text{contribution margin} \times \text{sales} = 0.21 \times \$100 \text{ million}$$
$$= \$21 \text{ million}$$

Price changes result in changes in unit contribution and contribution margin. Recall that the contribution margin of 21% was based on variable costs representing 79% of sales. Therefore, unit variable costs can be determined by multiplying the original price by this percentage: $168 × 0.79 = $132.72 per unit. If price is decreased by 10%, the new price is $151.20. However, variable costs do not change just because price decreased, so the contribution and contribution margin decrease as follows:

	Old	New (reduced 10%)
Price	$168	$151.20
− Unit variable cost	$132.72	$132.72
= Unit contribution	$35.28	$18.48
Contribution margin	$35.28/$168 = 0.21 or 21%	$18.48/$151.20 = 0.12 or 12%

So a 10% reduction in price results in a decrease in the contribution margin from 21% to 12%.[vi] To determine the sales level needed to break even on this price reduction, we calculate the level of sales that must be attained at the new contribution margin to achieve the original total contribution of $21 million:

$$\text{New contribution margin} \times \text{new sales level} = \text{original total contribution}$$

So,

$$\text{New sales level} = \frac{\text{original contribution}}{\text{new contribution margin}} = \frac{\$21,000,000}{0.12} = \$175,000,000$$

Thus, sales must increase by $75 million ($175 million − $100 million) just to break even on a 10% price reduction. This means that HD must increase market share to 7% ($175 million ÷ $2.5 billion) to achieve the current level of profits (assuming no increase in the total market sales). The marketing manager must assess whether or not this is a reasonable goal.

Extend the Product Line

As a final option, HD is considering extending its product line by offering a lower-priced model. Of course, the new, lower-priced product would steal some sales from the higher-priced model. This is called **cannibalization**—the situation in which one product sold by a company takes a portion of its sales from other company products. If the new product has a lower contribution than the original product, the company's total contribution will decrease on the cannibalized sales. However, if the new product can generate enough new volume, it is worth considering.

To assess cannibalization, HD must look at the incremental contribution gained by having both products available. Recall in the previous analysis we determined that unit variable costs were $132.72 and unit contribution was just over $35. Assuming costs remain the same next year, HD can expect to realize a contribution per unit of approximately $35 for every unit of the original product sold.

Assume that the first model offered by HD is called HD1 and the new, lower-priced model is called HD2. HD2 will retail for $250, and resellers will take the same markup percentages on price as they do with the higher-priced model. Therefore, HD2's price to wholesalers will be $140 as follows:

Retail price:	$250
minus retail margin (30%):	− $75
Retailer's cost/wholesaler's price:	$175
minus wholesaler's margin (20%):	− $35
Wholesaler's cost/HD's price	$140

If HD2's variable costs are estimated to be $120, then its contribution per unit will equal $20 ($140 − $120 = $20). That means for every unit that HD2 cannibalizes from HD1, HD will *lose* $15 in contribution toward fixed costs and profit (that is, contribution$_{HD2}$ − contribution$_{HD1}$ = $20 − $35 = −$15). You might conclude that HD should not pursue this tactic because it appears as though the company will be worse off if it introduces the lower-priced model. However, if HD2 captures enough *additional* sales, HD will be better off even though some HD1 sales are cannibalized. The company must examine what will happen to *total* contribution, which requires estimates of unit volume for both products.

Originally, HD estimated that next year's sales of HD1 would be 600,000 units. However, with the introduction of HD2, it now estimates that 200,000 of those sales will be cannibalized by the new model. If HD sells only 200,000 units of the new HD2 model (all cannibalized from HD1), the company would lose $3 million in total contribution (200,000 units × −$15 per cannibalized unit = −$3 million)—not a good outcome.

Cannibalization

The situation in which one product sold by a company takes a portion of its sales from other company products.

However, HD estimates that HD2 will generate the 200,000 of cannibalized sales plus an *additional* 500,000 unit sales. Thus, the contribution on these additional HD2 units will be $10 million (i.e., 500,000 units × $20 per unit = $10 million). The net effect is that HD will gain $7 million in total contribution by introducing HD2.

The following table compares HD's total contribution with and without the introduction of HD2:

	HD1 only	**HD1 and HD2**
HD1 contribution	600,000 units × $35 = $21,000,000	400,000 units × $35 = $14,000,000
HD2 contribution	0	700,000 units × $20 = $14,000,000
Total contribution	$21,000,000	$28,000,000

The difference in the total contribution is a net gain of $7 million ($28 million − $21 million). Based on this analysis, HD should introduce the HD2 model because it results in a positive incremental contribution. However, if fixed costs will increase by more than $7 million as a result of adding this model, then the net effect will be negative and HD should not pursue this tactic.

Now that you have seen these marketing tactic analysis concepts in action as they related to HD's new product, here are several exercises for you to apply what you have learned in this section in other contexts.

Marketing by the Numbers Exercise Set Three

3.1   Alliance, Inc. sells gas lamps to consumers through retail outlets. Total industry sales for Alliance's relevant market last year were $100 million, with Alliance's sales representing 5% of that total. Contribution margin is 25%. Alliance's sales force calls on retail outlets and each sales rep earns $50,000 per year plus 1% commission on all sales. Retailers receive a 40% margin on selling price and generate average revenue of $10,000 per outlet for Alliance.

   a. The marketing manager has suggested increasing consumer advertising by $200,000. By how much would dollar sales need to increase to break even on this expenditure? What increase in overall market share does this represent?

   b. Another suggestion is to hire two more sales representatives to gain new consumer retail accounts. How many new retail outlets would be necessary to break even on the increased cost of adding two sales reps?

   c. A final suggestion is to make a 10% across-the-board price reduction. By how much would dollar sales need to increase to maintain Alliance's current contribution? (See endnote 13 to calculate the new contribution margin.)

   d. Which suggestion do you think Alliance should implement? Explain your recommendation.

3.2   PepsiCo sells its soft drinks in approximately 400,000 retail establishments, such as supermarkets, discount stores, and convenience stores. Sales representatives call on each retail account weekly, which means each account is called on by a sales rep 52 times per year. The average length of a sales call is 75 minutes (or 1.25 hours). An average salesperson works 2,000 hours per year (50 weeks per year × 40 hours per week), but each spends 10 hours a week on non-selling activities, such as administrative tasks and travel. How many sales people does PepsiCo need?

3.3 Hair Zone manufactures a brand of hair-styling gel. It is considering adding a modified version of the product—a foam that provides stronger hold. Hair Zone's variable
costs and prices to wholesalers are:

	Current Hair Gel	New Foam Product
Unit selling price	$2.00	$2.25
Unit variable costs	$0.85	$1.25

Hair Zone expects to sell 1 million units of the new styling foam in the first year after
introduction, but it expects that 60% of those sales will come from buyers who normally
purchase Hair Zone's styling gel. Hair Zone estimates that it would sell 1.5 million units of
the gel if it did not introduce the foam. If the fixed cost of launching the new foam will be
$100,000 during the first year, should Hair Zone add the new product to its line? Why or
why not?

APPENDIX 3 Careers in Marketing

You may have decided you want to pursue a marketing career because it offers constant challenge, stimulating problems, the opportunity to work with people, and excellent advancement opportunities. But you still may not know which part of marketing best suits you—marketing is a very broad field offering a wide variety of career options.

This appendix helps you discover what types of marketing jobs best match your special skills and interests, shows you how to conduct the kind of job search that will get you the position you want, describes marketing career paths open to you, and suggests other information resources.

Marketing Careers Today

The marketing field is booming, with nearly a third of all working Americans now employed in marketing-related positions. Marketing salaries may vary by company, position, and region, and salary figures change constantly. In general, entry-level marketing salaries usually are only slightly below those for engineering and chemistry but equal or exceed starting salaries in economics, finance, accounting, general business, and the liberal arts. Moreover, if you succeed in an entry-level marketing position, it's likely that you will be promoted quickly to higher levels of responsibility and salary. In addition, because of the consumer and product knowledge you will gain in these jobs, marketing positions provide excellent training for the highest levels in an organization.

Overall Marketing Facts and Trends

In conducting your job search, consider the following facts and trends that are changing the world of marketing:

Focus on customers. More and more, companies are realizing that they win in the marketplace only by creating superior value for customers. To capture value from customers, they must first find new and better ways to engage customers, solve customer problems, and improve customer brand experiences. This increasing focus on the customer puts marketers at the forefront in many of today's companies. As the primary customer-facing function, marketing's mission is to get all company departments to "think customer."

Technology. Technology is changing the way marketers work. For example, internet, social media, mobile, and other digital technologies are rapidly changing the ways marketers interact with and service customers. They are also changing everything from the ways marketers create new products and advertise them to how marketers access information and recruit personnel. Whereas advertising firms have traditionally recruited "generalists" in account management, *generalist* has now taken on a whole new meaning—advertising account executives must now have both broad and specialized knowledge.

Diversity. The number of women and minorities in marketing continues to grow, and women and minorities also are advancing rapidly into marketing management. For example, women now outnumber men by nearly two to one as advertising account executives. As marketing becomes more global, the need for diversity in marketing positions will continue to increase, opening new opportunities.

Global. Companies such as Coca-Cola, McDonald's, Google, IBM, Facebook, Walmart, and Procter & Gamble have become multinational, with manufacturing and marketing operations in hundreds of countries. Indeed, such companies often make more profit from sales outside the United States than from within. And it's not just the big companies that are involved in international marketing. Organizations of all sizes have moved into the global arena. Many new marketing opportunities and careers will be directly linked to the expanding global marketplace. The globalization of business also means that you will need more cultural, language, and people skills in the marketing world of the twenty-first century.

Not-for-profit organizations. Increasingly, colleges, arts organizations, libraries, hospitals, and other not-for-profit organizations are recognizing the need for effectively marketing their "products" and services to various publics. This awareness has led to new marketing positions—with these organizations hiring their own marketing directors and marketing vice presidents or using outside marketing specialists.

Looking for a Job in Today's Marketing World

To choose and find the right job, you will need to apply the marketing skills you've learned in this course, especially marketing analysis and planning. Follow these eight steps for marketing yourself: (1) Conduct a self-assessment and seek career counseling; (2) examine job descriptions; (3) explore the job market, follow up, and assess opportunities; (4) develop search strategies; (5) prepare résumés; (6) write a cover letter and assemble supporting documents; (7) interview for jobs; and (8) take a follow-up interview.

Conduct a Self-Assessment and Seek Career Counseling

If you're having difficulty deciding what kind of marketing position is the best fit for you, start out by doing some self-testing or seeking career counseling. Self-assessments require that you honestly and thoroughly evaluate your interests, strengths, and weaknesses. What do you do well (your best and favorite skills) and not so well? What are your favorite interests? What are your career goals? What makes you stand out from other job seekers?

The answers to such questions may suggest which marketing careers you should seek or avoid. For help in completing an effective self-assessment, look for the following books in your local bookstore or online: Nicholas Lore, *The Pathfinder: How to Choose or Change Your Career for a Lifetime of Satisfaction and Success* (Touchstone, 2012); and Richard Bolles, *What Color Is Your Parachute? 2017* (Ten Speed Press, 2016; also see www.eparachute.com). Many online sites also offer self-assessment tools, such as the Keirsey Temperament Theory and the Temperament Sorter, a free but broad assessment available at Keirsey.com. For a more specific evaluation, CareerLeader.com offers a complete online business career self-assessment program designed by the Directors of MBA Career Development at Harvard Business School. You can use this for a fee.

For help in finding a career counselor to guide you in making a career assessment, Richard Bolles's *What Color Is Your Parachute? 2017* contains a useful state-by-state sampling. CareerLeader.com also offers personal career counseling. (Some counselors can help you in your actual job search, too.) You can also consult the career counseling, testing, and placement services at your college or university.

Examine Job Descriptions

After you have identified your skills, interests, and desires, you need to see which marketing positions are the best match for them. Two U.S. Labor Department publications available in your local library or online—the *Occupation Outlook Handbook* (www.bls.gov/ooh) and the *Dictionary of Occupational Titles* (www.occupationalinfo.org)—describe the duties involved in various occupations, the specific training and education needed, the availability of jobs in each field, possibilities for advancement, and probable earnings.

Your initial career shopping list should be broad and flexible. Look for different ways to achieve your objectives. For example, if you want a career in marketing management, consider the public as well as the private sector, and local and regional as well as national and international firms. Be open initially to exploring many options, then focus on specific industries and jobs, listing your basic goals as a way to guide your choices. Your list might include "a job in a start-up company, near a big city on the West Coast, doing new-product planning with a computer software firm."

Explore the Job Market and Assess Opportunities

At this stage, you need to look at the market and see what positions are actually available. You do not have to do this alone. Any of the following may assist you.

Career Development Centers

Your college's career development center and its website are excellent places to start. For example, the websites of the undergraduate career services center provide lists of career links that can help to focus your job search. Most schools also provide career coaches and career education courses. Also check the National Association of Colleges and Employers website (www.naceweb.org). It publishes a national forecast of hiring intentions of employers as they relate to new college graduates (search: "Job Outlook").

In addition, find out everything you can about the companies that interest you by consulting company websites, business magazine articles and online sites, annual reports, business reference books, faculty, career counselors, and others. Try to analyze the industry's and the company's future growth and profit potential, advancement opportunities, salary levels, entry positions, travel time, and other factors of significance to you.

Job Fairs

Career development centers often work with corporate recruiters to organize on-campus job fairs. You might also use the internet to check on upcoming career fairs in your region. For example, visit National Career Fairs at www.nationalcareerfairs.com or Coast to Coast Career Fairs listings at www.coasttocoastcareerfairs.com.

Networking

Networking—asking for job leads from friends, family, people in your community, and career centers—is one of the best ways to find a marketing job. Studies estimate that 60 to 90 percent of jobs are found through networking. The idea is to spread your net wide, contacting anybody and everybody.

Internships

An internship is filled with many benefits, such as gaining experience in a specific field of interest and building up a network of contacts. The biggest benefit: the potential of being offered a job shortly before or soon after graduation. According to a recent survey by the National Association of Colleges and Employers, employers converted 51.2 percent of last year's interns into full-time hires. In addition, 63 percent of the seniors who had paid internship experience and applied for a job received at least one job offer. Conversely, only 35.2 percent of seniors without internship experience who applied for a job received an offer. In addition, survey results show that the median accepted salary offer for seniors with a paid internship was 40 percent higher than the median accepted salary offered to non-intern seniors.

Many company internet sites have separate internship areas. For example, check out Internships.com, InternshipPrograms.com, MonsterCollege (college.monster.com/education), CampusCareerCenter.com, InternJobs.com, and GoAbroad.com (www.goabroad.com/intern-abroad). If you know of a company for which you wish to work, go to that company's corporate website, enter the human resources area, and check for internships. If none are listed, try emailing the human resources department, asking if internships are offered.

Job Hunting on the Internet

A constantly increasing number of sites on the internet deal with job hunting. You can also use the internet to make contacts with people who can help you gain information on and research companies that interest you. The Riley Guide offers a great introduction to what jobs are available (www.rileyguide.com). CareerBuilder.com, Monster.com, and Beyond.com are good general sites for seeking job listings. Other helpful sites are Disability.gov and Diversity.com, which contain information on opportunities for African Americans, Hispanic Americans, Asian Americans, and Native Americans.

Most companies have their own online sites on which they post job listings. This may be helpful if you have a specific and fairly limited number of companies that you are keeping your eye on for job opportunities. But if this is not the case, remember that to find out what interesting marketing jobs the companies themselves are posting, you may have to visit hundreds of corporate sites.

Professional Networking Sites

Many companies have now begun to take advantage of social networking sites to find talented applicants. From LinkedIn to Facebook to Google+, social networking has become professional networking. For example, companies ranging from P&G to BASF have career pages on LinkedIn (www.linkedin.com/company/procter-&-gamble/careers and www.linkedin.com/company/basf/careers) to find potential candidates for entry-level positions. For job seekers, online professional networking offers more efficient job targeting and reduces associated costs as compared with traditional interaction methods such as traveling to job fairs and interviews, printing résumés, and other expenses.

However, although the internet offers a wealth of resources for searching for the perfect job, be aware that it's a two-way street. Just as job seekers can search the internet to find job opportunities, employers can search for information on job candidates. Jobs searches can sometimes be derailed by information mined by potential employers from online social networking sites that reveals unintended or embarrassing anecdotes and photos. Internet searches can sometimes also reveal inconsistencies and résumé inflation. A recent study found that more than half of recruiters surveyed have reconsidered a candidate based on their social profile.

Develop Search Strategies

Once you've decided which companies you are interested in, you need to contact them. One of the best ways is through on-campus interviews. However, not every company you are interested in will visit your school. In such instances, you can write, email, or phone the company directly or ask marketing professors or school alumni for contacts.

Prepare Résumés

A résumé is a concise yet comprehensive written summary of your qualifications, including your academic, personal, and professional achievements, that showcases why you are the best candidate for the job. Because an employer will spend on average only 15 to 20 seconds reviewing your résumé, you want to be sure that you prepare a good one.

In preparing your résumé, remember that all information on it must be accurate and complete. Résumés typically begin with the applicant's full name, telephone number, and mail and email addresses. A simple and direct statement of career objectives generally appears next, followed by work history and academic data (including awards and internships), and then by personal activities and experiences applicable to the job sought.

The résumé sometimes ends with a list of references the employer may contact (at other times, references may be listed separately). If your work or internship experience is limited, nonexistent, or irrelevant, then it is a good idea to emphasize your academic and nonacademic achievements, showing skills related to those required for excellent job performance.

There are three main types of résumés. Reverse *chronological* résumés, which emphasize career growth, are organized in reverse chronological order, starting with your most recent job. They focus on job titles within organizations, describing the responsibilities and accomplishments for each job. *Functional* résumés focus less on job titles and work history and more on assets and achievements. This format works best if your job history is scanty or discontinuous. *Mixed,* or *combination,* résumés take from each of the other two formats. First, the skills used for a specific job are listed, then the job title is stated. This format works best for applicants whose past jobs are in other fields or seemingly unrelated to the position. For further explanation and examples of these types of résumés, see the Résumé Resource format page (www.resume-resource.com/format.html).

Many books can assist you in developing your résumé. A popular guide is Molly Mapes, *Cracking the Code: A Practical Guide to Getting You Hired* (Difference Press: 2016). Websites such as MyPerfectResume (www.myperfectresume.com) provide sample résumés and ready-to-use phrases while guiding you through the résumé preparation process. CareerOneStop (www.careeronestop.org/resumeguide/introduction.aspx) offers a step-by-step résumé tutorial, and Monster (http://career-advice.monster.com) offers résumé advice and writing services. Finally, you can even create your own personalized online résumé at sites such as optimalresume.com.

Online Résumés

The internet is now a widely used job-search environment, so it's a good idea to have your résumé ready for the online environment. You can forward it to networking contacts or recruiting professionals through email. You can also post it in online databases with the hope that employers and recruiters will find it.

Successful internet-ready résumés require a different strategy than that for paper résumés. For instance, when companies search résumé banks, they search key words and industry buzz words that describe a skill or the core work required for each job, so nouns are much more important than verbs. Two good resources for preparing internet-ready résumés are Goodwill Community Foundation (www.gcflearnfree.org/resumewriting/9/print) and the Riley Guide (www.rileyguide.com/eresume.html).

After you have written your internet-ready résumé, you need to post it. The following sites may be good locations to start: Monster (www.monster.com), LinkedIn (www.linkedin.com/job/home), and CareerBuilder.com (www.careerbuilder.com/jobseeker/postnewresume.aspx). However, use caution when posting your résumé on various sites. In this era of identity theft, you need to select sites with care so as to protect your privacy. Limit access to your personal contact information, and don't use sites that offer to "blast" your résumé into cyberspace.

Résumé Tips

- Communicate your worth to potential employers in a concrete manner, citing examples whenever possible.
- Be concise and direct.
- Use active verbs to show you are a doer.
- Do not skimp on quality or use gimmicks. Spare no expense in presenting a professional résumé.
- Have someone critique your work. A single typo can eliminate you from being considered.
- Customize your résumé for specific employers. Emphasize your strengths as they pertain to your targeted job.
- Keep your résumé compact, usually one page.
- Format the text to be attractive, professional, and readable. Times New Roman is often the font of choice. Avoid too much "design" or gimmicky flourishes.

Write Cover Letter, Follow Up, and Assemble Supporting Documents

Cover Letter

You should include a cover letter informing the employer that a résumé is enclosed. But a cover letter does more than this. It also serves to summarize in one or two paragraphs the contents of the résumé and explains why you think you are the right person for the position. The goal is to persuade the employer to look at the more detailed résumé. A typical cover letter is organized as follows: (1) the name and position of the person you are contacting; (2) a statement identifying the position you are applying for, how you heard of the vacancy, and the reasons for your interest; (3) a summary of your qualifications for the job; (4) a description of what follow-ups you intend to make, such as phoning in two weeks to see if the résumé has been received; and (5) an expression of gratitude for the opportunity of being a candidate for the job. CareerOneStop (www.careeronestop.org/ResumeGuide/Writeeffectivecoverletters.aspx) offers a step-by-step tutorial on how to create a cover letter, and Susan Ireland's website contains more than 50 cover letter samples (susanireland.com/letter/cover-letter-examples). Another popular guide is Jeremy Schifeling, *Get It Done: Write a Cover Letter* (Adams Media, 2016).

Follow Up

Once you send your cover letter and résumé to prospective employers via the method they prefer—email, their website, or regular mail—it's often a good idea to follow up. In today's market, job seekers can't afford to wait for interviews to find them. A quality résumé and an attractive cover letter are crucial, but a proper follow-up may be the key to landing an interview. However, before you engage your potential employer, be sure to research the company. Knowing about the company and understanding its place in the industry will help you shine. When you place a call, send an email, or mail a letter to a company contact, be sure to restate your interest in the position, check on the status of your résumé, and ask employers about any questions they may have.

Letters of Recommendation

Letters of recommendation are written references by professors, former and current employers, and others that testify to your character, skills, and abilities. Some companies may request letters of recommendation, to be submitted either with the résumé or at the interview. Even if letters of recommendation aren't requested, it's a good idea to bring them with you to the interview. A good reference letter tells why you would be an excellent candidate for the position. In choosing someone to write a letter of recommendation, be confident that the person will give you a good reference. In addition, do not assume the person knows everything about you or the position you are seeking. Rather, provide the person with your résumé and other relevant data. As a courtesy, allow the reference writer at least a month to complete the letter and enclose a stamped, addressed envelope with your materials.

In the packet containing your résumé, cover letter, and letters of recommendation, you may also want to attach other relevant documents that support your candidacy, such as academic transcripts, graphics, portfolios, and samples of writing.

Interview for Jobs

As the old saying goes, "The résumé gets you the interview; the interview gets you the job." The job interview offers you an opportunity to gather more information about the organization, while at the same time allowing the organization to gather more information about you. You'll want to present your best self. The interview process consists of three parts: before the interview, the interview itself, and after the interview. If you pass through these stages successfully, you will be called back for the follow-up interview.

Before the Interview

In preparing for your interview, do the following:

1. Understand that interviewers have diverse styles, including the "chitchat," let's-get-to-know-each-other style; the interrogation style of question after question; and the tough-probing "why, why, why" style, among others. So be ready for anything.
2. With a friend, practice being interviewed and then ask for a critique. Or videotape yourself in a practice interview so that you can critique your own performance. Your college placement service may also offer "mock" interviews to help you.
3. Prepare at least five good questions whose answers are not easily found in the company literature, such as "What is the future direction of the firm?" "How does the firm differentiate itself from competitors?" or "Do you have a new-media division?"
4. Anticipate possible interview questions, such as "Why do you want to work for this company?" or "Why should we hire you?" Prepare solid answers before the interview. Have a clear idea of why you are interested in joining the company and the industry to which it belongs.
5. Avoid back-to-back interviews—they can be exhausting, and it is unpredictable how long each will last.
6. Prepare relevant documents that support your candidacy, such as academic transcripts, letters of recommendation, graphics, portfolios, and samples of writing. Bring multiple copies to the interview.
7. Dress conservatively and professionally. Be neat and clean.
8. Arrive 10 minutes early to collect your thoughts and review the major points you intend to cover. Check your name on the interview schedule, noting the name of the interviewer and the room number. Be courteous and polite to office staff.
9. Approach the interview enthusiastically. Let your personality shine through.

During the Interview

During the interview, do the following:

1. Shake hands firmly in greeting the interviewer. Introduce yourself, using the same form of address that the interviewer uses. Focus on creating a good initial impression.
2. Keep your poise. Relax, smile when appropriate, and be upbeat throughout.
3. Maintain eye contact and good posture, and speak distinctly. Don't clasp your hands or fiddle with jewelry, hair, or clothing. Sit comfortably in your chair.
4. Along with the copies of relevant documents that support your candidacy, carry extra copies of your résumé with you.
5. Have your story down pat. Present your selling points. Answer questions directly. Avoid either one-word or too-wordy answers.
6. Let the interviewer take the initiative but don't be passive. Find an opportunity to direct the conversation to things about yourself that you want the interviewer to hear.
7. To end on a high note, make your most important point or ask your most pertinent question during the last part of the interview.
8. Don't hesitate to "close." You might say, "I'm very interested in the position, and I have enjoyed this interview."
9. Obtain the interviewer's business card or address and phone number so that you can follow up later.

A tip for acing the interview: Before you open your mouth, find out *what it's like* to be a brand manager, sales representative, market researcher, advertising account executive, or other position for which you're interviewing. See if you can find a "mentor"—someone in a position similar to the one you're seeking, perhaps with another company. Talk with this mentor about the ins and outs of the job and industry.

After the Interview

After the interview, do the following:

1. Record the key points that arose. Be sure to note who is to follow up and when a decision can be expected.
2. Analyze the interview objectively, including the questions asked, the answers to them, your overall interview presentation, and the interviewer's responses to specific points.
3. Immediately send a thank-you letter or email, mentioning any additional items and your willingness to supply further information.
4. If you do not hear from the employer within the specified time, call, email, or write the interviewer to determine your status.

Follow-Up Interview

If your first interview takes place off-site, such as at your college or at a job fair, and if you are successful with that initial interview, you will be invited to visit the organization. The in-company interview will probably run from several hours to an entire day. The organization will examine your interest, maturity, enthusiasm, assertiveness, logic, and company and functional knowledge. You should ask questions about issues of importance to you. Find out about the working environment, job role, responsibilities, opportunities for advancement, current industrial issues, and the company's personality. The company wants to discover if you are the right person for the job, whereas you want to find out if it is the right job for you. The key is to determine if the right *fit* exists between you and the company.

Marketing Jobs

This section describes some of the key marketing positions.

Advertising

Advertising is one of the most exciting fields in marketing, offering a wide range of career opportunities.

Job Descriptions

Key advertising positions include copywriter, art director, production manager, account executive, account planner, and media planner/buyer.

- *Copywriters* write advertising copy and help find the concepts behind the written words and visual images of advertisements.
- *Art directors,* the other part of the creative team, help translate the copywriters' ideas into dramatic visuals called "layouts." Agency artists develop print layouts, package designs, television and video layouts (called "storyboards"), corporate logotypes, trademarks, and symbols.
- *Production managers* are responsible for physically creating ads, either in-house or by contracting through outside production houses.
- *Account development executives* research and understand clients' markets and customers and help develop marketing and advertising strategies to affect them.
- *Account executives* serve as liaisons between clients and agencies. They coordinate the planning, creation, production, and implementation of an advertising campaign for the account.
- *Account planners* serve as the voice of the consumer in the agency. They research consumers to understand their needs and motivations as a basis for developing effective ad campaigns.
- *Digital content managers* plan and place digital and social media marketing and advertising content and coordinate it with traditional media content.
- *Media planners* (or *buyers*) determine the best mix of television, radio, newspaper, magazine, digital, and other media for the advertising campaign.

Skills Needed, Career Paths, and Typical Salaries

Work in advertising requires strong people skills in order to interact closely with an often-difficult and demanding client base. In addition, advertising attracts people with strong skills in planning, problem solving, creativity, communication, initiative, leadership, and presentation. Advertising involves working under high levels of stress and pressure created by unrelenting deadlines. Advertisers frequently have to work long hours to meet deadlines for a presentation. But work achievements are very apparent, with the results of creative strategies observed by thousands or even millions of people.

Positions in advertising sometimes require an MBA. But most jobs only require a business, graphic arts, or liberal arts degree. Advertising positions often serve as gateways to higher-level management. Moreover, with large advertising agencies opening offices all over the world, there is the possibility of eventually working on global campaigns.

Starting advertising salaries are relatively low compared to those of some other marketing jobs because of strong competition for entry-level advertising jobs. Compensation will increase quickly as you move into account executive or other management positions. For more facts and figures, see the online pages of *Advertising Age*, a key ad industry publication (www.adage.com, click on the Jobs link) and the American Association of Advertising Agencies (www.aaaa.org).

Brand and Product Management

Brand and product managers plan, direct, and control business and marketing efforts for their products. They are involved with research and development, packaging, manufacturing, sales and distribution, advertising, promotion, market research, and business analysis and forecasting.

Job Descriptions

A company's brand management team consists of people in several positions:

- *Brand managers* guide the development of marketing strategies for a specific brand.
- *Assistant brand managers* are responsible for certain strategic components of the brand.
- *Product managers* oversee several brands within a product line or product group.
- *Product category managers* direct multiple product lines in the product category.
- *Market analysts* research the market and provide important strategic information to the project managers.

- *Project directors* are responsible for collecting market information on a marketing or product project.
- *Research directors* oversee the planning, gathering, and analyzing of all organizational research.

Skills Needed, Career Paths, and Typical Salaries

Brand and product management requires high problem-solving, analytical, presentation, communication, and leadership skills as well as the ability to work well in a team. Product management requires long hours and involves the high pressure of running large projects. In consumer goods companies, the newcomer—who usually needs an MBA—joins a brand team as an assistant and learns the ropes by doing numerical analyses and assisting senior brand people. This person eventually heads the team and later moves on to manage a larger brand, then several brands.

Many industrial goods companies also have product managers. Product management is one of the best training grounds for future corporate officers. Product management also offers good opportunities to move into international marketing. Product managers command relatively high salaries. Because this job category encourages or requires a master's degree, starting pay tends to be higher than in other marketing categories such as advertising or retailing.

Sales and Sales Management

Sales and sales management opportunities exist in a wide range of profit and not-for-profit organizations and in product and service organizations, including financial, insurance, consulting, and government organizations.

Job Descriptions

Key jobs include consumer sales, industrial sales, national account managers, service support, sales trainers, and sales management

- *Consumer sales* involves selling consumer products and services through retailers.
- *Industrial sales* involves selling products and services to other businesses.
- *National account managers (NAMs)* oversee a few very large accounts.
- *Service support* personnel support salespeople during and after the sale of a product.
- *Sales trainers* train new hires and provide refresher training for all sales personnel.
- *Sales management* includes a sequence of positions ranging from district manager to vice president of sales.

Salespeople enjoy active professional lives, working outside the office and interacting with others. They manage their own time and activities. And successful salespeople can be very well paid. Competition for top jobs can be intense. Every sales job is different, but some positions involve extensive travel, long workdays, and working under pressure. You can also expect to be transferred more than once between company headquarters and regional offices. However, most companies are now working to bring good work–life balance to their salespeople and sales managers.

Skills Needed, Career Paths, and Typical Salaries

Selling is a people profession in which you will work with people every day, all day long. In addition to people skills, sales professionals need sales and communication skills. Most sales positions also require strong problem-solving, analytical, presentation, and leadership abilities as well as creativity and initiative. Teamwork skills are increasingly important.

Career paths lead from salesperson to district, regional, and higher levels of sales management and, in many cases, to the top management of the firm. Today, most entry-level sales management positions require a college degree. Increasingly, people seeking selling jobs are acquiring sales experience in an internship capacity or from a part-time job before graduating. Sales positions are great springboards to leadership positions, with more CEOs starting in sales than in any other entry-level position. This might explain why competition for top sales jobs is intense.

Starting base salaries in sales may be moderate but compensation is often supplemented by significant commission, bonus, or other incentive plans. In addition, many sales jobs include a company car or car allowance. Successful salespeople are among most companies' highest paid employees.

Other Marketing Jobs

Retailing

Retailing provides an early opportunity to assume marketing responsibilities. Key jobs include store manager, regional manager, buyer, department manager, and salesperson. *Store managers* direct the management and operation of an individual store. *Regional managers* manage groups of stores across several states and report performance to headquarters. *Buyers* select and buy the merchandise that the store carries. The *department manager* acts as store manager of a department, such as clothing, but on the department level. The *salesperson* sells merchandise to retail customers. Retailing can involve relocation, but generally there is little travel, unless you are a buyer. Retailing requires high people and sales skills because retailers are constantly in contact with customers. Enthusiasm, willingness, and communication skills are very helpful for retailers, too.

Retailers work long hours, but their daily activities are often more structured than in some types of marketing positions. Starting salaries in retailing tend to be low, but pay increases as you move into management or a retailing specialty job.

Marketing Research

Marketing researchers interact with managers to define problems and identify the information needed to resolve them. They design research projects, prepare questionnaires and samples, analyze data, prepare reports, and present their findings and recommendations to management. They must understand statistics, data analytics tools, consumer behavior, psychology, and sociology. As more and more marketing research goes digital, they must also understand the ins and outs of obtaining and managing online information. A master's degree helps. Career opportunities exist with manufacturers, retailers, some wholesalers, trade and industry associations, marketing research firms, advertising agencies, and governmental and private nonprofit agencies.

New Product Planning

People interested in new product planning can find opportunities in many types of organizations. They usually need a good background in marketing, marketing research, and sales forecasting; they need organizational skills to motivate and coordinate others; and they may need a technical background. Usually, these people work first in other marketing positions before joining the new product department.

Marketing Logistics (Physical Distribution)

Marketing logistics, or physical distribution, is a large and dynamic field, with many career opportunities. Major transportation carriers, manufacturers, wholesalers, and retailers all employ logistics specialists. Increasingly, marketing teams include logistics specialists, and marketing managers' career paths include marketing logistics assignments. Coursework in quantitative methods, finance, accounting, and marketing will provide you with the necessary skills for entering the field.

Public Relations

Most organizations have a public relations staff to anticipate problems with various publics, handle complaints, deal with media, and build the corporate image. People interested in public relations should be able to speak and write clearly and persuasively, and they should have a background in journalism, communications, or the liberal arts. The challenges in this job are highly varied and very people-oriented.

Not-for-Profit Services

The key jobs in not-for-profits include marketing director, director of development, event coordinator, publication specialist, and intern/volunteer. The *marketing director* is in charge of all marketing activities for the organization. The *director of development* organizes, manages, and directs the fundraising campaigns that keep a not-for-profit in existence. An *event coordinator* directs all aspects of fundraising events, from initial planning through implementation. The *publication specialist* oversees publications designed to promote awareness of the organization.

Although typically an unpaid position, the *intern/volunteer* performs various marketing functions, and this work can be an important step to gaining a full-time position. The not-for-profit sector is typically not for someone who is money-driven. Rather, most not-for-profits look for people with a strong sense of community spirit and the desire to help others. Therefore, starting pay is usually lower than in other marketing fields. However, the bigger the not-for-profit, the better your chance of rapidly increasing your income when moving into upper management.

Other Resources

Professional marketing associations and organizations are another source of information about careers. Marketers belong to many such societies. You may want to contact some of the following in your job search:

Advertising Women of New York, 28 West 44th Street, Suite 912, New York, NY 10036. (212) 221-7969 (www.awny.org)

American Advertising Federation, 1101 Vermont Avenue, NW, Washington, DC 20005. (202) 898-0089 (www.aaf.org)

American Marketing Association, 130 E Randolph Street, 22nd Floor, Chicago, IL 60601. (800) AMA-1150 (www.marketingpower.com)

The Association of Women in Communications, 1717 E Republic Road, Suite A, Springfield, MO 65804. (417) 886-8606 (www.womcom.org)

Market Research Association, 1156 15th Street NW, Suite 302, Washington, DC 20005. (202) 800-2545 (www.marketingresearch.org)

National Association of Sales Professionals, 555 Friendly Street, Bloomfield Hills, MI 48341. (866) 365-1520 (www.nasp.com)

National Management Association, 2210 Arbor Boulevard, Dayton, OH 45439. (937) 294-0421 (www.nma1.org)

National Retail Federation, 1101 New York Avenue NW, Washington, DC 20005. (800) 673-4692 (www.nrf.com)

Product Development and Management Association, 330 Wabash Avenue, Suite 2000, Chicago, IL 60611. (312) 321-5145 (www.pdma.org)

Public Relations Society of America, 33 Maiden Lane, Eleventh Floor, New York, NY 10038. (212) 460-1400 (www.prsa.org)

Sales and Marketing Executives International, PO Box 1390, Sumas, WA, 98295. (312) 893-0751 (www.smei.org)

Glossary

Adapted global marketing A global marketing approach that adjusts the marketing strategy and mix elements to each international target market, which creates more costs but hopefully produces a larger market share and return.

Administered VMS A vertical marketing system that coordinates successive stages of production and distribution through the size and power of one of the parties.

Adoption process The mental process through which an individual passes from first hearing about an innovation to final adoption.

Advertising Any paid form of nonpersonal presentation and promotion of ideas, goods, or services by an identified sponsor.

Advertising agency A marketing services firm that assists companies in planning, preparing, implementing, and evaluating all or portions of their advertising programs.

Advertising budget The dollars and other resources allocated to a product or a company advertising program.

Advertising media The vehicles through which advertising messages are delivered to their intended audiences.

Advertising objective A specific communication task to be accomplished with a specific target audience during a specific period of time.

Advertising strategy The strategy by which the company accomplishes its advertising objectives. It consists of two major elements: creating advertising messages and selecting advertising media.

Affordable method Setting the promotion budget at the level management thinks the company can afford.

Agent A wholesaler who represents buyers or sellers on a relatively permanent basis, performs only a few functions, and does not take title to goods.

Age and life-cycle segmentation Dividing a market into different age and life-cycle groups.

Allowance Promotional money paid by manufacturers to retailers in return for an agreement to feature the manufacturer's products in some way.

Alternative evaluation The stage of the buyer decision process in which the consumer uses information to evaluate alternative brands in the choice set.

Approach The sales step in which a salesperson meets the customer for the first time.

Attitude A person's consistently favorable or unfavorable evaluations, feelings, and tendencies toward an object or idea.

B-to-B digital and social media marketing Using digital and social media marketing approaches to engage business customers and manage customer relationships anywhere, anytime.

Baby boomers The 78 million people born during the years following World War II and lasting until 1964.

Basing-point pricing Pricing in which the seller designates some city as a basing point and charges all customers the freight cost from that city to the customer.

Behavioral segmentation Dividing a market into segments based on consumer knowledge, attitudes, uses of a product, or responses to a product.

Behavioral targeting Using online consumer tracking data to target advertisements and marketing offers to specific consumers.

Belief A descriptive thought that a person holds about something.

Benchmarking Comparing the company's products and processes to those of competitors or leading firms in other industries to identify best practices and find ways to improve quality and performance.

Benefit segmentation Dividing the market into segments according to the different benefits that consumers seek from the product.

Big data The huge and complex data sets generated by today's sophisticated information generation, collection, storage, and analysis technologies.

Blogs Online forums where people and companies post their thoughts and other content, usually related to narrowly defined topics.

Brand A name, term, sign, symbol, or design, or a combination of these, that identifies the products or services of one seller or group of sellers and differentiates them from those of competitors.

Brand community website A website that presents brand content that engages consumers and creates customer community around a brand.

Brand equity The differential effect that knowing the brand name has on customer response to the product or its marketing.

Brand extension Extending an existing brand name to new product categories.

Brand value The total financial value of a brand.

Break-even pricing (target return pricing) Setting price to break even on the costs of making and marketing a product or setting price to make a target return.

Broker A wholesaler who does not take title to goods and whose function is to bring buyers and sellers together and assist in negotiation.

Business analysis A review of the sales, costs, and profit projections for a new product to find out whether these factors satisfy the company's objectives.

Business buyer behavior The buying behavior of organizations that buy goods and services for use in the production of other products and services that are sold, rented, or supplied to others.

Business buying process The decision process by which business buyers determine which products and services their organizations need to purchase and then find, evaluate, and choose among alternative suppliers and brands.

Business portfolio The collection of businesses and products that make up the company.

Business promotions Sales promotion tools used to generate business leads, stimulate purchases, reward customers, and motivate salespeople.

Buyer-readiness stages The stages consumers normally pass through on their way to a purchase: awareness, knowledge, liking, preference, conviction, and, finally, the actual purchase.

Buyers People in an organization's buying center who make an actual purchase.

Buying center All the individuals and units that play a role in the purchase decision-making process.

Buzz marketing Cultivating opinion leaders and getting them to spread information about a product or a service to others in their communities.

By-product pricing Setting a price for by-products to help offset the costs of disposing of them and help make the main product's price more competitive.

Captive-product pricing Setting a price for products that must be used along with a main product, such as blades for a razor and games for a video-game console.

Catalog marketing Direct marketing through print, video, or digital catalogs that are mailed to select customers, made available in stores, or presented online.

Category killer A giant specialty store that carries a very deep assortment of a particular line.

Causal research Marketing research to test hypotheses about cause-and-effect relationships.

Channel conflict Disagreements among marketing channel members on goals, roles, and rewards—who should do what and for what rewards.

Channel level A layer of intermediaries that performs some work in bringing the product and its ownership closer to the final buyer.

Closing The sales step in which a salesperson asks the customer for an order.

Co-branding The practice of using the established brand names of two different companies on the same product.

Cognitive dissonance Buyer discomfort caused by postpurchase conflict.

Commercialization Introducing a new product into the market.

Communication adaptation A global communication strategy of fully adapting advertising messages to local markets.

Competition-based pricing Setting prices based on competitors' strategies, prices, costs, and market offerings.

Competitive advantage An advantage over competitors gained by offering greater customer value either by having lower prices or providing more benefits that justify higher prices.

Competitive marketing intelligence The systematic monitoring, collection, and analysis of publicly available information about consumers, competitors, and developments in the marketing environment.

Competitive marketing strategies Strategies that strongly position the company against competitors and give it the greatest possible competitive advantage.

Competitive-parity method Setting the promotion budget to match competitors' outlays.

Competitor analysis Identifying key competitors; assessing their objectives, strategies, strengths and weaknesses, and reaction patterns; and selecting which competitors to attack or avoid.

Competitor-centered company A company whose moves are mainly based on competitors' actions and reactions.

Complex buying behavior Consumer buying behavior in situations characterized by high consumer involvement in a purchase and significant perceived differences among brands.

Concentrated (niche) marketing A market-coverage strategy in which a firm goes after a large share of one or a few segments or niches.

Concept testing Testing new product concepts with a group of target consumers to find out if the concepts have strong consumer appeal.

Consumer buyer behavior The buying behavior of final consumers—individuals and households that buy goods and services for personal consumption.

Consumer market All the individuals and households that buy or acquire goods and services for personal consumption.

Consumer product A product bought by final consumers for personal consumption.

Consumer promotions Sales promotion tools used to boost short-term customer buying and engagement or enhance long-term customer relationships.

Consumer-generated marketing Brand exchanges created by consumers themselves—both invited and uninvited—by which consumers are playing an increasing role in shaping their own brand experiences and those of other consumers.

Consumer-oriented marketing A company should view and organize its marketing activities from the consumer's point of view.

Consumerism An organized movement of citizens and government agencies designed to improve the rights and power of buyers in relation to sellers.

Content marketing Creating, inspiring, and sharing brand messages and conversations with and among consumers across a fluid mix of paid, owned, earned, and shared channels.

Contract manufacturing A joint venture in which a company contracts with manufacturers in a foreign market to produce its product or provide its service.

Contractual VMS A vertical marketing system in which independent firms at different levels of production and distribution join together through contracts.

Convenience product A consumer product that customers usually buy frequently, immediately, and with minimal comparison and buying effort.

Convenience store A small store, located near a residential area, that is open long hours seven days a week and carries a limited line of high-turnover convenience goods.

Conventional distribution channel A channel consisting of one or more independent producers, wholesalers, and retailers, each a separate business seeking to maximize its own profits, perhaps even at the expense of profits for the system as a whole.

Corporate chains Two or more outlets that are commonly owned and controlled.

Corporate VMS A vertical marketing system that combines successive stages of production and distribution under single ownership—channel leadership is established through common ownership.

Cost-based pricing Setting prices based on the costs of producing, distributing, and selling the product plus a fair rate of return for effort and risk.

Cost-plus pricing (markup pricing) Adding a standard markup to the cost of the product.

Creative concept The compelling "big idea" that will bring an advertising message strategy to life in a distinctive and memorable way.

Crowdsourcing Inviting broad communities of people—customers, employees, independent scientists and researchers, and even the public at large—into the new product innovation process.

Cultural environment Institutions and other forces that affect society's basic values, perceptions, preferences, and behaviors.

Culture The set of basic values, perceptions, wants, and behaviors learned by a member of society from family and other important institutions.

Customer (or market) sales force structure A sales force organization in which salespeople specialize in selling only to certain customers or industries.

Customer equity The total combined customer lifetime values of all of the company's customers.

Customer insights Fresh marketing information-based understandings of customers and the marketplace that become the basis for creating customer value, engagement, and relationships.

Customer lifetime value The value of the entire stream of purchases a customer makes over a lifetime of patronage.

Customer relationship management The overall process of building and maintaining profitable customer relationships by delivering superior customer value and satisfaction.

Customer relationship management (CRM) Managing detailed information about individual customers and carefully managing customer touch points to maximize customer loyalty.

Customer satisfaction The extent to which a product's perceived performance matches a buyer's expectations.

Customer value analysis An analysis conducted to determine what benefits target customers value and how they rate the relative value of various competitors' offers.

Customer value marketing A company should put most of its resources into customer value–building marketing investments.

Customer value–based pricing Setting price based on buyers' perceptions of value rather than on the seller's cost.

Customer-centered company A company that focuses on customer developments in designing its marketing strategies and delivering superior value to its target customers.

Customer-centered new product development New product development that focuses on finding new ways to solve customer problems and create more customer-satisfying experiences.

Customer-engagement marketing Making the brand a meaningful part of consumers' conversations and lives by fostering direct and continuous customer involvement in shaping brand conversations, experiences, and community.

Customer-perceived value The customer's evaluation of the difference between all the benefits and all the costs of a marketing offer relative to those of competing offers.

Deciders People in an organization's buying center who have formal or informal power to select or approve the final suppliers.

Decline stage The PLC stage in which a product's sales fade away.

Deficient products Products that have neither immediate appeal nor long-run benefits.

Demand curve A curve that shows the number of units the market will buy in a given time period, at different prices that might be charged.

Demands Human wants that are backed by buying power.

Demographic segmentation Dividing the market into segments based on variables such as age, life-cycle stage, gender, income, occupation, education, religion, ethnicity, and generation.

Demography The study of human populations in terms of size, density, location, age, gender, race, occupation, and other statistics.

Department store A retail store that carries a wide variety of product lines, each operated as a separate department managed by specialist buyers or merchandisers.

Derived demand Business demand that ultimately comes from (derives from) the demand for consumer goods.

Descriptive research Marketing research to better describe marketing problems, situations, or markets, such as the market potential for a product or the demographics and attitudes of consumers.

Desirable products Products that give both high immediate satisfaction and high long-run benefits.

Differentiated (segmented) marketing A market-coverage strategy in which a firm decides to target several market segments and designs separate offers for each.

Differentiation Actually differentiating the market offering to create superior customer value.

Digital and social media marketing Using digital marketing tools such as websites, social media, mobile apps and ads, online video, email, and blogs to engage consumers anywhere, at any time, via their digital devices.

Direct and digital marketing Engaging directly with carefully targeted individual consumers and customer communities to both obtain an immediate response and build lasting customer relationships.

Direct investment Entering a foreign market by developing foreign-based assembly or manufacturing facilities.

Direct marketing channel A marketing channel that has no intermediary levels.

Direct-mail marketing Marketing that occurs by sending an offer, announcement, reminder, or other item directly to a person at a particular address.

Direct-response television (DRTV) marketing Direct marketing via television, including direct-response television advertising (or infomercials) and interactive television (iTV) advertising.

Discount A straight reduction in price on purchases during a stated period of time or of larger quantities.

Discount store A retail operation that sells standard merchandise at lower prices by accepting lower margins and selling at higher volume.

Disintermediation The cutting out of marketing channel intermediaries by product or service producers or the displacement of traditional resellers by radical new types of intermediaries.

Dissonance-reducing buying behavior Consumer buying behavior in situations characterized by high involvement but few perceived differences among brands.

Distribution center A large, highly automated warehouse designed to receive goods from various plants and suppliers, take orders, fill them efficiently, and deliver goods to customers as quickly as possible.

Diversification Company growth through starting up or acquiring businesses outside the company's current products and markets.

Dynamic pricing Adjusting prices continually to meet the characteristics and needs of individual customers and situations.

E-procurement Purchasing through electronic connections between buyers and sellers—usually online.

Economic community A group of nations organized to work toward common goals in the regulation of international trade.

Economic environment Economic factors that affect consumer purchasing power and spending patterns.

Email marketing Sending highly targeted, highly personalized, relationship-building marketing messages via email.

Environmental sustainability A management approach that involves developing strategies that both sustain the environment and produce profits for the company.

Environmental sustainability Developing strategies and practices that create a world economy that the planet can support indefinitely.

Environmentalism An organized movement of concerned citizens, businesses, and government agencies designed to protect and improve people's current and future living environment.

Ethnographic research A form of observational research that involves sending trained observers to watch and interact with consumers in their "natural environments."

Event marketing (or event sponsorships) Creating a brand-marketing event or serving as a sole or participating sponsor of events created by others.

Exchange The act of obtaining a desired object from someone by offering something in return.

Exclusive distribution Giving a limited number of dealers the exclusive right to distribute the company's products in their territories.

Execution style The approach, style, tone, words, and format used for executing an advertising message.

Experience curve (learning curve) The drop in the average per-unit production cost that comes with accumulated production experience.

Experimental research Gathering primary data by selecting matched groups of subjects, giving them different treatments, controlling related factors, and checking for differences in group responses.

Exploratory research Marketing research to gather preliminary information that will help define problems and suggest hypotheses.

Exporting Entering foreign markets by selling goods produced in the company's home country, often with little modification.

Factory outlet An off-price retailing operation that is owned and operated by a manufacturer and normally carries the manufacturer's surplus, discontinued, or irregular goods.

Fad A temporary period of unusually high sales driven by consumer enthusiasm and immediate product or brand popularity.

Fashion A currently accepted or popular style in a given field.

Fixed costs (overhead) Costs that do not vary with production or sales level.

FOB-origin pricing Pricing in which goods are placed free on board a carrier; the customer pays the freight from the factory to the destination.

Focus group interviewing Personal interviewing that involves inviting small groups of people to gather for a few hours with a trained interviewer to talk about a product, service, or organization. The interviewer "focuses" the group discussion on important issues.

Follow-up The sales step in which a salesperson follows up after the sale to ensure customer satisfaction and repeat business.

Franchise A contractual association between a manufacturer, wholesaler, or service organization (a franchisor) and independent businesspeople (franchisees) who buy the right to own and operate one or more units in the franchise system.

Franchise organization A contractual vertical marketing system in which a channel member, called a franchisor, links several stages in the production-distribution process.

Freight-absorption pricing Pricing in which the seller absorbs all or part of the freight charges in order to get the desired business.

Gatekeepers People in an organization's buying center who control the flow of information to others.

Gender segmentation Dividing a market into different segments based on gender.

General need description The stage in the business buying process in which a buyer describes the general characteristics and quantity of a needed item.

Generation X The 49 million people born between 1965 and 1976 in the "birth dearth" following the baby boom.

Generation Z People born after 2000 (although many analysts include people born after 1995) who make up the kids, tweens, and teens markets.

Geographic segmentation Dividing a market into different geographical units, such as nations, states, regions, counties, cities, or even neighborhoods.

Geographical pricing Setting prices for customers located in different parts of the country or world.

Global firm A firm that, by operating in more than one country, gains R&D, production, marketing, and financial advantages in its costs and reputation that are not available to purely domestic competitors.

Good-value pricing Offering just the right combination of quality and good service at a fair price.

Government market Governmental units—federal, state, and local—that purchase or rent goods and services for carrying out the main functions of government.

Group Two or more people who interact to accomplish individual or mutual goals.

Growth stage The PLC stage in which a product's sales start climbing quickly.

Growth-share matrix A portfolio-planning method that evaluates a company's SBUs in terms of market growth rate and relative market share.

Habitual buying behavior Consumer buying behavior in situations characterized by low consumer involvement and few significant perceived brand differences.

Handling objections The sales step in which a salesperson seeks out, clarifies, and overcomes any customer objections to buying.

Horizontal marketing system A channel arrangement in which two or more companies at one level join together to follow a new marketing opportunity.

Idea generation The systematic search for new product ideas.

Idea screening Screening new product ideas to spot good ones and drop poor ones as soon as possible.

Income segmentation Dividing a market into different income segments.

Independent off-price retailer An off-price retailer that is independently owned and operated or a division of a larger retail corporation.

Indirect marketing channel A marketing channel containing one or more intermediary levels.

Individual marketing Tailoring products and marketing programs to the needs and preferences of individual customers.

Industrial product A product bought by individuals and organizations for further processing or for use in conducting a business.

Influencers People in an organization's buying center who affect the buying decision; they often help define specifications and also provide information for evaluating alternatives.

Information search The stage of the buyer decision process in which the consumer is motivated to search for more information.

Innovative marketing A company should seek real product and marketing improvements.

Inside sales force Salespeople who conduct business from their offices via telephone, online and social media interactions, or visits from prospective buyers.

Institutional market Schools, hospitals, nursing homes, prisons, and other institutions that provide goods and services to people in their care.

Integrated logistics management The logistics concept that emphasizes teamwork—both inside the company and among all the marketing channel organizations—to maximize the performance of the entire distribution system.

Integrated marketing communications (IMC) Carefully integrating and coordinating the company's many communications channels to deliver a clear, consistent, and compelling message about the organization and its products.

Intensive distribution Stocking the product in as many outlets as possible.

Interactive marketing Training service employees in the fine art of interacting with customers to satisfy their needs.

Intermarket (cross-market) segmentation Forming segments of consumers who have similar needs and buying behaviors even though they are located in different countries.

Internal databases Collections of consumer and market information obtained from data sources within the company network.

Internal marketing Orienting and motivating customer-contact employees and supporting service employees to work as a team to provide customer satisfaction.

Introduction stage The PLC stage in which a new product is first distributed and made available for purchase.

Joint ownership A cooperative venture in which a company creates a local business with investors in a foreign market who share ownership and control.

Joint venturing Entering foreign markets by joining with foreign companies to produce or market a product or service.

Learning Changes in an individual's behavior arising from experience.

Licensing Entering foreign markets through developing an agreement with a licensee in the foreign market.

Lifestyle A person's pattern of living as expressed in his or her activities, interests, and opinions.

Line extension Extending an existing brand name to new forms, colors, sizes, ingredients, or flavors of an existing product category.

Local marketing Tailoring brands and marketing to the needs and wants of local customer segments—cities, neighborhoods, and even specific stores.

Macroenvironment The larger societal forces that affect the microenvironment—demographic, economic, natural, technological, political, and cultural forces.

Madison & Vine A term that has come to represent the merging of advertising and entertainment in an effort to break through the clutter and create new avenues for reaching customers with more engaging messages.

Management contracting A joint venture in which the domestic firm supplies the management know-how to a foreign company that supplies the capital; the domestic firm exports management services rather than products.

Manufacturers' and retailers' branches and offices Wholesaling by sellers or buyers themselves rather than through independent wholesalers.

Market The set of all actual and potential buyers of a product or service.

Market challenger A runner-up firm that is fighting hard to increase its market share in an industry.

Market development Company growth by identifying and developing new market segments for current company products.

Market follower A runner-up firm that wants to hold its share in an industry without rocking the boat.

Market leader The firm in an industry with the largest market share.

Market nicher A firm that serves small segments that the other firms in an industry overlook or ignore.

Market offerings Some combination of products, services, information, or experiences offered to a market to satisfy a need or want.

Market penetration Company growth by increasing sales of current products to current market segments without changing the product.

Market segment A group of consumers who respond in a similar way to a given set of marketing efforts.

Market segmentation Dividing a market into distinct groups of buyers who have different needs, characteristics, or behaviors and who might require separate marketing strategies or mixes.

Market targeting (targeting) Evaluating each market segment's attractiveness and selecting one or more segments to serve.

Market-centered company A company that pays balanced attention to both customers and competitors in designing its marketing strategies.

Market-penetration pricing Setting a low price for a new product in order to attract a large number of buyers and a large market share.

Market-skimming pricing (price skimming) Setting a high price for a new product to skim maximum revenues layer by layer from the segments willing to pay the high price; the company makes fewer but more profitable sales.

Marketing The process by which companies engage customers, build strong customer relationships, and create customer value in order to capture value from customers in return.

Marketing analytics The analysis tools, technologies, and processes by which marketers dig out meaningful patterns in big data to gain customer insights and gauge marketing performance.

Marketing channel (distribution channel) A set of interdependent organizations that help make a product or service available for use or consumption by the consumer or business user.

Marketing channel design Designing effective marketing channels by analyzing customer needs, setting channel objectives, identifying major channel alternatives, and evaluating those alternatives.

Marketing channel management Selecting, managing, and motivating individual channel members and evaluating their performance over time.

Marketing concept A philosophy in which achieving organizational goals depends on knowing the needs and wants of target markets and delivering the desired satisfactions better than competitors do.

Marketing control Measuring and evaluating the results of marketing strategies and plans and taking corrective action to ensure that the objectives are achieved.

Marketing environment The actors and forces outside marketing that affect marketing management's ability to build and maintain successful relationships with target customers.

Marketing implementation Turning marketing strategies and plans into marketing actions to accomplish strategic marketing objectives.

Marketing information system (MIS) People and procedures dedicated to assessing information needs, developing the needed information, and helping decision makers to use the information to generate and validate actionable customer and market insights.

Marketing intermediaries Firms that help the company to promote, sell, and distribute its goods to final buyers.

Marketing logistics (physical distribution) Planning, implementing, and controlling the physical flow of materials, final goods, and related information from points of origin to points of consumption to meet customer requirements at a profit.

Marketing management The art and science of choosing target markets and building profitable relationships with them.

Marketing mix The set of tactical marketing tools—product, price, place, and promotion—that the firm blends to produce the response it wants in the target market.

Marketing myopia The mistake of paying more attention to the specific products a company offers than to the benefits and experiences produced by these products.

Marketing research The systematic design, collection, analysis, and reporting of data relevant to a specific marketing situation facing an organization.

Marketing return on investment (marketing ROI) The net return from a marketing investment divided by the costs of the marketing investment.

Marketing strategy The marketing logic by which the company hopes to create customer value and achieve profitable customer relationships.

Marketing strategy development Designing an initial marketing strategy for a new product based on the product concept.

Marketing website A website that engages consumers to move them closer to a direct purchase or other marketing outcome.

Maturity stage The PLC stage in which a product's sales growth slows or levels off.

Merchant wholesaler An independently owned wholesale business that takes title to the merchandise it handles.

Microenvironment The actors close to the company that affect its ability to serve its customers—the company, suppliers, marketing intermediaries, customer markets, competitors, and publics.

Micromarketing Tailoring products and marketing programs to the needs and wants of specific individuals and local customer segments; it includes local marketing and individual marketing.

Millennials (or Generation Y) The 83 million children of the baby boomers born between 1977 and 2000.

Mission statement A statement of the organization's purpose—what it wants to accomplish in the larger environment.

Mobile marketing Marketing messages, promotions, and other content delivered to on-the-go consumers through their mobile devices.

Modified rebuy A business buying situation in which the buyer wants to modify product specifications, prices, terms, or suppliers.

Motive (drive) A need that is sufficiently pressing to direct the person to seek satisfaction of the need.

Multichannel distribution system A distribution system in which a single firm sets up two or more marketing channels to reach one or more customer segments.

Multimodal transportation Combining two or more modes of transportation.

Native advertising Advertising or other brand-produced online content that looks in form and function like the other natural content surrounding it on a web or social media platform.

Natural environment The physical environment and the natural resources that are needed as inputs by marketers or that are affected by marketing activities.

Need recognition The first stage of the buyer decision process, in which the consumer recognizes a problem or need.

Needs States of felt deprivation.

New product A good, service, or idea that is perceived by some potential customers as new.

New product development The development of original products, product improvements, product modifications, and new brands through the firm's own product development efforts.

New task A business buying situation in which the buyer purchases a product or service for the first time.

Nonpersonal communication channels Media that carry messages without personal contact or feedback, including major media, atmospheres, and events.

Objective-and-task method Developing the promotion budget by (1) defining specific promotion objectives, (2) determining the tasks needed to achieve these objectives, and (3) estimating the costs of performing these tasks. The sum of these costs is the proposed promotion budget.

Observational research Gathering primary data by observing relevant people, actions, and situations.

Occasion segmentation Dividing the market into segments according to occasions when buyers get the idea to buy, actually make their purchase, or use the purchased item.

Off-price retailer A retailer that buys at less-than-regular wholesale prices and sells at less than retail.

Omni-channel retailing Creating a seamless cross-channel buying experience that integrates in-store, online, and mobile shopping.

Online advertising Advertising that appears while consumers are browsing online, including display ads, search-related ads, online classifieds, and other forms.

Online focus groups Gathering a small group of people online with a trained moderator to chat about a product, service, or organization and gain qualitative insights about consumer attitudes and behavior.

Online marketing Marketing via the internet using company websites, online ads and promotions, email, online video, and blogs.

Online marketing research Collecting primary data through internet and mobile surveys, online focus groups, consumer tracking, experiments, and online panels and brand communities.

Online social networks Online social communities—blogs, online social media, brand communities, and other online forums—where people socialize or exchange information and opinions.

Opinion leader A person within a reference group who, because of special skills, knowledge, personality, or other characteristics, exerts social influence on others.

Optional-product pricing The pricing of optional or accessory products along with a main product.

Order-routine specification The stage of the business buying process in which the

buyer writes the final order with the chosen supplier(s), listing the technical specifications, quantity needed, expected time of delivery, return policies, and warranties.

Outside sales force (or field sales force) Salespeople who travel to call on customers in the field.

Packaging The activities of designing and producing the container or wrapper for a product.

Partner relationship management Working closely with partners in other company departments and outside the company to jointly bring greater value to customers.

Percentage-of-sales method Setting the promotion budget at a certain percentage of current or forecasted sales or as a percentage of the unit sales price.

Perception The process by which people select, organize, and interpret information to form a meaningful picture of the world.

Performance review The stage of the business buying process in which the buyer assesses the performance of the supplier and decides to continue, modify, or drop the arrangement.

Personal communication channels Channels through which two or more people communicate directly with each other, including face-to-face, on the phone, via mail or email, or even through an internet "chat."

Personal selling Personal presentation by the firm's sales force for the purpose of engaging customers, making sales, and building customer relationships.

Personality The unique psychological characteristics that distinguish a person or group.

Pleasing products Products that give high immediate satisfaction but may hurt consumers in the long run.

Political environment Laws, government agencies, and pressure groups that influence and limit various organizations and individuals in a given society.

Portfolio analysis The process by which management evaluates the products and businesses that make up the company.

Positioning Arranging for a market offering to occupy a clear, distinctive, and desirable place relative to competing products in the minds of target consumers.

Positioning statement A statement that summarizes company or brand positioning using this form: To (target segment and need) our (brand) is (concept) that (point of difference).

Postpurchase behavior The stage of the buyer decision process in which consumers take further action after purchase, based on their satisfaction or dissatisfaction.

Preapproach The sales step in which a salesperson learns as much as possible about a prospective customer before making a sales call.

Presentation The sales step in which a salesperson tells the "value story" to the buyer, showing how the company's offer solves the customer's problems.

Price The amount of money charged for a product or service, or the sum of the values that customers exchange for the benefits of having or using the product or service.

Price elasticity A measure of the sensitivity of demand to changes in price.

Primary data Information collected for the specific purpose at hand.

Problem recognition The first stage of the business buying process in which someone in the company recognizes a problem or need that can be met by acquiring a good or a service.

Product Anything that can be offered to a market for attention, acquisition, use, or consumption that might satisfy a want or need.

Product adaptation Adapting a product to meet local conditions or wants in foreign markets.

Product bundle pricing Combining several products and offering the bundle at a reduced price.

Product concept A detailed version of the new product idea stated in meaningful consumer terms.

Product concept The idea that consumers will favor products that offer the most quality, performance, and features; therefore, the organization should devote its energy to making continuous product improvements.

Product development Company growth by offering modified or new products to current market segments.

Product development Developing the product concept into a physical product to ensure that the product idea can be turned into a workable market offering.

Product invention Creating new products or services for foreign markets.

Product life cycle (PLC) The course of a product's sales and profits over its lifetime.

Product line A group of products that are closely related because they function in a similar manner, are sold to the same customer groups, are marketed through the same types of outlets, or fall within given price ranges.

Product line pricing Setting the price steps between various products in a product line based on cost differences between the products, customer evaluations of different features, and competitors' prices.

Product mix (or product portfolio) The set of all product lines and items that a particular seller offers for sale.

Product position The way a product is defined by consumers on important attributes—the place the product occupies in consumers' minds relative to competing products.

Product quality The characteristics of a product or service that bear on its ability to satisfy stated or implied customer needs.

Product sales force structure A sales force organization in which salespeople specialize in selling only a portion of the company's products or lines.

Product specification The stage of the business buying process in which the buying organization decides on and specifies the best technical product characteristics for a needed item.

Product/market expansion grid A portfolio-planning tool for identifying company growth opportunities through market penetration, market development, product development, or diversification.

Production concept The idea that consumers will favor products that are available and highly affordable; therefore, the organization should focus on improving production and distribution efficiency.

Promotion mix (marketing communications mix) The specific blend of promotion tools that the company uses to persuasively communicate customer value and build customer relationships.

Promotional pricing Temporarily pricing products below the list price, and sometimes even below cost, to increase short-run sales.

Proposal solicitation The stage of the business buying process in which the buyer invites qualified suppliers to submit proposals.

Prospecting The sales step in which a salesperson or company identifies qualified potential customers.

Psychographic segmentation Dividing a market into different segments based on lifestyle or personality characteristics.

Psychological pricing Pricing that considers the psychology of prices and not simply the economics; the price is used to say something about the product.

Public Any group that has an actual or potential interest in or impact on an organization's ability to achieve its objectives.

Public relations (PR) Building good relations with the company's various publics by obtaining favorable publicity; building up a good corporate image; and handling or heading off unfavorable rumors, stories, and events.

Pull strategy A promotion strategy that calls for spending a lot on consumer advertising and promotion to induce final consumers to buy the product, creating a demand vacuum that "pulls" the product through the channel.

Purchase decision The buyer's decision about which brand to purchase.

Push strategy A promotion strategy that calls for using the sales force and trade promotion to push the product through channels. The producer promotes the product to channel members who in turn promote it to final consumers.

Reference prices Prices that buyers carry in their minds and refer to when they look at a given product.

Retailer A business whose sales come primarily from retailing.

Retailing All the activities involved in selling goods or services directly to final consumers for their personal, nonbusiness use.

Return on advertising investment The net return on advertising investment divided by the costs of the advertising investment.

Sales force management Analyzing, planning, implementing, and controlling sales force activities.

Salesperson An individual who represents a company to customers by performing one or more of the following activities: prospecting, communicating, selling, servicing, information gathering, and relationship building.

Sales promotion Short-term incentives to encourage the purchase or sale of a product or a service.

Sales quota A standard that states the amount a salesperson should sell and how sales should be divided among the company's products.

Salutary products Products that have low immediate appeal but may benefit consumers in the long run.

Sample A segment of the population selected for marketing research to represent the population as a whole.

Secondary data Information that already exists somewhere, having been collected for another purpose.

Segmented pricing Selling a product or service at two or more prices, where the difference in prices is not based on differences in costs.

Selective distribution The use of more than one but fewer than all of the intermediaries that are willing to carry the company's products.

Selling concept The idea that consumers will not buy enough of the firm's products unless the firm undertakes a large-scale selling and promotion effort.

Selling process The steps that salespeople follow when selling, which include prospecting and qualifying, preapproach, approach, presentation and demonstration, handling objections, closing, and follow-up.

Sense-of-mission marketing A company should define its mission in broad social terms rather than narrow product terms.

Service An activity, benefit, or satisfaction offered for sale that is essentially intangible and does not result in the ownership of anything.

Service inseparability Services are produced and consumed at the same time and cannot be separated from their providers.

Service intangibility Services cannot be seen, tasted, felt, heard, or smelled before they are bought.

Service perishability Services cannot be stored for later sale or use.

Service profit chain The chain that links service firm profits with employee and customer satisfaction.

Service retailer A retailer whose product line is actually a service; examples include hotels, airlines, banks, colleges, and many others.

Service variability The quality of services may vary greatly depending on who provides them and when, where, and how they are provided.

Share of customer The portion of the customer's purchasing that a company gets in its product categories.

Shopper marketing Focusing the entire marketing process on turning shoppers into buyers as they approach the point of sale, whether during in-store, online, or mobile shopping.

Shopping center A group of retail businesses built on a site that is planned, developed, owned, and managed as a unit.

Shopping product A consumer product that the customer, in the process of selecting and purchasing, usually compares on such attributes as suitability, quality, price, and style.

Showrooming The shopping practice of coming into retail store showrooms to check out merchandise and prices but instead buying from an online-only rival, sometimes while in the store.

Social class Relatively permanent and ordered divisions in a society whose members share similar values, interests, and behaviors.

Social marketing The use of traditional business marketing concepts and tools to encourage behaviors that will create individual and societal well-being.

Social media Independent and commercial online social networks where people congregate to socialize and share messages, opinions, pictures, videos, and other content.

Social selling Using online, mobile, and social media to engage customers, build stronger customer relationships, and augment sales performance.

Societal marketing A company should make marketing decisions by considering consumers' wants, the company's requirements, consumers' long-run interests, and society's long-run interests.

Societal marketing concept The idea that a company's marketing decisions should consider consumers' wants, the company's requirements, consumers' long-run interests, and society's long-run interests.

Spam Unsolicited, unwanted commercial email messages.

Specialty product A consumer product with unique characteristics or brand identification for which a significant group of buyers is willing to make a special purchase effort.

Specialty store A retail store that carries a narrow product line with a deep assortment within that line.

Standardized global marketing A global marketing strategy that basically uses the same marketing strategy and mix in all of the company's international markets.

Store brand (or private brand) A brand created and owned by a reseller of a product or service.

Straight product extension Marketing a product in a foreign market without making any changes to the product.

Straight rebuy A business buying situation in which the buyer routinely reorders something without modifications.

Strategic group A group of firms in an industry following the same or a similar strategy.

Strategic planning The process of developing and maintaining a strategic fit between the organization's goals and capabilities and its changing marketing opportunities.

Style A basic and distinctive mode of expression.

Subculture A group of people with shared value systems based on common life experiences and situations.

Supermarket A large, low-cost, low-margin, high-volume, self-service store that carries a wide variety of grocery and household products.

Superstore A store much larger than a regular supermarket that offers a large assortment of routinely purchased food products, nonfood items, and services.

Supplier development Systematic development of networks of supplier-partners to ensure an appropriate and dependable supply of products and materials for use in making products or reselling them to others.

Supplier search The stage of the business buying process in which the buyer tries to find the best vendors.

Supplier selection The stage of the business buying process in which the buyer reviews proposals and selects a supplier or suppliers.

Supply chain management Managing upstream and downstream value-added flows of materials, final goods, and related information among suppliers, the company, resellers, and final consumers.

Survey research Gathering primary data by asking people questions about their knowledge, attitudes, preferences, and buying behavior.

Sustainable marketing Socially and environmentally responsible marketing that meets the present needs of consumers and businesses while also preserving or enhancing the ability of future generations to meet their needs.

SWOT analysis An overall evaluation of the company's strengths (S), weaknesses (W), opportunities (O), and threats (T).

Systems selling (or solutions selling) Buying a packaged solution to a problem from a single seller, thus avoiding all the separate decisions involved in a complex buying situation.

Target costing Pricing that starts with an ideal selling price, then targets costs that will ensure that the price is met.

Target market A set of buyers who share common needs or characteristics that a company decides to serve.

Team selling Using teams of people from sales, marketing, engineering, finance, technical support, and even upper management to service large, complex accounts.

Team-based new product development New product development in which various company departments work closely together, overlapping the steps in the product development process to save time and increase effectiveness.

Technological environment Forces that create new technologies, creating new product and market opportunities.

Telemarketing Using the telephone to sell directly to customers.

Territorial sales force structure A sales force organization that assigns each salesperson to an exclusive geographic territory in which that salesperson sells the company's full line.

Test marketing The stage of new product development in which the product and its proposed marketing program are tested in realistic market settings.

Third-party logistics (3PL) provider An independent logistics provider that performs any or all of the functions required to get a client's product to market.

Total costs The sum of the fixed and variable costs for any given level of production.

Total market strategy Integrating ethnic themes and cross-cultural perspectives within a brand's mainstream marketing, appealing to consumer similarities across subcultural segments rather than differences.

Trade promotions Sales promotion tools used to persuade resellers to carry a brand, give it shelf space, and promote it in advertising.

Undifferentiated (mass) marketing A market-coverage strategy in which a firm decides to ignore market segment differences and go after the whole market with one offer.

Uniform-delivered pricing Pricing in which the company charges the same price plus freight to all customers, regardless of their location.

Unsought product A consumer product that the consumer either does not know about or knows about but does not normally consider buying.

Users Members of the buying organization who will actually use the purchased product or service.

Value chain The series of internal departments that carry out value-creating activities to design, produce, market, deliver, and support a firm's products.

Value delivery network A network composed of the company, suppliers, distributors, and, ultimately, customers who partner with each other to improve the performance of the entire system in delivering customer value.

Value proposition The full positioning of a brand—the full mix of benefits on which it is positioned.

Value-added pricing Attaching value-added features and services to differentiate a company's offers and charging higher prices.

Variable costs Costs that vary directly with the level of production.

Variety-seeking buying behavior Consumer buying behavior in situations characterized by low consumer involvement but significant perceived brand differences.

Vertical marketing system (VMS) A channel structure in which producers, wholesalers, and retailers act as a unified system. One channel member owns the others, has contracts with them, or has so much power that they all cooperate.

Viral marketing The digital version of word-of-mouth marketing: videos, ads, and other marketing content that is so infectious that customers will seek it out or pass it along to friends.

Wants The form human needs take as they are shaped by culture and individual personality.

Warehouse club An off-price retailer that sells a limited selection of brand name grocery items, appliances, clothing, and other goods at deep discounts to members who pay annual membership fees.

Whole-channel view Designing international channels that take into account the entire global supply chain and marketing channel, forging an effective global value delivery network.

Wholesaler A firm engaged primarily in wholesaling activities.

Wholesaling All the activities involved in selling goods and services to those buying for resale or business use.

Word-of-mouth influence The impact of the personal words and recommendations of trusted friends, family, associates, and other consumers on buying behavior.

Zone pricing Pricing in which the company sets up two or more zones. All customers within a zone pay the same total price; the more distant the zone, the higher the price.

References

Chapter 1

1. Adam Lashinsky, "Nike's Master Craftsman," *Fortune*, December 1, 2015, pp. 95–102; Mark Fidelman, "Nike Is Dominating the World Cup—Here's Why," *Forbes*, July 1, 2014, www.forbes.com/sites/markfidelman/2014/07/01/nike-is-dominating-the-world-cup-heres-why/; Scott Cendrowski, "Nike's New Marketing Mojo," *Fortune*, February 13, 2012, http://fortune.com/2012/02/13/nikes-new-marketing-mojo/; Mary Lisbeth D'Amico, "Report Sends Nike and Adidas to Head of Digital Marketing Class," *Clickz*, September 25, 2012, www.clickz.com/clickz/news/2208172/report-sends-nike-and-adidas-to-head-of-digital-marketing-class; Marina Nazario, "An Underdog Is Taking Over the Sneaker Market," *Business Insider*, September 29, 2015, www.businessinsider.com/skechers-sales-are-on-fire-2015-9; and http://investors.nikeinc.com/Investors and https://secure-nike-plus.nike.com/plus/, accessed September 2016.

2. See "Taste the Feeling," January 25, 2016, www.coca-colacompany.com/stories/brands/2016/taste-the-feeling--watch-6-ads-from-coke-s-new-global-campaign/; "Market Share of Carbonated Beverages Worldwide as of 2015, by Company," www.statista.com/statistics/387318/market-share-of-leading-carbonated-beverage-companies-worldwide/, accessed February 2016; Facebook Newsroom, http://newsroom.fb.com/company-info/, accessed February 2016; and www.facebook.com/Amazon/info/?tab=page_info, accessed September 2016.

3. See Philip Kotler and Kevin Lane Keller, *Marketing Management*, 15th ed. (Hoboken, NJ: Pearson Education, 2016), p. 5.

4. The American Marketing Association offers the following definition: "Marketing is the activity, set of institutions, and processes for creating, communicating, delivering, and exchanging offerings that have value for customers, clients, partners, and society at large." See www.marketingpower.com/_layouts/Dictionary.aspx?dLetter=M, accessed September 2016.

5. See Kai Ryssdal, Mukta Mohan, and Julian Burrell, "'Big Chicken' Has Boston Market Flying Highers," *Marketplace*, June 22, 2015, www.marketplace.org/2015/06/22/business/big-chicken-has-boston-market-flying-higher; Daniel P. Smith, "Keep in Touch," *QSR Magazine*, July 2013, www.qsrmagazine.com/executive-insights/keep-touch; Phil Wahba, "Back on Target," *Fortune*, March 1, 2015, p. 86–94; and Jackie Crosby, "Target CEO Brian Cornell Visiting Homes of Customers," *StarTribune*, January 20, 2016, www.startribune.com/target-to-add-1-000-technology-jobs-in-year-ahead/365965181/.

6. See Samantha Shankman, "The Simple Message behind San Diego's $9 Million Ad Campaign," *Skift*, February 5, 2015, http://skift.com/2015/02/05/the-simple-message-behind-san-diegos-9-million-ad-campaign/; and http://stoptextsstopwrecks.org/#home, accessed September 2016.

7. See Theodore Levitt's classic article, "Marketing Myopia," *Harvard Business Review*, July–August 1960, pp. 45–56. For more recent discussions, see Roberto Friedmann, "What Business Are You In?" *Marketing Management*, Summer 2011, pp. 18–23; Al Ries, "'Marketing Myopia' Revisited: Perhaps a Narrow Vision Is Better Business," *Advertising Age*, December 4, 2013, http://adage.com/print/245511; and Charity Delich, "Best of Multimedia: Marketing Myopia in 120 Seconds," *strategy+business*, September 4, 2014, www.strategy-business.com/blog/Best-of-Multimedia-Marketing-Myopia-in-120-Seconds?gko=70a85.

8. See www.americangirl.com/stores/, accessed September 2016.

9. "The Difference in Creating Companies and Categories," *bright*, March 4, 2014, http://bright.stellaservice.com/uncategorized/column-the-difference-in-creating-companies-and-categories/.

10. See Michael E. Porter and Mark R. Kramer, "Creating Shared Value," *Harvard Business Review*, January–February 2011, pp. 63–77; Marc Pfitzer, Valerie Bockstette, and Mike Stamp, "Innovating for Shared Value," *Harvard Business Review*, September 2013, pp. 100–107; "About Shared Value," *Shared Value Initiative*, http://sharedvalue.org/about-shared-value, accessed September 2016; and "Shared Value," www.fsg.org, accessed September 2016.

11. Michael Krauss, "Evolution of an Academic: Kotler on Marketing 3.0," *Marketing News*, January 30, 2011, p. 12; and Simon Mainwaring, "Marketing 3.0 Will Be Won by Purpose-Driven, Social Brands," *Forbes*, July 16, 2013, www.forbes.com/sites/simonmainwaring/2013/07/16/marketing-3-0-will-be-won-by-purpose-driven-social-brands-infographic/.

12. Deborah Gage, "Online Grocer Door to Door Organics Reaps $25.5 Million to Grow," *Wall Street Journal*, November 10, 2014, http://blogs.wsj.com/venturecapital/2014/11/10/online-grocer-door-to-door-organics-reaps-25-5-million-to-grow/; and www.bcorporation.net/community/door-to-door-organics and www.doortodoororganics.com, accessed September 2016.

13. See "Acoustic Piano: Model and Pricing Guide," www.piano-buyer.com/fall15/acoustic-prices-steinway.html, accessed July 2016; "Steinway Composes Global Campaign to Reach Cultured Achievers," *Luxury Daily*, April 13, 2016, www.luxurydaily.com/steinway-composes-global-campaign-to-reach-cultured-achievers/; and www.steinway.com/about and www.steinwaypianos.com/kb/artists, accessed September 2016.

14. Based on information from "Company Values," www.llbean.com/customerService/aboutLLBean/company_values.html; www.llbean.com/customerService/aboutLLBean/company_history.html?nav=s1-ln; and other pages at www.llbean.com, accessed September 2016. Also see Pam Goodfellow, "L.L.Bean, Amazon and Nordstrom Are Customer Service Champions, According to Consumers," *Forbes*, March 29, 2016, www.forbes.com/sites/forbesinsights/2016/03/29/l-l-bean-amazon-and-nordstrom-are-customer-service-champions-according-to-consumers/#7fabb2ee7bc2.

15. "Delighting the Customer Doesn't Pay," *Sales & Marketing Management*, November 11, 2013, http://salesandmarketing.com/content/delighting-customers-doesnt-pay; Patrick Spenner, "Why Simple Brands are Profitable Brands," *Forbes*, February 20, 2014, www.forbes.com/sites/patrickspenner/2014/02/20/why-simple-brands-are-profitable-brands-2/#2b28be11b097; and Chad Quinn, "How IT Can Great an Effortless Experience," *CIO*, www.cio.com/article/3007770.

16. See "The Ultimate Guide to JetBlue TrueBlue," *LoungeBuddy*, www.loungebuddy.com/jetblue-trueblue-ultimate-guide/, accessed September 2016; and www.jetblue.trueblue.com, accessed September 2016.

17. See Gordon Wyner, "Getting Engaged," *Marketing Management*, Fall 2012, pp. 4–9; David Aponovich, "Powered by People, Fueled by Optimism," *Fast Company*, July 18, 2012, www.fastcompany.com/1842834/life-good-powered-people-fueled-optimism; Celia Brown, "Life Is Good Redefines Retailing through Joy," *Forbes*, January 17, 2014, www.forbes.com/sites/sap/2014/01/17/life-is-good-redefines-retail-through-joy/; and www.lifeisgood.com and www.lifeisgood.com/good-vibes/, accessed September 2016.

18. See https://ideas.lego.com and http://mystarbucksidea.force.com, accessed September 2016.

19. Benjamin Snyder, "Here's Why Doritos Is Ending Its 'Crash the Super Bowl' Contest," *Fortune*, January 29, 2016, http://fortune.com/2016/01/29/doritos-crash-the-super-bowl-contest/.

20. Lauren Johnson, "Mountain Dew Turns Tweets into Online Ads with the Return of Baja Blast," *Adweek,* April 9, 2015, www.adweek.com/print/163979.

21. See "#Bashtag: Avoiding User Outcry in Social Media," *WordStream,* March 8, 2013, www.wordstream.com/blog/ws/2013/03/07/bashtag-avoiding-social-media-backlash; and "What Is Hashtag Hijacking?" *Small Business Trends,* August 18, 2013, http://smallbiztrends.com/2013/08/what-is-hashtag-hijacking-2.html.

22. See www.stewleonards.com/about-us/company-story, accessed September 2016.

23. See Mai Erne, "Calculating Customer Lifetime Value," HaraPartners, www.harapartners.com/blog/calculating-lifetime-value/, accessed September 2016.

24. See Chris Isidore, "Amazon Prime Now Reaches Nearly Half of U.S. Households," *CNN Money,* January 26, 2016, http://money.cnn.com/2016/01/26/technology/amazon-prime-memberships/; Brad Stone, "What's in the Box? Instant Gratification," *Bloomberg Businessweek,* November 29–December 5, 2010, pp. 39–40; "Annual Number of Worldwide Active Amazon Accounts," *Statista,* www.statista.com/statistics/237810/number-of-active-amazon-customer-accounts-worldwide/, accessed September 2016; and www.amazon.com/b?ie=UTF8&node=8445211011, accessed September 2016.

25. For more discussions on customer equity, see Roland T. Rust, Valerie A. Zeithaml, and Katherine N. Lemon, *Driving Customer Equity* (New York: Free Press, 2000); Roland T. Rust, Katherine N. Lemon, and Valerie A. Zeithaml, "Return on Marketing: Using Customer Equity to Focus Marketing Strategy," *Journal of Marketing,* January 2004, pp. 109–127; Christian Gronroos and Pekka Helle, "Return on Relationships: Conceptual Understanding and Measurement of Mutual Gains from Relational Business Engagements," *Journal of Business & Industrial Marketing,* Vol. 27, No. 5, 2012, pp. 344–359; and Peter C. Verhoef and Katherine N. Lemon, "Successful Customer Value Management: Key Lessons and Emerging Trends," *European Management Journal,* February 2013, p. 1.

26. This example is based on one found in Rust, Lemon, and Zeithaml, "Where Should the Next Marketing Dollar Go?" *Marketing Management,* September–October 2001, pp. 24–28; with information from Grant McCracken, "Provocative Cadillac, Rescuing the Brand from Bland," *Harvard Business Review,* March 4, 2014, http://blogs.hbr.org/2014/03/provocative-cadillac-rescuing-the-brand-from-bland/; Christine Birkner, "Cadillac Ditches 'Generic Backdrop' and Other Car Ad Clichés in Its Oscar Spots," *Adweek,* February 28, 2016, www.adweek.com/print/169890, and www.dare-greatly.com, accessed September 2016.

27. Based on Werner Reinartz and V. Kumar, "The Mismanagement of Customer Loyalty," *Harvard Business Review,* July 2002, pp. 86–94. Also see Chris Lema, "Not All Customers Are Equal—Butterflies & Barnacles," April 18, 2013, http://chrislema.com/not-all-customers-are-equal-butterflies-barnacles/; Jill Avery, Susan Fournier, and John Wittenbraker, "Unlock the Mysteries of Your Customer Relationships," *Harvard Business Review,* July–August 2014, pp. 72–81, "Telling Customers 'You're Fired,'" *Sales and Marketing.com,* September/October 2014, p. 8; and Michele McGovern, "6 Rules for Firing a Customer," *Customer Insight Experience,* January 6, 2016, www.customerexperienceinsight.com/6-rules-for-firing-a-customer/.

28. "Internet Usage Statistics," *Internet World Stats,* www.internetworldstats.com/stats.htm; accessed June 2016; and "U.S. Smartphone Use in 2015," Pew Research Center, April 1, 2015, www.pewinternet.org/2015/04/01/us-smartphone-use-in-2015/.

29. "Digital Set to Surpass TV in Time Spent with US Media," *eMarketer,* August 1, 2013, www.emarketer.com/Article/Digital-Set-Surpass-TV-Time-Spent-with-US-Media/1010096; and Amanda Kooser, "Sleep with Your Smartphone in Hand? You're Not Alone," *CNET,* June 30, 2015, www.cnet.com/news/americans-like-to-snooze-with-their-smartphones-says-survey/.

30. See https://community.petco.com/ and http://community.us.playstation.com/, accessed September 2016.

31. See Calla Cofield, "Social Media: NASA's Not So Secret Weapon for the Orion Test Flight," *Space,* December 3, 2014, www.space.com/27912-nasa-orion-spacecraft-social-media-blitz.html; Laura Nichols, "NASA Soars on Social Media with Orion Spacecraft," *PRWeek,* December 18, 2015, www.prweek.com/article/1327011; "By the Letters EFT: Sesame Street Muppets Count Down to NASA Launch," *Collect Space,* November 24, 2014, www.collectspace.com/news/news-112514a-orion-eft1-muppets-countdown.html; and www.nasa.gov, accessed September 2016.

32. Bill Briggs, "M-Commerce Is Saturating the Globe," *Internet Retailer,* February 20, 2014, www.internetretailer.com/2014/02/20/m-commerce-saturating-globe; Mark Brohan, "Mobile Commerce Is Now 30% of All U.S. E-Commerce," *Internet Retailer,* August 18, 2015, www.internetretailer.com/2015/08/18/mobile-commerce-now-30-all-us-e-commerce; and Sandra Rand, "The Psychology of Mobile Usage & Its Impact on Advertising," *B2C,* February 15, 2016, www.business2community.com/mobile-apps/psychology-mobile-usage-impact-advertising-01453221#eXku1BSeQyf2SvyV.99.

33. "Mobile Marketing: How Redbox Drove 1.5 Million Texts and Added 200,000 Mobile Participants in 10 Days," *Marketing Sherpa,* October 6, 2011, www.marketingsherpa.com/article/case-study/how-redbox-drove-15-million; www.youtube.com/watch?v=c1nLbQeXAXc and www.redbox.com/textclub, accessed September 2016.

34. See John Gerzema, "How U.S. Consumers Are Steering the Spend Shift," *Advertising Age,* October 11, 2010, p. 26; Gregg Fairbrothers and Catalina Gorla, "The Decline and Rise of Thrift," *Forbes,* April 23, 2012, www.forbes.com/sites/greggfairbrothers/2012/04/23/the-decline-and-rise-of-thrift/; and Gillian B. White, "Household Finances Still Fragile Six Years after the Recession," May 20, 2015, www.theatlantic.com/business/archive/2015/05/household-finances-still-fragile-six-years-post-recession/393698/.

35. See "Purpose & Beliefs," https://corporate.target.com/about/purpose-beliefs, accessed September 2016.

36. Information from "The 50 Largest U.S. Charities: St. Judes Children's Research Hospital," *Forbes,* www.forbes.com/companies/st-jude-childrens-research-hospital/, accessed September 2016; and various pages at www.stjude.org, accessed September 2016. Finding Cures. Saving Children®, Up 'Til Dawn®, St. Jude Dream Home® Giveaway, and St. Jude Thanks and Giving® are registered trademarks of St. Jude Children's Research Hospital.

37. "100 Leading National Advertisers," *Advertising Age,* July 13, 2015, p. 15.

38. www.aboutmcdonalds.com/mcd and www.nikeinc.com, accessed September 2016.

39. See www.benjerry.com/values, www.benandjerrysfoundation.org, and www.unilever.com/brands-in-action/detail/ben-and-jerrys/291995, accessed September 2016.

Chapter 2

1. John Kell, "Starbucks Wants Your Phone as Much as It Wants to Sell You Coffee," *Fortune,* July 24, 2015, http://fortune.com/2015/07/24/starbucks-mobile-investments/; David Kaplan, "Starbucks: The Art of Endless Transformation," *Inc.,* June, 2014, pp. 82–86+; Laura Lorenzetti, "Fortune's World's Most Admired Companies: Starbucks, Where Innovation Is Always Brewing," *Fortune,* October 30, 2014, http://fortune.com/2014/10/30/starbucks-innovation-cafe-to-classroom/; "Starbucks Corporation: Fiscal 2007 Annual Report," http://media.corporate-ir.net/media_files/irol/99/99518/2007AR.pdf; Julia Hanna, "Starbucks, Reinvented: A Seven-Year Study on Schultz, Strategy, and Reinventing a Brilliant Brand," *Forbes,* August 25, 2014,

www.forbes.com/sites/hbsworkingknowledge/2014/08/25/starbucks-reinvented/; Bryan Pearson, "Starbucks Loyalty Program Change Brews Anger, Filters Out Value of Experience," *Forbes*, February 24, 2016, www.forbes.com/sites/bryanpearson/2016/02/24/starbucks-loyalty-change-brews-anger-filters-out-value-of-experience/print/; http://roastery.starbucks.com, accessed September 2016; and Starbucks annual reports and other information accessed at www.starbucks.com, September 2016.

2. The NASA mission statement is from www.nasa.gov/about/highlights/what_does_nasa_do.html, accessed September 2016.

3. See www.ritzcarlton.com/en/about/gold-standards, accessed September 2016. For more discussion of mission statements and examples, both good and bad, see Jack and Suzy Welch, "State Your Business; Too Many Mission Statements Are Loaded with Fatheaded Jargon. Play It Straight," *BusinessWeek*, January 14, 2008, p. 80; Setayesh Sattari et al., "How Readable Are Mission Statements? An Exploratory Study," *Corporate Communications*, 2011, p. 4; and www.missionstatements.com/fortune_500_mission_statements.html, accessed September 2016.

4. Information about CVS Health and its mission and activities from www.cvshealth.com/about, www.cvshealth.com/about/our-story, www.cvs.com/minuteclinic/visit/about-us/history, and www.cvshealth.com/about/our-offerings, accessed September 2016.

5. The following discussion is based in part on information found at www.bcg.com/documents/file13904.pdf, accessed September 2016.

6. See Jessica Stephans, "Gauging General Electric's Appliance Segment," February 9, 2016, http://marketrealist.com/2016/02/understanding-general-electrics-appliance-segment/; "General Electric Co.," *Reuters*, www.reuters.com/finance/stocks/companyProfile?symbol=GE.N, accessed September 2016; and www.ge.com/ar2015/assets/pdf/GE_AR15.pdf, www.ge.com/investor-relations/financial-reporting, and www.ge.com/products, accessed September 2016.

7. H. Igor Ansoff, "Strategies for Diversification," *Harvard Business Review*, September–October 1957, pp. 113–124.

8. Information about Under Armour in this section is from Palbir Nijjar, "The 3 Most Important Growth Drivers for Under Armour," *The Motley Fool*, February 16, 2016, www.fool.com/investing/general/2016/02/18/the-3-most-important-growth-drivers-for-under-armo.aspx; Sarah Meehan, "Here's How Much Under Armour Spent on Marketing Last Year," *Business Journal*, February 24, 2015, www.bizjournals.com/baltimore/news/2015/02/24/heres-how-much-under-armour-spent-on-marketing.html?page=all; George Slefo, "Under Armour Enters Wearable Tech with IBM's Watson and HTC," *AdAge*, January 8, 2016, http://adage.com/article/print/302041/; and various pages at www.underarmour.com and http://investor.underarmour.com, accessed September 2016.

9. See Michael E. Porter, *Competitive Advantage: Creating and Sustaining Superior Performance* (New York: Free Press, 1985); and Michael E. Porter, "What Is Strategy?" *Harvard Business Review*, November–December 1996, pp. 61–78. Also see "The Value Chain," www.quickmba.com/strategy/value-chain, accessed June 2015; and Philip Kotler and Kevin Lane Keller, *Marketing Management*, 15th ed. (Hoboken, NJ: Prentice Hall, 2016), Chapter 2.

10. Tom French and others, "We're All Marketers Now," *McKinsey Quarterly*, July 2011, www.mckinseyquarterly.com/Were_all_marketers_now_2834.

11. See www.gapinc.com/content/gapinc/html/aboutus/our-brands/gap.html, accessed September 2016.

12. "Ad Age's 200 Leading National Advertisers Report Shows Marketers Tightening and Reallocating Spending," *PR Newswire*, July 15, 2015, www.prnewswire.com/news-releases/ad-ages-200-leading-national-advertisers-report-shows-marketers-tightening-and-reallocating-spending-300113836.html.

13. The four Ps classification was first suggested by E. Jerome McCarthy, *Basic Marketing: A Managerial Approach* (Homewood, IL: Irwin, 1960). The four As are discussed in Jagdish Sheth and Rajendra Sisodia, *The 4 A's of Marketing: Creating Value for Customer, Company and Society* (New York: Routledge, 2012); and Philip Kotler and Kevin Lane Keller, *Marketing Management*, 15th ed. (Hoboken, NJ: Pearson Education, 2016), p. 26.

14. Tim Dunn, "Is the Era of CMO Over?" *Adweek*, March 2, 2015, p. 14; and Bob Evans, "The CMO Revolution: 10 Challenges That Will Rock the Marketing World in 2016," *Forbes*, February 1, 2016, www.forbes.com/sites/oracle/2016/02/01/the-cmo-revolution-10-challenges-that-will-rock-the-marketing-world-in-2016/#258c6a07e0c2.

15. For more on marketing dashboards and financial measures of marketing performance, see Ofer Mintz and Imran S. Currim, "What Drives Managerial Use of Marketing Financial Metrics and Does Metric Use Affect Performance of Marketing-Mix Activities?" *Journal of Marketing*, March 2013, pp. 17–40; and "Marketing Dashboard Examples," *Klipfolio*, www.klipfolio.com/resources/dashboard-examples, accessed September 2016.

16. For a full discussion of this model and details on customer-centered measures of marketing return on investment, see Roland T. Rust, Katherine N. Lemon, and Valerie A. Zeithaml, "Return on Marketing: Using Customer Equity to Focus Marketing Strategy," *Journal of Marketing*, January 2004, pp. 109–127; Roland T. Rust, Katherine N. Lemon, and Das Narayandas, *Customer Equity Management* (Upper Saddle River, NJ: Prentice Hall, 2005); Roland T. Rust, "Seeking Higher ROI? Base Strategy on Customer Equity," *Advertising Age*, September 10, 2007, pp. 26–27; Andreas Persson and Lynette Ryals, "Customer Assets and Customer Equity: Management and Measurement Issues," *Marketing Theory*, December 2010, pp. 417–436; and Kirsten Korosec, "'Toma- to, Tomäto'? Not Exactly," *Marketing News*, January 13, 2012, p. 8.

17. Molly Soat, "More Companies Require Revenue-Focused Marketing ROI Measures, Study Finds," *Marketing News Weekly*, www.ama.org/publications/eNewsletters/Marketing-News-Weekly/Pages/more-companies-require-revenue-focused-marketing-roi-measures.aspx#sthash.2zpUS7QR.npUibTEw.dpuf, accessed September 2016.

Chapter 3

1 Kim Severson, "Cereal, a Taste of Nostalgia, Looks for Its Next Chapter," *New York Times*, February 22, 2016, www.nytimes.com/2016/02/24/dining/breakfast-cereal.html?_r=0; Devin Leonard, "Bad News in Cereal City," *Bloomberg Businessweek*, March 2–8, 2015, pp. 42–47; John Kell, "Decline in Cereal Sales Bites into Kellogg's Results," *Fortune*, October 30, 2014, http://fortune.com/2014/10/30/kellogg-breakfast-sales-drop/; Annie Gasparro and Chelsey Dulaney, "Kellogg Sales Continue to Slide," *Wall Street Journal*, February 11, 2016, www.wsj.com/articles/kellogg-sales-continue-to-slide-1455200247; and http://investor.kelloggs.com/investor-relations/annual-reports/default.aspx and www.kellogg.com, accessed September 2016.

2. Ginger Christ, "Supplier Relationships Key to Honda's Healthy Profit Margins," *Industry Week*, May 23, 2012, www.industryweek.com/blog/supplier-relationships-key-hondas-healthy-profit-margins; "2014 Annual Automotive OEM-Supplier Relations Study Shows Toyota and Honda on Top," *PR Newswire*, May 12, 2014; and www.hondainamerica.com/parts-and-suppliers and http://world.honda.com/profile/philosophy/, accessed September 2016.

3. Information from Robert J. Benes, Abbie Jarman, and Ashley Williams, "2007 NRA Sets Records," www.chefmagazine.com, accessed September 2007; "Thought Leadership Begins with Experience," *fishbowl*, February 20, 2015, www.fishbowl.com/coca-cola-offers-restaurant-customers-new-digital-marketing-solutions-powered-by-fishbowl/; and www.cokesolutions.com, accessed September 2016.

4. See https://corporate.homedepot.com/corporateresponsibility/hdfoundation/pages/default.aspx and www.homedepot foundation.org, accessed September 2016.

5. World POPClock, U.S. Census Bureau, at www.census.gov/popclock/, accessed September 2016. This website provides continuously updated projections of the U.S. and world populations.

6. U.S. Census Bureau projections and POPClock Projection, at www.census.gov/main/www/popclock.html, accessed September 2016.

7. "U.S. Population," *Worldometers,* www.worldometers.info/world-population/us-population/, accessed September 2016.

8. See "50+ Facts and Fiction: Size, Wealth and Spending of 50+ Consumers," *Immersion Active,* March 9, 2015, www.immersionactive.com/resources/size-wealth-spending-50-consumers/; "Millennials Outnumber Baby Boomers and Are Far More Diverse, Census Bureau Reports," U.S. Census Bureau, June 25, 2015, www.census.gov/newsroom/press-releases/2015/cb15-113.html; and "Baby Boomers Will Control 70% of Disposable Income," Impact Business Partners, February 22, 2016, http://impactbp.com/baby-boomers.

9. Suzanne Vranica, "AARP Launches Baby Boomer Ad Firm despite Marketers' Obsession with Millennials," *Wall Street Journal,* August 13, 2015, http://blogs.wsj.com/cmo/2015/08/13/aarp-launches-baby-boomer-ad-firm-despite-marketers-obsession-with-millennials/.

10. "Generational Marketing: Tips for Reaching Baby Boomers," July 16, 2015, www.mayecreate.com/2015/07/generational-marketing-tips-for-reaching-baby-boomers/.

11. "Last Night's Ads: Walgreens Reassures Baby Boomers They Can Still Be Cool," *Advertising Age,* January 4, 2016, http://adage.com/print/301976/; "Walgreens TV Commercial, 'Carpe Med Diem,'" www.ispot.tv/ad/A7LR/walgreens-carpe-med-diem, accessed September 2016; and www.walgreens.com/topic/pharmacy/medicarepartd-info.jsp, accessed September 2016.

12. See Joe Ruiz, "How Lowe's Is Sustaining Customer Relationships," *Maximize Social Business,* January 27, 2014, http://maximizesocialbusiness.com/lowes-sustaining-customer-relationships-12506/; and www.lowes.com/mobile, www.lowes.com, www.youtube.com/watch?v=zbFX7p6ZGTk, and www.pinterest.com/lowes/, accessed September 2016.

13. See "AT&T's Catherine Borda Spills the Secrets to Millennial Marketing," *Adweek,* March 3, 2015, www.adweek.com/print/163219; and "10 Stats That Will Make You Rethink Marketing to Millennials," *WordStream,* February 2, 2016, http://www.wordstream.com/blog/ws/2016/02/02/marketing-to-millennials.

14. "Fifth Third Bank Invites You to 'Lose the Wait,'" Leo Burnett, February 12, 2016, http://leoburnett.us/chicago/article/fifth-third-bank-invites-you-to-lose-the-wait-/; and Adrianne Pasqarelli, "Another Bank Chases Millennials with Digital Games, Ads," *AdAge,* January 21, 2016, http://adage.com/print/302263/.

15. See Giselle Abramovich, "15 Mind-Blowing Stats about Generation Z," *CMO,* June 12, 2015, www.cmo.com/articles/2015/6/11/15-mind-blowing-stats-about-generation-z.html; and Jessica Geller, "Move Over, Millennials. Gen Z Is New Target Audience," *Boston Globe,* September 21, 2015, www.bostonglobe.com/business/2015/08/31/brands-turn-attention-towards-gen-wV99rNryDEEEhd06UjioFN/story.html; and Mahesh Rajagopalan, "Cracking the Code to Understand Gen Z," *Adweek,* March 9, 2016, www.adweek.com/print/635650.

16. See "GenZ: Digital in Their DNA"; Shannon Bryant, "'Generation Z' Children More Tech-Savvy; Prefer Gadgets, Not Toys," *Marketing Forecast,* April 3, 2013, www.ad-ology.com/tag/tech-savvy-children/#.U5d9avldV8E; and Brett Relander, "How to Market to Gen Z," *Entrepreneur,* November 4, 2014, www.entrepreneur.com/article/238998.

17. Robert Klara, "It's Not Easy Being Tween," *Adweek,* June 27, 2012, www.adweek.com/print/141378; Tim Feran, "Retailer Justice Shedding Brothers Brand," *The Columbus Dispatch,* February 19, 2015, www.dispatch.com/content/stories/business/2015/02/18/justice-shedding-brothers-brand.html; and www.shopjustice.com.

18. See http://neverstopexploring.com/2016/02/18/12068/ and http://neverstopexploring.com/2015/08/25/the-north-face-youth-design-team-seeks-inspiration-from-kids/, accessed September 2016.

19. For statistics on family composition, see U.S. Census Bureau, "Family Households," Table F1, www.census.gov/hhes/families/data/cps2015F.html; and U.S. Census Bureau, "Households by Type, Age of Members, Region of Residence, and Age of Householder: 2015," Table H2, www.census.gov/hhes/families/data/cps2015H.html, accessed September 2016.

20. Wendy Wang, "Interracial Marriage: Who Is 'Marrying Out'?" *Pew Research,* June 12, 2015, www.pewresearch.org/fact-tank/2015/06/12/interracial-marriage-who-is-marrying-out/; "The Changing American Family," *CBS News,* May 11, 2014, http://www.cbsnews.com/videos/the-changing-american-family/; and U.S. Census Bureau, "Table 1. Household Characteristics of Opposite-Sex and Same-Sex Couple Households," www.census.gov/hhes/samesex/, accessed September 2016.

21. See Department of Labor, "Facts Over Time: Women in the Labor Force," www.dol.gov/wb/stats/facts_over_time.htm; Pew Research Center, "Breadwinner Moms," May 29, 2013, www.pewsocialtrends.org/2013/05/29/breadwinner-moms/; U.S. Census Bureau, "America's Families and Living Arrangements: 2015," Table FG1, www.census.gov/hhes/families/data/cps2015FG.html, accessed March 2016; and U.S. Census Bureau, "Parents and Children in Stay at Home Parent Family Groups: 1994 to Present," Table SHP-1, www.census.gov/hhes/families/data/families.html, accessed September 2016.

22. See Cord Jefferson, "Cheerios Ad Starring Interracial Family Predictably Summons Bigot Wave," *Gawker,* May 30, 2013, http://gawker.com/cheerios-ad-starring-interracial-family-predictably-sum-510591871; Jessica Wohl, "Campbell Soup Shows 'Real, Real Life' in New Brand Campaign," *Advertising Age,* October 5, 2016, http://adage.com/print/300750; and www.youtube.com/watch?v=Z01qH-jqGBY and www.youtube.com/watch?v=7rZOMY2sOnE, accessed September 2016.

23. U.S. Census Bureau, "U.S. Mover Rate Remains Stable at About 12 Percent Since 2008, Census Bureau Reports," March 18, 2015, www.census.gov/newsroom/press-releases/2015/cb15-47.html; and U.S. Census Bureau, "Geographical Mobility/Migration," www.census.gov/population/www/socdemo/migrate.html, accessed September 2016.

24. See U.S. Census Bureau, "Metropolitan and Micropolitan Statistical Areas," www.census.gov/population/metro/data/index.html/, accessed September 2016; U.S. Census Bureau, "Census Estimates Show New Patterns of Growth Nationwide," April 5, 2012, www.census.gov/newsroom/releases/archives/population/cb12-55.html; and "The 536 Micropolitan Statistical Areas of the United States of America," *Wikipedia,* http://en.wikipedia.org/wiki/List_of_Micropolitan_Statistical_Areas, accessed September 2016.

25. "It's Unclearly Defined, but Telecommuting Is Fast on the Rise," *New York Times,* March 8, 2014, p. B5; and Jeffrey M. Jones, "In U.S., Telecommuting for Work Climbs to 37%," *Gallup,* August 19, 2015, http://www.gallup.com/poll/184649/telecommuting-work-climbs.aspx.

26. U.S. Census Bureau, "Educational Attainment," www.census.gov/hhes/socdemo/education/data/cps/2014/tables.html, accessed June 2016.

27. See U.S. Department of Labor, "Employment Projections: 2014–2024 Summary," www.bls.gov/emp/ep_table_103.htm, accessed September 2016.

28. See U.S. Census Bureau, "Projections of the Size and Composition of the U.S. Population: 2014 to 2060," March 2015, www.census.gov/content/dam/Census/library/publications/2015/demo/p25-1143.pdf; and "Multicultural Consumers by the Numbers," *Advertising Age,* April 6, 2015, p. 20.

29. See "Ads Targeting Asian Americans in the U.S., Multicultural Marketing Resources," http://multicultural.com/multicultural_markets/asian-american, accessed September 2016; Marilyn

Much, "More Firms Reach Out to Asian Americans," *Investors.com*, September 29, 2003, http://news.investors.com; and www.chineseparade.com/, www.southwest.com/asianoutreach/, accessed September 2016.

30. Witeck Communications, "America's LGBT 2014 Buying Power Estimated at $884 Billion," June 10, 2015, www.witeck.com/pressreleases/americas-lgbt-2014-buying-power-estimated-at-884-billion/; and David Gianatasio, "Agencies Eye Pot of Gold," *Adweek*, September 14, 2015, p. 26.

31. For more discussion, see Dominique Mosbergen, "Adidas Shuts Down Homophobic Commenters in the Best Way Possible," *Huffington Post*, February 18, 2016, www.huffingtonpost.com/entry/adidas-valentines-day-ad-same-sex-couple_us_56c56250e4b08ffac127b0eb; Jacob Passy, "Wells Fargo: Ad with Gay Couple Reflects 'Demographic Reality,'" *American Banker*, June 23, 2015, www.americanbanker.com/news/consumer-finance/wells-fargo-ad-with-gay-couple-reflects-demographic-reality-1075043-1.html; and https://www.youtube.com/watch?v=DxDsx8HfXEk, accessed September 2016.

32. "CDC: 53 Million Adults in the U.S. Live with a Disability," *CDC Newsroom*, July 30, 2015, www.cdc.gov/media/releases/2015/p0730-us-disability.html; Institute on Disability, "2014 Disability Statistics Annual Report," www.disabilitycompendium.org/docs/default-source/2014-compendium/annual-report.pdf; and "Disability Travel Generates $17.3 Billion in Annual Spending," *PR Newswire*, July 31, 2015, www.prnewswire.com/news-releases/disability-travel-generates-173-billion-in-annual-spending-300121930.html.

33. "We Can Change Attitudes with Disability in Advertising," *Advertising and Disability*, February 18, 2016, http://advertisinganddisability.com/2016/02/18/we-can-change-attitudes-with-disability-in-advertising/.

34. See Rob Walker, "Tiffany & Co: At What Point Does Affordable Luxury Prove Costly?" *Euromonitor International*, June 25, 2014, http://blog.euromonitor.com/2014/06/tiffany-co-at-what-point-does-affordable-luxury-prove-costly.html; "Tiffany Moves Down Market and Makes a Mint," *Bloomberg Businessweek*, May 21, 2014, www.bloomberg.com/bw/articles/2014-05-21/tiffany-moves-down-market-and-makes-a-mint; and www.tiffany.com, accessed September 2016.

35. See U.S. Census Bureau, "Income and Poverty in the United States: 2014," Table 2, p. 9, September 2015, www.census.gov/content/dam/Census/library/publications/2015/demo/p60-252.pdf.

36. Drew Harwell, "Meet the Secret Army of Meteorologists Who Keep Your Holiday Deliveries on Time," *The Washington Post*," December 8, 2014, www.washingtonpost.com/business/economy/meet-the-secret-army-of-meteorologists-who-keep-your-holiday-deliveries-on-time/2014/12/08/2d9d3c82-759d-11e4-9d9b-86d397daad27_story.html; Sally Herships, "Weather Information Is Big Business," *Marketplace*, October 28, 2015, www.marketplace.org/2015/10/28/tech/weather-information-big-business; and "UPS Meteorologists Use the Latest Technology to Ensure On-Time Delivery," http://thenewlogisticsasia.ups.com/customers/ontime-delivery/, accessed September 2016.

37. Sarah Begley, "UN Report Warns of Serious Water Shortages within 15 Years," *Time*, March 20, 2015, http://time.com/3752643/un-water-shortage-2030/; The 2030 Water Resources Group, www.2030wrg.org, accessed September 2016; and "The World's Water," *Pacific Institute*, www.worldwater.org/data.html, accessed September 2016.

38. See Joel Makower, "Walmart Sustainability at 10: The Birth of a Notion," *GreenBiz*, November 16, 2016, www.greenbiz.com/article/walmart-sustainability-10-birth-notion; Joel Makower, "Walmart Sustainability at 10: An Assessment," *GreenBiz*, November 17, 2016, www.greenbiz.com/article/walmart-sustainability-10-assessment; and http://corporate.walmart.com/global-responsibility/sustainability/ and www.walmartsustainabilityhub.com/, accessed September 2016.

39. See "Tracking Customers' Shopping Data: RFIDs, Barcodes or QR Codes?" April 6, 2015, www.bigdata-madesimple.com/tracking-customers-shopping-data-rfids-barcodes-or-qr-codes/; and Melissa Anders, "8 Retail Technologies to Watch in 2016," *RetailDIVE*, January 14, 2016, www.retaildive.com/news/8-retail-technologies-to-watch-in-2016/410567/.

40. See "A $1 Billion Project to Remake the Disney World Experience, Using RFID," www.fastcodesign.com/1671616/a-1-billion-project-to-remake-the-disney-world-experience-using-rfid#1; Brooks Barnes, "At Disney Parks, a Bracelet Meant to Build Loyalty (and Sales)," *New York Times*, January 7, 2013, p. B1; Claire Swedberg, "MagicBands Bring Convenience, New Services to Walt Disney World," *RFID Journal*, June 16, 2014, www.rfidjournal.com/articles/view?11877; and Christopher Palmeri, "Why Disney Won't Be Taking Magic Wristbands to Its Chinese Park," *BloombergBusiness*, January 10, 2016, www.bloomberg.com/news/articles/2016-01-10/why-disney-won-t-be-taking-magic-wristbands-to-its-chinese-park.

41. See www.shakeshack.com/tag/great-american-shake-sale/ and www.itcanwait.com, accessed September 2016.

42. See "Warby Parker: Do Good," www.warbyparker.com/do-good/#home, accessed June 2016.

43. John Biggs, "Three Things Warby Parker Did to Launch a Successful Lifestyle Brand," *TechCrunch*, May 7, 2013, http://techcrunch.com/2013/05/07/the-three-things-warby-parker-did-to-launch-a-successful-lifestyle-brand/; and "Warby Parker: Breaking 'Glasses' Ceiling," *CNBC*, February 2, 2016, http://video.cnbc.com/gallery/?video=3000490919.

44. See "Statistics Every Cause Marketer Should Know," www.causemarketingforum.com/site/c.bkLUKcOTLkK4E/b.6448131/k.262B/Statistics_Every_Cause_Marketer_Should_Know.htm, accessed September 2016.

45. Kristina Monllos, "Sperry Goes Back to Basics with a Campaign for Adventurous Millennials," *Adweek*, February 19, 2015, www.adweek.com/print/162983; Erik Oster, "mono Rebrands Sperry with 'Odysseys Await,'" *Adweek*, February 19, 2015, www.adweek.copm/print/81123; and www.sperry.com/en/our-story/ and https://mono-1.com/work/sperry-odysseys-await, accessed September 2016.

46. Sherry Turkle, "The Flight from Conversation," *New York Times*, April 22, 2012, p. SR1; and Turkle, "Stop Googling. Let's Talk," *New York Times*, September 27, 2015, p. SR1.

47. See Tim Nudd, "What the Famous Faces from Jeep's Super Bowl Ad Really Had to Do with the Vehicle," *Advertising Age*, February 7, 2016, www.adage.com/print/169489; "Apple Kicks Off 'Made in USA' Marketing Push with High-End Mac Pro," *Advertising Age*, December 19, 2013, http://adage.com/print/245765/; E.J. Schultz, "Coke Joins Patriotic Branding Boom with Flag Can," *Advertising Age*, May 26, 2016, www.adage.com/print/304186; and www.youtube.com/watch?v=wKn5K5V7tRo, accessed September 2016.

48. See "Natural and Organic Foods and Beverages in the U.S., 4th Edition," *PR Newswire*, December 22, 2014, www.prnewswire.com/news-releases/natural-and-organic-foods-and-beverages-in-the-us-4th-edition-300013041.html; and "Technavio Expects Natural and Organic Food Market in the US to Exceed $200 Billion by 2019," December 4, 2015, www.technavio.com/pressrelease/technavio-expects-natural-and-organic-food-market-us-exceed-200-billion-2019.

49. Based on information from various pages at www.annies.com, accessed September 2016.

50. The Pew Forum on Religion & Public Life, "Nones on the Rise," www.pewforum.org/Unaffiliated/nones-on-the-rise.aspx, accessed October 9, 2012; "America's Changing Religious Landscape," May 12, 2015, www.pewforum.org/2015/05/12/americas-changing-religious-landscape/; and www.pewforum.org/religious-landscape-study/, accessed July 2016.

51. For more discussion, see David Masci and Michael Lipka, "Americans May Be Getting Less Religious, but Feelings of Spirituality Are

on the Rise," Pew Research Center, January 21, 12016, www. pewresearch.org/fact-tank/2016/01/21/americans-spirituality/.

52. See Brad Tuttle, "McDonald's Made the Right Move in Response to Gross 'Pink Slime,'" *Time*, February 5, 2014, http://time.com/4680/mcdonalds-made-the-right-move-in-response-to-gross-pink-slime/; www.youtube.com/watch?v=Ua5PaSqKD6k, accessed September 2016; Bruce Horovitz, "McDonald's to Customers: Ask about Food Quality," *USA Today*, October 13, 2014, www.usatoday.com/story/money/business/2014/10/13/mcdonalds-fast-food-food-quality-restaurants/17213145/; and www.mcdonalds.com/us/en/your_questions/our_food.html, accessed September 2016.

Chapter 4

1. John Kell, "Lego Says 2015 Was Its 'Best Year Ever,' with Huge Sales Jump," *Fortune*, March 1, 2016, http://fortune.com/2016/03/01/lego-sales-toys-2015/; Jonathon Ringen, "When It Clicks, It Clicks," *Fast Company*, February 2015, pp. 72–78+; Andrew Jack, "How LEGO Took to Anthropology," *Financial Times*, February 26, 2014, www.ft.com/cms/s/0/b071990c-9d4c-11e3a599-00144feab7de.html#axzz3N8u6XIPH; "How 5 Massive Companies Changed Using Market Research," *SurveyPolice*, March 21, 2015, www.surveypolice.com/blog/how-5-massive-companies-changed-using-market-research/; Christian Madsbjerg and Mikkel B. Rasmussen, "An Anthropologist Walks into a Bar...," *Harvard Business Review*, March, 2014, pp. 80–88; Richard Milne, "Sales Jump Secures LEGO's Crown as World's Biggest Toymaker," *Financial Times*, September 2, 2015, www.ft.com/intl/cms/s/0/f03d0188-513d-11e5-9497-c74c95a1a7b1.html#axzz3szkTNfDv; and www.lego.com, September 2016.

2. See Craig Smith, "By the Numbers: 250 Amazing Pinterest Statistics," *Digital Marketing Ramblings*, October, 2015, http://expandedramblings.com/index.php/pinterest-stats/; Jacob Kastrenakes, "Pinterest Now Has 100 Million Monthly Users," *The Verge*, September 17, 2015, www.theverge.com/2015/9/17/9348519/pinterest-100m-monthly-users; and www.pinterest.com/llbean/, www.pinterest.com/nordstrom/, and www.pinterest.com/lowes/, accessed September 2016.

3. See "Big Data," *Wikipedia*, http://en.wikipedia.org/wiki/Big_data, accessed June 2016; Michael Lev-Ram, "What's the Next Big Thing in Big Data? Bigger Data," *Fortune*, June 16, 2014, pp. 233–240; and Peter Horst and Robert Duboff, "Don't Let Big Data Bury Your Brand," *Harvard Business Review*, November 2015, pp. 79–86.

4. Based on information from Shareen Pathak, "How PepsiCo Sweetens Up Consumer Insights," *Digiday*, June 8, 2015, http://digiday.com/brands/pepsico-sweetens-consumer-insights/.

5. See www.walmartstores.com/Suppliers/248.aspx, accessed September 2016; and "Retail Link 2.0," 8th & Walton, http://blog.8thandwalton.com/2014/08/retail-link-2-0/, accessed September 2016.

6. See Micah Solomon, "Crushing It via Customer-Centricity: How USAA Insurance Succeeds without Geckos and Flying Pigs," *Forbes*, August 13, 2015, www.forbes.com/sites/micahsolomon/2015/08/13/crushing-it-via-customer-centricity-not-geckos-and-flying-pigs-the-usaa-model/; Scott Horstein, "Use Care with That Database," *Sales & Marketing Management*, May 2006, p. 22; "Top 10 Customer-Centric Companies of 2014," *Desk Talk*, January 13, 2015, https://www.talkdesk.com/blog/top-10-customer-centric-companies-of-2014/; and www.usaa.com and www.usaa.com/inet/pages/reporttomembers_financialhighlights_landing, accessed September 2016.

7. George Chidi, "Confessions of a Corporate Spy," *Inc.*, February 2013, pp. 72–77.

8. For more on research firms that supply marketing information, see Laurence N. Gold, "The 2015 AMA Gold Global Top 50 Report," *Marketing News*, August 2015. Other information from www.

nielsen.com/us/en/solutions/measurement/retail-measurement.html and http://thefuturescompany.com/what-we-do/us-yankelovich-monitor, accessed September 2016.

9. See www.iriworldwide.com, accessed September 2016.

10. See www.fisher-price.com/en_US/ourstory/research-at-the-heart/index.html, accessed September 2016.

11. E. J. Schultz, "Tapping into the Secret Town," *Advertising Age*, June 17, 2013, pp. 12–13. For other discussions and examples of ethnographic research in marketing, see Christine Birkner, "C'est La Vie," *Marketing News*, June 2014, pp. 23–27.

12. See Birkner, "C'est La Vie"; and "Landor Families," http://landor.com/#!/talk/articles-publications/articles/landor-families/, accessed September 2016.

13. See Rebecca Greenfield, "How the Deepest, Darkest Secrets of Moms Shape the Products in Aisle 6," *Fast Company*, December 19, 2014, www.fastcompany.com/3039798/most-creative-people/how-the-deepest-darkest-secrets-of-moms-shape-the-products-in-aisle-6?utm_source; and www.momcomplex.com, accessed September 2016.

14. Molly Soat, "Everything in Moderation," *Marketing News*, April 2014, pp. 36–46, here p. 38.

15. See "Internet World Stats," www.internetworldstats.com/stats14.htm#north, accessed June 2016.

16. For more information, see www.focusvision.com and www.youtube.com/watch?v%3DPG8RZl2dvNY, accessed September 2016.

17. See www.nascarfancouncil.com, accessed September 2016; Sarah Sluis, "Beauty Marketers Must Put Their Best Face Forward," *CRM*, June 2014, www.destinationcrm.com/Articles/Editorial/Magazine-Features/Beauty-Marketers-Must-Put-Their-Best-Face-Forward-96977.aspx; and www.allurebeautyenthusiasts.com, accessed September 2016.

18. For more discussion, see "Do-Not-Track Online Act of 2013," www.congress.gov/bill/113th-congress/senate-bill/418; Fred B. Campbell, Jr., "The Slow Death of 'Do Not Track,'" *New York Times*, December 27, 2014, p. A17; Dustin Volz, "U.S. Regulators Reject Push for 'Do Not Track' Internet Rules," *Reuters*, November 6, 2015, www.reuters.com/article/2015/11/06/usa-tech-tracking-idUSL1N1311XW20151106; and "Do Not Track Legislation," http://en.wikipedia.org/wiki/Do_Not_Track_legislation, accessed September 2016.

19. Michael E. Smith, "The Brains behind Better Ads: Optimizing the Cute and Cuddly," June 18, 2014, www.nielsen.com/us/en/insights/news/2014/the-brains-behind-better-ads-optimizing-the-cute-and-cuddly.html; "The Shelter Pet Project," 2015 ARF Awards, http://thearf-org-aux-assets.s3.amazonaws.com/ogilvy/2015/studies/shelter-pet.pdf; and www.theshelterpetproject.org, accessed September 2016.

20. See Jennifer Alsever, "Technology Is the Best Policy," *Fortune*, November 18, 2013; "Built in Record Time, the MetLife Wall Knocks Down Barriers to Great Customer Service," October 23, 2013, www.metlifegto.com/news/Built-in-record-time-the-MetL; "5 Lessons Learned from the MetLife Wall," *Insurance Networking News*, www.insurancenetworking.com/gallery/5-lessons-learned-from-the-metlife-wall-34261-1.html, accessed June 2016; and "Rethinking the Customer Experience at MetLife," MongoDB, www.mongodb.com/customers/metlife, accessed June 2016.

21. Andrew Nusca, "Despite High Tech, the Future of Marketing Is Exactly the Same: Focus on Customers," *Fortune*, July 15, 2014, http://fortune.com/2014/07/15/big-data-future-marketing-customer-focus/; Phani Nagarjuna, "Seven Steps to Understanding Your Business and Monetizing Analytics," *Sales & Marketing Management*, January 9, 2015, http://salesandmarketing.com/content/seven-steps-understanding-your-business-and-monetizing-analytics; and Jon Cifuentes, "The State of Marketing Analytics: Insights in the Age of the Customer," *Venture Beat*, September 25, 2015, http://insight.venturebeat.com/report/state-marketing-analytics-insights-age-customer.

22. For more discussion, see Matt Ariker and others, "Quantifying the Impact of Marketing Analytics," *Harvard Business Review,* November 5, 2015, https://hbr.org/2015/11/quantifying-the-impact-of-marketing-analytics; and Martin Kihn, "What's Going On with Marketing Analytics?" Gartner, September 30, 2015, http://blogs.gartner.com/martin-kihn/whats-going-on-with-marketing-analytics-2/.

23. Avi Dan, "How Data Nourishes Agile Marketing at Kraft," *Forbes,* October 26, 2014, www.forbes.com/sites/avidan/2014/10/26/how-data-nourishes-agile-marketing-at-kraft-foods/; and Jack Neff, "Kraft Says Content Delivers Four Times Better ROI than Ads," *Advertising Age,* September 15, 2014, p. 8.

24. For examples, see Molly Soat, "Size Matters," *Marketing News,* June 2015, pp. 10–11; and Peter Horst and Robert Duboff, "Don't Let Big Data Bury Your Brand," *Harvard Business Review,* November 2015, pp. 79–86.

25. "1-800-Flowers.com Customer Connection Blooms with SAS Business Analytics," www.sas.com/success/1800flowers.html, accessed September 2016.

26. See Daryl Travis, "The Best Omni-Channel Brands Look More Like a Cause than a Business," *The Hub,* August 2014, www.hubmagazine.com/the-hub-magazine/zappos-omnivalues-082014/; and https://zuul.zappos.com/zuul/login, accessed September 2016.

27. Based on information in Ann Zimmerman, "Small Business; Do the Research," *Wall Street Journal,* May 9, 2005, p. R3; with additional information and insights from John Tozzi, "Market Research on the Cheap," *BusinessWeek,* January 9, 2008, www.businessweek.com/smallbiz/content/jan2008/sb2008019_352779.htm; "Understanding the Basics of Small Business Market Research," *All Business,* www.allbusiness.com/marketing/market-research/2587-1.html#axzz2K8T92eOR, accessed September 2016; and www.bibbentuckers.com, accessed September 2016.

28. For some good advice on conducting market research in a small business, search "conducting market research" at www.sba.gov or see "Researching Your Market," *Entrepreneur,* www.entrepreneur.com/article/43024-1, accessed September 2016.

29. See "The 2015 AMA Gold Global Top 25 Report," *Marketing News,* August 2015, pp. 34+; and www.nielsen.com/us/en/about-us.html and www.nielsen.com/us/en/about-us.html, accessed September 2016.

30. For these and other examples, see "From Tactical to Personal: Synovate's Tips for Conducting Marketing Research in Emerging Markets," *Marketing News,* April 30, 2011, pp. 20–22. Internet stats are from http://data.worldbank.org/indicator/IT.NET.USER.P2, accessed June 2016.

31. Subhash C. Jain, *International Marketing Management*, 3rd ed. (Boston: PWS-Kent, 1990), p. 338. For more discussion on international marketing research issues and solutions, see Warren J. Keegan and Mark C. Green, *Global Marketing*, 8th ed. (Upper Saddle River, NJ: Prentice Hall, 2015), pp. 170–201.

32. See Mary Madden, "Privacy and Cybersecurity: Key Findings from Pew Research," Pew Research, January 16, 2015, www.pewresearch.org/key-data-points/privacy/; and Natasha Singer, "Sharing Data, but Not Happily," *New York Times,* June 5, 2015, p. B1.

33. Based on information from Charles Duhigg, "Psst, You in Aisle 5," *New York Times,* February 19, 2012, p. MM30; Kashmir Hill, "How Target Figured Out a Teen Girl Was Pregnant before Her Father Did," *Forbes,* February 16, 2012, www.forbes.com/sites/kashmirhill/2012/02/16/how-target-figured-out-a-teen-girl-was-pregnant-before-her-father-did/; and "7 Big Data Blunders You're Thankful Your Company Didn't Make," Umbel, October 22, 2014, www.umbel.com/blog/big-data/7-big-data-blunders/?utm_content=buffer6a719&utm_medium=social&utm_source=twitter.com&utm_campaign=buffer.

34. See Kate Kaye, "The $24 Billion Data Business that Telcos Don't Want to Talk About," *Advertising Age,* October 26, 2015,

pp. 12–14; and "Mobile Data Analysis with SAP Consumer Insight 365," https://experience.sap.com/designservices/work/mobile-data-analysis-with-sap-consumer-insight-365, accessed September 2016.

35. See "Respondent Bill of Rights," www.marketingresearch.org/issues-policies/best-practice/respondent-bill-rights, accessed September 2016.

36. See www.casro.org/?page=TheCASROCode&hhSearchTerms=%22code+and+standards%22, accessed September 2016.

Chapter 5

1. Quotes and other information from Rich Duprey, "Can Harley-Davidson Inc. Stop Sliding Sales with This Strategy?" *The Motley Fool,* December 5, 2015, www.fool.com/investing/general/2015/12/05/can-harley-davidson-inc-stop-sliding-sales-with-th.aspx; Ben Popkin, "How Harley-Davidson, Inc. Hopes to Gain Market Share," *The Motley Fool,* February 5, 2014, http://www.fool.com/investing/general/2014/02/05/how-harley-davidson-inc-hopes-to-gain-market-share.aspx; Susanna Hamner, "Harley, You're Not Getting Any Younger," *New York Times,* March 22, 2009, p. BU1; "Thousands of Thundering Motorcycles Rumble through Milwaukee for Harley-Davidson 110th Anniversary Parade," PRNewswire, August 31, 2013, www.prnewswire.com/news-releases/thousands-of-thundering-motorcycles-rumble-through-milwaukee-for-harley-davidson-110th-anniversary-parade-221946591.html; Meredith Davis, "Harley-Davidson Third-Quarter Profit Falls, Stock Hits Two-Year Low," *Reuters,* October 20, 2015, www.reuters.com/article/us-harley-davidsonresults-idUSKCN0SE1BL20151020; "Harley Owners Group," www.harley-davidson.com/content/h-d/en_US/home/owners/hog.html, accessed September 2016; and various pages at www.harley-davidson.com, accessed September 2016.

2. Consumer expenditure figures from "Household Final Consumption Expenditure," *The World Bank,* http://data.worldbank.org/indicator/NE.CON.PRVT.CD, accessed September 2016. Population figures from the World POPClock, U.S. Census Bureau, www.census.gov/main/www/popclock.html, accessed September 2016. This website provides continuously updated projections of U.S. and world populations.

3. "Advertising Age Hispanic Fact Pack," August 3, 2015, pp. 30–31; Claudia "Havi" Goffan, "Hispanic Market Trends Forecast," *Target Latino,* http://targetlatino.com/hispanic-market-trends-forecast/, accessed September 2016; and "Population Projections," www.census.gov/population/projections/, accessed September 2016.

4. Lee Vann, "5 Predictions for Hispanic Online Marketing in 2015," *MediaPost,* November 13, 2014, www.mediapost.com/publications/article/238136; and Goffan, "Hispanic Market Trends Forecast."

5. Ann-Christine Diaz, "Toyota's 'Mas Que un Auto' Is More than Your Average Campaign," *Advertising Age,* April 7, 2015, http://adage.com/print/297904/; Laurel Wentz, "U.S. Hispanic Awards Honor Toyota, Volvo, California Milk," *Advertising Age,* April 29, 2015, http://adage.com/print/298296/; and www.masqueunauto.com, accessed September 2016.

6. See "Connecting through Culture: African Americans Favor Diverse Advertising," Nielsen, October 20, 2014, www.nielsen.com/us/en/insights/news/2014/connecting-through-culture-african-americans-favor-diverse-advertising.html; and U.S. Census Bureau, "U.S. Population Projections," www.census.gov/population/projections, accessed September 2016.

7. "U.S. Forest Service and Ad Council Launch New Multimedia Public Service Advertising Effort to Encourage African American Families to Discover Nature," June 7, 2012, www.multivu.com/mnr/62047-us-forest-service-ad-council-psa-african-american-families-discover-nature; "US Forest Service Discover the

Forest," National Environmental Justice Conference and Training Program, April 4, 2013, www.scribd.com/doc/134213528/ US-Forest-Service-Discover-The-Forest#scribd; "Discovering Nature (African-American Market)," www.adcouncil.org/ Our-Campaigns/Family-Community/Discovering-Nature-African-American-Market, accessed February 2015; and www.discovertheforest.org, accessed September 2016.

8. See "Nielsen: Asian-American Buying Power Increased by More than $50 Billion in One Year—Expected to Hit $1 Trillion by 2018," Nielsen, June 11, 2015; and U.S. Census Bureau, "U.S. Population Projections," www.census.gov/population/projections, accessed September 2016.

9. See Hannah Madans, "Retailers Step Up Luxury Goods during Lunar New Year as Asians Celebrate a Season of Shopping," *McClatchy-Tribune Business News*, February 24, 2015; Mitch Moxley, "Global Luxury Retailers Gear Up for Chinese New Year Shoppers," *Jing Daily*, January 29, 2014, https://jingdaily. com/global-luxury-retailers-gear-up-for-chinese-new-year-shoppers/#.Vmc1bnarRhF; and Tori Telfer, "Bloomingdale's Will Celebrate the Chinese New Year Again This Year," *Chicago Magazine*, www.chicagomag.com/style-shopping/ January-2015/Bloomingdales-Will-Celebrate-Chinese-New-Years-Again-This-Year/.

10. See Yuriy Boykiv, "What Leaders Need to Know about the 'Total Market' Approach to Diverse Audiences," *Inc.*, November 10, 2014, www.inc.com/yuriy-boykiv/what-leaders-need-to-know-about-the-total-market-approach-to-diverse-audiences.html; Tim Nudd, "Ad of the Day: Honey Maid Celebrates Fourth of July with an Immigrant Family's Story," *Adweek*, June 29, 2015, www.adweek.com/print/165626; and Laurel Wentz, "Welcome to the Multicultural Mainstream," *Advertising Age*, April 6, 2015, pp. 18+.

11. Barry Levine, "New Marketing Survey, It's the Trust, Stupid," *Venture Beat*, September 29, 2015, http://venturebeat. com/2015/09/29/new-marketing-survey-its-the-trust-stupid/.

12. "Mercedes-Benz: Take the Wheel," http://industry.shorty-awards.com/nominee/6th_annual/It/mercedes-benz-take-the-wheel, accessed September 2016; and Razorfish NYC, "Mercedes-Benz Take the Wheel Case Study," https://vimeo.com/81342429, accessed September 2016.

13. Kate Taylor, "For McRib Fans, Search for the Sandwich Is Worth the Effort," *Entrepreneur*, November 21, 2013, www.entrepreneur. com//article/230063#; and http://mcriblocator.com, accessed September 2016.

14. See "Dunkin' Donuts Taps Vine Star Logan Paul for Loyalty Program Jolt," *Advertising Age*, November 9, 2015, www.adage. com/print/310271.

15. See Andrew Adam Newman, "To Buoy Tourism in Bermuda, a Campaign Turns to Social Media," *New York Times*, December 3, 2014, www.nytimes.com/2014/12/04/business/media/to-buoy-tourism-in-bermuda-a-campaign-turns-to-social-media.html; and www.gotobermuda.com/default/, accessed September 2016.

16. See Sam Parr, "This Men's Fashion Startup is KILLING Content Marketing: 7 Tactics Learned from Chubbies Shorts," *The Hustle*, January 13, 2015, http://thehustle.co/mens-fashion-startup-killing-content-marketing-7-tactics-learned-chubbies-shorts; and www.chubbies.com and www.chubbiesshorts.com/pages/the-ambassadors, accessed September 2016.

17. Chris Slocumb, "Women Outspend Men 3 to 2 on Technology Purchases," *ClarityQuest*, January 3, 2013, www.clarityqst. com/women-outspend-men-3-to-2-on-technology-pur-chases/; "More Men Are Grocery Shopping, but They Do So Grudgingly, Reports NPD," November 12, 2014, www.npd. com/wps/portal/npd/us/news/press-releases/more-men-are-grocery-shopping-but-they-do-so-grudgingly/; Sarwant Singh, "Women in Cars: Overtaking Men on the Fast Lane," *Forbes*, May 23, 2014, www.forbes.com/sites/sarwantsingh/2014/ 05/23/women-in-cars-overtaking-men-on-the-fast-lane/;

and "Women Make Up 85% of All Consumer Purchases," *BloombergBusiness*, June 22, 2015, www.bloomberg.com/news/ videos/b/9e28517f-8de1-4e59-bcda-ce536aa50bd6.

18. See Jack Neff, "Move Over Mom, It's Dad's Turn," *Advertising Age*, January 26, 2014, p. 6; "Dad Gets a Makeover in Super Bowl Ads," *CNN*, January 31, 2015, www.cnn.com/2015/01/30/ living/feat-super-bowl-dads-ads/; "Cheerios Leverages the Power of 'Dadvertising,'" *Marketing News*, February 2015, pp. 4–5; and www.youtube.com/watch?v=6GYxH2-WeZY, accessed September 2016.

19. See "Kids Spending and Influencing Power: $1.2 Trillion Says Leading Ad Firm," Center for Digital Democracy, November 1, 2012, www.democraticmedia.org/kids-spending-and-influencing-power-12-trillion-says-leading-ad-firm; and "How Much Influence Do Teens Wield over Their Parents' Purchase Decisions?" *Marketing Charts*, June 23, 2015, www.marketingcharts.com/traditional/ how-much-influence-do-teens-wield-over-their-parents-purchase-decisions-56068/.

20. See www.redcap.com and www.redkapautomotive.com/Home/ Our-Story, accessed September 2016.

21. For more on the Nielsen PRIZM, visit https://segmentation solutions.nielsen.com/mybestsegments/, accessed September 2016.

22. See "Microsoft-Nokia Launches Cheap Lumia Phones for Price Sensitive Consumers," *Forbes*, January 15, 2015, www.forbes.com/sites/greatspeculations/2015/01/15/ microsoft-nokia-launches-cheap-lumia-phones-for-price-sensitive-consumers/; and Sanjay Sanghoee, "Can Apple Win in China in a Market of Cheaper Smartphones?" *Fortune*, February 24, 2015, http://fortune.com/2015/02/24/ can-apple-win-china-in-a-market-of-cheaper-smartphones/.

23. See Jennifer Aaker, "Dimensions of Measuring Brand Personality," *Journal of Marketing Research*, August 1997, pp. 347–356; and Philip Kotler and Kevin Lane Keller, *Marketing Management*, 15th ed. (Upper Saddle River, New Jersey: Pearson Publishing, 2016), p. 163.

24. Deborah Malone, *The Reinvention of Marketing* (New York: The Internationalist Press, 2014), Kindle location 142.

25. See Abraham H. Maslow, "A Theory of Human Motivation," *Psychological Review, 50* (1943), pp. 370–396. Also see Maslow, *Motivation and Personality*, 3rd ed. (New York: HarperCollins Publishers, 1987); and Michael R. Solomon, *Consumer Behavior*, 11th ed. (Upper Saddle River, NJ: Prentice Hall, 2014), pp. 132–134.

26. See "The Myth of 5,000 Ads," http://cbi.hhcc.com/writing/ the-myth-of-5000-ads/, accessed September 2016.

27. See "Does Subliminal Advertising Actually Work?" *BBC*, January 20, 2015, www.bbc.com/news/magazine-30878843.

28. See Erik Oster, "Jimmy Dean Moves beyond Breakfast in New Ads," *Adweek*, September 8, 2014, www.adweek.com/print/159972; Andrew Adam Newman, "Jimmy Dean Goes from Breakfast Nook to Dinner Table," *New York Times*, September 7, 2014, www. nytimes.com/2014/09/08/business/media/jimmy-dean-goes-from-breakfast-nook-to-dinner-table.html?_r=1; and Felicia Greiff, "Jimmy Dean's New Campaign Strikes Sunny Tone without Familiar Sunshine Mascot," *Advertising Age*, November 2, 2015, www.adage.com/print/301159.

29. See www.yelp.com and www.yelp.com/about, accessed September 2016.

30. The following discussion draws from the work of Everett M. Rogers. See his *Diffusion of Innovations*, 5th ed. (New York: Free Press, 2003).

31. Based on Rogers, *Diffusion of Innovation*, p. 281. For more discussion, see http://en.wikipedia.org/wiki/Everett_Rogers, accessed September 2016.

32. See "Electric Car Use by Country," *Wikipedia*, http://en.wikipedia. org/wiki/Electric_car_use_by_country, accessed September 2016; and "Plug-In Vehicle Tracker: What's Coming, When," www. pluginamerica.org/vehicles, accessed September 2016.

Chapter 6

1. See "Welcome to the Cognitive Era," www.slideshare.net/ibm/welcome-to-the-cognitive-era, accessed September 2016; Kate Kaye, "Tangled Up in Big Blue: IBM Replaces Smarter Planet with … Bob Dylan," *Advertising Age*, October 6, 2015, www.adage.com/print/300774; Jesi Hempel, "IBM's All-Star Salesman," *Fortune*, September 26, 2008, http://money.cnn.com/2008/09/23/technology/hempel_IBM.fortune/index.htm; "Virginia Rometty's Vision of How IBM Will Thrive," *Wall Street Journal*, October 26, 2015, www.wsj.com/articles/virginia-romettys-vision-of-how-ibm-will-thrive-1445911327; www.millwardbrown.com/brandz/top-global-brands/2015 and www.ibm.com/cognitive/outthink, accessed September 2016.

2. See www.corninggorillaglass.com/en/home, accessed September 2016.

3. Based on information from www.cargill.com, www.cargillcocoachocolate.com/about-us/index.htm, and www.cargillcocoachocolate.com/innovation/product-development-support/index.htm, accessed September 2016.

4. See www.cargill.com, www.cargillcocoachocolate.com/about-us/index.htm, and www.cargillcocoachocolate.com/innovation/product-development-support/index.htm, accessed September 2016.

5. This classic categorization was first introduced in Patrick J. Robinson, Charles W. Faris, and Yoram Wind, *Industrial Buying Behavior and Creative Marketing* (Boston: Allyn & Bacon, 1967). Also see Philip Kotler and Kevin Lane Keller, *Marketing Management* (Hoboken, NJ: Pearson Publishing, 2016), pp. 192–193.

6. Based on information from "Six Flags Entertainment Corporation: Improving Business Efficiency with Enterprise Asset Management," July 12, 2012, www-01.ibm.com/software/success/cssdb.nsf/CS/LWIS-8W5Q84?OpenDocument&Site=default&cty=en_us; and www-01.ibm.com/software/tivoli/products/maximo-asset-mgmt/, accessed September 2016.

7. See Frederick E. Webster Jr. and Yoram Wind, *Organizational Buying Behavior* (Upper Saddle River, NJ: Prentice Hall, 1972), pp. 78–80. Also see Philip Kotler and Kevin Lane Keller, *Marketing Management*, 15th ed. (Hoboken, NJ: Pearson Publishing, 2016), pp. 193–197.

8. See Marco Link and John H. Fleming, "B2B Companies: Do You Know Who Your Customer Is?" *Business Journal*, November 11, 2014, www.gallup.com/businessjournal/179309/b2b-companies-know-customer.aspx; and Karl Schmidt, Brent Adamson, and Anna Bird, "Making the Consensus Sale," *Harvard Business Review*, March 2015, pp. 107–113.

9. See Kate Maddox, "Seven B-to-B Marketing Trends That Will Shape 2015," *Advertising Age*, January 13, 2015, www.adage.com/print/296518; and "USG 'It's Your World. Build It,'" www.pinterest.com/gyroideasshop/usg-its-your-world-build-it/, accessed September 2016.

10. Robinson, Faris, and Wind, *Industrial Buying Behavior*, p. 14. Also see Kotler and Keller, *Marketing Management*, pp. 198–204.

11. For more ads in this series, see https://www.accenture.com/id-en/advertising-index, accessed September 2016.

12. See David Moth, "Q&A: How Maersk Line Created a Brilliant B2B Social Media Strategy," September 9, 2015, https://econsultancy.com/blog/66901-q-a-how-maersk-line-created-a-brilliant-b2b-social-media-strategy; Laurence Hebberd, "How Maersk Line Uses Social Media," October 19, 2015, http://linkhumans.com/case-study/maersk-line; and www.maerskline.com/ar-sa/social/our-social-media, accessed September 2016.

13. Information from www.shrinershospitalsforchildren.org/Hospitals.aspx; and www.chs.net/investor-relations/annual-reports/, accessed September 2016.

14. Thierry Goddard, "The Economics of the American Prison System," *SmartAsset*, October 21, 2015, https://smartasset.com/insights/the-economics-of-the-american-prison-system; Michael Myser, "The Hard Sell," *CNN*, March 15, 2007,

http://money.cnn.com/magazines/business2/business2_archive/2006/12/01/8394995/; and Michelle Ye Hee Lee, "Yes, the U.S. Locks People Up at a Higher Rate than Any Other Country," *Washington Post*, July 7, 2015, www.washingtonpost.com/news/fact-checker/wp/2015/07/07/yes-u-s-locks-people-up-at-a-higher-rate-than-any-other-country/.

15. See www.generalmillscf.com, accessed September 2016.

16. Niraj Chokshi, "There's about One 'Government Unit' for Every 3,566 People in the U.S.," *Washington Post*, September 4, 2013, www.washingtonpost.com/blogs/govbeat/wp/2013/09/04/theres-about-one-governmental-unit-for-every-3566-people-in-the-u-s/; and "State & Local Government Finances," http://factfinder.census.gov/faces/tableservices/jsf/pages/productview.xhtml?src=bkmk, accessed September 2016.

17. Charles S. Clark, "Federal Contract Spending Fell 3.1 Percent in 2014, Study Finds," *Government Executive*, June 5, 2015, www.govexec.com/contracting/2015/06/federal-contract-spending-fell-31-percent-2014-study-finds/114547/; and Wyatt Kash, "New Details Released on Proposed 2016 IT Spending," *FedScoop*, February 4, 2015, http://fedscoop.com/what-top-agencies-would-spend-on-it-projects-in-2016.

18. See "GSA Organization Overview," www.gsa.gov/portal/content/104438, accessed September 2016; "Defense Logistics Agency: Medical Supply Chain," www.dscp.dla.mil/sbo/medical.asp, accessed September 2016; and Department of Veterans Affairs Office of Acquisition & Material Management, www.va.gov/oal/business/dbwva.asp, accessed September 2016.

Chapter 7

1. Quotes and other information from "Strong Comparable Sales Growth in the U.S. Drives Q1 Revenues for Dunkin' Brands," *Forbes*, April 28, 2015, www.forbes.com/sites/greatspeculations/2015/04/28/strong-comparable-sales-growth-in-the-u-s-drives-q1-revenues-for-dunkin-brands/; Christine Champagne and Teressa Iezzi, "Dunkin' Donuts and Starbucks: A Tale of Two Coffee Marketing Giants," *Fast Company*, August 21, 2014, www.fastcocreate.com/3034572; Janet Adamy, "Battle Brewing: Dunkin' Donuts Tries to Go Upscale, but Not Too Far," *Wall Street Journal*, April 8, 2006, p. A1; "Dunkin' Donuts' Goes the Whole Nine Yards: Brand Keys Ranks Dunkin' Donuts Number One in Coffee Customer Loyalty for Ninth Straight Year," Dunkin' Donuts Newsroom, February 18, 2015, http://news.dunkindonuts.com; Khushbu Shah, "Starbucks or Dunkin' Donuts? Where America's Coffee Loyalty Lies," *Eater*, January 15, 2015, www.eater.com/2015/1/15/7551497/starbucks-dunkin-donuts-peets-coffee-spending-percent; and www.dunkindonuts.com and www.dunkinbrands.com, accessed September 2016.

2. Rebecca Cooper, "Target Aiming TargetExpress Format at Washington, D.C. Area," *Washington Business Journal*, January 21, 2015, www.bizjournals.com/twincities/news/2015/01/21/target-targetexpress-washington-dc-arlington.html; and Hayley Fitzpatrick, "Target Is Quietly Opening a New Kind of Store in Cities Across America," *Business Insider*, July 6, 2015, www.businessinsider.com/target-is-quietly-opening-a-new-kind-of-store-2015-7.

3. See "Macy's—Set for Healthy Performance in 2015," *Seeking Alpha*, January 21, 2015, http://seekingalpha.com/article/2836036; Cotton Timberlake, "With Stores Nationwide, Macy's Goes Local," *Bloomberg BusinessWeek*, October 4–10, 2010, pp. 21–22; Jim Tierney, "Macy's Confident in My Macy's, Magic Selling Customer Engagement Strategies," *Loyalty 360*, August 15, 2013, http://loyalty360.org/resources/article/macys-confident-in-my-macys-magic-selling-customer-engagement-strategies, and "Refinement of M.O.M Strategies," http://macysinc.com/macys/m.o.m.-strategies/default.aspx, accessed September 2016.

4. See www.dovemencare.com/, accessed September 2016.

5. Michael McCarthy, "Ad of the Day: Dick's Sporting Goods Goes the Extra Mile in Its First Campaign for Women," April 30, 2015, www.adweek.com/print/164418; Alana Vagianos, "'Who Will You Be?' Campaign Celebrates the Raw Strength of Women's Bodies," *Huffington Post,* May 8, 2015, www.huffingtonpost.com/2015/05/08/who-will-you-be-campaign-dicks-sporting-goods_n_7242320.html; and www.youtube.com/watch?v=Mf0_G1FS0l4, accessed September 2016.

6. "Inside a Department Store's Secret Shopping Service," *Wall Street Journal,* August 11, 2011, www.wsj.com/articles/SB10001424053111904140604576498733634049992; Alanna Greco, "A Day at Saks: Getting Personal with Their Personal Stylists," *Luxe Me Now,* March 12, 2014, http://lmnonline.com/saks-interview/; and www.saksfifthavenue.com/Saks-Stylist, accessed September 2016.

7. Andrew McMains, "Ad of the Day: Panera Gets into Lifestyle Branding with Manifesto about Healthy Living," *Adweek,* June 15, 2015, www.adweek.com/print/165330; Lisa Brown, "Panera Debuts New Ad Campaign: "Food as It Should Be," *St. Louis Post-Dispatch,* June 16, 2015, www.stltoday.com/business/local/panera-debuts-new-ad-campaign-food-as-it-should-be/article_28c506b9-1a71-508d-9166-b1da12850076.html; and www.panerabread.com/en-us/our-beliefs/food-as-it-should-be-nopt.html, accessed September 2016.

8. Clare O'Connor, "The Pumpkin Spice Economy: How Starbucks Lattes Fueled a $500 Million Craze," *Forbes,* November 10, 2015, www.forbes.com/sites/clareoconnor/2015/11/10/the-pumpkin-spice-economy-how-starbucks-lattes-fueled-a-500-million-craze/.

9. Based on information from www.fitbit.com, accessed September 2016.

10. See Lisa Jennings, "CKE: Advertising, Turkey Burgers Drive Sales," *Restaurant News,* April 12, 2013, http://nrn.com/latest-headlines/cke-advertising-turkey-burgers-drive-sales; and "Bikini Models Play Border Wall Volleyball in New Carl's Jr. Ad" *Fox News Insider,* September 30, 2015, http://insider.foxnews.com/2015/09/30/watch-models-bikinis-play-border-wall-volleyball-new-carls-jr-ad.

11. See www.patagonia.com/us/ambassadors, accessed September 2016.

12. For this and other information on the Mosaic USA system, see www.experian.com/marketing-services/consumer-segmentation.html and www.experian.com/assets/marketing-services/product-sheets/mosaic-usa.pdf, accessed September 2016.

13. See www.starbucksfs.com and http://starbucksocs.com/, accessed September 2016.

14. See Aaron Yaube, "5 Brands That Are Killing It on Spotify," *Contently,* March 20, 2015, https://contently.com/strategist/2015/03/20/5-brands-that-are-killing-it-on-spotify/; G. C. Francisco, "Coca-Cola: The AHH Effect," March 15, 2015, https://digitalcasestudies.wordpress.com/2015/03/11/coca-cola-the-ahh-effect/; and www.ahh.com and www.coca-colacompany.com/coca-cola-music/, accessed September 2015.

15. See Michael Porter, *Competitive Advantage* (New York: Free Press, 1985), pp. 4–8, 234–236. For a more recent discussion, see Philip Kotler and Kevin Lane Keller, *Marketing Management,* 15th ed. (Hoboken, NJ: Pearson, 2016), pp. 263–264.

16. See Jack Neff, "Laundry Bounces Back by Playing Both Ends against the Middle," *Advertising Age,* March 23, 2015, p. 28; Serena Ng, "New Tide Churns the Laundry Market," *Wall Street Journal,* September 26, 2013, http://online.wsj.com/news/articles/SB10001424052702304526204579099390487182058; Lauren Coleman-Lochner, "Laundry Detergent Maker Want More Suds," *Bloomberg Businessweek,* October 23, 2014, www.businessweek.com/articles/2014-10-23/laundry-detergent-sales-hurt-by-water-saving-washing-machines; and www.pg.com/en_US/investors/financial_reporting/annual_reports.shtml and www.pg.com/en_US/brands/index.shtml, accessed September 2016.

17. See Evie Nagy, "Putting Its Best Foot Forward," *Fast Company,* October 2015, pp. 46–48; Adam Tschorn, "How Stance Socks Got to Be on Rihanna's and NBA Players Feet," *Los Angeles Times,* October 19, 2015, www.latimes.com/fashion/la-ig-stance-20151018-story.html; and www.stance.com and www.stance.com/about/, accessed September 2016.

18. Denise Lee Yohn, "Stitch Fix Combines High Tech and High Touch to Transform Retail," *Forbes,* December 2, 2015, www.forbes.com/sites/deniselyohn/2015/12/02/stitch-fix-combines-high-tech-and-high-touch-to-transform-retail/; Sapna Maheshwari, "Stitch Fix and the New Science behind What Women Want to Wear," *BuzzFeed,* September 24, 2014, www.buzzfeed.com/sapna/stitch-fix-and-the-new-science-behind-what-women-want-to-wea#.jcA81lEoW; Bridget Brennan, "The Retailer Redefining Personal Service in Ecommerce," *Forbes,* December 4, 2014, www.forbes.com/sites/bridgetbrennan/2014/12/04/the-retailer-redefining-personal-service-in-ecommerce/; and www.stitchfix.com/referral/4097702 and www.stitchfix.com, accessed September 2016.

19. See Darren Dahl, "Partners in the Pursuit: Coke's VEB Unit Teams with Entrepreneurial Firms to Find Tomorrow's Hit Brands," September 22, 2015, www.coca-colacompany.com/stories/partners-in-the-pursuit-cokes-veb-unit-teams-with-entreprenerial-firms-to-find-tomorrows-hit-brands/.

20. See Amy Plitt, "What It Takes to Be a High-Level Hotel Concierge," *Conde Nast Traveler,* December 10, 2014, www.cntraveler.com/stories/2014-12-10/what-it-takes-to-be-a-high-level-hotel-concierge; "Renaissance Hotels Launches New Navigator Program to Help Guests Discover 'Hidden Gems' of Various Cities around the World," January 8, 2013, www.adweek.com/print/146321; and http://renaissance-hotels.marriott.com/navigators, accessed September 2016.

21. See James M. Loy, "Shopkick Achieves Tremendous Digital Customer Engagement for Major Brands," *loyalty360,* September 9, 2015, http://loyalty360.org/resources/article/shopkick-achieves-tremendous-digital-customer-engagement#sthash.osPi8JQK.dpuf; and www.shopkick.com/partners and www.shopkick.com/about, accessed September 2016.

22. Hannah Elliot, "With Bespoke Details, You Can Make Your Aston Martin or Rolls-Royce as Ugly as You Want," *Bloomberg Business,* February 18, 2015, www.bloomberg.com/news/articles/2015-02-18/with-bespoke-details-you-can-make-your-aston-martin-or-rolls-royce-as-ugly-as-you-want; Harvey Briggs, "For Rolls-Royce the Future Is Bespoke," *Purist,* http://pursuitist.com/for-rolls-royce-the-future-is-bespoke/, accessed September 2016; and www.rolls-roycemotorcars.com/en-GB/bespoke.html, accessed September 2016.

23. Mike Shields, "Nike and AKQA Turn People's Running Data into 100,000 Unique Videos," *Wall Street Journal,* January 7, 2015, http://blogs.wsj.com/cmo/2015/01/07/nike-and-akqa-turn-peoples-running-data-into-100000-unique-videos/.

24. See Carolyn Kellogg, "McDonald's Brings Back Happy Meals with Books," *Los Angeles Time,* January 8, 2015, www.latimes.com/books/jacketcopy/la-et-jc-mcdonalds-happy-meals-with-books-20150108-story.html.

25. Lucia Moses, "Kids and Ads," *Adweek,* March 18, 2014, p. 13; and Julia Greenberg, "Exposing the Murky World of Online Ads Aimed at Kids," *Wired,* April 4, 2015, www.wired.com/2015/04/exposing-murky-world-online-ads-aimed-at-kids/.

26. See "2014 Internet Crime Report," May 2015, www.fbi.gov/news/news_blog/2014-ic3-annual-report.

27. SUV sales data furnished by www.WardsAuto.com, accessed September 2016. Price data from www.edmunds.com, accessed September 2016.

28. See "Zappos Family Core Values," http://about.zappos.com/our-unique-culture/zappos-core-values; and http://about.zappos.com/, accessed September 2016.

29. David Rohde, "The Anti-Walmart: The Secret Sauce of Wegmans Is People," *The Atlantic,* March 23, 2012, www.theatlantic.com/

business/archive/2012/03/the-anti-walmart-the-secret-sauce-of-wegmans-is-people/254994/; and www.wegmans.com, accessed September 2016.

30. See www.heartsonfire.com/Learn-About-Our-Diamonds.aspx, accessed September 2016.

31. See Bobby J. Calder and Steven J. Reagan, "Brand Design," in Dawn Iacobucci, ed., *Kellogg on Marketing* (New York: John Wiley & Sons, 2001), p. 61. For more discussion, see Philip Kotler and Kevin Lane Keller, *Marketing Management*, 15th ed. (Hoboken, NJ: Pearson, 2016), Chapter 10.

Chapter 8

1. Based on information found in Jason Cipriani, "GoPro Rakes in More Profit Thanks to Surge in Overseas Demand," *Fortune*, July 22, 2015, http://fortune.com/2015/07/22/gopro-profit-overseas; Parker Thomas, "GoPro Market Shares and Earnings Trends," *Market Realist*, August 10, 2015, http://marketrealist.com/2015/08/gopros-market-shares-earnings-trend; Ryan Mac, "The Mad Billionaire behind GoPro: The World's Hottest Camera Company," *Forbes*, March 3, 2013, www.forbes.com/sites/ryanmac/2013/03/04/the-mad-billionaire-behind-gopro-the-worlds-hottest-camera-company/; Adam Levine-Weinberg, "GoPro Has an Earnings Wipeout: Why I'm Not Worried," *Motley Fool*, November 2, 2015, www.fool.com/investing/general/2015/11/02/gopro-inc-has-an-earnings-wipeout-why-im-not-worri.aspx; and www.gopro.com and http://-gopro.com/about-us/, accessed September 2016.

2. See "How Online Retailers Are Creating Immersive Brand Experiences in the Real World," *Advertising Age*, March 25, 2015, www.adage.com/print/297750; and apple.com/retail/ and www.apple.com/retail/learn/, accessed September 2016.

3. See "The B to B Best Awards 2015," *Advertising Age*, January 26, 2015, p. 28; and "Childlike Imagination—What My Mom Does at GE," www.ge.com/news/advertising, September 2016.

4. Chris Isidore, "How Nike Became King of Endorsements," *CNN Money*, June 5, 2015, http://money.cnn.com/2015/06/05/news/companies/nike-endorsement-dollars/.

5. See www.neworleansonline.com and www.australia.com/campaigns/nothinglike/us/index.html, accessed September 2016.

6. For more on social marketing, see Nancy Lee and Philip Kotler, *Social Marketing: Changing Behaviors for Good*, 5th ed. (Thousand Oaks, CA: SAGE Publications, 2015); and www.adcouncil.org and www.i-socialmarketing.org, accessed September 2016.

7. Quotes and definitions from Philip Kotler, *Marketing Insights from A to Z* (Hoboken, NJ: Wiley, 2003), p. 148; and www.asq.org/glossary/q.html, accessed September 2016.

8. Michael B. Sauter, Thomas C Frohlich, and Sam Stebbins, "Customer Service Hall of Fame," *24/7 Wall Street*, July 23, 2015, http://247wallst.com/special-report/2015/07/23/customer-service-hall-of-fame-2/4/.

9. See Nathaniel Wice, "Sonos: The Best Wireless Speakers," *Barrons*, January 3, 2015, http://online.barrons.com/articles/sonos-the-best-wireless-speakers-1420260626; Aaron Tilley, "Connected Speaker Market Heats Up with Super High-End Devialet Phantom," *Forbes*, June 8, 2015, www.forbes.com/sites/aarontilley/2015/06/18/super-high-end-speaker-devialet-phantom-looks-to/; and www.sonos.com, accessed September 2016.

10. See Gene Weingarten, "Pearls before Breakfast," *Washington Post*, April 8, 2007, www.washingtonpost.com/wp-dyn/content/article/2007/04/04/AR2007040401721.html; Jessica Contrera, "Joshua Bell's Metro Encore Draws a Crowd," *Washington Post*, September 30, 2014, www.washingtonpost.com/lifestyle/style/joshua-bells-metro-encore-draws-a-crowd/2014/09/30/c28b6c50-48d5-11e4-a046-120a8a855cca_story.html; and "Stop and Hear the Music," www.youtube.com/watch?v=hnOPu0_YWhw, accessed September 2016.

11. See http://cutiescitrus.com/products/ and http://cutiescitrus.com/about/, accessed September 2016.

12. See "3 in 4 Grocery Purchase Decisions Being Made In-Store," *MarketingCharts*, May 15, 2012, www.marketingcharts.com/direct/3-in-4-grocery-purchase-decisions-being-made-in-store-22094; "FMI—Supermarket Facts," www.fmi.org/research-resources/supermarket-facts, accessed September 2016; and "Our Retail Divisions," http://news.walmart.com/news-archive/2005/01/07/our-retail-divisions, accessed September 2016.

13. See www.tiffany.com/WorldOfTiffany/TiffanyStory/Legacy/BlueBox.aspx, accessed September 2016.

14. See Mary Mazzoni, "Amazon Continues Its Battle against 'Wrap Rage,'" *Triple Pundit*, December 9, 2013, www.triplepundit.com/2013/12/amazon-continues-battle-against-wrap-rage/; and www.amazon.com/b/?&node=5521637011, accessed September 2016.

15. Nora Naughton, "Lexus Rises to No. 1 in Customer Service Satisfaction Survey," *Automotive News*, August 25, 2015, www.autonews.com/article/20150825/RETAIL03/150829949/lexus-rises-to-no.-1-in-customer-satisfaction-study; Phil Nobile, "Consumer Reports' Best and Worst Car Brands in 2015," *Consumer Reposts*, December 21, 2015, www.newsday.com/classifieds/cars/consumer-reports-best-and-worst-car-brands-in-2015-include-lexus-mazda-and-toyota-1.10387053; and www.lexus-int.com/our-story/covenant.html and www.lexus-int.com/our-story/customer-care.html, accessed September 2016.

16. See Anna Rose Welch, "Lowe's Leverages Mobile Initiatives to Improve Customer Experience," *Integrated Solutions for Retailers*, November 21, 2013, www.retailsolutionsonline.com/doc/lowe-s-leverages-mobile-initiatives-to-improve-customer-experience-0001; Greg Petro. "Lowe's: The Home Improvement Retailer of the Future," *Forbes*, April 1, 2015, www.forbes.com/sites/gregpetro/2015/04/01/lowes-the-home-improvement-retailer-of-the-future/; and www.lowes.com/webapp/wcs/stores/servlet/ContactUsLandingPageView, www.lowes.com/how-to-library, and https://twitter.com/LowesCares, accessed September 2016.

17. See www.bmwgroup.com/com/en/brands/bmw.html and www.bmw.com/com/en/, accessed September 2016.

18. Information on the Colgate-Palmolive product mix is from www.colgatepalmolive.com/app/Colgate/US/CompanyHomePage.cvsp and www.colgate.com/en/us/oc/, accessed September 2016.

19. Devika Krishna Kumar, ""P&G to Sell Up to 100 Brands to Revive Sales, Cut Costs," *Reuters*, August 1, 2014, www.reuters.com/article/2014/08/01/procter-gamble-results-idUSL4N0Q745T20140801; P&G Brand Divestitures Will Be Bigger than Original Targets," *Advertising Age*, February 19, 2015, www.adage.com/print/297240; and Penny Morgan, "P&G Readies Its Divestiture of Beauty Brands to Coty," Yahoo! Finance, September 22, 2015, http://finance.yahoo.com/news/p-g-readies-divestiture-beauty-183549480.html.

20. See CIA World FactBook, www.cia.gov/library/publications/the-world-factbook, accessed September 2016; and "List of Countries by GDP Sector Composition," http://en.wikipedia.org/wiki/List_of_countries_by_GDP_sector_composition, accessed September 2016.

21. Based on information from Leonard Berry and Neeli-Bendapudi, "Clueing In Customers," *Harvard Business Review*, February 2003, pp. 100–106; Jeff Hansel, "Mayo Hits the Blogosphere," *McClatchy-Tribune Business News*, January 22, 2009; "Mayo Clinic Model of Care," www.mayo.edu/pmts/mc4200-mc4299/mc4270.pdf, accessed September 2016; and www.mayoclinic.org, accessed September 2016.

22. See James L. Heskett, W. Earl Sasser Jr., and Leonard A. Schlesinger, *The Service Profit Chain: How Leading Companies Link Profit and Growth to Loyalty, Satisfaction, and Value* (New York: Free Press, 1997); and Heskett, Sasser, and Schlesinger, *The Value Profit Chain: Treat Employees Like Customers and Customers Like Employees* (New York: Free Press, 2003). Also see John Marshall and Dave

Mayer, "Activate a Brand Internally," *Marketing Management*, Winter 2012, pp. 37–44; and The Service-Profit Chain Institute, http://serviceprofitchain.com/, accessed September 2016.

23. "Four Seasons Hotels and Resorts Named to Fortune List of the '100 Best Companies to Work for,'" March 2, 2015, http://press.fourseasons.com/news-releases/2015/fortune-100-best-companies-to-work-for/; and http://jobs.fourseasons.com and www.fourseasons.com/about_us/, accessed September 2016

24. See "United States: Prescription Drugs," www.statehealthfacts.org/profileind.jsp?sub=66&rgn=1&cat=5, accessed September 2016; and "Postal Facts," http://about.usps.com/who-we-are/postal-facts/welcome.htm, accessed September 2016.

25. See Terry Maxon, "Horrible Flight? Airlines' Apology Experts Will Make It Up to You," *McClatchy-Tribune News Service*, August 24, 2010; Katie Morell, "Lessons from Southwest Airlines' Stellar Customer Service," *ehotelier.com*, August 29, 2012, http://ehotelier.com/hospitality-news/item.php?id=23931_0_11_0M_C; and Adam Toporek, "Southwest Airlines: A Service Recovery Surprise," *B2C*, April 24, 2014, www.business2community.com/customer-experience/southwest-airlines-service-recovery-surprise-0886284#dri7dI4r5qW2ESBH.97.

26. See Martha White, "Lost Bags, at 140 Characters, and Airlines Respond," *New York Times*, October 20, 2015, p. B6.

27. See "McAtlas Shrugged," *Foreign Policy*, May–June 2001, pp. 26–37; and Philip Kotler and Kevin Lane Keller, *Marketing Management*, 15th ed. (Upper Saddle River: Pearson Publishing, 2016), p. 316.

28. See "For Sale: Hessian, A Brand without a Product," *Fast Company*, February 12, 2013, www.fastcodesign.com/1671819/for-sale-hessian-a-brand-without-a-product.

29. For more on BrandAsset Valuator, see Kotler and Keller, *Marketing Management*, Chapter 11; and "BrandAsset Valuator," www.yr.com/BAV, accessed September 2016.

30. See Millward Brown Optimor, "BrandZ Top 100 Most Valuable Global Brands," www.millwardbrown.com/BrandZ/2015/Global/2015_BrandZ_Top100_Chart.pdf, accessed September 2016. Also see "Best Global Brands," http://interbrand.com/best-brands/best-global-brands/2015/ranking/, accessed September 2016.

31. See Scott Davis, *Brand Asset Management*, 2nd ed. (San Francisco: Jossey-Bass, 2002). For more on brand positioning, see Kotler and Keller, *Marketing Management*, Chapter 10.

32. See Jack Neff, "How Whirlpool Heated Up Sales by Warming Up 'Cold Metal,'" *Advertising Age*, June 15, 2015, p. 38; "Every Day Care," www.multivu.com/players/English/7318751-whirlpool-announced-launch-of-every-day-take-the-chore-out-of-household-responsibilities/, accessed September 2016; and www.whirlpool.com/everydaycare/, accessed September 2016.

33. See Doug Grisaffe, "Feeling the Brand Love," *Marketing News*, February 2014, pp. 26–27; Simon Goodley, "Marketing Is Dead, Says Saatchi & Saatchi Boss—Long Live Lovemarks," *The Guardian*, March 3, 2015, www.theguardian.com/media/2015/mar/03/advertising-is-dead-says-saatchi-saatchi-boss-long-live-lovemarks; and www.saatchi.com/the_lovemarks_company and www.lovemarks.com, accessed September 2016.

34. "Why I Love Walt Disney World," https://ithoughtyouwereshorter.wordpress.com/2012/11/15/why-i-love-walt-disney-world/, accessed September 2016.

35. Leslie Scism, "Travelers Doesn't Want to Share Its Umbrella Logo," *Wall Street Journal*, May 25, 2015, www.wsj.com/articles/travelers-doesnt-want-to-share-its-umbrella-logo-1432598794.

36. "Best Store Brands at the Supermarket," *Consumer Reports*, April 8, 2015, www.consumerreports.org/cro/news/2015/04/the-best-store-brands/index.htm.

37. See "Best Store Brands at the Supermarket"; and Lindsey Rupp and Lauren Coleman, "How Kohl's Is Outperforming Its More Upscale Rivals," *BloombergBusiness*, March 30, 2015, www.bloomberg.com/news/articles/2015-03-30/kohl-s-backs-big-name-brands-to-boost-shares-faster-than-macy-s.

38. See Bonnie S. Benwick, "Store Brands, the (Now) Welcome Option," *Washington Post*, February 25, 2014, www.washingtonpost.com/lifestyle/food/store-brands-the-now-welcome-option/2014/02/24/be4808c6-99b0-11e3-80ac-63a8ba7f7942_story.html; Alexander Coolidge, "Kroger Using House Brands to Power Growth," *Cincinnati.com*, September 20, 2014, www.cincinnati.com/story/money/2014/09/20/kroger-using-house-brands-power-growth/15955797/; Thad Rueter, "Amazon Powers Ahead to 2015," *Internet Retailer*, December 31, 2014, www.internetretailer.com/2014/12/31/amazon-powers-ahead-2015; and Joe Springer, "Kroger to Introduce Premium Import Brand," *Supermarket News*, September 11, 2015, http://supermarketnews.com/private-label/kroger-introduce-premium-import-brand.

39. Lauren Coleman-Lochner, "Laundry Detergent Maker Want More Suds," *Bloomberg Businessweek*, October 23, 2014, www.businessweek.com/articles/2014-10-23/laundry-detergent-sales-hurt-by-water-saving-washing-machines.

40. Matthew Daneman, "Kodak Brand Is Returning to Store Shelves," *USA Today*, December 26, 2014, www.usatoday.com/story/tech/2014/12/26/kodak-branding/20910231/; and www.kodak.com/ek/US/en/Our_Company/Doing_Business_with_Kodak/Brand_Licensing.htm and www.kodak.com/ek/US/en/Home_Main_new/Brand_Partnerships/All_Licensed_Products.htm, accessed September 2016.

41. "Top 150 Global Licensors," *Global License*, May 2015, www.licensemag.com/license-global/top-150-global-licensors-1.

42. Julie Jaron, "McDonald's Wants to Speed Up with Smaller Drive-Through Menu," *Wall Street Journal*, May 11, 2015, www.wsj.com/articles/mcdonalds-simplifying-menu-adjusting-prices-1431376068; and John Kell, "McDonald's Is Working to Fix Screwups in Drive-Thru Windows," *Fortune*, November 23, 2015, http://fortune.com/2015/11/23/mcdonalds-drive-thru-windows/.

43. See "Sales of the Leading 10 Tortilla Chip Brands of the United States," *Statista*, www.statista.com/statistics/188233/top-tortilla-tostada-chip-brands/, accessed September 2016; and www.fritolay.com/our-snacks/doritos.html, accessed September 2016.

44. See Edward C. Baig, "Google's Nest to Open 'Works with Nest' Store for Nest-Compatible Smart Products," *USA Today*, October 1, 2015, www.usatoday.com/story/tech/columnist/baig/2015/10/01/googles-nest-open-works-nest-store-nest-compatible-smart-products/73136594/; and "Your Smart Home Shouldn't Be Dumb," https://nest.com/works-with-nest/, accessed September 2016.

45. For interesting lists of good and bad brand extension candidates, see Christina Austin, "See the 10 Worst Brand Extensions Currently on the Market," *Business Insider*, February 9, 2013, www.businessinsider.com/the-10-worst-brand-extensions-2013-2?op=1; and Brad Tuttle, "Why Some Brand Extensions Are Brilliant and Others Are Just Awkward," *Time*, February 7, 2013, http://business.time.com/2013/02/07/why-some-brand-extensions-are-brilliant-and-others-are-just-awkward/.

46. "100 Largest Global Marketers," *Advertising Age*, December 6, 2015, p. 26.

47. Stephen Cole, "Value of the Brand," *CA Magazine*, May 2005, pp. 39–40. Also see "The Power of Customer Service," *Fortune*, December 3, 2012, www.timeincnewsgroupcustompub.com/sections/121203_Disney.pdf; and "Customer Engagement," http://thewaltdisneycompany.com/citizenship/community/consumer-engagement, accessed September 2016.

Chapter 9

1. Shara Tibken, "Samsung Says the Future Is Here. It's Helping You Do the Laundry," *CNET*, January 7, 2016, www.cnet.com/news/samsung-says-the-internet-of-things-is-already-here-and-actually-helps-with-things-you-need/; "Samsung Receives Largest Number of Awards at IDEA 2015," August 23, 2015, http://

news.samsung.com/global/samsung-receives-largest-number-of-awards-at-idea-2015; "Apple Will Edge Closer to Samsung in Smartphone Market Share in 2016, Says TrendForce," November 19, 2015, http://press.trendforce.com/press/20151119-2179.html#rOR7UL2UdryVddwB.99; Jared Newman, "Samsung's $100 Million Internet of Things Bet Is Even Crazier Than You Think," *Fast Company*, January 28, 2015, www.fastcompany.com/3041104/app-economy/samsungs-100-million-internet-of-things-bet-is-even-crazier-than-you-think; "Samsung Introduces SleepSense, a Tracker for Better, Smarter Sleep," *CNET*, September 3, 2015, www.cnet.com/products/samsung-sleepsense/; and www.samsung.com, accessed September 2016.

2. "Apple Q4 2015 Financial Results," October 28, 2015, www.macworld.co.uk/news/apple/apple-q4-2015-financial-results-how-many-iphones-ipads-watches-macs-sold-revenue-results-3581769/; and "Share of Apple's Revenue from iPhone Sales Worldwide from 1st Quarter 2009 to 4th Quarter 2015," *Statista*, www.statista.com/statistics/253649/, accessed June 2016.

3. David Meer, Edward C. Landry, and Samrat Sharma, "Creating What Consumers Want," *Forbes*, January 26, 2015, www.forbes.com/sites/strategyand/2015/01/26/creating-what-consumers-want/.

4. See Michael Martinez, "Ford Opens Silicon Valley Innovation Center," *The Detroit News*, January 22, 2015, www.detroitnews.com/story/business/autos/ford/2015/01/22/ford-silicon-valley/22165837/; and "Chick-fil-A Innovation," Matchistic, http://matchstic.com/work/case-studies/chick-fil-a-innovation, accessed September 2016.

5. "The Ultimate Employee Collaboration Platform," www.att.com/Common/about_us/pdf/innovation_pipeline_092013.pdf, accessed September 2016.

6. See Jacob Morgan, "Five Uncommon Internal Innovation Examples," *Forbes*, April 15, 2015, www.forbes.com/sites/jacobmorgan/2015/04/08/five-uncommon-internal-innovation-examples/#477ce91c378b2ea63cd0378b; Kevin Scott, "The LinkedIn [in]cubator," December 7, 2012, http://blog.linkedin.com/2012/12/07/linkedin-incubator/; and www.linkedin.com/static?key=what_is_linkedin, accessed September 2016.

7. See Jonathan Ringen, "How LEGO Became the Apple of Toys," *Fast Company*, January 8, 2015, www.fastcompany.com/3040223/when-it-clicks-it-clicks; and https://ideas.lego.com, accessed September 2016.

8. See Jeff Beer, "Why Under Armour's Future Show Is Key to Its Brand Innovation Strategy," *Fast Company*, October 14, 2015, www.fastcocreate.com/3052298/why-under-armours-future-show-is-key-to-its-brand-innovation-strategy#13; Bruce Horovitz, "Under Armour Seeks Ideas for Its Next Big Thing," *USA Today*, October 20, 2013; and www.underarmour.com/en-us/future-show, accessed September 2016.

9. Guido Jouret, "Inside Cisco's Search for the Next Big Idea," *Harvard Business Review*, September 2009, pp. 43–45; Geoff Livingston, "Real Challenges to Crowdsourcing for Social Good," *Mashable*, October 12, 2010, http://mashable.com/2010/10/12/social-good-crowdsourcing; and "Creating Business Opportunities to the Tune of $1 Billion Plus," *Brightidea*, www.brightidea.com/Brightidea-Case-Studies-Cisco.bix, accessed September 2016.

10. See George S. Day, "Is It Real? Can We Win? Is It Worth Doing?" *Harvard Business Review*, December 2007, pp. 110–120.

11. This example is based on Tesla Motors and information obtained from www.teslamotors.com, accessed September 2016; "The Future of EV," www.chevrolet.com/culture/article/bolt-ev-concept-car.html, accessed September 2016; and "Electric Car," *Wikipedia*, http://en.wikipedia.org/wiki/Electric_car, accessed September 2016.

12. See www.carharttgroundbreakers.com and www.carhartt.com/GroundBreakersSignUpView?storeId=10201&langId=-1&catalogId=10551, accessed September 2016.

13. See Maureen Morrison, "Marketer of the Year: Taco Bell," *Advertising Age*, September 2, 2013, pp. 15–16; Susan Berfield,

"Baristas, Patrons Steaming over Starbucks VIA," *Bloomberg BusinessWeek*, November 13, 2009; and Tamara Walsh, "Starbucks Makes a Big Bet on New Product Mix in 2014," *The Motley Fool*, January 8, 2014, www.fool.com/investing/general/2014/01/08/starbucks-makes-a-big-bet-on-new-product-mix-in-20.aspx.

14. Austin Carr, "Starbucks Leap of Faith," *Fast Company*, June 2013, pp. 46–48; and "Starbucks' Mobile Transactions Top 8 Million Weekly," *PYMNTS.COM*, April 24, 2015, www.pymnts.com/news/2015/starbucks-mobile-transactions-top-8-million-weekly/.

15. See Jack Neff, "P&G Reinvents Laundry with $150 Million Tide Pods Launch," *Advertising Age*, April 26, 2011, www.adage.com/print/227208/; Sheila Shayon, "Microsoft Unleashes Global Marketing Blitz for Windows 8, New Devices," *BrandChannel*, October 25, 2012, www.brandchannel.com/home/post/2012/10/25/Microsoft-Global-Windows-8-Launch-102512.aspx; and Erik Sherman, "Apple Watch $38B Ad Spend a Drop in the Bucket," *CBS Money Watch*, April 10, 2015, www.cbsnews.com/news/apple-watch-38m-ad-spend-a-drop-in-the-bucket/.

16. "iPhone 6 & iPhone 6 Plus Arrive in 36 More Countries and Territories This Month," Apple press information, October 13, 2014, www.apple.com/pr/library/2014/10/13iPhone-6-iPhone-6-Plus-Arrive-in-36-More-Countries-and-Territories-This-Month.html.

17. See Gary P. Pisano, "You Need an Innovation Strategy," *Harvard Business Review*, June 2015, pp. 44–54; Robert G. Cooper, "Formula for Success," *Marketing Management*, March–April 2006, pp. 19–23; Christoph Fuchs and Martin Schreier, "Customer Empowerment in New Product Development," *Product Innovation Management*, January 2011, pp. 17–32; and Robert Safien, "The Lessons of Innovation," *Fast Company*, March 2012, p. 18.

18. See Brad Power and Steve Stanton, "How IBM, Intuit, and Rich Products Became More Customer-Centric," *Harvard Business Review*, June 17, 2015, https://hbr.org/2015/06/how-ibm-intuit-and-rich-products-became-more-customer-centric; Chris O'Brien, "How Intuit Became a Pioneer of 'Delight,'" *Los Angeles Times*, May 10, 2013; Brad Smith, "Intuit's CEO on Building a Design-Driven Company," *Harvard Business Review*, January–February 2015, pp. 35–38; and http://investors.intuit.com/financial-information/annual-reports/default.aspx and www.intuitlabs.com/about/, accessed September 2016.

19. This definition is based on one found in Bryan Lilly and Tammy R. Nelson, "Fads: Segmenting the Fad-Buyer Market," *Journal of Consumer Marketing*, Vol. 20, No. 3, 2003, pp. 252–265.

20. See Katya Kazakina and Robert Johnson, "A Fad's Father Seeks a Sequel," *New York Times*, May 30, 2004, www.nytimes.com; John Schwartz, "The Joy of Silly," *New York Times*, January 20, 2008, p. 5; "Drew Guarini, "11 Surprising Product Fads," *Huffington Post*, August 8, 2012, www.huffingtonpost.com/2012/08/22/product-fads_n_1819710.html#slide=1410262; and www.crazy-fads.com, accessed September 2016.

21. Based on information from Stuart Elliott, "3M Says, 'Go Ahead, Make Something of It,'" *New York Times*, January 28, 2013, www.nytimes.com/2013/01/28/business/mutfund/3m-says-go-ahead-make-something-of-it.html?pagewanted=2&tntemail0=y&_r=3&emc=tnt; and "Post-it Brand. Go Ahead," www.youtube.com/watch?v=j_zUZb4EJTk, accessed September 2016.

22. See www.crayola.com/fashionshow/, accessed September 2016.

23. Tanzina Vega, "Quaker Oats Prepares to Court Younger, More Diverse Moms," *New York Times*, December 21, 2012, p. B3; E. J. Schultz, "The Quaker Man Is Growing a Milk Mustache," *Advertising Age*, September 8, 2014, www.adage.com/print/294857; and www.quakerup.com and www.quakeroats.com, accessed September 2016.

24. See P&G Brand Divestitures Will Be Bigger than Original Targets," *Advertising Age*, February 19, 2015, www.adage.com/print/297240; and Penny Morgan, "P&G Readies Its Divestiture of Beauty Brands to Coty," Yahoo! Finance, September 22, 2015, http://finance.yahoo.com/news/p-g-readies-divestiture-beauty-183549480.html.

25. For a more comprehensive discussion of marketing strategies over the course of the PLC, see Philip Kotler and Kevin Lane Keller, *Marketing Management*, 15th ed. (Hoboken, NJ: Pearson Education, 2016), pp. 358.

26. Jaclyn Trop, "Toyota Will Pay $1.6 Billion over Faulty Accelerator Suit," *New York Times*, September 20, 2013, p. 3B; Mike Spector and Sara Randazzo, "GM Ignition-Switch Suit Is Dismissed," *Wall Street Journal*, January 22, 2016, www.wsj.com/articles/gm-ignition-switch-suit-dismissed-1453473564.

27. Information on McDonald's menus and operations found in Lucy Fancourt, Bredesen Lewis, and Nicholas Majka, "Born in the USA, Made in France: How McDonald's Succeeds in the Land of Michelin Stars," Knowledge@Wharton, January 3, 2012, http://knowledge.wharton.upenn.edu/article.cfm?articleid=2906; Richard Vines and Caroline Connan, "McDonald's Wins Over French Chef with McBaguette Sandwich," *Bloomberg*, January 15, 2013, www.bloomberg.com/news/2013-01-15/mcdonald-s-wins-over-french-chef-with-mcbaguette-sandwich.html; Rob Wile, "The True Story of How McDonald's Conquered France," *Business Insider*, August 22, 2014, www.businessinsider.com/how-mcdonalds-conquered-france-2014-8; and "McDonald's Food You Can't Get Here," *Chicago Tribune*, www.chicagotribune.com/business/ct-biz-mcdonalds-food-around-the-world,0,5168632.photogallery, accessed September 2016.

28. Information from www.db.com, accessed September 2016.

29. See "Global Powers of Retailing 2016," www2.deloitte.com/content/dam/Deloitte/global/Documents/Consumer-Business/gx-cb-global-powers-of-retailing-2016.pdf; "Walmart Corporate International," http://corporate.walmart.com/our-story/locations, accessed September 2016; and information from www.walmart.com and www.carrefour.com, accessed September 2016.

Chapter 10

1. Based on information from Kevin Kelleher, "Why Amazon Is Dominating Walmart Now," *Time*, September 18, 2015, http://time.com/4040160/amazon-walmart/; Spencer Soper, "Amazon Is Capturing Bigger Slice of U.S. Online Holiday Spending," *BloombergBusiness*, December 16, 2015, www.bloomberg.com/news/articles/2015-12-16/amazon-is-capturing-bigger-slice-of-u-s-online-holiday-spending; Tom Gara, "When Elephants Fight: The Great Wal-Mart-Amazon War of 2013," *Wall Street Journal*, March 28, 2013, http://blogs.wsj.com/corporate-intelligence/2013/03/28/when-elephants-fight-the-great-wal-mart-amazon-war-of-2013; Sally Banjo, Suzanne Kapner, and Paul Ziobro, "Can Wal-Mart Clerks Ship as Fast as Amazon Robots?," *Wall Street Journal*, December 18, 2014, www.wsj.com/articles/can-wal-mart-clerks-ship-as-fast-as-amazon-robots-1418930087; Brad Tuttle, "How Walmart Beat Amazon on Prime Day," *Money*, July 16, 2015, http://time.com/money/3961161/prime-day-amazon-walmart-review/; "U.S. E-Commerce Sales as Percent of Retail Sales," https://ycharts.com/indicators/ecommerce_sales_as_percent_retail_sales, accessed February 2016; and www.walmart.com and www.amazon.com, accessed September 2016.

2. For more on the importance of sound pricing strategy, see Thomas T. Nagle, John Hogan, and Joseph Zale, *The Strategy and Tactics of Pricing: A Guide to Growing More Profitably*, 5th ed. (Upper Saddle River, NJ: Prentice Hall, 2011), Chapter 1.

3. See Megan Willett, "How Swiss Watchmaker Patek Philippe Handcrafts Its Famous $500,000 Watches," *Business Insider*, July 12, 2013, www.businessinsider.com/how-a-patek-philippe-watch-is-made-2013-7; Stacy Perman, "Patek Philippe Crafts Its Future," *Fortune*, June 16, 2014, pp. 37–44; and www.patek.com/contents/default/en/values.html, accessed September 2016.

4. See Michael Johnsen, "Walmart Prepares to Expand Price First Launch," *Retailing Today*, August 21, 2014, www.retailingtoday.com/article/walmart-prepares-expand-price-first-nationwide; and www.walmart.com/c/brand/price-first and www.mbusa.

com/mercedes/vehicles/class/class-CLA/bodystyle-CPE, accessed September 2016.

5. See www.bose.com, accessed September 2016.

6. Accumulated production is drawn on a semilog scale so that equal distances represent the same percentage increase in output.

7. The arithmetic of markups and margins is discussed in Appendix 2, Marketing by the Numbers.

8. See Beth Kowitt, "Why Trader Joe's Needs to Stop Being So Secretive," *Fortune*, December 8, 2015, http://fortune.com/2015/12/08/trader-joes-milanos/; and www.traderjoes.com/our-story and www.traderjoes.com, accessed September 2016.

9. See www.sleepnumber.com and www.sleepnumber.com/jdpower-service-award?cm_re=Learn-_-JD-Power-_-Service-Award,accessed September 2016.

10. See Joseph Weber, "Over a Buck for Dinner? Outrageous," *BusinessWeek*, March 9, 2009, p. 57; Tom Mulier and Matthew Boyle, "Dollar Dinners from ConAgra's Threatened by Costs," *Bloomberg Businessweek*, August 19, 2010, www.businessweek.com; and Jessica Wohl, "ConAgra's Banquet Raises Prices, Brings Back Commercials," *Advertising Age*, December 9, 2015, www.adage.com/print/301684.

Chapter 11

1. Shira Ovide and Daisuke Wakabayashi, "Apple's Share of Smartphone Industry's Profits Soars to 92%," *Wall Street Journal (Online)*, July 12, 2015, www.wsj.com/articles/apples-share-of-smartphone-industrys-profits-soars-to-92-1436727458; Lance Whitney, "Thanks to Apple Watch, Smartwatch Sales Could Hit $11.5 Billion This Year," *CNet*, February 2, 2016, www.cnet.com/news/thanks-to-apple-watch-smartwatch-sales-could-hit-11-5-billion-this-year/; Harry McCracken, "Xiaomi vs. Apple," *Fast Company*, September, 2015, p. 74; Eva Dou, "Xiaomi Ends 2015 as China's Smartphone King," February 1, 2016, http://blogs.wsj.com/digits/2016/02/01/xiaomi-ends-2015-as-chinas-smartphone-king/; Charles Arthur, "Xiaomi, Vivo, and Oppo: The Challengers Leading China's Charge against Apple," *The Guardian*, January 30, 2016, www.theguardian.com/technology/2016/jan/30/apple-xiaomi-vivo-oppo-challengers-leading-charge-china; and http://fortune.com/fortune500/ and http://investor.apple.com/financials.cfm, accessed October 2016.

2. Ashlee Vance, "Smartphone Margins," *Bloomberg Businessweek*, October 12–18, 2015, pp. 33–34; and Jamal Carnette, "Who Is the World's Fastest-Growing Smartphone Vendor? (Hint: It's Not Apple or Samsung)," *The Motley Fool*, February 1, 2016, www.fool.com/investing/general/2016/02/01/who-is-the-worlds-fastest-growing-smartphone-vendo.aspx.

3. See David Sax, "Hang $99.99," *Bloomberg Businessweek*, November 2–8, 2015, pp. 43–44; and www.wavestormboards.com/about-us/, accessed October 2016.

4. Karis Hustad, "Kindle Fire HDX Keeps Amazon's Low Price, Adds Extra Features," *Christian Science Monitor*, September 26, 2013, www.csmonitor.com/Innovation/2013/0926/Kindle-Fire-HDX-keeps-Amazon-s-low-price-adds-extra-features; and David Gilbert, "Fire Tablet vs. iPad: Why Amazon's $50 Tablet Is Betting Content Is King," *IBT*, September 17, 2015, www.ibtimes.com/fire-tablet-vs-ipad-why-amazons-50-tablet-betting-content-king-2102347.

5. See information found at http://investor.keuriggreenmountain.com/annuals-proxies.cfm, accessed October 2016.

6. See Kathleen Elkins, "Using K-Cups Costs up to 5 Times More Than Getting Coffee from a Pot," *Business Insider*, March 13, 2015, www.businessinsider.com/keurig-cups-are-expensive-2015-3.

7. See Bill Campbell, "Cheese to the Rescue: Surprising Spray Melts Road Ice," *NPR*, January 21, 2014, www.npr.org/blogs/thetwo-way/2014/01/21/264562529/cheese-to-the-rescue-surprising-spray-melts-road-ice; "Four Foods That Help Prevent Slippery

Roads," *AccuWeather.com*, January 22, 2015, www.accuweather.com/en/weather-news/beet-cheese-and-potatoes-roads/22447484; and "Laval to Use Beets to Keep Roads Clear This Winter," *CBC News*, December 2, 2015, www.cbc.ca/news/canada/montreal/laval-beets-clear-snow-ice-1.3346675.

8. See Danielle Paquette, "Why You Should Always Buy the Men's Version of Almost Anything," *Washington Post*, December 22, 2015, www.washingtonpost.com/news/wonk/wp/2015/12/22/women-really-do-pay-more-for-razors-and-almost-everything-else/; and Rafi Mohammed, "You Can Charge Women More, but Should You?" *Harvard Business Review*, January 29, 2016, https://hbr.org/2016/01/you-can-charge-women-more-but-should-you?cm_sp=Article-_-Links-_-Comment.

9. For this and other examples and explanations, see Peter Coy, "Why the Price Is Rarely Right," *Bloomberg Businessweek*, February 1 & 8, 2010, pp. 77–78; and Utpal Dholakia, "What Shoppers Should Know about Reference Prices," *Psychology Today*, September 8, 2015, www.psychologytoday.com/blog/the-science-behind-behavior/201509/what-shoppers-should-know-about-reference-prices.

10. See Anthony Allred, E. K. Valentin, and Goutam Chakraborty, "Pricing Risky Services: Preference and Quality Considerations," *Journal of Product and Brand Management*, Vol. 19, No. 1, 2010, p. 54; Kenneth C. Manning and David E. Sprott, "Price Endings, Left-Digit Effects, and Choice," *Journal of Consumer Research*, August 2009, pp. 328–336; Travis Nichols, "A Penny Saved: Psychological Pricing," *Gumroad*, October 18, 2013, http://blog.gumroad.com/post/64417917582/a-penny-saved-psychological-pricing; and Bouree Lam, "The Psychological Difference between $12.00 and $11.67," *The Atlantic*, January 30, 2015, www.theatlantic.com/business/archive/2015/01/the-psychological-difference-between-1200-and-1167/384993/.

11. Trefis Team, "Bed Bath & Beyond Falls on Sales Miss, but Profit Decline Is a Bigger Problem," *Forbes*, January 9, 2015, www.forbes.com/sites/greatspeculations/2015/01/09/bed-bath-beyond-falls-on-sales-miss-but-profit-decline-is-a-bigger-problem/; and Sarah Halzack, "The Trouble with Those 20 Percent Off Coupons from Bed Bath & Beyond," *Washington Post*, September 30, 2015, www.washingtonpost.com/news/business/wp/2015/09/30/the-trouble-with-those-20-percent-off-coupons-from-bed-bath-beyond/.

12. See Justin D. Martin, "Dynamic Pricing: Internet Retailers Are Treating Us Like Foreign Tourists in Egypt," *Christian Science Monitor*, January 7, 2011; and Mike Southon, "Time to Ensure the Price Is Right," *Financial Times*, January 21, 2012, p. 30.

13. Jack Nicas, "Now Prices Can Change from Minute to Minute," *Wall Street Journal*, December 14, 2015, www.wsj.com/articles/now-prices-can-change-from-minute-to-minute-1450057990.

14. See Natalie Zmuda, "Best Buy Tries to Co-Opt 'Showrooming' This Holiday Season," *Advertising Age*, October 29, 2013, http://adage.com/print/244993/; and "How Best Buy Beat the Infamous Showrooming Effect," *The Motley Fool*, September 8, 2015, www.fool.com/investing/general/2015/09/08/how-best-buy-beat-the-infamous-show-rooming-effect.aspx.

15. Liza Lin, "Shhh…Luxury Goods Are Discounted in China," *Bloomberg Businessweek*, August 21, 2014, pp. 28–29.

16. Scheherazade Daneshkhu, "Emerging Market Woes Ease for Unilever but Deepen for Diageo," *FT.com*, April 16, 2015, www.ft.com/cms/s/0/c24dd624-e450-11e4-a4de-00144feab7de.html#axzz3vikZH9hh.

17. "Xiaomi Ends 2015 as China's Smartphone King," *Wall Street Journal*, February 1, 2016, http://blogs.wsj.com/digits/2016/02/01/xiaomi-ends-2015-as-chinas-smartphone-king/; and Charles Arthur, "Xiaomi, Vivo, and Oppo: The Challengers Leading China's Charge against Apple," *The Guardian*, January 30, 2016, www.theguardian.com/technology/2016/jan/30/apple-xiaomi-vivo-oppo-challengers-leading-charge-china.

18. See Serena Ng, "Toilet-Tissue 'Desheeting' Shrinks Rolls, Plumps Margins," *Wall Street Journal*, July 24, 2013, http://online.wsj.com/news/articles/SB10001424127887323971204578626223494483866; Serena Ng, "At P&G, New Tide Comes In, Old Price Goes Up," *Wall Street Journal*, February 10, 2014, http://online.wsj.com/news/articles/SB1000142405270230445090457936885298030157 2; and Conor Pope, "Shrinkflation: When Products Get Smaller but the Prices Don't," *The Irish Times*, April 27, 2015, www.irishtimes.com/news/consumer/shrinkflation-when-products-get-smaller-but-the-prices-don-t-1.2187869.

19. For discussions of these issues, see Dhruv Grewal and Larry D. Compeau, "Pricing and Public Policy: A Research Agenda and Overview of the Special Issue," *Journal of Public Policy and Marketing*, Spring 1999, pp. 3–10; Walter L. Baker, Michael V. Marn, and Craig C. Zawada, *The Price Advantage* (Hoboken, NJ: John Wiley & Sons, 2010), Appendix 2; and Thomas T. Nagle, John Hogan, and Joseph Zale, *The Strategy and Tactics of Pricing: A Guide to Growing More Profitably*, 5th ed. (Upper Saddle River, NJ: Prentice Hall, 2011).

20. See Joe Rossignol, "Apple Loses Appeal in E-books Price Fixing Lawsuit, Ordered to Pay $450 Million Fine," *MacRumors*, June 30, 2015, www.macrumors.com/2015/06/30/apple-ebooks-appeal-rejected-450m-fine; "Airlines Accused of Price-Fixing Conspiracy in Dallas Class-Action Lawsuit," *PRNewswire*, July 8, 2015, www.prnewswire.com/news-releases/airlines-accused-of-price-fixing-conspiracy-in-dallas-class-action-lawsuit-300110405.html.

21. Roger Lowenstein, "Why Amazon Monopoly Accusations Deserve a Closer Look," *Fortune*, July 23, 2015, http://fortune.com/2015/07/23/why-amazon-monopoly-accusations-deserve-a-closer-look/.

22. Jonathan Stempel, "Michael Kors Settles U.S. Lawsuit Alleging Deceptive Price Tags," *Reuters*, June 12, 2015, www.reuters.com/article/us-michaelkors-settlement-idUSKBN0OS2AU20150612.

23. "FTC Guides against Deceptive Pricing," www.ecfr.gov/cgi-bin/text-idx?c=ecfr&sid=dfafb89837c306cf5b010b5bde15f041&rgn=div5&view=text&node=16:1.0.1.2.16&idno=16, accessed October 2016.

Chapter 12

1. Eric Newcomer and Ellen Huet, "Battling Lyft for Market Share, Uber Again Turns to Discounting," *Skift*, January 22, 2016, http://skift.com/2016/01/22/battling-lyft-for-market-share-uber-again-turns-to-discounting/; Alan Murray, "Uber-nomics," *Fortune*, January, 2015, p. 6; Jim Edwards, "Uber Has Changed My Life and as God Is My Witness I Will Never Take a Taxi Again," *Business Insider*, January 22, 2014, www.businessinsider.com/uber-has-changed-my-life-and-as-god-is-my-witness-i-will-never-take-a-taxi-again-where-available-2014-1#ixzz3TYF7ZY29; Brad Stone, "Invasion of the Taxi Snatchers: Uber Leads an Industry's Disruption," *Businessweek*, February 20, 2014, pp. 38–42; Tracey Lien, "Lyft Defies Predictions by Continuing to Grow as a Rival to Uber," *Los Angeles Times*, January 5, 2016, www.latimes.com/business/technology/la-fi-0105-lyft-growth-20160105-story.html; Jon Russell, "Uber Makes First Big Expansion in China as It Aims to Reach 100 Cities in 2016," *Techcrunch*, January 18, 2016, http://techcrunch.com/2016/01/18/uber-sichuan-expansion/; and www.uber.com/our-story, accessed October 2016.

2. See Bryan Gruley and Leslie Patton, "McRevolt: The Frustrating Life of the McDonald's Franchisee: Not Lovin' It," *Bloomberg Business*, September 16, 2015, www.bloomberg.com/features/2015-mcdonalds-franchises/; "Is McDonald's Broken? Franchisees Are Furious," *Yahoo! Finance*, April 15, 2015, http://finance.yahoo.com/news/mcdonalds-broken-franchisees-furious-133644537.html; and Paul R. La Monica, "McDonald's: A Great American McComeback?" *CNN Money*, January 22, 2016, http://money.cnn.com/2016/01/22/investing/mcdonalds-earnings-comeback/.

3. See "The Kroger Co. Fact Book," http://ir.kroger.com/CorporateProfile.aspx?iid=4004136, accessed October 2016.

4. See "Is Competition in the Eyewear Segment Preying Over Luxottica's Bottom Line?" GuruFocus, February 24, 2015, www.gurufocus.com/news/318329; and www.luxottica.com and luxottica.com/en/company/quick_view, October 2016.

5. "Franchise Business Economic Outlook for 2016," January 2016, http://emarket.franchise.org/FranchiseOutlookJan2016.pdf.

6. See "Two Men and a Truck Wraps Up Successful 2014, Fuels Future Expansion in 2015," January 29, 2015, www.twomenandatruck.com/details.aspx?p=1EC0C69A41A54054&ppid=59896&naid=C0CACB36C71828B8; and www.twomenandatruck.com/history-of-two-men-and-a-truck, accessed October 2016.

7. See Eric Platt, "22 Companies That Are Addicted to Walmart," June 13, 2012, Business Insider, www.businessinsider.com/22-companies-who-are-completely-addicted-to-walmart-2012-6#; Dan Mitchell, "Say Goodbye to Your Supermarket," Fortune, March 14, 2014, http://fortune.com/2014/03/14/say-goodbye-to-your-supermarket/; and "Clorox CEO Shares Roadmap for Growth with Shareholders," Bizjournals.com, November 18, 2015, www.bizjournals.com/sanfrancisco/blog/2015/11/clorox-ceo-growth-clx-walmart-amazon-wmt-amzn-tgt.html.

8. See www.staralliance.com, www.oneworld.com, and www.skyteam.com, accessed October 2016.

9. See Joan E. Solsman, "Streaming Music Drowns Out CD Sales in US for the First Time," Cnet, March 19, 2015, www.cnet.com/news/streaming-music-drowns-out-us-cd-sales-for-the-first-time/; John Paul Titlow, "5 Ways Streaming Music Will Change in 2016," Fast Company, December 30, 2015, www.fastcompany.com/3054776/5-ways-streaming-music-will-change-in-2016; and Kimberly Kurimski, "Best Streaming Service," WeRockYourWeb, January 13, 2016, www.werockyourweb.com/spotify-vs-rhapsody-vs-pandora-vs-google-music-vs-rdio-vs-mog/.

10. Todd Bishop, "Nook Holiday Sales Plunge Another 25% to $41M as Barnes & Noble Falls Further Behind Amazon Kindle," GeekWire, January 7, 2016, www.geekwire.com/2016/nook-holiday-sales-fall-another-25-to-41-million-as-barnes-nobles-e-reader-business-keeps-slipping/.

11. Lawrence Frost, "Volvo to Launch Online Car Sales in Marketing Shift," Reuters, December 15, 2014, www.reuters.com/article/2014/12/15/us-volvo-internet-idUSKBN0JT0D020141215; and Diana Kuryiko, "Volvo Dealers Are Hungry for the Redesigned XC90," Automotive News, January 25, 2015, www.autonews.com/article/20150123/RETAIL06/301249995/volvo-dealers-are-hungry-for-the-redesigned-xc90.

12. Brad Tuttle, "America's Most Popular Supermarket Is Also Its Least Loved," Money, April 2, 2015, http://time.com/money/3769044/walmart-lowest-rated-groceries/.

13. See Colleen Kelleher, "Wegmans Top-Ranked Grocery in Consumer Reports," WTOP, April 2, 2015, http://wtop.com/food/2015/04/wegmans-top-ranked-consumer-reports-survey/; Ashley Lutz, "17 Reasons Why Wegmans Is America's Best Grocery Store," Business Insider, April 2, 2014, www.businessinsider.com/wegmans-grocery-is-americas-best-2014-4; "The 100 Best Companies to Work For," Fortune, March 15, 2016, pp. 143+; and "Wegmans," Yelp, www.yelp.com/biz/wegmans-fairfax, accessed October 2016.

14. See http://new.pamperedchef.com/company-facts and www.stelladot.com/trunkshow, accessed October 2016.

15. See Steven Butler, "Walmart China: Hitting Headwinds," CNNMoney, January 22, 2015, http://money.cnn.com/2015/01/22/news/economy/ozy-china-walmart/; and Greg Knowler, "China Logistics Reaps Rewards of Rising Trade, Domestic Consumption," Journal of Commerce, July 2, 2015, www.joc.com/international-logistics/china-logistics-reaps-rewards-rising-trade-domestic-consumption-barclays-says_20150702.html.

16. Based on information from Julie Jargon, "Asia Delivers for McDonald's," Wall Street Journal, December 13, 2011, http://online.wsj.com/article/SB10001424052970204397704577707498215 1549316.html; "Feel Like a Burger? Dial M for McDonald's Japan,"

Asia Pulse, January 23, 2012; and McDonald's annual reports, www.aboutmcdonalds.com/mcd/investors/annual_reports.html, accessed October 2016.

17. See Phil Wahba, "The Change Agent Inside CVS," Fortune, September 11, 2015, http://fortune.com/2015/09/11/cvs-health-helena-foulkes/; and Hope Nguyen, "Why We Didn't Quit CVS When CVS Quit Tobacco," NetBase, February 2016, http://info.cvscaremark.com/cvs-insights/cvs-quits.

18. See Marcus Williams, "Cutting Logistics Costs Key to GM Profit Targets," Automotive Logistics, October 2014, http://automotivelogistics.media/news/cutting-logistics-costs-key-to-gm-profit-targets; and Rosalyn Wilson, "26th Annual State of Logistics Report: Freight Moves the Economy," July 1, 2015, www.logisticsmgmt.com/article/26th_annual_state_of_logistics_freight_moves_the_economy.

19. Andy Brack, "Piggly Wiggly Center Offers Info-Packed Field Trip," Charleston Currents, January 4, 2010, www.charlestoncurrents.com/issue/10_issues/10.0104.htm; and information from http://en.wikipedia.org/wiki/Piggly_wiggly and http://corporate.walmart.com/_news_/news-archive/2005/01/07/our-retail-divisions, accessed October 2016.

20. Ian Lifshitz, "Sustainable Supply Chains and Bottom Lines—The Two Are No Longer Mutually Exclusive," Supply Demand Chain Executive, January 4, 2016, www.sdcexec.com/article/12154417/sustainable-supply-chains-and-bottom-lines-the-two-are-no-longer-mutually-exclusive.

21. Jessica Stillman, "Green Cred: Sustainability a Cost-Cutting Move for Suppliers," Forbes, December 11, 2012, www.forbes.com/sites/ups/2012/12/11/green-cred-sustainability-a-cost-cutting-move-for-suppliers/; and www.apparelcoalition.org/higgindex/, www.nikeresponsibility.com/, and www.nikeresponsibility.com/report/content/chapter/manufacturing, accessed October 2016.

22. Katherine Scott, "Amazon Expects to Shatter Its Own Cyber Monday Sales Record," November 30, 2015, http://6abc.com/shopping/amazon-expects-to-shatter-cyber-monday-records/1103662/; and "Working at Amazon," www.amazon.com/gp/help/customer/display.html?nodeId=200787540&view-type=stand-alone, accessed January 2016.

23. See Donna Tam, "Meet Amazon's Busiest Employee—the Kiva Robot," CNET, November 30, 2014, www.cnet.com/news/meet-amazons-busiest-employee-the-kiva-robot/; Eugene Kim, "Amazon Is Now Using a Whole Lot More of the Robots from the Company It Bought for $775 Million," Business Insider, October 22, 2015, www.businessinsider.com/amazon-doubled-the-number-of-kiva-robots-2015-10; and www.amazonrobotics.com, accessed October 2016.

24. Bureau of Transportation Statistics, "Pocket Guide to Transportation 2016," January 2016, http://www.rita.dot.gov/bts/sites/rita.dot.gov.bts/files/publications/pocket_guide_to_transportation/2016.

25. See Walmart's supplier requirements at http://corporate.walmart.com/suppliers, accessed October 2016.

26. www.oracle.com/webfolder/assets/infographics/value-chain/index.html, accessed October 2016.

27. For this and other UPS examples and information, see "Toshiba Laptop Repair," accessed at http://pressroom.ups.com/Video/Toshiba+Laptop+Repair, May 2013; and www.thenewlogistics.com and www.ups.com/content/us/en/about/facts/worldwide.html, accessed October 2016.

28. "3PL Customers Report Identifies Service Trends, 3PL Market Segment Sizes and Growth Rates," Armstrong & Associates, Inc., July 11, 2013, www.3plogistics.com/PR_3PL_Customers-2013.htm. Also see Robert C. Lieb, "25 Years of Third-Party Logistics Research & Studies," Supply Chain 247, December 31, 2014, http://www.supplychain247.com/article/25_years_of_third-party_logistics_research.

29. See John Langley Jr., "2016 Third-Party Logistics Study: The State of Logistics Outsourcing," Capgemini Consulting, www.kornferry.com/media/sidebar_downloads/2016_3PL_Study.pdf, accessed October 2016.

Chapter 13

1. Based on information from "Fortune Global 500," *Fortune,* http://fortune.com/global500/, accessed July 2016; Bryan O'Keefe, "The Chosen One," *Fortune,* June 15, 2015, pp. 134–144; Michael Barbano and Stuart Elliott, "Clinging to Its Roots, Wal-Mart Steps Back from an Edgy, New Image," *New York Times,* December 10, 2006, www.nytimes.com/2006/12/10/business/worldbusiness/10iht-walmart.3845671.html; "Top 250 Global Retailers," *National Retail Federation,* https://nrf.com/2016/global250-table, accessed July 2016; Phil Whaba, "Walmart Targets Affluent Shoppers to Shake Funk," *Fortune,* October 14, 2015, http://fortune.com/2015/10/14/walmart-affluent-consumers/; and annual reports and other information found at http://news.walmart.com/walmart-facts/corporate-financial-fact-sheet, http://corporate.walmart.com/newsroom/company-facts, and www.corporate.walmart.com, accessed October 2016.

2. See "Monthly and Annual Retail Trade," U.S. Census Bureau, www.census.gov/retail/, accessed October 2016.

3. See "Just Released: P&G 2014 Annual Report," P&G Corporate Newsroom, August 20, 2014, http://news.pg.com/blog/company-strategy/just-released-pg-2014-annual-report; "Procter & Gamble," *Growth Champions,* March 2016, http://growthchampions.org/growth-champions/procter-gamble/; and "ZMOT," *Google Digital Services,* www.zeromomentoftruth.com/, accessed October 2016.

4. For more on digital aspects of shopper marketing and omni-channel retailing, see Lisa R. Melsted, "Retailers Turn to Omnichannel Strategies to Remain Competitive," *Forbes,* February 9, 2015, www.forbes.com/sites/samsungbusiness/2015/02/09/retailers-turn-to-omnichannel-strategies-to-remain-competitive/print/; Susie Stulz, "The Splintered Moment of Truth," *Adweek,* July 22, 2015, pp. S9–S10; Jordy Leiser, "Think Tank: Why an Omnichannel Approach Can Help Retail Escape the Amazon," *WWD,* January 12, 2016, wwd.com/retail-news/forecasts-analysis/blazing-the-amazon-and-why-an-omnichannel-approach-can-help-retail-10312172/; and www.shoppermarketingmag.com/home/, accessed May 2016.

5. John Russell, "Grocery Wars Certain to Flair Up on North Side," *IndyStar,* January 27, 2015, www.indystar.com/story/news/2015/01/25/grocery-wars-certain-flare-north-side/22125353/.

6. See Jon Springer, "Kroger to Unveil New Fresh Concept: 'Main & Vine,'" *Supermarket News,* December 21, 2015, http://supermarketnews.com/kroger/kroger-unveil-new-fresh-concept-main-vine; and www.mainandvineshop.com/about/, accessed October 2016.

7. "How to Cater to the Fill-In Shopper," *Convenience Store Decisions,* August 14, 2015, www.cstoredecisions.com/2015/08/14/how-to-cater-to-the-fill-in-shopper/; "The Convenience Top 101," *Convenience Store and Fuel News,* January 7, 2016, www.cspnet.com/industry-news-analysis/top-convenience-stores/retailer/kroger-co-convenience-division-2016; and www.loafnjug.com/topic/in-our-stores, accessed October 2016.

8. http://corporate.walmart.com/our-story/our-business/locations/#/united-states, accessed June 2016; and "Supermarket Facts," www.fmi.org/research-resources/supermarket-facts, accessed October 2016.

9. See Mike Troy, "Dollar General to Open 730 Stores in 2015 as It Accelerates Expansion," *Chain Store Age,* March 12, 2015, www.chainstoreage.com/article/dollar-general-open-730-stores-2015-it-accelerates-expansion; Christopher Matthews, "Will Dollar Stores Rule the Retail World?" *Time,* April 1, 2013, http://business.time.com/2013/04/01/will-dollar-stores-rule-the-retail-world/; Wayne Duggan, "Dollar General Seen as Winner from Wal-Mart Store Closures," *Yahoo! Finance,* January 18, 2016, http://finance.yahoo.com/news/dollar-general-seen-winner-wal-181228126.html; and http://investor.shareholder.com/dollar/financials.cfm, accessed October 2016.

10. "How We Do It," http://tjmaxx.tjx.com/store/jump/topic/how-we-do-it/2400087, accessed October 2016.

11. Phil Wahba, "Macy's Mull Taking on T.J. Maxx, Nordstrom Rack in "Off-Price" Wars," *Fortune,* January 8, 2015, http://fortune.com/2015/01/08/macys-outlet-off-price/.

12. See "H&R Block," *Entrepreneur,* http://www.entrepreneur.com/franchises/hrblock/330827, accessed October 2016; and www.hrblock.com/corporate/tax-franchise/index.html, accessed October 2016.

13. Company and franchising information from "2015 Franchise Times Top 200 Franchise Systems," *Franchise Times,* October 2014, www.franchisetimes.com/Top-200/; www.score.org/resources/should-i-buy-franchise; and www.aboutmcdonalds.com/mcd/our_company.html, accessed October 2016.

14. Kristina Monllos, "The Gap's Biggest Problem Is That It Lost Its Brand Identity," *Adweek,* June 17, 2015, www.adweek.com/print/165367; Natalie Zmuda, "Under New Management, Gap Must Figure Out Way to Fix a Faded Icon," *Advertising Age,* February 7, 2011, pp. 2–3; Hannah Marriott, "Muddying the Gap: How the US Clothing Chain Has Failed to Uphold Its Identity," *Guardian,* June 19, 2015, www.theguardian.com/business/2015/jun/19/muddying-the-gap-us-clothing-chain-failed-uphold-identity-normcore; and www.gapinc.com, accessed June 2016.

15. Dina Berrta, "The Power List: Lynsi Snyder—Growing the Cult Chain Slow and Steady," *Nation's Restaurant News,* January 19, 2016, http://nrn.com/power-list-2016-Lynsi-Snyder; Robert Klara, "How In-N-Out Became the Small Burger Chain with the Massive Following," *Adweek,* November 17, 2015, www.adweek.com/print/168120; "In-N-Out Burger," http://nrn.com/top-100/n-out-burger, accessed October 2016, and www.in-n-out.com/, accessed October 2016.

16. See Betsy Riley, "A Sneak Peek at Buckhead's New Restoration Hardware Gallery," *Atlanta Magazine,* November 20, 2014, www.atlantamagazine.com/decorating/a-sneak-peek-at-buckheads-new-restoration-hardware-gallery/; Richard Mullins, "Restoration Hardware Building Meg-Mansion 'Gallery' in Tampa," *Tampa Tribune,* January 4, 2015, www.tbo.com/news/business/restoration-hardware-building-mega-mansion-gallery-in-tampa-20150104/; and Bridget Brennan, "Would You Like Champagne with That Sofa? Restoration Hardware Bets Big on Experiential Retail," *Forbes,* November 13, 2015, www.forbes.com/sites/bridgetbrennan/2015/11/13/would-you-like-champagne-with-that-sofa-restoration-hardware-bets-big-on-experiential-retail/#7b46683e579e67def966579e; and www.restorationhardware.com/content/promo.jsp?id=557012, accessed October 2016.

17. See Justine Sharrock, "How Manufactured Smells Are Making People Shop Longer and Kill Better," *BuzzFeed,* March 15, 2013, www.buzzfeed.com/justinesharrock/how-manufactured-smells-are-making-people-shop-longer-and-ki; Alexandra Sifferlin, "My Nose Made Me Buy It," *Time,* December 16, 2013, http://healthland.time.com/2013/12/16/my-nose-made-me-buy-it-how-retailers-use-smell-and-other-tricks-to-get-you-to-spend-spend-spend/; Sarah Nassauer, "Using Scent as a Marketing Tool, Stores Hope It—and Shoppers—Will Linger," *Wall Street Journal,* May 20, 2014, www.wsj.com/articles/SB10001424052702303468704579573953132979382; and www.scentair.com, accessed October 2016.

18. See various social media sites for Walmart and Fairway, accessed October 2016.

19. "CVS/pharmacy Revolutionizes the Way Customers Experience the Sales Circular with Launch of myWeekly Ad," October 17, 2013, http://info.cvscaremark.com/newsroom/press-releases/cvspharmacy-revolutionizes-way-customers-experience-sales-circular-launch; Stuart Elliott, "For CVS Regulars, Ads Tailored Just to Them," *New York Times,* October 10, 2013, www.nytimes.com/2013/10/11/business/media/for-cvs-regulars-ads-tailored-just-to-them.html?_r=0; and www.cvs.com, accessed October 2016.

20. For definitions of these and other types of shopping centers, see "Dictionary," *American Marketing Association,*

www.marketingpower.com/_layouts/Dictionary.aspx, accessed October 2016.

21. Nelson D. Schwartz, "The Economics (and Nostalgia) of Dead Malls," *New York Times,* January 3, 2015, www.nytimes.com/2015/01/04/business/the-economics-and-nostalgia-of-dead-malls.html; and Christine Birkner, "Retail's White Elephants," *Marketing News,* April 2015, pp. 48–59.

22. Jennifer Reingold and Phil Wahba, "Where Have All the Shopper Gone?" *Fortune,* September 3, 2014, http://fortune.com/2014/09/03/where-have-all-the-shoppers-gone/.

23. See Rick Brockmann, "Nike to Open Pop-Up Shop Near Barclays for NBA's All-Star Weekend," *The Real Deal,* February 9, 2015; and Lydia Dishman, "How American Department Stores Are Fighting Extinction," *Fortune,* January 20, 2016, http://fortune.com/2016/01/20/department-stores-reinvention/.

24. See www.gilt.com and www.zulily.com, accessed October 2016.

25. See www.rpminc.com/leading-brands/consumer-brands, accessed October 2016.

26. Matt Linder, "Global E-Commerce Sales Set to Grow 25% in 2015," *Internet Retailer,* July 29, 2015, www.internetretailer.com/2015/07/29/global-e-commerce-set-grow-25-2015; "U.S. E-Commerce Sales as Percent of Retail Sales," https://ycharts.com/indicators/ecommerce_sales_as_percent_retail_sales, accessed October 2016; and "U.S Retail Sales Growth," www.multpl.com/us-retail-sales-growth, accessed October 2016.

27. See Chuck Martin, "42% Mobile Commerce Growth; 33% Buy via Smartphone," *MediaPost,* February 20, 2015, http://www.mediapost.com/publications/article/244163/42-mobile-commerce-growth-33-buy-via-smartphone.html.

28. Lauren Johnson, "Target Turns Its Stores into One Big Mobile Game for the Holidays," *Adweek,* December 2, 2014, www.adweek.com/print/161727; and Greg Sterling, "Survey 90 Percent of Retail Shopper Use Smartphones in Stores," *MarketingLand,* July 20, 2015, http://marketingland.com/survey-90-percent-of-retail-shoppers-use-smartphones-in-stores-135759.

29. David P. Schulz, "Top 100 Retailers 2015," *NRF,* July 1, 2015, https://nrf.com/news/top-100-retailers-2015.

30. David P. Schulz, "Top 100 Retailers 2015," *NRF,* July 1, 2015, https://nrf.com/news/top-100-retailers-2015; George Anderson, "Will Omnichannel Keep Macy's Ahead of Amazon," *Forbes,* August 9, 2015, www.forbes.com/sites/retailwire/2015/08/09/will-omnichannel-keep-macys-ahead-of-amazon/2/#385905153143; and "Macy's Reorganizes for Omni-Channel Success," August 2015, www.thinkwithgoogle.com/interviews/macys-reorganizes-for-omni-channel-success.html.

31. See Jacqueline Renfrow, "AT&T Turns Michigan Avenue Flagship into a Museum," *Fierce Retail,* March 11, 2015, www.fierceretail.com/story/att-turns-michigan-avenue-flagship-museum/2015-03-11; Christopher Heine, "The Store of the Future Has Arrived," *Adweek,* June 3, 2013, www.adweek.com/print/149900; and www.callison.com/projects/att-%E2%80%93-michigan-avenue, accessed October 2016.

32. Brad Tuttle, "The Creepy New Way Macy's Tempts You to Make Impulse Purchases," *Time,* September 26, 2014, http://time.com/money/3432693/macys-shopkick-ibeacon/; and Kenny Kline, "How Bluetooth Beacons Will Transform Retail in 2016," *Huffington Post,* January 15, 2016, www.huffingtonpost.com/kenny-kline/how-bluetooth-beacons-wil_b_8982720.html.

33. See Sarah Halzack, "Ever Wanted to Base Jump? North Face Wants You to Try It—in Its Stores," *Washington Post,* www.washingtonpost.com/business/economy/virtual-reality-the-latest-weapon-in-the-battle-for-your-shopping-dollars/2015/05/10/07639f8c-e976-11e4-9767-6276fc9b0ada_story.html; and John Gaudiosi, "Audi Drives Virtual Reality Showroom with HTC Vive," *Fortune,* January 8, 2016, http://fortune.com/2016/01/08/audi-showroom-uses-vr/.

34. "Green MashUP: 7 Trends Transforming Retail Sustainability," *The Fifth Estate,* February 17, 2015, www.thefifthestate.com.au/business/trends/green-mashup-7-trends-transforming-

retail-sustainability/71455; and "The IKEA Group Sustainability Report," www.ikea.com/ms/en_US/pdf/sustainability_report/sustainability_report_2014.pdf accessed February 2016.

35. See www.staples.com/sbd/cre/marketing/easy-on-the-planet/recycling-and-eco-services.html, accessed October 2016.

36. See "Global Powers of Retailing 2016," *Deloitte,* January 2016, accessed at www2.deloitte.com/content/dam/Deloitte/global/Documents/Consumer-Business/gx-cb-global-powers-of-retailing-2016.pdf.

37. Grainger facts and other information are from the "Grainger: Beyond the Box Fact Book," accessed at http://invest.grainger.com/phoenix.zhtml?c=76754&p=irol-irFactBook and www.grainger.com, accessed October 2016.

38. Paul Demery, "W.W. Grainers Close in on Capturing 40% of Sales Online," *Internet Retailer,* www.top500guide.com/top-500/the-top-500-list, April 16, 2015; and www.grainger.com, accessed October 2016.

39. See Sysco 2015 Annual Report, www.sysco.com/aboutus/OnlineAnnual2015/Sysco-2015-Annual-Report.html; and www.sysco.com/, accessed October 2016.

40. Facts from "2014 Power 50," http://supermarketnews.com/2014-power-50-clickable-list, accessed June 2015; and www.supervalu.com, accessed October 2016.

Chapter 14

1. Tim Nudd, "Snickers Swaps Out Brand Name for Hunger Symptoms on Painfully Honest Packaging," *Adweek,* September 21, 2015, www.adweek.com/print/167061; Alfred Maskeroni, "Snickers' Brady Bunch Ad Is Here, and It's One of the Funniest Super Bowl Spots Ever," *Ad Week,* January 20, 2015, www.adweek.com/adfreak/snickers-brady-bunch-ad-here-and-its-one-funniest-super-bowl-spots-ever-162620; E. J. Schultz, "Behind the Snickers Campaign That Launched a Global Comeback," *Advertising Age,* October 4, 2013, www.adage.com/print/244593; Robert Klara, "How Snickers Fired a Quarterback, Hired a Zebra, and Tweaked One of Advertising's Most Famous Tag Lines," *Adweek,* February 27, 2014, www.adweek.com/print/155873; Andrea Jincks, "Snickers Executes Digital 'You're Not YouTube' Campaign & UGC Contest," Moosylvania, April 9, 2015, http://moosylvania.com/tracker/snickers-executes-digital-youre-not-youtube-campaign-ugc-contest/; and www.snickers.com, www.mars.com, www.youtube.com/snickers, and www.facebook.com/snickers, accessed October 2016.

2. For other definitions, see www.ama.org/resources/Pages/Dictionary.aspx, accessed October 2016.

3. "Digital Ad Spending to Surpass TV Next Year," *eMarketer,* March 8, 2016, www.emarketer.com/Article/Digital-Ad-Spending-Surpass-TV-Next-Year/1013671; Avi Dan, "Why P&G Is Quickly Shifting to a Digital-First Approach to Building Brands," *Forbes,* March 8, 2015, www.forbes.com/sites/avidan/2015/03/12/why-pg-is-quickly-shifting-to-a-digital-first-approach-to-building-brands/2/#552e75a03b68; Lara O'Reilly, "Almost a Quarter of Unilever's $8 Billion Ad Budget Is Now Spent on Digital," *Business Insider,* January 28, 2016, www.businessinsider.com/unilever-digital-advertising-budget-up-to-24-2016-1.

4. See Andrew Adam Newman, "With a French Accent, a Soap Brand Tells a Tale of Well-Scrubbed Lovers," *New York Times,* March 21, 2014, p. B4; Stuart Elliott, "Ad for Method Celebrates the Madness," *New York Times,* March 12, 2012, p. B1; and www.methodhome.com/cleanhappy/ and www.youtube.com/user/peopleagainstdirty, accessed October 2016.

5. Lesley Bielby, "The 'A' Word—Does Advertising Still Exist?" *Advertising Age,* April 22, 2016, www.adage.com/print/303678.

6. See "Advertisers Blend Digital and TV for Well-Rounded Campaigns," *eMarketer,* March 12, 2014, www.emarketer.com/Article/Advertisers-Blend-Digital-TV-Well-Rounded-Campaigns/1010670.

7. See Troy Dreier, "How Lowe's and Vine Build Social Video Success," *Streaming Media,* May 2014, www.streamingmedia.

com/Articles/Editorial/Featured-Articles/How-Lowes-and-Vine-Build-Social-Video-Success-96585.aspx; Alexxis Letozoa, "Lowe's Fix in Six," *-Ation*, December 1, 2014, http://ation.digitalmediauconn.org/lowes-fix-in-six/; https://vine.co/lowes, www.youtube.com/user/lowes, https://instagram.com/loweshomeimprovement/, www.pinterest.com/lowes/, and other Lowe's social media sites, accessed October 2015.

8. See "McCann New York Ask Parents to Love Cereal 'Again' in General Mills Campaign," *Little Black Book*, February 2016, http://lbbonline.com/news/mccann-new-york-asks-parents-to-love-cereal-again-in-general-mills-campaign/; Ashley Halladay, "General Mills Celebrates Milestone," *Taste of General Mills*, January 19, 2016, www.blog.generalmills.com/2016/01/cereal-team-celebrates-milestone/; Evan Ramstad, "General Mills Begins Marketing Cereals without Artificial Colors and Flavorings," *Star Tribune*, January 22, 2016, www.startribune.com/general-mills-begins-marketing-cereals-without-artificial-colors-flavors/366129821; and www.generalmills.com/en/Brands/Cereals/genmills-cereals?dclid=COTC76qAqcsCFVeqaQodHSsDKQ, accessed October 2016.

9. See Bethonie Butler and Maura Judkis, "The 10 Best Commercials of Super Bowl 50," *Washington Post*, February 8, 2016, www.washingtonpost.com/news/arts-and-entertainment/wp/2016/02/08/the-10-best-commercials-of-super-bowl-50/; and Matt Quigley, "Who Loved the Audi 'Starman' Super Bowl Ad Featuring David Bowie," *Statssocial Blog*, February 14, 2016, http://blog.statsocial.com/the-bowie-starman-ad-mild-with-bowie-fans-but-smash-with-car-nuts/.

10. "Global Trust in Advertising." Nielsen, September 28, 2015, www.nielsen.com/us/en/insights/reports/2015/global-trust-in-advertising-2015.html; and Barry Levine, "New Marketing Survey: It's the Trust Stupid," *Venture Beat*, September 29, 2015, http://venturebeat.com/2015/09/29/new-marketing-survey-its-the-trust-stupid/.

11. See Ami Iannone, "Netflix Is Joining the Influencer Marketing Movement," *Business 2 Community*, March 5, 2016, www.business2community.com/marketing/netflix-joining-influencer-marketing-movement-01474508#LzEQciHFLSsjVhpX.97; and http://grammasters.netflix.com/, accessed October 2016.

12. www.bzzagent.com and http://about.bzzagent.com/, accessed October 2016.

13. See T. L. Stanley, "Dancing with the Stars," *Brandweek*, March 8, 2010, pp. 10–12; and Chris Isidore, "Lance Armstrong: How He'll Make Money Now," *CNNMoney*, January 18, 2013, http://money.cnn.com/2013/01/16/news/companies/armstrong-endorsements/. Also see "Topic: Celebrity Endorsements," *Adweek*, www.adweek.com/topic/celebrity-endorsements, accessed October 2016.

14. For more on advertising spending by company and industry, see "100 Leading National Advertisers: U.S. Ad Spending by Category," *Advertising Age*, October 13, 2015, pp. 14–32; and "2016 Marketing Fact Pack," *Advertising Age*, December 29, 2015, pp. 8–12.

15. See Tim Nudd, "The 10 Most Watched Ads on YouTube in 2015," *Adweek*, December 9, 2015, www.adweek.com/print/168524; Tim Nudd, "The 10 Most Watched Ads on YouTube in January," *Adweek*, February 10, 2016, www.adweek.com/print/169570; and www.youtube.com/watch?v=Ho8lyiR0DrU, accessed October 2016.

16. See discussions at Mike Ishmael, "The Cost of a Sales Call," October 22, 2012, http://4dsales.com/the-cost-of-a-sales-call/; Jeff Green, "The New Willy Loman Survives by Staying Home," *Bloomberg Businessweek*, January 14–20, 2013, pp. 16–17; Scott Tousley, "107 Mind-Blowing Sales Statistics That Will Help You Sell Smarter," *HubSpot*, September 14, 2015, http://blog.hubspot.com/sales/sales-statistics; and "What Is the Real Cost of a B2B Sales Call?" www.marketing-playbook.com/sales-marketing-strategy/what-is-the-real-cost-of-a-b2b-sales-call, accessed October 2016.

17. Lara O'Reilly, "Almost a Quarter of Unilever's $8 Billion Ad Budget Is Now Spent on Digital," *Business Insider*, January 28, 2016, www.businessinsider.com/unilever-digital-advertising-budget-up-to-24-2016-1.

18. See Kristen Bellstrom, "Google and Pixar Are Teaming Up to Get Girls to Love Coding," *Fortune*, December 8, 2015, http://fortune.com/2015/12/08/pixar-and-google-girls-code/; Jordan Crook, "Google Invests $50 Million in 'Made with Code' Program to Get Girls Excited about CS," *Tech Crunch*, June 22, 2014, http://techcrunch.com/2014/06/22/google-invests-50-million-in-made-with-code-program-to-get-girls-excited-about-cs/; and www.madewithcode.com/about/, accessed October 2016.

Chapter 15

1. Quotes and other information from Ann-Christine Diaz, "Geico's 'Unskippable' from the Martin Agency Is Ad Age's 2016 Campaign of the Year," *Advertising Age*, January 25, 2016, www.adage.com/prit/302300; Scott Davis, "When GEICO Accelerated Past Allstate," *Forbes*, March 10, 2014, www.forbes.com/sites/scottdavis/2014/03/10/when-geico-accelerated-past-allstate/; E. J. Schultz, "Muscling Past Mayhem: GEICO Rides Giant Ad Budget Past Allstate," *Advertising Age*, July 8, 2013, www.adage.com/print/242980; "10 Most-Advertised Brands," Marketing Fact Pack 2016, *Advertising Age*, December 21, 2015, p. 7; www.geico.com and www.martinagency.com/work/its_what_you_do; accessed October 2016.

2. For these and other advertising spending facts, see *Advertising Age Marketing Fact Pack 2016*, December 21, 2015, and "200 Leading National Advertisers," *Advertising Age*, July 13, 2015, pp. 14–23.

3. See "200 Leading National Advertisers," *Advertising Age*, July 13, 2015, p. 16; John Tozzi, "The CDC's New Anti-Smoking Ads Target Tobacco Country," *Bloomberg Business*, January 20, 2016, www.bloomberg.com/news/articles/2016-01-20/the-cdc-s-new-anti-smoking-ads-target-tobacco-country; and www.cdc.gov/tobacco/campaign/tips/, accessed October 2016.

4. See E. J. Schultz, "Pepsi Ads Take Shot at Share-A-Coke, Polar Bears," *Advertising Age*, June 15, 2015, www.adage.com/print/298985.

5. See Michael Addady, "General Mills Sues Chobani for Advertising That Yoplain Contains 'Bug Spray,'" *Fortune*, January 12, 2016, http://fortune.com/2016/01/12/general-mills-sues-chobani/; and Christine Birkner, "'Scare Tactics' Used in Its Ads: Spots Imply Yoplait and Dannon Contain Pesticides, Chlorine," *Advertising Age*, January 20, 2016, www.adweek.com/print/169107.

6. See Jean Halliday, "Thinking Big Takes Audi from Obscure to Awesome," *Advertising Age*, February 2, 2009, http://adage.com/print/134234; Chad Thomas and Andreas Cremer, "Audi Feels a Need for Speed in the U.S.," *Bloomberg Businessweek*, November 22, 2010, p. 1; and Kyle Stock, "Audi Swipes BMW's Luxury Crown. Keeping It Will Be Harder," *Bloomberg BusinessWeek*, March 11, 2014, www.businessweek.com/articles/2014-03-11/where-audi-will-win-or-lose-the-luxury-car-race.

7. "Number of Magazines in the United States from 2002 to 2014," *Statista*, www.statista.com/statistics/238589/number-of-magazines-in-the-united-states/, accessed June 2016; and Andrew Burger, "Nielsen: Despite Hundreds of Choices, Average Number of TV Channels Watched Is 17," *Telecompetitor*, May 9, 2014, www.telecompetitor.com/nielsen-average-number-of-tv-channels-watched-is-17/.

8. Kelsey Libert and Kristen Tynski, "Research: The Emotions That Make Marketing Campaigns Go Viral," HBR Blog Network, October 24, 2013, http://blogs.hbr.org/2013/10/research-the-emotions-that-make-marketing-campaigns-go-viral/; and data from YouTube, Facebook, Instagram, and Twitter, accessed October 2016.

9. "How Much Does Television Advertising Really Cost," *Houston Chronicle*, http://smallbusiness.chron.com/much-television-advertising-really-cost-58718.html, accessed October 2016;

"AOL Says There Are More Ads on TV than Ever," *Wall Street Journal*, July 28, 2015, http://blogs.wsj.com/cmo/2015/07/28/aol-says-there-are-more-ads-on-tv-than-ever/; and "Cost for a 30-Second Commercial," *Marketing Fact Pack 2016*, *Advertising Age*, December 21, 2015, p. 18.

10. "Real Beauty Shines Through: Dove Wins Titanium Grand Prix, 163 Million Views on YouTube," *Google: Think Insights*, June2013, www.thinkwithgoogle.com/case-studies/dove-real-beauty-sketches.html; Nina Bahadur, "Dove 'Real Beauty' Campaign Turns 10: How a Brand Tried to Change the Conversation about Female Beauty," *Huffington Post*, February 6, 2014, www.huffingtonpost.com/2014/01/21/dove-real-beauty-campaign-turns-10_n_4575940.tml; "Dove's Latest Ad Shows That Grass Is Always Greener When It Comes to Body Image," *The Drum*, October 2, 2015, www.thedrum.com/news/2015/10/02/dove-s-latest-ad-shows-grass-always-greener-when-it-comes-body-image; and www.youtube.com/watch?v=XpaOjMXyJGk and www.youtube.com/watch?v=c96SNJihPjQ, accessed October 2016.

11. See Seth Fiegerman, "The New Way Brands Like Hostess Use Social Media: Playing Dumb," *Mashable*, April 6, 2015, http://mashable.com/2015/04/06/brands-play-dumb/; and Lindsay Kolowich, "Funny Tweets and Social Media Examples from 17 Real Brands," *Hubspot*, February 4, 2016, http://blog.hubspot.com/blog/tabid/6307/bid/33488/14-Funny-Brands-You-Can-t-Help-But-Follow-in-Social-Media.aspx.

12. See Joe Flint, "Pepsi Gets Taste of 'Empire' Drama," *Wall Street Journal*, November 9, 2015, www.wsj.com/articles/pepsi-gets-taste-of-empire-drama-1447902181.

13. Abe Sauer, "Announcing the 2016 Brandcameo Product Placement Awards," *BrandChannel*, February 24, 2016, www.brandchannel.com/2016/02/24/2016-brandcameo-product-placement-awards-022416/.

14. "Why *The Lego Movie* Is the Perfect Piece of Product Placement," *A.V. Club*, February 11, 2014, www.avclub.com/article/why-the-lego-movie-is-the-perfect-piece-of-product-201102; and Katarina Gustafsson, "LEGO Movie Helps Full-Year Revenue Growth Beat Rivals," *Bloomberg Business*, February 25, 2015, www.bloomberg.com/news/articles/2015-02-25/lego-movie-helps-toymaker-s-full-year-sales-growth-beat-rivals.

15. Michael Sebastian, "Nearly Two-Thirds of Marketers Plan to Increase Native-Ad Spending in 2015," January 29, 2015, *Advertising Age*, www.adage.com/print/296887; Joline Buscemi, "The Good and Evil of Native Advertising," *Hubspot*, March 1, 2016, http://blog.hubspot.com/marketing/good-and-evil-native-advertising; and David Cohen, "Native Advertising Dominates Facebook Audience Network (Study)," *Adweek*, April 5, 2016, www.adweek.com/print/637217.

16. Benjamin Snyder, "Here's Why Doritos Is Ending Its 'Crash the Super Bowl' Contest," *Fortune*, January 29, 2016, http://fortune.com/2016/01/29/doritos-crash-the-super-bowl-contest/.

17. Lauren Johnson, "This New Ad Format Helps Brands Insert Your Social Media Photos Into Facebook Ads," *Adweek*, March 6, 2015, www.adweek.com/print/163301.

18. Christopher Heine, "GoPro Marketing Gets Its Close-Up," *Adweek*, July 20, 2015, pp. 9–10; and www.licensing.gopro.com, accessed October 2016.

19. Lauren Johnson, "How Social and Email Helped Mazda's Limited-Edition Preorders Sell Out Crazy Fast," *Adweek*, May 28, 2014, www.adweek.com/print/157985.

20. See Evan Tarver, "What Makes the 'Share a Coke' Campaign So Successful," *Investopedia*, October 7, 2015, www.investopedia.com/articles/markets/100715/what-makes-share-coke-campaign-so-successful.asp.

21. See "Multitasking Is Changing Media Consumption Habits," *Screen Media Daily*, April 8, 2016, http://screenmediadaily.com/multitasking-is-changing-media-consumption-habits/.

22. *Forbes* and *Bloomberg Businessweek* cost and circulation data found online at www.bloombergmedia.com/magazine/businessweek/rates/ and www.forbesmedia.com/forbes-magazine-rates/, accessed October 2016.

23. Natalie Tadena, "With the New Year Approaching, Weight Loss Ad Barrage Has Commenced," *Wall Street Journal*, December 30, 2014, http://blogs.wsj.com/cmo/2014/12/30/with-the-new-year-approaching-weight-loss-ad-barrage-has-commenced/; and T. L. Stanley, "Peeps Do Their Best to Get Scary for Halloween," *Adweek*, www.adweek.com/print/161073.

24. For these and other examples, see Christopher Heine, "Lexus Nabs 100K Video Views on Facebook—in 10 Minutes," *Adweek*, January 23, 2013, www.adweek.com/news/technology/print/146726; Richard Nino, "Top 10 Examples of Great Real-Time Marketing," *Social Media Delivered*, January 22, 2015, www.socialmediadelivered.com/2015/01/22/top-10-examples-of-great-real-time-marketing/; and Tanya Dua, "You Can Still Dunk in the Dark, but You Don't Need a War Room," *Digiday*, February 4, 2016, http://digiday.com/agencies/super-bowl-war-room-rip/.

25. E. J. Schultz, "Fired Up; Need for Speed Is Putting Copy Testing to the Test," *Advertising Age*, September 14, 2015, pp. 20–23.

26. Information on advertising agency revenues from "Agency Report," *Advertising Age*, May 4, 2015, pp. 45+; and *Advertising Age Marketing Fact Pack 2016*, December 21, 2015, p. 24–25.

27. "OREO Brand Encourages Fans around the World to Open Their Hearts to Others in New Integrated Global Campaign, 'Open Up with OREO,'" *MultiVu*, January 19, 2016, www.multivu.com/players/English/7738651-open-up-with-oreo/.

28. Based on Glen Broom and Bey-Ling Sha, *Cutlip & Center's Effective Public Relations*, 11th ed. (Upper Saddle River, NJ: Prentice Hall, 2013), Chapter 1.

29. See "Healthcare Campaign of the Year 2015," *PR Week*, March 20, 2015, www.prweek.com/article/1337832; "CVS Health: CVS Quits for Good Campaign," (add)ventures, http://www.addventures.com/cvs-quits-good-campaign, accessed April, 2016; and www.cvs.com/quit-smoking/, accessed April 2016.

30. See Craig Giammona, "Long Live the King," *Bloomberg Businessweek*, October 5–11, 2015, pp. 23–24; Krushbu Shah, "Burger King Mascot Steals Show at Belmont Stakes," *Eater*, June 8, 2015, www.eater.com/2015/6/8/8746047/burger-king-mascot-steals-show-at-belmont-stakes; and http://mcwhopper.com/, accessed October 2016.

31. Quotes from Sarah Skerik, "An Emerging PR Trend: Content PR Strategy and Tactics," *PR Newswire*, January 15, 2013, http://blog.prnewswire.com/2013/01/15/an-emerging-pr-trend-content-pr-strategy-tactics/; and Mary Teresa Bitti, "The New Mad Men: How Publics Relations Firms Have Emerged from the Shadows," *Financial Post*, December 28, 2014, http://business.financialpost.com/entrepreneur/the-changing-role-of-public-relations-firms.

Chapter 16

1. Based on information from Dan Gallagher, "How Salesforce.com Can Keep Making It Rain," *Wall Street Journal*, February 25, 2016, www.wsj.com/articles/how-salesforce-com-can-keep-making-it-rain-1456429982; Heather Clancy, "Best Buyer for Salesforce?" *Fortune*, April 29, 2015, http://fortune.com/2015/04/29/best-buyer-for-salesforce/; David Whitford, "Salesforce.com: The Software and the Story," *Inc.*, September 2014, pp. 113–117; Whitford, "Selling, the Story: Four Strategies Salesforce.com Uses to Stay on Top," *Inc.*, September 2014, p. 116; "The World's Most Innovative Companies," *Forbes*, www.forbes.com/innovative-companies/list/, accessed October 2016; and www.salesforce.com, http://investor.salesforce.com/about-us/investor/financials/, and www.salesforce.com/company/, accessed October 2016.

2. See Molly Soat, "Four Best Practices to Ensure Sales/Marketing Alignment," *Marketing News*, December 2015, pp. 8–9; Chanin Ballance, "End Your Sales and Marketing Tug-of-War," *Sales & Marketing Management*, September 26, 2014, http://salesandmarketing.com/content/end-your-sales-and-marketing-tug-war; and Philip Kotler and Kevin Lane Keller,

Marketing Management, 15th ed. (Hoboken, NJ: Pearson Education, 2016), p. 644.

3. "Customer Business Development," http://we.experiencepg.com/home/customer_business_development_cbd_sales.html, accessed October 2016.

4. "500 Largest Sales Forces in America (2015) *Selling Power,* www.sellingpower.com/2015/selling-power-500/largest-sales-forces/manufacturing/, accessed October 2016.

5. See discussions in Mike Ishmael, "The Cost of a Sales Call," October 22, 2012, http://4dsales.com/the-cost-of-a-sales-call/; Kim Zimmerman, "B2B Inside Sales Teams Leverage Social, Video and Data to Reach Top Prospects," *Demand Gen,* January 20, 2016, www.demandgenreport.com/features/industry-insights/b2b-inside-sales-teams-leverage-social-video-and-data-to-reach-top-prospects; and "What Is the Real Cost of a B2B Sales Call?" www.marketing-playbook.com/sales-marketing-strategy/what-is-the-real-cost-of-a-b2b-sales-call, accessed October 2016.

6. Jeff Green, "The New Willy Loman Survives by Staying Home"; Andris A. Zoltners, PK Sinha, and Sally E. Lorimer, "The Growing Power of Inside Sales," *Harvard Business Review,* July 29, 2013, https://hbr.org/2013/07/the-growing-power-of-inside-sa/; Soat, "Four Best Practices to Ensure Sales/Marketing Alignment"; and Zimmerman, "B2B Inside Sales Teams Leverage Social, Video and Data."

7. See Kurt Shaver, "Why Inside Salespeople Make Great Social Sellers," November 12, 2014, http://blog.sellingpower.com/gg/2014/11/why-inside-salespeople-make-great-social-sellers.html; Matt Mayberry, "The Amazing Evolution and Power of Inside Sales," *Entrepreneur,* December 8, 2015; and Nick Hedges, "5 Trends Shaping the Sales Industry," *Velocify Blog,* January 13, 2016, http://velocify.com/blog/5_trends_shaping_the_sales_industry/.

8. Scott Fuhr, "Good Hiring Makes Good Cents," *Selling Power,* July/August/September 2012, pp. 20–21; "How Sales Rep Turnover Costs Your Company More Than You Think," *Insight Squared,* July 15, 2014, www.insightsquared.com/2014/07/how-sales-rep-turnover-costs-your-company-more-than-you-think; and Chris Young, "What Bad Sales Hiring Decisions Really Cost You," *Rainmaker Group Sales Wolf Blog,* January 23, 2015, www.therainmakergroupinc.com/human-capital-strategy-blog/what-bad-sales-hiring-decisions-really-cost-you.

9. For this and more information and discussion, see www.gallupaustralia.com.au/consulting/118729/sales-force-effectiveness.aspx, accessed July 2012; Donal Daly, "6 Things Successful Salespeople Do," *Salesforce.com,* April 17, 2015, www.salesforce.com/blog/2015/04/6-things-successful-sellers-do-cso-gp.html; and Brittney Helmrich, "8 Important Traits of Successful Salespeople," *Business News Daily,* January 25, 2016, www.businessnewsdaily.com/4173-personality-traits-successful-sales-people.html.

10. See Steve Denning, "The One Thing the Greatest Salespeople All Have," *Forbes,* November 29, 2012, www.forbes.com/sites/stevedenning/2012/11/29/the-one-thing-the-greatest-salespeople-all-have/.

11. "Strengths Based Selling," www.gallup.com/press/176651/strengths-based-selling.aspx, accessed October 2016.

12. Corporate Visions, Inc., "ADP Case Study," http://corporatevisions.com/v5/documents/secure_downloads/CVI_caseStudy_ADP.pdf, accessed October 2016; and Henry Canaday, "The Transformation of Enterprise Sales Training," *Selling Power,* www.adobe.com/content/dam/Adobe/en/products/adobeconnect/pdfs/elearning/transformation-of-enterprise-sales-training.pdf, accessed October 2016.

13. See Norman Behar, "Selecting the Best Sales Training Delivery Method," ATD, January 21, 2015, www.td.org/Publications/Blogs/Sales-Enablement-Blog/2015/01/Selecting-the-Best-Sales-Training-Delivery-Method.

14. See www.theknowledgeguru.com, www.theknowledgeguru.com/testimonials/case-studies/, and www.theknowledgeguru.com/solution/, accessed October 2016.

15. For more discussion, see Mark Roberge, "The Right Way to Use Compensation," *Harvard Business Review,* April 2015, pp. 70–75; and "Getting Beyond 'Show Me the Money,'" *Harvard Business Review,* April 2015, pp. 77–81.

16. See "2014 Sales Performance Optimization Study," CSO Insights, www.csoinsights.com/Publications/.

17. Lain Chroust Ehmann, "Sales Up!" *Selling Power,* January/February 2011, p. 40. Also see Tony J. Hughes, "Back to the Future of Sales in 2015," *LinkedIn,* December 27, 2014, www.linkedin.com/pulse/back-future-sales-2015-tony-j-hughes; Eliot Burdett, "Six Reasons Why Technology Won't Kill B2B Salespeople," *Business Review,* June 3, 2015, www.businessreviewusa.com/technology/4943/Six-reasons-why-technology-won't-kill-B2B-salespeople; and Pete Caputa, "47 Sales Experts Predict How to Radically Improve Sales Productivity in 2016," *HubSpot,* January 11, 2016, http://blog.hubspot.com/sales/sales-experts-predict-improve-sales-productivity.

18. See Scott Gillum, "The Disappearing Sales Process," *Forbes,* January 7, 2013, www.forbes.com/sites/gyro/2013/01/07/the-disappearing-sales-process/; and Paul Nolan, "Mapping the Buyer's Journey," *Sales & Marketing Management,* March/April 2015, pp. 32–34.

19. Neil Davey, "Using Social Media Marketing in B2B Markets," *Smart Insights,* February 16, 2015, www.smartinsights.com/b2b-digital-marketing/b2b-social-media-marketing/b2bsocialmediamarketing/. For more on Makino's social networking efforts, see www.facebook.com/MakinoMachine, www.youtube.com/user/MakinoMachineTools, and http://twitter.com/#!/makinomachine, accessed October 2016.

20. Example based on information from James C. Anderson, Nirmalya Kumar, and James A. Narus, "Become a Value Merchant," *Sales & Marketing Management,* May 6, 2008, pp. 20–23; and "Business Market Value Merchants," *Marketing Management,* March/April 2008, pp. 31+. For more discussion and examples, Ron Shapiro, "Selling While Holding Your Price," *Sales & Marketing Management,* January 5, 2015, www.salesandmarketing.com/content/selling-while-holding-your-price; and Julia Cupman, "Three Ways to Avoid a Price War," *B2B Marketing,* September 2015, www.ama.org/publications/eNewsletters/B2BMarketing/Pages/three-ways-to-avoid-a-price-war.aspx.

21. Kantar Retail, *Making Connections: Trade Promotion Integration across the Marketing Landscape* (Wilton, CT: Kantar Retail, July 2012), p. 5.

22. Jonathan Treiber, "Why Digital Promotions Are More Important Than Ever," *Retailing Today,* June 14, 2015, www.retailingtoday.com/article/why-digital-promotions-are-more-important-ever; and "Survey: The Vast Majority (87%) of Retail Marketers Plan to Invest More in Mobile Marketing in 2016," *PR Newswire,* March 3, 2016, www.prnewswire.com/news-releases/survey-the-vast-majority-87-of-retail-marketers-plan-to-invest-more-in-mobile-marketing-in-2016-300230162.html.

23. "Coupon Use Hits 40-Year Low," *Coupons in the News,* February 1, 2016, http://couponsinthenews.com/2016/02/01/coupon-use-hits-40-year-low.

24. See "Coupon Use Hits 40-Year Low" and "Improving Economy, Increasing Shopper Demand for Digital Offers Impacting Coupon Use," *Globe Newswire,* February 1, 2016, https://globenewswire.com/news-release/2016/02/01/806336/10159649/en/Improving-Economy-Increasing-Shopper-Demand-for-Digital-Offers-Impacting-Coupon-Use.html.

25. Hilary Milnes, "Walgreens Uses Mobile Apps to Solve In-Store Headaches," *Digiday,* May 4, 2015, https://digiday.com/brands/walgreens-uses-mobile-apps-solve-store-headaches/; "Entering the New Era of Digital Coupons," *Adweek,* June 16, 2014, p. S7; and www.walgreens.com/topic/apps/learn_about_mobile_browser_app.jsp and www.walgreens.com/coupons, accessed October 2016.

26. See www.happymeal.com, accessed October 2016.

27. See "The 2014 Estimate of Promotional Products Distributor Sales," *PPAI,* www.ppai.org/inside-ppai/research/Documents/2014SalesVolumeSheet.pdf.

28. Rachael Kirkpatrick, "Delta Sets Record with Mass Shower at Warrior Dash," *Event Marketer,* July 0, 2015, www.eventmarketer.com/article/delta-sets-new-world-record-331-person-shower-warrior-dash/; and "Mud Shower Station," *Adweek,* September 7, 2015, p. 38.

29. Kantar Retail, *Making Connections,* p. 10.

30. See "CES Attendee Audit Summary Results," https://www.cesweb.org/Why-CES/CES-by-the-Numbers, accessed June 2016; "New Logo for Bauma Ahead of 2016 Trade Fair," *World Cement,* July 5, 2015, www.worldcement.com/europe-cis/07052014/Bauma_new_look_ahead_of_2016_show_145/.

Chapter 17

1. See Krystina Gustafson, "Cyber Monday Sales Top $3 Billion," *Best Forecast,* www.cnbc.com/2015/12/01/cyber-monday-sales-top-3-billion-beat-forecast.html; Morten T. Hansen, Herminia Ibarra, and Urs Peyer, "The Best-Performing CEOs in the World," *Harvard Business Review,* January–February 2013, pp. 81–86; George Anders, "Jeff Bezos's Top 10 Leadership Lessons," *Forbes,* April 4, 2012, www.forbes.com/sites/georgeanders/2012/04/04/bezos-tips/; "Benchmarks by Company: Amazon," ACSI, www.theacsi.org/?option=com_content&view=article&id=149&catid=&Itemid=214&c=Amazon, accessed October 2016; "Number of Worldwide Active Amazon Customer Accounts from 1997 to 2015 (in Millions)," *Statista,* www.statista.com/statistics/237810/number-of-active-amazon-customer-accounts-worldwide/, accessed October 2016; and annual reports and other information found at www.amazon.com and walmart.com, accessed October 2016.

2. Stan Phelps, "Three Lessons from Mountain Dew on Leveraging Events to Create an Authentic Brand Experience," *Forbes,* October 18, 2014, www.forbes.com/sites/stanphelps/2014/10/18/three-lessons-from-mountain-dew-on-leveraging-events-to-create-an-authentic-brand-experience/; Natalie Tadena, "Mountain Dew Ads Go Global with Return of 'Do the Dew,'" *Wall Street Journal,* March 29, 2015, http://blogs.wsj.com/cmo/2015/03/29/mountain-dew-ads-go-global-with-return-of-do-the-dew/; and www.mountaindew.com, accessed October 2016.

3. See "Priceline Profit Tops Estimates as Bookings Rise," *Reuters,* February 20, 2014, www.reuters.com/article/2014/02/21/us-priceline-results-idUSBREA1J26X20140221; and http://ir.pricelinegroup.com/financials.cfm, accessed October 2015.

4. See Ginger Conlon, "2016 Will Be Growth Year in Marketing Spend," *Direct Marketing News,* February 1, 2016, www.dmnews.com/marketing-strategy/2016-will-be-a-growth-year-in-marketing-spending/article/469545/; George Slefo, "Digital Ad Spending Surges to Record High as Mobile and Social Grow More Than 50%," *Advertising Age,* April 21, 2016, www.adage.com/print/303650; and other information at www.thedma.org, accessed September 2016.

5. See "Internet Usage Statistics," *Internet World Stats,* www.internetworldstats.com/stats.htm; accessed October 2016; "Mobile Phone Users Worldwide," *Statista,* www.statista.com/statistics/274774/forecast-of-mobile-phone-users-worldwide/, accessed October 2016.

6. See Doug Heise "4 E-Commerce Predictions for 2016," *Internet Retailer,* January 7, 2016, www.internetretailer.com/commentary/2016/01/07/4-e-commerce-predictions-2016; "US Retail Sales to Near $5 Trillion in 2016," *eMarketer,* December 21, 2015, www.emarketer.com/Article/US-Retail-Sales-Near-5-Trillion-2016/1013368; Thad Rueter, "The Web's Influence on U.S. Retail Grows," *Internet Retailer,* July 25, 2014, www.internetretailer.com/2014/07/25/webs-influence-us-retail-grows; and Matt Linder, "Online Sales Will Reach $253 Billion by 2020 in the U.S.," *Internet Retailer,* January 29, 2016, www.internetretailer.com/2016/01/29/online-sales-will-reach-523-billion-2020-us.

7. See "Global Powers of Retailing 2016: Navigating the New Digital Divide," Deloitte, www2.deloitte.com/content/dam/Deloitte/global/Documents/Consumer-Business/gx-cb-global-powers-of-retailing-2016.pdf, pp. 36–37.

8. Mark Brohan, "Home Depot Hammers Away at Online Growth," *Internet Retailer,* January 20, 2016, www.internetretailer.com/2016/01/20/home-depot-hammers-away-online-growth; and Home Depot annual reports and other information found at www.homedepot.com and http://phx.corporate-ir.net/phoenix.zhtml?c=63646&p=irol-reportsannual, accessed October 2016.

9. See Roger Katz, "2015 Will Be the Year of the Brand Community—Here's Why," *ClickZ,* January 23, 2015, www.clickz.com/clickz/column/2391666/2015-will-be-the-year-of-the-brand-community-here-s-why; ComBlu, "The State of Online Branded Communities," http://comblu.com/downloads/ComBlu_StateOfOnlineCommunities_2012.pdf, November 2012, p. 19; and www.espn.com, accessed October 2016.

10. For these and other examples of rich media ads, see "Rising Starts: Display," *Jivox,* www.jivox.com/ad-gallery.php, accessed September 2016; and "Best Rich Media Online Ad," www.iacaward.org/iac/winners_detail.asp?yr=all&award_level=best&medium=Rich%20media%20Online%20Ad, accessed October 2016.

11. Alphabet annual reports, https://abc.xyz/investor/, accessed October 2016.

12. "Social Media Is the Hot New Thing, but Email Is Still the King," *Advertising Age,* September 30, 2013, p. 18.

13. See Greg Sterling, "Majority of Emails Opened on Apple Devices, Android Users Pay More Attention," *MarketingLand,* January 28, 2015, http://marketingland.com/majority-emails-opened-apple-devices-android-users-pay-attention-115945; Daniel Newman, "Alive and Kicking: Why Email Marketing Is Still a Huge Tool for Business," *Entrepreneur,* November 9, 2015, www.entrepreneur.com/article/252581.

14. See "The Top 100 Email Marketing Campaigns," www.campaignmonitor.com/best-email-marketing-campaigns/, accessed October 2016.

15. See Lindsey Kolowich, "12 of the Best Email Marketing Examples You've Ever Seen (and Why They're Great)," *Hubspot,* March 5, 2015, http://blog.hubspot.com/marketing/email-marketing-examples-list; and "The Top 100 Email Marketing Campaigns," www.campaignmonitor.com/best-email-marketing-campaigns/, accessed October 2016.

16. "Email: Unloved, Unbreakable," *Fortune,* May 1, 2015, pp. 54–55; Stephanie Mlot, "Email Spam Rates Dip below 50 Percent," *PC Magazine,* July 17, 2015, www.pcmag.com/article2/0,2817,2487933,00.asp; and Symantec Security Response Publications, www.symantec.com/security_response/publications/monthlythreatreport.jsp, accessed October 2016.

17. See "The 2016 Unroll.Me SPAMMY Awards," *Unroll.Me,* February 16, 2016, http://blog.unroll.me/the-2015-unroll-me-spammy-awards/; and Zach Brooke, "Who Is Winning—and Losing—the Inbox Battle?" American Marketing Association, March 1, 2016, www.ama.org/publications/eNewsletters/MarketingInsightsNewsletter/Pages/Who-is-Winning-and-Losing-the-Inbox-Battle.aspx.

18. Josh Constine, "Facebook Hits 8 Billion Daily Video Views, Doubling from 4 Billion in April," *Tech Crunch,* November 15, 2015, http://techcrunch.com/2015/11/04/facebook-video-views; Mark R. Robertson, "500 Hours of Video Uploaded to YouTube Every Minute [Forecast]," *Reelseo,* November 13, 2015, www.reelseo.com/hours-minute-uploaded-youtube/; "Statistics and Facts about Online Video Usage," *Statista,* www.statista.com/topics/1137/online-video/, accessed April 2016.

19. See Tim Nudd, "The 20 Most Viral Ads of 2015," *AdWeek,* November 19, 2015, www.adweek.com/news-gallery/advertising-branding/20-most-viral-ads-2015-168213; Abner Li, "Latest 'Be together. Not the same.' Android Ad Has a Strong and Charming Message," *9TO5 Google,* February 29, 2016, http://9to5google.com/2016/02/29/latest-be-together-not-the-same-ad/; and www.youtube.com/watch?v=vnVuqfXohxc, accessed October 2016.

20. See "Top 10 Branded Videos: Adidas Racks Up 21 Million YouTube Views in One Week," *Adweek,* February 25, 2015,

www.adweek.com/print/163145; and www.youtube.com/watch?v=N2TEZ8UOLMw, accessed October 2016.

21. Troy Dreier, "The Force Was Strong with This One," *Streaming Media Magazine*, April/May 2011, pp. 66–68. Also see Hilary Masell Oswald, "The Biology of a Marketplace Sensation," *Marketing News*, September 2013, pp. 31–35; "Why Some Videos Go Viral," *Harvard Business Review*, September 2015, pp. 34–35; and "Why Certain Things Go Viral," *HBR Video*, January 2016, https://hbr.org/video/4698519638001/why-certain-things-go-viral.

22. Kayleen Schafer, "How Bloggers Make Money on Instagram," *Harpers Bazaar*, May 20, 2015; Caitlin Keating, "The Fashion Blogger behind We Wore What," *New York Times*, January 20, 2016, www.nytimes.com/2016/01/21/fashion/weworewhat-danielle-bernstein.html; Laureen Indvik, "The 20 Most Influential Personal Style Bloggers: 2016 Edition," *Fashionista*, March 14, 2016; and http://weworewhat.com/, accessed October 2016.

23. Tom Pick, "47 Superb Social Media Marketing Stats and Facts," *Business2Community*, January 19, 2016, www.business2community.com/social-media/47-superb-social-media-marketing-stats-facts-01431126#TcQ1jRpYTOpYkQmo.97.

24. See http://newsroom.fb.com/company-info, www.youtube.com/yt/press/statistics.html, and www.statisticbrain.com/twitter-statistics/, accessed October 2016.

25. For these and other examples, see www.goodreads.com, www.farmersonly.com, www.birdpost.com, and www.cafemom.com, all accessed October 2016.

26. See "The 30 Most Brilliant Social Media Campaigns of 2015," *Salesforce.com*, December 14, 2015, www.salesforce.com/blog/2015/12/2015-most-brilliant-social-media-campaigns.html; and "TOMS One Day without Shoes," http://shortyawards.com/8th/toms-one-day-without-shoes-2015, 8th Annual Shorty Awards, accessed May 2016.

27. See www.instagram.com/etsy/, www.pinterest.com/etsy/, and www.etsy.com/about, accessed October 2016.

28. See Alison Griswold, "Why Would Companies Ever Think a Campaign Like #AskSeaWorld Is a Good Idea?" *Slate*, March 27, 2015, www.slate.com/blogs/moneybox/2015/03/27/_asksea-world_twitter_amas_are_a_terrible_idea_and_yet_companies_do_them.html; and Nicole Fallon Taylor, "5 Corporate Marketing Efforts That Seriously Backfired," *Business News Daily*, September 2015, www.businessnewsdaily.com/8385-corporate-marketing-fails.html.

29. Michael Bourne, "Sailing of 14 Social Cs," *Mullen Advertising*, February, 13, 2012.

30. "How the Starbucks Social Media Team Captures the Personality of a Beverage," May 4, 2015, https://news.starbucks.com/news/how-the-starbucks-social-media-team-captures-the-personality-of-a-beverage.

31. Melissa Allison, "Re-Creating the Coffee Klatch Online," *Raleigh News & Observer*, May 6, 2013, p. 1D; Todd Wassermann, *Mashable*, December 13, 2013, http://mashable.com/2013/12/05/starbuckss-tweet-a-coffee-180000/; and www.facebook.com/Starbucks and https://twitter.com/Starbucks, accessed June 2016.

32. Facts in this paragraph are from "The Daredevils without Landlines," *NPR*, December 3, 2015, www.npr.org/sections/alltechconsidered/2015/12/03/458225197/the-daredevils-without-landlines-and-why-health-experts-are-tracking-them; and Kenneth Olmstead and Michelle Atkinson, "Chapter 1: The Majorty of Smartphone Owners Download Apps," *Pew Research Center*, November 10, 2015, www.pewinternet.org/2015/11/10/the-majority-of-smartphone-owners-download-apps/.

33. Sarah Perez, "U.S. Consumers Now Spend More Time in Apps Than Watching TV," *Tech Crunch*, September 10, 2015, http://techcrunch.com/2015/09/10/u-s-consumers-now-spend-more-time-in-apps-than-watching-tv/; Lisa Eadicicco, "Americans Check Their Phones 8 Billion Times a Day," *Time*, December 15, 2015, http://time.com/4147614/smartphone-usage-us-2015/.

34. Lauren Johnson, "Target Turns Its Stores into One Big Mobile Game for the Holidays," *Adweek*, December 2, 2014, www.adweek.com/print/161727; and Sandy Rand, "The Psychology of Mobile Usage & Its Impact on Advertising," *B2C*, February 15, 2016, www.business2community.com/mobile-apps/psychology-mobile-usage-impact-advertising-01453221#VsZ6fOktj8Zm5kTP.99.

35. See "US Digital Display Ad Spending to Surpass Search Ad Spending in 2016," *eMarketer*, January 11, 2016 www.emarketer.com/Article/US-Digital-Display-Ad-Spending-Surpass-Search-Ad-Spending-2016/1013442#sthash.RcwOztEM.dpuf; and "IAB Internet Advertising Revenue Report," April 2016, www.iab.com/wp-content/uploads/2016/04/IAB-Internet-Advertising-Revenue-Report-FY-2015.pdf.

36. Lauren Johnson, "Taco Bell's Mobile Ads Are Highly Targeted to Make Users Crave Its Breakfast Menu," *Adweek*, March 14, 2016, www.adweek.com/print/170155.

37. See Ginger Conlon, "2016 Will Be a Growth Year in Marketing Spending," *DM News*, February 1, 2016, www.dmnews.com/marketing-strategy/2016-will-be-a-growth-year-in-marketing-spending/article/469545/; and "Stats & Facts: Direct Marketing," *CMO Council*, www.cmocouncil.org/facts-stats-categories.php?view=all&category=direct-marketing, accessed September 2016.

38. Julie Liesse, "When Times Are Hard, Mail Works," *Advertising Age*, March 30, 2009, p. 14; and Lois Geller, "If Direct Mail Is Dying, It's Sure Taking Its Time about It," *Forbes*, December 4, 2013, www.forbes.com/sites/loisgeller/2013/12/04/if-direct-mail-is-dying-its-sure-taking-its-time-about-it/; and Craig Simpson, "4 Reasons to Use Direct Mail Marketing Instead of Email," *Entrepreneur*, February 17, 2015, www.entrepreneur.com/article/242731.

39. Rebecca R. Ruiz, "Catalogs, after Years of Decline, Are Revamped for Changing Times," *New York Times*, January 26, 2015, p. B1; and Katie Ferguson, "The Big Payoff behind All Those Catalogs in the Mail," *MarketPlace*, February 11, 2016, www.marketplace.org/2016/02/03/world/big-payoff-behind-all-those-catalogs-mail.

40. Mike Ryan, "Print Is Dead? J.C. Penney Catalog Crunches the Data, Returns to Print," *Businesss2Community*, July 30, 2015, www.business2community.com/consumer-marketing/print-is-dead-j-c-penney-catalog-crunches-the-data-returns-to-print-01289952#kDooq0brVHlyjgym.97.

41. Ruiz, "Catalogs, after Years of Decline, Are Revamped for Changing Times"; and Molly Soat, "In the Mood to Peruse," *Marketing News*, July 2015, pp. 41–49.

42. Conlon, "2016 Will Be a Growth Year in Marketing Spending."

43. See Federal Trade Commission, "FTC Issues FY 2015 National Do Not Call Registry Data," November 19, 2015, www.ftc.gov/news-events/press-releases/2015/11/ftc-issues-fy-2015-national-do-not-call-registry-data-book; and www.donotcall.gov, accessed October 2016.

44. See Allison Collins, "Guthy-Renker Said to Be Considering Sale of Proactiv," *WWD*, March 23, 2016, http://wwd.com/beauty-industry-news/financial/guthy-renker-proactiv-sale-10397175/; and www.proactiv.com, accessed October 2016.

45. Barbara Seale, "Team Beachbody: Fit to Grow," *Direct Selling News*, May 1, 2015, http://directsellingnews.com/index.php/view/team_beachbody_fit_to_grow#.VwewNBjELbM.

46. See Jeanine Poggi, "H&M Super Bowl Ad Lets You Buy Beckham Bodywear by Remote Control," *Advertising Age*, January 6, 2014, www.adage.com/print/290915.

47. "Best Buy: Consumer Electronics Retailing on the Go," www.zoomsystems.com/our-partners/partner-portfolio/; and www.zoomsystems.com/about-us, accessed October 2016.

48. See Internet Crime Complaint Center, www.ic3.gov, accessed October 2016.

49. See "Fear and Worry in America? Identity Theft and Cybercrime," *Huffington Post*, November 5, 2014, www.huffingtonpost.com/creditsesamecom/fear-and-worry-in-america_b_6102910.html; and "2015 Data Breaches," *Identity Theft Resource Center*,

January 25, 2016, www.idtheftcenter.org/ITRC-Surveys-Studies/2015databreaches.html.

50. See "10 Completely Insane Social Media Statistics," *Content Factory*, www.contentfac.com/more-people-own-cell-phone-than-toothbrush-10-crazy-social-media-statistics/, accessed October 2016; and "BBC Newsround Uncovers Widespread Underage Social Media Usage," *The Drum*, February 9, 2016, www.thedrum.com/news/2016/02/09/bbc-newsround-uncovers-widespread-underage-social-media-usage.

51. See Zach Miners, "Your Control of Your Personal Info Is All but Dead, Pew Respondents Fear," *PCWorld*, November 12, 2014, www.pcworld.com/article/2846855; Hadley Malcolm, "Millennials Don't Worry about Online Privacy," *USA Today*, April 21, 2013; "2016 TRUSTe US Consumer Confidence Index," *TRUSTe*, www.truste.com/resources/privacy-research/ncsa-consumer-privacy-index-us/; and "Marketers, It's Time to Get Personal," Adobe, March 2016, www.adobe.com/content/dam/Adobe/en/news-room/pdfs/201603/032116AdobeGetPersonalReport-Final.pdf.

52. Based on information from Michael Bush, "My Life, Seen through the Eyes of Marketers," *Advertising Age*, April 26, 2010, http://adage.com/print/143479.

53. Kate Kane, "The $24 Billion Data Business That Telcos Don't Want to Talk About," *Advertising Age*, October 26, 2015, pp. 12–14, and "SAP Consumer Insight 365: Inleash Mobile Data Analytics on Carrier Networks," http://go.sap.com/product/crm/mobile-data-analytics.html#item_0; accessed October 2016.

54. See "Facebook to Make Targeted Ads More Transparent for Users," *Advertising Age*, February 4, 2013, http://adage.com/article/239564/; and www.aboutads.info/, accessed October 2016.

55. See Richard Byrne Reilly, "Feds to Mobile Marketers: Stop Targeting Kids, or Else," *Venture Beat*, March 27, 2014, http://venturebeat.com/2014/03/27/feds-to-mobile-marketers-stop-targeting-kids-or-else-exclusive/; and www.business.ftc.gov/privacy-and-security/childrens-privacy, accessed September 2016.

56. Information on TRUSTe at www.truste.com, accessed October 2016.

57. Information on the DMA Privacy Promise at www.the-dma.org/cgi/dispissue?article=129 and www.dmachoice.org/static/privacy_policy.php, accessed October 2016.

Chapter 18

1. Tom Warren, "Microsoft's 'Last Lumia' Reportedly Launching on February 1st," *The Verge*, January 18, 2016, www.theverge.com/2016/1/18/10785106/microsoft-lumia-650-last-lumia-rumors; Maribel Lopez, "Is Microsoft a Mobile Company?" *Forbes*, April 22, 2016, www.forbes.com/sites/maribellopez/2016/04/22/is-microsoft-a-mobile-company/#507ea0fa6157; Maribel Lopez, "7 Reasons To Give Microsoft's Strategy Another Look," *Forbes*, April 19, 2016, www.forbes.com/sites/maribellopez/2016/04/19/7-reasons-to-give-microsofts-strategy-another-look/#28b03eb46726; "CEO Satya Nadella," http://news.microsoft.com/ceo/announcement/index.html, accessed October 2016; and www.microsoft.com and www.microsoft.com/en-us/investor/, accessed October 2016.

2. Maureen Morrison, "Cinnabon's Recipe for Expansion: Licensing and Co-branding," *Advertising Age*, February 19, 2014, http://adage.com/article/news/cinnabon-expands-licensing-vodka-air-fresheners/291726/; and "New Tricks: How Old Brands Can Still Surprise Customers," *Knowledge@Wharton*, May 5, 2015, http://knowledge.wharton.upenn.edu/article/new-tricks-how-old-brands-can-still-surprise-consumers/; and www.cinnabon.com, accessed October 2016.

3. See www.lexus-int.com/models/LFA/ and www.fordgt.com/content/brand_ford/en_us/performance/gt/wired/application/welcome.html, accessed October 2016.

4. See "T-Mobile Busts Verizon's Balls…Ad," January 21, 2016, https://newsroom.t-mobile.com/news-and-blogs/ballbuster.htm; and Maureen Morrison, "T-Mobile's Mystery Super Bowl Star: Steve #Ballogize Harvey," *Advertising Age*, www.adage.com/print/302578.

5. "Alexa Top Sites in the U.S.," www.alexa.com/topsites/countries;1/US, accessed October 2016.

6. Adapted from information found in W. Chan Kim and Renée Mauborgne, *Blue Ocean Strategy, Expanded Edition: How to Create Uncontested Market Space and Make Competition Irrelevant* (Boston: Harvard Business Press, 2015). For other discussion, see Kim and Mauborgne, "Red Ocean Traps," *Harvard Business Review*, March 2015, pp. 68–73; and "Blue Ocean Strategy," www.blueoceanstrategy.com/, accessed October 2016.

7. See Eddie Yoon and Linda Deeken, "Why It Pays to Be a Category Creator," *Harvard Business Review*, March 2013, pp. 21–24; "Keurig Green Mountain Is Being Acquired for $13.9B," *Fox Business News*, December 7, 2015, www.foxbusiness.com/features/2015/12/07/keurig-green-mountain-to-be-acquired-for-2-per-share.html; and http://investor.keuriggreenmountain.com/financials.cfm and www.keurig.com/, accessed October 2016.

8. See "Sunstroke: Cirque du Soleil May Be Struggling, but the Cluster around It Is Thriving," *The Economist*, February 15, 2014, www.economist.com/news/business/21596583-cirque-du-soleil-may-be-struggling-cluster-around-it-thriving-sunstroke; and Renée Mauborgne and W. Chan Kim, "This Is How Cirque du Soleil Reinvented the Circus," *Quartz*, March 20, 2015, http://qz.com/366601/this-is-how-cirque-du-soleil-reinvented-the-circus/.

9. See Dinah Eng, "Samuel Adams's Beer Revolution," *Fortune*, April 8, 2013, pp. 23–26; and www.bostonbeer.com/phoenix.zhtml?c=69432&p=irol-overview and www.ab-inbev.com/go/investors/financial_information/our_key_figures.cfm, accessed October 2016.

10. For these and other examples, see Dan Schwabel, "Why Companies Want You to Become an Intrapreneur," *Forbes*, September 9, 2013, www.forbes.com/sites/danschawbel/2013/09/09/why-companies-want-you-to-become-an-intrapreneur/; and George Deeb, "Big Companies Must Embrace Intrapreneurship to Survive," February 18, 2016, www.forbes.com/sites/georgedeeb/2016/02/18/big-companies-must-embrace-intrapreneurship-to-survive/#43f1fdd8eb9e.

11. Michael E. Porter, *Competitive Strategy: Techniques for Analyzing Industries and Competitors* (New York: Free Press, 1980), Chapter 2; and Porter, "What Is Strategy?" *Harvard Business Review*, November–December 1996, pp. 61–78. Also see Stefan Stern, "May the Force Be with You and Your Plans for 2008," *Financial Times*, January 8, 2008, p. 14; and "Porter's Generic Strategies," www.quickmba.com/strategy/generic.shtml, accessed October 2016.

12. See Michael Treacy and Fred Wiersema, "Customer Intimacy and Other Value Disciplines," *Harvard Business Review*, January–February 1993, pp. 84–93; Treacy and Wiersema, *The Discipline of Market Leaders: Choose Your Customers, Narrow Your Focus, Dominate Your Market* (New York: Perseus Press, 1997); and Wiersema, *Double-Digit Growth: How Great Companies Achieve It—No Matter What* (New York: Portfolio, 2003). Also see Elaine Cascio, "Fast, Cheap, or Good—Pick Two," *Inter@ction Solutions*, January/February 2012, p. 8; Jürgen Kai-Uwe Brock and Josephine Yu Zhou, "Customer Intimacy," *Journal of Business and Industrial Marketing*, 2012, pp. 370–383; Joe Weinman, "How Customer Intimacy Is Evolving to Collective Intimacy, Thanks to Big Data," *Forbes*, June 4, 2013, www.forbes.com/sites/joeweinman/2013/06/04/how-customer-intimacy-is-evolving-to-collective-intimacy-thanks-to-big-data/; and Sue Troy, "Value Disciplines and the Operational Excellence Model for BPM," *Tech Target*, August 10, 2015, http://searchcio.techtarget.com/video/Value-disciplines-and-the-operational-excellence-model-for-BPM.

13. See Brett Berk, "The Chevy Bolt–Tesla Model 3 Rivalry Is Bullshit," *Yahoo! Autos*, April 15, 2016, www.yahoo.com/autos/chevy-bolt-tesla-model-3-191500497.html; and www.teslamotors.com, accessed June 2016.

14. For more discussion, see Philip Kotler and Kevin Lane Keller, *Marketing Management*, 15th ed. (Hoboken, NJ: Prentice Hall, 2016), Chapter 12.

15. Jonathan Chew, "How LEGO Finally Found Success with Girls," *Fortune*, December 30, 2015, http://fortune.com/2015/12/30/lego-friends-girls/; and http://friends.lego.com/en-us/products, accessed January 2016.

16. See "2000+ Uses," www.wd40.com/uses-tips/ and http://wd40.com/files/wd40-2000.pdf, accessed October 2016.

17. Tamara Walsh, "Is This Procter & Gamble's Secret Weapon?" *The Motley Fool*, July 7, 2015, www.fool.com/investing/general/2015/07/07/is-this-procter-gambles-secret-weapon.aspx; Jack Neff, "P&G Regains U.S. Diaper Lead—but in China, Kimberly Clark's Share Ticks Up," *Advertising Age*, March 25, 2015, p. 30; Lauren Coleman-Lochner, "P&G Studies 'Pee Points' to Maintain Edge in Diaper Wars," *Bloomberg*, March 24, 2014, www.bloomberg.com/news/articles/2014-03-04/p-g-studies-pee-points-to-maintain-edge-in-diaper-wars; "Pampers or Huggies: Innovations in Diaper Technology Creates Fierce Competition," *Technavio*, March 5, 2014, www.technavio.com/blog/pampers-or-huggies-innovations-in-diaper-technology-creates-fierce-competition; and "Global Diaper Market (Estimated Size of $52.7 billion in 2015) to Witness 5.5% CAGR during 2016–2022," *P&S Market Research*, February 2016, www.psmarketresearch.com/press-release/diaper-market.

18. See "Top Shampoo Players Clean Up," *Drug Store News*, April 2016, www.drugstorenews.com/sites/drugstorenews.com/files/PromoWatch_April2016_shampoo.pdf; and "Marketing Size of Soft Drinks in the United States," *Statista*, www.statista.com/statistics/422532/united-states-soft-drink-market-size/, accessed October 2016.

19. "Top Selling Energy Drink Brands," *Caffeine Informer*, www.caffeineinformer.com/the-15-top-energy-drink-brands, accessed October 2016; and www.redbull.com/us/en, accessed October 2016.

20. See Angela Chen, "The Rise of Niche Online Dating Sites," *Wall Street Journal*, October 15, 2013, http://online.wsj.com/news/articles/SB10001424052702304561004579137441269527948; Laura T. Coffey, "From Farmers to Salad Toppings: 26 Weirdly Niche Dating Sites," *USA Today*, August 5, 2013, www.today.com/health/farmers-salad-toppings-26-weirdly-niche-dating-sites-6C10843053; Jenny Morrill, "6 Unbelievably Niche Dating Sites," *Mental Floss*, October 2, 2015; and www.farmersonly.com, accessed October 2016.

21. Information from www.vfc.com, accessed October 2016.

Chapter 19

1. See Beth Kowitt, "It's IKEA's World," *Fortune*, March 15, 2015, pp. 166–175; Richard Milne in Leiden, "IKEA Thinks Outside the Big Box," *Financial Times*, December 4, 2015, www.ft.com/cms/s/2/44a495f6-9a68-11e5-bdda-9f13f99fa654.html#axzz47Ft78U7Q; Michael Wei, "In IKEA's China Stores, Loitering Is Encouraged," *Bloomberg Businessweek*, November 1, 2010, pp. 22–23; Emily Raulhala, "No, IKEA Hasn't Banned Customers from Sleeping in Its Chinese Stores," *Time*, April 10, 2015, http://time.com/3814935/ikea-china-customers-sleeping/; Preetika Rana, "IKEA's India Bet Runs into a Thicket of Rules," *Wall Street Journal*, February 24, 2016, www.wsj.com/articles/ikeas-india-bet-runs-into-thicket-of-rules-1456265878; and www.ikea.com/ms/en_JP/about-the-ikea-group/company-information/ accessed October, 2016.

2. Data from "*Fortune* 500," *Fortune*, June 2016, http://money.cnn.com/magazines/fortune/fortune500/; Douglas B. Fay, "Multinational Customers: Are Their Needs Really Being Met?" www.globexintl.com/corporate/?p=82, accessed October 2016; and "List of Countries by GDP: List by the CIA World Factbook," *Wikipedia*, http://en.wikipedia.org/wiki/List_of_countries_by_GDP_(nominal), accessed October 2016.

3. See "Trade Growth to Remain Subdues in 2016 as Uncertainties Weigh on Global Demand," *WTO*, April 7, 2016, www.wto.org/english/news_e/pres16_e/pr768_e.htm; and "Gross Domestic Product (GDP) at Current Prices from 2010 to 2020," *Statista*, www.statista.com/statistics/268750/global-gross-domestic-product-gdp/, accessed October 2016.

4. Information from www.michelin.com/eng/finance/institutional-investors-analysts/main-indicators, www.jnj.com, and www.caterpillar.com, accessed October 2016.

5. See www.otisworldwide.com/d1-about.html and UTC Annual Report, www.utc.com/Investors/Pages/Annual-Reports-and-Proxy-Statements.aspx, accessed October 2016.

6. Rob Schmitz, "Trade Spat between China and EU Threatens Exports of Solar Panels, Wine," *Marketplace*, June 6, 2013, www.marketplace.org/topics/world/trade-spat-between-china-and-eu-threatens-exports-solar-panels-wine; Ben Blanchard and Francesco Guarascio, "EU, China End Wine Dispute Ahead of Xi's European Tour," *Reuters*, March 21, 2014, www.reuters.com/article/idUSBREA2K0QE20140321; "EU to Benefit from China's 'New Normal' Economy: Ambassador," April 15, 2015, www.ecns.cn/voices/2015/04-15/161743.shtml; and "The European Union's Measures against Dumped and Subsidised Imports of Solar Panels from China," European Commission, February 29, 2016, http://trade.ec.europa.eu/doclib/docs/2015/july/tradoc_153587.pdf.

7. Gardiner Harris, "Wal-Mart Drops Ambitious Expansion Plan for India," *New York Times*, October 10, 2013, p. B3; Paul Ausick, "Walmart Still Struggles in India," *247wallst*, April 8, 2014, http://247wallst.com/retail/2014/04/08/walmart-still-struggles-in-india/; and Adi Narayan and Rajhkumar K. Shaaw, "Giving Shoppers Less Means Big Bucks for Indian Retailer," *Bloomberg*, February 17, 2016, www.bloomberg.com/news/articles/2016-02-17/watch-me-wal-mart-message-from-most-profitable-india-supermart.

8. "What Is the WTO?" www.wto.org/english/thewto_e/whatis_e/whatis_e.htm, accessed October 2016.

9. See "The Doha Round," www.wto.org/english/tratop_e/dda_e/dda_e.htm, accessed October 2016.

10. "The EU at a Glance," http://europa.eu/about-eu/index_en.htm; "EU Statistics and Opinion Polls," http://europa.eu/documentation/statistics-polls/index_en.htm; and "EU Position in World Trade," http://ec.europa.eu/trade/policy/eu-position-in-world-trade/, all accessed October 2016.

11. "France's Sapin: Euro's Weakening Phase Has Run Its Course," *Wall Street Journal*, April 17, 2015, www.wsj.com/articles/frances-sapin-euros-weakening-phase-has-run-its-course-1429300555; Chris Giles, "Former BoE Chief King Predicts Collapse of Eurozone," *Financial Times*, February 19, 2016, www.ft.com/intl/cms/s/0/5726e610-dec0-11e5-b7fd-0dfe89910bd6.html#axzz4720ff4j3; and "European Union: The Euro," http://europa.eu/about-eu/basic-information/money/euro/, accessed October 2016.

12. CIA, *The World Factbook*, www.cia.gov/library/publications/the-world-factbook, accessed October 2016.

13. Statistics and other information from CIA, *The World Factbook*; and North America Free Trade Agreement, www.international.gc.ca/trade-agreements-accords-commerciaux/agr-acc/nafta-alena/info.aspx?lang=eng, accessed October 2016.

14. See "Explainer: What Is UNASUR?" www.as-coa.org/articles/explainer-what-unasur; and http://en.wikipedia.org/wiki/Union_of_South_American_Nations, accessed October 2016.

15. "TPP: What Is It and Why Does It Matter?" *BBC*, February 3, 2016, www.bbc.com/news/business-32498715.

16. See Zeenat Moorad, "The Coca-Cola Company: Tapping Africa's Fizz," *Financial Mail*, May 4, 2015, www.financialmail.co.za/coverstory/2015/04/30/the-coca-cola-company-tapping-africas-fizz; Annaleigh Vallie, "Coke Turns 125 and Has Much Life Ahead," *Business Day*, May 16, 2011, www.bdlive.co.za/

articles/2011/05/16/coke-turns-125-and-has-much-more-life-ahead; Kate Taylor, "Coca-Cola Has Discovered an Untapped Market to Save the Soda Business," *Business Insider,* February 7, 2016, www.businessinsider.com/africa-is-the-future-of-coca-cola-2016-2; and Coca-Cola annual reports and other information from www.thecoca-colacompany.com, accessed October 2016.

17. See "2015 Investment Climate Statement—Russia," U.S. Bureau of Economic and Business Affairs, May 2015, www.state.gov/e/eb/rls/othr/ics/2015/241713.htm; and "Welcome to the U.S. Commercial Service in Russia," http://export.gov/russia/, accessed October 2016.

18. Jim Wyss, "Chicken for Diapers: Bartering Abounds in the Scarcity-Stricken Venezuela," *Miami-Herald,* December 1, 2015, www.miamiherald.com/news/nation-world/world/americas/venezuela/article47429270.html; and International Reciprocal Trade Association, www.irta.com/about/the-barter-and-trade-industry/, accessed October 2016.

19. For these and other examples, see Emma Hall, "Do You Know Your Rites? BBDO Does," *Advertising Age,* May 21, 2007, p. 22; and Michael R. Czinkota and Ilkka A. Ronkainen, *International Marketing* (Cincinnati, OH: South-Western College Publishing, 2013), Chapter 3.

20. Jamie Bryan, "The Mintz Dynasty," *Fast Company,* April 2006, pp. 56–61; Robert Mackey, "Coca-Cola Retreats from Social Media War Over Crimea," *New York Times,* January 6, 2016, www.nytimes.com/2016/01/07/world/europe/coca-cola-withdraws-from-social-media-war-over-crimea.html; and "Coke Holiday Ad Depicting Russia Stumbles into Geopolitical Row," *Wall Street Journal,* January 6, 2016, www.wsj.com/articles/coke-holiday-ad-depicting-russia-map-stumbles-into-geopolitical-row-1452122024.

21. For these and other examples, see Bill Chappell, "Bill Gates' Handshake with South Korea's Park Sparks Debate," *NPR,* April 23, 2013, www.npr.org/blogs/thetwo-way/2013/04/23/178650537/bill-gates-handshake-with-south-koreas-park-sparks-debate; "Managing Quality across the (Global) Organization, Its Stakeholders, Suppliers, and Customers," Chartered Quality Institute, www.thecqi.org/Knowledge-Hub/Knowledge-portal/Corporate-strategy/Managing-quality-globally, accessed October 2016.

22. See Rory Jones, "Foreign Retailers Bend to Conform to Saudi Religious Rules," *Wall Street Journal,* June 16, 2015, www.wsj.com/articles/foreign-retailers-bend-to-conform-to-saudi-religious-rules-1434421369; and www.marksandspencer.com, accessed October 2016.

23. Andres Martinez, "The Next American Century," *Time,* March 22, 2010, p. 1.

24. Thomas L. Friedman, *The Lexus and the Olive Tree: Understanding Globalization* (New York: Anchor Books, 2000); Michael Wei and Margaret Conley, "Global Brands: Some Chinese Kids' First Word: Mickey," *Bloomberg Businessweek,* June 19, 2011, pp. 24–25; and Nick Fraser, "How the World Was Won: The Americanization of Everywhere Review—a Brilliant Essay," *The Guardian,* November 2, 2014, www.theguardian.com/books/2014/nov/02/how-the-world-was-won-americanization-of-everywhere-review-peter-conrad.

25. Adam Chandler, "How McDonald's Became a Target for Protest," *The Atlantic,* April 16, 2015, www.theatlantic.com/business/archive/2015/04/setting-the-symbolic-golden-arches-aflame/390708/; and "McDonald's Set for Russia Expansion," *New Europe Investor,* August 26, 2015, www.neweuropeinvestor.com/news/mcdonalds-set-for-russia-expansion10522/.

26. "2015 BrandZ Top 100 Global Brands," Millward Brown, www.millwardbrown.com/mb-global/brand-strategy/brand-equity/brandz/top-global-brands/2015.

27. See Rachael Tepper, "Yum! Brands' International Product Strategy: How the Double Down Went Global," *Huffington Post,* March 11, 2013, www.huffingtonpost.com/2013/03/11/yum-brands-international-product-strategy_n_2814360.html;

Molly Osberg, "How Colonel Sanders Became Father Christmas in Japan," *TPM,* December 23, 2014, http://talkingpointsmemo.com/theslice/kfc-christmas-in-japan-colonel-sanders-history-12-23-2014; and Jason Johnson, "KFC Christmas Tradition in Japan," *Brain Skewer,* May 2015, http://brainskewer.com/bs/20150506/kfc-christmas-tradition-japan; and Megan Townsend, "Christmas in Japan," *Independent,* December 24, 2015, www.independent.co.uk/news/world/asia/christmas-in-japan-hundreds-queue-outside-of-kfc-branches-in-tokyo-for-japanese-christmas-tradition-a6785571.html.

28. See annual reports and other financial and review data from www.coca-colacompany.com/our-company/ and www.coca-colacompany.com/our-company/infographic-coca-cola-at-a-glance/, accessed October 2016.

29. For this and other information in this section on Amazon in India, see Vivienne Walt, "Amazon Invades India," *Fortune,* January 1, 2016, pp. 63–72; Jan Dawson, "Amazon's International Growth Challenge," *Re/Code,* May 11, 2015, http://recode.net/2015/05/11/amazons-international-growth-challenge/; Wang Qionghui, "In Tough China Market, Amazon Sells the World," *Caixin Online,* November 2, 2015, http://english.caixin.com/2015-11-02/100869131.html; and Leena Rao, "Amazon May Face Regulatory Hurdles in India," *Fortune,* April 8, 2016, http://fortune.com/2016/04/08/amazon-regulatory-hurdles-india/.

30. See Kate Taylor, "Coca-Cola Has Discovered an Untapped Market to Save the Soda Business," *Business Insider,* February 7, 2016, www.businessinsider.com/africa-is-the-future-of-coca-cola-2016-2; and www.olc.co.jp/en/ and www.coca-colahellenic.com/aboutus/, accessed October 2016.

31. See "Škoda and Volkswagen Group Russia: One Year of Successful Production in Nizhny Novgorod," December 11, 2013, www.volkswagenag.com/content/vwcorp/info_center/en/news/2013/12/Nizhny_Novgorod.html; and www.pg.com/en_IN/company/pg-india.shtml, accessed October 2016.

32. See http://en.wikipedia.org/wiki/Doubletree, accessed October 2016.

33. Rick Munarriz, "Shanghai Disney Hits a Few Hiccups," *The Motley Fool,* March 28, 2016, http://www.fool.com/investing/general/2016/03/28/shanghai-disney-hits-a-few-hiccups.aspx.

34. Christina Larson, "Intel Buys Its Way Deeper into China," *Bloomberg Businessweek,* March 8, 2015, pp. 33–34.

35. "Intel in China," *iLook China,* May 28, 2010, http://ilookchina.net/2010/05/page/2/; Christina Larson, "Intel Buys Its Way Deeper into China," *Bloomberg Businessweek,* March 8, 2015, pp. 33–34; and Stacey Higginbotham, "Qualcomm Forms Joint Venture in China to Take on Intel," *Fortune,* January 17, 2016, http://fortune.com/2016/01/17/qualcomm-server-china/.

36. Based on information from "Our Mission Is 'Beauty for All,' Says L'Oréal Global CEO Jean-Paul," *The Economic Times,"* January 30, 2015, http://articles.economictimes.indiatimes.com/2015-01-30/news/58625572_1_l-oreal-loreal-jean-paul-agon; Hae-Jung Hong and Yves Doz, "L'Oréal Masters Multiculturalism," *Harvard Business Review,* June, 2013, pp. 114–119; Liza Lin, "L'Oréal Puts on a Happy Face in China," *Bloomberg Businessweek,* April 1–7, 2013, pp. 25–26; and www.lorealusa.com/Article.aspx?topcode=CorpTopic_RI_CustomerInnovation, www.lorealusa.com/research-innovation/when-the-diversity-of-types-of-beauty-inspires-science/stories-of-multicultural-innovations.aspx, and www.loreal-finance.com/eng/annual-report, accessed October 2016.

37. See Warren J. Keegan and Mark C. Green, *Global Marketing,* 8th ed. (Hoboken, NJ: Pearson, 2015), pp. 303–308.

38. Toshiro Wakayama, Junjiro Shintaku, and Tomofumi Amano, "What Panasonic Learned in China," *Harvard Business Review,* December 2012, pp. 109–113.

39. "Dunkin' Donuts Enters India," *Business Standard,* May 9, 2012, www.business-standard.com/article/companies/dunkin-donuts-enters-india-112050900069_1.html; Preetika Rana, "Dippin into India, Dunkin' Donuts Changes Menu," *Wall Street Journal,* November 8, 2014, www.wsj.com/articles/dipping-into-india-dunkin-donuts-changes-menu-1417211158; Mallory Schlossberg,

"Dunkin' Donuts Is Plotting a Huge Expansion," *Business Insider*, December 30, 2014; and www.dunkinbrands.com, accessed October 2016.

40. See Normandy Madden, "In China, Multinationals Forgo Adaptation for New-Brand Creation," *Advertising Age*, January 17, 2011, p. 10; Susan Adams, "The 10 Companies Considered 'Best for the World,'" *Forbes*, March 31, 2014, www.forbes.com/sites/susanadams/2014/03/31/10-companies-considered-best-for-the-world/; Meg Cichon, "Solar Making Big Strides to Power the Developing World," *Renewable Energy World*, May 7, 2014, www.renewableenergyworld.com/rea/news/article/2014/05/solar-making-big-strides-to-power-the-developing-world; and www.dlightdesign.com/, accessed October 2016.

41. Jeffrey N. Ross, "Chevrolet Will 'Find New Roads' as Brand Grows Globally: Aligns around the World behind Singular Vision," January 8, 2013, http://media.gm.com/media/us/en/gm/news.detail.html/content/Pages/news/us/en/2013/Jan/0107-find-new-roads.html; and Dale Buss, "Chevy Wins at Sochi by Giving Dimension to 'Find New Roads,'" *Forbes*, February 24, 2014, www.forbes.com/sites/dalebuss/2014/02/24/chevrolet-wins-at-sochi-as-find-new-roads-theme-gets-traction/.

42. See Sophia Yan, "What's in a Brand Name? In China, Everything," *CNN Money*, September 7, 2015, http://money.cnn.com/2015/09/07/news/foreign-firms-china-branding/; Michael Wines, "Picking Brand Names in China Is a Business Itself," *New York Times*, November 12, 2011, p. A4; Carly Chalmers, "12 Amazing Translations of Chinese Brand Names," *todaytranslations*, August 27, 2013, www.todaytranslations.com/blog/12-amazing-translations-of-chinese-brand-names/; and Alfred Maskeroni, "Can You Identify All These Famous Logos Redesigned by an Artist into Chinese?" *Adweek*, February 10, 2015, www.adweek.com/print/162867.

43. "Nike Faces Ultimate Marketing Challenge in China: Make Running Cool," *Advertising Age*, October 31, 2011, pp. 1+; "Firms Help Spur a Running Craze in China," *China Sports News*, December 30, 2013, www.chinasportsbeat.com/2013/12/firms-help-spur-running-craze-in-china.html; "Nike Faces Tough Competition in Europe and China," *Forbes*, March 4, 2014, www.forbes.com/sites/greatspeculations/2014/03/04/nike-faces-tough-competition-in-europe-and-china/; and Jerry Clode, "Our New Digital Report—Nike's China Run Club," *Social Brand Watch*, March 21, 2016, http://socialbrandwatch.com/new-digital-report-nikes-china-run-club/.

44. See Warren J. Keegan and Mark C. Green, *Global Marketing*, 8th ed. (Hoboken, NJ: Pearson Publishing, 2015), pp. 413–414.

45. See Nikhil Subramaniam, "Motorola Beats Nokia in India Smartphone Sales Thanks to Moto G, Moto E," *Tech 2*, August 4, 2014, http://tech.firstpost.com/news-analysis/motorola-beats-nokia-in-india-smartphone-sales-thanks-to-moto-g-moto-e-228420.html; Luke Jones, "Motorola Moto G Brazil's Best-Selling Smartphone," *Mobile Burn*, March 29, 2015, www.mobileburn.com/24405/news/motorola-moto-g-brazils-best-selling-smartphone; and Ina Fried, "Lenovo Plans to Keep Moto Brand, Continue Moto E and Moto G Lines," *recode*, February 22, 2016, www.recode.net/2016/2/22/11588092/lenovo-plans-to-keep-moto-brand-continue-moto-e-and-moto-g-lines.

46. Drew Hinshaw, "Burgers Face a Tough Slog in Africa," *Wall Street Journal*, December 10, 2013, www.wsj.com/articles/SB10001424052702304607104579214133498585594.

47. See www.nestle.com.br/portalnestle/nestleatevoce/abordo_sobre_projeto.aspx, accessed October 2016.

48. Anita Chang Beattie, "Catching the Eye of a Chinese Shopper," *Advertising Age*, December 10, 2013, pp. 20–21.

49. Hae-Jung Hong and Yves Doz, "L'Oréal Masters Multiculturalism," *Harvard Business Review*, June, 2013, pp. 114–119; and "L'Oréal around the World," www.loreal.com/group/our-activities/l%E2%80%99or%C3%A9al-around-the-world, accessed October 2016.

Chapter 20

1. See Jessica Lyons Hardcastle, "How Unilever, GE, Ikea Turn a Profit from Sustainability," *Environmental Leader*, January 16, 2016, www.environmentalleader.com/2016/01/07/how-unilever-ge-ikea-turn-a-profit-from-sustainability/#ixzz4921RtMGH; "Unilever Named as an Industry Leader in DJSI," October 9, 2015, www.unilever.com/news/press-releases/2015/Unilever-named-as-an-industry-leader-in-DJSI.html; Andrew Saunders, "Paul Polman of Unilever," *Management Today*, March 2011, pp. 42–47; Adi Ignatius, "Captain Planet," *Harvard Business Review*, June 2012, pp. 2–8; "Unilever: Key Trends to Watch in 2015," *Forbes*, March 5, 2015, www.forbes.com/sites/greatspeculations/2015/03/05/unilever-key-trends-to-watch-in-2015/; Joi Sears, "Unilever Develops Groundbreaking Sustainable Packaging," *TriplePundit*, May 12, 2016, www.triplepundit.com/2016/05/unilever-develops-groundbreaking-sustainable-packaging/#; and www.unilever.com/sustainable-living/, accessed October 2016.

2. See www.mcdonalds.com/content/us/en/food/food_quality/nutrition_choices.html, www.aboutmcdonalds.com/mcd/sustainability.html, and www.mcdonalds.com/us/en/food/meal_bundles/favoritesunder400.html, accessed October 2016.

3. Brad Tuttle, "More Retailers Accused of Misleading Customers with Fake Price Schemes," *Money*, January 7, 2016, http://time.com/money/4171081/macys-jc-penney-lawsuit-original-prices/.

4. Tony T Liu, "Overstock.com Receives $6.8 Million Fine for False Advertising," *Orange Country Business Attorney Blog*, February 11, 2014, www.orangecountybusinessattorneyblog.com/2014/02/11/overstock-com-receives-6-8-million-fine-false-advertising/; and David Streitfeld, "It's Discounted, but Is It a Deal? How List Prices Lost Their Meaning," *New York Times*, March 6, 2016, p. A1.

5. See "FTC Charges Lumosity with Deceptive Advertising," *The Beacon*, January 14, 2016, http://bbbconsumereducation.com/ftc-charges-lumosity-with-deceptive-advertising/; and "Luminosity to Pay $2 Million to Settle FTC Deceptive Advertising Charges for Its 'Brain Training' Program," *FTC*, January 5, 2016, www.ftc.gov/news-events/press-releases/2016/01/lumosity-pay-2-million-settle-ftc-deceptive-advertising-charges.

6. Dan Mitchell, "Americans Don't Buy Enough Soda—Here's the New Targets," *Fortune*, February 19, 2016, http://fortune.com/2016/02/19/soda-emerging-nations-sales/; and Center for Science in the Public Interest, "Carbonating the World," www.cspinet.org/carbonating/, accessed October 2016.

7. Brian Clark Howard, "Planned Obsolescence: 8 Products Designed to Fail," *Popular Mechanics*, www.popularmechanics.com/technology/planned-obsole scence-460210#slide-5, accessed September 2015.

8. Rob Walker, "Replacement Therapy," *Atlantic Monthly*, September 2011, p. 38. For another interesting discussion, see Homa Khaleeli, "End of the Line for Stuff That's Built to Die?" The Guardian, March 3, 2015, www.theguardian.com/technology/shortcuts/2015/mar/03/has-planned-obsolesence-had-its-day-design.

9. See U.S. Department of Agriculture, "Creating Access to Healthy, Affordable Food," http://apps.ams.usda.gov/fooddeserts, accessed October 2016.

10. See Maanvi Singh, "Why a Philadelphia Grocery Chain Is Thriving in Food Deserts," NPR, May 14, 2015, www.npr.org/sections/thesalt/2015/05/14/406476968/why-one-grocery-chain-is-thriving-in-philadelphias-food-deserts.

11. See www.newdream.org/, www.newdream.org/about/mission, and www.newdream.org/blog/more-fun-less-stuff-photos, accessed October 2016.

12. See Erik Oster, "Erwin Penland, L.L. Bean Take on Disposable Fashion with 'When,'" Adweek, April 21, 2016, www.adweek.com/print/107497.

13. See Texas Transportation Institute, "Annual Urban Mobility Report," http://mobility.tamu.edu/ums/report/, accessed October 2016.

14. Mimi Kirk, "A Prius Costs $154,000 in Singapore and People Are Still Buying Them," Quartz, June 18, 2013, http://qz.com/95429/a-prius-costs-154000-in-singapore-and-people-are-still-buying-them/; and Jeff Cuellar, "What Is the True Cost of Owning a Car in Singapore? You Don't Want to Know," MoneySmart.sg, August 21, 2014, http://blog.moneysmart.sg/car-ownership/the-true-cost-of-owning-a-car-in-singapore/.

15. For this and more information about the Google antitrust example, see Nathan Newman, "EU Antitrust Action Today Is Just the Beginning of Google's Troubles in Europe," Huffington Post, April 15, 2015, www.huffingtonpost.com/nathan-newman/eu-antitrust-action-today_b_7070568.html; James Kanter and Mark Scott, "Europe Challenges Google, Seeing Violations of Its Antitrust Law," New York Times, April 16, 2015, p. B1; and Mark Scott, "Google's Antitrust Woes in Europe Are Likely to Grow," Wall Street Journal, April 20, 2016, p.A1.

16. See Philip Kotler, "Reinventing Marketing to Manage the Environmental Imperative," Journal of Marketing, July 2011, pp. 132–135; and Kai Ryssdal, "Unilever CEO: For Sustainable Business, Go against 'Mindless Consumption,'" Marketplace, June 11, 2013, www.marketplace.org/topics/sustainability/consumed/unilever-ceo-paul-polman-sustainble-business.

17. Andrew Lord, "Adidas Created a Shoe That Is Literally Made Out of Trash," Huffington Post, June 30, 2016, www.huffingtonpost.com/2015/06/30/adidas-shoe-made-of-ocean-trash_n_7699632.html; "Adidas Group Sustainable Materials," www.adidas-group.com/en/sustainability/products/materials/#/recyceltes-polystyrol/sustainable-better-cotton/pvc-and-phthalates/, accessed October 2016; and www.adidas-group.com/en/sustainability/managing-sustainability/general-approach/ and http://www.adidas-group.com/en/sustainability/planet/green-company/#/green-teams/, accessed October 2016.

18. See Alan S. Brown, "The Many Shades of Green," Mechanical Engineering, January 2009, http://memagazine.asme.org/Articles/2009/January/Many_Shades_Green.cfm; and www-03.ibm.com/financing/us/recovery/, accessed October 2016.

19. Based on information from "Local Insights Leasing to Globally Valid Innovations," Coca-Cola India, May 7, 2015, www.coca-colaindia.com/2015/05/07/local-insights-leading-globally-valid-innovations/; "Coca-Cola Installs 1 Millionth HFC-Free Cooler Globally, Preventing 5.25MM Metric Tons of CO2," January 22, 2014, www.coca-colacompany.com/press-center/press-releases/coca-cola-installs-1-millionth-hfc-free-cooler-globally-preventing-525mm-metrics-tons-of-co2; and www.coca-colacompany.com/stories/position-statement-on-climate-protection; www.coca-colacompany.com/stories/our-2020-environment-goals-infographic and www.coca-colacompany.com/press-center/, accessed October 2016.

20. Information from "The North Face 2014 Sustainability Report," http://neverstopexploring.com/2014/07/22/north-face-2014-corporate-responsibility-report/, accessed September 2015; Leon Kaye, "The North Face Sustainability Report," Triple Pundit, July 29, 2014, www.triplepundit.com/2014/07/the-north-face-sustainability/; and www.thenorthface.com/about-us/responsibility.html, accessed October 2016.

21. See www.thenorthface.com/about-us/responsibility.html, accessed October 2016.

22. See "Johnson & Johnson's Share of the Baby Care Market Worldwide from 2013 to 2021," Statista, www.statista.com/statistics/258429/johnson-und-johnsons-share-of-the-baby-care-market-worldwide/, accessed October 2016; Jack Neff, "Johnson's Baby Turns to Social-Media Transparency to Woo Millennial Moms," Advertising Age, July 30, 2014, www.adage.com/print/294376; "Our Promise," www.johnsonsbaby.com/difference/our-promise, accessed October 2016; and "The IKEA Way," www.ikea.com/ms/en_SA/about_ikea/the_ikea_way/index.html, accessed October 2016.

23. "SC Johnson's CEO on Doing the Right Thing, Even When It Hurts Business," Harvard Business Review, April 2015, pp. 33–36; and "We Commit to What Matters Most," http://scjohnson.com/en/commitment/overview.aspx, accessed October 2016.

24. See Transparency International, "Bribe Payers Index," www.transparency.org/research/bpi/overview; and "Global Corruption Barometer 2013," www.transparency.org/gcb2013. Also see Michael Montgomery, "The Cost of Corruption," American RadioWorks, http://americanradioworks.publicradio.org/features/corruption/, accessed October 2016.

25. See www.marketingpower.com/AboutAMA/Pages/Statement%20of%20Ethics.aspx, accessed October 2016.

26. See https://abc.xyz/investor/other/google-code-of-conduct.html, accessed June 2016.

27. David A. Lubin and Daniel C. Esty, "The Sustainability Imperative," Harvard Business Review, May 2010, pp. 41–50; and Roasbeth Moss Kanter, "It's Time to Take Full Responsibility," Harvard Business Review, October 2010, p. 42.

Appendix 2

i   This is derived by rearranging the following equation and solving for price: Percentage markup = (price − cost) ÷ price.

ii Again, using the basic profit equation, we set profit equal to ROI × I: ROI × I = (P × Q) − TFC − (Q × UVC). Solving for Q gives Q = (TFC + (ROI × I)) ÷ (P − UVC).

iii U.S. Census Bureau, available at http://quickfacts.census.gov/qfd/states/00000.html, June 13, 2014.

iv See Roger J. Best, Market-Based Management, 4th ed. (Upper Saddle River, NJ: Prentice Hall, 2005).

v   Total contribution can also be determined from the unit contribution and unit volume: Total contribution = unit contribution × unit sales. Total units sold in 2017 were 595,238 units, which can be determined by dividing total sales by price per unit ($100 million ÷ $168). Total contribution = $35.28 contribution per unit × 595,238 units = $20,999,996.64 (difference due to rounding).

vi Recall that the contribution margin of 21% was based on variable costs representing 79% of sales. Therefore, if we do not know price, we can set it equal to $1.00. If price equals $1.00, 79 cents represents variable costs and 21 cents represents unit contribution. If price is decreased by 10%, the new price is $0.90. However, variable costs do not change just because price decreased, so the unit contribution and contribution margin decrease as follows:

	Old	New (reduced 10%)
Price	$1.00	$0.90
− Unit variable cost	$0.79	$0.79
= Unit contribution	$0.21	$0.11
Contribution margin	$0.21/$1.00	$0.11/$0.90
	= 0.21 or 21%	= 0.12 or 12%

Index

Subject Index

Note: Page numbers in italic indicate a figure or table appears on that page.